Dante, Petrarch, Boccaccio
Literature, Doctrine, Reality

LEGENDA

LEGENDA is the Modern Humanities Research Association's book imprint for new research in the Humanities. Founded in 1995 by Malcolm Bowie and others within the University of Oxford, Legenda has always been a collaborative publishing enterprise, directly governed by scholars. The Modern Humanities Research Association (MHRA) joined this collaboration in 1998, became half-owner in 2004, in partnership with Maney Publishing and then Routledge, and has since 2016 been sole owner. Titles range from medieval texts to contemporary cinema and form a widely comparative view of the modern humanities, including works on Arabic, Catalan, English, French, German, Greek, Italian, Portuguese, Russian, Spanish, and Yiddish literature. Editorial boards and committees of more than 60 leading academic specialists work in collaboration with bodies such as the Society for French Studies, the British Comparative Literature Association and the Association of Hispanists of Great Britain & Ireland.

The MHRA encourages and promotes advanced study and research in the field of the modern humanities, especially modern European languages and literature, including English, and also cinema. It aims to break down the barriers between scholars working in different disciplines and to maintain the unity of humanistic scholarship. The Association fulfils this purpose through the publication of journals, bibliographies, monographs, critical editions, and the MHRA Style Guide, and by making grants in support of research. Membership is open to all who work in the Humanities, whether independent or in a University post, and the participation of younger colleagues entering the field is especially welcomed.

ALSO PUBLISHED BY THE ASSOCIATION

Critical Texts
Tudor and Stuart Translations • *New Translations* • *European Translations*
MHRA Library of Medieval Welsh Literature

MHRA Bibliographies
Publications of the Modern Humanities Research Association

The Annual Bibliography of English Language & Literature
Austrian Studies
Modern Language Review
Portuguese Studies
The Slavonic and East European Review
Working Papers in the Humanities
The Yearbook of English Studies

www.mhra.org.uk
www.legendabooks.com

SELECTED ESSAYS

Each title in *Selected Essays* presents influential, but often scattered, papers by a major scholar in the Humanities. While these essays will, we hope, offer a model of scholarly writing, and chart the development of an important thinker in the field, the aim is not retrospective but to gather a coherent body of work as a tool for future research. Each volume contains a new introduction, framing the debate and reflecting on the methods used.

Selected Essays is curated by Professor Susan Harrow (University of Bristol).

Managing Editor
Dr Graham Nelson, 41 Wellington Square, Oxford OX1 2JF, UK

www.legendabooks.com

Dante, Petrarch, Boccaccio

Literature, Doctrine, Reality

ZYGMUNT G. BARAŃSKI

LEGENDA

Selected Essays 6

Modern Humanities Research Association

2020

Published by Legenda
an imprint of the Modern Humanities Research Association
Salisbury House, Station Road, Cambridge CB1 2LA

ISBN 978-1-78188-879-7 *(HB)*
ISBN 978-1-78188-880-3 *(PB)*

First published 2020

Copy-Editor: Charlotte Brown

CONTENTS

PART V: WRITING REALITY

LIST OF SOURCES

The essays included here originally appeared in the following publications, and are reprinted with the kind permission of the publishers and editors.

'On Dante's Trail', *Italian Studies*, 72 (2017), 1–15. Published by Taylor & Francis.

'Dante and Doctrine (and Theology)', in *Reviewing Dante's Theology*, ed. by Claire Honess and Matthew Treherne, 2 vols (Bern: Peter Lang, 2013), I, 1–63

'(Un)Orthodox Dante', in *Reviewing Dante's Theology*, ed, by Claire Honess and Matthew Treherne, 2 vols (Bern: Peter Lang, 2013), II, 253–330

'Canto XXII', in *Lectura Dantis Turicensis. Paradiso*, ed. by Georges Güntert and Michelangelo Picone (Florence: Cesati, 2002), pp. 339–62

'Dottrina degli affetti e teologia: la rappresentazione della beatitudine in *Paradiso*', in *Dante poeta cristiano e la cultura religiosa medievale: in ricordo di Anna Maria Chiavacci Leonardi*, ed. by Giuseppe Ledda (Ravenna: Centro Dantesco dei Frati Minori Conventuali, 2018), pp. 259–312

'"Tres enim sunt manerie dicendi...": Some Observations on Medieval Literature, Dante, and "Genre"', in *'Libri poetarum in quattuor species dividuntur': Essays on Dante and 'Genre'*, ed. by Zygmunt G. Barański, special supplement 2 to *The Italianist*, 15 (1995), 9–60

'"Primo tra cotanto senno": Dante and the Latin Comic Tradition', *Italian Studies*, 46 (1991), 1–31. Published by Taylor & Francis.

'The Poetics of Meter: *terza rima*, "canto", "canzon", "cantica"', in *Dante Now*, ed. by Theodore Cachey Jr (Notre Dame, IN, and London: Notre Dame University Press, 1995), pp. 3–41

'Purgatorio XXV', in *Lectura Dantis Turicensis. Purgatorio*, ed. by Georges Güntert and Michelangelo Picone (Florence: Cesati, 2001), pp. 389–406

'Petrarch, Dante, Cavalcanti', in *Petrarch and Dante*, ed. by Zygmunt G. Barański and Theodore J. Cachey Jr (Notre Dame, IN: University of Notre Dame Press, 2009), pp. 50–113

'"Io mi rivolgo indietro a ciascun passo" (*Rvf* 15. 1): Petrarch, the *fabula* of Eurydice and Orpheus, and the Structure of the Canzoniere', in *Cultural Reception, Translation and Transformation from Medieval to Modern Italy: Essays in Honour of Martin McLaughlin*, ed. by Guido Bonsaver, Brian Richardson, and Giuseppe Stellardi (London: Legenda, 2017), pp. 1–24

'"Piangendo" e "cantando" con Orfeo (e con Dante): strutture emotive e strutture poetiche in *Rerum vulgarium fragmenta* 281–90', in *Il Canzoniere: lettura micro e macrotestuale*, ed. by Michelangelo Picone (Ravenna: Longo, 2007), pp. 617–40

'Guido Cavalcanti and his First Readers', in *Guido Cavalcanti*, ed. by Maria Luisa Ardizzone (Fiesole: Cesati, 2003), pp. 149–75

'The Ethics of Ignorance: Petrarch's Epicurus and Averroes and the Structures of the *De sui ipsius et multorum ignorantia*', in *Petrarch in Britain: Interpretations, Appropriations, Translations*, ed. by Martin McLaughlin and Letizia Panizza (London: The British Academy, 2007), pp. 39–59

'"Alquanto tenea della oppinione degli Epicuri": The *auctoritas* of Boccaccio's Cavalcanti (and Dante)', in *Mittelalterliche Novellistik im europaischen Kontext*, ed. by Mark Chinca,

Timo Reuvekamp-Felber, and Christopher Young (Berlin: Erich Schmidt Verlag, 2006), pp. 280–325

'Boccaccio and Epicurus', in *Caro Vitto: Essays in Memory of Vittore Branca*, ed. by Jill Kraye and Anna Laura Lepschy, special supplement to *The Italianist*, 27 (2007), 10–27

'Guido Cavalcanti tra le *cruces* di *Inferno* IX– XI, ovvero Dante e la storia della ragione', in *Versi controversi: letture dantesche*, ed. by Domenico Cofano and Sebastiano Valerio (Foggia: Edizioni del Rosone, 2008), pp. 39–112

'"E cominciare stormo": Notes on Dante's Sieges', in *'Legato con amore in un volume': Essays in Honour of John A. Scott*, ed. by John Kinder and Diana Glenn (Florence: Olschki, 2013), pp. 175–203

'Scatology and Obscenity in Dante', in *Dante For the New Millennium*, ed. by Teodolinda Barolini and H. Wayne Storey (New York: Fordham University Press, 2003), pp. 259–73

ABBREVIATIONS AND EDITIONS

The following editions are used throughout, unless otherwise stated.

Albert the Great's works are cited from *Alberti Magni Opera omnia*, ad fidem codicum manuscriptorum edenda curavit Institutum Alberti Magni Coloniense, 41 vols (Cologne: Aschendorff, 1951–).

Bernard of Clairvaux's works are cited from *Sancti Bernardi Opera*, ed. by Jean Leclerq and others, 8 vols in 9 (Rome: Editiones cistercienses, 1957–77).

Bonaventure's works are cited from *Opera Omnia*, 10 vols (Quaracchi: Ex typographia Collegii S. Bonaventurae, 1882–1902).

Thomas Aquinas's works are cited from Thomas Aquinas, *Opera omnia*, 25 vols (Parma: Fiaccadori, 1852–73); I have used the reprint (New York: Musurgia, 1948–50).

Classical Latin authors, unless stated otherwise, are cited from the Loeb Classical Library.

AP	Horace, *The 'Ars Poetica'*, ed. by Charles Oscar Brink (Cambridge: Cambridge University Press, 1971)
Ben. maj.	Richard of St Victor, *Benjamin major*, in PL, vol. CXCVI, cols 63–192
Bible	*Biblia Sacra iuxta vulgatam versionem*, ed. by Robert Weber and Roger Gryson, 5th edn (Stuttgart: Deutsche Bibelgesellschaft, 2007)
CCSL	Corpus Christianorum Series Latina
CCCM	Corpus Christianorum Continuatio Mediaevalis
Commedia	Dante Alighieri, *La Commedia secondo l'antica vulgata*, ed. by Giorgio Petrocchi, 2nd edn, 4 vols (Florence: Le Lettere, 1994)
Conv.	Dante Alighieri, *Convivio*, ed. by Franca Brambilla Ageno, 3 vols (Florence: Le Lettere, 1995)
De civ. Dei	Augustine, *De civitate Dei*, in PL, vol. XLI
De doc. chr.	Augustine, *De Doctrina Christiana*, ed. and trans. by R. P. H. Green (Oxford: Clarendon Press, 1995)
Dec.	Giovanni Boccaccio, *Decameron*, ed. by Vittore Branca (Turin: Einaudi, 1987)
De ign.	Francesco Petrarca, *De sui ipsius et multorum ignorantia*, ed. by Enrico Fenzi (Milan: Mursia, 1999)
Detto	*Il Fiore e il Detto d'Amore attribuibili a Dante Alighieri*, ed. by Gianfranco Contini (Milan: Mondadori, 1984), pp. 483–512
DDP	Dartmouth Dante Project: <https://dante.dartmouth.edu/> [accessed 10 August 2019]
DSAM	*Dictionnaire de spiritualité, ascétique et mystique*, 17 vols (Paris: Beauchesne, 1932–95)
DTC	*Dictionnaire de théologie catholique*, 15 vols in 21 (Paris: Letouzey & Ané, 1923–50)
Dve	Dante Alighieri, *De vulgari eloquentia*, ed. by Pier Vincenzo Mengaldo, in *Opere minori*, 2 vols (Milan and Naples: Ricciardi, 1979–88), II, 1–237

Ecl. Dante Alighieri, *Egloge*, ed. by Gabriella Albanese, in *Opere*, 3 vols (Milan: Mondadori, 2011–), II, 1593–783

ED *Enciclopedia dantesca*, 5 vols + Appendix (Rome: Istituto della Enciclopedia Italiana, 1970–78)

Ep. Dante Alighieri, *Epistole*, ed. by Claudia Villa, in *Opere*, 3 vols (Milan: Mondadori, 2011–), II, 1417–1592

Etym. Isidore of Seville, *Libri Etymologiarum sive Originum*, ed. by Wallace M. Lindsay, 2 vols (Oxford: Clarendon Press, 1911)

Fam. Francesco Petrarca, *Rerum familiarium libri*, ed. by Vittorio Rossi and Umberto Bosco, 4 vols (Florence: Sansoni, 1933–42)

Faral *Les Arts poétiques du XIIe et du XIIIe siècle*, ed. by Edmond Faral (Paris: Champion, 1971)

Fiore *Il Fiore e il Detto d'Amore attribuibili a Dante Alighieri*, ed. by Gianfranco Contini (Milan: Mondadori, 1984), pp. 1–467

Huygens *Accessus ad auctores, Bernard d'Utrecht, Conrad d'Hirsau*, ed. by Robert B. C. Huygens (Leiden: Brill, 1970)

Inf. Dante Alighieri, *Inferno*

Itin. Bonaventure, *Itinerarium mentis in Deum*

Keil *Grammatici latini*, ed. by Heinrich Keil, 8 vols (Leipzig: Teubner, 1855–70)

LPQSD *'Libri poetarum in quattuor species dividuntur': Essays on Dante and 'Genre'*, ed. by Zygmunt G. Barański, special supplement 2 of *The Italianist*, 15 (1995)

MLTC *Medieval Literary Theory and Criticism c. 1100–c. 1375: The Commentary Tradition*, ed. by A. J. Minnis and A. B. Scott with the assistance of David Wallace, rev. edn (Oxford: Oxford University Press, 1991)

Mon. *Monarchia*, ed. by Prue Shaw (Florence: Le Lettere, 2009)

Par. Dante Alighieri, *Paradiso*

PL *Patrologiae cursus completus: Series latina*, ed. by Jacques Paul Migne, 221 vols (Paris: Migne, 1844–64)

Purg. Dante Alighieri, *Purgatorio*

Questio *Questio de aqua et terra*, ed. by Francesco Mazzoni, in Dante Alighieri, *Opere minori*, 2 vols (Milan and Naples: Ricciardi, 1979–88), II, 693–880

Rer. mem. Francesco Petrarca, *Rerum memorandarum libri*, ed. by Giuseppe Billanovich (Florence: Sansoni, 1943)

Rime *Rime*, ed. by Domenico De Robertis (Florence: Edizioni del Galluzzo, 2005)

Rvf Francesco Petrarca, *Canzoniere. 'Rerum vulgarium fragmenta'*, ed. by Rosanna Bettarini, 2 vols (Turin: Einaudi, 2005)

SCG Thomas Aquinas, *Summa contra Gentiles*

Sen. Francesco Petrarca, *Res seniles*, ed. by Silvia Rizzo and Monica Berté, 3 vols (Florence: Le Lettere, 2006–17)

Secretum Francesco Petrarca, *Secretum*, ed. by Enrico Fenzi (Milan: Mursia, 1992)

ST Thomas Aquinas, *Summa theologiae*

TLL *Thesaurus linguae latinae* (Leipzig: Teubner; Berlin: de Gruyter, 1900–)

Tr. Francesco Petrarca, *Triumphi*, in *Trionfi, Rime estravaganti, Codice degli abbozzi*, ed. by Vinicio Pacca and Laura Paolino (Milan: Mondadori, 1996)

Vn Dante Alighieri, *La vita nuova*, rev. ed. by Michele Barbi (Florence: Bemporad, 1932)

Commentaries on the *Commedia* and on the *Rvf* are referred to by the name or names of the editors.

Bellomo	Dante Alighieri, *Inferno*, ed. by Saverio Bellomo (Turin: Einaudi, 2013)
Bosco-Reggio	Dante Alighieri, *La Divina Commedia*, ed. by Umberto Bosco and Giovanni Reggio (Florence: Le Monnier, 1979)
Chiavacci Leonardi	Dante Alighieri, *Commedia*, ed. by Anna Maria Chiavacci Leonardi, 3 vols (Milan: Mondadori, 2003–08)
Durling-Martinez	Dante Alighieri, *The Divine Comedy*, ed. by Ronald L. Martinez and Robert M. Durling, 3 vols (Oxford: Oxford University Press, 1996–2011)
Hollander	Dante Alighieri, *The Inferno*; *Purgatorio*; *Paradiso*, ed. by Robert Hollander (New York: Anchor Books, 2000–07)
Inglese	Dante Alighieri, *Commedia*, ed. by Giorgio Inglese, 3 vols (Rome: Carocci, 2007–16)
Momigliano	Dante Alighieri, *La Divina Commedia*, ed. by Attilio Momigliano, 3 vols (Florence: Sansoni, 1946)
Pasquini-Quaglio	Dante Alighieri, *Commedia*, ed. by Emilio Pasquini and Antonio Quaglio, 3 vols (Milan: Garzanti, 1982–86)
Sapegno	Dante Alighieri, *La Divina Commedia*, ed. by Natalino Sapegno, 3 vols (Florence: La Nuova Italia, 1978)
Bettarini	Francesco Petrarca, *Canzoniere. 'Rerum vulgarium fragmenta'*, ed. by Rosanna Bettarini, 2 vols (Turin: Einaudi, 2005)
Santagata	Francesco Petrarca, *Canzoniere*, ed. by Marco Santagata (Milan: Mondadori, 1996)

All translations are my own, unless otherwise stated.

to

Al, Dave, Fogey, Ian, Liam, Paul, Pip, Ravi,
Student, Suttie, and the three Steves,

and in memory of

Mick B., Mick S., and Stuart

INTRODUCTION

'A Contrariness in It':
Seven 'Fragmented' Reflections

I.

The nineteen articles brought together in this collection originally appeared between 1991 and 2017. They constitute an accurate representative record of the development of my principal academic interests in the area of medieval Italian literature and culture in this period, and especially since the start of the new millennium (sixteen of the pieces belong to this time frame). Although the studies largely coincide with my time in Cambridge (2002–11) and then at Notre Dame (2011–), their roots stretch back to Reading, and even more remotely to Aberdeen and to Hull. Twelve, a clear majority, deal with Dante. The remainder are divided between four articles on Petrarch, two on Boccaccio, and a solitary contribution on Cavalcanti's late-medieval reception — a distribution, I must confess, that, however crudely, conforms to my personal sense of the four authors' relative literary merits and importance. Nonetheless, I would hope that the studies that follow might offer a degree of vindication for my heavily Dante-weighted appreciation.

Despite the impression that might be created by the studied balance between title and subtitle, *Dante, Petrarch, Boccaccio: Literature, Doctrine, Reality* does not forge a close and exclusive link between author and corresponding category. Rather, if taken together, the essays highlight the distinct, yet also overlapping ways in which each of the *tre corone* dealt with literature, doctrine, and reality. Specifically, the volume explores how Italy's three major authors strove to create and establish their literary authority and identity while developing new ideas about literature, and, especially in Dante's case, forging and legitimating new literary forms. Each tested (vernacular) literature's epistemological status, its possibilities and its limits, as well as its ethical, social, and personal functions and ramifications. To put it simply, they tested its place in the world. Likewise, their self-authorizing strategies often involved treating other poets — Orpheus and Guido Cavalcanti are good cases in point — and thinkers, such as Epicurus, polemically and selectively as foils to their own self-portraits. At the same time, even if their reactions were different, both Petrarch and Boccaccio found it difficult to come to terms with Dante's extraordinary yet suffocating success as a 'modern' vernacular *auctor* in fourteenth-century Italy.

My approach to literature and authorship is predicated on close consideration of context — whether literary, linguistic, historical, cultural, or intellectual. Such persistent attention is what underpins and unites the book's different chapters. It is what grants them a degree of cohesion and permits the collection to develop over-arching and, I believe, integrated accounts of 'fragments' — Petrarch's designation is spot on — of the careers of three outstanding writers, as well as of key moments of late-medieval (Italian) culture. Moreover, my approach is complemented by an equally watchful awareness of the scholarly tradition on the questions addressed — the context within which I think, teach, research, and write. To be a historian of literature also means being a historian of one's subject; and, in due course, I intend to return to consider these matters, as well as those touched on in the next paragraph, in greater detail and from a less sanguine and more critical perspective.

   Dante, Petrarch, Boccaccio: Literature, Doctrine, Reality is thus defined and delimited by its steady historicist and philological focus. Although, at times, the two epithets are treated as synonymous, this is not the case here. Indeed, as ought to become clear below, I prefer to see them as existing in tension. By 'historicism', I mean an understanding of texts, authors, institutions, events, ideas, practices that grants primary and determining significance to the time and place of their existence. I use the term 'philology' in the loose Italian sense of a historically inflected appre-ciation, first, of language, especially as regards its morphological and semantic developments, and second, of literature as a communicative and 'self-contained' macrosystem made up of a plurality of interconnecting yet discrete microsystems: Boccaccio's *œuvre*, Romance literature, comedy, etc.[1] In its substance, the collection ranges quite widely across decisive foundational moments of one such microsystem which, at least since Francesco De Sanctis, has been termed 'letteratura italiana', namely, the literature, which is deemed to have begun warily with the so-called *scuola siciliana*, that has been composed in an Italian vernacular or has been written in other languages, most notably Latin, by authors who also employ Italian or whose origins are rooted in the peninsula and its islands. Consequently, and quite conventionally, the book engages with the 'three crowns'; with Guido Cavalcanti, for whom a solid case can be made that he ought to be recognized as medieval Italy's fourth literary and intellectual *corona*; and with a significant array of issues — from Averroes and Averroism to vernacular *auctoritas*, from popular piety to scholastic controversies, from heresy to the legacy of antiquity, and from conventions of 'reading' to violence — that characterized and structured the culture of late Due- and Trecento Italy, as well as that of medieval Christendom more generally. Yet, *Dante, Petrarch, Boccaccio: Literature, Doctrine, Reality* also has a 'narrow' remit. Given that Dante returns, often vitally, in all seven non-expressly Dantean chapters, it is ultimately, and I'd say primarily, a book about the poet. And this is as it should be. I have long felt that, if I can claim to have any sort of academic expertise, it is not as an Italianist, nor as a medievalist, but, restrictedly, as a Dantist.

---

1   The Italian term *filologia* also embraces the critical editing and annotating of literary works. As my studies only touch extremely fleetingly on such matters, this aspect of philology is not really relevant when discussing the main methodological parameters of my scholarship. For a witty and apposite critique of the Italian academy's obsession with the editing of texts, see Paolo Cherchi, 'Edizioni in condizioni critiche', in his *Erudizione e leggerezza: saggi di filologia comparativa*, ed. by Giuliana Adamo (Rome: Viella, 2012), pp. 215–35.

II.

I first read the *Commedia* — or rather, as at the time I had no reason to doubt the validity of the designation, the *Divina Commedia* — in the mid-1960s, at around the age of fifteen. The edition was: Dante Alighieri, *La Divina Commedia, Testo critico della Società Dantesca Italiana riveduto, col commento scartazziniano rifatto da Giuseppe Vandelli, aggiuntovi il Rimario perfezionato da L. Polacco e Indice de' nomi proprii e di cose notabili.* It was the 'quindicesima edizione (completa)' — the original edition dates to 1893, although this only included the drastically reduced 'edizione minore' of Scartazzini's excellent, if woefully underused, three-volume commentary. The *Rimario* was added in 1896, the *Indice* in 1899, while Vandelli offered the results of his first stab at revising both text and commentary in 1903. Ulrico Hoepli, Editore-Libraio of Milan, was the publisher, as he had been of every reprint since 1893. The edition I held in my hands, the fifteenth as I've mentioned, had appeared — with the benefit of hindsight, I now appreciate 'fatefully' — in 1951, the year of my birth. It was printed on cheap, coarse off-white paper with a flimsy yellowish cover, although someone had had the good sense to bind it sturdily. The copy is here with me in our home in Reading, and, as I handle it, I'm struck that the poor quality of its external appearance was almost certainly a result of post-war austerity, that same war that was the ultimate cause for its being apprehensively opened and examined in a modest home in a nondescript South Manchester street. My father was Polish and a political emigré who had met my mother in a small Italian town in the Marche having been billeted in one of the nearby farms at the war's end. The United Kingdom became the preferred destination of many among General Anders's troops who had decided not to return to communist-run Poland. They were reassured by Britain's standing as the 'mother of parliaments', as well as its reputation for fairness and for welcoming political exiles. They were also impressed, although this is something that is rarely noted, by the planned welfare reforms of the newly elected Labour government. My father arrived in 1947, my mother in 1949, and I, two years later. A few years after that, the Scartazzini–Vandelli *Divina Commedia* joined us, a gift from my mum's zia Francesca, who, with her brother Amerigo, had brought her up in the last house on the road to Cerreto d'Esi on the edge of Matelica. They had taken responsibility for my mum since her own mother, my nonna Matilde, was struggling to bring up five children with her husband, nonno Guido, in and out of prison for anti-fascist activities.

Our family life was in many ways eccentric, but also invigorating. My father, when not at work, was ever taken up with obscure, nostalgic, and inevitably irrelevant political doings (I have quite a bit of sympathy for Dante's sons who, through no fault of their own, also ended up having to share their 'obsessed' father's exile). My mother was often distracted, resentful towards my dad, and pining for Matelica. My brothers and I quite soon learned to look after ourselves. The three of us remain extremely close. I trace something of my independence of thought, my strong sense of personal responsibility, and my self-confidence — traits that people have been kind enough to note in my life and in my contributions as an academic — as well as much else, to that strange upbringing and to that unconventional heritage: a mix of Polish nationalism, Italian left-wing radicalism, (Irish) Catholicism, a rejection of prejudice and authoritarianism, an unshakable naive veneration for 'high culture', and, most of all, an ironcast sense that beliefs should not be compromised. Henryk, my dad, aggressively anti-communist, and Guido, my grandad, first a socialist, then a communist, and finally an anarchist, never met (nonno died in 1941 as a result of wounds suffered in the Great War and years of fascist mistreatment). Yet, as I write this paragraph on a snowy Chicago morning, I imagine that, if they had, they would have respected and understood each other's visceral and unflinching moral and political commitment. Even though this was a process that took time to reach fruition, perhaps more than anything, my upbringing and heritage helped me to appreciate and to draw benefit from my 'otherness'. In narrow and prosaic scholarly terms — and yes, it is, of course, on these that I should concentrate in this introduction, except that my scholarship has distinctly non-academic beginnings and then debts — my upbringing and heritage, I repeat, have led me to recognize the advantages, especially when doing research, not just of reflecting on things from outside the mainstream, but also of striving to develop and then to defend a firmly independent voice. And my heritage and upbringing had a powerful ally in all this...

I know that, even if my mum and dad were far from ideal parents, I owe to them something of my temperament, certainly my intellectual energy and my *forma mentis*, and, ultimately, the fact that I became an academic. They shared their mother tongues and their cultures with me. If it had not been for my mum, I would not have studied Italian, never mind become a Dantist. Thanks to my parents' insistence that we kids should speak to them only in their own language — Italian, tellingly, was their *lingua franca* — I could read the *Divina Commedia* and the Scartazzini–Vandelli annotations, and, occasionally, even follow text and notes. Overall, however, my first stab at reading Dante's masterpiece left me perplexed, in awe, and deeply dissatisfied. I still remember the sense of being in contact with something uncommon and remarkable, but which I was quite incapable of grasping beyond a vague and frustrating intuition of, yes, its greatness. I'm not sure whether it was then that I had the first inklings that it might be worth seriously engaging with the *Commedia*, or whether, as I kept returning to the poem, it was an idea that developed during my sixth-form years at the academically excellent but humanly defective St Bede's College, and later at the University of Hull, whose Italian department was both intellectually outstanding and sensitive to the needs of its students. In many ways, it doesn't matter. Ever since that first, fateful encounter (grazie, zia Checca!), part of my life has been a sustained attempt to overcome that artless dissatisfaction and frustration by justifying, first to myself and then to others, the *Commedia*'s and Dante's exceptionality.

However, before I digress yet further, I need to finish acknowledging my debts to my parents. Thus, my enduring conviction that, without an appreciation of history, our understanding of literature (and much else) is inescapably diminished, comes first, and possibly foremost, from my dad, an outstanding orator who, rather than tell fairy tales or read from children's books, would memorably recount to the pre-school Bol, Jajo, and me the vicissitudes of centuries of doomed, dysfunctional Polish history and read to us from Henryk Sienkiewicz's bloody epic-historical *Trylogia* — heady, disturbing, unforgettable stuff. I still ponder, especially as I shudder at today's Law and Justice [PiS] party's right-wing, xenophobic nationalism, the lasting effects of the partitions and elimination of the Polish-Lithuanian Commonwealth at the end of the eighteenth century: traumatizing circumstances that, for over two hundred years, have defined 'Polishness' and have brought out both the best and the worst in Poles. And there is more for which I'm beholden to my parents. 'Dziękuję ojcze' and 'grazie mamma' for having books haphazardly scattered around our home (more books in fact, as our neighbours liked to remark, than could be found in all the other houses around us put together). Thanks, too, for having encouraged my studies. And thanks, most of all, for moving from Nottingham to Manchester in December 1959.

III.

I have been extremely fortunate in my career as a scholar. Things have worked out even when they could easily have not. About the only thing that I knew when I applied to university was that I wanted to read Italian (thank you, Dante). I went to Hull because it had a reputation for radical politics, for having, at the time, the largest working-class student body of any university in the UK, and for putting on great gigs. I was going where I would feel comfortable. Academic considerations played no part in my decision. Yet, as I soon recognized, if, in 1969 Britain, one had an interest in things Italian, it would have been difficult to find a more conducive and intellectually invigorating environment than Hull's Department of Italian. I had as my teachers, interlocutors, and increasingly friends, some outstanding British Italianists. Suffice it to say that I was able to learn from John Barnes, Peter Brown, Judith Bryce, John Gatt-Rutter, Gwyn Griffith, Peter Hainsworth, June Salmons, John Woodhouse, and then, after John's departure to Oxford, from his namesake, Frank Woodhouse. I received a thorough and illuminating grounding in Italian literature, the history of the language, and Italian culture more generally, as well as some idea of their complex, interweaving connections. As had been the norm in Italian scholarship since the humanists, before passing through Vico, De Sanctis, and then Croce, Gramsci and beyond, and as largely continues to this day, the predominant approach, was loosely and flexibly historical (my father's early imprint was being intensified). This was coupled to an emphasis on close reading: a mix of New Criticism, stylistics, and a burgeoning awareness of structuralism. By the early to mid-1970s, some of us in Hull — my Single Honours in Italian was complemented by a five-term Subsidiary in American Literature — were reading and discussing what would come to be termed 'critical theory'. This wasn't an official part of the syllabus, not least because not everyone felt that such 'new' developments were relevant to the study of literature. I'm glad to have read Barthes and Metz, Jakobson and the often exhilarating pages of the early *Screen*, Goldmann and the 'Gramscian' Stuart Hall, Lukács and Bernard Williams, the early Eco and Pasolini *eretico*. There is no question that these demanding, at times startling, generally thought-provoking encounters have made me better responsive to the nuances of language and to the complexities of texts. To put it simply, they have helped me to read better. And as a scholar of literature, can one really ask for more? To this day, I take an interest in the kaleidoscopic approaches to understanding and interpreting texts that characterize contemporary literary and cultural studies. Given that I have been teaching courses in film and supervising Doctorates in Italian cinema since 1979, this is a professional obligation. In addition, I feel that, as a professor of literature, it is my responsibility to have an inkling of what my colleagues are doing and of what is happening in our field. Much of the work being done is fascinating and suggestive; a small part of it is obfuscatory and lacking that feel for history, for context, and for cultural minutiae towards which I have always been drawn. Indeed, one vital effect of my, if I'm generous, tangential relationship to 'critical theory' has been to confirm that what fundamentally interests me is analysing texts and textual traditions from a historicist and philological perspective. As ought to be apparent from some of the names listed above, I have tended to be drawn to theorists who have allowed a sense of history to inflect their thinking. I have always much preferred Foucault to Lacan, Benjamin to Derrida. And yet, overall, the impact of these great minds on my scholarship has been marginal, imperceptible, but undoubtedly present in ways that are difficult to pin down but which, even if no one else can discern them, I know are there.

I should like to make one thing clear. I do not think, never mind believe, that the way I study texts is somehow 'superior' to other forms of interpretation. In very simple terms, it's the manner of reading that suits me best; and I hope that what I have indicated about my heritage and formation explains why this is so. I've also been fortunate that generations of students, both undergraduate and graduate, have recognized some validity in the ways I have tried to discuss with them Italian literature, whether medieval or modern, and film. If I feel anything akin to pride about my academic career, it is that my classes have normally been oversubscribed and that I have successfully supervised a very high number of Doctoral students. To put it differently, it has been my students who, above all, have granted a degree of validation to my scholarship, especially since, as ought to become apparent in due course, I have long been conscious of the limitations of my way of reading.

For now, it's time to go back to 1973. On graduating, I was offered funding to study for a Doctorate in Oxford. I was supposed to prepare a critical edition of Jacopo Alighieri's commentary to the *Inferno* under the supervision of Cecil Grayson. I lasted a week. Oxford back then was not an environment in which I felt comfortable. Nor was I convinced that textual criticism was my metier. In my final year as an undergraduate, I had become fascinated by Kenelm Foster and Pat Boyde's commentary to Dante's lyric poetry and, in particular, by Pat's *Dante's Style in his Lyric Poetry*, which originally and suggestively fused medieval rhetoric and twentieth-century stylistics to provide a description and analysis of the character and development of the poet's style in his *rime*. Thus, in 1974, I returned to Hull: my naive aim to do something similar for the style of the *Commedia*. Despite the excellent supervision I received from John Barnes, my research wasn't really going anywhere, and I was extremely fortunate, on the basis of a couple of articles that I'd written (one jointly with John on Dante's *Montanina*), to be appointed to a lectureship in Aberdeen half-way through my second year. In Scotland, I continued to wrestle, mostly ineffectively, with my ever more slippery PhD topic. I did at least have the good sense to publish a few, mostly short, articles on questions largely unrelated to my thesis (Dante's imagery, Italo-Polish cultural relations, Montale, Dante's twentieth-century reception, and First-World-War literature), so that, in 1979, I became the Dantist, in John Scott's Australia-bound wake, at the University of Reading.

The Reading Department of Italian had a quasi-mythic status. Thanks to Gigi Meneghello's acumen, nous, and foresight, it had pioneered the study of Italian not as a staid pairing of language and literature, but, inspired by the Warburg Institute's approach to the Renaissance, as an organic fusion of history, history of the language, history of art, history of ideas, literature, and film. It was, to use the parlance that would start to be popular in the 1980s, an *avant-la-lettre* department of 'Italian studies' — a model for studying a foreign language that would increasingly become the norm in universities in the English-speaking world. Given my interests, I had come home. And I would stay at Reading for twenty-three years. I owe an incalculable debt to the invigorating, at times spiky, but always intellectually stirring and challenging life in the department, for many years the foremost centre for the study of Italian culture outside Italy. I worked with many outstanding colleagues. To list them is to demean them. As someone who has studied epic catalogues, I am all too aware of the hollow distortions of banalizing inventories. Dryly naming names would only belittle what I think of you, my friends, and the deep gratitude that I feel for the time we spent together. I also hope that you won't be offended if I briefly do say something about two of you. You've probably already guessed who they are. Giulio Lepschy, not just a great linguist but probably the best all-round Italianist of his generation, is the only person I would consider my *maestro* in the Italian sense of the term. Giulio has taught me to think rigorously and to write clearly and precisely; he has instilled in me the need to keep paring away at a problem until I am confident that what I'm left with is essential; and, most of all, he has convinced me of the absolute need to 'know things' — 'le cose bisogna saperle' — and hence to avoid *chiacchiere*. Thank you, Giulio, for your unstinting support and example. Chris Wagstaff — mercurial, brilliant, frustrating — thank you for always challenging what I did. Even when you were at your most irritatingly unreasonable, what you said and annotated was not without merit. To be an Italianist at Reading in the eighties and nineties was a privilege, even if a slightly equivocal one. You couldn't but do good work: the standards were set high and one's immediate 'referees' were demanding, knowledgable, and generously honest. But it was also tiring. At times, everything could become just a bit too edgy; and it would be dishonest to pretend that these tensions did not affect personal relations and what we were doing as academics. I was not unhappy to leave for Cambridge in 2002, where my colleagues in Italian were just as talented as those in Reading, but the communal atmosphere was more relaxed, more collegial, ultimately, I discovered, more conducive to reflection. And exactly the same is true of Italian at Notre Dame, where I have been since 2011. Indeed, it would be fair to say that I have completed most of my best work since leaving Reading; although it was

Reading that largely gave me the tools, the intellectual energy, and the know-how
to be able to recognize the need for this research, and then to do it.

IV.

So, what happened to my study of the style of the *Commedia*? Well, let me begin by
admitting that I have never been awarded a PhD. During my first years in Reading,
I kept trying to find ways to make my lists of metaphors, similes, repetitions, rhyme
words, all dutifully subdivided, critically meaningful. Yet, however I organized and
reorganized them, they were always dully uninteresting. They bore no ostensible
relationship to the *Commedia*'s formal complexity, to its lexical richness, never mind
to the breathtaking originality of how Dante used language — by then I had read
enough classical and medieval literature to be able to appreciate the fundamental
force and significance of his *novitas*. To put it bluntly, they offered no insight into
the extraordinary allure of Dante's poetry — that poetry that had enthralled me
back in Manchester, but which I was still failing to come close to understanding.
I could 'dismantle' Dante's tercets into some of their constituent parts; I could sort
these according to medieval rhetorical categories; and I could recognize that the
Commedia's formal make-up was quite unlike that of the *Aeneid*, of the Vulgate, of
the *Roman de la rose*, and of his own past as an author of lyric and prose. And yet,
there was something of all of them in his verses; as well as a lot more... The problem
was to find a way of bringing the various elements that I was amassing, as well as
the largely unformed intuitions that had started to accompany them, into some
sort of coherent 'whole' that not just was accessible to analysis (and, of course, was
worth analysing), but was also able to lead to some sort of explanatory hypothesis
as to why Dante had composed the *Commedia* in the manner that he had. I now
realize, as I peruse my publications of the early to mid-1980s, that I must have been
deeply disheartened: almost none deals directly with Dante. There is little doubt
that I was beginning to drift away from Dante, from the *Commedia*, and from being
a *dantista*.

I have always read a lot. I am also an efficient reader with a long and systematizing
memory. In order to help me comprehend rhetoric's position in the late-medieval
world, I read manuals of rhetoric (my copy of Faral is now held together by
rubber bands); scholastic commentaries (including those of the fourteenth-century
commentators on the *Commedia*, who would become a major research interest); and
scholars, from Ernst Curtius to Erich Auerbach, from Edgar De Bruyne to Henri
de Lubac, and from Gianfranco Contini to Beryl Smalley, as well as more recent
contributions by Judson Boyce Allen, James J. Murphy, Richard H. Rouse, Brian
Stock, and Winthrop Wetherbee, all of whom looked at medieval literature, and
especially at its structures, from broad and overarching perspectives. And something
finally clicked. And what clicked was really very straightforward. As I had no idea
either what Dante or what the Middle Ages understood by 'style', I was failing
to think about, and so to assess, the style of the *Commedia* in a manner that was
historically and philologically sensitive, namely, that had some connection to how
a medieval poet may have thought about what he was doing. Once I grasped this,

everything changed. In extremely reductive terms, my whole career as a scholar, certainly as a Dantist, is built on that intuition, or better, on the ways that I have drawn on it to guide my research. I had allowed myself to become trapped in a double cul-de-sac. On the one hand, for rather too long, I had been thinking of the *Commedia*'s style in too much of a vacuum: in dryly and abstracting formalist terms — the legacy, I suspect, of my readings in stylistics, structuralism, and semiotics. On the other, and like nearly every other literary medievalist, I had left unchallenged the truism that, by the early thirteenth century, if not actually long before then, 'literary theory [had] died or at least [had gone] underground'.[2] The Middle Ages was the epoch 'without criticism', just as, in post-Crocean Italian literary historiography, and equally misleadingly, the Quattrocento is designated 'il secolo senza poesia'.

Things fell into place; or better, I remembered that *stilus*, and what seemed to be related terms, such as *modus, maneria, figura*, kept cropping up in the medieval texts that I had been reading. That first essential realization was then very quickly followed by the concomitant and startling apprehension that, far from being 'dead', literary theory and criticism had been very much alive in the Middle Ages. Indeed, this could not but have been the case in a culture whose educational and religious systems were predicated on the interpretation of texts, both human and divine. Medieval textual reflection was thus pervasive, sophisticated, and determining. More importantly, I grasped that Dante's works were run through with what could only be termed literary criticism and theory, and that these elements appeared to have their roots in the critical discourses of his day. Such insights are manna for the historicist scholar. Even though, already in the late 1930s, Contini had remarked that 'una costante della personalità dantesca *è* questo perpetuo sopraggiungere della riflessione tecnica accanto alla poesia',[3] Dantists had largely failed to consider the consequences of his claim.[4] I thus found myself — I did say I was lucky — in a field that was basically unexplored and that I could begin to map and contour. I left behind, definitively, the futile attempt systematically and formalistically to describe the poet's style, and instead began to develop what would become one of my major research interests: the study of Dante's relationship to medieval literary theory and criticism and his highly original reworkings of both traditions. This is now a major area in Dante scholarship. However, back in the late 1980s, it was extremely

---

2   Alastair Minnis, *Medieval Theory of Authorship: Scholastic Literary Attitudes in the Later Middle Ages*, 2nd edn (Philadelphia: University of Pennsylvania Press, 2010), p. 3. Alastair's groundbreaking book came out in 1984 and the second edition in 1988. When I first read *Medieval Theory of Authorship, c.* 1986–87, beyond all that I learned from it, I was reassured that the new direction that my research on Dante had taken was not a personal anomaly. Alastair and I subsequently became friends, have collaborated, and continue to wonder how the Middle Ages, a culture where textual exegesis was 'everything', could have been so mischaracterized.

3   Gianfranco Contini, 'Introduzione alle Rime di Dante' [1939], in his *Un'idea di Dante* (Turin: Einaudi, 1976), pp. 3–20 (p. 4). For an assessment of the impact of this study on my work as a Dantist, see Zygmunt G. Barański, 'Dante *poeta* e *lector*: "poesia" e "riflessione tecnica" (con divagazioni sulla *Vita nova*)', in *Dante oggi*, vol. I, ed. by Roberto Antonelli, Annalisa Landolfi, and Adriana Punzi, special issue of *Critica del testo*, 14:i (2011), 81–110.

4   For a discussion of the slow appreciation among *dantisti* of Contini's groundbreaking contention, see below.

exciting to be almost alone in focusing on issues such as the poet's radical challenge to contemporary poetics; his original development of new exegetical forms and metaliterary discourses; his unconventional reutilization of standard critical notions and terminology (most notably the seemingly 'inappropriate' designation 'comedía' for his masterpiece); his re-interpretation of the classical canon; and his constant concern with self-legitimation and self-authorization not simply as the 'modern' vernacular *auctor* par excellence but also as a divinely inspired *scriba Dei*. Vitally, at least for me, I was beginning to sense that I was, at last, getting some sort of grip on the poet and his *œuvre*; and, in 1996, I published a set of revised and interconnected articles on *Dante critico* with the title '*Sole nuovo, luce nuova': saggi sul rinnovamento culturale in Dante* (Turin: Scriptorium, 1996). I have never really thought in terms of 'books' but always with reference to 'problems'; and I have largely dealt with these 'problems' singly, in article-length studies (some of quite considerable length). Later on, I would come to realize that, jointly, several of my discrete contributions might actually have a 'book-like' coherence. But, by then, I had moved on to some other new and riveting problem.

In some ways, even more important than my fortuitous stumbling across *Dante critico*, has been the lesson in scholarly scepticism that I learned. Ever since the mid-1980s, I have made it my purpose as a researcher to test the validity of the critical orthodoxies, the truisms both small and large, that delimit and sustain the areas within which I work. And such an attitude has proved both necessary and productive. In general, Dante studies is an unexpectedly 'conservative' field — I discuss some of the reasons for this below and in the present volume's opening chapter — and so it is teeming with accepted and (long) untested critical and historical tenets. I firmly believe that my best work as a Dantist has been powered by a pragmatic imperative to doubt, that has been accompanied by a handy aptitude to ask questions which *dantismo* has tended to pass over. For instance, as may be read in Chapter 8, simply to ask 'Why did Dante call a *canto* a "canto"?' can lead to some remarkable answers. In September 1993, I gave the commemorative lecture in Ravenna to mark the anniversary of Dante's death. The lecture attempted to answer the twinned questions 'Where did Dante go to school, and what were the educational institutions of late-thirteenth-century Florence?'. From these questions grew what is now increasingly termed the study of Dante's intellectual formation: how, where, when, and by what means did the poet come to know the things that he did, and, by extension, what the implications might be for his *œuvre* of what was an unsystematic, eclectic, and haphazard learning process. Indeed, and I hope that this does not sound too self-aggrandizing, it is not unreasonable to maintain that I markedly affected this area of study in the 1990s, and especially so after the publication of my 2000 book *Dante e i segni: saggi per una storia intellettuale di Dante Alighieri* (Naples: Liguori). After a bumpy start, the book was very positively received. Colleagues have generally agreed that it presents a better nuanced interpretation of the poet's intellectual development than that which had held sway for roughly a century in Dante studies. The prevailing view, before the book's appearance, was that the poet was primarily, if not overwhelmingly, influenced by rationalist, specifically Aristotelian traditions. *Dante e i segni*, by contrast, argues that, throughout his career, Dante was also significantly drawn to Scripturally-inflected symbolic and exegetical currents which placed considerable emphasis on faith, revelation, and divine inspiration. Rather than allow any single intellectual tendency or epistemology to control his thinking, the poet amalgamated different traditions into original syntheses, thereby evaluating their relative efficacy as forms of knowledge and enlightenment. Since the appearance of *Dante e i segni*, Dantists in Italy and especially in the English-speaking world have used its intuitions to help them to develop major studies and research projects on the nature of the poet's education and readings (especially in Florence in the 1280s and 1290s); on the character of his syncretism; on his fundamental debts to the Bible and its commentary tradition; on the profound theological imprint that marks his *œuvre*; on his ties to contemplative, liturgical, confessional, and affective traditions; and, therefore, on his status as a religious writer. I see myself working on these and related questions for the foreseeable future.

V.

I hope that I have neither a naive view of our relationship to the past nor a serenely optimistic appreciation of the hermeneutic possibilities of historicism and philology. Let me focus on a concrete example to illustrate my sense of the efficacy (or otherwise) of both methodologies with respect to an understanding of what has gone before — an example which ought also to tie off several of the issues already discussed.[5]

For rather too long, although the situation is slowly beginning to change, it has been the norm in Dante studies when addressing the issue of the poet's sources to pay scant attention to the complexities of the context in which Dante would have read or come to learn about other writers and thinkers, and this despite the fact that the medieval world of books was staggeringly amorphous and that its most obvious characteristic was precisely that reading was a highly mediated, haphazard, and often fragmentary activity. Instead, the standard position among *dantisti* has been to postulate an impossible direct, one-to-one relationship between, arguably, the supreme literary classic, Dante Alighieri, and another remarkable figure, such as Terence, whose writings, it is almost automatically assumed, the poet could not but have known (see Chapter 7). For someone like myself, who, at school in the 1960s, was taught English literature by a cadre of Cambridge-educated masters, this way of thinking about Dante-*lettore* recalls nothing as much as a variation on the Leavisite unmediated and timeless encounter between an intellectually exceptional and refined individual and a great author and his or her texts. It is as if a *grande* like Dante, the 'father of the Italian language' and *celui qui a lu tous les livres* could not but remain untouched by the niggling, messy realities of his culture: his presumed 'uniqueness' dependent on his somehow transcending the limitations — I was tempted to write the 'darkness' — of an environment where books were few,

5   I draw on Zygmunt G. Barański, '"With Such Vigilance! With Such Effort!" Studying Dante "Subjectively"', *Italian Culture*, 33 (2015), 55–69, for much of the present 'fragment'.

hard to come by, and the preserve of elites. Moreover, the attitude continues to predominate that the poet 'must have' read widely, especially if we today deem it 'necessary' for him to have read a particular text that we consider important. It is an attitude that is effectively captured in the recurring refrain in Dante scholarship, *Dante non poteva che conoscere...* and its variants — a refrain that is rather too often not accompanied by hard documentary evidence. *Ecco*: the insidiously pervasive, and not just in the popular imagination, Dante the 'solitary' genius, the creator of works without precedent, unfettered by the practical constraints holding down the rest of his contemporaries. Put in such stark and ironic terms, the anachronism of this mode of studying the poet's relationship to his literary and doctrinal sources is self-evident. In place of a historically nuanced idea of Dante *medievale*, we find an image of exceptionality — one that has its present-day roots in the nineteenth century — being uncritically introduced as the basic and controlling analytical matrix for studies of the poet's intellectual and artistic debts. To claim as much is not to suggest that the figure of the extraordinary individual was irrelevant to the Middle Ages. Quite the opposite, in fact. Medieval culture was more than capable of creating myths of *illustres viri*: it is enough to recall the *vitae* and the notion of *auctoritas*. Equally, it is not my intention to deny that, in all his major writings, Dante worked hard to fashion himself as both 'authoritative' and peerless. However, neither the medieval fascination with 'somma e altissima autoritade' (*Conv.* IV. 6. 5) nor the poet's subjective presentation of himself as special should lull us into a comfortable, unreflective acceptance of the view that to study Dante we need to treat him as a 'special' case, as somehow different from all other medieval readers when it came to his relationship with books and to his modes of reading. Of course, what distinguish Dante are the remarkable and original ways in which he bent his culture to his artistic and intellectual ambitions; and this despite the many obstacles that, in practice, he must have faced, as a relatively poorly educated *laicus*, in gaining access to and in coming to grips with the intricacies of that culture: a knotty problem, also largely neglected by generations of *dantisti*. Indeed, if we wish to appreciate how and why Dante is special, then we can best achieve this, I believe, by integrating him ever more effectively and accurately with what we are able, however partially, to reconstruct of his world, or better, of those facets of the Middle Ages that can reasonably be said to have touched him.

At the same time, we also need to be sensitive to the many impediments that prevent us from ever satisfactorily arriving at such an integration, beginning with our own subjectivity, as well as all the other subjectivities, whether communal or individual, namely, the cultural, intellectual, professional, and methodological assumptions, often left undetected and unacknowledged, that mar our efforts to achieve a measured appreciation of the past. Indeed, it is by unmasking such assumptions, and just as importantly, persuading others of their deleterious effects, that significant scholarly progress can be attained. Let me offer a magisterial example. Although, as I have suggested, the image of Dante the solitary genius rising above his time is deeply rooted in the study of his influences, that same image received a decisive rebuttal, and interestingly in a field not-too-distant from that of source studies. Contini's proposal in his 1939 Introduction to Dante's *Rime*, that I have already cited, was revolutionary. Instead of celebrating, as had been the norm since the nineteenth century, the ahistorical exceptionality of Dante's writings, Contini suggested that, in literary terms, these were the product of subtle and sustained reflection on medieval ideas about literature and its practices. The poet's works were exceptional thanks to their complex ties to the literary thinking and procedures of his time and not despite these, as was customarily implicit in earlier views. Although the notion of Dante as both *auctor* and *lector* is today a given in Dante scholarship, it took until the 1960s for Contini's insight even to begin to have some impact on a few other critics. I suspect that his proposals were just too disturbing: they challenged too many comfortable and cherished assumptions about Dante, too many established ways of reading, talking, and writing about the poet, to be readily accepted. And this is another problem that bedevils our work as Dantists: most colleagues, as I have also already adumbrated, are rather too cautiously conformist in their opinions, and far too frequently find it difficult to react positively and creatively to innovative, paradigm-changing research. In part, this is because studying Dante is hugely demanding. Not only are his texts extraordinarily complex but they also presuppose a quite considerable degree of familiarity with broad swathes of medieval history, culture, and thought. In order to pursue our own researches, we rely on fundamental fixed points, which we treat as somehow 'objectively' legitimate, and hence 'absolute', despite the 'subjectivity' of their origins, and feel uncomfortable when these are called into doubt since they are the foundations upon which we construct our own proposals. I was well aware of colleagues' uneasy irritation when *Dante e i segni* first appeared. As I noted, my re-evaluation of Dante's 'rationalist' roots and identity has now been widely accepted, at least in general terms. One might say it has become a new 'orthodoxy'. Thus, as I reconsider the work that I did in the 1990s from the vantage point of a further twenty or so years of research, I am regularly struck by its limitations, its provisionality, and, yes, its subjectivity. As I learn and understand more, I have also sought to submit my own earlier work to the same probing scepticism that I apply to the work of other scholars. Consequently, my recent research may in part be read as a revision and critique of my own earlier work. Hence, in this same spirit, I have rewritten, in some instances significantly, many of the chapters included in the present collection.

I have no doubt that Contini's insights into Dante as a quintessentially self-reflective writer capture something essential — I had to stop myself from writing 'objective' — about the poet. At the same time, it is also necessary to acknowledge that Contini's formulation was developed at the service of a distinctly subjective view of Dante's *rime*: one largely in opposition to Barbi's, that interpreted the poems as 'closed' formal structures whose points of reference were effectively, if not exclusively, those of the contemporary Romance lyric. Although the elaborately wrought literariness of the *rime* is extremely powerful, Contini's interpretation is reductive. It banalizes the poems, separating them from an array of other elements, from biography to history, and from philosophy to echoes of the 'schools of the religious' (*Conv.* II. 12. 7), that also characterize them. Contini was of course the emblematic *filologo*. However, even someone of his acute sensitivity to the obligations of linguistic and literary context when studying works of literature was limited by his subjectivity: most especially, by his artistic, namely 'expressionist', preferences and by his professional formation as a Romance philologist. We should never forget that even the most stringent *filologismo* is not a guarantee of objectivity. In a scholarly tradition such as that of Italian literary studies, in which philology is granted centre stage, it is vital not to ignore the subjectivity that inevitably accompanies the endeavours of the philologist; and it is vital precisely because there is a tendency to equate the 'philological' with the 'objective', thereby introducing that debilitating absolutism that should have no place in our research if we want scholarship to progress. In the end, it is the subjectivity of every critical, historical, and methodological proposal that permits us to call them into question, and hence to assert the intellectual prerogatives of our own subjectivity.

A couple of clarifications: first, my preceding comments are not to be taken as a ludic postmodern deconstruction of academic knowledge and scholarly practice. In fact, I have limited sympathy for what I judge to be, in some cases, an essentially frivolous, if not actually mischievous, and hence 'amoral' way of reading and relating to the past. And this would seem to be the appropriate place to note that it is striking how little success modern 'critical theory' has had in coming to grips with Dante. I have often thought about this, and do not have any answers for this failure, although I suspect that these need to be sought in the nature of Dante's texts and in the remarkable control that the poet managed to exercise over these: the force of the author's power countering the critic's efforts to assert her or his exegetical prerogatives. Thus, even when we try to read against the grain and highlight tensions and contradictions in his texts, the impression lingers that this is exactly what Dante wants us to do (see Chapter 17). I apologize for being so vague; however, these seem to be questions that, as early-twenty-first-century *dantisti*, we ought to be examining, especially if we want the study of Dante to intersect with contemporary critical-theoretical concerns. Second, my earlier reservations are even less an attack on the historicist contextualizing mode of reading the poet. As evidenced by my entire scholarly career, I remain convinced that this still offers an effective means of approaching and understanding Dante and his *œuvre*. At the same time, I also feel that, as *italianisti* — the problem goes well beyond the study of Dante — we are normally reluctant to assess critically the strengths and weaknesses of philology and historicism, and so to challenge their acquisitions. There is in fact a somewhat contradictory tendency both to fetishize such methods as the only ones proper for the study of literature, and to consider the archaeological uncovering of contextual information relevant to the understanding of a text as sufficient in itself.[6] There is thus something of a resistance to move from philological reconstruction to hermeneutics, from what is deemed to be 'objective' to what is clearly 'subjective' (although this last is a distinction which, as ought to be clear by now, is not one that I believe can easily be averred in the study of literature). Ultimately, I believe

6   This is a failing that is especially characteristic of scholarship done in Italy. Indeed, what primarily distinguishes scholars in the English-speaking world from those in Italy is the willingness of the former both to document and to interpret. Strangely, as far as I am concerned, this is deemed a flaw by some Italian colleagues.

that one of our fundamental responsibilities as scholars is to ask hard questions about the nature of the inter-relationship between authors, their works, and the contexts that shaped them, and, more significantly, to do our best to explain what the implications of such interconnections might be. To put it bluntly, we have a duty to interpret and not just to document; and, in interpreting, we must interrogate not just text and context, but also our own critical tools and how others have dealt with the same problems.[7]

VI.

I had earlier observed that I was especially grateful to my parents for having moved to Manchester in late 1959. And yes, Manchester *c'entra, e come*, in all this.

When asked, given my heritage, how I define myself, I explain curtly that I don't feel either Polish or Italian, never mind English or British. Instead, I assert, 'I'm Mancunian and United'. Mancs are a strange breed. We share a sense of our innate difference ('This is Manchester, we do things differently here'[8]), as well as a belief in our capacity to do things 'better' than others, especially if those others come from thirty or so miles west on the East Lancs Road, or from two hundred miles south along the M1 and M6, or from anywhere in fact. Ever since the eighteenth century, people, both insiders and outsiders, have remarked on the gutsy distinctiveness of Mancunian self-sufficiency and self-confidence. It is what has fostered the city's long and honourable history of radicalism and its everyday belligerence; its entrepreneurship and its energetic need to engage; its scientific inventiveness and its artistic creativity. And what unites all these activities, I like to imagine, is what is encapsulated in a phrase that resounds around Manchester and among Mancunians: 'That's bollocks'. Originally, I had thought provocatively (Mancunianly...) to use it as the title of this piece, before substituting it with Jeanette Winterson's — another Mancunian — more elegant formulation of the same underlying idea: 'It was a good place to be born. Manchester is in the south of the north of England. Its spirit has a contrariness in it — a south and north bound up together — at once untamed and unmetropolitan; at the same time, connected and worldly'.[9] 'That's bollocks' is the battle-cry that challenges what is trite, accepted, orthodox, or what others deem difficult and impossible — a challenge that is then trailed by the Mancunian-forged solution to the matter — and nothing is too banal or too complex to be left unquestioned. It was in Manchester that I learned to accept and appreciate my 'otherness', and to meld it with the city's 'contrariness'. It was Manchester that taught me to question and to test. It was Manchester that gave me the assurance to appreciate, develop, substantiate, and defend what that slightly neurotic, ceaselessly

---

7   I haven't forgotten about Petrarch and Boccaccio. At the same time, in my academic career, they play a largely subsidiary role. They are either spin-offs from my work on Dante or 'footnotes' to my studies of the poet.

8   The phrase is attributed to Tony Wilson, broadcaster, commentator, socialist, and of course backbone of the Manchester music scene, but it could have been uttered by any Manc.

9   Jeanette Winterson, *Why Be Happy When You Could Be Normal?* (New York: Grove Press, 2011), p. 13. Winterson's is a quintessentially Mancunian title.

twitchy probing brings to the surface. It was Manchester that crystallized and empowered what I had assimilated from my Italo-Polish heritage. In simple terms, I took on 'the Manchester habit'.[10]

VII.

It is one thing to acknowledge what I owe a city — even one that is more 'glorious', more 'vital', more 'romantic', more 'adventurous' than Athens, Paris, Cairo, and Bruges.[11] It is of a quite different order of complication to record properly the deep debts that I owe to my family and friends, some of whom have already made an appearance in these pages, and do so again, together with others so far unnamed, in the remainder of the book. I am who I am thanks to you.

Maggie, Anna, and Ed, to articulate the capillary intricacies of our life together is so overwhelming that anything I might say will be an ugly distortion. I think — a sad case of *déformation professionnelle* — of Dante struggling to describe Beatrice's transcendental beauty on the brink of the Empyrean:

> Da questo passo vinto mi concedo
> più che già mai da punto di suo tema
> soprato fosse comico o tragedo. (*Par.* xxx. 22–24)

That quotation and a simple 'Thank you' will need to suffice.

Bol and Jajo, best friends and arch Mancs, and who, more than anyone, have kept me honest as an academic. There's little that we haven't done together, but the most meaningful, of course, is more than fifty years of following United. It's a run, now that Ed and Joe have joined us, that we need to keep going...

The friends to whom this collection is dedicated span my life from 1960s Manchester to the present day, passing especially through Hull and Reading, and with the odd stop-off in Melbourne. We have known each other for decades. Three are United fans, and they can stand emblematically for all the match-going United fans that I have known and know; though a heartfelt and unique thanks must go to Ravi, from Košice to Cape Town, from Anfield to Yeovil, from Ann Arbor to... The majority are Chelsea supporters. We hardcore fans, whatever team we may support, understand and appreciate each other and our need to be there. These are the people that I go to the pub with to talk football, music, politics; to reminisce; to share problems and celebrate achievements; to grieve and to laugh. Our families are close. Only three — all scientists — are academics (one now 'lapsed'), while

---

10   'For Manchester is the place where people do things. || It is good to talk about doing things, but better still to do them. [...] "Don't talk about what you are going to do — do it." That is the Manchester habit. And in the past through the manifestation of this quality the word Manchester became a synonym for energy and freedom, and the right to do and to think without shackles'. This assessment was made by a Londoner, Sir Edward Abbott Parry, who was Judge of Manchester County Court, 1894–1911. The passage comes from his *What the Judge Saw Being Twenty-five Years in Manchester by One Who Has Done It* (London: Smith, Elder & Co, 1912), pp. 311–12.

11   Gerald Cumberland (pseudonym for Charles Frederick Kenyon), *Set Down in Malice: A Book of Reminiscences* (New York: Brentano's, 1919), pp. 153–54. The association with Athens may also be found in Benjamin Disraeli, *Coningsby* [1844] (London: J. M. Dent & Sons Ltd, 1911), p. 127.

several left school in their mid-teens. Spending time with you, my friends, is vital. Indeed, in many ways, it is more important for my scholarly work than the sound advice of experts in my field. Thanks to you I have an uncluttered vantage point from which to reflect on my doings as an intellectual. Thanks to you I am able to place a healthy distance between myself and the at times petty, narcissistic, and inward-looking world of academe.

I have of course benefitted much from my academic friendships. The essays collected here have been improved thanks to the comments, suggestions, and corrections of Ted Cachey, Glauco Cambon, Ambrogio Camozzi, George Corbett, Enrico Fenzi, Simon Gilson, Unn Falkeid, Peter Hainsworth, Claire Honess, Amilcare Iannucci, Daniela La Penna, Giulio and Laura Lepschy, Giuseppe Ledda, Martin McLaughlin, Giuseppe Mazzotta, Christian Moevs, Vittorio Montemaggi, Paola Nasti, Emilio Pasquini, Lino Pertile, Michelangelo Picone, Brian Richardson, Matthew Treherne, Jon Usher, Shirley Vinall, and Chris Wagstaff.

Claire, Lino, Paola, Simon, and Ted, a special thanks for having been my privileged interlocutors and collaborators.

More than any colleague, Maggie has taught me to write lucidly and accessibly.

I'm profoundly grateful to Susan Harrow for having invited me to contribute to 'Selected Essays', thereby prodding me to think how my essays might fit together, and allowing me to write about things that would have remained unwritten.

For being involved with all aspects of this volume's coming-into-being, I'm deeply indebted to the indefatigable Graham Nelson, vastly more than a general editor.

This collection has also benefitted from the sensitive translating skills both of Elisabetta Drudi, who disentangled and rendered into English occasionally quasi-intractable passages of medieval Latin, and of Demetrio Yocum, who transformed my attempts at writing academic Italian into acceptable English. Finally, I'm very pleased to express my warmest gratitude to the Institute for Scholarship in the Liberal Arts at the University of Notre Dame, and especially to its Director, my colleague in French, Alison Rice, for its generous financial support towards the costs of the translations.

The previous paragraph was meant conventionally and staidly to close this Introduction. As I was typing my acknowledgement of ISLA's consideration, our daughter Anna called from London to tell Maggie and me that she and Tony had decided to marry. To close with such joyous news seems entirely apt given the tenor of this piece.[12]

Zyg Barański
Reading, Chicago, and the CrossCountry train to Manchester
December 2018–January 2019

---

12   I should like to thank Anna Barański, Edward Barański, Henryk Barański (Jajo), Lilli Barański, Maggie Barański, Marek Barański (Bol), Ted Cachey, Simon Gilson, Susan Harrow, Claire Honess, Tony Marsden, Graham Nelson, and Ravi Doorgachurn for their comments on an earlier version of this Introduction.

PART I

Debating Doctrine

CHAPTER 1

On Dante's Trail:
From 1295 to 2018

1. Historicizing Dante and *dantismo*

Dante today, at least in scholarly terms, appears as an arresting, stately, and somewhat foreboding presence.[1] An effective comparison may be drawn between our academically hewn prodigy and those post-Unification effigies of the poet that dominate the public spaces of various Italian cities, merging patriotic zeal with the desire to commemorate the 600th anniversary of his birth. It is enough to recall probably the most famous such monument, the statue which, since 1865, has mainly stood in Florence's Piazza Santa Croce, the work of the Ravennate sculptor Enrico Pazzi.[2] Head wreathed in a laurel crown and firmly grasping the *Commedia* in his right hand, Dante looms pensive and somewhat scornful as he gazes into the distance ignoring his surroundings, left arm supporting a long swathing mantle. Chiselled out of white Carrara marble, the statue has a clearly delineated and imposingly solid monumentality that both fascinates and daunts. We are faced with a Dante who appears not just fixed but also set apart, and hence difficult to approach. Not dissimilarly, the Dante that now confronts us as scholars looks like an intimidating affirmation of permanency, or rather and paradoxically, of permanencies. The *sommo poeta* may not be elevated, as in the past, on a plinth of patriotic symbols as in Piazza Santa Croce; instead his canonicity is now underpinned by an irresistible

1   This essay was first given as one of the keynote addresses at the Society for Italian Studies Biennial Conference held at the University of Oxford from 28 to 30 September 2015. In the text that appeared in *Italian Studies*, which was somewhat closer to the original oral address than the present version which, as far as possible, I have tried to harmonize with the stylistic register of the book as a whole, I tried to be economical when listing secondary sources. Given that this chapter now serves to frame and contextualize a number of the issues explored in the current volume, while also establishing important elements of its overall approach, I deemed it appropriate to augment the references to Dante scholarship.

2   See Silvia Paccassoni, 'L'impresa di Enrico Pazzi "statuario": un monumento per Santa Croce', *Romagna Arte e Storia*, 25:74 (2005), 53–62; Thies Schulze, *Dante Alighieri als nationales Symbol Italiens (1793–1915)* (Tübingen: Niemeyer, 2005); Bruno Tobia, 'La statuaria dantesca nell'Italia liberale: tradizione, identità e culto nazionale', in *Mélanges de l'École Française de Rome. Italie et Méditerranée*, 109:1 (1997), 75–87; *Dante vittorioso: il mito di Dante nell'Ottocento*, ed. by Eugenia Querci (Turin: Allemandi & C., 2011); *Le bandiere di Dante: l'inaugurazione del monumento a Dante in Firenze Capitale*, ed. by Laura Cirri and others (Pisa: Edizioni Il campano, 2014).

and unruly mass of exegesis stretching back to the fourteenth century that, in recent years, has grown faster than ever: works of reference; an extensive assortment of annotated and critical editions that, like the *Convivio*, overwhelm the text they are supposed to elucidate; myriad collections of *letture*; a fertile flourishing of websites; and tens of thousands of books and articles on every conceivable topic and detail of his *œuvre*. Unsurprisingly, one major effect of scholars seeking ways to orient themselves amidst this bibliographic whirl has been the rise and consolidation of deeply engrained critical orthodoxies. In addition, the field of Dante studies has become increasingly fragmented as particular orthodoxies have become the preserve of distinct academic 'schools', national traditions, and interest groups that confidently affirm the cogency of their respective positions, while, not infrequently, failing to engage with the work of those who might challenge their views. Finally, exacerbating yet further the lack of a reliable critical compass, nearly all the 'Dantes' — what I earlier termed 'permanencies' — that have emerged give the impression of having valid credentials, backed up as they are by substantial and seemingly authoritative scholarship.[3]

This is not an ideal state of affairs. Indeed, since the late 1980s, various efforts, albeit with limited success, have been and continue to be made to address this fraught situation.[4] The remainder of this chapter could be given over to explaining why contemporary *dantismo* finds itself in some difficulty: national and 'campanilistic' prickliness, academic politicking, scholarly formation and lineage, linguistic deficiencies, individual ambition, the reluctance to question the contributions of leading figures, innate conservatism and hence an unwillingness to challenge prevailing attitudes, outside interference, and, perhaps most significantly, that overpowering, debilitating accumulation of scholarship that can serve as a brake as academics endeavour to move their teaching and research forward.[5] In what follows, while continuing to touch on aspects of present-day *dantismo*, my principal

---

3   What I am describing are broad trends. For many years, various individual scholars, especially in the United Kingdom and Ireland, have taken forward original research initiatives that manage to steer successfully between different critical orthodoxies and the *mare magnum* of Dante criticism.

4   Two such notable initiatives, tellingly both now defunct, were the *Lectura Dantis Virginiana* bravely and polemically launched by Tibor Wlassics and the more sedate and ecumenical International Dante Seminar.

5   I very much hope that my observations are not read as the jeremiads of a senior colleague at the end of his career. In truth, I am anything but alone in being troubled about the shape of modern Dante studies. In a valuable and insightful essay, which shares several important points of contact with the present article, Albert Russell Ascoli writes 'that we have reached a difficult turning point in our collective researches, at which we should examine closely some of the key assumptions that have governed the posing and exploration of such questions': 'Reading Dante's Readings: What? When? Where? How?', in *Dante and Heterodoxy: The Temptations of 13th Century Radical Thought*, ed. by Maria Luisa Ardizzone (Newcastle upon Tyne: Cambridge Scholars Publishing, 2014), pp. 126–44 (p. 127). Although Ascoli is specifically referring to the question of Dante's orthodoxy and unorthodoxy, a problem which continues to be studied with a lack of adequate attention to the medieval context, his discussion in fact ranges widely across the present condition of Dante studies. For critiques of the manner in which the poet's heterodoxy (or otherwise) has been studied, see Chapter 3; and Luca Bianchi, 'L'averroismo di Dante: qualche osservazione critica', *Le tre corone*, 2 (2015), 71–109.

aim is to offer, even if not without the occasional detour, some basic, and I hope not entirely unoriginal, observations on a defining moment in Dante's personal, poetic, and intellectual development, while at the same time using the discussion of the poet's circumstances *c.* 1295, and of the ways in which the question of Dante's intellectual formation has generally been examined, to conclude by suggesting a few ways in which the critical deadlock affecting Dante studies might begin to be eased, especially as what I plan to discuss touches on matters that underpin our subject.

Pazzi's statue can continue to serve for a while longer as an instructive point of reference. At first sight, the Dante represented seems to embody several familiar features that guarantee and affirm his formidable presence. Yet, in reality, these elements are either incorrect or at best open to question. Dante was never crowned, although, already during his lifetime, there were those, such as Giovanni del Virgilio, who supported his laureation (*Ecl.* 1. 35–40); he almost certainly never had the satisfaction of holding in his hands the finished *Commedia*, since it was his son Jacopo who likely prepared the complete copy of the poem after his father's death; and the idea that he was disdainful and self-absorbed is a commonplace of early accounts of his temperament that conforms to standard classical and medieval notions regarding the mind-set of great intellects.[6] Even the well-known physiognomy — aquiline nose, prominent jaw, long face — come from Boccaccio who never actually saw his hero: 'Il suo volto fu lungo, e il naso aquilino [...], le mascelle grandi [...] e sempre nella faccia malinconico e pensoso'.[7] The Dante up to whom we raise our eyes in Piazza Santa Croce is a fiction — one, more specifically, that, while drawing on long-established iconographic details associated with the poet's representation, chimes well with the patriotic aspirations of Risorgimento intellectuals and the civic sensibilities of many Florentines, whose city a few months earlier had become the new nation's capital. Contextualized, the statue is transformed into something very different from what it first seemed. It is an illusion of solidity. Rather than consolidating the historical Dante and his achievements, the sculpture points to the obfuscating qualities of his canonization, and in particular to the obstacles that stand in the way of the academic study of the poet and his writings. Furthermore, the key role that Boccaccio's *vita* plays in transmitting information about Dante raises questions about the nature and reliability of the documentary evidence relating to the poet that has survived.

Remembering the points that I have just made about the vehicle of my comparison, I should like to revisit its tenor, namely, the part which I am somewhat keener to illustrate and examine: the Dante critical tradition, and especially the condition —

---

6   On Dante's haughtiness, see the examples listed in Simon Gilson, *Dante and Renaissance Florence* (Cambridge: Cambridge University Press, 2005), p. 248. On the tradition of the *vitae*, see at least Huygens; Johannes Bartuschat, *Les 'Vies' de Dante, Pétrarque et Boccace en Italie (XIV–XV siècles)* (Ravenna: Longo, 2007), pp. 13–29; Giuseppe Billanovich, 'La leggenda dantesca del Boccaccio: dalla lettera di Ilaro al *Trattatello in laude di Dante*', *Studi danteschi*, 28 (1949), 45–144; Margarita Egan, 'Commentary, *vita poetae*, *vida*: Latin and the Old Provençal "Lives of Poets"', *Romance Philology*, 37 (1983–84), 36–48; *Creative Lives in Classical Antiquity: Poets, Artists and Biography*, ed. by Richard Fletcher and Johanna Haninck (Cambridge: Cambridge University Press, 2016).

7   Giovanni Boccaccio, *Trattatello in laude di Dante Alighieri*, ed. by Pier Giorgio Ricci (Milan: Mondadori, 2002), red. I, 112 (p. 31).

at least as I perceive it — of present-day *dantismo*. The issue regarding this on which I want mainly to focus is made up of two closely related elements: first, the extent to which scholars have shown themselves sensitive to the nature of the sources on which our knowledge of Dante and our interpretations of his works is based, and in particular how significant and valuable these might actually be; and second, the degree to which our critical assumptions and the manner in which we utilize these sources can be said to be conditioned by 'extraneous' interference. Before I proceed, it goes without saying that I do not believe in an 'untainted' historicism able to negotiate unproblematically with the past — what in Italy not uncommonly goes under the name of *filologia*. Historically inflected research, analysis, and interpretation inescapably involves a mediated and, ultimately, an anachronistic act of reconstruction; and I say this as someone who essentially has spent the whole of his academic career working within this one paradigm. The problem is whether and how far we, as *filologi* or historicists, are willing to acknowledge the limitations of our approach and the partiality of our scholarship.

2. Sources

Historically modulated scholarship is able to draw on four main types of antique source that directly relate to Dante and his works; and the perspective from which I am discussing the poet, his career, and his artistic and intellectual achievements brings together the biographical and the textual, while endeavouring to set each aspect and their relationship within a historically attentive and critically informed framework. The four sources are: historical documents that mention the poet and members of his family; Dante's self-presentations and self-exegesis; contemporary and near-contemporary texts that introduce, discuss, and elucidate the man and his *œuvre*; and finally, of course, Dante's writings. The efficacy and value of each category as documentary evidence is complex and problematic, although it would not be unfair to state that Dantists do not normally acknowledge this fact. Furthermore, the recourse that has often been made to this evidence is disappointing.

I shall briskly deal with each group in turn. Few documents concerning Dante have survived, not least because both the Alighieris and the poet himself were minor players in the world of late-medieval Italy. Most of the documents relate to financial, economic, and other practical matters, such as Dante's betrothal to Gemma Donati, while others are connected to his political activities, most notably his contributions to formal debates and decision-making, as well as official declarations that have some bearing on his banishment.[8] What is obvious is that the surviving documents do not account for large swathes of his life (for instance, most of his movements during his exile) and, significantly, cast no light on his education

---

8   See principally Renato Piattoli, *Codice diplomatico dantesco* (Florence: Gonelli, 1940). On this edition and Piattoli's subsequent four *Aggiunte*, see Teresa De Robertis and Laura Regnicoli, 'Lo stato dei lavori sul Codice diplomatico dantesco', in *Dante attraverso i documenti. 1. Famiglia e patrimonio (secolo XII–1300 circa)*, ed. by Giuliano Milani and Antonio Montefusco, special issue of *Reti medievali rivista*, 15:2 (2014), 189–201. Now see also the excellent *Codice diplomatico dantesco*, ed. by Teresa De Robertis and others (Rome: Salerno, 2016).

and on his intellectual formation more generally — issues that dominate much of what follows. As might be expected, Dantists have used the documents in their accounts of his life — something to which I shall return shortly — and to elucidate passages in his writings. In both instances, and this is important, the documents have been largely subordinated either to preconceived schemas regarding Dante's biography or to the claims the poet makes about himself in his writings. What has not normally been done is for the documents to be contextualized and evaluated in themselves before they are put in contact with other possible sources of information. For instance, in light of Dante's customary high moral tone, his fulminating attacks on all sorts of venality, his impassioned self-defence as an innocent man falsely accused, and his grotequely dismissive treatment of the sin of barratry, it has long been the standard view that the accusation of political corruption, which was the official reason for his banishment, was a groundless accusation trumped up by his political enemies. Very recently, however, and reviving seminal research completed around a century ago,[9] it has been demonstrated, convincingly in my view, that such a narrowly Dante-centric reaction to the *bando* is almost certainly distorting, if not quite plainly wrong: it decontextualizes the charges, the legal process, and the realities of political life and office in Duecento Florence.[10] The time has come to recognize, and most *dantisti* bridle at the idea, that Dante the politician may not have been as virtuous as he himself later claimed, and thus to accept the consequences of this when we interpret his moralizing and, more generally, read his works.

The most obvious implication that arises from the example just cited, and one that conveniently leads me to the second type of source, is the need to question the trustworthiness of what Dante writes about himself. In stark contrast to the paucity of independent documentary evidence relating to the poet, his writings are chock-full of details about himself. Indeed, Dante rarely desists from speaking about himself, as he carefully constructs self-portraits that are meant to present him in authoritative and exemplary guises, that furthermore conform to the overarching logic of the texts in which they appear. The complex cultural, ideological, and literary operation underpinning Dante's obsessive autobiographism ought to serve as the key point of reference when estimating what the poet has decided to reveal about himself. Yet, such an approach is not especially common in Dante studies. Scholars rather too often prefer to accept as factual what Dante tells us, not just about himself but also about other historical matters, especially if a revelation can be adapted to support a cherished interpretation. In addition, with one or two noteworthy exceptions, biographers of the poet uncritically accept his personal tidbits in order to help them construct and pad out their narratives, thereby introducing a troubling degree of fictionality into their accounts of Dante's life.[11]

---

9   See Robert Davidsohn, *Storia di Firenze. III. Le ultime lotte contro l'Impero* (Florence: Sansoni, 1960; original ed. 1912), pp. 274–94 & 312–23; Bernardino Barbadoro, 'La condanna di Dante e le fazioni politiche del suo tempo', *Studi danteschi*, 2 (1920), 5–74, and 'La condanna di Dante e la difesa di Firenze guelfa', *Studi danteschi*, 8 (1924), 111–27.

10   See Giuliano Milani, 'Appunti per una riconsiderazione del bando di Dante', *Bollettino di italianistica*, 8:2 (2011), 42–70.

11   For noteworthy exceptions, see Giorgio Inglese, *Vita di Dante: una biografia possibile* (Rome:

In reality, extreme care needs to be exercised when assessing the truth-content of his self-disclosures, as the ensuing example ought to illuminate.

Since my aim is to offer a contribution, however fleeting, on the vexed question of the poet's career in the aftermath of completing the *Vita nova*, a time which, already in the *libello*, is presented as dedicated to study and to discovering new artistic solutions — 'apparve a me una mirabile visione, ne la quale io vidi cose che mi fecero proporre di non dire più di questa benedetta infino a tanto che io potesse più degnamente trattare di lei. E di venire a ciò io studio quanto posso' (XLII. 1–2) — I would like to linger briefly on Beatrice's assessment in the Earthly Paradise of roughly this same moment in her wayward lover's life:

> 'Perché conoschi', disse, 'quella scuola
> c' hai seguitata, e veggi sua dottrina
> come può seguitar la mia parola;
>   e veggi vostra via da la divina
> distar cotanto, quanto si discorda
> da terra il ciel che più alto festina'. (*Purg.* XXXIII. 85–90)

Beatrice is adamant that, rather than aiding the pilgrim to celebrate her in new ways, his 'studies' in the 1290s led him badly astray. The nature of this *traviamento* has long fascinated the poet's readers. In order to fix its details, scholars begin by merging the historical Dante with his fictional namesake. As a result, Beatrice's charge appears to offer unambiguous evidence that, before composing the *Commedia*, there had been a period in the poet's life when he had been enthralled by the intellectually unorthodox, which he was now recanting. Yet, despite the sinful gravity of the intellectual lapse, what does Dante actually tell us about it? Very little indeed. Beatrice reveals that he had adhered to an intellectual current ('scuola') whose teaching ('dottrina') and method ('via') were both different from and at odds with her 'word' and the 'divine'. It is clear, therefore, that, given the allusiveness of Beatrice's description of the errant 'scuola' and the complexity of the intellectual world in the late Middle Ages, we need to move with caution when trying to establish the possible identity of the ideological current that had led Dante-*personaggio* astray in the 1290s. Yet, it is a commonplace confidently to assert that the poet is alluding to his extensive philosophical studies, in particular to his fascination with Aristotle and other rationalist currents, most notably with 'Averroistic' positions that encouraged him to accept that human reason was self-sufficient. This conclusion is troubling for all sorts of reasons. For instance, historians of ideas have definitively demonstrated that, for a long time now, Dantists have been mistaken in their use of the term 'Averroism', not to mention the claims they make about the standing of Averroes in medieval culture.[12] Just as troubling is the manner in

Carocci, 2015); Lino Pertile, 'Life', in *Dante in Context*, ed. by Zygmunt G. Barański and Lino Pertile (Cambridge: Cambridge University Press, 2015), pp. 461–74.

12   See in particular Bianchi, 'L'averroismo di Dante', and '"Ultima perfezione" e "ultima felicitade": ancora su Dante e l'averroismo', in *Edizioni, traduzioni e tradizioni filosofiche (secoli XII–XVI)*, ed. by Luca Bianchi and others, 2 vols (Rome: Arachne, 2018), I, 315–28. See also Angelo M. Mangini, 'Guido, Averroè e il "granchio" di Platone: considerazioni sull'averroismo in Cavalcanti e in Bruno Nardi', in *'Il mondo errante': Dante tra letteratura, eresia e storia*, ed. by Marco Veglia and

which a historical person and a literary character are treated as if they were one and the same entity. It is at the very least perplexing that scholars of literature should confuse life and art so blithely. In any case, the nature of the relationship between Dante Alighieri and Dante-*personaggio*, and hence the nature and extent of any possible biographism in the *Commedia*, is far from having been satisfactorily established. In narrative terms, that the protagonist should have sinned intellectually certainly chimes with the overriding logic of the story of his past behaviour that emerges in the poem. Whether, during the 1290s or at some other time, Dante Alighieri, too, had behaved like his character is not something, I believe, that can be straightforwardly maintained on the basis of a poetic declaration. Nonetheless, most Dantists would affirm that, thanks to the *Convivio*, evidence of such intellectual erring is available; and so pilgrim and poet are necessarily one. Without going into the question whether the *Convivio* can be read as 'unorthodox', 'rationalist', or 'Aristotelian', even accepting the biographism of the *Commedia*, the 'quasi comento' (*Conv.* I. 3. 2) is not narratively germane to the pilgrim, since, at the time of his great otherworldly adventure, the *Convivio* had not yet been written. It thus follows that the 'disposizione' (I. I. 15) cannot play a role in the events that occurred in the decade after her death to which Beatrice refers.[13] Furthermore, as the manuscript evidence confirms — and this should probably be deemed to offer a fifth antique documentary source — , it is almost certain that Dante had no intention of making the *Convivio* public, thereby, raising extremely serious questions regarding how it might be used in relation to the *Commedia*.[14] Substantial difficulties, it is fair to say, affect and delimit the presentation of the 'scuola' in *Purgatorio* XXXIII. It is thus probably impossible to be precise about the complexion of the pilgrim's *traviamento*, never mind that of the poet, that is if evidence from the canto can actually be used as the basis for laying charges of heterodoxy against him — something which I very seriously doubt. Indeed, as we shall see, what little evidence we have for Dante's intellectual interests in the 1290s suggests a very different state of affairs — evidence, furthermore, that raises stimulating questions about how we might draw on the *Convivio* to help us understand the poet's doctrinal formation in the years immediately preceding his exile.

The Dante *vitae*, a key component of the third category of documentary source, provide almost no help as regards either his education in general or his intellectual activities during the 1290s in particular. Following Giovanni Villani and Boccaccio,

others (Spoleto: Fondazione Centro italiano di studi sull'alto Medioevo, 2013), pp. 243–56.

13   See Lino Pertile, 'Dante's *Comedy* beyond the Stilnovo', *Lectura Dantis Virginiana*, 13 (1993), 47–77.

14   See Luca Azzetta,'La tradizione del *Convivio* negli antichi commenti alla *Commedia*: Andrea Lancia, l'"Ottimo commento" e Pietro Alighieri', *Rivista di studi danteschi*, 5 (2005), 3–34, and 'Il *Convivio* e i suoi più antichi lettori', *Testo*, 61–62 (2011), 225–38; Saverio Bellomo, *Filologia e critica dantesca*, 2nd edn (Brescia: La scuola, 2012), pp. 110–18; Claudio Ciociola, 'Dante', in *Storia della letteratura italiana. X. La tradizione dei testi*, ed. by Enrico Malato (Rome: Salerno, 2001), pp. 137–99 (pp. 157–61); Guglielmo Gorni, 'Appunti sulla tradizione del *Convivio*: a proposito dell'archetipo e dell'originale dell'opera', *Studi di filologia italiana*, 55 (1997), 239–51; Andrea Mazzucchi, 'Per una nuova edizione commentata del *Convivio*', in *Leggere Dante oggi*, ed. by Enrico Malato and Andrea Mazzucchi (Rome: Salerno, 2012), pp. 81–107 (pp. 82–100).

the early biographers and commentators make grandiose but unsubstantiated claims about the poet's intellectual formation whose main scope is not historical accuracy but the desire to transform Dante into an outstanding 'modern' *sapiens*, the equal, if not the superior, of the great thinkers and poets of the past. Villani declares: 'e andossene [after his *sbandimento*] a lo Studio di Bologna e poi a Parigi, e in più parti del mondo. Questi fue grande letterato quasi in ogni scienza, tutto fosse laico; fue sommo poeta e filosafo';[15] while Boccaccio is even more exaggeratedly celebratory:

> E così come in varie etadi varie scienze furono da lui conosciute studiando, così in varii studii sotto varii dottori le comprese.
>
> Egli li primi inizii [...] prese nella propria patria, e di quella, sì come a luogo più fertile di tal cibo, n'andò a Bologna; e già vicino alla sua vecchiezza andò a Parigi, dove, con tanta gloria di sé, disputando, più volte mostrò l'altezza del suo ingegno, che ancora, narrandosi, se ne meravigliano gli uditori. E di tanti e sì fatti studii non ingiustamente meritò altissimi titoli: perciò che alcuni il chiamarono sempre 'poeta', altri 'filosofo', e molti 'teologo', mentre visse. (red. I. 24–25; pp. 9–10)

It is not difficult to appreciate why both writers should want to associate Dante with two of the major universities of the time and, in Boccaccio's case, to present him as close to the *doctores*, the professional intellectuals of his day.[16] Nonetheless, the reality, as Villani lets slip when he terms him a 'laico' — in fact, the 'maggior laico della nostra letteratura'[17] — namely someone without much formal education,[18] is that the poet almost certainly had little schooling, a crucial fact that brings to the forefront the issue that is at the core of my chapter, namely, how, when, and by what means did Dante acquire the doctrinal, literary, and cultural knowledge that is unquestionably evident in his writings.[19] In general, Dantists have tended to accept uncritically the indications of the *vitae*, especially as they much prefer, in harmony with Boccaccio, to think of the poet as a well-educated and widely read genius — a position that demonstrates little appreciation either of contemporary educational structures or of the messy, fragmentary, and unpredicatable ways in

---

15   Giovanni Villani, *Nuova cronica*, ed. by Giuseppe Porta, 3 vols (Parma: Fondazione Pietro Bembo, 1991), IX. 136 (I, 337).

16   On the myth of Dante's visit to Paris, see Francesco Longo, 'Il viaggio di Dante a Parigi: un mito biografico', *Studi (e testi) italiani*, 18 (2006), 31–77. For an insightful analysis of this passage, see Lorenzo Dell'Oso, 'Per la formazione intellettuale di Dante: i cataloghi librari, le tracce testuali, il *Trattatello* di Boccaccio', *Le tre corone*, 4 (2017), 129–61 (pp. 156–57).

17   Carlo Dionisotti, 'Chierici e laici', in his *Geografia e storia della letteratura italiana*, 11th edn (Turin: Einaudi, 2011), pp. 55–88 (p. 58).

18   See Ruedi Imbach, *Dante, la philosophie et les laïcs* (Fribourg: Éditions Universitaires; Paris: Éditions du Cerf, 1996). On the implications of Dante's status as a *laicus* and on ways in which late-medieval Florentine lay culture might be reconstructed, see Dell'Oso, whose study is deeply indebted to Armando Antonelli's research into the archives of medieval cities and his investigations of lay culture in the communes. See also Luca Lombardo, ' "Ed imaginava lei fatta come una donna gentile": Boezio, Brunetto Latini e la prima formazione intellettuale di Dante', *Le tre corone*, 5 (2018), 39–71.

19   See Andrea A. Robiglio, 'Philosophy and Theology', in Barański and Pertile, pp. 137–58 (p. 143).

which knowledge was transmitted in the Middle Ages.[20] I shall return to these latter problems too in due course. For the moment, I would like to say something more about the ways in which scholars have turned to the early lives. As with the historical documents and the annotations of the Trecento commentators of the *Commedia*, the information contained in the *vitae* has been used uncritically to bolster Dante's self-serving assertions and to support a priori critical positions. Despite excellent research that has demonstrated the underlying ideological premises that structure the biographies — premises that cannot but introduce serious doubts about the lives' reliability, their limitations as 'objective' documents continue to be ignored.[21] Indeed, it is not unusual for their veracity to be maintained on the flimsy basis of a *vita*'s antiquity and of whether or not a particular detail is mentioned elsewhere. Nevertheless, as with Villani's 'laico', there is valuable information in the lives, although this needs to be approached not just with care and integrated with other materials, but also on occasion by being read flexibly. For instance, the myth of the quasi-miraculous discovery of the closing cantos of the *Paradiso* may conceal a hint of the late completion of the third canticle and of the dismembered state of the poem at the time of Dante's death.

By now the question might fairly be asked whether my aim is to propose that it may not actually be possible to make any reasonably dependable claims about Dante's intellectual formation. This is not in fact what I believe. My view rather is that the ways in which this fundamental issue has tended to be studied are unsatisfactory and lead to faulty conclusions. Thus, the poet's texts, our fourth source, can certainly aid us in establishing the substance of his knowledge, while tracing its shifting and evolving character. It is not so much what Dante admits about himself that we ought to draw on, although, as we shall very soon see, even elements of his self-presentation can yield valuable clues; rather we ought to pay

---

20   See in particular Filippo Gianferrari, 'Dante and Thirteenth-century Latin Education: Reading the "auctores minores"' (unpublished PhD thesis, University of Notre Dame, 2017), which includes an insightful discussion of methodological issues related to the study of Dante's education and a very good bibliography, as well as his '*Pro patria mori*: From the *Disticha Catonis* to Dante's Cato', *Dante Studies*, 135 (2017), 1–30. See also Robert Black, *Humanism and Education in Medieval and Renaissance Italy: Tradition and Innovation in Latin Schools from the Twelfth to the Fifteenth Century* (Cambridge: Cambridge University Press, 2001), and 'Education' and 'Classical Antiquity', in *Dante in Context*, pp. 260–76 & 297–318; Charles T. Davis, 'Education in Dante's Florence', *Speculum*, 40 (1965), 415–35, as well as the revised version in Italian, 'L'istruzione a Firenze nel tempo di Dante', in his *L'Italia di Dante* (Bologna: il Mulino, 1988), pp. 135–66; Silvia Diacciati and Enrico Faini, 'Ricerche sulla formazione dei laici a Firenze nel tardo Duecento', *Archivio Storico Italiano*, 175 (2017), 205–37; Paul Gehl, *A Moral Art: Grammar, Society, and Culture in Trecento Florence* (Ithaca, NY, and London: Cornell University Press, 1993); M. Michèle Mulchahey, 'Education in Dante's Florence Revisited: Remigio de' Girolami and the Schools of Santa Maria Novella', in *Medieval Education*, ed. by Ronald B. Begley and Joseph W. Koterski (New York: Fordham University Press, 2005), pp. 143–81; Helene Wieruszowski, 'Rhetoric and the Classics in Italian Education of the Thirteenth Century', *Studia Gratiana*, 11 (1967), 169–207. On earlier Florentine education, see Enrico Faini, 'Prima di Brunetto: sulla formazione intellettuale dei laici a Firenze ai primi del Duecento', *Reti medievali rivista*, 18:1 (2017), 189–218.

21   See in particular Bartuschat, pp. 31–149; Gilson, pp. 21–32, 40–53. See also *Fra biografia ed esegesi: crocevia danteschi in Boccaccio e dintorni*, ed. by Emilio Pasquini (Ravenna: Longo, 2014), special issue of *Letture classensi*, 42.

serious attention to the intertextual make-up of his works. For instance, in recent years, it has become increasingly clear that a far from insubstantial number of the poet's quotations are probably not evidence of his first-hand familiarity with the texts from which they come. On account of their status as cultural commonplaces, *sententiae*, it is more likely that Dante came across passages of this type in works of synthesis and compilation, such as commentaries, encyclopaedias, collections of *auctoritates*, and *florilegia*, as well as hearing them during sermons and quodlibetal disputations. Indeed, constructing arguments on the basis of the bringing together of authoritative passages was a standard scholastic procedure. This discovery has led to a reconsideration, at least by some scholars, of the cherished idea, which, as we have noted, has its origins in the Trecento, of Dante as a widely-read font of all wisdom. Indeed, mediated and bitty knowledge is precisely what a *laicus* would have had. At the same time, there is also little doubt that, by the time he was composing the *Commedia*, Dante had read relatively widely, although this probably occurred after his exile rather than before.

3. *c.* 1295

The time has come to bring all that I have said so far to bear on what Dante may have been doing and intellectually assimilating in and around 1295. The year marks a crucial stage in what little we know about Dante's life and development. The poet had recently completed the *Vita nova*, probably during 1294, and had begun to receive the public recognition which, inter alia, the *libello* was meant to foster.[22] In the wake of the *prosimetrum*, as both this in its *explicit* and chapter 12 of Book II of the *Convivio* make clear, their author had become intent on developing new intellectual interests and expanding his literary range, although the declared ultimate goal of these endeavours was unquestionably different: respectively, the celebration of Beatrice and that of Lady Philosophy. That Dante had indeed set himself novel objectives is confirmed by the innovative shift to moral, doctrinal, and possibly 'allegorizing' concerns characteristic of the *canzoni* and other poems that he began to write around the mid-1290s, some of which (it is enough to think of the *petrose*) also demonstrate new formal directions. In addition, 1295 marks the year when Dante, for reasons that remain unclear, unexpectedly entered into political life.[23] This action raises a host of questions,[24] concerning his motives, his possible backers, the relationship between his new intellectual interests and his new public role,[25] that can only be answered cautiously and hypothetically, even if, until

22   Justin Steinberg, *Accounting for Dante: Urban Readers and Writers in Late Medieval Italy* (Notre Dame: University of Notre Dame Press, 2007), pp. 62–66 & 81.

23   Despite some oversimplification, Edward Peters, 'The Shadowy, Violent Perimeter: Dante Enters Florentine Political Life', *Dante Studies*, 113 (1995), 69–87, includes useful information and suggestive insights. For powerful corrective analyses and accounts, see the studies cited in the next three notes.

24   See Giuliano Milani, 'Dante politico fiorentino', *Reti medievali rivista*, 18:1 (2017), 511–63 (pp. 517 & 525).

25   Paolo Borsa, 'Identità sociale e generi letterari: nascita e morte del sodalizio stilnovista', *Reti medievali rivista*, 18:1 (2017), 271–303; Marco Grimaldi, 'La poesia della rettitudine: sul rapporto tra canzoni morali e impegno politico in Dante', *Reti medievali rivista*, 18:1 (2017), 305–26.

recently, scholars have preferred to sidestep such issues, explaining his move into politics as an instance of his exceptional moral rigour.[26] Yet, the questions cannot be so easily dismissed: for example, to what extent might Dante's sudden commitment to politics be tied to the Cerchi's ambitions and machinations? Could there have been specifically cultural reverberations to his behaviour? In late 1293, Florence's outstanding 'public intellectual', Brunetto Latini had died, which created a significant cultural-political void in the city. One possible way in which we might think about Dante's career up to 1294 is as calculatedly in opposition to Brunetto's literary and intellectual profile.[27] Dante wrote for an elite, Brunetto for a broad audience; Dante concentrated on love, Brunetto on a wide range of doctrinal and practical questions; Dante primarily had recourse to lyric poetry, Brunetto to prose and narrative verse; Dante wrote self-commentary, Brunetto glossed and vernacularized the works of the *auctores*. The contrasts are striking; and I could have listed others. I have become increasingly convinced that a re-evaluation of Dante's relationship to Brunetto can yield important insights into his cultural activities during his time in Florence. If initially Dante was careful to forge an authorial identity that was clearly distinct from Brunetto's, once the older man had died, he felt able to begin to take over the latter's public mantle. I do not have the space to develop this hypothesis, but, as I said, I strongly believe that it would be worth doing so, especially if Guittone and Guido Cavalcanti, as well as Bono Giamboni, were thrown into the mix.[28] Thus, it is not difficult to read 'Le dolci rime d'amor', with its investigation of the nature of nobility, as an attempt to mediate between contending positions on a concept that had become highly contentious in Florentine political life during the 1290s. In addition, the overtly doctrinal character of the canzone, in particular the modelling of its structure on that of a scholastic *quaestio* and its appeal to Aristotle, is an attempt, as with several of the other poems that Dante wrote after the *Vita nova*, to confirm to his contemporaries that his intellectual interests were no longer narrowly erotic but, like Brunetto's, were broadly based, communally useful, and drew on a substantial and up-to-date body of knowledge.[29]

26   See in particular Silvia Diacciati, 'Dante: relazioni sociali e vita pubblica', in *Dante attraverso i documenti*, pp. 1–28; Milani, 'Dante politico fiorentino'. The challenge now facing scholars is to explore the inter-relationship between what might be termed the 'cultural' and the 'political' during this period (1295–1301) of the poet's life. This is the aim of this chapter, as it is of the two excellent collections of essays edited by Giuliano Milani and Antonio Montefusco as special issues of *Reti medievali rivista* under the general designation *Dante attraverso i documenti*. The first appeared in 2014 with the subtitle *Famiglia e patrimonio (secolo XII–1300 circa)* as volume 15:2 of the journal, while the second in 2017 (volume 18:1) and is subtitled *Presupposti e contesti dell'impegno politico a Firenze (1295–1302)*.

27   See in particular Enrico Fenzi, '*Sollazzo* e *leggiadria*: un'interpretazione della canzone dantesca *Poscia ch'Amor*', *Studi danteschi*, 63 (1991), 191–280 (p. 215). See also Diacciati, 'Dante: relazioni sociali', p. 263.

28   See especially Antonio Montefusco, 'La linea Guittone-Monte e la nuova parola poetica', *Reti medievali rivista*, 18:1 (2017), 219–70.

29   Claiming that, in the mid 1290s, the poet aspired to a balanced cultural approach fits in well with Milani's highly suggestive conclusion regarding Dante's political stance in 1295: 'Nel luglio del 1295 si inaugurò quindi un regime popolare in cui gli equilibri risultavano ridefiniti rispetto al passato. Se [...] Dante fece il suo ingresso nelle istituzioni proprio per sostenere e difendere queste

4. Aristotle and/or Remigio de' Girolami

But how and where might Dante have acquired this new knowledge, and how substantial were his new intellectual acquisitions? The view persists that the poet was able to read widely and to assimilate considerable amounts of fresh information as a result of being granted access to the Florentine 'libraries' of the three mendicant *studia*, of attending their courses, and of his ties to the University of Bologna.[30] Supporters of this position, who consider Dante's intellectual shift as occurring under the aegis of Aristotle, cite as evidence the Aristotelian character of 'Le dolci rime'; the references to the philosopher and his works in the *Vita nova*; the influence of the *Nicomachean Ethics* on his moral system; the identity of the 'donna [...] fera e disdegnosa' (LXXXI. 75–76) who, in several poems, is presented as challenging Beatrice, a figure that, with the benefit of the hindsight offered by the *Convivio*, is adjudged to be a personification of Aristotelian philosophy; and, of course, Beatrice's accusation in *Purgatorio* XXXIII. 'Le dolci rime' includes what some have claimed to be the first extant translation in the Romance lyric of a passage from Aristotle:

> Dico ch'ogni vertù principalmente
> vien da una radice:
> vertute, dico, che fa l'uom felice
> in sua operazione.
> Questo è, secondo che l'Etica dice,
> un abito eligente
> lo qual dimora in mezzo solamente,
> e tai parole pone. (81–88)

Dante places considerable emphasis on the fact that lines 86 and 87 — 'un abito eligente | lo qual dimora in mezzo solamente' — repeat Aristotle's actual 'words' in *Ethics* II. 6. In Robert Grosseteste's Latin version, which had become the vulgate from around the middle of the thirteenth century, the phrase reads 'Est ergo virtus habitus electivus in medietate existens', before continuing 'que ad nos determinata racione; et ut utique, sapiens determinabit' [Thus virtue is a deliberating disposition that exists in the middle, and with respect to us is determined by reason; and, particularly, as the wise will determine].[31] The poet possibly wished to distinguish

riforme, egli mise la propria capacità di argomentare e persuadere al servizio di un programma politico volto alla moderazione e al compromesso' ('Dante politico fiorentino', p. 519; see also pp. 529–30, 556–57). According to Milani, and his is a view with which I concur, Dante's entry into politics was thus significantly conditioned by the end of Giano Della Bella's supremacy: 'Nel primo biennio testimoniato (1295–1296) [of Dante's political activity] a dominare nettamente fu il dibattito relativo ai modi di ristrutturare la politica e la giustizia comunale dopo il biennio "rivoluzionario" dominato da Giano Della Bella' (p. 555). 1295 marked a watershed both for the poet and for his city. At the same time, Milani notes that 'Molto di ciò che fece Dante può essere considerato posto sul confine tra il legittimo e l'illegittimo' (pp. 558–59; and see n. 10).

30   In recent years this position has been most energetically defended by Luciano Gargan, *Dante, la sua biblioteca e lo studio di Bologna* (Rome and Padua: Antenore, 2014). Various reviewers have expressed historically nuanced reservations about Gargan's claims.

31   Robertus Grosseteste, *Ethica Nicomachea: Libri I–III; VIII.1–5. Recensio pura*, ed. by René A. Gauthier, in *Aristoteles latinus*, vol. XXVI, tome 3 (Leiden and Brussels: Brill and Desclée de Brouwer,

himself from Guittone who had referred to the philosopher in the canzone 'Degno è che che dice omo',[32] but who, without giving a source, had synthesized rather than translated the definition of happiness which Dante too, strategically and somewhat more accurately, reiterates immediately before his direct quotation from Aristotle.[33] Nor is it difficult to grasp why, if Dante had been intent on establishing his credentials as a worthy successor to Brunetto, he would have wished to underscore his first-hand familiarity with the leading philosophical *auctoritas* of his day, whose contributions constituted knowledge at its most cutting-edge, as well as his superiority to Guittone, the leading Tuscan poet-intellectual of the previous generation, who still held cultural sway in Florence. Accordingly, as many *dantisti* have averred, the evidence would indeed appear to confirm that, in the mid-1290s, Dante had been reading Aristotle, and that, consequently, Beatrice's charges are biographically accurate. Such a conclusion, however, takes almost no heed of contemporary realities.

Around the middle of 1295, and probably not long before the composition of 'Le dolci rime', the Dominican friar, Remigio de' Girolami, who for many years taught and preached in Santa Maria Novella, gave a sermon on justice which, with an eye on Florentine political factionalism, was a paean to civic concord. Remigio's aim was not that different to Dante's attempt in his canzone to mediate between the city's warring groups.[34] In the written version of the homily, when assessing justice and mercy as virtues, Remigio declares: 'secundum philosophum in ii Ethic. [...] virtus est habitus electivus in medietate consistens et cetera' [according to the philosopher in *Ethics* II [...] virtue is a deliberating disposition that consists in a middle, etc.].[35] The coincidences between poet and preacher are eye-catching. In any case, even if Dante had not heard Remigio speak, the phrase that he translated was a self-standing commonplace, present in its full form in writers as different as Thomas Aquinas and the anonymous author of the *Legenda de origine Ordinis fratrum Servorum Virginis Marie*.[36] Suggestively, it is in fact only Remigio and Dante who just cite

---

1972), p. 171.

32   '[S]egondo che 'l saggio Aristotel dice | e mostra omo felice | vertù ovrando' (54–56). I cite from *Le rime di Guittone d'Arezzo*, ed. by Francesco Egidi (Bari: Laterza, 1940).

33   On Guittone's reliance on Aristotle, see Sonia Gentili, 'Letture dantesche anteriori all'esilio: filosofia e teologia', in *Dante fra il settecentocinquantenario della nascita (2015) e il settecentenario della morte (2021)*, ed. by Enrico Malato and Andrea Mazzucchi, 2 vols (Rome: Salerno, 2016), I, 303–25 (pp. 313–15); Claude Margueron, *Recherches sur Guittone d'Arezzo* (Paris: PUF, 1966), pp. 321–32.

34   On possible political points of contact between Dante and Remigio, see Delphine Carron, 'Remigio de' Girolami dans la Florence de Dante (1293–1302)', *Reti medievali rivista*, 18:1 (2017), 443–71.

35   Remigio de' Girolami, 'Tractatus de iustitia', in Ovidio Capitani, 'L'incompiuto "Tractatus de iustitia" di fra' Remigio de' Girolami († 1319)', *Bullettino dell'Istituto storico italiano per il Medio Evo e Archivio muratoriano*, 72 (1960), 91–134 (p. 126).

36   For Thomas Aquinas, and limiting my references to the *ST*, see I. 2. 63. 2; I. 2. 64. 1. arg. 2 and 2. arg. 4; I. 2. 59 1 co; II. 2. 47. 5. obj. 1 and arg. 1; II. 2. 58. 1. arg. 2 and 2. arg. 4, and 10. obj. 1; II. 2. 59. 1 co. For the *Legenda*, see *Legenda de origine Ordinis fratrum Servorum Virginis Mariae*, ed. by Ermanno M. Toniolo (Rome: Centro di Cultura Mariana, 1982), pp. 628–31. Vincenzo Valente notes that the passage from *Ethics* II. 6 cited by Dante is a 'formula scolasticamente ripetuta dai trattatisti morali': 'elettivo', in *ED*, II, 652–53 (p. 653).

the first part of the locution. The probability that, in 'Le dolci rime', the poet was quoting directly from Aristotle is thus extremely unlikely, especially as his other contemporaneous citations from the philosopher, such as the canzone's definition of happiness, the allusion at the close of the *Vita nova* to the 'secondo de la Metafisica' (*Vn* XLI. 6), and his Aristotelian-sounding moral affirmations, are also all cultural commonplaces.[37] Thus, it would not seem unreasonable to conclude, especially in light of what I am about to say about Dante's likely relationship to Florentine and Bolognese educational establishments, that, during the 1290s, the poet had begun to show a growing interest in Aristotle, but that this interest was based on meagre and secondhand knowledge of the philosopher's writings, although, as the structure of 'Le dolci rime' demonstrates, he did have a better appreciation of scholastic forms of argumentation. Before I move on to the *scuole*, I should like to stress something that Dante scholarship has all too rarely done. If we wish to begin to appreciate the poet's intellectual formation before his exile, the most reliable sources that we have are the *Vita nova* and his lyric poetry,[38] as I hope I have been able to demonstrate, albeit cursorily, with respect to 'Le dolci rime'.[39] Moreover, the evidence these works provide needs to be carefully tested both against what we can establish about

37   On happiness, see the passage cited from Guittone and 'Et puis que felicitez est en huevre de vertu': Brunetto Latini, *Tresor*, ed. by Pietro G. Beltrami *et al.* (Turin: Einaudi, 2007), II. 47. 4 (p. 432). On *Met.*, II. 1, see Paolo Falzone, *Desiderio della scienza e desiderio di Dio nel 'Convivio' di Dante* (Naples: Società editrice il Mulino, 2010), pp. 126–30, 257–77. On the 'popularization' of Aristotle's *Ethics*, see in particular Sonia Gentili, *L'uomo aristotelico alle origini della letteratura italiana* (Rome: Carocci, 2005), pp. 27–55, and 'La vulgarisation de l'*Éthique* d'Aristote en Italie aux XIIIe et XIVe siècles: enjeux littéraires et philosophiques', *Médiévales*, 63 (2012), 47–58; and see also Anthony Celano, *Aristotle's 'Ethics' and Medieval Philosophy: Moral Goodness and Practical Wisdom* (Cambridge: Cambridge University Press, 2016). As regards the reference to 'lo Filosofo' and the general 'philosophizing' register of *Vn* XXV. 1–2, see Donato Pirovano's excellent annotations highlighting 'la diffusione' of the concepts Dante introduces: Dante Alighieri, *Vita nuova. Rime*, ed. by Donato Pirovano and Marco Grimaldi (Rome: Salerno, 2015), pp. 207–09 (p. 209). See more generally Lorenzo Minio-Paluello, 'Dante's Reading of Aristotle', in *The World of Dante*, ed. by Cecil Grayson (Oxford: Clarendon Press, 1980), pp. 61–80 (esp. pp. 65–68); Andrea A. Robiglio, 'Dante e le *Auctoritates Aristotelis*', in *Les 'Auctoritates Aristotelis', leur utilisation et leur influence chez les auteurs médiévaux: état de la question 40 ans après la publication*, ed. by Jacqueline Hamesse and José Meirinhos (Barcelona and Madrid: Fédération Internationale des Instituts d'Études Médiévales, 2015), pp. 187–202. Sonia Gentili asserts that Dante's 'fu una lettura [of the *Nicomachean Ethics*] complessiva e approfonditissima, iniziata sin dall'epoca fiorentina' ('Letture dantesche', p. 312), yet provides no concrete and convincing evidence based in the poet's pre-exilic writings for her claim. Indeed, as regards the two examples that she presents of Dante's direct knowledge of the *Ethics* during his time in Florence, one, as she recognizes herself, is mediated ('La nozione aristotelica di virtú compare in vari testi poetici anteriori all'esilio. Essa si deve supporre veicolata anzitutto dal dibattito stilnovistico sulla natura dell'amore e dal contatto con il primo amico Guido Cavalcanti'; p. 311), while the other, the allusion in the *Vita nova* to the 'divine' Beatrice — 'certo di lei si potea dire quella parola del poeta Omero: "Ella non parea figliuola d'uomo mortale, ma di deo"' (II. 8) — , has long been recognized not as a direct borrowing from *Ethics* VII. 1, as Gentili suggests, but, as Pirovano notes, a 'citazione [...] mediata' (p. 85).

38   See Roberto Antonelli, 'Le letture fiorentine: le letterature volgari', in Malato and Mazzucchi, *Dante fra il settecentocinquantenario della nascita*, 1, 255–72 (p. 255).

39   For an important reading of the canzone that has some points of contact with my argument, see Paolo Borsa, '"Le dolci rime" di Dante: nobiltà d'animo e nobiltà dell'anima', in *Le dolci rime d'amor ch'io solea*, ed. by Rosario Scrimieri Martín (Madrid: La Biblioteca de Tenzone, 2014), pp. 57–112.

the transmission and institutions of knowledge in central Italy at the time, and against any other clues that Dante may have left.

5. A Florentine Education: *Conv.* II. 12

In this regard, the *Convivio* provides a suggestive sketch of how the poet's new intellectual interests developed. While remembering to treat what Dante says about himself with caution, let us fleetingly consider some of the principal lines that he traces. The key fixed point is Beatrice's death on 8 June 1290. Using a complex astronomical periphrasis centred on the movement of Venus in its epicycle, Dante reveals that his new doctrinal interests, which resulted in a spiritual and intellectual crisis and conversion, began in late August 1293, a date that fits well with the later stages of the *libello*'s composition, and indeed with its recourse to Aristotle in chapters XXV and XLI:

> Cominciando adunque, dico che la stella di Venere due fiate rivolta era in quello suo cerchio che la fa parere serotina e matutina secondo diversi tempi, apresso lo trapassamento di quella Beatrice beata che vive in cielo colli angeli e in terra colla mia anima, quando quella gentile donna [di] cui feci menzione nella fine della Vita Nova, parve primamente, acompagnata d'Amore, alli occhi miei e prese luogo alcuno nella mia mente. (*Conv.* II. 2. 1)

Yet, nowhere in his subsequent account of these crucial experiences in the same Book of the *Convivio* does Dante mention the philosopher:

> (1) Poi che la litterale sentenza è sufficientemente dimostrata, è da procedere alla esposizione allegorica e vera. E però, principiando ancora da capo, dico che, come per me fu perduto lo primo diletto della mia anima, dello quale fatta è menzione di sopra, io rimasi di tanta tristizia punto, che conforto non mi valeva alcuno. (2) Tuttavia, dopo alquanto tempo, la mia mente, che si argomentava di sanare, provide, poi che né 'l mio né l'altrui consolare valea, ritornare al modo che alcuno sconsolato avea tenuto a consolarsi; e misimi a leggere quello non conosciuto da molti libro di Boezio, nel quale, cattivo e discacciato, consolato s'avea. (3) E udendo ancora che Tulio scritto avea un altro libro, nel quale, trattando dell'Amistade, avea toccate parole della consolazione di Lelio, uomo eccellentissimo, nella morte di Scipione amico suo, misimi a leggere quello. (4) E avegna che duro mi fosse nella prima entrare nella loro sentenza, finalmente v'entrai tanto entro, quanto l'arte di gramatica ch'io avea e un poco di mio ingegno potea fare; per lo quale ingegno molte cose, quasi come sognando, già vedea, sì come nella Vita Nova si può vedere. (5) E sì come essere suole che l'uomo va cercando argento e fuori della 'ntenzione truova oro, lo quale occulta cagione presenta; non forse sanza divino imperio, io, che cercava di consolar me, trovai non solamente alle mie lagrime rimedio, ma vocabuli d'autori e di scienze e di libri: li quali considerando, giudicava bene che la filosofia, che era donna di questi autori, di queste scienze e di questi libri, fosse somma cosa. (6) Ed imaginava lei fatta come una donna gentile, e non la poteva imaginare in atto alcuno se non misericordioso; per che sì volentieri lo senso di vero la mirava, che appena lo potea volgere da quella. (7) E da questo imaginare cominciai ad andare là dov'ella si dimostrava veracemente, cioè nelle scuole delli religiosi e alle disputazioni delli filosofanti; sì che in picciolo tempo, forse

di trenta mesi, cominciai tanto a sentire della sua dolcezza, che lo suo amore cacciava e distruggeva ogni altro pensiero. (8) Per che io, sentendomi levare dal pensiero del primo amore alla vertù di questo, quasi maravigliandomi apersi la bocca nel parlare della proposta canzone, mostrando la mia condizione sotto figura d'altre cose: però che della donna di cu' io m'innamorava non era degna rima di volgare alcuna palesemente poetare; né li uditori erano tanto bene disposti che avessero sì leggiere le [non] fittizie parole apprese; né sarebbe data [per] loro fede alla sentenza vera come alla fittizia, però che di vero si credea del tutto che disposto fosse a quello amore, che non si credeva di questo. (9) Cominciai dunque a dire: *Voi che 'ntendendo il terzo ciel movete*. E perché, sì come detto è, questa donna fu figlia di Dio, regina di tutto, nobilissima e bellissima Filosofia, è da vedere chi furono questi movitori, e questo terzo cielo. E prima [dirò] del cielo, secondo l'ordine trapassato. E non è qui mestiere di procedere dividendo e a littera esponendo; ché, volta [la] parola fittizia di quello ch'ella suona in quello ch'ella 'ntende, per la passata esposizione questa sentenza fia sufficientemente palese. (*Conv.* II. 12)

Instead of Aristotle, Dante introduces Boethius's *Consolatio philosophiæ* and Cicero's *De amicitia*, texts that he insists he read ('e misimi a leggere'; *Conv.* II. 12. 2), as the triggers for his new interests. At the same time, he admits that 'duro mi fosse nella prima entrare nella loro sentenza, finalmente v'entrai tanto entro, quanto l'arte di gramatica ch'io avea e un poco di mio ingegno potea fare' (4) — an admission that would confirm that he had probably received a basic formal education, since he highlights the limitations of his 'gramatica', namely his Latin, and the difficulties he had in interpreting both texts ('entrare nella loro sentenza'; 4). Finally, his efforts led to his discovering 'vocabuli d'autori e di scienze e di libri' (5), that is to say, simply the 'names of authors and of disciplines' and the 'titles of books', further evidence of how restricted and challenging, as with any *laicus*, was his access to information.[40] These occasional readings and tidbits of knowledge, nonetheless, encouraged him 'ad andare là dov'ella [Philosophy] si dimostrava veracemente, cioè nelle scuole delli religiosi e alle disputazioni delli filosofanti' (7).[41] I can think of few other passages in Dante that have occasioned as much unsatisfactory scholarship

---

40   The conventional interpretation of 'vocabuli' is *lessico*, a definition which does not make much sense in the context of chapter 12; see Alessandro Niccoli and Pier Vincenzo Mengaldo, 'vocabolo', in *ED*, V, 1107–10. Vasoli's gloss — 'cioè, gli autori, i testi e le dottrine citati nel *De consolatione philosophiae* e nel *De amicitia*' — endeavours to contextualize the phrase, but without explaining the value of 'vocabuli': Dante Alighieri, *Convivio*, ed. by Cesare Vasoli (Milan and Naples: Ricciardi, 1988), p. 204. In his turn, Fioravanti only explains the first part of the expression before offering an unnecessarily convoluted and grammatically questionable explanation of the remainder of the phrase: 'vocabuli d'autori...: "nomi di autori", cioè, ancora una volta di coloro che hanno trovato e sistematizzato le varie scienze (fisica, astronomia, medicina...) rendendole poi disponibili in opere scritte ("libri")': Dante Alighieri, *Convivio*, in *Opere*, 2 vols (Milan: Mondadori, 2011–14), II, 3–805 (p. 301). The interpretation I offer not only conforms to the rest of Dante's account, but also matches his usage elsewhere of *vocabulo* with the meaning of 'name', 'denomination': *Conv.* IV. vi. 14; *Purg.* V. 97; XIV. 26; *Par.* VIII. 11. On the basis of a search of the texts contained in the OVI database, it would appear that Dante is the first Italian vernacular writer to use *vocabulo* with the meaning of 'name'.

41   For a suggestive discussion of the same two passages from the *Convivio* discussed here that focuses on matters of chronology, see Alberto Casadei, 'Dalla *Vita nova* al *Convivio*', *Dante*, 12 (2015), 29–40.

as this phrase. Thus, although the poet makes no mention of Bologna, the allusion to 'schools' and 'disputations' has been interpreted as Dante disclosing not just that he had studied at its university, but also that he had attended classes taught both by theologians ('religiosi') and by arts masters ('filosofanti'). Yet, there is absolutely no evidence to support such claims. At the same time — and this raises a whole set of other questions that I am unable to address here — Dante had probably spent time in the city during the late 1280s, even if not during the 1290s. Besides, the *Convivio* is clear: the events that Dante evokes all occurred in Florence. In addition, what the poet states conforms to what we know from other sources about the places where Filosofia 'si dimostrava veracemente' (7) in the city.

As I have already intimated, there were at least three mendicant *studia* in the city:[42] the Augustinians at Santo Spirito, about whom we currently know very little, the Dominicans at Santa Maria Novella, and the Franciscans at Santa

---

42   On the *studia*, see in particular Charles T. Davis, 'The Early Collection of Books of S. Croce in Florence', *Proceedings of the American Philosophical Society*, 107 (1963), 399–414, 'L'istruzione a Firenze', and 'The Florentine *studia* and Dante's "Library"', in *The 'Divine Comedy' and the Encyclopedia of Arts and Sciences*, ed. by Giuseppe Di Scipio and Aldo Scaglione (Amsterdam and Philadelphia: Benjamins, 1988), pp. 339–66. See also Giuseppina Brunetti and Sonia Gentili, 'Una biblioteca nella Firenze di Dante: i manoscritti di Santa Croce', in *Testimoni del vero: su alcuni libri in biblioteche d'autore*, ed. by Emilio Russo, special issue of *Studi (e testi) italiani*, 6 (2000), 21–55; Sonia Gentili and Sylvain Piron, 'La bibliothèque de Santa Croce', in *Frontières des savoirs en Italie médiévale à l'époque des premières universités (XIIIe–XVe siècles)*, ed. by Joël Chandelier and Aurélien Robert (Rome: École française de Rome, 2015), pp. 481–507; Mulchahey; Sylvain Piron, 'Le Poète et le théologien: une rencontre dans le *studium* de Santa Croce', *Picenum Seraphicum. Rivista di studi storici e francescani*, 19 (2000), 87–134, then in *'Ut philosophia poesis': questions philosophiques dans l'œuvre de Dante, Pétrarque et Boccace*, ed. by Joël Biard and Fosca Mariani Zini (Paris: Vrin, 2008), pp. 73–112, and 'Un couvent sous influence: Santa Croce autour de 1300', in *Économie et religion: l'expérience des ordres mendiants (XIIIe–XVe siècle)*, ed. by Nicole Bériou and Jacques Chiffoleau (Lyon: Presses Universitaires de Lyon, 2009), pp. 331–55; Gabriella Pomaro, 'Censimento dei manoscritti della Biblioteca di S. Maria Novella. 1. Origini e Trecento', *Memorie domenicane*, n.s. 11 (1980), 325–470.

The most significant and authoritative contribution on Santa Croce is Anna Pegoretti, '"Nelle scuole delli religiosi": materiali per Santa Croce nell'età di Dante', *L'Alighieri*, 58 (2017), 5–55. In addition, her cautious methodological approach chimes well with my arguments in this chapter. Thus, as regards the books found in the *studia* and Dante, Pegoretti correctly counsels caution: 'l'esperienza (tutta da divinare) che può averne [of the manuscripts] fatta Dante' (p. 8). More generally, '[l]'obiettivo [of her study] non è quello di identificare la sfuggente *silhouette* dantesca. Più modestamente si cercherà di perimetrare un ambiente, identificandone le possibili vie d'accesso e alcune tendenze generali, nella convinzione che solo pazienti ricognizioni possano restituirci un quadro con il quale fare efficacemente dialogare l'opera del Nostro. Questo, infatti, ritengo sia lo scopo principale da perseguire: l'individuazione delle linee generali espresse dalla didattica, dalla predicazione, dall'approvvigionamento di testi, persino dalla posizione politica ed economica del convento di Santa Croce. Un approccio globale che sia allo stesso tempo il più preciso possibile, corroborato da dati (per quanto incompleti) e alieno da qualunque feticismo di sapore positivista. Solo così potremo renderci conto se, in che modo e fino a che punto la cultura dei frati abbia portato linfa alla letteratura del Duecento fiorentino, al suo più grande esponente e in generale a una classe di intellettuali che appare peculiare per estrazione sociale e interessi politici e professionali [...] e a prima vista distante dagli *studia* mendicanti, che erano comunque i centri di più alta formazione a Firenze. Ebbene: come si colloca la cultura teologica e filosofica degli *studia* in relazione a questa "cultura dei laici"? Che cosa voleva dire, in concreto, frequentare una "scuola dei religiosi"? Che cosa ci si poteva aspettare di trovare? Domande come queste potranno trovare risposte solo a seguito di indagini pazienti su ambienti specifici' (pp. 8–9).

Croce.[43] Our information about the latter two orders is much fuller. Nevertheless, the oft-repeated contention that, given Dante's close ties to the *studia*, we can reconstruct his reading in the early to mid-1290s on the basis of what we know about their manuscript collections is essentially without foundation. As is the related claim that he attended their classes. The evidence against both assertions, if not quite conclusive, is pretty overwhelming. First, each order restricted access to its books to its own members.[44] Second, it has very recently been conclusively demonstrated that the terms 'religiosi' and 'filosofanti' are not to be interpreted, as conventionally has been done, with reference to respectively ecclesiastical and secular intellectuals.[45] *Phylosophans* was in fact anyone involved in intellectual activity: 'dunque, i *filosofanti* del *Convivio* possono ben essere tutti coloro dediti, nei contesti delle dispute, alla speculazione razionale dei fenomeni' (Pegoretti, 'Filosofanti', p. 37). Furthermore, the designation was rarely used to distinguish between different groups of intellectuals or different intellectual traditions. Given that Florence had no secular *studia*, Dante's 'filosofanti' were in all likelihood also his 'religiosi'. That this fundamental proposal is almost certainly correct is further confirmed by the fact that, unlike philosophical lectures in universities, including Bologna, some theological presentations, in particular quodlibetal 'disputations',[46]

43   Anna Pegoretti has highlighted the potential importance for Dante of the Servites: '*Civitas diaboli*: forme e figure della religiosità laica nella Firenze di Dante', in *Dante poeta cristiano: in ricordo di Anna Maria Chiavacci Leonardi*, ed. by Giuseppe Ledda (Ravenna: Centro Dantesco dei Frati Minori Conventuali, 2018), pp. 65–116 (pp. 84–98).

44   See Davis, 'The Florentine *studia*', pp. 344 & 353, Pegoretti, 'Materiali', pp. 21–27, who notes: 'Restano però i dubbi sulla disponibilità di questi materiali di studio a laici esterni' (p. 23, but see also pp. 40–41). See also Neslihan Senocak, 'Circulation of Books in the Medieval Franciscan Order: Attitude, Methods, and Critics', *The Journal of Religious History*, 28 (2004), 146–61, and *The Poor and the Perfect: The Rise of Learning in the Franciscan Order, 1209–1310* (Ithaca, NY, and London: Cornell University Press, 2012), pp. 201–08. On 'Firenze e i cataloghi librari: oltre le collezioni di Santa Croce e Santa Maria Novella', see Dell'Oso, pp. 137–41 (as well as pp. 155–56). See also Donatella Nebbiai, 'Les Bibliothèques dans la société italienne (XIIIe–XVe siècles)', in Chandelier and Robert, pp. 453–80.

45   Anna Pegoretti, 'Filosofanti', *Le tre corone*, 2 (2015), 11–70 (especially pp. 33–37). Pegoretti's excellent article includes a detailed discussion of the different ways in which 'I due sintagmi "scuole delli religiosi"/"disputazioni delli filosofanti" sono stati letti' (p. 12). In addition, she too notes 'la profonda "fiorentinità" del quadro fornito da Dante' (p. 14) in *Convivio* II. 12.

46   See Bernardo C. Bazàn and others, *Les Questions disputées et les questions quodlibétiques dans les facultés de théologie, de droit et de médecine* (Turnhout: Brepols, 1985); Palémon Glorieux, *La Littérature quodlibétique de 1260 à 1320*, 2 vols (Le Saulchoir, Kain: Revue des sciences philosophiques et théologiques, 1925; and Paris: Vrin, 1935), and 'La disputa teologica all'università di Parigi', in *Filosofi e teologi: la ricerca e l'insegnamento nell'università medievale*, ed. by Luca Bianchi and Eugenio Randi (Bergamo: Lubrina, 1989), pp. 153–68; Emilio Panella, 'Nuova cronologia remigiana', *Archivum Fratrum Praedicatorum*, 40 (1990), 145–311 (pp. 180–82), and '"Ne le scuole de li religiosi e a le disputazioni de li filosofanti" (Dante Alighieri). *Lectio, disputatio, predicatio*', in *Dal convento alla città: filosofia e teologia in Francesco da Prato O.P. (XIV secolo)*, ed. by Fabrizio Amerini (Florence: Zella, 2008), pp. 115–31 (pp. 116–21); Olga Weijers, *La 'disputatio' dans les Facultés des arts au moyen âge* (Turnhout: Brepols, 2002); *Disputatio 1200–1800: Form, Funktion und Wirkung eines Leitmediums universitärer Wissenskultur*, ed. by Marion Gindhart and Ursula Kundert (Berlin and New York: de Gruyter, 2010); *Theological Quodlibeta in the Middle Ages: The Thirteenth Century*, ed. by Christopher Schabel (Leiden and Boston: Brill, 2006); *Theological Quodlibeta in the Middle Ages: The Fourteenth Century*, ed. by Christopher Schabel (Leiden and Boston: Brill, 2007).

were, as Dante accurately states in the *Convivio*, open to the public.[47] Contrary to a longheld belief, Dante is most unlikely to have enjoyed a privileged relationship with the intellectual environments of the Florentine mendicant orders, though this does not mean that these did not exercise an important influence on the poet. In the *Convivio*, therefore, Dante is straightforwardly announcing that, like others among his fellow-citizens, he attended the public *disputationes* of learned friars.[48] Moreover, as with Remigio's lesson on justice delivered in Santa Maria Novella, preaching would also have played an important role in disseminating the friars' learning, since a *lector* was normally also a *praedicator*.[49] Consequently, if we wish to begin to arrive at an appreciation, however tentative, of what Dante might have learned from the mendicants during the 1290s, we need to establish who was present in each convent, what their interests were at the time, and what books were actually part of their collections during this time.[50] Dante's non-literary 'schooling' in Florence would thus have been principally, even if not exclusively, religious in orientation, although this 'education' would likely have afforded him some insight

Robiglio writes that 'the standard courses were available only to friars, and were not open to the public, although there may have been exceptions to this rule. Courses on the Bible, on the other hand, were possibly accessible to a larger audience and, as is evident from scholastic commentaries to the books of the Bible, these courses could include a generous amount of logic and natural philosophy. The laity could certainly attend and probably even contribute to the so-called disputed *quaestiones de quolibet*' ('Philosophy', p. 145). Unfortunately, we currently do not know whether exceptions were made in the Florentine *studia* or whether their courses on the Bible were open to outsiders. See also Pegoretti, 'Materiali', p. 13.

47   'Le dispute a cui Dante ha assistito sono certamente di natura accademica e, visto quanto abbiamo capito dei filosofanti, potevano tenersi tanto nelle scuole dei frati [...] quanto in altri contesti istituzionali' (Pegoretti, 'Filosofanti', p. 39). Paolo Falzone is of a similar opinion: 'nulla prova [...] che delle "disputazioni delli filosofanti" Dante abbia fatto esperienza in contesti accademici di necessità diversi dalle "scuole delli religiosi"': 'Il *Convivio* di Dante', in *La filosofia al tempo di Dante*, ed. by Carla Casagrande and Gianfranco Fioravanti (Bologna: il Mulino, 2016), pp. 225–64 (p. 227).

48   On the importance of the *quodlibeta* for Dante's intellectual formation, see Simon A. Gilson, 'Appunti metodologici su teologia e scolastica nel *Paradiso*', in *Le teologie di Dante*, ed. by Giuseppe Ledda (Ravenna: Centro dantesco dei frati minori conventuali, 2015), pp. 99–115 (pp. 104, n. 12, 106–07; the present chapter concurs on many historical and methodological points with this fine essay); Paola Nasti, '"Vocabuli d'autori e di scienze e di libri" (*Conv.* II xii 5): percorsi sapienzali di Dante', in *La Bibbia di Dante: esperienza mistica, profezia e teologia biblica in Dante*, ed. by Giuseppe Ledda (Ravenna: Centro Dantesco dei Frati Minori Conventuali, 2011), pp. 121–78 (p. 164–71); Pegoretti, 'Materiali', pp. 13–14. See also, but to be consulted with care, Piron, 'Le Poète'. On the quodlibetal character of the pilgrim's examination in the heaven of the Fixed stars, see, Matthew Treherne, 'Reading Dante's Heaven of the Fixed Stars (*Paradiso* XXII–XXVII): Declaration, Pleasure and Praise', in '*Se mai continga...*': Exile, Politics and Theology in Dante, ed. by Claire E. Honess and Matthew Treherne (Ravenna: Longo, 2013), pp. 11–26 (pp. 20–23).

49   On Dante and preaching, see Nicolò Maldina, *In pro del mondo: Dante, la predicazione e i generi della letteratura religiosa medievale* (Rome: Salerno, 2017).

50   See in particular Nasti, '"Vocabuli d'autori e di scienze e di libri"', and 'Storia materiale di un classico dantesco: la *Consolatio Philosophiae* fra XII e XIV secolo tradizione manoscritta e rielaborazioni esegetiche', *Dante Studies*, 134 (2016), 142–68. See also Simon A. Gilson, 'Dante and Christian Aristotelianism', in *Reviewing Dante's Theology*, ed. by Claire E. Honess and Matthew Treherne, 2 vols (Oxford: Peter Lang, 2013), I, 65–109 (pp. 84–86), and 'Appunti metodologici', pp. 112–13; Mulchahey; Panella, 'Nuova cronologia remigiana'; Piron, 'Le Poète'. Raffaella Zanni, 'Una ricognizione per la biblioteca di Dante in margine a alcuni contributi recenti', *Critica del testo*, 17 (2014), 161–204, is generally unhelpful as it is too narrow and overly tendentious.

into Aristotle's *libri naturales* and the *Nicomachean Ethics*, given that the mendicants drew on these when addressing quodlibetal questions, as well as when preaching and glossing the Sapiential and other biblical books.[51]

The religious slant of Dante's Florentine formation is confirmed by the heavily Scriptural and Christian character of the *Vita nova*, in which allusions to Aristotle and Aristotelian, loosely understood, moral and scientific thought are, as I have intimated, few and hackneyed. Indeed, the evidence of Dante's pre-exilic literary production points to an intellectual formation that was largely dependent on the Romance vernacular tradition, on the Bible and its exegesis, and, as the poet recognizes in the *Convivio*, on Boethius's *Consolatio*, with some (limited) debts to Brunetto's ethical Aristotelianism and civic Ciceronianism,[52] and possibly even more restricted debts to the classical *auctores*.[53] If we focus specifically on Dante's lyric production after 1295, we find clear continuities with the *Vita nova*. In it there is very little Aristotle but a lot of Boethius and his commentators, as well as religious and Scriptural echoes, as has been established with regard in particular to 'Amor che movi tua vertù dal cielo' and the *petrose*. Indeed, together with the biblical and the erotic, the third element that determines the ideological patina of Dante's writing in the 1290s is a Christianizing cosmological Neoplatonism with its roots in the rich tradition that had flourished around Boethius's great popular hymn from the third book of the *Consolation*, 'O qui perpetua mundum ratione gubernas' [Oh you who govern the world by perpetual reason].[54]

6. *Donne*

Dante claims that he spent 'picciolo tempo, forse di trenta mesi' (*Conv.* II. 12. 7) learning from the friars before totally giving himself to his new 'philosophical' love. Recalling that he had first gone to their 'scuole' in late August 1293, this would

---

51   See Nasti, '"Vocabuli d'autori e di scienze e di libri"', pp. 159–72; Pegoretti, 'Materiali', pp. 40–41. Aristotle, and in particular the *Ethics*, of course also had a non-religious circulation; see the following note.

52   The question of Dante's possible debts to Brunetto's *Trésor*, whether the original Old French text or one of its 'vernacularizations', remains largely unexplored. Alongside what I term Brunetto's 'ethical Aristotelianism', one should align the Latin and vernacular compendia of Aristotelian *sententiae* circulating in Florence and more generally in Italy; see Gentili, *L'uomo aristotelico*, pp. 27–55, 'La vulgarisation de l'*Éthique*', and 'Letture dantesche', p. 313; see also notes 37 and 41.

53   See Zygmunt G. Barański, 'The Roots of Dante's Plurilingualism: "Hybridity" and Language in the *Vita nova*', in *Dante's Plurilingualism: Authority, Knowledge, Subjectivity*, ed by Sara Fortuna and others (Oxford: Legenda, 2010), pp. 98–121 (pp. 109–10). See also Giuseppina Brunetti, 'Lucano, i libri di Dante e un ritrovato sonetto di Petrarca (*RVF* 102)', *Studi e problemi di critica testuale*, 90 (2015), 55–71, and 'Le letture fiorentine: i classici e la retorica', in Malato and Mazzucchi, *Dante fra il settecentocinquantenario della nascita*, I, 225–53.

54   See, in particular, Robert M. Durling and Ronald L. Martinez, *Time and the Crystal: Studies in Dante's 'Rime petrose'* (Berkeley: University of California Press, 1990); Claudio Giunta, 'Dante: l'amore come destino', in *Dante the Lyric and Ethical Poet*, ed. by Zygmunt G. Barański and Martin McLaughlin (Leeds: Legenda, 2010), pp. 119–36; Luca Lombardo, *Boezio in Dante: la 'Consolatio philosophiae' nello scrittoio del poeta* (Venice: Edizioni Ca' Foscari, 2014); Nasti, 'Storia materiale di un classico dantesco'.

have occurred in late 1295 or very early 1296, which coincides neatly with the new intellectual shift marked by 'Le dolci rime', as well as with his entry into political life that occurred in November 1295. It is time to acknowledge the reliability, at least in general terms, of the *Convivio*'s account of Dante's intellectual development, which can be deemed trustworthy because external evidence would seem to support its contentions. However, there are two important details mentioned in the *Convivio* that do not conform to what we can read in the *rime*. In the 'almost commentary', Dante describes the transition from his love of Beatrice to that of 'Filosofia' as reasonably evolutionary and largely unproblematic: 'sentendomi levare dal pensiero del primo amore alla vertù di questo' (8). In the poems, on the other hand, we find a more painful struggle:

> Suol esser vita de lo cor dolente
> un soave penser, che se ne gia
> molte fiate a' pie' del nostro Sire,
> ove una donna gloriar vedia,
> di cui parlava me sì dolcemente
> che l'anima dicea: 'Io men vo' gire'.
>   Or apparisce chi lo fa fuggire
> e segnoreggia me di tal virtute,
> che 'l cor ne trema che di fuori appare.
> Questi mi face una donna guardare. (LXXIX. 14–23)

Equally, in the *Convivio*, the new lady is defined as 'figlia di Dio, regina di tutto, nobilissima e bellissima Filosofia' (9), whereas, in the lyrics, on occasion she appears with similar luminous attributes — 'Questa è colei ch'umilia ogni perverso: | costei pensò chi mosse l'universo' (LXXXI. 71–72) —, at other times she assumes 'darker' lineaments: 'Tanto disdegna qualunque la mira, | che fa chinare gli occhi di paura' (LXXX. 5–6). The first discrepancy can be explained in terms of the fact that the *rime* describe the unfolding of the predicament assailing the poet, while the *Convivio* focuses on its outcome. The second inconsistency is more complicated. The description that Dante offers of his new lady in the commentary as 'daughter of God, queen of everything, most noble and most beautiful' is culturally highly indicative. It defines her not as Artistotelian *Philosophia* but conventionally as Scriptural-Boethian *Sapientia* — a characterization, which, as we have seen, is in keeping with the intellectual make-up of the later Florentine lyrics.[55] However, the *Vita nova* too fits into the same paradigm, thereby raising many questions, that once more I cannot discuss here, regarding the connections between Beatrice and the *donna*. What is essential to grasp is that, unlike many Dantists, the poet is not positing a sharp break between the intellectual world of the *libello* and what comes immediately after.[56] If this is indeed the case, and the textual evidence would

---

55   See Peter Dronke, *Dante's Second Love: The Originality and the Contexts of the 'Convivio'* (Leeds: Society for Italian Studies, 1997); Paola Nasti, *Favole d'amore e 'saver profondo': la tradizione salomonica in Dante* (Ravenna: Longo, 2007), pp. 93–130.

56   It is enough to remember what Dante announces in *Conv*, II. 12. 4: 'E avegna che duro mi fosse nella prima entrare nella loro sentenza, finalmente v'entrai tanto entro, quanto l'arte di gramatica ch'io avea e un poco di mio ingegno potea fare; per lo quale ingegno molte cose, quasi come

appear to support such a view, then, where does this leave 'Le dolci rime'? If, on the one hand, the ethical-political thrust of the canzone certainly marks a new departure in Dante's interests and writing, though less than has generally been maintained — very recently the ethical, social, and political nuances of the *Vita nova* have begun to be recognized[57] —, on the other, the 'manifesto' poem's basic ideological framework, for all its foregrounding of Aristotle, cannot be said to constitute proof of a substantial intellectual shift. Rather it implies an ambition, a hope even, that such a shift can occur. Let me explain. It has long been maintained that, in his doctrinal poetry, Dante represents the struggle between Beatrice and a new woman, Philosophy, who, in keeping with the confusion that he feels, oscillates between appearing as 'umile' and as 'fera'. I wonder, however, whether the struggle depicted is somewhat more complicated: a threeway conflict between Beatrice, a glorious *Sapientia* with close ties to the poet's first love, and a new and distinct brand of rationally rigorous 'severe' *Philosophia* whose supreme *auctor* was Aristotle and of whose existence Dante was only slowly and haphazardly becoming aware in the mid-1290s. Such a hypothesis might not only account for the seeming inconsistencies and tensions recorded in the post-*Vita nova* poems, but also, and more importantly, would appear to find support in the poems' textual weave, in which we discern little Aristotle but clear ideological continuities between them and the 'little book'.

7. A Florentine Education

There is little doubt that around 1295 a shift occurred in Dante's sense of his responsibilities and standing as a poet-intellectual, which stimulated him to modify his poetic *materia* and encouraged him to expand his learning. His poetry offers clear testimony of this. Likewise, albeit at the service of their respective local concerns, the *Vita nova*, the *Convivio*, and the *Commedia* also all indicate that the mid-1290s constituted a key moment in Dante's life and career. It would thus seem reasonably safe to treat this as one of the relatively few 'fixed' points in our knowledge of his biography. I would further add that the account in the *Convivio*, since it appears to be supported by autonomous contextualizing evidence, may be deemed, at least for now, to be not unreliable. That this is indeed so finds additional confirmation when we recall that, inter alia, in the *Convivio*, Dante was endeavouring to rehabilitate his reputation, and so was addressing, in the first instance, his fellow-citizens, who would likely have known about his activities during the closing years of the Duecento. To lie would have undermined the *Convivio*'s vindicating goals. As with everything I have said so far, this is a hypothesis; and I hope that I might be permitted one last hypothesis. As I fleetingly alluded earlier, I tend to believe

sognando, già vedea, sì come nella Vita Nova si può vedere'.
57   See Borsa, 'Identità sociale'; Dante Alighieri, *Dante's Lyric Poetry. Poems of Youth and of the 'Vita Nuova'*, ed. with a general introduction and introductory essays by Teodolinda Barolini (Toronto, Buffalo, and London: University of Toronto Press, 2014); Jeffrey Turco, 'Restaging Sin in Medieval Florence: Augustine, Brunetto Latini, and the Streetscape of Dante's *Vita nuova*', *Italian Studies*, 73 (2018), 15–21.

that, given the relatively restricted uniformity of Dante's Florentine intellectual influences, he only began to read more widely during the early years of his exile. Consequently, I wonder whether this was because he was able to take advantage of books owned by individuals, access to which would not have been hampered by institutional restrictions as occurred with the volumes housed in the Florentine *studia*. Indeed, the question that now arises is whether private book collections existed in late-Duecento Florence (Dell'Oso, pp. 137–41). To date, unfortunately, no such collection has come to light. In any case, we should never forget that, as scholars, hypotheses are all that we can propose, and hence why it is vital that we treat the available evidence cautiously and with respect, which, for me, as a textual historicist, means by contextualizing it. Accordingly, it is time to recognize that there is no substantive support for the claim that the poet's intellectual pursuits during his last years in Florence led him to unorthodoxy; or even that, in ideological terms, much actually changed in the transition from the *Vita nova* to the post-*libello* poems. The precise relevance of Beatrice's condemnation in Eden is thus exclusive to the narrative and intellectual demands of the *Commedia*.

8. *c.* 2018

I should like to close by finally clarifying my title. It is obviously a calque on Dante's image of 'hunting' (*Dve* I. 11. 1) for the most elegant Italian vernacular, that 'panther' whose 'tracks he follows' without ever 'finding' or 'seeing' it (16. 1).[58] Similarly, as my argument implies, it is impossible for us ever ultimately to catch up with the poet, and if we believe that we have achieved this, then, what we are actually seeing is a variation of Pazzi's statue. His solidity is in fact a mirage. All we can do is doggedly stay on his trail. Moreover, the signs that we uncover when following him are few, tantalizing, and overwhelmingly problematic, which does not mean that they are not also fascinating, intellectually invigorating, and aesthetically remarkable. Indeed, there is much, and there always will be, that can still be said about them. However, we ought also to recognize not simply what they can, but also what they cannot signify. To put it simply, we must not set them in stone. The time has come for us as a community of scholars to converge around certain points which even if hypotheses, in light of the historical and textual evidence currently available, seem difficult to challenge: Dante is not alluding to Bologna in *Convivio* II. 12; he did not spend time reading in the Florentine mendicant libraries;

58   'Quam multis varietatibus latio dissonante vulgari, decentiorem atque illustrem Ytalie venemur loquelam; et ut nostre venationi pervium callem habere possimus, perplexos frutices atque sentes prius eiciamus de silva' [Amidst the many clashing varieties of vernacular, let us hunt for a more elegant and illustrious language of Italy; and that we may have a free path in our hunt, let us first remove from the forest the intricate and thorny bushes] (I. 11. 1), and 'Postquam venati saltus et pascua sumus Ytalie nec panteram quam sequimur adinvenimus, ut ipsam reperire possimus, rationabilius investigemus de illa ut, solerti studio redolentem ubique et necubi apparentem nostris penitus irretiamus tenticulis' [After we have searched the woodlands and pastures of Italy and have not found the panther we were tracking, in order to catch her, let us examine her more rationally so that through clever scrutiny we may ensnare in our trap the creature whose scent is everywhere but who nowhere appears] (I. 16. 1).

indeed, to term these 'libraries' is a misnomer, since what we are actually talking about are books for the friars' exclusive use that were kept in cells and *armaria* and not in monastic libraries; Dante's knowledge of Aristotle before the exile was extremely restricted; to speak of him as an 'Averroist' makes little sense in terms of late-medieval culture; etc., etc.[59] How we then use such historically and textually validated conclusions in our own work will of course be a matter of personal choice. What we should not do is cling to positions that, in light of the best available evidence, have been demonstrated to be unsatisfactory. We ought not to forget that not all hypotheses are equally valid. As a younger colleague has very recently urged, we need to return to basics and begin to rebuild our work as Dantists on firmer and common foundations.[60] Such a move needs to be based not just on a better informed appreciation of the medieval context and of the Dante-specific documentary evidence, but also of the critical tradition, recognizing without favour what is and is not useful and valid. This would certainly be one way of making the mass of Dante scholarship more manageable and less daunting. Much of what I have discussed in these reflections draws on the work of others — that relatively small group of *dantisti* who have eschewed the temptation of belonging to a 'school', but who have preferred to grant primacy to the poet rather than subordinate him to other interests. If I have one exhortation to make to my fellow-Dantists, it is: 'Read more, write with precision and perhaps less, and, please, please, question your assumptions as you think carefully about the evidence'.[61]

---

59 'La biblioteca di Santa Croce non era al tempo di Dante una biblioteca come la intendiamo noi: di sicuro non era un luogo. Caso mai era un fondo librario il cui statuto era ancipite fra il patrimonio collettivo e l'uso privato': Pegoretti, 'Materiali', p. 40.

60 Anna Pegoretti, 'Bonjour tristesse: Possibilities and Limits of Historicism in Dante Studies', paper given at the conference *Dante Alighieri — Quo vadis? Neue Perspektiven im Dialog der Disziplinen* (Göttingen, 27–29 May 2015). I can think of few other scholars who, in recent years, have suggested and explored more effectively than Anna Pegoretti the ways in which we might 'individuare in prossimità di Dante un territorio comune di studio e divulgazione dottrinale, che tracci anche la sinopia di un insegnamento teologico per lo più irrecuperabile': Anna Pegoretti, '"Oltre la spera che più larga gira": l'Empireo e la "divina scienza"', in *'Theologus Dantes': tematiche teologiche nelle opere dantesche e nei primi commenti*, ed. by Luca Lombardo and others (Venice: Edizioni Ca' Foscari, 2018), pp. 161–88 (p. 165, n. 10).

61 Readers may be perplexed why I have not cited in this essay various studies that, at first blush, might appear relevant to the present discussion. I am aware of this work, and I have deliberately not cited it since I deem it to bear the marks of those limitations that have been highlighted here. By citing I would have courted controversy; and throughout my academic career I have tried to avoid polemicizing, since, in my experience, this is not the way in which to make one's point effectively. At the same time, my hope is that at least one or two colleagues might reconsider their work in light of my observations...

CHAPTER 2

Dante and Doctrine
(and Theology)

1. De doctrina et theologia, quales sint[1]

To treat the (inter-related) concepts of 'doctrine' and 'theology' in Dante is fraught with complications.[2] Both notions are difficult, slippery even, on account of — as we shall see — their rich range of connotation in the poet and in medieval culture. Thus, how best to approach them and what stress to give them is far from straightforward. Equally, the nature of their relationship is perplexing. In particular, it is far from a given that priority should be granted to 'theology', as one might not unreasonably expect in light of the religious concerns of much of Dante's *œuvre*. Two things, however, can already be stated with a degree of certainty. First, *dottrina/doctrina* in Dante cannot be restricted to 'Christian doctrine' and its dissemination. The notion of 'doctrine', despite its strong religious associations, has long had more general connotations:

> Taken in the sense of 'the act of teaching' and 'the knowledge imparted by teaching', this term [Christian doctrine] is synonymous with CATECHESIS and CATECHISM. [...] The word katechesis means instruction by word of mouth, especially by questioning and answering. Though it [doctrine] may apply to any subjectmatter, it is commonly used for instruction in the elements of religion, especially preparation for initiation into Christianity.[3]

Second, Christian doctrine and theology have traditionally been seen as closely connected:

1   The subheading calques and adapts the title of the opening *quaestio* of Thomas Aquinas's *ST* — 'Quaestio 1. de sacra doctrina, qualis sit et ad quae se extendat' [on the nature and extent of sacred doctrine] — a question which has some bearing on matters discussed in this chapter. My reliance on Thomas and on medieval forms of analysis is also meant to highlight the strongly historicist and philological emphasis of my discussion.

2   The present essay originally constituted the opening chapter of the groundbreaking multi-author collection *Reviewing Dante's Theology*, ed. by Claire E. Honess and Matthew Treherne, 2 vols (Oxford: Peter Lang, 2013), and was supposed to serve as a contextualizing framework for the other contributions by clarifying the inter-relationship between 'theology' and 'doctrine'. On account of the complications discussed in what follows, I remain unconvinced that I adequately dispensed my obligations.

3   Thomas B. Scannell, 'Doctrine, Christian', in *The Catholic Encyclopedia*, ed. by Charles G. Hebermann and others, 15 vols (New York: Universal Knowledge Foundation, 1907–12), v, 75–88 (p. 75).

> A systematic exposition of Christianity is [...] demanded by the needs of instruction and preaching. Theological science deals with revelation primarily from the standpoint of truth, whereas catechetics stresses the goodness of the teaching, but the two cannot be divorced, and the theoretical has to be associated with the practical since there is a danger that doctrine may be isolated from vital problems.[4]

Nonetheless, as I hope to demonstrate, this latter fact does not substantially affect the essential validity of my first claim regarding the inappropriateness of limiting Dante's thinking about doctrine to its specifically Christian dimension or, indeed, of restricting his treatment of theology to its doctrinal effects.

In light of the complexity of the definitional, historical, and intellectual issues involved, it is probably not surprising that, not just when I first wrote this piece, but still now, the questions associated with doctrine and theology should be a source of puzzlement: What might be the precise nature of the relationship between 'doctrine' and 'theology', never mind the relationship between 'doctrine' and a specifically Dantean branch of theology, 'Dante's theology'? What meaning should be ascribed to the two words? Should I return them to the medieval context? Trace their presence in Dante? Or rely on their modern characterizations? In an artist and thinker as ambitious, wide-ranging, innovative, and syncretic as Dante, how can the relative status of 'doctrine' and 'theology' be established? Such questions are not the result of some sophistic 'deconstructive' urge — not least because I am acutely conscious of Dante's warnings about relying on 'ingegno di sofista' (*Par.* xxiv. 81). As far as I am concerned, my uncertainties are precisely the type of interrogation that Dantists have a bit too often failed to carry out when addressing the poet's intellectual formation and interests. That 'doctrine' and 'theology' ought to be subsumed under the 'intellectual' goes, of course, without saying; nonetheless, to be exact, both — and the matter is far from inconsequential — need also to be considered among his spiritual and affective concerns. The critical failure to define,[5] I regret to say, has had, on the whole, a reductive and distorting effect on

---

4   M. E. Williams, 'Doctrine', in *New Catholic Encyclopedia*, ed. by an Editorial Staff at the Catholic University of America, 17 vols (New York: McGraw-Hill, 1967–74), v, 939–40 (p. 939). It is worth remembering that the modern notion of doctrine is somewhat narrower than the medieval sense of the concept, given that 'since the Reformation, Catholics have more often understood the word doctrine of [*sic*] a body of truths and used other words to express the active teaching of the faith' (p. 940). It is also useful to keep in mind that '[c]oncerning the system of Christian doctrine, early summaries and creeds soon coalesced into the present form of the creed, where there is expressed: first, belief in God the Father of all; then belief in Christ the Redeemer, involving an account of salvation history especially as seen in the mysteries of His Passion, death, Resurrection, and Ascension; and, finally, belief in the Holy Spirit and His work of sanctification in the Church, which will continue until the end of the world' (p. 940).

5   Eugenio Garin, too, in commenting on Étienne Gilson, 'Poésie et théologie dans la *Divine Comédie*', in *Atti del Congresso Internazionale di Studi Danteschi*, 2 vols (Florence: Sansoni, 1965–66), I, 197–223, usefully declares that '[i]l testo gilsoniano [...] meriterebbe, senza dubbio, molte chiose, e innanzitutto un esame rigoroso a proposito dei concetti di "filosofia" e di "arte" che sottintende, e di quelli che in realtà devono supporsi validi per i secoli XII al XVI': Eugenio Garin, 'Dante e la filosofia', *Il veltro*, 18 (1974), 281–93 (p. 283). However, and tellingly, during the course of his valuable study, Garin makes no attempt to define his own use of the term 'philosophy', never mind that of

the ways in which scholars have approached the matter of Dante's thought.[6] To put it another way, they have treated as essentially unproblematic that which, in reality, is overwhelmingly complex and difficult.[7]

---

other scholars, apart from a fleeting allusion to Nardi (p. 286; and see n. 21 below), or its meaning in the Middle Ages.

6   The present chapter touches, in some cases fleetingly, on all the questions that I have just raised (for fuller discussions, see Chapters 1, 3, and 4). Its main emphasis, however, as I have mentioned, is historical and historiographical: to assess philologically Dante's usage of the terms 'theology' and 'doctrine', and to examine the ways in which Dante scholarship over the last century or so has discussed the poet's engagement with intellectual and ideological issues, in particular his relationship to theology and philosophy.

7   The leading scholars of Dante's thought, beginning with Bruno Nardi, have always been sensitive to the historical and cultural specificities of Dante's individual ideas. On the other hand, however, they have demonstrated considerably less concern with defining in a philologically refined manner the poet's understanding of the scope and nature of particular broad areas of knowledge, epistemology, and intellectual activity, such as 'philosophy', 'theology', 'wisdom', etc., and hence have tended to underplay the implications of the character and reverberations of his ideological preferences. My studies of Dante's relationship to medieval semiotics and symbolic thought constituted an attempt to begin to address some of the issues arising from this neglect; see, in particular, Zygmunt G. Barański, *Dante e i segni: saggi per una storia intellettuale di Dante* (Naples: Liguori, 2000). Simon Gilson, too, has become increasingly and sophisticatedly aware of questions of definition and of the complex implications of Dante's ideological sympathies; see his 'Medieval Science in Dante's *Commedia*: Past Approaches and Future Directions', *Reading Medieval Studies*, 27 (2001), 39–77, 'Rimaneggiamenti danteschi di Aristotele: *gravitas* e *levitas* nella *Commedia*', in *Le culture di Dante: studi in onore di Robert Hollander*, ed. by Michelangelo Picone and others (Florence: Cesati, 2004), pp. 151–77, and 'Dante and Christian Aristotelianism', in Honess and Treherne, 1, 65–109. It is interesting (and, for me, profoundly reassuring) that, despite what some might consider Simon's and my antithetical approaches to Dante's intellectual formation, given that his point of departure is medieval Aristotelianism, our analyses share many substantive points in common, in particular, as regards Dante's syncretism, the complex nature of his intellectual and artistic itinerary, the vital need to define key terms, the importance of the heaven of the Sun, the complex ways in which knowledge was mediated in the Middle Ages, and, most important of all, the fact that the poet's doctrine cannot be separated from the textual forms through which he transmitted his ideas. Robert Hollander too has noted the proximity between our perspectives; see 'Dante's *Paradiso* as Philosophical Poetry', *Italica*, 86 (2009), 571–82 (pp. 578–79). On Dante's ideological preferences, see also Garin; Alfonso Maierù, 'Dante di fronte alla Fisica e alla Metafisica', in Picone and others, pp. 127–49; Giuseppe Mazzotta, *Dante's Vision and the Circle of Knowledge* (Princeton: Princeton University Press, 1993); and most especially Christian Moevs's exemplary *The Metaphysics of Dante's 'Comedy'* (Oxford: Oxford University Press, 2005). Finally, I should like to make it clear that, in general, I remain sceptical of the recent scholarly trend which, on scant evidence and with an easy disregard for the integrity of Dante's works and for the poet's powerful and repeated affirmations of orthodoxy, insists on associating him with what are blithely deemed to have been unorthodox thinkers and heterodox positions. This tradition has its roots primarily in the work of Maria Corti, though it should be noted that Corti herself was rather more cautious than some of those who appeal to her considerable scholarly authority to legitimate their work on Dante as intellectually deviant. Thus, in the 'Premessa' to her collection of writings on Cavalcanti and on Dante, she noted that '[a] differenza di Cavalcanti Dante nel *Convivio* non uscì mai, tutto sommato, dai territori dell'ortodossia': *Scritti su Cavalcanti e Dante* (Turin: Einaudi, 2003), pp. 5–6 (p. 5). For an extended discussion of orthodoxy and unorthodoxy in the Middle Ages and of Dante's relationship to these notions, as well as a critical analysis of modern claims regarding the poet's heterodoxy, see the next chapter.

2. De theologia 1

Let me be more specific and give some examples, with reference to the notion of theology, of what I have in mind; and, in singling out certain studies, I should like to stress that I am focusing on these not because they are in some way eccentric or especially flawed, overall the opposite is in fact true, but because of their typicality. In each of the three most recent broad-based, synthetic, and generally valuable discussions of 'Dante and theology' in English, not one of the authors feels the need to explain or specify with any sort of rigour what she or he means by theology, never mind what Dante, not to mention the Middle Ages, might have meant by the term. The concept of theology is treated as though it were limpidly clear and straightforward, and common not just to all modern readers of the poet, but also, and more generally, to Dante and his shifting readership across space and time. Like God, theology is one and eternal; although, unlike God, it seems to be easily definable and readily accessible. Yet, it is almost certain that such an attitude would have been met with incredulity, and probably disdain, at the end of the thirteenth and at the beginning of the fourteenth centuries, when major debates raged as regards the status and remit of theology and its relationship to other, indisputably rationalist, intellectual disciplines.[8] However, today too, the notion is rich in nuance, ranging from the study of theistic religion to a system of theoretical principles, from the science of God or religion to, more specifically, 'the science which treats of the existence, character, and attributes of God, his laws and government, the doctrines we are to believe, and the duties we are to practice', and from revealed truth to the rational analysis of a religious faith.[9] To use the term without at least acknowledging the historical and semantic difficulties that it brings in its wake is unlikely, I

---

8   See Marie-Dominique Chenu, *La Théologie comme science au XIIIe siècle*, 3rd rev. edn (Paris: Vrin, 1957), and 'The Masters of the "Theological" Science' and 'Tradition and Progress', in his *Nature, Man, and Society in the Twelfth Century* (Chicago and London: University of Chicago Press, 1968), pp. 270–309 & 310–30; Gillian R. Evans, *Old Arts and New Theology: The Beginnings of Theology as an Academic Discipline* (Oxford: Clarendon Press, 1980), and 'Theology. The Vocabulary of Teaching and Research 1300–1600: Words and Concepts', in *Vocabulary of Teaching and Research between Middle Ages and Renaissance*, ed. by Olga Weijers (Turnhout: Brepols, 1995), pp. 118–33; Ulrich Köpf, *Die Anfänge der theologischen Wissenschaftstheorie im 13. Jahrhundert* (Tübingen: Mohr, 1974); Albert Lang, *Die theologische Prinzipienlehre der mittelalterlichen Scholastik* (Freiburg: Herder, 1964); Jean Leclercq, 'La Théologie comme science dans la littérature quodlibétique', *Recherches de théologie ancienne et médiévale*, 11 (1939), 351–74; Pasquale Porro, 'Tra l'oscurità della fede e il chiarore della visione: il dibattito sullo statuto scientifico della teologia agli inizi del XIV secolo', in *Forme e oggetti della conoscenza nel XIV secolo: studi in ricordo di Maria Elena Reina*, ed. by Luca Bianchi and Chiara Crisciani (Florence: SISMEL and Edizioni del galluzzo, 2014), pp. 195–256; Aimé Solignac, 'Théologie', in DSAM, xv, cols 463–87 (cols 463–81); *Storia della teologia nel Medioevo*, ed. by Giulio D'Onofrio, 3 vols (Casale Monferrato: Piemme, 1996), in particular vol. III: *La teologia delle scuole*; Christian Trottmann, *Théologie et noétique au XIIIe siècle* (Paris: Vrin, 1999). For useful historical syntheses of the medieval use of *theologia*, see Gillian R. Evans, *Philosophy and Theology in the Middle Ages* (London and New York: Routledge, 1993), pp. 10–16; Jean Rivière, 'Theologia', *Revue des sciences religieuses*, 16 (1936), 47–57. See also Francis Schüssler Fiorenza, 'Systematic Theology: Task and Method', in *Systematic Theology: Roman Catholic Perspectives*, ed. by Francis Schüssler Fiorenza and John P. Galvin, 2nd edn (Minneapolis: Fortress Press, 2011), pp. 1–78.
9   *Websters Unabridged Dictionary.*

believe, to bring clarity to the question, and a vital one at that in Dante studies, of the poet's relationship to and view of theology. Only a disregard for theology's connotative wealth could have led Christopher Ryan, in the first edition of *The Cambridge Companion to Dante*, to claim subjectively and without corroboration that 'one way' — and this is of course the 'way' taken in his chapter — 'to sketch Dante's theology in outline [...] is to trace some of the main features of [the poet's] conviction' that 'there is for man no better way to discover God than to attend to that human nature shared by and restored by Christ'.[10] Equally, Amilcare Iannucci, in his entry on 'Theology' for *The Dante Encyclopedia*, restricts his presentation to discussing some of the theologians whose ideas are likely to have influenced the poet and to alluding to the fact that Dante's 'use of theology [...] has been studied by modern scholars chiefly from the perspective of the poem's truth claims',[11] namely, the *Commedia*'s allegory and the ways in which the poet established ties between his poetry and theology.[12] Iannucci's purview is certainly an improvement on

10   Christopher Ryan, 'The Theology of Dante', in *The Cambridge Companion to Dante*, ed. by Rachel Jacoff (Cambridge: Cambridge University Press, 1993), pp. 136–52 (p. 136).
11   Amilcare A. Iannucci, 'Theology', in *The Dante Encyclopedia*, ed. by Richard Lansing (New York and London: Garland, 2000), pp. 811–15 (p. 814). I am not persuaded that Iannucci is correct to state that Dantists have principally studied the poet's recourse to theology in light of his concern to establish the truthfulness of the *Commedia*. The most common way in which modern scholars have discussed Dante and theology, as already was the case among his Trecento commentators, is by highlighting the presence of possible theological sources and influences in the *Commedia* and his other works, namely, borrowings from and links with the writings and positions of figures whom we term 'theologians'. Whether Dante would also have considered all such intellectuals as theologians is a matter to which I shall return in due course.
12   It is certainly the case that considerable work has been and continues to be done on the relationship in the *Commedia* between 'poetic practice and theological thought' as evidenced most recently by the excellent collection of essays edited by Vittorio Montemaggi and Matthew Treherne, *Dante's 'Commedia': Theology as Poetry* (Notre Dame, IN: University of Notre Dame Press, 2010); the quotation is taken from Vittorio Montemaggi and Matthew Treherne, 'Introduction: Dante, Poetry, Theology', pp. 1–13 (p. 4). Indeed, the volume editors go so far as to suggest that the *Commedia* 'is firmly rooted in the medieval tradition of reflection on the nature of theological language, and at the same time presents us with an unprecedented piece of sustained poetic experimentation, which appears to attempt to move beyond traditional theological assessments of the status and value of poetry. Understood in this way, Dante's might be seen as one of the most original theological voices of the Middle Ages' (p. 8). Montemaggi and Treherne's claim is not without value and insight; at the same time, however, it raises at least three major questions if considered in strictly philological terms. First, what is meant by 'the medieval tradition of reflection on the nature of theological language'? Second, what would have been understood by 'theological voice' at the beginning of the fourteenth century? And third, is there any evidence in the *Commedia* to indicate that Dante actually deemed his 'voice' as 'theological' rather than as 'poetic'? For all its many merits, *Dante's 'Commedia': Theology as Poetry* too normally falls short when it comes to historicizing Dante's perception of theology. The one obvious exception is Paola Nasti, '*Caritas* and Ecclesiology in Dante's Heaven of the Sun', pp. 210–44, who, in keeping with what we shall see were substantially Dante's own views, develops her analysis from the fact that 'in the Middle Ages theology was not so much a scientific enterprise as an affective meditation on the word of God' (p. 210); but see also John Took, 'Dante, Conversation, and Homecoming', pp. 308–17 (esp. pp. 309–10). See also *Le teologie di Dante*, ed. by Giuseppe Ledda (Ravenna: Centro dantesco dei frati minori conventuali, 2015), which includes an excellent discussion of the methodological issues related to study of 'Dante and theology' that is also an authoritative survey of the major scholarly contributions in this area: Simon A. Gilson, 'Appunti

Ryan's; however, its limitations are still self-evident. Anna Williams's chapter, 'The Theology of the *Comedy*', which justifiably takes the place of Ryan's in the second edition of the *Companion*, goes further in its assessment of the poem's theological purview than the contributions of its two predecessors. With a welcome degree of historical acumen, it focuses on a relatively wide series of purportedly theological issues, such as humanity's end and what it means to be human, the Last Things, creation, love, and salvation — all issues which, undoubtedly, are of some weight in the *Commedia*. Yet, in Williams's rich survey as well, we find no overarching appraisal of Dante's thinking about theology, no attempt at definition, or even at establishing whether or not the poet actually judged the problems highlighted as theological in character. As Ryan had done, Williams too has recourse to a personal and untested generalization in order to organize her argument: 'the conviction that human beings can affect their own, and even others', salvation, is the dominant theological idea in the *Comedy*'.[13]

Scholars writing in English on Dante and theology are in no way unique. Cesare Vasoli's excellent critical assessment of the notable achievements attained in the study of Dante's thought during the first half of the twentieth century,[14] especially as regards the mapping of his philosophical and, to a lesser extent, his theological sources, is, in this regard, both revealing in itself and a useful guide to the approaches which in particular Bruno Nardi and Étienne Gilson took to investigate the poet's intellectual interests.[15] As is common in the Italian tradition, Vasoli treats

metodologici su teologia e scolastica nel *Paradiso*', pp. 99–115. For a very recent judicious assessment, see Abigail Rowson, 'Theologians as Persons' (unpublished PhD thesis, University of Leeds, 2018).

13   Anna N. Williams, 'The Theology of the *Comedy*', in *The Cambridge Companion to Dante*, ed. by Rachel Jacoff, 2nd edn (Cambridge: Cambridge University Press, 2007), pp. 201–17 (p. 202).

14   Cesare Vasoli, 'Filosofia e teologia in Dante', in *Dante nella critica d'oggi: risultati e prospettive*, ed. by Umberto Bosco (Florence: Le Monnier, 1965), pp. 47–71.

15   In general, Nardi, and in his wake scholars such as Kenelm Foster, Patrick Boyde, Vasoli himself, and Maria Corti, have tended to focus primarily on scholastic Aristotelian thinkers. This emerges clearly when, for once, Nardi defined what he meant by philosophy: 'Col nome di Filosofia dal secolo XIII al XVI s'intese il compatto e organico sistema di dottrine di Aristotele intorno alla natura e composizione del mondo, alle sue cause e alle sue finalità': Bruno Nardi, 'Filosofia e teologia ai tempi di Dante', in *Atti del Congresso Internazionale di Studi Danteschi*, I (1965), 79–175 (p. 79). As a result of this concentration — Nardi's definition fits uncomfortably with Dante's treatment of *Filosofia* in the *Convivio*; see Peter Dronke, *Dante's Second Love: The Originality and the Contexts of the 'Convivio'* (Leeds: Maney, 1997); Paola Nasti, *Favole d'amore e 'saver profondo': la tradizione salomonica in Dante* (Ravenna: Longo, 2007), pp. 93–130 — broad swathes of Dante's religious culture, from Augustine to Alan of Lille and from Gregory the Great to the *Glossa ordinaria*, were, until quite recently, pushed into the shadows when not actually ignored. This is not the place to examine in detail the history of the study of Dante's intellectual formation, but see Barański, esp. pp. 9–39, as well as my 'Sulla formazione intellettuale di Dante: alcuni problemi di definizione', *Studi e problemi di critica testuale*, 90:1 (2015), 31–54, and ' "With such vigilance! With such effort!" Studying Dante "Subjectively" ', *Italian Culture*, 33 (2015), 55–69, and Chapter 1; Garin; Simon Gilson's studies quoted in n. 7. Suffice it to say that, while there have always been scholars who have drawn attention to the poet's ties to non-Aristotelian traditions (if I may be permitted such a loose categorization), their work, until the last fifteen or so years, has tended not to be seen as part of the mainstream of the study of his philosophical and theological formation. *Reviewing Dante's Theology* marks an important stage in arriving at a better appreciation of Dante's relationship not just to Christian culture but also to the world of medieval ideas more generally.

filosofia and *teologia* together, a mark, I would suggest, of the failure of many secular Italian academics to come properly to terms with the strongly religious character of so much of Dante's *œuvre*.[16] As a result, they have not infrequently downplayed and at times actually elided the importance of the poet's Christianity, even when, as in the *Vita nova* and in the *Commedia*, this certainly constitutes the works' vital element, as is obvious from their emphasis on salvation and on the primacy of the transcendent.[17] Vasoli warns in fact of the dangers of approaching Dante with an '*ardor theologicus*' (p. 48).[18] As we have come to expect, at no stage in his largely meticulous presentation does Vasoli feel the need to define either theology or philosophy. Indeed, for much of the essay, the distinction between the two is blurred, which would not have pleased the masters in thirteenth- and fourteenth-century theological and arts university faculties who were intent on safeguarding the integrity and independence of their respective disciplines. Nor would such an approach have met with the approval of a leading theologian such as Bonaventure of Bagnoregio:

> Philosophia quidem agit de rebus, ut sunt in natura, seu in anima secundum notitiam naturaliter insitam, vel etiam acquisitam: sed theologia, tanquam scientia supra fidem fundata et per Spiritum sanctum revelata, agit et de eis quae spectant ad gratiam et gloriam et etiam ad Sapientiam aeternam. Unde ipsa, substernens sibi philosophicam cognitionem et assumens de naturis rerum,

---

16   Elsewhere, in fact, Vasoli revealed himself sensitive to Dante's religious culture and beliefs; see 'La Bibbia nel *Convivio* e nella *Monarchia*', in *Dante e la Bibbia*, ed. by Giovanni Barblan (Florence: Olschki, 1986), pp. 19–39; 'Introduzione' and annotations to Dante Alighieri, *Convivio*, ed. by Cesare Vasoli and Domenico De Robertis, in Dante Alighieri, *Opere minori*, 2 vols (Milan and Naples: Ricciardi, 1979–88), II.1 (1988).

17   It would not be reasonable, however, to see this as an exclusively Italian failing. Thus, the widespread interest in North America in an 'unorthodox' Dante, *mutatis mutandis*, has similar secular and secularizing roots. I return below to the weighty question of the inter-relationship between theology and philosophy in Dante and in medieval culture.

18   In using this phrase, Vasoli was referring in particular to the work of two scholars: first, the influential book of the French Dominican historian, Pierre Mandonnet, *Dante le théologien* (Paris: Desclée de Brouwer, 1935); and second the various studies of the important Jesuit scholar, Giovanni Busnelli, who, throughout his career, doggedly persisted, even against definitive evidence to the contrary, in maintaining that Dante's primary intellectual influence was Thomas Aquinas, a view which no serious Dantist would now support; see in particular, his annotations to Dante Alighieri, *Il Convivio ridotto a miglior lezione e commentato*, ed. by Giovanni Busnelli and Giuseppe Vandelli, 2 vols (Florence: Le Monnier, 1934–37; rev. edn by Antonio Enzo Quaglio, 1964–68). Gilson effectively assesses the value of Busnelli and Vandelli's commentary: 'It will [...] be profitable to consult the numerous philosophical and theological works cited in notes by these two editors; but such works may be utilized without danger only on condition that one discerns clearly, beneath their analogies or their verbal coincidences with the text of Dante, the profound differences of thought due to the clearly defined use which Dante makes of them. Dante did not envisage, or we are not sure that he envisaged, anything save what he says in his text, certainly not anything of what the other authors cited by way of comment say. This has sometimes been forgotten': Étienne Gilson, *Dante the Philosopher* (London: Sheed & Ward, 1948), p. 85 n. 1. Much of Nardi's work was a deliberate counter to Busnelli's claims; see 'Il tomismo di Dante e il p. Busnelli S.J.', in his *Saggi di filosofia dantesca*, 2nd edn (Florence: La Nuova Italia, 1967), pp. 341–80. It is not hard to think that the extensive downplaying of Dante's religious sentiments and interests is in part a lasting reaction to Busnelli's and Mandonnet's dogmatism.

quantum sibi opus est ad fabricandum speculum, per quod fiat repraesentatio divinorum.[19]

[Philosophy is concerned with things as they are in nature, or in the soul according to innate, or acquired, knowledge; but theology, as a science rooted in faith and revealed through the Holy Spirit, is concerned also with things that pertain to grace, glory, and eternal Wisdom. Therefore this one [theology] subordinates philosophical knowledge to itself and gathers from the nature of things what it needs to make a mirror, through which divine things may be represented.]

The failure to establish the remit of theology and of philosophy, whether in Dante or in late medieval culture, is not simply a failure of definition, of appreciating the subjective and historical dimension of both notions, but is also a rather more serious failure affecting the elucidation and understanding of Dante's texts and his intellectual and artistic development. Thus, the relative status of philosophy and theology fundamentally constrains interpretations of several of the poet's works. For instance, according to Nardi, in the *Convivio*, the two disciplines are close, representing two intertwined tendencies: 'una apertamente mistica, l'altra tendenzialmente razionalistica [...] formata di elementi filosofici frammisti a elementi teologici, non ancora ben fusi fra loro, anzi spesso discordanti gli uni tra gli altri'.[20] Gilson, on the other hand, maintained that, in the treatise, Dante presented theology and philosophy as distinct, with the latter, and contrary to Thomas Aquinas's opinion, not in fact subordinated to the former.[21] Whatever

19   Bonaventure, *Breviloquium*, Prologus 3. 2, in *Doctoris Seraphici Sancti Bonaventurae [...] Opera omnia*, 10 vols (Quaracchi: Collegium S. Bonaventurae, 1882–1902), v, 205.

20   Bruno Nardi, *Nel mondo di Dante* (Rome: Edizioni di Storia e Letteratura, 1944), p. 228.

21   Étienne Gilson's claim regarding the relationship of philosophy and theology in the *Convivio* has garnered considerable consensus: 'Il fatto, poi, che D. abbia messo (come, del resto, tutto il Medioevo) la Teologia al di sopra delle altre scienze, secondo il Gilson non comporta subordinazione della f[ilosofia] alla teologia, nell'ambito della distinzione tra gerarchia di valori e di giurisdizione': Vincenzo Placella, 'Filosofia', in *ED*, ii, 881–85 (p. 881). See also Vasoli, 'Filosofia', pp. 53–55, 59, and edn, p. 262. Eugenio Garin too recognized that establishing the relative standing in the *Convivio* of philosophy and theology, which once again he too does not define, is crucial when attempting to describe and understand the work; see Eugenio Garin, 'Il pensiero di Dante', in his *Storia dei generi letterari italiani. La filosofia. I. Dal Medioevo all'Umanesimo* (Milan: Vallardi, 1947), pp. 133–56 (p. 142). For Garin, philosophy's role in Dante is secondary, since the poet's intellectual striving is normally directed towards the divine: 'Non deve infatti dimenticarsi che la *donna gentile* del *Convivio* non può identificarsi *sic et simpliciter* con la filosofia aristotelica, escludente da sè la conquista della rivelazione cristiana. I termini in cui Dante ce la rappresenta, connettendola insieme con la Sapienza dei *Proverbi* e col Verbo giovanneo, coincidono con quelli con cui i più ortodossi teologi ci parlano del Figlio di Dio come mondo delle idee esemplari' (p. 140; and see also pp. 145–46). Garin's views thus separate him from both Gilson and Nardi. Although I find myself largely in sympathy with Garin's position, as ought to become clear below (and see also my *Dante e i segni*), I also believe that Gilson's stress on the (relative) independence of philosophy and Nardi's emphasis on the *frammischiato* character of the different doctrinal elements in the *Convivio* are also essentially correct. To recognize the self-sufficient distinctiveness of philosophy in the treatise, as well as its 'intermingling' of sources, does not invalidate the idea that, in it, theology holds pride of place. In his 'rationalist' reading of the *Convivio*, Gilles Meersseman refers to Dante's position in the treatise as 'teologia filosofica' and 'teologia [...] della ragione', highly questionable designations, which do nothing to help resolve and counter the terminological confusion and inattentiveness bedeviling this area of Dante studies; see

the merits of Nardi's and Gilson's positions, without a proper sense of what each meant by theology and philosophy, and what, according to them, Dante judged each of these to embrace, then, in the final analysis, it remains difficult adequately to evaluate their claims, never mind their responses to each other's work. The problems are, of course, the same when gauging the effectiveness of the different trajectories each traces of Dante's ideological development.[22]

3. De theologia 2

That Dantists, some of whom elsewhere in their work have shown themselves to be acutely sensitive to historical and textual nuance, should nonetheless demonstrate limited philological discernment when addressing the poet's thinking about theology (and philosophy) is surprising; and it is even more so when we remember that definitions of *theologia* and discussions of its status proliferated in the Middle Ages, and that Dante himself offered a clear and authoritative explanation of *doctrina sacra*. In illuminating the analogies between the 'sciences' and the heavens in the *Convivio*, Dante writes:

> Lo Cielo empireo per la sua pace simiglia la divina scienza, che piena è di tutta
> pace: la quale non soffera lite alcuna d'oppinioni o di sofistici argomenti, per la

Gilles G. Meersseman, 'Dante come teologo', in *Atti del Congresso Internazionale di Studi Danteschi*, I, 177–95 (p. 185).

22   Scholars have tended to present the history of Dante's intellectual development either as progressive and evolutionary (for Nardi, the movement goes from the 'intermingling' of philosophy and theology in the *Convivio* to the primacy of the former in the *Monarchia* — Nardi mistakenly believed that the political treatise preceded the *Commedia*, rather than having been written while the poet was composing *Paradiso* — before the definitive triumph of the theological in the 'sacrato poema', *Par.* XXIII. 62), or as largely consistent and coherent, given that, according to this view, the different moments of the poet's career are characterized by significant ideological continuity. This is, of course, the interpretation championed by Gilson and Garin, as well as by Kenelm Foster and John Scott. I have not yet examined Foster's generally balanced and terminologically not unaware contributions, since they fit better with my discussion of *teologia* and *dottrina* below. In recent years, both types of 'orderly' accounts of Dante's intellectual history have begun to be called into question. In particular, as the idea of Dante as a syncretist has taken hold, so it has become increasingly difficult to present his thought as tidily packaged. See Barański, *Dante e i segni*, esp. pp. 30–32, and passim; Simon A. Gilson, 'Sincretismo e scolastica in Dante', *Studi e problemi di critica testuale*, 90:1 (2015), 317–39; Moevs, pp. 86, 214–15. It is interesting, not to say ironic, that, together with Gianfranco Contini's now canonical definition of the *Commedia* as a plurilingual 'encyclopaedic' poem (*Un'idea di Dante* (Turin: Einaudi, 1976), p. 272), the other main influence behind modern syncretic readings of Dante should be Bruno Nardi, who regularly highlighted the range of the poet's doctrinal sources and the personal stress he gave to these: 'egli non è averroista e neppure tomista; non esclusivamente aristotelico, né soltanto neoplatonico, o agostiniano puro': Bruno Nardi, 'Sigieri di Brabante nella *Divina Commedia* e le fonti della filosofia di Dante', *Rivista filosofica neo-scolastica*, 3 (1911), 187–95, 526–45, and 4 (1912), 73–90, 225–39 (also in book form, Spianate [Pescia]: *presso l'autore*, 1912; the quotation is found on p. 69). Nardi correctly linked Dante's approach to the fact that the poet was 'un uomo di cultura del XIII secolo, non teologo e non filosofo "di professione", non legato alla "routine" della scuola o alla osservanza di una unica direttiva speculativa' (Vasoli, 'Filosofia', p. 50). In medieval terms, and crucially, Dante was not a *clericus* but a *laicus*; see Ruedi Imbach, *Dante, la philosophie et les laïcs* (Fribourg: Editions Universitaires, 1996). For an important, new, and polemical reading of Dante's intellectual trajectory, see George Corbett, *Dante and Epicurus: A Dualistic Vision of Secular and Spiritual Fulfilment* (Leeds: Legenda, 2013).

eccellentissima certezza del suo subietto, lo quale è Dio. E di questa dice esso alli suoi discepoli: 'La pace mia do a voi, la pace mia lascio a voi' [John 14: 27], dando e lasciando a loro la sua dottrina, che è questa scienza di cu' io parlo. Di costei dice Salomone: 'Sessanta sono le regine, e ottanta l'amiche concubine; e delle ancille adolescenti non è numero: una è la colomba mia' [Song of Songs 6: 7–8]. Tutte scienze chiama regine e drude e ancille; e questa chiama perfetta perché perfettamente ne fa il vero vedere nel quale si cheta l'anima nostra. (*Conv.* II. 14. 19–20)[23]

The basic substance of Dante's treatment of theology is not difficult to grasp. Like the Empyrean's relationship to the other heavens — 'Veramente, fuori di tutti questi, li catolici pongono lo cielo Empireo' (*Conv.* II. 3. 8) — 'la scienza divina, che è Teologia appellata' (*Conv.* II. 13. 8) is distinct from the other *scientiae*, which,

---

23   For a valuable analysis of this passage that both has its explicit basis in the current chapter and yet also departs from it, see Anna Pegoretti, 'L'Empireo in Dante e la "divina scienza" del *Convivio*', in '*Theologus Dantes': tematiche teologiche nelle opere dantesche e nei primi commenti*, ed. by Luca Lombardo and others (Venice: Edizioni Ca' Foscari, 2019), pp. 147–74 (pp. 158–71). My friend Anna goes 'in una direzione diversa e ancora più radicale' than my Scripturally circumscribed reading of Dante's idea of theology. Consequently, she maintains that 'Questa dottrina di cui Dante parla sembra essere solo ed esclusivamente la Parola del Cristo, il Verbo trasmesso dai Vangeli; ancora meglio, l'auto-Rivelazione che è operata per il tramite dell'Incarnazione e che troverà il suo compimento ultimo nell'invio dello Spirito Santo. La sua piena comprensione non appare mediata da metodo alcuno, ma è resa possibile solo dal dono pentecostale dello Spirito, unico "assistente" del *magister* Cristo, in un'aula che è il *cuore* del discente [...]. L'esperienza conoscitiva che emerge è di tipo rivelatorio e ha poco a che fare con una scienza discorsiva e dimostrativa (come inevitabilmente è invece il sapere umano, esegesi biblica compresa)' (pp. 163–64). Pegoretti's interpretation depends fundamentally on granting primacy to Dante's quotation of John 14: 27, as well as to related passages from John 14 and 16, including their exegesis, especially by Thomas Aquinas. However, as I hope the discussion here of *Conv.* II. 14. 19–20 makes evident, there are implications that go beyond the *sententia* from John. At the same time, as someone who has long stressed the importance in Dante, including for our understanding of his notion of theology, of what Pegoretti terms knowledge that is 'given as a gift', namely, of revelation and of divinely inspired forms of knowledge, I am naturally strongly supportive of her 'affective' standpoint. Indeed, I suspect that the differences in our respective interpretations of Dante's treatment of theology in the *Convivio* are far from unresolvable. Anna brings her argument to a close as follows: 'Sulla base di una lettura *ex parte obiecti* dell'intera descrizione dantesca delle scienze, ho cercato di limitare al minimo i riferimenti al ruolo del soggetto conoscente, ovvero dell'eventuale "discente" di questa peculiare dottrina, la quale va prima compresa in sé. Mi sono limitata a identificarlo come il destinatario della mediazione dello Spirito Santo, che lo rende — come gli apostoli, ma anche "i dottori della Chiesa come Agostino e altri", "a Spiritu Sancto adiutos" nella stesura delle loro opere (*Mon.* III, III, 13) — *capacis*, gli permette cioè di comprendere in modo certo la natura di Dio, della Trinità e della loro unione con i fedeli (il corpo mistico di Cristo). Il fatto che una tale grazia sia *data* permette anch'esso di tralasciare — almeno per il momento, e per necessità metodologica — l'analisi delle elaborazioni umane di una simile scienza, compresa l'esegesi biblica di quanti Dante chiama "teologi". Sia concesso a tale proposito semplicemente ipotizzare che solo in seconda istanza si possa allargare lo sguardo all'approccio — più o meno arduo e contrastato — dei mortali alla "divina scienza", ai *documenta Christi* tramandati sì dalle Sacre Scritture, ma inerti al di fuori di un quadro trinitario' (pp. 170–71). My reading of *Conv.* II. 14. 19–20, and hence the view of Dante's idea of theology that it proposes, is largely fixed on 'the human elaborations of a similar science'. One might say that, in writing this chapter, the 'second instance' was for me the 'first'. Our responsibility as scholars is now to bring 'peace', as Dante surely would have wanted, to his two overlapping iterations of theology included in his definition — iterations that are not just interconnected but also have their being in and through the revealed Word.

as Solomon asserts, and the exegetical tradition concurred, are all subordinate to it: 'una est columba mea perfecta mea una est matris suae electa genetrici suae viderunt illam filiae et beatissimam praedicaverunt reginae et concubinae et laudaverunt eam' [one is my dove, my perfect one, the only one of her mother, the favourite of the one who bore her. The daughters saw her, and declared her most blessed: the queens and concubines praised her] (Song of Songs 6: 8). Having God as its 'subject', and hence dealing with 'the most excellent certainty', theology is 'perfect', reveals the 'truth', and permits no controversy or sophistry. In addition, its appeal and the satisfaction it provides are affective rather than intellectual: 'ne fa il vero vedere nel quale si cheta l'anima nostra'. Fittingly, 'peace' is what binds together the various strands of Dante's presentation; and the poet leaves no doubt as to the centrality of 'pace' in his conception of theology by drawing on the authority of Jesus's words — 'Pacem relinquo vobis, pacem meam do vobis' [I leave you peace, my peace I give to you] — words which, neatly, become emblematic of 'la sua [Christ's] dottrina, che è questa scienza'.[24] Theology thus finds its expression in and through 'la voce del verace autore, | [...] di sé parlando' (*Par.* XXVI. 40–41), which, as the two exemplary and strategic *sententiae* from the Old and New Testaments confirm, reaches us thanks to the miracle of Scripture. In essence, for Dante, theology is revelation of the divine as mediated through 'la divina Scrittura' (*Par.* XXIX. 90), the supreme *vestigium Dei* (see Chapter 9). Its methods are those of exegesis, as Dante confirms when, rather than conventionally speaking of *allegoria in factis* to allude to Biblical hermeneutics,[25] he associates the interpretation of Scripture specifically with 'theologians': 'Veramente li teologi questo senso [l'allegorico] prendono altrimenti che li poeti' (*Conv.* II. 1. 4).[26]

---

24   On the importance of peace for Dante, see Claire E. Honess, '"Ecce nunc tempus acceptabile": Henry VII and Dante's Ideal of Peace', *The Italianist*, 33 (2013), 482–502. See also the essays by Spencer Pearce (pp. 115–40), Matthew S. Kempshall (pp. 141–72), Elena Lombardi (pp. 173–930), Vittorio Montemaggi (pp. 195–225), and Pamela Williams (pp. 227–49) in *War and Peace in Dante*, ed. by John C. Barnes and Daragh O'Connell (Dublin: Four Courts Press, 2014). A major influence on Dante's treatment of peace is Augustine's *sententia* 'inquietum est cor nostrum, donec requiescat in te' (*Conf.* I. 1; our heart is restless, until it may rest in You) which the poet calques in the phrase 'nel quale [il vero] si cheta l'anima nostra'. I am grateful to George Corbett for this reference. For the importance of Augustine's dictum and the ideas associated with it in the *Commedia*, see Elena Lombardi, *The Wings of the Doves: Love and Desire in Dante and Medieval Culture* (Montreal and Ithaca, NY: McGill-Queens University Press, 2012), pp. 113–14.

25   On medieval allegory, see Marie-Dominique Chenu, *La Théologie au douzième siècle* (Paris: Vrin, 1957); Henri de Lubac, *Exégèse médiévale*, 2 vols (Paris: Aubier, 1959–64), English translation: *Medieval Exegesis: The Four Senses of Scripture*, 3 vols (Grand Rapids, MI: Eerdmans, 1998–2009); Beryl Smalley, *The Study of the Bible in the Middle Ages*, 3rd edn (Oxford: Blackwell, 1983); Ceslas Spicq, *Esquisse d'une histoire de l'exégèse latine* (Paris: Vrin, 1944); Armand Strubel, '*Allegoria in factis* et *Allegoria in verbis*', *Poétique*, 23 (1975) 342–57, and '*Grant senefiance a': allégorie et littérature au Moyen Âge* (Paris: Campion, 2002); Jon Whitman, *Allegory: The Dynamics of an Ancient and Medieval Technique* (Oxford: Clarendon Press, 1987).

26   I am mystified how Meersseman can conclude that, in the *Convivio*, 'per teologia Dante intende quella che dai moderni viene chiamata teodicea, cioè scienza del Dio della ragione, non di quello della fede. [...] Però è più probabile che con teologia Dante fece allusione al *Libro delle cagioni* di Proclo [...] spesso citato nel *Convivio*' (p. 185).

So far so clear; now, however, come the problems. About the same time as Dante was composing the *Commedia*, the Dominican Durandus of Saint Pourçain noted, in the prologue to his commentary on the *Sentences* of Peter Lombard, that, in his era, three main theological traditions were discernible. The first and long-established position, which can loosely be considered as Augustinian in character, equated theology with Scripture and revelation.[27] The second and, at the time, increasingly influential tradition inaugurated by St Thomas, which Durandus energetically opposed, stressed the 'scientific' nature of *theologia*, namely its recourse to the logical structures of Aristotelianism, which meant, in practice, treating the articles of faith as 'first principles' from which to depart in order to arrive by deduction at further, more accessible, truths as conclusions.[28] The third current, which Durandus discussed second since it had ties to the first *habitus*, concentrated on the principles of theology treated in themselves rather than on the conclusions, and hence on the new knowledge, that might be drawn from those same principles.[29] Durandus felt strongly that, despite Thomas Aquinas's standing and their belonging to the same order, his predecessor had seriously erred when he argued that theology was a *scientia*.[30] Indeed, as is discernible from the polemical tones of Durandus's presentation, relations in the early fourteenth century between those who tied *theologia* to Scripture and those who approached it with the 'modes of the philosophers' were anything but straightforward and harmonious.[31] Dante's explicit emphasis on the equation between Scripture and theology thus unambiguously locates him among the ranks of the traditionalists and, at least implicitly, in opposition to the theological rationalists. The poet's

27 'Theologia videtur posse accipi tripliciter: Vno modo pro habitu, quo solum vel principaliter assentimus his, quae in sacra scriptura traduntur, et prout in ea traduntur' [It is clear that Theology can be understood in three ways: one way as a lasting disposition of the soul which alone or principally moves us to accept the things handed down in Sacred Scripture and to accept them as they are handed down in it]: Durandus of St Pourçain, *In Petri Lombardi Sententias Theologicas Commentariorum libri IIII* (Venice: Ex officina Gasparis Bindoni, 1586), Prologus 1. 6.

28 'Tertio accipitur Theologia communius (nescio si verius) pro habitu eorum, quae deducuntur ex articulis fidei, et ex dictis sacrae scripturae, sicut conclusiones ex principiis: et hic modus nunc vertitur communiter in ore loquentium' [Third, Theology can be understood more commonly (I don't know whether more truly) as a systematic understanding of those things that are deducted from the articles of faith, and from the words of Sacred Scriptures, as conclusions from principles: and this way is now commonly adopted in the words of those who speak]: *In Petri Lombardi Sententias*, Prologus 1. 8.

29 'Secundo accipitur Theologia, pro habitu, quo fides, et ea quae in sacra scriptura traduntur, defenduntur, et declarantur, ex quibusdam principiis nobis notioribus' [The second way in which Theology is understood is as a lasting disposition of the soul by means of which faith and the things handed down in Sacred Scripture are defended and clarified by relying on principles that we know better]: *In Petri Lombardi Sententias*, Prologus 1. 7.

30 See Maria Teresa Beonio Brocchieri Fumagalli, *Durando di S. Porziano: elementi filosofici della terza redazione del 'Commento alle Sentenze'* (Florence: La Nuova Italia, 1969), pp. 1–51; Elizabeth Lowe, *The Contested Theological Authority of Thomas Aquinas: The Controversies between Hervaeus Natalis and Durandus of St. Pourçain* (New York and London: Routledge, 2003), pp. 99–106. See also Isabel Iribarren, *Durandus of St Pourçain: A Dominican Theologian in the Shadow of Aquinas* (Oxford: Oxford University Press, 2005). See below for a fuller discussion of Thomas's conception of theology.

31 See Chenu, *Théologie comme science*, pp. 15–32, 85–100.

stress on the affective character of theology is especially significant in this respect. Nor, in itself, does the fact that he labels *teologia* a *scienza* necessarily attenuate his intellectual and religious *prise de position*, since *scientia*, in its broad acceptation of 'knowledge', had long been used by both sides to refer to theology. In fact, already in Augustine, theology is termed a science: 'Theologia est scientia de rebus quae ad salutem hominis pertinent' [Theology is a science about things that pertain to man's salvation] (*De Trinitate* XIV. I).[32]

In light of the tensions marring early Trecento religious culture, it is tempting to conclude that Dante's description of the nature and remit of theology was, beyond its strictly definitional ends, also an affirmation of partisanship. Yet, for all its seeming plausibility, such an interpretation is almost certainly wrong, doing scant justice to the subtlety, originality, and equanimity of the poet's presentation. If, on the one hand, Dante is quite clear about which idea of theology he considers correct and makes little attempt to blur the divergences between different positions, on the other, as befits a definition centred so fixedly on peace, his treatment of theology is noteworthy for its sincere effort to mitigate conflict rather than to foster it. What underpins the poet's assessment of theology is the sad awareness that the 'divine science' had become an intellectual and institutional battlefield — hence his almost immediate declaration that it 'non soffera lite alcuna d'oppinioni o di sofistici argomenti' (*Conv.* II. 14. 19). Such a statement, as far as I have been able to ascertain, is exceptional in contemporary treatments of theology (in fact, as will become apparent shortly, it is far from the only 'quirkiness' in Dante's characterization of the 'colomba').[33] Kenelm Foster, in his important discussion of the poet's understanding of theology, remarks that 'questa nozione di T[eologia] [Dante's privileging of peace] è, a dir poco, assai inconsueta'.[34] He then goes on specifically to contrast Dante's 'peaceful' perspective with Thomas Aquinas's viewpoint, styling the former as 'certamente non tomista'.[35]

32   On the slippery notion of *scientia*, see Patrick Boyde, 'L'esegesi di Dante e la scienza', in *Dante e la scienza*, ed. by Patrick Boyde and Vittorio Russo (Ravenna: Longo, 1995), pp. 9–23 (pp. 20–21); Gilson, 'Medieval Science', pp. 39–44; Eileen Serene, 'Demonstrative Science', in *The Cambridge History of Later Medieval Philosophy*, ed. by Norman Kretzmann and others (Cambridge: Cambridge University Press, 1982), pp. 496–517.

33   Dante's position, however, does have connections with concerns expressed about the current state of theological studies by Thomas Aquinas in his Prologue to the *ST*: 'Consideravimus namque hujus doctrinae novitios in his quae a diversis scripta sunt plurimum impediri, partim quidem propter multiplicationem inutilium quaestionum, articulorum, et argumentorum' [For we have considered novitiates in this doctrine are often impeded by what has been written by different authors, partly because of the multiplication of useless questions, articles, and arguments]. It also appears to hark back to Augustine's dictum: 'Homo timens deum voluntatem eius in scripturis sanctis diligenter inquirit. Et ne amet certamina, pietate mansuetus' [The person who fears God diligently seeks His will in the sacred scriptures. He is made gentle by piety, lest he like disputes] (*De doctr. chr.* III. I. I).

34   Kenelm Foster, 'Teologia', in *ED*, V, 564–68 (p. 565). Foster had previously noted, when speaking about the role Dante had accorded to revelation in his description, that '[f]in qui, non c'è dubbio, si tratta del consueto insegnamento cattolico, ma tuttavia importanti differenze emergono non appena andiamo più a fondo' (p. 564).

35   Foster, p. 565. For Thomas, 'come del resto per tutti i teologi del suo tempo, presupposto fondamentale della *sacra doctrina* (come egli preferisce chiamare la T.) è la rivelazione divina quale fu

There is little doubt that Foster's is the most helpful evaluation of Dante and theology that I have read. Contrary to the general trend, it largely focuses on what the poet actually said about theology; and, in addition, as is evident from the passage quoted above, it does this by trying to contextualize Dante's presentation.[36] Yet, despite its usefulness, Foster's encyclopaedia entry is nonetheless problematic, contradictory, and, at times, wrong, as with the assertion that 'all theologians' in the Middle Ages deemed a 'rationalist' approach to theology as 'indispensable', when, in fact, a tradition that had its roots in the Greek Fathers, and which was still strong at the start of the fourteenth century, like Dante, equated theology primarily, when not exclusively, with Christ and Scripture, and considered it an affective experience.[37] As a result of this misrepresentation, Foster is able to treat Dante's discussion of theology in the *Convivio* as eccentric since, in it, as far as he is concerned, the poet leaves no space for reason:

> Di contro le opinioni dei due grandi teologi [Thomas and Bonaventure], la nozione dantesca di T. può essere caratterizzata, negativamente, come la rimozione della ragione dall'ambito della T., e positivamente, come l'identificazione della T. con l'insegnamento di Cristo, cioè come una sorta di adombramento sulla terra, accolto solo per fede, di verità che trascendono la "presente" capacità della ragione e che saranno svelate in una vita futura. (p. 565)

According to Foster, it is only as regards theology's basis in revelation that Dante is part of the mainstream: 'Dove invece c'è differenza è nel modo in cui D. mette rivelazione cristiana e T. in rapporto con l'operare della ragione naturale in

trasmessa nella Scrittura ed esposta dalla Chiesa negli *articuli fidei* (*Sum. theol.* I 1 1 8 ad 2, II II 1 8 e 9, 2 6). Ma tutto ciò — *revelatio*, Scrittura, *articuli fidei* — costituisce soltanto i *principia* della T. in senso tecnico, soltanto il punto di partenza da cui essa inizia a operare. In questo operare, la ricerca e il dibattito razionale svolgono un ruolo pur sempre subordinato, ma indispensabile: "sacra doctrina est argumentativa" (*Sum. theol.* I 1 8, cfr. *In Boet. de Trinitate* 3, 7)' (Foster, p. 565).

36   It is remarkable that, for all their overwhelming, not to say obsessive, concern to establish sources for Dante's views in the *Convivio*, the four major annotated editions of the text pay little attention to the possible sources of Dante's definitions of theology (in addition to *Conv.* II. 14. 19–20, the poet seems to refer to theology at *Conv.* II. 8. 14–15, a passage which I examine in the subsection *De doctrina*) and largely fail to evaluate these in relation to medieval discussions of sacred doctrine. I am of course thinking of the editions by Busnelli and Vandelli, by Cesare Vasoli, by Thomas Ricklin of Book II — Dante Alighieri, *Das Gastmahl*, ed. by Thomas Ricklin, Francis Chevenal, Ruedi Imbach, and Roland Béhar, 4 vols (Hamburg: Meiner, 1996–2004), II (1996) — and by Gianfranco Fioravanti: Dante Alighieri, *Convivio*, in *Opere*, 2 vols (Milan: Mondadori, 2011–14), II, 3–805. Vasoli's is by far the best treatment of *Conv.* II. 14. 19–20, see edn, pp. 261–63.

37   See, with numerous examples, Solignac, cols 466–67, 471, 475–76, 478–79. See also nn. 58 & 66 below. A convenient presentation of theology as 'affective', which furthermore distinguishes this from the 'speculative' and the 'practical' may be found in Hervaeus Natalis, *In quatuor libris sententiarum commentaria* (Paris: apud viduam Dyonisii Moreau & Dyonisium Moreau filium, 1647), Prologus I. 4: 'ista scientia [Theologia] non sit speculativa nec practica loquendo de fine principali [...] quia ista scientia [...] est affectiva [...] Sed scientia affectiva nec est practica nec speculativa [...] quia practicum et speculativum pertinent ad habitus intellectus, sed affectivum pertinet ad voluntatem' [this science is neither speculative nor practical since it speaks of the first end, because this science is affective. But affective science is neither practical nor speculative because the practical and the speculative pertain to intellectual dispositions, but the affective pertains to the will]; but see the whole of the fourth prefactory *quaestio* which deals with '[u]trum Theologia sit speculativa vel practica' [whether Theology is speculative or practical] (p. 10).

questa vita' (p. 564). In truth, as well as his description of late-medieval attitudes to theology, there are other aspects of Foster's claims that I find questionable. Although Dante does not address reason directly in *Conv.* II. 14. 19–20, neither does he deny its relevance in relation to theology. If anything, his definition would seem to imply the opposite. Thus, in a writer as linguistically attentive as Dante, the fact that he should use the same term, *scienza*, to describe both theology and the other, rationally based, intellectual disciplines is unlikely to be simply an instance of conventional inert usage. Rather, I believe, Dante is hinting that there might be ways in which, despite their differences, they might be viewed as parts of a unified system,[38] just as the Empyrean, at least in Christian Aristotelian cosmology, is not entirely separate from the other heavens — and what unites them, as *scienze*, a term which the poet employs three times in his definition, is their 'scientificity', namely, their ties to human reason and knowledge. The use of the technical idiom, 'subietto'/ *subiectum*, which refers to the topic of a discipline, would seem to point in this same direction. That this is indeed the case is confirmed when Dante considers what 'doing' theology entails in practice. As he had explained in the opening of Book II of the *Convivio*, theologians are those who interpret Scripture,[39] a quintessentially rational activity.[40] Furthermore, in Book IV, Dante makes it apparent that there is a theological 'method', which, while distinct from philosophical inquiry, offers 'knowledge' and 'clarification' in the here and now. Discussing human nobility, he writes:

> Acciò che più perfettamente s'abbia conoscenza della umana bontade secondo che in noi è principio di tutto bene, la quale nobilitade si chiama, da chiarire è in questo speziale capitolo come questa bontade discende in noi; e prima per modo naturale, e poi per modo teologico, cioè divino e spirituale. (IV. 21. 1)

And when Dante, at the end of the chapter, examines the question, '[p]er via teologica' (11), he offers a description of God endowing 'his creature' with the 'Doni di Spirito Santo', which is a rationally deduced distillation of Scriptural *loci*, beginning with 'Isaia profeta' (12) — the reference is to Isaiah 11: 2–3[41] — and authoritative statements taken from the writings of theologians.[42] Furthermore, in

---

38   For a fuller discussion of this point, see the subsection *De doctrina*.

39   Although Dante does not state this openly in the *Convivio*, when he refers there to theologians interpreting Scripture, he naturally means that they do this in an orthodox manner, namely, in line with and in support of the 'fidei fundamentum' (*Mon.* III. 3. 10; foundation of faith). It is in the *Monarchia*, when challenging the erroneous Biblical exegesis of the hierocrats, that Dante makes the point openly; see the paragraph that follows.

40   'Deinde illa quae in eis [the canonical books of the Bible] aperte posita sunt, vel praecepta vivendi vel regulae credendi, sollertius diligentiusque investiganda sunt. Quae tanto quisque plura invenit quanto est intellegentia capacior' [Then those things that are openly set down in them, whether precepts for how to live or rules for what to believe, should be examined more intelligently and more diligently. The greater a person's intellectual capability, the more of these he finds] (Augustine, *De doc. chr.* II. 9. 14).

41   Dante also alludes to 1 Corinthians 12: 8 & 11; 1 John 4: 8 & 16.

42   Dante appears to be drawing on Pseudo-Dionysius, *De divinis nominibus*, ed. by Beate Regina Suchla (Berlin and New York: de Gruyter, 1990), IV. 10. 159; Thomas Aquinas, *ST* I–II. 68. 2 and 7; *CG* IV. 19 & 21.

this regard, it is of some import that the chapter as a whole interweaves the two *modi*, as occurs with the association between 'santo Augustino, e [...] Aristotile nel secondo de l'Etica' (14).[43]

Although I still have a number of things to say about Dante's definition of theology, having introduced the question of the *modus theologicus*, a short *digressio* is in order. The other text besides the *Convivio* in which Dante has recourse to the word 'theology' and its cognates is the *Monarchia*. Discussing the relationship between ignorance and dispute, he remarks that the 'theologus vero numerum angelorum ignorat: non tamen de illo litigium facit' [in truth the theologian does not know the number of angels: however he does not make it into a matter of dispute] (III. 3. 2), a declaration which, via Daniel 7: 10, indicates the limits of Scriptural exegesis, limits which are willingly accepted by the orthodox theologian who acknowledges that the Bible raises matters that are 'inexplicable' since they go beyond the capacities of human reason — a view of the work of the *theologus* obviously in harmony with that presented in the *Convivio*.[44] Later, in the same chapter, Dante introduces those groups that deny that the Emperor receives his authority directly from God. Among these, '[s]unt etiam tertii — quos decretalistas vocant — qui, theologie ac phylosophie cuiuslibet inscii et expertes, suis decretalibus [...] tota intentione innixi' [there is also a third group — whom they call decretalists — who ignorant and entirely bereft of theology and philosophy, rest their whole argument on their decretals] (9). Once again, tellingly, Dante suggests that theology and philosophy have attributes in common, necessarily rational ones given the substance, limits, and methods of the latter, and that each has basic elements that can be learned and which define them.[45] He also conveniently provides a list of the authorities

43   I have long felt enormous respect for Kenelm Foster's work as a Dantist, and so am uncomfortable about belabouring the point regarding the flaws in his contribution on theology (especially as a critique of his entry is not the purpose of this chapter). However, given its authoritative standing, I do consider it necessary to highlight some of the entry's other principal weaknesses. Thus, Foster, without explanation, equates theology with faith, while also declaring that, in *Mon.* III. 15, '[a]ll'anima in quanto destinata alla vita ultraterrena (e in quanto dotata d'intelletto) non rimane che la nuda fede, una fede a cui non corrisponde alcuna virtù intellettuale, una fede, cioè, priva di Teologia' (p. 566). Despite recognizing the importance of Dante's discussion of theology in the *Convivio*, Foster too ends up by using the term loosely and with a variety of meanings (I return to this and related issues below). Foster's most important contributions on Dante's thought are the judiciously even-handed *The Two Dantes and Other Studies* (Berkeley and Los Angeles: University of California Press, 1977) and 'Tommaso d'Aquino', in *ED*, V, 626–48.

44   See *Dante's 'Monarchia'*, trans. and ed. by Richard Kay (Toronto: Pontifical Institute of Mediaeval Studies, 1998), pp. 206–07. Especially in the *Paradiso*, Dante develops at length the implications of the inadequacy of human reason in the face of revelation. Thus, his statement of poetic humility in *Par.* XXIII. 55–60 points to his limpid appreciation of 'the ethical implications of the fact that certain things may not be capable of being explained', so that 'because certain things are not even in principle open to explanation, all one's words and deeds ought to be an expression of that love which truth itself is': Vittorio Montemaggi, '"La rosa in che il verbo divino carne si fece": Human Bodies and Truth in the Poetic Narrative of the *Commedia*', in *Dante and the Human Body: Eight Essays*, ed. by John C. Barnes and Jennifer Petrie (Dublin: Four Courts Press, 2007), pp. 159–94 (p. 186).

45   Dante's position appears to have some points of contact with Thomas Aquinas's view that 'the principles and premises of theology differ from those of secular reasoning — but theology,

which he considers to be divinely inspired, and which thus constitute the texts the theologian studies, since they provide the 'fidei fundamentum' [foundation of faith] (10):

> Est advertendum quod quedam scriptura est ante Ecclesiam, quedam cum Ecclesia, quedam post Ecclesiam. Ante quidem Ecclesiam sunt vetus et novum Testamentum, quod 'in ecternum mandatum est' ut ait Propheta [Psalms 111: 9]; hoc enim est quod dicit Ecclesia loquens ad sponsum: 'Trahe me post te' [Song of Songs 1: 3]. Cum Ecclesia vero sunt veneranda illa concilia principalia quibus Cristum interfuisse nemo fidelis dubitat, cum habeamus ipsum dixisse discipulis ascensurum in celum 'Ecce ego vobiscum sum in omnibus diebus usque ad consummationem seculi' [Matthew 28: 20], ut Matheus testatur. Sunt etiam scripture doctorum, Augustini et aliorum, quos a Spiritu Sancto adiutos qui dubitat, fructus eorum vel omnino non vidit vel, si vidit, minime degustavit. (*Mon.* III. 3. 11–13)

> [One needs to be aware that there is a certain scripture that preceded the Church, a certain one contemporary to the Church, and a certain one that followed the Church. Before the Church are the Old and New Testament, which 'are sent in eternity' as the Prophet says; for this is what the Church says speaking to the bridegroom: 'Draw me after you'. Contemporary to the Church are those venerable principal councils at which no believer doubts Christ participated, since we know that he said to the disciples as he was about to ascend to Heaven: 'Behold I am with you all days until the consummation of the world', as Matthew attests. There are also the writings of the doctors, of Augustine and of the others; and who doubts that they were helped by the Holy Spirit has either completely not seen their fruits or, if he has seen them, has never tasted them.]

Everything else, Dante insists, is not *fundamentalis Scriptura* (14). Nonetheless, for all their miraculous character, such Scriptures need to be the object of human study: 'oportet enim, hanc veritatem [the source of Imperial authority] venantes, ex hiis ex quibus Ecclesie manat auctoritas investigando procedere'[46] [in fact those who hunt for this truth must go forward with their investigation by starting from those things from which comes the Church's authority] (16).[47] In the six chapters that follow (4–9), Dante highlights how such study of the Bible must avoid 'error' when interpreting the 'mystical sense', 'aut querendo ipsum ubi non est, aut accipiendo aliter quam accipi debere' [either seeking for it where it is not to be found, or taking it in a manner other than that in which it ought to be taken] (III. 4. 6). Otherwise,

---

insofar as it uses reason, does not offer "alternative modes of reason"': Paul O'Grady, 'Philosophical Theology and Analytical Philosophy in Aquinas', in *The Theology of Thomas Aquinas*, ed. by Rik Van Nieuwenhove and Joseph Wawrykow (Notre Dame, IN: University of Notre Dame Press, 2005), pp. 416–41 (p. 422). See in particular *ST* I. 1. 2.

46   The image of 'hunting for truth' was a scholastic commonplace, which again associates the *modus theologicus* with other forms of intellectual endeavour; see Dante Alighieri, *Monarchia*, ed. by Gustavo Vinay (Florence: Sansoni, 1950), p. 152; Dante Alighieri, *Monarchia*, ed. by Diego Quaglioni, in *Opere*, II, 807–1415 (p. 1141).

47   Dante's discussion of Scriptural and Church authority in *Mon.* III. 16 has interesting links with several of Augustine's works; see, for instance, *Contra Faustum* XI. 2 and 5; *De doc. chr.* II. 8. 12; *De Trinitate* III. 2. 22.

God is offended[48] and '"Titubabit fides, si *Divinarum Scripturarum* vacillat auctoritas"' [faith will totter, if the authority of the Divine Scriptures wavers] (9). The last phrase is a quotation from Augustine's *De doctrina christiana* (I. 37. 41), the pre-eminent guide in the Middle Ages to the correct reading of the Bible.[49] However much this part of the *Monarchia* is a refutation of 'asserentes auctoritatem Imperii ab auctoritate Ecclesie dependere' [those who assert that the authority of the Empire depends on the authority of the Church] (1), it also serves as a carefully constructed methodological statement, based appropriately on Augustine (7–9), on how a theologian ought to carry out his duties as Scriptural exegete.[50] Indeed, in demolishing his opponents' interpretations of key Biblical *sententiae*, and in establishing the correctness of his own reading, Dante demonstrates in practice how this task ought to be undertaken.[51] His approach, significantly, is quintessentially rational: drawing both on the authority of other Biblical passages and on the logical argumentative structures of philosophy.

At the very close of the *Monarchia*, however, when discussing what would become one of the most controversial questions in Dante studies, namely, his theory of humanity's two goals, the poet appears decisively to separate philosophy from theology:

> Ad has quidem beatitudines, velut ad diversas conclusiones, per diversa media venire oportet. Nam ad primam per phylosophica documenta venimus, dummodo illa sequamur secundum virtutes morales et intellectuales operando; ad secundam vero per documenta spiritualia que humanam rationem transcendunt, dummodo illa sequamur secundum virtutes theologicas operando, fidem spem scilicet et karitatem. Has igitur conclusiones et media, licet ostensa sint nobis hec ab humana ratione que per phylosophos tota nobis innotuit, hec a Spiritu Sancto qui per prophetas et agiographos, qui per coecternum sibi Dei filium Iesum Cristum et per eius discipulos supernaturalem veritatem ac nobis necessariam revelavit. (*Mon.* III. 16. 8–9)

> [In fact, these forms of happiness, just like different ends, must be reached by different means. For we reach the first through philosophical teachings, as long as we follow them putting into practice the moral and intellectual virtues; whereas the second through spiritual teachings that transcend human reason, as long as we follow them putting into practice the theological virtues, namely

---

48   'O summum facinus, etiamsi contingat in sompniis, ecterni Spiritus intentione abuti! Non enim peccatur in Moysen, non in David, non in Iob, non in Matheum, non in Paulum, sed in Spiritum Sanctum qui loquitur in illis. Nam quamquam scribe divini eloquii multi sint, unicus tamen dictator est Deus, qui beneplacitum suum nobis per multorum calamos explicare dignatus est' [Oh supreme villainy, even if it should occur in dreams, to abuse the intention of the eternal Spirit! For this is a sin not against Moses, not against David, not against Job, not against Matthew, not against Paul, but against the Holy Spirit who speaks in them. Although there are in fact many scribes of the divine word, however the only one who dictates it is God, who deigns to reveal to us His gracious purpose through the pens of many] (11).

49   See *Reading and Wisdom: The 'De doctrina christiana' of Augustine in the Middle Ages*, ed. by Edward D. English (Notre Dame, IN, and London: University of Notre Dame Press, 1995).

50   See in particular the excellent Paola Nasti, 'Dante and Ecclesiology', in Honess and Treherne, II, 43–88.

51   Foster notes correctly that 'da *Mn* II x alla fine del III libro D. ragiona da teologo' ('Teologia', p. 566).

faith, hope, and charity. Accordingly these ends and means are allowed to be shown to us, the first by human reason which has been fully made known to us through the philosophers, the other by the Holy Spirit, who through the prophets and agiographos, through Jesus Christ the Son of God, coeternal with Him, and through His disciples, has revealed the supernatural truth that we need.][52]

It is important to recognize, however, that Dante here is not alluding to the 'sciences' of philosophy and theology, but to their teachings and authorities (*documenta*), to their sources of origination (*ostendere; revelare*), and to the means whereby they are apprehended (exercise of virtues).[53] Tellingly, the adjective *theologicus* is restricted to the virtues of faith, hope, and charity, and is meant to help distinguish them from the 'moral and intellectual virtues'. The 'theological' is thus carefully removed from the sphere of knowledge to that of action (*operare*).[54] As he had done in *Conv.* II. 14.

52   On the technical value of the term *agiographos*, see Quaglioni, pp. 1401–02.

53   On the meaning of *documenta*, see Kay's annotation to *Mon.* III. 15. 8 (p. 313), and in particular Quaglioni, p. 1398.

54   Compare Bonaventure, *Breviloquium*, Prologus 1. 2: 'Recte autem sacra Scriptura dividitur in vetus et novum testamentum, et non in theoricam et practicam, sicut philosophia: quia, cum Scriptura fundetur proprie super cognitionem fidei, quae virtus est et fundamentum morum et iustitiae et totius rectae vitae, non potest in ea sequestrari notitia rerum sive credendorum a notitia morum. Secus autem est de philosophia, quae non tantum de veritate morum, verum etiam agit de vero nuda speculatione considerata. Quoniam igitur Scriptura sacra est notitia movens ad bonum et revocans a malo; et hoc est per timorem et amorem: ideo dividitur in duo testamenta, quorum "brevis differentia est timor et amor" [Augustine, *Contra Adimantum* 17. 2]' [And the Holy Scripture is befittingly divided into the Old and New Testament, and not into theoretical and practical writings, as is philosophy: because, since Scripture is essentially founded on the knowledge stemming from faith, which is a virtue and the foundation of morality and justice and of the whole righteous life, there cannot be in it any separation between the knowledge of the arguments of faith and the knowledge of morals. Not so for philosophy, which is concerned not only with moral truths, but also with truth inquired by pure speculation. And because the Holy Scripture is knowledge that leads to good and draws away from evil, specifically through fear and love: it is therefore divided in two Testaments, of which one could say 'there is little difference between fear and love'] (p. 203); and also Robert of Kilwardby, *Quaestiones in librum primum Sententiarum*, ed. by Johannes Schneider (Munich: Bayerischen Akademie der Wissenschaften, 1986), p. 3: 'Similiter in proposito est, quia theologia non sistit in speculatione, sed intendit actionem finaliter. Virtutes enim theologicae idem habent pro obiecto et fine, ut fides summum verum, caritas summum bonum' [Likewise for the intent, since theology does not consist of speculation, but finally aims to an action. Indeed the theological virtues have one same thing for their object and their end, as faith has the supreme truth, and love the supreme good] (p. 10). Dante's view of theology is closer to Bonaventure's than to Thomas's, given that, in his discussion of theology, the latter privileges the 'speculative' over the 'practical' (*ST* I. 1. 4). Indeed, 'Thomas's idea that theology is a speculative science was always a minority view in the middle ages. William of Auxerre, Alexander of Hales and Bonaventure thought it was a practical science dealing with knowledge which leads us to love God and attain salvation, and this was the view later expounded by Duns Scotus': Geoffrey Turner, 'St Thomas Aquinas on the "Scientific" Nature of Theology', *New Blackfriars*, 78 (1997), 464–76 (p. 473). Closer to Thomas was Henry of Ghent, who, in his *Summa quaestionum ordinarium*, expressed the 'conviction that theology is not primarily affective (an idea found in the *Summa Alexandri* and elaborated by Henry's arch-opponent Giles of Rome) but speculative': Alastair J. Minnis, 'The *Accessus* Extended: Henry of Ghent on the Transmission and Reception of Theology', in *'Ad Litteram': Authoritative Texts and their Medieval Readers*, ed. by Mark D. Jordan and Kent Emery Jr (Notre Dame, IN, and London: University of Notre Dame Press, 1992), pp. 275–326 (p. 288).

19–20, Dante is alluding to the affective impact of the 'documenta spiritualia', an experience open to anyone who 'follows' the three theological virtues. It thus seems that, with the term 'theology', Dante was actually alluding to two different, though inter-related, types of knowledge and of activity. In its essential form, theology denotes the affective and spiritual apprehension of revelation which is a possibility made available to every Christian. At the same time, and more restrictively, it denotes the work of the theologian, an intellectual 'method' that is dedicated to the interpretation of the 'books' of revelation and which aids others in their pursuit of salvation, complementing their affective experience of the divine. The former is of course much more important than the latter, and Dante's definition in *Conv.* II. 14. 19–20 reflects this fact, while, suggestively, also offering some clues to the existence of the latter. *Explicit digressio.*

4. De theologia 3

Dante's twofold sense of theology, irrespective of their differences as regards other aspects of the nature of *theologia*, is not unlike Aquinas's similar two-part distinction.[55] As Joseph Wawrykow writes:

> In his *Summa theologiae* Thomas Aquinas discusses this technical discipline [of *theologia*] as part of his analysis of the broader concept, *sacra doctrina*. In Thomas's *Summa*, *sacra doctrina* and the technical discipline of 'theology' are not identical; *sacra doctrina* includes this 'theology' but also covers God's revelation, patterned on God's self-knowledge, which is conveyed in Scripture.[56]

At the same time, however, as we have begun to see, Dante's sense of *teologia* in *Conv.* II. 14. 19–20 is fundamentally different from that of Thomas.[57] In fact, although in

---

55   Both Thomas's and Dante's twofold distinction of a clearly Christian theology in both its acceptations ought to be distinguished from that other categorization of two types of theology that Aquinas described and to which Dante does not make direct reference: 'Et per hunc modum tractantur res divinae secundum quod in seipsis subsistunt, et non solum prout sunt rerum principia. Sic igitur theologia, sive scientia divina, est duplex. Una, in qua considerantur res divinae non tamquam subiectum scientiae, sed tamquam principium subiecti; et talis est theologia quam philosophi prosequuntur, quae alio nomine Metaphysica dicitur. Alia vero quae ipsas res divinas considerat propter seipsas ut subiectum scientiae; et haec est theologia quae Sacra Scriptura dicitur' [In this way we address divine things as they subsist in themselves, and not only in so far as they are the principles of things. Thus, there are two kinds of theology or divine science. One in which divine things are considered not as the subject of the science but as the principle of the subject; and this is the kind of theology pursued by philosophers which is also called Metaphysics. There is, however, another one that considers these divine things in themselves as the subject of the science; and this is the theology that is called Sacred Scripture] (*Super Boetium De Trinitate* III. 5. 4. 4). The association between metaphysics and theology has its origins in Aristotle. *Met.* I. 2, 983a, where the 'first philosophy' is termed 'divine science'. Given the clear separation that Dante establishes in the *Convivio* between theology and metaphysics, I do not believe that the phrase 'divina scienza' (II. 14. 19) can be deemed to have Aristotelian associations.

56   Joseph Wawrykow, 'Reflections on the Place of the *De doctrina christiana* in High Scholastic Discussions of Theology', in English, pp. 99–125 (p. 115). Bonaventure, too, in the *Brevilioquium* had a similar understanding of theology; see Jacques Guy Bougerol, *Introduction to the Works of Bonaventure* (Paterson, NJ: St Anthony Guild Press, 1964), pp. 88–94 & 108–12.

57   See also Gilson, *Dante*, pp. 115–20.

general terms his presentation can be conveniently and unproblematically associated with the traditionalist Augustinian view of theology, in its detail and focus, Dante's treatment of *teologia* constitutes a personal consideration and synthesis. To put it simply, I have not found any medieval definition of theology quite like his.[58] And yet, for all its originality, in addition to its 'Augustinianism' and its ties to Thomas's distinction, *Conv.* II. 14. 19–20 carefully also maintains other links with current opinion on *theologia*.

Before attempting to suggest some possible reasons for Dante's ambivalent treatment of theology, I reproduce again, for the reader's convenience, Dante's exposition of the 'divine science':

> Lo Cielo empireo per la sua pace simiglia la divina scienza, che piena è di tutta pace: la quale non soffera lite alcuna d'oppinioni o di sofistici argomenti, per la eccellentissima certezza del suo subietto, lo quale è Dio. E di questa dice esso alli suoi discepoli: 'La pace mia do a voi, la pace mia lascio a voi' [John 14: 27], dando e lasciando a loro la sua dottrina, che è questa scienza di cu' io parlo. Di costei dice Salomone: 'Sessanta sono le regine, e ottanta l'amiche concubine; e delle ancille adolescenti non è numero: una è la colomba mia' [Song of Songs 6: 7–8]. Tutte scienze chiama regine e drude e ancille; e questa chiama perfetta perché perfettamente ne fa il vero vedere nel quale si cheta l'anima nostra. (*Conv.* II. 14. 19–20)

In essence, Dante's definition, as we have begun to recognize, has two principal emphases. On the one hand, it is adapted to and serves personal ends; on the other, it remains part of the mainstream debate on theology. From this perspective, the poet's approach is identical to his normal attitude to the various strands of his culture — innovation from within the tradition. The elements in his presentation of *teologia* that are almost certainly new and individual are three: first, the equation with the Empyrean,[59] which is unprecedented;[60] second, the emphasis on peace, which I have not found elsewhere; and third, the allusion to 'strife', which again is idiosyncratic, and is of course closely connected to the concern with 'pace'. Indeed,

58   In saying this I am not trying to suggest that my reading has been in any way exhaustive — far from it. I have, however, looked at the principal sources, and, at least in this respect, my claim, and the argument that I am about to develop from it, has some, however limited, philological validity.

59   On Dante's views of the Empyrean, see in particular Moevs, pp. 15–35 & 193–201. See also Gianfranco Fioravanti, 'Aristotele e l'Empireo', in *Christian Readings of Aristotle from the Middle Ages to the Renaissance*, ed. by Luca Bianchi (Turnhout: Brepols, 2011), pp. 25–36; Étienne Gilson, 'À la recherche de l'Empyrée', *Revue des études italiennes*, 11 (1965), 147–61; Attilio Mellone, *La dottrina di Dante Alighieri sulla prima creazione* (Nocera Superiore: Convento S. Maria degli Angeli, 1950), pp. 22–57, and 'Empireo', in *ED*, II, 668–71; Bruno Nardi, 'La dottrina dell'Empireo nella sua genesi storica e nel pensiero dantesco', in *Saggi*, pp. 167–214; Pegoretti, pp. 158–71. For a useful synthesis, see Vasoli edn, pp. 133–36.

60   As Dante acknowledges, the authority of Scripture encouraged him to associate theology with the Empyrean: 'Questa è quella magnificenza della quale parlò il Salmista, quando dice a Dio: "Levata è la magnificenza tua sopra li cieli" [Psalms 8: 2]' (*Conv.* II. 3. 11). See also Psalms 18: 2; Job 38: 37; Isaiah 34: 4; Revelation 6: 14. The poet may also have been influenced by Alan of Lille's positioning of the 'puella poli residens in culmine' [the young woman who resides at the summit of the [celestial] pole], namely Theology, at the boundaries of the universe: *Anticlaudianus*, ed. by Robert Bossuat (Paris: Vrin, 1955), v. 83–174 (the quotation is found at l. 83).

all three elements are interdependent; and, whatever their other implications, all
have functions that are peculiar to the *Convivio*.

Among the key concerns of the 'quasi comento' (*Conv.* I. 3. 2) is the investigation
of the differences and points of contact between an earthbound, partial, and
fractured knowledge and divine absolute wisdom. The analogy Dante establishes
between the ten heavens of the Christianized Aristotelian-Ptolemaic universe and
the seven liberal arts plus physics, metaphysics, ethics, and theology is an attempt
to give his untutored readers, the *Convivio*'s avowed audience, a schematized and
accessible idea of the nature and specificities of individual 'sciences', including
theology, as well as a sense of their ties and of the complex totality of knowledge.
At the same time, however, by recognizing that 'il vero' is 'perfettamente'
embodied in theology, Dante could not but raise doubts about the accuracy and
value of his schematization. Indeed, he went further than this, openly and fittingly
deconstructing his model from within the definition of theology. The allusion to
the sixty queens, the eighty concubines, and the numberless handmaidens makes it
abundantly clear that, for all its flaws, earthly knowledge, never mind theology, is
in reality much more complex than the straightforward equation with the heavens
might imply. Thus, it is telling that Dante did not employ the eleven 'sciences' to
organize the *Convivio*, a procedure that was well established in the Middle Ages.
Instead he had recourse to more fluid structures, interlacing different problems and
doctrines — I haven't forgotten the chapter's other primary topic — not just in each
book but also within single chapters, an approach that anticipates the freedom with
which doctrinal matters are presented in the *Commedia*.[61]

Given the vastness of knowledge and the constraints of human reason, it is
not surprising that our intellectual activity should be marked and marred by
disagreements and sophistry. Dante himself in the *Convivio* regularly assesses
competing claims, attempting to establish which might have the greatest validity
by coming closest to the truth. In stark contrast, knowledge in its absolute sense,
as it exists in the mind of God, is one and 'pieno di tutta pace'; and theology, like
the tenth heaven, since 'its subject is God' and its 'mode' is revelation, through its
'perfection' offers a miraculous intimation of the mystery of divine wisdom. Divine
knowledge thus could not be more different from earthly knowledge, so that, while
the other 'sciences' can be apprehended rationally and imperfectly, theology is
experiential, bringing tranquillity to 'l'anima nostra' on account of its 'perfection'
and 'peace'.[62] Yet earthly knowledge and the exercise of human reason are not

---

61   See Barański, *Dante e i segni*, pp. 84–90.

62   Compare Bonaventure, *Breviloquium* I. I. 3: 'Ipsa [Theologia] etiam sola est *sapientia perfecta*,
quae incipit a causa summa, ut est *principium* causatorum, ubi terminatur cognitio philosophica; et
transit per eam, ut est *remedium* peccatorum; et reducit in eam, ut est *praemium* meritorum et finis
desideriorum. Et in hac cognitione est sapor perfectus, vita et salus animarum; et ideo ad eam
addiscendam inflammari debet desiderium omnium Christianorum' [This [Theology] is also the
only perfect wisdom, which begins from the supreme cause, as this is the principle of all things
caused, where philosophical knowledge ends; and goes on through it, for it is the remedy of sinners;
and leads back to it, for it is the reward of merits and the goal of desires. And in this knowledge is
the perfect savour, the life and salvation of the souls; and all Christians should burn with desire to
gain this knowledge] (p. 210).

distinct from divine wisdom — what Moevs terms 'the connaturality between human intelligence and divine intellect' (p. 82) — since the former represent a 'lesser' version of the latter.[63] As the analogy of the heavens establishes, theology, like the Empyrean, is 'fuori di tutti questi [cieli/scienze]' (*Conv.* II. 3. 8); nonetheless it is also part of a coherent unified system which has its origin and being in God: 'Questo è lo soprano edificio del mondo, nel quale tutto lo mondo s'inchiude, e di fuori dal quale nulla è; ed esso non è in luogo ma formato fu solo nella Prima Mente, la quale li Greci dicono Protonoè' (II). Furthermore, both systems are hierarchical, as the cosmological exemplar reveals, with the lower heavens and 'sciences' subordinated to and dependent upon the highest:

> Veramente, fuori di tutti questi, li catolici pongono lo cielo Empireo, che è a dire cielo di fiamma o vero luminoso; e pongono esso essere immobile per avere in sé, secondo ciascuna [sua] parte, ciò che la sua materia vuole. E questo è cagione al Primo Mobile per avere velocissimo movimento; ché per lo ferventissimo appetito ch'è ['n] ciascuna parte di quello nono cielo, che è [im]mediato a quello, d'essere congiunta con ciascuna parte di quello divinissimo ciel quieto, in quello si rivolve con tanto desiderio, che la sua velocitade è quasi incomprensibile. (*Conv.* II. 3. 8–9)[64]

Theology is everything (or almost) that the other 'sciences' are not. Dante had

---

63   '[F]ilosofia è uno amoroso uso di sapienza, lo quale massimamente è in Dio, però che in lui è somma sapienza e sommo amore e sommo atto: che non può essere altrove se non in quanto da esso procede. È adunque la divina filosofia della divina essenzia, però che in esso non può essere cosa alla sua essenzia aggiunta; ed è nobilissima, però che nobilissima è la essenzia divina; [ed] è in lui per modo perfetto e vero, quasi per etterno matrimonio. Nell'altre intelligenze è per modo minore, quasi come druda della quale nullo amadore prende compiuta gioia, ma nel suo aspetto [mirando], contenta[se]ne la loro vaghezza' (*Conv.* III. 12. 12–13).

64   '[L']Empireo è il luogo immobile dell'universo, il termine al quale si possono riferire tutti i movimenti, compreso quello della prima sfera mobile' (Nardi, 'Dottrina', pp. 194–95), which is the source of the motion of all the other spheres. Given the poet's understanding and presentation of the workings of the cosmological system, and hence of the interconnections between the 'sciences', it is difficult to accept Étienne Gilson's contention that 'Dante has nowhere said or suggested that the philosophical sciences are in any way subordinate to this supposed queen, theology' (*Dante*, p. 120). Gilson arrives at his conclusion by comparing Dante narrowly and exclusively to Thomas Aquinas's discussion of the same problem in *ST* I. 1. 5 (pp. 115–19). There is no doubt that, in the round, Dante's views and the manner in which he expounded these are not the same as Thomas's; at the same time, both would appear to agree as regards the basic nature of the inter-relationship between philosophy and theology. Thus, it is interesting to note that, when Dante asserts the truth of the Empyrean by appealing to the authority of the Church, he should also remark 'e Aristotile pare ciò sentire, a chi bene lo 'ntende, nel primo Di Cielo e Mondo' (II. 3. 10), thereby both pointing to philosophy as providing a 'service' (*pace* Gilson, p. 117) to theology and as offering insights that are subordinate to those of the 'divine science'. Theology 'cannot lie'; Aristotle, the emblem of philosophy, on the other hand, 'appears to sense'. On Thomas Aquinas's view of theology, see at least Chenu, *Théologie comme science*, pp. 67–100; Brain Davies, 'Is *Sacra Doctrina* Theology?', *New Blackfriars*, 71 (1990), 141–47; Thomas Gilby, 'Theology as Science', in St Thomas Aquinas, *Summa theologiae. Volume I (1a. 1). Christian Theology*, ed. by Thomas Gilby (Blackfriars in conjunction with New York: McGraw-Hill; London: Eyre & Spottiswoode, 1964), pp. 67–87; Turner; James A. Weisheipl. 'The Meaning of *Sacra Doctrina* in *Summa theologiae* I, q. 1', *The Thomist*, 38 (1974), 49–80. The subordination of philosophy to theology was the standard position among late medieval theologians; see, for instance, Bonaventure, *Breviloquium*, Prologus 3. 2; and see Chenu, *Théologie comme science*, pp. 71–85.

diligently prepared its 'otherness' when discussing the Empyrean before offering his actual definition of the 'divine science' in *Conv.* II. 14. 19–20: 'Li numeri, li ordini, le gerarchie narrano li cieli mobili, che sono nove, e lo decimo annunzia essa unitade e stabilitade di Dio' (II. 5. 12; and see 3. 8–9). Equally, he had earlier associated the tenth heaven with Catholic thought ('li catolici pongono lo cielo Empireo', II. 3. 8) and with the infallible teachings of the Church ('Questo loco è di spiriti beati, secondo che la Santa Chiesa vuole, che non può dire menzogna', II. 3. 10), hinting already at its (and, by extension and subsequently, theology's) links to revealed truth; links which become explicit in chapter 14.[65]

65   Any discussion of the inter-relationship between theology and philosophy in the *Convivio* is complicated by Dante's enthusiastic and effusive outbursts in praise of *Filosofia*. He thus declares that the *donna gentile* can offer an intimation of celestial beatitude: 'E dico che nello suo aspetto apariscono cose le quali dimostrano de' piaceri *di Paradiso; ed intra li altri di quelli*, lo più nobile, e quello che è *frutto* e fine di tutti li altri, si è contentarsi, e questo si è essere beato; e questo piacere è veramente, avegna che per altro modo, nell'aspetto di costei. Ché, guardando costei, la gente si contenta, tanto dolcemente ciba la sua bellezza li occhi de' riguardatori; ma per altro modo che per lo contentare in Paradiso, [ché lo contentare in Paradiso] è perpetuo, che non può ad alcuno essere questo' (*Conv.* III. 8. 5; and cf. 15. 2–3, 5–6, 15–16). This is of course a great claim to make, and one which touches on an area that was normally seen as the preserve of Scripture. At the same time, Dante is careful to acknowledge the limitations of this rational experience of the supernatural — a point to which he returns and further clarifies in chapter 15: 'Dunque si vede come nell'aspetto di costei delle cose di Paradiso appaiono [...] Poi, quando si dice: *Elle soverchian lo nostro intelletto*, escuso me di ciò, che poco parlar posso di quelle per la loro soperchianza. Dove è da sapere che in alcuno modo queste cose nostro intelletto abbagliano, in quanto certe cose [si] affermano essere, che lo 'ntelletto nostro guardare non può, cioè Dio e la etternitate e la prima materia: che certissimamente si veggiono e con tutta fede si credono essere, e pur quello che sono intender noi non potemo, se non cose negando si può apressare alla sua conoscenza, e non altrimenti' (6). In addition, Dante never portrays philosophy as in any way creating problems for theology or the divine. Indeed, as we have noted, *Filosofia* is closely and harmoniously associated with God, a view that masks contemporary controversies regarding the relative standing of and the inter-relationship between theological and philosophical knowledge; see Luca Bianchi, *Pour une histoire de la 'double vérité'* (Paris: Vrin, 2008). However, despite Dante consistently affirming the uniqueness and superiority of divine wisdom and of theology, a position which I believe needs to serve as the starting-point for any analysis of the *Convivio*'s epistemology and intellectual sympathies, his celebratory treatment of *Filosofia*, the shifting terminology that he utilizes to refer to wisdom and knowledge, and the corrupt nature, and hence questionable reliability, of the text, especially in *Conv.* III. 8, undoubtedly raise problems of some substance. Unfortunately, I do not have the space here to examine these important matters in any sort of detail, except to note that, at least since Augustine, many Christian thinkers had recognized that unenlightened human reason could touch on some Christian truths. At the same time, by the start of the fourteenth century, this idea had become fraught with controversy as a result of disputes between academic philosophers and theologians regarding disciplinary boundaries; see, for instance, Luca Bianchi, *Il vescovo e i filosofi: la condanna parigina del 1277 e l'evoluzione dell'aristotelismo scolastico* (Bergamo: Lubrina, 1990); Evans, *Philosophy*, pp. 10–16; Alessandro Ghisalberti, *Medioevo teologico* (Bari: Laterza, 1990), pp. 85–145; Étienne Gilson, *History of Christian Philosophy in the Middle Ages* (London: Sheed & Ward, 1980), pp. 325–485; Martin Grabmann, 'Il concetto di scienza secondo S. Tommaso d'Aquino e le relazioni della fede e della teologia con la filosofia e le scienze profane', *Rivista di filosofia neo-scolastica*, 26 (1934), 127–55; J. M. M. H. Thijssen, *Censure and Heresy at the University of Paris: 1200–1400* (Philadelphia: University of Pennsylvania Press, 1998); Fernand van Steenberghen, *La Philosophie au XIIIe siècle* (Louvain and Paris: Publications universitaires, 1966). On Dante's attitude to these disputes, see Barański, *Dante e i segni*; Mazzotta; Angela Meekins, 'Reflecting on the Divine: Notes on Dante's Heaven of the Sun', *The Italianist*, 18 (1998), 28–70.

Dante's treatment of the 'divina scienza' is thus both effectively adapted to the basic expositional needs of the *Convivio* and skilfully integrated with its overarching idea and illustration of divine and human knowledge and of their inter-relationship. At the same time, however, it is vital to recognize that, by bending theology to his immediate, local needs, Dante in no way undermined either the supreme 'science' in itself or his ability to treat it in an orthodox and coherent manner. The opposite is in fact true. Dante could not have defined theology more orthodoxly than by linking it to Scripture and Christ; although the fact that he did not do this through an explicit statement but through the use of quotations is a further personal imprint.[66] Even those theologians, such as Aquinas, who favoured a 'scientific' *modus* for theology, never doubted its basis in the Bible.[67] Equally conventional are the declarations that 'its subject is God',[68] that it deals with 'certainty' and truth,[69] that its influence is affective,[70] and that other forms of knowledge are 'ancillary' to it, as the Solomonic *sententia* from the Song of Songs succinctly affirms.[71] Finally, the use of superlative adjectives to refer to theology ('eccellentissima' in Dante's case) was a commonplace,[72] as were designations such as 'divina scienza', 'scienza', and 'dottrina'.[73] *Conv.* II. 14. 19–20 is thus built on a solid traditional

---

66   See, for instance, Roger Bacon, *Opus majus*, ed. by John Henry Bridges, 2nd edn, 3 vols (Frankfurt: Minerva, 1964), I, 32; Bonaventure, *Breviloquium*, Prologus, 1–2; Gregory IX, *Ab Aegyptiis*, in *Chartularium Universitatis Parisiensis*, ed. by Henri Denifle and Émile Chatelain, 4 vols (Paris: ex typis fratrum Delalain, 1891–99), I, 114–15; Chenu, *Théologie comme science*, pp. 15–17, 23, 27–28, 31, 38–39, 51, 53–57, 61 (with many examples); Solignac, col. 467.

67   Thomas Aquinas, *ST* I. 1. 2 and 8. See also Solignac, col. 480; Wawrykow, p. 100; Weisheipl, pp. 79–80.

68   See, for instance, Alexander of Hales, *Summa theologica*, 4 vols (Quaracchi: ex Typographia Collegii S. Bonaventurae, 1924–48), I. 2; Bonaventure, *Breviloquium*, Prologus 6. 6; I. 1. 1–2; Odo Rigaldus, *Quaestiones* I, quoted from Basilius Pergamo, 'De Quaestionibus ineditis Fr. Odonis Rigaldi, Fr. Gulielmi de Melitona et Codicis Vat. Lat. 782 circa naturam theologiae deque earum relatione ad Summam theologicam Fr. Alexandri Halensis', *Archivum Franciscanum Historicum*, 29 (1936), 3–54 & 308–64 (pp. 20–24); Thomas Aquinas, *ST* I. 1. 7. But see also Weisheipl, p. 75.

69   Thomas Aquinas, *ST* I. 1. 4 and 5. See also Chenu, *Théologie comme science*, pp. 41 & 59.

70   See, for instance, Alexander of Hales, *Summa theologica* I. 2; Bonaventure, *Commentaria in quatuor libros Sententiarum*, III. 35. 2, in *Opera omnia*, III (1887), 775–76; Guy de l'Aumône, *Summa de diversis questionibus theologie*, Paris, Bibliothèque nationale. MS fonds latins 14891, fol. 176ʳ; Robert Kilwardby, *Quaestiones in librum primum Sententiarum* 7 and 14. See also Chenu, *Théologie comme science*, pp. 40–41, 68, 94; Martin Grabmann, *I divieti ecclesiastici di Aristotele sotto Innocenzo III e Gregorio IX* (Rome: Libreria SALER, 1941), pp. 75–77, 79–80; Nasti, *Favole*, pp. 105–06.

71   See Bernard Baudoux, 'Philosophia "Ancilla Theologiae"', *Antonianum*, 12 (1937), 293–326; Malcolm de Mowbray, 'Philosophy as Handmaid of Theology: Biblical Exegesis in the Service of Scholarship', *Traditio*, 59 (2004), 1–37 (pp. 1–29). See also Franz Jakob Clemens, *De scholasticorum sententia philosophiam esse theologiae ancillam commentatio*, in Antonio Piolanti, *Un pioniere della filosofia cristiana della metà dell'ottocento: Franz Jakob Clemens (m. 1862) con la riedizione della 'Commentatio' 'Philosophia theologiae ancilla'* (Vatican City: Pontificia Accademia di S. Tommaso e di Religione Cattolica and Libreria Editrice Vaticana, 1988), pp. 77–155. Although the idea of philosophy as *ancilla theologiae* was a commonplace, when Dante cited Song of Songs 6: 7–8 as his supporting Scriptural *auctoritas*, the quotation was another sign of the personal emphasis that he gave his presentation of theology. The customary *sententiae* were Genesis 16: 1; Deuteronomy 21: 10–14; Proverbs 9: 3.

72   Chenu, *Théologie comme science*, pp. 47–48.

73   See, for instance, Alexander of Hales, *Summa theologica* I. 1–2; Bonaventure, *Breviloquium*, Prologus 6. 6; I. 1. 2; Guy de l'Aumône, fol. 176ʳ; Thomas Aquinas, *ST* I. 1. 1. See Chenu, *Théologie*

foundation. Indeed, the personal elements that the poet adds — the comparison to the tenth heaven, peace, the exclusion of controversy, and the use of an unusual New Testament *auctoritas* (I have not found John 14: 27 in other classifications of theology) — do not destabilize or damage the solidity of his construction, but integrate perfectly with the traditional features. As a whole, Dante's presentation confirms his excellent familiarity with the substance, forms, and vocabulary of contemporary definitions of *theologia*, and, by extension, with the institutional and doctrinal controversies that, as he insinuated, were ravaging its divine integrity. The sophistication and functionality of Dante's definition is remarkable, though it is also typical of the knowing subtlety of his writing and of his cultural operations. Thus, the definition allows him to pass judgment, as so often, on contemporary squabbling; to express a view that, while personal, effectively contributes directly and meaningfully to the issue at hand (compare his treatment of beatitude discussed in Chapter 5); to suggest a solution to the problem (a return to Scripture); and to establish his own disinterested independence as someone who, from the outside, is endeavouring to understand and bring order to the world around him — a position which fits well with his self-presentation in the treatise. At the same time, *Conv.* II. 14. 19–20 allows him to transition from the general to the particular, namely, as we have seen, to the illustrative requirements and ideological concerns of his text. I am tempted, in fact, to conclude by noting that, *per analogiam*, theology's charitable uplifting universalism is appositely captured in the totalizing role that Dante assigned it in the structure of the *Convivio*, a work whose aim is disinterestedly to enlighten and improve all who wish to read it...

5. De doctrina

Especially in light of my earlier comments regarding possible interconnections between *doctrina* and *theologia*, it goes without saying that I have not failed to notice that, in the passage explaining the similarities between the Empyrean and 'divine science', on which I have largely focused my attention so far, Dante steadfastly equates 'doctrine' with theology: 'la sua [Christ's] dottrina, che è questa scienza'. Indeed, unlike Thomas Aquinas's use of *theologia* and *sacra doctrina* in the *Summa theologiae*, in the *Convivio* the two notions are indisputably synonymous. Their association, at first sight, would seem to resolve the question of the relationship between the two, especially as their interchangeability appears to be confirmed when *Conv.* II. 14. 19–20 is brought together with an earlier passage from the same Book that can be read as a kind of preparatory gloss to its discussion of theology-doctrine:

> La dottrina veracissima di Cristo, la quale è via, veritade e luce: via, perché per essa sanza impedimento andiamo alla felicitade di quella immortalitade; veritade, perché non soffera alcun errore; luce, perché alumina noi nella tenebra della ignoranza mondana. Questa dottrina dico che ne fa certi sopra tutte altre ragioni. (*Conv.* II. 8. 14–15)

comme science, p. 58. Unlike Thomas and other theologians, Dante does not use the popular designation *sacra doctrina* for theology.

Indeed, the close inter-relationship between the two passages — they can almost be read as two parts of a single statement — is confirmed by the fact that the earlier extract includes several elements that were standard in contemporary definitions of theology, but which Dante, with his usual aversion to unnecessary repetition, decided not to introduce into *Conv.* II. 14. 19–20. Most obviously, in chapter 8, the poet lays considerable stress on salvation, '*la felicitade di quella immortalitade*', which was frequently depicted as the end of theology but of which no mention is made in chapter 14.[74] Furthermore, he utilizes a pair of metaphors, of the 'way' and of the 'light', which regularly found a place in treatments of *sacra doctrina*, but which, once again, he omitted in the later passage.[75] It is only the idea of theology as the source of truth and certainty that Dante repeats in chapter 14 — a repetition that appears to underscore the key role that *teologia* plays in the *Convivio*'s presentation of knowledge. At the same time, taken together, the two passages highlight the poet's rich understanding of contemporary thinking about theology, which thus grants considerable authority to his handling of 'sacred doctrine', to his analysis of its relationship to the other 'sciences', and to his criticism of theological quarrelling.

Although it is obvious that, in the two passages from the *Convivio*, doctrine and theology do overlap, their correlation is not consistently posited by the poet — far from it in fact. *Dottrina/doctrina*, whether in Dante or in medieval culture, was a much more flexible and wide-ranging concept than *teologia/theologia*.[76] Even if Dante nowhere offers the stock explanation of 'doctrine' based on Augustine's *De doctrina christiana* — 'Omnis doctrina vel rerum est vel signorum, sed res per signa discuntur' [All doctrine [teaching] is either of things or of signs, but things are learnt through signs] (I. 2. 2)[77] — the ways in which he employed the term reflect the connotative flexibility and cultural ramifications implied by the Bishop of Hippo's terse yet totalizing phrase. Already in the two *Convivio* passages dealing

---

74   See, for instance, Bonaventure, *Breviloquium*, Prologus 3–4; 4. 5; Robert Kilwardby, *Quaestiones* 10; Thomas Aquinas, *ST* I. 1. 1.

75   See, for instance, Alexander of Hales, *Summa theologica*, Introd. 2. 3. 4; Bonaventure, *Breviloquium*, Prologus 5; 6. 1; William of Auxerre, *Summa aurea*, ed. by Jean Ribaillier and others, 5 vols (Paris: Editions du Centre national de la recherche scientifique and Rome: Editiones Collegii S. Bonaventurae ad Claras Aquas, 1980–87), Prologue. See also Andrea Aldo Robiglio, 'Christ as the Common Doctor and John Duns Scotus's Place in the History of Hermeneutics', in *'Vera Doctrina': zur Bergriffsgeschichte der Lehre von Augustinus bis Descartes*, ed. by Philippe Büttgen and others (Wiesbaden: Harrassowitz in Kommission, 2009), pp. 85–113 (pp. 109–11).

76   On *doctrina* see Sebastiano Aglianò, 'dottrina', in *ED*, I, 590–91; Gilby, pp. 58–66; Maarten J. F. M. Hoenen, 'Categories of Medieval Doxography: Reflections on the Use of "Doctrina" and "Via" in 14th and 15th Century Philosophical and Theological Sources', in Büttgen and others, pp. 62–84; Adriano Oliva, '*Doctrina* et *sacra doctrina* chez Thomas d'Aquin', in Büttgen and others, pp. 35–61; Dante Alighieri, *De l'éloquence en vulgaire*, trans. and ed. by Irène Rosier-Catach (Paris: Fayard, 2011), pp. 284–85. See also Alain Hus, *'Docere' et les mots de la famille de 'docere': étude de sémantique latine* (Paris: PUF, 1965).

77   'Distinguit autem Magister [Peter Lombard] sic, per quamdam propositionem sumptam ab Augustino, libro *De doctrina christiana*: "Omnis doctrina vel est de rebus vel signis"' [Moreover the Master differentiated thus on the basis of a certain proposition taken from Augustine's book *On Christian Doctrine*: 'All doctrine is either about things or signs']: Alexander of Hales, *Glossa in quatuor libros Sententiarum Petri Lombardi*, 4 vols (Quaracchi: Collegium S. Bonaventurae, 1951–57), I, [Introitus] 2 (p. 1).

with 'Christ's doctrine',[78] *dottrina* can also, and most accessibly, be interpreted as 'teaching';[79] this same sense, necessarily, is also present in those utilizations of *theologia* that associate it with Scripture and its effects.[80] And it is with the meaning of 'teaching' that the poet uses the term in a variety of contexts and generally in keeping with contemporary usage. When taken together, since they include both divine and earthly instruction, these different instances of 'doctrine' in Dante embrace knowledge as a whole. Indeed, 'doctrine' can range from the general to the particular. Thus *dottrina* is any kind of teaching ('Se quantunque s'acquista | giù per dottrina', *Par.* XXIV. 79–80);[81] it is allegorical teaching ('la dottrina che s'asconde | sotto 'l velame de li versi strani', *Inf.* IX. 62–63); it is a particular teaching of a specific individual (Averroes 'per sua dottrina fé disgiunto | da l'anima il possibile intelletto', *Purg.* XXV. 64–65);[82] it is a certain and substantial axiom ('sicut verum et falsum ab esse rei vel non esse in oratione causatur, ut doctrina *Predicamentorum* nos docet' [just as truth and falsehood in speech depend on the being of the thing or its non-being, as the doctrine of the *Categories* teaches us], *Mon.* III. 15. 9). The term can also refer to a complete intellectual system — 'e tiene questa gente [i Peripatetici] oggi lo reggimento del mondo in dottrina per tutte parti, e puotesi appellare quasi catolica oppinione' (*Conv.* IV. 6. 16) — or to a single major branch of knowledge, such as ethics, the 'morale dottrina' (*Conv.* III. 15. 12), or to a specific ideological current ('"Perché conoschi," disse, "quella scuola | c'hai seguitata, e veggi sua dottrina | come può seguitar la mia parola"', *Purg.* XXXIII, 85–87), or to

78   In the Middle Ages, as today, the image of Christ as a teacher was conventional and deeply embedded in Christian culture on the authority of the Gospels; see, for instance, Matthew 7: 29; Luke 9: 26; John 3: 13, 5: 17, 8: 25–27.

79   In the *De doctrina christiana*, normally 'the sense of *doctrina* must be "teaching" [...] The work is about teaching Christianity; hence "Christian teaching", referring both to the process and the content of teaching': R. P. H. Green, 'Introduction', in Augustine, *De Doctrina Christiana*, ed. and trans. by R. P. H. Green (Oxford: Clarendon Press, 1995), pp. ix–xxiii (pp. ix–x). See also Kurt Flasch, 'Doctrina bei Augustin', in Büttgen and others, pp. 23–33.

80   '[T]he teaching of Christ [...] was never merely a theoretical communication of knowledge or information about certain salvific events. It was always directed beyond knowledge to a change of heart; it became effective in action' (Williams, 'Doctrine', p. 939).

81   At the beginning of the *Convivio*, Dante highlights the 'usefulness' of his 'teaching' by comparing it to Augustine's: 'L'altra [reason] è quando, per ragionare di sé, grandissima utilitade ne segue altrui per via di dottrina; e questa ragione mosse Agustino nelle sue Confessioni a parlare di sé, ché per lo processo della sua vita, lo quale fu di [meno] buono in buono, e di buono in migliore, e di migliore in ottimo, ne diede essemplo e dottrina, la quale per [altro] sì vero testimonio ricevere non si potea. Per che, se l'una e l'altra di queste ragioni mi scusa, sofficientemente lo pane del mio comento è purgato della prima sua macula. Movemi timore d'infamia, e movemi disiderio di dottrina dare, la quale altri veramente dare non può' (*Conv.* I. 2. 14–15). Compare too 'convienesi amare li suoi maggiori, dalli quali ha ricevuto ed essere e nutrimento e dottrina' (*Conv.* IV. 26. 10). *Dottrina* in Dante, as in medieval culture, most frequently signifies teaching; see also 'E quinci nasce che mai a dottrina non vegnono; credendo da sé sufficientemente essere dottrinati, mai non domandano, mai non ascoltano, disiano essere domandati, e anzi la domandagione compiuta, male rispondono. E per costoro dice Salomone nelli Proverbii: "Vedesti l'uomo ratto a rispondere? Di lui stoltezza più che correzione è da sperare"' (*Conv.* IV. 15. 13). *Dottrinato* thus means 'educated', and compare 'conoscenza [...] non [...] dottrinata' (*Conv.* IV. 12. 16).

82   '"Doctrina" denotes the teaching or doctrine of a master or school of thought': Hoenen, p. 62, and see also p. 65.

any discipline ('la medicina o vero sotto più nobile dottrina', *Conv.* IV. 9. 13),[83] or to a highly specialized area of technical expertise: 'de rithimorum doctrina' [the doctrine of rhyme] (*Dve* II. 13. 12).[84] *Dottrina* is the source of our intellectual joy — 'E però si dice nel libro di Sapienza: "Chi gitta via la sapienza e la dottrina, è infelice"' (*Conv.* III. 15. 5; the term here refers either to teaching or to knowledge or indeed alludes to both simultaneously) — and what distinguishes us from the beasts: 'Costoro [the pusillanimous] sempre come bestie in grossezza vivono, d'ogni dottrina disperati' (*Conv.* IV. 15. 14).

It is clear that Dante customarily employed *dottrina/doctrina* without religious associations. However, in *Paradiso*, as in *Convivio* II, the term does take on specifically spiritual values. As one great Christian intellectual speaking about another, in his encomium of the founder of the Dominicans, Bonaventure expresses his appreciation of the saint's learning:

> Non per lo mondo, per cui mo s'affanna
> di retro ad Ostïense e a Taddeo,
> ma per amor de la verace manna
> in picciol tempo gran dottor si feo. (*Par.* XII. 82–85)

Instead of dedicating himself to the study and interpretation of the Decretals and canon law — a charge that Dante regularly laid against contemporary religious intellectuals — Dominic concentrated on 'the true manna', namely God's word which he approached affectively ('for love'). The saint thus opened himself to Scripture and became expert in its interpretation.[85] Instead of, like 'nowadays', pursuing corrupt earthbound ends, he deployed his learning in defence of the faith and to destroy 'li sterpi eretici' (100):

> ma contro al mondo errante
> licenza di combatter per lo seme
> del qual ti fascian ventiquattro piante.
>   Poi, con dottrina e con volere insieme,
> con l'officio apostolico si mosse
> quasi torrente ch'alta vena preme. (*Par.* XII. 94–99)

Dominic's 'doctrine' is thus the same as that celebrated in *Convivio* II. It is *teologia*; and by extension 'dottor' stands for 'theologian', in keeping with conventional usage, whereby *doctor* was someone who was both skilled in a *doctrina* and able to promulgate it.[86] As he had done in *Conv.* II. 8. 14–15 and 14. 19, Dante once again asserted the connection between 'doctrine' and Scripture by referring to

---

83   And compare 'in ciascuna dottrina si dee avere rispetto alla facultà del discente' (*Conv.* IV. 17. 12), where the emphasis is on the instruction of each discipline.

84   'When Augustine does use the word in the context of classical learning [...] he uses it in the plural, clearly referring to discrete branches of learning or culture' (Green, p. ix).

85   On the link between manna, Scripture, and exegesis, see de Lubac, I, 63, and II, 27, 156, 166, 204.

86   See Astrik L. Gabriel, 'The Ideal Master of the Mediaeval University', *The Catholic Historical Review*, 60 (1974), 1–40 (p. 5 and passim); Gabriel Le Bras, '"Velut splendor firmamenti": le docteur dans le droit de l'Eglise médiévale', in *Mélanges offerts à Étienne Gilson* (Toronto: Pontifical Institute of Medieval Studies; Paris: Vrin, 1959), pp. 373–88 (pp. 374–75).

'l'evangelica dottrina' (*Par.* XXIV. 144) in his powerful affirmation of the foundations of his Biblically revealed faith: 'per Moïse, per profeti e per salmi, | per l'Evangelio e per voi che scriveste' (136–37). Moreover, as in the *Convivio*, in *Paradiso* XXIV too, Dante contrasts 'doctrine' as Scripture and theology with other lesser forms of 'doctrine', which do not enjoy the privilege of 'certainty' but can be undermined by false premises:

> Allora udi': 'se quantunque s'acquista
> giù per dottrina, fosse così 'nteso,
> non li avria loco ingegno di sofista'. (*Par.* XII. 79–81)[87]

Fittingly, Dante's final utilization of 'doctrine' in the *Commedia* is religious: to refer to Bernard's knowledge of Mary and the archangel Gabriel, thereby highlighting the understanding the saint had acquired through contemplation: 'Così ricorsi ancora a la dottrina | di colui ch'abbelliva di Maria' (*Par.* XXXII. 106–07).[88]

Nevertheless, and in keeping with his preferred usage of the term, Dante's most suggestive deployment of 'doctrine' has no connections with spiritual, never mind theological, matters. At the opening of the *De vulgari eloquentia*, the aspiring *praeceptor* announces:

> Cum neminem ante nos de vulgaris eloquentie doctrina quicquam inveniamus tractasse, atque talem scilicet eloquentiam penitus omnibus necessariam videamus — cum ad eam non tantum viri sed etiam mulieres et parvuli nitantur, in quantum natura permictit — volentes discretionem aliqualiter lucidare illorum qui tanquam ceci ambulant per plateas, plerunque anteriora posteriora putantes: Verbo aspirante de celis locutioni vulgarium gentium prodesse temptabimus, non solum aquam nostri ingenii ad tantum poculum aurientes, sed, accipiendo vel compilando ab aliis, potiora miscentes, ut exinde potionare possimus dulcissimum ydromellum.

87   It is difficult not to hear behind this tercet an echo of 'la divina scienza [...] la quale non soffera lite alcuna d'oppinioni o di sofistici argomenti, per la eccellentissima certezza del suo subietto, lo quale è Dio. E di questa dice esso alli suoi discepoli [...], dando e lasciando a loro la sua dottrina' (*Conv.* II. 14. 19).

88   I have increasingly begun to suspect that an earlier instance of *dottrina* ought perhaps to be interpreted in a religious key. 'O voi ch'avete li 'ntelletti sani, | la dottrina che s'asconde | sotto 'l velame de li versi strani' (*Inf.* IX. 61–63) is a tercet that has attracted considerable critical attention (see Chapter 17). What has not been noted, as far as I am aware, is the peculiar value that Dante here gives to 'dottrina'. While the idea of the 'veil' was a commonplace of allegorical vocabulary, 'doctrine' was not. The standard term to allude to the 'concealed' 'other senses' was, of course, *sententia*, as Dante well knew: 'Sotto la quale rubrica io trovo scritte le parole le quali è mio intendimento d'assemplare in questo libello; e se non tutte, almeno la loro sentenzia' (*Vn* I. 1). What is also striking is the proximity of *sano* to 'dottrina', which, at least as far as I am concerned, makes me think immediately of the hugely influential Augustinian 'sana doctrina': 'sed qualis esse debeat qui in doctrina sana, id est Christiana, non solum sibi sed aliis etiam laborare studet' [but the sort of person he ought to be who strives in cultivating sound doctrine, namely Christian [doctrine], not only for his own sake but for the sake of others] (*De doc. chr.* IV. 31. 64; and compare IV. 16. 33; 27. 59; see also *Conf.* VII. 19; *Comm. in Ps.* LXVII. 39), which develops from the Scriptural 'amplectentem eum qui secundum doctrinam est fidelem sermonem ut potens sit et exhortari in doctrina sana et eos qui contradicunt arguere' [embracing that faithful speech which is according to doctrine, so that he may be able to exhort in sound doctrine and to censure those who contradict] (Titus I: 9); and 'Christian teaching' is precisely what lies behind the *lictera* of *Inferno* IX; see Chapter 17.

Sed quia unamquanque doctrinam oportet non probare, sed suum aperire subiectum, ut sciatur quid sit super quod illa versatur, dicimus, celeriter actendentes, quod vulgarem locutionem appellamus eam qua infantes assuefiunt ab assistentibus cum primitus distinguere voces incipiunt; vel, quod brevius dici potest, vulgarem locutionem asserimus quam sine omni regula nutricem imitantes accipimus. (*Dve* I. I. I–2)

[Since we find that no one before ourself has dealt in any way with the doctrine of vernacular eloquence, and since we see clearly that such eloquence is deeply necessary to everyone — for not only men but also women and children strive towards it, in as far as nature permits — wishing to illuminate somewhat the discernment of those who walk the streets like the blind, generally thinking that what is behind them lies ahead, inspired by the Word from Heaven, we will endeavour to benefit the language of illiterate people, not only drawing the water of our intellect to [fill] so large a cup, but, taking and compiling from others, we shall mix what is more useful, so that we can then offer to drink the sweetest mead.

But since any doctrine is not required to demonstrate its subject, but to clarify it, so that it may be known what it is that it reflects upon, we say, hastening to address the question, that we call vernacular language that which infants acquire from those who take care of them when they first begin to differentiate sounds; or, as can be said more briefly, we declare that vernacular language is that which we receive without any rule imitating our nurse.]

Dante's intent is clear: he portrays himself as the bold founder of a new branch of knowledge, a claim that serves as the basis for his self-construction as an *auctoritas* in the treatise.[89] He begins by confirming the absolute necessity for the new *doctrina* and by deflecting any possible accusations of *praesumptio*. *Talis eloquentia* will satisfy a universal need. The fundamental importance of the *De vulgari* is thus immediately established, as is the generosity of its author, who fulfills a divinely sanctioned undertaking 'inspired by the Word from Heaven'. As in the *Convivio*, Dante presents his task as an act of *caritas* on behalf of a majority whose needs are largely ignored by other intellectuals. Indeed, even though his work is without precedent, his aim is to rely not simply on his own *ingenium* but also on the contributions of others. He humbly presents himself as a *compilator* ('accipiendo vel compilando ab aliis')[90] rather than as an *auctor*. His new 'doctrine', as always occurs when Dante innovates, maintains links with the tradition. In addition, the poet demonstrates his competence for the task at hand by revealing that he is fully and conventionally aware of how to proceed in establishing the parameters of the new discipline — 'Sed quia unamquanque doctrinam oportet non probare, sed suum aperire subiectum, ut sciatur quid sit super quod illa versatur' — a declaration

---

89   All commentators of the opening of the *Dve* note its 'annuncio di novità assoluta' (Mengaldo, p. 26). They fail to recognize, however, that Dante is not simply and conventionally highlighting his work's *novitas*, but is presenting it as the founding text of a new intellectual discipline.

90   See Mengaldo's excellent note (p. 29), as well as the equally excellent annotations in Dante, *De vulgari eloquentia*, ed. by Enrico Fenzi, with the collaboration of Luciano Formisano and Francesco Montuori (Rome: Salerno, 2012), pp. 7–8. On the *Convivio* as a *compilatio*, see Zygmunt G. Barański, ' "Oh come è grande la mia impresa": Notes towards Defining Dante's *Convivio*', in *Dante's 'Convivio': Or How to Restart a Career in Exile*, ed. by Franziska Meier (Oxford: Peter Lang, 2018), pp. 9–26.

whose technical precision and aptness would have met with the approval of even the most exacting *magister*.[91] And yet, a flaw inexorably undermines Dante's assertion that his aim is to serve the needs of the *vulgares gentes*: if they are 'illiterate' how can they read a work in a language which only 'few' ('pauci') can master, 'quia non nisi per spatium temporis et studii assiduitatem regulamur et doctrinamur in illa [grammatica, namely, Latin]' [because only with time and assiduous study can we know its rules and be instructed in it] (3)? Rather than an act of altruism, the *De vulgari* has precise cultural ambitions: to establish Dante's 'authoritativeness' and its own uniqueness: 'Unde nos doctrine operi intendentes doctrinatas eorum poetrias emulari oportet' [Thus we who are aiming at a work of doctrine, it is proper for us to emulate their doctrinally rich [learned] handbooks on poetry] (II. 4. 3). The eye-catching word play *doctrina/doctrinatus* confirms once again the importance that Dante ascribed to the new 'doctrine'. Indeed, the declaration in Book II supplements effectively the emphasis that he had placed on his 'vulgaris eloquentie doctrina' [doctrine of vernacular eloquence] not just in the incipit of the treatise, as we saw, but also at the close of Book I: 'Et quia intentio nostra, ut polliciti sumus in principio huius operis, est doctrinam de vulgari eloquentia tradere' [And since our aim, as we promised at the beginning of this work, is to transmit/teach the doctrine of vernacular eloquence] (I. 19. 2). Such strategic structuring in Dante is never without significance. The rhetorical force of the polyptoton *doctrina/doctrinatus* also strengthens the ties between his vernacular *poetria* and established Latin poetic manuals.[92] At the same time, the poet hints that his work will go beyond these, since it will 'emulate' rather than 'imitate' them. Indeed, the perplexing reference to *poetriae* rather than to a single *poetria*, as one would expect from the allusion in the following paragraph to the *Ars poetica* — 'Hoc est quod Magister noster Oratius precipit cum in principio Poetrie' [This is what our Master Horace advises at the beginning of the *Ars poetica*] (II. 4. 4) — which has so exercised scholars, can probably be explained in terms of Dante's desire to underscore the uniqueness of his treatise. An alternative designation for the *De vulgari eloquentia* could easily be *Dantis Doctrina*.

Rather than become simpler, as the association between *dottrina* and *teologia* in Book II of the *Convivio* had initially suggested might be the case, the problem of 'Dante and doctrine' has actually become more complicated. The slipperiness and semantic potential of the term is probably best captured in another famous, yet somewhat baffling, passage from the *De vulgari eloquentia*. Dante describes the achievements of Old French literature as 'Biblia cum Troianorum Romanorumque gestibus compilata, et Arturi regis ambages pulcerrime et quamplures alie ystorie ac doctrine' [collections from the Bible together with the deeds of Trojans and Romans, and the wonderful adventures of King Arthur and many other works of history and doctrine] (I. 10. 2), where 'doctrine' have been interpreted as 'opere

---

91   On the 'scientific' character of Dante's phrase, see Fenzi, pp. 8–9; Mengaldo, p. 30. See also Dante Alighieri, *De vulgari eloquentia*, ed. by Mirko Tavoni, in *Opere*, I, 1065–547 (pp. 1130–32).
92   'Dante intende, senza intaccare la naturalità del volgare [...], regolarne la poesia e in generale l'eloquenza producendo una *doctrina* [...] equivalente alle *doctrinate poetrie* latine' (Tavoni, p. 1415).

didattiche' (Mengaldo, p. 85), as 'trattati' (Tavoni, p. 1237), as 'prose [...] dottrinali' (Fenzi, p. 69), and as 'ouvrages [...] de science', namely 'la composition savant en prose', all meanings which seem eminently reasonable.[93] At the same time, what I find particularly significant for the present discussion is the subtle manner in which Dante here shifts the sense of *doctrina* from an area of knowledge to the works, and even the genre, in which that knowledge is propagated. Although, unlike 'theology', the poet does not offer a formal definition and systematic treatment of 'doctrine', nonetheless, his *œuvre* provides a telling record of the connotative flexibility of the term, as well as of its creative possibilities at the hands of a remarkable wordsmith such as Dante.[94]

In truth, given the equation that the poet established between *dottrina* and knowledge in general, the scope of my chapter has grown dramatically. Doctrine's breadth of reference raises additional questions: most notably, questions about the nature of the relationship between theological and non-theological doctrine, which I have already touched on when examining Dante's treatment of theology. Despite the clear demarcation that the poet drew between them — the 'colomba' on one side of the divide, the 'regine e drude e ancille' firmly on the other — both, in practice, can be subsumed under an overarching *dottrina*. That a degree of permeability exists between theology and other intellectual disciplines, as we have noted, is undoubtedly apparent in the *Convivio* and in the *Monarchia*. It is essential, I believe, to remember that Dante saw human knowledge as stratified and composite — and I shall return fleetingly to this vital fact — since it reminds us of three things: first, that no area of human knowledge is self-standing; second, that every 'science' is part of a larger whole; and third, that, ultimately, every discipline can only properly be understood in light of all the other disciplines and of the whole. Theology is, naturally, unique and 'apart'; nevertheless, it is also a component of an all-embracing larger intellectual totality, which, in Dante, is given different designations: *dottrina*, *Sapienza*, *scienza*, *Filosofia*, *verità*, and, of course, *Dio*. Yet, as we saw, God is the 'subietto' of 'la divina scienza'... In attempting to understand what Dante might have meant by 'theology' (and to a lesser extent by 'doctrine'), it thus becomes imperative to establish the meanings and interconnections of those

93   Rosier-Catach edn, p. 121. On the use of *doctrina* in the titles of didactic works, see Mengaldo edn, pp. 84–85; Tavoni edn, pp. 1236–37.

94   In the Epistle to Cangrande, we find the extremely rare late-classical Latin and medieval Latin adjective *doctrinalis* (see Lewis and Short, *A Latin Dictionary*, in which the term is translated as 'theoretical' and just two examples are cited, one from Isidore and the other from Cassiodorus; Niermeyer, *Mediae Latinitatis Lexicon*, where the meanings given are 'concerned with teaching' and 'relating to religious doctrine'): 'Sex igitur sunt que in principio cuiusque doctrinalis operis inquirenda sunt' [Therefore there are six topics that need to be examined first as regards any doctrinal work] (XIII. 6. 18). What the author might have meant by *doctrinalis opus*, and how the *Commedia* might be defined as such, are both problems that are not easy to resolve. As occurs fairly frequently in the letter, the use of technical vocabulary is not only imprecise and impressionistic, but also does not conform to Dante's normal usage; see Chapter 6, pp. 251–56). *Dottrina* appears twice in the *Fiore*: 'La Vec[c]hia, che sapea ben la dottrina, | Ché molte volte avea studiato l'arte' (137. 12–13, where *arte* equals 'discipline' and *dottrina* means 'knowledge of that discipline'); 'Se non per insegnarti mia dottrina' (152. 2; where *dottrina* has the meaning of 'body of knowledge').

key concepts that might either overlap with the 'divine science' or, in some way, share or touch on some of its attributes.[95] As Dante was evidently aware, and as is clear from the striking convergence between 'Wisdom' and 'Philosophy', *Sapientia* and *scientia*, notions which historians of ideas have tended to present as discrete and antagonistic, medieval culture and thought were rather more flexible, malleable, and porous than much modern scholarship has been willing to acknowledge.[96]

6. On Synthesis

Still, distinctions were fundamental in the Middle Ages; and difference defined identity, allegiance, and intellectual sympathy. Thus, Dante's definition of theology, which, as I mentioned earlier, is limpid in its clarity, becomes transformed into something rather more problematic, yet also more significant, when judged against competing contemporary definitions of *theologia*. The implications of Dante's declaration of ideological allegiance, as well as of his treatment of *Sapienza* and *Filosofia*, for establishing the *Convivio*'s aims and intellectual sympathies and identity lie well beyond the scope of these terminological observations, although we have noted how Dante's definition of theology helps clarify and structure the treatise's overarching idea of knowledge. Instead, what is vital to note here is that it is almost certain that, in the years that followed, the poet never modified or abandoned the view of theology that he had expressed in the *Convivio*. We cannot definitively be sure that this is the case since Dante never again addressed the issue directly and only employed *teologia* and its cognates very infrequently; although when he did this, as we have seen, his usage tidily conformed to what he had said in the *Convivio*. Interestingly, and almost certainly significantly, the term finds no place in the *Commedia* — a detail which perhaps should advise caution when we endeavour to understand the poem's theological qualities. What there can be no doubt about is that, in the *Commedia*, and also in the *Monarchia*, Dante continued to grant unmistakable primacy to Scriptural revelation over the achievements of human reason, namely, to the 'documenta spiritualia que humanam rationem transcendunt' [spiritual teachings that transcend human reason] (*Mon.* III. 16. 8).[97] In fact, there is further evidence in the 'sacrato poema' (*Par.* XXIII. 62) to confirm that Dante's sense of theology had not altered since the early years of his exile, and that he still harboured serious doubts about those who wished to treat it as a 'science'. The pilgrim's examination on faith in *Paradiso* XXIV is not just an elucidation of the virtue and a personal assertion that he is a man of faith, but also a declaration of his thinking about 'sacred doctrine', and so of his (and his author's) theological

---

95   Once more this is a task that lies beyond the remit of the present chapter, not least because it would need to start by defining with care all those notions, such as *Sapienza, scienza, filosofia*, etc., which in some way come into contact with *teologia*.

96   Augustine established the distinction between the two in *De Trinitate* XII–XIV.

97   I thus find it difficult to accept Foster's claim, which he admittedly presents as a personal extrapolation, that 'a nostro avviso [...] la concezione dantesca della T[eologia] [...], quale appare nella *Commedia*, non differisce sostanzialmente da quella espressa da Tommaso in *Cont. Gent.* I. 9' ('Teologia', p. 567).

sympathies. This is not the occasion to go into the details of the relationship between *fede* and *teologia* in the *Commedia* and elsewhere in Dante; suffice it to say that the idea of the strict proximity between theology and faith was deeply embedded in medieval Christian culture.[98] In any case, by means of the pilgrim's answers, Dante deliberately evoked contemporary debates about the status of theology. In particular, by translating at the start of the exchange the incipit of chapter 11 of Paul's Epistle to the Hebrews — 'fede è sustanza di cose sperate | e argomento de le non parventi' (64–65) — a pivotal *sententia* in the dispute, he clearly established the key role that he wished theology to play in the episode.[99] Equally importantly, throughout the interrogation, the *viator* utilizes the technical terminology of Aristotelianism in his answers. However, unlike 'scientific' theologians, who used this same vocabulary and its attendant methods directly as the basic supports for their argumentation, Dante embeds the terminology in declarative poetic affirmations and prayers asserting his faith in God, the miracles, and Scripture:

> 'La larga ploia
> de lo Spirito Santo, ch'è diffusa
> in su le vecchie e 'n su le nuove cuoia,
>   è silogismo che la m'ha conchiusa
> acutamente sì, che 'nverso d'ella
> ogne dimostrazion mi pare ottusa'. (*Par.* XXIV. 91–96)

The technical language is used metaphorically and in a position of clear subordination and contrast both to '[l]e profonde cose' (69) and to the style in which the poet-pilgrim speaks, thereby highlighting its epistemological limitations. At the same time, by having recourse to such vocabulary, and subsequently admitting that 'a tal creder non ho io pur prove | fisice e metafisice' (133–34), Dante allowed a degree of validity to rationalist approaches to understanding the mysteries of the divine, as he had already done in the *Convivio*. The poet is clearly trying to go beyond the controversies surrounding theology, and attempting to synchronize the different positions.[100] As is well known, this is a typical Dantean approach, especially in the *Commedia*, which, as far as the poet's attitude to the world of human intellectualism is concerned, finds its most telling expression in the harmonious coming together of thinkers of very different stripe in the heaven of the Sun. What is especially striking about Dante's treatment of the souls of the wise is that none is given a specific tag associating him with a particular discipline, but each is defined in terms of some aspect of their intellectual attainment — some aspect of their 'doctrine', I should have said. Avoiding using potentially loaded terms such as 'theologian', Dante attempted to transcend contemporary animosities and to underscore the unity of knowledge and truth — a unity which finds its origin and legitimacy in God: 'nel vero in che si queta ogne intelletto' (*Par.* XXVIII. 108). From this perspective, and

---

98 See Chenu, *Théologie comme science*, pp. 15–16, 33–37, 48, 59, 64–66, 69–76, 79–90, 96.

99 'Est autem fides sperandorum substantia rerum argumentum non parentum'. See also Chenu, *Théologie comme science*, pp. 34–37, 61, 85–92.

100 See Matthew Treherne, 'Reading Dante's Heaven of the Fixed Stars (*Paradiso* XXII–XXVII): Declaration, Pleasure and Praise', in *'Se mai continga...': Exile, Politics and Theology in Dante*, ed. by Claire E. Honess and Matthew Treherne (Ravenna: Longo, 2013), pp. 11–26.

as the poet acknowledged recognizing the value of 'prove | fisice e metafisice' in illuminating the divine, all 'correct' intellectual striving, even if to differing degrees, is 'theological' in nature, since its ultimate 'subietto [...] è Dio'.

7. Conclusion

Dottrina and *teologia* thus, ultimately, do coincide; and the concept of the divine harmony of Wisdom is, of course, pleasing religiously, intellectually, and aesthetically. It lies at the very basis of the *Commedia*'s all-embracing plurilingualism. However, it also raises serious questions as regards where to set the boundaries of any endeavour to 'review Dante's theology'. *Mutatis mutandis*, the poet's 'narrow' association of theology with Scripture is equally a source of difficulties when trying to fix the parameters of any such investigation. Thus, adhering strictly to this latter perspective, Dante would not have considered Christian Aristotelians as theologians, even though they would have considered themselves as such. It is thus probably unsurprising that, in an *avant la lettre* spirit of ecumenism, the poet should have avoided classifying Christian thinkers in the *Commedia*. The complications we face when approaching the matter of Dante and theology are considerable but not insurmountable. In each instance, I would suggest, a thinker, a doctrine, a practice that we decide to designate as 'theological' ought to be evaluated in terms of Dante's theological perceptions and those of medieval culture in general. Moreover, we ought to establish the sense in which the objects of our study saw and presented themselves theologically. Finally, we need to decide whether or not to bring modern theological sensibilities and insights into the mix.

I should like to bring this chapter to a close, however, by returning one last time to Dante himself. At several points I have fleetingly touched on the question of the relationship between theology and poetry, or better, between theology and the poetry of the *Commedia*. We must never forget that we are dealing with a poet and not a theologian. Indeed, it is crucial to remember that, while he made many and varied claims for his poetic prowess, Dante never once presented himself in the guise of a *theologus* — at most, he introduced himself as 'inter vere phylosophantes minimus' (*Questio* 1).[101] It was others, such as Giovanni del Virgilio, who, as part of their own cultural programmes, elevated him to the rank of theologian.[102] Thus,

---

101 Although it is not uncommon to read that the simile of the 'bachelor' — 'Sì come il baccialier s'arma e non parla | fin che 'l maestro la question propone, | per approvarla, non per terminarla' (*Par.* XXIV. 46–48) — employed by Dante to describe the pilgrim readying himself to answer St Peter on Faith refers specifically to a scholar in a Faculty of Theology, this is in fact incorrect. The designation *baccalarius* was common to different faculties; see Gordon Leff, *Paris and Oxford Universities in the Thirteenth and Fourteenth Centuries: An Institutional and Intellectual History* (New York: Wiley, 1968), pp. 147–67; Jacques Verger, 'Baccalarius', in *Lexikon des Mittelalters* (Munich and Zurich: Artemis, 1980), I, col. 1323. Although matters theological weigh heavily on the events described in the heaven of the Fixed Stars, it is telling that Dante should leave the specialization of his 'bachelor' undeclared.

102 'Theologus Dantes nullius dogmatis expers, | quod foveat claro philosophia sinu: | gloria musarum, vulgo gratissimus auctor' [Dante the theologian lacking no doctrine that philosophy may foster in her illustrious bosom, glory of the Muses, author most pleasing to the unlearned] (ll. 1–3); the opening of Giovanni's epitaph is quoted from Philip H. Wicksteed and Edmund G. Gardner,

the *Commedia*'s theological *materia* should, in the first instance, be judged in light of poetry and of its poetic transformation. Whether the poet thought, as some have suggested, that, in the hierarchy of knowledge too, the *doctrina sacra* was inferior to the 'poema sacro' (*Par.* xxv. 1) is yet something else that I am unable to tackle here.[103] However, the answer, once again, as with so much that I have touched on, may very well depend on questions of definition. *Ah definitiones, refugium peccatorum.*

Dante and Giovanni del Virgilio (Westminster: Constable, 1902), p. 174. The promotion of Dante to the status of *poeta-theologus* by del Virgilio, Boccaccio, and others was part of a wide-ranging defence of poetry that was a key feature of fourteenth-century Italian cultural life; see Francesco D'Episcopo, *Il poeta-teologo tra Medioevo e Rinascimento* (Pomigliano d'Arco [Naples]: Oxiana, 2001); Simon A. Gilson, *Dante and Renaissance Florence* (Cambridge: Cambridge University Press, 2005), pp. 30–31 and passim; Robert Hollander, 'Dante *Theologus-Poeta*', *Dante Studies*, 94 (1976), 91–136; Craig W. Kallendorf, 'From Virgil to Vida: The *Poeta Theologus* in Italian Renaissance Commentary', *Journal of the History of Ideas*, 56 (1995), 41–62; Claudio Mésoniat, *Poetica Theologia: la 'Lucula Noctis' di Giovanni Dominici e le dispute letterarie tra '300 e '400* (Rome: Edizioni di storia e letteratura, 1984); Ronald Witt, 'Coluccio Salutati and the Conception of the *Poeta Theologus* in the Fourteenth Century', *Renaissance Quarterly*, 30 (1977), 538–63. It is important to remember that, despite what some scholars have maintained, Dante did not present himself as a 'poet-theologian'. The closest he may have come to doing this was through his treatment of Orpheus, the archetypical *poeta-theologus*; see Zygmunt G. Barański, 'Notes on Dante and the Myth of Orpheus', in *Dante: mito e poesia. Atti del secondo Seminario Dantesco Internazionale*, ed. by Michelangelo Picone and Tatiana Crivelli (Florence: Cesati, 1999), pp. 133–62. The primary literary identity that Dante constructed for himself in the *Commedia* was that of the *scriba Dei*, and specifically of the *poeta Dei*, namely of the divinely inspired poet akin to the authors of the books of Scripture. Dante's emphasis on being 'God's poet' was likely to distinguish himself from the traditional *scribae Dei*.

103 I am also unable to address here the question, increasingly posed by theologians with a keen interest in Dante, whether and to what extent the 'sacrato poema' might develop an understanding of poetry that is 'theological', namely, affectively, spiritually, and salvifically transformative. See in particular Vittorio Montemaggi, *Reading Dante's 'Commedia' as Theology* (Oxford: Oxford University Press, 2016). See also the following essays in *Dante's 'Commedia'*, ed. by Montemaggi and Treherne: Oliver Davies, 'Dante's *Commedia* and the Body of Christ', pp. 161–79; David F. Ford, 'Dante as Inspiration for Twenty-First-Century Theology', pp. 318–28; Douglas Hedley, 'Neoplatonic Metaphysics and Imagination in Dante's *Commedia*', pp. 245–66; Vittorio Montemaggi, 'In Unkowability as Love: The Theology of Dante's *Commedia*', pp. 60–94; Denys Turner, 'How to Do Things with Words: Poetry as Sacrament in Dante's *Commedia*', pp. 286–305. See also Vittorio Montemaggi, 'Contemplation, Charity and Creation *ex nihilo* in Dante's *Commedia*', *Modern Theology*, 29.2 (2013), 62–82.

CHAPTER 3

(Un)Orthodox Dante

'tolto per essemplo dal buono frate Tommaso d'Aquino, che a
un suo libro, che fece a confusione di tutti quelli che disviano
da nostra Fede' (*Conv.* IV. 30. 3)

1. *Scuola*

Reunited with Beatrice at the top of Mount Purgatory, the pilgrim is made to
confront and acknowledge his intellectual and moral errors — errors which had
led him to reject his beloved and to 'give himself to another': 'questi si tolse a me,
e diessi altrui' (*Purg.* XXX. 126).[1] Beatrice invokes a strikingly apt image to describe

---

1   The present chapter is an implicit dialogue with many Dante scholars and with various traditions
of Dante studies. Most specifically it is a sort of conversation with one of the most important books
on Dante of the recent past: Christian Moevs, *The Metaphysics of Dante's 'Comedy'* (Oxford and New
York: Oxford University Press, 2005), a conversation which, mutatis mutandis, mirrors the exchanges
that Christian and I have travelling between Chicago and Notre Dame. Although our emphases
are not the same, we both firmly believe in Dante's fundamental and constant orthodoxy (see, for
instance, Moevs, p. 86). This does not mean that there are not instances, as I discuss below, when
Dante's ideas stray into areas whose ideological acceptability in terms of contemporary Christian
belief is at the very least doubtful. The question of the poet's intellectual formation has not always
been addressed with due scholarly detachment. I thus consider it important to be clear from the start
as to my basic premise, approach, and personal perspective. Given the at times overly forceful, not to
say emotive, manner in which the question of the poet's ideological sympathies and influences has
been approached, I have largely avoided making direct reference to particular scholars and studies.
Moreover, I have endeavoured to minimize any tones that might be taken as polemical, especially
against an individual. I am grateful to the contributions of all Dantists in helping me formulate
my thoughts. This does not mean that I do not strongly argue for a particular interpretation: I do,
and with a degree of insistence, since I consider the matter of the poet's intellectual allegiances of
profound importance for the study of his *œuvre*. My hope is to stimulate dialogue. Polemic, on the
other hand, all too often seems to close off discussion. Finally, several of those who, over the years,
have written on the matter of Dante's thought have allowed unacknowledged personal sympathies
and concerns to intrude a bit too much into their academic work. I am thus happy to declare that
my perspective is coloured by a strong secularism and religious agnosticism, both of which, however,
are indelibly tinged by the Catholicism of my parents and of the immigrant communities in which
I grew up, and by the very good pre-university Catholic education that I received at schools in
Manchester, in particular at St Bede's Grammar School.
     The chapter originally brought *Reviewing Dante's Theology* to a close. Thus, together with the
preceding essay, it served to bookend the collection. I leave it to others to decide to what extent the
two chapters complement each other. The chapter bore the following dedication: 'In memory of
Massi Chiamenti, a true unorthodox'.
     Around the time when this chapter first appeared, the following three studies were also

the damaging and obfuscating effects of the *traviamento* on her wayward lover's intelligence:

> io veggio te ne lo 'ntelletto
> fatto di pietra e, impetrato, tinto,
> sì che t'abbaglia il lume del mio detto.
> (*Purg.* XXXIII. 73–75; and compare 67–69)

Dante-character's error was of such magnitude and obduracy that it was as if his mind had been transformed into rock; and 'obscured' rock at that. The assertion is deeply troubling: if the pilgrim's 'intellect' had indeed become like a dark stone then he had imperilled his very humanity, since the loss of the divinely infused rational soul meant an inevitable drop to a lower order of being.[2] Yet, it is difficult to deny that Beatrice's adynaton succinctly encapsulates the horror and enormity of the *viator*'s intellectual transgression. Sin had so brutalized him that his *anima intellectiva*, and hence his whole being, was as if entombed in stone. Not dissimilarly, though now in fact and not just metaphorically, to mark the nature of their evildoing and to affirm how sin had destroyed their humanity, divine justice transformed Pier delle Vigne into a tree and Ulysses into a flame. By following the wrong 'via' (88), the pilgrim's intellect, puffed up by Odyssean *praesumptio*, had committed intellectual and spiritual suicide. The association with the *Inferno*'s two finest thinkers and rhetoricians is chilling and instructive. Beatrice, however, does not restrict her condemnation to the pilgrim's failure to appreciate the stylistic

---

published: '*Il mondo errante*': *Dante tra letteratura, eresia e storia*, ed. by Marco Veglia and others (Spoleto: Fondazione Centro italiano di studi sull'alto Medioevo, 2013); *Dante and Heterodoxy: The Temptations of 13th Century Radical Thought*, ed. by Maria Luisa Ardizzone (Newcastle upon Tyne: Cambridge Scholars Publishing, 2014); *Ortodossia ed eterodossia in Dante Alighieri*, ed. by Carlotta Cattermole and others (Alpedrete [Madrid]: Ediciones de la Discreta, 2014). For two very different approaches to mine to the question of Dante and (un)orthodoxy, see Adriano Comollo, *Il dissenso religioso in Dante* (Florence: Olschki, 1990); *Dante & the Unorthodox: The Aesthetics of Transgression*, ed. by James Miller (Waterloo, ON: Wilfrid Laurier University Press, 2005).

  Yet more recently, the following study, that has several striking points of contact with the present chapter, appeared: Paolo Falzone, 'Eresia ed eterodossia nella *Commedia*: equivoci, punti fermi, zone d'ombra', in *Letture classensi*, 47 (2018), 41–72. Yet, as the author himself made me aware in a personal email of 2 October 2018, no reference is made in it to my work. Paolo further acknowledges that this was an unfortunate oversight. I am grateful for and impressed by his candour, and should like publicly to thank him for his exemplary and generous collegiality.

2   It was a commonplace in the Middle Ages to use stones as examples when distinguishing between different orders of being: 'Quodcumque vero nomen huiusmodi perfectiones exprimit cum modo proprio creaturis, de Deo dici non potest nisi per similitudinem et metaphoram, per quam quae sunt unius rei alteri solent adaptari, sicut aliquis homo dicitur lapis propter duritiam intellectus. Huiusmodi autem sunt omnia nomina imposita ad designandum speciem rei creatae, sicut homo et lapis: nam cuilibet speciei debetur proprius modus perfectionis et esse' [But when any name expresses such perfections together with a mode that is proper to a creature, it can be said about God only through resemblance and metaphor, by which what belongs to one thing is adapted to another, as when a man is said to be a stone because of the hardness of his intellect. Moreover all such names are used to designate the species of a created thing, such as man and stone: for to each species belongs its own mode of perfection and being] (Thomas Aquinas, *SCG* I. 30. 2). Compare also I. 26. 9; I. 31. 2; III. 48. 10; III. 104. 9). See also *Conv.* IV. 8. 13–14. There are, of course, also Medusan overtones to the *viator*'s 'being turned to stone'.

subtleties of her 'parola ornata' (*Inf.* II. 67). Like any good moralist, she makes public Dante-*personaggio*'s erring that is the ultimate cause of his incomprehension:

'Perché conoschi', disse, 'quella scuola
c'hai seguitata, e veggi sua dottrina
come può seguitar la mia parola:
    e veggi vostra via da la divina
distar cotanto, quanto si discorda
da terra il ciel che più alto festina.' (*Purg.* XXXIII. 85–90)

There is much that is problematic in these two tercets, as well as in the earlier lines 67–75. First and foremost, in narrative terms, both Beatrice's description and explanation of why the *viator*'s ''ngegno' is 'asleep' (64) and the entire episode of which these clarifications are part do not make logical sense. The pilgrim has reached the Earthly Paradise, is spiritually cleansed, and has been bathed in Lethe; yet, nonetheless, Beatrice accuses him of being distracted by 'pensier vani' (68) and describes his mind as 'petrified'. Indeed, Dante-*personaggio* himself stresses his intellectual limitations, confessing that he cannot follow her 'parola disïata' (82–84), which spurs Beatrice to explain that the cause of his Edenic shortcomings can be traced back to 'that school he had followed' on earth. But 'vain thoughts' and earthly errors, however grave, can have no direct part to play in that privileged place where 'è l'uom felice' (*Purg.* XXX. 75), as Beatrice herself corroborates:

'E se tu ricordar non te ne [his 'estrangement' (92) from her] puoi',
    sorridendo rispuose, 'or ti rammenta
come bevesti di Letè ancoi.' (*Purg.* XXXIII. 94–96)

It is not surprising that the pilgrim, and we with him, should be confused. He is obviously aware that it is Eastertime 1300 and that he is in the Earthly Paradise; and yet Beatrice treats him as if he were still in Florence, in the years after her death, when he had betrayed her: 'colpa ne la tua voglia altrove attenta' (99). To highlight dramatically the enormity of the *viator*'s past rejection of his blessed beloved, the poet performs a literary sleight of hand. He momentarily abandons narrative and ideological coherence by conflating two distinct moments in the relationship between Beatrice and her inconstant lover. Yes, we are, of course, in Eden. However, in a sort of 'pseudo–flashback', what Dante has his character anachronistically enact, in order to define and evaluate it, is his past, rather than present, behaviour.

That the poet should have gone to such extraordinary lengths, with their inherent danger of undermining the carefully constructed verisimilitude of his otherworldly account, confirms the crucial importance of the intellectual *traviamento* in the pilgrim's biography. Indeed, if we feel inclined to merge the historical Dante with his fictional namesake — and most Dantists are so inclined — then Beatrice's charge appears to offer unambiguous evidence that, before composing the *Commedia*, there had been a period in the poet's life when he had been tempted and enthralled by the intellectually unorthodox, which, like the pilgrim in Eden, he was now regretting and recanting. Yet, despite the sinful gravity of the intellectual lapse, what does Dante actually tell us about it? If we are honest, not very much at all. Beatrice reveals that he had adhered to an intellectual current ('scuola') whose teaching ('dottrina') and method ('via') were both dramatically different from and at odds with her 'word' and the 'divine'.[3] In light of the revealed qualities of Beatrice's speech ('la mia narrazion buia', 46) which closely imitate the revealed nature of divine forms of communication, both of which depend on an affective and inspired reception and exegesis ('conosceresti [...] moralmente', 72) which are beyond the 'stony' pilgrim, the 'school' he had 'followed' was decidedly earthbound in perspective and distinctly rationalist in approach.[4] That, especially in the universities and the schools, significant tensions existed during the second part of the thirteenth century and the early part of the fourteenth century between 'doctors' who placed different emphases on the role that reason, 'science', dialectic, disputation, Scripture, faith, inspiration, *Sapientia*, and revelation ought to have in intellectual work is well known.[5] At the same time, the oppositions that emerged were anything but straightforward. To reduce these, say, to conflicts between rationalists and exegetes or between philosophers and theologians means grossly to banalize a highly complex and nuanced intellectual environment. It is enough to remember that neither the philosophers nor the theologians constituted homogenous blocks — thus serious disagreements regarding the status of 'sacred doctrine' created rifts among theologians[6] — and that all medieval intellectuals were essentially commentators. It was their respective readings of the texts that they chose to gloss, from the Bible to Aristotle, and from Peter Lombard's *Sentences* to canon law, that both distinguished and divided them. Dante's trenchant presentation in *Mon.* III. 4 of the exegetical errors committed by supporters of papal power when interpreting Scripture is impressively instructive in this regard.[7] The hierocrats recognized the authority of the Bible and the fundamental need to elucidate God's word. However, according to Dante, when they did this, they were insensitive to

3   Beatrice's choice of words is technically precise. ' "Doctrina" denotes the teaching or doctrine of a master or school of thought, whereas "via" refers to the method used in solving problems when commenting on texts': Maarten J. F. M. Hoenen, 'Categories of Medieval Doxography: Reflections on the Use of "Doctrina" and "Via" in 14th and 15th Century Philosophical and Theological Sources', in *'Vera Doctrina': zur Bergriffsgeschichte der Lehre von Augustinus bis Descartes*, ed. by Philippe Büttgen and others (Wiesbaden: Harrassowitz in Kommission, 2009), pp. 62–84 (p. 62). For an analysis of Dante's use of the term *dottrina/doctrina*, see the preceding chapter.

4   See Zygmunt G. Barański, *Dante e i segni: saggi per una storia intellettuale di Dante Alighieri* (Naples: Liguori, 2000), pp. 41–76.

5   See, for instance, Luca Bianchi, *Il vescovo e i filosofi: la condanna parigina del 1277 e l'evoluzione dell'aristotelismo scolastico* (Bergamo: Lubrina, 1990); Gillian R. Evans, *Philosophy and Theology in the Middle Ages* (London and New York: Routledge, 1993), pp. 10–16; Alessandro Ghisalberti, *Medioevo teologico* (Bari: Laterza, 1990), pp. 85–145; Étienne Gilson, *History of Christian Philosophy in the Middle Ages* (London: Sheed & Ward, 1980), pp. 325–485; Martin Grabmann, 'Il concetto di scienza secondo S. Tommaso d'Aquino e le relazioni della fede e della teologia con la filosofia e le scienze profane', *Rivista di filosofia neo-scolastica*, 26 (1934), 127–55; J. M. M. H. Thijssen, *Censure and Heresy at the University of Paris: 1200–1400* (Philadelphia: University of Pennsylvania Press, 1998); Fernand van Steenberghen, *La Philosophie au XIIIe siècle* (Louvain and Paris: Publications universitaires, 1966).

6   See n. 8 in the preceding chapter.

7   For an excellent analysis of Dante's treatment of the conventions of Scriptural exegesis in *Monarchia* III, see Paola Nasti, 'Dante and Ecclesiology', in *Reviewing Dante's Theology*, ed. by Claire E. Honess and Matthew Treherne, 2 vols (Oxford: Peter Lang, 2013), II, 43–88.

the true meaning and purpose of the text since they bent it to contingent earthly needs: 'si vero industria, non aliter cum sic errantibus est agendum, quam cum tyrampnis, qui publica iura non ad comunem utilitatem secuntur, sed ad propriam retorquere conantur. O summum facinus, etiamsi contingat in sompniis, ecterni Spiritus intentione abuti!' [however if [such errors are committed] intentionally, one should behave towards those who err no differently than with tyrants, who do not follow the public rights for the common benefit, but endeavour to twist them to their own advantage. Oh supreme villainy, even if it should occur in dreams, to abuse the intention of the eternal Spirit!] (10–11). Such opportunistic Scriptural exegetes, as much as the most secularizing of philosophers at the University of Paris, were deaf to Beatrice's 'parola' and found themselves at an enormous distance from the 'via [...] divina'. In fact, given the gravity of their error, they were almost certainly further away than their philosophizing counterparts. Instead of allowing the Holy Spirit to guide their exegesis, they deliberately misapplied their reason, distorting and exploiting the word of God — aberrant behaviour which reduced them to 'fleshly servitude'.[8]

It is clear, therefore, that, given the allusiveness of Beatrice's description of the errant 'scuola' and the complexity of the medieval intellectual world at the beginning of the Trecento, we need to move with caution when trying to establish the possible identity of the ideological current that had led Dante-*personaggio* astray in the 1290s. By extension, any discussion of the poet's actual or presumed unorthodoxy needs also to be extremely sensitive to the historical, philological, and contextual evidence. Much of what follows deals precisely with such matters. For the moment, however, I should like to continue to focus on Beatrice's exposure of the pilgrim's past intellectual waywardness.

Whenever Dante leaves things vague, it is because he wants us to employ our 'intelletti sani' (*Inf.* IX. 61) and engage critically with his text.[9] As with so many of the *Commedia*'s cruces, Dantists have eagerly taken up the challenge of attempting to pinpoint the intellectual and institutional parameters of the 'school'. Allow me to cite some recent authoritative suggestions:

> *Scuola*: è certamente un'allusione (e lo conferma la parola *dottrina* del verso successivo) agli studi filosofici seguiti da Dante con grande entusiasmo, di cui è ricordo esplicito nel *Convivio*. Si tratta di una dottrina al di fuori e completamente indipendente dagli studi teologici. Che tale dottrina fosse ad un certo momento interpretata dal poeta come una specie di traviamento intellettuale, sembra da questo passo indubitabile, senza che per questo si arrivi all'assurda tesi di un Dante eretico o, per lo meno, sfiorante l'eresia. (Bosco-Reggio, p. 565)

---

8   See, for instance, 'Legenda est ergo Scriptura divina, et Spiritus sancti dispensatio cognoscenda, et intuenda prophetia; et rejicienda carnalis servitus, et liberalis intellegentia retinenda' [Therefore one should read divine Scripture, and recognize the dispensation of the Holy Spirit, and pay attention to prophecy; and reject fleshly servitude and retain the intelligence of a free person] (Augustine, *Contra Adimantum Manichaei* XV. 3, in PL XLII, col. 155).

9   See *Versi controversi: letture dantesche*, ed. by Domenico Cofano and Sebastiano Valerio (Foggia: Edizioni del Rosone, 2008).

La *scuola* seguita da Dante a cui qui si allude è certo una scuola di pensiero, una filosofia, come dice la parola *dottrina* al verso seguente, e tutto il senso del contesto. Non può tuttavia intendersi della filosofia in senso assoluto, che di per sé non era da considerarsi tendenza colpevole (come appare questa ai vv. 94–9) e che non è comunque una *scuola*. È molto probabile che si parli qui di quella passione filosofica esclusiva che prese Dante nella sua giovinezza e lo avvicinò alle posizioni averroistiche, che portavano a ritener la ragione umana di per sé sufficiente a intendere la verità dell'universo (cfr. vv. 87–90). Questa tendenza, propria dell'ambiente intellettuale fiorentino (averroista fu Cavalcanti, il *primo amico*), fa certamente parte del traviamento di Dante denunciato a questo punto del suo cammino. (Chiavacci Leonardi, II, 974)

L'accenno alla **dottrina** fa pensare che Beatrice si riferisca ad una 'deviazione' intellettuale di Dante, la quale per alcuni studiosi consisterebbe nella vicinanza giovanile (anche per l'influenza di Guido Cavalcanti) a posizioni averroistiche. Al riguardo, però, può essere sufficiente prendere in considerazione l'approccio del *Convivio*, che, pur non derogando dalla fede, presentava un'ambigua sovrapposizione o indistinzione fra dominio della filosofia e dominio della teologia [...]; si tenga presente che la prima 'accoglienza' che Beatrice riserva al suo fedele nell'Eden allude alla aleatorietà della *beatitudo* raggiungibile *in hac vita* [...], e che nel *Convivio* [...] circola l'idea di una felicità terrena che, pur entro i suoi limiti, può dirsi perfetta.[10]

What 'school' Dante refers to here is much debated [...]. Views arguing that a specific intellectual error is meant, such as that supposedly represented by Lady Philosophy in the *Convivio*, or Averroism [...], seem too restrictive: as the pilgrim's limitations are associated with universal history and the Fall of Adam, Beatrice may be noting the pilgrim's share in Adamic arrogance. (Durling-Martinez, II, 579)

There is much that I find troubling, because inaccurate and problematic, in the first two explanations, and to a lesser extent in the third proposal, regarding the 'school' and its consequences. Of greatest concern is the way in which a historical person and a literary character are treated as if they were one and the same entity. It is at the very least perplexing that scholars of literature should confuse life and art so blithely. Durling and Martinez are unusual in carefully sidestepping this all-too-common pitfall of Dante studies. In any case, the nature of the relationship between Dante Alighieri and Dante-*personaggio*, and hence the nature and extent of any possible biographism in the *Commedia*, is far from being satisfactorily established and resolved.[11] In narrative terms, that the protagonist should have sinned intellectually is certainly coherent with the overriding logic of the story of his past behaviour that emerges in the poem. Whether, during the 1290s or at some other time, Dante Alighieri, too, had behaved like his character is not something, I believe, that can be straightforwardly maintained on the basis of a poetic declaration. Nonetheless, most

10   The words are Nicola Fosca's, whose excellent annotations to the *Commedia* have still, alas, not found a publisher. I cite his commentary from the text uploaded to the Dartmouth Dante Project database, <http://dante.dartmouth.edu> [accessed 11 August 2019].

11   Given the crucial need to distinguish between author and character, I employ 'Dante', 'Dante Alighieri', and 'the poet' to refer to the historical author, and 'pilgrim', 'Dante-*personaggio*', 'Dante-character', *viator*, and similar designations to denote the *Commedia*'s protagonist.

Dantists would affirm, as indeed do some of the commentators in the quotations above, that, thanks to the *Convivio*, evidence of such intellectual erring is available; and so pilgrim and poet are naturally and necessarily one. Such a position too is not without its dangers. If one compares Bosco and Reggio's description of the *Convivio* as embodying 'una dottrina al di fuori e completamente indipendente dagli studi teologici' with Fosca's cautious characterization of the treatise as a work 'che, pur non derogando dalla fede, presentava un'ambigua sovrapposizione o indistinzione fra dominio della filosofia e dominio della teologia', it is immediately obvious that we are confronted with two contrasting interpretations of the 'esposizione' (*Conv.* I. 2. 1) and its ideology, and hence with two conflicting views of its possible 'erring'. Indeed, it is questionable whether, according to Fosca's definition, one can even talk about 'error'; and if this is indeed the case, then, the *Convivio* is significantly less relevant when discussing Dante's supposed unorthodoxy than is generally asserted. In any case, even accepting the biographism of the *Commedia*, the *Convivio* is not narratively germane to the pilgrim, since, at the time of his great otherworldly adventure, the 'quasi comento' (*Conv.* I. 3. 2) had not yet been written. It thus follows that the *Convivio* cannot play a role in the events that occurred in the decade after her death to which Beatrice refers.[12] Furthermore, as the manuscript evidence confirms, it is almost certain that Dante had no intention of making the *Convivio* public, thereby, raising extremely serious questions regarding how it might be used in relation to the *Commedia*.[13] Obviously, this does not mean that we cannot have recourse to the *Convivio* when endeavouring to establish Dante's intellectual formation and sympathies (see Chapter 1, pp. 27 and 35–40), including any possible unorthodoxies in his thought, especially in the years immediately after his exile; and I shall be doing as much in due course.

Substantial difficulties affect and delimit the presentation of the 'scuola' in *Purgatorio* XXXIII.[14] It is thus probably impossible to be precise about the complexion of the pilgrim's *traviamento*, never mind that of the poet (that is if evidence from the canto can actually be used as the basis for laying charges of heterodoxy against him — something which I very seriously doubt). Beatrice is deliberately allusive, while the intellectual world of the Middle Ages was extremely complex. Consequently we should proceed with care, as Durling and Martinez commendably do, when explicating her words. Dogmatism, with its assertions of 'certainty', is unwarranted and unhelpful. Where is the hard proof to conclude that, in *Purgatorio* XXXIII,

12   See Zygmunt G. Barański, 'The "New Life" of "Comedy": The *Commedia* and the *Vita Nuova*', *Dante Studies*, 113 (1995), 1–29; Peter Dronke, *Dante's Second Love: The Originality and the Contexts of the 'Convivio'* (Leeds: Maney, 1997), pp. 26, 72–76; Lino Pertile, 'Dante's *Comedy* beyond the *stilnovo*', *Lectura Dantis Virginiana*, 13 (1993), 47–77 (pp. 56–61). See also the exchange in the Electronic Bulletin of the Dante Society of America, <www.princeton.edu/~dante/ebdsa/index.html> [accessed 11 August 2019]: Robert Hollander, 'Dante's Deployment of *Convivio* in the *Comedy*', 7 October 1996; Lino Pertile, 'Lettera aperta di Lino Pertile a Robert Hollander sui rapporti tra *Commedia* e *Convivio*', 8 October 1996; and Robert Hollander, 'Dante's Quarrel with his own *Convivio* (Again)', 23 March 2008.

13   See Chapter 1, n. 14.

14   On the 'scuola', see also John A. Scott, 'Beatrice's Reproaches in Eden: Which "School" Had Dante Followed?', *Dante Studies*, 109 (1991), 1–23.

Beatrice is talking about 'studi filosofici seguiti da Dante con grande entusiasmo'; or about the *Convivio*; or about 'quella passione filosofica esclusiva che prese Dante nella sua giovinezza e lo avvicinò alle posizioni averroistiche, che portavano a ritener la ragione umana di per sé sufficiente a intendere la verità dell'universo'? As far as I have been able to ascertain, definitive evidence in support of such assertions is not available either in the *Commedia* in general or in the close of *Purgatorio* in particular.

2. Contra fidem

Yet, the fact that the *Commedia* provides limited insight into the 'school', and even less into Dante's intellectual interests before he began to write the poem, does not mean that his masterpiece cannot contribute to elucidating the thorny question of the poet's (un)orthodoxy. It is a commonplace of a substantial part of modern Dante scholarship to depict the *Convivio* and the *Commedia* as works in ideological opposition: the former teetering on the brink of a dangerous irreligious rationalism; the latter returning triumphantly to Christian intellectual and spiritual order — to orthodoxy, in other words. Regardless of what one might think about the nature of the relationship between the 'almost commentary' (*Conv.* I. 3. 2) and the 'sacred poem' (*Par.* XXIII. 62 and XXV. 1), the idea that, in the *Commedia*, all is approved doctrinal harmony is, in fact, far from straightforward. The fourteenth-century commentators of the poem — never mind the learned Dominicans in Trecento Bologna and Florence — who were normally more sensitive than we are today to what might and might not be problematic in Christian terms, would have had little doubt how to answer if questioned about the *Commedia*'s ties to accepted religious belief. They would have acknowledged, almost certainly with a ready explanation to hand, that not everything in the poem, at first sight at least, was 'secondo [...] vera teologia'.[15] The reason I can confidently make such a bold assumption is the evidence of the commentators' own words.[16] Graziolo Bambaglioli was actually quite blunt about the matter when glossing:

> Sappie che, tosto che l'anima trade
>   come fec'ïo, il corpo suo l'è tolto
> da un demonio, che poscia il governa
> mentre che 'l tempo suo tutto sia vòlto. (*Inf.* XXXIII. 129–32)

---

15   *L'Ottimo Commento della 'Divina Commedia': testo inedito d'un contemporaneo di Dante citato dagli Accademici della Crusca*, ed. by Alessandro Torri, 3 vols (Pisa: Capurro, 1827–29), I, 251.

16   On the ways in which the fourteenth-century commentators dealt with ideological difficulties posed by the *Commedia*, see Zygmunt G. Barański, '*Chiosar con altro testo*': *leggere Dante nel Trecento* (Fiesole: Cadmo, 2001), pp. 23–31; Simon Gilson, *Dante and Renaissance Florence* (Cambridge: Cambridge University Press, 2005), pp. 48–49; Robert Wilson, '"Quandoque bonus dormitat Dantes"? The Treatment of Dante's Errors in the "Trecento" Commentaries', *Rassegna europea di letteratura italiana*, 29–30 (2007), 141–56, and 'Allegory as Avoidance in Dante's Early Commentators: "bella menzogna" to "roza corteccia"', in *Interpreting Dante: Essays on the Traditions of Dante Commentary*, ed. by Paola Nasti and Claudia Rossignoli (Notre Dame, IN: University of Notre Dame Press, 2013), pp. 30–52.

'Sed quamvis hec ita scripta sint, tamen simpliciter non sunt vera, quia falsum est, et contra naturam et fidem' [Yet however much these [words] may be written in this way, nevertheless they are simply not true, because it is false, and against nature and faith].[17] The Bolognese commentator's unequivocal judgement concerns Dante's startling revelation that it is possible for souls to be cast down to Tolomea while they are still alive, their bodies remaining on earth in the thrall of a devil and functioning as if nothing awry has happened (*Inf.* XXXIII. 124–32). Such a claim, Graziolo asserts, is untrue in terms both of natural science and of Christian faith. As we have already noted, deprived of the *anima intellectiva*, a person ceases to be a living human being; and Bambaglioli too stresses this commonplace fact.[18] Furthermore, as the poet would very soon establish in the opening cantos of *Purgatorio*, it is a fundamental Catholic tenet that, as long as we have a single breath left in our bodies, repentance, and hence salvation, both remain a concrete possibility. To suggest otherwise was (and continues to be) 'contra [...] fidem'.

There is much that at first sight is troubling, whether narratively or ideologically, about frate Alberigo's 'unfeasible' existence across two worlds — and I shall return quite soon to some of these complications.[19] For the present, however, I want to focus on something that might come as a surprise to those modern scholars who anachronistically assume that, in the Middle Ages, whatever could be deemed nonconformist was automatically problematic: an inevitable and glaring challenge to authority that would have been aggressively countered, and which would have inexorably led to the proponent of the doctrinal eccentricity (and any apologist) being condemned as a heretic.[20] The reality on the ground, however, was rather more complicated, pliant, and, yes, forgiving. Although he recognized the unorthodoxy of Dante's 'living dead', at the same time Graziolo had no difficulty or concern about putting forward an ideologically acceptable explanation for the *scripta non vera*: 'Hec siquidem sunt figurative ab auctore descripta; nam hoc nichil aliud significat vel figurat nisi quod tanta est gravitas prodicionis et proditoris, quod statim ex peccati pondere pena sequitur' [Nevertheless these matters are figuratively described by the author; for this signifies or figures nothing other than how great

---

17   Graziolo Bambaglioli, *Commento all'*'Inferno' di Dante, ed. by Luca Carlo Rossi (Pisa: Scuola Normale Superiore, 1998), p. 212.

18   '[Q]uod anima separata a corpore corpus aliqualiter gubernetur et vivat: hec est ratio quia, cum anima <sit> regulatrix et motrix et vivificativa ac perfectio totius corporis, sequitur quod, ipsa descedente et recedente de corpore, corpus moveri et vivificari non possit; et hoc est quod dicit testus' [because when the soul is separated from the body, the body by no means may be governed and live: this is the reason why, since the soul is the regulator and the mover and the life-giver and the completion of the whole body, it follows that, when it [the soul] separates and departs from the body, the body cannot be moved and restored to life; and this is what the text says] (Bambaglioli, p. 212).

19   See the next subsection '*Disgiunto*'.

20   Such a view is reductive not just on account of its sweeping nature but also because its proponents normally fail to explain what they — never mind different communities during the course of the Middle Ages — might mean by 'unorthodox'; who and what institutions had the power to censure, and how such acts of denunciation might formally be expressed and executed; and whether all social and professional groups were deemed to have the same relationship to nonconformity. What follows touches on some of these key issues; see in particular the subsection '*Eresïarche* and *fines*'.

is the seriousness of treachery and of traitors, because immediately from the gravity of a sin follows its punishment].[21] Dante, the commentator explains, is not speaking literally but allegorically (*figurative* and *figurare*): his aim is to underscore both the seriousness of the sin of treachery and its resulting appropriately harsh punishment. The poet's allegorizing solution is thus, self-evidently, an expression of religious propriety. In any case, earlier in his commentary, Bambaglioli had already dealt with another case of heterodoxy by appealing to the difference between the *Commedia*'s literal and allegorical senses. In the wood of the suicides, Pier delle Vigne reveals that, at the Last Judgement, 'Come l'altre verrem per nostre spoglie, | ma non però ch'alcuna sen rivesta' (*Inf.* XIII. 103–04), a disconcerting admission that runs counter to the key doctrine of the resurrection of the flesh, according to which everyone's body and soul will be reunited for eternity. In this instance, the commentator discussed the poet's highly problematic claim not just in terms of allegory, but also, and more significantly, by explicitly legitimating it in terms of mainstream belief, before concluding that Dante was a 'faithful Catholic' who accepted the Church's teachings (subsequently, in *Inferno* XXXIII, having previously established the fact of the poet's orthodoxy in canto XIII, Graziolo had not felt the need to repeat himself on these matters):

> Sed quamvis hec verba sic sint ab auctore descripta, nichilominus teneo quod aliud scriptum fuerit et alia fuerit auctoris intencio: Scriptura siquidem sic rigide sic singulariter et vituperose punit et ponit de hiis qui, velud desperate cecitatis filii, perdiderunt sponte se ipsos ad terrorem et instructionem mortalium, ut sibi precaveant ab huiusmodi perdictione inposterum, per quam

---

21   Bambaglioli, p. 212. It was well established in medieval culture that creative writers enjoyed a considerable degree of artistic and imaginative licence, especially as the substantial meaning of their writings was not found at the literal level but 'integumentally', namely 'poetically'. Guido da Pisa is very clear on this point from the very start of his commentary: 'Ubi est notandum quod Virgilius in hoc loco tenet figuram et similitudinem rationis humane, qua mediante autor penas peccatis adaptat. Unde, si in aliquo loco vel passu videatur contra catholicam fidem loqui, non miretur aliquis, quia secundum rationem humanam poetice pertractando dirigit vias suas. Et ego, simili modo exponens et glosans, non nisi itinera sua sequar, quia ubi loquitur poetice, exponam poetice [...]. Quia si in ista *Comedia* esset aliquod hereticum quod per poesiam seu aliam viam sustineri non posset, non intendo illud tale defendere vel fovere; immo potius, viso vero, totis conatibus impugnare. Rogo te autem, o lector, ut autorem non iudices sive culpes si tibi videatur quod ipse autor in aliquo loco vel passu contra captolicam fidem agat, quia poetice loquitur et fictive' [Here it is to be noted that Virgil in this place is a figure and analogy of human reason, by means of which the author adapts the punishments to the sins. Thus if in any place or passage he seems to speak against Catholic faith, let nobody be surprised, because treating things poetically he orders his ways according to human reason. And I in a similar way explaining and glossing, shall do nothing other than follow his path. Because where he speaks poetically, I will explain poetically. Because if in this *Comedy* there should be anything heretical, which cannot be supported poetically or in another way, I do not intend to defend or foster such a thing, but rather, in all honesty, to attack it with all my strength. Indeed I ask you, o reader, not to judge and blame the author, if it may seem to you that this author in any place or passage acts against Catholic faith, because he is speaking poetically and fictively]: Guido da Pisa, *Expositiones et Glose. Declaratio super 'Comediam' Dantis*, ed. by Michele Rinaldi, 2 vols (Rome: Salerno, 2013), I, 270. On the Trecento commentators' allegorization of the *Commedia*'s problematic passages, see Wilson, 'Allegory as Avoidance in Dante's Early Commentators', an important study which usefully historicizes the practice of allegorical 'avoidance'.

inremediabiliter et preter spem alicuius misericordie Deus graviori offensione offenditur: nam nullum est gravedinis tante delictum cuius divina misericordia misereri non possit, excepto desperationis delicto que sola mederi nequit. Hoc est quod probat et dicit; credo autem auctorem prefatum, ta*m*quam fidelem captolicum et omni prudentia et scientia clarum, suo tenuisse iudicio quod Ecclesia santa tenet videlicet. (Bambaglioli, *Commento all''Inferno' di Dante*, p. 106)

[Yet however much these words were written thus by the author, nonetheless I maintain that one thing was written and the author's intention was another: Scripture likewise inflexibly likewise uniquely likewise vituperatively punishes and depicts those who, just as the sons of desperate blindness, have lost themselves of their own accord to the terror and teaching of mortals, that henceforth they guard themselves against such perdition, through which irremediably and beyond hope of any mercy God is offended by a highly grievous offence: for no sin is of such gravity that divine mercy cannot have compassion for it, except for the sin of despair which alone cannot be restored. This is what he demonstrates and says: indeed I believe the aforementioned author, as a faithful Catholic and renowned for his prudence and all-encompassing knowledge, to have maintained by his own discernment what the holy Church manifestly maintains.]

At the same time, the resurrection of the body was a matter of considerable doctrinal significance. Indeed, Augustine had remarked that 'In nulla ergo re tam vehementer, tam pertinaciter, tam obnixe et contentiose contradicitur fidei christianae, sicut de carnis resurrectione' [On no other matter is Christian faith contradicted so vehemently, so tenaciously, so strenuously and obstinately as the resurrection of the flesh].[22] Nonetheless, there is no escaping the fact that Dante had decided that it was acceptable and appropriate for him to 'contradict Christian faith' on precisely this point, offering a description of the ultimate eternal condition of the suicides that was undeniably heretical: 'Or se l'auctore sentisse come la lettera dice non v'è dubio che farebbe heresia però che col corpo come ora siamo sia ciascuna anima al Judicio'.[23] In his own commentary, unlike his 'friend', the Ottimo had avoided any mention of heresy, glossing *Inf.* XIII. 103–05 as a well known universal truth:

Nelle predette parole è da notare due cose: l'una, che le parti d'alcuna cosa non hanno loro perfezioni se non sono insieme congiunte; e questo vegiamo e nelle cose artificiali, e nelle materiali. Onde le parti d'una cosa allora hanno compiuto essere, quando il fondamento con le parti, e col t[u]tto insieme sono congiunte; e se per esse[re] abbiamo alcuna parte, non l'a[bbiam]o in quanto parte, se non quando che 'l tutto si compone delle parti son congiunte. E imperò che l'uomo hae in sè due parti, secondo la verità, e vera teologia, e vera filosofia, cioè l'anima e il corpo; l'anima non ha suo propio essere se non

---

22   Augustine, *Enarrationes in Psalmos* LXXXVIII (2). 5, in PL XXXVII, col. 1134.
23   *L'ultima forma dell'Ottimo commento: chiose sopra la Comedia di Dante Alleghieri fiorentino tracte da diversi ghiosatori. Inferno*, ed. by Claudia Di Fonzo (Ravenna: Longo, 2008), p. 151. It is most unlikely that what Di Fonzo terms the 'last version' of the Ottimo's commentary was actually written by the commentator of that soubriquet. Contrary to a view long held by scholars, it has recently been established that the philological and textual evidence points to a different exegete for this set of glosses. The anonymous commentator, however, did unquestionably base his own commentary on the Ottimo's. Furthermore, both of them almost certainly belonged to the same Florentine intellectual circle.

> è congiunta col propio corpo: del corpo sanza l'anima, è chiaro. (*L'Ottimo Commento*, 1, 250–51)

The logic of the Ottimo's approach is not difficult to fathom: by presenting *Inf.* XIII. 103–05 as quintessentially orthodox — 'secondo la verità, e vera teologia, e vera filosofia', a case of normalizing overkill if ever there was one — he hoped to camouflage their deviance. His 'friend', however, must have been troubled by his source's interpretive tactic. In his commentary, he openly stated that the 'letter' of *Inf.* XIII. 103–05 was heretical, but, as Graziolo had similarly noted, the literal sense should not be taken as a statement of the 'author's intention'. Furthermore, the anonymous commentator makes clear that others too think as he does. He thus points out that the *Commedia*'s readers had proposed a variety of doctrinally acceptable explanations for Dante's eccentric treatment of the suicides, thereby dismissing any suggestion that the poet may have harboured heretical intentions:

> Ma elli poetiza et argumentando come si fa in questi nostre materiale cose. Et alli dipintori et alli poeti è attribuita cotale balia. Altri dicono che ciò fece per terrore dare a' mortali che non venissoro a tale desperatione. Udendo lo straccio ch'era facto de l'anime perse et poi del corpo per sé. Alcuno theologo dice che l'auctore essendo fornito de theologia et di phylosophia parloe con altro intendimento cioè che queste anime avranno doppia pena doppo la resurrectione universale, nella quale avranno li corpi loro cioè la pena positiva che ora sostegnono et la pena privativa di vedere li corpi suoi allato a sé col quale desiderano de riunirse. Et questo desiderio accrescerae le pene però che i lloro desiderio sia loro defraudato. (*L'ultima forma dell'Ottimo commento*, p. 151)

It is striking that the Ottimo's 'friend' deemed it necessary to involve the entire community of Dante's contemporary readers in legitimating the poet's unconventional treatment of the resurrection of the body. Indeed, he was careful to establish that even theologians concurred that Dante was not a heretic; and first among these, tellingly, was an 'inquisitor of heretical perverseness', Accursio Bonfantini,[24] best known for his role in the condemnation of Cecco d'Ascoli for heresy.[25] This would strongly indicate that, in the first half of the Trecento, the passage from *Inferno* XIII was generally considered to be problematic, though not a mark of its author's nonconformism. To put it simply, lines 103–05 could be orthodoxly defended and explicated, so that there could be no question that Dante's and the *Commedia*'s 'opinion was plainly the same as that held by the Church' (Bambaglioli, p. 106). The recourse to allegoresis and to a writer's real rather than

---

24 Di Fonzo notes, 'La chiosa relativa alla doppia pena dei suicidi "positiva" e "privativa" è la chiosa attribuita espressamente ad Accursio Bonfantini nel codice Magliabechiano Conventi Soppressi I V 8 a c. 130. Nella nostra redazione del commento il frate francescano inquisitore *hereticae pravitatis* in Toscana dal 1326 al 1329 è designato genericamente con l'epiteto di "alcuno teologo". E se il commento Magliabechiano *ad locum* parla di "Expositione sopra questo caso di frate Accorso Bonfantini" la nostra redazione usa la locuzione: "come dice alcuno teologo" rafforzando l'ipotesi del Mehus circa un ciclo di letture e commenti alla *Commedia* affidate al frate' (p. 151); the reference is to *Vita Ambrosii Traversarii*, ed. by Lorenzo Mehus (Florence: ex typographio Caesareo, 1759; reprinted Bologna: Forni, 1968), pp. 137, 182, 340.

25 See Eugenio Ragni, 'Bonfantini, Accursio', in *Dizionario Biografico degli Italiani* (Rome: Istituto della Enciclopedia Italiana, 1960–), XII, 10–11.

apparent *intentio* were standard devices that medieval intellectuals regularly used when attempting to normalize the ideologically challenging. In this regard, it is worth remembering that it was only the younger Dominicans, namely those who had not yet learned how to interpret properly, who were prevented from reading Dante's poem. Religiously motivated attacks against the *Commedia* were in fact rare.[26] Guido Vernani's uncompromising, albeit clichéd, assault on the poem was very much an exception, and one of course whose real target was the *Monarchia*:

> Inter alia vero talia sua [the devil's] vasa quidam fuit multa fantastice poetizans et sophista verbosus, verbis exterioribus in eloquentia multis gratus, qui suis poeticis fantasmatibus et figmentis, iuxta verbum philosophie Boetium consolantis, scenicas metriculas adducendo, non solum egros animos, sed etiam studiosos dulcibus sirenarum cantibus conducit fraudulenter ad interitum salutifere veritatis.[27]

> [Indeed among the devil's other such vases was a certain one who poeticizing wrote many fantastic things and was a wordy sophist, with his superficial words pleasing many through his eloquence, who with his vain poetic things and fictions, according to the word of Philosophy consoling Boethius, brought theatrical whores, and not only fraudently led sick minds with sweet siren songs, but also learned ones to the annihilation of salubrious truth.]

In the Trecento, the poem was much more likely to be judged a repository, rather than a 'destroyer', of 'Catholic truth': 'Fu adunque il nostro poeta, sì come gli altri poeti sono, nasconditore, come si vede, di così cara gioia, come è la catolica verità, sotto la volgare corteccia del suo poema'.[28] Modern and medieval readers of the *Commedia* thus ultimately concur as regards its orthodoxy. Yet, the former arrive at this position largely uncritically; the latter thanks to a keen corrective and standardizing eye. Neither, it seems to me, does justice to the letter of the text. The problem remains: is the *Commedia*, even if only occasionally, heterodox? And if it is, what might the implications be for both poet and poem?

3. *Disgiunto*

Although the *Commedia*'s fourteenth-century readers were keen to recognize its religious conformity and, faced with the outwardly heretical, were skilled at deftly transforming the heterodox into the orthodox, when the poet wrote his masterpiece,

---

26   See Roberto Antonelli, 'L'ordine domenicano e la letteratura nell'Italia pretridentina', in *Letteratura italiana. 1. Il letterato e le istituzioni*, ed. by Alberto A. Rosa (Turin: Einaudi, 1982), pp. 681–728 (p. 714). Giorgio Padoan, 'Il Boccaccio "fedele" di Dante', in his *Il Boccaccio, le Muse, il Parnaso e l'Arno* (Florence: Olschki, 1982), pp. 229–46 (pp. 236–37); Maria Picchio Simonelli, 'L'inquisizione e Dante: alcune osservazioni', *Dante Studies*, 118 (2000), 303–21.

27   Guido Vernani, *De reprobatione Monarchiae*, in Nevio Matteini, *Il più antico oppositore politico di Dante: Guido Vernani da Rimini: Testo critico del 'De reprobatione Monarchiae'* (Padua: CEDAM, 1958), p. 93. See also Anthony K. Cassell, *The 'Monarchia' Controversy* (Washington, DC: Catholic University of America Press, 2004); Roberto Lambertini, 'Guido Vernani contro Dante: la questione dell'universalismo politico', in Veglia and others, pp. 359–69; Simonelli.

28   Giovanni Boccaccio, *Esposizioni sopra la Comedia*, ed. by Giorgio Padoan, 2 vols (Milan: Mondadori, 1965), I, 57.

he must have known that there were no guarantees that his future readers would react to his doctrinal manipulations in the wary, though largely accepting way that the majority of them actually did in the Trecento, and as they have essentially continued to do ever since. Dante, it thus seems, was taking a serious risk — one that could have fatally damaged the ideological, cultural, and religious foundations underpinning ''l poema sacro | al quale ha posto mano e cielo e terra' (*Par.* xxv. 1–2). In the Middle Ages, a heretic was someone who, despite being cognizant of definitive evidence to the contrary, irrationally persisted in propagating falsehoods regarding the tenets of the faith.[29] A heretic could thus neither be 'authoritative', namely worthy of trust, and hence of imitation, nor a source of 'scientific' and ethical truths, never mind a *scriba Dei*, providentially ordained to guide errant humanity back to the 'diritta via' (*Inf.* I. 3).[30] Instead of serving as a counter to '*il* mondo che mal vive' (*Purg.* xxxii. 103), a heretical *Commedia* would have made a dire situation catastrophic, especially as it would have insinuated pernicious unorthodoxies among undoubted affirmations of obedient piety. Nearly as problematically, the 'sickness' of heresy would have fatally devastated the poem's vital claim to offer a historically true account of a divinely sanctioned otherworldly journey.[31] As I said, Dante was taking a serious risk.

To put it simply, why might — and I stress 'might', since what follows is necessarily a hypothesis — why might, I repeat, have the poet considered it profitable and acceptable to introduce matters heretical into his 'sacrato poema' (*Par.* xxiii. 62)? The question is ominously weighty; and it is surprising that Dantists have not posed it more regularly, and thus, as a consequence, have not endeavoured to deal

---

29   See Annelise Maier, *Ausgehendes Mittelalter: Gesammelte Aufsätze zur Geistesgeschichte*, 3 vols (Rome: Storia e letteratura, 1964–77), II, 59–81. On heresy in the Middle Ages, see Jennifer Kolpacoff Deane, *A History of Medieval Heresy and Inquisition* (Lanham, MD: Rowman & Littlefield, 2011); Herbert Grundmann, *Religious Movements in the Middle Ages* (Notre Dame, IN: University of Notre Dame Press, 1995); Malcolm D. Lambert, *Medieval Heresy: Popular Movements from the Gregorian Reform to the Reformation*, 3rd edn (Oxford: Blackwell, 2002); Raoul Manselli, *Studi sull'eresie del secolo XIII*, 2nd edn (Rome: Istituto storico per il Medio Evo, 1975); Albert Michel, 'Hérésie. Hérétique', in DTC, VI, cols 2208–57; Walter Leggett Wakefield and Austin Patterson Evans, *Heresies of the High Middle Ages* (New York and London: Columbia University Press, 1969); *The Concept of Heresy in the Middle Ages (11ᵗʰ–13ᵗʰ C.)*, ed. by Willem Lourdaux and Daniel Verhelst (Leuven: University Press; The Hague: Nijhoff, 1976); *Heresy and Authority in Medieval Europe*, ed. by Edward Peters (Philadelphia: University of Pennsylvania Press, 1980). For the specifically Italian context see Claudio Giunta, 'Letteratura ed eresia nel Duecento italiano: il caso di Matteo Paterino', *Nuova rivista di letteratura italiana*, 3 (2000), 9–97; Carol Lansing, *Power and Purity: Cathar Heresy in Medieval Italy* (Oxford: Oxford University Press, 1998); Grado Giovanni Merlo, 'L'eresia all'epoca di Bonifacio VIII, ovevero l'illusione della fine', in Veglia and others, pp. 229–41; Lorenzo Paolini, 'Italian Catharism and Written Culture', in *Heresy and Literacy, 1000–1530*, ed. by Peter Biller and Anne Hudson (Cambridge: Cambridge University Press, 1994), pp. 83–103; Riccardo Parmeggiani, *L'Inquisizione a Firenze nell'età di Dante* (Bologna: il Mulino, 2018); Augustine Thompson, *Revival Preachers and Politics in Thirteenth–century Italy: The Great Devotion of 1233* (Oxford: Oxford University Press, 1992); Felice Tocco, *L'eresia nel Medio Evo* (Florence: Sansoni, 1884).

30   On Dante's self–construction as an *auctoritas* and a *scriba Dei*, see Albert R. Ascoli, *Dante and the Making of a Modern Author* (Cambridge: Cambridge University Press, 2008). See also Zygmunt G. Barański, '*Sole nuovo, luce nuova': saggi sul rinnovamento culturale in Dante* (Turin: Scriptorium, 1996).

31   See Robert Ian Moore, 'Heresy as a Disease', in Lourdaux and Verhelst, pp. 1–12.

with its unnervingly troublesome implications, preferring instead to seek out and recognize unorthodoxies and doctrinal complications in the poet's *œuvre* where none may necessarily exist. This last issue I leave for later; for the present, the 'stench' of heresy in the *Commedia*.[32]

It is noteworthy that both instances of apparent heterodoxy in the *Inferno* should involve the soul, and more specifically the relationship between the soul and the body. As is well known, when Dante composed the first canticle, the problem of the soul, in the wake of competing interpretations of Aristotle's *De anima* III. 5, continued to be a key area of dispute among intellectuals.[33] In particular, the immortality of the individual soul had been called into doubt by those who accepted Averroes's controversial thesis regarding the possible intellect — an interpretation that Dante, loyal to standard Christian belief, dismissed as incorrect:

> Ma come d'animal divegna fante,
> non vedi tu ancor: quest'è tal punto,
> che più savio di te fé già errante,
>   sì che per sua dottrina fé disgiunto
> da l'anima il possibile intelletto,
> perché da lui non vide organo assunto. (*Purg.* XXV. 61–66)

Already in the *Convivio*, Dante had energetically insisted that no reputable thinker had denied the eternity of the individual soul: 'Dico che intra tutte le bestialitadi quella è stoltissima, vilissima e dannosissima, chi crede dopo questa vita non essere altra vita; però che, se noi rivolgiamo tutte le scritture, sì de' filosofi come delli altri savi scrittori, tutti concordano in questo, che in noi sia parte alcuna perpetuale' (II. 8. 8).[34] To claim otherwise, as far as Dante was concerned, was to lapse into heresy. Indeed, although he conventionally acknowledged that there were many heresies ('Qui son li eresïarche | con lor seguaci, d'ogne setta', *Inf.* IX. 127–28), one group of heretics more than any other encapsulated for him doctrinal deviance: those, of course, who 'l'anima col corpo morta fanno' (*Inf.* X. 15). Given his personal stern inflexibility regarding the immortality of the soul and his lucid awareness of the intellectual and fideistic tangles in which the soul had become enmeshed, it makes Dante's decision to embroil the soul in problematic reworkings of significant issues of dogma especially perplexing.

---

32   On Dante and heresy, see at least Felice Tocco, *Quel che non c'è nella 'Divina Commedia' o Dante e l'eresia* (Bologna: Zanichelli, 1899), and *L'eresia*. The recent collection edited by Veglia, Paolini, and Parmeggiani, '*Il mondo errante*', includes some noteworthy studies, but, in general, suffers from a failure adequately to define the notion of heresy in the late Middle Ages. It is enough to think of the startling claim that Averroism might be deemed an 'eresia dotta': Marco Veglia and Lorenzo Paolini, 'Prefazione', pp. IX–XV (p. XII). In addition, the relationship between the subject-matter of several of the chapters and the question of heresy is at best tangential.

33   See Alain de Libera, 'Introduction', in Thomas Aquinas, *Contre Averroès*, ed. by Alain de Libera (Paris: Flammarion, 1994), pp. 9–73.

34   Dante then goes on to substantiate his point and begins by stating that 'E questo massimamente pare volere Aristotile in quello dell'Anima; questo pare volere massimamente ciascuno Stoico' (II. 8. 9). It is indicative, in light of contemporary controversies, that his first reference should be to Aristotle and the *De anima*, thereby affirming that he rejected the views of those who in any way drew on the Greek philosopher to refute personal immortality.

And yet, I believe, it was precisely on account of his customary orthodox intransigence regarding questions relating to the soul that Dante probably felt that, for reasons of didactic and dramatic efficacy, he could exceptionally take some carefully circumscribed doctrinal liberties. In the sixth circle of Hell, Virgil, an unlikely yet striking model of Catholic orthodoxy in contrast to Epicurus and 'tutti suoi seguaci' (*Inf.* x. 14), many of whom it will soon become apparent were Christians, explains that the 'sepulchres' (7) in which the heretics are imprisoned

> [t]utti saran serrati
> quando di Iosafàt qui torneranno
> coi corpi che là su hanno lasciati. (*Inf.* x. 10–12)

Dante thus strategically rebuts in advance the deplorable view that the 'soul dies with the body' (15); and, to emphasize the absurdity of the error, he returns to the Last Judgment later in the same canto (103–08). Lines 10–12 are actually the second time in the canticle that the poet had mentioned the resurrection of the body. Previously, on seeing Ciacco collapse back into the infernal mud, Virgil had declared:

> Più non si desta
> di qua dal suon de l'angelica tromba,
> quando verrà la nimica podesta:
>   ciascun rivederà la trista tomba,
> ripiglierà sua carne e sua figura,
> udirà quel ch'in etterno rimbomba. (*Inf.* vi. 94–99)

And Dante restated his belief in the reunion of body and soul in each of the next two canticles (*Purg.* i. 75; xxx. 13–15; *Par.* xiv. 43–66; xxv. 91–93 and 124–26; and see also *Par.* xxx. 129). The resurrection of the flesh is one of the great themes of the *Commedia*, which complements the poem's emphasis on the 'physical' appearance of the souls that culminates in the principle of the aerial body (see Chapter 9).[35] There is thus not the slightest doubt about Dante's deepfelt orthodoxy as regards the final restoration of the body; although it is equally likely that one reason why he kept underscoring his faith in the *miraculum* was his keen awareness that, if read superficially and unsympathetically, the doctrinal breach he had seemingly committed in *Inferno* xiii could potentially have dangerous consequences both for him and for his poem. The inadequacy of my earlier frame of reference for assessing *Inf.* xiii. 103–05 (and xxxiii. 124–32) has been exposed. Rather than ask why Dante might have introduced the heretical into the *Commedia*, the question I ought to have asked is the extent to which the suicides' uniquely divided condition after the end of time can actually be considered an authentic challenge to orthodoxy.

Let us reconsider what Dante reveals will happen to the suicides at the Second Coming. First and foremost, he conventionally states that, like everyone else, the suicides will be judged for a second time and will have their bodies restored to

---

35   See Anna Maria Chiavacci Leonardi, '"Le bianche stole": il tema della resurrezione nel *Paradiso*', in *Dante e la Bibbia*, ed. by Giovanni Barblan (Florence: Olschki, 1986), pp. 249–71. See also Caroline Walker Bynum, *The Resurrection of the Body in Western Christianity, 200–1336* (New York: Columbia University Press, 1995).

them ('Come l'altre verrem per nostre spoglie', 103). No doctrinal problems so far. At the same time, and problematically, what the suicides will not be permitted to do is 'reclothe' (*rivestire*, 104) — the metaphor is technical[36] — themselves with their resurrected bodies, 'ché non è giusto aver ciò ch'om si toglie' (105). Yet, it is anything but straightforward to regard the separation of body and soul as a challenge to revealed truth given that their being 'disgiunto' is 'just', the avowal, in fact, of another and higher mystery, the extraordinary and largely incomprehensible, as far as we humans are concerned, operation of God's justice:

> Però ne la giustizia sempiterna
> la vista che riceve il vostro mondo,
> com' occhio per lo mare, entro s'interna. (*Par.* XIX. 58–60)

The 'alcuno theologo' cited by the Ottimo's 'friend', like the good orthodox thinker that he was, had got it right when he referred to the appropriateness of the suicides' 'double punishment'. Equally, as a dutiful *scriba Dei*, Dante had accurately reported what he had seen and learned — the astonishing revelation, lest we forget, is Pier's not his — even when his account might strain belief: 'Ma nondimen, rimossa ogne menzogna, | tutta tua visïon fa manifesta' (*Par.* XVII. 127–28). Far from undermining his and the *Commedia*'s *auctoritas* and orthodoxy, the exceptionality and fitting coherence of the suicides' ultimate punishment are guarantors of truth. They highlight and affirm the measured uniqueness of God's actions, whose unflinching fairness is momentously evident throughout Hell. Almost paradoxically, the suicides' 'disjointed' state allows Dante to assert his orthodoxy by upholding the resurrection of the flesh and extolling the perfect execution of divine justice.

The peculiar condition of the inhabitants of Tolomea too can be orthodoxly resolved in light both of divine justice and of accepted belief. In *Paradiso* XX, Dante recounts the famous story of Trajan's miraculous revivification (which, among many sources, is also described in *Novellino* 69):

> Ché l'una de lo 'nferno, u' non si riede
> già mai a buon voler, tornò a l'ossa;
> e ciò di viva spene fu mercede.
> (*Par.* XX. 106–08, but see the whole account as far
> as line 117)

The idea that the dead could be restored fully to life was deeply engrained in Christian culture, with memorable instances documented in the Old and New Testaments — it is enough to think of Elias raising the widow of Sarephta's son (III Kings 17: 17–24) and Jesus reviving Lazarus (John 11: 1–46)[37] — as well as in various subsequent exemplary accounts, normally lives of saints, in which the later miracles closely follow the norms established in the Bible.[38] Academic theologians

36   See, for instance, I Corinthians 15: 53–54.
37   See also IV Kings 4: 32–37; Mark 5: 41–42; Luke 7: 14–15; Acts 9: 40–42.
38   See, for instance, Eugippius, *Vita sancti Seuerini*, ed. by Hermann Sauppe (Berlin: Weidmann, 1961), 6; Gregory the Great, *Dialogi libri IV*, ed. by Umberto Morrica (Turin: Bottega d'Erasmo, 1966), I. 2. 5–6; 10. 18; 12. 2; II. 32. 3; III. 17. 3–4; 33. 1; Sulpicius Severus, *Vita sancti Martini* 7 and 8,

too recognized the occurrence and divine legitimacy of such extraordinary events. Thomas Aquinas wrote:

> Ad quintum dicendum, quod idem est de Trajano qui forte post quingentos annos suscitatus est, et de aliis qui post unum diem suscitati sunt; de omnibus enim dicendum est, quod non finaliter damnati erant: praesciebat enim Deus eos sanctorum precibus a poenis liberandos, et vitae restituendos; et sic ex liberalitate bonitatis suae eis veniam contulit, quamvis aeternam poenam meruissent. Non enim est simile de ipso in quem solum peccatur, et de alio judice. Unde et Deus libere remittere potest sine ullius offensa; non alius judex qui punire habet culpam in alium, vel in rempublicam, vel in Deum commissam; unde et poenam licite remittere non potest.[39]

> [To address the fifth point, the same thing can be said of Trajan who was raised from the dead after almost five hundred years, and of the others who were raised after one day; it should in fact be said of all that they were not condemned for good: for God knew beforehand that they were to be freed from their punishments and brought back to life by the prayers of saints, so He granted them mercy by his generous benevolence, even though they deserved eternal punishment. There is in fact a difference between a judge who may only receive offences, and any other judge. God can accordingly forgive freely without commiting offence; but not any other judge who must punish a sin committed against another person, against the state, or against God; he cannot accordingly remit a sin rightfully.]

The miraculous raising of the dead, as is clear from Trajan's experience, entails the restoration of the departed soul to the body, so that the revived person is once again fully human and able to participate for a second time in the process of salvation:

> L'anima glorïosa onde si parla,
> tornata ne la carne, in che fu poco,
> credette in lui che potëa aiutarla;
>   e credendo s'accese in tanto foco
> di vero amor, ch'a la morte seconda
> fu degna di venire a questo gioco (*Par.* xx. 112–17).

and *Dialogi* ii. 4, both in *Lettere e dialoghi*, ed. by Davide Fiocco (Rome: Città nuova, 2007).

39   Thomas Aquinas, *Scriptum super libros Sententiarum* i. 43. 2. 2. 5; and compare 'de facto Traiani in hoc modo potest probabiliter aestimari: quod precibus beati Gregorii ad vitam fuerit revocatus, et ita gratiam consecutus sit, per quam remissionem peccatorum habuit, et per consequens immunitatem a poena; sicut etiam apparet in omnibus illis qui fuerunt miraculose a mortuis suscitati, quorum plures constat idololatras et damnatos fuisse. De omnibus enim similiter dici oportet quod non erant in inferno finaliter deputati, sed secundum praesentem iustitiam propriorum meritorum. Secundum autem superiores causas, quibus praevidebantur ad vitam revocandi, erat aliter de eis disponendum' [concerning the incident of Trajan it can probably be supposed in this way: that he was recalled to life by the prayers of blessed Gregory, and in this manner obtained grace, thanks to which he received the remission of his sins, and consequently exemption from punishment; and furthermore the same is evident in all those who were miraculously raised from the dead, many of whom were indisputably idolaters and damned. For it is necessary to declare likewise about all such persons that they were not finally consigned to Hell, but as was due to their own merits according to justice. Indeed according to higher causes, by which it was foreseen that they would be recalled to life, they were to be disposed of differently] (*ST* Suppl. iii. 71. 5).

However, not all the dead who, according to medieval lore, returned among the living were so fortunate.[40] Most were simply bodies in the thrall of an evil spirit, namely possessed corpses, or, more regularly, corpses that, despite being separated from their souls, had marvellously returned to life.[41] The revenants were not infrequently evildoers in life. The dwellers of Dante's Tolomea establish suggestive links with the first two groups of resuscitated dead. They most obviously recall the demonically possessed: 'il corpo suo l'è tolto | da un demonio, che poscia il governa' (*Inf.* XXXIII. 130–31), even if the takeover occurs at quite different points in their respective life-death cycles.[42] Furthermore, in sharp contrast to the resurrected, they are sentient soulless bodies; yet, like the resurrected, they marvellously die twice: once when 'tosto che l'anima trade | [...] il corpo suo l'è tolto' (129–30), and then, for a second time, when ''l tempo suo tutto sia vòlto' (132). Both the traitors and the resurrected are *exempla* of God's total power over life and death:

> Ille suscitavit hominem, qui fecit hominem; ipse enim est Unicus Patris, per quem, sicut nostis, facta sunt omnia. Si ergo per illum facta sunt omnia, quid mirum est si resurrexit unus per illum, cum tot quotidie nascantur per illum? Plus est homines creare quam resuscitare. Dignatus est tamen et creare et resuscitare; creare omnes, resuscitare quosdam.[43]

> [He raised from the dead a man, who made man; for He is the Only-begotten Son of the Father, through Whom, as you know, everything was made. Thus, if through Him everything was made, how is it a cause of wonder if one is raised up through Him, when each day so many are born through Him? It is a greater thing to create humans than to raise them from the dead. Notwithstanding he

---

40   The belief in the 'living dead' was widespread in the Middle Ages. In addition, such beings were deemed to be anything but uncommon; see Nancy Caciola, 'Wraiths, Revenants, and Ritual in Medieval Culture', *Past and Present: A Journal of Historical Studies*, 152 (1996), 3–45, 'Spirits Seeking Bodies: Death, Possession, and Communal Memory in the Middle Ages', in *The Place of the Dead: Death and Remembrance in Medieval and Early Modern Europe*, ed. by Bruce Gordon and Peter Marshall (Cambridge: Cambridge University Press, 2000), pp. 66–86, and *Discerning Spirits: Divine and Demonic Possession in the Middle Ages* (Ithaca, NY: Cornell University Press, 2003). See also Jane Gilbert, *Living Death in Medieval French and English Literature* (Cambridge: Cambridge University Press, 2011).

41   'Indeed, many tales of the undead explicitly reject the demonic interpretation. The demonic-possession school of thought about revenants, as best represented by Thomas of Cantimpré and the hagiographer of Ida of Louvain, was distinctly a minority viewpoint. Texts such as chronicles and histories, which lack the same didactic agenda as exempla collections or hagiographies, universally reject or ignore the possibility of demonic animation in regard to revenants. For these more historical authors, the transgression involved in a corpse coming back to life is one between life and death, rather than between flesh and unclean spirit. For example, several entries in Walter Map's twelfth-century English chronicle *De nugis curialium* tell of the predations of living, not possessed, corpses. The chronicler's tone gives these tales in particular an air of immediacy: for Walter and his contemporaries, these were strange, but real events' (Caciola, 'Wraiths, Revenants, and Ritual in Medieval Culture', p. 19).

42   The traitors also recall another widespread tradition: that of the living person taken over by a demon, of which there are many examples especially in the New Testament; see, for instance, Matthew 8: 28–34, 17: 18; Mark 1: 23–28, 5: 1–17; Luke 4: 35–36. As regards these unfortunates, there is no suggestion that their souls were cast down to Hell. In fact, once the evil spirit has been exorcized, their lives return to normal and salvation once more becomes an option.

43   Augustine, *In Evangelium Ioannis tractatus centum viginti quatuor* XLIX. 1, in PL XXXV, col. 1746. See also 1 Samuel 2: 6; Psalms 139: 12–16.

deigned both to create and to raise from the dead; to create all, to raise some from the dead.]

At the same time, frate Alberigo and his companions also grotesquely parody the divine life-restoring miracle — yet another dramatic reversal of the holy that is a constant feature of Dante's representation of Hell.[44] In particular, although they are notionally alive, salvation is no longer an option for those who betrayed their guests. Their bodies may function normally, but, spiritually, sin has killed them. As Dante makes memorably clear, they have lost their souls and 'inside them is death'. In any case, the poet had an authoritative precedent for his invention. The idea that one might be dead while still living, metaphorically at least, was well established in Christian thought: 'et intelligamus detestabiliores mortes, omnis qui peccat moritur. Sed mortem carnis omnis homo timet, mortem animae pauci. [...] Delectavit quod malum est, consensisti, peccasti; consensio illa occidit te: sed intus est mors' [and if we were to understand the more detestable [spiritual] deaths, [we would appreciate that] all who sin die. Yet, every person fears the death of the flesh, few the death of the soul. [...] He delighted in what is evil, you have assented, you have sinned; that assent has killed you: but death is inside].[45]

Although, ultimately, the precise condition of Dante's traitors is unprecedented, it is in fact a careful amalgam of well-established Scriptural, theological, exemplary, and popular traditions, which the poet subtly tweaked — a textbook example of his syncretism.[46] The poet actualized the doctrinally metaphorical on the basis of documented instances of demonic possession and of the dead returning to life as a result of a variety of exceptional interventions whether divine or satanic.[47] To put it somewhat differently, by textually and culturally contextualizing the inhabitants of Tolomea, the unorthodoxy of Dante's view is (largely) dispelled.[48] In a text which

44 Dante's Hell is full of perverted forms of the divine, disturbing instances of sin's deviant effects; see in particular Anthony K. Cassell, *Dante's Fearful Art of Justice* (Toronto, Buffalo, and London: University of Toronto Press, 1984).

45 Augustine, *In Evang. Ioannis* XLIX. 2–3; see also paragraph 15 in the same Tractate. See too Wisdom 1: 12–13, 2: 24; Romans 5: 12, 7: 13; and see *Conv.* IV. 7. 10–14. For Pietro Alighieri's recourse to the idea of the 'two deaths' to explain the divided condition of frate Alberigo, see Luca Fiorentini, 'Per il lessico esegetico di Pietro Alighieri e Benvenuto da Imola (in rapporto all'*Epistola a Cangrande* e ad altre fonti)', *Bollettino di italianistica*, 7:2 (2010), 120–55 (pp. 141–48).

46 In addition, Dante is careful to leave a degree of uncertainty regarding the state in which the traitors find themselves; see *Inf.* XXXIII. 121–23 & 133–35. He also presents the arrival of the soul in Hell before death as not affecting all the inhabitants of Tolomea (124–26).

47 Virgil's strange tale of his first journey to the pit of Hell 'per trarne un spirto del cerchio di Giuda' (*Inf.* IX. 27), 'congiurato da quella Eritón cruda | che richiamava l'ombre a' corpi sui' (23–24) also belongs to the tradition of the living dead. Boccaccio is unusual in vehemently denying the possibility that the 'corpi [...] d'alcuni morti' can be brought back to life; see *Esposizioni*, I, 475–76.

48 Dante's decision to synthesize the metaphor of sin as death with the tradition of the dead being returned to life was probably conditioned by their earlier integration in the exegesis of the raising of Lazarus, as is apparent from the passages that I have quoted from Augustine's commentary to John 11. Interestingly, though unsurprisingly, in discussing Lazarus, the Bishop of Hippo also addressed the resurrection of the flesh ('Audisti enim quia Dominus Iesus mortuum suscitavit: sufficit tibi ut scias quia si vellet, omnes mortuos suscitaret. Et hoc quidem sibi ad finem saeculi reservavit' [For you have heard that the Lord Jesus brought back to life a dead person: it is enough for you to know that if He wanted, He could have brought all the dead back to life. And in truth he has reserved this

persistently asserts and depicts the fundamental possibility of redemption, those who betrayed their guests, like the suicides, are the exception that proves the rule, while highlighting, once again, the enigma of divine judgment and the authenticity of the *Commedia*'s *lictera*.[49] In any case, as the author of the *Supplementum* to the third book of Aquinas's *Summa theologica* averred when discussing Trajan's return to life: 'alia sunt quae lege communi accidunt, et alia quae singulariter ex privilegio aliquibus conceduntur: sicut *alii sunt humanarum limites rerum, alia divinarum signa virtutum*, ut Augustinus dicit, in libro *de Cura pro mortuis agenda* [16]' [one thing is what happens according to common law, and another what is permitted in particular instances by privilege: indeed one thing are the limits of human affairs, another the signs of divine power, as Augustine says, in his book *De cura pro mortuis agenda*] (*ST* Suppl. III. 71. 5). Part of Dante's responsibility in the *Commedia* was to offer a sense of God's mystery and power — a mystery and power which at times appear to transcend, although without disturbing them, the very principles of faith. Indeed, it was precisely because he was a *scriba Dei* that his poem, like Scripture, is able to provide a glimpse into divine mysteries: 'Monumentum Christi est divina Scriptura, in qua divinitatis et humanitatis ejus mysteria densissima veluti quadam muniuntur petra' [The sepulchre of Christ is divine Scripture, in which the most profound mysteries of His divinity and humanity are defended as if by a sort of rock].[50] Furthermore, as was common knowledge in the Middle Ages, it was a fundamental attribute of the Bible to be characterized by what might appear to uninitiated eyes as conflicting positions: 'In Scripturis enim divinis quaedam inveniuntur tam diversa, ut sibi invicem videantur adversa' [For in divine Scripture certain things are found

---

for the end of time], xlix. 1, but see the whole paragraph). It is significant in helping us appreciate Dante's treatment of the suicides and the traitors against guests that the two groups are united as a result of the fact that both have ties to the same eschatological traditions — traditions concerned with the relationship between life and death and between body and soul. As they say in Italy, Dante's eccentrically orthodox presentation of their punishments *fa sistema*, and that system is closely involved with God's uniqueness.

49   The best discussion that I know of the strange condition of the traitors in Tolomea is Simon Gilson, 'Medieval Magical Lore and Dante's *Commedia*: Divination and Demonic Agency', *Dante Studies*, 119 (2001), 27–66 (pp. 45–48). Although our analyses share a number of points of contact, especially as regards the poet's willingness 'in certain circumstances [...] to invoke miraculous forms of divine intervention' (p. 47), we differ substantially as regards the ideological and artistic implications of the poet's presentation. For Simon, the traitors' punishment constitutes 'one of Dante's most radically unorthodox and highly personal fabrications' (p. 45), a mark that 'Dante is not always a theologically orthodox poet' (p. 48), while my emphasis, in keeping with the overarching argument in the present chapter, is to attempt to explain their *contrapasso* in as orthodox terms as possible. See also Arturo Graf, 'Demonologia di Dante', in *Miti, legende e superstizioni del Medioevo*, 2 vols (Turin: Loescher, 1892–93), II, 77–139 (pp. 98–100). While the correlation between the suicides' sin and their final punishment is self-evident, I am not at all clear why Dante should have inflicted the strange retribution on the traitors against guests that he did. The best explanation I have read is centred on Psalm 54; however, as Gilson admits, 'the biblical passage is in itself [not] a wholly adequate precedent for the demonic action described by Dante' (p. 47).

50   John Scottus Eriugena, *Homilia in Prologum Sancti Evangelii secundum Joannem*, in PL cxxii, col. 284. See also Henri de Lubac, *Medieval Exegesis: The Four Senses of Scripture*, 3 vols (Grand Rapids, MI: Eerdmans, 1998–2009), I, 30, 32, 34, 63, 101; Jean Leclercq, *The Love of Learning and the Desire for God* (London: SPCK, 1978), pp. 251–52.

that are so different, that they appear to be mutually contradictory].[51] Naturally, no contradiction exists: 'In his autem omnibus quae inspicienda ponere institui, quaecumque inter se videbuntur esse contraria, postea propositis quaestionibus exponenda atque solvenda sunt' [Indeed in all [the passages] which I undertook to place for consideration, any of the things that will seem to be mutually contradictory, must be explained and resolved subsequently when questions have been proposed].[52] Rather it was the responsibility of the exegete, illuminated by Christ, humbly to seek out and elucidate their harmony.[53] Dante's 'sacred poem', in this too, dutifully and accurately 'imitates' its divine model, so that, tellingly, not to say paradoxically, the closer it might seem to heterodoxy the nearer in fact it is to orthodoxy. The onus falls on us, its readers, to sort out the order and coherence of the *Commedia*'s 'divine' message: 'Sententia divina numquam absurda, numquam falsa esse potest, sed cum in sensu [...] multa inveniantur contraria, sententia nullam admittit repugnantiam, semper congrua est, semper vera' [Divine meaning can never be absurd, can never be false, yet although in the [literal] sense many things are found to be contrary, the [deeper] meaning allows no contradiciton, is always harmonious, always true].[54]

4. *Eresïarche* and *fines*

'È qui da credere che l'autore non ha qui fatte narrar queste parole a questo spirito [Pier delle Vigne], sì come ignorante degli articoli della nostra fede, per ciò che tutti esplicitamente gli seppe, sì come nel *Paradiso* manifestissimamente appare' (Boccaccio, *Esposizioni*, I, 619). Despite the somewhat anxious hyperbole of the two adverbs, Boccaccio is correct: Dante was an orthodox Catholic and the *Commedia*, like the *Vita nova* before it, is a work of Catholic orthodoxy. The evidence is irresistible. Thus, the overall ideological tenor of the poem, expressed most explicitly and fervently, if far from exclusively, as Boccaccio recognized, in the final canticle, is one of profound and sincere religious conformity. It is enough to recall the pilgrim's answers on faith, hope, and charity in the heaven of the Fixed Stars;[55] or the regular affirmations regarding the primacy of Scripture and the authority of the great canonical figures of the Church; or the equally frequent avowals of the

---

51   Philip of Harvengt, *Epistola* I. I, in PL CCIII, col. I.

52   Augustine, *De Scriptura sacra Speculum*, Preface, in PL XXXIV, col. 889. As the formula declared, matters that appeared contradictory were in fact *diversa sed non adversa*; see Henri de Lubac, 'À propos de la formule *Diversi, sed non adversi*', in *Mélanges Jules Lebreton*, 2 vols, II, 27–40, special issue of *Recherches de science religieuse*, 39:2–4 (1951) and 40:1–2 (1952); Hubert Silvestre, 'Diversi, sed non adversi', *Revue de théologie ancienne et médiévale*, 31 (1964), 124–32.

53   See de Lubac, *Medieval Exegesis*, I, 60, 79–89, 225–67. See also Catherine Brown, *Contrary Things: Exegesis, Dialectic and the Poetics of Didacticism* (Stanford: Stanford University Press, 1998), especially pp. 15–35.

54   Hugh of St Victor, *Didascalicon*, ed. by Charles Henry Buttimer (Washington: Catholic University Press, 1939), VI. II.

55   'The theological examination the pilgrim takes in *Paradiso* 24–26 [...] is [...] a well-timed occasion for the poet to pass the test of orthodoxy, colors flying': Peter S. Hawkins, 'Poema Sacro', in *Literature, Religion, and the Sacred*, ed. by Dino S. Cervigni, special issue of *Annali d'Italianistica*, 25 (2007), 177–201 (pp. 177–78).

subordination of the human to the divine. This does not mean, as we have just seen and as the *Commedia*'s earliest readers immediately recognized, that everything in it is tranquilly uncomplicated. Far from it. Nonetheless, and as we have also just noted, whatever might appear to go against established and approved doctrine ought not be assessed in itself, namely in isolation, but considered and, if possible, explained and legitimated in terms both of contemporary Christian culture and of the poem's dominant spiritual and intellectual creed. In particular, the relative status of any seemingly problematic element needs to be carefully judged so that it is not granted overblown significance. To do otherwise — and we ought to remember this when evaluating some of Dante's more overtly 'scientific' works[56] — is, I suspect, to misrepresent the poet's views.

Of course, as I have discussed, there were excellent artistic and didactic reasons why Dante may have wanted at times to challenge his readers' doctrinal expectations; and it is certain that he would have been aware of the licence which creative writers were accorded. Yet, despite his well-known inventiveness and independence, when it came to matters of belief, and I extend this claim to all his works, Dante was only rarely doctrinally quirky; and, when he was, contrary to *Inferno* XIII and XXXIII, he normally avoided touching on matters of faith. Thus, his treatment of Limbo, while undoubtedly personal, was in no way heterodox, never mind heretical. In the fourteenth century, the nature of Limbo, and with it the ultimate fate of the unbaptized, was not fixed as a tenet of faith. Like much else in medieval Christianity, it was an area of intellectual investigation, debate, and disagreement.[57] Embracing and propagating a minority view that did not challenge the dogmas of faith was not the same as promulgating doctrinal unorthodoxies — it was simply that: a minority, and not an untenable, opinion.[58] Indeed, it was a standard position that a single passage of Scripture would generate different interpretations.[59] Just as the apparently eccentric in Dante should always be properly contextualized, so substantially more research needs to be done on medieval attitudes and solutions to competing and conflicting viewpoints, error, intellectual irregularity and, naturally, unorthodoxy before blanket judgments are made regarding what was and was not ideologically acceptable in the Middle Ages, and in particular during Dante's lifetime.[60] Alas, it cannot be said that Dante studies have been especially sensitive to such issues. The poet, on the other hand, was acutely aware of what boundaries of belief could or could not be crossed, and how best to insulate his occasional truly challenging invention from accusations that it was *contra fidem*.

56   See Subsection 5, 'Invidïosi veri', below.
57   de Lubac has described this situation as 'what would, in our day and age, be called theological pluralism within the unifying matrix of faith. At that time, this idea derived its foundations from the multiplicity of senses offered by a Scriptural text that could never be directly comprehended in all its depths': *Medieval Exegesis*, I, 31. See also de Lubac, *Medieval Exegesis*, I, 31–66.
58   Ibid., I, 80–82.
59   Richard of St Victor's assertion is typical: 'Et saepe fit ut una eademque Scriptura, dum multipliciter exponitur, multa nobis in unum loquatur' [And it often happens that the one and same Scripture, when it is explained in various ways, speaks to us many meanings in one] (*Ben. maj.* IV. 14 [col. 151]). See also Brown, pp. 24–35.
60   I shall return to these matters, albeit fleetingly, in the remainder of this chapter.

Some intellectual attitudes, however, as far as Dante was concerned, were never acceptable: those which willfully and persistently called into question any aspect of the faith. Heresy and heretics, as *Inferno* IX–XI makes abundantly clear, were always wrong, and the inevitable end of those who upheld such abhorrent views was eternal damnation:

> Qui son li eresïarche
> con lor seguaci, d'ogne setta, e molto
>   più che non credi son le tombe carche.
> Simile qui con simile è sepolto,
> e i monimenti son più e men caldi. (*Inf.* IX. 128–32)

Dante was unswerving in his condemnation of heresy, whose defeat is symbolically described in the Earthly Paradise through the traditional image of the 'fox', which, its errors confounded by the *vox Dei*, is put to 'flight' (*Purg.* XXXII. 118–23).[61] Equally, St Dominic is praised for having violently overwhelmed 'li sterpi eretici' (*Par.* XII. 100). Dante resolutely and consistently rejected current heretical opinion, whether as regards the immortality of the soul, or the eternity of the world, or the independence of free will. What is striking about the poet's reaction to such errors of doctrine is that he refrained from attacking the individuals who held them in order to focus attention on the ideas themselves. It was the heresies rather than the heretics that needed combatting, since it was the former that inflicted damage on the faith: 'Titubabit fides, si *Divinarum Scripturarum* vacillat auctoritas' [Faith will totter, if the authority of the Divine Scriptures wavers] (*Mon.* III. 4. 9).[62] In addition, Dante probably wished to distinguish himself from those, especially within the Church, who used accusations of heresy as an indiscriminate weapon against their enemies. At the same time, there is no doubt that the poet took an unflinchingly hard line against heresy — one which aligned him squarely with doctrinaire Church policy. The astonishing appearance in Ante-Purgatory of Manfred, against whom Pope Clement IV instigated a trial for heresy shortly before the king's death at Benevento, in no way weakens Dante's intransigence. It was established doctrine that, as long as they repented their sins, however 'orribil' (*Purg.* III. 121), heretics and excommunicates could hope for salvation. Indeed, by placing Manfred among the excommunicate penitent, Dante openly recognized the validity, in this instance at least, of the papal condemnation against him.[63]

61   The image is Scriptural: 'capite nobis vulpes vulpes parvulas quae demoliuntur vineas' [Catch us foxes, the little foxes that destroy the vines] (Song of Songs 2: 15). See also Jean Leclercq, 'L'Hérésie d'après les écrits de S. Bernard de Clairvaux', in Lourdaux and Verhelst, pp. 12–26 (p. 19).

62   The phrase is a quotation from Augustine's *De doc. chr.* (I. 37. 41), the pre-eminent guide in the Middle Ages to the correct reading of the Bible; see *Reading and Wisdom: The 'De doctrina christiana' of Augustine in the Middle Ages*, ed. by Edward D. English (Notre Dame, IN, and London: University of Notre Dame Press, 1995).

63   Dante's treatment of Manfred is, of course, much more nuanced than my brief aside intimates; and part of the poet's purpose is to condemn Clement IV's behaviour towards the king. However, it is precisely because his judgment of the Pope is so withering that Dante's acknowledgment of the legality of the censure against Manfred is so striking. On excommunication, see Elisabeth Vodola, *Excommunication in the Middle Ages* (Berkeley, Los Angeles, and London: University of California Press, 1986).

In the medieval imaginary, heretics were obstinate, intellectually arrogant, deceitful, and, of course, invariably wrong. They lacked the capacity — refined by faith and humility — to discern the truth (*Par.* XIII. 123):

> sì fé Sabellio e Arrio e quelli stolti
> che furon come spade a le Scritture
> in render torti li diritti volti. (*Par.* XIII. 127–29)

Deliberately to misinterpret Scripture, Dante concurred with orthodox Catholic opinion, was a heinous sin and a hallmark of the heretic. It had led Sabellius and Arius, despite evidence to the contrary, doggedly to promote anti-trinitarian positions. The rigour, vehemence, orthodoxy, and consistency of the poet's views against heresy meant that he had no need to repeat himself, so that actual references to heretics and heresies in the *Commedia* are few (I believe that I have cited the most significant instances).[64] No one can doubt where he stands on heresy: foursquare with every canonical Catholic *auctoritas*, from Augustine to Aquinas. At the same time, Dante refined and personalized his attitude in one particular regard. He presented the calculated exploitation of Scripture as one of the great ills of his day, thereby implying that those who undertook such malpractice — often on behalf of ecclesiastical authorities — even if not condemned as such, were in reality akin to heretics. His denunciation of the *impii atque mendaces* [impious and liars] (*Mon.* III. 1. 3), both terms were commonly applied to heretics,[65] is especially withering in the final book of the *Monarchia*. Although, as I discussed earlier, in the treatise, Dante was specifically challenging the ways in which the hierocrats misinterpreted the Bible in order to assert the Pope's supremacy over the Emperor, the polemic is also the poet's major statement, in line with Augustine's *De doctrina christiana*, on the supreme cognitive authority of Scripture and on the attitude, responsibilities, and methods of the orthodox exegete. In chapters 4–9, Dante highlights how the study of the Bible must avoid 'error' when interpreting the 'mystical sense': 'aut querendo ipsum ubi non est, aut accipiendo aliter quam accipi debere' [either searching for it where it is not, or interpreting it differently from how it should be interpreted] (4. 6).[66] And in her great diatribe on contemporary intellectual life in *Paradiso* XXIX, Beatrice too presents the 'twisting' of Scripture as the rational activity which most offends Heaven (88–95).

According to Dante, human reason, a marvellous divine gift, must be directed towards apprehending truth, whose ultimate expression is of course in God: 'omnis sapientia a Deo Domino est et cum illo fuit semper et est ante aevum' [All wisdom is from the Lord God and has always been with Him and is before time].[67] The aims of intellectual inquiry are ethical, cognitive, and ultimately salvific. Reason should not be used to undermine truth by propagating lies whether for personal

---

64   I have decided not to discuss the case of fra Dolcino, whom Dante presents as a schismatic, since this would require an elucidation of medieval debates on the inter-relationship and differences between heresy and schism, which would distract from my present purpose.

65   See, for example, Augustine, *Contra mendacium liber unus* VI. 13–IX. 18, in PL XL, cols 187–90.

66   For a brilliant overarching reading of *Monarchia* III, see Nasti, 'Dante and Ecclesiology'.

67   Ecclesiasticus 1: 1. The phrase was a standard in medieval discussions of different types of intellectual work; see de Lubac, *Medieval Exegesis*, I , 43. See also *Conv.* III. 12. 13.

or instututional gain; nor should the exercise of reason be treated as an end in itself. Beatrice's attacks against those who use their intellectual faculties simply as a means of self-aggrandizement without any regard for the 'purity' of 'la verità' (73–74) dominate her celestial *vituperatio* in canto XXIX. She lambasts those who 'non credendo dicer vero' (83) on account of their obsession with wishing to appear original (86–87). To this end, they are happy to exploit 'la divina Scrittura' (90) as a means of showing off: 'Per apparer ciascun s'ingegna e face | sue invenzioni' (94–95). However, like denounced heretics such as Sabellius and Arius, they 'lie' (100). Beatrice's charges are highly conventional, echoing the concerns, language, and tropes of conservative medieval Catholic thinkers troubled by what they deemed new and questionable intellectual practices. Thus, at least since Abelard's time, the pursuit of *novitas* was attacked and discouraged.[68] Equally worthy of censure were those who used Scripture as a means to achieve professional advancement.[69] What lay behind such criticisms was a deep anxiety about the negative effects of the growing interest in dialectics which had resulted in the dangerous proliferation of different teachings. Beatrice shares in this apprehension ('Voi non andate giù per un sentiero | filosofando', *Par.* XXIX. 85–86; and compare 94–100, 104–05),[70] an unease which she efficiently captures at the beginning of her invective in the verb *equivocare* ('la verità che là giù si confonde, | equivocando in sì fatta lettura', 74–75) which tersely highlights the power of dialectic pointlessly and uncritically to accommodate conflicting and erroneous opinion,[71] what Beatrice terms 'waking dreams' (82), 'invenzioni' (95), 'favole' (104), and 'ciance' (110).[72] Most worryingly, the explosion in competing views could only sow confusion among the ordinary faithful: 'sì che le pecorelle, che non sanno, | tornan dal pasco pasciute di vento' (106–07).[73]

---

68   See Brown, p. 33; de Lubac, *Medieval Exegesis*, I, 34, 62, 64, 69, 72; Leclercq, *The Love of Learning*, pp. 245–49, 255.

69   See de Lubac, *Medieval Exegesis*, I, 49–50, 62; Leclercq, *The Love of Learning*, pp. 255–56.

70   *Filosofare* here is technical and pointedly alludes to the behaviour of medieval intellectuals. Originally I had incorrectly restricted the verb to 'scholastics in arts faculties' (p. 290, n. 78). Anna Pegoretti correctly comments: 'un simile restringimento del focus alle sole Arti appare francamente ingiustificato […]. Tanto più che si sta parlando, in *Paradiso* XXIX, di una materia squisitamente teologica come l'angelologia': 'Filosofanti', *Le tre corone*, 2 (2015), 11–70 (p. 36). As further evidence in support of my friend's claim, I would suggest that the line 'l'amor de l'apparenza e 'l suo pensiero!' (87) alludes to the problem of the tension and disjuncture between appearance and reality which, since at the least the thirteenth century, had fascinated both theologians and philosophers who probed questions of vision; visual error; the limitations of the senses; the nature and limits of knowledge; the intimate connection between sight, truth, and knowledge; and the relationship between viewer and thing viewed; see at least Dallas G. Denery, *Seeing and Being Seen in the Later Medieval World: Optics, Theology and Religious Life* (Cambridge: Cambridge University Press, 2005); Katherine Tachau, *Vision and Certitude in the Age of Ockham* (Leiden: Brill, 1988).

71   On religious worries about dialectic, see Brown, pp. 36–64; de Lubac, *Medieval Exegesis*, I, 55–74; Leclercq, *The Love of Learning*, pp. 245–51, 256–58.

72   Compare 'stultas autem quaestiones et genealogias et contentiones et pugnas legis devita sunt enim inutiles et vanae' [but avoid foolish questions and genealogies and contentions and conflicts about the law for they are pointless and vain] (Titus 3: 9). The passage from Paul was a commonplace and the phrase *vanae quaestiones* had a wide circulation. 'Ciance' is an extremely apt rendering of this in the vernacular.

73   See de Lubac, *Medieval Exegesis*, I, 57 & 313. It is interesting to note that Dante's presentation

Beatrice contrasts the *modus* of the arrogant dialectician with that of the good Christian who 'humbly' pursues his intellectual activities: 'e quanto piace | chi umilmente con essa [la divina Scrittura] s'accosta' (92–93; and compare 109–14). At the same time, it is important to recognize that, however much she might be focusing on the disuse into which the Bible has fallen in the present — 'e 'l Vangelio si tace' (96) — , her attack, as the references to 'philosophizing', to the 'putting aside of Scripture' (89–90), to 'inventions' (95), and to fantastical and comic preaching (103–05 and 115–17) make evident, takes in every type of intellectual pursuit that is error-strewn and inappropriate, and hence not a means, as it should be, to arriving at 'pure truth'. Dante is not against the pursuit of knowledge, the asking of questions. Far from it. Indeed, one way of thinking about the pilgrim's experience in the afterlife is as a succession of questions that only comes to an end once his intellectual 'desires' find ultimate satisfaction in the union with God (see Chapter 5). What Dante rejects out of hand, and this is true of the *Convivio* as much as of the *Commedia*, is knowledge whose ends are exclusively earthbound, deliberately selfish, and, of course, quite simply wrong — knowledge, to be precise, that fails to acknowledge that 'all wisdom is from the Lord God' (Ecclesiasticus 1. 1): 'l'ardore | ch'i' ebbi a divenir del mondo esperto | e de li vizi umani e del valore' (*Inf.* XXVI. 97–99; and compare 112–20). *Praesumptio, cupiditas sciendi, superbia*: these are the sins of the intellect that the poet found unacceptable, as did the mainstream Christian tradition as a whole.[74] It is thus extremely unlikely that Dante would have been persuaded by the ideas and methods of those masters of arts, especially at the University of Paris, who may have championed the independence of reason and philosophical inquiry and the relative self-sufficiency and fulfilment of philosophical principles and conclusions.[75] There are certainly no assertions in his

---

of the behaviour of contemporary intellectuals recalls the conduct of heretics: 'Non enim disputare amant haeretici, sed quoquo modo superare impudentissima pervicacia, ut congregent, sicut hic dixit, quae non pepererunt. Christianos enim, quos maxime Christi nomine seducunt, iam per ipsius Christi Evangelium natos inveniunt, et faciunt illos divitias suas: non sane cum iudicio, sed cum temeritate inconsiderata. Non enim intellegunt ibi esse veram et salubrem, et quodam modo germanam atque radicalem christianam societatem, unde istos separaverunt, quos ad suas divitias congregarunt' [For heretics do not like to debate, but to win in any way with the most impudent obstinacy, in order to gather, as he said, those goods that they had not gained. For they find Christians, whom they seduce especially with Christ's name, who have already been born thanks to the Gospel of that Christ himself, and they make them into their own riches: not with healthy judgment, but with inconsiderate temerity. For they do not understand that there is the true and healthy, and in a certain way the true and rooted Christian community, from which they have separated those that they have gathered into their riches] (Augustine, *Contra Faustum Manichaeum libri triginta tres* XIII. 12, in PL XLII, col. 289). Equally, for Bernard of Clairvaux, heretics express eccentric opinions because of their desire for personal success: 'Omnibus una intentio haereticis semper fuit, captare gloriam de singularitate scientiae' [All heretics have always had one single purpose, to acquire glory through the originality of doctrine] (*Sermones super Cantica* LXV. 2). On the heretic as a cypher for intellectual erring in general, see below pp. 113 and 556–62.

74   See, for instance, Edward Peters, '*Libertas inquirendi* and the *vitium curiositatis* in Medieval Thought', in *La Notion de liberté au moyen âge: Islam, Byzance, Occident*, ed. by George Makdisi and others (Paris: Les Belles Lettres, 1985), pp. 91–98.

75   See Gyula Klima, '*Ancilla Theologiae* vs. *Domina philosophorum*: St. Thomas Aquinas, Latin Averroism and the Autonomy of Philosophy', in *What is Philosophy in the Middle Ages? Proceedings of*

œuvre, not even in the *Convivio* (or in the *Monarchia*), that definitively point in this direction. This does not mean, of course, that the poet was not sensitive to what, within limits, human reason might achieve on its own without the aid of divine illumination, as his treatment of the pagan world makes more than apparent. Nor did he deny that reason could be a source of 'happiness' in this life. Nonetheless, such appreciation, I should like to stress, is not the same as asserting the autonomy of reason and its acquisitions.[76]

In truth, Dante's presentation of the 'two ends' of humanity in the *Convivio* and in the *Monarchia* is not especially radical, though it does have some interesting original inflections. Nor does the poet claim that total satisfaction is attainable in this life. Now that the fires of the overheated polemic on the matter stoked by Nardi and his neo-Thomist opponents have burnt out, it is possible to recognize that the notion that human beings are uniquely destined to a *duplex finis* was solidly part of thirteenth- and fourteenth-century theological thought. As a result, agreement existed that a circumscribed form of earthly intellectual happiness was possible; and Dante could have found support for these positions not only in Albertus Magnus, but also, as has become increasingly apparent in recent years, *pace* Nardi, in Thomas Aquinas.[77] In any case, the parameters within which the poet treated the *duo fines*

the Tenth International Congress of Medieval Philosophy, ed. by Jan A. Aertsen and Andreas Speer (Erfurt: Akademie Gemeinnütziger Wissenschaft zu Erfurt, 1997), pp. 393–402.

76   A number of scholars has unhelpfully confused the two perspectives when examining Dante's intellectual positions.

77   See Dante, *Monarchia*, trans. and ed. by Richard Kay (Toronto: Pontifical Institute of Medieval Studies, 1998), pp. 308–14; Patrick M. Gardner, 'Thomas and Dante on the *duo ultima hominis*', *The Thomist*, 75 (2011), 415–59 (esp. pp. 418–25); and especially Mario Trovato, 'Dante and the Tradition of the "Two Beatitudes"', in *Lectura Dantis Newberryana*, ed. by Paolo Cherchi and Antonio Mastrobuono (Evanston, IL: Northwestern University Press, 1988), pp. 19–36. These recent contributions have their point of origin in Maccarrone's and Vinay's somewhat underappreciated studies. For a recent treatment of the question that continues to present it as problematic, see Gianfranco Fioravanti, 'A Natural Desire Can Be Fulfilled in a Purely Natural Manner: The Heresy of Dante', in Ardizzone, pp. 35–46. By far the fullest assessments of *Conv.* III. 15 are: Paolo Falzone, *Desiderio della scienza e desiderio di Dio nel 'Convivio'* (Naples: Società editrice il Mulino, 2010), pp. 101–256; and Pasquale Porro, 'Tra il *Convivio* e la *Commedia*: Dante al "forte dubitare" intorno al desiderio naturale di conoscere sustanze separate', in *1308: ein Topographie historischer Gleichzeitigkeit*, ed. by Andreas Speer and David Wirmer (Berlin and New York: De Gruyter, 2010), pp. 631–59. See also Luca Bianchi, 'L'averroismo di Dante: qualche osservazione critica', *Le tre corone*, 2 (2015), 71–109 (pp. 103–09); Christian Moevs, 'The Metaphysical Basis of Dante's Politics', in *Le culture di Dante: studi in onore di Robert Hollander*, ed. by Michelangelo Picone and others (Florence: Cesati, 2004), pp. 215–41. Adriana Diomedi, *Il principio di perfezione nel pensiero dantesco* (Leicester: Troubador, 2005; reprinted 2012), despite its promising title, not only casts little, if any, new light on the question of 'perfection', but also needs to be read with extreme caution. As regards Thomas, see in particular 'Respondeo dicendum quod nomine beatitudinis intelligitur ultima perfectio rationalis seu intellectualis naturae, et inde est quod naturaliter desideratur, quia unumquodque naturaliter desiderat suam ultimam perfectionem. Ultima autem perfectio rationalis seu intellectualis naturae est duplex. Una quidem, quam potest assequi virtute suae naturae, et haec quodammodo beatitudo vel felicitas dicitur. Unde et Aristoteles [*Ethics* x] perfectissimam hominis contemplationem, qua optimum intelligibile, quod est Deus, contemplari potest in hac vita, dicit esse ultimam hominis felicitatem. Sed super hanc felicitatem est alia felicitas, quam in futuro expectamus, qua videbimus Deum sicuti est. Quod quidem est supra cuiuslibet intellectus creati naturam' [I reply by saying that by the name of

are personal and specific, and, contrary to what Bruno Nardi maintained, his discussion is carefully worded to avoid the impression that, thanks to the exercise of human reason in the here and now, an individual can 'termin*are* ogni desiderio, e così è beato' (*Conv.* III. 15. 4).[78] Thus, it is important to recognize that, in *Mon.* III. 15. 5–10, Dante nowhere argues for the independence, self-sufficiency, or perfection of the 'beatitude of this life' (7). He simply states:

> Si ergo homo medium quoddam est corruptibilium et incorruptibilium, cum omne medium sapiat naturam extremorum, necesse est hominem sapere utranque naturam. Et cum omnis natura ad ultimum quendam finem ordinetur, consequitur ut hominis duplex finis existat: ut, sicut inter omnia entia solus incorruptibilitatem et corruptibilitatem participat, sic solus inter omnia entia in duo ultima ordinetur, quorum alterum sit finis eius prout corruptibilis est, alterum vero prout incorruptibilis.
>
> Duos igitur fines providentia illa inenarrabilis homini proposuit intendendos: beatitudinem scilicet huius vite, que in operatione proprie virtutis consistit et per terrestrem paradisum figuratur; et beatitudinem vite ecterne, que consistit in fruitione divini aspectus ad quam propria virtus ascendere non potest, nisi lumine divino adiuta, que per paradisum celestem intelligi datur. (*Mon.* III. 15. 5–7)
>
> [If then man is, so to speak, a middle between corruptible and incorruptible things, since everything that stands in between knows the nature of the extremes, man necessarily knows both natures. And since every nature is directed toward some ultimate end, there is accordingly a twofold end of man: that, as among all beings he alone partakes in corruptibility and incorruptibility, so among all beings he alone is directed to two ends, of which one is his end as corruptible, the other as incorruptible.
>
> That ineffable providence has thus set two ends for man to aim to: the happiness of this life, which consists in the exercise of our own virtue and is figured in the earthly paradise; and the happiness of eternal life, which consists in the experience of the divine vision to which our own virtue cannot rise, unless aided by divine light, and which can be understood through the heavenly paradise.]

Rather than distinct, the two 'ends', as they are too in Albertus Magnus, are intimately, though hierarchically, inter-related.[79] It is only the 'beatitude of eternal life'

---

beatitude is understood the ultimate perfection of rational or of intellectual nature, and hence it is what is naturally desired, since everything naturally desires its ultimate perfection. Indeed ultimate perfection of rational or of intellectual nature is twofold. The first is one which it can attain by its own natural power; and this is in a certain manner called beatitude or happiness. Hence Aristotle says that man's ultimate happiness consists in his most perfect contemplation, whereby in this life he can behold the best intelligible object, and that is God. However above this happiness there is another happiness, which we look forward to in the future, whereby we shall see God as He is. This is beyond the nature of every created intellect] (*ST* I. 62. 1 resp.). See also Gerald F. Stanley, 'Contemplation as Fulfillment of the Human Person', in *Personalist Ethics and Human Subjectivity*, ed. by George F. McLean (Washington, DC: Council for Research in Values and Philosophy, 1996), pp. 363–420.

78   See Bruno Nardi, *Dante e la cultura medievale: nuovi saggi di filosofia dantesca*, 2nd edn (Bari: Laterza, 1949), pp. 67–68. See below for a contextualized analysis of the phrase from the *Convivio*.

79   'The Albertian double beatitude implies no dualism: it points out only the coexistence in man of a double order related, subordinated, and integrated in one operation' (Trovato, p. 24).

that, thanks to revelation (8–9), guarantees satisfaction (*fruitio*).[80] Earthly *beatitudo* is an exclusively human 'mechanistic' activity (*operatio*), the workings of an imperfect *humana ratio*, that is bounded by philosophical 'conclusiones et media' [conclusions and means] (9), which are inescapably 'transcended' by the *documenta spiritualia* (8). Moreover, as Vasoli has expertly concluded, Dante is less interested in the *duo ultima* in themselves than in the differing 'means' necessary to arrive at these.[81]

Mutatis mutandis, the same is true as regards the earlier treatment in *Conv.* III. 15 of how 'l'umano desiderio' achieves a state of 'beatitude' (7) 'in questa vita' (9). The principal thrust of Dante's argument is not the 'two ends', but to clarify the limits of earthly knowledge in relation to a higher form of enlightenment and vision. Thus, even as he declared that reason could bring about 'human perfection' on earth, so he immediately underscored its deficiencies with respect to the divine:

> E in questo sguardo [of the *donna gentile*/Sapienza] solamente l'umana perfezione s'acquista, cioè la perfezione della ragione, dalla quale, sì come da principalissima parte, tutta la nostra essenza depende; e tutte l'altre nostre operazioni — sentire, nutrire, e tutte — sono per questa sola, e questa è per sé, e non per altre, sì che, perfetta sia questa, perfetta è quella, tanto cioè che l'uomo, in quanto ello è uomo, [v]ede terminato ogni [suo] desiderio, e così è beato. [...] Dunque si vede come nell'aspetto di costei delle cose di Paradiso appaiono. E però si legge nel libro allegato di Sapienza, di lei parlando: 'Essa è candore della etterna luce e specchio sanza macula della maestà di Dio.'
>
> Poi, quando si dice: *Elle soverchian lo nostro intelletto*, escuso me di ciò, che poco parlar posso di quelle per la loro soperchianza. Dove è da sapere che in alcuno modo queste cose nostro intelletto abbagliano, in quanto certe cose [si] affermano essere, che lo 'ntelletto nostro guardare non può, cioè Dio e la etternitate e la prima materia: che certissimamente si veggiono e con tutta fede si credono essere, e pur quello che sono intender noi non potemo, se non cose negando si può apressare alla sua conoscenza, e non altrimenti. (*Conv.* III. 15. 4–6)

Indeed, Dante had prefaced the above discussion by stressing first, that, for all its wondrousness and efficacy, earthbound Sapienza is partial: 'li occhi della Sapienza sono le sue dimostrazioni, colle quali si vede la veritade certissimamente; e lo suo riso sono le sue persuasioni, nelle quali si dimostra la luce interiore della Sapienza sotto alcuno velamento' (2); and second, that 'in queste due cose [the eyes and smile of Wisdom] si sente quel piacere altissimo di beatitudine lo quale è massimo bene in Paradiso' (2). These caveats, as with what the poet would almost immediately go on to say especially in paragraph 6, inescapably inhibit earthly intellectual 'perfection' as a limited terrestrial experience which, however satisfying in strictly

---

80   Albertus defined *fruitio* as 'Frui est amore inherens alicui rei propter se [...] Frui autem dicit delectationem ultimam et perfectam et optimam' [To enjoy is to adhere by love to something for its own sake [...]. Indeed to enjoy is termed the ultimate and perfect and best delight] (*Summa theologiae sive de mirabili scientiae Dei* I. 2. 7. 3). It is noteworthy that, in order to restrict as much as possible the 'beatitude of this life', Dante only associated 'fruition' with the divine, even though, following Albert, he could have presented earthly intellectual beatitude as the relative *fruitio secundum quid* distinct from the absolute *fruitio proprie dicta/simpliciter* (see the same chapter of his *Summa*). See Trovato, pp. 23–24.

81   Cesare Vasoli, 'Filosofia e politica in Dante fra *Convivio* e *Monarchia*', *Letture classensi*, 9–10 (1982), 11–37 (p. 31).

human terms, is simply that, a narrow transient satisfaction 'in quanto ello è uomo' — one that cannot comprehend what is truly important and at most can offer a 'negative' intimation of the divine. In any case, as Vasoli makes clear when glossing paragraph 2, earthly knowledge for the poet is significant not in itself, but in so far as it provides a sense of the divine:

> Dante sembra [...] dire che la massima felicità raggiungibile in questa vita consiste nella cognizione dimostrativa data dalla scienza e nella persuasione o intuizione analogica e allegorica delle cose divine; e che tale felicità sarà compiutamente perenne nell'altra vita e nella beatitudine dell'eterna contemplazione di Dio di cui fruiscono i beati.[82]

Furthermore, as Beatrice will demonstrate in detail in *Paradiso* XXIX, human intellectual striving is dangerously prone to 'error', especially when it transgresses its limits: 'E però l'umano desiderio è misurato in questa vita a quella scienza che qui avere si può, e quello punto non passa se non per errore, lo quale è di fuori di naturale intenzione' (9). The point is central to Dante's argument, and he further defines and insists on it in the following paragraph: 'Onde, con ciò sia cosa che conoscere di Dio, e di certe altre cose, quello esso è, non sia possibile alla nostra natura, quello da noi naturalmente non è desiderato di sapere' (10). Constraints encircle constraints: chapter 15 is hardly that ringing endorsement of earthly philosophy and of the autonomy of human reason that some have claimed it to be.[83]

Throughout his career, Dante was always acutely aware of the restrictions and pitfalls of human reason, as well as its responsibilities towards and subservience to the divine. Indeed, it is noteworthy that he should have blurred, as we have seen, the boundaries between heretics and other intellectual transgressors.[84] All willful error, as far as the poet was concerned, by detracting from truth, was an offence against God. It was a form of heresy, as he appropriately made clear through his treatment of the heretics in *Inferno* IX–XI. By denying the immortality of the soul, Epicurus and 'his followers' (*Inf.* X. 14) adamantly refused to raise their intelligence towards matters celestial. On account of the extremism of their views, they could thus serve as powerful symbols of intransigent materialism and rationalism; and Dante certainly intended his heretics to have a broad function and connotation.[85] Thus,

---

82   See Dante Alighieri, *Convivio*, ed. by Cesare Vasoli and Domenico De Robertis (Milan and Naples: Ricciardi, 1988), p. 470.

83   For an excellent and balanced synthesis of the major competing interpretations of *Conv.* III. 15, see Vasoli's annotations, pp. 465–83. I shall consider more fully issues relating to the ties between faith and reason in Dante in Subsection 5, 'Invidïosi veri'. Chapter 15 ought also be read in light of *Conv.* III. 14; IV. 13. 7–9; 22. 17–18.

84   On the elasticity of the term 'heresy' in the Middle Ages, see Mariano d'Alatri, ' "Eresie" perseguite dall'Inquisizione in Italia nel corso del Duecento', in Lourdaux and Verhelst, pp. 211–24 (pp. 222–24); Robert Ian Moore, *The Birth of Popular Heresy* (London: Edward Arnold, 1975), pp. 1–7; Thijssen, pp. 1–2.

85   'In *Inferno* 10 [...] Dante systematically attacks and subverts the perspective of those Epicureans who, like Farinata and Cavalcanti, sustain the autonomy of human history as a field of action. Their commitment to historical temporality has led to blindness and damnation. In other words, Dante pointedly rejects secularism and its modes of representing earthly existence' (Ascoli, p. 49). See also Chapter 17.

rather than focus on specifically Christian 'eresïarche | con lor seguaci, d'ogne setta' (*Inf.* IX. 127–28), and thereby restrict attention to a particular doctrinal irregularity such as Arianism or Manichaeism, he instead, and provocatively, concentrated on an emblematic pagan philosopher and his adherents (although it is worth recalling that, in the Middle Ages, heretics were those who, regardless when they may have lived, doggedly rejected a tenet of the faith).[86] In medieval culture, as is confirmed, for instance, by commentaries to the Psalms and to Ecclesiastes, *epicureus* was employed as a generic term to refer not only to heretics but also to anyone who used their intellect incorrectly and especially for wholly materialist ends (see Chapter 15, pp. 443 and 563). Epicurus and the Epicureans thus represented the worst of philosophy. As occurs in *Inferno*, they were rational extremists who, solely concerned with earthly things, showed 'disdegno' (*Inf.* x. 63) for everything else — an attitude which for most medieval intellectuals, including Dante, had little to do with the proper practice of philosophy. That Epicurus and his supporters could effectively embody the (ir)rational 'anti-philosopher' was an idea deeply embedded in the medieval world. Their reputation as mortalists and unbridled hedonists, sceptical about the gods, dismissive of divine providence, and pessimistic about the human condition, was a commonplace. In the *Commedia*, their rejection of the immortality of the soul functions as a synecdoche for all their errors. Thus, the Epicureans both signify themselves and all those who abuse the gift of reason. As ought to be clear, even from my rapid résumé, in the Middle Ages, *epicureus* was a highly elastic term, which meant it could be applied to a broad range of sins and suspect intellectual behaviours — something which likely encouraged Dante to elect the Epicurean as a general symbol of the heretic and the deluded thinker.[87]

Dante's consistently uncompromising attitude towards heresy in particular and towards intellectual heterodoxy in general, together with the scrupulous conformity of his overarching ideology, are the parameters within which, as I have already begun to intimate, any discussion of the unconventional and the seemingly unorthodox present in his *œuvre* should be considered and appraised. Some of these problematic elements were unquestionably thorny, especially when they involved a doctrinal mainstay such as the soul; others, however, were rather less challenging than we

---

86   In this regard, it is important to note that Dante's choice of the Epicureans has nothing to do with their supposedly explicit ties to Averroism in medieval culture, as Italianists have mistakenly claimed for far too long. To put it simply, there is no documentary evidence to support the idea that, in the late Middle Ages, the designations 'Epicurean' and 'Averroist' were synonymous. On the question of the unlikelihood that, in the Middle Ages, a strict relationship existed between Epicurus and Averroes, see Subsection IV, 'Exploiting Epicurus'.

87   On the medieval reception of Epicurus, in addition to George Corbett, *Dante and Epicurus: A Dualistic Vision of Secular and Spiritual Fulfilment* (Leeds: Legenda, 2013), see Howard Jones, *The Epicurean Tradition* (London and New York: Routledge, 1989); Valerio Lucchesi, 'Epicurus and Democritus: The Ciceronian Foundations of Dante's Judgement', *Italian Studies*, 42 (1987), 1–19; Alexander Murray, 'The Epicureans', in *Intellectuals and Writers in Fourteenth–century Europe*, ed. by Piero Boitani and Anna Torti (Tübingen and Cambridge: Gunter Narr and Brewer, 1986), pp. 138–63; Maria Rita Pagnoni, 'Prime note sulla tradizione medievale ed umanistica di Epicuro', *Annali della Scuola Normale Superiore di Pisa. Classe di Lettere e Filosofia*, 3:4 (1974), 1443–77; Wolfgang P. Schmid, *Epicuro e l'epicureismo cristiano* (Brescia: Paideia Editrice, 1984).

moderns might imagine.[88] All, nevertheless, can be resolved, I believe, in approved terms. In addition, Dante's ideological orthodoxy should not be treated as evidence that he reluctantly adapted himself to an oppressive ideology and environment. Where precisely in his works can one discover the proof of such an attitude? In any case, the idea that the Middle Ages was a 'persecuting society' has,[89] in recent years, been authoritatively disputed.[90] Indeed, already many earlier accounts of heresy, intolerance, and persecution that antedate Moore's present a rather different, more nuanced, and less doom-laden picture of medieval society than his. Bernard Hamilton, the well-known historian of the crusades, can confidently write that, by the fourteenth century, 'dissent had become part of the western tradition'.[91] Thus, the extent to which ideological controls were actually imposed, and when they were, that these were implemented as a result of ideological factors, is seriously open to question (it is enough to remember the Church's reactions to Manfred). In any case, as we have previously ascertained, creative writers were certainly one group afforded quite considerable leeway, and allegoresis was a tool of extraordinary ideological flexibility. Equally, the acceptance of the validity of pagan, especially classical and Islamic, culture by the end of the thirteenth century was a given. Moreover, although there is a tendency among scholars of medieval Italian literature romantically to present the philosophizing masters of arts at the Universities of Paris or of Bologna, the so-called radical Aristotelians and neo-Averroists, and their sympathizers as a beleaguered minority, the reality of their situation was somewhat different.[92] To put it simply, despite formal condemnations, such as those issued in

88   See the following subsection, 'Invidïosi veri'.

89   Robert Ian Moore, *The Formation of a Persecuting Society: Power and Deviance in Western Europe, 950–1250* (Oxford: Blackwell, 1987). I have always been struck by the ambiguity of some of the evidence Moore adduces in support of his thesis. However, now see also his *The War on Heresy* (Cambridge, MA: Belknap Press of Harvard University Press, 2012).

90   See in particular Mario Condorelli, *I fondamenti giuridici della tolleranza religiosa nell'elaborazione canonistica dei secoli XII–XIV: contributo storico-dogmatico* (Milan: Giuffré, 1960); Cary J. Nederman, *Worlds of Difference: European Discourses of Toleration, c. 1100–c. 1550* (University Park: Pennsylvania State University Press, 2000); Klaus Schreiner, 'Toleranz', in *Geschichtliche Grundbegriffe: Historisches Lexicon zur politisch–sozialen Sprache in Deutschland*, ed. by Otto Brunner and others, 9 vols (Stuttgart: Klett–Cotta, 1972–97), VI, 445–605; *Beyond the Persecuting Society. Religious Toleration before the Enlightenment*, ed. by John Christian Laursen and Cary J. Nederman (Philadelphia: University of Pennsylvania Press, 1998), pp. 1–91: *Difference and Dissent: Theories of Tolerance in Medieval and Early Modern Europe*, ed. by Cary J. Nederman and John Christian Laursen (Lanham, MD, Boulder, New York, and London: Rowman & Littlefield, 1996), pp. 1–82.

91   Bernard Hamilton, *Religion in the Medieval West* (London: Edward Arnold, 1986), p. 178. He also notes that 'the Inquisition was far less bloodthirsty and oppressive than it is often represented as being. The vast majority of those whom it found guilty were dismissed with canonical penances, and a substantial minority were detained in the Inquisition's prisons, but the number of unrepentant heretics handed over to the secular authorities and burned at the stake was small' (p. 177). On the Inquisition, see at least Grado Giovanni Merlo, *Inquisitori e inquisizione del Medioevo* (Bologna: il Mulino, 2008). See also Caterina Bruschi, 'Falsembiante-Inquisitor? Images and Stereotypes of Franciscan Inquisitors between Literature and Juridical Texts', in Veglia and others, pp. 99–136.

92   On the problematic notion of thirteenth-century Averroism as a historiographical category, see Gianfranco Fioravanti, 'Boezio di Dacia e la storiografia sull'"Averroismo"', *Studi medievali*, 7 (1966), 283–332; Guido Giglioni, 'Introduction', in *Renaissance Averroism and its Aftermath: Arabic Philosophy in Early Modern Europe*, ed. by Guido Giglioni (Dordrecht: Springer, 2013), pp. 1–34. On the generally

Paris in 1270 and 1277, university teachers were granted not inconsiderable latitude and significant institutional effort was made to allow proponents of unorthodoxies to regularize their views.[93] Such an attitude of accommodation had long been a feature of official Church reaction to intellectuals and their contrasting opinions, even as regards matters of theological doctrine.[94] Debate, and hence contrasting opinion, not least because of the centrality of *disputatio* in scholasticism, was far from discouraged.

Instead of recognizing the complex, stratified character of the late-medieval intellectual environment, where differing and competing ideas, not infrequently of questionable conformity, vied for attention and legitimacy, too often Dantists have blithely reduced this hugely sophisticated and shifting world to two monolithic camps: the orthodox and the unorthodox.[95] This is not to suggest that intellectually everything was open to question and revision. The centrality of Scripture, the authority of the Church Fathers, and, of course, the tenets of the faith as essentially established in the Nicene Creed were inviolate. Around this core, however, there was, and there had been for centuries, a remarkable intellectual ferment, beginning with how best to read Scripture whether in general or in its details. Opinion was

problematic and misleading use of the term 'Averroism' in Dante studies, see Bianchi, 'L'averroismo di Dante' (pp. 71–78 address historiographical and terminological issues), and ' "Ultima perfezione" e "ultima felicitade": ancora su Dante e l'averroismo', in *Edizioni, traduzioni e tradizioni filosofiche (secoli XII–XVI)*, ed. by Luca Bianchi and others, 2 vols (Rome: Arachne, 2018), I, 315–28. Bianchi writes: 'Ciò che rende problematiche le discussioni sull'"averroismo" di Dante *non* è dunque l'anacronismo di questa categoria storiografica, ma il fatto che essa ci appare tanto indefinita quanto carica di sottintesi giudizi di valore poiché — implicitamente ma inesorabilmente — rimanda a nozioni, anch'esse vaghe, come "razionalismo", "eterodossia", "miscredenza" ' ('L'averroismo di Dante', p. 71)

93   See in particular Thijssen, a key study which casts much new light on the complex relationship between what today we term academic freedom and religious authority in the thirteenth and fourteenth centuries. See also Luca Bianchi, 'Censure, liberté et progrès intellectuel à l'Université de Paris au XIIIe siècle', *Archives d'histoire doctrinale et littéraire du moyen âge*, 63 (1996), 45–93; William J. Courtenay, 'Inquiry and Inquisition: Academic Freedom in Medieval Universities', *Church History*, 58 (1989), 168–82; Mary M. McLaughlin, *Intellectual Freedom and its Limitations in the University of Paris in the Thirteenth and Fourteenth Centuries* (New York: Arno, 1977); Peters, *Heresy*, pp. 217–19. It has been suggested, though more research needs to be done on the matter, that intellectuals in Bologna and Padua enjoyed greater intellectual freedom than those in Paris; see Emanuele Coccia and Sylvain Piron, 'Poésie, sciences et politique: une génération d'intellectuels italiens (1290–1330)', *Revue de synthèse*, 129 (2008), 549–86 (p. 556).

94   See Janet Coleman, 'The Science of Politics and Late Medieval Academic Debate', in *Criticism and Dissent in the Middle Ages*, ed. by Rita Copeland (Cambridge: Cambridge University Press, 1996), pp. 181–214; Constant J. Mews, 'Philosophy and Theology 1100–1150: The Search for Harmony', in *Le XIIe Siècle: mutations et renouveau en France dans la première moitié du XIIe Siècle*, ed. by Françoise Gasparri (Paris: Le Léopard d'or, 1994), pp. 159–203.

95   It might be objected that, in light of my earlier point regarding Dante's homologizing treatment of heresy, the poet too divided the world of ideas into two camps. At a general and polemical level, this is undoubtedly the case. At the same time, he was also sensitive to the fact that most intellectual transgressions were not strictly speaking heretical; and, from Ulysses to the Decretalists, he presented many examples of his attentive sense of discrimination in this regard. Furthermore, unlike the poet, we are not writing as polemicists but as historians of literature. We thus bear the responsibility, whatever the obstacles, to reconstruct the past as accurately as possible, so that, in turn, we can hope to arrive at a degree of precision when we make claims for the poet.

not fixed or conveniently pigeonholed; and what, at one point, was problematic, subsequently could become acceptable, or vice versa. The very notions of ortho-doxy, heterodoxy, error, irregularity were intricate and fluid;[96] and medieval thinkers prided themselves on their ability to make 'distinctions'. The difference between 'untrue' (*falsus*), 'erroneous' (*erroneus*), and 'heretical' (*hereticus*) was clearly perceived by medieval intellectuals. The theologian Godfrey of Fontaines, for instance, observed that errors are faults that endanger our salvation; they become heresies when they are defended with pertinacity (Thijssen, p. 2). Given the short-comings of human reason, error is inevitable.[97] Even the greatest minds, as Dante confirmed, err:

> Ma Gregorio da lui [Dïonisio] poi si divise;
> onde, sì tosto come li occhi aperse
> in questo ciel, di sé medesmo rise. (*Par.* XXVIII. 133–35)

It is how we react once we become aware that we have made a mistake that is crucial, as the poet succinctly captures in Gregory the Great's smile. To put it differently, what is vital is how we respond to the 'ver' (XXVIII. 136 and 139) when it runs counter to our own positions:

> Quest' è tal punto,
> che più savio di te fé già errante,
> Sì che per sua dottrina fé disgiunto
> da l'anima il possibile intelletto,
> perché da lui non vide organo assunto.
> Apri a la verità che viene il petto. (*Purg.* XXV. 62–67)

And Averroes too must have 'opened his breast to truth', according to Dante, or otherwise he would not be in Limbo. Genuine wisdom was in part defined by the ways in which one dealt with error and correction. Indeed, the pilgrim stumbles from one misunderstanding to another throughout his journey. However, as soon as the truth is presented to him, he accepts it unconditionally and error is left behind.

Every intellectual, even the most sophisticated, could blunder, or be considered by some to have done so, as negative reaction to Thomas Aquinas, from Bishop Stephen Tempier to Durandus of St Pourçain, incontrovertibly testifies.[98] Yet, when we speak about Dante and unorthodoxy, we tend to forget that this should include Thomas. Our modern perceptions of the saint as the bastion of established Catholic

---

96   'A formal definition of orthodoxy was precisely what was lacking in many cases of academic censure. Academics were not censured for disseminating views that had already been formally condemned by ecclesiastical authorities as heretical. Rather, they were engaged in running scholastic debate during which they incurred accusations of false teaching. [...] academics charged with suspect teaching did not adhere to views that overtly contradicted faith, or that had already been formally condemned' (Thijssen, pp. 4–5). See also Luca Bianchi, *Censure et liberté intellectuelle à l'Université de Paris (XIIIe–XIVe siècles)* (Paris: Les Belles Lettres, 1999), pp. 14–16, 61–62, as well as his 'A "Heterodox" in Paradise? Notes on the Relationship between Dante and Siger of Brabant', in Ardizzone, pp. 78–105.

97   See Gillian R. Evans, *Getting it Wrong: The Medieval Epistemology of Error* (Leiden: Brill, 1998).

98   See Bianchi, 'A "Heterodox" in Paradise?', pp. 90–92.

doctrine cloud our sense of history. In any case, it was not the person but his ideas that were the issue. It was the validity of particular viewpoints that was evaluated. The individual only became a problem when he obstinately insisted that his errors were legitimate. To have held seriously questionable opinions, even when these were not modified in life, was not a bar to salvation — obviously as long as such opinions had not led to the intractable denial of a precept of the faith and were part of genuine debate. Thus, in the *Paradiso*, Thomas is exalted in the Heaven of the Sun, but he is also among those who, as far as Dante was concerned, were quite wrong to insist on a scientific explanation for the eclipse that had occurred at Jesus's death:

> Un dice che la luna si ritorse
> ne la passion di Cristo e s'interpuose,
> per che 'l lume del sol giù non si porse;
> e mente. (*Par.* xxix. 97–100)[99]

If on the one hand, medieval religious authorities reacted energetically to falsehood, as did Dante himself, on the other, both were also conscious of the complexity, variety, volatility, and inevitability of error and were willing, whenever possible, to handle it with a fair degree of understanding and commonsense. Until we begin properly to appreciate how official medieval culture and Dante reacted to and dealt with that broad and diverse swathe of opinion that we clumsily lump together under a catch-all tag of 'unorthodoxy', in particular how officialdom and poet discriminated between different types of irregularity, our discussions of Dante's relationship to problematic areas, ideas, and figures of his world, as well as of his possible recourse to dubious opinions, will remain mired in imprecision and, worse, unhelpful anachronism.

5. *Invidïosi veri*

To examine the question of heterodoxy in the Middle Ages requires a sharp sensitivity to context — historical, cultural, institutional, and, unquestionably, textual. It thus should not be treated piecemeal. Yet, this is precisely the way in which the problem has been regularly approached in Dante studies. Individual details are both detached from the overarching framework of the text of which they are part, and freed from the specific constraints of the episode, argument, etc. in which they are embedded, as well as insulated from the equally determining pressures of the poet's *œuvre* and of the medieval setting. This, in my view, has led not only to poor readings, but also to tenuous assumptions. Allow me to linger briefly on a couple of well-known, though usefully distinct, examples.

To elucidate the creation and nature of angels, Beatrice, appropriately and orthodoxly, considers their coming into being in relation to the act of creation in its totality:

---

99 'Era questa l'opinione di Dionigi pseudo-Areopagita, seguita da molti teologi, tra cui anche Tommaso (*S. T.* iii, q. 44 a. 2)': Chiavacci Leonardi, iii, 809.

> Forma e materia, congiunte e purette,
> usciro ad esser che non avia fallo,
> come d'arco tricordo tre saette.
>   E come in vetro, in ambra o in cristallo
> raggio resplende sì, che dal venire
> a l'esser tutto non è intervallo,
>   così 'l triforme effetto del suo sire
> ne l'esser suo raggiò insieme tutto
> sanza distinzïone in essordire.
>   Concreato fu ordine e costrutto
> a le sustanze; e quelle furon cima
> nel mondo in che puro atto fu produtto;
>   pura potenza tenne la parte ima;
> nel mezzo strinse potenza con atto
> tal vime, che già mai non si divima. (*Par.* xxix. 22–36)

These are lines of substantial difficulty and density, which have generated no little controversy among Dantists. However, they may not be quite as complicated and controversial as is normally claimed, especially if individual doctrinal elements are not judged in isolation. Even if, for reasons of space, I intend to focus on just one aspect of doctrine alluded to in the tercets — the most important one in terms of the canto, the coming into being of the angelic intelligences — my approach, I hope, is not in contradiction with my immediately preceding assertion, as I shall endeavour to understand the question contextually. My aim is thus to offer a mode of reading and an interpretive structure that might also not be irrelevant to other disputed ideological issues in the tercets, most notably Dante's understanding of prime matter. The poet refers to the angels both as 'pure form' (22) and as 'pure act' (33). Dante's choice of terms has led to accusations of inconsistency, misperception, and, most worryingly, but also most pertinently for my present discussion, unorthodoxy. Indeed, it is maintained that not one but two instances of heterodoxy trouble his treatment of the angels. First, by defining the angels as 'forma puretta', Dante appears to be confusing them with God, since, according to established Christian belief, only God is pure actuality. Second, by terming them 'pure form' and 'pure act', he compounds the muddle by treating the angels, together with God, as first causes — an unorthodoxy seemingly confirmed in the *Monarchia* when the poet speaks of the angels as being 'essentie [...; quae] quedam sunt intellectuales et non aliud, et earum esse nichil est aliud quam intelligere quod est quod sunt' [essences that are a certain type of intellectual species and nothing else, and their being is nothing other than understanding what they are] (1. 3. 7), given that, as Moevs lucidly explains 'only in God is understanding, or the "power of sight" (*intelligere*), identical with the act of existence itself (*esse*)'.[100] Yet, it is almost certainly incorrect to impute heterodoxy to Dante's formulations.

100 Moevs, *The Metaphysics of Dante's 'Comedy'*, p. 150. My discussion here, especially as regards matters of medieval thought, is heavily dependent on Moevs's balanced and reliably informed account of divine creation, being, act, etc. See also Susanna Barsella, *In the Light of the Angels: Angelology and Cosmology in Dante's 'Divina Commedia'* (Florence: Olschki, 2010); Stephen Bemrose, *Dante's Angelic Intelligences* (Rome: Edizioni di storia e letteratura, 1983), pp. 56–76, 185–201.

As the *Convivio* documents ('l'oro, le margherite e li campi perfettamente forma e atto abbiano in loro essere', IV. 11. 4), *forma* and *actus* were often used as synonyms in medieval philosophy,[101] a usage which had its origins in Aristotle, where the theory of matter and form is transformable to that of potentiality and act (*De anima* II. 1).[102] Thus, when Beatrice remarks that the angels are pure form or pure act, she is simply and correctly highlighting the fact that they are immaterial, and hence unchangeable and unaffected by time and space. Elsewhere, Dante was less allusive, terming the angelic intelligences 'sustanze partite da materia' (*Conv.* III. 4. 9), and stressing that they are 'sanza grossezza di materia, quasi diafani per la purità della loro forma' (*Conv.* III. 7. 5). Equally, the supposedly contentious phrase in the *Monarchia*, as paragraphs 6 and 7 confirm when read unitarily, repeats the general and non-contentious Aristotelian generalization that *intelligere intelligentibus est esse* [to understand for intellectual creatures is being].[103] In any case, elsewhere in the *Monarchia*, and in perfect conformity with *Par.* XXIX. 28–30, Dante stresses that God has the exclusive power of creation: 'Nec etiam possent omnia sibi [to the Pope] commicti a Deo, quoniam potestatem creandi et similiter baptizandi nullo modo Deus commictere posset, ut evidenter probatur' [Nor is it even possible for all things to be delegated to him by God, for God can in no way delegate the power of creating and similarly of baptizing, as is clearly demonstrated] (III. 7. 6).[104]

One thing is evident. In both *Paradiso* XXIX and *Mon.* I. 3, Dante is not saying anything especially remarkable, although, as Luca Bianchi has recently demonstrated, there are 'minor' elements in Dante's presentation of the nature and knowledge of separated substances that are ideologically 'delicate', even if not 'specificamente "rušdian*i*", né [...] "averroist*i*"'.[105] He is in fact repeating commonplaces about

---

101 Nardi, *Dante e la cultura medievale*, p. 117.

102 See Frederick Charles Copleston, *Medieval Philosophy: An Introduction* (Mineola, NY: Dover Publications, 2001), p. 88; William Thomas Jones, *A History of Western Philosophy. I. The Classical Mind*, 2nd edn (Fort Worth, TX: Harcourt Brace Jovanovich, 1970), p. 222; Moevs, *The Metaphysics of Dante's 'Comedy'*, pp. 43–45, 50, 82, 150.

103 James H. Robb, '*Intelligere Intelligentibus Est Esse*', in *An Étienne Gilson Tribute*, ed. by Charles J. O'Neil (Milwaukee, WI: Marquette University Press, 1959), pp. 209–27.

104 In light of what I say above about reaction to error and questionable opinion in medieval theological culture, it is interesting to dwell a moment on Dante's observation that Peter Lombard ('Magister contrarium dixerit in quarto' [the Master said the contrary in the fourth [book]], 6) disagrees with his claim regarding God's creative power. The Lombard's view, which he expressed in *Sentences* IV. 5. 3, was certainly eccentric and was energetically refuted by Thomas Aquinas (*ST* I. 45. 5 resp.). Nonetheless, this did not prevent author and text from being hugely influential in the Middle Ages. Indeed, the *Sentences* was a standard schoolroom text which inspired an enormous commentary tradition. Dante celebrates Peter in the Heaven of the Sun: 'quel Pietro fu che con la poverella | offerse a Santa Chiesa suo tesoro' (*Par.* X. 107–08). The Lombard's error was much more troubling than, say, Gregory's; and yet both he and his great work of synthesis are beatified. On controversies connected to Peter, see Pietro B. Rossi, '*Contra Lombardum*: reazioni alla cristologia di Pietro Lombardo', in *Pietro Lombardo* (Spoleto: Centro italiano di studi sull'Alto Medioevo, 2007), pp. 123–91.

105 Bianchi, 'L'averrosimo di Dante', pp. 87–93 (pp. 88 & 91). For an energetic reaffirmation of the problematic status of Dante's treatment of the angels, see Paolo Falzone, 'La dottrina delle intelligenze separate come "puri atti" in Dante (*Convivio* II 4, *Paradiso* XXIX, *Monarchia* I 3)', in *Il 'Convivio' di Dante*, ed. by Johannes Bartuschat and Andrea Aldo Robiglio (Ravenna: Longo, 2015), pp. 165–89.

creation, angels, being, intellection, etc. — commonplaces which, furthermore, chime harmoniously with what he says more directly and expansively elsewhere about the same issues. There is no unorthodoxy here; and to claim otherwise is unnecessarily to seek out complications where none exist, and hence to do violence to Dante's texts, *œuvre*, thought, and religious belief. Yet, one might reasonably wonder why, given the importance of his subject-matter in *Paradiso* XXIX, the poet had not been limpidly and unambiguously clear when dealing with topics of such delicacy. The answer, in truth, is obvious: Dante was writing (vernacular) poetry and not scientific (Latin) prose. *Par.* XXIX. 22–36 builds on and extends the stupendous imagistic writing with which the canto had opened, evoking in simile 'li figli di Latona' (1). Beatrice's speech from its inception (10) is constellated with metaphor, before fully finding its descriptive voice in the rich concentration of similes and metaphors that constitute our lines: bows, arrows, glass, amber, crystal, light, peaks, bindings. As with other terms, Dante is using the technical vocabulary too *poetice*; and as we have seen, medieval poets were granted a degree of semantic leeway. Contextualizing *Par.* XXIX. 22–36 highlights levels of relevant complexity within orthodoxy — the episode's, the canticle's, and the poem's undoubted frame of reference. It is not enough simply to assert, even when this is accompanied by an array of learned quotations, that Dante's treatment of angels and creation is heterodox. What needs also to be done, and which as far as I am aware has not been attempted by any scholar who has argued for the lines' unorthodoxy, is to explain why, in a situation where doctrinal orthodoxy is a key theme, as the latter part of Beatrice's speech confirms, and where our lines are immediately preceded by a rigorously conformist declaration denying the eternity of the world (19–21), which functions as a kind of emblem of the canto's celebration of established doctrine, the poet should have wished to undermine Beatrice, the *Commedia*, and himself as a *scriba Dei* by 'lying' (100).[106] The tenets of the faith may seem absurd to the secular modern mind; for a medieval believer, such as Dante, they were a hallowed mystery, worthy of the most profound respect.

Some have claimed that *Paradiso* XXIX's treatment of the angels reveals the influence of Averroes, and this conveniently leads me to my second example. That the great Arab philosopher had a considerable impact on medieval thought is indisputable; and Dante dutifully acknowledged his importance by citing him as an *auctoritas*, by presenting him as an individual of exceptional intelligence and erudition (*Purg.* XXV. 63), and by locating him in Limbo and emphasizing the 'greatness' of his work as a commentator of Aristotle (*Inf.* IV. 144). As far as thirteenth- and fourteenth-century intellectual culture was concerned, such appreciation of Averroes was unexceptionable. Yes, as Dante too underscores in *Purg.* XXV. 62–66, the philosopher had made some mistakes, including some dangerously heretical ones.[107] However,

---

106 On the controversy see *Thomas d'Aquin et la controverse sur 'L'Éternité du monde'*, ed. by Cyrille Michon (Paris: Flammarion, 2004).

107 I do not have the space to examine in depth Dante's reference to Averroes in *Mon.* 1. 3: 'Et quia potentia ista per unum hominem seu per aliquam particularium comunitatum superius distinctarum tota simul in actum reduci non potest, necesse est multitudinem esse in humano genere, per quam quidem tota potentia hec actuetur; sicut necesse est multitudinem rerum generabilium ut potentia

in general, he was deemed an excellent and authoritative interpreter of Aristotle, many of whose opinions were not in any way at odds with Christianity. It is enough to remember that, despite sharply criticizing him on matters relating to the possible intellect and creation, Thomas Aquinas made ready recourse to Averroes, not least when attacking Avicenna. Yet, it has become increasingly the case among Dantists to use the name Averroes as a marker of the poet's supposed unorthodoxy. To put it somewhat differently, whenever an echo of the Arab philosopher is heard in Dante,[108] this has also been taken as evidence that the poet had heterodox leanings,

tota materie prime semper sub actu sit: aliter esset dare potentiam separatam, quod est inpossibile. Et huic sententie concordat Averrois in comento super hiis que *De anima*. Potentia etiam intellectiva, de qua loquor, non solum est ad formas universales aut speties, sed etiam per quandam extensionem ad particulares: unde solet dici quod intellectus speculativus extensione fit practicus, cuius finis est agere atque facere' [And because that power cannot fully and simultaneously be reduced into act in any one person or in any one of the particular communities distinguished above, it is necessary for a multitude to be in the human race through which the whole of this power can be actualized, just as a multitude of things that can be generated is necessary so that the whole power of prime matter can always be actualized; otherwise one would be postulating a power separate [from actualization], which is impossible. And Averroes agrees with this opinion in his commentary on the *De anima*. Yet the intellective power, about which I am speaking, is not only concerned with universal forms or species, but also by a sort of extension with particulars: consequently it is usually said that the speculative intellect by extension becomes practical, whose end is doing and making] (8–9).

Three recent studies have authoritatively dismantled the Averroistic reading of this passage; see Bianchi, 'L'averrosimo di Dante', pp. 80–84 & 92–93; Jean-Baptiste Brenet, 'Théorie de l'intellect et organisation politique chez Dante et Averroès', *Rivista di filosofia neoscolastica*, 98 (2006), 467–87; Iacopo Costa, 'Principio di finalità e fine nella *Monarchia* dantesca', in *'Ad ingenii acuitionem': Studies in Honour of Alfonso Maierù*, ed. by Stefano Caroti and others (Louvain-la-Neuve: FIDEM, 2006), pp. 39–65. Suffice it to say that I too do not believe that, in the treatise, Dante accepted Averroes's doctrine of a single possible intellect for the whole of humanity. As is well known, the poet always affirmed the immortality of the individual soul. The idea that he might have casually claimed otherwise is unthinkable; not least, because as I have attempted to demonstrate, he was acutely aware of the pitfalls of unorthodoxy. It is extremely difficult to imagine what might have been the purpose in the *Monarchia* of such a dangerously radical claim. John Marenbon has attempted to provide an answer to this conundrum. He writes: 'in a philosophical argument of the sort found throughout *Monarchia* i, Dante should be expected to argue in earnest the positions, which, in philosophical terms, he thought convincing'; consequently, he 'held the Averroist position on the single possible intellect *as the right position within philosophical discussion*': John Marenbon, 'Dante's Averroism', in *Poetry and Philosophy in the Middle Ages: A Festschrift for Peter Dronke* ed. by John Marenbon (Leiden, Boston, and Cologne: Brill, 2001), pp. 349–74 (p. 371; Bianchi is particularly critical of Marenbon's claims). I remain unpersuaded by this explanation. Nowhere in his *œuvre* did Dante show the slightest sympathy for the claims and methods of those contemporary philosophers who wished to insulate their thinking and conclusions from the higher insights provided by revelation, although even such philosophers were careful to present problematic claims as erroneous when considered in light of faith (see below n. 110). In fact, for Dante, a philosophical truth could only be true if it did not challenge the tenets of faith. As I document at some length in this chapter, he always took care to subordinate reason to revelation and not to treat philosophy as self-sufficient. Now see also Donatella Stocchi Perucchio, 'The Limits of Heterodoxy in Dante's *Monarchia*', in Ardizzone, pp. 197–223.

108 It is not my intention here to evaluate the validity of such echoes. On the one hand, there is no doubt that Dante had read some Averroes (how much is a matter that is still far from established); on the other, there is little question that the extent of his knowledge of and recourse to Averroes has been exaggerated. Rather too frequently, when an influence from the philosopher on the poet is posited, this is not supported by hard philological and intertextual evidence. Bianchi, '"Ultima perfezione"' provides an excellent example of how to undertake research into Dante's 'Averroism'.

a reaction that has its origins in Bruno Nardi and which, in the early 1980s, was given a hefty boost by Maria Corti.[109] I hope that I need not linger any longer on the deficiencies of this perspective.

Another consequence of the fascination with Averroes is to associate Dante with the so-called radical Aristotelians or neo-Averroists, those intellectuals, usually masters of arts at the Universities of Paris and Bologna in the thirteenth and fourteenth centuries, who, inspired by aspects of Averroes's reading of Aristotle, privileged the independence of rational philosophical inquiry, while acknowledging that this could lead to interpretations that were different from what might be found in Scripture and thus from the tenets of the faith, although, in such instances, they were also careful to acknowledge that the truth resided in revelation.[110] In addition, they believed that a life dedicated to philosophy constituted a self-sufficient earthly ideal that could lead to satisfaction (happiness) in the here and now. That, from circa the mid-1200s, the Church and orthodox theologians considered such thinkers as problematic, error-ridden, and hence heterodox, especially as regards their views on the unity of the possible intellect, the eternity of the world, astrological determinism, the mortality of the individual soul, and free will, is well known. Thus, if it could be shown that Dante accepted even some of their ideas and viewpoints, then, proponents of the poet's heterodoxy would have potent and historically pertinent evidence in support of their case. However, it is of no little consequence that, on the contentious questions just listed, Dante always expressed himself orthodoxly, firmly rejecting Averroistic positions on the soul, creation, and free will.[111]

His study establishes how what might be deemed an instance in the incipit of the *Convivio* of the poet borrowing from the philosopher in fact 'non consente di dimostrare una diretta dipendenza testuale di Dante da Averroè, né di confermare, sul piano dottrinale, la controversa ipotesi del suo averroismo' (p. 328).

109 I should like to stress that I have a high regard for both Nardi and Corti. In particular, it is impossible to think about Dante's intellectual formation and development without having recourse to Nardi's researches. At the same time, we should not be blind to the limitations of his scholarship, beginning with his personal biases, his love of polemic, his unacknowledged shifts in opinion, his deafness to poetry, and, most notoriously, his failure to account for the contradictory nature of some of his claims. Thus, as regards creation, Nardi presented Dante as orthodoxly Christian, as sympathetic to Avicennian emanation, and as tinged by Averroism — all positions the poet is supposed to have held in the *Commedia*. Corti, in her turn, was profoundly affected by her discovery of the *modistae* and radical Aristotelian circles in Paris and Bologna, so that it is not unfair to say — because it can be, and has been, documented — that her enthusiasm clouded her customary philological caution.

110 See, for instance, Boethius of Dacia, *De aeternitate mundi* 335–36. 1–27 and 364–66. 805–60, in *Opera. Topica-Opuscula*. VI.ii. *De aeternitate mundi; De summo bono; De somniis*, ed. by Nicolaus Georgius Green-Pedersen (Copenhagen: Gad, 1976). Fernand Van Steenberghen writes about Siger of Brabant: 'chaque fois qu'il expose une doctrine contraire au dogme chrétien, il déclare que, conformément à son rôle de professeur de philosophie, il présente les opinions d'Aristote et des autres philosophes, sans prétendre qu'elles soient vraies. Au contraire, il laisse entendre que ces opinions sont erronées dans la mesure où elles sont contredites par les enseignements de la foi, lesquels sont toujours vrais': *Maître Siger de Brabant* (Louvain and Paris: Publications Universitaires and Vander-Oyez, 1977), p. 232.

111 Dantists should also take note of the fact that 'La critica recente ha infatti chiarito che dal 1270 in avanti vennero chiamati *averroistae* i difensori di una *molteplicità* di tesi filosofiche' (Bianchi, 'L'averroismo di Dante', pp. 75–76).

At the same time, the neo-Averroists were not a homogenous movement, but individuals who reacted personally, and so differently, to Averroes's teachings, a fact that is confirmed by the imprecision and elasticity in the late-medieval culture of the term 'Averroist'.[112] Thus, if we wish to argue for their influence on Dante, we need to demonstrate his ties to specific figures. Yet, despite the far from infrequent references in Dante scholarship to the significance of medieval Averroism for the poet, such detailed work is largely missing. This is true even as regards Siger of Brabant,[113] the only unquestionably Averroistic *magister* whom Dante mentions:

> Questi onde a me ritorna il tuo riguardo,
> è 'l lume d'uno spirto che 'n pensieri
> gravi a morir li parve venir tardo:
>   essa è la luce etterna di Sigieri,
> che, leggendo nel Vico de li Strami,
> silogizzò invidïosi veri. (*Par.* x. 133–38)

The presentation of Siger and his presence in Paradise are suggestive and potentially problematic, especially as the philosopher was formally summoned to appear before the inquisitor of France, Simon du Val, in 1276 to account for his errors and thirty of the articles censured by Bishop Tempier in 1277 apparently relate to his opinions. At first sight, the beatification of Siger would point to Dante's sympathy for the philosopher, and, by extension, for his unconventional views. However, in reality, matters are rather more complex and indefinite. First and foremost, the lines cannot be taken as evidence that Dante had firsthand knowledge of any of Siger's writings; or even that he was aware that some of the philosopher's positions were unconventional.[114] Instead, we have a portrait of an intense, troubled, and powerful intellect (*Par.* x. 134–35 & 138), a master of arts at the University of Paris (137) who 'commenting' (*leggere*) — presumably on the works of Aristotle — employed dialectical methods (*silogizzare*)[115] to arrive at 'truths' which, as is not unusual in

112 For an excellent survey of the scholarship on medieval Averroism, which highlights how historians of ideas have been uncovering a highly complex and individuated reality, see Valeria Sorge, *Profili dell'averroismo bolognese: metafisica e scienza in Taddeo di Parma* (Naples: Luciano, 2001), pp. 13–38. See also Libera, 'Introduction'; Dag N. Hasse, ' "Averroica secta": Notes on the Formation of Averroist Movements in Fourteenth-century Bologna and Renaissance Italy', in *Averroès et les averroïsmes juif et latin*, ed. by Jean-Baptiste Brenet (Turnhout: Brepols, 2007), pp. 307–31.

113 However, see Luca Bianchi's excellent 'A "Heterodox" in Paradise?' cited at n. 96. Although our emphases are different, our essential conclusions regarding Dante's treatment of Siger are close; as are our views regarding how problems of 'unorthodoxy' in general and of the poet's connections to supposedly heterodox traditions in particular, with 'Averroism' to the fore, have been addressed by Dantists.

114 Bianchi, 'A "Heterodox" in Paradise?", pp. 80–81, refers to recent research that has documented the extremely limited presence of neo-Averroistic writings, including Siger's *De anima intellectiva* and *De causis*, in Bolognese and Paduan circles with which Dante may possibly have had some contact. There is, however, no evidence that the poet had access to the library of Tommaso d'Arezzo or that of Antonio da Parma.

115 It has been noted that 'Siger était un bon logicien' (Libera, p. 45). In light of this, to argue from Dante's use of the verb *silogizzare* that the poet must have had firsthand knowledge of Siger's work would be excessive. *Silogizzare* is what masters of arts did as a matter of course; see Lino Pertile, 'Sigieri e l'invidiosa sapienza di Salomone', *Studi e problemi di critica testuale*, 90:1 (2015), 241–56 (pp. 243–46).

academic circles, created resentments among his less able colleagues (137–38).[116] Naturally, the emphasis on 'pensieri | gravi' might imply that Dante was hinting at Siger's interest in unorthodox ideas which brought about such a serious crisis in him that death appeared as the only way of resolving it. Yet, Siger must have overcome his despair, otherwise he would not be an 'eternal light'; and his 'veri', for the same reason, cannot relate to issues that challenged Christian dogma.

Nonetheless, given the allusiveness of Dante's description, we need to tread carefully when maintaining that the poet was aware of Siger's intellectual biography and especially of his heterodoxy. Indeed, the medieval context encourages such caution. Although it is a commonplace in Dante criticism to state that Thomas and Siger were adversaries on earth who are reconciled in eternity,[117] Thomas never referred to his opponent by name.[118] On the other hand, in his *De anima intellectiva*, Siger did respectfully mention Aquinas, together with Albertus Magnus:

> Per quem autem modum anima intellectiva sit unita corpori, et separata ab eodem, dicunt praecipui viri in philosophia Albertus et Thomas quod substantia animae intellectivae unita est corpori dans esse eidem, sed potentia animae intellectivae separata est a corpore, cum per organum corporeum non operetur.[119]

> [By what means moreover the intellective soul is united to the body, and separated from it, the pre-eminent experts in philosophy Albert and Thomas state that the substance of the intellective soul is united to the body because it gives to it being, but the power of the intellective soul is separated from the body, since it does not function through a corporeal organ.]

(Dante's knowledge of this *opusculum* has not been established.)[120] The *De anima*

---

116 Luca Bianchi suggestively relates the epithet *invidiosi* to late thirteenth-century Parisian philosophical complaints about intellectual harassment triggered by envy: 'A "Heterodox" in Paradise?', pp. 93–99. See also Pertile, 'Sigieri e l'invidiosa sapienza di Salomone', pp. 250–55.

117 On Dante and Siger, see at least Francesco Bausi, *Dante fra scienza e sapienza: esegesi del canto XII del 'Paradiso'* (Florence: Olschki, 2009), pp. 215–27 ; Bryan Brazeau, ' "I fight auctoritas, auctoritas always wins": Siger of Brabant, *Paradiso* x and Dante's Textual Authority', in Ardizzone, pp. 106–25; M. B. Crowe, '*Paradiso* x: Siger of Brabant', in *Dante Soundings: Eight Literary and Historical Essays*, ed. by David Nolan (Dublin: Irish Academic Press, 1981), pp. 146–63; Peter Dronke, *Dante and Medieval Latin Traditions* (Cambridge: Cambridge University Press, 1986), pp. 96–100; Kenelm Foster, *The Two Dantes and Other Studies* (Berkeley and Los Angeles: University of California Press, 1977), pp. 135–36; Ruedi Imbach, *Dante, la philosophie et les laïcs* (Fribourg: Editions Universitaires, 1996), pp. 141–48; Bruno Nardi, *Sigieri di Brabante nella 'Divina Commedia'* (Spianate [Pescia]: Presso l'Autore, 1912); Antonio Petagine, 'L'elogio di Dante', in Sigieri di Brabante, *Anima dell'uomo* (Milan: Bompiani, 2007), pp. 355–59 ; Salomon Reinach, 'L'enigme de Siger', *Revue historique*, 151 (1926), 34–47; John A. Scott, 'Il Sigieri dantesco rivisitato', *Letteratura italiana antica*, 9 (2008), 193–217; Giampiero Tulone, 'Gli "invidïosi veri" nella *Commedia* e nelle fonti dantesche', *Lettere italiane*, 52 (2000), 345–78; Marco Veglia, 'Per un'ardita umiltà: l'averroismo di Dante tra Guido Cavalcanti, Sigieri di Brabante e San Francesco d'Assisi', *Schede umanistiche*, n.s. 1 (2000), 67–106, and 'Da Sigieri al "venerabile Bernardo": su *Par.* X–XI', *Studi danteschi*, 68 (2003), 113–29.

118 Bonaventure, too, in his anti-Averroistic writings, does not mention Siger.

119 *De anima intellectiva* III (p. 81, ll. 78–82; and see also ll. 83–95), in Siger de Brabant, *Questiones in tertium de anima; De anima intellectiva; De aeternitate mundi*, ed. by Bernardo Bazán (Louvain and Paris: Publications Universitaires and Béatrice–Nauwelaerts, 1972).

120 Maria Corti makes much of the fact that Siger broke off the *De anima intellectiva* with the

intellectiva, however, is not a polemical work but a careful response to Thomas's *De unitate intellectus contra averroistas*. It represents in fact an important moment in Siger's fluctuating accommodation to orthodoxy, in which he departs from Averroes's interpretation of a single separate intellect, admits the failure of philosophy to deal with the question, and submits to the authority of faith (see especially chapter 7, p. 108). Furthermore, nowhere in his *œuvre*, does Dante offer even a hint that he was aware of Bishop Tempier and his condemnations; and even if he had known about the censures, it is almost certain that he would not have necessarily associated the errors with Siger, since only one manuscript of the 1277 condemnation, Paris BN lat. 4391, fol. 68, introduces the 219 errors as 'contra Segerum et Boetium hereticos' [against the heretics Siger and Boethius].[121] Indeed, explicit contemporary references to Siger as a heterodox thinker are rare. In addition to the annotation just quoted below, there is one mention in a chronicle of 1320 (quoted on pp. 126–27); another in a manuscript of Ramon Llull;[122] and in two out of the over fifty extant manuscripts

following phrase: 'Sed qualiter tunc debeat intelligi quod scientia est qualitas de prima specie qualitatis in praedicamentis, vigiles et studeas atque legas, ut ex hoc dubio tibi remanente exciteris ad studendum et legendum, *cum vivere sine litteris mors sit et vilis hominis sepultura*' [But then just as one ought to understand that science is a quality of the first species among categories of quality, you be vigilant, and study and read, so that, by the doubt that remains in you, you are roused to study and read, *since to live without study is death and an unworthy tomb for a man*] (p. 112; my emphasis). Corti considers the emphasized phrase as evidence that Dante had read the *De anima intellectiva* — 'Dante sapeva bene di cosa stava parlando' — by deeming the phrase 'a morir li parve venir tardo' (*Par.* x. 135) a reference to Siger's words: Maria Corti, *Dante a un nuovo crocevia* (Florence: Libreria Commissionaria Sansoni, 1981), p. 98. This is most unlikely. Not only are the contexts very different, but the phrase itself, rather than a heartfelt personal 'testamentario intellettuale' (100), is a wellworn and longstanding Scriptural and classical commonplace; see Chapter 15, pp. 494 and 507–15; Alfonso Maierù, 'Dante al crocevia', *Studi medievali*, 24 (1983), 735–48. Siger's formulation is in fact close to the most influential classical version of the saying. Offering advice to Lucilius on how best to lead his life, Seneca noted: 'Deinde idem delicati timent, [mors] cui vitam suam fecere similem. [...] Puto, aeque qui in odoribus iacet mortuus est quam qui rapitur unco; *otium sine litteris mors est et hominis vivi sepultura*' [Next the voluptuaries fear the very thing [death] to which they have likened their life. [...] One who lies covered in perfumes, I think, is as dead as one who is dragged by the hook; *leisure without study is death and a burial of man alive*]: Lucius Anneus Seneca, *Epistulae morales ad Lucilium*, ed. by Leighton Durham Reynolds (Oxford: Oxford University Press, 1965), LXXXII. 2–3 (my emphasis; and compare *Conv.* IV. 7. 11–12). It saddens me to conclude that most of Corti's short presentation of Siger's career and Dante's reactions to him is exaggerated, imprecise, and incorrect (pp. 98–101). In 'A "Heterodox" in Paradise?', Luca Bianchi too is critical of Corti's work, including her discussion of the *De anima intellectiva* (pp. 80 and 82); see also his 'L'averroismo di Dante', pp. 85–86.

121 Thijssen, p. 139. The thirty articles associated with Siger condemned in 1277 are a modern reconstruction and are not linked to him in the original document.

122 'Raymond Lulle prend le parti de Tempier dans un ouvrage intitulé "Declaratio per modum dialogi edita contra aliquorum philosophorum et eorum sequacium opiniones erroneas et damnatas a Venerabili Patre Domino Episcopo Parisiensi." [Exposition in the form of a dialogue against the false beliefs — which have been condemned by the Venerable Father and Master Bishop of Paris — of some philosophers and their followers] Dans le catalogue des œuvres de Raymond Lulle (Paris, Bibl. Nat. fonds lat. 16.533 f. 60) de 1311 cet ouvrage est intitulé "Liber contra errores Boetii et Sigerii" [The book against the errors of Boethius and Siger]': Severinus Skovgaard Jensen, 'Introduction', in Boethius of Dacia, *Opera. Modi significandi sive Quaestiones super Priscianum maiorem*, ed. by Severinus Skovgaard Jensen (Copenhagen: Gad, 1969), pp. ix–xxxix (p. xxxi).

of Thomas's *De unitate intellectus*.[123] None of the early Dante commentators, except for the author of the so-called *Chiose Vernon*, dated to around 1390, who terms him 'infedele', makes any mention of Siger's unorthodoxy. The *Chiose cagliaritane* go so far as to describe him as a 'grandissimo sancto maestro'.[124] One very simple reason as to why Siger was not generally considered a controversial figure in the Middle Ages is that, as now seems reasonable to surmise, since no documentary evidence of a conviction for heresy exists, he was acquitted of the charges laid against him by the inquisitor.[125] But what of the reference to Siger in the *Fiore*?

> Mastro Sighier non andò guari lieto:
> A ghiado il fe' morire a gran dolore
> Nella corte di Roma, ad Orbivieto. (*Fiore* XCII. 9–11)

Even if the *poemetto* is not by Dante, it surely reveals that, in the mid 1280s, news of Siger's violent death, and so about his flight from Paris in late November 1276 to plead his case before Pope John XXI after Simon du Val had issued summons against him, was circulating in Florence? The first assumption is certainly not unreasonable. As regards the second, there is absolutely no trace in what Falsembiante says that Siger had abandoned Paris and was in Orvieto on account of his questionable opinions. If the author of the *Fiore* had known this, given his well-known anti-French views and his particular animus against the theologians at the university (XCII. 12–14 and XCII. 5–8), it is not unlikely that he would have mentioned it, just as he did William of St Amour's treatment:

> Mastro Guglielmo, il buon di Sant'Amore,
> Fec'i' di Francia metter in divieto
> E sbandir del reame a gran romore. (*Fiore* XCII. 12–14)

In fact, what is rarely appreciated is that, if the first mention of Siger being in Italy is found in the *Fiore*, the earliest reference that he had fled Paris because his views had been 'confuted' appears *c*. 1320:

> Hujus tempore floruit Albertus, de ordine Praedicatorum, qui multa scripsit praeclare de theologia, qui magistrum Sygerum in scriptis suis multum rearguit. Qui Sygerus, natione Brabantinus, eo quod quasdam opiniones contra fidem

---

123 In ms. Munich, Bayerische Staatsbibliothek, Clm 8001, end of thirteenth century, at fol. 29r the title is given as 'Tractatus fratris Thome contra magistrum Sogerum.de vnitate intellectus' [Friar Thomas's treatise against master Siger on the unity of the intellect]; while in ms. Oxford, Corpus Christi College 225, fourteenth century, at fol. 67v the colophon states: 'Hec scripsit tl'r [Thomas] contra magistrum sig'md' de barbantia et alios plurimos parisius in philosophia regentes anno domini m°.cc°.70' [This work was written by Thomas against master Siger of Brabant and many other professors in philosophy in Paris in the year of Our Lord 1270].

124 Quotations are taken from the texts uploaded to the invaluable Dartmouth Dante Project. My conclusion regarding the commentators' view of Siger is also based on the same source. The following commentators and commentaries make no allusion to his holding 'opiniones contra fidem': Jacopo della Lana, the Ottimo, Pietro Alighieri, *Chiose ambrosiane*, *Chiose cagliaritane*, Benvenuto da Imola, Francesco da Buti, Anonimo fiorentino, and Giovanni da Serravalle.

125 René-Antoine Gauthier, 'Notes sur Siger de Brabant. II. Siger en 1272–1275. Aubry de Reims et la scission des Normands', *Revue des sciences philosophiques et théologiques*, 68 (1984), 3–49 (pp. 26–28); Thijssen, p. 48.

tenuerat, Parisius subsistere non valens, Romanam curiam adiit, ibique post parvum tempus a clerico suo quasi dementi perfossus periit.[126]

[At that time came to excel Albertus, from the order of the Preachers, who wrote brilliantly and extensively on theology, and argued strongly against master Siger in his writings. Siger who, originally from Brabant, for the fact that he had held certain beliefs against the faith, and could no longer be a Parisian, fled to the Roman curia, and here after a little time was stabbed to death by one of the clergy who was quite out of his mind.]

The reliability of this account, given the erroneous indication of Albertus Magnus and of the amount of time that elapsed between Siger's supposed departure (late 1276) and murder (between 1281 and 1284), is suspect. Indeed, one cannot but wonder at the extent of the reliability of the information provided in the *Fiore*, since its source is the deceitful Falsembiante. Thus, it comes as little surprise that recent research has seriously called into question Siger's flight to the papal court and his appeal.[127]

What is clear from my presentation — which is quite different in its focus from the version of Siger's career that holds sway in Dante studies — is that, in line with medieval *communis opinio*, it is most unlikely that the poet would have deemed the philosopher a heretical thinker.[128] The question thus arises of the implications of Siger's presence in the Heaven of the Sun. I believe that, in broad terms, these are relatively straightforward. The conflicts between the masters of theology and of philosophy, especially in Paris, were widely known. In keeping with the spirit of intellectual harmony that marks his presentation of the inhabitants of the fourth heaven, Dante was emblematically bringing together an exemplary teacher from each faculty, namely, Thomas and Siger, hence the precise reference to the 'Vico de li Strami' (*Par.* x. 137) where the philosophers taught at the university of Paris, in order to place a seal on the otherworldly reconciliation of the once litigious academics. In order properly to assess Dante's intellectual sympathies and to define the syncretic nature of his attitude to the medieval world of ideas, an in-depth study of *Paradiso* x–xiv, which I do not have the space to undertake here, would be necessary.[129] At the same time, on the basis of the figures Dante does introduce, it is extremely unlikely that any of them would disturb my basic contention regarding the fundamental ideological orthodoxy of the *Commedia*. And I most certainly include Joachim of Fiore in this assertion. Given the contradictory reaction to and the wealth of conflicting information circulating about him in the Middle Ages, much more research needs to be done before we can state with a degree of certainty

---

126 *Continuationes chronici Martini Oppaviensis: Continuationes Brabantina*, ed. by Ludwig Weiland, in *Monumenta Germaniae Historica. Scriptores*, vol. XXIV (1879), pp. 259–65.

127 Gauthier, pp. 26–28; Thijssen, pp. 46–48. If Siger had not fled to Orvieto, why was he there at some point during the first half of the 1280s? Louis-Jacques Bataillon, 'Bulletin d'histoire des doctrines médiévales: le treizième siècle (fin)', *Revue des sciences philosophiques et théologiques*, 65 (1981), 101–22 (p. 107), argues that he was there on business relating to his chapter. That the *Fiore*'s 'Sighier' is indeed Siger of Brabant appears to be confirmed by his being termed a 'gra·litterato' (XCII. 6).

128 See also Bianchi, 'A "Heterodox" in Paradise?', pp. 89–90; Davide Canfora, 'Sul canto x del *Paradiso*', *L'Alighieri*, 50 (2009), 65–80 (p. 80).

129 For the present, see Bausi; Bianchi, 'A "Heterodox" in Paradise?'.

what Dante's attitude towards the Abbot and his views may have been.[130] Like many of his contemporaries, in the *Paradiso*, Dante too accepts Joachim's prophetic powers: 'il calavrese abate Giovacchino | di spirito profetico dotato' (*Par.* XII. 140–41). The phrase describing Joachim's divine gift, translates verbatim a section of the liturgy, the Antiphon to Vespers, with which his order would commemorate him. Tellingly, since Dante appears to have known the text, the Antiphon goes on to affirm that 'blessed Joachim' was 'far from heretical error': 'Beatus Joachim, spiritu dotatus prophetico, decoratus intelligentia errore procul haeretico, dixit futura et praesentia' [Blessed Joachim, endowed with prophetic spirit, adorned with intelligence far from heretical error, spoke about future and present things].[131] Equally, although there is little doubt that Dante had some sympathy for Spiritual positions, only the most extreme of which were officially condemned, he was careful to distance himself from the radicalism of Ubertino da Casale, and to align himself with Bonaventure's moderate Franciscanism:

> Ben dico, chi cercasse a foglio a foglio
> nostro volume, ancor troveria carta
> u' leggerebbe 'I' mi son quel ch'i' soglio;'
>   ma non fia da Casal né d'Acquasparta,
>   là onde vegnon tali a la scrittura,
>   ch'uno la fugge e altro la coarta. (*Par.* XII. 121–26)[132]

In any case, as with Joachim, and as with several of the other figures and intellectual traditions that make an appearance in the Heaven of the Sun, considerably more philological research needs to be done before we can begin to have a sense of Dante's (and the medieval world's) standpoint on them.

A probable general reason why the poet associated Thomas and Siger was to underscore his belief that theology and philosophy, and so faith and reason, were not in opposition. Indeed, in *Paradiso* XXIX, Beatrice reiterates this point:

> ma questo vero [the creation of the angels] è
>   scritto in molti lati
>   da li scrittor de lo Spirito Santo,

130 For an excellent presentation of Joachim's medieval reception, see Marjorie Reeves, *The Influence of Prophecy in the Later Middle Ages: A Study in Joachimism* (Notre Dame, IN, and London: University of Notre Dame Press, 1993), pp. 3–132.
131 *Commentarius Praevius* I. 3, in *Acta Sanctorum*, vol. VII, p. 90.
132 On the variety of medieval reaction, including that of the Church, to the Franciscans and Dante's relationship to medieval Franciscanism, see Nicholas R. Havely, *Dante and the Franciscans: Poverty and the Papacy in the 'Commedia'* (Cambridge: Cambridge University Press, 2004). On Dante and Ubertino, see Davide Bolognese, '"Et miror si iam non est": l'*Arbor vitae* di Ubertino da Casale nella *Commedia*', *Dante Studies*, 126 (2008), 57–88. Among Dantists, Ubertino is frequently associated with his teacher Peter John Olivi, with whom he came into contact at Santa Croce. On their time in Florence, see Antonio Montefusco, 'Autoritratto del dissidente da giovane: gli anni della formazione di Ubertino da Casale nel primo Prologo dell'*Arbor Vitae*', in *Ubertino da Casale: Atti del XLI Convegno internazionale: Assisi, 18–20 ottobre 2013* (Spoleto: CISAM, 2014), pp. 27–81. On Dante and Peter John Olivi, see Alberto Forni, 'Pietro di Giovanni Olivi e Dante: un progetto di ricerca', *Collectanea Franciscana*, 82 (2012), 87–156, which, however, should be read with Antonio Montefusco, 'Segnalazione del sito web di Alberto Forni', *Oliviana*, 4 (2012), available at <http://oliviana.revues. org/599> [accessed 12 August 2019].

> e tu te n'avvedrai se bene agguati;
>
> e anche la ragione il vede alquanto. (*Par.* XXIX. 40–43)

In asserting as much, Dante was upholding an idea that was deeply rooted in Christian thought: reason, as long as it recognized both its boundaries, as that delimitative 'alquanto' declares, and its subordination to revelation, then, it could have an important supporting role to play in human life, especially as its origins are divine.[133] Reason — and by extension philosophy, the exercise of the human intellect — only became problematic when it was deemed to be self-sufficient and its focus was restricted solely to contingent and earthly matters with little or no concern for the transcendent. In the *Commedia*, Dante provides several examples of those who, 'presumptuously' or to gain material advantage or for reasons of expediency, misdirect and overestimate their rational faculties: from the heretics to Ulysses and from the Decretalists to those who are not 'content' to curb their speculations to the '*quia*' (*Purg.* III. 37). Human reason, and hence the knowledge and satisfaction this can provide, is extremely limited, especially when faced by the divine, as, pointedly, Virgil admits, since true knowledge can only come through Christ:

> Matto è chi spera che nostra ragione
>
> possa trascorrer la infinita via
>
> che tiene una sustanza in tre persone.
>
> State contenti, umana gente, al quia;
>
> ché, se potuto aveste veder tutto,
>
> mestier non era parturir Maria. (*Purg.* III. 34–39)

As the earlier discussion of *Conv.* III. 15 had made evident, this had been Dante's position in the 'almost commentary' too. Admittedly, there, the function of the Incarnation and revelation are left substantially implicit. However, by the close of Book III, Christ's fundamental role and the inadequacy of reason had already been definitively established in the treatise, and, tellingly, in connection with a matter of the highest import: 'la immortalità dell'anima' (II. 8. 7), a reality which, even if affirmed by 'tutte le scritture, sì de' filosofi come delli altri savi scrittori' (8), 'noi non potemo perfettamente vedere mentre che 'l nostro immortale col mortale è mischiato; ma vedemola per fede perfettamente, e per ragione la vedemo con ombra d'oscuritade' (15). The close of this passage is in perfect harmony with Beatrice's declaration in *Par.* XXIX. 40–43. Indeed, it accurately distills Dante's steadfast view on the relationship between faith and reason. And, with dutiful precision, the poet had orthodoxly established what he meant by *fede* in the preceding paragraph: 'la

---

133 See, for instance, Fernand Brunner, 'Philosophie et religion ou l'ambiguité de la philosophie', in *Historia philosophiae medii aevi: Studien zur Geschichte der Philosophie des Mittelalters*, ed. by Burkhard Mojsisch and Olaf Pluta, 2 vols (Amsterdam and Philadelphia: Grüner, 1991), I, 129–44; Chenu, *La Théologie comme science*; Edward Grant, *God and Reason in the Middle Ages* (Cambridge: Cambridge University Press, 2001); Toivo Holopainen, *Dialectic and Theology in the Eleventh Century* (Leiden: Brill, 1996); Joseph W. Koterski, *Medieval Philosophy: Basic Concepts* (Malden, MA, and Oxford: Wiley-Blackwell, 2009), pp. 9–36. However, see also Gerard Verbeke, 'Philosophy and Heresy: Some Conflicts between Reason and Faith', in Lourdaux and Verhelst, pp. 172–97. See also Alexander Murray, *Reason and Society in the Middle Ages* (Oxford: Clarendon Press, 1985).

dottrina veracissima di Cristo, la quale è via, veritade e luce: via, perché per essa sanza impedimento andiamo alla felicitade di quella immortalitate; veritade, perché non soffera alcuno errore; luce, perché allumina noi nella tenebra della ignoranza mondana' (14).

Certainly, the emphases of the *Convivio* and of the *Commedia* are not always the same, including as regards the efficacy of human reason; while Christ and revelation play a less prominent role in the former than in the latter. However, the controlling ideological purview in both works is that of a conformist medieval Christian. Philosophy, as might be expected from the heavily Aristotelian character of the *Convivio*, is granted an important status. Yet, as recent research has shown, *documenti alla mano*, the treatise is far from that Aristotelian monolith that some used to maintain (and others doggedly still do). As a result, the notion of philosophy in the commentary is unstable and fluid, its contours in a state of flux. It is not narrowly equivalent to the dialectical and demonstrative study of the *ordo naturalis*, as it would have been in rigorist Aristotelian circles.[134] Dante's *Filosofia* — the editorial oscillation between capitalization and non-capitalization is an immediate mark of the term's semantic breadth — brings together ethical, erotic, Scriptural, divine, and contemplative associations.[135] Until such time as we have a study which thoroughly explores the term's different and connotatively stratified applications in the *Convivio*,[136] as well as its ties to closely related notions such as *Sapienza*, *scienza*, *veritade*, *ragione*, and, of course, *Dio*, we should try to refrain from making easy assumptions about its, and hence the treatise's laicizing values, which, in any case, in the wake especially of Vasoli's, of Dronke's, and of Nasti's work, are unquestionably religiously imprinted and orthodoxly circumscribed.[137] At the same time, the celebration of *Filosofia*, and by extension of the working of the human intellect, is more forceful in the *Convivio* than in the *Commedia*. Thus, if on the one hand, the intellectual 'sciences' are subordinated to an affective all-encompassing theology (see the previous chapter), on the other, Dante pushes philosophy as close as he can to the sphere of faith, so that it can offer meaningful support to the former:

---

134 'Col nome di Filosofia dal secolo XIII al XVI s'intese il compatto e organico sistema di dottrine di Aristotele intorno alla natura e composizione del mondo, alle sue cause e alle sue finalità': Bruno Nardi, 'Filosofia e teologia ai tempi di Dante', in *Atti del Congresso Internazionale di Studi Danteschi*, 2 vols (Florence: Le Monnier, 1965–66), I, 79–175 (p. 79).

135 See Dronke, *Dante's Second Love*; Moevs, *The Metaphysics of Dante's 'Comedy'*, p. 85; Paola Nasti, *Favole d'amore e 'saver profondo': la tradizione salomonica in Dante* (Ravenna: Longo, 2007), pp. 93–130; Vasoli's annotations to the *Convivio*. It is unlikely that anyone would now write, as Kenelm Foster did in the 1970s that, in the *Convivio*, 'the two components, the philosophical and the Christian are merely juxtaposed' (p. 246).

136 For the present see Moevs, 'The Metaphysical Basis of Dante's Politics', pp. 229–30, and *The Metaphysics of Dante's 'Comedy'*, pp. 82–90; Vincenzo Placella, 'Filosofia', in *ED*, II, 881–85. See also Imbach.

137 See also Zygmunt G. Barański, '"Oh come è grande la mia impresa" (*Conv.* IV. vii. 4): Notes Towards Defining the *Convivio*', in *Dante's 'Convivio' or, How to Restart Writing in Exile*, ed. by Franziska Meier (Bern: Peter Lang, 2018), pp. 9–26; Nicolò Maldina, 'Raccogliendo briciole: una metafora della formazione dantesca tra *Convivio* e *Commedia*', *Studi danteschi*, 81 (2016), 131–64.

Onde, sì come per lei molto di quello si vede per ragione, e per consequente *si vede poter essere*, che sanza lei pare maraviglia, così per lei si crede ogni miracolo in più alto intelletto pote[r] avere ragione, e per consequente pote[r] essere. Onde la nostra buona fede ha sua origine; dal[la] quale viene la speranza, ch'è 'l proveduto desiderare; e per quella nasce l'operazione della caritade. (*Conv.* III. 14. 14; and see also III. 8. 5; 15. 2–3, 5–6, 15–16)

Dante's positions at the close of chapter 14 of Book III could not be further from those of philosophers following closely in Averroes's wake. Thus, the poet's belief that philosophy can provide confirmation of the miraculous runs directly counter to the view widely held among the *philosophi* that this was just not possible — a view that Siger pithily summarized as 'Sed nihil ad nos nunc de Dei miraculis, cum de naturalibus naturaliter disseramus' [But we are not concerned with God's miracles, when we examine the things of nature according to the principles of nature].[138] Dante never portrays philosophy as in any way creating problems for theology or the divine. Indeed, as we have just seen, *Filosofia* is closely and harmoniously associated with God ('E dico che nello suo aspetto appariscono cose le quali dimostrano de' piaceri *di Paradiso*', III. 8. 5), a view which challenges contemporary controversies regarding the relative standing of and the inter-relationship between theological and philosophical knowledge.[139] Consequently, one way of reading the *Convivio* is as a work which confirms how the proper exercise of reason not only leads to intellectual and ethical improvement but also to insights about the transcendent. Indeed, the stamp of the theological virtues is discernible in the treatise. The purpose of the work is charitable: 'intendo fare un generale convivio' (I. 1. 11).[140] Unlike the *philosophi*, who considered their discipline to be the preserve of an elite, for Dante it was potentially accessible to everyone: 'Ed essa Filosofia non solamente alberga [... alberga] non pur nelli sapienti, ma eziandio, come provato è di sopra in altro trattato, essa è dovunque alberga l'amore di quella' (IV. 30. 5).[141] And the *Convivio* is a means to enflame that love.

---

138 Siger, *De anima intellectiva* III (p. 84, ll. 47–48); and compare Albertus Magnus, *De generatione et corruptione* I. 1. 22; Boethius of Dacia, *De aeternitate mundi* 335–36. 1–27 and 364. 805–09. See also Bruno Nardi, *Dal 'Convivio' alla 'Commedia'* (Rome: Alla sede dell'Istituto, 1960), pp. 64–67.

139 See Luca Bianchi, *Pour une histoire de la 'double vérité'* (Paris: Vrin, 2008).

140 See Barański, '"Oh come è grande la mia impresa"'.

141 See Boethius of Dacia, *De summo bono* 373. 111–12. Boethius does somewhat temper his position in the *opusculum*'s close (377. 226–44), where, in a precautionary move, he also gives his strongly 'humanistic' argument a conventional final religious flourish. See also Bianchi, *Il vescovo e i filosofi*, pp. 149–95, 'La felicità intellettuale come professione nella Parigi del Duecento', *Rivista di filosofia*, 78 (1987), 181–99, and 'Filosofi, uomini e bruti: note per la storia di un'antropologia "averroista"', *Rinascimento*, 32 (1992), 185–201 (Bianchi usefully stresses the intricate transmission of the idea of philosophical superiority, including Albertus Magnus's key role in its dissemination, and the fact that, ultimately, it was not as elitist a notion as some formulations might suggest. As far as I am aware, the extent to which Dante might have been aware of the complex history of the idea and its ramifications has not even begun to be considered by Dante studies); Gianfranco Fioravanti, 'Desiderio di sapere e vita filosofica nelle *Questioni sulla Metafisica* del ms. 1386 Universitätsbibliothek Leipzig', in Mojsisch and Pluta, I, 271–83.

6. Conclusion

I'm far from certain that this chapter merits a conclusion. The argument it develops, probably at too great a length, is straightforward: throughout his career, Dante's fundamental and controlling intellectual premises conformed to the tenets of the faith.[142] His acceptance of religious orthodoxy was anything but a restriction, not least because his cultural context granted an 'independent' artist-intellectual such as him not inconsiderable room in which to manoeuvre. His philosophical and theological interests ranged widely. Indeed, one point on which most of us who have studied Dante's thought and intellectual development can agree is that he cannot be associated with any single ideological current. As Cacciaguida acknowledged, Dante was his own man politically. However, morally, intellectually, and, of course, poetically he also made 'parte per se stesso' (*Par.* XVII. 69). Dante was a great syncretist; and only in recent years have we begun to appreciate the rich ideological and artistic implications of his synthesizing eclecticism.[143] There is much that still needs to be done in this regard. Nonetheless, I am confident of one thing: Dante's syncretism needs to be understood, in the first instance, in terms of his faith. More specifically, his 'encyclopaedism' is closely tied to his firm belief that Truth resides solely in God, while here on earth, on account of our limitations — of the mind, of the body, of temporality — we can at best glimpse a multitude of scrappy *veri*. Our responsibility, not unlike that shouldered by the author of the *Convivio*, is to gather together these 'truthful' 'crumbs' in order to try to transcend the fragmentariness of our knowledge and achieve a somewhat fuller intimation, even though this will always amount to no more than an approximation, of the absolute Truth that is God. Dante's loyalty was determinedly to the divine, never to any particular human doctrine. This is one reason why all his major works, beginning with the *Vita nova* — and if it is in fact his, already as early as the *Fiore* — are works of wide-ranging synthesis.

In positing two determining constants for Dante's entire career — religious orthodoxy and artistic-cum-intellectual fusion produced by a powerful experimental energy — am I not essentially rehearsing a variation on the old flawed idea of the poet's coherently evolving progress? My perspective is most decidedly not evolutionary. In any case, we should not forget that this is the image that, across his *œuvre*, was first carefully and consistently constructed by the poet himself. To put it bluntly, it is an idealized fiction, which fits in well with the conventions of the *vitae* of great men, whether lay or religious. My point is rather different. Dante's development is profoundly, at times contradictorily, marked by change — change brought about by external events and by personal variations in interests,

---

142 In the past, I accepted, if not especially forcefully, that the *Convivio* represented a rationalizing 'break' in Dante's intellectual development. I was wrong; and this study explains why I was wrong.
143 See at least Simon Gilson, 'Medieval Science in Dante's *Commedia*: Past Approaches and Future Directions', *Reading Medieval Studies*, 27 (2001), 39–77, 'Rimaneggiamenti danteschi di Aristotele: *gravitas* e *levitas* nella *Commedia*', in Picone and others, pp. 151–77, 'Dante and Christian Arstotelianism', in Honess and Treherne, I, 65–109, and 'Sincretismo e scolastica in Dante', *Studi e problemi di critica testuale*, 90:1 (2015), 317–39; Giuseppe Mazzotta, *Dante's Vision and the Circle of Knowledge* (Princeton: Princeton University Press, 1993).

understanding, learning, taste, and sympathies. It is not neatly progressive. As Paolo Falzone has somewhat dryly, though not incorrectly, put it, the poet's texts record 'le asimmetrie del pensiero dantesco'.[144] Yet, I believe, for all the 'asymmetries', which are unquestionably not the same as unorthodoxies or even contradictions, Dante ensured that his shifts were always controlled by a deepseated and, one can only assume, genuine adherence to and belief in the tenets of medieval Catholicism. This is, at least, what I have increasingly, in the last fifteen or so years, found when reading his works; and it is his texts that have to provide the basis for any account of Dante's intellectual and spiritual biography, and for any statement regarding his beliefs. Conversely, what we should not rely on are the compromised self-portraits that Dante paints in and between his works — compromised, first, because normally they are not supported by independent documentary evidence, and, second, because they are subordinated to the needs and structures of the text in which they appear (see Chapter 1). The fact that Beatrice accuses the pilgrim of having betrayed her does not necessarily mean that Dante actually underwent a spiritual and intellectual crisis in life. Her account has to be treated *poetice*. It certainly cannot be used as a yardstick with which to determine the *Convivio*'s ideological make-up. That really would be muddling up art and life! In any case, as Étienne Gilson trenchantly noted over seventy years ago, and as I have attempted to illustrate, 'if Dante really experienced a crisis of pure philosophism, that crisis was over when he wrote the *Banquet*'.[145]

The time is probably overdue for a major reassessment of the *Convivio*'s ideological parameters and its textual identity (and it is reassuring that this is precisely what is happening). Such a re-evaluation will need to begin by recognizing the difficulties and constraints posed by its compromised textual state. For instance, as a rapid glance at Vasoli's notes will confirm, several of the passages which, ever since Nardi and Busnelli locked horns, scholars have used to argue that Dante was expressing support for a particular intellectual position — not infrequently the same passage has been made to bear diametrically opposing views — are, in fact, textually corrupt, and thus should be treated with great caution. Before making significant claims on the basis of such passages, we need to establish what can be confirmed with a degree of certainty about the *Convivio* and what sort of overarching concerns, if any, define and unite it. Given the *Convivio*'s tentative state, we cannot even be certain to what degree the views Dante expressed therein can be taken as definitive or as expressing his actual opinions. He may very well have been exploring and testing different doctrinal possibilities. What the *Convivio* might have contained if Dante had ever prepared a version for publication we shall never know. However, I am willing to hazard one last hypothesis. Indeed, I feel quite relaxed in stating — on the basis of his practice in his other texts — that Dante would have ironed out potential ideological contradictions and incongruities, and that, if he had included elements

144 Falzone, *Desiderio della scienza e desiderio di Dio nel 'Convivio'*, p. 256; the reference is to the *Convivio*, nonetheless, the notion can be usefully extended to Dante's other works and their interconnections.
145 Étienne Gilson, *Dante the Philosopher* (London: Sheed & Ward, 1948), p. 159.

which, at first sight, might seem questionable, he would have offered the means for their orthodox resolution in the pages of the *Convivio* itself.[146]

146 I leave it to readers of this chapter to decide whether or not I claim that 'Dante and radical thought are incompatible', as has been suggested as regards a shortened version of this study; see Teodolinda Barolini, 'Contemporaries Who Found Heterodoxy in Dante, Featuring (But Not Exclusively) Cecco d'Ascoli', in Ardizzone, pp. 259–75 (p. 260). My 'The Temptations of a Heterodox Dante' also appeared in Ardizzone, pp. 164–96.

CHAPTER 4

'Reflecting' on the Divine and on the Human: *Paradiso* XXII

1. Looking and Reading

As is common in adventure and travel narratives, the *Commedia* is organized around moments of passage and transition.[1] In Dante, however, such episodes are not simply stages that 'mechanically' punctuate the course of the journey. Rather, and more significantly, they often function as invitations, both to the pilgrim and to the reader, to reflect on what has already happened so as to prepare for what will happen next — Singleton's famous 'vistas in retrospect'.[2] In such instances, the *viator*'s progress from one otherworldly zone to another represents a quintessentially didactic experience that improves him intellectually, psychologically, and spiritually. Thus, thanks to an overarching backward 'look', he arrives at a fuller understanding of the implications of what God has miraculously established that he should see and hear 'in pro del mondo che mal vive' (*Purg.* XXXII. 103). In the same way, and imitating the *exemplum* of the meditative *viator*, the *lettor* has the obligation, as the poet emphasizes, to reflect on the *Commedia*'s divinely inspired *materia*. It is in the act of reconsidering and synthesizing large narrative, poetic, and ideological blocks, of the dimension of a canto, of an episode, and even of an entire *cantica*,

---

1   Preparing this chapter for publication in the present volume has been difficult. On the one hand, the manner in which I had originally written it in Italian made it difficult to translate into English. To put it bluntly, the register and forms of argumentation of my Zurich *lectura* are too close to academic Italian, something that I normally try to avoid when I write in my mother's language. The present English version, therefore, is more of an adaptation and rewriting of the original than a translation. However, there is another and more substantial reason why the chapter has not been easy to update and adapt. Since its publication, my reading has had an impact on the critical reception of *Paradiso* XXII (see nn. 8, 12, & 13 below). Thus, in general, the criticisms that I made regarding the scholarship on the canto are no longer as pertinent as they were around 2001. Indeed, in recent years, colleagues have been making important new discoveries (especially as regards *Paradiso* XXII's sources) and have been proposing new suggestive interpretive hypotheses. The present version reflects, mostly in the footnotes, these recent scholarly acquisitions, while also maintaining, as best as I could, the logic of the original argument. If I had not done as much, I would have needed to prepare a new *lectura* of the canto. I'm not satisfied with what I've done. There is something unbalanced and 'limping' about this chapter, for which I apologize.

2   Charles S. Singleton, 'The Vistas in Retrospect', in *Atti del Congresso internazionale degli studi danteschi*, 2 vols (Florence: Olschki. 1965–66), I, 279–303. See also Zygmunt G. Barański, '*Sole nuovo, luce nuova': saggi sul rinnovamento culturale in Dante* (Turin: Scriptorium, 1996), pp. 255–79.

that the attentive reader will come to appreciate better the lesson of moral reform and of literary renewal that is at the heart of the 'sacrato poema' (*Par.* XXIII. 62). Moreover, making us aware of the rigorous coherence and order both of the journey and of the *Commedia*, Dante highlights their divine character, as well as his own artistic prowess in 'far manifesta tutta *s*ua visïon' (*Par.* XVII. 128) in imitation of the creative *ordo* of the *Deus artifex*. In this regard, if I may anticipate one of this chapter's conclusions, I believe that, among various interpretive possibilities, the pilgrim who, soon after entering the Starry heaven, looks down at the earth and at the planetary spheres prefigures his later self, in the Empyrean, reading the 'book of the universe' in preparation for when, in his guise as poet, he will come to pen his own text. Creation, in its bookish forms — and by extension the Bible — is the key text that Dante imitates in the *Commedia* (and not Virgil's *Aeneid*, as is still regularly maintained):

> Nel suo profondo vidi che s'interna,
> legato con amore in un volume,
> ciò che per l'universo si squaderna. (*Par.* XXXIII. 85–87)

Paradiso XXII closes dramatically and memorably with the most famous of the *Commedia*'s retrospective looks. Prompted by Beatrice, the pilgrim *ritorna* (133) his gaze down through the first seven spheres of the Ptolemaic universe before finally reaching '[l']aiuola che ci fa tanto feroci' (151). Reviewing the whole course of his journey, and thus also its various stages, Dante-character precisely appreciates the relative value of the different parts of creation — an essential premise for someone who very soon will be blissfully enjoined with the Creator (124–25):

> 'Tu se' sì presso a l'ultima salute',
> cominciò Bëatrice, 'che tu dei
> aver le luci tue chiare e acute;
>   e però, prima che tu più t'inlei,
> rimira in giù'. (*Par.* XXII. 124–28)

Given that the pilgrim is moving ever nearer to experiencing the *visio Dei*, the reasons why, when he passes from the heaven of Saturn to that of the Fixed Stars, he needs to 'rimirare in giù' so as to proceed further are obvious.[3] Less clear, however, particularly at first blush, are the reasons why the reader should strive to acquire a retrospective and global vision both of this canto and of this moment of transition. In fact, the need for such a perspective is open to question. Unlike other 'reflective' cantos, there is no 'appeal' here to the reader to perform such a task.[4] After all, *Paradiso* XXII is divided into two distinct and separate parts — a structure that would seem to undermine, or at least to weaken, the possibility that the canto might offer overarching viewpoints and unifying ideological perspectives, which, in addition, might illustrate what is to come.[5] The first part, which takes place in the heaven

---

3   On the nature of the pilgrim's beatitude, and on Dante's ideas regarding the beatific vision, a contentious topic in fourteenth-century religious culture, see the chapter that follows.
4   Employing the term 'appeal', I am of course referring to Erich Auerbach, 'Gli appelli di Dante al lettore', in his *Studi su Dante* (Milan: Feltrinelli, 1966), pp. 292–304.
5   Chiavacci Leonardi maintains that the arrival of the *viator* in the eighth heaven not only divides

of Saturn (1–99), continues the subject-matter and approach of the previous canto. Rooted in the world of monastic contemplation, it focuses on major themes of universal import that concern theology and religious culture (the nature of Paradise and particularly of the Empyrean; the mystical ladder; the connections between Heaven and earth), as well as the history of the Church (St Benedict; ecclesiastical corruption). The second part, which takes place in the heaven of the Fixed Stars (100–54), despite its sweeping overview of the seven planetary spheres, is strictly personal. It concentrates on the biography, on the feelings, and on the behaviour of the pilgrim — a fitting purview given the intimate connecion between the *viator* and the constellation of Gemini:

> O glorïose stelle, o lume pregno
> di gran virtù, dal quale io riconosco
> tutto, qual che si sia, il mio ingegno,
>   con voi nasceva e s'ascondeva vosco
> quelli ch'è padre d'ogne mortal vita,
> quand' io senti' di prima l'aere tosco. (*Par.* XXII. 112–17)

Despite what might be deemed signals to the contrary, given the consequence of Dante-*personaggio*'s totalizing gaze, which, along the course of the poem, regularly provides valuable hints as to how we should read, it seems reasonable to assume that the poet is encouraging us to 'look downwards once more'. Sweeping our eyes back over *Paradiso* XXII's *terzine*, it is not unlikely that we are meant to recognize both the role that the canto plays in the *Commedia*'s structure and the elements that might unite its seemingly varied *materia*.[6] Thus, even if, unlike Beatrice, Dante does not explicitly invite us to look back, it is nonetheless striking that he should involve us directly in the pilgrim's experiences in the Starry heaven (and also in those of the poet on his return to earth):

> S'io torni mai, lettore, a quel divoto
> trïunfo per lo quale io piango spesso
> le mie peccata e 'l petto mi percuoto,
>   tu non avresti in tanto tratto e messo
> nel foco il dito, in quant' io vidi 'l segno
> che segue il Tauro e fui dentro da esso. (*Par.* XXII. 106–11)

However, the problem remains of establishing the ideological and literary links that might bind *Paradiso* XXII together — a difficult task given the lack of obvious

---

the canto into two halves, but also cuts the third canticle in two: 'questo passaggio dai cieli dei pianeti al cielo Stellato o delle stelle fisse, vera cerniera nella struttura della cantica' (III, 618).

6   It is a well-established convention of the *lectura Dantis* to interpret each canto as if it were self-sufficient and organic. Although this approach has resulted in many fundamental readings, it tends to 'flatten' the identity of the hundred cantos, since it presumes that all of them are organized in the same manner within the *Commedia*'s macrostructure. I am not persuaded by this critical and methodological truism. My approach is to allow, as much as possible, a canto itself to dictate how it might be read. I thus try to avoid constraining a canto by imposing on to it an external and a priori way of reading. Consequently, there should be nothing troubling in recognizing that a canto, rather than homogenous, is fragmentary and even 'disorganized'. In light of this note, one may wonder why I seem so keen to stress *Paradiso* XXII's unitary coherence. My answer is banal: the canto itself, as I hope to demonstrate, demands it.

elements of continuity between, but also within, the different parts of the canto. *Paradiso* XXII's perspective is complex and eclectic. The canto ranges across a wide array of themes, each of which is intellectually demanding: the effects of the cry of the blessed souls on the human *viator*; the latter's relationship to Beatrice; the contrast and the connections between the human and the divine; the pilgrim's various 'disi*i*' (26); St Benedict's self-presentation; the request to see the saint's 'imagine scoverta' (60); the description of the Empyrean; the sinful state of the contemporary Church and the relationship between its past and present condition; Benedict's prophecy of an imminent providential intervention in earthly affairs; the ascent to the Starry heaven; the invocation to the constellation of Gemini and celestial determinism; Dante-character's self-presentation; Beatrice's request to 'rimir*are* in giù'; the description of the earth and the seven planets. In general, and perhaps not surprisingly, scholars have found themselves puzzled by this disjointed range of subjects. The majority of *lecturae* offers little more than a prose paraphrase of the canto's content, adding occasional stylistic and literary observations and some historical and astronomical clarifications.[7] There are almost no readings that try to assess *Paradiso* XXII in its entirety and in relation to the rest of the poem.[8] Little

7   The original version of this *lectura*, which I wrote in 2001, had taken the following studies into consideration: Salvatore Accardo, 'Dante e San Benedetto', in *Miscellanea di studi artistici e letterari in onore di Giovanni Fallani*, ed. by Dante Balboni (Naples: De Dominicis, 1982), pp. 305–19; Giuliana Angiolillo, 'Canto XXII: San Benedetto', in her *La nuova frontiera della tanatologia: le biografie della 'Commedia'*, 3 vols (Florence: Olschki, 1996), III, 213–29; Marcello Aurigemma, 'Tra gli spiriti contemplanti: San Benedetto', in *Lectura Dantis Modenese. 'Paradiso'* (Modena: Banca Popolare dell'Emilia, 1985), pp. 187–99; Massimo Bontempelli, 'Il canto XXII del *Paradiso*', in *Letture dantesche. 'Paradiso'*, ed. by Giovanni Getto (Florence: Sansoni, 1970), pp. 449–65; Alberto Chiari, 'San Benedetto cantato da Dante (*Par.* XXII, 1–99)', in his *Saggi danteschi e altri studi (1980–1990)* (Florence: Le Lettere, 1991), pp. 89–101; Eurialo De Michelis, 'Il canto XXII del *Paradiso*, in *Nuove letture dantesche*, 8 vols (Florence: Le Monnier, 1968–76), VII, 35–66; Dante Della Terza, 'L'incontro con S. Benedetto (*Paradiso* XXII)', in his *Strutture poetiche, esperienze letterarie, percorsi culturali da Dante ai contemporanei* (Naples: Edizioni Scientifiche Italiane, 1995), pp. 65–81; Roberto Durighetto, 'Il simbolo della Scala di Giacobbe e le figure di S. Pietro Damiano e di S. Benedetto nel XXI e nel XXII canto del *Paradiso*', in *Atti della Dante Alighieri a Treviso 1989–1996*, ed. by Arnaldo Brunello, 2 vols (Mestre: Ediven, 1996), II, 145–55; Peter S. Hawkins, ' "By gradual scale sublimed": Dante and the Contemplatives', in his *Dante's Testaments: Essays in Scriptural Imagination* (Stanford: Stanford University Press, 1999), pp. 229–43; Annibale Ilari, 'Il canto XXII del *Paradiso*', in *'Paradiso': letture degli anni 1979–'81*, ed. by Silvio Zennaro (Rome: Bonacci, 1989), pp. 573–624; Giuseppe Mazzotta, 'Language and Vision (*Paradiso* XXI and XXII)', in his *Dante's Vision and the Circle of Knowledge* (Princeton: Princeton University Press, 1993), pp. 154–73; Ettore Paratore, 'S. Benedetto e S. Bernardo', in *Rivista di cultura classica e medievale*, 23 (1981), 3–15; Silvio Pasquazi, *Il canto XXII del 'Paradiso'* (Turin: SEI, 1964); Emilio Pasquini, 'Canto XXII', in *Lectura Dantis Neapolitana. 'Paradiso'*, ed. by Pompeo Giannantonio (Naples: Loffredo, 2000), pp. 431–40; Pasquale Vannucci, *Il canto XXII del 'Paradiso'* (Turin: SEI, 1965); Giorgio Varanini, 'Canto XXII', in *Lectura Dantis Scaligera. III. 'Paradiso'* (Florence: Le Monnier, 1971), pp. 156–74; William Wilson, 'XXII', in *Dante's 'Divine Comedy'. III. 'Paradiso'*, ed. by Tibor Wlassics (Charlottesville: University of Virginia Printing Service, 1995), pp. 318–28. *Lecturae* that in part escape the criticisms that I make are those by Della Terza, Hawkins, Mazzotta, Pasquazi, and Pasquini; and see n. 12 below.
8   On the importance of *Paradiso* XXII in the structure of the *Commedia*, see Claudia Di Fonzo, *Dante e la tradizione giuridica* (Rome: Carocci, 2016), pp. 144–46; Carlo Vecce, 'Canto XXII: San Benedetto e il "mondo sotto li piedi"', in *Lectura Dantis Romana. Cento canti per cento anni. III. 'Paradiso'. 2. Canti XVIII–XXXIII*, ed. by Enrico Malato and Andrea Mazzucchi (Rome: Salerno, 2015), pp. 642–70 (pp. 648–51, 655–57, 659, 668); both scholars, *inter alia*, stress the contrastive links

critical energy has been expended in attempting to see the canto 'tutto quanto' (133), in imitation of the pilgrim gazing on the cosmic vision.[9]

My aim is to offer a possible comprehensive interpretation of the canto in order to begin to clarify its ideological and structural parameters. In truth, this study represents the first, 'introductory' section of a broader two-part research project on *Paradiso* XXII, whose second, and major section will consist of an examination of the canto's literary, philosophical, and theological sources.[10] Indeed, when I originally 'read' *Paradiso* XXII, the question of its sources constituted a further flaw in its critical reception. The few intertexts that Dantists had recognized — the *Dialogues* of St Gregory, St Benedict's *Regula*, the *Somnium Scipionis* and the medieval tradition of fantastic flights that this had inspired, some quotations from Boethius's *Consolation of Philosophy*, and a handful of Scriptural echoes — had long become ossified critical clichés.[11] Scholars mechanically reconfirmed the presence of these echoes in the canto, but without asking what their functions and possible inter-relationships might be, or what may have been their ideological and cultural force in the early fourteenth century. Furthermore, fresh sources had not been proposed for many years.[12] Reading *Paradiso* XXII at the start of the new millennium, was to find oneself in a situation of exegetical 'closure': the final word seemed to have been said about the canto's intellectual parameters and, therefore, about its meaning.[13]

to Ulysses. More generally, Mira Mocan notes that 'in questo quadro figurale [of the Heaven of Saturn] sono sintetizzati alcuni dei temi più importanti del poema': Mira Mocan, 'Sulla "scala della contemplazione": i canti XXI–XXIII del *Paradiso*', in her *L'arca della mente. Riccardo di San Vittore nella 'Commedia' di Dante* (Florence: Olschki, 2012), pp. 191–231 (pp. 192–93). Finally, Domenico Cofano examines connections between our canto and several episodes in *Purgatorio*, in particular the encounter with Statius: Domenico Cofano 'Paradiso XXII: un canto "cenobitico"', in *Non di tesori eredità. Studi di letteratura italiana offerti ad Alberto Granese*, ed. by Rosa Giulio, 2 vols (Naples: Guida, 2015), I, 93–108.

9   Della Terza and Pasquini address this question in passing.

10   *Mea culpa*. Despite having largely completed the relevant research, as with the piece I mention on p. 493, I have also not written this second study. The distractions of academic life...

11   See Chiavacci Leonardi for a useful compendium of these sources.

12   In recent years, Marco Ariani has highlighted classical and Christian precedents for the pilgrim's 'sguardo complessivo alla *machina mundi*' and for 'la sublime oltranza del viaggio astrale': Marco Ariani, 'La visione dall'alto: *parvitas mundi* (canto XXII)', in his *'Lux inaccessibilis': metafore e teologia della luce nel 'Paradiso' di Dante* (Rome: Aracne, 2010), pp. 269–75 (pp. 270–72; the two quoted passages may be read on p. 270). Referring to Patrice Sicard, *Diagrammes médiévaux et exégèse visuelle: le 'Libellus de formatione arche' de Hugues de Saint-Victor* (Paris and Turnhout: Brepols, 1993), Mocan has noted the influence in our canto of the 'visione del cosmo' coming from the 'tradizione vittorina' (p. 193). However, the most significant aspect of her chapter convincingly demonstrates the dependence of the heaven of Saturn on Richard of St Victor. In his turn, Carlo Vecce has highlighted more fully than has been done previously Dante's debts to Boethius's *Consolatio philosophiæ* (pp. 643–45 & 667), to the Bible (pp. 657–58), and, in Pasquazi's wake, to Gregory's *Dialogues* (II. 35), especially as regards the pilgrim's look down to see the earth (p. 664).

13   Since the publication of my reading, the following studies of *Paradiso* XXII have appeared: Ariani; Silvano Ciprandi, 'Canto XXII', in his *Le mie lecturae Dantis. III. 'Paradiso'* (Pavia and Milan: Selecta and Società Dante Alighieri, Comitato di Milano, 2006), pp. 295–307; Cofano; Elena Landoni, 'S. Benedetto e il modello di lettura della *Commedia*: Par. XXII', *L'Alighieri*, 47 (2006), 91–111; Giuseppe Ledda, 'Truth, Autobiography and the Poetry of Salvation', in *Vertical Readings in Dante's 'Comedy'*, ed. by George Corbett and Heather Webb, 3 vols (n.p.: Open Book Publishers, 2015–18), II, 237–58;

As a result, a broad collection of texts and authors had been left undisturbed to gather dust in the weave of *Paradiso* XXII's *terzine*. Yet, these are texts and authors that not only substantially expand the canto's range of interests, but are also ideologically and intertextually interconnected. To put it a bit differently, the sources, as our Italian colleagues like to say, *fanno sistema*, and therefore serve as one of the principal means with which Dante unified the canto. In this chapter, as I mentioned earlier, I will only be able to touch lightly on *Paradiso* XXII's cultural and ideological background; although I do discuss a handful of previously unrecognized borrowings that can perhaps offer some sense of the complexity of its cultural infrastructure. Instead, my goal is to offer a preliminary assessment of *Paradiso* XXII. As befits an 'introduction', I focus mainly on an analysis of the canto itself — a sort of *explication de texte* — in order to evaluate the extent to which its multiform *materia* might actually converge and cohere around common clusters of ideas. When I linger on a source, I do this to assess whether or not it highlights the same ideological concerns that emerge from the 'surface' of *Paradiso* XXII, and therefore whether or not it functions in line with the canto as a whole.

2. Descending, Reflecting, Ascending

The look that the pilgrim casts 'in giù' (128) over the 'le sette spere' (134), despite its drama, is little more than a commonplace in *Paradiso* XXII. Even in a poem in which the protagonist's *vedere* functions as one of its key structuring devices ('Però ti son mostrate', *Par.* XVII. 136), the canto is noteworthy for being chock-full of gazes.[14] Lines 19–23 offer a telling example of this concern, not to say obsession, with looking:

> 'Ma rivolgiti omai inverso altrui;
> ch'assai illustri spiriti vedrai,
> se com' io dico l'aspetto redui'.
>   Come a lei piacque, li occhi ritornai,
> e vidi cento sperule.

At the strictly narrative level, the lines offer a redundancy of information. One can easily go from line 19 to line 23 without losing the thread of the story. In a poet as rigorous as Dante, who, in the *Commedia*, normally avoids prolixity, wasted words, and stylistic vanities, such a flagrant tautology is striking. On account of its rarity, it requires special critical attention. Even though the lines reconnect

Giuseppe Mazzotta, 'Canti XXI–XXII: contemplazione e poesia', in *Esperimenti danteschi. 'Paradiso' 2010*, ed. by Tommaso Montorfano (Genoa and Milan: Marietti, 2010), pp. 201–12; Mocan; Matthew Treherne, 'Reading Dante's Heaven of the Fixed Stars (*Paradiso* XXI–XXVII): Declaration, Pleasure and Praise', in *'Se mai continga...': Exile, Politics and Theology in Dante*, ed. by Claire E. Honess and Matthew Treherne (Ravenna: Longo, 2013), pp. 11–26; Vecce. Several of these studies, and most especially Domenico Cofano's, Mira Mocan's, and Carlo Vecce's *lecturae*, use my reading as a point of reference. It would be fair to say that more recent *lecturae* have tended to recognize, and hence address, the canto's complexities.
14   On the canto's emphasis on seeing, see Della Terza, pp. 79–80, and Pasquazi, p. 8, for some preliminary observations.

with the elegant simile describing a 'parvol's' (2) reliance on his mother (2–6) with which the canto had opened, their purpose is more than simply a device with which to restate Beatrice's 'maternal' behaviour and Dante-character's reaction as an obedient 'figlio' (5). Nor is their function exhausted in underlining the importance of the new group of souls in general and, among them, of St Benedict, 'la maggiore e la più luculenta | di quelle margherite' (28–29), in particular. Such reiterative and highlighting strategies are too common in the *Paradiso* (and in the rest of the *Commedia*) to merit being granted exceptional stress. However, what is uncommon, and hence it would seem to be this that the lines are especially emphasizing, is the intimate relationship that they evoke between the pilgrim and the act of seeing. Above all, the circumlocutions at lines 21 and 22 — 'l'aspetto redui' and 'li occhi ritornai' — both in rhyme position, sharing the same syntactic structure, and semantically marked in relation to the two cases of the simple use of the verb *vedere* that 'bookend' them, draw attention not only to themselves and to the act of looking, but also, and more specifically, to the role, in this process, of the *viator*, who has the responsibility of 'ricondurre' his gaze where his guide urges him. Although lines 19–23 do not represent the first reference in the canto to the act of seeing — the first appears two *terzine* earlier, 'la vendetta | che tu vedrai innanzi che tu muoi' (14–15) — given the emphasis that they place on seeing and given their proemial position, they function as one of the keys with which *Paradiso* XXII can be interpreted.[15] In addition, the importance of seeing is explicitly confirmed at the close of the canto ('poscia rivolsi li occhi a li occhi belli', 154), another of the privileged spaces of the Dantean canto that tend to determine its meaning. Moreover, between line 23 and the one with which *Paradiso* XXII closes, there are fifteen other references to looking, of which all, bar two, refer, as in lines 19–23, to the pilgrim.[16]

The theme of seeing and its relationship to Dante-character are evidently at the centre of *Paradiso* XXII's concerns. At the same time, given the complexity of the concept of sight in the Middle Ages, it remains to establish which aspects of looking and which totalizing category of seeing the poet wished to address in our canto.[17]

15   On medieval prologues, see Chapter 14, p. 483, n. 38.

16   'Se tu vedessi' (31); 'La buona sembianza | ch'io veggio' (33–34); 'ti veggia' (60); 'dal viso ti s'invola' (69); 'vide il patriarca' (70); 'se guardi 'l principio' (91); 'riguardi' (92); 'vederai' (93); 'mirabile a veder' (96); 'io vidi 'l segno' (110); 'le luci tue chiare e acute' (126); 'rimira in giù' (128); 'col viso ritornai' (133); 'Vidi la figlia' (139); 'e vidi' (143). There are thus twenty-one references to seeing in the canto. In structural terms, what is especially striking is their distribution. There are fourteen allusions in the heaven of Saturn and seven in that of the Fixed Stars. The 2:1 proportion is almost identical to the ratio of lines assigned to each heaven: ninety-nine and fifty-five — a further indicator of the close ties between *Paradiso* XXII's two parts.

17   See Dallas G. Denery II, *Seeing and Being Seen in the Later Medieval World: Optics, Theology and Religious Life* (Cambridge: Cambridge University Press, 2005); Simon A. Gilson, *Medieval Optics and Theories of Light in the Works of Dante* (Lewiston, NY, Queenston, and Lampeter: Edwin Mellen Press, 2000); David C. Lindberg, *Theories of Vision from Al-Kindi to Kepler* (Chicago and London: University of Chicago Press, 1976); Katherine Tachau, *Vision and Certitude in the Age of Ockham* (Leiden: Brill, 1988); *La visione e lo sguardo nel Medioevo / View and Vision in the Middle Ages*, special issue of *Micrologus*, 5–6 (1997–98); *Visuality Before and Beyond the Renaissance*, ed. by Robert Nelson (Cambridge: Cambridge University Press, 2000).

The problem is far from straightforward, since *Paradiso* XXII presents various and, seemingly, contrasting ways of looking. Thus, Dante highlights the differences between the sight of the blessed souls and that of the living ('Se tu vedessi | com' io la carità', 31–32); and then, by referring to Jacob's dream, he alludes to visionary seeing (70–72). Later, when St Benedict invites the pilgrim to 'look at' how the saints behaved in the past ('se guardi 'l principio di ciascuno', 91), the poet is adding intellectual reflection to the mix. Likewise, the description of the *viator* who studies the planets recalls the manner of the astronomer observing the heavens, which might be defined as 'scientific looking' (see Subsection 4 below). Finally, the pilgrim who focuses his attention on Beatrice's 'occhi belli' (154) recalls mystics directing their gaze at God.

To better understand what might unite these different ways of seeing, it is useful to begin by establishing whether there are other elements which, like the preoccupation with seeing, are a constant in *Paradiso* XXII, and so serve to characterize it. A formal and semantic trait immediately catches the eye: the high frequency of verbs with the prefix *re-/ri-*. We thus find 'ricorre' (2), 'rivolgiti' (19), 'redui' (21), 'ritornai' (22), 'relusse' (43), 'ritrassi' (44), 'riguardi' (92), 'rimira' (128), 'ritornai' (133), and 'rivolsi' (154). Except for two of them (43 and 44), the verbs are once more associated with the *viator* and, apart from line 2, with his acts of looking. The verbs, therefore, constitute an important element within Dante's broad treatment of seeing. The prefixes *re-* and *ri-* of course express repetition: in particular, a return to an earlier phase.[18] First, and in general terms, the verbs emphasize the intellectual, reflective aspect that is an integral part of seeing — an aspect to which Dante explicitly alludes, for example, in lines 54 ('ch'io veggio e noto')[19] and 91–93. Second, and much more specifically, they spotlight that, repeatedly and not just at the end of the canto, the pilgrim moves his gaze between two distinct points to reconsider what he has already seen — an emblematically reflective movement that confirms the centrality of the relationship between sight and intellect not only as regards the *agens*, but also the canto as a whole. Hence, all the different ways of seeing illustrated in *Paradiso* XXII, from the scientific to the visionary and from the mystical to the recapitulatory, are based on the same relationship, thereby reiterating the importance of the links between the eyes and the mind.

The representation of Dante-character who changes the focus of his attention is articulated in four main moments. The first, and the most conventional, because typical of his behaviour in the *Paradiso*, describes the *viator* who *rivolge* his eyes from Beatrice to the ranks of the blessed (19–24). The second involves the pilgrim in a complicated mnemonic gaze that takes in several moments along the span of providential history: 'Se guardi 'l principio di ciascuno | poscia riguardi là dov' è trascorso' (91–92). The broad perspective established in lines 91–92 anticipates the third moment, when Dante-*personaggio* casts a look from the Starry heaven to

---

18   The importance of the verbs with this form is affirmed by the inclusion in the canto of words that begin with re- and ri- but in which the prefix does not suggest repetition: 'ridendo' (11); 'represe' (25); 'risposta' (35); 'regola' (74); 'retroso' (94); 'riconosco' (113).

19   '[V]eggio è degli occhi, osserva Torraca, *noto* è della mente' (Chiavacci Leonardi, III, 610)

'questo globo' (134) that takes in the vast cosmic panorama of the planets and the earth. The final gaze rises back up from the earthly 'aiuola' (151) to return to the eighth heaven, and in particular to Beatrice's face. Consequently, *Paradiso* XXII — and as is rarely the case in the *Commedia* — is perfectly symmetrical: it opens with the pilgrim who *si volge alla sua guida* (1–2), and ends with him as he *si rivolge agli occhi belli* (154), a further mark that the poet intended the canto to be read in a unified manner.

Anyhow, the canto's emphasis on *guardare* and *riguardare* does not end with the theme of reflection. In itself, this latter concern is too generic and somewhat too far from the theological, historical, astronomical, and autobiographical interests of *Paradiso* XXII to provide a mechanism subtle enough with which to undertake the exegesis of the canto. At the same time, it would seem to confirm, as I suggested earlier, that the *lettor* needs to read the canto 'reflectively'. We begin with Beatrice's 'smile' (11) and motherly words and return to her 'beautiful eyes' at the end. In *Paradiso* XXII's narrative and ideological development, this movement of return is, in fact, a sign of growth. On the surface, by 'presumptiously' requesting to view Benedict's 'imagine scoverta' (60) ahead of time, it may seem that the pilgrim is in danger of losing the correct perspective on what he sees.[20] Yet, the canto's ending indicates that, despite the many visual and intellectual distractions, Dante-*personaggio*, thanks to the saint's and Beatrice's interventions, continues to advance in harmony with the principal driving motor of his heavenly voyage, his desire for the divine: 'il tuo alto disio | s'adempierà in su l'ultima spera' (61–62). Throughout *Paradiso*, the emphasis on desire is a standard motif.[21] However, in a canto whose attention is trained in so many different directions, the relationship between desire and knowledge inevitably takes on special significance. Thus, *Paradiso* XXII spans ambitiously across the universe and across providential history: from the first human generations, 'il patriarca | Iacobbe' (70–71), to the corruption of the present (73–93), in the process passing through crucial moments, such as the Exodus (95), the Incarnation (41–42), and the ministries of Saints Peter (88), Benedict (37–51, 89), and Francis (90). Scholars have failed to notice that, alongside *Paradiso* XXII's broad cosmological perspective, which is predicated on the *viator* properly evaluating each planet in relation to the other six (148–50), Dante has introduced a corresponding and equally broad evaluative vision of history that helps to contextualize his memorable judgment on the relative insignificance of the earth.[22] Moreover, the fact that the pilgrim *rimiri* both creation and providential history as he prepares for the final part of his heavenly vision confirms that, far from being distractions, both, when integrated with his *disio*, play a fundamental role in refining his intellect as he advances on his *itinerarium in Deum*. Once again, Dante-character finds himself

20   On the problems inherent in lines 58–63, see Attilio Mellone, 'Il desiderio dantesco di vedere il volto di S. Benedetto (*Pd* XXII 58–60)', in his *Saggi e letture* dantesche (Angri: Gaia, 2005), pp. 359–70; Fernando Salsano, 'Per l'esegesi di *Paradiso* XXII 58–63', *Studi e problem di ciritica testuale*, 9 (1974), 21–28.

21   See Lino Pertile, *La punta del disio: semantica del desiderio nella 'Commedia'* (Fiesole: Cadmo, 2005); Giuliano Rossi, '*Disio* nella *Commedia*', *La parola del testo*, 9 (2005), 99–124.

22   See Alfonso Traina, '"L'aiuola che ci fa tanto feroci": per la storia di un topos', in his *Poeti latini (e neolatini): note e saggi filosofici* (Bologna: Patron, 1986), pp. 305–35.

among divine *signa*; and a concern with signs and their interpretation has dominated the *Paradiso* at least since the heaven of the Sun.[23]

From what has just been said, it would seem that, in addition to reflection, two other connected elements help bring together *Paradiso* XXII's spectating concerns, according them additional depth and nuance. These elements are movement and hierarchy — the latter resulting from a visual and intellectual act of discrimination. Both, of course, are closely associated with the processes of reflection. To re-view what had been seen in the past or what is already known involves an act of movement and of judgment through which to relativize what is being reconsidered from a new perspective. The main effect of such a process is to offer the observing subject the possibility to advance intellectually and spiritually. The whole canto and in particular the pilgrim's experience (but also the reader's) are constructed around this cluster of ideas. Dante seems to suggest that to proceed along the 'diritta via' (*Inf.* I. 3), the *homo viator* — one of the load-bearing concepts of the *Commedia* and Christianity — needs to have a clear appreciation of the past and of the world around him. Again, as with his interest in divine *signa*, Dante is touching on matters of great contemporary ideological signficance. Indeed, the idea that life is a pilgrimage is indissolubly involved with the appreciation and interpretation of the *vestigia Dei*, two prime instances of which are providential history and creation. In particular, the emphasis on seeing and reflecting indicates how Dante believes that we should approach, and hence interpret, history and the work of the *Deus artifex*. *Rimirare* what we already know is quintessentially an exegetical act. To understand ever more fully the things that we see and think, we need regularly to re-examine and reinterpret them. The fact that the pilgrim is able to see and understand the entire planetary system ('tutto', 148) and the whole of the earth ('tutta', 153) reveals the remarkable intellectual and spiritual progress that, by harmonizing his reflective efforts to grace and faith, he has managed to achieve during the course of his journey. Vision, movement, and enlightenment become one:

> L'aiuola che ci fa tanto feroci,
> volgendom' io con li etterni Gemelli,
> tutta m'apparve da' colli a le foci. (151–53)

As the bridge between the 'inhabited' heavens and those without communities of souls, *Paradiso* XXII enjoys a pivotal position in the unfolding of the *Commedia*. Consequently, it addresses crucial themes, such as sight and thought, in an appropriately rigorous manner. In keeping with the canto's exacting structural and ideological logic, as well as his aim to grant the *Commedia* a coherent and recognizable overarching *ordo* modelled on that of creation (see Chapter 8), Dante further connected *Paradiso* XXII's principal motifs to the major intellectual strands of the third *cantica*: most notably the centrality of divine signification and its exegesis as the basis for humanity's relationship to God. To underscore the nature and

---

23   See Zygmunt G. Barański, *Dante e i segni: saggi per una storia intellettuale di Dante Alighieri* (Naples: Liguori, 2000); Angela G. Meekins, 'Reflecting on the Divine: Notes on Dante's Heaven of the Sun', *The Italianist*, 18 (1998), 28–70; Paola Nasti, *Favole d'amore e 'saver profondo': la tradizione salomonica in Dante* (Ravenna: Longo, 2007), pp. 160–229. See also Chapters 5, 9, and 17.

importance of the canto's principal notions, Dante synthesized them in a symbol which, in medieval culture, embraced ideas of motion, hierarchy, reflection, the order of creation, and cognitive and spiritual development, while subsuming these to the concept of sight. This symbol, of course, is Jacob's ladder:

> e nostra scala infino ad essa [the last heaven] varca,
> onde così dal viso ti s'invola.
>   Infin là sù la vide il patriarca
> Iacobbe porger la superna parte,
> quando li apparve d'angeli sì carca.
>   Ma, per salirla, mo nessun diparte
> da terra i piedi. (68–74)

Stretching from earth up to the Empyrean, the 'scaleo' (*Par.* XXI. 29) offers to anyone who ascends its rungs a carefully graded and hierarchized set of visions of the divine. Each vision depends on the prior assimilation of the previous ones, and dramatically impacts on the intellect, the emotions, and the spirit, before finally culminating in the *visio Dei*.[24] Dante 'personalizes' the ladder's values and functions by presenting the *viator*'s connections to it. Thus, the pilgrim's relationship to the 'scaleo' serves emblematically to measure his evolving relationship to God and his progression along his miraculous *itinerarium in Deum*. Where the *agens* finds himself on the ladder indicates both what he has already achieved during the course of his ascent, as well as what he still needs to achieve. Thus, his becoming one with the heaven of the Fixed Stars ('volgendom' io con li etterni Gemelli', 152), a condition that the pilgrim has attained thanks to his rapid 'volo' up the ladder (100–05), prefigures, as confirmed by the repetition of the verb *volgere*, his none-too-distant arrival at the top of the 'scaleo', and hence his union with God, thanks to which, as Benedict announces (61–65), all his desires will be totally satisfied (for an extended discussion of the *Commedia*'s closing lines, see the following chapter):

> ma già volgeva il mio disio e 'l *velle*,
> sì come rota ch'igualmente è mossa,
>   l'amor che move il sole e l'altre stelle.
>   (*Par.* XXXIII. 143–45)

At the same time, and Dante places considerable stress on this aspect, the *viator*'s continuing 'reflective' experience in the heaven of the Fixed Stars — the look that he casts down can equally be interpreted as evidence that he has profitably assimilated the lessons of the previous 'grades' and that he is now ready to face new revelations — underlines that, even if the goal of his journey is near, there are

---

24   On the ladder, see at least E. Bertaud and André Rayez, 'Echelle spirituelle', in DSAM, VI:I, cols 62–86; Warren Ginsberg, 'Dante's Dream of the Eagle and Jacob's Ladder', *Dante Studies*, 100 (1982), 41–69; Claudia Di Fonzo, '"La dolce donna dietro a lor mi pinse | con un sol cenno su per quella scala" (*Par.* XXII, 100–101)', *Studi danteschi*, 68 (1991), 141–75; Alessandro Ghisalberti, 'La scala dei contemplativi: da San Benedetto a Dante Alighieri', in *Peccato, penitenza e santità nella 'Commedia'*, ed. by Marco Ballarini and others (Rome and Milan: Bulzoni and Biblioteca Ambrosiana, 2016), pp. 33–46; Christian Heck, 'Du songe de Jacob aux visions de saints dans l'art médiéval: théophanie et géographie sacrée', *Micrologus*, 6 (1998), 43–57; Mocan, pp. 216–26; Georg Rabuse, 'Saturne et l'échelle de Jacob', *Archives d'histoire doctrinale et littéraire du Moyen Âge*, 45 (1978), 7–31.

still several steps to climb, as Benedict had indicatively declared (68–69). Thus, the pilgrim needs to make further intellectual and spiritual efforts before he is ready to achieve *deificatio*, as is immediately affirmed by his ensuing examinations on faith, hope, and charity. It is not surprising that 'La dolce donna dietro a lor [the blessed] mi pinse | con un sol cenno su per quella scala' (100–01). Her action reveals that, unlike the base attitudes of the 'monaci [...] folli' (81), who are exclusively fixated on earthly matters, the *viator*'s 'reflective' behaviour harmonizes with the demands of the ascent to God, as is confirmed by the miraculous speed with which he passes from one heaven to the next:

> né mai qua giù dove si monta e cala
> naturalmente, fu sì ratto moto
> ch'agguagliar si potesse a la mia ala. (103–05)

Yet, despite the wealth of its connotations — and to those already discussed I will add others, and potentially of greater interest — readers of *Paradiso* XXII have tended to underestimate the importance of Jacob's ladder. Essentially, they have failed to appreciate its strategic and totalizing functions in the canto's organization. In general, they have limited themselves to noting its traditional links with the contemplative tradition, thereby narrowly resolving its meaning, almost as if it were an 'inevitable' symbolic presence given the canto's monastic focus. As a result, they have not recognized that the ladder's values are actually the same as the ones that dominate *Paradiso* XXII as a whole. By linking the two heavens (100–02), and hence the canto's two parts, the 'scaleo' provides further (and conclusive) evidence of *Paradiso* XXII's unity and the commonality of interests between the heavens of Saturn and of the Fixed Stars.

3. 'Cognitio caelestium corporum'

Two interdependent questions arise at this juncture. The more substantial one concerns the extent to which it is appropriate to stress the importance of 'reflection' on earthly and human matters in a setting where 'tutti contemplanti | uomini fuoro' (46–47). As scholars have long recognized, *Paradiso* XXII is marked by mystical impulses of desire for the divine, which are accompanied by a recognition of the *viltà* (134) of this world (134–35 & 151). The second question concerns my stress on the close links between the two parts of *Paradiso* XXII. Specifically, the problem focuses on why Dante decided to bring together two seemingly contrasting situations: the collective vision of the heaven of Saturn, which is deeply absorbed in 'pensier contemplativi' (*Par.* XXI. 117), with the autobigraphical individualism of the heaven of the Fixed Stars. In particular, if the *Commedia*'s first readers were to appreciate his rapprochement — and Dante was always acutely aware of his immediate audience — it needed to have cultural resonance.[25] In the absence of such cultural anchoring, the hypothesis about *Paradiso* XXII's structural and ideological coherence would find

25   On Dante's self-conscious and reader-directed poetics, see Barański, *'Sole nuovo, luce nuova'*, and 'Dante Alighieri: Experimentation and (Self-)Exegesis', in *The Cambridge History of Literary Criticism*. II. *The Middle Ages*, ed. by Alastair Minnis and Ian Johnson (Cambridge: Cambridge University Press, 2005), pp. 561–82. See also Chapters 6–8.

support exclusively in the canto itself, or rather, in my interpretation of the canto — a type of circular argument whose hermeneutic inadequacies are achingly self-evident. The two questions are therefore of a certain weight; and to answer them adequately is complicated.

I should like to begin by offering a partial explanation of the second problem, and by straightaway declaring that, in the Middle Ages, strong connections were deemed to unite the heavens of Saturn and of the Fixed Stars. Both spheres, in fact, were associated with contemplation. It is widely recognized that medieval astrology posited a specific link between Saturn and *meditatio* and, more generally, between the planet and the workings of the human intellect.[26] What does not seem to have been equally acknowledged is that, at least as far as contemplation is concerned, the same is true of the heaven of the Fixed Stars. Thus, an important hermeneutic tradition considered the two brothers of the Gemini constellation as a symbol of the relationship between the active and the contemplative life:

> Legimus hos duos fratres de eadem matre et diversis patribus, mortali scilicet et deo, idoque alterum mortalem, alterum deum. Ledam itaque sciendum est zelum vel invidiam interpretari. Pollucem perditionem, Castorem extremum malum. Mens quidem humana zelo bono felicitatem appetens non immerito Leda, id est zelus dicitur. In hac Iuppiter Pollucem gignit dum ipsa amore Dei contemplativam vitam in se capit. In eadem a mortali Castor generatur dum hec amore carnali activam amplexatur. Vita contemplativa Pollux, id est perditio dicitur, quia bona hec relinquendo animam suam perdit, ut eam invenire mereatur. Activa vita extremum malum dicitur quia terminus corporee volup-tatis esse perhibetur. Inter voluptatem namque et contemplationem media est actio. Ille immortalis esse ex hoc monstratur, quia morte corporali non ita contemplatio ut accio terminatur. Unde Dominus dicit Mariam eam elegisse partem, que ab ea non auferetur. Castori Pollux confert deitatem, quia accio ad contemplationem transiens assequitur immortalitatem.[27]

> [We read that these two brothers, who had the same mother but different fathers, that is one a mortal and the other a god, were themselves one mortal and the other a god. We must know that Leda is interpreted as zeal and jealousy, Pollux as loss, Castor as extreme evil. Leda is — rightly so — the human mind that seeks happiness with good zeal, that is, she represents zeal. Jupiter procreates Pollux with her, while she, by loving God, receives in herself the contemplative life. From a mortal she has Castor, while she embraces the active life by means of carnal love. Pollux is the contemplative life, he represents, that is, loss, because by abandoning material goods she loses her soul, so that she may deserve to find it again. The active life is called extreme evil because it is said to be the limit of bodily pleasure. For action is halfway between pleasure and contemplation. A man is shown to be immortal by the fact that contemplation does not end with the death of the body, as instead does action. Thus the Lord says that Mary chose that part which could not be taken away from her.

---

26   Richard Kay, *Dante's Christian Astrology* (Philadelphia: University of Pennsylvania Press, 1994), pp. 232–33; Raymond Klibansky, Edwin Panofsky, and Fritz Saxl, *Saturn and Melancholy* (New York: Basic Books, 1964), pp. 155–56.

27   *The Commentary on Martianus Capella's 'De nuptiis Philologiae et Mercurii' Attributed to Bernardus Silvestris*, ed. by Haijo J. Westra (Toronto: PIMS, 1986), x. 473–90 (p. 240).

Pollux grants Castor divine nature, because action, when it transforms into contemplation, achieves immortality.]

The divinizing interpretation of Pollux clarifies why Dante would have thought it appropriate to draw together the seventh and eighth spheres. It also confirms that *Paradiso* XXII's seemingly divided structure is actually in harmony. Just as important, however, is the light that the exegesis of the demigod and his brother casts on the figure of the pilgrim. It is a critical commonplace, seemingly in keeping with the poet's own words, that the invocation to the constellation constitutes a public declaration of the stars' influence on his poetic genius:

> O glorïose stelle, o lume pregno
> di gran virtù, dal quale io riconosco
> tutto, qual che si sia, il mio ingegno. (112–14)

Although, in the Middle Ages, it was commonly accepted that the Gemini's 'virtù' manifested itself through the gift of writerly prowess, Dante here is not specifically speaking of his poetic abilities, but, more broadly, of 'tutto [...] il *suo* ingegno'. The poet thus seems to be alluding to his intellectual abilities in general. The *cogitationis vis*, as we have just seen, was traditionally associated with Saturn. However, as a result of the connection between the Gemini and Mercury, the constellation of Dante's birth too was related to the functioning and achievements of the human mind: 'Gemini [...] è casa di Mercurio, che è significatore, secondo li astrolaghi, di scrittura e di scienza e di conoscibilitade: e così dipone quelli che nascono, esso ascendente: e maggiormente quando il Sole vi si truova'.[28] As his use of 'ingegno' affirms, Dante invokes the Gemini to thank them for having shaped his entire intellectual make-up and not just his abilities as a writer. Once more, the differences between the seventh and the eighth sphere are blurred. In fact, the Gemini also confirm the relevance in *Paradiso* XXII of another of the canto's elements that had emerged from my earlier textual analysis: the importance of earthly matters, and, in particular, their relationship to the heavenly. Thus, in the myth of the two brothers, medieval readers also recognized an allegory of the link between the human and the divine:

> Ideo dicit *nexa* (id est iuncta) *complexu* (proportione) *sacro*, quia ad tempus divinum mortali, ut in eternum mortale iungatur divino. Quod tibi illud de Polluce et Castore apte figurat. Pollux enim perditio. Castor vero extremum malum interpretatur. Perditio dicitur spiritus humanus quia, sicut semina terre mandata prius moriuntur ut postmodum vivant, sic anima corpori iuncta. Corpus autem extremum malum dicitur quia [...] parcientibus omne quod est, nichil inferius humano corpore occurrit. [...] Et Pollux quidem dicitur deus, quia est spiritus substantia rationalis et immortalis; Castor mortalis, quia corpus substantia hebes et dissolubilis. Deus mortalis mortem recipit, ut suam deitatem ei conferat, quia spiritus ad tempus moritur, ut corpus in eternum vivat. (*The Commentary on Martianus Capella's 'De nuptiis Philologiae et Mercurii'*, III. 615–31 [p. 69])

---

28 *L'Ottimo commento della 'Divina Commedia'*, ed. by Alessandro Torri, 3 vols (Pisa: presso Niccolò Capurro, 1827–29), III, 498.

[Therefore he says *connected* (that is joined) by *sacred ties* (relation), because they are mortals for a divine time, so that the 'mortal' may be joined to the 'divine' in eternity. This is what the story of Pollux and Castor clearly shows you. Pollux is the loss. And Castor is interpreted as extreme evil. The 'loss' refers to the human soul because, as the seeds planted in the earth first die so that later they live, so the soul is connected to the body. And 'extreme evil' refers to the body because [...] to those who divide everything that is, there is nothing lower than the human body. [...] And Pollux is called god, because the spirit is a rational and immortal substance; Castor is called mortal, because the body is a heavy and dissoluble substance. The god experiences the death of the mortal, in order to grant him his own divine nature, because the spirit dies to time, so that the body may live in eternity.]

In due course, I intend to say something more about the role of the earthly and the human in our canto. For now, however, I should like to continue to focus on how the traits shared by Saturn and the Fixed Stars clarify the nature of Dante-character's intelligence (and consequently also provide further reasons as to why the poet conjoined the two heavens). As the pilgrim moves ever closer to God, so the essence of his individuality is increasingly revealed. The intense interrogation that he undergoes in the cantos that follow offers unambiguous evidence of this process of (self-)disclosure. *Paradiso* XXII not only 'reflects' on the nature of history and the universe, but also on that of the *viator*. Moreover, it is a mark of Dante-*personaggio*'s growing spiritual and intellectual maturity that he merges ever more with the rest of creation — a condition that symbolically anticipates the end of the journey. The *viator* is attaining, in and outside himself, that harmony which is one of the fundamental elements of salvation and of the divine, and which is vitally necessary in order to arrive at the *visio Dei*. By defining the pilgrim's *ingenium* in relation to the Gemini, Dante was emphasizing that his intellectual abilities are profoundly marked by *actio* and *contemplatio*, and hence combine the two principal modes of human behaviour.[29] The implications of Dante's claim are complex. In the immediate context of *Paradiso* XXII, the poet institutes a continuity between the 'pensier contemplativi' (*Par.* XXI. 117) of the *viator* and those of the blessed inhabitants of the seventh sphere. Thanks to the progress he has made on his journey, Dante-character is now ready to become a member of their monastic community, which on earth, as I shall very shortly discuss, was characterized by efforts to integrate meditation and work. The pilgrim is inducted into this heavenly community by its highest authority. On addressing the *viator*, Benedict calls him 'Frate' (61), the term which, in his *Rule*, the saint had decreed that older monks should use to address younger ones.[30]

29   The myth of Castor and Pollux also confirms the importance of the theme of harmony in *Paradiso* XXII, since the medieval exegesis of the twins was predicated on the idea of the reconciliation of opposites; see Robert M. Durling and Ronald L. Martinez, *Time and the Crystal: Studies in Dante's 'Rime Petrose'* (Berkeley, Los Angeles, and London: University of California Press, 1990), p. 89. On the role of the brothers in Dante, see Hans-Friedrich Bartig, '"feltro e feltro" — Die Dioskuren Castor und Pollux in der *Divina Commedia*', *Deutsches Dante-Jahrbuch*, 89–90, (2004–05), 73–101; Vincenzo Vitale, '"Se tu segui tua stella": postille sugli argonauti di Dante', *Le tre corone*, 5 (2018), 97–120.
30   Benedict, *Regula*, in Gregorio Magno, *Vita di San Benedetto e la Regula* (Rome: Città Nuova, 1999), LXIII (p. 224).

It is becoming ever more apparent, as I will consider in the penultimate sub-section of this chapter, that *Paradiso* XXII is fascinated by the question of *contemplatio*, and hence, as this analysis has been accentuating, of sight in its various modalities. Yet, in resolving the problem of the nature of the connections between the pilgrim and the 'contemplanti uomini', as well as that of the continuity between the two heavens, other intriguing issues emerge. In particular, given *Paradiso* XXII's concern with mapping the pilgrim's intellectual and spiritual identity, in what ways, beyond the canto's immediate monastic boundaries, might the pilgrim be defined as a contemplative? Alongside this question, another one emerges regarding the relationship between the *viator*'s 'reflective' and contemplative activities. I will return to this tangle of problems having examined the ways in which *Paradiso* XXII deals with contemplation, since the idea that Dante offers of this necessarily determines the traits of 'Dante the contemplative'.

However, before dealing with these matters, and in order to cement further the heaven of Saturn to that of the Fixed Stars, it is useful to recognize that, in the Middle Ages, it was not only the Gemini constellation that was associated with contemplation but also the entire Starry heaven. In Aquinas's *Summa Theologiae*, specifically and suggestively, in the *quaestio* that deals with *De raptu* and comments on the famous Pauline *sententia*: 'Scio hominem [...] raptum huiusmodi usque ad tertium caelum' [I know that the man [...] was thus raptured up to the third heaven] (II Corinthians 12: 2), the great theologian institutes the following set of comparisons:

> Ad quartum dicendum quod nomine tertii caeli potest uno modo intelligi aliquid corporeum. Et sic tertium caelum est caelum Empyreum, quod dicitur tertium respectu caeli aerei et caeli siderei; vel potius respectu caeli siderei et respectu caeli aquei sive crystallini. Et dicitur raptus ad tertium caelum, non quia raptus sit ad videndum similitudinem alicuius rei corporeae, sed propter hoc quod locus ille est contemplationis beatorum. [...] Alio modo per tertium caelum potest intelligi aliqua visio supermundana. Quae potest dici tertium caelum triplici ratione. Uno modo, secundum ordinem potentiarum cognoscitivarum, ut primum caelum dicatur visio supermundana corporalis, quae fit per sensum, sicut visa est manus scribentis in pariete, Dan. V; secundum autem caelum sit visio imaginaria, puta quam vidit Isaias, et Ioannes in Apocalypsi; tertium vero caelum dicatur visio intellectualis [...]. Secundo modo potest dici tertium caelum secundum ordinem cognoscibilium, *ut primum caelum dicatur cognitio caelestium corporum; secundum cognitio caelestium spirituum; tertium, cognitio ipsius Dei.* Tertio potest dici tertium caelum contemplatio Dei secundum gradus cognitionis qua Deus videtur, quorum primus pertinet ad Angelos infimae hierarchiae, secundus ad Angelos mediae, tertius ad Angelos supremae, ut dicit Glossa, II ad Cor. XII. (*ST* II–II. q. 175. a. 3. resp. 4)

> [To the fourth point I reply that by the name of 'third heaven' we can understand in one way something corporeal. And the third heaven is the Empyrean, which is called third with respect to the aerial and the sidereal heavens; or rather with respect to the sidereal heavens and the aequous or crystalline heavens. And Paul is said to be raptured to the third heaven, not because he was raptured to see the resemblance of something corporeal, but because that is the place appointed for the contemplation of the blessed. [...] Otherwise, by 'third heaven' we may

understand an ultramundane vision, which can be called third heaven for three reasons. First, according to the order of the cognitive powers, so that the first heaven would indicate a bodily ultramundane vision, which occurs through the senses, as the hand of the writer is seen on a wall, Dan. v; the second heaven would be an imaginary vision, such as Isaiah saw it, and John in the Apocalypse; and the third heaven would be an intellectual vision. Second, the third heaven may be interpreted according to the order of things knowable, so the first heaven would be the knowledge of the celestial bodies; the second would be the knowledge of the celestial spirits; the third, the knowledge of God himself. Third, the third heaven could be interpreted as the contemplation of God according to the degree of knowledge whereby God is seen: the first of these degrees belongs to the Angels of the lowest hierarchy, the second to the Angels of the middle hierarchy, the third to the Angels of the highest hierarchy, as the *Glossa* explains, in II Cor. 12.]

The passage helpfully casts light on *Paradiso* XXII. Thus, as in our canto, when describing the ascent to God, Thomas organizes his presentation around notions of sight, hierarchy, and knowledge. Its connections with the second part of *Paradiso* XXII, which takes place in the *coelum sidereum*, are especially instructive. The *responsio* consolidates the link between the heaven of the Fixed Stars and contemplation by equating the former with the contemplative capacities of the lowest of the angelic hierarchies. In addition, it elucidates various key aspects of the pilgrim's behaviour and condition on his arrival in the Starry heaven. Aquinas's comments explain why the *viator* is still so dependent on his eyes and on creation: he continues to see 'per sensum'. They also explicate why Beatrice should invite him to study the planets: the 'primum coelum dicatur cognitio coelestium corporum' [the first heaven would mean the knowledge of the celestial bodies]; and his intellectual abilities must adapt to this type of knowledge before proceeding further. The passage from the *Summa* thus offers important cultural coordinates with which to define *Paradiso* XXII's ideological parameters, together with precise explanations for the logic of the action in the heaven of the Fixed Stars and for the protagonist's *forma mentis*. Indeed, Aquinas is able to provide an idea of the basic structure that unites *Paradiso*'s last three heavens: 'ut primum caelum dicatur cognitio caelestium corporum; secundum cognitio caelestium spirituum; tertium, cognitio ipsius Dei' [so the first heaven would be the knowledge of the celestial bodies; the second would be the knowledge of the celestial spirits; the third, the knowledge of God himself]; and, in the last part of the canticle, Dante-character passes from an understanding of the universe to an appreciation of the angels, before finally arriving at the *visio Dei*.[31]

What makes Thomas's *responsio* especially valuable for the present analysis is the fact that it synthesizes widely circulating notions. The ideas around which *Paradiso* XXII is constructed were thus an integral part of contemporary culture. Although the canto's poetry is impressively rich and original (particularly striking are its

31   It would be instructive to examine the links between *Paradiso* XXII and the close of the *Commedia*, since, appropriately, our canto appears to 'prefigure' various elements belonging to the representation of the final moments of the pilgrim's journey. As well as 'reflective', *Paradiso* XXII is also proleptic, underscoring its structural complexity and importance. See Vecce, p. 644, and n. 8 above.

accumulation of images, its syntactic rigour, and its lexical inventiveness), the concepts that Dante presents were part of well-established systems of thought, and therefore accessible to his readers.[32] In relying on them, what becomes evident is the transformative power of Dante's writing: on the one hand, his extraordinary ability to modify abstract ideas into poetic and narrative matter, and on the other, the controlled confidence with which he knits together in a restricted textual space a wide range of concepts. We have already seen that *Paradiso* XXII deals with the intellectual and spiritual identity of the pilgrim, along with semiotics, providential history, forms of knowledge, the *itinerarium mentis in Deum*, sight, the order of the universe, monasticism, and contemplation. And it is on contemplation that I should now like to dwell.

4. *Contemplatio*[33]

Among the several noteworthy elements in Aquinas's passage, there is one that is particularly suggestive. His *responsio* ends with a description of different modes of contemplating: 'contemplatio Dei secundum gradus cognitionis qua Deus videtur' [the contemplation of God according to the degree of knowledge whereby God is seen]. In Dante scholarship, however, there is a long-established tendency to treat contemplation as if it were a monolith and equivalent to mysticism, which, in its turn, given the mind's focus on God, is seen as a form of *contemptus mundi*. Any standard account of medieval contemplation underscores the inadequacies of treating *contemplatio* in this manner.[34] As Thomas averred, *contemplatio* embraced 'Humana vero studia, quae ordinantur ad considerationem veritatis' [The human studies, which are directed towards the examination of truth] (*ST* II–II. q. 179. a. 2. resp. 3) — and those plural *studia* are of course highly significant. Thus, from nearly their inception, the cantos of Saturn also conventionally highlight contemplation's multifacetedness. *Paradiso* XXI's solitary simile, whose uniqueness underlines its importance, compares the movements of the souls on the golden ladder to those of jackdaws in flight:

> E come, per lo natural costume,
> le pole insieme, al cominciar del giorno,
> si movono a scaldar le fredde piume;

32   To date, there is still no in-depth study of *Paradiso* XXII's stylistic profile.

33   Mira Mocan's *lectura* substantially adds to my discussion of the function of *contemplatio* in *Paradiso* XXII.

34   See, for instance, Jacques Leclercq, *L'Amour des lettres et le désir de Dieu* (Paris: Éditions du Cerf, 1957), *Études sur le vocabulaire monastique du moyen âge* (Rome: Herder, 1961), and *'Otia monastica': études sur le vocabulaire de la contemplation au moyen âge* (Rome: Herder, 1963). See also Jules Lebreton, 'Contemplation dans la Bible', in DSAM, II, cols 1644–1715; René Arnou, 'La Contemplation chez les anciens philosophes du monde gréco-latin', in DSAM, II, cols 1715–42; Jean-Loup Lemaitre and others, 'Contemplation chez les Grecs et autres orientaux chrétiens', in DSAM, II, cols 1762–1911; Jacques Leclercq and Michel Olphe-Galliard, 'Contemplation dans la littérature chrétienne latine', in DSAM, II, cols 1911–47; Jean-Marie Déchanet, 'Contemplation au XIIe siècle', in DSAM, II, cols 1947–66; P. Philippe, 'Contemplation au XIIIe siècle', in DSAM, II, cols 1966–88; François Vandenbroucke, 'Contemplation au XIVe siècle', in DSAM, II, cols 1988–2001; Georges Frénaud, 'Dans l'école bénédictine', in DSAM, II, cols 2119–38.

> poi altre vanno via sanza ritorno,
> altre rivolgon sé onde son mosse,
> e altre roteando fan soggiorno;
>   tal modo parve me che quivi fosse
> in quello sfavillar che 'nsieme venne,
> sì come in certo grado si percosse. (*Par.* XXI. 34–42)

Edmund Gardner had already noted that the image recalls one that Richard of St Victor had employed to illustrate different forms of contemplation by equating them to birds in flight. The basic idea had its origins in the pseudo-Dionysius's concept of the three movements of the contemplative soul, namely, circular, linear, and 'oblique'.[35] Thus, as Dante's choice of simile confirms, from the first appearance of the 'tanti splendori' (*Par.* XXI. 32), he was intent on stressing the variety of contemplation. Once more, these are ideas that enjoyed wide cultural currency. Indeed, accompanied by the same aviary image, Thomas discusses both the Areopagite and Richard in the *Summa theologica* at a short distance from his analysis of the third heaven.[36] Having signposted *contemplatio*'s importance at the beginning of *Paradiso* XXI, Dante then devotes the rest of the canto,[37] and especially the following one, to analyzing contemplation's complex multiplicity.[38]

As the poet often does in the *Commedia*, and as I have begun to document, the abstract problem is not expounded directly by means of a dry doctrinal disquisition. Instead, it is disclosed via the *narratio* and through the poetic fabric, both of which demand an act of exegetical engagement on the reader's part:

> O voi ch'avete li 'ntelletti sani,
> mirate la dottrina che s'asconde
> sotto 'l velame de li versi strani. (*Inf.* IX. 61–63)

In *Paradiso* XXII, the most striking element of Dante's treatment of contemplation is the strong bond that he posits between this and the active life. Conversely, Dante scholarship has a bit too often preferred to insist on the distinctiveness of the two *vitae*.[39] Yet, as Aquinas explains with his customary precision, the Middle Ages

---

35   Edmund G. Gardner, *Dante and the Mystics* [1913] (New York: Haskell House, 1968), pp. 173–75. See also Jean Châtillon, 'Les Trois Modes de la contemplation selon Richard de Saint Victor', *Bulletin de littérature écclésiastique*, 41 (1940), 3–26. Mocan provides an excellent analysis of Dante's image (pp. 201–15). For the passage from Richard of St Victor, see *Ben. maj.* I. 5; for that from the pseudo-Dionysius, see *De divinis nominibus* IV. 8–10, in *Mistica teologia = De mystica theologia; Epistole I–V*, ed. by A. M. Ritter (Rome: San Clemente; Bologna: Studio domenicano, 2011). Dante appropriately reprises Richard's image in describing the pilgrim's union with God which brings to completion the experiences of the 'contemplating' *viator* that had begun in the heaven of Saturn; see Chapter 5, p. 193.

36   *ST* II–II. q. 180. a. 6. The whole section that includes *quaestiones* 179–82 constitutes a wide-ranging assemblage of medieval ideas on contemplation (including its relationship to the active life).

37   On contemplation in *Paradiso* XXI, see Gabriele Muresu, 'Lo specchio e la contemplazione (*Paradiso* XXI)', *L'Alighieri*, n.s. 8 (1996), 7–39.

38   Both Hawkins and Mazzotta, 'Language and Vision', note the importance of contemplation in *Paradiso* XXII.

39   Della Terza, Hawkins, Mazzotta, 'Language and Vision', and Pasquazi recognize the interconnections between the active and the contemplative life in *Paradiso* XXII. See also Tommaso Leccisotti, *Il canto di San Benedetto* (Turin: SEI, 1965), p. 14.

considered the two to be interdependent:

> Ad secundum dicendum quod media conficiuntur ex extremis, et ideo virtute continentur in eis, sicut tepidum in calido et frigido, et pallidum in albo et nigro. Et similiter sub activo et contemplativo comprehenditur id quod est ex utroque compositum. Et tamen sicut in quolibet mixto praedominatur aliquod simplex, ita etiam in medio genere vitae superabundat quandoque quidem contemplativum, quandoque vero activum.[40]

> [On the second point I answer that a mean is made of a combination of the extremes, thus it is by virtue contained in them, as warm in hot and cold, or pale in white and black. Similarly, active and contemplative comprehend what is made of both. Nonetheless, just as in any mixture one of the simple elements dominates, so even in the mean state of life sometimes the contemplative element, and sometimes the active abounds.]

Recounting the course of his own life rich in work and prayer (37–45, 89) and celebrating 'i fiori e' frutti santi' (48), the thoughts and deeds of the contemplatives, Benedict too affirms the intimate connection between *actio* and *contemplatio*.[41] The saint's words chime with the dictates of his *Rule* which emphasize the need to *laborare, legere et orare*.[42] Yet, in Dante's time, that same *Regula* 'rimasa è per danno de le carte' (75). It is now the divinely ordained responsibility of the pilgrim through his behaviour and the poet through the *Commedia* to re-establish the proper balance between active and contemplative. Equally, we his readers, by first interpreting the poem and then acting on its lessons, will ensure that our 'lives are adequately divided into active and contemplative'.

There is little doubt that, for Dante and the Middle Ages, contemplation was complex and wide-ranging, offering different ways to arrive at the truth and at an experience of God.[43] This is underlined by the different forms of looking evoked

---

40   *ST* II–II. q. 179. a. 2. resp. 2. Aquinas defines the two 'lives' as follows: 'Intellectus autem dividitur per activum et contemplativum, quia finis intellectivae cognitionis vel est ipsa cognitio veritatis, quod pertinet ad intellectum contemplativum; vel est aliqua exterior actio, quod pertinet ad intellectum practicum sive activum. Et ideo vita etiam sufficienter dividitur per activam et contemplativam' [The intellect is divided into active and contemplative, because the aim of intellectual knowledge is either the very knowledge of truth, which pertains to the contemplative intellect, or some kind of external action, which belongs to the practical, or active, intellect. Thus life is adequately divided into active and contemplative] (*ST* II–II. q. 179. a. 2).

41   Compare: 'Si autem dicatur fructus hominis id quod ex homine producitur, sic ipsi actus humani fructus dicuntur. [...] Opera igitur nostra, in quantum sunt effectus quidam Spiritus sanctis in nobis operantis, habent rationem fructus; sed in quantum ordinantur ad finem vitae aeternae, sic magis habent rationem florum' [If then what is produced by man is called the fruit of man, human actions themselves are called fruits. [...] All of our works, therefore, inasmuch as they are consequences, so to speak, of the Holy Spirit that operates in us, can be considered fruits; but inasmuch as they are directed to the end which is eternal life, they are rather considered flowers] (*ST* I–II. q. 70. a. 1).

42   See Jacques Leclercq, 'Otium monasticum as a Context for Artistic Creativity', in *Monasticism and the Arts*, ed. by Timothy G. Verdon and John Dally (Syracuse, NY: Syracuse University Press, 1984), pp. 63–80.

43   On the inter-relationship between seeing and knowing in medieval thought, see Giacinta Spinosa, 'Visione sensibile e intellettuale: convergenze gnoseologiche e linguistiche nella semantica della visione medievale', *Micrologus*, 5 (1997), 119–34; Giorgio Stabile, 'Teoria della visione come teoria della conoscenza', *Micrologus*, 5 (1997), 225–46.

in *Paradiso* XXII. Furthermore, as contemplation's links with the active life make clear, it is incorrect to think of it as being insulated from the things of this world. Contemplation is not simply a one-way system, from the earth up to Heaven, but also functions in the opposite direction — it is a fundamentally 'reflective' system. This quality is emblematically summarized in Jacob's ladder, which serves not only as a means to 'dipart*ire* | da terra i piedi' (*Par.* XXII. 73–74). but also to 'scender giuso' (*Par.* XXI. 31). It serves as a bridge between the human and the divine: on the one hand, as a medium to reach God; on the other, as an intermediary through which God can reach humanity. This two-way movement is more than evident in the patriarch's dream: 'Viditque in somnis scalam stantem super terram, et cacumen illius tangens caelum: angelos quoque Dei ascendentes et descendentes per eam' [In my dream I saw a ladder standing on the ground, and its top touched the sky: and the angels of God were going up and down on it] (Genesis 28: 12). Indeed, the exegetical tradition stressed the bilateral functions of the 'scaleo', as one of the two protagonists of the heaven of Saturn made explicit: 'Tu scala illa Jacob, quae homines vehis ad coelum, et angelos ad humanum deponis auxilium' [You, famous ladder of Jacob, which carries men to Heaven, and sends angels to man's aid].[44]

The double function of Jacob's ladder allows us to appreciate why, in the heaven of contemplation, Dante should devote so much space to earthly matters. Looking downward is one of the obligations of those who find themselves on high. It is enough to remember St Peter's anguish at the state of the contemporary papacy in *Paradiso* XXVII. More significantly, this two-way process also allows us better to grasp the subtle and contrasting implications of the disdain with which the poet describes the 'vil sembiante' (135) of our 'aiuola' (151). The incongruity between the ways in which the poet presents life on earth is striking. On the one hand, Dante declares peremptorily that 'quel consiglio per migliore approbo | che l'ha [the earth] per meno' (136–37), and supports his claim with telling instances of human corruption (73–87, 91–93) On the other, however, he celebrates illustrious examples of human greatness by alluding to saints of the calibre of Peter, Benedict, and Francis. What might seem a contradiction is resolved in light of the basic symbolism of the ladder. The 'scaleo' establishes that creation is structured not as a series of separate realities, but as a carefully hierarchized continuum — a fact that is confirmed by the pilgrim's privileged discriminating view of the universe. Consequently, along this continuum, 'questo globo' (134) finding itself at the bottom, is irrefutably the 'meno' (137). However, being located on the lowest rung of the ladder, does not mean that all that is found there is worthless. On earth, in keeping with an ethical hierarchy appropriate to human behaviour, each individual can choose between 'il bianco' and 'il bruno' (93). Notions such as 'more' and 'less' are highly relative, and are inevitably affected by the rung of the ladder from which one looks. What I am alluding to here is of course tied to what I noted earlier about the system of values related to sight and, henceforth, it is probably better to speak of contemplation rather than of sight. On earth, to perceive the truth, we must rely on

---

44 Peter Damian, *Dominus vobiscum*, in *Die Briefe des Petrus Damiani*, ed. by Kurt Reindel, 4 vols (Munich: Monumenta Germaniae Historica, 1983–93), I, no. 28 (p. 274). For an important discussion of this aspect of the ladder, see Di Fonzo, '"La dolce donna"'.

our contemplative intellect. At the same time, Dante reminds us of the limits that restrict any earthly contemplative effort and, hence, our apprehension of the truth — issues that the poet had earlier investigated as regards the cognitive efficacy of different epistemologies in the heavens of the Sun and Jupiter.[45] As Benedict states, the truth, in its absolute sense, exists only in God (61–67). Thus, being 'sì presso a l'ultima salute' (124), the pilgrim must 'aver le luci [...] chiare e acute' (126) in order properly to contemplate 'l'alta luce che da sé è vera' (*Par.* XXXIII. 54). Again, Dante reminds us of the many different forms into which the search for truth, and hence contemplation, are refracted.

In *Paradiso* XXII, Dante never calls into doubt that religious life offers the best environment in which to exercise the *intellectus contemplativus*. Yet, as is apparent from the fact that the pilgrim is so intimately involved with contemplation, the poet also underscores that contemplation, namely, the *consideratio veritatis*, cannot be restricted to those who 'dentro ai chiostri | fermar li piedi e tennero il cor saldo' (50–51). St Benedict reiterates this same point when he addresses the *viator* as 'Frate'. One of the many functions of *Paradiso* XXII, therefore, is to focus on the similarities and differences between the pilgrim who looks and the monks that contemplate, and, by extension, between 'secular' and 'religious' *contemplatio*, namely, between the different forms of looking, thinking, and learning evoked in the canto.

The ladder's symbolism again offers evidence in support of this reading. *Paradiso* XXII opens with an explicit borrowing from Boethius's *Consolatio philosophiae*. 'Oppresso di stupore' (1) echoes 'sed te, ut video, stupor oppressit' [but you, as I can see, are oppressed by wonder] (1. prose 2), the words that Philosophy, soon after appearing, addresses to her disciple. Boethius had earlier concentrated on the appearance of the mysterious woman:

> Statura discretionis ambiguae. Nam nunc quidem ad communem sese hominum mensuram cohibebat, nunc vero pulsare caelum summi verticis cacumine videbatur; quae cum altius caput extulisset, ipsum etiam caelum penetrebat respicientiumque hominum frustrabatur intuitum. Vestes erant tenuissimis filis subtili artificio [...] Harum in extremo margine π Graecum, in supremo vero θ, legebatur intextum. Atque inter utrasque litteras in scalarum modum gradus quidam insigniti videbantur, quibus ab inferiore ad superius elementum esset ascensus. (*Cons. phil.* 1. prose 1, pp. 132–34)

> [Her height was hard to determine, for at times she kept to the ordinary measure of men, other times she seemed to touch the heaven with the highest point of her head; and when she raised her head higher, she could penetrate the heaven itself and subtract herself from the sight of men looking. Her garments were made of the finest fabrics, and of accurate craftsmanship [...] their bottom edge showed a woven Greek π, and the top edge showed a θ. And between the two letters steps were marked that resembled a ladder, through which one might climb from the lower to the higher letter.]

The similarities that Dante programmatically evokes between Jacob's ladder and Philosophy with her embroidered vestment are striking. The allusion to the *Con-*

45   See Barański, *Dante e i segni*; Meekins; Nasti. See also Pamela Williams, 'Dante's Heaven of the Sun and the Wisdom of Solomon', *Italica*, 82 (2005), 165–79.

solatio further corroborates that, in *Paradiso* XXII, the poet was intent on treating contemplation broadly, in relation to different *studia humana*. As is well known, the two Greek letters decorating *Philosophia*'s dress were associated with the two parts of philosophy, the practical and the theoretical. Neoplatonic circles, where the *Consolatio* enjoyed considerable popularity, developed a definition of the two philosophical branches, and in particular of the theoretical, that circulated extensively. I quote here a version that not only explicitly refers to Philosophy's vestment, but is also taken from a text that Dante may possibly have known first-hand: Bernardus Silvestris's commentary on Virgil's *Aeneid*.[46] In glossing VI. 42 ('Excisum Euboicae latus ingens rupis in antrum' [The massive side of the Euboean rock is cut into a cavern]), Bernardus opens a long digression:

> *EXCISUM:* Ponit topografiam describens mistice philosophiam quia ad eam dicebat Sibillam advocare Eneam. *LATUS:* Pars quedam *EUBOICE RUPIS*, id est philosophie, non ipsa scientia, sed ipsa ars. Ideo autem dicuntur rupes philosophice artes quod inrefragibiles sunt. Tante namque integritatis sunt artes philosophice quod nulla est earum ratio que falli possit. Unde Boetius ait, 'vestes philosophie indissolubili materia factas'. Euboice autem dicuntur ille rupes quia in Euboa, id est in scientia, sunt. Pars Euboice rupis, id est pars artium philosophicarum, est theorica; alia pars practica. Illa pars philosophie, id est theorica, ita est excisa, id est a se separata. Dividitur enim per theologiam et mathematicam et phisicam. Theorica namque ea contemplatur in quibus practica nequit agere, id est incorporalia. Et quoniam incorporeorum tria sunt genera, tres sunt species theorice contemplantis ipsa. Est enim primum incorporeorum genus a corporibus penitus remotum, in quo genere est creator, eius sapientia, anima mundi, angelus, quod contemplatur theorica per primam speciem suam, theologiam, unde sic dicta est theologia, id est divinorum ratio. Secundum autem genus est incorporeorum, id est ille incorporeum quod est circa corpora secundum multitudinem magnitudinemque, quod contemplatur secunda species theorice, id est mathematica. Tercia species theorice tercium genus comprehendit incorporeorum, id est phisica natura rerum. Contemplatur namque theologia invisibiles substantias, mathematica visibiles visibilium quantitates, phisica invisibiles visibilium causas. Itaque theorica per tres species est excisa.[47]

> [CUT: Virgil gives a topography which mystically describes philosophy, because the Sybil is said to call Aeneas into it. SIDE: one part of the *EUBOEAN ROCK*, that is philosophy, not as philosophical knowledge, but as the art of philosophy itself. The philosophical arts are in fact called rocks that cannot be destroyed. The philosophical arts are of such perfection that there is no reasoning in them that may fail. Thus Boethius says: 'the garments of philosophy are made of indissoluble material'. Those rocks are called Euboean because they are in Euboea, that is

---

46   See Giorgio Inglese, *L'intelletto e l'amore* (Milan: La Nuova Italia, 2000), pp. 146–48. See also Giorgio Padoan, 'Bernardo Silvestre', in ED, vol. I, pp. 606–07.

47   *The Commentary on the First Six Books of the 'Aeneid' of Virgil Commonly Attributed to Bernardus Silvestris*, ed. by Julian W. Jones and Elizabeth F. Jones (Lincoln and London: University of Nebraska Press, 1977), pp. 40–41. In their notes to this passage, the editors cite works by William of Conches and by Ralph of Longchamp that include very similar definitions of philosophy. See also Boethius, *De Trinitate*, in *The Theological Tractates*, II. 5–21 (pp. 8–10), and Hugh of St Victor, *In Hierarchia coelestis* I. 1, in PL, vol. CLXXV, cols 927–28. Bernard's distinctions are commonplaces.

scientific knowledge. Part of the Euboean rock, that is part of the philosophical arts, refers to theory, the other to practice. The theoretical part of philosophy is cut into smaller parts, and is separate from philosophy itself. It is in fact divided into theology, mathematics, and physics. The theoretical concerns the things which practical philosophy cannot concentrate on, that is non-material things. And since there are three kinds of non-material, there are also three species of theoretical philosophy. The first kind of non-material things is completely separated from the bodies, and to this kind belong the creator, his wisdom, the soul of the world, the angels, what theoretical philosophy can oversee through its first species, theology, and thus it is called theology, that is the knowledge of divine things. The second kind still comprises non-material things, but that type of 'non-material' that concerns elements in their number and size, which the second species of theoretical philosophy, that is mathematics, studies. The third species of theoretical philosophy includes the third kind of non-material, that is physics which includes the nature of things. Thus theology studies the invisible substances, mathematics studies the visible quantity of things visible, and physics the invisible causes of things visible. Theoretical philosophy is therefore divided into three species.]

As is the case with the ladder, so this passage too clarifies *Paradiso* XXII's ideological parameters. It confirms that medieval *contemplatio*, by embracing Boethian philosophy, stretched from the *divinorum ratio* to mathematical and scientific investigations. Although *Paradiso* XXII as a whole shares in this comprehensive sense of *contemplatio*, it is the pilgrim's conduct in the heaven of the Fixed Stars that most explicitly dramatizes contemplation's range.

In the Platonic tradition, as documented by the *Timaeus*, the only one of the philosopher's texts that Dante may have known, and this in Calcidius's version, human philosophical thought directly results from the divine gift of sight that enables the study of the heavens. Once again, close links unite *Paradiso* XXII and a text that exercised considerable sway on medieval culture — a further sign of the canto's crucial status in the *Commedia*'s ideological structure. Both Plato and Dante place the same emphasis on sight and on the observation of the heavens:

Uisus enim iuxta meam sententiam causa est maximi commodi plerisque non otiose natis atque institutis ob id ipsum quod nunc agimus. neque enim de uniuersa re quisquam quaereret nisi prius stellis sole caeloque uisis. At nunc diei noctisque insinuata nobis alterna uice menses annorumque obitus et anfractus nati sunt, eorumque ipsorum dinumeratio et ex dinumeratione perfectus et absolutus extitit numerus. tum temporis recordatio, quae naturam uniuersae rei quaerere docuit curamque inuestigationis iniecit mentibus quasi quoddam seminarium philosophiae pandens, quo bono nihil umquam maius ad hominum genus diuina munificentia commeauit. Hoc igitur maximum beneficium uisus oculorumque esse dico. Minora alia praetereo quibus, qui a philosophia remoti sunt, carentes debiles caecique maestam uitam lugubremque agunt. Nobis uero causa dicenda demonstrandaque uidetur diuini muneris, quod prouidentia commenta est salubriter hactenus. Deum oculos hominibus idcirco dedisse, ut mentis prouidentiaeque circuitus, qui fiunt in caelo, notantes eorum similes cognatosque in usum redigerent suae mentis circuitusque animae, qui animaduersiones seu deliberationes uocantur, quam simillimos efficerent diuinae mentis prouidis motibus placidis tranquillisque perturbatos licet, confirmatoque ingeneratae rationis examine, dum imitantur aplanem mundi intellegibilis circumactionem, suae mentis motus erraticos corrigant.[48]

[For sight, in my opinion, is the cause of the greatest satisfaction for many whose birth was not meaningless and who were educated for the very thing that we are now doing. Nobody would indeed inquire about the universe without having seen first the stars, the sun, and the heaven. In fact because of the alternating succession of day and night which we have to face, the months and the cyclical progression of the years have come to be, and their calculation, and from their calculation a perfect and whole number has arisen. Then came the idea of time, which taught us to investigate the nature of the universe and instilled in our minds the concern for examination, as if expanding, as it were, a nursery-garden of philosophy; and the divine benevolence has never made a greater gift than this to humankind. Thus I say that the benefit of our eyes and sight is the most valuable. I omit other minor ones, for the lack of which those who are far away from philosophy are weak and blind, and live a sad and mournful life. Nonetheless, we should evidently articulate and explain the reason of the divine gift, which providence so far has devised for our own well-being: God has given men eyes so that, by noticing the circlings of mind and providence that happen in heaven, they might retrieve to the use of their own mind circlings that are very similar to these, and make the circlings of their own soul, which are called considerations or deliberations, as similar as possible — even if confused — to the cautious, calm, and peaceful motions of the divine mind, and so that with the reinforced consideration of their ungenerated reason they may correct the inconsistent motions of their own mind, while imitating the steady rotation of the intelligible world.]

Already in Calcidius's commentary, and then consistently in medieval Neoplatonism, the philosophy of which Plato speaks is divided into two, 'consideratio et item actus: consideratio quidem ob adsiduam contemplationem rerum diuinarum et inmortalium nominata, actus uero, qui iuxta rationabilis animae deliberationem progreditur in tuendis conseruandisque rebus mortalibus' [consideration and act: the term 'consideration' comes from the constant contemplation of divine and immortal things, and act is what after the deliberation of the rational soul proceeds in the observation and conservation of mortal things]. *Consideratio* is then further subdivided, 'in theologiam et item naturae sciscitationem praestandaeque etiam rationis scientiam' [into theology, the study of nature, and the science of performing calculations], specifically, the three disciplines that, over time, became the three parts of *theorica*: theology, physics, and mathematics.[49] Thus, it is not difficult to recognize in the pilgrim who *rimira* the spheres the Platonic philosopher, even if the direction of their gazes is diametrically opposed:

> Quindi m'apparve il temperar di Giove
> tra 'l padre e 'l figlio: e quindi mi fu chiaro
> il variar che fanno di lor dove;

48   *Platonis Timaeus interprete Chalcidio cum eiusdem commentario*, ed. by Johannes Wrobel (Leipzig: Teubner, 1876), 47a–c (pp. 56–57).

49   Calcidius, *In Platonis Timaeum Commentarius*, in *Platonis Timaeus*, XII. 264 (p. 295). See also Bernard of Chartres, *Glosae super Platonem*, ed. by Paul E. Dutton (Toronto: PIMS, 1991), pp. 214–15.

> e tutti e sette mi si dimostraro
> quanto son grandi e quanto son veloci
> e come sono in distante riparo. (145–50)

In particular, he behaves like the 'ideal' mathematician and physicist, who comprehends in their totality the 'visible quantities of visible things' and the 'invisible causes of visible things'. The *viator* fully assimilates the knowledge of two of the branches of contemplation in preparation to being granted access to the third branch of *contemplatio*: theology and the contemplation of the invisible substances; and invisible substances of course predominate in the remaining *canti* of *Paradiso*.

The pilgrim's contemplative comportment in the heaven of the Fixed Stars confirms *Paradiso* XXII's structural coherence and the continuities uniting its two halves. It also establishes the evolutionary and hierarchical character of the relationship between what I earlier termed 'secular' and 'religious' contemplation. At the end of *Paradiso* XXII, after his look backwards, which assesses both his journey's achievements and the efforts that he still needs to make, the pilgrim, imitating the example of the holy monks, prepares to fix his gaze on theological *contemplatio*: 'poscia rivolsi li occhi a li occhi belli' (154). In addition, thanks to the truths that the pilgrim-'scientist' perceived and absorbed as he contemplated the nature of the universe, the poet, in his turn, having returned to earth will be able to compose a work worthy of the lofty material for which God has made him responsible.[50] Finally, the fact that the *viator* contemplates the heavens from above, while we look at them from below, underlines the miraculous uniqueness of his mission; and his wondrous celestial condition ought to be integrated with the revelation regarding the heavenly origins of his 'ingegno' (114).[51] Yet, in his role as Everyman, the pilgrim reminds us that, in this life, we also have the obligation to behave as contemplatives. In the first instance, we need to reflect on *Paradiso* XXII, and then on the entire 'sacred' text that we are privileged to read, which, like the heavens, is ultimately the work of the *Deus artifex*. In so doing, we can be confident that, scrutinizing and then interpreting the divine *vestigia* with intelligence and from the appropriate perspective, as when we 'contemplate' *Paradiso* XXII, a canto that celebrates the extraordinary potential and remit of *contemplatio*, we will discover the harmonious order that lies behind elements that, at first glance, appear unrelated.

5. Conclusion

The basic principle behind *Paradiso* XXII's organization is directed at establishing that contemplation unveils the congruent orderliness of being. The most sophisticated manifestation of this structural and ideological imperative is apparent in Dante's careful interweaving of major strands of contemporary thought. *Paradiso*

---

50   On the relationship between *poetare* and *contemplare*, see Mocan, pp. 226–31.
51   In *Paradiso* XXII, Dante paints a much richer and more nuanced portrait of the pilgrim than I am able to sketch here. For instance, as a consequence of his asking St Benedict to reveal his face to him, the *viator* is linked to the key doctrine of *Nosce teipsum*. Unfortunately, I do not have the space to investigate this important issue.

XXII's poetic fabric is coherently made up of a complex yet ordered pattern of inter-related threads of Neoplatonic discourse. In this weave, Plato is connected to his medieval commentators, to Boethius, to the school of Chartres, and, of course, to Macrobius, whose commentary on the *Somnium Scipionis* serves as yet another indicator of the fundamental pertinence of Neoplatonic reflection on sight, philosophy, and contemplation in the canto's make-up.[52] Furthermore, to assure the orthodoxy of his treatment, Dante merges his 'secular' sources with religious tropes close to Neoplatonism, such as mystical ascent, the ties between Heaven and earth, and the doctrine of active and contemplative life, as well as precise connections to Neoplatonicizing Christian authors, most notably Richard of St Victor.[53] By associating contemplation with Neoplatonic thought which, like Scriptural exegesis, saw the surface of creation as a 'veil' behind which higher truths can be discovered, Dante unmbiguously located *contemplatio* within the medieval symbolic and hermeneutic tradition.[54] At the same time, by having recourse to Chartrian Neoplatonism, which had a serious scientific interest in the physical causes of the natural world, the poet underlined that the universe concealed not only eschatological truths but, as the pilgrim realizes looking downwards, also truths of a different order. It is of course *contemplatio* that binds together this 'ladder' of truths, or rather reveals that such truths are there to be contemplated.[55]

The textual clues regarding the importance of sight which served as my point of departure have allowed us to travel far. During the course of this journey up and down *Paradiso* XXII, which itself functions as a *signum* of the pilgrim's journey down and then up creation, it has been possible to appreciate, if not *tutto*, at least Dante's extraordinary ability to tie together, around the concept of *contemplatio*, the different formal, semantic, and ideological strands of his exposition. That the canto is overwhelmingly concerned with contemplation is 'obvious' if one recalls the basic values that the Middle Ages assigned to its two heavens. Yet, Dante's greatness also

---

52   See, in particular, Claudia Di Fonzo, 'Il *Somnium* di Cicerone e la scala di Giacobbe: politica e poetica del *trasumanar*', *Studi danteschi*, 80 (2015), 23–48.

53   See Mocan, p. 193. More specifically, she argues that Dante 'aderi*sce* a una concezione della *contemplatio* più vicina a quella di ascendenza dionisiano-agostiniana sostenuta dai Vittorini e dallo stesso Riccardo' (p. 212).

54   'Looking backwards' from our canto along the *Paradiso*'s tercets, a highly suggestive pattern emerges. In the heaven of the Sun, Dante assesses different epistemologies and grants primacy to semiotic exegesis; in the heaven of Jove, he examines different types of *signa* and organizes these hierarchically; and, finally, in the heaven of Saturn, and especially in *Paradiso* XXII, he introduces *contemplatio* as the best *ars* with which to interpret signs.

55   Again Mira Mocan's conclusions are close to mine and refine them: 'La conseguenza sul piano dottrinale [of cleaving close to Dionysian and Ricardian mysticism] è significativa: non escludere dalla contemplazione le attività esercitate dalle altre facoltà dell'anima, quali la ragione e soprattutto l'immaginazione, vuol dire tra l'altro poter attribuire alla *contemplatio* una natura visiva, ovvero definirla come una forma di visione superiore "costruita" sulla base dell'ascensione progressiva attraverso le modalità "inferiori" della visione sensibile. [...] l'adesione dell'*auctor* a quella tradizione di pensiero, e soprattutto al *sistema epistemologico* [...] derivato sostanzialmente dal modello emanzionista neoplatonico, secondo cui le realtà sensibili, segni del "libro della natura", necessitano di un'operazione interpretativa ed ermeneutica che restituisca loro il senso superiore, di verità, di cui sono portatrici' (pp. 212–13).

lies in his ability to transform what is obvious into something new, unexpected, and exciting. As the pilgrim's experience dramatically makes known, contemplation, when properly exercised, always leads to new insights. This is *Paradiso* XXII's vital lesson, whose cogency is confirmed by our *contemplatio* of its *terzine*.

CHAPTER 5

'Affectivity' and Theology:
The Representation of Beatitude
in Dante's *Paradiso*

Sempre quello che massimamente dire intende lo dicitore sì dee
riservare di dietro; però che quello che ultimamente si dice, più
rimane nell'animo dello uditore.
(*Conv.* ii. 8. 2)

1. Feeling (and Thinking) 'Medievally'

In recent years,[1] particularly in the English-speaking world, but also in France, medievalists have been paying sustained attention to the emotions and affections: to mental states that arise spontaneously rather than from an intellectual process, and that can be associated with the senses.[2] At the core of this important research

---

1   The original Italian version of this chapter bore the following dedication: 'To Edward, my son, who, thanks to his interest, ensured I got to the end'.

2   See, for example, Thomas H. Bestul, *Texts of the Passion: Latin Devotional Literature and Medieval Society* (Philadelphia: University of Pennsylvania Press, 1996); Damien Boquet and Piroska Nagy, *Sensible Moyen Âge: une histoire des émotions dans l'Occident médiéval* (Paris: Seuil, 2015); Carla Casagrande and Silvana Vecchio, *Passioni dell'anima: teorie e usi degli affetti nella cultura medievale* (Florence: SISMEL and Edizioni del Galluzzo, 2015); Jessica Brantley, *Reading in the Wilderness: Private Devotion and Public Performance in Late Medieval England* (Chicago and London: University of Chicago Press, 2007); Boyd Taylor Coolman, 'The Medieval Affective Dionysian Tradition', *Modern Theology*, 24 (2008), 615–32; Daisy Delogu, '"Ala grant temps de douleur languissant": Grief and Mourning in Giraut d'Amiens' *Istoire le roy Charlemaine*', *Speculum*, 93 (2018), 1–26; Anne Derbes, *Picturing the Passion in Late Medieval Italy* (Cambridge: Cambridge University Press, 1996); Michelle Karnes, *Imagination, Meditation, and Cognition in the Middle Ages* (Chicago: University of Chicago Press, 2011); Peter King, 'Emotions in Medieval Thought', in *The Oxford Handbook of Philosophy of Emotion*, ed. by Peter Goldie (Oxford: Oxford University Press, 2009), pp. 167–87; Laurelle LeVert, '"Crucifye hem, crucifye hem": The Subject and Affective Response in Stories of the Passion', *Essays in Medieval Studies*, 14 (1997), 73–87; Sarah McNamer, *Affective Meditation and the Invention of Medieval Compassion* (Philadelphia: University of Pennsylvania Press, 2010); Éric Palazzo, *L'Invention chrétienne des cinq sens dans la liturgie et l'art au Moyen Âge* (Paris: Cerf, 2010); Barbara H. Rosenwein, *Emotional Communities in the Early Middle Ages* (Ithaca, NY, and London: Cornell University Press, 2006), and 'Modernity: A Problematic Category in the History of Emotions', *History and Theory*, 53 (2014), 69–78; Anastasia P. Scrutton, *Thinking through Feeling: God, Emotion and Passibility* (New York: Continuum, 2011); James Simpson, 'From Reason to Affective Knowledge: Modes of Thought and Poetic Form in *Piers Plowman*', in *Medium Ævum*, 55 (1986), 1–23; *Cultures of Religious Reading in the Late Middle Ages: Instructing the Soul, Feeding the Spirit, and Awakening the Passion*, ed. by Sabrina Corbellini (Turnhout: Brepols, 2013);

lies the idea that affections and emotions not only are generated biologically and psychologically, but are also cultural facts, whose values change across time, space, and circumstance. It is enough to recall a state of mind such as idleness, which, under different conditions, encompasses discrete concepts such as spiritual and intellectual apathy, sloth, negligence, but also *otium*, the stillness of spirit and mind that facilitates study or contemplation. Likewise, an emotional outburst like anger can have bloody and irrational results, as Dante reveals in *Inferno* XII. However, it can also arise from a just and morally upright reaction, as when Jesus responded angrily to the merchants in the temple, or when the pilgrim challenged the corrupt popes: 'Io non so s'i' mi fui qui troppo folle' (*Inf.* XIX. 88). To say nothing of pain: gruesome and self-sustaining torment or spiritual and salvific correction, as Dante dramatically illustrates in the transition from Hell to Purgatory and, then, via the reference to the 'buon dolor' (*Purg.* XXIII. 81).[3]

From an early date, Christian thinkers were sensitive to the complexity and richness of the emotions, recognizing their implications for salvation and damnation. Dante's *Commedia* offers an emblematic example of the profound medieval attention to human feelings. It is enough to remember the centrality in the poem of love, as well as the problem of the relationship between body and soul, between desire and knowledge, between the senses and the intellect — all issues that fundamentally involve the emotions, which, moreover, according to the poet and the Christian tradition, are at the heart of our relationship to God and to others. More specifically, the emotions determine Dante's representation of the second kingdom, in which repentance and compassion are intimately connected. Consequently, Purgatory can be considered, to use the term coined by historians of the emotions, as an 'emotional community',[4] namely, a community that shares the same emotional values.[5] In actual fact, Dante's whole otherworldly journey presents a polychromatic gallery of emotions: from those in continuous movement of the wayfarers to those, less mobile but, when taken together, spanning a multiplicity of states, of the inhabitants of the netherworld. Furthermore, the moral system of Dante's afterlife is tightly linked to contemporary reflection on the vices and virtues, in which the passions — always apt to impose themselves — and their

Emotion and Cognitive Life in Medieval and Early Modern Philosophy, ed. by Martin Pickavé and Lisa Shapiro (Oxford: Oxford University Press, 2012); *'Ragionar d'amore': il lessico delle emozioni nella lirica medievale*, ed. by Alessio Decaria and Lino Leonardi (Florence: SISMEL and Edizioni del Galluzzo, 2015); *La expresión de las emociones en la lirica románica medieval*, ed. by Mercedes Brea (Alessandria: Edizioni dell'Orso, 2015); *Les Cinq sens au Moyen Âge*, ed. by Éric Palazzo (Paris: Cerf, 2016); *The Spirit, the Affections, and the Christian Tradition*, ed. by Dale M. Colter and Amos Yong (Notre Dame, IN: University of Notre Dame Press, 2016). See also Valentina Atturo, *Emozioni medievali: bibliografia degli studi 1941–2014 con un'appendice sulle risorse digitali* (Rome: Bagatto Libri, 2015). For an important contribution on the role of non-affective forms in medieval religious literature, see Cristina M. Cervone, *Poetics of the Incarnation: Middle English Writing and the Leap of Love* (Philadelphia: University of Pennsylvania Press, 2012).

3   See in particular Lino Pertile, 'Sul dolore nella *Commedia*', in *Letteratura e filologia fra Svizzera e Italia: studi in onore di Guglielmo Gorni. I. Dante: la 'Commedia' e altro*, ed. by Maria Antonietta Terzoli and others, 3 vols (Rome: Edizioni di Storia e Letteratura, 2010), I, 105–20.

4   See in particular Rosenwein, *Emotional Communities*.

5   See Jeremy Tambling, *Dante in Purgatory: States of Affect* (Turnhout: Brepols, 2010).

control played a vital role.[6]

It should be clear, even on the basis of these few examples, that the emotions were a central issue both in medieval culture and in Dante's *opera omnia*. Indeed, at least from the second half of the nineteenth century, Dantists have regularly focused on individual emotions, above all love, and on individual 'emotive' characters, such as the irascible Filippo Argenti and the envious Sapia. Yet, in spite of many particularized analyses, almost no studies exist that aim to clarify, from a historical and overarching perspective that acknowledges the complexity of the emotions in medieval culture, their presence and implications in Dante.[7] This chapter can be no more than a first uncertain step in helping us to arrive — quite a long distance into the future, I suspect — at a more complete understanding of a key aspect of Dante's cultural and intellectual make-up. For the moment, I should like to begin by fleetingly touching on two general problems that, in my view, circumscribe the question of the relationship between the poet and medieval reflection on the emotions. Subsequently, I intend to concentrate on one high-profile example — Dante's representation of the *visio Dei* — that constitutes the culminating moment of the pilgrim's experience of the afterlife, while, from a poetic point of view, it stands as the pinnacle of the artistic and intellectual problems associated with Dante's treatment of the otherworld. I hope that, as part of an in-depth investigation of beatitude in the *Commedia*, the example of the *viator*'s miraculous union with God might be able to offer a sense of how studying the emotions can enrich our understanding of the poem.

The first general point concerns the main sources for Dante's knowledge of the emotions.[8] As might be expected, with regard to the purely psychological and physiological aspects of feelings, Dante follows the Aristotelian and medical

6   See Rosenwein, *Emotional Communities*, pp. 46–49, 81–91; Tambling, pp. 13–60.

7   See however John Alcorn, 'Suffering in Hell: The Psychology of Emotions in Dante's *Inferno*', *Pedagogy*, 13 (2013), 77–85; Marco Ariani, 'Mistica degli affetti e intelletto d'amore: per una ridefinizione del canto xxiv del *Paradiso*', *Rivista di studi danteschi*, 9 (2009), 29–55, then revised in *Cento canti per cento anni. III. 'Paradiso'. 2. Canti XVIII–XXXIII*, ed. by Enrico Malato and Andrea Mazzucchi (Rome: Salerno, 2015), pp. 698–722; Lina Bolzoni, 'Dante o della memoria appassionata', *Lettere italiane*, 60 (2008), 169–93; Daniela Castelli, 'L'errore rigorista e la "fisica dell'anima" in una *Commedia* senza *lex talionis*', *Studi danteschi*, 78 (2013), 154–95; Paolo Falzone, 'Psicologia dell'atto umano in Dante: problemi di lessico e di dottrina', in *Filosofia in volgare nel Medioevo*, ed. by Nadia Bray and Loris Sturlese (Louvain-La-Neuve: Fédération internationale des instituts d'études médiévales, 2003), pp. 331–66; Mira Mocan, '"Ratio ab amore illuminatur": sulla mistica affettiva in Dante e nella letteratura romanza delle origini', in *'Tutto il lume della spera nostra': studi per Marco Ariani*, ed. by Giuseppe Crimi and Luca Marcozzi (Rome: Salerno, 2018), pp. 125–35; Arianna Punzi, '*Animos movere*: la lingua delle invettive nella *Commedia*', in *Dante, oggi*, ed. by Roberto Antonelli and others, 3 vols (Rome: Viella, 2011), II, 11–42; Tambling; Heather Webb, *Dante's Persons: An Ethics of the Transhuman* (Oxford: Oxford University Press, 2016). On Dante and the senses the bibliography is more substantial, although in general the studies do not reveal much interest in the affective and emotive dimension of the senses; however see Marco Ariani, 'Dante, la *dulcedo* e la dottrina dei "sensi spirituali"', in *Miscellanea di studi in onore di Claudio Varese*, ed. by Giorgio Cerboni Baiardi (Rome: Vecchiarelli, 2001), pp. 113–39.

8   For an idea of the complications relating to Dante's sources as regards this aspect of medieval culture, see Subsection 4, 'The Sources of Beatitude', below.

traditions.[9] At the same time, as I have already noted as regards the vices and virtues, emotions were part of a wide array of religious discourses, from confessional manuals to accounts of contemplative experiences, from theological treatises on love to literary and iconographic representations of the Passion and of the sufferings of martyrs (see n. 2). It is therefore imperative — and this is my second point — not to posit in Dante, as has often been done, a bland opposition between reason and the emotions in which reason has positive valences while the emotions are judged negatively. One might object that it is Dante himself who establishes such a clear opposition. It is enough to remember his presentation of the sins of incontinence and violence in the *Inferno*, as well as the many references in the poem to the bestiality of a life subject to the passions. In the *Convivio* too, he affirms the superiority of reason over the senses:

> È da sapere che le cose deono essere denominate dall'ultima nobilitade della loro forma: sì come l'uomo dalla ragione, e non dal senso né d'altro che sia meno nobile. Onde, quando si dice l'uomo vivere, si dee intendere l'uomo usare la ragione, che è sua speziale vita ed atto della sua più nobile parte. E però chi dalla ragione si parte e usa pure la parte sensitiva, non vive uomo ma vive bestia: sì come dice quello eccellentissimo Boezio: 'Asino vive'. Direttamente, dico, però che lo pensiero è propio atto della ragione, per che le bestie non pensano, ché non l'hanno; e non dico pur delle minori bestie, ma di quelle che hanno apparenza umana e spirito di pecora o d'altra bestia abominevole. (*Conv.* II. 7. 3–4)

Yet, there are also instances in which the relationship between reason and the emotions is not only more nuanced but also bent to the advantage of the latter. For Dante, therefore, knowledge is not simply an intellectual attainment, but, in conformity with almost the whole Christian tradition, it is also the effect of divinely inspired 'affective' processes, which, by definition, transcend a simply rational wisdom which, in Aristotelian terms, stems from the physio-psychological relationship between the senses and the intellect:[10]

> O imaginativa che ne rube
> talvolta sì di fuor, ch'om non s'accorge
> perché dintorno suonin mille tube,
>   chi move te, se 'l senso non ti porge?
> Moveti lume che nel ciel s'informa,
>   per sé o per voler che giù lo scorge. (*Purg.* XVII. 13–18)

Equally, and again in harmony with the main currents of Christianity, in describing the pilgrim's intellectual experiences, Dante presents them as the fruit of desire: 'L'alto disio che mo t'infiamma e urge, | d'aver notizia di ciò che tu vei' (*Par.*

---

9   See Natascia Tonelli, *Fisiologia della passione: poesia d'amore e medicina da Cavalcanti a Boccaccio* (Florence: Edizioni del Galluzzo, 2015), pp. 71–145.

10   See Zygmunt G. Barański, *Dante e i segni: saggi per una storia intellettuale di Dante Alighieri* (Naples: Liguori, 2000). However, more than forty years before my book appeared, Charles Singleton had alluded to the importance in the *Commedia* of Christian *Sapientia*, which 'touches the will and the affective life most profoundly': Charles S. Singleton, *Journey to Beatrice* (Cambridge, MA: Harvard University Press, 1958), p. 132.

xxx. 70–71). This process reaches its climax in the final canto of *Paradiso*, where, in conformity with theologians ranging from Augustine to Thomas Aquinas, the experience of God 'in su l'ultima spera' entails that 's'adempie | [...] ciascuna disïanza' (*Par.* xxII. 62–63, 65), so that immersion in the divine is joy, delight, sweetness, love.[11]

2. *Cognitio Dei* and/or *affectus in Deum*: Some Problems of Method

Does this mean that, in enjoying the *visio Dei*, there is no role nor space for the intellect? The answer is complicated. In very simple terms, according to many late-medieval theologians, it was thanks to the intellect being divinely illuminated that human beings can achieve beatitude, namely, the absolute joy of eternal life that results from union with God. For these thinkers, therefore, intellectual knowledge of God constitutes an experiential stage superior to the affective appreciation of the *visio Dei*. For others, however, heavenly joy is the exact opposite. In fact, the nature of beatitude was one of the most debated questions among thirteenth- and fourteenth-century theologians, as it had been since the dawn of Christianity.[12] The first position, that is now designated as 'intellectualist', had illustrious supporters especially in Dominican circles. According to Aquinas, 'eternal life is the ultimate goal [...]. Man's beatitude thus consists of the knowledge of God, which is an act of the intellect. [...] Accordingly, then, the essence of beatitude consists in an act of the intellect, but the delight/joy which results from beatitude pertains to the will'.[13] But what is the *voluntas*, and how might it be distinguished

---

11   See in particular Lino Pertile, *La punta del disio: semantica del desiderio nella 'Commedia'* (Fiesole: Cadmo, 2005); Giuliano Rossi, '*Disio* nella *Commedia*', *La parola del testo*, 9 (2005), 99–124.

12   The most ample study of the question is Christian Trottmann, *La Vision béatifique: des disputes scolastiques à sa définition par Benoît XII* (Rome: École française de Rome, 1995), on which one ought to consult Kent Emery Jr, 'A Forced March towards Beatitude: Christian Trottmann's *Histoire* of the Beatific Vision', *Vivarium*, 37 (1999), 258–82. See also the fundamental Brian McGinn, '*Visio dei*: Seeing God in Medieval Theology and Mysticism'', in *Envisaging Heaven in the Middle Ages*, ed. by Carolyn Muessig and Ad Putter (London: Routledge, 2007), pp. 15–33. I also found helpful J. Baschet, 'Vision béatifique et représentations du Paradis (xie–xve siècle)', *Micrologus*, 6 (1998), 73–93; Maria C. Bertolani, *Petrarca e la visione dell'eterno* (Bologna: il Mulino, 2005).

13   It is useful to quote the complete passage from which the translated passages (printed in bold) have been excerpted: 'Sed contra est quod dominus dicit, Ioan. xvii, *haec est vita aeterna, ut cognoscant te, Deum verum unum.* **Vita autem aeterna est ultimus finis, ut dictum est. Ergo beatitudo hominis in cognitione Dei consistit, quae est actus intellectus.** Respondeo dicendum quod ad beatitudinem, sicut supra dictum est, duo requiruntur, unum quod est essentia beatitudinis; aliud quod est quasi per se accidens eius, scilicet delectatio ei adiuncta. Dico ergo quod, quantum ad id quod est essentialiter ipsa beatitudo, impossibile est quod consistat in actu voluntatis. Manifestum est enim ex praemissis quod beatitudo est consecutio finis ultimi. Consecutio autem finis non consistit in ipso actu voluntatis. Voluntas enim fertur in finem et absentem, cum ipsum desiderat; et praesentem, cum in ipso requiescens delectatur. Manifestum est autem quod ipsum desiderium finis non est consecutio finis, sed est motus ad finem. Delectatio autem advenit voluntati ex hoc quod finis est praesens, non autem e converso ex hoc aliquid fit praesens, quia voluntas delectatur in ipso. Oportet igitur aliquid aliud esse quam actum voluntatis, per quod fit ipse finis praesens volenti. [...] **Sic igitur essentia beatitudinis in actu intellectus consistit, sed ad voluntatem pertinet delectatio beatitudinem consequens**; secundum quod Augustinus dicit, x Confess., quod beatitudo

from the *intellectus*? Again, in highly schematic terms, the will can be defined as an appetite, the tendency to good as such and the ability to enjoy the *delectatio* that comes from what is good.[14] More precisely, we can speak of a rational appetite that exercises control over choice and is part of the spiritual soul. Being an appetite, the will is distinguished from the intellect as a strictly ratiocinative capacity, even if, as Aquinas explicitly clarifies, there is a relationship of reciprocal influence and connection between the two faculties. The basic problem, the source of energetic disagreements, was whether to assign, in the beatific process and in the condition of bliss, ultimate priority to the intellect, as Aquinas does, or to the will, as, in the wake of the great mystical tradition of the previous two centuries, the Franciscans did. Such thinkers embraced what has been termed a 'voluntarist' idea of eternal happiness. St Bonaventure writes: '*On mental and mystical ecstasy,*[15] *in which rest is given to the intellect, when through ecstasy affection totally passes over into God.* [...] However in this passing over, if it is to be perfect, it is necessary for all intellectual operations to be relinquished, and for the height of affection to be totally transferred and transformed into God'.[16]

est gaudium de veritate; quia scilicet ipsum gaudium est consummatio beatitudinis' [But on the other hand the evangelist says (John 17): *this is eternal life, that they may know you, the only true God.* **Now, eternal life is the ultimate goal, as it is said. Man's beatitude thus consists of the knowledge of God, which is an act of the intellect.** I reply by saying that, as was mentioned above, two things are required for the achievement of beatitude, one which is the essence of beatitude; the other which is, as it were, its attribute, that is the delight connected with it. I say then that, as to what this beatitude is in essence, it is impossible that it consists of an act of the will. For it is evident from the premises that beatitude is the attainment of the ultimate end. And the attainment of the end does not consist of the very act of the will. The will is indeed driven toward the end both when this is absent, as a desire for it, and when it is present, as a delight born from resting therein. It is clear that this desire of the end is not the attainment of the end, but a motion toward the end. And the delight of the will occurs because the end is present, and not, on the contrary, because something becomes present as the will delights in it. It must therefore be something different from an act of the will, that through which the end itself becomes present for him who desires it. [...] **Accordingly, then, the essence of beatitude consists of an act of the intellect, but the delight which results from beatitude pertains to the will**; as stated by Augustine, *Confess.* x, beatitude is rejoicing about the truth; because joy itself is the accomplishment of happiness] (*ST* I–II. q. 3. a. 4, sed contra + resp.). See also *SCG* III. 60. 2.

14   On the will, see at least Aimé Solignac, 'Volonté', in DSAM, XVI, cols 1220–48; Giorgio Stabile, 'Volontà', in ED, V, 1134–40.

15   The term *excessus*, as well as the phrase *excessus mentis*, are extremely difficult to translate. A handy compendium of the rich range of its meaning may be found in *Angelic Spirituality: Medieval Perspectives on the Ways of Angels*, trans. and intro. by Steven Chase (New York and Mahwah: Paulist Press, 2002), p. 337: '[*excessus*] was used often from the time of Ambrose to denote rapture, stupor, or ecstasy of the senses, spirit, or mind. [...] It carried as well the implication of a vision or appearance, even a trance. Finally, it indicated a departure from this life, a death. [...] *Excessu mentis* carried the weight of most if not all of the meanings listed above, but the implication of a "higher state" encountered while "standing outside the mind" is particularly appropriate'.

16   In this instance too I reintegrate the translated passage, highlighted in bold, into its original context: '*De excessu mentali et mystico, in quo requies datur intellectui, affectu totaliter in deum per excessum transeunte* [...] In hoc autem transitu, si sit perfectus, oportet quod relinquantur omnes intellectuales operationes, et apex affectus totus transferatur et transformetur in Deum. Hoc autem est mysticum et secretissimum, quod *nemo novit, nisi qui accipit*, nec accipit nisi qui desiderat, nec desiderat nisi quem ignis Spiritus sancti medullitus inflammat, quem Christus misit in terram.

For a poet who had set himself the daring task of representing not just the union between the Creator and a living being, but specifically the union between himself and God, the question of how the otherworldly *viator* might have attained beatitude and whether he ultimately experienced it intellectually or emotionally, had to pose considerable difficulties. The problem went beyond artistic considerations to involve significant ideological matters. It could not straightforwardly be resolved by offering an account of the fulfilment of a miraculous personal experience, since it touched on one of the major mysteries of the Catholic faith: 'Oh quanto è corto il dire e come fioco | al mio concetto' (*Par.* XXXIII. 121–22). In practice, it meant navigating and choosing between conflicting beatific options. More specifically, in an environment of heated doctrinal tensions, it meant moving towards, if not actually adhering to, one strand of religious thought rather than another, with all that — in ideological and institutional terms — such a choice would have implied. Moreover, it would have been a decisive choice, since it would have brought the 'poema sacro' (*Par.* XXV. 1) to a close and, thereby, would have sanctioned the ultimate nature of the relationship between God and humanity.

Obviously, Dante did not refrain from choosing. With his usual self-confidence — a self-confidence that allowed him to present himself as a *scriba Dei* who had witnessed the otherworld first hand — the poet chose with inventive energy and, as we shall see, with subtle doctrinal sophistication. At the same time, the precise ideological parameters of this choice, which has been the source of recurrent critical perplexities, are complicated, at times allusive, and seemingly contradictory. Overall, they are marked by tensions and hesitancy, a situation that evocatively recalls contemporary disputes on the character of the beatific vision.[17] It is therefore not surprising that, among *dantisti*,[18] the question of how the poet dealt with the

Et ideo dicit Apostolus, hanc mysticam sapientiam esse per Spiritum sanctum revelata' [*On mental and mystical ecstasy, in which rest is given to the intellect, when through ecstasy affection totally passes over into God*. [...] However in this passing over, if it is to be perfect, it is necessary for all intellectual operations to be relinquished, and for the height of affection to be totally transferred and transformed into God. And this is mystical and utterly secret, and nobody knows what it is except one who has experienced it, and nobody experiences it except one who desires it, and nobody desires it unless his heart is inflamed by the fire of the Holy Spirit, which Christ sent into the world. So the Apostle says: this mystical knowledge is revealed through the Holy Spirit] (*Itin.* VII, chapter title and par. 4). See also Elizabeth Dreyer, '*Affectus* in St. Bonaventure's Theology', *Franciscan Studies*, 42 (1982), 5–20.

17   In line with what the poet asserts throughout the *Paradiso*, the complications and uncertainties that envelop the representation of the *visio Dei* can be explained by the fact that he finds it almost impossible to recall his heavenly experiences. At the same time, as I go on to argue, there are also other and, in some ways, more substantial reasons for his allusiveness. On ineffability in the *Commedia*, see at least Manuela Colombo, *Dai mistici a Dante: il linguaggio dell'ineffabilità* (Florence: La Nuova Italia, 1987), esp. pp. 11–60; Giuseppe Ledda, *La guerra della lingua: ineffabilità, retorica e narrativa nella 'Commedia' di Dante* (Ravenna: Longo, 2002).

18   At various points in this chapter, I express reservations about earlier discussions of the beatific vision in Dante (among the most curious claims that I have read is the following: 'Non ci sono dubbi che la visione di Dio in questa vita entra nell'Occidente cristiano per opera di Averroè': Antonio Gagliardi, 'Dante e Averroè: la visione di Dio: *Par.* XXXIII', *Tenzone*, 5 (2004), 39–78 (p. 51)). I do this, however, without normally citing specific studies. I have become more and more convinced that it is much more fruitful to map the principal coordinates characterizing the critical tradition on

a problem than to concentrate on individual studies. At the same time, I do feel that it is appropriate to signal analyses that have made a significant contribution, as well as to recognize studies and intuitions that have positively influenced my research. Proceeding in this manner, I believe that one is more likely to address a problem with a degree of equanimity and critical clarity.

Those who would like to evaluate the accuracy and fairness of my claims regarding the work that has been done on *Paradiso* XXXIII and the *visio Dei* should read, together with the other relevant studies cited in these notes, the following works: Mario Apollonio, 'Canto XXXIII', in *Lectura Dantis Scaligera. Paradiso* (Florence: Le Monnier, 1971), pp. 1195–23; Valentina Atturo, 'Il *Paradiso* dei sensi: per una metaforologia sinestetica in Dante', in Antonelli and others, II, 425–64, and 'Contemplating Wonder: *Admiratio* in Richard of St. Victor and Dante', *Dante Studies*, 129 (2011), 99–124; Mario Aversano, 'La conclusione della *Commedia*', in his *La quinta ruota: Studi sulla 'Commedia'* (Turin: Tirrenia Stampatori, 1988), pp. 189–221; Luca Azzetta, 'La geometria e il volto — *Paradiso* XXXII–XXXIII', in *Esperimenti danteschi: Paradiso 2010*, ed. by Tommaso Montorfano (Genoa: Marietti, 2010), pp. 311–50; Salvatore Battaglia, 'L'umano e il divino nell'ultimo canto del Paradiso', in his *Esemplarità e antagonismo nel pensiero di Dante* (Naples: Liguori, 1967), pp. 201–21; Stephen Bemrose, '"Una favilla sol della tua gloria": Dante Expresses the Inexpressible', *Forum for Modern Language Studies*, 27:2 (1991), 126–37; Piero Boitani, 'The Sybil's Leaves: A Study of *Paradiso* XXXIII', *Dante Studies*, 96 (1978), 83–126; Steven Botterill, *Dante and the Mystical Tradition: Bernard of Clairvaux in the 'Commedia'* (Cambridge: Cambridge University Press, 1994), pp. 194–241; Jean Canteins, *Dante. I. L'Apothéose* (Paris: Archè, 2003), pp. 159–81; Giuliana Carugati, 'La visione mancata', in her *Dalla menzogna al silenzio* (Bologna: il Mulino, 1991), pp. 113–39; Gino Casagrande, 'Le teofanie di *Paradiso* XXXIII', *Studi danteschi*, 74 (2009), 199–224; Mario Casella, 'Il canto XXXIII del '*Paradiso*', in *Letture dantesche. Paradiso*, ed. by Giovanni Getto (Florence: Sansoni, 1970), pp. 673–92; Siro A. Chimenz, *Il canto XXXIII del 'Paradiso'* (Rome: Signorelli, 1951); Leone Cicchitto, 'Il canto XXXIII del *Paradiso*', *Miscellanea francescana*, 49 (1949), 375–402; Andrea Consoli, 'Incontro con Dio (c. XXXIII)', in his *Dante ecumenico* (Naples: Fratelli Conte, 1973), pp. 345–67; Peter Dronke, 'The Conclusion of Dante's *Commedia*', *Italian Studies*, 49 (1994), 21–39; Giovanni Fallani, '*Visio beatifica*', in ED, V, 1070–71, 'La visione beatifica', in his *L'esperienza teologica di Dante* (Lecce: Milella, 1976), pp. 119–35, and 'Il canto XXXIII del *Paradiso*', in *Paradiso. Letture degli anni 1979–'81*, ed. by Silvio Zennaro (Rome: Bonacci, 1989), pp. 849–68; Paolo Falzone, 'Visione beatifica e circolazione celeste negli ultimi versi del *Paradiso*', *Bollettino di italianistica*, 7:2 (2010), 46–77; Diego Fasolini, '"E io ch'al fine di tutt'i disii appropinquava": un'interpretazione teologica del *desiderium* nel XXXIII canto del *Paradiso*', *Forum Italicum*, 37 (2003), 297–328; Paolo Fedrigotti, *Esprimere l'Inesprimibile: la concezione dantesca della beatitudine* (Bologna: Edizioni Studio Domenicano, 2009), special isse of *Divus Thomas*, 52 (2009), 7–194; Kenelm Foster, 'Dante's Vision of God', in his *The Two Dantes and Other Studies* (Berkeley and Los Angeles: University of California Press, 1977), pp. 66–85; Mario Fubini, 'L'ultimo canto del *Paradiso*', in his *Il peccato di Ulisse e altri scritti danteschi* (Milan and Naples: Ricciardi, 1966), pp. 101–36; Edoardo Fumagalli, 'L'ardor del desiderio in me finii', in *Marco Prarolan 1955–2011: studi offerti dai colleghi delle università svizzere*, ed. by Silvia Calligaro and Alessia Di Dio (Pisa: Edizioni ETS, 2013), pp. 3–9; Edmund G. Gardner, *Dante and the Mystics* [1913] (New York: Haskell House, 1968), pp. 314–23; Simon Gilson, *Medieval Optics and Theories of Light in the Works of Dante* (Lewiston, NY: Edwin Mellen Press, 2000), pp. 250–56; Georges Güntert, 'Canto XXXIII', in *Lectura Dantis Turicensis. Paradiso*, ed. by Georges Güntert and Michelangelo Picone (Florence: Cesati, 2002), pp. 505–18; Angelo Jacomuzzi, '"L'imago al cerchio": nota sul canto XXXIII del *Paradiso*', in his *L'imago al cerchio: invenzione e visione nella 'Divina Commedia'* (Milan: Silva Editore, 1968), pp. 5–27; Ledda, *La guerra della lingua*, pp. 243–319, and '"Vergine madre, figlia del tuo figlio": Paradiso, XXXIII 1–57', in *Lectura Dantis Scaligera 2005–2007*, ed. by Ennio Sandal (Rome and Padua: Antenore, 2008), pp. 97–135; Enrico Malato, *Dante al cospetto di Dio* (Rome: Salerno, 2013); Bortolo Martinelli, 'Dante: la preghiera, la supplica e la visione finale (*Paradiso* XXXIII)', *Letteratura italiana antica*, 13 (2012), 209–317, and 'La *Commedia*: preludio ed epilogo', *Letteratura italiana antica*, 15 (2014), 239–324; Andrea Mazzucchi, '"Multa videmus per intellectum quibus signa vocalia desunt": Par. XXXIII', in *Lectura Dantis Nolana: un'introduzione al 'Paradiso'*, ed. by Andrea Mazzucchi (Nola: Scala, 1999), pp. 65–84; Mira Mocan, 'L'"alta fantasia" alla fine del poema', in her *La trasparenza e il riflesso: sull'"alta*

problem of the 'essence of beatitude' (*ST* I–II. q. 3. a. 4) in *Paradiso* XXXIII[19] has long been controversial and, I would say, unresolved.[20] At the end of the pilgrim's journey, we might have expected resolution and 'l'etterna pace' (*Par.* XXXIII. 8), also because, 'ultimamente' (*Conv.* II. 8. 2), Dante is conventionally describing a condition of harmony between Creator and creature. Yet, at the formal and ideological levels, we find the opposite: complications, obscurity, and irresolution. Suffice to mention the syntactic, lexical, and semantic problems involving the last three lines of the *Commedia*, as well as the issues regarding their possible sources:[21]

> ma già volgeva il mio disio e 'l *velle*,

fantasia' in Dante e nel pensiero medievale (Milan: Bruno Mondadori, 2007), pp, 147–87, and *L'arca della mente: Riccardo di San Vittore nella 'Commedia' di Dante* (Florence: Olschki, 2012,) pp. 246–54; Carlo Ossola, 'La poesia mistica della terza cantica', in *Dante poeta cristiano*, ed. by Società Dante Alighieri: Comitato di Firenze (Florence: Polistampa, 2001), pp. 133–54; Adriano Pennacini, 'Retorica e teologia nel canto XXXIII del *Paradiso*', in *La parola del testo: scritti per Bice Mortara Garavelli*, ed. by Gian Luigi Beccaria and Carla Marello, 2 vols (Alessandria: Edizioni dell'Orso, 2002), II, 933–42; Pertile, *La punta del disio*, pp. 247–81; Tamara Pollack, 'Light, Love and Joy in Dante's Doctrine of Beatitude', in *Reviewing Dante's Theology*, ed. by Claire E. Honess and Matthew Treherne, 2 vols (Oxford: Peter Lang, 2013), I, 263–319; Antonio Rossini, *Dante, il nodo e il volume: una 'lectura' di 'Paradiso' XXXIII* (Pisa and Roma: Fabrizio Serra, 2011); Aleardo Sacchetto, 'Il canto XXXIII del *Paradiso*', in *Nuove letture dantesche*, 8 vols (Florence: Le Monnier, 1968–76), VII, 265–87; Selene Sarteschi, 'Il canto XXXIII del *Paradiso*', in her *Il percorso del poeta cristiano* (Ravenna: Longo, 2006), pp. 173–92; Mirko Tavoni, 'La visione di Dio nell'ultimo canto del *Paradiso*', in *Dire l'indicibile: esperienza religiosa e poesia dalla Bibbia al Novecento*, ed. by Cesare Letta (Pisa: ETS, 2009), pp. 65–112; Webb, pp. 192–205. I have also consulted the following commentaries on canto XXXIII: Chiavacci Leonardi; Durling-Martinez; Hollander; Inglese; Pasquini-Quaglio.

19 It is appropriate to distinguish Marco Ariani's work on the *Paradiso* from the remainder of modern studies on the canticle. Even if rather too dense, his contributions constitute the major analysis of Dante's representation of Heaven of the last thirty or so years. Ariani touches on the *visio Dei* on various occasions, but always in relation to other and broader issues. His perspective, therefore, blurs the differences between the beatific vision and other, albeit related aspects of the pilgrim's *itinerarium in Deum* (other analyses that touch on Dante's treatment of beatitude share this same flaw). See Ariani's following studies listed in chronologral order: '"Abyssus luminis": Dante e la veste di luce', *Rivista di letteratura italiana*, 11 (1993), 9–71; 'Dante, la *dulcedo*'; '"E sì come di lei bevve la gronda | de le palpebre mie"' (*Par.*, XXX, 88): Dante e lo Pseudo Dionigi Areopagita', in *Leggere Dante*, ed. by Lucia Battaglia Ricci (Ravenna: Longo, 2002), pp. 131–52; '"La forma universal di questo nodo": *Paradiso*, XXXIII 58–105', in Sandal, pp. 137–81; 'I "metaphorismi" di Dante', in *La metafora in Dante*, ed. by Marco Ariani (Florence: Olschki, 2009), pp. 1–57; 'La luce nel *Paradiso*', *Filologia e critica*, 34 (2009), 3–41; *Mistica degli affetti*; *'Lux inaccessibilis': metafore e teologia della luce nel 'Paradiso' di Dante* (Rome: Aracne, 2010); 'Canto I. "Alienatus animus in corpore": deificazione e ascesa alle sfere celesti', in *Cento canti*, III:1, 27–60; 'Canto XXIV: mistica degli affetti e intelletto d'amore', in *Cento canti*, III:2, 698–722; 'Canto XXX: La "transformatio viatoris per claritatem"', in *Cento canti*, III:2, 894–916; 'Canto XXXIII: La mistica preterizione: il "dicer poco" dell'"ultimus cantus"', in *Cento canti*, III:2, 971–1011.

20 'Nonostante l'ingegno profuso dagli interpreti, non mi pare si sia ancora riusciti a scandire precisamente le fasi dell'estrema esperienza di D., secondo l'una o l'altra delle varie graduazioni che i teologi riconoscevano nelle *visiones* o nel *raptus*' (Inglese, p. 405).

21 See, for example, Chiavacci Leonardi, III, 928; Durling-Martinez, III, 739–41; Pertile, *La punta del disio*, pp. 265–81. I deal with the cruces present in lines 143–45 only in so far as they affect issues relating to the beatific vision. It is surprising to read that 'Non sarebbe esatto dire che il senso generale di questi versi [*Par.* XXXIII. 142–45] sia stato oggetto di controversia fra i critici': Raffaele Pinto, 'Il viaggio di ritorno: *Pd.* XXXIII, 142–145', *Tenzone*, 4 (2003), 199–226 (p. 199).

>   sì come rota ch'igualmente è mossa,
>   l'amor che move il sole e l'altre stelle. (*Par.* XXXIII. 143–45)

The divergences between what is narrated and the formal and figurative means by which this *materia* is evoked are striking.

It is thus a critical cliché to acknowledge the difficulties that envelop the poem's ending. Yet, despite this, the tradition of studies on the *visio Dei* in *Paradiso* XXXIII has preferred, perplexingly, to insist on absolute and exclusive solutions. To put it simply, in individual contributions, Dante is often presented in an excessively mechanistic and peremptory manner: either as a supporter of 'voluntarist' positions or as a champion of 'intellectualist' solutions. In truth, there are various indications — in particular, the fact that it has been possible to recognize, quite correctly, the presence of conflicting traditions in the last canto[22] — which would suggest that one-eyed dogmatism is probably not the approach to take if we want to arrive at a more accurate idea of how, in the last lines of the *Paradiso*, Dante addressed the thorny *quaestio* of beatitude. In any case, the standard view on the beatific vision that dominates in Dante studies is too narrow. Focusing almost exclusively on the last canto of the *Commedia* and on the problem of whether the intellect or affection has priority at the moment of the *visio Dei*, scholars have lost sight of the scope and complexity of the problem. Thus, *Paradiso* XXXIII does not present the poet's definitive statement on the *visio beatifica*, as would appear from a perusal of Dante scholarship. The canto, in fact, brings to a close a rich analysis of *beatitudo*, in which *Par.* XXXIII. 136–45 constitutes the last stage — an analysis that extends along the entire length of the third canticle.[23]

Dante's approach to the *visio Dei* in the *Paradiso* assimilates with his customary synthesizing skill several tricky, correlated, and controversial *quaestiones*. From the dawn of Christianity, since it is a contradiction present both in the Old and in the New Testament, the debate raged whether or not it is possible for a created being to see God. The standard *auctoritas* in favour of such an experience was the evangelical 'beatitude' 'beati mundo corde quoniam ipsi Deum videbunt' [blessed are the pure in heart, for they will see God] (Matthew 5: 8), which, however, clashed with another passage from the Gospels: 'Deum nemo vidit umquam unigenitus Filius qui est in sinu Patris ipse enarravit' [Nobody has ever seen God: the only begotten Son who is in the Father's bosom has declared Him] (John 1: 18). Similar antithetical *sententiae* are found in the Old Testament: on the one hand, 'vocavitque Iacob nomen loci illius Phanuhel dicens vidi Deum facie ad faciem et salva facta est anima mea' [and Jacob called the name of that place Phanuhel [Peniel] saying: I saw God face to face and yet my life has been saved] (Genesis 32: 30), and on the

---

22   See, in particular, Subsection 4, 'The Sources of Beatitude', below.

23   For an analysis of the principal passages in the *Paradiso* that examine the *visio Dei* and their interconnections, see Subsection 5, 'Beatitudes', below. Furthermore, analysing these passages, caution ought to be exercised when proposing direct sources. Given its popularity, the *visio beatifica* belonged to the interdiscursive patrimony of late-medieval culture (the quotations from Aquinas and Bonaventure that I cited earlier ought to be read, at least for now, as illustrative of general attitudes and not specific to Dante's treatment of beatitude); see Subsection 4, 'The Sources of Beatitude', below.

other, 'rursumque ait non poteris videre faciem meam non enim videbit me homo et vivet' [but He said: you cannot see my face, for no man will look at me directly and still live] (Exodus 33: 20).[24] On 13 January 1241, in Paris, William of Auvergne affirmed a stance that, a century later, ended up being decisive, by condemning as erroneous the idea that God would not be seen directly in Paradise:

> Primus [error], quod divina essentia in se nec ab homine nec ab angelo videbitur.
> Hunc errorem reprobamus et assertores et defensores auctoritate Wilhermi episcopi excommunicamus. Firmiter autem credimus et asserimus, quod Deus in sua essentia vel substantia videbitur ab angelis et omnibus sanctis et videbitur ab animabus glorificatis.[25]

> [The first [error] is the claim that the divine essence will not be seen in itself neither by men nor by angels.
> We condemn this error and excommunicate its advocates and defenders under the authority of bishop William. We firmly believe and claim that God will be seen in His essence or substance by the angels and all the saints and will be seen by the souls who have been glorified.]

William's implicit target was John Scottus Eriugena, who, in the wake of the pseudo-Dionysius, had declared that 'diuinam essentiam nulli corporeo sensui, nulli rationi, nulli seu humano seu angelico intellectui per se ipsam comprehensibilem esse' [the divine essence cannot be grasped in itself by any corporeal senses, any reasoning, any faculty of either human or angelic intellect].[26] However, thanks in particular to the efforts of the Dominicans, and then to the intervention of Pope Benedict XII on 29 January 1336 with the encyclical Benedictus Deus, William's position became doctrinally canonical. Nevertheless, the idea that it was impossible to see God directly continued to circulate, partly on account of the great popularity of Dionysius in the thirteenth century. According to the Areopagite, the divine essence is absolutely unknowable. At the same time, as Eriugena pointed out, even though God can never be seen in Himself, He is perceptible in His theophanies, the illuminations through which God reveals Himself, and which are the graces that deify the human being. Moreover, in keeping with St Augustine, the majority of thinkers sharply distinguished between the visio Dei granted to a living being, like Dante the pilgrim, and that enjoyed by the angels and the blessed (hence the question arises whether it is appropriate, as is done regularly among dantisti, to refer to Beatrice's explanation of angelic beatitudo in Par. XXVIII. 106–14 to clarify the viator's beatific visio).[27] Complicating matters further, it was also generally

---

24   See also Isaiah 6: 5; I Corinthians 13: 12; II Corinthians 3: 18; and I John 3: 2, all of which declare that God can be seen directly, and so contradict Matthew 11: 27; John 6: 46; I Timothy 6: 16; I John 4: 12.

25   Chartularium Universitatis Parisiensis, edited by Heinrich Denifle, 4 vols (Paris: Delalain, 1889–97), I, 170 (n. 128). On the condemnation of 1244, see Trottmann, pp. 175–97.

26   Periphyseon, ed. by Édouard A. Jeauneau, CCCM 161–65, 5 vols (Turnhout: Brepols, 1996–2003), I, 11.

27   'Alio modo cognoscitur Deus in se; et hoc dupliciter, aut clare et hoc modo a solo Filio et a Beatis; alio modo in caligine, sicut dicit beatus Dionysius de Mystica Theologia; et sic vidit Moyses et sublimiter contemplantes, in quorum aspectu nulla figitur imago creature. Et tunc revera magis

accepted that, among those who have been granted the privilege of miraculously approaching God *in via*, some — Moses and Paul, but also John the Apostle — had had a transcendent experience close to that which the saints and the angels enjoy *in patria*.[28] The *quaestio* of the *visio beatifica* thus involved far more than the problem of the roles played in it by the intellect and by the will.[29]

It would thus appear appropriate for research on Dante's meditation on the *visio Dei* to be guided by the fact that, since the time of the Church Fathers, the problem had been a source of controversy; and that subsequently, between the thirteenth and fourteenth centuries, following the condemnations of 1241 and 1277 and the assertion of Aristotelianism, the solutions increased in number and complexity, while the disagreements intensified.[30] Dante was not just a great syncretist, but, as is evident, for example, in the heaven of the Sun, he also felt the need to harmonize conflicting ideological opinion. It would not be surprising, therefore, if the poet had felt this responsibility with particular urgency in relation to the conflicts circulating around the beatific vision — a metaphysical truth on which everyone agreed, but whose nature and whose experiential mode were causes of controversy and disagreement. In any case, if we re-read the passage from Aquinas quoted above — 'Sic igitur essentia beatitudinis in actu intellectus consistit, sed ad voluntatem pertinet delectatio beatitudinem consequens' [the essence of beatitude consists in an act of the intellect, but the delight/joy which results from beatitude pertains to the will] — it is not difficult to recognize an attempt by the *Doctor angelicus* to smooth out the differences between 'knowing' and 'loving' God in the beatific vision. And Dante does something similar when he describes, not the *visio Dei* in itself, but the Empyrean:

> Luce intellettüal, piena d'amore;
> amor di vero ben, pien di letizia;
> letizia che trascende ogne dolzore. (*Par.* XXX. 40–42)[31]

sentiunt quam cognoscant' [God Himself can be known in a different way; and this way is twofold, either clearly — and this is possible only for his Son and for the Blessed; or otherwise in obscurity, as blessed Dionysius says in the Mystical Theology; and this is how God was seen by Moses and those who live in full contemplation, whose sight was not mediated by the image of any creature. And in this case it is more correct to say that they sense rather than know God] (Bonaventure, *Commentarius in Evangelium Ioannis* I. 43). See also Barbara Faes de Mottoni, 'La conoscenza di Dio di Adamo innocente nell'*In II Sententiarum* d. 23, a. 2, q. 3 di Bonaventura', in *Archivum franciscanum historicum*, 91 (1998), 3–32.

28   See Barbara Faes de Mottoni, 'Mosè e Paolo: figure della contemplazione e del rapimento nelle teologie del secolo XIII', in her *Figure e motivi della contemplazione nelle teologie medievali* (Florence: SISMEL and Edizioni del Galluzzo, 2007), pp. 17–48.

29   Thanks to the *auctoritas* of John 14: 2 ('In domo Patris mei mansiones multae sunt' [In the house of my Father there are many rooms]), the question of the different degrees of beatitude to which Piccarda refers in *Paradiso* III does not appear to have been the source of polemics. For a recent discussion of the problem, See George Corbett, 'Moral Structure', in *The Cambridge Companion to Dante's 'Commedia'*, ed. by Zygmunt G. Barański and Simon Gilson (Cambridge: Cambridge University Press, 2018), pp. 61–78.

30   Bernard McGinn correctly underlines the heavily conflictual character of the debate (p. 16).

31   Although Dante presents the Empyrean as immaterial, and hence beyond time and space (*Par.* XXII. 61–67), and associates it, on the one hand, with beatitude and, on the other, with the splendour of the divine mind (*Par.* XXX. 100–08), it is also the case that, in describing the last moments of the

Examples such as these should warn us against falling into the trap of easy and schematic oppositions that end up trivializing complex and refined theological disqui-
sitions, as well as the efforts of a poet finely attuned to the nuances of his culture.[32]

And the problems do not end here. Throughout the *Paradiso*, and with particular
force in the last canto, Dante insistently reiterates that it is impossible for human
reason and language even minimally to come to terms with God, and hence to offer
an account and explanation of the divine:

> Da quinci innanzi il mio veder fu maggio
> che 'l parlar mostra, ch'a tal vista cede,
> e cede la memoria a tanto oltraggio. (*Par.* XXXIII. 55–57)

Any attempt on our part to *intendere* (125–26), and then to represent the 'luce
etterna' (124), even if this is the product of a divinely inspired mind, can at most
merely be partial and imprecise:

> O somma luce che tanto ti levi
> da' concetti mortali, a la mia mente
> ripresta un poco di quel che parevi,
>   e fa la lingua mia tanto possente,
> ch'una favilla sol de la tua gloria
> possa lasciare a la futura gente. (*Par.* XXXIII. 67–72)

Human language, and this in privileged cases such as Dante's, manages to
communicate no more than a 'spark' of the transcendent heavenly 'luce'.[33] The poet
insists on the constraints delimiting his presentation of Paradise in general and the
beatific vision in particular. By extension, Dante's admonitions also bear upon the
efforts of all those — theologians, preachers, poets, artists — who attempt to speak
de Deo. Yet, to speak *de Deo* is the responsibility that, as a *scriba Dei*, he has been
providentially assigned. Whittling down what Dante tells us about his enjoyment
of the *visio Dei* to simplistic critical solutions presented as 'definitive' ends up by

---

pilgrim's voyage into God, the poet seems to present these as temporal successions and the last heaven
as if it were a 'place'. Dante does this, I would say, for two reasons. The heavenly experiences of the
viator, living being, are inevitably circumscribed by time, space, and the movement that brings him
progressively closer to God. In addition, the poet wants to distinguish between the pilgrim who sees
the reality and complexity of the Empyrean — a vision that occurs in different phases — and the
pilgrim who enjoys the *visio Dei*. Christian Moevs, who has written the best recent assessment of
Dante's Empyrean, notes: '[i]f we wish to conceive the reality in which all desire ends as the "last
sphere", it is a sphere that "is not in place and has no poles" [*Par.* XXII. 62 and 67]. If we wish to
picture it (for example, as a gigantic rose full of seats, children and sages), we must be aware that all
that is appearance (*parvenza* [*Par.* XXX. 106]), and the reality is light, however understood': Christian
Moevs, *The Metaphysics of Dante's 'Comedy'* (Oxford: Oxford University Press, 2005), p. 24, but see
also pp. 15–35. It does not seem to me that Dante scholarship has addressed the problem of the 'double
reality' of the Empyrean in the *Paradiso*.

32   For analyses that emphasize the syncretic nature of Dante's treatment of the *visio Dei*, see
Fedrigotti; Mocan, *L'alta fantasia'*, pp. 171–72; Pertile, *La punta del disio*, pp. 247–81; Pollack, pp.
279 & 295. Ariani, 'La mistica preterizione', refers to an imposing number of passages taken from
different writers and traditions. However, he does not assess their possible inter-relationship in the
structure of *Paradiso* XXXIII.

33   See Filippo Gianferrari, '"Poca favilla, gran fiamma seconda" (*Par.* I, 34): riscrivere un proverbio
tra Cino, San Giacomo e San Girolamo', *Le tre corone*, 7 (forthcoming).

weakening not just the idea of the divine that underpins the *Commedia*, but also the *modi* with which the poet decided to 'trattar' (*Inf.* I. 8) his extraordinary encounter with 'l'amor che move il sole e l'altre stelle' (*Par.* XXXIII. 145). When Dante arrived at the poem's culminating moment, as had been the case throughout the *Paradiso*, the challenge facing him was to find ways of speaking about God which, given the denotative limitations of any *modus tractandi*, did not end up by undermining the *Commedia*'s artistic and intellectual foundations.

Among the paradoxes delimiting the endeavour to speak *de Deo*, the inevitable slippage from the divine, the inexpressible, to the human, namely, to what can be expressed linguistically about the divine holds pride of place. As Dante frequently reiterated, whatever formal solution is adopted to deal with the ineffability of the transcendent, it is by definition inadequate. It is simply a way of speaking 'darkly' (I Corinthians 13:12), whereby one engages not with the divine but with the ways in which the divine has been treated. When reduced to human capabilities, the problem of talking about God becomes one of representation and culture, both of which, unlike the divine, are accessible to us. Consequently, in examining beatitude in the *Commedia*, as well as the entire metaphysical system of the poem, it is important to recognize that we are dealing not with the divine, but with the representation of the divine.[34] Our task, therefore, is to evaluate how Dante gave linguistic form to, and therefore thought about, the *visio Dei*. All this may seem obvious. Yet, all too often, scholars treat the *viator*'s heavenly experiences described in the *Commedia* as events and not as representations of events. The difference, to say the least, is fundamental.

I undertake the analysis of the *visio Dei* in four stages. In the first of four subsections ('Reading *Par.* XXXIII. 136–45'), in light of their popularity among Dantists and of their structural importance, I offer an *explication de texte* of the *Commedia*'s final ten lines. Moreover, *Paradiso* XXXIII in general and lines 136–45 in particular tie off the separate threads of Dante's treatment of the beatific vision. Finally, it is only in lines 140–41 and 143–45 that the union between God and the pilgrim is evoked. To be precise, *beatitudo* stems directly from the failure of the wayfarer's normal intellectual operations, a traumatic event recorded in lines 136–39 and 142.[35] Yet, as far as I am aware, such a partition of the last ten lines has never before been proposed, even if the evidence in its favour would seem to be relatively secure. Perhaps the main reason why scholars have not studied the *deificatio* with due care is to be sought, as

---

34   In their commentary, Durling and Martinez write: 'Our view is that the entire intellectual vision [...] has been derived from Dante's reading and, however vividly imagined, has been represented in images' (III, 681). Marguerite Mills Chiarenza, 'The Imageless Vision and Dante's *Paradiso*', *Dante Studies*, 90 (1972), 77–91, is of the opposite opinion.

35   Aquinas and Bonaventure agree on this basic point. Thomas affirms: 'Intellectus autem hominis, in statu viae, necesse est quod a phantasmatibus abstrahatur, si videat Dei essentiam' [The human intellect, while *in via* [transition into God], must necessarily withdraw from sensible images, if it is to see the essence of God] (*ST* II–II. q. 175. a. 4, resp.), while the *Doctor seraphicus* declares that 'In hoc autem transitu [in Deum], si sit perfectus, oportet quod relinquantur omnes intellectuales operationes' [In this transition into God, if it is to be perfect, it is necessary for all intellectual operations to be relinquished] (*Itin.* VII. 4). For a discussion of this question, see the following subsection.

I have begun to suggest, in a failure adequately to appreciate the philological and historical ramifications of the problem. For example, despite the fact that Dante seems clear on this point, there is no agreement as to where, in the *Paradiso*, the pilgrim's *visio Dei* may actually begin. Thus, even if in contradiction with Dante's text and with medieval theological and philosophical thought, and, in addition, without providing supporting evidence, the start of the *visio* has, time and again, been located before its actual occurrence: at *Par.* XXX. 49, at *Par.* XXXIII. 50–51, or 52–54, but also at lines 57, 76, 85, 94, and 97 of the last canto, all undoubtedly significant moments along the wayfarer's *appropinquarsi* (47) to God (Cicchitto, pp. 394–400), but which are markedly distinct from beatitude itself.[36] Next, Subsection 4, titled 'The Sources of Beatitude', focuses on the heterogeneous array of texts and authors that have been proposed as sources for Dante's representation of beatitude in *Paradiso* XXXIII, and evaluates their relevance. In doing so, I concentrate on intertexts that have been proposed not just for lines 136–45 but also for the whole canto, since, on occasion, scholars have used the latter to define Dante's idea of the *visio Dei*. Subsection 5, 'Beatitudes', examines the presentation of the beatific vision in lines 140–41 and 143–45 along with other passages of the *Commedia* in which Dante refers to *beatitudo*. As mentioned earlier, in the poem's explicit, the poet brings to a close a broad ideological enquiry into the *quaestio de beatitudine* that he distributed across several cantos. Finally ('Di dietro'), I hope to make some general observations on how Dante dealt with the issue of *deificatio*.

3. Reading *Par.* XXXIII. 136–45

I should like to begin my detailed investigation of 'Dante and *beatitudo*' re-reading the last ten lines of the *Commedia*:

> tal era io a quella vista nova:
> veder voleva come si convenne
> l'imago al cerchio e come vi s'indova;
>   ma non eran da ciò le proprie penne:
> se non che la mia mente fu percossa
> da un fulgore in che sua voglia venne.
>   A l'alta fantasia qui mancò possa;
> ma già volgeva il mio disio e 'l velle,
> sì come rota ch'igualmente è mossa,
>   l'amor che move il sole e l'altre stelle. (*Par.* XXXIII. 136–45)

To describe the pilgrim 'ch'al fine di tutt'i disii | appropinquava' (46–47), Dante evokes a process that occurs in three distinct yet logically linked phases. The first depicts Dante the character immediately before the union with God, and who still behaves according to human norms and with a degree of autonomy (136–39 & 142).[37] The second constitutes the moment of the union itself: of the definitive

---

36   The tercet 'E' mi ricorda ch'io fui più ardito | per questo [the reaction of the pilgrim struck by the 'vivo raggio', 77] a sostener, tanto ch'i' giunsi | l'aspetto mio col valore infinito' (*Par.* XXXIII. 79–81) does not mark the start of the *visio* but functions as a proleptic marker for the miracle.

37   In general, when assessing the pilgrim's behaviour in Paradise, it is important to remember

transition from the human to the divine (140–41); while the third illustrates the condition of the *viator* following his miraculous transformation (143–45). The last two phases, therefore, present Dante's idea of *beatitudo*.

At the same time, the three stages should not be taken as conventionally distinct from one another. As we shall see, the wondrous experience that, at the close of the *Commedia*, the poet strives to record by means of his 'lingua' (70) does not follow the norms of an earthly experience in which one state automatically follows another in time and space. Instead, the different moments that make up the experience are best thought of as simultaneous. The three final phases, in keeping with a standard contemplative trope, are preceded by many earlier ones, that go back at least to the beginning of the *viator*'s journey through Paradise. Especially significant are the occurrences that immediately precede the events described in the last ten lines. Thus, after St Bernard's prayer, the pilgrim is granted the privilege of 'giung*ere* | l'aspetto [...] col valore infinito' (80–81), which permits him to distinguish three different characteristics of the 'luce etterna' (83 & 124): the mysteries of creation (85–93), of the Trinity (115–20), and of the Incarnation (127–32). In fact, before his 'occhi' (129) are able to contemplate ('circunspetta', 129) the miracle present in the second 'circulazion' (127), he had *visto* (85) 'il mistero dell'unità del molteplice' (Chiavacci Leonardi, III, 919), which was followed by the 'tre giri | di tre colori' (116–17). The closing lines of the *Commedia*, and the events they clarify, although fundamentally dependent on these two prefiguring manifestations of the divine, are especially connected to the third revelation: to the vision of the Incarnation, and hence to Christ (I will return to this important point in due course).

The final three moments of Dante-character's *itinerarium in Deum* begin with the *voler veder* (137), namely, with his desire to understand how 'la nostra effige' (131) 's'indova' (138) in God. There is a tendency among Dantists to equate here and elsewhere in Paradise the *vedere* of the wayfarer exclusively with Aristotelian noesis, and specifically with the explanation that Aquinas gave of this. Yet, *videre*, together with related terms, is also the word that the 'voluntarist' tradition empoyed to refer to the ascent of the 'mente' (140) — another technical term that unites the two currents — into God.[38] Therefore, without the support of additional evidence, it does not seem appropriate to restrict the scope of this terminology by associating it univocally with either one or the other tradition.[39] For now, it is enough to recognize that the *viator* desires to understand the mystery of the Incarnation by resorting to the power of his own reason.

The failure of this rash attempt, whose lack of success had been anticipated by the

---

that, apart from his fleeting experience of beatitude, he continues here, as he does in the other two otherworldly realms, to behave as a living person, and that the blessed treat him as such. It is also necessary to recall that 'at no point does he [Dante] ever give the reader to understand that, as was often made clear in medieval accounts of otherworld journeys, his experience was of the disembodied variety': David Ruzicka, '"Uno lume apparente di fuori secondo sta dentro": The Expressive Body in Dante's *Commedia*', *The Italianist*, 34 (2014), 1–22 (p. 1).

38   Barbara Newman, 'What Did it Mean to Say "I Saw"? The Clash between Theory and Practice in Medieval Visionary Culture', *Speculum*, 80 (2005), 1–43.

39   I examine this and related points in the following subsection.

famous simile of the 'geomètra' (133), is inevitable: 'ma non eran da ciò le proprie penne' (139). Faced with the 'vista nova' (136) of the transcendent, the pilgrim has reached the extreme limits of the power of the *intellectus*.[40] However, and this is crucial, he has reached this condition without having yet attained beatitude, one of whose indisputable traits is the immersion in 'lo bene | di là dal qual non è a che s'aspiri' (*Purg.* XXXI. 23–24). Thus, before he can definitively participate in the *visio Dei*, the pilgrim must satisfy his desire to understand the miracle of the Incarnation and, given the context, that of the bond that unites humanity to God. But achieving this is beyond 'le proprie penne' (139).

The three lines that follow the failure of the wayfarer's intellectual wings — lines that document the happy resolution of the impasse and clarify the reason for the failure, do not make for easy reading:

> Se non che la mia mente fu percossa
> da un fulgore in che sua voglia venne.
> A l'alta fantasia qui mancò possa. (*Par.* XXXIII. 140–42)

Their logical, doctrinal, and narrative connections are, to say the least, slack. Line 142, relegated grammatically to the next sentence, in conceptual terms is problematically separated from the preceding two lines and, more significantly, from line 139. Thus, line 142 not only defines line 139 in terms of late-medieval science, since it offers the theoretical explanation for the failure of the 'penne', but also anticipates chronologically lines 140–41, which, strictly speaking, describe the second of the three concluding moments. In Aristotelian terms, the reason why the pilgrim's 'mente' (140) is incapable of functioning is because 'la fantasia venia meno allo 'ntelletto' (*Conv.* III. 4. 11). As Michele Rak explains:

> La f[antasia] è [...] una virtù organica che fornisce i materiali sui quali può muoversi il vario discorso dell'intelletto. Essa è in diretto contatto con la percezione e si pone come luogo intermedio tra questa e il pensiero, compie quindi un'opera di sintesi attraverso il 'senso comune' rendendo stabili nella mente quei 'fantasmi' che rappresentano punti fermi nel fluire dell'esperienza. La f[antasia] costituisce il fondamento del conoscere, poiché il fantasma da essa elaborato è l'aspetto materiale del concetto, attraverso il quale soltanto l'intendere acquista concretezza.[41]

Hence, it does not seem correct to maintain, as is often the case, that 'fantasia' ceases to function only *after* the 'mente' has been struck by the 'fulgore' (140–42). If phantasy had not failed in the attempt to 'veder' (137), there would have been no need for a miraculous intervention since there would have been no 'difetto della virtù dalla quale trae quello ch'el [l'intelletto] vede, che è virtù organica, cioè la fantasia' (*Conv.* III. 4. 9). It is because, when faced by the mystery of the 'imago al

---

40   'Trinitas personarum non est cognoscibilis per creaturas, sed tantum trinitas appropriatorum, scilicet unitas, veritas, bonitas' [The trinity of the persons cannot be known through creatures, but only the trinity of their attributes, that is unity, truth, goodness] (Bonaventure, *Commentaria in quatuor libros Sententiarum* I. d. 3. a. unique. q. 4).
41   Michele Rak, 'Fantasia', in ED, II, 793–94 (p. 793). See also Mocan, *La trasparenza*, pp. 93, 98–106, 109–87.

cerchio' (138), as the passage from the *Convivio* goes on to explain ('la fantasia nol [l'intelletto] puote aiutare, ché non ha lo di che'), that the miracle is essential. In logical and 'scientific' terms, phantasy's failure cannot but precede the *venuta* of the 'fulgore'.

Dante's presentation of the last moments of his approach to God is conceptually demanding and connotatively complex. Disrupting its logical order, the poet lets us participate, albeit indirectly and fleetingly, in the disconcerting otherness of the pilgrim's experience and in the difficulties that he must overcome in trying to record what little he can remember.[42] More significantly, he makes us understand that the rational and linguistic norms on which we habitually rely have little or nothing to do with the experience of the divine. He emphasizes that our trust, like that of the 'geomètra' (133), in the 'principi' of *pensare* (135) is ultimately misplaced. Yet, paradoxically, if, on the one hand, we need to read in a manner that appropriately recognizes the miraculous *novità* (136) that the poet presents, on the other, here on earth, we can only do this by resorting to reason. Granting priority to the 'fulgore', Dante emphasizes what 'qui' (142) was truly essential: the miracle that put an end to the 'voglia' (141), thereby ensuring that the pilgrim is allowed to enjoy the *visio Dei*. In such a metaphysically elevated context, the psycho-physiological explanation of the imperfection of human thought is justifiably relegated to a banalizing afterthought — an addition that adds nothing to the miracle, but which, firmly addressed to our 'concetti umani' (68), helps us to appreciate the wayfarer's extraordinary circumstances. In truth, line 142 is redundant because, in light of Aristotelian science, the failure of the intellectual 'penne' also necessarily involves the failure of phantasy — a tautology that would confirm the highly elaborate nature of lines 139–42. In any case, imagining the *viator*'s experience as if it were a transparent and rigidly ordered succession of events, one loses its exceptional transcendent nature. Before God, time and space lose their prerogatives, so that different experiences are lived as simultaneous. From this perspective, the conjunction 'se non che', which connects the failure and the *percuotere* of the 'mente' (140), indicates their concomitance: the two states, rather than successive, are interdependent. Even the chronologically dislocated structure of lines 139–42 alludes to this simultaneity, suggesting that at such a heavenly height to think humanly in terms of 'before' and 'after' makes little sense. Therefore, unlike those who in the 'qui' (142) recognize a precise point that follows the effect of the 'fulgore' — an 'inexistent' moment since the miraculous illumination is necessitated by the insufficiency of Dante-character's 'fantasia' — it would seem more appropriate to interpret the adverb as having an 'indefinite' value, indicating the whole moment that not only directly anticipates the beatific vision but also without interruption and effort dissolves in the *visio Dei*, as the 'già' of line 143 appears to confirm.

Dantists generally maintain that phantasy continues to act when the 'fulgore' reveals the mystery of the Incarnation, because they believe that, according to

---

42   Katherine Powlesland, 'Invitations to Participate: Bernard's Sign', *Le tre corone*, 4 (2017), 97–115, examines in detail another instance of 'cognitive dissonance' (pp. 102–03) in the structure of *Paradiso* XXXIII.

Dante, who on this point would be following Aquinas, the *visio Dei* is experienced thanks to the intellect.[43] Putting aside for now the question of whether or not in lines 136–45 we can recognize 'intellectualist' views, such an interpretation of the role of phantasy is almost certainly incorrect, not least because, to put it bluntly, it goes against what Aquinas himself would have affirmed. According to the *Doctor angelicus*, as well as the whole theological tradition, the Incarnation could not be understood by means of the normal operations of the intellectual faculties: 'de ipso nunc incarnationis mysterio restat dicendum. Quod quidem inter divina opera maxime rationem excedit: nihil enim mirabilius excogitari potest divinitus factum quam quod verus Deus, Dei filius, fieret homo verus' [Now I have to speak about the very mystery of the Incarnation. Which, among the divine works, is the one that most exceeds human reason: for there is nothing of divine making conceivably more marvellous than the fact that the real God, the son of God, became a real man] (*SCG* IV. 27. 1). Thus, it is axiomatic that the revelation of the hypostatic union, like the *visio Dei* in which the Incarnational miracle is resolved, 'exceeds human reason' and its related functions:

> Respondeo dicendum quod divina essentia non potest ab homine videri per aliam vim cognoscitivam quam per intellectum. Intellectus autem humanus non convertitur ad sensibilia nisi mediantibus phantasmatibus, per quae species intelligibiles a sensibilibus accipit, et in quibus considerans de sensibilibus iudicat et ea disponit. Et ideo in omni operatione qua intellectus noster abstrahitur a phantasmatibus, necesse est quod abstrahatur a sensibus. Intellectus autem hominis, in statu viae, necesse est quod a phantasmatibus abstrahatur, si videat Dei essentiam. Non enim per aliquod phantasma potest Dei essentia videri; quinimmo nec per aliquam speciem intelligibilem creatam, quia essentia Dei in infinitum excedit non solum omnia corpora, quorum sunt phantasmata, sed etiam omnem intelligibilem creaturam. Unde impossibile est quod homo in statu viae videat Deum per essentiam sine abstractione a sensibus. (*ST* II–II. q. 175. a. 4, resp.)

> [I reply by saying that the divine essence cannot be seen by man through any other cognitive power than the intellect. Now, the human intellect does not turn to intelligible objects except by the mediation of sensible images, through which it gathers the intelligible species of the objects, and in considering these images it defines and arranges the objects. Accordingly, in any operation in which our intellect withdraws from the sensible images, it must also withdraw from the senses. Thus the human intellect, while *in via* [transition into God], must withdraw from the sensible images, if it is to see the essence of God. For the essence of God cannot be seen through any sensible image; not indeed through any created intelligible species, because the essence of God infinitely

---

43   But see 'La *caduta* della fantasia rimane [...] negativa, perché segna il confine della visibilità, ma si configura nel contempo come positiva e necessaria a consentire l'apertura a un'altra dimensione, quella in cui viene totalmente rimosso il "velo" tra creatore e creatura, nella quale soltanto è resa possibile l'armonizzazione perfetta con l'Amore eterno nel movimento circolare delle sfere'; and 'Quella che viene meno, che "fallisce", è [...] proprio la facoltà che *vede* per l'intelletto, cioè la fantasia, la quale, guardando direttamente nella fonte originaria della luce, *cade*, si smarrisce, "disvia"' (Mocan, *L'alta fantasia*', pp. 172 & 174, and also 181). See also Mocan, *L'arca della mente*, pp. 107–37.

exceeds not only all bodies of which we have sensible images, but all intelligible things created. It is therefore impossible, while *in via*, for a man to see God in His essence without withdrawing from the senses.]

If Dante's goal was to present the revelation of the 'mystery of the Incarnation' as part of the 'intellectualist' 'elevation' to the highest vision of the divine essence, presenting phantasy as involved in the experience would have compromised not only the representation of the *visio Dei*, but also the entire artistic and ideological structure of the *Commedia*. Committing such a gross error, Dante would have called into question the truth claims carefully introduced throughout the poem, as well as his own status as *scriba Dei*. Of course, Dante did nothing of the sort. Unlike modern scholars, the poet knew very well what were the limits of phantasy, and that, according to the proponents of the beatific vision as an intellectual experience, this experience was perceived by the intellect thanks to God and not the *phantasmata*.

In keeping with my argument so far, I prefer to read 'voglia', in the phrase 'in che sua voglia venne' (41), not as 'l'oggetto della sua voglia' — a common interpretation that was first proposed by Francesco Torraca and which, in Thomistic terms, proposes the final satisfaction of desire in the intellect — but, more generally, as desire itself.[44] By restricting the semantic scope of the noun, there is the danger of positing the end of the pilgrim's journey not in the *visio Dei* but in understanding the mystery of the Incarnation,[45] and thereby treating lines 142–45 as if they were almost an addition of secondary importance.[46] Yet, as regards the *visio Dei* — and again, on this point, there was no disagreement — what is theologically fundamental is not so much a matter of appreciating the mystery of the Incarnation, or any other divine mystery, but to *venire* to the end of all desires, namely, to the absolute satisfaction of the 'voglia' in God. As usual, Dante's formulation is precise, ideologically nuanced, and connotatively complex: 'se non che la mia mente fu percossa | da un fulgore in che sua voglia venne' (140–41). The lines allow a double reading: on the one hand, the satisfaction that results from *seeing* the miracle of the 'imago al cerchio' (137–38), and on the other, the fulfilment of every desire. The two satisfactions would seem to be different but, in reality, they are closely connected. Moreover, that we should give priority to the second interpretation seems to be confirmed by the fact that Dante does not allude to the gratification of *seeing* — the verb is here associated with human intellectual processes — but to the fulfilment of the 'voglia'. In any case, the end of desire inevitably also brings with it the resolution of the mystery of

44 Francesco Torraca, *Commento alla 'Divina Commedia'*, ed. by Valerio Marucci, 3 vols (Rome: Salerno, 2008), I, 1640.

45 '[U]n poema [la *Commedia*] che si fonda e culmina nella visione della presenza di Dio nella carne e nella storia' (Jacomuzzi, p. 25). On the basis of the incipit of John's first letter ('quod fuit ab initio quod audivimus quod vidimus oculis nostris quod perspeximus et manus nostrae temptaverunt de verbo vitae' [what was from the beginning, what we have heard, what we have seen with our eyes, what we have looked upon and our hands have touched concerns the word of life]) Christ was assigned a fundamental role in the unfolding of the *visio Dei*. At the same time, as in Dante, Christ does not represent the end but the last stage before *beatitudo*. I will have something more to say on this question

46 A similar tendency characterizes interpretations that read lines 142–45 exclusively or principally in a metaliterary key; not to mention those that fail entirely to consider the closing lines.

the Incarnation.[47] The 'fulgore' is the *visio Dei* thanks to which the 'voglia' of the 'mente' of the *viator* finds absolute satisfaction.

The third phase represents an attempt, however minimal and inadequate, to offer an impression of the beatific condition reached by the pilgrim. The last three lines are introduced by one of Dante's typically blunt 'ma' that signal a fundamental turning point in the development of the otherworldly journey: 'ma già volgeva il mio disio e 'l *velle* | [...] | l'amor'. With the failure of the *intellectus*, the harmonious immersion in God occurs or rather, to be precise, has 'already' (143) miraculously happened, as is evident from lines 140 and 141. What fundamentally characterizes the state of glory reached by the pilgrim is the new relationship between his 'disio' and his will — '*velle*' is the present infinitive of the Latin verb *volo*, 'I want', used as a noun[48] — which, for the first time, are found in perfect harmony and finally affectively fulfilled in divine love.[49] The state that Dante sketches is not, as Aquinas would have argued, beatitude as an 'act of the intellect' (*ST* I–II.ʼ q. 3. a. 4, sed contra + resp.), in which the will's loving delight plays a secondary and ancillary role, but, in line with Bonaventure, beatitude as the 'passing over [in which] all intellectual operations *are* relinquished', thanks to which 'the affection — or the

47 Dante had anticipated in *Paradiso* II that, at the moment of the *visio Dei*, the reality of the Incarnation would be revealed to him: 'accender ne dovria più il disio | di veder quella essenza in che si vede | come nostra natura e Dio s'unio. | Lì si vedrà ciò che tenem per fede, | non dimostrato, ma fia per sé noto | a guisa del ver primo che l'uom crede' (40–45).

48 'Caduta anche l'"alta fantasia" resteranno a Dante, e a noi con lui, solo i livelli non intellettuali dell'anima, i suoi aspetti emozionali, gli *affectus* che Agostino e gli agostiniani, soprattutto i Vittorini, hanno ricollocato al centro dell'interiorità umana: il "disio" e il "velle", la volontà coniugata al desiderio in una perfetta fusione di volere e desiderare': Corrado Bologna, 'Canto XVI: al centro del libro e del viaggio', in *Cento canti per cento anni. II. 'Purgatorio'. 1. Canti I–XVII*, ed. by Enrico Malato and Andrea Mazzucchi (Rome: Salerno, 2014), pp. 446–83 (p. 449); and see Pinto, pp. 215–16. Dronke, p. 37, is of a similar view. In addition, he convincingly criticizes Freccero's proposal to interpret 'disio' as 'intellectual desire': John Freccero, 'The Final Image: *Paradiso* XXXIII, 144', in his *Dante: The Poetics of Conversion* (Cambridge, MA: Harvard University Press, 1986), pp. 245–57 (p. 255). Frecero's position is typical of those who have insisted that the pilgrim's beatific vision is 'intellectualist' in nature. To do this, they need to introduce an intellectual dimension into the *viator*'s experience. They thus maintain that 'disio' 'si riferisce all'intelletto (come desiderio di conoscere) e il secondo alla volontà (come amore del bene), le due facoltà cioè dell'anima razionale' (Chiavacci Leonardi, III, 929). The problem is that there is no evidence in the text that 'disio' might have such a meaning. The comparison that is regularly made with the perfect balance of '[l]'affetto e 'l senno' (*Par.* XV. 73, but see 73–78) of the blessed is theologically misleading, since their beatific condition cannot be paralleled to Dante-*personaggio*'s; and see n. 101 below. In any case, there is a clear semantic distinction between 'senno' e 'disio'. This is the crux of the matter: it is far from easy to impose 'intellectual' connotations on desire. Furthermore, the formal and ideological make-up of lines 136–45 goes against an intellectual 'disio'. Similar objections can be levied against proposals that read '*velle*' as the will determined by the intellect, a meaning that finds no support in the explicit of the *Paradiso*.

49 'What defeats the pilgrim [who endeavours to understand the mystery of the Incarnation] is that the understanding he seeks is not conceptual: there is no "how" involved. The understanding comes in a flash of illumination or experience, canceling concept and image (*l'alta fantasia*) and with them the last trace of autonomous desire and will, which are now integrated into the harmony of creation, into the experience of self and all things as the self-expression of divine love. This firsthand knowledge of Truth or reality, of all as oneself, alone quenches the thirst for understanding' (Moevs, p. 81).

'buona voglia' to which the poet alludes in *Par.* XXVIII. 113 — is totally transferred and transformed into God'.[50] Furthermore, in agreement again with the *Doctor seraphicus*, Dante assigns to desire a key role: without 'disio' it is impossible to reach the goal of total satisfaction *in Deum*, which 'nec accipit nisi qui desiderat' (nobody experiences except one who desires it). In a manner similar to the whole contemplative tradition, from St Bernard to Richard of St Victor and from William of St Thierry to the Franciscans, for Dante too the condition of beatitude attained by the *viator* seems to 'consist' 'in actu voluntatis' [in an act of the will] (*Itin.* VII, chapter title and paragraph 4): an affective, and therefore emotive, experience.[51]

4. The Sources of Beatitude

Yet, this conclusion is partial and potentially misleading. Given the complexities of the medieval debate on the beatific vision, it is difficult to imagine how, by itself, the ending of the *Commedia* might be read as resolving Dante's thinking on the *visio Dei*. *Paradiso* XXXIII's take on the problem, in spite of its prominent structural position, is limited. The canto presents the subjective memories of the encounter with the divine of Dante the character, a living being, filtered through the artistic and intellectual sensibilities of Dante the poet. At most, it makes a contribution to contemporary discussions about the ways in which God can be experienced in this life.[52] Taken individually, neither *Par.* XXXIII. 136–45 nor any of the other passages on the *visio beatificata* that I examine in the next subsection is able fully to illustrate Dante's thought on the beatific vision. By privileging a single passage or favouring a group of mutually reinforcing passages, we end up discarding, omitting, and marginalizing other pertinent indications which, while present in the *Commedia*, do not fall within the ideological scope of the chosen text or texts. Dante was an all-encompassing and syncretistic poet, and hence an 'inclusive' thinker, who was always ready to propose totalizing solutions that could embrace the different ramifications of a problem. In our turn, if we want to arrive at an idea of Dante's reflections on the *visio Dei* in the *Commedia*, we need to recognize, assessing its

50   The miraculous process described by Dante recalls quite closely the phases presented by St Bonaventure, for whom '[a]n intimate experience of God begins with knowledge and is consummated in love' given the 'strict subordination of reason to love', even if '[b]oth acts are necessary, but the goal of the cognitive is to lead to that which is higher and more perfect, namely, the affective': Dreyer, pp. 14 & 19; and see also Coolman, pp. 615–18, 621, & 624. On the relationship between the close of the *Paradiso* and the *Itinerarium*, see the last part of the following subsection.

51   'As he [Dante] says in line 142, the previous precision of his imaginings has ceased, and, according to 33.58–63, he can remember only the sweetness left of the vision. We are to understand the pilgrim to be completely integrated affectively into harmony with God and with the cosmos': Durling-Martinez, III, 741, and see p. 682; while Pertile, *La punta del disio*, notes that '[i] suoi [del pellegrino] affetti sono [...] rimasti sani' (p. 262). Botterill, p. 238, provides an explanation close to mine: 'Here, at last [*Par.* XXXIII. 142–45], divine love acts on Dante-character's will, to bring it into accord with God's; here, for the first time, imagination loses its power, and language fails; here — and not before — Dante is deified'. See also Atturo, 'Il *Paradiso* dei sensi', pp. 442–44 & 464; Mocan, *L'alta fantasia*', pp. 171–74.

52   Pollack notes that, in Bonaventure, the emphasis on the will and affection as means with which to achieve the *visio Dei* 'relates chiefly to mystical union in this life' (p. 290).

consequences, that the poet's various statements on *beatitudo* function as a single system.

I have divided the analysis of this system in two. The following subsection, 'Beatitudes', analyzes the ways in which, thanks to the web of passages on the *visio Dei,* whose first thread begins in *Paradiso* III and which stretches as far as the last lines of the poem, Dante intervenes in the contemporary debate on the beatific vision, confirming, but also resolving, at times in an 'eccentric' manner, some key issues. Before that, in the present subsection, I explore how Dante dealt with and presented the theme of *beatitudo* in rhetorical and poetic terms, laying particular stress on interdiscursive and intertextual elements. In accordance with the emphasis given so far, I concentrate on the explicit of the *Commedia* to determine the formal strategies that Dante normally employed when addressing the union with God. An examination of the sources and intellectual traditions involved in the structure of *Paradiso* XXXIII, and specifically of lines 136–45, helps establish with a degree of precision the nature of the experience presented 'ultimamente' (*Conv.* II. 8. 2). As a result, it becomes easier to answer the question whether or not Dante is here actually advocating for 'voluntarist' positions, as would seem to be the case from the *explication* of the *lictera* of the poem's ending. Finally, and most significantly, the analysis permits us to take a further step forward in appreciating both the rich and shifting complexity of Dante's thought on the *visio Dei* and its relationship to late-medieval debates on the beatific vision.

In *Paradiso* XXXIII, one element in the presentation of the *viator*'s approach to and then immersion in God stands out: Dante formally moulds the *materia* in a decidedly personal way. First of all, he avoids much of the technical language that, at the beginning of the fourteenth century, was associated with the *visio beatifica,* and, therefore, also the connotations that this specialist language brought with it. Let's take the case of the concept of *raptus*. It is a commonplace among Dantists that, at the end of the *Commedia*, Dante describes the pilgrim's 'rapture' in a manner that recalls Paul's heavenly experience — a state that, in harmony with Aquinas, would reinforce the idea that the poem ends on an 'intellectualist' note (see in particular Foster, pp. 70–72, 78). Although there is no doubt that, from the beginning of the journey, the poet resorts to the apostle in fashioning Dante-*personaggio*, in the Empyrean in general and in *Paradiso* XXXIII in particular, Paul's influence is in fact restricted.[53] In support of the hypothesis that the *viator*'s beatific vision is equivalent to Paul's, passages from the *Summa theologica* are aligned with *Paradiso* XXXIII. 139–42 — passages such as 'mens humana divinitus rapitur ad contemplandam veritatem divinam, tripliciter. [...] Tertio, ut contempletur eam in sua essentia. Et

---

53   In addition to the discussion in the remainder of this paragraph, see also pp. 189–90 & 196–97. Despite the explicit Pauline echo at *Par.* XXX. 49 — 'così mi circunfulse luce viva' that repeats 'subito de caelo circumfulsit me lux copiosa' [suddenly an abundant light from heaven resplended around me] (Acts 22: 6) — explicit allusions to the saint are rare; see for example the poverty of evidence to support the idea of a Pauline Empyrean in Giuseppe Di Scipio, *The Presence of Pauline Thought in the Works of Dante* (Lewiston, NY: Edwin Mellen Press, 1975). Not even Hollander, energetic supporter of the equivalence between Paul and the pilgrim in the *Commedia*, provides concrete indications of the Pauline character of the Empyrean and of the final vision.

talis fuit raptus Pauli, et etiam Moysi' [the human mind is raptured towards heaven to contemplate divine truth in three ways. [...] Third, that it may contemplate it in its essence. And this is how Paul's, and even Moses's, rapture occurred] (*ST* II–II. q. 175. a. 3. ad 1); and:

> Divina essentia non potest ab homine videri per aliam vim cognoscitivam quam per intellectum. [...] Intellectus autem hominis, in statu viae, necesse est quod a phantasmatibus abstrahatur, si videat Dei essentiam. [...] Oportet autem, cum intellectus hominis elevatur ad altissimam Dei essentiae visionem, ut tota mentis intentio illuc advocetur, ita scilicet quod nihil intelligat aliud ex phantasmatibus, sed totaliter feratur in Deum. (*ST* II–II. q. 175. a. 4, resp.)[54]

> [The divine essence cannot be seen by man through any other cognitive power than the intellect. [...] The human intellect, while *in via*, must necessarily withdraw from sensible images, if it is to see the essence of God. [...] When the human intellect is elevated to the highest vision of the essence of God, all of the mind's effort ought to be directed there, so that it may not infer anything else from sensible images, but be carried completely into God.]

However, the links between Dante's verses and Aquinas's *responsiones* are, to say the least, problematic. Neither here nor elsewhere in the *Commedia*, does Dante use the term *raptus* and related terms to indicate the pilgrim's heavenly experience.[55] Moreover, at the end of the poem, there are no references to the *intellectus* and to the divine *essentia*, notions which, together with that of *raptus*, determine and delimit the 'intellectualist' theory of the *visio Dei*.[56] It seems unlikely, therefore, that, at the end of the *Commedia*, Dante is describing an intellectual *raptus*, is equating Dante the character to St Paul, and is claiming that 'knowledge [is] eclipsing claims of love' (Hollander, III, 844), also because the last three lines, those in which the *viator* is finally in harmony with God, speak of love, desire, and will.

At the same time, although not specifically in lines 136–45, in *Paradiso* XXXIII and elsewhere in the cantos of the Empyrean, these (and similar) 'intellectualist' notions do persist, although Dante accompanies them — as we shall soon see — with others that come from different traditions, thereby contextualizing and relativizing their meanings, and, ultimately, complicating them. Indeed, in the *Paradiso* in general, Dante either employs, moderately and in a targeted manner (see the next subsection), technical language associated with the 'intellectualist' tradition, or, as we have just noted, avoids it altogether. A further example of the second of these strategies is the way in which Dante presents the celestial light that facilitates the pilgrim's movement towards God. This mediating light plays a central role in Aquinas's thought on *beatitudo*. It is a metaphysical reality, that Thomas designates as *lumen gloriae*, without which God cannot be seen:

54   When examining the *visio Dei*, Dantists lean heavily on *quaestio* 175, 'De raptu', as well as on other passages taken from the *ST* (for example, I. q. 12; I–II. q. 5. a. 4; II–II. q. 24. a. 2).

55   In the *Commedia*, Dante's sole use of the verb *rapire* is to refer to the effect of the singing of the blessed on the *viator*: 'così da' lumi che lì m'apparinno | s'accogliea per la croce una melode | che mi rapiva, sanza intender l'inno' (*Par.* XIV. 121–23).

56   Foster, pp. 71–72, 74–76, 81; L. Malevez, 'Essence de Dieu', in DSAM, IV:2, cols 1333–45; L. Reypens, 'Âme', in DSAM, I:1, cols 433–69 (cols 436–49).

Lumen istud non requiritur ad videndum Dei essentiam quasi similitudo in qua Deus videatur, sed quasi perfectio quaedam intellectus, confortans ipsum ad videndum Deum. Et ideo potest dici quod non est medium in quo Deus videatur, sed sub quo videtur. Et hoc non tollit immediatam visionem Dei. [...] lumen gloriae non potest esse naturale creaturae, nisi creatura esset naturae divinae, quod est impossibile. Per hoc enim lumen fit creatura rationalis deiformis. (*ST* I. q. 12. a. 5. 2–3)[57]

[This light is required in the vision of God not as a similitude in which God may be seen, but as a sort of perfection of the intellect, strengthening it to see God. So it can be said that [this light] is not a means in which God may be seen, but by which He is seen. And this medium does not take away the immediate vision of God. [...] The light of glory cannot be natural to the creature, unless the creature be of divine nature, which is impossible. For through this light the rational creature is made godlike.]

Nevertheless, in spite of the fundamental importance of the *lumen gloriae* for 'intellectualist' theorizing, Dante never uses the term — a decision of undoubted significance. The way that Dante presents light in the Empyrean is flexible and non-sectarian. Consider lines such as:

> ché la mia vista, venendo sincera,
> e più e più intrava per lo raggio
> de l'alta luce che da sé è vera. (*Par.* XXXIII. 52–54)

The 'alta luce' can be 'the light of glory' of the 'intellectualists', but it can equally be the affective *lux*: 'postquam mens nostra contuita est Deum [...] supra se per divinae lucis similitudinem supra nos relucentem et in ipsa luce' [after our mind has looked into God [...] over itself through a resembling image of the divine light which shines over us and in that very light] (*Itin.* VII. 1). As a result, light is another element that, in the wake of the Psalmist ('in lumine tuo videbimus lumen' [in Your light we will see the light], Psalm 35: 10), unites the 'voluntarists' and the 'intellectualists', and which Dante uses to smooth out polemical and contrasting elements between the two traditions.[58] Equally, as we saw above, the failure of the 'alta fantasia' (142) before God, that is, of the normal intellectual functions, was also a position shared by Thomas and Bonaventure.

And there is more. Just as Dante avoids specialist 'intellectualist' language when treating the *visio Dei*, so he also eschews typical 'voluntarist' terminology, in particular *excessus* or *exstasis* (Newman, pp. 9–10). Furthermore, he avoids other technical

---

57   Casagrande (p. 211) asserts that the light that leads the pilgrim to God in *Paradiso* XXXIII is not the *lumen gloriae*; of the opposite view are: Mauro Gagliardi, *'Lumen gloriae': studio interdisciplinare sulla natura della luce nell'Empireo dantesco* (Vatican City: Libreria editrice vaticana, 2010); Marco Signori, 'Sulla distinzione di luce e gloria nel *Paradiso* dantesco', *Italianistica*, 45:2 (2016), 51–65 (pp. 57–59). In truth, it is impossibile to define precisely the nature of the light that the *viator* sees in the Empyrean, since Dante fails to provide the means with which to do this.

58   On light in the *Paradiso*, see Simon Gilson, pp. 151–256; Signori. To be read with caution Pablo García Acosta, 'Follow the Light: *Lumen gloriae* and *visio Dei* in the Works of Dante Alighieri and Marguerite *dicta* Porete', *Eikón Imago*, 6:2 (2014), 51–76.

vocabulary, such as *deificatio, deiformis*,[59] *dotes animae*,[60] and *sensus spiritales*,[61] that was utilized across different intellectual traditions.[62] Dante's decision to renounce the technical language relating to the beatific vision is very likely to have been deliberate, as is confirmed by the fact that the poet had no qualms about flexibly using the concepts that this jargon conveyed and in creatively 'vernacularizing' it with personal inflections.[63] For example, the famous neologism 'trasumanar' (*Par.* I. 70) would seem to be close to *deificatio/deificari*;[64] while the *oltraggio* evoked in the line 'e cede la memoria a tanto oltraggio' (*Par.* XXXIII. 57) 'traduce l'*excessus humanae mentis* della contemplazione mistica, [ma anche] ne innova profondamente

59   Dante employs the adjective to describe the Empyrean: 'La concreata e perpetüa sete | del deïforme regno cen portava | veloci quasi come 'l ciel vedete' (*Par.* II. 19–21).
60   See Pollack, pp. 277–97. See also Nikolaus Wicki, *Die Lehre von der himmlischen Seligkeit in der mittelalterlichen Scholastik von Petrus Lombardus bis Thomas Aquinas* (Freiburg: Universitätsverlag, 1954). Pollack remarks that 'Dante himself does not use the term "dowries" in specific connection with the three elements of beatitude' (p. 278).
61   On the *sensus spiritales*, see at least *The Spiritual Senses: Perceiving God in Western Christianity*, ed. by Paul L. Gavrilyuk and Sarah Coakley (Cambridge: Cambridge University Press, 2012). See also Ariani, 'Dante, la *dulcedo*'.
62   In truth, in the Middle Ages, the debate on the *visio Dei* was marked by considerable terminological fluidity that brought together different authors and traditions. For instance, the concept of *raptus*, which certainly played a key role in 'intellectualist' discourses, is also present in St Bernard: 'Sed aliquando homo interior rationem excedit et supra se rapitur, et dicitur excessus mentis' [But at times the inner man exceeds his reason and is raptured beyond himself, and this is called a mental ecstasy] (*Sermones de diversis*, CXV). In his turn, Bonaventure associates *raptus* and *ecstasis*: 'amplexabile per ardentissimam caritatem, quae mentem nostram per ecstasim et raptum transire facit ex hoc mundo ad Patrem' [it can be comprehended through a most fervent love, which through ecstasy and rapture brings our mind from this world to the Father] (*Breviloquium* V. 6. 6). When I distinguish between the technical language of the two traditions, I am aware of the approximate nature of my affirmations. As we will see, Dante exploits this fluidity for personal ends. See also Barbara Faes de Mottoni, '*Excessus mentis, alienatio mentis*, estasi, *raptus* nel Medioevo', in *Per una storia del concetto di mente*, ed. by Eugenio Canone (Florence: Olschki, 2005), pp. 167–84; Paul L. Gavrilyuk and Sarah Coakley, 'Introduction', in *The Spiritual Senses*, pp. 1–19 (pp. 2–4); Newman, pp. 9–10.
63   Botterill notes: 'it must be admitted that neither Aquinas nor any other source in the deification tradition seems to have supplied Dante with the technical vocabulary he employs for the evocation of his character's adventures in mysticism: neither Aquinas' *raptus* nor Bernard's *deificari* nor Maximus Confessor's (Latinized) *excessus* has left any verbal traces in the text of *Paradiso*' (p. 221). My late-lamented friend Steven Botterill then adds that 'when he, as poet, comes to render the experience for which tradition offered him so many and such authoritative precedents, he does so in terms, both conceptual and lexical, that are resoundingly his own'. Fallani, 'La visione beatifica', arrives at a similiair conclusion: 'la sintesi dantesca [...] è sì debitrice alla cultura del tempo, ma non è riducibile al punto di partenza di una fonte unica' (p. 125). See also Pollack, p. 279. My chapter at this point develops these important insights.
64   Botterill; and Rosetta Migliorini Fissi, 'La nozione di *deificatio* nel *Paradiso*', *Letture classensi*, 9–10 (1982), 39–72. Botterill correctly states: '"Trasumanar" is, in fact, only the *beginning* of a protracted and arduous education in mystical experience and spiritual growth, which Dante *personaggio* is required to undergo in Paradise. [...] and this fact alone is fatal to the correlation of *deificatio* and "transumanar"' (pp. 236–37). Nevertheless, if one interprets *Par.* I. 70–72 in broad terms, since the *terzina* can be read both as referring specifically to the pilgrim and as a general statement regarding the possibility that any believer has of attaining beatitude, then, even if only partially, the connections between the two terms can be revived.

il significato e la portata poetica'.[65] At the same time, it is necessary to specify that with *oltraggio* Dante does not refer to the moment of the beatific vision, to that *excessus* which constitutes, for example, the subject of the seventh chapter of Bonaventure's *Itinerarium*, but to an earlier and preparatory 'ecstatic' state, even if one that is very close to the ultimate *visio* itself. In the contemplative tradition, it is normal to present the ascent to God as a progressive series of distinct yet balanced states in which the soul is refined. The *viator*'s itinerary too is progressive. However, the clear distinctions that characterize the mystical experience disappear during his journey through the celestial spheres, so that this ends up being divided into three structurally distinct experiential phases: the nine spheres of the Ptolemaic universe, the Empyrean, and the extremely brief *visio beatifica*. Yet, in composing the *Paradiso*, Dante regularly draws on the mystical-contemplative tradition, adapting it to his own needs. Thus, on the one hand, it is almost certain that the poet borrowed elements taken from Richard of Saint Victor's *Benjamin major*, but, on the other, it is rare for these to conform tidily to the particular situation that Dante describes.[66] For example, Pertile states that 'sembra indubbio che Dante traesse spunti per la composizione dell'ultima grande scena del *Paradiso* dal v libro del *Benjamin Major*', citing two indicative passages from chapters five and nine (Pertile, *La punta*, p. 256, n. 17). In both, however, Richard is defining the *excessus mentis* that results from *admiratio*,[67] a condition different from and preceding that which Dante evokes in *Paradiso* XXXIII. Likewise, the poet, who laments the effects on his 'memoria' (*Par.* XXXIII. 57) of gazing on 'lo raggio | de l'alta luce' (53–54) 'ché quasi tutta cessa | mia visïone, e ancor mi distilla | nel core il dolce che nacque da essa' (61–63), seems to recall St Paul, who, according to Aquinas:

> Postquam cessavit videre Deum per essentiam, memor fuit illorum quae in illa visione cognoverat, per aliquas species intelligibiles habitualiter ex hoc in eius intellectu relictas, sicut etiam, abeunte sensibili, remanent aliquae impressiones in anima, quas postea convertens ad phantasmata, memorabatur. Unde nec totam illam cognitionem aut cogitare poterat, aut verbis exprimere. (*ST* II–II. q. 175. a. 4. ad 3)

> [After he ceased to see God in His essence, he remembered those things that he had seen in that vision, through some intelligible species which after this experience were left in his intellect as if by habit, just as, when the sensible object is gone, certain impressions remain in the soul, which this one recalls when it turns to the sensible images. He could not, accordingly, think over the whole of that knowledge, or express it in words.]

And yet, Anna Maria Chiavacci Leonardi notes: '[t]uttavia, nella somiglianza dei due testi, c'è una fondamentale differenza: per Tommaso restano in Paolo delle "specie intelligibili", cioè delle immagini; per Dante resta solo una *passione* [59], cioè un sentimento provato. Ciò che vide non è ricordabile, e quindi non esprimibile'

---

65   Pertile, *La punta del disio*, pp. 255–56; see also Chiavacci Leonardi, III, 914.
66   On Dante and Richard, see in particolar Atturo, 'Contemplating Wonder'; Salvatore Battaglia, 'La visione divina', in his *Esemplarità e antagonismo*, pp. 223–26; Colombo, pp. 61–71; Gardner, pp. 166–83; Mocan, *L'arca della mente*; Pertile, *La punta del disio*, pp. 255–56.
67   On Richard's *admiratio* in *Par.*, see Atturo, 'Contemplating Wonder'.

(Chiavacci Leonardi, III, 915–16). Indeed, the differences between Dante and Thomas outweigh the *somiglianze*. Unlike Paul, the pilgrim has not yet arrived at the *visio Dei*; the emphasis on *dolcezza* and 'passione' distance the experience described from 'intellectualist' norms and recalls instead 'affective' *topoi*; and the same can also be said of the apophatic dimension of the 'somma luce' (67). What is crucial about lines 55–63 is their syncretic character. In fact, Dante does not limit himself to synthesizing elements taken from different and contrasting traditions, but adapts them to the new context that he is describing. Thus, the affective-apopathic implications of the failed 'visïone' that 'quasi tutta cessa' (61–62) normally characterize the mental 'impressions' of a living being once the *visio Dei* is over, and not the memory of the moments immediately preceding the *visio beatifica*:[68]

> Qual è colüi che sognando vede,
> che dopo 'l sogno la passione impressa
> rimane, e l'altro a la mente non riede' (*Par.* XXXIII. 58–60)

The examples just discussed are typical of the ways in which Dante resorts to the mystical tradition to fashion his Paradise in general and the beatific vision in particular. Texts and *topoi* constitute a storehouse of images, situations, discourses, and *sententiae* from which the poet draws at will, refurbishing the mystical-contemplative legacy in an accumulative-syncretic and explicitly personal key. In this way, Dante eases the tensions between conflicting positions, recognizing the value, but also the limits and the provisional nature of each. At the same time, the bold eclecticism of his approach and the care with which he avoids technical terminology, both strategies that guarantee that the poet cannot be too closely associated with a single current and its proposals, have not served him well among Dante scholars. On the one hand, his solutions have fostered that impression of ambiguity and even uncertainty that some have claimed distinguishes the manner in which the poet deals with the divine vision. On the other, they have encouraged those who do not recognize the rich and integrated stratification of his treatment of *beatitudo* to focus solely on those aspects that allow them to insist that Dante had championed only one particular ideological position (usually of an 'intellectualist' stripe).

At this point a question arises: is Dante's goal to present a generalizing idea of the beatific vision that transcends, and therefore neutralizes, doctrinal disputes, so that, in the *Commedia*, it would be pointless to try to align the poet with a particular ideological current? As usual with Dante, it is not easy to offer a definitive answer — even if the remainder of this chapter has precisely this aim. And it is not easy because the answers are many and interconnected, sometimes in ways that are apparently 'impossible'.

Everything depends on the angle from which one considers the issues that my question raises. It is legitimate to start by answering in the affirmative. By integrating and resemanticizing elements taken from different traditions and reusing them in new contexts, Dante indicates their limitations as means with which to describe

---

68 What obviously unites Paul and Dante is the general problem of how, once they have returned to earth, they might be able to recall the encounter with the divine.

the *visio Dei*. Regardless of the tradition, its images, lexicon, and suggestions are simply human 'inventions' and 'approximations'. They are, as I noted earlier, subjective representations whose relationship to the reality of the transcendent is negligible. Therefore, insisting on the determining validity of any solution makes little sense in the face of the mystery of the divine. Rather, as he does with other burning issues, Dante attempts to resolve, through a work of synthesis, the differences between discrete positions. It is thanks to the assimilation of different ideological and formal solutions that one can perhaps arrive at some intuition of heavenly realities, as Dante proposes in the heaven of the Sun. At the same time, he does not cease to emphasize the fundamental 'pointlessness' of every effort to grasp the divine with rational and linguistic human means — a truth that, in the *narratio*, Dante avers when he describes the trauma that overwhelms the pilgrim at the end of the *Paradiso*. Therefore, and in a highly significant manner, describing the union with God experienced by the *viator*, the poet does not resort to any of the *sententiae* and the *auctoritates* that were normally associated with the literature on the *visio Dei*. Lines 140–41 are avowedly 'nuovi'. If I am not mistaken, the lines do not have formal and textual precedents. The one exception may be the unlikely reprise of Gregory the Great's phrase '[f]ulgur [...] mentes percutit' [a flashing light struck my mind],[69] that Dante could have translated as 'la mia mente fu percossa | da un fulgore'.[70] Immediately afterwards, and in clear contrast to what happens

---

69   See Mario Aversano, *Dante, Iacopone da Todi e il canto XXXIII del 'Paradiso'* (Manocalzati (AV): Edizioni il Papavero, 2015), pp. 175–76. Gregory is glossing Ezechiel 1: 13 ('et similitudo animalium aspectus eorum quasi carbonum ignis ardentium et quasi aspectus lampadarum haec erat visio discurrens in medio animalium splendor ignis et de igne fulgor egrediens' [and as for the likeness of the living creatures, their appearance was like a fire of burning coals and as the appearance of lamps; this was the vision, a bright fire running to and fro among the creatures and a flashing light springing from the fire]; but see also the following line: 'et animalia ibant et revertebantur in similitudinem fulguris coruscantis' [and the living creatures were coming and going in the likeness of a flashing light]): 'Splendor ergo ignis, et de igne fulgur egrediens inter pennata animalia discurrit, quia Spiritus sanctus simul singulis atque omnibus praesto fit, et incendit quos contigerit, et illuminat quos incendit, ut post frigus pristinum accensi ardeant, et per ignem amoris quem acceperint flammas exemplorum reddant. Fulgur quippe de hoc igne egrediens torpentes mentes percutit, easque percutiendo excitat et inflammat, ut post amorem illus ardentes pariter et lucentes currant' [thus the brightness of the fire, and the flashing light springing from the fire runs to and fro among the winged creatures, because the Holy Spirit manifests itself at once to each individual and to all, and inflames all whom it touches, and brightens those whom it inflames, that once inflamed after the previous coldness they may burn, and may give back flames of examples through the fire of love which they have received. Then the flashing light that springs from this fire strikes the torpid minds, and by striking them it reawakens them and inflames them, that in the wake of such love they may run equally burning and shining] (Gregory the Great, *Homiliarum in Ezechielem prophetam*, PL vol. LXXVI, cols 824D–25A). Given the undoubted presence of the first chapter of Ezechiel in the explicit of *Paradiso*, it is likely that Dante's 'fulgore' is an echo of the prophet. At the same time, it is important to recognize that both the Scriptural passages and Gregory's exegesis are far from *Paradiso* XXXIII's visionary context and that, like the intertexts of lines 143–45, on which immediately below, they do not belong to mystical language.

70   Casagrande (pp. 216–17) suggests as precedents the *simpli fulgores* of pseudo-Dionysius mediated by Hugh of St Victor (*Commentariorium in Hierarchiam coelestem*, VI. 7, in PL, vol. CXLLV, col. 1033D); however, not only are the contexts different — the fundamental difference between theophany and the *visio Dei* — but the Areopagite is also speaking of *fulgori* in the plural. Equally, the passage from

in lines 140–41, in lines 143–45, Dante relies on readily recognizable intertexts. However, Ezekiel 1: 16–21 and 10: 2–19, as well as their exegetical tradition, and *Consolatio philosophiae* II. metre 8. 28–30,[71] to which Dante adds the occasional generalizing Aristotelian reference,[72] are all cited 'inappropriately', since none of

Thomas Aquinas that some have cited ('Unde etiam quidam ponentes divinam essentiam solum per hunc modum videri, dixerunt quod ipsa essentia non videbitur sed quidam fulgor, quasi radius ipsius' [Thus even those claiming that the divine essence can be seen only in this way, said that the essence will not be seen in itself, but as a shining light, as it were, almost as a ray coming from it], *ST* suppl., q. 92. a. 1) does not refer to the *visio Dei* but to theophany as the extreme limit of the experience of the divine, a viewpoint that Dante rejects in the wake of Thomas himself: 'Unde nec iste modus sufficit ad visionem divinam, quam querimus' [Therefore not even this way is adequate for the divine vision which we long for]. The proposal that, instead of *fulgore*, we should read *folgore* is unconvincing: Richard Kay, 'Flash or Effulgence: Mental Illumination in Dante's *Paradiso* 33. 141', in *Medieval Paradigms: Essays in Honor of Jeremy duQuesnay Adams*, ed. by Stephanie Hayes-Healey, 2 vols (New York: Palgrave Macmillan, 2005), I, 169–80.

71   At the start of the canto, Dante had already made recourse to Boethius alluding to the great hymn 'O qui perpetua', which, like the close of the *Commedia*, celebrates the order of creation. The lines 'perché tu ogne nube li disleghi | di sua mortalità co' prieghi tuoi' (*Par.* XXXIII. 31–32) calque 'Dissice terrenae nebulas et pondera molis | Atque tuo splendore mica!' [Disperse the dim heaviness of this earthly weight and shine forth in your brightness!] (*Cons. phil.* III. metre 9. 25–26). As Giuseppe Ledda correctly notes, the image is also 'un ulteriore ribaltamento del motivo del *Deus absconditus*' (*La guerra della lingua*, p. 309, n. 29). See also Francesco Tateo, 'Il "punto" della visione e una reminiscenza da Boezio', in his *Questioni di poetica dantesca* (Bari: Adriatica, 1972), pp. 201–16.

72   On the sources of lines 143–45, see at least Aversano, *Dante, Iacopone da Todi*, pp. 178–85; Dronke, p. 38; Freccero; Gardner, pp. 321–22; Martinelli, 'La *Commedia*', p. 311 (on the commentaries to the *Cons. phil.*); Pertile, *La punta del disio*, pp. 274–81 (with references to Jerome's commentary on Ezechiel; and see also Aversano, 'La conclusione', pp. 194–95, 198). Claudia Di Fonzo's recent suggestion that the final line of the *Commedia* recalls Cicero, *De amicitia* VII. 24 — 'Agrigentium quidem doctum quendam virum carminibus Graecis vaticinatum ferunt, quae in rerum natura totoque mundo constarent quaeque moverentur, ea contrahere amicitiam' [Indeed, it is said that a certain learned man from Agrigentum [Empedocles] celebrated in Greek verse that in nature and the whole universe whatever things are at rest and whatever are in motion are united in friendship] (Cicero, *De senectute, De amicitia, De divinatione*, trans. by William A. Falconer (Cambridge, MA and London: Harvard University Press, 1923) — is suggestive, especially as it conforms to Dante's intertextual strategies at the close of the poem; see Claudia Di Fonzo, *Dante e la tradizione giuridica* (Rome: Carocci, 2016), p. 135. See also Peter Dronke, '"L'amor che move il sole e l'altre stelle"', *Studi medievali*, 6 (1965), 389–422. The problem of the Aristotelianism of the closing lines is complicated. According to Dronke, 'The Conclusion of Dante's *Commedia*', pp. 23, 31, and 34, at various points in *Paradiso* XXXIII, Dante deliberately rejects Aristotelian solutions, even though the 'moto' of the final scene conforms to Aristotelian *scientia* (p. 37). Pertile, *La punta del disio*, p. 266, remarks that in the 'ultimi versi del poema si annida il problema dei rapporti tra aristotelismo e neoplatonismo'; while Ariani, 'La mistica preterizione', without resolving the apparent contradiction, first asserts that Dante 'chiude la *Commedia* con un'adesione alla teologia francescana degli *affectus*' (p. 1006), but then declares that '[l]'adozione [...] di un formulario aristotelico-tomistico [which is not defined] proprio all'*explicit* del "poema sacro" indicherebbe una scelta precisa che conferma *in extremis* la sintesi aristotelico-neoplatonica dell'impianto teologico del *Paradiso*' (p. 1007). Insisting too energetically on the Aristotelian dimension of the close of the *Commedia*, leads to underplaying the overwhelming non-Aristotelian character of the closing lines, in which there is little that might be termed Aristotelian. At most, it is possibile to indicate the physics of movement, which was a doctrinal commonplace, and perhaps the 'igualmente' (144), another *communis opinio*, if it is the case that Dante is here translating Aristotle's and his commentators' technical term *aequaliter*; see Bruno Nardi, '"Sì come rota ch'igualmente è mossa"', *Studi danteschi*, 19 (1935), 83–96, and Falzone, 'Visione beatifica', pp. 49–56. At the same time, Pertile's proposal on this point is more persuasive. He writes that 'in

them was part of the conventional language on beatitude.[73] Dante implies that there
are no 'definitive' ways to talk about the miracle of the beatific union. Equally, by
extension, no theological tradition exists that in some way has a privileged access
to the mystery.[74] Hence, the highly independent, even 'eccentric' ways in which
he seeks to define the *viator*'s ultimate experience are as legitimate as any other
treatment. In addition, the decidedly personal stamp that marks the ending of the
Commedia affirms for the last time the uniqueness of Dante-character's experience.
Indeed, given that the poet stresses that his version stems from personal memories,
however opaque, of an event that he actually experienced, the impression begins
to take shape that his representation, for all its subjectivity and inadequacy, may
perhaps have some minimal validity...

The analysis that I have been expounding obviously goes against the conclusion
to which I had arrived, on the basis of a careful reading of the *lictera* of the final

Ezechiele [an undoubted source of the closing lines] [...] la sincronicità [of movements] viene espressa
per mezzo dell'avverbio *pariter*: come appunto fa Dante con *igualmente*' (*La punta del disio*, p. 277).
Gregory B. Stone, 'Dante as Celestial Soul: The Final Verses of *Paradiso* in the light of Avicenna's
Metaphysics', in '*Tra amici*': *Essays in Honor of Giuseppe Mazzotta*, ed. by Walter Stephens and others,
supplement to *MLN*, 127:1 (2012), S99–S109, is largely unconvincing. See also the interesting but
improbable hypothesis in Sandra Rizzardi, 'Dante e l'orologio', *Studi e problemi di critica testuale*, 60
(2000), 51–70. For a possible pseudo-Dionysian substratum to *Par.* XXXIII. 143–45, see Stefano Prandi,
'Dante e lo Pseudo-Dionigi: una nuova proposta per l'immagine finale della *Commedia*', *Lettere
italiane*, 61 (2009), 1–29 (pp. 20–29).

73   The only link with the contemplative tradition is the circular motion with which the poem
closes. See, for example, Richard of St Victor: 'Contemplatio autem omnia circumvolat, et cum
voluerit se in summis librat' [Contemplation flies around all things, and whenever it pleases it swings
up to the top] (*Ben. maj.* I. 3), even if the second clause describes a state that is diametrically different
to that of the pilgrim *volto* by *Amore*. See also I. 5: 'Nam vivacitas illa intelligentiae in contemplantis
animo mira agilitate modo it atque redit, modo se quasi in gyrum flectit' [For that intellectual vigour
with marvellous agility now comes and goes, now turns itself, as it were, in a circle, in the soul of
the one who contemplates]. This movement is compared to that of birds: 'Hujus sane rei formam si
recte perpendimus, in coeli volatilibus quotidie videmus' [and certainly if we examine carefully the
shape of this movement, we see it everyday in the birds of the sky] — an image which, together with
the passage cited from I. 3, might be present in the background of line 139: 'ma non eran da ciò le
proprie penne'. *Ben. maj.* I. 5 includes other references to the circular motion of the contemplatives.
See also Coolman, pp. 627–28, who cites passages from the pseudo-Dionysius and Thomas Gallus,
to which can be added Thomas Aquinas, *ST* II–II. q. 180. a. 6. ad 3 and *In librum beati Dionysii de Div.
Nom.* IV. 7. Suggestive links between the explicit of the *Commedia* and the 'mystical' Iacopone have
been put forward by Aversano, *Dante, Iacopone da Todi*, pp. 180–81 & 184, and by Paolo Canettieri,
'Intertesti ideologici e rimici: tasselli per Iacopone e Dante', in *Prassi intertestuale*, ed. by Simonetta
Bianchini (Rome: Bagatto, 1996), pp. 55–80 (pp. 73–74). However, the connections between the two
great religious poets would seem to be interdiscursive rather than intertextual.

74   The range of sources with which Dante concludes the *Commedia* is further enriched, in addition
to the allusions to the Dionysian tradition, by references to Alan of Lille and to Joachim of Fiore in
the descriptions of the theophanies: Dronke, 'The Conclusion of Dante's *Commedia*', p. 36; André
Pézard, 'La vision finale du *Paradis*', in his *Dans le sillage de Dante* (Paris: Société d'Études Italiennes,
1975), pp. 481–91 (pp. 486–91); Marjorie Reeves and Beatrice Hirsch-Reich, *The 'Figurae' of Joachim
of Fiore* (Oxford: Clarendon Press, 1972), pp. 317–29. Very recently, Anna Pegoretti has highlighted
the possibility of 'una maggiore diffusione, almeno a Firenze, dell'iconografia delle sfere trinitarie':
'"Nelle scuole delli religiosi": materiali per Santa Croce nell'età di Dante', *L'Alighieri*, 58 (2017), 5–55
(p. 36). Finally, Boitani (p. 113) proposes connections between the 'volume' (86) and some passages
from Aquinas's commentary to *De divinis nominibus* of the pseudo-Dionysius.

lines, at the end of the previous subsection, namely, that Dante presents the pilgrim's experience as affective. In effect, the contrast between the two positions is more apparent than real; and let us not forget that paradox and oxymoron are among the basic *modi tractandi* of medieval mystical discourse.[75] In the interplay of sources that bear upon the ending of the *Commedia*, the three nouns — 'disio', '*velle*', and 'amor' — markers of the 'voluntarist' tradition, continue to exert an influence. On the one hand, Dante calls into serious doubt the accuracy and effectiveness of every reflection on the divine, including his own, and poses the *quaestio* of the *visio Dei* in terms that are *supra partes* and reconciliatory. On the other, however, he also has the responsibility to provide some sort of intimation, however vague, of what had in fact happened to the pilgrim at the end of the journey. Thus, 'quanto' of this encounter the poet 'poté far tesoro' (*Par.* I. 10–11) would seem to suggest that, with all due reservation that his repeated assertions of ineffability demand, his experience was of an affective rather than of an intellectual nature.

Moreover, the entire intertextual, formal, ideological, and narrative structure of *Paradiso* XXXIII is dominated by 'voluntarist' elements that prepare the way for the affective ending. In contrast, 'intellectualist' features are scarce, even if, for the reasons that I have noted, they do not disappear. Nonetheless, the disparity between the two traditions is stark. The overwhelming majority of sources, as Dante scholarship has established, comes from affective *auctoritates*.[76] The figure of St Bernard of Clairvaux not only directs the pilgrim towards union with God, but also serves, for us, as an ideological and textual guide. Although precise intertextual reprises from his works have not been identified in *Paradiso* XXXIII, it is not difficult to recognize elements belonging to Bernardian mysticism, from the commentaries to the Psalms to the *De diligendo Deo*.[77] In addition, as I have already indicated, Richard of Saint Victor, in particular thanks to the *Benjamin major*, exercises a similar influence on the canto, as do his confrère Hugh and William of St. Thierry.[78] The atmosphere of *Paradiso* XXXIII, even if not its intertextual weave, is heavily affective and 'voluntarist'. In truth, a Franciscan text is explicitly quoted in it. Back in 1924, in a note that Dante scholarship has almost entirely forgotten, Étienne Gilson had traced a system of borrowings taken directly from Bonaventure's *Itinerarium mentis in*

75   On the oxymoronic character of *Paradiso*, see Rachel Jacoff, 'Introduction to *Paradiso*', in *The Cambridge Companion to Dante*, ed. by Rachel Jacoff, 2nd edn (Cambridge: Cambridge University Press, 2007), pp. 107–24 (pp. 119–23); Rebecca West, 'XXXIII', in *Dante's 'Divine Comedy': Introductory Readings. III. 'Paradiso'*, ed. by Tibor Wlassics (Charlottesville: University of Virginia Printing Service, 1995), pp. 504–18.

76   Although the presence of the 'voluntarist' tradition in *Paradiso* XXXIII has been extensively documented, as is clear from the notes that follow, in general, scholars have concentrated on one or two texts and writers. These are then normally put forward as the exclusive models for the canto, and so for the beatific vision. Such an approach is reductive, since it fails to assess the problem of the *visio Dei* and its sources in *Paradiso* XXXIII and in the *Commedia* in broad and syncretic terms.

77   Botterill; Fausta Drago Rivera, *S. Bernardo e l'ascesa mistica del Paradiso* (Milan: Società Dante Alighieri, 1995); Dronke, 'The Conclusion of Dante's *Commedia*', pp. 22–23; Gardner, pp. 111–43; Richard Kay, 'Dante in Ecstasy: *Paradiso* 33 and Bernard of Clairvaux', *Mediaeval Studies*, 66 (2004), 183–212; Rizzardi, pp. 68–70.

78   On Hugh, see Casagrande, pp. 216–19. On William, see Botterill, pp. 213–14. Aversano, 'La conclusione', has stressed, unconvincingly, the influence of Gregory the Great.

Deum that allowed him to conclude that '[l']*Itinerarium* de saint Bonaventure, dont le dernier chant de Dante suit pas à pas la méthode, aboutit à une extase d'où toute connaissance est exclue et qui ne réalise le contact qu'entre la volonté humaine et Dieu', so that the contemplative manages to 'éprouver la présence de Dieu par la joie de l'amour, mais sans le voir par l'intellect'.[79] Gilson's contribution is fundamental if we wish to understand the ideological background of *Paradiso* XXXIII. At the same time, the study's overarching perspective is too serene and orderly. The great historian of philosophy does not recognize the tensions and complications that characterize Dante's treatment of the beatific vision, as he does not recognize the fact, which ought to become better evident in the next subsection, that, in the *Paradiso*, and always in the circumscribed manner that I have suggested, Dante also affords space to 'intellectualist' solutions. For Gilson, on the contrary, the *visio Dei* in the *Commedia* has 'un sens précis' that is neatly resolved through 'une extase d'amour transcendante à toute connaissance' (pp. 55 & 63).

In *Paradiso* XXXIII, Bonaventure stands at the head of an extensive system of allusions to the affective tradition — allusions to writers and texts, but also to commonplaces, which, since they prepare the way for the final act, anticipate it in a crescendo and contextualize it doctrinally. For instance, Bernard prays to the Virgin, and prayer was considered among the *modi affectivi* par excellence,[80] to 'conserv*are* sani, | dopo tanto veder, li affetti' (35–36) of the pilgrim; the approach to God is presented as an entry, 'la mia vista [...] | e più e più intrava' (52–53), a metaphor typical of the language of contemplative ascent;[81] the general system of metaphors, from sweetness to taste to fluidity, belongs to contemplative imagery (Casagrande, pp. 216–17 on tasting and sweetness; Dreyer, p. 19); and the simile of

---

79   Étienne Gilson, 'La Conclusion de la *Divine Comédie* et la mystique franciscaine', *Revue d'histoire franciscaine*, I (1924), 55–63; the quotation may be read on p. 57. See also pp. 59–60, 63 for a detailed comparison between *Paradiso* XXXIII and Bonaventure's text. To Gilson's examples should be added Dante's use of *circunspetto*: 'Quella circulazion che sì concetta | pareva in te come lume reflesso, | da li occhi miei alquanto circunspetta' (127–29). According to Gilson, 'Dante et la mystique dont il décrit l'expérience en sont donc alors à ce moment préparatoires de l'extase que saint Bonaventure nomme la "circumspectio", c'est à dire le point culminant de la méditation avant le passage en Dieu' (p. 59, with reference to *Hexaemeron* XXII. 39). Dante's use of the term is technically and theologically precise, given that, immediately afterwards, the pilgrim enjoys the *visio Dei*. Gilson associates the *Ben. major* to the *Itinerarium* as the main sources — 'source immédiate' (p. 56) — of *Paradiso* XXXIII and of the final vision (pp. 56 and 61). However Gilson's points of contact between Richard and Dante are not as convincing as the ones linking the poet to Bonaventure. The present chapter is deeply indebted to Gilson's work. I have often wondered whether the scholarly discussion of the pilgrim's *visio* would have developed along different lines if colleagues had been aware of Gilson's article. Not even Edward Hagman, 'Dante's Vision of God: The End of the *Itinerarium Mentis*', *Dante Studies*, 106 (1988), 1–20, refers to Gilson's study.

80   See Rachel Fulton Brown, '*Oratio*/Prayer', in *The Cambridge Companion to Christian Mysticism*, ed. by Amy Hollywood and Patricia Z. Beckham (Cambridge: Cambridge University Press, 2012), pp. 167–77.

81   See 'Contemplatio est libera mentis perspicacia in sapientiae spectacula [...]. Contemplatio est perspicax et liber animi contuitus in res perspiciendas usquequaque diffusus' [Contemplation is a free looking of the mind into the wonders of wisdom [...] Contemplation is a penetrating and free observation of the soul which altogether considers the objects of examination] (Richard of Saint Victor, *Ben. maj.* I. 4); and 'ibi [in Dio] non intrat intellectus sed affectus' [and here [in God] the intellect does not enter but affection] (Bonaventure, *Hexaemeron* II. 32–34).

the dreamer fuses various elements associated with mystical ecstasy: dreaming as the image of the highest contemplative state along with the declaration that such experience is affective, 'la passione impressa', and not intellectual, 'e l'altro a la mente non riede':[82]

> Qual è colüi che sognando vede,
> che dopo 'l sogno la passione impressa
> rimane, e l'altro a la mente non riede. (*Par.* XXXIII. 58–60)

And there's more. Anticipating the *viator*'s beatific union with God, Dante insists on the vital importance of the will in experiencing beatitude:

> però che 'l ben, ch'è del volere obietto,
> tutto s'accoglie in lei [la luce], e fuor di quella
> è defettivo ciò ch'è lì perfetto. (*Par.* XXXIII. 103–05)

Furthermore, that the pilgrim should arrive at the beatific vision while concentrating on the mystery of the Incarnation (130–38), recalls the affective *topos* that saw in Christ the privileged means through which beatitude is reached.[83] And the three final visions, as has been correctly argued,[84] have strong theophanic implications that evoke the Dionysian tradition,[85] which had considerable influence on

---

82   See, for example, 'ipsa quidem dormit, sed cor ejus vigilat, quo utique interim veritatis arcana rimiratur: quorum postmodum memoria statim ad se reditura pascatur. Ibi videt invisibilia, audit ineffabilia, quae non licet homini loqui' [she sleeps, but her heart is vigilant, and meantime with it she admires the mysteries of truth: the memory of these nourishes her when a little later it will come back at once. Here she sees things that cannot be seen and hears things that cannot be heard, things which man is not allowed to speak] (Bernard of Clairvaux, *De gradibus humilitatis et superbiae* VII. 21). To these passages should be added those on the 'equivalenza tra sonno ed estasi teorizzata da Riccardo da San Vittore': Ariani, 'La mistica preterizione', p. 981; and see also the references to Augustine, Bernard, and Bonaventure he lists in n. 27. See also Colombo, p. 67; Ledda, *La guerra della lingua*, p. 285. Less convincing is the attempt to read the simile of the dreamer in a Thomistic vein. Like other scholars had previously done, Ariani (*La mistica preterizione*, p. 1009) connects the image to 'Paulus, postquam cessavit videre Deum per essentiam, memor fuit illorum quae in illa visione cognoverat, per aliquas species intelligibiles habitualiter ex hoc in eius intellectu relictas, sicut etiam, abeunte sensibili, remanent aliquae impressiones in anima, quas postea convertens ad phantasmata, memorabatur' [Paul, after he ceased to see God in His essence, remembered those things that he had seen in that vision, through some intelligible species which after this experience were left in his intellect as if by habit, just as, when the sensible object is gone, certain impressions remain in the soul, which this one recalls when it turns to the sensible images] (*ST* II–II. q. 175. a. 4. resp. 3). Ariani is followed by Malato, pp. 43–45. In truth, the passage from Aquinas, together with *De veritate* q. 8. a. 5. ad 5–6 and q. 13. a. 3. ad 4, had already been highlighted by Giovanni Busnelli, *Il concetto e l'ordine del Paradiso dantesco* (Città di Castello: S. Lapi, 1911), pp. 252–53. The hypothesis that the close of *Paradiso* is the account of a *visio in somniis* does scant justice to the cultural and ideological, as well as ontological, complexity of Dante's representation; see Tavoni; however, see also his 'Dante "Imagining" his Journey through the Afterlife', *Dante Studies*, 133 (2015), 70–97.

83   *Benj. maj.* IV. 18; *Itin.* VI. See also Étienne Gilson, pp. 56–57; and Cicchitto, pp. 391–93.

84   See Casagrande. To be read with caution: Jason Aleksander, 'The Problem of Theophany in *Paradiso* 33', *Essays in Medieval Studies*, 27 (2011), 61–78. See also Coolman.

85   Dante's recourse to the pseudo-Dionysius at the close of *Paradiso* is very suggestive. On the one hand, the poet recognizes the importance of theophany as a means for mediating the beatific vision. On the other, however, he rejects the Areopagite's view that our experience of God can only be indirect.

Franciscanism: 'Thomas [Gallus] produced a series of commentaries on the whole corpus [of the pseudo-Dionysius] by reinterpreting negative theology in terms of the priority of supreme affectivity over all intellectual contact with God'.[86] Thus, in *Paradiso* XXXIII, Dante ends by implying that, even though his memories are inferior to those 'd'un fante | che bagni ancor la lingua a la mammella' (107–08), nonetheless, these imply, as he hints in particular by means of a rich array of interdiscursive elements, that the pilgrim's satisfaction in God involved an absolute and supreme enhancement, not of his *intellectus*, but of his *affectus*.[87]

5. Beatitudes

As was perhaps to be expected, the analysis of the allusive and ideological system of *Paradiso* XXXIII brings us back to the general conclusion, even if now strictly circumscribed and revised, which the *explication* of lines 136–45 had already reached. Despite the serious reservations that Dante expresses regarding the human possibility of speaking *de Deo* in general and of *beatitudo* in particular, in the end, the poet appears to have decided, when it came to the *visio Dei*, to align himself with the 'voluntarists'. At least this might seem to be the case, if it were not for what Peter Damian had earlier revealed to the *viator* in the heaven of Saturn:

> Luce divina sopra me s'appunta,
> penetrando per questa in ch'io m'inventro,

---

86   McGinn, p. 21. On the importance of Thomas Gallus in Dante, see Zygmunt G. Barański, ' "With such vigilance! With such effort!" Studying Dante "Subjectively" ', *Italian Culture*, 33:1 (2015), 55–69 (pp. 55–56).

87   'Bonaventura [...] nel medesimo contesto della *Theologia Mystica* distingue due conoscenze: quella degli estatici (più frequente) e quella dei rapiti rarissima ['excessus in experimento divinae dulcedinis potius est laudabilis quam vituperabilis, secundum quod patet in viris sanctis et contemplativis, qui prae nimia dulcedine modo elevantur in ecstasim, modo sublevantur usque ad raptum, licet hoc contingat paucissimis' [ecstasy in the experience of divine sweetness is laudable rather than blameworthy, according to what is visible in saintly and contemplative men, who for an abundance of sweetness are now elevated in ecstasy, now are raised up in rapture, even though this happens to very few] (*In III Sententiarum* 35 un. 1. resp.)]. La prima è la conoscenza di Dio *in caligine* di natura affettiva, ovvero la conoscenza di amore estatico, sperimentata da Mosè nei suoi "eccessi anagogici" [*In II Sententiarum* 23. 2. 3. ad 6]. Essa che è la più alta *in via*, non fa vedere Dio in sé, più precisamente nella chiarezza della sua essenza, ma nell'effetto della grazia e nell'esperienza della sua soavità attraverso l'unione anagogica [*In III Sententiarum* 24. dub. 4]. La seconda è conoscenza (momentanea) di Dio in sé, nella sua essenza, visione faccia a faccia, per avere la quale il rapito oltrepassa in quel attimo il suo stato di viatore' (Faes de Mottoni, 'Mosè e Paolo', pp. 38–39). The first 'conoscenza' is very close to that described by Dante in the closing lines of *Paradiso* XXXIII, which would confirm the importance of the *Doctor seraphicus* for the representation of the pilgrim's experience. Furthermore, and this is intriguing, it would associate Dante-*personaggio* with Moses rather than with Paul, who, according to Bonaventure, had been exceptionally 'sollevato' to his *raptus*. This would help explain the marginalization of Pauline elements in the last canto, as well as the dominance of 'affective-Mosaic' elements. The implications of a *viator* suspended between Moses and Paul remain hitherto unstudied. Finally, it is striking that Dante leaves unresolved the question of whether or not the pilgrim's vision was that of God *in essentia*, regardless of the fact that he had gone beyond the limits of theophany — a position that distinguishes him from Aquinas, according to whom, both Moses and Paul saw 'ipsam Dei essentiam' (*ST* II–II. q. 174. a. 3. resp.).

> a cui virtù, col mio veder congiunta,
> mi leva sopra me tanto, ch'i' veggio
> la somma essenza de la quale è munta.
>   Quinci vien l'allegrezza ond'io fiammeggio;
> per ch'a la vista mia, quant'ella è chiara,
> la chiarità de la fiamma pareggio. (*Par.* XXI. 83–90)

In these tercets, we find an accurate account of the beatific vision in 'intellectualist' terms, even if Dante avoids the tradition's jargon and enriches Peter's speech with maternal and feminine metaphors, such as *inventrare* (84) and *mungere* (87), that evoke rhetorical forms belonging to affective sensuality.[88] Lines 83–87 describe the function of the *lumen gloriae*, which, significantly, is transformed into the 'luce divina' of St Bonaventure ('postquam mens nostra contuita est Deum [...] supra se per divinae lucis similitudinem supra nos relucentem et in ipsa luce' [after our mind has looked into God [...] over itself through a resembling image of the divine light which shines over us and in that very light], *Itin.* VII. 1), which descends from above to unite with human visual and intellectual capabilities to elevate them to *vedere* God's *essentia* — the only strictly technical term, but again one that was common to the two currents, employed by the saint. Moreover, in strict conformity with Albert the Great and Aquinas, Dante clearly distinguishes between the light and God, who is the source of the former and the sole object of the vision.[89] Subsequently, and as a secondary effect of the visual and intellectual experience (the *visio beatificans*), as lines 88–90 affirm, 'l'allegrezza' (88), namely, the *delectatio consequens*, arrives.[90]

It is remarkable that, among those who have concentrated on the beatific vision in Dante, Peter Damian's revelation has been almost completely overlooked.[91] Yet, here is definitive proof — proof that the *viator*'s experience cannot offer — that, according to the poet, the *visio Dei* is reached thanks to the intellect. The contradiction between the means by which the living pilgrim and the blessed spirit find fulfillment in God is tangible. It is a contradiction, in fact, that I have not found in the medieval *auctoritates* that deal with the *visio beatifica*. At the same time, as clarified earlier, it was generally accepted that the *beatitudo* of the angels and saints was of a different complexion to that of a living being. Dante too orthodoxly recognizes the truth of this distinction. However, while the standard position on the question of the difference between the beatific vision *in patria* and *in via* was

---

88   Patricia Dailey, 'The Body and its Senses', in Hollywood and Beckham, pp. 264–76 (pp. 274–76).

89   Albertus Magnus, *Super Caelestem Hierarchiam*, p. 71, lines 20–25; *ST* I. q. 12. a. 5 and *SCG* III. 53. See also Trottmann, pp. 283–302.

90   'Et quia visio Dei non potest esse sine delectatione, propterea non solum se dicit raptum ad tertium caelum, ratione contemplationis, sed etiam in Paradisum, ratione delectationis consequentis' [And since the vision of God cannot but imply delight, on that account he not only says that he is raptured into the third heaven, by reason of the contemplation, but also into Paradise, by reason of the delight that follows] (*ST* II–II. q. 175. a. 3. ad 4).

91   The only exception to this trend that I am aware of is Pollack, pp. 303–11, where she usefully synthesizes the saint's words: 'Damian's speech [...] pictures the beatific vision as a descent and an ascent: above gathers the divine light, which penetrates into the soul below, lifting up the soul's faculty of sight all the way to the Source of light. The reciprocity of divine descent (grace, self-revelation, theophany) and human ascent (beatific vision, deification) recalls the famous patristic formula that "God became man, so that man might become God"' (pp. 306–07).

to propose different experiential states either of an 'intellectualist' or a 'voluntarist' character, Dante illustrates the distinction in a new and personal manner. His solution conforms to that syncretistic imperative thanks to which the poet hoped to be able to reconcile the ideological disputes on the *visio Dei*, by recalling not only the limits of any human proposal on the matter but also the validity of seemingly conflicting theological hypotheses, which, when made to converge, enrich each other. By presenting his own experience as affective rather than intellectualist, Dante provides a persuasive explanation as to why his memories of Heaven, as he insists throughout the cantica, are so inadequate. Finally, out of pure pedantry, I should like to recall that it is inappropriate to rely on passages from the *Commedia*, at least those of an 'intellectualist' stamp, that deal with the state of the blessed or of the angels, to clarify the pilgrim's *deificatio*.

At this point, one might think that the problems associated with Dante's reflections on that medieval theological conundrum that was the *visio Dei* have been 'solved', and all that remains for me to do is draw a few conclusions. But when, in Dante, are *quaestiones* ever resolved in such a tranquil manner? Well before Peter Damian described his eternal happiness, Piccarda Donati had explained her own celestial condition in strictly 'voluntarist' terms, as is immediately evident from her insistence on *volontà*, *volere*, and *voglia*, which she appropriately associates with terms connected to love and desire:

> Frate, la nostra volontà quïeta
> virtù di carità, che fa volerne
> sol quel ch'avemo, e d'altro non ci asseta.
>   Se disïassimo esser più superne,
> foran discordi li nostri disiri
> dal voler di colui che qui ne cerne;
>   che vedrai non capere in questi giri,
> s'essere in carità è qui necesse,
> e se la sua natura ben rimiri.
>   Anzi è formale ad esto beato esse
> tenersi dentro a la divina voglia,
> per ch'una fansi nostre voglie stesse;
>   sì che, come noi sem di soglia in soglia
> per questo regno, a tutto il regno piace
> com'a lo re che 'n suo voler ne 'nvoglia.
>   E 'n la sua volontade è nostra pace:
> ell'è quel mare al qual tutto si move
> ciò ch'ella crïa o che natura face. (*Par.* III. 70–87)

As a result, Piccarda can conclude her presentation by declaring that the 'essential'[92] condition of beatitude — 'esto beato *esse*' — consists in the union with 'la divina voglia'.[93] The startling discrepancy between the statements of the two saints is

---

92 '[L]a forma determina una cosa per ciò che è: in questo senso, *formale* è lo stesso che "essenziale"': Inglese, p. 64.

93 Piccarda anticipates the substance of her 'voluntarist' speech when she explains that 'Li nostri affetti, che solo infiammati | son nel piacer de lo Spirito Santo, | letizian del suo ordine formati' (52–54), a statement that recalls Bonaventure's words when he presents the *visio Dei* in an affective

arresting, also because, in theological terms, it is disconcerting. How is it possible that Piccarda and Peter Damian, on both of whom 'la grazia |del sommo ben [...] vi piove' (89–90), are contradicting each other? Is Dante actually asserting that different blessed souls enjoy the *visio Dei* in different, even contrasting ways?

To complicate matters further, the angels too seem to be distinguished between those who enjoy the *visio beatifica* through the intellect and those who experience it through affection. In *Paradiso* XXVIII, during her *lectio magistralis* on angelology, and, like Piccarda, having recourse to the rhetoric of repetition, in this instance centred on *vedere* and related terms, Beatrice asserts:

> e dei saper che tutti [i primi tre ordini angelici] hanno diletto
> quanto la sua veduta si profonda
> nel vero in che si queta ogne intelletto.[94]
>   Quinci si può veder come si fonda
> l'esser beato[95] ne l'atto che vede,
> non in quel ch'ama, che poscia seconda;
>   e del vedere è misura mercede,
> che grazia partorisce e buona voglia:
> così di grado in grado si procede. (*Par.* XXVIII. 106–14)

Her explanation conforms perfectly to what Peter Damian had previously asserted: the beatific vision is primarily an intellectual experience which is 'followed' by love. However, immediately afterwards, in the following canto in fact, Beatrice seems to state the opposite:

> Quelli che vedi qui furon modesti
> a riconoscer sé da la bontate
> che li avea fatti a tanto intender presti:
>   per che le viste lor furo essaltate
> con grazia illuminante e con lor merto,
> sì c'hanno ferma e piena volontate;
>   e non voglio che dubbi, ma sia certo,
> che ricever la grazia è meritorio
> secondo che l'affetto l'è aperto. (*Par.* XXIX. 58–66)

key at the climax of the *Itinerarium*: 'nec desiderat [the beatific vision] nisi quem ignis Spiritus sancti medullitus inflammat' [and nobody desires it unless his heart is inflamed by the fire of the Holy Spirit] (VII. 4).

94   However, it is important to recognize that line 108 — 'nel vero in che si queta ogne intelletto' — translates almost literally Bonaventure's 'in quo [mental and mystical ecstasy] requies datur intellectui' [in which rest is given to the intellect] (*Itin.* VII, chapter title).

95   The phrase 'l'esser beato' repeats Piccarda's 'esto beato *esse*' (*Par.* III. 79). The repetition establishes that in each case the 'essential' nature of beatitude is being specifically and directly discussed — of an 'intellectualist' stamp the first, of a 'voluntarist' character the second. In both accounts, and with exemplary parallelism, the parameters of the beatific experience are presented clearly and with technical precision. If there might be links, on the one hand, between the seraphim, cherubim, and thrones and the intellect and, on the other, between the failure to keep a vow and the will, these are certainly issues that, as Dantists, we ought to examine. Nevertheless, however these problems might be resolved, what does not change is that both Beatrice and Piccarda are presenting 'self-sufficient' states, namely, they are providing definitions of the *visio Dei* which, in line with the leading contemporary theological authorities, are valid in themselves.

As is often the case in the *Commedia*, the ways in which, in this passage, Dante synthesizes and transforms complex theological doctrines into poetry are highly distilled, and consequently not easy to interpret. At the same time, several salient points do emerge that establish its ideological parameters. As noted above, it is crucial to remember that vision, the intellectual faculties, and light are not exclusively concepts that define the 'intellectualist' experience of *beatitudo*, but are common to different contemplative currents. Thus, it is important to distinguish, case by case, the implications that, in different contexts, these key notions may have. So, 'le viste [...] essaltate | con grazia illuminante' of the humble angels match the 'mens veri contemplativi plena illustratione supernae sapientiae valeat sursum agi' [the mind of a true contemplative, overwhelmed by the vivid image of heavenly wisdom, is enabled to rise on high] (*Itin.* VII. 1). According to Bonaventure, '[i]n hoc autem transitu, si sit perfectus, oportet quod relinquantur omnes intellectuales operationes, et apex affectus totus transferatur et transformetur in Deum' [however in this passing over, if it is to be perfect, it is necessary for all intellectual operations to be relinquished, and for the height of affection to be totally transferred and transformed into God] (VII. 4). Likewise, Dante's angels achieve fulfilment in God thanks to 'l'affetto' so that 'hanno ferma e piena volontate'.[96]

It is difficult to ignore that, at times, the blessed explain that their condition 'si fonda | [...] ne l'atto che vede' (*Par.* XXVIII. 110), while, at other times, that it consists in 'tenersi dentro a la divina voglia' (*Par.* III. 80).[97] However, to speak of 'contradiction', as if one were dealing with earthly realities, is pointless. For Dante, the beatific vision enjoyed by the inhabitants of the 'candida rosa' (*Par.* XXXI. 1) is fundamentally characterized by a perfect and indistinguishable harmony between love and knowledge, between intellect and affection: a mystery that neither human reason nor human language is able to understand or represent. Where the human mind demands a sequence of states and a causal and temporal succession, the divine miracle, the 'fulgore', abolishes every trace of distinction and priority between love and intellect, as well as any causal relationship between them:

> L'affetto e 'l senno,
> come la prima equalità v'apparse,
> d'un peso per ciascun di voi si fenno,
>   però che 'l sol che v'allumò e arse,
> col caldo e con la luce è sì iguali,
> che tutte simiglianze sono scarse. (*Par.* XV. 73–78)

The normal logical, existential, communicative, and descriptive processes — as

---

96   In concluding her *lectio*, Beatrice explains that in the angels 'a l'atto che concepe | segue l'affetto, d'amar la dolcezza | diversamente in essa [the angelic order] ferve e tepe' (*Par.* XXIX. 139–41), a tercet that Chiavacci Leonardi glosses as follows: 'Se l'atto dell'intendere lo precede e lo fonda, non c'è dubbio che quello di amare prende il maggior spazio e il maggior rilievo in questa raffigurazione' (III, 815).

97   A fuller study of the *visio Dei* in the *Commedia* than the present one would also need to take into consideration the following passages: *Par.* XIV. 34–60; XV. 34–36, 61–66, 73–84; XVII. 13–18; XXX. 100–02. Although I am here unable to assess these passages, I can declare with confidence that none of them affects the general conclusions reached in this study.

occurs with the representation of the pilgrim's *visio* — are no longer valid. The poet can only proceed by recognizing and accepting this situation. In fact, he can go no further than acknowledge, as best he can, the 'transhuman' implications of an impasse that exceeds his expressive and intellectual capacities. At most, Dante, who was extremely sensitive to the absolute otherness of the transcendent, can try to provide a *vestigium* of this difference by subverting the rational structures with which earthly realities are normally considered and represented. Mechanically alternating, at the level of the *lictera*, the focus of attention between the two ecstatic possibilities — first on the blessed's affective state and then on their intellective one, thereby suggesting, in turn, the 'priority' and the 'superiority' of one and then the other — Dante emphasizes the arbitrariness of what he is describing and, therefore, that the separation that he is presenting, as well as the impressions that emerge from what he is evoking, can only be unreliable.[98] The poet thus definitively affirms his incapacity to represent the reality of heavenly beatitude,[99] as, in fact, he had peremptorily declared at the beginning of the cantica: 'Trasumanar significar *per verba* | non si poria' (*Par.* I. 70–71). What he is able to offer is an 'essemplo' (71), a symbolic approximation of a truth that can only be appreciated in all its immediacy by those 'a cui esperïenza grazia serba' (72).[100]

Recognizing his failure in dealing with the *visio Dei*, Dante also highlights the inevitable limitations of the ways in which other traditions — theological,

98   In Solomon's speech on the resurrection of the body, the chiasmatic structure that describes the condition of the blessed before and after the miracle anticipates in minor key the way in which Dante, by alternating 'intellectualist' and 'voluntarist' solutions, highlights how arbitrary it is to insist on the priority either of love or of knowledge in the 'festa | di paradiso': 'La sua [of the *vesta*] chiarezza séguita l'ardore; | l'ardor la visïone [...] | [...] | onde la visïon crescer convene, | crescer l'ardor che di quella s'accende, | crescer lo raggio che da esso vene' (*Par.* XIV. 37–38, 40–41, & 49–51). It is suggestive, however, that, once again, the source of lines 40–41 seems to be a passage from Bonaventure: 'Tantum gaudebunt quantum amabunt; tantum amabunt, quantum cognoscent' [Their joy will match their love, and their love will match their knowledge] (*Soliloquium* IV. 5. 27). Another aspect relating to Dante's treatment of the *visio Dei* that needs further investigation is the one that Solomon raises here; for now see Paola Nasti, *Favole d'amore e 'saver profondo': la tradizione salomonica in Dante* (Ravenna: Longo, 2007), pp. 199–208.

99   'The Pilgrim and Poet are hamstrung by this a-verbal experience, as well as by a memory that cannot recall even a fraction of what he witnessed. What ensues in Canto XXXIII is a monument to paradox, metaphor, simile, and periphrasis. Time, of the essence, flickers between past, present, future, and eternity. The distinction between beginning and end "dissolves" (*disigilla*, 64; lit. unseals)': Arielle Saiber, 'Song of the Return: *Paradiso* XXXIII', in *Lectura Dantis: Paradiso*, ed. by Allen Mandelbaum and others (Berkeley: University of California Press, forthcoming). I should like to thank my friend Arielle for allowing me to read a typescript version of her excellent *lectura*. Signori, too, is sensitive to the problems facing the poet when he attempts to describe his final experiences of Paradise. On the representation of *Paradiso* in general, see in particular Teodolinda Barolini, *The Undivine 'Comedy': Detheologizing Dante* (Princeton: Princeton University Press, 1992), pp. 166–256. On the lack of pictorial representations of the *visio Dei* in medieval art, see Lucy Sandler, 'Face to Face with God: A Pictorial Image of the Beatific Vision', in *England in the Fourteenth Century: Proceedings of the 1985 Harlaxton Symposium*, ed. by W. M. Ormrod (Woodbridge, Boydell Press, 1986), pp. 224–35.

100   In an important article — Arielle Saiber and Aba Mbirika, 'The Three "giri" of *Paradiso* 33', *Dante Studies*, 131 (2013), 237–72 — the authors examine in detail 'one of the very last imagistic puzzles [that of the 'tre giri' (116)] to express God's ineffability in the poem' (p. 238).

contemplative, literary — have dealt with the beatific vision. Any human presentation of the divine is merely an *exemplum*, whose expository and connotative efficacy is not only limited, but also fundamentally misleading. To insist on the exclusive validity of one particular solution as to how we attain beatitude makes no sense. The only minimally appropriate way of addressing the question, according to Dante, is to acknowledge the inscrutability of the miracle by drawing attention to the intellectual and communicative crisis that it engenders on earth. If one cannot analyse the reality of the beatific vision, it is however more than possible to assess how it has been represented. Thus, Dante implicitly criticizes the positions of both the 'intellectualist' and the 'voluntarist' tradition. At the same time, he recognizes that both provide valid 'vestigge' (*Purg.* XXXIII. 108) of the *visio*'s reality. Subsequently, by going beyond the contrasting approaches of the theological schools, the poet hints at the ultimate but ineffable simultaneity of affection and intellect in the union with God.[101] Although Dante 'deconstructs' the rhetorical and expressive possibilities of his own poetry in the face of the divine, he leaves us with the disconcerting feeling that it is in fact the syncretism of his *comedía*,[102] which harmonizes different 'ombre' (*Par.* I. 23) and which integrates and adapts different *modi tractandi* in new plurilingual structures, that may perhaps offer the most reliable *signum* of the *visio beatifica*.[103]

6. 'Di dietro'

If Dante does not seem to have been persuaded by the ideological and formal solutions of the individual theological schools regarding the means by which we reach *beatitudo*, it is equally clear that he fully accepted the basic parameters of the debate on the *visio Dei*. According to the poet, the main *quaestiones* that theologians probed were the right ones. Thus, he aligned himself with those who maintained

---

101 The pilgrim states as much in the heaven of Mars: 'L'affetto e 'l senno, | come la prima equalità v'apparse, | d'un peso per ciascun di voi si fenno, | però che 'l sol che v'allumò e arse, | col caldo e con la luce è sì iguali, | che tutte simiglianze sono scarse' (*Par.* XV. 73–78). As Lino Pertile has convincingly demonstrated, the pilgrim's entire voyage through the heavens is based on the synthesis of love and knowledge, and hence prefigures the character of the final vision: 'Il desiderio del pellegrino nel Paradiso è duplice: c'è il desiderio di conoscere Dio come Amore, e il desiderio di vederlo come Verità. Sono due approcci alla divinità corrispondenti a due forme distinte di contemplazione: l'una affettiva e l'atra intellettuale. [...] le due vie, in quanto espressioni della medesima tensione psicologica, sono inestricabilmente intrecciate' (*La punta del disio*, p. 153).

102 As I was completing the Italian version of this chapter in the Spring of 2017, I read what I consider to be one of the most significant books on the medieval intellectual world that has appeared in the last few years: Joel Kaye, *A History of Balance, 1250–1375: The Emergence of a New Model of Equilibrium and its Impact on Thought* (Cambridge: Cambridge University Press, 2014). As I read, I kept wondering to what extent Dante's syncretism may have been influenced by the new ideas on balance and equilibrium developed by the scholastics, and which Kaye examines with exemplary sophistication. In particular, I became more and more convinced that it might be worth assessing Dante's concluding 'igualmente' (144) in light of the new thinking on *aequalitas*.

103 Luca Azzetta has appropriately underlined the fact that, at the end of the *Commedia*, Dante 'afferma la certezza di un'esperienza unitiva con Dio che non ha confronti nella tradizione letteraria' (p. 341). This too is a question that deserves further study.

that, before the Last Judgment, the blessed not only perceive God but also perceive God in His essence. He recognized the difference between the experience of God *in patria* and *in via*; and he accepted the importance of theophanies, the illuminations that 'mostrano di Dio [...] sembiante' (*Par.* XXXII. 93), as preparatory steps for those who, in life, are miraculously lifted up to Paradise. The ideological positions that Dante embraces — in every instance, he subscribes to the majority solution — allow him to organize with rigour and in orthodox terms the *narratio* of his miraculous journey. In particular, they emphasize the uniqueness of his experience as a living person dependent on 'sembiant*i*' (93) and whose union with God is necessarily different from that of the inhabitants of Paradise. Unlike the bliss of the saints and angels, his momentary contact with God was principally affective in nature. It was thus distinct from the condition of eternal and harmonious affective and intellectual simultaneity enjoyed by the blessed. Proposing that the distinction between *deificatio in via* and *in patria* involves intellectual potentiality, Dante afforded a degree of precision to an idea of broad and fundamental significance in contemporary theological culture. In addition, the insight provides the key reason why the poet's 'memoria [...] cede' (*Par.* XXXIII. 57), so that what 'remains' is merely 'la passione' (59–60) and 'il dolce' (63). Moreover, his purpose, as with other controversial doctrinal issues, was to harmonize different positions relying on a syncretism that was not only ideological but also, and I would say primarily, formal. As we have seen, Dante freely drew on the *modi* of both the 'intellectualists' and the 'voluntarists'. Furthermore, what appears to be crucial in Dante's presentation of the beatific vision is the inexorable incommunicability of its real substance. Hence, returning one last time to *Par.* XXXIII. 136–45, it is possible to suggest a further elucidation. Lines 140–41 affirm ('se non che la mia mente fu percossa | da un fulgore in che sua voglia venne'), establishing the instance of its occurrence, that the pilgrim definitely experienced the *visio Dei*.[104] Next, putting aside its literal and ideological connotations, in the narrative unfolding of the *Commedia*, the 'aberrant' line 142 ('A l'alta fantasia qui mancò possa') is located at the precise point where the poet should have described the *viator* miraculously enjoying the beatific condition. However, Dante can neither remember nor describe the experience. Instead, all he can do is strive to leave at least a *vestigium* of the event in the poem's make-up, regardless of the fact that his 'essemplo' (*Par.* I. 71) cannot but be totally inappropriate, misleading, and insufficient. Yet, in rhetorical terms, Dante's refined solution, which stresses both the limitations and the creative possibilities of language and thought, constitutes a notable apophatic invention. Finally, lines 143–45:

> Ma già volgeva il mio disio e 'l velle,
> sì come rota ch'igualmente è mossa,
>   l'amor che move il sole e l'altre stelle.

They do not describe the *visio* itself, but its cosmological, universal, and affective impressions on the *viator*.

---

104 On the ways in which, in the last canto, the poet 'afferma la verità della sua visione', see Azzetta, pp. 341–44.

As I too arrive at the end of my *iter*, I have not forgotten where this rather too long chapter started:[105] the importance of emotions in medieval culture. Had it not been for the prod that I felt coming from work on the *passiones* and, specifically, on the *affectus*, it is unlikely that I would have been prompted to undertake this research. There is much more to learn from the 'emotional' Dante. Just think of St Bernard: 'Affetto al suo piacer, quel contemplante | libero officio di dottore assunse' (*Par.* XXXII. 1–2). The question immediately arises: What might be the relationship between affection, contemplative delight, and the didactic responsibilities of a *doctor*?[106]

---

105 Other matters affecting Dante's representation of the *visio Dei* are: its relationship to Scriptural sources; its ties to the interpretation of *Paradiso* put forward in the letter to Cangrande; and the connections between Dante's investiture as prophetic *scriba Dei* and his privileged enjoyment of the beatific vision.

106 For the beginnings of an answer, see Chapter 2, pp. 73–74.

PART II

Inventing Literature

'Tres enim sunt manerie dicendi...': Some Observations on Medieval Literature, 'Genre', and Dante

1. When is a Genre not a Genre?[1]

> Tres enim sunt manerie dicendi, quas alii stilos, alii figuras, alii caracteres appellant: humilis stilus, mediocris et altus. Humilis stilus est quando aliquis de humilibus personis humilibus prosequitur uerbis, ut in comedia. Mediocris stilus est quando de mediocribus personis mediocribus agitur uerbis, ut in satira. Altus stilus est quando de altis personis altis agitur uerbis, ut in tragedia.[2]

> [There are three manners of speaking, which some call styles, some call figures, and others characters: the humble/simple/low, the middle, and the high style. The humble style is when someone describes humble/simple people [low status] with humble/simple/low words, as in comedy. The middle style is when someone talks of ordinary people [middle status] with ordinary words, as in satire. The high style is when someone talks of highborn people with high/lofty/grand words, such as in tragedy.]

At first glance, there may not appear to be anything especially remarkable about the above passage taken from a twelfth-century French school-room *accessus* by an unknown author which serves to introduce his commentary on Horace's *Ars poetica*.[3] As medievalists and Dantists, we have all read many similar such statements and have used them to help us understand the nature of writing in the Middle Ages. Indeed, *mutatis mutandis*, we find a comparable tripartite categorization in Dante himself: in a famous set of definitions which, in the *De vulgari eloquentia*, help to establish the remit of the 'illustrious vernacular' (II. 4. 5–6). As might be expected, I shall have something more to say about Dante's definitions during the course of

---

1   I wrote this essay as an 'introduction' to a collection of articles that I edited on medieval genre that appeared as a supplement to *The Italianist* in 1995.

2   'Glose in Poetriam Horatii' [now commonly known as the 'Materia' commentary], p. 337, in Karsten Friis-Jensen, 'The *Ars Poetica* in Twelfth-century France: The Horace of Matthew of Vendôme, Geoffrey of Vinsauf, and John of Garland', *Cahiers de l'Institut du Moyen-Âge Grec et Latin*, 60 (1990), 319–88 (pp. 336–84).

3   For more information on this important commentary which may have served as a key source for the *artes poetriae*, see Friis-Jensen, pp. 319–29.

this chapter. For the moment, however, I wish to remain with the more humble figure of the anonymous French master.

The most common way in which we draw on typologies such as that which appears in the 'Materia' commentary (or even in Dante's treatise) is to use them as the foundation stones for constructing an idea of medieval literary theory and practice based on genre differences. Such an approach is quite understandable. It permits us to bring a degree of order to the many distinct categories of writing circulating in the Middle Ages — it is enough to think of the wealth of different lyric types fashioned by the Occitan poets — and to do this according to taxonomic principles which appear to be firmly rooted in contemporary usage.[4]

The methodological steps that modern scholars take to arrive at genre-based views of medieval literature are not only fairly easy to retrace, but also, at first sight, appear to have a powerful logical inevitability about them. Discovering the presence of canonical terminology like 'comedy' and 'tragedy' in medieval discussions of literature, namely of terms which at least since the time of Aristotle have been used to refer to the 'types' of poetry (*Poetics* I), they conclude (a) that, in the Middle Ages, too, the terms necessarily referred to genres; (b) that other tags, such as *stilus* and *genus* which often accompanied discussions of comedy and tragedy, endorse the latters' status as genre categories; and (c) that, since the terms are applied to specific texts (as occurs with the classic description of the *Aeneid* as a 'tragedy'), this usage too confirms their generic credentials. Medievalists therefore, somewhat uncritically and unproblematically, if not unsurprisingly given the terms' histories, assimilate the medieval variants of 'tragedy'[5] and 'comedy', as well as related labels, into the broad notion of 'genre' — a decision which undoubtedly has the sanction of the authority of centuries.[6] As a consequence of this, and bolstered by the widespread medieval fascination with classification, the literary variant of which found expression, for example, in the designations that medieval authors introduced into their own works as means to their definition and interpretation, many critics have made two further assumptions: first, that the Middle Ages had a notion of literature which was underpinned by a strong sense of genre; and second, given the preceding premise, that it is incumbent on modern scholarship to fashion new terms for groups of medieval texts that seem to lack contemporary generic tags (this is the reason for such anachronistic designations as 'elegiac comedy', 'allegorical-didactic literature', etc.).[7] In a similar manner, when medievalists have felt uncomfortable

---

4   See Alfred Jeanroy, *La Poésie lyrique des Troubadours*, 2 vols (Toulouse: Privat; Paris: Didier, 1934), in particular II; Pierre Bec, *Lyrique française au moyen-âge (XIIe-XIIIe siècles): contribution à une typologie des genres poétiques médiévaux*, 2 vols (Paris: A. & J. Picard, 1977).

5   On tragedy, see Chapter 7, n. 53.

6   On comedy, see Chapter 7, n. 38.

7   On this type of self-definition, see, for instance, Pierre Gallais, 'Recherches sur la mentalité des romanciers français du moyen âge', *Cahiers de civilisation médiévale*, 13 (1970), 333–47; Paul Strohm, '*Storie, Spelle, Geste, Romaunce, Tragedie*: Generic Distinctions in the Middle English Troy Narratives', *Speculum*, 46 (1971), 348–59; Jean Charles Payen and F. N. M. Diekstra, *Le Roman* (Turnhout: Brepols, 1975), pp. 20–23; Pierre Bec, 'Le Problème des genres chez les premiers troubadours', *Cahiers de civilisation médiévale*, 25 (1982), 31–47 (in particular pp. 33–36); Luciano Rossi, '*Cantar, canczun et flabla de cuczun*: sur le sens du dernier vers de la *Sainte Foy*', in *Mélanges de philologie et de littérature*

with the label or labels that authors actually gave to their works, they have overcome their unease either by granting the texts a new generic status or by simply ignoring their original designations.[8]

This state of affairs may appear — at first sight at least — to constitute a perfectly reasonable way of trying to make sense of medieval literature. Indeed, historians of literature have always enjoyed, and seen it as their duty, to bring order to the undisciplined, occasionally anarchic, world of literary creativeness (and this is especially so in medieval studies, where considerable effort has been expended to pigeonhole 'aberrant' works, such as the *Roman de la rose*, the *Fiore*, and the *Commedia*). It is my contention, however, that the validity and usefulness of the interpretive scheme that many medievalists have embraced are open to question. I thus believe that too great a reliance on genre as a critical tool can — philologically speaking[9] — end up by offering a misleading representation of medieval textuality and of medieval thinking about literature. The reason why I have doubts about this approach is because it relies on notions and assumptions that are, in fact, far from easy to discern in medieval reflection on literature.[10]

médiévales offerts à Michel Burger, ed. by Jacqueline Cerquiglini-Toulet and Olivier Collet (Geneva: Droz, 1994), pp. 245–54. See also the discussion below of the use of definitional labels by Occitan poets and by Dante.

8   Probably the two most notorious instances of this tendency are the perplexed, and consequently distorting, reactions to Dante's definition of his masterpiece as 'la mia comedía' (*Inf.* XXI. 2) and to Chaucer's description of *Troilus and Criseyde* as 'litel myn tregedie' (v. 1786). On the latter see Lee Paterson, '*Troilus and Criseyde*: Genre and Source', in *Answerable Style: The Idea of the Literary in Medieval England*, ed. by Frank Grady and Andrew Galloway (Columbus: Ohio State University Press, 2013), pp. 244–62.

9   My emphasis on the philological inappropriateness of generic descriptions of medieval literature may come as a surprise. As is well known, it was late nineteenth- and twentieth-century philologists who developed this approach. It is my view, however, that, in this instance, their philological acumen was subordinated to their classificatory fervour.

10   I am aware that my presentation of modern reactions to medieval genre is little more than a faint sketch. However, it would not be difficult to transform the sketch into a detailed picture, such is the popularity of the critical approach I have described. Indeed, others before me have expressed reservations similar to those articulated here. See, in particular, Strohm, p. 348; Henry A. Kelly, 'Interpretation of Genres and by Genres in the Middle Ages', in *Interpretation: Medieval and Modern*, ed. by Piero Boitani and Anna Torti (Cambridge: D. S. Brewer, 1993), pp. 107–22. See also Hans Robert Jauss, 'Theory of Genres and Medieval Literature', in *Toward an Aesthetic of Reception*, trans. by Timothy Bahti (Minneapolis: University of Minnesota Press, 1982), pp. 76–109 (this translation is based on 'Theorie der Gattungen und Literatur des Mittelalters', in *Grundriss der romanischen Literaturen des Mittelalters. I. Généralités*, ed. by Maurice Delbouille (Heidelberg: Winter, 1972), pp. 107–38; an earlier version of the same study appeared in French: 'Littérature médiévale et théorie des genres', *Poétique*, 1 (1970), 79–101). Jauss's influential contribution is problematic. On the one hand, he is aware of the philological deficiencies of most discussions of medieval genre; on the other hand, he tries to resolve these shortcomings not by making recourse to historically sanctioned evidence, but by introducing a new set of anachronistic genre categorizations largely shaped by structuralist concerns. This latter tendency becomes especially acute in his subsequent theoretical contribution on medieval genre: 'Cinq modèles d'identification esthétique: complément à la théorie des genres littéraires au Moyen Âge', in *Atti del XIV Congresso Internazionale di Lingue e Letterature Romanze*, 5 vols (Naples: Macchiaroli; Amsterdam: Benjamins, 1976–81), I, 145–64.

Since this study appeared, unsurprisingly, little has changed regarding how genre is discussed in relation to medieval literature. Thus, even in generally authoritative studies, one finds the following

Given the tenor of my objections, it is therefore reassuring to find immediate support for my claims in our French schoolmaster. In addition, like any effective teacher (which is what his commentary on Horace clearly reveals him to have been), his words are able to offer a way out of the impasse in which modern discussions of medieval genre largely find themselves. His observations succinctly highlight the shortcomings of our fascination with medieval genre, while also pointing to ways in which these limitations may be attenuated and even superseded.

However, before focusing on the 'Materia' commentary, I need to deal with another important issue. As most medievalists tend to do, I have so far employed the term 'genre' without attempting to define it, as if the concept were basically unproblematic. This may well be the case as far as general usage is concerned today (although whether this was equally true in the Middle Ages is among the questions that this chapter attempts to answer). Examining the ways in which 'genre' is used and discussed by theorists of the concept[11] and by medievalists in general, it is

type of assertion: 'The architectonic principles of rhetorical theory take us from the divisions and the arrangement of the speech to the division and classification of narrative into genres, and the division of rhetoric itself into genres. The emergence of the very concept of literary genre as a system of classification based on formal properties as well as content can be traced in the passage of ancient rhetorical thought into the Middle Ages': Rita Copeland and Ineke Sluiter, 'General Introduction', in *Medieval Grammar and Rhetoric: Language Arts and Literary Theory, AD 300–1475*, ed. by Rita Copeland and Ineke Sluiter (Oxford: Oxford University Press, 2009), pp. 1–60 (p. 42; but see also pp. 42–47 which include useful observations on how literature was classified in the Middle Ages). See also, among others, Élisabeth Gaucher, *La Biographie chevaleresque: typologie d'un genre (XIIIe–XVe siècle)* (Paris: Champion, 1994); Einar Már Jónsson, *Le Miroir: naissance d'un genre littéraire* (Paris: Belles Lettres, 1995); Julie Orlemanski, 'Literary Genre, Medieval Studies, and the Prosthesis of Disability', *Textual Practice*, 30:7 (2016), 1253–72; Robin Waugh, *The Genre of Medieval Patience Literature* (New York: Palgrave Macmillan, 2012); Kevin S. Whetter, *Understanding Genre and Medieval Romance* (Aldershot and Burlington, VT: Ashgate, 2008); *Gattungsinterferenzen: der Artusroman in Dialog*, ed. by Cora Dietl and others (Berlin and Boston: De Gruyter, 2016).

11   See, in particular, Eric D. Hirsch, *Validity in Interpretation* (New Haven, CT, and London: Yale University Press, 1969); Tzvetan Todorov, *Introduction à la littérature fantastique* (Paris: Seuil, 1970); Jauss, 'Theory of Genres and Medieval Literature'; Klaus W. Hempfer, *Gattungstheorie* (Munich: Fink, 1973); Maria Corti, 'Generi letterari e codificazioni', in *Principi della comunicazione letteraria* (Milan: Bompiani, 1976), pp. 151–81; Tzvetan Todorov, 'The Origin of Genres', *New Literary History*, 8 (1976), 159–70; Gérard Genette, *Introduction à l'architexte* (Paris: Seuil, 1979); Alastair Fowler, *Kinds of Literature: An Introduction to the Theory of Genres and Modes* (Oxford: Clarendon Press, 1982); *Théorie des genres*, ed. by Gérard Genette and Tzvetan Todorov (Paris: Seuil, 1986). See also Bec, 'Le Problème des genres chez les premiers troubadours', p. 32. Although the term 'genre' is constantly, usually unreflectively, being employed in present-day literary criticism, the efficacy of this usage is questionable. As most students of genre note, the term, because of the haphazard manner in which it is normally applied, raises more problems than it solves. For an excellent early (1931) assessment of the usefulness and limitations of the concept, see Karl Viëtor, 'L'Histoire des genres littéraires', in Genette and Todorov, pp. 9–35. Jauss has trenchantly remarked that 'the generic divisions of the handbooks [from which medievalists draw their genre terminology] rest on a convention of the discipline that is scarcely called into question any longer, according to which one promiscuously uses original characterizations, classical genre concepts, and later classifications' ('Theory of Genres and Medieval Literature', p. 77). Among recent studies on genre, see Anis Bawarshi and Mary Jo Reiff, *Genre: An Introduction to History, Theory, Research, and Pedagogy* (West Lafayette, IN: Parlor Press and WAC Clearinghouse, 2010), which includes an excellent bibliography; *Genres in the Internet: Issues in the Theory of Genre*, ed. by Janet Giltrow and Dieter Stein (Amsterdam and Philadelphia:

clear that, if one leaves aside the more 'sociologically' oriented applications of the term,[12] a high degree of consensus exists as regards the meaning of the term. Thus, it signifies a particular system of interconnexions between formal and thematic elements that defines a set of texts and which distinguishes one class of texts from other, similarly distinctively structured textual groupings. In addition, each genre is deemed to establish distinct and specific relationships with its audience, with other texts and genres, with language, and with its subject-matter (which is often the same across different genres, and, in this respect, since I am dealing primarily with medieval vernacular literature, it is enough to recall the multifaceted manner in which *Amor* was presented).

Keeping in mind the modern ideas that delimit our understanding of genre, let us return to the medieval school-room and to the lecture on the *Ars poetica*:

> Tres enim sunt manerie dicendi, quas alii stilos, alii figuras, alii caracteres appellant: humilis stilus, mediocris et altus. Humilis stilus est quando aliquis de humilibus personis humilibus prosequitur uerbis, ut in comedia. Mediocris stilus est quando de mediocribus personis mediocribus agitur uerbis, ut in satira. Altus stilus est quando de altis personis altis agitur uerbis, ut in tragedia.

A question immediately springs to mind: which of the terms and definitions used by the commentator can actually be deemed as analogous to our notion of genre? There is little doubt that *stilus* (and its synonyms), with its stress on the fundamental links between form and content, would qualify as a likely equivalent. Yet, if this is the case, where does such a conclusion leave those archetypal generic tags *comedia*, *satira*, and *tragedia*? It is evident from the clauses beginning in *ut* that the three terms are not meant to be taken as synonyms for the particular *stilus* with which each one is associated — as is not infrequently done in modern scholarship — but simply as an example of that 'style', thereby implying that each *stilus* can also embrace other literary types. This key detail is also obvious from the fact that the main thrust of both the *Ars poetica* and its commentary is to offer general advice 'de arte poetica' [on the art of poetry] — 'dat generalia precepta quibuslibet poetis pertinentia' [gives general precepts that concern any poet] (p. 336) — rather than to concentrate on any particular group or groups of poems.[13] Indeed, the lack of a precise and exclusive

Benjamins, 2009); *Matrices of Genre: Authors, Canons and Society*, ed. by Mary Depew and Dirk Obblink (Cambridge, MA: Harvard University Press, 2000); *The Work of Genre: Selected Essays from the English Institute*, ed. by Robyn Warhol (Cambridge, MA: English Institute in Collaboration with ACLS, 2011).

12   These have significantly grown in number in the last twenty to thirty years, and can loosely be categorized under the designation 'gender theory'; see *Genre and the Performance of Publics*, ed. by Anis Bawarshi and Mary Jo Reiff (Logan: Utah State University Press, 2016).

13   As was typical, the commentator acknowledges that Horace also had a 'private', restricted end in mind when he wrote his poem: 'Materia huius auctoris in hoc opere est ars poetica. Intentio uero est dare precepta de arte poetica. Causa huius intentionis est duplex: est enim communis, est specialis. Communis ut doceat quoslibet poetas in arte poetica aberrantes. Specialis, id est priuata, ut doceat Pisones [...] idcirco dat quedam precepta specialia in comediam et quedam specialia in satiram' [The subject-matter of this author in this work is the art of poetry. But his aim is to give precepts on the art of poetry. The reason of this aim is twofold: it is public, and it is particular. Public so that it may teach any poets who go astray in the art of poetry. Particular, that is, private, that it may teach the

equivalence between the three 'styles' and the three classes of works introduced to illustrate the *stili* is confirmed later in the commentary. The glosses to lines 73–98 of the *Ars poetica*,[14] a *locus classicus* for describing different categories of writing and for defining the differences between comedy and tragedy, make clear that *comedia* and *tragedia* (and implicitly *satira*) represent only three out of a much larger group of 'metrical' types.[15] This group equally embraces, inter alia, elegy, invective, and lyric song — all forms which, logically, would also need to be accommodated within one or other of the three basic 'styles', if their authors were to avoid, as was their duty as poets, the '[q]uartum vitium [quod] est incongrua stili mutatio' [the fourth error [that] is the incoherent change of style] (p. 337):

> EXIGUOS dicit respectu heroici, ELEGOS dicit secundum primam inuentionem, quia tantum elegia illo metro scribebatur. [...] Primum tamen ad inuectiva iambus inuentus est, postea uero comedi et tragedi sibi hunc pedem assumpserunt [...] Ecce causa quare hunc pedem sibi ceperint. Inter omnes scripturas iste due sole, scilicet comedia et tragedia, gestu ostendebantur. Ibi itaque persone introducebantur, ibi erat alternitas sermonum, ubi scilicet unus interrogabat et alius repondebat. Iambus autem pes breuis est et citus. Interrogatio uero et responsio breuitate gaudent. [...] Supradictas materias

Pisones [...] accordingly, it provides some particular precepts on comedy and some particular ones on satire] (p. 336). Yet, despite the work's dual 'intention', the commentary's attention is principally directed towards the *communia* of poetic composition.

14   *AP*, 73–98: 'res gestae regumque ducumque et tristia bella | quo scribi possent numero, monstrauit Homerus. | uersibus impariter iunctis querimonia primum, | post etiam inclusa est uoti sententia compos; | quis tamen exiguos elegos emiserit auctor, | grammatici certant et adhuc sub iudice lis est. | Archilocum proprio rabies armauit iambo: | hunc socci cepere pedem grandesque coturni | alternis aptum sermonibus et popularis | uincentem strepitus et natum rebus agendis. | Musa dedit fidibus diuos puerosque deorum | et pugilem uictorem et equum certamine primum | et iuuenum curas et libera uina referre. | descriptas seruare uices operumque colores | cur ego si nequeo ignoroque poeta salutor? | cur nescire pudens praue quam discere malo? | uersibus exponi tragicis res comica non uult; | indignatur item priuatis ac prope socco | dignis carminibus narrari cena Thyestae. | singula quaeque locum teneant sortita decentem. | interdum tamen et uocem comoedia tollit, | iratusque Chremes tumido delitigat ore | et tragicus plerumque dolet sermone pedestri, | Telephus et Peleus cum, pauper et exsul, uterque | proicit ampullas et sesquipedalia uerba, | si curat cor spectantis tetigisse querella' [In which metre the deeds of kings and heroes and the sorrowful wars may be written, Homer has shown. The lines incongruously joined first expressed lament, then the voice of love vows was included; but which author first published humble elegiacs the erudite dispute, and the matter is still under judgment. Rage armed Archilocus of its own iambic: the slippers [comedy] and the mighty sandals [tragedy] took this measure suitable for dialogue and successful over the noise of the crowd and born for actions. The Muse has allotted to the lyre to celebrate the gods and the heroes, and the victorious wrestler, and the horse that wins the race, and the troubles of youth and carefree drinking-songs. If I cannot and do not know how to observe the different types and styles of poetic works as established why am I called a poet? Why do I not prefer the modesty of ignorance to a distorted knowledge? Comic subjects do not want to be sung in tragic verses; likewise the banquet of Thyestes disdains to be narrated in verses familiar and worthy of the slipper. Let each single choice [of writing] keep its appropriate place. But sometimes even comedy raises her voice, and furious Chremes rails with tumid words and a tragic character often expresses grief with ordinary speech, Telephus and Peleus when, poor and exiled, both cast aside their six-footed words and swelling speech, if they care for their laments to touch the heart of the audience].

15   See Franz Quadlbauer, *Die antike Theorie der 'Genera dicendi' im lateinischen Mittelalter* (Vienna: Hermann Bohlaus Nachf., 1962).

talibus metris describes. Si uero materia tua fuerit himnus deorum et consimilia, lirico carmine describas, et hoc auctoritate sapientium. [...] DESCRIPTAS. Diceret ille: Tot varietates metrorum numquam potero obseruare. Ad hoc Horatius: Si non poteris obseruare, non debes dici poeta. [...] Uere diuerse materie diuersa expostulant metra, quia etiam diuersa expostulant uerba. Et hoc est: RES, id est materia, COMICA, scilicet comedia, et cetera. Comos, id est uilla, oda cantus uel sermo, inde comedia villanus sermo, eo quod sit affinis cottidiane locutioni et scribitur humili stilo. Tragos hircus, tragedia hircinus, id est fetidus, sermo. Nam tragedia est de crudelibus interfectionibus [...] Et scribitur tragedia alto stilo. ('Materia' commentary, pp. 348–49)

[He uses HUMBLE in comparison with the heroic metre, ELEGIACS he uses according to the initial creation, because only elegy was written in that metre. [...] First, however, the iambic was created for invectives, then comedians and tragedians adopted this metre [...] Here is the reason why they selected this metre. Among all the kinds of writings these two alone, that is comedy and tragedy, were performed. Now some characters were introduced, now there was a dialogue, where of course one character questioned and the other responded. But the iambic is a short and swift measure. Question and answer delight indeed in brevity. [...] You will write the abovementioned subjects in these metres. If then your subject were a hymn to the gods and the like, you would write a lyric poem, and this is according to the authority of wise men. [...] DESCRIBED [metres]. One may say: I will never be able to observe these many varieties of metres. To this, Horace: If you cannot observe them, you should not be called a poet. [...] Different subjects in fact require different metres, because they require different words. And then: RES, that is the subject, COMICA, that is comedy, etc. *Comos*, that is a country-house, *oda* is an ode or a speech, thus comedy is a lowly kind of speech, since it is similar to common expression and it is written in the humble style. *Tragos* is a goat, and tragedy is a goatish, that is disgusting, kind of speech. Indeed tragedy speaks of savage murders [...] And tragedy is written in the high style.]

To complicate further the search for the medieval equivalent of our term genre, the 'Materia' commentary — as is evident from the above quotation — not only includes comedy and tragedy under the general heading of *stili*, but also under those of *scripturae* and *metra*. Both these last two categories, as is apparent from what the *lector* explains, also establish their particular characteristics, just like *stilus*, on the basis of subject-matter and form — something which is equally true of *comedia* and *tragedia*. At the same time, the use of the iambic metre rather than discriminate between tragedy and comedy draws the two together (and associates both of them with the 'invective'); and the same occurs as a result of their common dependence on 'gestuality' and dialogue. What firmly emerges from the 'Materia' commentary is that its author did not have a clearcut sense of textual difference and specificity based on generic distinctions. This is especially evident when his glosses are compared to the lines from the *Ars poetica* which they interpret. For all the points of contact between text and gloss, it is far from insignificant that Horace's lines 73–98 make no mention of different literary categories but only of different poetic genres: 'descriptas servare vices operumque colores | cur ego si nequeo ignoroque poeta salutor?' [If I cannot and do not know how to observe

the alternation described and the colours of the works why am I called a poet?]
(86–87). Conversely, in comparison to Horace, the French commentator seems to
have had a rather more complex and stratified idea of poetry in which notions of
(textual) difference play a secondary, and even a limited role. His poetic reflection
is based on the premise that a variety of separate yet interconnected taxonomic
literary systems exist, and that individual texts and groups of texts can, to a lesser
or greater extent, be defined in relation to each of these. Such an approach not only
established the particular composite identity of a type of poetry, but also, in good
medieval totalizing and harmonizing fashion, it pinpointed the elements which
conjoined, as well as divided, different classes of works. It was this fundamentally
organic system of contrast and interdependence between texts and between the
typological schemes used to categorize them that constituted *poesia* and gave it a
recognizable unity and cohesion. To put it another way, the Middle Ages held that
no single textual category could exhaust a text's possibilities. Consequently, a work,
for all its peculiarities, could have features in common with other works — even
those, as occurs in the relationship between tragedy and comedy, to which it was
commonly opposed.

Before objections are raised that my description of medieval attitudes to literature
is based on an exceptional viewpoint, let me stress, once and for all, that the
perspective offered by our French schoolmaster is in no way unique. As we shall
see in greater detail in the next subsection, his presentation (as one would expect
from a teacher of grammar) is circumscribed by commonplaces, even if he does
demonstrate commendable skill in synthesizing these (Friis-Jensen, pp. 321, 323–25).
Indeed, given the commentator's fondness for *topoi,* there is, as I suggested earlier,
nothing 'especially remarkable' about the ways in which he talks about poetry. What
is noteworthy, however, is the way in which modern scholars have oversimplified
his ideas on literature and those of his peers. In essence, what they have done is to
conflate notions, such as *stilus, metrum,* and *tragedia,* which the Middle Ages took as
discrete. They have then further compounded their miscalculation by subsuming
these same notions under the single concept of 'genre': a concept which — as we
have begun to see — appears to bring various problems in its wake when applied
to medieval literature.

The problems become more acute when one recalls that I have not yet been
able to discover a precise equivalent of our 'genre' in the 'Materia' commentary's
'typical' broad assessment of literature. On the contrary, my research would suggest
that our idea of genre 'dissolves' on coming into contact with medieval literary
theory. The meanings we concentrate in the single controlling concept of genre
were diluted in the Middle Ages across a diversity of commonly used critical
categories. It is thus questionable whether the terms, *stilus* and *genus,* which we
most frequently translate as 'genre', can actually be interpreted in this manner.
When applied to literature, the medieval meanings of both words are vague rather
than specific.[16] This is not only apparent from the differing contexts in which *stilus*

---

16   As regards *stilus,* see Claudia Villa, 'Il lessico della stilistica fra XI e XIII sec.', in *Vocabulaire des
écoles et des méthodes d'enseignement au moyen âge,* ed. by Olga Weijers (Turnhout: Brepols, 1992), pp.

and *genus* were actually employed,[17] but also from the fact that, as a result of their mutual semantic indeterminacy, they could be employed interchangeably with several other words.[18] The 'Materia' commentary provides telling confirmation of this fact: 'Tres enim sunt manerie dicendi, quas alii stilos, alii figuras, alii caracteres appellant' (p. 337). We find an even more interesting instance of such synonymic listing in another Horatian manuscript:

> Species huius artis dicuntur tria genera stilorum qui a quibusdam vocantur figure, a quibusdam caracteres, aut stili figure appellantur quasi compositiones verborum. Tres sunt figure; dicitur una figura humilis, idest compositio verborum pertinentium modo ad parvas, ut in bucolicis invenitur;[19] dicitur alia figura mediocris, idest alia composicio verborum pertinentium ad parvas res, modo ad magnas; dicitur alia figura alta, idest compositio verborum pertinentium ad magnas res et altas. Hec, inquam, figure dicuntur species a similitudine quadam, quia sicut genus numquam extra suarum specierum aliqua reperitur, sic nullus poema reperitur extra aliqua istarum figurarum.[20]

> [The categories of this art are called the three types of style, which some name figures, some characters, or they are called figures of style as if they were compositions of words. There are three figures, one is called humble figure, that is a composition of words suitable only for little things, as it is found in bucolic poetry; the second is called middle figure, that is a composition of words suitable for little things, but sometimes for great things; the third is called

---

42–59; as regards *genus*, see Quadlbauer, as well as the next two notes.

17   For examples of the literary usage of *genus* with the indeterminate meanings 'kind', 'type', 'way', 'level', etc., see: 'Sunt igitur tria genera, quae genera nos figuras appellamus' [There are therefore three kinds, which kinds we call figures] (*Ad Her.* IV. 8. 11); compare also IV. 14. 21; for a fuller discussion of the former passage which controls the tradition of reflection on the 'styles', see below § i); 'poematos genera sunt tria. Aut enim activum vel imitativum est, quod Graeci dramaticon vel mimeticon appellant' [three are the kinds of poems. It is indeed either active or imitative, which the Greeks call dramatic or mimetic] (Bede, *De arte metrica*, in Keil, VII, 259; see § vi below for a discussion of this manner of classifying texts). An excellent example of the fluctuating meaning of *stilus* may be found, in a matter of a few lines, in an *Accessus Lucani*: 'Tres sunt stili: humilis, mediocris, grandiloquus [...] Sunt enim tres stili, dragmaticon [...] exagematicon [...] misticon' [There are three styles: humble, middle, and high [...] Indeed there are three styles, dramatic [...] narrative [...] mixed] (129–44, in Huygens, pp. 43–44). Thierry of Chartres, as Dante would do more fully and systematically over 150 years later (see below pp. 239–42), endeavoured to distinguish between the different terms used in discussions of the *genera dicendi*: 'genera orationis alii stilos, alii figuras, alii characteres appellarunt: sed proprie figura ad orationem, genus ad elocutionem refertur' [some call the types of discourse styles, some call them figures, and others characters: but strictly speaking *figura* refers to the speech itself, *genus* refers the delivery of the speech]: *Commentarius super Rhetoricam ad Herennium*, in *The Latin Rhetorical Commentaries by Thierry of Chartres*, ed. by Karin M. Fredborg (Toronto: Pontifical Institute of Medieval Studies, 1981), 4. 8. 11, ll. 71–73.

18   Thanks to the excellent 'Index of Latin Terms' in Copeland and Sluiter (pp. 922–37), it is possible to track the use and dissemination of technical terms related to literary classification, as well as their semantic instabilities.

19   The use of bucolic verse to illustrate the 'humble figure' confirms my earlier point that each of the three 'styles' embraces several different textual types (*qualitates carminum*).

20   The quotation, in Villa's transcription (pp. 44–45), is taken from Vatican MS Reg. lat. 1431, fol. 36r–v. The manuscript was copied in the twelfth century and is of French provenance; see Birger Munk Olsen, *L'Étude des auteurs classiques latins aux XI et XII siècles*, 4 vols (Paris: Editions du CNRS, 1982–2014), I, 501.

high figure, that is a composition of words suitable for serious and grand things. These figures, I may say, are called categories by a certain analogy, because just as a kind is never found outside any of its own categories, so no work of poetry is found outside any of these figures.]

This passage is especially noteworthy because of the double presence in it of *genus*. The word's first appearance confirms some of my earlier points about the loose manner in which it was utilized in medieval literary discourse. In addition, its lack of a precise technical force in such contexts is further displayed by its second, technically specific, philosophical usage: 'sicut genus numquam extra suarum specierum aliqua reperitur' [just as a kind is never found outside any of its own categories].[21] Rather than translate *stilus* and *genus*, when these refer to differing modes of composition, with the misleading and, for us, highly suggestive 'genre', we should think of rendering them, more neutrally and properly, as 'manner', or 'type', or 'way' [of writing].[22]

To appreciate how medieval writers dealt both with textual diversity and with literature as a system, it is important to be sensitive to their linguistic choices. Equally, it is vital to recognize the implications of the links, and also the differences, that medieval writers regularly established between, for instance, 'style', 'metre', and 'writing', as well as the subordinate position in which they placed comedy and tragedy in respect of these. Recognizing as much calls into doubt the totalizing pre-eminence that modern scholarship grants to genre in discussions of the ways in which medieval intellectuals constructed and discussed their notion of literature. Since, in medieval critical discourse, it is difficult to establish with a degree of certainty the presence of a word for genre or indeed the existence of the concept as an interpretive and descriptive tool, it would seem that the Middle Ages examined and perceived literature in relation to categories other than that of genre (see the next subsection). As Pierre Bec, one of the major students of genre and medieval vernacular literature, has noted: 'les hommes du moyen âge [...] ne paraissent pas avoir eu l'idée que les textes poétiques pouvaient être rangés en ensembles génériques'.[23] Thus, to claim that tragedy and comedy were understood as referring

---

21   See Aristotle, *Metaphysics* v. 28, 1024ab.

22   In this respect, it is noteworthy that Occitan critical language prefers *maneria* to either *genus* or *stilus* when alluding to the 'type' or 'sort' of a poem. See 'Index of Technical Terms': *maniera*, in *The 'Razos de Trobar' of Raimon Vidal and Associated Texts*, ed. by John Henry Marshall (London: Oxford University Press, 1972), p. 176. Indeed, Occitan *maneyra* rather than overlap with Latin *stilus* and related terms, which tend to refer to formal questions (see below § i), is closer to Latin *qualitates carminum*, 'kinds of poems' (see below § ii). Like *maneyra*, *qualitas carminum* (and similar terms) was used as the general tag to designate 'poetic types' which, both in the Latin and in the Occitan traditions, were distinguished according to their content (see, for instance, 'Two Anonymous Treatises from MS. Ripoll 129', in Marshall, pp. 101–05). What is yet more noteworthy about Occitan critical theory is that it did not seem intent on distinguishing texts in relation to their *manerie dicendi*. Thus, the 'styles' do not appear in Occitan treatises; instead theorists discriminate between types of poems on the basis of their *materia* and between *trobar clus* and *leu* as regards their formal properties (see below § xii). This fact serves as an important corrective to our modern obsession with the *stili* and with genre. (The present note anticipates some of the principal lines of argument that I develop in the rest of this chapter.)

23   Bec, 'Le Problème des genres chez les premiers troubadours', p. 31. A handful of other critics has

to genres by medieval writers and their audiences means not only to ignore the ways in which the terms were used in practice, but also to downgrade unjustifiably the other classificatory terminology so richly present in medieval reflection on literature.

The lack of an effective sense of genre in the Middle Ages emerges not just from the ways in which ties were created between different groups of works, but also from the fact that terms such as 'comedy', 'tragedy', and 'satire' (just like *stilus*, *genus*, etc.) did not have fixed meanings and did not consistently designate one particular kind of text. Time and again, and this is especially true of non-'tragic' designations, we find such terms qualifying or referring to similar, if not actually to identical, forms and subjects.[24] To tag a work as a comedy or a tragedy in medieval critical parlance did not mean to provide an 'exhaustive' description of its basic textual properties. From the ways in which the labels are glossed in the 'Materia' commentary, it is clear that they only partially characterize a text. The discomfort with which Dante's first readers reacted to the title of his great poem can, to some extent, be explained by what they would have deemed to be *comedia*'s conventional limitations as a descriptive label.[25] It was solely when comedy and tragedy were examined in light of other typologies, such as *metrum* or *scriptura*, that their textual lineaments became better defined. Thus, as I have suggested, it is not so much any single category that defined a work, but the whole, interlocking system of such descriptive categorizations.

It is the fluidity at the heart of the medieval sense of literature, a fluidity confirmed by the lack of a fixed critical vocabulary, that, I believe, the modern fascination with genre has obscured. Paradoxically, the more categories and definitions the Middle Ages proliferated, the more it attenuated the differences between texts, since it introduced additional ways in which these could be drawn together as well as differentiated. The *De vulgari eloquentia* presents a striking

---

expressed doubts as to whether the Middle Ages had an idea of genre. Yet, paradoxically, once these scholars have expressed their reservations, several of them go on to discuss medieval literature in light of generic classifications. See Strohm, pp. 348, 356–57; Jauss, 'Theory of Genres and Medieval Literature', p. 77; Payen and Diekstra, pp. 20–23; Karl Uitti, 'Foi littéraire et création poétique: le problème des genres littéraires en ancien français', in *Atti del XIV Congresso*, I, 165–76 (p. 165); James J. Murphy, 'Poetry without Genre: The Metapoetics of the Middle Ages', *Poetica*, 11 (1979), 1–8; Bec, 'Le Problème des genres chez les premiers troubadours', pp. 31, 37–47; Rossella D'Alfonso, 'Fra retorica e teologia: il sistema dei generi letterari nel basso medioevo', *Lingua e stile*, 17 (1982), 269–93 (pp. 276–78); Kelly, p. 112; Costanzo Di Girolamo, 'Premessa', in *La letteratura romanza*, ed. by Costanzo Di Girolamo (Bologna: il Mulino, 1994), pp. 11–16 (p. 12). Jeffrey Schnapp makes some interesting observations about the distorting effects of imposing anachronistic notions of genre onto medieval literature: 'Tragedy and the Theatre of Hell', in *LPQSD*, pp. 100–27 (p. 115–16). See also Suzanne Reynolds's comments regarding the ways in which satire could 'cut across [...] fixed generic distinctions' in the same volume: 'Orazio satiro (*Inferno* IV, 89)', pp. 128–44 (p. 134).

24   See the examples discussed in Chapter 7, pp. 275–83.

25   It is my sense, however, that Dante's use of *comedía* does have some links to modern 'totalizing' applications of comedy as a genre label; see p. 240 below and Chapter 7. Given the typical ways in which the term was used in the Middle Ages, it is understandable that Dante's first readers should largely have failed to appreciate the new ways in which he was expanding the word's critical and semantic range.

instance of this phenomenon in its second Book. It is often forgotten that, as well as the 'stylistically'-based categories of chapter 4, the treatise in its close also discusses an exclusively content-based distinction: 'Nam cum ea que dicimus cuncta vel circa dextrum aliquid vel sinistrum canamus' [Indeed, since all of our words in poetry can be sung either positively or negatively] (II. 14. 2). This distinction cuts across and ignores the particular features that demarcate the treatise's 'tragic', 'comic', and 'elegiac' *stili*. As a result, it not only establishes a different order of possible inter-connections between the works subsumed under each of the three 'styles', but it also delimits the classificatory import of the *stili* as a system for describing literature.[26] In the Middle Ages, the theory of the *genera dicendi* did not have that absolute definitional force that modern scholarship often ascribes to it. Indeed, no category could claim to have had such totalizing authority. Instead, the medieval text slides between categories and, in doing this, it fashions different identities for itself, while at the same time forging and breaking links between itself and other texts.

If my claims about medieval thinking about literature have a degree of merit, then, we should be wary of laying too great a stress on ideas of difference when describing the literary universe of the Middle Ages. It is rather the interplay between difference and similarity which is its key feature; and it is this characteristic which should serve as our point of departure when examining medieval texts or defining medieval thinking about literature. Genre's contrastive bias is especially unsuited for capturing such a nuanced view of *scriptura*. Where we place our interpretive faith in one overarching system, our medieval forebears — as we shall soon see in greater detail in the following subsection — fashioned many competing yet complementary systems with which to attempt to categorize, describe, and discuss the communicative and aesthetic ends to which language could be bent. I suspect that this proliferation of definitional categories owed much both to the preceptive character of medieval education and to the existence of competing *auctoritates* (in particular, the clash between a Ciceronian-rhetorical tradition and a Horatian-poetic one). However, I am rather more certain that it was also profoundly conditioned by a clear-eyed sense of the complexity and creative possibilities of literature — a sense which was both empirically determined and encouraged by a deepseated fascination with the symbolic potential of writing.[27] In such circumstances, it should not come as a surprise that medieval literature was propelled by considerable experimental ambitions. As is well known, these found expression in a wealth of new or hybrid textual forms and in the discovery of a novel kind of language, the vernacular, for literary composition.[28] And it is especially fitting that the fundamental creativity

26 For a discussion of the two classificatory systems present in the *De vulgari eloquentia* and of their inter-relationship, see Subsection 3. See also pp. 275–76 below.

27 On the 'book as symbol', see at least Ernst Robert Curtius, *European Literature and the Latin Middle Ages* (London and Henley: Routledge & Kegan Paul, 1979), pp. 302–47. See also John Ahern, 'Binding the Book: Hermeneutics and Manuscript Production in *Paradiso* 33', *PMLA*, 97 (1982), 800–09; David A. Orsbon, 'The Universe as Book: Dante's *Commedia* as Image of the Divine Mind', *Dante Studies*, 132 (2014), 87–111; Philippe Sollers, *L'Écriture et l'expérience des limites* (Paris: Seuil, 1968), pp. 14–47.

28 On the hybridity of medieval literature, see, for instance, Zygmunt G. Barański, '"The Roots of Dante's Plurilingualism: "Hybridity" and Language in the *Vita nova*', in *Dante's Plurilingualism,*

of the Middle Ages should have achieved its most sustained apotheosis in, arguably, the most original book that Western culture has ever produced, Dante's *Commedia*. Such consistent striving after *novitas* could not have found its inspiration in a restrictive notion of literature. It could only have stemmed from a notion that allowed writers a considerable degree of freedom — a notion which was sustained by a highly flexible idea of the text as something in constant flux between different possibilities (possibilities which found their theoretical and critical expression in different categorizations).

The tendency to circumscribe medieval texts within single genres thus lies at the opposite pole to the way in which a medieval reader would have classified these same texts. The idea that a work could be reduced to one particular category seems to have been quite alien to the Middle Ages. Thus Dante's 'comedía' is adorned with a series of other names: 'poema sacro', 'sacrato poema', 'poesí', 'canzon', 'cantica', 'canto', not to mention the allusions it makes to its 'rime aspre e chiocce' or to 'dolce stil novo'.[29] The effect of all these tags is to establish a range of distinct relations between the *Commedia* and different areas of the literary universe. Although Dantists have long been aware that a key feature of the poem is the interconnexions it establishes with literature and language in general, it has not been recognized that, by forging such links, Dante was giving supreme practical expression to an idea that can be traced back to the basic sense that the Middle Ages had of the fluidity of textual relations. As I never tire of declaring, even Dante's most radical experiments are inevitably grounded in contemporary thinking about literature. For all the medieval desire to establish rules for writing 'correctly' and for all the emphasis that was placed on the distinctiveness of the *genera dicendi*, authors actually had considerable freedom when composing their works. It is this freedom which our concern with genre has unnecessarily curtailed, thereby making us insensitive to the fundamental hybridity of so much medieval literature, as well as irritable with the medieval application of critical terminology.

The 'Materia' commentary clearly and typically documents how the Middle Ages dealt with the complexities of literature. In the rest of this chapter, I shall attempt to provide some more details about the various categories that the Middle Ages developed in order to classify and analyse both literature in general and individual compositions. In addition, I shall try to assess Dante's views regarding such categories, as well as their impact on his art and thought. My overriding aim is to begin to understand the effects that such a 'fragmented' yet organic sense of textuality had on medieval ideas about literature, on the practices of literary production, and most especially on Dante's artistic career.

If we allow the 'Materia' commentary to guide us, we cannot but leave behind, however reluctantly, our faith in the convenience of genre. Indeed, it should be

---

Authority, Knowledge, Subjectivity, ed. by Sara Fortuna and others (Oxford: Legenda, 2010), pp. 98–121; Jauss, 'Littérature médiévale et théorie des genres', p. 83; Uitti, 'Foi littéraire et création poétique', pp. 171–73; Di Girolamo, p. 12.

29   See Lino Pertile, '*Canto-cantica-Comedía* e l'*Epistola a Cangrande*', *Lectura Dantis Virginiana*, 9 (1991), 105–23, and '*Cantica* nella tradizione medievale e in Dante', *Rivista di storia e di letteratura religiosa*, 18 (1992), 389–412; and Chapter 8.

obvious by now when a genre is not a genre. Philologically speaking, a genre is not a genre when — regardless of what other ages may think — a particular community of writers and readers does not recognize it as such; and this is doubly so, if the strict concept of genre does not appear to belong to their intellectual baggage. Ultimately, this chapter is no more than a plea that heed be taken of what our anonymous French *magister* and his peers are trying to tell us about their view of literature.[30]

2. Fifteen Medieval Literary Categories

Discussions of literature and of the categories into which it might be divided were ubiquitous in medieval culture: from the school-room to the *compilatio*, and from the commentary, whether religious or lay, to manuals of instruction (which themselves ranged from a work of the sophistication of Hugh of St Victor's *Didascalicon*, which engages with the broad sweep of human knowledge, to practical handbooks on letter-writing, preaching, etc.). The impact and influence of such classifications were all-pervasive. They belonged to the 'interdiscursive' cultural memories of any literate medieval person.[31] To put it another way, given their key role in the educational curriculum — especially as regards the interpretation of the *auctores* and the teaching of composition — they formed one of the key supports on which literacy was built.[32] This state of affairs finds immediate and eloquent

30   On medieval literary categorization, in addition to the studies cited in nn. 10 & 23, see Udo Kindermann, 'Gattungsysteme im Mittelalter', in *Kontinuität und Transformation der Antike im Mittelalter*, ed. by Willi Erzgräber (Sigmaringen: Verlag GmbH & Co, 1988), pp. 303–13; Henning Krauss, 'Sistema dei generi e scuola siciliana', in *La pratica sociale del testo: scritti di sociologia della letteratura in onore di E. Köhler*, ed. by Carlo Bordoni (Bologna: CLUEB, 1982), pp. 123–58. On Dante and 'genre', see Theodore J. Cachey Jr, 'Title, Genre, Metaliterary Aspects', in *The Cambridge Companion to Dante's 'Commedia'*, ed. by Zygmunt G. Barański and Simon Gilson (Cambridge: Cambridge University Press, 2019), pp. 79–94; Ambrogio Camozzi Pistoja, 'Il quarto trattato del Convivio: O della satira', *Le tre corone*, 1 (2014), 27–53; Rossella D'Alfonso, *Il dialogo con Dio nella 'Divina Commedia'* (Bologna: CLUEB, 1988), pp. 79–108; Amilcare A. Iannucci, 'Dante's Theory of Genres in the *Divina Commedia*', *Dante Studies*, 91 (1973), 1–25; Henry A. Kelly, *Tragedy and Comedy from Dante to Pseudo-Dante* (Berkeley, Los Angeles, and London: University of California Press, 1989); Pier Vincenzo Mengaldo, 'L'elegia "umile" (*De vulgari Eloquentia* II iv 5–6)' [1966], in *Linguistica e retorica di Dante* (Pisa: Nistri-Lischi, 1978), pp. 200–22; Michelangelo Picone, 'Songbook and Lyric Genres in the *Vita Nuova*', in *LPQSD*, pp. 158–70; Antonio Pioletti, 'Il romanzo nella *Commedia*', *Letture classensi*, 17 (1988), 87–111; Reynolds, 'Orazio satiro' and 'Dante and the Medieval Theory of Satire: A Collection of Texts', in *LPQSD*, pp. 145–57; Vittorio Russo, 'Strutture innovative delle opere letterarie di Dante nella prospettiva dei generi letterari', *L'Alighieri*, 20:2 (1979), 46–63; Schnapp; and Chapter 7.

31   Cesare Segre, 'Intertestuale/interdiscorsivo: appunti per una fenomenologia delle fonti', in *La parola ritrovata*, ed. by Costanzo Di Girolamo and Ivano Paccagnella (Palermo: Sellerio, 1982), pp. 15–28.

32   The bibliography on medieval education is extensive: see in particular Filippo Gianferrari, 'Dante and Thirteenth-century Latin Education: Reading the "auctores minores"' (unpublished PhD thesis, University of Notre Dame, 2017), which includes an insightful discussion of methodological issues related to the study of medieval education, as well as a very good bibliography; see also Chapter 1, n. 20. As far as the points I am making here are concerned, it is enough to see Friis-Jensen, pp. 321–22; Douglas Kelly, *The Arts of Poetry and Prose* (Turnhout: Brepols, 1991), especially pp. 111–16; Villa, pp. 42–43. See also Paul M. Clogan, 'Literary Genres in a Medieval Textbook', *Medievalia et*

confirmation, for instance, in an introductory pedagogical work such as Conrad of Hirsau's *Dialogus super auctores* (just as it does inter alia, in the commentary tradition to Horace). In order to satisfy the request of his *Discipulus* to clarify 'secularis disciplinae [...] rudimenta' [the first principles of this long-standing doctrine] (29–30) and to provide 'quorum omnium [questions relating to the nature of writing] brev*em* solutio*nem*' that can serve as 'qua*m*dam ad auctores intelligendos magnos vel minimos introductio*nem*' [a brief explanation of all of these [...] an introduction, as it were, to the understanding of major and minor authors] (58–59; but see also the Pupil's complete speech, 44–59), Conrad's *Magister* accumulates literary categories and carefully lists the sub-classifications which go to make up each of these. He refers to the different types of 'book': 'Constat autem liber prosa, rithmo vel metro' [A book consists of prose, rhythmic prose or verse] (106; and see the full definitions, 108–14); he notes that 'sunt autem metrorum plura genera' [but there are many kinds of verses] (114–15, and see also 115–21); he explains the determining characteristics of various types of writer (135–49); and he distinguishes between factual, fictional, and 'mixed' accounts (136–40, 149). Next, spurred on by his demanding student (150–51), the *Magister* provides an impressive list of different 'kinds of poems' [*qualitates carminum*], which includes *carmen bucolicum, comicum, tragicum, satyricum, liricum, apollogeticum, panagericum, epithalamium, epitaphium, cronicum,* and *elegiacum* (152–69).[33] It is particularly significant for my claim regarding the absence of a clear idea of genre in the Middle Ages that the Teacher should exclusively define these poetic forms in terms of their content — for example, 'cronicum carmen id est temporum descriptio' [poetry on time, that is the description of the ages] (167–68) — and that there should be a marked overlap of concerns between some of these metrical types, for instance, both satire and panegyric deal with praise (161 & 165–66). The *Magister* then goes on to differentiate between works whose 'order' is 'artificial' and those which begin 'naturally' (191–98). Finally, he asserts that 'sunt etiam tres modi in stilo scribentis, humilis, mediocris, grandiloquus, ubi iuxta materiae qualitatem auctor sui stili temperat ordinem' [There are also three ways of writing, the humble, the middle, and the high style, when the author, according to the character of his subject-matter, determines the type of style he uses] (208–10), thereby, confirming yet again the fundamental lack of a precise correspondence between the three 'styles' and an open-ended complex of 'kinds of verse' to which comedy and tragedy belong. Indeed, this fact is even more explicit in Conrad's 'dialogue' than in the commentaries to the *Ars poetica*, since, as the *Magister* elucidates, *stilus* relates to form, while each *qualitas carminis* is determined by its specific *qualitas materiae*. It

---

Humanistica, 11 (1982), 199–209 (it should not come as a surprise that I dissent from Clogan's use of genre in his study).

33 Although satire is primarily that *qualitas carminis* which 'vitia cuncta reprehendit' [rebukes every vice] (157), it is further subdivided into other types of verse: 'hoc autem opus dicitur satyra, in qua sunt odae vel laudes vel contra viciosos validae reprehensiones' [that work is called a satire, which has odes or praises or fitting rebukes against those who are immoral] (160–62). The medieval appreciation of literature lies in these categories within categories whose proliferation ends up by managing both to distinguish and to bring together even those supposed irreconcilables, 'praise' and 'blame'. See § xi below.

is thus difficult to see where one might locate the notion of genre in such a starkly demarcated view of textuality.

Medieval literature is not just a matter of texts and authors. It is also that system of classifications and sub-classifications of which the *Magister* offers a first glimpse to his eager *Discipulus*. In fact, it is this system that provides the building-blocks out of which the medieval reader constructed his sense not just of literature in general, but also of the complexion of individual texts and authors. Thus, several of the questions around which literary prefaces were built, especially those regarding a work's author, title, form, and content, could only be answered by having recourse to the sort of categories presented in Conrad's compilation. The interpretive demands of the *accessus* guaranteed and reaffirmed the centrality of classification in literary criticism.[34] It is thus no coincidence that a collection of prologues to the *auctores*, which is what constitutes the bulk of the *Dialogus super auctores*, should open with a discussion of some of the most important categorizations into which literature might be divided.

How many systems for classifying literature were in circulation by Dante's time? I have discerned fifteen discrete schemes. At the same time, I should like to stress that this number should not be taken as definitive. Equally, my presentation is not a methodical study and history of these fifteen medieval literary categories (such an assessment would need to be based on several large-scale philological studies of individual terms and categories and of their inter-relationships).[35] My aims are quite modest. I should like to build on the examples that I have already provided and draw up a checklist — largely to confirm the claims made so far — of the various classifications under which a medieval text could be subsumed.

The following constitute the fifteen literary categories:

i. The most famous and widespread category was that of the *genera dicendi*, namely, that of the three 'styles', which, as we have seen, were also referred to as *figurae*, *caracteres*, *genera*, *maneriae*, and *species*, or were indicated by means of a combination of two of these terms (for example, 'manerie dicendi', 'genera stilorum', 'stili figure'),[36] or by other composite phrases such as 'genera locutionis'.[37] The earliest extant division of the 'styles' into three is that found in the *Rhetorica ad Herennium*:

> Sunt igitur tria genera, quae genera nos figuras appellamus, in quibus omnis oratio non vitiosa consumitur: unam gravem, alteram mediocrem, tertiam extenuatam vocamus. Gravis est quae constat ex verborum gravium levi et ornata constructione. Mediocris est quae constat ex humiliore neque tamen ex infima et pervulgatissima verborum dignitate. Adtenuata est quae demissa est usque ad usitatissimam puri consuetudinem sermonis. (IV. 8. 11; but see the full discussion at IV. 8. 11–IV. 10. 15)

34   On the *accessus* tradition, see Alastair J. Minnis, *Medieval Theory of Authorship*, 2nd edn (Aldershot: Scolar Press, 1988), pp. 9–72; *MLTC*, pp. 12–15.

35   Two important studies of this kind are Quadlbauer and Villa.

36   The first example is taken from the 'Materia' commentary, p. 337, while the remaining two may be found in Vatican MS Reg. lat. 1431, fol. 36r (quoted from Villa, p. 44).

37   London, British Library, MS Harley 3534, fol. 69r (quoted from Reynolds, 'Dante', p. 147). The letter to Cangrande employs 'in modo loquendi'/'ad modum loquendi' [manner of speaking] (*Ep.* XIII. 30 & 31).

[There are then three kinds of style, which we call figures, in which every speech, if not faulty, is divided: we call the first high, the second middle, the third simple/plain. The high style consists of weighty words ordered in a smooth and adorned structure. The middle consists of a quality of words that is more humble yet not base or highly colloquial. The simple/plain is very modest, up to the most ordinary use of standard speech.]

It is important to note that, in the *Ad Herennium*, the 'styles' are exclusively formal categories not associated with any particular kind of text or subject-matter.[38] Indeed, even as regards form, they appear to be solely concerned with the differing qualities of words. Although, in later definitions, classes of text — normally, tragedy, satire, and comedy (Mengaldo, 'L'elegia') — particular works,[39] social groups, and topics (though these were much less fixed than the *qualitates carminum*) were used to illustrate specific 'styles', the main focus of attention of the *genera dicendi* continued to be on matters of form.[40] Thus, the emphasis on diction remained just about constant from the time of Cicero to the fourteenth century. Despite other modifications, especially as regards the terms used to describe each of the *stili* (for instance, the *gravis* was more commonly known as the *altus* or the *grandiloquus*, and occasionally as the *sublimis*), the influence of the *Ad Herennium*'s tripartite stylistic division, not least because it became closely involved with the exegetical tradition of the *Ars poetica*, spread into every corner of medieval written culture. Of all the classifications it was not just the most influential, but also, because of its emphasis on the need for authors to ensure that, in general though not absolutely, the three *stili* were to be kept separate, it was the one that most affected and determined the formal character of medieval literature. It was against its perceived constraints that Dante directed much of his energy when he composed the *Commedia*.[41]

---

38   It is striking that in the *Orator* (XXI. 69) Cicero associates each of the 'styles' with one of the canonical duties of the orator, thereby delimiting a particular end for each 'manner': 'Sed quot officia oratoris, tot sunt genera dicendi: subtile in probando, modicum in delectando, vehemens in flectendo' [But as many are the duties of an orator, so many are the styles of speech: low in demonstrating, modest in delighting, impetuous in moving].

39   See, for instance, 'Generales ergo figure dictaminum tres dicuntur, que stili etiam nuncupantur, scilicet humilis, mediocris et sublimis. Humilis est illa que usque ad usitatissimam puri sermonis consuetudinem est demissa, ut in Evangelis et Sacra Scriptura sepe videmus. At mediocris censetur que constat ex altiore neque tamen ex summa et hornatissima dignitate verborum, ut in epistolis Pauli et elegis Ovidianis. Sublimis ex magna et hornata verborum constructione conficitur, ut in Gregorii Moralibus et Lucano' [The general figures of the *dictamen* are said to be three, which also take the name of styles, that is humble, middle, and sublime. The humble is as low as the most ordinary use of plain speech, such as we often see in the Gospels and in Scripture. The one that consists of a higher quality of words, yet not grand and greatly adorned, is considered middle, as in St. Paul's epistles and in Ovid's elegies. The sublime is made of a refined and adorned structure of words, as in Gregory's *Moralia* and in Lucan]: Bene da Firenze, *Candelabrum*, ed. by Gian Carlo Alessio (Padua: Antenore, 1983), I. 6.

40   Douglas Kelly exaggerates the importance of the association between the *stili* and social groups, an association that he labels 'material style' (pp. 71–78).

41   The classic study of the *genera dicendi* is Quadlbauer. On Dante's critique of the doctrine of the 'three styles' in the *Commedia*, see pp. 250–51 below and Chapter 7. Finally, it is interesting to note that John of Garland, following Bernard de Meung, distinguishes between poetic and prose 'style', namely, between rhythmic verse and the *cursus*: *The Parisiana Poetria of John of Garland*, ed.

Nonetheless, despite the success of the *genera dicendi*, there existed other effective stylistic classifications which focused on formal features different to those privileged by the three *stili*.[42] What is especially interesting about these categories is that they cut across the divisions established by the *manerie dicendi*, thereby creating alternative formally-based systems of textual relations (see §§ xii–xiv below).

ii. All forms of writing came under the category of *scriptura*: for instance, 'Titulus autem libris inscribitur [...] a scripturae genere, ut epistolae, commenta' and 'Tres enim sunt scripturae caracteres' [The title of the book is assigned [...] by the kind of writing, such as epistles, commentaries; For there are three characters of writing] (Bernard of Utrecht, 64–68 and 176–77, for a fuller analysis of this passage, see § vi below); 'Inter omnes scripturas iste due sole, scilicet comedia et tragedia' [Of all types of writing, these two alone, that is comedy and tragedy] ('Materia' commentary, p. 337). *Liber* appears to have had a meaning not dissimilar to *scriptura*: 'Dicitur etiam liber orationum contextus, historiarum, commentariorum in unum corpus collectio vel de his similibus [...] Constat autem liber prosa, rithmo vel metro' [A series of writings, a collection in one corpus of histories, commentaries or similar things is called a book [...] A book consists of prose, rhythmic prose or metre] (Conrad of Hirsau, 102–06). The lists of different poetic and prose types — Conrad's *qualitates carminum* (see p. 223 above) — constituted subdivisions of *scriptura*. It is the various textual categories collected under, say, *libri poetarum* or the Occitans' 'maneres de rimes' (Ripoll, l. 145, in Marshall, p. 105) and distinguished principally according to their subject-matter that we describe, problematically in my view, as 'genres'. If modern scholars could not point to actual groups of texts as constituting separate genres, they would be unable to claim that the *genera dicendi* served the Middle Ages as a theory of genre.

iii. *Scriptura* was not simply divided into the opposition between prose and poetry. There were four main types of 'writing':

> Et liber quidem prosa vel rithmo vel metro vel horum duobus constat. Prosa est oratio metri lege soluta, dicta a proson quod productum vel diffusum sonat; rithmus est ubi syllabarum tantum consideratur numerus: rithmus enim numerus interpretatur; metrum est quod certis pedum mensuris discurrit, nam metron mensura interpretatur. (Bernard of Utrecht, 6–11)

> [And a book consists of prose, rhythmic prose, metre, or two of these together. Prose is a kind of writing not subject to metrical rules, named after the Greek *proson* ('long') because it sounds extended or diffused; rhythmic prose is when only the number of syllables is considered: rhythm is indeed interpreted as 'number'; metre is what flows with regular measures of metrical feet, and it is called *metron* from 'measure.]

It should also be noted, especially in the light of the claims I am making about the

by Traugott Lawler (New Haven, CT, and London: Yale University Press, 1974), v. 402–67, and see Lawler's long note discussing this passage, pp. 256–58.
42   On the three 'styles', see also Paul B. Salmon, 'The Three Voices of Poetry in Medieval Literary Theory', *Medium Ævum*, 30 (1961), 1–18.

harmonizing bias of medieval literary categories, that, while recognizing the formal differences between prose and verse, contemporary critics also underlined the fact that both prose and verse depended on the same 'principles of art' (*ars eadem*) (see, for example, Geoffrey of Vinsauf, *Poetria nova*, ll. 1853–82, especially ll. 1873–76, in Faral) and on the same types of 'narration' (*Parisiana Poetria*, v. 303–04).

iv. As well as constituting the two most famous and frequently cited *qualitates carminum*, and in fact almost certainly as a result of their notoriety, *tragedia* and *comedia*, taken together, came to be considered as embracing the whole of literature. Although comedy and tragedy were deemed primarily to incorporate literature's stylistic possibilities, matters of *materia* also seem to have been involved. Tragedy stood for all that was 'high', comedy for everything else (see Mengaldo, in *Dve*, pp. 164–65). This bipolar distinction appears to have its origins in *Ars poetica* 89–98.

v. With the emergence of literature in the vernacular, a new totalizing twofold categorization was established. The relationship between texts written in Latin and those composed in the vernacular was not simply contrastive. As Dante demonstrated several times, vernacular authors and their works had much in common with their classical counterparts (for instance, *Vn* XXV; *Dve* II. 4).

While employing different general criteria, each of the above five categories attempts to circumscribe 'good' literature in its entirety ('in quibus omnis oratio non vitiosa consumitur' [in which every form of speech, if not faulty, is divided], *Ad Her.* IV. 8. 11). Indeed, further classifications existed whose function was also that of providing notions which, when taken together, could embrace any kind of text. However, such systems relied on specific, often highly detailed, structural and ideological elements to accommodate textuality's many forms within a single system; for instance, John of Garland, when presenting the three *species narrationum* (see § vi below), states: 'Aliquo istorum trium utitur quicumque loquitur' [And whoever speaks uses one of these three] (v. 310–11).

vi. Texts could be categorized according to their forms of address (*modus recitandi, species narrationum*):[43]

> Tres enim sunt scripturae caracteres, dicton vel exegematicon, id est enarrativum, in quo auctor solus, dramaticon, id est activum, id est imitativum vel fabulosum, in quo solae personae, micticon, id est mixtum vel cenon, id est commune, in quo poeta et personae loquuntur: primo Terentius et Salemon in Canticis, secundo Lucretius et Salemon in Parabolis,[44] tercio Virgilius in Eneidis utitur et Theodulus. (Bernard of Utrecht, 176–82)

> [For there are three characters/types of writing, *dicton* or *exegematicon*, that is narrative, in which the author alone speaks, *dramaticon*, that is active, or imitative, or fictional, in which only the characters speak, *misticon*, that is mixed, or *caenon*, that is common, in which the poet and the characters speak:

---

43   The term *modus recitandi* is taken from the *Accessus Lucani*, 128–29 (in Huygens, p. 43), while *species narrationum* from *Parisiana Poetria* v. 303.

44   Bernard has transposed the examples relating to the first two 'characters'. For more examples of this category, see Huygens, p. 65; see also *Parisiana Poetria* v. 303–11 and Lawler's note, p. 254.

the first is used by Terence and by Solomon in the Canticles, the second is used by Lucretius and by Solomon in the Parables, the third is used by Virgil in the Aeneid and by Theodolus.]

vii. Texts were categorized according to the ontology of their plots: 'Et quia narrationum [...] tres accepimus species, fabulam, quae versatur in tragoediis atque carminibus, non a veritate modo sed etiam a forma veritatis remota; argumentum, quod falsum sed vero simile comoediae fingunt; historiam, in qua est gestae rei expositio' [And because [...] we have three species of narrative: a fable, which is found in tragedies and poems, detached not only from truth but even from the appearance of truth; a plot, which is the false but verisimilar representation of comedy; history, where we have the narration of deeds] (Quintilian, *Instit. orat.* II. 4. 2).[45] In addition, both *fabulae* and *historiae* were subdivided according to their subject-matter:

> Fabula autem aut est *esopica*, ubi muta finguntur inter se sermocinantia, aut *libistica*, ubi cum animalibus locuntur animalia, aut mixta, quae dicitur mixtologica id est humanae similitudinem vitae retinens [...] Historiae [...] species sunt quatuor, cottidiana qua quod cottidie, kalendaria, ubi quod a kalendis usque ad kalendas, annua ubi quod toto anno, cronica ubi quod multis temporibus fit adnotatur. (Bernard of Utrecht, 129–39)

> [A fable is either *esopica* [from Aesop], where things usually speechless are represented as conversing, or *libistica* [from Libya], where animals speak with animals, or mixed, which is called *mixtologica*, that is which maintains an analogy with human life [...] There are four kinds of history, daily history which records daily events, monthly history, which records the events from one month to the next, annual history, which records the events of an entire year, and the chronicle, which records events over a long period of time.]

Historia was also divided into different *qualitates carminum* (*Parisiana Poetria* v. 333–70, and see pp. 254–55) among which are listed the once 'fictional' tragedies (v. 365–66). Such taxonomic instability, like the flexibility of much of the technical vocabulary, is typical of medieval literary criticism.

viii. Texts were categorized according to the status of their characters: 'Illa species narracionis que consistit in posicione personarum, ne sit uiciosa, vi exquirit proprietates a sex rebus sumptis, que sunt: fortune condicio, etas, sexus, officium, natio, ydioma; quod notatur hiis uersibus in Poetria [*AP* 114–18]' [That species of narrative which is based on the status of its characters, to avoid being faulty, seeks diligently their qualities within the six categories, which are: social status, age, sex, office, birth, and language; as it is explained in these lines of the *Ars poetica*] (*Parisiana Poetria* v. 373–76; see also the note accompanying this passage, p. 256). This classification, while having its point of origin in Cicero (*De inventione* I. 24. 34–25.

---

45   See also Isidore, *Etym.* I. 44. For discussions of this set of distinctions, see Curtius, pp. 452–55; Heinrich Lausberg, *Handbuch der literarischen Rhetorik*, 2 vols (Munich: Max Hueber Verlag, 1960), I, 165–66; Päivi Mehtonen, *Old Concepts and New Poetics: Historia, Argumentum and Fabula in the Twelfth and Early Thirteenth-Century Latin Poetics of Fiction* (Helsinki: Finnish Society of Sciences and Letters, 1996).

36) and in Horace, is also closely related to the doctrine which associated each of the *stili* with a particular social class (see § i above). The attributes of characters were most frequently discussed as part of *descriptio* (see, for instance, Matthew of Vendôme, *Ars versificatoria* I. 74–92, in Faral, pp. 135–43).

ix. Texts were categorized according to their narrative structure (*dispositio, ordo*):

> Artificialis est dispositio, cum materia arte et compendio disponitur, ut in Eneidis, ubi Eneae naufragium prius describitur, postmodum Troiae excidium, cum hoc prius illo factum sit. Naturalis est cum eo ordine quo gestae sunt vel geri potuerunt res describuntur, ut in Lucano primum Cesar de Gallia redire, deinde Italiam invadere, tune Romam dicitur capere, post Pompeium vincere. Communis est cum partim arte, partim prout gestae sunt vel geri potuerunt res scribuntur. (Bernard of Utrecht, 149–57)[46]

> [The narrative structure is 'artificial', when the events are arranged by artistry and abridgment, as in the Aeneid, where first Aeneas's shipwreck is described, and only afterwards the destruction of Troy, even though the latter comes first. It is 'natural', when the events are described in the order in which they have happened or might have happened, as in Lucan Caesar is first said to come back from Gaul, then to invade Italy, then to conquer Rome, and finally to triumph over Pompey. It is 'common', when the events are arranged partly by artistry and partly as they have happened or might have happened.]

x. Texts were categorized according to the ways in which they could be interpreted:

> Dico che [...] questa esposizione conviene essere litterale ed allegorica. E a ciò dare a intendere, si vuol sapere che le scritture si possono intendere e deonsi esponere massimamente per quattro sensi. L'uno si chiama litterale, e questo è quello che [... L'altro si chiama allegorico, e questo è quello che] si nasconde sotto 'l manto di queste favole, ed è una veritade ascosa sotto bella menzogna: sì come quando dice Ovidio che Orfeo facea colla cetera mansuete le fiere, e li arbori e le pietre a sé muovere: che vuol dire che lo savio uomo collo strumento della sua voce faccia mansuescere ed umiliare li crudeli cuori, e faccia muovere alla sua volontade coloro che [non] hanno vita di scienza e d'arte; e coloro che non hanno vita ragionevole alcuna sono quasi come pietre. [...] Veramente li teologi questo senso prendono altrimenti che li poeti [...] Lo terzo senso si chiama morale, e questo è quello che li lettori deono intentamente andare apostando per le scritture ad utilitade di loro e di loro discenti: sì come apostare si può nello Evangelio, quando Cristo salio lo monte per transfigurarsi, che delli dodici Apostoli menò seco li tre: in che moralmente si può intendere che alle secretissime cose noi dovemo avere poca compagnia. Lo quarto senso si chiama anagogico, cioè sovrasenso; e questo è quando spiritualmente si spone una scrittura, la quale ancora [che sia

---

46 For an excellent discussion of narrative 'disposition' (with many examples), see Faral, pp. 55–59. See also Edoardo Vineis, 'La linguistica medioevale: linguistica e grammatica', in *Storia della linguistica*, ed. by Giulio C. Lepschy, 3 vols (Bologna: il Mulino, 1990–94), II, 13–101 (pp. 77–78). Both Matthew of Vendôme and Geoffrey of Vinsauf provide one or two examples of how a work may be brought to a close: see, respectively, *Ars versificatoria* IV. 49–51 and *Documentum* III. 1–6, in Faral, pp. 191–93 & 319–20.

> vera] eziandio nel senso litterale, per le cose significate significa delle superne cose dell'etternal gloria: sì come vedere si può in quello canto del Profeta che dice che nell'uscita del popolo d'Israel d'Egitto Giudea è fatta santa e libera: che avegna essere vero secondo la lettera sia manifesto, non meno è vero quello che spiritualmente s'intende, cioè che nell'uscita dell'anima dal peccato, essa sia fatta santa e libera in sua potestate. (*Conv.* II. I. 2–7)[47]

xi. In line with a rhetorical tradition that went back at least as far as Aristotle, texts could be categorized according to their primary ethical 'intention': 'Nam cum ea que dicimus cuncta vel circa dextrum aliquid vel sinistrum canamus — ut quandoque persuasorie quandoque dissuasorie, quandoque gratulanter quandoque yronice, quandoque laudabiliter quandoque contemptive canere contingit' [Indeed, since all of our words in poetry can be sung either positively or negatively — as we happen to write sometimes to persuade sometimes to dissuade, sometimes to congratulate, sometimes to mock, sometimes to praise and sometimes to blame] (*Dve* II. 14. 2; and see Mengaldo's annotations, pp. 236–37; see also chapters 4 and 5). A work's *intentio* was not only determined by its content but also by its audience and 'style':

> Oratius in suis operibus tripertitis formam humane etatis exprimit; in lirico enim adolescentie dissolutionem; in sermonibus iuventutis castigationem; in epistolis viribus moralitatis edificationem. Differt autem liber sermonum a libro epistolarum quia ibi intendit Oratius de viciorum reprehensione et eradicatione; hic autem de morum sui virtutum instructione et eruditione, ibi ad presentes, hic ad absentes, ibi humili stilo, hic alti loco.[48]

> [In his works that can be divided into three Horace shows the trajectory of human life; in the lyrics he shows the licentiousness of youth, in the satires he shows the correction of youth, and in the letters edification through moral virtues. And the book of satires differs from the book of letters, because in the first Horace draws attention to the condemnation and the obliteration of vices; in the second, he draws attention to the instruction and knowledge of the qualities of his own virtues; there he talks to a present audience, here to an absent one; in the first case with a humble style, in the second with a high style.]

Closely related to categories vi–xi are those classifications, based on precise stylistic criteria, that provide alternative ways of appraising literary style, and hence literary works, to the descriptive model offered by the system of the three *genera dicendi*.

xii. The most important such classification was the distinction between *ornatus facilis* and *ornatus difficilis* ('Unus modus est utendi ornata facilitate, alius modus est utendi ornata difficultate' [One way is to use an adorned simplicity, the other way is to

---

47   Vasoli provides a first-rate commentary to this passage in Dante Alighieri, *Convivio*, ed. by Cesare Vasoli and Domenico De Robertis, in *Opere minori*, 2 vols (Milan and Naples: Ricciardi, 1979–88), I:2, 108–16. See also *Dante e le forme dell'allegoresi*, ed. by Michelangelo Picone (Ravenna: Longo, 1987); *MLTC*, pp. 65–164.

48   Biblioteca Apostolica Vaticana, MS Reg. lat. 1780, fol. 92r, quoted from Reynolds, 'Dante', p. 150.

use an adorned complexity], Geoffrey of Vinsauf, *Documentum* ii. 3. 1). Its difference and independence from the *genera dicendi* are immediately signalled by the fact that it describes literary style in terms of a binary rather than a tripartite distinction and opposition. More significantly, where the 'styles' addressed questions of diction and tended to deal with these in a somewhat vague manner, the *ornatus* were concerned with highly codified issues of rhetorical ornamentation. Thus, the *ornatus difficilis* is based on the use of tropes, while the *ornatus facilis* relies on figures of thought and of words and, additionally, according to Geoffrey of Vinsauf and to John of Garland, on determinations.[49] Although Faral appears to associate 'difficult' ornamentation with the 'high style', since both were referred to by means of the epithet *gravis* (pp. 86–89), there is little doubt that, in medieval criticism, the *stili* and the *ornatus* were considered to be discrete systems and were discussed separately. For instance, John of Garland deals in depth with the *ornatus* in Book ii of his treatise and with the *stili* in Book v. However, what is more significant is the fact that, when he alludes *en passant* to the *rota Vergilii* and the three 'styles' during his presentation of 'difficult' and 'easy' ornamentation, he makes no effort to connect the two types of classification (ii. 116–23).[50] Lawler effectively summarizes the fundamental differences between the two categories: 'one can deal with a low subject, choosing words appropriate to the low style; if the words are tropes, that is *ornatus difficilis*, but it is still low style' (*Parisiana Poetria*, p. 237).[51] This key aspect is especially clear

49   On the *ornatus*, see Faral, pp. 89–97; Lawler, in *Parisiana Poetria*, pp. 236–37; Douglas Kelly, pp. 79–82. Faral provides a clear definition of *determinatio*: 'l'opération par laquelle on adjoint au nom soit un verbe, soit un adjectif, soit un autre nom qui lui sert de complément; ou par laquelle on adjoint soit à l'adjectif, soit au verbe l'un des compléments qu'ils ont l'habitude d'admettre' (p. 97). Geoffrey discusses determination in *Poetria nova* 1761–841 and *Documentum* ii. 3. 48–102, while John examines it in *Parisiana Poetria* ii. 147–265.

50   As I hope is becoming clear from the various examples cited so far, medieval critical terminology was denotatively volatile, so that the same word could often have different meanings and designate different textual characteristics. For instance, without in any way referring to the same textual features, the *Ad Herennium*'s definition of the 'high' style — 'Gravis est quae constat ex verborum gravium levi et ornata constructione' [The high style consists of weighty words ordered in a smooth and adorned structure] — not only shares with discussions of rhetorical ornamentation the term *gravis* but also the term *levis* (which was an alternative for *facilis*; see, for example, Geoffrey of Vinsauf, *Poetria nova* l. 1094: 'sermo [...] levis' [simple speech]). Whenever we attempt to understand a term's significance, we have to begin by considering the kind of text in which it appears, the category or topic to which it is referring, the intended audience, and the date of its usage (see Douglas Kelly, pp. 103–04; Henry A. Kelly; Lucia Lazzerini, 'La trasmutazione insensibile: intertestualità e metamorfismi nella lirica trobadorica dalle origini alla codificazione cortese', *Medioevo romanzo*, 18 (1993), 153–205 (p. 187)). What makes the situation even more confusing is that, while, in medieval culture in general, critical language was semantically highly unstable, within a single text or author, terminological usage could be precise and consistent. A further complication stems from the fact that a particular textual feature was rarely defined by a single term. As the author of the 'Materia' commentary reminds us, synonyms proliferated: 'Tres enim sunt manerie dicendi, quas alii stilos, alii figuras, alii caracteres appellant' [There are three manners of speaking, which some call styles, some call figures, and others characters].

51   Faral is not alone in connecting the *ornatus difficilis* with the 'high style' (see, for instance, Douglas Kelly, pp. 79–81, whose presentation is difficult to follow and shows little sensitivity to the kind of issues connected to medieval literary jargon highlighted in the previous footnote). Although, in the *poetriae*, as we have seen, the relationship between the two *ornatus* and the three *stili* is fluid,

in the ways in which Occitan poets used the terms *clus* and *leu* (as well as their synonyms) to describe literary practices that had little to do with the formal concerns connected to the three 'styles'.[52] Finally, as further evidence of that fluid tension between harmony and contrast that lies at the basis of medieval critical theory and which is the main reason why a medieval text could shift between literary identities, it is noteworthy that 'sunt quaedam alia documenta [*conversiones*] quae valent ad ornatum, sive ornatus ille pertineat ad facilitatem, sive ad difficultatem' [there are certain other constructions [conversions/transformations] that are very strong in the *ornatus*, whether this concerns simplicity, or complexity] (Geoffrey of Vinsauf, *Documentum* II. 3. 103, and see his presentation as far as 131). Indeed, the relationship between 'easy' and 'difficult' ornamentation was potentially so precarious that an experimental poet such as Guiraut de Bornelh increasingly blurred their differences (Di Girolamo, *I trovatori*, p. 118). There is little doubt that the *facilis-difficilis* categorization finds its most interesting and sophisticated expression in vernacular poetic theory. Rather than simply addressing matters of rhetorical presentation, the two terms were also employed to describe a text's interpretability — the extent to which a work was or was not easy to understand. For instance, following Occitan precedents linked to discussions of *clus* forms of writing, Dante defines the 'subtle style' as follows: 'e ["Le dolci rime"] dice "sottile" quanto alla sentenza delle parole, che sottilmente argomentando e disputando procedono', *Conv.* IV. 2. 13); and it is important to note that matters of understanding were not (necessarily) related to matters of style (see the discussion of 'subtlety' in § xiii). As a result of including within their remit issues of both form and content, and following a development which recalls the system centred on tragedy and comedy, the two types of *trobar* came to stand for poetry *tout court*. In the canzone to Giacomo da Leona, when Guittone praises his addressee as the incarnation of the ideal writer, he declares:

there is one early fourteenth-century text which appears to imply that the *ornatus difficilis* is the special preserve of the *superior stilus*. In Book II of the *De vulgari eloquentia*, Dante explains that of the four 'gradus constructionum' (6. 4) only the fourth, which is based on the *transumptio*, the most sophisticated of the tropes, is fit for the 'tragic' canzone: 'est et sapidus [gradus] et venustus etiam et excelsus, qui est dictatorum illustrium, ut "Eiecta maxima parte florum de sinu tuo, Florentia, nequicquam Trinacriam Totila secundus adivit". Hunc gradum constructionis excellentissimum nominamus, et hic est quem querimus cum suprema venemur, ut dictum est. Hoc solum illustres cantiones inveniuntur contexte' [This [degree of syntactic construction] is flavoured and elegant, and also the highest, and it is typical of illustrious writers, as in 'With the majority of flowers having been cast out of your bosom, Florence, the second Totila advanced in vain towards Trinacria'. I call this degree of syntactic construction the most excellent, and this is what we seek when we hunt for the best. Illustrious *canzoni* are found to be composed only with this degree of sophistication] (*Dve* II. 6. 4–6; and see Mengaldo's notes, pp. 182–84). As I shall discuss in more detail in the next subsection, in trying to give precise and exclusive characteristics to poetry in the 'illustrious vernacular', Dante attempted to counter the flexibility inherent in medieval literary categorizations by forcing these into a new system centred on the *genera dicendi* and which rested on the notion that particular elements were exclusively tied to particular 'styles'.

52 See, in particular, Ulrich Mölk, *Trobar clus tobar leu: Studien zur Dichtungstheorie der Trobadors* (Munich: Fink, 1968). This seminal study ranges well beyond the troubadours to offer, inter alia, an excellent analysis of Latin *difficultas* and *facilitas*. See also Costanzo Di Girolamo, *I trovatori* (Turin: Bollati Boringhieri, 1989), pp. 100–19; Elena Landoni, *La teoria letteraria dei provenzali* (Florence: Olschki, 1989), pp. 29–46. See also n. 22 above.

> Tu, frate meo, vero bon trovatore
> in piana e 'n sottile rima e 'n cara
> e in soavi e saggi e cari motti.[53]

The same idea appears to be present in Dante's 'manifesto' poem, 'Le dolci rime d'amor ch'i' solia', where the creative possibilities open to a poet are two: the 'soave stile' (10) and the 'rima aspr' e sottile' (14). It returns again, albeit in a more complex guise, in *Purgatorio* XXVI's assessment of Romance poetry. Thus, the canto, which serves as Dante's main statement in the *Commedia* on the vernacular poetic tradition in general, presents Arnaut Daniel as the supreme representative of *trobar clus*, while introducing Guido Guinizzelli as an 'authority' in the alternative way of writing: the 'rime d'amor [...] dolci e leggiadre' (99) and the 'dolci detti' (112).[54] Dante's use of the terminology relating to *facilitas* and *difficultas* is highly complex. It involves some of the most cherished aspects of his work such as his experimentation, the 'illustrious vernacular', and, most notably, his 'comedía'. Given that Dante often applied the same terms drawn from this tradition to different areas of his *œuvre*, as well as to the works of others, their meaning and value are not constant. It is a limitation of Dante scholarship that in-depth diachronic studies of terms such as *dolce*, *aspro*, *soave*, etc. and of their shifting inter-relationships have still to be undertaken.[55]

xiii. Texts were categorized according to their phonic qualities. Dante explains this system when glossing the line, 'con rima aspr' e sottile': 'dice aspra quanto al suono de lo dittato, che a tanta materia non conviene essere leno' (*Conv.* IV. 2. 13). Consequently, there were texts whose sound was 'sweet' and others that were characterized by the 'harshness' of their timbres. As with other categories, this system too did not correlate conveniently with any other classification. Hence, while Dante alludes to 'rima aspr' e sottile' in 'Le dolci rime', in the *De vulgari eloquentia*, he refers to Cino and himself as poets 'qui dulcius subtiliusque poetati vulgariter sunt' [who have written vernacular poetry more sweetly and elegantly] (I. 10. 2). It goes without saying that terms such as *dolce* and *aspro* could also refer to textual properties other than exclusively phonic ones.[56]

xiv. In a system that combined both structural and stylistic criteria, texts could be categorized according to whether they 'amplified' (*amplificatio*) or 'abbreviated' (*abbreviatio, brevitas*) their subject-matter:

---

53 'Comune perta fa comun dolore' (XLVI), in *Le rime di Guittone d'Arezzo*, ed. by Francesco Egidi (Bari: Laterza, 1940).

54 See Lino Pertile, 'Dante's *Comedy* Beyond the *Stilnovo*', *Lectura Dantis Virginiana*, 13 (1993), 47–77.

55 Useful preliminary observations on this vocabulary may be found in *Dante's Lyric Poetry*, ed. by Kenelm Foster and Patrick Boyde, 2 vols (Oxford: Clarendon Press, 1967), II, 213–14, 274–75; Mengaldo's annotations in *Dve*, pp. 86–87; De Robertis's annotations in *Conv.*, pp. 494 and 497.

56 For instance, on the wealth of connotations associated with the notion of sweetness, see Jean Chatillon, 'Dulcedo, Dulcedo Dei', in DSAM, III, 1777–95; Siegfried Heinimann, 'Dulcis: Ein Beitrag zur lateinisch-romanischen Stilgeschichte des Mittelalters', in *Studia Philologica: homenaje ofrecido a Dámaso Alonso par sus amigos y discipulos con ocasión de su 60º aniversario*, 3 vols (Madrid: Editorial Gredos, 1961), I, 215–32; Claudia Villa, *La 'Lectura Terentii'* (Padua: Antenore, 1984), pp. 39–42.

> Principio varium dedit ars praescripta tenorem:
> Te vocat ulterior progressus. Dirige gressum
> Ulterius cursumque viae, premente figura.
> Curritur in bivio: via namque vel ampla vel arta,
> Vel fluvius vel rivus erit; vel tractius ibis,
> Vel cursim salies; vel rem brevitate notabis,
> Vel longo sermone trahes
> (Geoffrey of Vinsauf, *Poetria nova*, ll. 203–9)

[At the beginning, the abovementioned principles of art have suggested various paths: the next part calls you onward. Direct your steps and your course further, with the image firmly in mind. The journey is at a crossroads: and the road will be wide or narrow, a river or a brook it will be; you will proceed at a moderate pace, or leap swiftly; you will write about the subject with brevity, or you will stretch it in a long discourse.]

As with the 'difficult'–'easy' distinction, both types of effect were achieved through the selection and application of rhetorical figures. 'Amplification' was attained by having recourse to repetition, periphrasis, comparison, apostrophe, personification, digression, description, and opposition (*Poetria nova*, ll. 219–689). 'Abbreviation', on the other hand, resulted from the use of *emphasis, articulus,* the ablative absolute, 'prudentia docti | In dictis non dicta notet' [let the discretion of the skilled convey the implicit in the explicit] (ll. 697–98), asyndeton, the fusion of clauses, and from the avoidance of repetition (ll. 690–736). Although the present category and the *ornatus* are both closely tied to the figures of rhetoric, they constitute two quite different systems. Not only do they define the formal character of a text in quite separate ways (although both also cut across the distinctions established by the *manerie dicendi*), but each also undermines the other's key contrastive characteristics, As Geoffrey notes:

> Sit brevis aut longus, se semper sermo coloret
> Intus et exterius, sed discernendo colorem [*difficilis* or *facilis*]
> Ordine discreto. (Geoffrey of Vinsauf, *Poetria nova*, ll. 737–39)

[Be it brief or long, a discourse should always be adorned in meaning and form [within and without], but choosing the ornament [complex or simple] according to discretion.]

Thus, for instance, a *brevis* text can be categorized as either 'difficult' or 'easy'; while a *facilis* one can be either 'brief' or 'long' depending on whether it employs *articulus* (ll. 1122–23) or description (ll. 1238–40). Telling proof, once again, of how inadvisable it is to attempt to constrain a medieval text within any single descriptive critical category.[57]

xv. Finally, texts could be categorized with respect to their authors. This mode of classification was divided into two: (a) according to specific classes of writers, and (b) according to the status and literary competence of particular writers.

---

57   On 'amplification' and 'abbreviation', see Rita Copeland, *Rhetoric, Hermeneutics, and Translation in the Middle Ages: Vernacular Traditions and Academic Texts* (Cambridge: Cambridge University Press, 1991), pp. 21–32, 56–62, 82–96, 158–78; Faral, pp. 61–85; Lawler, *Parisiana Poetria*, pp. 246–50.

The first of these two schemes categorized authors in terms of different ways of writing and different types of texts. It had close links with the various textual forms listed under *scripturae* (see § ii):

> Qui libros componunt vel exponunt auctores vel poetae vel vates vel commentatores id est expositores dicuntur, auctores eo quod latinam augeant linguam vel quod acta, id est historias, scribant, vel a greco *autenten* quod est principale; poetae sunt qui falsa immiscent veris: *poetes* enim fictor vel formator sonare videtur, unde poema unius et poesis multorum opus librorum traditur; vates a vi mentis qua futura predicebant dicuntur, vel quia insani habebantur vel a viendis id est flectendis carminibus: viere enim flectere dicitur, unde et vietus, vimen, vitis. (Bernard of Utrecht, 27–35).[58]

> [Those who write or explain books are called authors, poets, seers, commentators that is expositors; authors because they 'augment' the Latin language, or else because they write what has been done, that is history, or from the Greek *autenten*, which means primary; poets are those who mix falsity and truth: *poetes* indeed seems to mean one who creates or moulds, thus by poem is meant a single book and by poesis (poetic art) a work of many books; seers are so called from the ability of their mind to foresee the future, or because they were considered insane, or from *viendis* [binding], that is stretching, the texts: *viere* in fact means to stretch, hence *vietus* [wrinkled], *vimen* [twig], and *vitis* [vine].]

The second scheme, categorizing literature according to the status and capabilities of particular writers, was based on two main taxonomies. The first distinguished between 'major' and 'minor' authors: 'Secularis disciplinae congrua meae tarditati dare spoponderas olim rudimenta, quibus a minoribus quibuscumque auctoribus inciperem et per hos ad maiores pervenirem et gradus auctorum inferiorum occasio mihi fierent in discendo superiorum' [You had once promised that you would provide the basic principles of this long-standing discipline which would be fit for my slowness of mind, which minor authors or whichever authors I should start from and through them reach the major authors, and how the levels of the more humble authors would provide me with the occasion to learn the greater authors] (Conrad of Hirsau, 29–32). What is less clear is which *auctores* belonged to which group. Birger Munk Olsen tentatively concluded that 'come ipotesi di lavoro è [...] possibile delimitare un gruppo di dieci autori maggiori, cioè otto poeti: Giovenale, Lucano,

---

58   For a different categorization of writers to that proposed by Bernard, see: 'quadruplex est modus faciendi librum. Aliquis enim scribit aliena, nihil addendo vel mutando et iste mere dicitur scriptor. Aliquis scribit aliena addendo, sed non de suo; et iste compilator dicitur. Aliquis scribit et aliena et sua, sed aliena tamquam principalia, et sua tamquam annexa ad evidentiam; et iste dicitur commentator non auctor. Aliquis scribit et sua et aliena, sed sua tamquam principalia, aliena tamquam annexa ad confirmationem et talis debet dici auctor' [there are four ways of writing a book. One writes somebody else's ideas, without adding or changing anything; and such a one is called a mere scribe. Another writes somebody else's ideas and adds something, but not of his own; and such a one is called a compiler. Another writes both somebody else's and his own ideas, but he primarily writes the former and his own as reinforcing the evidence; and such a one is called a commentator, not an author. Finally, one writes both his own and somebody else's ideas, but he primarily writes his own and those of others as confirmation of the evidence, and such a one should be called an author] (Bonaventure, *In librum Sententiarum*, *prooemium*, *quaest.* 4, *conclusio*, in vol. I, p. 14, col. 2). See also, Isidore, *Etym.* VIII. 7. 4–9.

Orazio, Ovidio, Persio, Stazio, Terenzio e Virgilio, e due prosatori: Cicerone e Sallustio'.[59] As regards the 'minor' authors the situation is more fluid (see Munk Olsen, pp. 6–7, 57–74; Gianferrari). It has been suggested that by distributing his classical authors between *Inferno* IV and *Purgatorio* XXII, Dante was drawing up his own list of *maiores* and *minores*.[60] The second scheme into which the *auctores* were organized associated an author or a group of authors with each of the three 'styles' of the *genera dicendi*. As is well known, Dante's presentation of the poets of the 'bella scola' is based on this distinction (see p. 292 below). In line with the amorphousness of other categorizations, except as regards Terence, who was closely tied to comedy, and Virgil, who was either linked to tragedy or, via the *rota Vergilii*, to all the *genera*, the relationship between most other authors and the three *stili* was far from fixed (see the discussion of Horace and satire in Reynolds, 'Orazio satiro' and 'Dante').

More generally, and in contrast to the two preceding codified authorial systems, particular writers and/or their texts were most frequently employed in the Middle Ages simply as storehouses of examples with which to illustrate a wide array of textual features. Texts and authors could be used as *exempla* in this manner because they were the concrete manifestations of a view of literature whose central tenet — as I hope my catalogue of fifteen categories has demonstrated — was the belief in the fundamental complexity and richness of writing.[61] The Middle Ages proliferated different descriptive critical classifications as evidence of this fact. No single category could encompass a text's complexity and define its identity. Indeed, I suspect that the success and development of particular categories were to a large degree conditioned not only by the extent to which they were able to cover areas left untouched by other classifications, but also — as we have seen — by the extent to which they could stand in clear opposition to these other classifications. It was only by considering a work in terms of the many available systems that some idea of its nature would emerge. This is especially clear when we consider discussions of individual texts. Thus, medieval critics underlined the composite character of a text vis-à-vis the different classificatory groupings. When he examines the *De bello civile*, the unknown author of an *accessus* to Lucan observes: 'Liber iste habet stilum grandiloquuum et mixtum modum; est etiam historicus et tamen satyricus [...] Ordinem quoque habet naturalem' [This book has a grand style and a mixed mode; it is historical and yet satyrical [...] And it has a natural [narrative] structure] (*Accessus Lucani*, 145–49, in Huygens, p. 44). This manner of analysing and describing a text is particularly evident in Bernard of Utrecht's *Commentum in Theodolum*:

59   Birger Munk Olsen, *I classici nel canone scolastico altomedievale* (Spoleto: Centro Italiano di Studi sull'Alto Medioevo Italiano, 1991), p. 6, and see also pp. 4–7, 21–73.

60   On Dante and the *auctores*, see, for instance, *Dante e la 'bella scola' di poesia*, ed. by Amilcare A. Iannucci (Ravenna: Longo, 1993); Michelangelo Picone, 'Dante e il canone degli *Auctores*', *Rassegna europea di letteratura italiana*, 1 (1993), 9–26. See also Chapter 9.

61   Other catalogues of medieval textual categorizations, though less substantial than the one presented here, and often based on modern critical notions, may be found in Jauss, 'Littérature médiévale et théorie des genres', p. 92, 'Theory of Genres and Medieval Literature', pp. 83–87, and 'Cinq modèles d'identification esthétique'; Douglas Kelly, pp. 68–88, 141–44.

Carminis qualitas bucolicon est, id est pastorale, a digniori parte tractum id est boum custodia, quamvis opilionum et caprariorum vel subulcorum hic referantur verba [...] Haec tria in Theodolo possunt inveniri: argumentum est a principio usque *Primus Creteis,* fabula autem et historia donec prope finem, ubi et argumentum esse videtur. Intentio Theodoli esse videtur quasdam de ecclesiasticis et paganis scriptis conferre sententias [...] Ordo autem, qui et dispositio a plerisque vocatur, artificialis est in Theodolo [...] Explanatio etiam in libris necessaria creditur, quam quadrifariam accipiunt: ad literam, ad sensum, allegoricos et moraliter [...] Hae omnes non semper in eodem simul inveniuntur, in Theodolo tamen, licet non ubique, inveniri possunt [...] Tres enim aiunt orationis esse stilos, humilem, quo iste et Virgili ut in Bucolicis utuntur [...] tercio [form of speech] Virgilius in Eneidis utitur et Theodolus hic. (81–83, 141–45, 148–50, 160–62, 164–65, 167–69, 182)

[The kind of poetry is bucolic, that is pastoral, which is drawn from the more honourable element, namely the care of oxen, although there are passages about shepherds, goatherds, and swineherds [...] These three categories can be found in Theodolus: *argumentum* is found from the beginning until *First of the Cretans,* *fabula* and *historia* until almost the end, where it seems to become *argumentum* again. Theodolus's intention, as it seems, is to convey certain observations about sacred and pagan writings [...] But in Theodolus the structure, which is also called disposition by many, is artificial [...] Explanation is believed to be necessary even in books, which may include four different kinds of explanation: literal, as to meaning, allegorical, and moral [...] all of these kinds are not always found together in the same work, but in Theodolus they can be, although not everywhere [...] Indeed they say that there are three forms of speech, humble which both our author and Virgilius use in the *Eclogues* [...] the third is used by Virgil in the *Aeneid* and by Theodolus here.]

What is striking about this description of the eclogue is that it underlines that a text, as well as spanning different categories, may, in its various parts, actually embrace the discrete constituent elements that go to make up a particular classification. This is especially interesting because, in the abstract, medieval critics tended to underline the *differenciae* separating such elements, thereby implying that they would not be found together in the same text — a claim that was undermined when actual works were examined. Medieval commentators and writers were fascinated by the composite, even hybrid character of texts. It is thus not difficult to appreciate how, in such a cultural context, Dante would have been stimulated to compose the *Commedia,* the 'hybrid', composite work par excellence.

Ultimately, it was not the categories that defined a text; instead each text defined itself in terms of these, as well as the various shifting contacts it established, potentially at least, with every other text. Although similar works were often brought together, as in the vernacular lyric manuscript collections (see Picone, 'Songbook'), the dominant stress was, on the one hand, on the uniqueness of each text and, on the other, on its inter-relationship with the tradition as a whole rather than with any delimited group of works — a dual perspective that the rich system of classifications obviously made possible and encouraged. Our modern notion of genre, together with the new tags that have been invented to categorize the literature of the Middle Ages, fails to capture this key feature of medieval thinking about literature. On account of its emphasis on exclusion rather than on inclusion, such modern terminological usage goes against that highly stratified, nuanced, composite, and all-embracing view of literature and textuality that dominated in the Middle Ages (and which became yet more complex and rich with the advent of vernacular literature and vernacular critical terminology). It is surely noteworthy that such an idea of literature neatly dovetails with the dominant medieval organic conception of reality as plurality in oneness. It also conforms to the 'compilatory' character of medieval summatic writing and of many manuscript books.[62] Medieval thinking about literature thus conforms to the great ideological structures of the day; and it would have been odd, not least given the intimate relationship between textuality and knowledge, if the opposite had been the case.

Despite the expositional usefulness of my approach, it is artificial and misleading to treat the different categories separately. Together the categories formed that overarching system for defining literature that we have largely transferred and restricted to the notion of genre. Together they constituted the medieval idea of literature and served as the means with which to establish the identity of any text. They allowed both writers and readers considerable room to manoeuvre when composing or analysing a text. As long as authors followed the basic dictates regarding the proper relationship between form and content (the doctrine of *convenientiae*), they had considerable freedom when it came to deciding how to present and develop the remainder of their works. Such a view of composition fits in well with the creative and independent emphasis that the Middle Ages gave to the practices of *imitatio* and *aemulatio*. Similarly, *lectores* had considerable freedom as regards which aspects of a text to concentrate on in their critical work. By relying on genre, we have taken an extremely blunt instrument to a literary universe whose hallmark is its nuanced fluidity, its sensitivity to individual expression, and its constant awareness of writing in general.

Yet, paradoxically, despite everything that I have said so far, one category did seem to go against that flexible sense of literature which, I strongly believe, dominated medieval literary reflection. The principle of the *genera dicendi*, with its dogmatic

---

62   See *L'enciclopedismo medievale*, ed. by Michelangelo Picone (Ravenna: Longo, 1994). See also Zygmunt G. Barański, ' "Oh come è grande la mia impresa" (*Conv.* IV. vii. 4): Notes Towards Defining the *Convivio*'', in *Dante's 'Convivio' or How to Restart Writing in Exile*, ed. by Franziska Meier (Bern: Peter Lang, 2018), pp. 9–26; Bernard Guenée, 'Lo storico e la compilazione nel XIII secolo', in *Aspetti della letteratura latina nel secolo XIII*, ed. by Claudio Leonardi and Guido Orlandi (Perugia: Regione dell'Umbria; Florence: La Nuova Italia, 1986), pp. 57–76; Alastair J. Minnis, 'Late-medieval Discussions of *Compilatio* and the Role of the *Compilator*', *Beiträge zur Geschichte der deutschen Sprache und Literatur*, 101 (1979), 385–421, and '*Nolens auctor sed compilator reputari*: The Late-medieval Discourse of Compilation', in *La Méthode critique au Moyen Âge*, ed. by Mireille Chazan and Gilbert Dahan (Turnhout: Brepols, 2008), pp. 47–63; Malcolm B. Parkes, 'The Influence of the Concepts of *Ordinatio* and *Compilatio* on the Development of the Book', in *Medieval Learning and Literature: Essays Presented to Richard William Hunt*, ed. by Jonathan James Graham Alexander and Margaret T. Gibson (Oxford: Clarendon Press, 1975), pp. 115–41; Richard H. Rouse and Mary A. Rouse, '*Ordinatio* and *Compilatio* Revisited', in *'Ad litteram': Authoritative Texts and Medieval Readers*, ed. by Mark D. Jordan and Kent Emery Jr (Notre Dame, IN: University of Notre Dame Press, 1992), pp. 113–34. But see also Neil Hathaway, '*Compilatio*: From Plagiarism to Compiling', *Viator*, 20 (1989), 19–44.

insistence on the need to keep the 'styles' apart, even when it acknowledged the possibility of some limited contamination between them, appears to have curtailed a writer's creative freedom, especially in the light of the doctrine's wide popularity; or, rather, writers who relied on the *genera* as their principal point of reference could create the impression that they were needlessly retricting their artistic powers. And saying this, I have at last moved squarely into Dante's orbit.

3. Dante and the 'Qualities' of Literature

The history of Dante's relationship to the literary classifications of his day and to the technical language on which these were based is still far from being written. This is largely due to two causes. First, Dantists, like other medievalists, have tended not to acknowledge (at least not until relatively recently) the complexity and sophistication of medieval literary theory and criticism. Second, those interested in Dante's thinking about literature have preferred to emphasize the originality of the poet's reflections rather than to explain their ties to contemporary critical discourses and attitudes. Given the considerable amount of work that still needs to be done with respect to this area of Dante's *œuvre* (but see Chapter 8), in this section, I want simply to indicate some general lines that might be followed when endeavouring to assess the impact on the poet of medieval definitions of literature.

Any discussion of Dante's relationship to the critical ideas of his day needs to begin by recognizing that for all the poet's seeming 'objectivity' when examining matters of literature — for instance, in chapter XXV of the *Vita nova* or in the *De vulgari eloquentia* — his aims were in fact highly 'subjective'. Dante was concerned to exploit current literary values, conventions, and approaches in order to establish his own poetic *auctoritas* and to legitimate his experimentation and his claims regarding the nature of language and literature, claims that were generally linked not so much to contemporary literary and linguistic practices but to the nature of his own art. Thus, in itself, the presence in Dante's *œuvre* of the categorizations listed in the previous section is unremarkable. Indeed, given that the categorizations constituted the basic terms in which matters of literature were understood and discussed in the Middle Ages, it would be astonishing if they had not left their mark on Dante and his writings (accordingly, I was able to illustrate several of the categories with examples drawn from the poet's works). What is significant, however, are the means by which Dante bent and adapted the categories, and hence the view of literature that they supported, to conform to personal ends. In the poet's self-centred literary universe, the categories no longer serve the general aims of criticism; instead they are made to serve a singular, often idiosyncratic, poetics (in a manner that recalls the ways in which Dante distorted and minimized Guittone's far from inconsiderable achievements so that they might fit with his account of the character and history of the vernacular poetic tradition). Nor did Dante approach the various categorizations in a consistent manner. For example, as we shall see, in the *De vulgari eloquentia*, Dante championed the *genera dicendi* as the most effective scheme for encouraging and defining literary activity; in the *Commedia*, on the other hand, he attacked the *genera dicendi* as the chief obstacle to literary progress and artistic independence.

Dante was ever ready to modify his views and to accommodate these to the specific needs of individual works. His career was marked by changes in points of view (although what has not yet been adequately studied are the means by which Dante vindicated his reversals of opinion, while, at the same time, claiming an overarching coherence for his artistic and intellectual experiences). Consequently, when examining the poet's debts to medieval systems of classifying and discussing literature, it is necessary to contextualize his borrowings and especially the transformations that particular classifying systems underwent at his hands.

Nevertheless, one aspect of Dante's relationship to the critical discourses of his day remained consistent. He was keenly aware of the room to manoeuvre that contemporary literary theory and practice afforded a writer who wished to experiment. Indeed, it is reasonable to surmise that it was as a result of the flexibility with which literature was typically approached that Dante felt authorized to shift between different critical positions. Equally, his consistent pursuit of innovation in his writings reveals a confidence that his striving after *novitas* did not overstep the boundaries of contemporary literary ideology and would be appreciated by at least the more sophisticated among his readers. If this had not been the case, Dante ran the danger of having his work ignored or dismissed as aberrant.[63] To emphasize the strength of the poet's ties to his culture does not mean to diminish his achievements or to deny his originality. Rather it means to attempt to explain these aspects of his art in light of the possibilities and conventions of his world; even if, in practice, Dante pushed those conventions and possibilities to their very limits. For all Dante's 'modernity', for all the uniqueness of each of his major works, and for all the sharply distinctive individuality of his vision, his art remains rooted in the intellectual soil of the late Middle Ages. Indeed, the foundations of Dante's unique attainments can be said to lie in his having recognized the considerable freedoms that his culture offered a writer and intellectual prepared to take calculated risks.

How did Dante think theoretically about literature as a system? More specifically, how did he categorize literature? One thing is certain. Like the rest of his culture, he did not have a sense of genre comparable to that which modern scholarship anachronistically imposes on the Middle Ages. At the same time, the manner in which he applied his concept of *comedía* to the 'poema sacro' (*Par.* xxv. 1) does, *mutatis mutandis*, reveal some interesting similarities (as well as fundamental dissimilarities) with the modern idea of genre. Consequently, Dante did not have recourse to a technical term akin to our notion of genre. Thus, as we shall see, neither his use of *genus/genere* nor that of *stilus/stilo,-e* bear such a meaning. Where Dante does differ from many other medieval literary critics, however, is in the care, consistency, and discrimination with which he employed vocabulary such as *genus* and *stilus*. Although it was common in medieval literary criticism to treat these and related terms as synonyms, Dante rejected such lax usage. In keeping with his customary linguistic rigour and sensibility — a rigour and a sensibility that were particularly acute when it came to technical language — he attentively distinguished between the terms, using each one for specific and distinct purposes.

63   For a fuller discussion of these matters, see Chapter 7.

Thus, to allude generically to the 'manner', 'type', or 'way of writing', Dante utilized *modo*.[64] In the *Convivio*, he employed *maniera* with a meaning closely related to *modo*. However, it is far from insignificant, especially in the context of my present argument, that the poet should have employed *maniera* with a restricted sense rather than with the flexible value typical of vernacular usage, where the term could designate the manner of any kind of communicative act (see n. 22). Dante, on the other hand, utilized *maniera* to indicate exclusively spoken rather than written language: 'ne li quali [the prophets], per molte maniere di parlare e per molti modi, Dio avea loro parlato' (II. 5. 1), and 'Ma però che in ciascuna maniera di sermone lo dicitore massimamente dee intendere a la persuasione' (II. 6. 6).[65]

In the established canon of the poet's works, *genus/genere* — like *maniera* — is never applied to matters of literature, but is solely used with its philosophical and scientific meanings. In line with Aristotle's definitions in the *Metaphysics* (V. 28, 1024ab), Dante's *genus/genere*:

> Sta sia per l'ininterrotta generazione di una specie di viventi, sia per la totalità di coloro che discendono da un'unica causa, sia per indicare il sostrato delle differenze specifiche e quindi il primo elemento della definizione, sia, infine, per categoria, perché tutte le categorie sono di genere diverso in quanto nessuna è riducibile a un'altra.[66]

Stilus/stilo, too, is utilized by the poet with considerable care and precision. Unlike the somewhat loose usage of *stilus* in texts such as the 'Materia' commentary, Dante, in keeping with the Ciceronian tradition, restores to the term its exclusively formal connotations (indeed, it is just about synonymous, I would say, with our modern notion of 'style'). And he is unswerving in this. 'Lo stilo de la sua loda' (*Vn* XXVI. 4) refers to the form in which the praise of Beatrice is to be expressed; both the 'più alto stilo' (*Conv.* I. 4. 13) and 'lo mio soave stilo' (*Conv.* IV. canzone, 10) in which the poet had talked about love ('trattar d'amore', 11) can be glossed as 'modo' (IV. 2. 11), namely, as the 'manner' in which a subject is formally presented;[67] while

---

64   See Antonietta Bufano, 'modo', in ED, III, 983–85 (p. 984).

65   See Bruna Cordati Martinelli, 'maniera', in ED, III, 805. See also Anon., 'maneries', in ED, III, 801; Mengaldo's annotations in *Dve*, p. 190. In the *Commedia*, Dante used *modo* to refer to speech: 'parlare in modo soave e benigno' (*Purg.* XIX. 44); 'Ed ecco piangere e cantar s'udíe | "Labia mëa, Domine" per modo | tal' (*Purg.* XXIII. 10–12); 'e a quel modo | ch'e' ditta dentro' (*Purg.* XXIV. 53–54). However, even though the poet replaces the *Convivio*'s *maniera* with *modo*, his usage continues to be consistent and clear, since both terms are used exclusively with reference to the *vox*. Consequently, as regards Justinian's famous monologue which is introduced as follows: 'e cosí chiusa chiusa mi rispuose | nel modo che 'l seguente canto canta' (*Par.* V. 138–39), it seems likely that 'canto' refers to the Emperor's speech rather than to the metrical structure that reports it.

66   Alfonso Maierù, 'genere', in ED, III, 108–09 (p. 108). See also Alfonso Maierù, 'generazione', in ED, III, 107–08. In a similar manner, Dante limits *species/specie* to its philosophical meanings; see Alfonso Maierù, 'specie', in ED, V, 367–69. For additional discussion of these terms, see the next subsection.

67   In light of the association between *stilo* and *modo*, one might conclude that Dante considered the two words to be synonymous: 'Dico: "poi che d'aspettare mi pare, diporroe", cioè lascerò stare, "lo mio stilo", cioè modo, "soave" che d'amore parlando [ho]e tenuto' (*Conv.* IV. 2. 11). Yet, given the ways in which he normally applies the terms, this is unlikely. *Stilo*, in Dante, refers exclusively to literary form, while *modo* is less semantically specific. However, when he needed to gloss *stilo*, in

the 'dolce stil novo' (*Purg.* XXIV. 57) is the form in which the 'inspiration' (53) of the 'dittator' (59) is granted poetic shape, as the technical verb *significare* (54), namely, to give symbolic, in this instance linguistic, form, underlines.[68]

Dante's use of *stilus* in the *De vulgari eloquentia*, although consistent with his usage in the rest of his *œuvre*, presents some distinctive and interesting nuances. The poet employs *stilus* to designate the formal elements in which different *materiae* are 'sung': 'ea que digna sunt illo [the illustrious vernacular] cantari discrevimus [...] et modum cantionarium selegimus illis [...] et, ut ipsum perfectius edocere possimus, quedam iam preparavimus, stilum videlicet atque carmen, nunc de constructione agamus' [I have determined what subjects are worthy of being sung in that vernacular [...] and I have selected for these the form of the canzone [...] and, in order to teach the use of the vernacular more accurately, I have already laid out some of its elements, such as style and verse, now let me talk about its construction] (II. 6. 1). As Dante mentions, he had indeed already discussed *stilus* (II. 4. 5–8). However, that presentation cannot be said to belong to the most limpid pages that he wrote.[69] He begins by unmistakeably distinguishing between subject-matter and 'style':

> Deinde in hiis que dicenda occurrunt [the topics of poetry] debemus discretione potiri, utrum tragice, sive comice, sive elegiace sint canenda. Per tragediam superiorem stilum inducimus, per comediam inferiorem, per elegiam stilum intelligimus miserorum. Si tragice canenda videntur, tunc assumendum est vulgare illustre, et per consequens cantionem ligare. Si vero comice, tunc quandoque mediocre quandoque humile vulgare sumatur [...] Si autem elegiace, solum humile oportet nos sumere. (*Dve* II. 4. 5–6)

> [Then in dealing with the topics of poetry we must make a choice of whether we are to sing them in the tragic, comic, or elegiac style. By 'tragedy' I mean the higher style, by 'comedy' I mean the lower, by 'elegiac' I mean the style of the afflicted. If the topics are to be sung in the tragic style, you must employ the illustrious vernacular, and accordingly you must bind together a canzone. But if they are to be sung in the comic style, an alternation of middle and humble vernacular should be used [...] Finally, if they are to be sung in elegiac style, we should only use the humble.]

It is important to note too that here 'tragedy', 'comedy', and 'elegy' not only cannot be taken to stand for genres, but the first two cannot even be taken as *qualitates carminum*. Only *elegia*, thanks to its allusion to the *miseri*, makes a passing reference

terms of his personal lexical usage, *modo* was the word that best approximated to 'style'.

68   The other three instances of *stilo* in the *Commedia* also refer to artistic form: 'tu se' solo colui da cu' io tolsi | lo bello stilo che m'ha fatto onore' (*Inf.* I. 86–87); 'Qual di pennel fu maestro o di stile | che ritraesse l'ombre e' tratti' (*Purg.* XII. 64–65); and, discussing the 'sweet new style', Bonagiunta concludes: 'e qual più a gradire oltre si mette, | non vede più da l'uno a l'altro stilo' (*Purg.* XXIV. 61–62). See also Zygmunt G. Barański, '"Infiata labbia" and "dolce stil novo": A Note on Dante, Ethics, and the Technical Vocabulary of Literature", in *Sotto il segno di Dante: scritti in onore di Francesco Mazzoni*, ed. by Domenico De Robertis and Leonella Coglievina (Florence: Le Lettere, 1998), pp. 17–35.

69   For an excellent analysis of these famous paragraphs of the *De vulgari eloquentia*, which in part also deals with their logical difficulties, see Mengaldo, 'L'elegia', and his commentary in *Dve*, pp. 164–67. On account of our differing understanding of genre, my discussion diverges in several instances from that of Mengaldo.

to matters of content. Ultimately, all three are just formal categories defined by the particular type of vernacular with which each one is associated.[70] And, as is well known, Dante described the *vulgare illustre* in quintessentially formal terms. Although paragraphs 5 and 6 unmistakably enunciate a formally based idea of 'style', paragraph 7, while indicating some of the features that constitute literary style, introduces a degree of confusion: 'de stilo tragico pertractemus. Stilo equidem tragico tunc uti videmur quando cum gravitate sententie tam superbia carminum quam constructionis elatio et excellentia vocabulorum concordat' [Let us discuss the tragic style. We seem to be using the tragic style when the loftiness of the verse, the sophistication of the structure, and the excellence of the lexicon all agree with the seriousness of the subject-matter]. The phrase 'cum gravitate sententie' is problematic. It can be taken as suggesting that tragedy embraces both 'superior' form and 'superior' content. Yet, such an interpretation is dubious. There is another possible reading that, in the context, is likely to be preferred. 'Cum gravitate sententie' need not be considered as part of the definition of the 'tragic style'. The expression, in keeping with the doctrine of *convenientia*, alludes in extremely general terms to the kind of *materia* that ought to be presented *tragice*.[71] The whole sentence may be read as a gloss on the earlier statement which claimed that 'Si tragice canenda videntur, tune assumendum est vulgare illustre, et per consequens cantionem ligare' [If the topics are to be sung in the tragic style, you must employ the illustrious vernacular, and accordingly you must bind together a canzone] (II. 4. 6). For Dante, *stilus tragicus* and *gravitas sententie* are two separate if complementary paradigms which the true poet 'cautiously' and 'with discernment' (II. 4. 9–10) 'accords' (*concordare*, 7); and this interpretation gains considerable support from paragraph 8. Dante appropriately brings his discussion on the three 'styles' to a close by explaining the relationship between form and content in literary composition,

---

70 In his commentary, Mengaldo succinctly explains Dante's strategy in paragraphs 5 and 6, as well as its cultural antecedents: 'Nella determinazione del fondamentale rapporto materia-stile s'incrociano, senza fondersi appieno, due diverse prospettive: la contrapposizione bipolare di un livello stilistico alto e di uno inferiore, antonomasticamente indicati [...] con *tragedia* e *comedia* [my category iv] secondo la tradizione [...], che permette a Dante di isolare, come per ora gli preme, l'esperienza stilistica "tragica" della canzone illustre dalle altre, inferiori; e d'altra parte il diffusissimo schema [my category i] della tripartizione degli stili [...], i cui attributi tradizionali sono però riferiti a un grado del volgare e non a un livello stilistico' (*Dve*, p. 164).

71 The vagueness of the phrase is confirmed if its original collocation is recalled. 'Cum gravitate sententie' [with the seriousness of the subject-matter] is taken directly from the *Ad Herennium*'s discussion of the 'tria genera' (IV. 8. 11; three kinds of style). Indeed, it is the only overt echo in Dante's presentation of the rhetorical *auctoritas*. As in the *De vulgari eloquentia*, among an array of precise formal observations, the Latin work makes a fleeting allusion to a seemingly wide range of 'grave thoughts' which, in any case, on the basis of the examples cited, are defined through a mix of stylistic and emotive terms: 'et si graves sententiae quae in amplificatione et commiseratione tractantur eligentur' [and if serious thoughts are chosen, such as those used in *amplificatio* [amplification] and *commiseratio* [appeal to compassion]]. The same fusion of formal and thematic concerns returns in the commentary tradition: 'Graves id est commotivae. In *amplificatione* id est indignatione. *Commiseratione* id est conquestione' [Serious, that is moving. In *amplificatio*, that is an expression of indignation. *Commiseratio*, that is lamentation]: Thierry of Chartres, *Commentarius super Rhetoricam ad Herennium* 4. 8. 11.

a question that, until this point, he had left in the background, as well as rather vague and confused:

> Quare, si bene recolimus summa summis esse digna iam fuisse probatum, et iste quem tragicum appellamus summus videtur esse stilorum,[72] illa que summe canenda distinximus isto solo sunt stilo canenda: videlicet salus, amor et virtus et que propter ea concipimus, dum nullo accidente vilescant. (*Dve* II. 4. 8)

> [Therefore, if we rightly recall the previous demonstration that the highest are worthy of the highest, and this which we call tragic seems to be the highest style, those topics which — as we have identified — require the highest style, should be sung in that style alone: for example salvation, love, and virtue, and the thoughts they inspire in us, provided they are not corrupted by any unexpected circumstance.]

Even if Dante was more rigorous than the norm when discussing literature, and even though his criticism was driven by personal concerns, his basic presentation of the *genera dicendi* and that of the relationship between form and content were firmly rooted in medieval critical discourses. Similarly, and as has already been noted, the terms in which he thought about literature and, in particular, about its complex make-up were unmistakably the same ones in which any literate person in the Middle Ages thought about these matters. This fact is especially clear in the *Commedia*. Thus, during the course of the poem, Dante alludes, both explicitly and implicitly, to most of the competing and complementary categories that were normally used to define *scriptura* in general. For instance, the *Commedia* makes reference to the opposition between prose and poetry (most notably in the opening to *Inferno* XXVIII; see Chapter 7, pp. 264–65); to the relationship between Latin and vernacular culture; to the ontology of narrative plots; to systems of allegorical interpretation;[73] to its 'artificial' narrative structure ('Nel mezzo del cammin di nostra vita'); and to *facilis* and *difficilis* types of writing (see § XII above).

---

72   The other references to *stilus tragicus/tragedia* in the *De vulgari eloquentia* confirm the terms' exclusive formal connotations. Thus, they reappear when Dante discusses the structure of the canzone (II. 8. 8), the verses that ought to be employed in it (II. 12. 5–8), and its rhymes (II. 13. 13). There is one statement, however, that may seem to cast doubt on my interpretation of the meaning of *tragedia*: 'Sed si ad eorum [canzoni beginning with a *settenario*] sensum subtiliter intrare velimus, non sine quodam elegie umbraculo hec tragedia processisse videbitur' [But if we want to examine more subtly the meaning of these *canzoni*, it will be clear that this tragic verse unfolded with some elegiac tinge] (II. 12. 6). In my view, this sentence does not suggest, as some have claimed, that Dante believed *canzoni* to be tragedies. *Tragedia*, as the poet himself had explained, 'signifies' *superior stilus* (II. 4. 5). Keeping this definition in mind, the main clause might be rendered as follows: 'it is clear that this particular use of the tragic style [as embodied in the three canzoni — 'Di fermo sofferire', 'Donna, lo fermo core', and 'Lo meo lontano gire' — cited by Dante] advanced not without some shadow of elegy'. The *canzoni* are therefore not tragedies; if anything, given their 'unhappy' subject-matter as evidenced by their openings — and in Dante elegy always bears characteristics of a *qualitas carminis* — they are, more properly, elegies written in a tragic style which accommodates some traces of the *stilus humilis*. As we shall see, in the *Commedia*, Dante abandoned his earlier, purely formal understanding of comedy and tragedy.

73   For a discussion of the ways in which Dante presents the two principal allegorical systems and adapts them to the needs of the *Commedia*, see Zygmunt G. Barański, *Dante e i segni: saggi per una storia intellettuale di Dante* (Naples: Liguori, 2000), pp. 103–26.

In the poem, however, such notions are not primarily introduced to discuss the character of literature, but to define the *Commedia*. By underlining the presence not just of different literary systems in the tercets of his poem, but also that of the different, frequently mutually exclusive elements that made up a particular system (for example, the *Commedia*'s style includes both 'harsh' and 'sweet' forms), Dante suggests the all-embracing range of his 'sacrato poema' (*Par.* XXIII. 62), a human work that 'providentially' is able to cover the whole space normally assigned to all the 'qualities' of 'writing'.[74]

However, among these various *qualitates*, three play an especially important role in Dante's œuvre. These are the *genera dicendi*, the distinction between *clus* and *leu*, and the system of the *auctores*; and Dante's approach to each of these undergoes important changes during the course of his career — changes, in fact, that are closely tied to the shifts in his literary experimentation.

In the *Vita nova*, the *genera dicendi* do not appear to exert a determining influence. Beyond the obvious general importance for the *libello* of the categories that considered *scriptura* in terms of prose and verse and of Latin and vernacular, the most obvious literary paradigm that plays a key role in determining the character of the *Vita nova*, as it does for so many other vernacular Romance texts, is the one that opposed *clus* and *leu* forms. In the proemial stanza of 'Donne ch'avete intelletto d'amore', Dante left no doubt that he considered the 'stilo de la loda' as a type of *trobar leu*. He stated categorically that he 'non vo' parlar sì altamente' (9), namely using *clus forms*, but intended 'trattare [...] | di lei [Beatrice] leggeramente' (11–12), using the *leu* register, which is certainly the one that most prominently colours both the *libello*'s prose and its poetry. Furthermore, Dante underscored the fundamental relationship between literary clarity and moral uprightness. Thus, the 'stilo de la loda' resolves the growing obscurity of the lover's poetry, an obscurity that parallels the increasingly negative nature of his relationship with Beatrice:

> Vero è che tra le parole dove si manifesta la cagione di questo sonetto ['Con l'altre donne'), si scrivono dubbiose parole, cioè quando dico che Amore uccide tutti li miei spiriti, e li visivi rimangono in vita, salvo che fuori de li strumenti loro. E questo dubbio è impossibile a solvere a chi non fosse in simile grado fedele d'Amore; e a coloro che vi sono è manifesto ciò che solverebbe le dubitose parole: e però non è bene a me di dichiarare cotale dubitazione, acciò che lo mio parlare dichiarando sarebbe indarno, o vero di soperchio. (*Vn* XIV. 14)

The same ethical interpretation of poetic clarity and obscurity returns in *Purgatorio* XXVI. As Lino Pertile has demonstrated ('Dante's *Comedy*'), Arnaut Daniel's *leu* speech on the *girone* of lust highlights the moral limitations of the self-indulgent hermetic poetry that he wrote on earth. Indeed, I wonder whether one of the errors that Dante committed after Beatrice's death, and for which she condemns him so energetically in the Earthly Paradise, was that of having written poetry 'con rima aspr' e sottile' ('Le dolci rime', 14), most notably in the allegorical-didactic *canzoni*

---

74 For a discussion of how Dante creates an equivalence between literature *tout court* and his *comedía*, see Chapter 7, pp. 282–83.

and in the *petrose*.[75] In contrast to such 'subtle' and elitist solutions, the *Commedia* aspires to accessibility, even when its author is aware, as in *Paradiso*, that he is dealing with matters that make extraordinary demands on the human intellect. Such matters, because of their divine origins, can only be expressed as a type of 'narrazion buia' (*Purg.* XXXIII. 46). However, their cryptic nature does not stem from an act of rhetorical posturing and of intellectual snobbery — attitudes that result in an unnecessary failure to communicate, and hence that deny literature's fundamental moral *utilitas*, since they privilege obscurity as an end in itself.[76] On the other hand, the 'via [...] divina' (*Purg.* XXXIII. 88), because of our 'vista rude' (*Purg.* XXXIII. 102) — as St Paul noted (1 Corinthians 13:12) — appears to us as deeply 'enigmatic'. Hence, when Dante was obliged to deal with divine mysteries, it was axiomatic that, as in *Purg.* XXXIII. 31–102, he would end up making recourse to *clus* techniques. In addition, by combining *leu* and *clus* forms in the *Commedia*, the poet once again emphasized its totalizing character. Dante's esotericism, unlike that of his Occitan predecessors or that of his own youth, is ethically and poetically necessary. It is characterized by a proper balance between *materia* and *stilus* which come together as the *convenientiae* demanded. Indeed, obscurity becomes the 'clearest' way of imparting an impression of God's unfathomability (see Chapter 5). Despite its difficulties, the 'poema sacro' (*Par.* XXV. 1) continues to communicate and to fulfil its moral responsibilities. If this were not the case, and if the *Commedia* were in fact ultimately inaccessible to its readers, the poet would have failed in his God-given mission to restore humanity to the path of righteousness. Just as troublingly, the poem that he had composed would also have failed as literature.[77]

Dante had previously stressed the fundamental need to write clearly in chapter XXV of the *Vita nova*:

> Però che grande vergogna sarebbe a colui che rimasse cose sotto vesta di figura o di colore rettorico, e poscia, domandato, non sapesse denudare le sue parole da cotale vesta, in guisa che avessero verace intendimento. E questo mio primo amico e io ne sapemo bene di quelli che cosi rimano stoltemente. (*Vn* XXV. 10)

The importance of the *clus-leu* system in the *prosimetrum* is confirmed by the fact that reference to it is made in the chapter which more than any other discusses and synthesizes the key literary categories that structure and define the *Vita nova*. These are of course — in addition to *clus-leu* — Latin-vernacular, prose-poetry, and, of course, the *auctores*. I shall examine the implications for the *libello* of this last category in due course. For the moment, however, I intend to focus on the *genera dicendi*, which make their memorable entrance in the *De vulgari eloquentia*, and which, once they have entered on to the stage of Dante's *œuvre*, continue to play a leading role right up to the close of the *Commedia*.

---

75   On the accusations levied by Beatrice against the pilgrim in Eden, see Chapter 3.
76   On the fundamental relationship between literature and ethics in medieval literary criticism and theory, see Judson Boyce Allen, *The Ethical Poetic of the Later Middle Ages* (Toronto: University of Toronto Press, 1982).
77   For a fuller discussion of the points raised in this paragraph, see Barański, *Dante e i segni*, pp. 41–76.

The shock and the new demands of living in exile forced Dante to modify many of his views. In the *De vulgari eloquentia*, he abandoned that stalwart of the *Vita nova* and of Romance vernacular thinking about literature, the opposition between *clus* and *leu*. In its place, Dante introduced the *genera dicendi*, which he treated as quintessentially formal and linguistic categories. At first sight, this change may seem strange in a work that aims to assess the Romance literary tradition. However, the implications of this substitution are extremely revelatory. There seem to be two main reasons why Dante made the switch. First, in order to confirm the literary sophistication of vernacular poetry, or rather of *canzoni* written in the 'illustrious vernacular', and in particular of those *canzoni* which he himself had penned (I. 17. 3), he associated such poems with a system that, unlike the opposition between *clus-leu*, had an unambiguous classical aura and authority about it. In the treatise, Dante was intent on demonstrating the sophistication of vernacular 'tragic' poetry by highlighting its close links to Latin culture: 'Idcirco accidit ut, quantum illos [classical poets] proximius imitemur, tantum rectius poetemur' [Therefore, it happens that the more accurate our imitation of those poets, the more noble our poetry will be] (II. 4. 3). Unlike the *Vita nova,* in which, as chapter XXV underlines, Latin and vernacular literature are ultimately presented as distinct, the *De vulgari eloquentia* aims to blur the contrasts between works written in different languages yet which share the same *superior stilus*.[78] It was, in fact, not from Latin culture but from the vernacular tradition in general that Dante wished to detach his 'illustrious' *canzoni*. The *genera* — and this is the second reason why he gave them prominence — offered, hypothetically at least, the means by which precise distinctions could be drawn between texts, and consequently enabled barriers to be erected between them. In wishing to privilege poetry in the *vulgare illustre* above any other type of vernacular composition, Dante attempted to isolate such 'tragic' verse from works written either in the 'comic' or in the 'humble' vernacular. By doing so, and in this instance the poet was breaking with tradition, he transformed a not entirely inflexible tripartite stylistic system, whose details, since different emphases were placed on these (see § i above), were somewhat vague, into a rigid tripartite linguistic-cum-stylistic scheme, in which the formal and thematic elements that were to be conveyed through the *superior stilus* were carefully catalogued. For Dante, keen to present the 'illustrious vernacular' as the special linguistic vehicle for all that was best in literature, such elements were what distinguished 'tragedy' from the other two 'styles': they were *tragedia*'s special preserve.

The *De vulgari eloquentia* is a work of considerable dogmatism. In his effort to define and isolate the 'illustrious vernacular', Dante became increasingly prescriptive. Given the disjunction between, on the one hand, the elitism of his sense of the 'tragic' and, on the other hand, the flexibility of medieval critical discourse and literary practice, his preceptive turn is not surprising. Equally unsurprising is the poet's choice of the *genera* as the classification around which

---

78   Zygmunt G. Barański, 'Dante *poeta* e *lector*: "poesia" e "riflessione tecnica" (con divagazioni sulla *Vita nova*)', in *Dante, oggi*, ed. by Roberto Antonelli and others, 3 vols (Rome: Viella, 2011), I, 81–110.

to organize his definition of the *vulgare illustre*. Despite the asides about the cross-contamination of 'styles', the *stili* were the only category that consistently focused on the specific characteristics of groups of texts and on the need to keep such texts separate from each other. And this emphasis was especially apparent in a mnemonic system like the *rota Vergilii* and, more generally, in the Horatian tradition, under whose *auctoritas*, tellingly, the *De vulgari eloquentia* as a whole was composed and Dante's interpretation of the *genera dicendi* in particular was legitimated: 'hoc est quod magister noster Oratius precipit [...] in principio Poetrie' [This is what our master Horace teaches at the beginning of the *Ars poetica*] (II. 4. 4).[79] Dante wanted to show that language and literature were highly codified and ordered systems — systems, in fact, that could serve as models for how society could properly be organized, thereby helping to overcome the political chaos which, after his exile, the poet saw as the typical condition of his world.[80] To fulfil his cultural and civic ambitions, Dante needed to create an image of literature in the treatise which, with its stress on clear hierarchies and distinctions between texts, authors, and linguistic traditions, went against that fluidity and amorphousness which actually characterized medieval writing and criticism. The poet's view of literature in the *De vulgari eloquentia*, just like his notion of the *vulgare illustre*, is an idealization: a 'fiction'. As a result, rather than highlight ways in which art and life might intersect, the treatise ends up by not even being able to deal 'realistically' with language and literature, the specific objects of its analysis.

As Dante proceded with his description of what constituted poetry written in the 'illustrious vernacular', the inescapable weaknesses in his approach became increasingly apparent. The problems stemmed from his having idiosyncratically organized his assessment of literature around a single all-controlling category, which itself is then exploited to define one particular linguistic register, the *vulgare illustre*. The poet further compounded his problems by applying the *genera dicendi*, at least as far as his presentation of *superior* features was concerned, in an inflexible manner. The 'styles', as we have seen, were never meant to serve as the starting-point for a totalizing and rigid description of literature. Indeed, Dante himself was aware of this, as is evident from the fact that, in chapter 4, he limited the *genera* to linguistic matters, and acknowledged that the 'comic' style could include both the *mediocris* and the *humilis*. Nevertheless, in Book II, he doggedly went forward with listing 'tragic' features until the artificiality of his enterprise could no longer be concealed. In chapter 12, he acknowledged that literary practice did not conveniently fit into the kind of schematizing that he was proposing. Even the canzone, that most 'illustrious' of metrical forms, could contaminate two 'styles': 'Sed si ad eorum [the three canzoni just cited] sensum subtiliter intrare velimus, non sine quodam elegie umbraculo hec tragedia processisse videbitur' [But if we want to examine more

---

79   On the 'Virgilian wheel', see Anker Teilgard Laugesen, 'La Roue de Virgile: une page de la théorie littéraire du moyen âge', *Classica et mediaevalia*, 23 (1962), 248–73. On the Horatian tradition and the *genera dicendi*, see Quadlbauer.

80   For political readings of the *De vulgari eloquentia*, see Zygmunt G. Barański, 'I trionfi del volgare: Dante e il plurilinguismo' [1986], in *'Sole nuovo, luce nuova': saggi sul rinnovamento culturale in Dante* (Turin: Scriptorium, 1996), pp. 41–77; Marianne Shapiro, *De vulgari eloquentia: Dante's Book of Exile* (Lincoln and London: University of Nebraska Press, 1990).

subtly the meaning of these *canzoni*, it will be clear that this tragic verse unfolded with some elegiac tinge] (6). With this admission, Dante's optimism regarding the efficacy of the *genera* as means for classifying literature begins to fade. And his optimism vanishes completely a few paragraphs later. In chapter 14, the poet deliberately showed up the limitations both of the *genera dicendi* as a classificatory scheme and of the use to which he had put them in the *De vulgari eloquentia*. Against the flow of his argument in the chapter, and also against his earlier discussion of 'tragic' subject-matter, he interrupted his analysis of the *ars* of the canzone to raise a general and well-known literary issue — one, significantly, that the doctrine of the *stili* could not elucidate. In addition, he articulated this problem in terms which could not but highlight the fact that, contrary to his earlier claims regarding the totalizing classificatory efficacy of the *genera dicendi*, the aspect of literature to which he was referring had, in fact, for centuries, been accorded its own category:

> Nostra igitur primo refert discretionem facere inter ea que canenda occurrunt, quia quedam stantie prolixitatem videntur appetere, quedam non. Nam cum ea que dicimus cuncta vel circa dextrum aliquid vel sinistrum canamus — ut quandoque persuasorie quandoque dissuasorie, quandoque gratulanter quandoque yronice, quandoque laudabiliter quandoque contemptive canere contingit — que circa sinistra sunt verba semper ad extremum festinent, et alia decenti prolixitate passim veniant ad extremum. (*Dve* II. 14. 2)

> [First, then, I must necessarily draw a distinction between the topics of poetry, because if some seem to require a certain length of the stanza, some others do not. Indeed, since all of our words in poetry can be sung either positively or negatively — as we happen to write sometimes to persuade sometimes to dissuade, sometimes to congratulate sometimes to mock, sometimes to praise and sometimes to blame —, those verses which sing something negative should hasten towards the end, while the others should always come to an end at a moderate pace.]

In a matter of a few lines, Dante undermined the logic of his interpretation and recourse to the *genera*. He destroyed the idea that the three *stili* cannot share the same *materia*; that they could not cross-fertilize each other; that the 'illustrious vernacular' was the only language fit for the true poet; that literature was made up of neatly packaged segments; and that any single categorization could exhaust its possibilities. Most of all, Dante destroyed the entire *raison d'être* and value-system of the *De vulgari eloquentia*. The treatise and the *genera*, on account of their reductiveness and artificiality, could no longer reconcile his literary aims and his political ambitions (which, in any case, were by now taking on an increasingly imperial rather than 'curial' flavour). Indeed, the *De vulgari eloquentia*'s elitist theorizing was driving a wedge between literature and the complexities of life. To put it another way, the treatise's literary ideology was making it difficult for the poet to fulfil his moral duties of 'praising' and 'blaming'. It was right, therefore, that, having understood the error of his critical thinking, Dante should have dramatically abandoned the *De vulgari eloquentia* in mid-sentence before wholeheartedly embracing his culture's fluid sense of literature.[81]

81 Chapter 7 explores in greater detail the ways in which Dante may have become aware of less

The shift was crucial for the composition of the *Commedia*. Becoming aware of *scriptura*'s flexibility provided Dante with the necessary framework within which he could attempt to match the variety of life with the wealth of expressive possibilities inherent in language and literature. Equally crucial was the poet's continued attack on the *genera dicendi*. In order to highlight the originality of his plurilingual 'sacrato poema' (*Par.* XXIII. 62), and, I suspect, to underplay the degree to which his poem owed a debt to that flexible notion of *scriptura* which underpinned medieval textuality, Dante, in the *Commedia*, presented the *genera dicendi* as the antithesis of his syncretic and encyclopaedic poetry. Indeed, in a move that recalls his strategy in the *De vulgari eloquentia*, but whose aim is precisely the opposite of that intended in the treatise, he once again presented the *genera* as his culture's dominant and controlling critical axiom. However, in this instance, Dante persistently underlined that it was a principle whose effects were fundamentally negative, since they constrained artistic freedom — a point that the *Commedia* makes over and over again (see Chapter 7). From this perspective, therefore, the *comedía*, stands as the supreme example of how the constraining chains of convention can successfully be broken.

Once again, Dante exaggerates the *genera dicendi*'s remit and influence in order to establish the uniqueness and exemplary character of his own poetry. It is this striving after 'authority' which, from the time of the *Vita nova*, ceaselessly propels Dante's poetics and experimentation.[82] Dante could only establish his own status as an *auctoritas* if his artistic activities could be described and explained in terms of the critical values that could grant a writer this exalted rank. Thus, paradoxically, the more Dante strove to distinguish the singularity of his art, the more he had to ensure that its ties to the tradition were made explicit. For a writer trying to convince his audience that they ought to treat him as 'authoritative', probably none of the categories through which literature was understood in the Middle Ages was more significant than the system of the *auctores*. As the doctrines of *imitatio* and *aemulatio* made plain, any writer, in the last analysis, had to measure his achievements against those of other writers. In particular, he had to measure his writings against those of the recognized maestros in the different *qualitates scripturae*.

The *auctores* are thus the ultimate yardstick against which Dante wants both himself and his works to be judged. They are constantly present in his *œuvre*. In the *Vita nova*, next to his vernacular models, most notably, the two Guidi, Dante, in chapter XXV, introduces the great classical authors, with whose works the *libello* is boldly and originally associated.[83] In the *De vulgari eloquentia*, any distinction

---

dogmatic ways of discussing literature. For a fuller discussion of the *De vulgari eloquentia*'s elitism and the problems which this raises for its analysis of literature, see Barański, 'I trionfi del volgare', pp. 63–68. On the importance of the *laus/vituperatio* distinction in *Inferno* IV, see Reynolds, 'Orazio satiro', pp. 137–40.

82　On Dante's self-construction as an *auctoritas*, see in particular Albert R. Ascoli, *Dante and the Making of a Modern Author* (Cambridge: Cambridge University Press, 2008). See also Barański, 'Sole nuovo, luce nuova'.

83　See Zygmunt G. Barański, '"Valentissimo poeta e correggitore de' poeti": A First Note on Horace and the *Vita nova*', in *Letteratura e filologia fra Svizzera e Italia: studi in onore di Guglielmo Gorni. I. Dante: la 'Commedia' e altro*, ed. by Maria Antonietta Terzoli and others, 3 vols (Rome: Edizioni di Storia e Letteratura, 2010), I, 3–17, and 'Dante *poeta e lector*', pp. 93–101.

that may still persist between the the 'dicitori d'amore in lingua volgare' and the 'poete in lingua latina' (*Vn* xxv. 3) disappears. What becomes significant is less a matter of whether a poet wrote in Latin or in the vernacular, but rather whether or not he could be counted among the *Dei dilecti*, whether or not he was one of the soaring *astripetae aquilae* (II. 4. 11) who glory in the *superior stilus*, and whose principal vernacular representative was Cino's 'friend' (I. 10. 2). In the *Commedia*, by introducing the *auctores* as part of the cast of his exemplary story, Dante acknowledged their cultural and historical importance. At the same time, as has been extensively documented, he also regularly displayed the incomparability of his own poem, and thereby of his own 'authoritativeness'. And he defined his supremacy in terms of the literary limitations of the traditional *auctoritates*. Unlike their works, his *comedía* was no longer restricted by the *genera dicendi* (see Chapters 7 and 9). The impact and effectiveness of Dante's metaliterary positions owe much to the tidy manner in which he develops and structures his arguments — the neat way in which their different elements 'logically' merge together to demonstrate the poet's uniqueness. Within the *Commedia*'s critical system, any work that is in any way artificially constrained is deemed artistically and ideologically flawed.

Finally, back to the question of genre. In the 'poema sacro' (*Par.* xxv. 1), notions such as 'tragedy' (*Inf.* xx. 113) and 'satire' (*Inf.* iv. 89) involve both form and content, and hence can be said to begin to take on some of the traits of more recent thinking about genre.[84] In the last analysis, however, it is difficult to cite these usages as evidence that Dante had evolved an *avant la lettre* theory of genre. Thus, although his concept of 'comedy' also brought together *materia* and *stilus*, an unbridgeable gap separated it from *tragedia, satira,* and any other literary type. The *Commedia*'s range was potentially limitless, while that of 'tragedy' and 'satire' was restricted by the *genera dicendi*. More importantly, *comedía* embraced both *stili*, as it did the *genera* and every other literary and linguistic form.[85] It is the all-encompassing character of the *Commedia*, which is predicated on an idea of literature not as a system of differences but as a structure which, despite its variety, could be integrated harmoniously in a single work, that most militates against any claim that Dante shared our sense of genre. It was not genre, but the fluid medieval sense of *scriptura* that Dante championed and celebrated in his *comedía*.

4. Concluding Remarks: The Epistle to Cangrande

To bring my analysis of 'medieval literature, "genre", and Dante' to a close, and as a way of gathering together the various strands of my argument, I should like to consider briefly the treatment of 'genera narrationum poeticarum' [kinds of poetic

---

84   See Reynolds, '*Orazio satiro*'; Schnapp.

85   Although Dante's new sense of 'comedy', as I have already mentioned, is equivalent to *scriptura* in its broadest acceptation, on one level, it continues to maintain a link with contemporary modes of categorization. It connects, in ways that are explored in Chapter 7, with that wide-ranging idea of *comedia* whereby the twinning of comedy and tragedy was deemed equivalent to literature in general. What is interesting, and this too is discussed in Chapter 7, is why Dante should have deemed comedy, rather than tragedy, as best suited for his totalizing ends.

narration] (32) in paragraph X of the epistle to Cangrande. This section of the letter raises a number of questions not only as regards Dante's customary modes of thinking and writing about the *stili*, but also, though to a lesser degree, as regards the ways in which matters of literary categorization were normally presented in medieval critical writing.

Once again I should like to start with the key term *genus*. The author of the letter refers to 'comedia' as a 'genus [...] poetice narrationis' [kind of poetic narration] (29) before alluding to 'genera narrationum poeticarum' [kinds of poetic narration] (32). Previously, when listing the *sex inquirenda*, the 'anonimo' writes that the last of these clarifies the 'genus phylosophie' [philosophical kind] (18)) to which the poem belongs, subsequently explaining that 'Genus vero phylosophie sub quo hic in toto et parte proceditur, est morale negotium, sive ethica' [But the philosophical kind, in which this is included as a whole or in part, is a matter of morality, or ethics] (XIII. 40).[86] Finally, when glossing the prologue to the *Paradiso*, he observes that 'ad bene exordiendum tria requiruntur, ut dicit Tullius in Nova Rethorica, scilicet ut benivolum et attentum et docilem reddat aliquis auditorem; et hoc maxime in admirabili genere cause' [three things are necessary to make a good beginning, as Tullius [Cicero] says in the New Rhetoric [*Rhetorica ad Herennium*], namely that the speaker cause the audience to be benevolent, attentive, and well disposed; and this especially in the kind of case which is uncommon] (XIII. 49). It is clear from the passages cited that, in the epistle, *genus* is utilized, as was typical in medieval usage, in a very broad manner as a catch-all term signifying 'kind', 'type', 'sort', 'manner', etc. Both this loose, non-specific use of *genus* and the contexts in which it is introduced raise significant problems if the *epistola* is to be assigned to Dante's pen. The author of the letter and the poet of the *Commedia* have a different idea of its meaning, and hence of how and where to employ it. In contrast to Dante's careful and precise application of the term, the author of the letter employs it slackly. As we saw, in both his Latin and vernacular writings, Dante never utilized *genus/genere* in a non-technical manner but always in keeping with philosophical, specifically Aristotelian usage. Indeed, it is far from insignificant that, nowhere in his *œuvre*, Dante should make recourse to the term in order to discuss matters of literature,

86 I term the author of the letter the 'anonimo' as I continue to harbour doubts that it was written by Dante; see Zygmunt G. Barański, '*Comedía*: Notes on Dante, the Epistle to Cangrande and Medieval Comedy', *Lectura Dantis Virginiana*, 8 (1991), 26–55. For recent contributions on the controversial *epistola*, see Luca Azzetta, '*Epistola XIII*', in *Epistole. Egloge. Questio de aqua et terra*, ed. by Marco Baglio and others (Rome: Salerno, 2016), pp. 271–487; Saverio Bellomo, 'L'Epistola a Cangrande, dantesca per intero: "a rischio di procurarci un dispiacere"', *L'Alighieri*, 56 (2015), 5–19, and '"Una finestretta da niuno mai più veduta": e l'Epistola a Cangrande', *Studi e problem di critica testuale*, 90 (2015), 341–52; Alberto Casadei, 'Il titolo della *Commedia* e l'Epistola a Cangrande', *Allegoria*, 60 (2009), 167–81, then in his *Dante oltre la 'Commedia'* (Bologna: il Mulino, 2013), pp. 15–43, 'Sull'autencità dell'"Epistola a Cangrande"', in *Ortodossia ed eterodossia in Dante Alighieri*, ed. by Carlotta Cattermole and others (Alpedrete [Madrid]: Ediciones de la Discreta, 2014), pp. 803–30, 'Essential Issues Concerning the *Epistle to Cangrande*', in *Medieval Letters: Between Fiction and Document*, ed. by Christian Høgel and Elisabetta Bartoli (Turnhout: Brepols, 2015), pp. 381–92, and 'Sempre contro l'autenticità dell'Epistola a Cangrande', *Studi danteschi*, 81 (2016), 215–45; Giorgio Inglese, 'Dante (?) a Cangrande: postille', in *Giornale storico della letteratura italiana*, 191 (2014), 121–23; Thomas Ricklin, 'Indagine su un disguido epistolare: l'*Epistola a Cangrande* fra Verona e Padova', in Høgel and Bartoli, pp. 369–79.

or to distinguish between different areas of philosophy, or to discriminate between different types of forensic case, even though phrases such as *genera dicendi*, *genera carminum*, and *genera causarum* were deeply embedded in contemporary usage. With his customary lexical sensibility and feel for terminological accuracy, Dante reserved *genus/genere* for philosophical issues, while drawing on other, equally apposite vocabulary to present those self-same topics that the author of the epistle felt could all be categorized under *genus*. Thus, when discussing different branches of philosophy, rather than *genus*, the poet relied on *pars/parte*, which was the standard and technically appropriate way of referring to such distinctions.[87] Similarly, when Dante, like the *anonimo*, addressed the question of rhetorical 'persuasion' and drew on the self-same 'authority', Cicero's *De inventione*, the poet — differently from the author of the letter — carefully avoided the original's use of *genus*. Such differing reactions to the the same source point to different intellectual and linguistic sensibilities, and hence to different authors.[88] In addition, they are reactions that are consistent with what may be adduced about each one's writerly practices. It is useful to quote both authors in full, as well as their source, so that their differences can properly emerge:

> Exordium est oratio animum auditoris idonee comparans ad reliquam dictionem; quod eveniet, si eum benivolum, attentum, docilem confecerit. Quare qui bene exordiri causam volet, eum necesse est genus suae causae diligenter ante cognoscere. Genera causarum quinque sunt: honestum, admirabili, humile, anceps, obscurum [...] In adrnirabili genere causae, si non omnino infesti auditores erunt, principio benivolentiam comparare licebit [...] Attentos autem faciemus, si demonstrabimus ea, quae dicturi erimus, magna, nova, incredibilia esse. (Cicero, *De inventione* I. 15. 20–21 and 16. 23)

> [The *exordium* [introduction] is a discourse which prepares the mind of the audience to listen to the rest of the speech; and this happens, if the speaker makes the audience benevolent, attentive, and well disposed. Therefore, one who wants to begin his subject properly must know thoroughly in advance the kind of case he is presenting. There are five kinds of case: honorable, uncommon, humble, ambiguous, obscure [...] In the kind of case that is uncommon, if the audience is not altogether hostile, it will be possible to obtain their benevolence by an introduction [...] And we will make them attentive, if we show that the things we are about to say are great, original, and out of the ordinary.]

> Ma però che in ciascuna maniera di sermone lo dicitore massimamente dee intendere a la persuasione, cioè a l'abbellire, de l'audienza, sì come a quella ch'è principio di tutte l'altre persuasioni, come li rettorici [s]anno; e potentissima persuasione sia, a rendere l'uditore attento, promettere di dire nuove e grandissime cose. (*Conv.* II. 6. 6)

> Propter primam partem notandum quod ad bene exordiendum tria requiruntur,

---

87   See *Conv.* III. 15. 14. On the wide dissemination of the phrase *pars philosophiae*, see Minnis, *Medieval Theory*, pp. 26–27.
88   In his commentary to the epistle, Giorgio Brugnoli underlines other important factors regarding section 49 of the letter that do not fit in with Dante's customary intellectual and compositional practices: Dante Alighieri, *Epistole*, ed. by Arsenio Frugoni and Giorgio Brugnoli, in *Opere minori*, II, 505–643 (pp. 626–28).

ut dicit Tullis in Nova Rethorica, scilicet ut benivolum et attentum et docilem reddat aliquis auditorem; et hoc maxime in admirabili genere cause, ut ipsemet Tullius dicit. (*Ep.* XIII. 49)[89]

[With respect to the first part, it must be observed that three things are necessary to make a good beginning, as Tullius [Cicero] says in the New Rhetoric [*Rhetorica ad Herennium*], namely that the speaker cause the audience to be benevolent, attentive, and well disposed; and this especially in the kind of case which is uncommon.]

The difference in their use of *genus* is typical of a fundamental and determining difference between Dante and the *anonimo*. Thus, where the former develops a complex, nuanced, and ultimately personal way in which to talk about literature and, in particular, his own writings, the latter tends to lack a sense of discrimination and sophistication when using critical language, preferring instead to rely on the commonplaces and clichés of medieval literary theory and criticism, such as 'genera [...] poeticarum' and 'genere cause' (see Barański, '*Comedía*'). The conventional critical abilities of the *anonimo* clearly emerge in his presentation of 'comedy' in light of other textual forms:

Et est comedia genus quoddam poetice narrationis ab omnibus aliis differens. Differt ergo a tragedia in materia [...] Et per hoc patet quod Comedia dicitur presens opus. Nam si ad materiam respiciamus, a principio horribilis et fetida est, quia Infernus, in fine prospera, desiderabilis et grata, quia Paradisus; ad modum loquendi, remissus est modus et humilis, quia locutio vulgaris in qua muliercule comunicant. Sunt et alia genera narrationum poeticarum, scilicet carmen bucolicum, elegia, satira, et sententia votiva,[90] ut etiam per Oratium patere potest in sua Poetria; sed de istis ad presens nichil aliud dicendum est. (*Ep.* XIII. 29 & 31–32)

[And comedy is a kind of poetic narration which differs from any other kind. It differs indeed from tragedy in its subject-matter [...] And on this account it is clear that the present work is called a Comedy. For if we look carefully at the subject-matter, at the beginning it is horrific and disgusting, because it is the Inferno, at the end it is rich, desirable, and pleasing, because it is the Paradiso; if we look at its manner of speaking, it is composed and moderate and humble, because it uses the vernacular language in which women-folk communicate. There are other kinds of poetic narration, as for example bucolic songs, elegy, satire, and prayers and hymns, as Horace explains in his *Ars poetica*, but at present I shall add nothing else about these.]

89   Although the *anonimo* refers to the *Rhetorica ad Herennium*, his source is in fact the *De inventione*, since in the former there is no mention of the *admirabilis causa*; see *Ad Her.* I. 4. 6 and 7. 11. This error too raises questions regarding Dante's authorship of the letter.

90   For a good discussion of the make-up of this list of 'poetic narrative types', see Brugnoli, p. 623. I am not persuaded, however, that Brugnoli is correct in asserting that the first five *genera* 'derivano dalla tradizione scolastica adeguata a Diomede', while 'il sesto, la "sentenza votiva", è ricavato arbitrariamente da Orazio' (from *Ars poetica* 76). It would seem more likely that all six terms come from Horace as the phrase 'ut etiam per Oratium patere potest in sua Poetria' [as Horace explains in his *Ars poetica*] underlines. Indeed, except for 'carmen bucolicum', the remaining five types are examined in *AP*. As regards 'bucolic song', it is more than likely that reference to it would be found in many glossed manuscripts of Horace's poem (see, for instance, the passage quoted at p. 223 above).

The author of the epistle treats *comedia*, as is obvious from the manner in which he equates it with 'alia genera narrationum poeticarum' [other kinds of poetic narration], as if it were simply a *qualitas carminis*. His emphasis on its specificities in no way highlights the uniqueness of Dante's *Commedia* but simply uses an established formula to distinguish comedy from other types of poetry. Exactly the same 'differentiating' phrase — 'a kind of poetic narration which differs from any other kind' — can be applied to the other *genera* that the *anonimo* goes on to list.[91] *Comedia*, and by extension Dante's poem, are tidily separated from the other poetic types, while, at the same time, they are all presented as particular compartmentalized expressions of 'genera narrationum poeticarum'. Such a conservative view of *comedia* is the opposite of Dante's all-embracing conception of comedy in the 'sacrato poema' (*Par.* XXIII. 62). Indeed, while the *Commedia* is the kind of text that can accommodate any *qualitas carminis*, the epistle to Cangrande asserts that not only is comedy unable to take over the literary space occupied by other *genera*, but also that both its narrative and stylistic possibilities are necessarily constrained by the fact of its comic identity. The letter's restrictive and banalizing conclusions regarding the *Commedia*'s status as a comedy are in harmony with the general thrust of its *lectura*. As I have argued elsewhere (Barański, '*Comedìa*'), it is the *anonimo*'s aim to downplay the originality and uniqueness of Dante's masterpiece.

91   I am not persuaded by recent attempts to argue that the discussion in the *accessus* section of the letter to Cangrande is original. The evidence put forward in support of such claims is problematic. For instance, it is an overstatement to claim that 'la precisazione — "Et est comedia genus quoddam poetice narrationis ab omnibus aliis differens. Differt ergo a tragedia in materia" [And comedy is a kind of poetic narration which differs from any other kind. It differs indeed from tragedy in its subject-matter] — non ha riscontri nella tradizione medievale' (Azzetta, p. 359). Already in Diomedes *Grammaticus* an almost identical discriminating construction and presentation may be found, and not exclusively with reference to comedy, but also (as I note above would have been the case) as regards other 'kinds of poetic narration': 'Comoedia a tragoedia differt, quod in tragoedia introducuntur heroes duces reges, in comoedia humiles atque privatae personae; in illa luctus exilia caedes, in hac amores, virginum raptus' [Comedy differs from tragedy, because in tragedy heroes, leaders, kings are introduced, in comedy humble and ordinary people; in tragedy sorrows, exiles, bloodshed, in comedy love, and the abduction of maidens], and 'togata praetextata a tragoedia differt [...] togata tabernaria a comoedia differt [...] Latina Atellana a Graeca satyrica differt' [The Roman kind of tragic drama [*fabula praetexta*] differs from tragedy [...] And the Roman kind of comedy [*fabula tabernaria*] differs from comedy] (*Ars grammatica*, in Keil, I, 488 & 490). Similar phraseology may be found in a popular late thirteenth-century work of compilation, Johannes Balbus's *Catholicon*: 'Comedia [...] differt a tragedia' [Comedy [...] differs from tragedy], and 'Differunt tragedia et comedia, quia comedia privatorum hominum continent facta, tragedia regum et magnatum; item comedia humili stilo describitur, tragedia alto; item comedia a tristibus incipit sed cum letis desinit, tragedia e contrario; unde in salutatione solemus mittere et aptare tragicum principium et comicum finem' [Comedy and tragedy are different, because comedy involves the deeds of ordinary people, tragedy those of kings and prominent people; moreover, comedy is written in the humble style, tragedy in the high style; and again, comedy starts with a sad situation but has a happy ending, in tragedy it is the opposite; thus in greetings we usually send and wish a tragic beginning and a comic end]: Johannes Balbus, *Catholicon* (Mainz: n.pr., 1460), V [De littera]. Balbus's definitions of *comedia* and *tragedia* had first been cited in relation to *Ep.* XIII by Giuseppe Boffito, 'L'epistola di Dante Alighieri a Cangrande della Scala: saggio d'edizione critica e di commento', *Memorie della Reale Accademia delle Scienze di Torino*, ser. 2, 57 (1907), 1–39 (p. 27). There is obviously nothing particularly remarkable about the *anonimo*'s treatment of the 'differences' between comedy and tragedy in paragraph 29.

The letter does not just reveal a limited understanding of the *Commedia*; it also reveals an equally limited sense of literature in general. Thus, we do not discover in it that wide-ranging sense of *scriptura*'s many and interweaving categories that was a typical feature even of school-room texts such as the 'Materia' commentary and Conrad of Hirsau's *Dialogus super auctores*. The epistle to Cangrande's critical purview seems primarily to be based on Horace's *Ars poetica*, a fact that its author twice acknowledges (30 and 32). Although Horace had long been a major and broad *auctoritas* in matters of literature, the *anonimo*'s sense of the Roman poet's teachings is narrow. He did not share the wide-ranging interpretation of the *Ars poetica* as developed, for instance, in the 'Materia' commentary. Instead, as in some of the *poetriae*, he considered it a source of prescriptions with which to draw clear distinctions between texts especially in terms of the *genera dicendi*. This was precisely the sort of reading of Horace and the *Ars poetica* which, after having flirted with it in the *De vulgari eloquentia*, Dante categorically rejected in the *Commedia*.

The world of medieval literary criticism was both unique and complex. And to appreciate this complexity and uniqueness, as well as the different yet interconnected ways in which a French schoolmaster, a great poet, and a polemical fourteenth-century reader of the *Commedia* thought about literature, it is necessary — as I have attempted to suggest — to approach the critical language of the Middle Ages with considerable philological care. A fascinatingly fluid and rich theory of literature awaits us if we are prepared to appreciate the nuances of medieval critical discourse. 'Tres enim sunt manerie dicendi, quas alii stilos, alii figuras, alii caracteres appellant'...

CHAPTER 7

'Primo tra cotanto senno':
Dante and the Latin Comic Tradition

Faciam ut commixta sit; sit tragico [co]moedia.
(Plautus, *Amphitruo* I. 59)[1]

1. Introduction

The study of Dante's relationship to the Latin comic tradition may be divided into two main areas: his possible links with the Roman comedians and the significance of his thought-provoking decision to give his masterpiece the title 'comedía' (*Inf.* XVI. 128 and XXI. 2).[2]

---

1   [I shall make it a mix; let it be a tragicomedy.]
2   On the title of the *Commedia* and the poem's 'comic style', see Pio Rajna, 'Il titolo del poema dantesco', *Studi danteschi*, 4 (1921), 5–37; Erich Auerbach, 'L'oggetto della *Commedia*' [1929], in his *Studi su Dante* (Milan: Feltrinelli, 1978), pp. 62–91 (pp. 83–84); Manfredi Porena, 'Il titolo deIla *Divina Commedia*', *Rendiconti della R. Accademia Nazionale dei Lincei. Classe di scienze morali, storiche e filologiche*, ser. 6, 9 (1933), 114–41; André Pézard, *Dante sous la pluie de feu* (Paris: Vrin, 1950), pp. 339–54; Alfredo Schiaffini, 'A proposito dello "stile comico" in Dante' [1953], in *Italiano antico e moderno*, ed. by Tullio de Mauro and Paolo Mazzantini (Milan and Naples: Ricciardi, 1975); Gianfranco Contini, review of Mario Marti, *Cultura e stile nei poeti giocosi* (Pisa: Nistri-Lischi, 1953), in *Giornale storico della letteratura italiana*, 131 (1954), 220–26; Siro A. Chimenz, 'Per il testo e la chiosa della *Divina Commedia*', *Giornale storico della letteratura italiana*, 133 (1956), 161–88 (pp. 168–69); Ignazio Baldelli, 'Sulla teoria linguistica di Dante', in *Dante nella critica d'oggi*, ed. by Umberto Bosco (Florence: Le Monnier, 1965), pp. 705–13; August Buck, 'Gli studi sulla poetica e sulla retorica di Dante e del suo tempo', in *Atti del Congresso internazionale di studi danteschi*, 2 vols (Florence: Sansoni, 1965–66), II, 249–78 (p. 267); Gianfranco Contini, 'Un'interpretazione di Dante' [1965], in his *Un'idea di Dante* (Turin: Einaudi, 1976), pp. 69–111 (pp. 93, 102–04); Ettore Paratore, 'L'eredità classica di Dante', in *Dante e Roma* (Florence: Le Monnier, 1965), pp. 3–50 (pp. 37–42); Bruno Nardi, *Saggi e note di critica dantesca* (Milan and Naples: Ricciardi, 1966), pp. 161–63; Manlio Pastore Stocchi, 'Dante, Mussato e la tragedia', in *Dante e la cultura veneta*, ed. by Vittore Branca and Giorgio Padoan (Florence: Olschki, 1966), pp. 251–62; Franco Ferrucci, 'Comedia', *Yearbook of Italian Studies*, I (1971), 29–52; Robert S. Haller, 'Introduction', in *Literary Criticism of Dante Alighieri* (Lincoln: University of Nebraska Press, 1973), pp. ix–xlvii (pp. xxxvi–xxxvii); Otello Ciacci, *Nuove interpretazioni dantesche* (Perugia: Volumnia, 1974), pp. 5–26; L. Jenaro-Maclennan, *The Trecento Commentaries on the 'Divina Commedia' and the Epistle to Cangrande* (Oxford: Clarendon Press, 1974), pp. 68–70, 92–104, 121–23; Sesto Prete, 'Dante e gli *Excerpta De Comoedia*', in *Dante nel pensiero e nella esegesi dei secoli XIV e XV* (Florence: Olschki, 1975), pp. 127–36; Antonio E. Quaglio, 'Titolo', in '*Commedia*', in ED, II, 79–81; Giorgio Agamben, '*Comedía*: la svolta comica di Dante e la concezione della colpa', *Paragone*, 29 (1978),

It is evident from his writings that Dante knew something about Plautus, Caecilius Statius, and Terence. However, the quality and the extent of his knowledge remain a matter of critical uncertainty. In general, scholars agree that it is unlikely that Dante would have been aware of much else beside the names of Plautus and Caecilius and the cultural commonplaces that had become attached to them. They are recalled only once in his *œuvre*, and then fleetingly, in the catalogue of pagans in *Purgatorio* XXII ('Cecilio e Plauto', 98). On the other hand, less accord exists on the nature of the undoubtedly more complex bonds uniting Dante and Terence. It is noteworthy, however, that even those who most staunchly advocate that the poet enjoyed a goodish acquaintance with the Roman writer have not actually managed to bolster their belief with convincing new evidence, but have continued to build their case on the long-established, standard three 'Terentian' allusions: namely, the appearance, in *Inferno* XVIII, of a quite idiosyncratic Thais when measured against her original namesake in the *Eunuchus*; Statius's request for information concerning 'Terrenzio nostro antico' (*Purg.* XXII. 97); and the introduction of the playwright's name as an *auctoritas* in the letter to Cangrande: 'ut patet per Terentium in suis comediis' [as it is shown by Terence in his comedies] (XIII. 29). In comparison to the poet's contacts with other classical authors, from Virgil to Statius and from

3–27; Amilcare A. Iannucci, 'Dante's Theory of Genre', *Dante Studies*, 91 (1975), 1–25; L. Jenaro-Maclennan, '*Remissus est modus et humilis* (Epistle to Cangrande)', *Lettere italiane*, 31 (1979), 406–18; Aldo Rossi, 'Il "serio-comico" dantesco', *Paragone*, 30 (1979), 32–48; Rossella D'Alfonso, ' "Comico" e "commedia": appunti sul titolo del poema dantesco', *Filologia e critica*, 7 (1982), 3–41; Lucia Battaglia Ricci, *Dante e la tradizione letteraria medievale* (Pisa: Giardini, 1983), pp. 220–23; Robert Hollander, *Il Virgilio dantesco* (Florence: Olschki, 1983), pp. 117–54; Teodolinda Barolini, *Dante's Poets* (Princeton: Princeton University Press, 1984), pp. 213–18, 228–37, & 270–86; Vittorio Russo, *Il romanzo teologico* (Naples: Liguori, 1984), pp. 13–30; Claudia Villa, *La 'Lectura Terentii'* (Padua: Antenore, 1984), pp. 137–89; Mauda Bregoli-Russo, 'Le *Egloghe* di Dante: un'analisi', *Italica*, 62 (1985), 34–40; Zygmunt G. Barański, ' "Significar *per verba*": Notes on Dante and Plurilingualism', *The Italianist*, 6 (1986), 5–18, and 'Re viewing Dante', *Romance Philology*, 42 (1988), 51–76; Carlo Paolazzi, *Dante e la 'Comedia' nel Trecento* (Milan: Vita e Pensiero, 1989). Since this article appeared in 1991, the following studies on the *Commedia*'s title have appeared: Zygmunt G. Barański, '*Comedìa*: Notes on Dante, the Epistle to Cangrande, and Medieval Comedy', *Lectura Dantis Virginiana*, 8 (1991), 26–55; Lino Pertile, '*Canto-cantica-Comedìa* e l'Epistola a Cangrande', *Lectura Dantis Virginiana*, 9 (1991), 103–23; Zygmunt G. Barański, '*La Commedia*', in *Manuale di letteratura italiana. I. Dalle origini alla fine del Quattrocento*, ed. by Franco Brioschi and Costanzo Di Girolamo (Turin: Bollati Boringhieri, 1993), pp. 492–560; Albert R. Ascoli, 'Access to Authority: Dante in the Epistle to Cangrande', in *Seminario Dantesco Internazionale/International Dante Seminar 1*, ed. by Zygmunt G. Barański (Florence: Le Lettere, 1996), pp. 309–52; Mirko Tavoni, 'Il titolo della *Commedia*', *Nuova rivista di letteratura italiana*, 1 (1998), 9–34; Silvia Conte, 'Le finalità del comico: una nuova proposta per l'interpretazione della *intitulatio* della *Commedia*', *Critica del testo*, 4 (2001), 559–74; Claudia Villa, ' "*Comoedia: laus in canticis dicta*": schede per Dante: *Paradiso*, XXV I e *Inferno*, XVIII', *Rivista di studi danteschi*, 1 (2001), 316–31; Zygmunt G. Barański, 'Dante Alighieri: Experimentation and (Self-)Exegesis', in *The Cambridge History of Literary Criticism. II. The Middle Ages*, ed. by Alastair Minnis and Ian Johnson (Cambridge: Cambridge University Press, 2005), pp. 561–82; Francesco Tateo, 'Il canone dantesco dei poeti comici e la moderazione di Stazio', *L'Alighieri*, 47 (2006), 89–103; Alberto Casadei, 'Il titolo della *Commedia* e l'Epistola a Cangrande', *Allegoria*, 60 (2009), 167–81, then in his *Dante oltre la 'Commedia'* (Bologna: il Mulino, 2013), pp. 15–43 (from which I cite); Villa commentary in *Ep.*, pp. 1568–78; Mirko Tavoni, *Qualche idea su Dante* (Bologna: il Mulino, 2015), pp. 335–69. See also Chapters 6 and 8 that, respectively, were first published in 1995 and 1994.

Cicero to Horace, his apparent interest in and familiarity with the *comici* were unimpressive.

Yet this state of affairs cannot but strike one as odd. Leaving aside, at least for the moment, the implications for Dante of Terence's considerable popularity in the Middle Ages, the marginal standing of the Roman, hence the most illustrious, 'comic' tradition in a work that declares in its very title to be a *comedía* is disconcerting.[3] This is all the more so, when one remembers not only the insistence with which the poem affirms its metaliterary concerns, but also how such a dimension is typical of medieval literature in general. Perhaps, instead of laboriously seeking for other traces of Terence in Dante's *œuvre*, scholars should turn the question on its head and ask why the poet should have granted so little space to Roman comedy in his writings. The problem is all the more intriguing since it is clear that, possibly from as early as the *Fiore*, and certainly from the *tenzone* with Forese, through the *De vulgari eloquentia*, and culminating in the *Commedia*, Dante must have had, to say the least, an interest in and an appreciation of 'comic' forms.[4] In any case, knowledge of the 'comic' was almost certainly 'inevitable', as it belonged to the interdiscursive culture of the poet's era.[5] In the Middle Ages, with its confused and partial understanding of dramatic forms, the combination of comedy and tragedy had come to stand for literature *tout court*, whereby each of the two major *stili* embraced a variety of other literary forms and situations. For example, comedy was primarily associated with difficult beginnings and happy endings, with the 'middle' and 'low' styles, and with low-class characters, private events, and realistic themes — a view that was bolstered by the word's etymology, 'country [*comos*] song [*oda*]' (paragraphs 29–32 of the letter to Cangrande presents a handy compendium of these standard positions, and, as also was customary, contrasts them with 'tragic' characteristics; and see Chapter 6). Discussions and definitions of the 'comic' and the 'tragic' permeated every corner of medieval culture, ranging from theology to rhetoric and from exegesis to philosophy, and could be heard in every classroom.[6] Yet, in the *Commedia*, as with

---

3   Evidence for the poem's title comes, first, from its manuscript tradition, in particular, from copyists' rubrics and, second, from its exegesis in the Trecento; see Quaglio, p. 79; but see also Casadei, p. 22. Both traditions have as their point of reference the two passages in *Inferno* where Dante terms his poem 'comedía'. Further confirmation of the title from Dante's own pen may be found in a (controversial) passage in the *Monarchia*: 'sicut in Paradiso *Comedie* iam dixi' [as I said already in the Paradise of the *Comedy*] (I. 12, 6). Porena's suggestion that the poet intended to call only the first *cantica* 'comedía' continues to find little support (but see Casadei, also as regards the reference in *Monarchia*, pp. 107–27); for an immediate critique, see Giovanni Vandelli, review of 'Il titolo della *Divina Commedia*', *Studi danteschi*, 9 (1935), 141–49.
4   I am not simply thinking of the definition of 'comedy' given in the treatise (II. 4. 5–6), but also of the examples of different regional languages that Dante presents in Book I, and which may be read as an anthology 'in disguise' of the 'comic' style, as Contini acutely noted: 'ma importa rilevare nel *De vulgari* [...] anche la fondazione d'una teoria della poesia dialettale riflessa, antitetica a quella di tono alto': 'La poesia rusticale come caso di bilinguismo', in his *Ultimi esercizî ed elzeviri* (Turin: Einaudi, 1988), pp. 5–21 (pp. 14–15).
5   See Cesare Segre, 'Intertestuale-interdiscorsivo: appunti per una fenomenologia delle fonti', in *La parola ritrovata*, ed. by Costanzo Di Girolamo and Ivano Paccagnella (Palermo: Sellerio Editore, 1982), pp. 15–28.
6   For a more detailed discussion of tragedy and comedy in the Middle Ages, see Subsections 6

its marginalized presence of Plautus, Caecilius, and Terence, explanations for its title do not seem to abound. The poem's 'style' is simply underlined twice in quick succession, though apparently without comment:

> ma qui tacer nol posso; e per le note
> di questa comedía, lettor, ti giuro,
> s'elle non sien di lunga grazia vòte (*Inf.* XVI. 127–29)

and:

> Così di ponte in ponte, altro parlando
> che la mia comedía cantar non cura,
> venimmo. (*Inf.* XXI. 1–3)

The matter is then allowed to drop, except for one paradoxical aside in *Paradiso*:

> Da questo passo vinto mi concedo
> più che già mai da punto di suo tema
> soprato fosse comico o tragedo. (*Par.* XXX. 22–24)

These three references obviously belong to the second area of Dante's relationship to the 'comic', namely, the technical definition of the *Commedia*. This revolves not so much around the interaction between poets, but around one poet's view of the cultural and artistic ramifications of the literary and rhetorical tradition of his time, and of his own position within it.

Dante's approach to the 'comic', as I hinted earlier, combines poetry with poetics. The same is true of his treatment of every (classical) writer and school. Thus, given that Dante authored a 'comedy', the bond between literature and reflection on literature is likely to be especially powerful in his presentation of the 'comic'. There was nothing unusual in such an approach — poetry and poetics were constantly brought together by the education system and the modes of exegesis (not least in the commentaries and glosses that accompanied the manuscripts of the *auctores*). What is original are the ways in which Dante expanded and adapted the metaliterary discourses of his day. Thus, ever since Contini's pioneering discoveries, it has become a critical standard to affirm that, in a strikingly novel turn, Dante developed a sophisticated range of textual strategies to unmask deficiencies in the works and practices of other authors in order to boost and highlight the intellectual and poetic achievements of his own compositions.[7] It is because the poet normally made regular and careful use of this dialectical approach to measure and define his artistic solutions against those of others — that structure of 'authority and challenge' which this chapter aims to explore — that the *Commedia*'s seeming lack of interest both in the 'comic' tradition and in Roman comedy is so perplexing. Thus, remembering the self-evident discrepancies between the *Commedia* and the customary definitions of 'comedy' in the Middle Ages, and Dante's own near silence on the matter, it is perhaps not surprising that scholars should have failed to put forward adequate explanations as to why the poet chose to refer to his work

and 7, which also include bibliographies.

7 Gianfranco Contini, 'Dante come personaggio-poeta della *Commedia*', in *Un'idea*, pp. 33–62, and 'Un'interpretazione'.

as 'comedía'. The 'mystery' of the title remains as tantalizing as when, about six hundred years ago, Francesco da Buti, clearly at the end of his tether, irritatingly conceded: 'Sarebbe dubbio, se questo poema dell'autore si dé chiamare comedia o no ma poiché li è piaciuto di chiamarla comedia, desili concedere'.[8]

My aim obviously is to try to offer some new hypotheses concerning the perplexing problem of Dante and comedy. I shall begin by trying to see whether, in the *Commedia*, despite the paucity of explicit references, Dante did, in fact, address the 'comic' through other means. In the light of this investigation, I shall go on to explore the connections, on the one hand, between the poem's title and its literary character and, on the other, between the title and the poem's exegesis by looking at the cultural, ideological, and artistic reasons that might have led Dante to define "l poema sacro | al quale ha posto mano e cielo e terra' (*Par.* xxv. 1–2) as 'questa comedía' (*Inf.* xvi. 128). Having established the ideological parameters within which reflection on comedy may have taken place in late-medieval Italy and Dante's views on and application of the *stilus*, I shall then focus on the specific question of the poet's (and his culture's) attitude towards the Roman comedians. Finally, I shall examine the possible interconnections between the two sides of the problem — a perspective that, surprisingly, has rarely been attempted — in the hope of clarifying further Dante's encounter with the 'comic'.

2. The Question of the Title

Although satisfactory explanations for the *Commedia*'s title have remained elusive (for a discussion of the various proposals, see Subsection 6 below), it was in fact a critical commonplace in the Middle Ages that special attention be paid to a work's *titulus*. This point was most influentially affirmed in the tradition of the *accessus ad auctores*: 'In exponendis auctoribus haec consideranda sunt: poetae vita, titulus operis, qualitas carminis, scribentis intentio, numerus librorum, ordo librorum, explanatio' [These are the things to be considered in commenting on the authors: the life of the poet, the title of the work, the quality of the verse, the intention of the writer, the number of books, their arrangement, and explanation].[9] It is thus unremarkable that several of the Trecento commentators should have focused on Dante's title. What is more significant, however, is that, with the notable exception of Jacopo Alighieri[10] and of the second version of the Ottimo, none managed to

---

8   Francesco da Buti, 'Il "Commento" di Francesco da Buti alla "Commedia". "Inferno"', ed. by Claudia Tardelli (unpublished PhD thesis, Scuola Normale Superiore di Pisa, 2010–11), p. 851.

9   *Servii Grammatici qui fertur in Vergilii carmina commentarii*, ed. by Georg Thilo and Hermann Hagen, 3 vols (Leipzig: Teubner, 1881–87), *In Verg. Aen.*, vol. I, Praef. 1–3. See also Denis van Berchem, 'Poètes et grammariens: recherches sur la tradition scolaire d'explication des auteurs', *Museum Helveticum*, 9 (1952), 79–87 (pp. 79–82); Alastair J. Minnis, *Medieval Theory of Authorship*, 2nd edn (Aldershot: Scolar Press, 1988), pp. 15–16, 19–20.

10   'Io Iacopo suo figliuolo per maternale prosa dimostrare intendo parte del suo profondo e autentico intendimento, incominciando in prima a quello che ragionevolmente pare che si convegnia, cioè che suo titol sia [...]. // Il cui ordine brievemente così comincio che, secondo quello che ciertamente appare in quattro stili ogni autentico parlar si conchiude, de' quali: [...]. Il secondo, commedia, sotto il quale generalmente, e universalmente si tratta di tutte le cose, e quindi il titol

offer an adequate explanation for the poet's slippery designation.[11] In fact, like Buti, they express reservations about the appropriateness of the poem being labelled a *comedía*, even when they cleave close to the widely circulating, and not entirely inappropriate as far as the *Commedia* is concerned, structural definition of comedy — a definition which, as with similar 'comic' commonplaces, is conventionally (and conveniently) repeated in the letter to Cangrande: 'Et per hoc patet quod Comedia dicitur presens opus. Nam si ad materiam respiciamus, a principio horribilis et fetida est, quia Infernus, in fine prospera, desiderabilis et grata, quia Paradisus' [it is clear that the present work is called a Comedy. For if we look carefully at the subject-matter, at the beginning it is horrific and disgusting, because it is the Inferno, at the end it is rich, desirable, and pleasing, because it is the Paradiso] (XIII. 31–32).[12]

If the commentators' strictures are valid, then the implications are quite startling. Dante was not just demonstrating little discrimination and sensitivity when he gave his poem the title *Comedía*, but he could also be accused of having been wilfully misleading in light of the *titulus*'s accepted exegetical functions. Such a conclusion, however, is most unlikely. Dante is famous for his critical sophistication and for the care with which he brought together reflection on literature with literary creativity. Furthermore, throughout his writings, the poet always revealed an incisively lucid appreciation of his culture's complex reactions both to the composition and to the consumption of literature. It would be more reasonable to surmise, therefore, that Dante chose his title with care, and that it was the commentators who failed adequately to grasp the implications of what he was trying to convey with his bold choice of *titulus*. The same can in fact be said about their explanations of the *Commedia*'s formal and stylistic characteristics in general. With the possible exception of Benvenuto da Imola, they consistently fail to account for the poem's *novitas*. Thus, even though Dante was almost certainly employing the term *comedía* in a new and unconventional manner, this does not mean that he would have expected his readers, trained in the ways of the *accessus*, to ignore his title. If anything, given its striking unusualness, the opposite would hold true. Nor would Dante have been intentionally and flippantly obscure as regards an element that was normally readily accessible to a medieval audience. He must have believed that, despite the difficulties, his use of 'comedía' would still be open to interpretation.

The question of the *Commedia*'s title, therefore, remains a key critical problem.[13] An answer to how and why Dante's poem is a 'comedy' might help both to define it

del presente volume procede': Jacopo Alighieri, *Chiose all''Inferno'*, ed. by Saverio Bellomo (Padua: Antenore, 1990), pp. 85–86.

11   *L'Ottimo commento della Divina Commedia*, ed. by Alessandro Torri, 3 vols (Pisa: Niccolò Capurro, 1827–29), I, 97.

12   For a survey of the commentators' views on comedy and tragedy, see Henry A. Kelly, *Tragedy and Comedy from Dante to Pseudo-Dante* (Berkeley, Los Angeles, and London: University of California Press, 1989).

13   Since its publication in 1991, this analysis has been received positively and has exercised a certain influence on Dante studies. However, as with all scholarship, its conclusions can only ever be provisional. As the noteworthy assortment of new studies confirms (see in particular the contributions cited in the latter part of n. 2), the *Commedia*'s title continues to perplex.

and to offer clues as to the ways in which it should be read.[14] Given the traditionally close inter-relationship between a text and its title, the fact that the *Commedia* boldly and immediately displays its status in its *titulus* suggests that, far from being parsimonious with his technical clarifications regarding the 'comic', Dante was actually being quite generous. Since the term *comedía* embraces the poem as a whole, it is not unreasonable to surmise that all its metaliterary features — which proliferate in the *Commedia* — in some way go towards explaining Dante's use of the term. To put it simply, the whole of the poem, to a greater or lesser extent, clarifies its 'comic' qualities. And one aspect is visible straightaway. By associating the well-known, probably hackneyed concept of *comedia* with his stylistically radically innovative poem, Dante underlined not only the novelty of his work but also its connections with the literary tradition. We are once again close to that fundamental ideological framework of 'authority and challenge'.

Before I proceed, however, a brief explanatory aside. It might be wondered why I have so far made little mention of the letter to Cangrande. This is not so much the result of my doubts regarding Dante's authorship of the epistle. In support of my reservations, I would highlight, for example, the conservatism of its technical explanations when compared both to the poem's artistic practices and, as we shall see, to its metaliterary statements. Indeed, as regards the *Commedia*'s title, Giorgio Brugnoli has argued persuasively that, of the various solutions so far put forward, 'quella del "lieto fine" proposta nell'Epistola e la meno accertabile'.[15] Rather, even if the letter were by Dante, this would not alter one basic fact. When Dante wrote and circulated the bulk of his poem, he could not count on the epistle's exegetical support (1317 has been proposed as its earliest possible date of composition).[16] Suggestions on how the *Commedia* might be read and on how its title might be interpreted need to be sought in the poem itself, especially in light of the richly shaded, text-based interpretive tradition (*poetarum enarratio*; the exegesis of the poets) that the Middle Ages had developed.[17]

14   Gérard Genette is typical in reacting with bafflement at the poem's formal textual status: 'à quel genre appartient la *Divine Comédie?*', *Palimpsestes* (Paris: Seuil, 1982), p. 11.

15   Giorgio Brugnoli, annotations to *Epistole*, ed. by Arsenio Frugoni and Giorgio Brugnoli, in Dante Alighieri, *Opere minori*, 2 vols (Milan and Naples: Ricciardi, 1979–88), II, 505–643 (p. 616). See also the preceding chapter.

16   For my reservations regarding the letter's authenticity, see Barański, '*Comedía*', and 'The *Epistle to Cangrande*', in Minnis and Johnson, pp. 583–89. See also, Chapter 6.

17   See, in particular, Martin Irvine, *The Making of Textual Culture: 'Grammatica' and Literary Theory, 350–1100* (Cambridge: Cambridge University Press, 1994); *Medieval Grammar & Rhetoric: Language Arts and Literary Theory, AD 300–1475*, ed. by Rita Copeland and Ineke Sluiter (Oxford: Oxford University Press, 2009); *MLTC*; *The Cambridge History of Literary Criticism. II. The Middle Ages*, ed. by Minnis and Johnson.

3. From *imitatio* to *novitas*

In the *Commedia*, Dante frequently emphasizes the artistic difficulties that faced him as he composed his poem; for example:

> Chi poria mai pur con parole sciolte
> dicer del sangue e de le piaghe a pieno
> ch'i' ora vidi, per narrar più volte?
>   Ogne lingua per certo verria meno
> per lo nostro sermone e per la mente
> c' hanno a tanto comprender poco seno. (*Inf.* XXVIII. 1–6)

To highlight his predicament as he tried to describe the grotesque horrors of the bolgia of the schismatics, the poet, in seemingly conventional terms, brings together two clearly signposted rhetorical commonplaces. The belief that prose was more flexible than verse — 'parole sciolte' is here a technical term — is integrated with a pair of ineffability *topoi*.[18] Thus, according to Dante, not even prose would be able adequately to represent what he saw. The infernal spectacle that met his eyes was more shocking than the combined bloody massacres recorded in classical and contemporary historiography:

> S'el s'aunasse ancor tutta la gente
> che già, in su la fortunata terra
> di Puglia, fu del suo sangue dolente
>   per li Troiani e per la lunga guerra
> che de l'anella fé sì alte spoglie,
> come Livïo scrive, che non erra,
>   con quella che sentio di colpi doglie
> per contastare a Ruberto Guiscardo;
> e l'altra il cui ossame ancor s'accoglie
>   a Ceperan, là dove fu bugiardo
> ciascun Pugliese, e là da Tagliacozzo,
> dove sanz'arme vinse il vecchio Alardo;
>   e qual forato suo membro e qual mozzo
> mostrasse, d'aequar sarebbe nulla
> il modo de la nona bolgia sozzo. (*Inf.* XXVIII. 7–21)

In medieval texts, such claims were not unusual: they were part of the hyperbole of rhetorically nuanced literary composition. Yet, in *Inferno* XXVIII, their function is neither straighforwardly decorative nor a sop to tradition. Despite the lengthy preamble asserting the contrary, Dante of course goes on to fill the remainder of the canto with one of his graphically most successful and powerful descriptions. We thus have the astonishing situation — in medieval terms — whereby a poem shows itself to be more elastic and better able to record experience than prose, and historiographical prose at that, which was believed to be the secular literary form that came closest to the truth of the real event. To define Livy, even if conventionally, as a writer 'who does not err' is to remind the reader unambiguously

---

18   On *verba soluta* and prose in general, see Isidore, *Etym.* I. 38. See also Chapter 6, p. 244.

of this fact.[19] Yet, while Dante praised the Roman writer as the *auctoritas* in the field of historical writing in a manner consonant with current perceptions, at the same time he felt it necessary to underscore Livy's limitations — and by extension that of historiography in general — as a model that might help him deal with the reality of his eschatological journey. Whatever the achievements of the literary tradition, Dante needed to go beyond its conventions and standard solutions. Furthermore, the emphasis on history also serves to recall that the account found in the *Commedia* records events that are neither fictional nor belong to secular history; hence, the inadequacy of historiography as a model for 'imitation'. Dante clearly established in *Inferno* I, the prologue to the poem as a whole, that the *Commedia* tells of things that are part of providential history, and which thus need to be interpreted according to Scriptural *allegoria in factis*.[20] The reasons why the poet is only able to depend in part on secular literature and its norms are becoming clearer, as are the experimental bias of Dante's formal procedures and the tension that these create between his poem and the tradition.

As is now generally accepted, the *Commedia* constitutes Dante's major challenge to established contemporary literary theory and practice. Yet, as *Inferno* XXVIII goes on to make clear, the full extent of this challenge is more radical than the already startling fact that the *Commedia* is poetry that is more flexible than prose and 'truer' than history.[21] Dante describes a sinner's mutilated body:

> Già veggia, per mezzul perdere o lulla,
> com'io vidi un, così non si pertugia,
> rotto dal mento infin dove si trulla.
>   Tra le gambe pendevan le minugia;
> la corata pareva e 'l tristo sacco
> che merda fa di quel che si trangugia. (*Inf.* XXVIII. 22–27)

The shock of this passage for a medieval reader cannot be overestimated. The accumulated lexical violence of the colloquialisms, of the scatological terms (see Chapter 19), and of the semi-technical vocabulary of Florentine barrel-makers would have been deemed quite inappropriate for poetry, even that written in the

---

19   On medieval notions of *historia* and historiography, see Pierre Courroux, *L'Écriture de l'histoire dans les chroniques françaises (XIIe–XVe siècle)* (Paris: Garnier, 2016); Henri de Lubac, *Exégèse médiévale*, 2 vols (Paris: Aubier, 1959–64), I:2, 425–78; Bernard Guenée, *Histoire et culture historique dans l'Occident médiéval* (Paris: Aubier Montaigne, 1980); A. Seifert, 'Historia im Mittelalter', *Archiv für Begriffsgeschichte*, 21 (1977), 226–84; Beryl Smalley, *Historians in the Middle Ages* (London: Thames and Hudson, 1974); Peter von Moos, 'Poeta und Historicus im Mittelalter: Zum Mimesis-Problem am Beispiel einiger Urteile über Lucan', *Beiträge zur Geschichte der deutschen Sprache und Literatur*, 98 (1976), 93–130; *Historiography in the Middle Ages*, ed. by Deborah M. Deliyannis (Leiden: Brill, 2003); *L'Écriture de l'histoire au Moyen Âge: contraintes génériques, contraintes documentaires*, ed. by Étienne Anheim and others (Paris: Garnier, 2015); *Le Métier d'historien au Moyen Âge*, ed. by Bernard Guenée (Paris: Publications de la Sorbonne, 1977); *The Writing of History in the Middle Ages*, ed. by Ralph H. C. Davis and John M. Wallace-Hadrill (Oxford: The Clarendon Press, 1981).

20   See Zygmunt G. Barański, *Dante e i segni: saggi per una storia intellettuale di Dante Alighieri* (Naples: Liguori, 2000), pp. 103–26.

21   As Dante himself recognized, poetry was commonly associated with fiction: *poesis* 'nihil aliud est quam fictio rethorica musicaque poita' [is nothing else than a fiction based on rhetoric and music] (*Dve* II. 4. 2).

'low' style. Such richly seasoned verbal expressionism could neither find support in the lexicon conventionally associated with the *stilus humilis* in rhetorical and grammatical handbooks and in the commentary tradition, nor in the practices of, say, the so-called *comico-realistici*. An even greater *vitium* is the mingling of 'styles' in the opening nine *terzine* of canto XXVIII, which directly contravenes the doctrine of the *genera dicendi* on which contemporary grammatical education, aesthetics, and poetics were all substantially based: 'Quartum uitium est incogrua stili mutatio' [The fourth mistake is the incoherent change of style].[22] In 'stylistic' terms, Dante has unjustifiably — to be precise, erroneously — modified his register from a recognizably 'high' style and 'tragic' subject-matter in the first twenty-one lines (the presentation of martial themes) to an idiosyncratic form of the 'low' style. What is more: the poet could not even claim that he was treating a different topic, as he was still presenting wounds inflicted by the sword, though, obviously, with reference to very different circumstances. The 'stylistic' eclecticism and experimentation at the start of *Inferno* XXVIII draw attention to the fact that, not just historical prose, but even the 'tragic' style as a whole is inadequate to deal with the concerns of Dante's 'comedía': a perspective that overturns the traditional hierarchy between tragedy and comedy. This is further underlined, when it is recalled, as John of Garland had advised, that if, as in canto XXVIII, a shift in subject-matter and *stilus* was unavoidable, then, the 'higher' *forma* had always to be adopted throughout.[23] At the same time, on account of his recourse to a most peculiar 'low' style to paint the portrait of Mohammed, Dante was also emphasizing his reservations as regards traditional *humilis* forms. By skilfully integrating poetry and reflection on the poetic, a standard procedure in the *Commedia* and often used for the same effect as here (see Subsection I), Dante points to one of the central pillars on which he constructed his poem — one, furthermore, that is close to the heart of his vision of the 'comic': his sense of the unnecessary restrictiveness of the doctrine of the *genera dicendi* and of the literary tradition that this had engendered and sustained. He begins to describe the infernal massacre by 'imitating' established rhetorical and literary conventions. However, he is soon forced to abandon these as they prove unsatisfactory for the task at hand. 'Stylistic' syncretism — the opposite of the enshrined belief that insisted on 'stylistic' separation — was his solution. To put it simply, Dante had to break the rules in order to write 'questa *sua* comedía' (see Chapters 6 and 8).

---

22 'Glose in Poetriam Horatii' (more commonly known as the 'Materia' commentary), p. 337, in Karsten Friis-Jensen, 'The *Ars Poetica* in Twelfth-century France: The Horace of Matthew of Vendôme, Geoffrey of Vinsauf, and John of Garland', *Cahiers de l'Institut du Moyen-Âge Grec et Latin*, 60 (1990), 319–88 (pp. 336–84), now reprinted in Karsten Friis-Jensen, *The Medieval Horace*, ed. by Karin M. Fredborg and others (Rome: Edizioni Quasar, 2015), pp. 51–99. On the *genera*, the fundamental study remains Franz Quadlbauer, *Die antike Theorie der 'Genera dicendi' im lateinischen Mittelalter* (Vienna: Hermann Bohlaus Nachf., 1962). See also Chapter 6, pp. 224–26.
23 John of Garland, *The 'Parisiana Poetria' of John of Garland*, ed. by Traugott Lawler (New Haven, CT, and London: Yale University Press, 1974), V. 51–54.

4. Reading the New Comedy

To explain the *Commedia*'s hybrid, and thus rhetorically 'deficient' style, a number of scholars has insisted, in contrast to my argument in the preceding subsection, that the answer to Dante's experimentation is nevertheless to be found in the precepts of the *artes poetriae*. For them, the poem is original because it exploits rhetorically established *convenientiae* in a flexible manner and embraces the whole of the *rota Vergilii*. While limited, this claim is not invalid. At the same time, as far as I have been able to establish, no rhetorical work or treatise on poetics circulating in the late Middle Ages provides a justification for the sort of experimentation that Dante pursued in the *Commedia*.[24] In addition, the implications of the poet's formal choices should not be viewed so much as a further sign of the all-embracing power of contemporary rhetoric and poetics, but as evidence of Dante's sense of their limitations. The poet made his position limpidly clear throughout the *Commedia*, but perhaps rarely as pointedly as in *Paradiso* XXIII.

Once again, Dante asks his reader to be indulgent. In this instance, he is accounting for his failure to re-evoke the beauty of Beatrice's smile illuminated by Christ in His triumph:

> Ma chi pensasse il ponderoso tema
> e l'omero mortal che se ne carca,
> nol biasmerebbe se sott'esso trema. (*Par.* XXIII. 64–66)

It is a critical commonplace to recognize the source of this *terzina* in Horace's *Ars poetica*:

> Sumite materiam vestris, qui scribitis, aequam
> viribus et versate diu, quid ferre recusent,
> quid valeant umeri. cui lecta potenter erit res,
> nec facundia deseret hunc nec lucidus ordo.
> ordinis haec virtus erit et venus, aut ego fallor,
> ut iam nunc dicat iam nunc debentia dici,
> pleraque differat et praesens in tempus omittat,
> hoc amet, hoc spernat promissi carminis auctor. (*AP* 38–45)

[Pick a subject, you writers, equal to your strength and consider carefully what your shoulders refuse and what they are able to bear. Whoever will have made a skilful choice, will not lack eloquence nor elegant arrangement. This will be the virtue and elegance of the arrangement, unless I'm mistaken, that the author of the promised poem will say at the moment what at that moment should be said, and delaying and omitting much at present, loving this, scorning that.]

However, it has not been adequately noted that Dante is openly subverting Horace's teaching. Given the uniqueness of the subject-matter of his 'comedía', not even one of the most basic poetic and rhetorical rules is deemed to apply. More generally, the poet is also calling into question Horace's famous and highly influential precepts on artistic unity and discretion with which the *Ars poetica* opens, and to

---

24 At the same time, it is the case that a sense of literature's 'flexibility' is implicit in the ways in which medieval criticism categorized *scriptura*; see Chapter 6.

which the above lines are a kind of appendix. More specifically, Dante is revising his own earlier adherence to such doctrines. Horace's theories were at the centre of contemporary *poetriae*, including the *De vulgari eloquentia*: 'Ante omnia ergo dicimus unumquenque debere materie pondus propriis humeris coequare, ne forte humerorum nimio gravata virtute in cenum cespitare necesse sit: hoc est quod Magister noster Oratius precipit cum in principio Poetrie "Sumite materiam" dicit' [I say therefore that first and foremost any writer should match the weight of his subject-matter to his own shoulders, lest he stumble in the mud because the strength of his shoulders is excessively burdened: this is what our master Horace teaches when at the beginning of the *Ars poetica* he says 'Pick a subject'] (*Dve* II. 4. 4). In particular, in line with Horace, the lines were used to vindicate the doctrine of the division of styles (see, in particular, *Dve* II. 4. 5–6), whose constraints Dante was concerned to highlight in the *Commedia*.[25] What is suggestive, however, is that while the poet was underlining rhetoric's failure to account for his poem, he was quite willing to carry on exploiting individual traditional elements, as may be seen in his choice of title and in his composition of both *Inferno* XXVIII and *Paradiso* XXIII.

This seemingly ambivalent attitude is probably the most vital aspect in understanding the *Commedia*'s poetics and ultimately Dante's choice of title. Although the poet relentlessly stressed the *novitas* of his work, nevertheless, he was acutely aware that he needed to communicate within a culture that set great store by convention and which, almost unconsciously, associated particular formal procedures with certain meanings and values. Thus, in the broadest comparative terms, Dante did rhetorically 'raise' his stylistic register as he moved from one *cantica* to the next. He similarly made constant recourse to the works and the standard contemporary images of other authors. Quite simply, if his great work of reform was to succeed, he needed to communicate in an accessible manner. Dante was not an 'avant-garde' artist in the twentieth-century sense: his respect for the tradition was deep (it is enough to remember his treatment of Virgil). On the other hand, he was aware of the unnecessary, even unreasonable, constraints that a dogmatically preceptive approach could impose, and not just on a poem with the *Commedia*'s 'unique' concerns. His artistic aim was to innovate — and also to criticize — in a measured and reasoned manner from inside the tradition, rather than to rebut what had gone before. In fact, if Dante had not created tensions, from within the poem itself, between the rhetorically sanctioned literary models and his own personal solutions, he would have found it difficult to draw attention to the originality of the *Commedia*. Although he challenged the dominant rhetorical *forma mentis*, his basic appreciation of what constituted rhetoric's concerns remained that which he would have learned when he first began to study *grammatica*.

25   On Dante and Horace, see Zygmunt G. Barański, '*Magister satiricus*: Preliminary Notes on Dante, Horace and the Middle Ages', in *Language and Style in Dante*, ed. by John C. Barnes and Michelangelo Zaccarello (Dublin: Four Courts Press, 2013), pp. 13–61, which includes an extensive bibliography of Horace's influence on Dante and on his medieval reception. See in addition Zygmunt G. Barański, '*Inferno* I', in *Lectura Dantis Bononiensis*, ed. by Emilio Pasquini and Carlo Galli (Bologna: Bononia University Press, 2011), pp. 11–40 (pp. 21–26); Tavoni, *Qualche idea su Dante*, pp. 335–69; Piermario Vescovo, 'La via dei satiri. ("Oratius satyrorum scriptor")', *L'Alighieri*, 58 (2017), 6–28.

Dante was well aware of the interpretive difficulties that his experimentation was likely to cause. However, not unreasonably, he expected his readers to engage in deciphering his poem by drawing on the methods that they had been taught in their grammar classes — a manner of reading that the exegetical tradition constantly reaffirmed. His addresses to the ubiquitous *lettor* are simply the most accessible examples of this design. Dante believed that, in order to make apparent the *Commedia*'s original features, he would be able to count on the refined literary-technical memories and exegetical skills of, at least, the most sophisticated among his audience. To help and guide his readers in this operation, the poet introduced, as we have already noted, a remarkable array of metaliterary elements — elements that range from the reworking of standard literary models to the use of critical language. He hoped that these would illuminate his poem's *novitas*, since his approach would be recognizable to his contemporaries. Thus, his use of metaliterary features as stimuli to exegesis is typical of medieval literature. Yet, both their number (there is scarcely a canto that does not include several such references) and the carefully planned way in which these are introduced distinguish Dante's approach from that of other writers. Furthermore, if one considers, for example, the metrical definition of *Purgatorio* ('questa cantica seconda', *Purg.* XXXIII. 140) the distance between Dante's and other current uses of the term *cantica* is soon apparent, though the poet also wanted some connection between these to be recognized.[26] Dante referred to the *Commedia* in a language and in narrative, exegetical, and poetic micro-structures familiar to his time (it is especially noteworthy that, as far as I know, he did not invent a single new technical term with which to describe his disturbingly innovatory poem).[27] Yet, a semantic and artistic discrepancy is almost always apparent between the subject-matter and style of the passages in which he re-elaborated his literary sources or into which he introduced his technical statements, and the customary uses to which these same traditional elements were normally put (my analyses of *Inferno* XXVIII and *Paradiso* XXIII offer some insight into the nature and ramifications of this procedure; but see especially Subsection 6; indeed most of the chapters on Dante in this volume touch on these same matters). Thus, in the semantic and ideological 'gap' that would be created between a reader's conventional literary expectations in being told that 'Livy does not err' and the *Commedia*'s unexpected exploitation of this claim, Dante believed elucidations for his experiments would begin to emerge. To overcome her or his confusion, the reader would be forced to interpret, and as a result, the poem's distinctive standing vis-à-vis the tradition would emerge and be justified.

---

26   On *cantica* in particular and on the general point being made here, see Chapter 8.
27   This claim still holds good as I revise this chapter almost thirty years after I began researching the *Commedia*'s peculiar *titulus*.

5. 'e cielo e terra'

It is likely that Dante's choice of title can also be resolved in light of the general interpretive scheme that I have just delineated; and that his attitude towards the Roman comedians too will become clearer if viewed from this perspective. However, before I come to these matters (see Subsections 6, 7, and 8), I need to consider one last major question as I seek to establish the complexity of the term 'comedy' in Dante. Given his challenge to the rhetorical and literary traditions, how might the poet have sought to authorize his new 'comic' style?

If we return once more to *Inferno* XXVIII's *prooemium*, it would not be unreasonable to suggest that, having so effectively dismissed not just Livy but also the *auctores tragici et comici* in general, Dante, in medieval terms, is actually attempting the 'impossible' — writing *sine auctoritatibus*.[28] As is often the case, however, appearances are deceptive: not least because Dante was keenly aware of the need to vindicate his work in a manner that would not offend his audience's sensibilities. To have done otherwise, would have meant to countermand the *Commedia*'s fundamental moral purpose:

> In pro del mondo che mal vive,
> [...] e quel che vedi,
> ritornato di là, fa che tu scrive. (*Purg.* XXXII. 103–05)

According to Dante, there were two principal reasons, closely related to each other, why the literature that preceded the *Commedia* could not offer an appropriate model for his poem. One, as I have argued, was its rigid attachment to the *genera dicendi*; the other, as I hinted earlier, was that no human text was as directly involved in God's providential scheme of things as his 'comedy'. Unlike his literary predecessors, Dante had the divinely ordained duty to report 'all' that he had learned on his eschatological journey (*Purg.* XXXIII. 52–57), an experience that seems to have touched upon every aspect of 'ciò che per l'universo sì squaderna' (*Par.* XXXIII. 87); and he had to do this as accurately as possible:

> Ma nondimen, rimossa ogne menzogna,
> tutta tua visïon fa manifesta;
> e lascia pur grattar dov'è la rogna. (*Par.* XVII. 127–29)

Consequently, Dante could only achieve his purpose if he were free to use those linguistic solutions that his discrimination — sharpened by his journey and his artistic gifts (*Par.* XXII. 112–14) — suggested as most suitable for achieving his momentous ends. Quite simply, Dante claimed to be using language and literature to do God's work. It thus no longer made sense for him to be limited by human conventions, in particular, given the breadth of his *materia*, by something as artificially restrictive as the partitions of the *genera dicendi*. These perforce had to be remodified as a result of their contact with the divine, since, as the *Commedia*

---

28   On Dante's profound and sensitive concern with *auctoritas*, see Albert R. Ascoli, *Dante and the Making of a Modern Author* (Cambridge: Cambridge University Press, 2008). See also Zygmunt G. Barański, *'Sole nuovo, luce nuova': saggi sul rinnovamento culturale in Dante* (Turin: Scriptorium, 1996). I also touch on this matter at various points in this collection.

explains, the principal authority for Dante's revolutionary poetics came from Heaven (see in particular Chapter 9).

Dante takes care to substantiate and to explain the workings and implications of these formidable claims. Thus, in *Paradiso* XXIII, the poet indicates some of the problems involved in 'figurando il paradiso' (61). *Figurare* here means 'to represent figuratively', and is an apt term with which to describe the style of the *Paradiso* given its dependence on tropes and imagery.[29] In addition, *figurare* offers an insight into the *cantica*'s underlying poetics. Dante insisted that, on account of the limitations of the human mind, his memory of Paradise was both extremely limited and highly mediated. All that he could recall was 'l'ombra del beato regno' (*Par.* I. 23). This intellectual failure has two compositional consequences. First, the account proffered in *Paradiso* is not based on first-hand recollections, as in *Inferno* and *Purgatorio*, but on a memorial trope, a 'shadow' of the original experience — this is the case as regards the Empyrean (approximately *Par.* XXX–XXXIII). Second, the bulk of the third canticle describes the poet's reminiscences of a 'figurative' representation of celestial realities that he would finally experience directly in the 'celestial rose' before largely forgetting them: the ascent up the heavens of the Ptolemaic cosmos (see Chapter 5).

And *figurare* has still other, equally noteworthy resonances in the *Commedia*. A couple of cantos further on, it is used, in an explicitly Scriptural allusion, to refer to the symbolic status that James the Apostle has in the New Testament as the representative of Hope:

> fa risonar la spene in questa altezza:
> tu [James] sai, che tante fiate la figuri,
> quante Iesù ai tre fé più carezza. (*Par.* XXV. 31–33)

Dante is drawing attention to the commonplace belief in the Bible's symbolic character. In particular, through the use of *figurare*, he is pointing to its allegory.[30] Yet, since he utilizes the same verb with a similar meaning first in *Paradiso* XXIII and then in *Paradiso* XXV, he also appears to hint at a possible inter-relationship between the techniques and allegory of his poem and those of the divine book. The equation

---

29   *Figurare* was extensively used with this meaning in allegorical, rhetorical-grammatical, and exegetical writing; see, for instance, 'Si vero contra argumentetur [on the question of animals' inability to speak] quis de eo quod Ovidius dicit in quinto Metamorfoseos de picis loquentibus, dicimus quod hoc figurate dicit, aliud intelligens' [But if somebody should argue against what Ovid says in the fifth book of the *Metamorphoses* about the talking fish, I reply that he speaks figuratively, and means something different] (*Dve* I. 2. 7); and, in general, see the entry in *TLL*. Modern Dante commentators generally fail to grasp the complex semantic range of the verb in line 61, since they take it as a simple equivalent of 'to describe'.

30   On Biblical figurative allegory, see at least Marie-Dominique Chenu, *La Théologie au douzième siècle* (Paris: Vrin, 1957); Henri de Lubac, *Exégèse médiévale*, 2 vols (Paris: Aubier, 1959–64), English translation: *Medieval Exegesis: The Four Senses of Scripture*, 3 vols (Grand Rapids, MI: Eerdmans, 1998–2009); Beryl Smalley, *The Study of the Bible in the Middle Ages*, 3rd edn (Oxford: Blackwell, 1983); Ceslas Spicq, *Esquisse d'une histoire de l'exégèse latine* (Paris: Vrin, 1944); Armand Strubel, 'Allegoria in factis et Allegoria in verbis', *Poétique*, 23 (1975) 342–57, and 'Grant senefiance a': allégorie et littérature au Moyen Âge (Paris: Champion, 2002); Jon Whitman, *Allegory: The Dynamics of an Ancient and Medieval Technique* (Oxford: Clarendon Press, 1987).

is, in fact, strongly supported by *Paradiso* xxv as a whole. The canto highlights some of the ways in which the *Commedia* imitates and assimilates Biblical forms.[31] The special links uniting the work of the divine artist, source for every book, and Dante's poem are further strengthened when we recall the magnificent 'speaking' sculptures that God had fashioned on the first *girone* of Purgatory. Here, too, Dante chose *figurare* to define the Creator's artistry when he depicted the effigies of punished pride in terms of earthly sepulchral carvings:

> sì vid'io lì, ma di miglior sembianza
> secondo l'artificio, figurato
> quanto per via di fuor del monte avanza. (*Purg.* xii. 22–24)

Although *figurare* occurs on two other occasions in the *Commedia* (*Inf.* xviii. 43 and *Purg.* xxv. 107), neither of these instances has aesthetic connotations. Among all that wealth and variety of human art that Dante evokes in his poem, only his 'comedía' shares in divine 'figuring'.

Yet, despite his divine election, Dante remains a quintessentially human poet, and hence inescapably depends, as he makes immediately evident in *Inferno* i when he meets Virgil, on earthly literary 'authorities'. Indeed, together with pinpointing the *Commedia*'s Scriptural traits, *Paradiso* xxiii draws attention to its engagement with the works of human authors: 'e così, figurando il paradiso, | convien saltar lo sacrato poema' (61–62). While the definition 'sacrato poema' plainly ties the *Commedia* to the divine (this is confirmed in the *incipit* of the 'Scriptural' *Paradiso* xxv: ''l poema sacro | al quale ha posto mano e cielo e terra', 1–2), it nonetheless also ties it to Virgil thanks to Macrobius's description of the *Aeneid* as *sacrum poema* (*Sat.* i. 24. 13).[32] Dante seems to be implying that his *Commedia* is a synthesis in the vernacular of God's mode of 'writing' and secular literary culture, especially as exemplified by Virgil (or the Latin *auctores* in general), who, in fact, can stand for the entire tradition, on account of his magisterial contribution to each of the three 'styles'. It would seem that Dante's claim that the *Commedia* has debts to 'both heaven and earth' is to be taken seriously; and it is difficult to think of more potent *auctoritates* for a fourteenth-century literary work than God and Virgil or, more generally, the classical 'authors'. Dante thus persists with his usual metaliterary scheme. He grounds his explanations in accepted notions as regards both the *Deus artifex* and the classics, but then, especially through their rapprochement, he modifies their

---

31   See, for example, Kevin Brownlee, 'Why the Angels Speak Italian: Dante as Vernacular *poeta* in *Paradiso* xxv', *Poetics Today*, 5 (1984), 597–610; Stefano Prandi, 'Canto xxv: "Ritornerò poeta"', in *Lectura Dantis Romana. Cento canti per cento anni. III. 'Paradiso'. 2. Canti XVIII–XXXIII*, ed. by Enrico Malato and Andrea Mazzucchi (Rome: Salerno, 2015), pp. 723–46.

32   Very recently, doubts have been cast on the likelihood that Dante could have known Macrobius's description of the *Aeneid*: Federico Rossi, '"Poema sacro" tra Dante e Macrobio: una verifica sulla tradizione italiana dei *Saturnalia*', *L'Alighieri*, 58 (2017), 29–51. I am generally persuaded by Rossi's case. However, his study not only does not invalidate the claims that I had made in 1991, and which I restate here, but provides supporting evidence for my argument. Rossi writes: 'il significato della formula ['poema sacro'], che potrà [...] essere messa in parallelo con le tradizionali designazioni di *sacrum carmen* o *sacra carmina* associate a singoli libri della Bibbia', but which can also be associated with '*la* letteratura classica, all'interno della quale non di rado troviamo la poesia indicata sotto l'etichetta di *sacra*' (pp. 47–48).

customary terms of reference to pinpoint the *Commedia*'s peculiarities. For instance, it is intriguing that God alone cannot serve as his 'authority'.

In writing the *Commedia*, given its synthesizing eclecticism (and despite the press of secular literary allusion), Dante's most direct structural models could only be God's two 'books': the universe which includes the whole of creation 'in un volume' (*Par.* XXXIII. 86), into whose pages the pilgrim had been granted the unique privilege of looking, and the Bible which is written according to the stylistically all-embracing conventions of the *sermo humilis*.[33] Dante, in his turn, dutifully strove to create a similar synthesis by constraining and integrating the different rhetorical 'styles', literary genres, and languages of his culture within a numerically harmonious structure of threes and tens that could serve as a textual *exemplum* of the principles and *ordo* of God's creation. It was also meant to exhibit the divine hand behind the *Commedia*'s genesis. By imitating the divine artist, Dante drew legitimacy for his experimentation from the one source where no pedantic and conservative schoolmaster could find fault. Humanity's duty, inspired by the *Commedia*, was to follow the lead of its author and adhere to the divine lesson, thereby achieving a properly ordered balance in all its activities. By claiming God as his *auctoritas*, Dante was able to weave his artistic and didactic concerns into a single skein.

Dante's 'theological poetics' instituted and subscribed to a 'new rhetoric' — one that, in opposition to the 'old rhetoric' with its discrete *genera dicendi*, made a virtue of plurality in oneness.[34] This was the only literary ideal fit for one of Western culture's most committed syncretists; and it is, thus, inevitable that Dante's attitude in his poem whether to grammar, or to rhetoric, or to the literary tradition, or most especially to the world, was always a synthesizing one. At every level of the *Commedia*, Dante relied on his human reworking of the macroscopic syncretist model of divine origin. It is evident too, for example, in the poem's allegorical superstructure which fuses *allegoria in factis* with that *in verbis*, and both of these with conventional and personification allegory (Barański, *Segni*, pp. 103–26). Once again, Dante's aim was to meld religious and secular culture; or, to put it more starkly, the Bible with Virgil — the mix that essentially delimits the *Commedia*'s poetics.

One of the main reasons why Dante forged a privileged allegorical and intertextual bond between his poem and the Bible was to sanction the truth of his account. Since the twelfth century, the literal-historical sense of the holy book had once again become crucial. On the other hand, however, thanks in no small part to Thomas Aquinas's strictures, the 'letter' of secular writing was increasingly called into question.[35] To complicate matters further, while the events described

33   See Erich Auerbach, *Literary Language and its Public in Late Latin Antiquity* (London: Routledge & Kegan Paul, 1965), and 'Sacrae scripturae sermo humilis', in his *Studi su Dante* (Milan: Feltrinelli, 1978), pp. 165–73; Edgar de Bruyne, *Études d'esthétique médiévale*, 3 vols (Bruges: 'De Tempel', 1946), II, 314–18. See also Sarah Elliott Novacich, *Shaping the Archive in Late Medieval England* (Cambridge: Cambridge University Press, 2017).

34   See Zygmunt G. Barański, 'Re-viewing Dante', *Romance Philology*, 42 (1988), 51–76.

35   See Thomas Aquinas, *Quaestiones quodlibetales* VII. art. 15–16, and *ST* I. I. 10 resp. See also de Bruyne, II, 304, 307–13; Robert Hollander, 'Dante *theologus-poeta*', in his *Studies in Dante* (Ravenna: Longo, 1980), pp. 39–89.

in the Bible, as well as its allegorical senses, were regarded as divinely inspired, many exegetes, on account of the renewed interest in Scripture's *sensus licteralis*, had begun to recognize and praise the literary prowess that human authors displayed in fashioning the *lictera* of individual books (see Minnis, *Medieval Theory*). Thus, for Dante, the 'Biblical' status of his 'letter' — the fact that his literal sense was to be read according to the fourfold 'allegory of the theologians' — was a guarantee that his literary skill too would be appreciated and not ignored Thomistically as the suspect coating for 'belle menzogne' (*Conv.* II. I. 3) whose essential value lay in their moral explication. In addition, as I mentioned earlier, one of the ways in which Dante demonstrated the insufficiency of the other literary traditions that he recalled in the *Commedia* was by measuring them against the Bible. Hence, only his poem was able to capture something of the formal, ideological, and ontological range of God's book. In Dante's literary pantheon dominated by the Bible, one other text, besides the *Commedia*, gains some advantage when associated with Scripture. Not surprisingly, this text is the *Aeneid*, since, as Statius memorably reveals, it too has the power to save (*Purg.* XXIII. 37–45), and, by recording the foundation of Rome, recounts providential history.[36] Thanks to this 'comparative' literary process, Dante succeeds in honouring his favoured trinity of texts (and it is unlikely that the number is fortuitous). Indeed, the unique quality of each work is underscored: the Bible is the pinnacle of ideological and formal achievement that only God can fully appreciate; the *Aeneid* represents the finest possible example of an ideologically and rhetorically constrained text; while the *Commedia* takes all that is best from the latter and endeavours, however falteringly, to follow the lead of the former.

Dante never even comes close to implying that the *Commedia* might be deemed a 'new Bible'. The poem's subordination to the *vox Dei* is absolute. Conversely, the *Commedia* is not simply a 'new — because Christian and plurilingual — *Aeneid*'. It is a new, and possibly unique, way of doing literature: "l poema sacro | al quale ha posto mano e cielo e terra' (*Par.* XXV. 1–2), where 'earth' does not simply point to Dante's literary skills as was the case with the Scriptural *auctores*, but also indicates the synthesis in it of secular literary traditions. The *Commedia*'s subordination to the Bible is immediately evident, since it can never achieve that perfect synthesis of *verba*, *res*, and *signa* that is the Bible's divinely sanctioned hallmark.[37] Given his human limitations, it would have been fruitless for Dante merely to try 'to imitate' God's 'writing'. Instead, he drew on every human literary tradition in order to make his weak human voice fit to carry God's redemptive message. And although the exceptional demands of his poem meant that it transcended the standard 'temi' of conventional 'comici o tragedi' (*Par.* XXX. 23–24), Dante was nevertheless ready to acknowledge his debts to these, even as he indicated their flaws. His treatment of Virgil is exemplary in this respect. The complex tensions that emerge between

---

36   More conventionally, Statius also acknowledges the 'Christian' message of Virgil's Fourth Eclogue (*Purg.* XXII. 67–73). However, this is the only instance in the *Commedia* that Dante grants a position of note to this text. Instead, throughout the poem, he stresses, in an original move, the *Aeneid*'s privileged status in God's plan for humanity; see also Giuseppe Mazzotta, *Dante Poet of the Desert* (Princeton: Princeton University Press, 1979). On the *Aeneid* as 'divine' poetry, see Chapter 9.
37   See Battaglia Ricci, pp. 90–100; de Bruyne, II, 302–13.

his poem and God's 'books', and between it and the literary tradition, are crucial. In the space that emerges between the divine *verbum* and Dante's human language, and between the conventions of the *genera dicendi* and his 'comic' style, not only does the poet reveal his personal *auctoritates*, but he also highlights the uniqueness of his own poem and his own divinely ordained *auctoritas*. In order to appreciate the singularity of the *Commedia*, it is necessary to keep in mind the rich range of its allusiveness and the constant interplay between its plurality of sources. Of such stuff are the schemes of the divinely ordained syncretist.

6. Which Comedy?

An assessment of the *Commedia*'s poetics and of the formal solutions that this motivated can help elucidate what Dante may have meant by the term 'comedía'. However, what remains unexplained is how these highly original, even idiosyncratic ideas and forms relate to standard contemporary views on the 'comic'.[38] Several major problems quickly emerge when Dante's and the tradition's contrasting perceptions of comedy are brought together. How can a comedy embrace both secular and religious forms? How can it have contacts with, even surpass, the literary tradition as a whole? How can it be the *stilus* best suited for experimentation? Most crucially, how can a concept so firmly embedded in the doctrine of formal and thematic separation (see Chapter 6, Subsection 2:i) have anything to do with Dante's poem?

The beginnings of an answer to all these questions may be found in the poet's *œuvre*. There are seven passages (I naturally exclude the discussion in the letter to Cangrande from the Dantean canon) in which the poet analyses or makes reference to comedy.[39] The most interesting is the discussion in the *De vulgari eloquentia*:

> Deinde in hiis que dicenda occurrunt debemus discretione potiri, utrum tragice, sive comice, sive elegiace sint canenda. Per tragediam superiorem stilum inducimus; per comediam inferiorem; per elegiam stilum intelligimus miserorum. Si tragice canenda videntur, tunc adsumendum est vulgare illustre, et per consequens cantionem oportet ligare. Si vero comice, tunc quandoque mediocre, quandoque humile vulgare sumatur [...]. Si autem elegiace, solum humile nos oportet sumere. (*Dve* II. 4. 5–6)

---

38   On medieval perceptions of comedy, see Fabian Alfie, *Comedy and Culture: Cecco Angiolieri's Poetry and Late Medieval Society* (Leeds: Northern University Press, 2001); Karl-Heinz Bareiss, *Comoedia: die Entwicklung der Komödiendiskussion von Aristotles bis Ben Jonson* (Frankfurt and Bern: Peter Lang, 1982); Wilhelm Cloetta, *Komödie und Tragödie im Mittelalter*, vol. 1 of *Beiträge zur Litteraturgeschichte Mittelalters und der Renaissance* (Halle a. S.: Max Niemeyer, 1890); Paul M. Clogan, 'Literary Genres in a Medieval Textbook', *Medievalia et Humanistica*, n.s. 11 (1982), 199–209; Kelly; Philip A. McMahon, 'Seven Questions on Aristotelian Definitions of Tragedy and Comedy', *Harvard Studies in Classical Philology*, 40 (1929), 97–198; Quadlbauer; Joachim Suchomski, *'Delectatio' und 'utilitas': ein Beitrag zum Verständnis mittelalterlicher romischer Literatur* (Bern and Munich: Francke Verlag, 1975); Claudia Villa, *'Lectura'*, 'Il lessico della stilistica fra XI e XIII sec.', in *Vocabulaire des écoles et des methodes d'enseignement au moyen âge*, ed. by Olga Weijers (Turnhout: Brepols, 1992), pp. 42–59, and 'Terenzio e (Orazio) in Toscana fra IX e XIV secolo', *Studi italiani di filologia classica*, ser. III, 10 (1992), 1103–15; *L'eredità classica nel Medioevo: il linguaggio comico*, ed. by Centro di Studi sul Teatro Medioevale e Rinascimentale (Viterbo: Agnesotti Editore, n.d.); *Versions of Medieval Comedy*, ed. by Paul G. Ruggiers (Norman: University of Oklahoma Press, 1977).

39   *Dve* II. 4. 5–6; 8. 8; *Conv.* I. 5. 8; *Inf.* XVI. 127–29; XXI. 1–3; *Par.* XXX. 24; *Ecl.* II. 51–54.

[Then in dealing with the topics of poetry we must make a choice of whether we are to sing them in the tragic, comic, or elegiac style. By 'tragedy' I mean the higher style, by 'comedy' I mean the lower, by 'elegiac' I mean the style of the afflicted. If the topics are to be sung in the tragic style, you must employ the illustrious vernacular, and accordingly you must bind together a canzone. But if they are to be sung in the comic style, an alternation of middle and humble vernacular should be used [...] Finally, if they are to be sung in elegiac style, we should only use the humble.]

What is immediately striking about Dante's definition of *comedia*, especially after his conservative recourse to 'le comedie e tragedie latine' as a metonymy for Roman literature in the *Convivio* (I. 5. 8), is its inventiveness. In the *De vulgari eloquentia*, Dante tried, if not quite successfully, to fuse into a single system two of the major critical models used to define literature as a whole: the tripartite division of 'styles' and the binary opposition between 'tragedy' and 'comedy'.[40] Furthermore, he granted the 'comic' a much wider range than either of the other two *formae* by having it embrace both the *mediocris* and the *humilis* registers. In contrast, as I indicated earlier, the discussion of these same matters in Epistle XIII is marked by its trite and commonplace explanations. The etymological definition of comedy ('comedia dicitur a "comos" villa et "oda" quod est cantus, unde comedia quasi "villanus cantus"' [it is called 'comedy' from *comos* — a country-house — and *oda*, which is a song, thus comedy is, as it were, a lowly song]) and the structural-thematic one ('Comedia vero inchoat asperitatem alicuius rei, sed eius materia prospere terminatur' [Comedy begins with harsh circumstances, but its subject-matter ends favourably]) are old favourites.[41] Equally, the epistle's stylistic interpretation of comedy is not simply standard, but, with the loss of *mediocris* — 'modus loquendi: [...] comedia vero remisse et humiliter' [the manner of speaking: [...] that of comedy is unrefined and humble] — also constitutes an evident reduction, not to say banalization, of the *De vulgari eloquentia*'s presentation. Just as regressive is the disappearance in Epistle XIII of any allusion to the doctrine of the 'styles'. In fact, given its flexible presentation of the 'comic', the treatise is a much better guide to the *Commedia* than the letter to Cangrande.[42] If the latter were genuine, then the problem arises why Dante should have wanted to analyse and define his innovatory poem in unquestionably hackneyed terms (for a fuller discussion of these matters, see Chapter 6, pp. 251–56). Since, as far as I am aware, exegesis was to be read literally, such a decision would have undermined the *Commedia*'s carefully constructed metaliterary system whose end was to develop new critical modes with which to elucidate the poem's originality. In addition, the letter countermands the poet's precise and unambiguous claim that 'questa *mia*

40   See Mengaldo, pp. 164–65. For a discussion of these and other similar categories, see Chapter 6, in particular Subsection 2:i and ii.

41   See, for instance, Diomedes, *Artes grammaticae libri III*, in Keil, I, 488; Bernard of Utrecht, *Commentum in Theodulum, Accessus ad Auctores,* ed. by R. B. C. Huygens, 2nd edn (Leiden: Brill, 1970), pp. 85–94; Giovanni da Genova, *Catholicon* (Lyons: J. Dupré, 1492), s.v. *tragedia*. See also Cloetta, pp. 26–30, 33, 46–48, 112–14, 150.

42   This is especially paradoxical given the *De vulgari eloquentia*'s normally conservative views on literature, and the fact that, in general, the *Commedia*'s poetics constitutes a challenge to the treatise's theorizations.

comedía' (*Inf.* XVI. 128 and XXI. 2) goes beyond the concerns of ordinary 'comici o tragedi' (*Par.* XXX. 24). Just as astonishingly, if Dante were the author of Epistle XIII, then his largely conventional lyric poetry would be attended by a more original and apt 'commentary' — the *De vulgari eloquentia* — than his great epic poem. All this seems, at least to me, most unlikely.

Indeed, other elements in paragraphs 29–32 militate against the letter's authenticity. The equation this establishes between the vernacular and the 'comic' ('ad modum loquendi, remissus est modus et humilis, quia locutio vulgaris in qua et muliercule comunicant' [if we look at its manner of speaking, it is composed and moderate and humble, because it uses the vernacular language in which womenfolk communicate]) is baffling when one recalls Dante's treatment of his 'maternal' language in the *Convivio* and the *De vulgari eloquentia*, as well as the ways in which he employed and celebrated it in the *Commedia*. Nor, as some scholars have tried, can *Eclogue* II be used to bolster the letter's claim. Tityrus's reply ought not be taken as Dante's judgement on the vernacular, but as a polemical calque on Giovanni del Virgilio's reservations regarding the *Commedia* (*Ecl.* I. 5–24). In fact, Dante's reponse vindicates his choice of language in the poem:

> 'Mopsus' tunc ille 'quid?' inquit.
> 'Comica nonne vides ipsum reprehendere verba,
> tum quia femineo resonant ut trita labello,
> tum quia Castalias pudet acceptare sorores?' (*Ecl.* I. 51–54)

['Mopsus,' he said, 'what about him?'. 'Don't you see that he scorns the words of comedy, because they sound common on the lips of females, and because the Castalian sisters blush to receive them?']

Finally, other scholars have claimed that, when the letter to Cangrande quotes *Ars poetica* 93–96, the aim is to vindicate the *Commedia*'s hybrid style:

Similiter differunt in modo loquendi: elate et sublime tragedia; comedia vero remisse et humiliter, sicut vult Oratius in sua Poetria, ubi licentiat aliquando comicos ut tragedos loqui, et sic e converso:

> Interdum tamen et vocem comedia tollit,
> iratusque Chremes tumido delitigat ore;
> et tragicus plerunque dolet sermone pedestri
> Telephus et Peleus, etc.

Et per hoc patet quod Comedia dicitur presens opus. (*Ep.* XIII. 30–31)

[Likewise, they differ in the manner of speaking: tragedy is lofty and sublime; comedy is lowly and humble, as Horace instructs in his *Ars poetica*, where sometimes he allows comedians to speak like tragedians, and viceversa:

> But sometimes even Comedy raises her voice,
> and furious Chremes rails with tumid words;
> and tragic Telephus and Peleus express their grief
> with prosaic speech, etc.

And this shows that the present work is called comedy.]

Yet, if the goal were indeed to legitimate the *Commedia*'s formal variety, then

Horace is being poorly used. Not only does the Roman poet (and the author of the letter with him) advise caution when mingling 'styles', but he also grants licence to both comedians and tragedians.[43] There is little in his precept that can explain and authorize the *Commedia*'s radical and unique plurilingualism. Yet, Horace's lines are revealing. They suggest that the division between *genera* was not necessarily as rigid as might appear from many medieval definitions and much medieval literary usage. In fact, Cicero, Horace, Quintilian,[44] and Augustine all encouraged a degree of artistic freedom and stylistic variety.[45] The fact that this advice was relatively little

43   This very same point is made in the 'Materia' commentary: 'Dixi comediam nolle exponi tragicis uerbis, tragediam comicis. Sed tamen et comedia quandoque extollit uocem et tragedia quandoque deprimit, sed causa interueniente' [I have said that comedy does not want to be expressed in tragic verses, nor does tragedy want to be expressed in comic verses. However, even comedy at times raises her voice and tragedy lowers it, but only for a specific reason] (p. 350). It is noteworthy that none of the late-classical and early medieval traditions of Horatian glosses to the *Ars poetica* interpret lines 93–96 as legitimating stylistic licence, at most they paraphrase the original; see Acro, *Acronis et Porphyrionis Commentarii in Q. Horatium Flaccum*, ed. by Ferdinand Hauthal, 2 vols (Berlin: J. Springer, 1864–66), II, 592; Porphyrio, in *Acronis*, II, 654; Pseudo-Acro, *Pseudoacronis scholia in Horatium vetustiora*, ed. by Otto Keller, 2 vols (Leipzig: Teubner, 1902–04), I, 325; *Scholia in Horatium*, ed. by H. J. Botschuyver, 4 vols (Amsterdam: H. A. Van Bottenburg, 1935–42), I, 4–9 and IV, 462–63; *Scholia Vindobonensia ad Horatii Artem Poeticam*, ed. by J. Zechmeister (Vienna: Apud C. Geroldum Filium Bibliopolam, 1877), p. 10. Interestingly, in the *Scholia Vindobonensia*, which wholeheartedly sustain the doctrine of stylistic separation, a gloss to lines 7 and 8 of the *Ars poetica* ('cuius, velut aegri somnia, vanae | fingentur species' [whose idle pictures shall be fashioned like the dreams of an ill man]) also acknowledges the need for flexibility: 'haec tria genera scribendi debere servari in omnibus orationibus, ita ut quaeque oratio habeat suum genus. non negatur tamen, quin aliquando etiam in una oratione possit fieri descensus a gravi in mediocre vel a mediocri in humile, aut ascensus ab humili in mediocre vel a mediocri in grave, ita ut una sola oratio aliquando contineat haec tria genera' [these three kinds of writing must be preserved in all speeches, so that each speech may have its own kind. It is possible, however, that even a single speech may sometimes descend from the high to the middle style, or from the middle to the humble, or may rise from the humble to the middle or from the middle to the high, to the point that one single speech sometimes includes these three styles] (p. 2). At the same time, given the Horatian pedigree of the *Scholia*, it is not unlikely that this claim will have had its origins in lines 93–96, and possibly also in lines 9–11.

44   On the diffusion of Quintilian in the Middle Ages, see Birger Munk Olsen, *L'Étude des auteurs latins aux XIe et XIIe siècles*, 4 vols (Paris: Editions du CNRS, 1982–2014), II, 289–305; Michael Winterbottom, 'Quintilian. *Institutio oratoria*', in *Texts and Transmission*, ed. by Leighton D. Reynolds (Oxford: Clarendon Press, 1983), pp. 332–34.

45   Cicero: 'Sed figuram in dicendo commutare oportet, ut gravem mediocris, mediocrem excipiat adtenuata, deinde identidem commutentur, ut facile satietas varietate vitetur' [But we should switch figure in a speech, so that the middle follows the high, and the simple follows the middle, and then interchange them again, in order for satiety to be easily avoided through differentiation] (*Ad Her.* IV. II. 16); 'Est enim finitimus oratori poeta, numeris astrictior paulo, verborum autem licentia liberior, multis vero ornandi generibus socius, ac paene par; in hoc quidem certe prope idem, nullis ut terminis circumscribat aut definiat ius suum, quo minus ei liceat eadem illa facultate et copia vagari, qua velit' [The poet is indeed very close to the orator, a little more constrained with regard to rhythm, but freer in the choice of words, while in the use of many types of embellishments he is his fellow, and almost his equal; in this one aspect by all means they are almost the same, that he does not limit or define his own claims in any respect, which would prevent him from wandering at his will with the same authority and freedom of the other] (*De oratore* I. 16. 70, and see III. 8. 30 & 32); 'Magni igitur iudici, summae etiam facultatis esse debebit moderator ille et quasi temperator huius tripertitae varietatis. Nam et indicabit quid cuique opus sit et poterit, quocumque modo postulabit causa dicere' [The one who controls and balances, as it were, this threefold variety will need to

heeded in subsequent centuries reveals how grammar and rhetoric had become increasingly taxonomic and prescriptive, culminating in the lists of poetic do's and don'ts of the twelfth- and thirteenth-century *artes poetriae*. Consequently, despite its original resonances, the *De vulgari eloquentia* normally subscribes to the doctrine of literary separation, not least because it primarily depends on medieval traditions and reinterpretations, rather than (directly) on classical rhetoric.[46]

Nonetheless, the more flexible outlook found in Cicero, Horace, Quintilian, and Augustine would seem to be of some consequence for the *Commedia*. The problem immediately arises of the extent to which, or even if at all, their doctrines on stylistic contamination may have exercised an influence on Dante. It is almost certain that he was familiar with Horace's *Ars poetica*, and probably with Augustine's *De doctrina cristiana*, when he composed the *Vita nova*. Equally, it is extremely unlikely that, at any point in his career, Dante enjoyed a firsthand appreciation of Cicero's *Orator* and *De oratore* and of Quintilian's *Institutiones*. At the same time, as we have begun to see, evidence exists to confirm that the idea that a text's defining *stilus* could admit a degree of limited interference from another 'style' continued to circulate during the Middle Ages. Indeed, before he composed the *Commedia*, Dante had already begun to test the limits of 'stylistic' exclusivity: in practice in the *Vita nova* and in some of his lyric poems (for instance, 'Io sento sì d'Amor la gran possanza'),[47] and in theory in the *Convivio*.[48] Naturally, the formal and ideological differences between these texts and the *Commedia* are substantial. Yet, it should

possess bright judgment and extreme ability. For he will indicate what is needed at any point, and will be able to speak in any way which the case requires] (*Orator* III. 70, and see XXII. 74, XXVIII. 97–99, XXXI. 110–11). Horace, *Ars poetica* 9–11 and 93–96. Quintilian: 'Nec augenda semper oratio sed summittenda nonumquam est. Vim rebus aliquando verborum ipsa humilitas adfert' [The speech should not always be embellished, it should sometimes be moderated. Humility of words may itself on occasion lend vigour] (*Instit. orat.* VIII. 3. 21) and 'Neque illud tamen est nefas, ut aliquem vel omnia vel plura [styles] deceant' [And it is not abominable, when all or many [styles] befit a person] (*Instit. orat.* XI. 3. 181). Augustine: 'Nec quisquam praeter disciplinam esse existimet ista miscere, immo quantum congrue fieri potest, de omnibus generis dictio varianda est. Nam quando prolixa est in uno genere, minus detinet auditorem. Cum vero fit in aliud ab alio transitus, etiamsi longius est, decentius procedit oratio, quamvis habeant singula genera varietates suas in sermone eloquentium, quibus non sinuntur in eorum, qui audiunt, frigescere vel tepescere sensibus' [Let nobody think that combining these [styles] is an artistic failure, for indeed as far as it can be done coherently, a speech should combine all styles. For when it stretches too long in one style, it is less compelling for the audience. But when it shifts from one style to the other, even if it is long, the speech proceeds more elegantly, although even each single style in the orators' speech has its own variations, which prevent the audience's attention from dropping or becoming languid] (*De doc. chr.* IV. 22, and see 22–23 in their entirety). Echoes of these doctrines may be heard in the Middle Ages especially in the commentary tradition associated with the *Ad Her.*; see Quadlbauer, passim.

46 The *De vulgari eloquentia* reveals particular debts to the medieval reception of Horace; see Barański, '*Magister satiricus*', pp. 47–58.

47 See Zygmunt G. Barański, 'La canzone "anomola" di Dante: *Io sento sì d'Amor la gran possanza*', in *Dante Alighieri. Le Quindici Canzoni. Lette da diversi. I, 1–7* (Lecce: Pensa Multimedia, 2009), pp. 145–211, and 'The Roots of Dante's Plurilingualism: "Hybridity" and Language in the *Vita nova*', in *Dante's Plurilingualism, Authority, Knowledge, Subjectivity*, ed. by Sara Fortuna and others (Oxford: Legenda, 2010), pp. 98–121.

48 See Zygmunt G. Barański, 'Il *Convivio* e la poesia: problemi di definizione', in *Lectura Dantis Federiciana*, ed. by Francesco Tateo and Daniele M. Pegorari (Bari: Palomar, 2004), pp. 9–64.

also be recognized, and rather more than scholars normally do, that Dante was a 'hybrid' experimental writer throughout his career and not just in the 'sacrato poema' (*Par.* XXIII. 62). As is now generally acknowleged, the early years of his exile not only allowed Dante to broaden his literary and doctrinal knowledge, but also to reflect on the strengths and weakesses of his culture, as well as on his world's political, social, and ecclesiastical institutions and on the role of divine providence. As, among others, Ulrich Leo, Bruno Nardi, and Maria Corti successfully argued, Dante's deep consideration and critique of contemporary literary and intellectual traditions led directly to the composition of the *Commedia*.[49] Matters of poetics, as evidenced both by the *Convivio* and by the *De vulgari eloquentia*, were at the forefront of his concerns. Building on the hints regarding the opportunity to experiment with the *stili* that occasionally made an appearance in late-medieval literary theory and criticism, as well as his own earlier cautious endeavours in this regard, Dante developed, probably around 1305, a new bold and 'unconstrained' way of thinking about and hence composing literature. This process is typical of Dante. He was generally careful to root his most challenging experiments and proposals in practices and ideas that had their point of origin in contemporary culture. Finally, and this is crucial for my present argument, close connections exist, as we shall soon see, between Dante's major shift in poetics — his refusal to be bound by the exclusive and elitist dogmatisms of the medieval literary system — and his choice of the *Commedia*'s title.[50]

When one considers the proposals that scholars have put forward to explain why Dante decided to designate his poem a 'comedía', their variety is impressive. Thus, inter alia, it has been suggested that 'comedy' is a humility *topos*;[51] that it is used to underline the difference between Dante's poem and Virgil's 'alta [...] tragedía' (*Inf.* XX. 113; Schiaffini, p. 75); that it highlights the poem's links to satire, and thus its political preoccupations and its *materia reprehensoria*;[52] that it points to the poem's structure and, by extension, to its allegory (Iannucci); that it attests to the *Commedia*'s veracity, given the associations between comedy and truth (D'Alfonso, p. 41); and that it serves to suggest that Dante's 'comic' style, unlike the usual conventionally constrained *stilus medius*, was a truly 'middle' style where every idea, subject, and formal register could come together (Barański, 'Re-viewing'). What is immediately noteworthy about these explanations is that they all appropriately draw on contemporary authorities to support their proposals.

49   See Ulrich Leo, 'The Unfinished *Convivio* and Dante's Rereading of the *Aeneid*', *Mediaeval Studies*, 13, (1951), 41–64; Bruno Nardi, *Dal 'Convivio' alla 'Commedia'* (Rome: Nella sede dell'Istituto, 1960); Maria Corti, *La felicità mentale* (Turin: Einaudi, 1983).

50   I have substantially rewritten this paragraph. In light of our understanding in 1991 of Dante's intellectual formation and of his artistic priorities, as well as of the circulation of classical works in late medieval Italy, the hypothesis I had originally delineated — the poet 're-rea*din*g or perhaps rea*din*g for the very first time' during the early years of his exile the works of the four rhetorical *auctoritates* — was not entirely illegitimate.

51   Gianfranco Contini, 'Introduzione alla *Cognizione del dolore*', in his *Varianti e altra linguistica* (Turin: Einaudi, 1970), pp. 601–19 (p. 614).

52   Benvenuto da Imola, *Comentum super Dantis Aldigherij 'Comoediam'*, ed. by James Philip Lacaita, 5 vols (Florence: G. Barbèra, 1887), I, 151–52. See also D'Alfonso; Tavoni, 'Il titolo della *Commedia*'.

As might have been intuited from the stylistic discussion of *comedia* in the *De vulgari eloquentia* ('quandoque mediocre quandoque humile vulgare sumatur'; an alternation of middle and humble vernacular should be used), medieval comedy was a wide-ranging *stilus*. In fact, it was by far the most flexible of all the literary 'styles'.[53] It would, thus, not have been difficult for Dante to have recognized in *comedia* the category that could complement the rhetoricians' teaching on 'stylistic' hybridity. And while they approached this thorny issue with considerable caution, in the *Commedia*, Dante boldly pushed it, both theoretically and practically, to its all-embracing logical limits.

Examining presentations of comedy from Cicero to the fourteenth century, one finds that different definitions proliferate, and that all of them establish suggestive connections with the *Commedia*. For example, in addition to the interpretations I have already mentioned, comedy is linked to the kind of narrative found in an *argumentum*, namely 'res ficta, quae tamen fieri potuit' [a fiction, which may nonetheless occur] (Cicero, *De inv.* I. 19. 27) thanks to an act of divine intervention;[54] it proliferates with characters of every stripe and deals with every type

---

53   On comedy see n. 38. On the other *qualitates carminum*, see Bernhard Bischoff, 'Living with the Satirists', in *Classical Influences on European Culture A.D. 500–1500*, ed. by Robert R. Bolgar (Cambridge: Cambridge University Press, 1971), pp. 83–94; Ambrogio Camozzi Pistoja, 'Il quarto trattato del *Convivio*: o della satira', *Le tre corone*, 1 (2014), 27–53; Cloetta; Clogan; D'Alfonso; Vincent Gillespie, 'From the Twelfth Century to c. 1450', in Minnis and Johnson, pp. 145–238; Jenaro-MacLennan, *Trecento*, and 'Remissus'; Henry A. Kelly, 'Aristotle-Averroes-Alemannus on Tragedy: The Influence of the *Poetics* in the Latin Middle Ages', *Viator*, 10 (1979), 161–209, and *Ideas and Forms of Tragedy from Aristotle to the Middle Ages* (Cambridge: Cambridge University Press, 1993); Udo Kindermann, *Satyra. Die Theorie der Satire im Mittellateinischen: Vorstudie zu einer Gattungsgeschichte* (Nuremberg: Verlag Hans Carl, 1978); McMahon; John F. Mahoney, 'Chaucerian Tragedy and the Christian Tradition', *Annuale medievale*, 3 (1962), 81–99; Jill Mann, 'La poesia satirica e goliardica', in *Lo spazio letterario del Medioevo. I. Il Medioevo latino. v. La produzione del testo*, ed. by Guglielmo Cavallo and others (Rome: Salerno, 1993), pp. 73–109; Pier Vincenzo Mengaldo, 'L'elegia umile (*De vulgari Eloquentia* II iv 5–6)', in his *Linguistica e retorica di Dante* (Pisa: Nistri-Lischi, 1978), pp. 200–22; Paul S. Miller, 'John Gower, Satiric Poet', in *Gower's 'Confessio Amantis': Responses and Reassessments*, ed. by Alastair J. Minnis (Cambridge: Cambridge University Press, 1983), pp. 79–105; Alastair J. Minnis, *'Magister Amoris': The 'Roman de la Rose' and Vernacular Hermeneutics* (Oxford: Oxford University Press, 2001), and 'Medieval Imagination and Memory', in Minnis and Johnson, pp. 239–74; Francesco Mosetti Casaretto, 'Alle origini del genere pastorale cristiano: l'*Ecloga Theoduli* e la demonizzazione del paganesimo', *Studi medievali*, 33 (1992), 456–536; Giovanni Orlandi, 'Classical Latin Satire and Medieval Elegiac Comedy', in *Latin Poetry and the Classical Tradition: Essays in Medieval and Renaissance*, ed. by Peter Godman and Oswyn Murray (Oxford: Clarendon Press, 1990), pp. 97–114; Ben Parsons, ' "A Riotous Spray of Words": Rethinking the Medieval Theory of Satire', *Exemplaria*, 21 (2009), 105–28; Quadlbauer; Suzanne Reynolds, ' "Orazio satiro " (*Inferno* IV, 89): Dante, the Roman Satirists, and the Medieval Theory of Satire', in *LPQSD*, pp. 128–44; Charles A. van Rooy, *Studies in Classical Satire and Related Literary Theory* (Leiden: Brill, 1965).

54   'Argumentum est res ficta que tamen fieri potuit, ut contingit in comediis. Item in comedia non debet fieri invocacio, nisi fuerit difficultas in materia, sicut dicit Horacius: "Nec deus intersit, nisi dignus vindice nodus | Inciderit". Idest non fiat invocatio divina nisi difficultas inciderit' [The subject-matter is a fiction which may nonetheless occur, as happens in comedies. Moreover, comedy must not have an invocation, unless there will be complications in the plot, as Horace says: 'Let not a god intervene, unless there is a knot worthy of a judge'. That is to say, let there be no divine invocation unless a complication occurs] (John of Garland, *Parisiana poetria* v. 327–31). See also Paolazzi, pp. 81–110.

of emotion;[55] it is associated with prose;[56] it deals with amorous themes;[57] and it embraces a wide range of registers: rising from 'pedestrus' (prosaic) to 'grandis et elegans et venustus' (high and elegant and charming) before descending once again to 'humilis' (humble).[58] The 'comic' seems to touch on every subject and style; it seems to stand for literature *tout court*,[59] and this equation becomes nearly explicit when comedy is tied to ethics, since this characteristic was deemed to be the basic feature of any literary work.[60] Comedy was thus the only form fit for a poet bent on tackling the multiplicity of 'ciò che per l'universo si squaderna' (*Par.* XXXIII. 87). Indeed, *comedia*'s links to the Bible and Christian literature leave no doubts about this. Thus, Jerome praised comedy for its moral force (*Ep.* LIV. 9); furthermore, Scriptural *sermo humilis* forged an obvious bond with 'comic' *stilus humilis*. By the Duecento, as in Bene da Firenze's *Candelabrum*, which Dante may well have known (Mengaldo, *Linguistica*, p. 45), the Bible was introduced as an example of both the 'middle' and 'low' 'styles' — the same *stili*, of course, as those to which comedy had been traditionally harnessed.[61]

55   'Comoediae, quae plurimum conferre ad eloquentiam potest, cum per omnes et personas et adfectus est' [As to comedy, which can contribute a lot to eloquence, since it goes through all types of characters and emotions] (Quintilian, *Instit. orat.* I. 8. 7).

56   'Alia [prosa] ystorialis, qua utitur ecclesia, et tragedi et comedi aliquando, et alii nonnulli philosophi' [Another is historical prose, which the Church uses, and sometimes tragedians and comedians, and even some other philosophers] (John of Garland, *Parisiana poetria* I. 51–52).

57   '[On *Aen.* IV. I] est autem paene totus in affectione, licet in fine pathos habeat, ubi abscessus Aeneae gignit dolorem. Sane totus in consiliis et subtilitatibus est; nam paene comicus stilus mirum, ubi de amore tractatur' [it is almost all about love, and of course it has pathos at the end, where the departure of Aeneas causes pain. It is however all about schemes and subtleties; it is indeed little wonder that the style is comic where the subject is love]: *Servii grammatici qui feruntur in Vergilii carmina commentarii*, ed. by Georg Thilo and Hermann Hagen, 3 vols (Leipzig: Teubner, 1881–87), I, 459. See also Claudia Villa, 'Il canone poetico mediolatino (e le strutture di Dante, *Inf.* IV e *Purg.* XXII)', in her *La protervia di Beatrice* (Florence: SISMEL-Edizioni del Galluzzo, 2009), pp. 17–37 (p. 28).

58   See, for instance, Horace, *AP* I. 95; Quintilian, *Instit. orat.* X. 1. 65; Matthew of Vendôme, *Ars versificatoria* II. 7, in Faral, p. 153.

59   As with my earlier discussion of the critical debate on Dante's use of 'comedía', I have merely presented a sample of the many different definitions of comedy that were circulating at the beginning of the Trecento. However, see Villa, 'Il lessico della stilistica'.

60   'Quid est ethicum genus? In quo moralitas quaedam est, id est ubi mores hominum considerantur, ut sunt comoediae' [What is an ethical kind of work? One in which there is a certain morality, where, that is, human behaviours are considered, as in comedies]: Fortunantianus, *Ars rhetorica* I. 10, in *Rhetores latini minores*, ed. by Karl Halm (Leipzig : Teubner, 1863), p. 88. See also Villa, '*Lectura*', pp. 53 and 121; and, in general, Judson B. Allen, *The Ethical Poetic of the Later Middle Ages* (Toronto: University of Toronto Press, 1982); Gillespie, pp. 161–78 & 189–206.

61   'Generales ergo figure dictaminum tres dicuntur, que stili etiam nuncupantur, scilicet humilis, mediocris et sublimis. Humilis est illa que ad usitatissimam puri sermonis consuetudinem est demissa, ut in Evangeliis et Sacra Scriptura sepe videmus. At mediocris censetur que constat ex altiore neque tamen ex summa hornatissima dignitate verborum, ut in epistolis Pauli et elegis Ovidianis. Sublimis ex magna et hornata verborum constructione conficitur, ut in Gregorii Moralibus et Lucano' [The general figures of the *dictamen* are said to be three, which also take the name of styles, that is humble, middle, and sublime. The humble is as low as the most ordinary use of plain conversation, such as we often see in the Gospels and in Scripture. The one that consists of a higher quality of words, yet not grand and greatly adorned, is considered middle, as in St Paul's epistles and in Ovid's elegies. The sublime is made of a refined and adorned structure of words, as in Gregory's *Moralia* and in Lucan]:

'Comedía' embraces the same wide breadth of concerns as the *Commedia*'s totalizing *materia*, its formal pluralism, and its metaliterary system. With one bold move, Dante integrated in a single text the many features of the 'comic' that the tradition recognized but which it never conflated either in its texts or in its criticism. Perhaps only a syncretist of Dante's calibre was able properly to appreciate comedy's range and potential. The vagueness of the two references to 'comedía' in the poem offer a clue to the wealth of the term's connotations (thus the precision and narrowness of the letter to Cangrande's definitions would seem to be yet more evidence against its authenticity). If, as was his custom, Dante wished to offer a concise traditional label through which to suggest the *Commedia*'s new poetics and poetry, then he could not have found a more apt and convenient term than 'comedía'. His poem, as its title openly declares, is quintessentially 'comic'; and, from this perspective, a 'comedía' is equivalent to a 'poema sacro' (*Par.* xxv. 1), given that both draw inspiration from divine forms, and, at the same time, surpasses any 'alta [...] tragedía' (*Inf.* xx. 113).

7. The 'Comic' Presence: Plautus, Caecilius, Terence

Dante's lack of enthusiasm for the Roman comedians should probably not cause surprise. For him, comedy was equivalent to literature in general, and consequently could not be the special preserve of any particular artistic group. Furthermore, I remain convinced that, as has always been recognized with respect to Plautus and Caecilius, Dante almost certainly never had direct knowledge of Terence.[62] Indeed,

Bene Florentinus, *Candelabrum*, ed. by Gian Carlo Alessio (Padua: Antenore, 1983), i. 6. On the ties between comedy and the *Canticum canticorum*, see Lino Pertile, '*Cantica* nella tradizione medievale e in Dante', *Rivista di storia e di letteratura religiosa*, 18 (1991), 389–412.
62   On Dante and Terence, see Cesare Beccaria, 'Dante e Terenzio', *Il Borghini*, 2 (1875–76), 324–26; Salvatore Betti, *Postille alla 'Divina Commedia' qui per la prima volta edite di su il manoscritto dell'autore da Giuseppe Cugnoni*, 4 vols (Città di Castello: S. Lapi Tipografo-Editore, 1893), I, 97; Edward Moore, *Scripture and Classical Authors in Dante* [1896] (Oxford: Clarendon Press, 1969), vol. I of *Studies in Dante*, ed. by Colin Hardie, 4 vols (1968–69), pp. 12 and 261–62; Michele Scherillo, *Alcuni capitoli della biografia di Dante* (Turin: Ermanno Loescher, 1896), p. 109; Umberto Cosmo review of Paget Toynbee, *Dante Dictionary*, in *Giornale dantesco*, 7 (1899), 313–14; Paget Toynbee, *Dante Studies and Researches* (London: Methuen, 1902), p. 103; Paride Chistoni, *La seconda fase del pensiero dantesco: periodo degli studi sui classici e filosofi antichi e sugli espositori medievali* (Livorno: Raffaello Giusti Editore, 1903), p. 96; Ernesto G. Parodi, 'La lettura di Dante in Orsanmichele', *Bullettino della Società Dantesca italiana*, 8 (1908), 281–90 (p. 283); Francesco D'Ovidio, *Studi sulla 'Divina Commedia'*, 2 vols (Naples: Guida, 1931), II, 259; J. Russo, 'Did Dante Know Terence?', *Italica*, 24 (1947), 212–18; André Pézard, 'Du *Policraticus* à la *Divine Comédie* (premier article)', *Romania*, 70 (1948), 1–36 (pp. 4–20); Paul Renucci, *Dante disciple et juge du monde gréco-latin* (Paris: Société d'édition les Belles Lettres, 1954), pp. 46, 98–99, 122, & 180; Marino Barchiesi, *Un tema classico e medievale: Gnatone e Taide* (Padua: Antenore, 1963); Giorgio Brugnoli, '*Ut patet per Senecam in suis tragediis*', *Rivista di cultura classica e medievale*, 5 (1963), 146–63; Giorgio Padoan, 'Il *Liber Esopi* e due episodi dell'*Inferno*' [1964], in his *Il pio Enea, l'empio Ulisse* (Ravenna: Longo, 1977), pp. 151–69; Ezio Raimondi, 'Noterella dantesca (a proposito di Taide)', *Lettere italiane*, 17 (1965), 443–44; Felicina Groppi, *Dante as Translator* (Rome: Herder, 1966); Marino Barchiesi, 'Arte del prologo e arte della transizione', *Studi danteschi*, 44 (1967), 115–207; Ettore Paratore, *Biografia e poetica di Persio* (Florence: Le Monnier, 1968), pp. 213–14; Roberto Mercuri, 'Terenzio nostro antico', *Cultura neolatina*, 29 (1969), 84–116; Giorgio Brugnoli, 'Cecilio', in

echoes of his plays in Dante, with the exception of the time-honoured reference to Thais, quite simply cannot be heard.

As regards Terence, my conclusion may cause some eyebrows to be raised. Scholars have unequivocally demonstrated — none better than Claudia Villa in her excellent investigation of the twists and turns of the medieval and early humanist *lectura Terentii* — that, ever since the end of the eighth century, the dramatist was widely read and commented.[63] His position in the school-room as one of the *auctores*

ED, I, 900–01; Ettore Paratore, 'Terenzio', in ED, v, 569–70; Manlio Pastore Stocchi, 'Taide', in ED, v, 509–10; Prete, p. 135; Brugnoli annotations to *Epistole*, pp. 618–19; Villa, *Lectura*', pp. 137–91 and passim; Villa, 'Terenzio e (Orazio)'; Zygmunt G. Barański, 'Dante e la tradizione comica latina', in *Dante e la 'bella scola' della poesia*, ed. by Amilcare A. Iannucci (Ravenna: Longo, 1993), pp. 225–45; Mario Picchi, 'Quando Dante ride', in *L'informazione bibliografica*, 20, (1994), 365–73; John N. Grant, 'Taide in *Inferno* 18 and *Eunuchus* 937', *Quaderni d'italianistica*, 15 (1994), 151–55; Tavoni, 'Il titolo della *Commedia*'; Villa, 'Il canone poetico mediolatino' [2000], pp. 20–33; Conte; Raffaele Giglio, 'Dante fra Terenzio e Cicerone (La fonte latina per *If* XVIII 133–135)', in *Mathesis e Mneme: studi in memoria di Marcello Gigante*, ed. by Salvatore Cerasuolo and others, 2 vols (Naples: Arte Tipografica, 2004), II, 305–11, then in his *Il lettore innamorato: studi danteschi* (Naples: Loffredo, 2017), pp. 489–95; Tiziano Zanato, 'Lettura del canto XVIII dell'*Inferno*', *Per leggere*, 6 (2004), 5–47 (pp. 40–43); Tateo; Robert Black, 'Classical Antiquity', in *Dante in Context*, ed. by Zygmunt G. Baranski, and Lino Pertile (Cambridge: Cambridge University Press, 2015), pp. 297–318 (pp. 314–15). See also note 2.

63   On Terence's reception in the Middle Ages, in addition to the studies cited at the previous note, see Rudolf Peiper, 'Vermischte Bemerkungen und Mittheilungen zu römischen Dichtern zum Theil ans Handschriften', *Rheinisches Museum für Philologie*, n.s. 32 (1877), 516–37; Karl Dziatzko, 'Zu Terentius im Mittelalter', *Neue Jahrbücher für Philologie und Paedagogik*, 149 (1894), 465–77; Remigio Sabbadini, 'Il Commento di Donato a Terenzio', *Studi italiani di filologia*, 2 (1894), 465–77, and 'Biografi e commentatori di Terenzio', *Studi italiani di filologia*, 5 (1897), 289–327; Edward K. Rand, 'Early Medieval Commentaries on Terence', *Classical Philology*, 4 (1909), 359–89; Harald Hagendahl, *Latin Fathers and the Classics* (Goteborg: Elanders Boktr. Aktiebolag, 1958), pp. 269–74; Paul Lehmann, *Die Parodie im Mittelater* (Stuttgart: Hiersemann, 1963); Remigio Sabbadini, *Le scoperte dei codici latini e greci ne' secoli XIV e XV*, 2 vols (Florence: Sansoni, 1967); Yves-François Riou, 'Essai sur la tradition manuscrite du *Commentum Brunsianum* des comédies de Térence', *Revue d'histoire des textes*, 3 (1973), 79–113; Giuseppe Billanovich, 'Terenzio, Ildemaro, Petrarca', *Italia medioevale e umanistica*, 17 (1974), 1–60; Yves-François Riou, 'Gloses et commentaires des comédies de Térence dans les manuscrits de la bibliothèque du monastère San Lorenzo el real de l'Escorial', in *Lettres latines du Moyen Âge et de la Renaissance*, ed. by Guy Cambier and others (Brussels: Latomus, 1978), pp. 5–55; Giuseppe Billanovich, 'Petrarca, Pietro da Moglio e Pietro da Parma', *Italia medioevale e umanistica*, 22 (1979), 367–95 (pp. 373–90); Claudia Villa, '*Denique Terentia dultia legimus acta...*: una *lectura Terentii* a S. Faustino di Brescia nel secolo IX', *Italia medioevale e umanistica*, 22 (1979), 1–44; Gian Carlo Alessio, 'Hec Franciscus de Buti', *Italia medioevale e umanistica*, 24 (1981), 64–122; Munk Olsen, II, 583–653; Michael D. Reeve, 'Terence', in Reynolds, pp. 412–20; Villa, '*Lectura*', and 'Petrarca e Terenzio', *Studi petrarcheschi*, n.s. 6 (1989), 1–22; John N. Grant, *Studies in the Textual Tradition of Terence* (Toronto: University of Toronto Press, 1986); Birger Munk Olsen, *I classici nel canone scolastico altomedievale* (Spoleto: Centro Italiano di Studi sull'Alto Medioevo, 1991); Villa, 'Terenzio (e Orazio)'; Yves-François Riou, 'Les Commentaires médiévaux de Térence', in *Medieval and Renaissance Scholarship*, ed. by Nicholas Mann and Birger Munk Olsen (Leiden: Brill, 1997), pp. 33–49; Benjamin Victor and Bruno Quesnel, 'The Colometric Evidence for the History of the Terence-Text in the Early Middle Ages', *Revue d'histoire des textes*, 29 (1999), 141–68; Claudia Villa, 'I censimenti dei manoscritti e il regesto delle fonti' [2000], in her *La protervia*, pp. 3–16 (pp. 6–11); *Terentius Poeta*, ed. by Peter Kruschwitz and others (Munich: Beck, 2007), pp. 1–49; Benjamin Victor, 'The Transmission of Terence', and Chrysanthi Demetriou, 'Aelius Donatus and His Commentary on Terence's Comedies', both in *The Oxford Handbook of Greek and Roman Comedy*, ed. by Michael Fontaine and Adele C. Scafuro (Oxford: Oxford University Press, 2014), pp. 699–716; 782–99; Enara

facilitated his dissemination (Villa, 'Lectura', pp. 138–39). He was extensively cited as an 'authority' by generations of writers from Cicero to Priscian, from Jerome to John of Salisbury, and from the anonymous authors of the Horace commentaries to Brunetto Latini. He was presented, together with Virgil, as one of the two pinnacles of Roman literature, and his name was intimately associated with the 'comic'.[64] Indeed, Villa has established the existence of a specifically Tuscan-Emilian reception of Terence ('Lectura', pp. 137–89). All these facts can obviously be used to challenge my claim regarding Dante's lack of firsthand knowledge of Terence, except that, in the late Middle Ages, the poet was not alone in revealing little awareness of the dramatist's œuvre. For example, several of the Commedia's commentators are just as uninformed, or even more so, than Dante (Padoan, 'Liber', p. 154, n. 1). In addition, despite her extensive and sophisticated understanding of the medieval Terence tradition, Claudia Villa has been unable to establish decisively that Dante knew Terence. As she admits herself, her evidence is circumstantial, although her aim is to entangle Dante in the web of the lectura Terentii.[65] In fact, two of the elements that she presents as possible instances of the poet's ties to this tradition seem to me to point rather to the paucity of his knowledge.

In his first 'eclogue', Giovanni del Virgilio criticizes Dante for having chosen the 'comic' style:

> Ante quidem cythara pandum delphyna movebis,
> Davus et ambigue Sphyngos problemata solvet,
> Tartareum preceps quam gens ydiota figuret
> et secreta poli vix experata Platoni:

San Juan Manso, 'About the Origins of the Commentum Monacense Terence', Euphrosyne, 41 (2013), 259–76; Terence between Late Antiquity and the Age of Printing, ed. by Giulia Torello Hill and Andrew Turner (Leiden: Brill, 2015).

64   'Cum omnes poetae virtutem oratoriam semper versibus exequantur, tum magis duo viri apud Latinos, Virgilius et Terentius. Ex quibus, ut suspicio nostra est, magis Terentii virtus ad rationem rhetoricae artis accedit, cuius potentiam per comedias singulas ut possumus explicabimus' [As every poet always matches with his verses the ability of an orator, then especially those two men among the Romans, Virgil and Terence. And between the two of them, Terence's style, as I believe, got closer to the nature of the art of rhetoric, and I will explain his strength, as I can, in each single comedy]: Eugraphius, Prol. 1–6, vol. III of Aeli Donati Quad Fertur Commentum Terenti, ed. by Paul Wessner, 3 vols (Leipzig: Teubner, 1902–08). See also Giorgio Brugnoli, Per suo richiamo (Pisa: Opera Universitaria di Pisa, 1981), pp. 12–13.

65   Villa, 'Lectura', pp. x, 140, 153, 162–63, 165, 186–88, 191. In her more recent studies, Villa is less cautious than in her book, even though she does not offer new evidence in support of her claims that Dante knew Terence's works. Thus, her assertion that 'nella Firenze dell'età di Dante [...] nelle scuolette di grammatica [...] il comico latino era ampiamente diffuso come termine di confronto e modello stilistico' (Villa, '"Comoedia"', p. 327), is problematic since no concrete proof exists that the comedian circulated in the city or was used in its schools, as Robert Black has confirmed in his monumental study on education in Florence: 'Other authors, including Juvenal, Persius and Terence, who had been notable in the twelfth-century curriculum, now [in the Duecento] seem to have disappeared': Humanism and Education in Medieval and Renaissance Italy: Tradition and Innovation in Latin Schools from the Twelfth to the Fifteenth Century (Cambridge: Cambridge University Press, 2001), p. 197, but see also pp. 190, 192, 200, 209, 247, 254. Paul F. Gehl had previously arrived at a similar conclusion: A Moral Art: Grammar, Society, and Culture in Trecento Florence (Ithaca, NY, and London: Cornell University Press, 1993), p. 54.

> que tamen in triviis nunquam digesta coaxat
> comicomus nebulo, qui Flaccum pelleret orbe. (*Ecl.* I. 8–13)

[For sooner will you move the curved dolphin with your lyre, and Davus solve the riddles of the ambiguous Sphynx than the illiterate people imagine the precipice of Tartarus and the secrets of the pole scarcely hoped for by Plato, which, although never digested, are croaked at street corners by a shock-haired buffoon, who would drive Horace from the world.]

Villa expertly establishes the connections between these lines and the *lectura Terentii* ('*Lectura*', pp. 171–82). She explains that the rapprochement between Davus and the Sphinx can be elucidated thanks to the customary gloss on *Andria* 194 — 'e [...] una delle postille più conosciute e diffuse, presente nei codici terenziani fin dal x secolo' (p. 171). However, in his reply, Dante does not reveal the slightest intimation of having recognized Giovanni's Terentian allusion. Instead, as is well known, he resolves the question of the *Commedia*'s register by having recourse to Virgil. It is almost certain, given the conventions of poetic correspondence, that, if Dante had recognized the reference to Terence, he would have indicated as much in his response.[66]

   Villa suggests too that paragraph 29 of the letter to Cangrande, not least because it nods to Terence's 'authority', may have contacts with the Tuscan *lectura Terentii* ('*Lectura*', pp. 142–53). In light of the fact that direct borrowings from the comedian do not seem to be present in Dante's undisputed works, the epistle's dependence on Terence would provide further evidence against its having come from the poet's pen. Similarly, paragraph 29's reliance on the mundane definitions and methods of the *lectura Terentii* would appear to add force to my earlier argument regarding the conservatism of its discussion of comedy, which is so different from the *Commedia*'s uniquely inventive all-embracing overview. Finally, if the letter were by Dante, the references to Seneca ('ut patet per Senecam in suis tragediis' [as it is shown by Seneca in his tragedies]) and to Terence ('ut patet per Terentium in suis comediis' [as it is shown by Terence in his comedies]) would correlate poorly with the *Commedia*'s presentation of the 'authorities' on the two *stili*: namely, Virgil for 'tragedy' and Dante himself for 'comedy'.[67]

---

66   In discussing Giovanni del Virgilio's eclogue, Villa fleetingly notes another possible link between Dante and the *lectura Terentii*: 'il personaggio di Gnatone si imponeva a Giovanni del Virgilio come paradigma dello stile comico perchè proprio verso di lui è pronunciato, in *Eun.* 229, il "pape", la "interiectio admirantis" che dalla "lectura Terentii", dove è glossa sempre presente, passa ai repertori lessicali e in cui i contemporanei di Dante dovevano riconoscere ii "pape" di Pluto, in *Inf.* VII I' (p. 179). As Villa herself acknowledges by mentioning the 'repertori lessicali', *pape* was a term that circulated widely in medieval culture. Thus, the fact that it makes an appearance in Dante cannot in itself offer proof that the poet knew the gloss and hence Terence's play.
67   On Dante and Seneca, see Toynbee, *Dante*, pp. 150–56; Ernesto G. Parodi, 'Le tragedie di Seneca', *Bullettino della Società Dantesca*, 21 (1914), 41–52; Santore Debenetti, 'Dante e Seneca filosofo', *Studi danteschi*, 6 (1923), 5–24; Rocco Montano, *Suggerimenti per una lettura di Dante* (Naples: Quaderni di Delta, 1956), pp. 175–78; Giulio Marzot, 'Dante e Seneca "morale"', in *Dante e Roma* (Florence: Le Monnier, 1965), pp. 263–82; Brugnoli, '*Ut patet*'; Ettore Paratore, 'Seneca', in ED, V, 156–59; Brugnoli annotations to *Epistole*, pp. 617–18; Cristina Zampese, '"Pisa novella Tebe": un indizio della conoscenza di Seneca tragico da parte di Dante', *Giornale storico di letteratura italiana*, 166

I should like to be clear: my aim is not to determine that Dante only had scant appreciation of Terence, and thereby reduce his standing in the poet's *œuvre* to that of Plautus and Caecilius. Dante's relationship to the comedian is actually quite complex. My sense is that, without knowing his writings, Dante nevertheless built up quite an intricate idea of Terence as an author — as both *Inferno* XVIII and *Purgatorio* XXII document — out of asides relating to the dramatist that he is likely to have come across in a broad swathe of writings that conventionally drew on Terence's authoritative and exemplary status.

Statius's question and Virgil's answer on the otherwordly fate of some of their fellow writers is revealing from this point of view:

> 'dimmi dov'è Terrenzio nostro antico,
> Cecilio e Plauto e Varro, se lo sai:
> dimmi se son dannati, e in qual vico'.
>   'Costoro e Persio e io e altri assai,',
> rispuose il duca mio, 'siam con quel Greco
> che le Muse lattar più ch'altri mai,
>   [...]
> Euripide v'è nosco e Antifonte,
> Simonide, Agatone e altri piùe
> Greci che già di lauro ornar la fronte.' (*Purg.* XXII. 97–108)

Most Dantists concur that this catalogue of names, with the probable exception of Persius,[68] does not indicate that Dante had read any of the works of the writers listed, particularly as this would have been impossible as regards the Greeks and Caecilius. At the same time, he certainly picked up titbits of information about them from other written sources, as may be documented for both Plautus and Caecilius.[69]

(1989), 1–22; Giuseppina Mezzadroli, *Seneca in Dante* (Florence: Le Lettere, 1990); Ronald de Rooy, 'On Anthropophagy in Dante's *Inferno*', *Lectura Dantis*, 8 (1991), 64–84; Andreas Heil, 'Ugolino una Andromache: ein Senecazitat bei Dante?', *Deutsches Dante-Jahrbuch*, 75 (2000), 57–65; Steno Vazzana, 'L'*Hercules Furens* secondo modello dell'*Inferno* dantesco', in his *Dante e 'la bella scola'* (Rome: Edizioni dell'Ateneo, 2002), pp. 163–90; Enrico Fenzi, 'Seneca e Dante: da Alessandro Magno a Ulisse', in *Studi sul canone letterario del Trecento. Per Michelangelo Picone*, ed. by Johannes Bartuschat and Luciano Rossi (Ravenna: Longo, 2003), pp. 67–78; Claudia Villa, 'Rileggere gli archetipi: la dismisura di Ugolino', in *Leggere Dante*, ed. by Lucia Battaglia Ricci (Ravenna: Longo, 2004), pp. 113–29; Tobias Leuker, 'L'"orazion picciola" dell'Ulisse dantesco e un'invettiva di Seneca', *L'Alighieri*, 49 (2008), 91–94; Black, 'Classical Antiquity', pp. 311–12; Enrico Fenzi, 'Il mondo come patria: da Seneca a Dante, *De vulgari eloquentia*, I 6, 3', *Letture classensi*, 44 (2015), 85–95; Elisa Lucchesi, 'Echi di "Seneca morale" nel XIII canto dell'*Inferno*', *Italianistica*, 45 (2016), 99–106; Enrico Fenzi, 'Dante e Seneca', in *I classici di Dante*, ed. by Paola Allegretti and Marcello Ciccuto (Florence: Le Lettere, 2018), pp. 177–213.

68   Giorgio Brugnoli, 'Omero sire', *Cultura neolatina*, 27 (1967), 120–36 (pp. 130–35). See also Black, 'Classical Antiquity', pp. 312–13.

69   On Dante and Plautus, see Roberto Mercuri, 'Plauto', in ED, IV, 555, and 'Terenzio'. Moore notes the 'remarkable resemblance' between *Bacchides* III. 1–3 and *Inf.* III. 1–9; though he goes on to point out that 'If Dante had seen this passage, I should suppose that he may have met with it in a Florilegium' (p. 261). On Dante and Caecilius, see Brugnoli, 'Cecilio'. Information on both writers was available in the Trecento; see, for instance, the biographical-critical descriptions given by the Dante commentators in their annotations to *Purgatorio* XXII. See also Alessio, pp. 117–18; Giorgio Brugnoli, 'Teatro latino medioevale', *Rivista di cultura classica e medievale*, 3 (1961), 114–20 (pp. 115–16);

In general, these lines, together with the following two *terzine* (109–14), are most commonly deemed a sort of addendum in minor key to the lists of pagan worthies presented in *Inferno* IV (see in particular Tateo, pp. 89–94). More specifically, the reference to the Latin authors who accompany Homer complements the 'bella scola' (*Inf.* IV. 94) of Limbo. I would also note that, given its stress on 'comic' writers, *Purgatorio* XXII fills a space that had apparently been left empty in the earlier episode. Finally, if 'Varro', as is almost certain, is Virgil's friend, the tragedian and epic poet, Rufus Lucius Varius, then, in lines 97–100, Dante introduced one or more exemplary authors for each of the three 'styles', given Persius's standing as a leading satirist.[70] The scant attention he grants them, however, intimates his dissatisfaction with the *genera dicendi*, and with traditional perceptions of comedy in particular.

What is just as interesting about this passage is what it reveals about the nature of Dante's knowledge of Terence. Giorgio Brugnoli has recognized in lines 97–98 a quotation — 'una citazione di rito da Orazio' (*Richiamo*, p. 50). As other scholars have done, he equates the lines with *Ars poetica* 53–55:

> quid autem
> Caecilio Plautoque dabit Romanus ademptum
> Vergilio Varioque? (*AP* 53–55)

> [What then will a Roman grant Caecilius and Plautus yet deny to Virgil and Varius?]

The two texts are undoubtedly connected. Yet, it is also striking that Dante should have substituted 'Terrenzio nostro antico' in place of Virgil. Nor is this change simply an effect of narrative demands. Brugnoli is not wrong in claiming that Dante is quoting in lines 97–98. However, their source is not to be found in any single work but in a range of texts that allude to Terence. Dante's name-dropping establishes particularly suggestive links with a passage in St Jerome — 'Terentius Menandrum, Plautus et Caecilius veteres comicos' [Terence took Menander as a model, Plautus and Caecilius the old comedians] (*Ep.* LVII. 5) — and with a similar one in Isidore of Seville: 'Duo sunt autem genera comicorum, id est veteres et novi. Veteres, qui ex ioco ridiculares extiterunt, ut Plautus, Accius, Terentius. Novi et satirici a quibus generaliter vitia carpuntur, ut Flaccus, Persius, Iuvenalis et alii' [There are two kinds of comedians, the old and the new. The old stood out as buffoons for their jokes, as Plautus, Accius, and Terence. The new, and satirical, capture vices in general, as Flaccus, Persius, Juvenal and others] (*Etym.* VIII. 7. 7).[71] Both passages, beyond the names that they share with Dante, reveal how the

---

Hagendahl, pp. 269–70; Munk Olsen, *L'Étude des auteurs latins aux XIe et XIIe siècles*, II, 229–41, and *I classici nel canone scolastico altomedievale*, pp. 5, 81–82, 106, 120; Rudolf Peiper, 'Die profane Komoedie des Mittelalters', *Archiv für Litteraturgeschichte*, 5 (1876), 493–542 (pp. 494–95, 519–22), and 'Vermischte', pp. 516–17; Richard J. Tarrant, 'Plautus', in Reynolds, pp. 302–07.

70   On Dante and Varius, see Alan G. Ferrers Howell, 'Should "Vario" or "Varro" Be Read in *Purgatorio* XXII, 98', *The Academy*, 9 (November 1895), p. 389; Umberto Bosco, 'Varo, Vario, Varro (*Purg.* XXII, 98)', in his *Dante vicino* (Caltanisetta and Rome: Salvatore Sciascia Editore, 1966), pp. 391–98; Roberto Mercuri, 'Vario', in ED, V, 887; Tateo, 'Il canone dantesco dei poeti comici e la moderazione di Stazio', pp. 90–91; Villa, 'Il canone poetico mediolatino', p. 33.

71   Jerome, *Epistulae*, ed. by Isidoreus Hilberg, 4 vols (Vienna: Verlag der Österreichischen

poet transformed the technical *vetus* into a personal epithet. Dante may also owe a debt to John of Salisbury's 'nostri Terentii' [our Terence].[72] In any case, the use of the possessive pronoun with the dramatist's name was far from uncommon, as is confirmed by St Augustine: 'Indignum videlicet fuit, ut Plautus aut Naevius Publio et Gn. Scipioni aut Caecilius M. Catoni malediceret, et dignum fuit, ut Terentius vester flagitio Iovis optimi maximi adulescentium nequitiam concitaret' [It was clearly intolerable that Plautus or Naevius defamed Publius and Gnaeus Scipio or Cecilius defamed M. Cato, but it was appropriate that your Terence should incite the immorality of young people with the passion of Jupiter best and greatest] (*De civ. Dei* II. 12). Lines 97–98 also have possible points of contact with other passages in Horace (*Ep.* II. 1. 58–59) and in Quintilian (*Instit. orat.* X. 1. 98–99). The stratified conventional allusions that lie behind the lines would appear to confirm the second-hand quality of Dante's knowledge of Terence (and of the other comedians). And further proof can be adduced in support of this position. In Conrad of Hirsau's *Dialogus super auctores*, one finds a catalogue of authors which, remembering that Juvenal is alluded to in *Purg.* XXII. 14, includes many of the writers who appear in the canto: 'Sed quid de ceteris auctoribus: Terentio, Iuvenali, Statio maiore vel minore, Persio, Homero vel Virgilio' [but what about the other authors: Terence, Juvenal, 'major' Statius or 'minor' Statius, Persius, Homer, or Virgil] (1385–87).[73] Without wanting to claim that Dante was familiar with Conrad, I should like to underline that an extensive tradition existed, stretching back to classical antiquity, in which Terence's name was prominent in lists of *auctores*. The examples that I have just discussed amply substantiate this point.[74] In *Purgatorio* XXII, therefore, Dante was replicating a widely disseminated convention, which reveals the schematic and meditated nature of his appreciation of Terence.

This is confirmed by the notorious Thais episode in *Inferno* XVIII:

> Appresso ciò lo duca 'Fa che pinghe',
> mi disse, 'il viso un poco più avante,
> sì che la faccia ben con l'occhio attinghe
> di quella sozza e scapigliata fante
> che là si graffia con l'unghie merdose,
> e or s'accoscia e ora è in piedi stante.
> Taïde è, la puttana che rispuose
> al drudo suo quando disse "Ho io grazie
> grandi apo te?": "Anzi maravigliose!".' (*Inf.* XVIII. 127–35)

At least since Benvenuto da Imola, Dante's readers have been perturbed by his translation of *Eunuchus* III. 391–92. The poet erroneously placed into Thais's mouth Gnatho's original reply ('ingentis' [infinite]) to Thraso's question ('Magnas

---

Akademie der Wissenschaften, 1996). See also Diomedes, *Artes grammaticae libri III*, in Keil, I, 490, which is part of an extensive discussion of tragedy, comedy, and satire that, as in Dante, brings together Greek and Latin authors (pp. 487–91).

72 John of Salisbury, *Policraticus*, I. 8; ed. by K. S. B. Keats-Rohan, in CCCM, vol. CXVIII, p. 53.

73 Conrad of Hirsau, *Dialogus super auctores*, in Huygens, pp. 71–131.

74 See also Bernard of Utrecht, *Commentum*, 172–74; Bene da Firenze, *Candelabrum*, p. 297; Villa, *'Lectura'*, pp. 138–39.

vero agere gratias Thais mihi?' [did Thais really send me many thanks?]). The misquotation constitutes the strongest evidence available against Dante's direct knowledge of Terence in general and of the *Eunuchus* in particular. Furthermore, his whorish Thais bears little resemblance to the character in the Roman comedy, nor can Thraso properly be called her 'drudo'. Various explanations have been advanced to account for the poet's apparent 'error'. Thus, it has been maintained that, since the parasite is reporting the courtesan's reaction, his phrase can stand for Thais's actual answer.[75] More outlandishly, as it goes against the textual evidence, it has been claimed that Dante's exchange does not refer to *Eunuchus* III. 391–92 but to a later scene involving Thais and Thraso (III. 454–56) (Beccaria). The most convincing explanations, however, have stressed that Dante found Terence's lines in an intermediary source. Pride of place has justly been accorded to the *De amicitia*, given its important standing in Dante's intellectual biography: 'Nec parasitorum in comoediis adsentatio faceta nobis videretur nisi essent milites gloriosi. "Magnas vero agere gratias Thais mihi?" Satis erat respondere: "magnas"; "ingentes" inquit' [Nor would the flattery of parasites in comedies look facetious to us if there were no glorious soldiers. 'Did Thais really send me many thanks?' It would have been enough to answer: 'many', but he said 'infinite'] (XXVI. 98).[76] On reading the passage, scholars have suggested, Dante either mistakenly took 'Thais' as a vocative (Pastore Stocchi, 'Taide', p. 510), or, read it correctly as a nominative, but then interpreted the question as a third person address. Yet, the *De amicitia*, unless one hypothesizes a fairly complex set of glosses, does not present 'Taide' as a 'puttana'.[77] To remedy this problem, John of Salisbury's *Policraticus* has been proposed as a supplementary source, given that it quotes the lines from Terence (III. 4), but also summarizes the plot (VIII. 3), in which Thais is presented as a *meretrix*, Thraso can be interpreted as her lover, and Terence is presented as the author of the *Eunuchus*.[78] It has also been suggested that Dante could have found another dissolute portrait of Thais in the widely disseminated tradition of the *Liber Aesopi* (Padoan, '*Liber*'). In fact, negative representations of the courtesan were commonplace in the fourteenth century: Thais and *meretrix* had become almost synonymous, regardless of the fact that the pseudo-biographical details associated with her name varied dramatically, as the Trecento Dante commentaries on this episode amply demonstrate. Indeed, the most economical explanation for Dante's presentation of the prostitute at the close of *Inferno* XVIII is that he integrated the quotation from the *De amicitia* with the standard medieval image of Thais.[79]

Like *Purgatorio* XXII, *Inferno* XVIII thus depends on second-hand Terentian sources. However, the implications of the Thais episode in the *Commedia* are rather more

---

75   See Benvenuto da Imola, *Comentum*, II, 30; Barchiesi, *Un tema classico e medievale*, p. 130; Pastore Stocchi, 'Taide', p. 509; Villa, '*Lectura*', pp. 167–68.

76   See Barchiesi, *Un tema classico e medievale*; Betti.

77   See Villa, '*Lectura*', p. 153; and see Elisabeth Pellegrin, 'Quelques *accessus* au *De amicitia* de Ciceron', in *Hommages à Andre Boutemy*, ed. by Guy Cambier (Brussels: Latomus, 1976), pp. 274–98.

78   See Pézard, '*Policraticus*'; Paul Renucci, 'Une source de Dante: le *Policraticus* de Jean de Salisbury' (unpublished PhD dissertation, University of Paris Sorbonne, 1951).

79   The best overview of the 'scapigliata fante', remains Barchiesi, *Un tema classico e medievale*.

significant than the allusion to the dramatist in the second canticle. As Barchiesi has demonstrated in his excellent book, it is very likely that Dante would have been aware that the quotation in Cicero came from Terence's comedy (pp. 84–86). Thus, the *explicit* of *Inferno* XVIII can be read as a challenge to the Roman comedian. Barchiesi sees it as an act of *aemulatio*, whereby, in contrast to Terence, Dante elevated his register by introducing 'tragic' elements such as the Latinism 'apo' (pp. 144–49) into a 'comic' context. On the other hand, Villa focuses exclusively on the 'comic' dimension of the rapprochement: 'il personaggio di Taide è qui, credo, significante di Terenzio, il comico classico con il quale Dante si impegna in un confronto regolato dallo stesso registro stilistico [...]. [N]el primo dei canti di Malebolge, cioè dei grandi esercizi dello stile comico, Taide assolve a una funzione di cifra' (*'Lectura'*, pp. 168–70). Although these are important insights, I believe that more can be said about Dante's Thais.

It is evident that, in *Inferno* XVIII, Dante is not composing a conventional 'comic' vignette. The canto as a whole, as Caretti first revealed, is an amalgam of distinct stylistic registers;[80] and the Thais episode continues and brings to a climax *Inferno* XVIII's formal eclecticism by melding 'low' 'comic' elements (none more so than 'merdose' — a word well outside the Terentian lexicon) with 'tragic' Latinizing ones (most notably the translation from Terence). Dante's 'comic' style, as I have argued elsewhere in this chapter, has few effective points of contact with the traditional — in this case, Terentian — conventions of comedy. As Dante's exemplary treatment of Thais discloses, his 'comedía' is a rich and subtle blend of 'styles' and texts. Yet, unlike, say, his approach to Virgil, Ovid, and Lucan, the poet does not seem to be intent on openly 'challenging' the established 'comic' tradition and its major *auctor*. His 'comedy' is so different from, so superior to theirs that no meaningful contest is possible. Consequently, in *Inferno* XVIII, Terence is totally marginalized. He is not even named, never mind bidden to 'stay silent'. Tellingly, he is evoked indirectly via an allusion to one of medieval culture's most distasteful characters. Finally, and almost in passing, given the episode's brevity, Dante reveals to his supposedly 'authoritative' 'comic' predecessor (and to the *Commedia*'s readers) the properly nuanced manner in which a prostitute like Thais ought to be addressed poetically. By relying on a single *stilus*, Terence's treatment, in sharp contrast to Dante's divinely legitimated plurilingualism, is too reductive and mechanistic, lacking both ethical rigour and realistic toughness.

Terence, therefore, can no longer represent the 'comic' in Dante's new *Commedia*: neither at the incipit of the supposedly conventionally 'comic' Malebolge nor anywhere else. As I have tried to show, the poem as a whole is quintessentially and originally 'comic'. Although it is perhaps true that, considered in conventional 'generic' terms, the cantos of Malebolge are the most recognizably 'comic' part of the poem, what is more significant is that Dante continued to experiment with his new style throughout the ten *bolge*. Even those seeming paragons of the 'comic' — the

---

80 Lanfranco Caretti, 'Il canto XVIII dell'*Inferno*', in *Lectura Dantis Scaligera*, 3 vols (Florence: Le Monnier, 1967–68), I, 583–616. See also Zygmunt G. Barański, *Language as Sin and Salvation: A 'lectura' of 'Inferno' XVIII* (Binghamton, NY: MRTS, 2014).

cantos of barratry — are constructed out of a range of registers.[81] More specifically, just as, in his treatment of Thais, Dante showed up the insufficiencies of comedy, so, elsewhere in Malebolge, he referred to other well-established 'comic' traditions in order to highlight their deficiencies too: from the popularizing presentation of devils[82] to the cultural activities of jongleurs;[83] from the anti-courtly, bourgeois 'realist' tradition to the 'favole d'Isopo' (*Inf.* XXIII. 4);[84] and from the 'comic-realist' tenzone (so memorably evoked in Sinon and maestro Adamo's spat) to the 'rime aspre e chiocce' (*Inf.* XXXII. 1). It is, of course, his own 'comedía', and not the comedies of others, that Dante was constantly and energetically preoccupied to vindicate and to extol.

8. The 'Comic' Absence: Terence

Dante's presentation of Terence may appear unnecessarily harsh, especially when compared to his customary appreciative attitude towards classical culture. It recalls the ways in which he treated two other important writers: Guittone d'Arezzo and Guido Cavalcanti. They too are marginalized and 'trivialized' in the *Commedia*. Dante seemed intent on ensuring that his work could in no way be overshadowed by or confused with the writings of his foremost Italian competitors. Equally, Terence's cultural standing as the *comicus* par excellence constituted a threat to Dante's endeavours to establish his own exceptional 'modern' 'comic' *auctoritas*. Just as, in the *Commedia*, Dante stands in Guittone's stead as an experimental poet and in Cavalcanti's as a philosophical one, so, in the poem, he takes over too Terence's cultural position. Similar to the literary catalogue in *Purgatorio* XXII, the 'bella scola' in Limbo symbolizes the tripartite division of 'styles'. Homer, Virgil, Ovid, and Lucan, as is evident from the *Vita nova* (XXV. 9) and the *De vulgari eloquentia* (II. 6. 7), represent the 'tragic' register, while Horace ('Orazio satiro', *Inf.* IV. 89) stands for the 'satirical'. Consequently, Dante, 'sesto tra cotanto senno' (102), fills the 'comic' space normally assigned to Terence (Villa, *'Lectura'*, p. 84). In fact, the *Commedia* establishes that his 'comic' style embraces and surpasses the achievements of his five great predecessors, and calls into question the doctrine of the *genera dicendi* upon which their fame was in part built and which they 'authoritatively' embodied. The Christian 'comic' poet, thanks to divine illumination and his God-given gifts and responsibilities, is 'sesto' only out of modesty and chronologically. It is clear that what Dante attempted in his 'comedía' went far beyond traditional forms of 'imitation' and 'emulation', as well as beyond conventional disputes between 'ancients and

81   Aurelio Roncaglia, 'Lectura Dantis: Inferno XXI', *Yearbook of Italian Studies*, 1 (1971), 3–28.
82   See Piero Camporesi, *Il paese della fame* (Bologna; il Mulino, 1978); Guido Favati, 'Il "jeu di Dante": interpretazione del canto XXI dell'Inferno', *Cultura neolatina*, 25 (1965), 34–52; Leo Spitzer, 'Gli elementi farseschi nei canti XXI–XXII dell'*Inferno*', in his *Studi italiani*, ed. by Claudio Scarpati (Milan: Vita e Pensiero, 1976), pp. 185–90.
83   Michelangelo Picone, 'Baratteria e stile comico in Dante (*Inferno* XXI–XXII)', in *Saggi danteschi americani*, ed. by Gian Carlo Alessio and Robert Hollander (Milan: Franco Angeli, 1989), pp. 63–86.
84   Domenico De Robertis, 'In viaggio coi demoni: canto XXII dell'*Inferno*', *Studi danteschi*, 50 (1981), 1–29.

moderns'. Dante's purpose was to develop and legitimate a radically new way of writing — one which, nonetheless, would still be appropriate, 'useful', and ultimately familiar to his contemporaries. In this complex and ambitious endeavour, where Dante's main interlocutors, *per necessitatem*, could only be God and Virgil, the Roman comedians were, understandably, consigned to the margins.[85]

85   Nardi claimed that Dante had read Latin 'elegiac comedy', but without providing any supporting evidence: *Saggi e note di critica dantesca* (Milan and Naples: Ricciardi, 1966), pp. 161–63. In addition, the three parallelisms that Stefano Pittalunga has noted between Riccardo da Venosa's *De Paulino et Polla* and Dante are all commonplaces: *Commedie latine del XII e XIII secolo*, 5 vols (Genoa: Istituto di Filologia Classica e Medievale, 1976–86), III, 149.

CHAPTER 8

The Poetics of Metre: *Terza rima*, 'canto', 'canzon', 'cantica'

1. The Problem of the *Canto*

An arresting detail catches the eye in the Trecento commentaries to Dante's *Commedia*. With the exception of Guido da Pisa, Giovanni Boccaccio, and Francesco da Buti, the rest of the commentators are uncomfortable with the poet's choice of 'canto' to refer to the poem's one hundred constituent parts: 'e dar matera al ventesimo canto' (*Inf.* xx. 2); 'e li altri due che 'l canto suso appella' (*Inf.* xxxiii. 90); 'Sì cominciò Beatrice questo canto' (*Par.* v. 16); and 'nel modo che 'l seguente canto canta' (*Par.* v. 139; but see p. 241). In place of the poet's designation, they substitute *capitulum* or *capitolo*. For instance, Pietro Alighieri explains that 'Forma tractatus est divisio ipsi libri, qui dividitur et partitur per tres libros; qui libri postea dividuntur per centum capitula; quae capitula postea dividuntur per suas partes et rhythmos' [the form of the treatise is the division of the books themselves, which is divided and distributed into three books: these books are then divided into one hundred chapters: these chapters are then divided into their own parts and verses];[1] while the Ottimo paraphrases *Par.* v. 139 as follows: 'come contiene nel seguente capitolo'.[2] That the commentators should have rejected Dante's terminology is far from unjustified. Ever since classical times, *cantus*, when applied to literature, had simply meant a poetic composition.[3] It had never been utilized as a precise technical term with which to tag the discrete parts of a long narrative poem (whether written in Latin or in the vernacular). The proper term for such major divisions — as the commentators and Dante himself well knew[4] — was of course *capitulum* or,[5]

---

1   *Il 'Commentarium' di Pietro Alighieri*, ed. by Roberto Della Vedova and Maria Teresa Silvotti (Florence: Olschki, 1978), p. 3.

2   *L'ottimo commento della Divina Commedia*, ed. by Alessandro Torri, 3 vols (Pisa: Niccolò Capurro, 1827–29), iii, 103.

3   'Cantus', in TLL, iii, 295.

4   Dante employed 'capitolo' with a certain regularity to refer to the various parts of the four books of the *Convivio*, while he used 'capitulum' in *De vulgari eloquentia* and *Monarchia*. In the *Convivio*, he also labels the constituent elements of the Book of Proverbs by means of this term: 'nel vigesimo secondo capitolo delli Proverbi' (iv. 7. 9).

5   'Capitulum', in *TLL*, iii, 251.

possibly, *liber*.[6] In their annotations, as the two examples that I have just cited reveal, the poet's fourteenth-century readers normally responded to his use of canto by providing a clarificatory synonym for it — a procedure typical of the commentary tradition. They rarely posed themselves the question, however, why Dante should have decided to apply such an idiosyncratic label to the one hundred units making up his 'comedía' (*Inf*. XVI. 128; XXI. 2).[7] The commentators obviously appreciated the peculiarity of Dante's usage, hence their literal gloss, but they then did not take the matter beyond this first basic interpretive level.

In their turn, modern Dantists do not even go so far. The term *canto* has become so closely involved with the *Commedia* that it no longer seems to require an explanation, never mind be the cause of surprise. Indeed, it would be correct to say that neither the origins of the *canto*, nor its status as a metrical, epistemological, and structural form, nor the reasons for Dante's strange choice of the term have

---

6   'Liber', in *TLL*, VII:2, 1274–75.

7   Unlike the other commentators, Boccaccio, Benvenuto, and Francesco da Buti, and subsequently Giovanni da Serravalle, do try to account for Dante's selection of the term 'canto': (1) 'sì come i musici ogni loro artificio formano sopra certe dimensioni di tempi lunghi e brievi, e acute e gravi, e delle varietà di queste con debita e misurata proporzione congiunta, e quello poi appellano "canto" così i poeti: non solamente quegli che in latino scrivono, ma eziandio coloro che, come il nostro autore fa, volgarmente dettano, componendo i loro versi, secondo la diversa qualità d'essi, di certo e diterminato numero di piedi intra se medesimi [...] per che pare che a questi cotali versi, o opere composte per versi, quello nome si convenga che i musici alle loro invenzioni danno, come davanti dicemmo, cioè "canti", e per conseguente quella opera, che di molti canti è composta, doversi "cantica" appellare, cioè cosa in sé contenente più canti': Giovanni Boccaccio, *Esposizioni sopra la 'Comedia' di Dante*, ed. by Giorgio Padoan (Milan: Mondadori, 1965), *Accessus* 15–16; and 'Chiamano [...] i comedi le parti intra sé distinte delle loro comedìe "scene" [...] dove il nostro autore chiama "canti" le parti della sua Comedìa': Boccaccio, *Esposizioni*, *Accessus* 23; (2) 'perché si chiamano cantiche le suoe principali parte. Ad che si può dire ch'è perché sono composte di diversi canti, come dicto fu di sopra, et ciascun canto di versi misurati con certo numero di sillabe distinti per ternario sì che cantare si possano. Et cusì, tornando da l'ultimo al primo perché sono li versi distinti in ternario sì che cantare si possano, si chiamano li capituli canti': Francesco da Buti, 'Il "Commento" di Francesco da Buti alla '"Commedia". "Inferno"', ed. by Claudia Tardelli (unpublished PhD thesis, Scuola Normale Superiore di Pisa, 2010–11), pp. 11–12; (3) 'Quorum librorm quilibet dividitur per capitula, quae appellantur cantus propter consonantiam rhythmorum; et quilibet cantus per rhythmos' [any of these books is divided into chapters, which are called *canti* because of the consonance of their verses, and any canto is divided into verses]: Benvenuto da Imola, *Comentum super Dantis Aldigherij 'Comoediam'*, ed. by James Philip Lacaita, 5 vols (Florence: G. Barbèra, 1887), I, 21; and (4) 'Quare dicitur cantus, dictum fuit in uno preambulorum, scilicet propter dulcedinem modi dicendi in carminibus, vel in rithymis' [Thus it is called canto, and was so called in one of the introductions, evidently because of the sweetness of the narration in verses, or rhymes]: Giovanni di Serravalle, *Translatio et Comentum totius libri Dantis Aldigherii*, ed. by Marcellino da Civezza and Teofilo Domenichelli (Prato: Giachetti, 1891), p. 252. Although the explanations provided by the four commentators, as will become clear from my discussion, barely touch on the implications of Dante's choice of 'canto', the effort and ingenuity they put into clarifying the term is evidence of the sense they had of its importance.

The novelty of the poet's usage of 'canto' can also be gauged from the fact that, as far as I have been able to ascertain from the standard works of reference, his is the earliest attested use of the term in the medieval Latin tradition with the meaning of 'each of the parts into which a poem is divided'. It is, of course, through Dante's vernacular application of 'canto' that Latin *cantus* came to acquire the same meaning (as is confirmed by a perusal of classical and medieval Latin dictionaries in which, surprisingly, no mention is made of this important technical usage).

aroused much scholarly interest. The entry for 'canto' in the *Enciclopedia dantesca* emblematically records this indifference; it simply notes that '[i]l termine indica ciascuna delle parti in cui si divide ogni cantica della *Commedia*'.[8] Such critical neglect is odd in light of the key position which the canto enjoys in the organization of the poem, and thereby the importance it would appear to have for our appreciation of the *Commedia*.[9] I should like to suggest that, given Dante's customary careful use of technical literary terminology, and given his obvious familiarity with the normal language of textual division, he purposely employed 'canto' in a new and seemingly 'inappropriate' manner so as to draw attention to his use of the word. In my work on Dante's poetics, I have noted that it is a commonplace of his self-exegesis always to talk about the *Commedia* in a vocabulary that a contemporary audience would have known.[10] Yet, at the same time, a semantic discrepancy is invariably apparent between the conventional values of a term and the way in which Dante applied the concept to his poem. As a result, his readers are encouraged to reflect on his peculiar usages and thus begin to appreciate the *novitas* of his work, as well as its idiosyncratic, but continuing, relationship to the tradition. And this last factor is crucial. Dante must have believed that, despite first appearances to the contrary, something did link his experimental *canto* to current notions of the term. If this had not been the case, his use of 'canto' to describe and define his poetry would have been pointless, not to say meaningless, and therefore uninterpretable. It is thus in

8   Lucia Onder, 'Canto', in ED, II, 795. Ignazio Baldelli's excellent entries on Dante's metrics in the ED, as well as his synoptic overview of the poet's stylistic development ('Lingua e stile delle opere in volgare di Dante', in ED, Appendix, pp. 55–112), pay no attention to Dante's *canto*. However, see Zygmunt G. Barański, 'Canto', in *The Dante Encyclopedia*, ed. by Richard Lansing (New York and London: Garland, 2000), pp. 139–40, as well as Margaret Bent, 'Songs Without Music in Dante's *De vulgari eloquentia*: *Cantio* and Related Terms', in *'Et facciam dolçi canti': Studi in onore di Agostino Ziino*, ed. by Bianca Maria Antolini and others, 2 vols (Lucca: LIM, 2003), I, 161–82.

9   Notable exceptions to the general lack of critical interest in Dante's *canto* are: Teodolinda Barolini, *The Undivine Comedy: Detheologizing Dante* (Princeton: Princeton University Press, 1992), pp. 21–47, 257–65; Pietro G. Beltrami, *La metrica italiana*, 5th edn (Bologna: il Mulino, 2011), pp. 110–11; Guido Di Pino, *Pause e intercanti nella 'Divina Commedia'* (Bari: Adriatica, 1982), pp. 11–38; Joan Ferrante, 'A Poetics of Chaos and Harmony', in *The Cambridge Companion to Dante*, ed. by Rachel Jacoff, 2nd edn (Cambridge: Cambridge University Press, 2007), pp. 181–200 (pp. 181–86); Guglielmo Gorni, 'La teoria del cominciamento', in his *Il nodo della lingua e il Verbo d'Amore* (Florence: Olschki, 1981), pp. 164–86; Ettore Paratore, 'Analisi "retorica" del canto di Pier della Vigna', *Studi danteschi*, 42 (1965), 281–336 (pp. 281–85); Ernest H. Wilkins, 'Cantos, Regions, and Transitions in the *Divine Comedy*', in his *The Invention of the Sonnet and Other Studies in Italian Literature* (Rome: Edizioni di storia e letteratura, 1959), pp. 103–10. See also Marino Barchiesi, 'Arte del prologo e della transizione', *Studi danteschi*, 44 (1967), 115–207; Gianfranco Contini, *Un'idea di Dante* (Turin: Einaudi, 1976), pp. 123–25; Giovanni Getto, 'Lettura del canto XXIX del *Paradiso*', *Aevum*, 22 (1948), 257–77 (p. 257); Edoardo Sanguineti, *Interpretazioni di Malebolge* (Florence: Olschki, 1971), p. 71, n. 4. See also John Ahern's studies cited below in n. 64. The recent collections of 'vertical' readings of the *Commedia* have helped to refocus attention on the *canto*, as well as on the functioning of individual canticles; see *Vertical Readings in Dante's 'Comedy'*, ed. by George Corbett and Heather Webb, 3 vols (n.p.: Open Book Publishers, 2015–18).

10   See Zygmunt G. Barański, *'Sole nuovo, luce nuova': saggi sul rinnovamento culturale in Dante* (Turin: Scriptorium, 1996), and 'Dante Alighieri: Experimentation and (Self-)Exegesis', in *The Cambridge History of Literary Criticism. II. The Middle Ages*, ed. by Alastair Minnis and Ian Johnson (Cambridge: Cambridge University Press, 2005), pp. 561–82. See also Chapter 7.

contemporary usage and in the *Commedia* itself (especially in those sections of the poem where the word actually appears) that we need to seek the beginning of an answer to the problem of Dante's *canto*.

The poet first mentions the division of his poem into cantos in the *exordium* to *Inferno* xx, where he defines the *Commedia*'s major metrical and narrative units:

> Di nova pena mi conven far versi
> e dar matera al ventesimo canto
> de la prima canzon, ch'è d'i sommersi. (*Inf.* xx. 1–3)

Since the early 1960s, most critics have underlined the technical precision of these lines and their importance for Dante's metaliterary self-reflection.[11] The poet, in fact, made this feature of the *terzina* explicit by modelling it on the *accessus ad auctores,* the general prologues to literary and philosophical commentaries. Thus, lines 1–3 are typical of discussions of the *forma tractatus* and of the *materia* of a text.[12] Previously, scholars, disturbed by the tercet's 'prosaic' tone, tended, on the contary, to downgrade its importance;[13] although, fortunately, only Herbert Douglas Austin was so discomforted by it as to suggest that it should be expunged from the *Commedia* as an interpolation.[14]

---

11   For a detailed discussion of *Inf.* xx. 1–3 (though with few effective points of contact with my analysis), see Marino Barchiesi, 'Catarsi classica e "medicina" dantesca', in *Letture classensi*, 4 (1973), 9–124 (pp. 14–33). See also Ignazio Baldelli, 'Il canto xx dell'*Inferno*', in '*Inferno': letture degli anni 1973–'76*, ed. by Silvio Zennaro (Rome: Bonacci, 1977), pp. 477–93 (pp. 478–80); Giorgio Barberi Squarotti, *L'artificio dell'eternità* (Verona: Fiorini, 1972), pp. 235–39 (pp. 235–39); Teodolinda Barolini, 'xx', in *Dante's 'Divine Comedy'. Introductory Readings. 1. 'Inferno'*, ed. by Tibor Wlassics (Charlottesville: University of Virginia Printing Service, 1990), pp. 262–74 (p. 263); Ettore Caccia, 'Canto xx', in *Lectura Dantis Scaligera*, 3 vols (Florence: Le Monnier, 1967–68), I, 675–724 (pp. 675–77); Robert Hollander, 'The Tragedy of Divination in *Inferno* xx', in his *Studies in Dante* (Ravenna: Longo, 1980), pp. 131–218 (pp. 133–40); Ettore Paratore, 'Il canto xx dell'*Inferno*', *Studi danteschi*, 52 (1979–80), 149–69 (p. 169); Silvio Pasquazi, 'Il canto xx dell'*Inferno*', in *Nuove letture dantesche*, 8 vols (Florence: Le Monnier, 1966–76), II, 183–204 (183–84, 187–89); Raffaello Ramat, 'Lezione sul xx dell'*Inferno*', *L'Alighieri*, 2 (1965), 27–41 (pp. 27–28); Sanguineti, pp. 69–72; Achille Tartaro, *Canto xx dell'*Inferno*' (Naples: Loffredo, 1982), pp. 6–7. The various post-1960 commentaries to the *Commedia* that I consulted when researching this chapter do not include anything that may not be found in the above *lecturae*. See also Leo Spitzer, 'The Addresses to the Reader in the *Commedia*', *Italica*, 32 (1955), 143–65 (pp. 162–63, n. 3); Chandler B. Beall, 'Dante and his Readers', *Forum Italicum*, 13 (1979), 299–343 (p. 308). For readings of *Inf.* xx. 1–3 that have been published since 1993, see n. 15 below.

12   On the *accessus* tradition, see Alastair J. Minnis, *Medieval Theory of Authorship*, 2nd edn (Aldershot: Scolar Press, 1988), pp. 9–72; *MLTC*, pp. 12–15.

13   See Guido Marco Donati, *Il canto xx dell'*Inferno*' (Florence: Sansoni, 1906); Francesco D'Ovidio, 'Esposizione del canto xx dell'*Inferno*', in his *Nuovo volume di studi danteschi* (Caserta and Rome: APE, 1926), pp. 313–55 (pp. 316–17); Luigi Pietrobono, *Il canto xx dell'*Inferno*' [1916] (Rome: SEI, 1965). The idea of the tercet's 'prosaicness' has persisted into more recent times; see, for instance, Dante, *The Divine Comedy*, trans. and ed. by Mark Musa, 3 vols (Harmondsworth: Penguin Books, 1984), I, 255. Another way in which scholars have dismissed these fundamental lines is by describing them as the product of a 'tired' poet; see, for instance, Chiavacci Leonardi, I, 599; Momigliano, I, 147; Pietrobono, p. 5. The fourteenth-century commentators, too, as they did with so much of the *Commedia*'s metaliterary infrastructure, only paid, at best, scant attention to *Inf.* xx. 1–3.

14   Herbert Douglas Austin, '"The Submerged" (*Inf.* xx. 1–3)', *Romanic Review*, 23 (1932), 38–40 (pp. 39–40).

While recognizing the lines' breadth of reference, recent discussions have preferred to fragment the *terzina* rather than to analyse it as a single unit. In particular, attention is separately paid to the possible meanings of 'nova', of 'mi conven far versi', of 'canzon', and of 'sommersi'.[15] Yet it would appear that Dante intended these lines to be read in quite a different way. In order to elucidate the organization and the poetics of the *Commedia*, he established a sophisticated system of interconnections among the tercet's various elements. At the most basic level, the syntax of the sentence confirms that at least the opening two-and-a-half lines need to be read as one — a detail that modern editors acknowledge by introducing a single pause into the sentence, a comma after 'canzon'. As a result of this, special emphasis is placed on the term; and it is further highlighted by its position at the end of the hemistych. That Dante should underline his choice of 'canzon' is not surprising. His use of the word here seems even more aberrant, and therefore potentially more significant, than his use of 'canto'; and it is worth noting that this latter term, too, is placed in a metrically marked position at the end of the line. Indeed, by continuing to exploit the formal characteristics of the hendecasyllable, the poet also draws attention to the tercet's two remaining literary terms — 'versi' appears at the end of the line, while 'matera' is found at the end of the hemistych. The skill with which Dante constructs the opening of *Inferno* XX and the parallels which he creates between its four technical words are clear evidence both of the terms' interconnections and of their importance. Such attention to its composition befits a *terzina* which, it should be recalled, stands as Dante's first explicit internal definition of the *Commedia*'s metre and structure.[16] To put it simply, he declares that

---

15   This trend has largely continued since I completed the research on this chapter in 1993. See Bellomo, p. 319; Piero Boitani, '*Inferno* XX: Tiresias and the Soothsayers', in *'Legato con amore in un volume': Essays in Honour of John A. Scott*, ed. by John J. Kinder and Diana Glenn (Florence: Olschki, 2013), pp. 205–19; Stefano Carrai, 'Il corteo degli indovini: lettura del XX dell'*Inferno*', *L'Alighieri*, 46 (2005), 49–62; Paolo Chiesa, 'Canti XVIII–XIX–XX: il comico e il politico', in *Esperimenti danteschi. Inferno 2008*, ed. by Simone Invernizzi (Genoa and Milan: Marietti, 2009), pp. 141–55; Silvano Ciprandi, 'Canto XX', in his *Le mie lecturae Dantis. I. 'Inferno'* (Milan and Pavia: Società Dante Alighieri. Comitato di Milano and Selecta, 2007), pp. 249–60; Durling-Martinez, p. 312; Enzo Esposito, '*Inferno* XX', *L'Alighieri*, 40 (1999), 7–16; Sonia Gentili, 'Canto XX: deformità morale e rottura dei vincoli sociali: gli indovini', in *Lectura Dantis Romana. Cento canti per cento anni. II. 'Inferno. 2. Canti XVIII–XXXIV*, ed. by Enrico Malato and Andrea Mazzucchi (Rome: Salerno, 2013), pp. 642–70 (pp. 646–47); Georges Güntert, 'Canto XX', in *Lectura Dantis Turicensis. 'Inferno'*, ed. by Georges Güntert and Michelangelo Picone (Florence: Cesati, 2000), pp. 276–90; Inglese, p. 226; H. A. Mason, 'A Journey Through Hell: Dante's *Inferno* Re-visited. An Early Draft? Canto XX', *The Cambridge Quarterly*, 22 (1993), 155–83; Marilyn Migiel, 'The Diviners Truncated Vision: Sexuality and Textuality in *Inferno* XX', in *Dante. Summa Medievalis: Proceedings of the Symposium of the Center for Italian Studies*, ed. by Charles Franco and Leslie Morgan (Stony Brook, NY: Forum Italicum, 1995), pp. 134–46; Valter Puccetti, 'La galleria fisiognomica del canto XX dell'*Inferno*', *Filologia e critica*, 19 (1994), pp. 177–210; Giancarlo Rati, 'La pietà negata (il canto XX dell'*Inferno*)', in *Miscellanea di studi danteschi in memoria di Silvio Pasquazi*, ed. by Alfonso Paolella and others, 2 vols (Naples: Federico & Ardia, 1993), II, 739–57. Noteworthy exceptions are Hollander, I, 370; Claudia Rossignoli, 'Prediction, Prophecy and Predestination: Eternalizing Poetry in the *Commedia*', in Corbett and Webb, II, 193–215 (p. 212).

16   At this juncture, the problem arises of what, if any, technical information concerning the structure of his poem Dante may have included in the incipit to the *Commedia*. A similar problem is

his poem has a most unusual form of organization; in Pietro Alighieri's commonplace language, it is divided into both *libri* and *capitula* — a unique arrangement for an epic poem (I shall return shortly to this crucial issue). And Dante immediately refines his description. The precision with which he affirms that we are about to read 'il ventesimo canto | de la prima canzon' also reveals for the first time that this first *canzone* will have its numerical counterpart or counterparts elsewhere in the text. Up to this point, the poem provides no clue that it is to have such an unexpected and original design.[17] Further and more generally, Dante's eccentric use of 'canto' and 'canzon' affords immediate proof of the uniqueness of the 'comedía' in relation to established literary canons, just as his conventional recourse to 'versi' and 'matera' serves as an equally timely reminder of its debts to the tradition. *Inferno* XX's incipit revitalizes the hoary *topos* of the novelty of the 'matera' which the writer is about to present. The newness of Dante's 'nova pena' spreads to every part of this crucial *terzina*, and, by extension, to the *Commedia* itself.

All that I have said so far is not difficult to discern; it involves what might be termed the surface meaning of the lines. However, what is more intriguing and important, if the complexity and originality of the *Commedia* are to be appreciated, are the reasons, first, why Dante should have felt it necessary to organize his poem in the peculiar manner that he did; second, why he decided to raise these matters at this particular juncture in his poem; and third, why he chose to describe his work with the strange terms found in *Inferno* XX. The remainder of this chapter attempts to provide some answers to these three questions. However, given the considerable degree of overlap among my proposed solutions, my answers will not be as neatly compartmentalized as the three questions which they hope to elucidate. The history of Dante's 'canto' and 'canzon', as befits the all-embracing ambitions of his 'comedía', is one of synthesis and variety, as well as of order.

2. 'Canzon' and 'canto' — *De vulgari eloquentia* and the *Commedia*

Not unexpectedly, unlike his use of 'canto', Dante's choice of 'canzon' has attracted considerable critical attention. The infernal *canzone* not only sits uneasily with the synonymous 'cantica' utilized at the end of *Purgatorio* (XXXIII. 140), but its

---

whether he prefaced each *cantica* and *canto* with a rubric of the type printed between square brackets in Petrocchi's critical edition (such a decision, it should be noted, would have necessitated the poet revealing in advance not only the terminology so dramatically unveiled in *Inferno* XX but also the peculiar structure of his work). The manuscript evidence regarding the *Commedia*'s rubrication is inconclusive: see Giuseppe Vandelli, *Per il testo della 'Divina Commedia'*, ed. by Rudi Abardo (Florence: Le Lettere, 1989), pp. 277–92, 297–301; Giorgio Petrocchi, 'Introduzione', in *Com.*, I, 472–73; Antonio E. Quaglio, 'Titolo', in '*Commedia*', in ED, II, 79. However, in light of the carefully programmed manner, as I shall discuss, in which Dante introduced *Inf.* XX. 1–3 into the structure of the *Commedia*, I believe that it is highly unlikely that he would have spoilt the tercet's effect by anticipating its substance. Lino Pertile adduces other telling evidence as to why it would have been difficult for Dante to have written the kind of rubrics published by Petrocchi; see his '*Canto-cantica-Comedía* e l'Epistola a Cangrande', *Lectura Dantis Virginiana*, 9 (1991), 103–23 (pp. 115–18).

17 *Inf.* XX. 1–3 is likely to have had a startling impact on the *Inferno*'s first readers, even though this is not recorded in the Trecento commentators, given the canticle's original independent dissemination.

relationship to the illustrious lyric genre of the same name also seems especially problematic. It is now widely, and not unreasonably, accepted that, by means of 'canzon', Dante was suggesting some kind of, probably contrastive, analogy between his 'lyric' and 'comic' poetry. However, less agreement exists as to what such an analogy might actually involve. Some critics claim that, given the *canzone*'s traditional association with the *stilus altus*, Dante's infernal 'canzon' is simply a pointer to *Inferno* XX's 'tragic' register, especially in the light of the *canto*'s debts to classical literature.[18] This is an unsatisfactory explanation since it ignores, first, that 'canzon' refers primarily to structural and thematic features rather than to stylistic

18   See Barberi Squarotti, p. 237; Sanguineti, p. 72. For a telling critique of these positions, see Pasquazi, pp. 187–89. Robert Hollander also argues that 'at this point [*Inf.* XX], as at perhaps no other point in the *Inferno*, Dante's poetry is tragic' ('Tragedy of Divination in *Inferno* XX', p. 139), while, at the same time, acknowledging the canto's stylistic hybridism. However, his list of *Inferno* XX's 'tragic' characteristics — 'First, it [the canto] is about to narrate the bitterly painful experience of its protagonist; second, the subject of the entire *cantica* is seen as being "i sommersi," those whose lives on earth have ended in the ultimate unhappiness of damnation; third, it occurs in the canto which more than any other in the *Commedia* addresses the question of Virgil's status as tragic poet' (p. 139) — relates somewhat tangentially to medieval notions of tragedy, especially as reworked by the poet in the *De vulgari eloquentia*, which Hollander recognizes, correctly, as having a determining effect on any interpretation of 'canzon' (pp. 138–39): 'Per tragediam superiorem stilum inducimus [...] Si tragice canenda videntur, tunc assumendum est vulgare illustre, et per consequens cantionem ligare [...] Stilo equidem tragico tunc uti videmur quando cum gravitate sententie tam superbia carminum quam constructionis elatio et excellentia vocabulorum concordat [...] illa que summe canenda distinximus isto solo sunt stilo canenda: videlicet salus, amor et virtus et que propter ea concipimus, dum nullo accidente vilescant' [By 'tragedy' I mean the higher style [...]. If the topics are to be sung in the tragic style, you must employ the illustrious vernacular, and accordingly you must bind together a canzone. [...] We seem to be using the tragic style when the loftiness of the verse, the sophistication of the structure, and the excellence of the lexicon all agree with the seriousness of the subject-matter [...] those topics which — as we have identified — require the highest style, should be sung in that style alone: for example salvation, love, and virtue, and the thoughts they inspire in us, provided they are not corrupted by any unexpected circumstance] (II. 4. 5–8). Furthermore, by explaining Dante's use of 'canzon' with reference solely to *Dve* II. 8. 3–4, Hollander delimits much too narrowly, as we shall see, the connotative and exegetical potential of the equation between *De vulgari eloquentia* and *Commedia* (see also n. 20 below). On the concept of tragedy, see Chapter 7, nn. 12 & 53. By dissenting from the proposals put forward by the proponents of *Inferno* XX's *stilus tragicus*, I do not wish to create the impression that the canto does not include 'lofty' elements. I object to the totalizing and dominant slant which they give to the 'tragic'. My view is that the 'high' is only one register among many, and that, as is usual in the *Commedia*, Dante's main focus in the *canto* is on the 'comic'. I am less inclined to disagree, however, with Hollander and with Lino Pertile, '*Cantica* nella tradizione medievale e in Dante', *Rivista di storia e di letteratura religiosa*, 18 (1991), 389–412 (p. 412), when they suggest that, in line with the widely current structural definition of tragedy as a narrative that begins well and ends badly, 'canzon' highlights the common 'tragic' ending of Hell's inhabitants. On the other hand, it is problematic to label *Inferno* a tragedy in structural terms, since more than any of the three parts of the *Commedia*, it has a quintessentially 'comic' organization, since it begins badly in the dark wood and ends positively with the travellers exiting to 'riveder le stelle' (XXXIV. 139). *Inferno* is thus a comedy that embraces a whole series of mini-tragedies (as well as a whole host of other *stili*). In this manner, too, Dante underlined the dominant 'comic' character of his poem. Other scholars are more nuanced when talking about *Inferno* XX's 'tragic' register. They note that the canto synthesizes 'un tono popolare ma non privo di una sua larghezza epica', and that 'canzone [...] è la spia stilistica più significativa ad indicare lo sliricarsi del tono e insieme il suo epicizzarsi' (Caccia, p. 676). See also Bellomo, p. 332; Gentili.

ones, and, second, that it embraces the *Inferno* as a whole and, as Dante makes clear by his use of the epithet 'prima', it can be applied to each of the *Commedia*'s major constituent parts and thus has a bearing on the poem as a whole. Furthermore, this suggestion fails to account for the *canto*'s stylistic variety which cannot easily be subsumed under the category of the 'tragic'. Other scholars argue more persuasively that, by means of 'canzon', Dante was deliberately recalling the *De vulgari eloquentia*, his major critical and theoretical contribution on this lyric form.[19] Telling support for this position comes from *Inferno* XX's closing line — 'Sì mi parlava, e andavamo introcque' (130) — which ends with a word that Dante had condemned in the treatise as unfit for the *volgare illustre* of the *canzone tragica* (I. 13. 2).[20] Thus, thanks to the verbal rapprochements between the *Commedia* and the *De vulgari eloquentia*, scholars go on to conclude, the poet underlined the ideological and artistic differences that distinguish the two principal moments of his poetic career. From this perspective, 'canzon' touches on the *Commedia* in its entirety: 'Il teorizzatore cioè della canzone come propria della poesia tragica si serve del termine — canzone — per indicare poesia comica per eccellenza'.[21]

Though I largely agree with this line of argument, I also believe that *Inferno* XX has more to reveal about the metaliterary interplay between the *De vulgari eloquentia* and the *Commedia* than has been recognized so far. To date, critics have restricted themselves to drawing broad comparisons between the two works — comparisons which, paradoxically, they have based on single words considered in isolation from the rest of the canto and of the chapters of the treatise from which they have been taken (and this is a trend that has continued to this day). Yet, as with its opening tercet, the whole thrust of Dante's presentation in *Inferno* XX is towards a totalizing reading. It is surely not by chance that, in the canto, Dante should have strategically brought together technical vocabulary, allusions to the *De vulgari eloquentia*, an evaluation of classical *tragedie*, and a startling synthesis of 'high' and 'low' stylistic forms.[22] As we shall see, these elements illuminate each other in turn, thereby

19 See Ignazio Baldelli, 'Canzon', in ED, I, 801, and 'Il canto XX', pp. 478–80; Barchiesi, 'Catarsi classica e "medicina" dantesca', pp. 28–29, 119; Hollander, 'Tragedy of Divination in *Inferno* XX', pp. 138–39; Paratore, 'Il canto XX', p. 168. For a wide-ranging analysis of the poetics of the *Commedia* in terms of the *De vulgari eloquentia*, see Antonino Pagliaro, *Ulisse: ricerche semantiche sulla 'Divina Commedia'*, 2 vols (Messina and Florence: D'Anna, 1967), II, 529–83.

20 Several critics, usually to defend their 'tragic' reading of the canto, have tried — unconvincingly in my opinion — to loosen the links between 'introcque' and the rest of *Inferno* XX. They argue that the Latinism, rather than an integral part of *canto* XX, in fact connects with the three cantos of barratry that follow, since it acts as a stylistic signpost for their 'low' register; see Caccia, p. 719, n. 2; Sanguineti, p. 97. Their arguments fail to persuade because 'introcque' is such a fundamental component of *Inferno* XX. Although Dante is certainly establishing a bridge between *Inferno* XX and XXI, what is most striking about his strategic usage of 'introcque' is the way in which he encloses the 'ventesimo canto' between two words that unambiguously recall the *De vulgari eloquentia*. For better-balanced discussions of 'introcque', see Barchiesi, 'Catarsi classica e "medicina" dantesca', p. 119; Hollander, 'Tragedy of Divination in *Inferno* XX', pp. 214–15.

21 Baldelli, '"Il canto XX', p. 479 (and compare his 'Canzon', p. 801, and 'Terzina', in ED, V, 583–94 (p. 584)). See also Barchiesi, 'Catarsi classica e "medicina" dantesca', pp. 28–29; Paratore, 'Il canto XX', pp. 168–69.

22 See the *lecturae* listed in nn. 11 & 15 above. In addition, see Robert Hollander, *Il Virgilio dantesco:*

providing both an explantion for Dante's original use of literary terminology in the canto's incipit, and general insights into the workings of his 'comedía'.

Dante placed the formal description of his poem at the head of a group of cantos which, stretching from *Inferno* XX to *Inf.* XXIII. 57, represents an unusual section in the make-up of the cantica. It constitutes the most explicitly 'anti-tragic' part of the poem, and thus it crucially serves to illustrate Dante's new ideas on the 'comic' register (see Chapters 6 and 7). More specifically, and in keeping with the concerns of their *exordium*, these cantos yield considerable information on the structure of the *Commedia*. Indeed, they could be said to offer an extended practical commentary on aspects of *Inf.* XX. 1–3.

The three cantos of barratry (*Inf.* XXI–XXIII) are the most conspicuous, if not actually the first, instance in the *Inferno* of a lack of correspondence between the structure of the canto and that of another narrative unit, such as a division of the afterlife, an infernal inhabitant, a group of sinners, etc.[23] As the poem moves from *Inferno* XXI to *Inferno* XXIII, the 'space' created between the close of a canto and the opening of the following one ceases to be employed as a kind of break — a brief pause, like that enjoyed by Virgil and the pilgrim by the sepulchre of Pope Anastasius (XI. 1–15) — in the onward flow of the story. Instead, a more fluid relationship, akin to enjambment, is established between the beginnings and the endings of these three cantos. This is a striking new development in the organization of the *Commedia*, and it is a ploy which becomes typical in the *Purgatorio* and the *Paradiso*.[24] Nevertheless, that such a shift should occur precisely at this point cannot but cause a degree of perplexity. Dante, it should not be forgotten, has just highlighted the specificity of the canto ('il ventesimo canto | de la prima canzon'), a fact which, somewhat bewilderingly, he almost immediately calls into question. If, on the one hand, the image of the canto presented by *Inferno* XX as a fairly well-defined unit conforms, in general terms, to the image which can be extrapolated from Dante's practice up to this point, then the next three *canti*, on the other hand, underscore its structural fragility and go some way to deconstruct its aura of self-sufficiency. Indeed, by doing this, and despite their particular narrative continuity, *Inferno* XXI– XXIII help to bring to the fore the fact that, unlike the *laisses* of, say, the *Chanson de Roland* (see Subsection 4, 'Epic Structures', below), none of Dante's cantos so far can claim to have a single narrative or stylistic focus. Despite the clearcut individuality of each canto, a feature confirmed by the organization of their rhyme scheme (a point to which I shall return in greater detail in this section and below in Subsection 3, 'The Flexible *Canto*') the cantos are not self-standing compositions but subordinate parts of larger textual, narrative, and stylistic entities.

Approximately two-thirds of the way through the first cantica, Dante felt it was time to exploit that knowledge and those expectations of his poem's organization which, by this point, he could reasonably expect his readers to have acquired, in

---

tragedia nella 'Commedia' (Florence: Olschki, 1983), pp. 81–115; Ernesto G. Parodi, 'La critica della poesia classica nel ventesimo canto dell'*Inferno*', *Atene e Roma*, 11 (1908), 183–95 & 237–50.

23   See, in particular, the transitions between *Inferno* VI and VII, and then VII, VIII, IX, X, and XI; on the latter panel of cantos, see Chapter 17. See also Barolini, *Undivine Comedy*, pp. 258–61.

24   See Barolini, *Undivine Comedy*, pp. 257–65; Ferrante, p. 158; Gorni; Wilkins.

order to stimulate reflection on the nature of the canto (and of the *Commedia* in general). He prefaced this operation by defining it in relation to the *Commedia*'s other metrical components, and by finally giving a name to this new form (and the canto's *novitas* could not have escaped notice, since nothing quite like it had previously graced the epic tradition).[25] In particular, Dante appeared to be raising a number of fundamental questions: if the *canto* is, narratively and stylistically, a diffuse, flexible, and possibly even arbitrary form, why does he bother to use it instead of an open-ended and continuous structure like that of the *romans*? In fact, why does he further complicate his poem by introducing an additional system of subdivision and another original organizational tier — the canzone? Yet again, Dante is prodding his readers to interpret, to act as commentators of his poem — a duty which he openly exhorts them to undertake a few lines later on: 'Se Dio ti lasci, lettor, prender frutto | di tua lezione, or pensa per te stesso' (*Inf.* XX. 19–20). And to succeed in this task, he provides them with an authoritative guide.

As might be imagined, this guide is the *De vulgari eloquentia*.[26] If this were not the case, it is difficult to understand why Dante should have made such an effort to evoke the treatise in this already crowded metaliterary context. The metrical term which most powerfully, because most unexpectedly, unites the treatise with the *Commedia* is, as we have seen, *cantio/canzone*. Thus, in keeping with Dante's standard self-exegetical procedures, it seems feasible that the 'comic' 'canzon' not only establishes a contrastive relationship with its 'tragic' counterpart (whose *caposcuola*, Virgil's *Aeneid*, is *Inferno* XX's principal intertext), but also, *mutatis mutandis*, has certain facets in common with the traditional 'high' canzone. And the poet's discussion of the *cantio* in the *De vulgari eloquentia* does indeed have uncanny links with *Inf.* XX. 1–3. It is obvious that, like the lyric *canzone*, Dante's epic 'canzon' is the shell which contains other structures: 'cantio [...] est equalium stantiarum sine responsorio ad unam sententiam tragica coniugatio' [a canzone [...] is a series of equal stanzas in tragic style without a refrain and with a single subject] (*Dve* II. 8. 8). In fact, if we ignore for the moment the two epithets — 'equalium' and 'tragica' — which most obviously drive a wedge between them, the structural similarities between the two kinds of *canzone* are quite striking. Both do not include refrains (*responsoria*) between their main constituent units (*stantia/canto*), and each is dedicated to a single concern (*una sententia*); as regards the 'prima canzon', this is naturally the 'sommersi'.[27] Furthermore, the specific structural relationship that exists between 'cantio' and 'stantia' also holds good for 'canzon' and 'canto': 'Nam quemadmodum cantio [/'canzon'] est gremium totius sententie, sic stantia [/'canto'] totam artem

25   On the novelty of the *canto* as an epic form, see Subsection 4, 'Epic Structures', below.

26   The vital role that the *De vulgari eloquentia* plays with respect to *Inferno* XX–XXIII is evidence that, unlike the *Convivio*, Dante intended to disseminate his treatise; or rather, he intended to do so when he was composing the *Inferno*. On the composition and transmission of the *Convivio*, see Chapter 1, n. 14; on those of the *De vulgari eloquentia*, see Zygmunt G. Barański, 'Textual Transmission', in *Dante in Context*, ed. by Zygmunt G. Barański and Lino Pertile (Cambridge: Cambridge University Press, 2015), pp. 509–17 (p. 516).

27   In this context, it is noteworthy that Barchiesi suggests that the phrase 'ch'è d'[i sommersi]' is equivalent to the Latin formula used in titles: *quae est de* ('Catarsi classica e "medicina" dantesca', pp. 24–25).

ingremiat' [for just as the canzone is the bearer of the whole of its subject-matter, so the stanza bears the whole poetic art] (*Dve* II. 9. 2). *Inferno* XX's *ars* is how it gives poetic form ('dar versi') to the 'matera' of the 'nova pena'. And the 'comic' *canto* has other affinities with the *canzone* stanza. Metrically and structurally they are both independent organic units: 'stantiam esse sub certo cantu et habitudine limitatam carminum et sillabarum compagem' [a stanza is a composition of verses and syllables defined by a certain melody and a certain arrangement] (*Dve* II. 9. 6), while the confines of the *canto* are fixed, first, by its opening and closing with a double rhyme (the so-called *rime rilevate*) rather than with a triple one, and, second, by ending with the single line of a new tercet[28] — effects that are achieved thanks to the 'artistic' manipulation of its 'versi'.[29] Finally, as well as both being 'closed'

---

28   See Baldelli, 'Terzina', p. 585; Zygmunt G. Barański, 'Re-viewing Dante', *Romance Philology*, 42 (1988), 51–76 (pp. 65–66); Beltrami, pp. 109–12; Gorni, pp. 164–65, 181–82, 207. For an important 'allegorical' reading of the *terza rima* and its assimilation into the *canto*, see John Freccero, 'The Significance of *terza rima*', in *Dante, Petrarch, Boccaccio: Studies in the Italian Trecento in Honor of Charles S. Singleton*, ed. by Aldo S. Bernardo and Anthony L. Pellegrini (Binghamton: State University of New York Press, 1983), pp. 3–17. See also Luisa Ferretti Cuomo, 'Per un modello della terza rima dantesca: "l'autonomia del significante"', *Tenzone*, 5 (2004), 11–38; Jean-Marie Kauth, 'The Shaping of Dante's Cosmos', *Medievalia et Humanistica*, 32 (2006), 7–24.

29   The precise value of 'versi' in this context is far from clear. It seems to cover three main areas of meaning: (1) 'far versi' is equivalent to the generic 'to compose poetry' which 'tria videtur consistere: primo circa cantus divisionem, secundo circa partium habitudinem, tertio circa numerum carminum et sillabarum' [seems to centre around three elements: first, around the division into cantos, second around the arrangement of their parts, third around the number of verses and syllables] (*Dve* II. 9. 4); (2) more specifically, 'versi', as is clear from the quotation just given, equals *carmina* and probably also, by extension, *sillabae*, given the close association of these last two terms in Dante (see *Dve* II. 9. 6; 12. 4); (3) in the particular context of the *Commedia*, 'versi' may stand for what we now call *terza rima* or *terzina*, and what the early commentators at times labelled *ternario*. 'Versi', thus, appears to focus on the 'line', the hendecasyllables of the *Commedia*, one of the three elements, together with the 'canto' and the 'canzon', which constitutes the poem's *forma tractatus*. In addition, some of the poem's fourteenth-century readers gloss 'versi' as *rithimi* (see, for instance, the passage from Benvenuto quoted in n. 7 above) — I do not find this interpretation especially persuasive, given the care with which Dante always keeps *rithimus* distinct from *carmen* and *sillaba* in the *De vulgari eloquentia* (see, in particular, II. 9. 4–5). It may equally be the case, however, that Benvenuto, who did not know the *De vulgari eloquentia*, could have been using the term not with the meaning of 'rhymes' but with that of 'verses', since both meanings were current in the Middle Ages: '*Rithimus* sonus cantilene, et *rithimus* grece numerus, quia in numero quodam sillabarum vel vocum; unde *rithimus-a-um*, dulciter sonans, vel quia fit ex rithimis, et *rithimor -aris* id est consonare, vel rithimos facere' (Uguccione's definition of *rithimus* quoted in Brugnoli's notes to Epistle XIII, in *Opere minori*, II, 612–13; *Rithimus* means the sound of a song, and *rithimus* also means 'number' in Greek, because it consists of a certain number of syllables or words; thus *rithimus-a-um*, 'with a sweet sound', or because it is made of verses, and *rithimor -aris*, that is 'to be consonant', or 'to create rhymes'). The fact that, in the epistle to Cangrande, under the *accessus* heading which deals, in a manner that recalls *Inf.* XX. 1–3, with the *forma tractatus* of the *Commedia*, the letter's author should state that 'quilibet cantus dividitur in rithimos' (26; any canto is divided into verses) would be further evidence, at least for me, of the epistle's inauthenticity. It seems unlikely, not to say pointless, that Dante, who certainly did know the *De vulgari eloquentia*, would have described the basic organization of his poem by intentionally going against his own previously carefully established usage of *carmen-verso* in opposition to *rithimus*. First, it would have meant repudiating the terminology which had been fixed, in part — as we have seen — by means of a rapprochement with the *De vulgari eloquentia*, within the *Commedia* itself. Second, if Dante were the author of the letter, it is not at all clear why he would have wanted to alter

structures, they are also 'open' ones, since they respectively unite with other *stantiae* and cantos to create *canzoni*. By exploring the possible analogies (and we should not forget the centrality which deduction *per analogiam* enjoyed in the Middle Ages) between chapters 8 and 9 of Book II of the *De vulgari eloquentia* and lines 1–3 of *Inferno* XX, we can gain illuminating insights into the character of the *Commedia*'s principal constituent parts.[30]

At this point, however, if the 'comic' and the 'lyric' are not to be perceived as somehow synonymous, it is imperative to restore the two 'missing' adjectives, 'equalium' and 'tragica', to the treatise's definition of *cantio* in chapter 8. In the following chapter, Dante goes on to explain what he means by 'equalium stantiarum': 'nee licet aliquid artis sequentibus arrogare, sed solam artem antecedentis induere' [and the following stanzas should not try to add any new poetic device, but should only wear the art of the previous ones] (*Dve* II. 9. 2); and his definition of the *stilus*

---

the terms in which he had already defined his poem, thereby creating terminological confusion, and this at a crucial point: the presentation of his poem's *forma tractatus*. In the *Commedia*, it is important to remember the basic nature of the line remains constant. The *verso* is not a key issue, its definition is not linked to the formal and ideological changes that the poem undergoes, such as the changes signalled by the terminological switch from 'canzon' to 'cantica', a process which, in any case, occurs not outside, but inside, the *Commedia*. To have used *rithimus* instead of *carmen* would have suggested that the line, like the *cantica*, alters its character during the course of the poem. Furthermore, in the light of the three meanings of *rithimus* current in the fourteenth century, Dante would have only compounded the confusion caused by his switch, since it is not at all clear what 'rithimos' stands for in the letter. For Dante, to have substituted the precise *carmen* for the imprecise *rithimus* seems to make little sense and goes against the consistently sophisticated coherence of his metaliterary practices. Such exegetical sloppiness, on the other hand, is far from untypical of the anonymous author of the Epistle; see Zygmunt G. Barański, '*Comedía*: Notes on Dante, the Epistle to Cangrande, and Medieval Comedy', *Lectura Dantis*, 8 (1991), 26–55, as well as Chapter 7. Let me offer another example of the gap in critical and writerly perception that separates Dante from the author of the letter. If one compares *Inf.* XX. 1–3 with paragraph 26 ('Forma tractatus est triplex, secundum triplicem divisionem. Prima divisio est, que totum opus dividitur in tres canticas. Secunda, qua quelibet cantica dividitur in cantus. Tertia, que quilibet cantus dividitur in rithimos' [the structure of the work is triple, according to a triple division. The first is that the whole work is divided into three canticles. The second, that each canticle is divided into *canti*. The third, that each *canto* is divided into verses]) what is immediately striking is the fact that they present the poem's *forma tracatus* in diametrically contrasting modes. Dante, with his poet's sensibility and experience, works his way up from the line, while the poetically inexperienced author of the Epistle works his way down, grandiosely but unrealistically, from the *cantica*. For an excellent discussion of Dante's use of *rithimus* and *rima*, see Brugnoli, annotations to *Ep.* XIII, pp. 612–13. See also Mario Pazzaglia, *Il verso e l'arte della canzone nel 'De vulgari eloquentia'* (Florence: La Nuove Italia Editrice, 1967), pp. 141–76; Antonio da Tempo, *Summa Artis Rithimici Vulgaris Dictaminis*, ed. by Richard Andrews (Bologna: Commissione per i testi di lingua, 1977), pp. 118, 120, 128–29. See also Alessandro Niccoli, 'Verso', in ED, V, 981–82.

30   As regards my discussion in this subsection, it is noteworthy that Beltrami should assert that, in the light of *Inf.* XX. 1–3, 'l'uso terminologico di Dante [...] spinge a credere che Dante pensi il canto come una stanza di canzone *sui generis*; una canzone "comica" nello stile, che consente una relativa elasticità nella misura delle stanze-canti' (p. 111). A final similarity between the stanza and the *canto* may be noted in the fact that just as, in a canzone, the first stanza establishes the basic metrical patterns for the *stanze* that follow it (*Dve* II. 9. 2), so *Inferno* I fixes such patterns for the remaining ninety-nine cantos. On Dante's theoretical reflection on the *canzone*, see Baldelli, 'Canzone', pp. 796–802; Gérard Gonfroy, 'Le Reflet de la *canso* dans le *De vulgari eloquentia* et dans les *Leys d'amors*', *Cahiers de civilisation médiévale*, 25:3–4 (1982), 187–96; Pazzaglia.

tragicus is equally restrictive: 'illa que summe canenda distinximus isto solo sunt stilo [tragico] canenda: videlicet salus, amor et virtus et que propter ea concipimus, dum nullo accidente vilescant' [those topics which, as we have identified, require the highest style, should be sung in that style alone: for example salvation, love, and virtue, and the thoughts they inspire in us, provided they are not corrupted by any unexpected circumstance] (*Dve* II. 4. 8; and see II. 2. 1–9). It is the *De vulgari eloquentia*'s championing of a formally balanced and restricted treatment of a narrow subject-matter which immediately discloses the abyss that divides the 'tragic' *cantio* and its *stantiae* from the equivalent components of the 'comedía'. Thus, if one undertakes a general assessment of the canto based on any small consecutive number of these, what emerges is a stylistic, structural, and thematic variety quite alien to the conventions of the lyric canzone. It is enough to think, since we are in its vicinity, of the richness of that group of eight cantos that begins with *Inferno* XVI (where Dante first introduces the title of his poem) and ends with *Inferno* XXIII.[31] The cantos supply the concrete evidence of the novelty of Dante's epic poetry, especially in contrast to the monotony of the *stantiae*. In fact, the formal and ideological polyvalence of the cantos is what distinguishes the 'comedía' from all other human books.

3. The Flexible *Canto*

The epistemological effectiveness of medieval analogy lay in its potential to highlight variance as well as similarity between things. The ways in which Dante took advantage of the *De vulgari eloquentia* in *Inferno* XX is a classic example of how he worked both with and against the tradition to explain his experimentation. In a similar manner, while pinpointing the features common to his hundred *canti*, Dante also indicated the uniqueness of each of these, as his lapidary 'ventesimo canto | de la prima canzon' enshrines. Like the stanza, the cantos are self-contained. However, Dante's new 'comic' outlook, as their changes in length testify, no longer permits 'harmony' between them.[32] The *Commedia* depends for its very artistic and ideological existence and resolution on their differences: the 'nova [...] matera' in the ever new 'versi' of each new canto. The single *canti*, however, are not left isolated. They are organically and logically integrated, first, into the scheme of their particular 'canzon', and, then, into the totalizing and unifying embrace of the 'comedía'. It is obvious that traditional literary conventions, like those examined in the *De vulgari eloquentia*, could only tangentially provide the forms for the *Commedia* and account for its *novitas*. Dante had to seek new models and new points of reference. He thus turned — as is well known — to God's two all-embracing books, the universe and the Bible (see Chapters 7 and 9). In imitation of what he

---

31   As well as *Inf.* XVI. 128, Dante alludes to the title and *stilus* of his poem in *Inf.* XXI. 2. After providing the structural and metrical description of his poem in the incipit to *Inferno* XX, he repeats the term *comedía*, which defines its register and subject-matter. Dante appears to have wanted the two *exordia* to be read together as a major metaliterary statement on the *Commedia*. See also Chapter 7.

32   A breakdown, in table form, of the length of each canto may conveniently be found in Ferrante, p. 154; Charles S. Singleton, 'The Poet's Number at the Center', *MLN*, 80:1 (1965), 1–10 (p. 5).

had learned from the synthesizing conventions of Scriptural *sermo humilis* and from the 'volume' which 'binds' the plurality of 'ciò che per l'universo si squaderna' (*Par.* XXXIII. 86–87), Dante similarly tried to incorporate 'everything' into a single text and to present this, in each instance, according to the style that he deemed most appropriate. This radical literary intent found formal fulfilment in the invention of the *canto*, a structure that, unlike conventional poetic frameworks subservient to the *genera dicendi*, was both all-receptive and able to establish links with God's 'writing'. Thus, the *dispositio* of the cantos into structures based on the numbers three and ten has its artistic and symbolic point of origin in the *ordo* and character of divine creation; and the same claim can be made for their wide-ranging style and content.[33] It is thus indicative that, just before and after he defined the structure of his poem in *Inferno* XX, Dante should have laid special emphasis on God's artistry:

> O somma sapïenza, quanta è l'arte
> che mostri in cielo, in terra e nel mal mondo,
> e quanto giusto tua virtù comparte! (*Inf.* XIX. 10–12)

and 'non per foco ma per divin' arte' (XXI. 16).

The *canto* is a form of enormous flexibility. This seems to be the main lesson of *Inf.* XX. 1–3. Its strength lies, first, in its structural ability both to stand alone and to become part of a larger whole, and, second, in its compositional possibility not to be tied to any one style or subject. Indeed, the canto is able to perform stylistic and thematic switches and syntheses at will, unconstrained by traditional notions of *convenientia* or of metrical 'harmonization', but driven only by the divinely willed demand that the poet 'tutta sua visïon fa manifesta' (*Par.* XVII. 128). A less ambitious poet than Dante would have restricted himself to instituting stylistic shifts between cantos rather than within them. It goes without saying, however, that such a solution would have singularly failed to provide a proper sense both of the complexity of the created universe and of the import of the poem's God-given message.

The other three references to the *canto* in the *Commedia* all similarly emphasize its flexibility. In *Inf.* XXXIII. 90 ('e li altri due [Ugolino's children] che 'l canto suso appella') the poet highlights the continuity, despite the changes in tone, time, and speaker, between Ugolino's story and Dante-*poeta*'s invective against Pisa. The two allusions in *Paradiso* V ('Sí cominciò Beatrice questo canto' (16) and 'nel modo che 'l seguente canto canta', 139) underscore the limits of the individual *canto* while recognizing its contacts with the rest of the poem and its role in the narrative

---

33   See Ernst Robert Curtius, *European Literature and the Latin Middle Ages* (London and Henley: Routledge & Kegan Paul, 1979), pp. 501–09; Singleton, p. 10. Curtius remarks that 'the wonderful harmony of Dante's numerical composition is the end and the acme of a long development. From the enneads of the *Vita nuova* Dante proceeded to the elaborate numerical structure of the *Commedia*: 1 + 33 + 33 + 33 = 100 cantos conduct the reader through the three realms, the last of which contains ten heavens. Triads and decads intertwine into unity. Here number is no longer outer framework, but a symbol of the cosmic *ordo*' (p. 509). However, now see the intriguing Catherine S. Adoyo, 'Dante Decrypted: *Musica universalis* in the Textual Architecture of the *Commedia*', *Bibliotheca Dantesca*, 1 (2018), 37–69. See also the discussion below on the relationship between music and the *Commedia*. I am unconvinced by Mattia Mantovani's suggestion that the structural model for the *Commedia* should be sought in the *liber mortis*: 'Le "lettere mozze" di Federico III di Sicilia e il *liber mortis* di Dante', *Dante Studies*, 135 (2017), 31–73.

unfolding of the *Commedia*.[34] The *canto* is the fundamental artistic and ideological unit of the poem. Just as every part of creation is a 'trace' of the Creator, each canto, on account of its versatility, stands as a microcosm of the all-embracing 'comedía'.[35] By hinting once again at his work's debts to the *Deus artifex*, Dante neatly and consistently clarifies and legitimates his literary experimentation and its forms.

Although the analogy I have suggested between the *exordium* of *Inferno* xx and the *De vulgari eloquentia* helps to cast light on the *Commedia*'s arrangement, and partly also on the reason for Dante's choice of 'canzon' as the tag with which to describe and explain his poetry (but see below), it fails to illuminate his thinking behind the selection of the term 'canto'. If anything, Dante's statement in the treatise that 'Tota [...] ars cantionis circa tria videtur consistere: primo circa cantus divisionem' [the whole artistic technique of the *canzone* seems to centre around three elements: the first is the arrangement of the melody] (*Dve* II. 9. 4), where 'cantus' is equivalent to *melodia* (see Mengaldo's annotations in *Dve*, p. 207), merely serves to underline the very different *divisio cantuum* of the *Commedia*. It is noteworthy, however, that Boccaccio, followed by Buti, did justify Dante's *canto* in terms of the similarities between musical and poetic scansion (see the passages cited in n. 7 above). This interpretation is, of course, unsatisfactory since it ignores the structural, ideological, and stylistic functions of the 'comic' *canto*. In any case, Dante leaves no doubt in the *Commedia* that he is sensitively aware of the different possible meanings of 'canto'.[36] When he appeals to the 'sante Muse' for help in *Pur.* I. 8, he draws a precise demarcation between poetry ('canto') and music ('suono') — 'seguitando il mio canto con quel suono | di cui le Piche misere sentiro | lo colpo tal' (10–12) — which recalls his technically more explicit discussion of the same distinction in the *De vulgari eloquentia*:

> Preterea disserendum est utrum cantio dicatur fabricatio verborum armonizatorum, vel ipsa modulatio. Ad quod dicimus quod nunquam modulatio dicitur cantio, sed sonus, vel thonus, vel nota, vel melos. Nullus enim tibicen, vel organista, vel cytharedus melodiam suam cantionem vocant, nisi in quantum nupta est alicui cantioni; sed armonizantes verba opera sua cantiones vocant, et etiam talia verba in cartulis absque prolatore iacentia cantiones vocamus. (*Dve* II. 8. 5)

> [Furthermore we should discuss whether the word 'canzone' may mean a composition of harmonious words, or a piece of music itself. On this point I say that music is never referred to as 'canzone', but 'sound', or 'tone', or 'note', or 'melody'. For no flute-player, or organist, or lyre-player calls his music a 'canzone', unless it accompanies a real canzone; but those who arrange their words harmoniously call their works 'canzoni', and even in the absence of the performer we call 'canzoni' such words when they are on the page.]

34   See also Fausto Montanari, 'Canto v', in *Letture dantesche*, III, 73–89 (pp. 79–81); Manlio Pastore Stocchi, 'Il canto v del *Paradiso*', in *Nuove letture dantesche*, v, 341–74 (p. 373).

35   See Zygmunt G. Barański, *Dante e i segni: saggi per una storia intellettuale di Dante* (Naples: Liguori, 2000). See also Chapters 4 and 9.

36   As well as using 'canto' to refer to the subdivisions of the *Commedia*, Dante employed it to mean 'poetry' and 'poetic composition', and the human voice singing or articulating melodiously; see Onder.

If Boccaccio's reading of Dante's use of 'canto' were correct, then it would necessarily mean that, on the one hand, Dante employed the term to associate the *Commedia* with 'modulatio' (for instance, in *Inferno* XX), while, on the other, he used *canto* to present his work as a 'fabricatio verborum armonizatorum' in opposition to music (as he did in the prologue to the *Purgatorio*). This seems extremely unlikely, as it would require Dante to have defined his poem in two mutually exclusive ways while utilizing the same word. Indeed, when Dante directly applied *canto* to his poem, it was always with expressly literary connotations.[37] Thus, I believe that he chose the term to refer to each of the one hundred parts of the *Commedia* precisely because of its traditional meaning as poetry or poetic composition in general. The all-embracing character of the *canto*, as we have seen, can potentially contain within its boundaries any type of poetry. Dante's new plurilingual *canto*, *vestigium* of the 'comedía', makes concrete in a similar microcosmic and symbolic manner the abstract notion of 'poetry', which, hitherto, on account of the precepts of the rhetorical *convenientiae*, had found practical expression in a fragmented manner through a system of discrete, as well as stylistically and thematically constrained, literary forms.

My suggestion that Dante selected 'canto' because of its broad connections with poetry finds immediate support in his choice of 'canzon', which, tellingly, can be justified for exactly the same reason. With his customary acumen and eye for detail, Gianfranco Contini was the first, as far as I know, to point out that, in *Inferno* XX, and once again thanks to the *De vulgari eloquentia*, 'canzon' should be associated with poetry in general, since 'ballates et sonitus et omnia cuiuscunque modi verba sunt armonizata vulgariter et regulariter, cantiones esse dicemus' [we call 'canzoni' all ballads and sonnets and all the words that are in any way arranged in harmony in the vernacular or in the regulated language] (*Dve* II. 8. 6; and see II. 3. 4).[38] Nor

---

37   Further evidence against Boccaccio's explanation of 'canto' in terms of the *Commedia*'s dependence on music comes from Dante's definition of *poesis* in *De vulgari eloquentia* as 'fictio rethorica musicaque poita' [a fiction based on rhetoric and music] (II. 4. 2). At no stage in his career did Dante modify the view that it is not music which subsumes poetry, as was widely deemed among his contemporaries, but that it is poetry which embraces music; see Gonfroy, p. 196; Pazzaglia, pp. 177–204. If anything, this position became even more entrenched in the *Commedia*; see Zygmunt G Barański, 'Teoria musicale e legittimazione poetica nella *Commedia* di Dante', in *Letteratura italiana e la musica*, ed. by Jorn Moestrup and others, 2 vols (Odense: Odense University Press, 1997), I, 75–82. In general on Dante and music, see Francesco Ciabattoni, *Dante's Journey to Polyphony* (Toronto, Buffalo, and London: University of Toronto Press, 2010). On the influence of *musica universalis* on the *Commedia*'s composition and structure, see Adoyo, pp. 64–69.

38   Contini, p. 124. In this context, Dante's words of praise for the lyric canzone in *Dve* II. 3. 3–9, and especially for its range, can take on revealingly suggestive new meanings when applied to his 'comic', all-embracing 'canzon'. This is particularly so as regards evaluations such as 'Quod autem tota comprehendatur in cantionibus ars cantandi poetice, in hoc palatur, quod quicquid artis reperitur in omnibus aliis et in cantionibus reperitur, sed non convertitur hoc' [In this we see that the whole art of poetic composition is included in the *canzoni*: that any poetic device that is found in any other type of compositions is found also in the *canzoni*, but the opposite is not true] (8), and 'quicquid de cacuminibus illustrium capitum poetantium profluxit ad labia, in solis cantionibus invenitur' [anything that has flown to the lips of illustrious men of poetry from their minds is found only in *canzoni*] (9). In addition, such statements furnish further proof of *De vulgari eloquentia*'s crucial role in clarifying the *Commedia*. As regards the relationship between Dante's 'comic' *canzone* and the

is Dante's definition unorthodox; similar usages of *cantio/canzone* can be found in a range of Italian writers from Brunetto to Bembo (Mengaldo's annotations in *Dve*, p. 204). Dante's 'canto' and 'canzon' come together in an effective alliance to sustain the idea of the literary all-inclusiveness of the *Commedia*. Furthermore, as I discuss in Chapter 7, Dante's decision to describe his poem as a 'comedía' stems from the fact that, among all the medieval *stili*, only 'comedy' was associated with such a wealth of literary situations that, akin to the meaning of 'canto' and 'canzone' as poetry in general, it could stand for literature *tout court*. The precision, coherence, and skill with which Dante clarifies his poem, as I like to remark, is impressive.

Before I leave the matter of the poet's possible reasons for applying *canto* and *canzone* to the *Commedia*, I should like to rectify any possible misconceptions which may have arisen from the sharp distinctions that I earlier drew between poetry and music. While I am far from persuaded that Dante intended any narrow or too specific associations between his versifying and the practices of musicians, I have little doubt that, by having recourse to *canto*, *canzone*, and *cantica*, given their traditional associations with song, he did aim to imply certain broad similarities between the *Commedia* and music. In particular, since musical harmony with its mathematical basis had long been equated with the order of divine creation, the poem's 'musical' qualities were yet another means of bringing to the fore both the *Commedia*'s dependence on the *Deus artifex* and its own numerically balanced organization (Barański, 'Teoria musicale'). As I hope is becoming clear, Dante reiterated in different ways certain basic facts about his great poem in order to ensure their implications would not be lost. Repetition is a fundamental characteristic of the *Commedia* (it is enough to think of the canto's structural functions or the narrative recapitulations which punctuate the pilgrim's journey; see Chapter 4, pp. 135–40). At the same time, variety, the poem's other key pole, can only be fully appreciated and offset in opposition to paradigms of sameness. *Variatio*, the interplay between coincidence and diversity, was a technique that Dante was more than happy to borrow from traditional rhetorical practice.

4. Epic Structures

Thus, *per variationem*, Dante's unique decision to arrange the *Commedia* into cantos and *canzoni* also helps highlight another aspect of its poetics. These two peculiar structures, precisely because of their peculiarity, cannot but draw attention to the problematic relationship that pertains between them and the traditional divisions of other literary texts circulating at the beginning of the Trecento. To note this fact is not something new. For instance, Ignazio Baldelli has stated that:

lyric form of the same name, if one recalls that 'con l'esperienza dantesca [as a lyric poet] si attua una decisiva grammaticalizzazione della canzone volgare, di cui verrà mortificato l'impressionante potenziale di polimorfismo vivo nel Duecento, promuovendo canoni e modelli in base illustre' (Guglielmo Gorni, 'Le forme primarie del testo poetico', in *Letteratura italiana*, ed. by Alberto Asor Rosa [Turin: Einaudi, 1984], III:1, 439–518 (p. 456)), then, the infernal 'canzon' represents a return, on Dante's part, to the less rigid and more 'open' view of the canzone.

> L'idea [...] di costruire un'unità metricamente autonoma, dell'estensione [...]
> del canto, è indubbiamente nuova, anche se può trovare un suggerimento
> nei 'canti' in cui è divisa la grande poesia epica o narrativa latina (classica e
> medievale). Rispetto infatti anche a quei 'canti latini', Dante innova in senso
> romanzo, attraverso l'invenzione di una struttura variabile, ma conclusa.
> (Baldelli, 'Terzina', p. 585)

However, like many analyses of the *Commedia's* metrical forms, this assessment is
too reductive. It offers no evidence for the claim that Dante was adapting Latin
models, nor does it explain what it means by 'Romance renewal'.[39] Furthermore
it remains silent about the implications of Dante's inventiveness (the aspect on
which my discussion has tended to concentrate). Like the glosses of the Trecento
commentators, it barely goes beyond the 'literal' level of Dante's *canto* and *canzone*.

Once again the *exordium* to *Inferno* xx helps to disentangle the knotty issue of the
nature of the contacts between the organization of the *Commedia* and that of other
works. Achille Tartaro observes that, in lines 1–3, Dante 'si procura d'identificare la
propria opera, segnalandone le coordinate culturali accanto alle unità compositive'
(p. 6). In line with this comment, therefore, it is suggestive that other scholars have
associated this troublesome *terzina* with a range of different poetic genres. D'Ovidio
and Parodi felt that it had a 'popularizing' bias; the former declared that 'il capitolo
comincia alla buona, con una prefazioncella un po' da cantastorie' (p. 316), while
the latter asserted that 'il canto comincia con un'intonazione un po' da poemetto
popolare'.[40] And this line of analysis has been accompanied by the idea that 'canzon'
is supposed to recall the *chansons de geste*.[41] Conversely, as I mentioned earlier, other
critics have interpreted *Inferno* xx's incipit, and especially the value of 'canzon', in
terms of the loftiest, 'tragic' creations of the classical tradition. The diversity of
literary echoes that may be heard in the opening tercet — echoes that find support
in the stylistic and thematic *variatio* of the rest of the *canto* — encourages the
view that, in *Inf.* xx. 1–3, Dante was underlining the need to measure his poem's
structures against those of other texts, both Latin and vernacular; an approach
which, naturally, also finds support in the association of 'canto' and 'canzon' with
poetry in general.

As is now widely recognized, the canto of the soothsayers stands as one of Dante's
major statements on classical literature. During the course of his evaluation, the
poet reveals what he considers to be the ideological and rhetorical limitations of
pagan Latin writing, especially in relation to his Christian poetry. However, Dante
did not restrict his criticism of classical poetry to these two aspects. I believe that,
in the light of *Inf.* xx. 1–3, he also highlighted its structural deficiencies. The
lengthy (often stretching for nearly a thousand lines), cumbersome, and narratively
amorphous 'books' of Virgil, Ovid, Lucan, and Statius, adopted also by their later

---

39   Baldelli, in 'Lingua e stile' (p. 81), does qualify the phrase 'in senso romanzo, attraverso
l'invenzione di una struttura variabile, ma conclusa' by adding 'quindi avvicinabile alla canzone con
congedo', an interesting suggestion in light of my 'lyric' analysis of the *canto*.

40   Ernesto G. Parodi, 'Il canto xx dell'*Inferno*', in *Letture dantesche*, ed. by Giovanni Getto
(Florence: Sansoni, 1962), pp. 379–91 (p. 379).

41   See, for instance, Bellomo, p. 319; Caccia, p. 676; Pasquazi, p. 183.

Latin imitators, are supplanted by the short, nimble, and narratively better focused
cantos of his *Commedia* which rarely run to more than fifty *terzine*. The form
of the *canto* is the first mark of the radical differences between the two types of
epic: the 'monolingualism' of the *tragedie* has no need for that sophisticated sense
of structural discrimination that is the *sine qua non* of the 'plurilingual' 'comedía'.
Dante's cantos may well owe something to the *libri* of his Latin predecessors, since
he probably took from them the idea that epics ought to be subdivided. However,
both the number and the stylistic and thematic span of his cantos, as well as their
assimilation into three *canzoni*, disclose that Dante had a more developed awareness
of *dispositio* than other epic writers. Nor is it fortuitous that, given the relatively
marginal concern with *dispositio* in much classical and medieval literary theory and
practice, Dante should have emphasized structural matters as part of his strategy to
fix his own artistic primacy.[42]

If few links can usefully be forged between the *canto* and the Latin epic *liber*,
its ties with the *laisse* of the *chanson de geste* appear, at first sight, to be made of
stronger stuff. Both the 'comedía' and the *chanson* are fashioned from a large
number of metrically independent units incorporating differing numbers of lines
of the same length; and, in both cases, these units are significantly shorter than
their Latin counterparts.[43] However, they are also crucially distinguished by two
major formal discrepancies: first, unlike the *canto*, all the lines of the *laisse* have the
same assonantic ending or are based on the same rhyme; and, second, the length
of the *laisse* is both much shorter — seldom reaching one hundred lines — and
much less stable than that of the *canto*. Though the span of the *laisse* did increase
with the passage of time, it is most unlikely that Dante knew poems, such as the
Couronnement de Louis and the *Moniage Guillaume*, where this happens (Monteverdi,
p. 129; Rychner, pp. 68–69, 107–25). In fact, the *Roland* is the only *chanson de geste*
which it is generally accepted that Dante had read.[44] If this is indeed the case, then,

---

42   See Faral, pp. 55–60. See also Douglas Kelly, 'The Scope of Treatment of Composition in
the Twelfth- and Thirteenth-century Arts of Poetry', *Speculum*, 41 (1966), 261–78, and 'Theory of
Composition in Medieval Narrative Poetry and Geoffrey of Vinsauf's *Poetria nova*', *Mediaeval Studies*,
31 (1969), 117–48. See also Ana Calvo Revilla, 'Tratamiento del *ordo* en la teorización poética
medieval: *Poetria nova*, de Godofredo de Vinsauf', in *Le 'poetriae' del medioevo latino: modelli, fortuna,
commenti*, ed. by Giancarlo Alessio and Domenico Losappio (Venice: Edizioni Ca' Foscari, 2018), pp.
69–89.

43   On the *laisse*, see Wilhelm T. Elwert, *Traité de versification française des origines à nos jours* (Paris:
Klincksieck, 1965), pp. 153–56; Angelo Monteverdi, 'La Laisse épique', in his *La Téchnique littéraire
des chansons de geste* (Paris: Les Belles Lettres, 1959), pp. 127–39; Jean Rychner, *La Chanson de geste:
essai sur l'art épique des jongleurs* (Geneva and Lille: Droz and Librairie Giard, 1955), pp. 68–125; Paul
Zumthor, *Semiologia e poetica medievale* (Milan: Feltrinelli, 1973), pp. 325–33. On the limited use of
lasse in medieval Italy, see Beltrami, pp. 106–07, 294–97.

44   On Dante and the *Chanson de Roland*, see Mark Balfour, '"Orribil furon li peccati miei":
Manfred's Wounds in *Purgatorio*, III', *Italian Studies*, 48 (1993), 4–17 (p. 8); Hollander, I, 576–77;
Angelo E. Mecca, 'Il veltro di Dante e la *Chanson de Roland*', *Nuova rivista di letteratura italiana*, 5
(2002), 213–26. See also Bellomo, p. 496; Inglese, p. 227. More generally, see Giovanni Palumbo, *La
'Chanson de Roland' in Italia nel Medioevo* (Rome: Salerno, 2013). On Dante's possible relationship to
the *chansons de geste*, see at least Giovanni Palumbo, 'Dante, le leggende epiche e i commenti antichi
alla *Commedia*', *Rivista di studi danteschi*, 6, (2006), 280–320; Paolo Rinoldi, 'Textes et traditions

the critical distinctions that Dante wished to draw between the *chansons* and the *Commedia* are all the more striking given the brevity of the *Roland*'s *laisses* and the almost perfect correspondence between these and narrative divisions — a correspondence whose rigidity recalls the narrow inflexibility of the equally censored lyric *stantia* (Rychner, p. 124). Thus, even before the fluid presentation of the episode of barratry, simply the *canto*'s greater length guarantees a narrative diversity that the *Roland* cannot match. As Erich Auerbach succinctly put it when discussing *Inferno* X's shifts of focus:

> The scenes [of the canto] are not set stiffly side by side and in the same key — we are thinking of [...] the *Chanson de Roland* — they rise from the depths as particular forms of the momentarily prevailing tonality and stand in contrapuntal relation to one another [...]. The events are not — as we put it in connection with the *Chanson de Roland* [...] — divided into little parcels; they live together, despite their contrast and actually because of it.[45]

Yet again, thanks to his structural inventiveness, Dante has little difficulty in asserting the fuller and more complex view of things which the *canto* and his 'comedía' can offer in comparison to the *laisse* and the *chanson*.

As befits the brainchild of an arch-syncretist, the *canto* succeeds in integrating the diffuseness of the Latin *liber* with the highly restricted purview of the French *laisse*. By being able to absorb and supersede two such diametrically different forms, the *canto* makes a clear declaration of its literary uniqueness and its superiority in relation to both traditions. In addition, neither the structure of the classical epic nor that of the *chanson* can even begin to compete with that numerically significant and subtle synthesis between the parts and the whole that characterizes the *Commedia*'s organization as it strives to 'imitate' the unity of God's art — a synthesis that is made possible largely thanks to the flexibility and range of the *canto*. From this perspective it also becomes clear why Dante rejected a *roman*-type structure for his poem. The uninterrupted, monotonous, and repetitive flow of the octosyllabic rhyming couplets of the *romans* presents an undifferentiated view of things which is contrary to the *Commedia*'s highly nuanced yet totalizing sense of structure and of the complexity of reality.[46] As Dante's sustained critique of conventional literary

épiques chez Dante (*Par.* XVIII)', in *La tradizione epica e cavalleresca in Italia (XII–XVI sec.)*, ed. by Claudio Gigante and Giovanni Palumbo (Brussels: Peter Lang, 2010), pp. 73–106.

45   Erich Auerbach, *Mimesis* (Princeton: Princeton University Press, 1968), pp. 178–80.

46   On Dante and the *romans* tradition, and in particular his contacts with the *Roman de la rose*, see Contini, pp. 245–83; Enrico Fenzi, 'Dante e il *Roman de la Rose*: alcune note sulla "candida rosa dei beati e sulla questione del libero arbitrio', *Critica del testo*, 19 (2016), 205–51; John Took, 'Dante and the *Roman de la Rose*', *Italian Studies*, 27 (1982), 1–25. Luigi Vanossi, *Dante e il 'Roman de la rose': saggio sul 'Fiore'* (Florence: Olschki, 1979); *Lettura del 'Fiore'*, ed. by Zygmunt G. Barański and others (Ravenna: Longo, 1993), special issue of *Letture classensi*, 22; *Sulle tracce del 'Fiore'*, ed. by Natascia Tonelli (Florence: Le Lettere, 2016); *The 'Fiore' in Context: Dante, France, Tuscany*, ed. by Zygmunt G. Barański and Patrick Boyde (Notre Dame, IN, and London: University of Notre Dame Press, 1997). To be read with caution: Gabriella I. Baika, *The Rose and Geryon: The Poetics of Fraud and Violence in Jean de Meun and Dante* (Washington, DC: Catholic University of America Press, 2014); Earl J. Richards, *Dante and the 'Roman de la Rose': An Investigation into the Vernacular Narrative Context of the 'Commedia'* (Tübingen: Max Niemeyer Verlag, 1981).

forms reveals, none of them could even begin to accommodate his 'vision' (*Par.* XVII. 128). Only his *canto* could do this, not least because it was based on and incorporated the different dominant architectonic features of the principal narrative verse forms of his day. Thus, as the poet had succeeded in bringing together the *liber* and the *laisse*, so he also managed to meld the *chanson* and the *roman*. One effect of Dante's decision to divide the *Commedia* into cantos is that it allowed him to fuse the pauses of the *chanson de geste* with the flow of the *roman*, thereby giving his poem a cogent, orderly, and harmonized narrative development. Tradition and innovation, as is typical of Dante's art and self-commentary, achieve a perfect balance in the *canto*, whose invention is not presented merely as a piece of poetic bravura but is cogently legitimated as a desideratum in the light of the deficiencies of other forms. Finally, the ways in which Dante redimensions French narrative poetry through his creation of the *canto* is consistent with his overall limitative assessment of Gallic culture in the *Commedia*. The *canto*, like the poem as a whole, is the practical confirmation of that victory of Italian literature over French writing which Dante had promised, albeit obliquely, in the *De vulgari eloquentia*.[47]

5. Lyric Structures

There is little doubt that, in *Inferno* XX, 'canzon' effectively and efficiently recalls both the Latin and the vernacular epic. However, it also has the further function, which I have already begun to discuss, of drawing attention to the Italian lyric tradition. It is thus suggestive when examining the *canto*'s structural properties vis-à-vis this tradition that the works which most closely approximate to its average length are two of Dante's own erotic allegorical *canzoni*, 'Le dolci rime' of 146 lines and 'Poscia ch'amor' of 133 lines, and three of his experimental and ethical poems written after his exile — 'Io sento sì d'Amor la gran possanza' of 106 lines, 'Tre donne' of 107 lines, and 'Doglia mi reca' of 158 lines.[48] In the Duecento lyric, *canzoni* of more than one hundred lines are extremely rare. The only other Italian poet to compose them with any sort of regularity is Guittone d'Arezzo.[49] It is thus not at all improbable that, as far as the basic shape of the cantos of the new extended 'canzon' is concerned, this finds its likeliest points of reference, first, in Dante's own lyric poetry and, second, in opposition to Guittone's versifying. At one level, the *canto* acknowledges the key role that the poet's lyric experience had in his artistic and intellectual journey to the *Commedia*. Especially in 'Tre donne' and 'Doglia mi reca', Dante showed himself a master at manipulating narrative and didactic forms of over one hundred lines — a skill which is at the basis of the composition of his 'comedía'. At another level, however, by transferring the

---

47   See Zygmunt G. Barański, ' "Significar *per verba*": Notes on Dante and Plurilingualism', *The Italianist*, 6 (1986), 5–18; Contini, p. 106.

48   For my arguments in favour of the canzone's composition after the exile, see Zygmunt G. Barański, 'La canzone "anomola" di Dante: *Io sento sì d'Amor la gran possanza*', in *Dante Alighieri. Le Quindici Canzoni. Lette da diversi. I, 1–7* (Lecce: Pensa Multimedia, 2009), pp. 145–211.

49   See Teodolinda Barolini, *Dante's Poets: Textuality and Truth in the 'Comedy'* (Princeton: Princeton University Press, 1984), p. 107, n. 21. Barolini makes the important observation for my present argument that the *Commedia* is 'the equivalent of many canzoni stitched together' (p. 108).

structures of the *canzone tragica* (including the hendecasyllable) to the new *canzone comica*, Dante was revealing his dissatisfaction with the older form; a dissatisfaction which, once again, was almost certainly conditioned by the established *canzone*'s stylistic and thematic restrictiveness (*Dve* II. 4. 6–8).[50] At the same time, Dante was also rejecting the claim he had earlier made in the *De vulgari eloquentia* concerning the literary primacy of 'tragic' poetry (*Dve* II. 3. 2–3). He emblematically enshrined this 'transfer of power' both by bequeathing the name of the erstwhile favourite to his new creation and by dramatically changing the appearance of the form that traditionally had gone under this designation. And such a bequest was, to say the least, inappropriate. It made over a term, *canzone*, which the poet himself had closely united with the 'high' style, to another *stilus*, the 'comic', which, as far as the tradition was concerned, most certainly had no right to it. In these circumstances, it is indeed difficult to think how Dante could have made more categorical his rejection of the oppressive precepts of the *genera dicendi* and of the literature which these sustained (see, in general, on this point Chapter 7).

The possible allusion to Guittone discernible in Dante's use of 'canzon' and in the length of the *canto* helps better to focus his critique of the vernacular lyric. Specifically, it provides a delimitative assessment of the most inventive and wide-ranging Italian poet writing in the *volgare* before Dante. This is not the place to go into the thorny question of Dante's relationship to Guittone. Suffice it to say that, in the *Commedia*, Dante not only criticized Guittone explicitly during the course of the pilgrim's encounter with Bonagiunta da Lucca, but also did this implicitly by means of the poem's structure. He revealed the proper form — the *canzone comica* and not the lyric canzone — in which the older poet and his followers should have carried out their artistic experimentation.[51]

6. The Problem of the *cantica*

By concentrating on the metaliterary reverberations of *Inf.* XX. 1–3 and on the interplay in the tercet both between 'canto' and 'canzon', and between these and the secular literary tradition, I have neglected the third term with which Dante, just as unexpectedly and originally, defined the structure of the *Commedia*:

50   I do not have the space here to go into the implications of the *Commedia* being written in hendecasyllables. Suffice it to say that, as the supreme Italian verse form (*Dve* II. 5. 3), the hendecasyllable subsumes all the other types of poetic line. It thus has the same totalizing character as the 'canto', the 'canzon', the 'comedía', and, as we shall soon see, the *terza rima*.

51   Contini makes some suggestive observations about the ways in which 'canzon' in *Inferno* XX serves as a 'bridge' connecting the *Commedia* with the structures of lyric poetry in general (pp. 58–59). I believe that two particularly important areas for future researchers to explore as regards this field are (1) the links in organization between the *Commedia* and the *corone* of sonnets, and (2) the formal and ideological ties between the 'sacrato poema' and a narrative sequence in sonnet form such as the *Fiore*. It would be astonishing if Dante had not established significant and revealing interconnections between the *Commedia* and the sonnet, given the latter's traditional standing as the lyric 'comic' metre (*Dve* II. 3. 2 and 4. 1). Unfortunately, as with the hendecasyllable, I am unable to explore these fascinating matters in this chapter. See, however, Contini, p. 107; Lino Leonardi, 'Sonetto e terza rima (da Guittone a Dante)', in *Omaggio a Gianfranco Folena*, 3 vols (Padua: Editoriale Programma, 1993), I, 337–51.

> ma perché piene son tutte le carte
> ordite a questa cantica seconda,
> non mi lascia più ir lo fren de l'arte. (*Purg.* XXXIII. 139–41)

There are two reasons for my omission. First, *Inf.* XX. 1–3 provides a much fuller description of the character and logic of the *Commedia*'s structure, style, and content than does *Purg.* XXXIII. 139–41. Second, when I originally wrote this chapter, Lino Pertile had very recently published two important articles on a number of the principal reasons behind Dante's choice of this term ('Canto' and 'Cantica'). Essentially, what Pertile showed, is that the poet's use of 'cantica' is closely tied to the rich commentary tradition to the *Canticum Canticorum*, not least because of the traditional association between the biblical book and comedy. The present chapter and particularly what follows complement Pertile's work. Just as 'canzon' highlights the role played by the secular literary tradition in the *Commedia*, so 'cantica' divulges its connections with the religious one. More importantly, by introducing the two terms as synonyms for one of the primary structures of the *Commedia*, Dante declares that his poem constitutes a balanced synthesis of both literary currents. Although 'cantica' underscores the special links that the 'comedía' enjoys with Scriptural *sermo humilis* — something in fact that the medieval concept of 'comedy' also does, but in other ways (see Chapter 7, pp. 282–83 and Chapter 9, pp. 330–33) — like 'canto' and 'canzon', *canticum* also refers to poetry in general.[52] The carefully programmed manner in which Dante selected the terms with which to define the *Commedia*, whereby these both complement and confirm each other's clarificatory functions in relation to the poem, can find no better illustration than this. Finally, 'cantica' introduces a further set of important metaliterary religious connotations into the *Commedia*. By means of its links with the biblical *canticum novum*, it suggests that the poem is a celebration of God and His creation — to use Dante's terminology, that it is a 'teodia' (*Par.* XXV. 73).[53] Furthermore, the association with *canticum novum* also pinpoints the role which God wants the poem to play in his scheme of earthly

---

52   'Canticum' in *TLL*, III, 284–85. Indeed, and obviously significant as far as Dante's choice of the term is concerned, *canticum* was used to refer both to the secular comedians, Plautus and Terence, and to the biblical one, Solomon (284). If I have a criticism to make of Pertile's excellent work on 'cantica', it is that he ties Dante's usage of the term a bit too closely to the Song of Songs (but see 'Cantica', 404–05), when, in fact, like the concept of comedy, *canticum* in medieval literary criticism was associated with a variety of different forms, thereby making it an especially apt tag with which to describe the *Commedia*. Bellomo makes the important point that '*cantio* e *canticum* in *Ps* CXXXVI 3 sono sinonimi' (p. 319). His observation, however, needs some qualification. It is only in the Septuagint that the two terms are brought together: 'quia illic interrogaverunt nos qui captivos duxerunt nos verba cantionum | et qui abduxerunt nos hymnum cantate nobis de canticis Sion | quomodo cantabimus canticum Domini in terra aliena' [because those who kept us in captivity there questioned us about the words of the songs, and those who took us away said: sing to us a hymn from the songs of Sion. How shall we sing a song of God in a land of strangers?] (3–4). The Vulgate associates *carmen* with *canticum*. When annotating 'canzon', Inglese makes the strange assertion that '[l]a denominazione vera e propria della più ampia partizione del poema è *cantica*' (p. 226). Not only is there no evidence to support such a claim, but it reveals scant appreciation of the complexity both of Dante's terminological choices in general and of *Inf.* XX. 1–3 in particular.

53   See, for instance, Psalms 95: 1 and 97: 1; Bernard of Clairvaux, *Sermones super Cantica Canticorum* I. 9, in *Opera*, ed. by Jean Leclercq and others, 8 vols (Rome: Editiones Cistercenses, 1957), I, 6–7. I return to the question of celebrating God in the next subsection.

spiritual renewal.[54] As Cacciaguida explains to the pilgrim, it is the latter's duty to report his otherworldly experiences as precisely as possible because, by doing this, he would be fulfilling his divinely ordained responsibilities (*Par.* XVII. 124–42). In fact, Dante's ancestor gives him a practical lesson in the kind of language he is to use by veering between Latin (XV. 28–30) and the vulgarities of the *parlato* (XVII. 129); and it is a plurilingualism — it should be remembered — which is sanctioned by God, since, as Cacciaguida speaks, he is in communion with his Maker (XV. 61–69). Dante's experimentalism is no mere artistic whim. It is the direct result of his miraculous journey and mission: 'Et [Dominus] immisit in os meum canticum novum' [and God put a new song on my lips] (Psalm 39: 4).

6. Biblical Structures

As I have already discussed, the *Commedia*'s style and structure are the tangible guarantors of its closeness to the divine; and this is especially so as regards its numerically significant two-tiered organization into cantos and *cantiche* However, this structure also has specifically textual implications. To put it starkly, the *Commedia*'s division into cantos and *canzoni* is, arguably, its most original formal feature, since, as far as I have been able to ascertain, no other narrative poem before Dante's had been organized in this manner. Given the poet's claim, for instance in *Inferno* XXVIII (see Chapter 7, p. 264), that his poem is superior to prose, and in particular to historical prose, and given its dialectical relationship with the philosophical *summa*, the encyclopedia, the compilation, and the 'dictionary' (Barański, *Dante e i segni*, pp. 77–101), it is not unlikely that Dante was trying to show that part of the success of his poetry was that, like prose, it could be flexibly and rationally compartmentalized. In this context, it is important to remember that, during the course of the thirteenth century, the *ordinatio* and *compilatio* of texts, with their attendant emphasis on subdivision, had become increasingly central in the production of books.[55] As a result, the *Commedia*'s structure was also a sign of its 'modernity' and literary sophistication.

54   See Pertile, 'Cantica', pp. 409–11. See also Domenico De Robertis, *Il libro della 'Vita Nuova'*, 2nd edn (Florence: Sansoni, 1970), pp. 117–20; Henri Rondet, 'Le Thème du cantique nouveau chez Saint Augustin', in *L'Homme devant Dieu: mélanges offerts au père Henri de Lubac*, 3 vols (Paris: Aubier, 1963–64), I, 341–53.

55   Bernard Guenée, 'Lo storico e la compilazione nel XIII secolo', in *Aspetti della letteratura latina nel secolo XIII*, ed. by Claudio Leonardi and Guido Orlandi (Perugia: Regione dell'Umbria and Florence: La Nuova Italia, 1986), pp. 57–76; Alastair J. Minnis, 'Late-medieval Discussions of *Compilatio* and the Role of the *Compilator*', *Beiträge zur Geschichte der deutschen Sprache und Literatur*, 101 (1979), 385–421, and '*Nolens auctor sed compilator reputari*: The Late-medieval Discourse of Compilation', in *La Méthode critique au Moyen Âge*, ed. by Mireille Chazan and Gilbert Dahan (Turnhout: Brepols, 2008), pp. 47–63; Malcolm B. Parkes, 'The Influence of the Concepts of *Ordinatio* and *Compilatio* on the Development of the Book', in *Medieval Learning and Literature: Essays Presented to Richard William Hunt*, ed. by Jonathan James Graham Alexander and Margaret T. Gibson (Oxford: Clarendon Press, 1975), pp. 115–41; Richard H. Rouse and Mary A. Rouse, '*Ordinatio* and *Compilatio* Revisited', in *'Ad litteram': Authoritative Texts and Medieval Readers*, ed. by Mark D. Jordan and Kent Emery Jr (Notre Dame, IN: University of Notre Dame Press, 1992), pp. 113–34. But see also Neil Hathaway, '*Compilatio*: From Plagiarism to Compiling', *Viator*, 20 (1989), 19–44. On Dante's sensitive appreciation of 'compilation', see Zygmunt G. Barański, '"Oh come è grande la mia impresa" (*Conv.* IV. vii. 4): Notes Towards Defining the *Convivio*', in *Dante's 'Convivio', or, How to Restart Writing in Exile*, ed. by Franziska Meier (Bern: Peter Lang, 2018), pp. 9–26.

Even if no secular poem can serve as a model for the *Commedia*'s structure, there is a type of poetry with which it does have a noticeable affinity. The Bible, too, gathers up a considerable number of independent poetic texts into larger structures, which then unite with other *libri* to constitute the divine book as a whole. This characteristic of Scripture, which the new contemporary concern with textual division could not but highlight, is especially apparent as regards the Book of Psalms and the Song of Songs.[56] I have already noted the metaliterary interplay that Dante established between the *Canticum Canticorum*, the 'cantica', and the 'comedía'. It is thus satisfying to recognize that, as the poet assiduously cultivated his poem's links with the Bible, he created, as he did for the Canticles, a similarly fascinating set of connections between his work and the Psalms. Indeed, I should like to suggest that the very idea of giving the *Commedia* a tripartite structure which is narratively and morally based on the three realms of the afterlife may have come to Dante from the hermeneutic tradition to the Psalms. In the prologue to Thomas Aquinas's commentary, after categorizing the 'modus seu forma' [manner or form] of the book as 'deprecativus vel laudativus' [expressing disapproval or praise], the great Doctor divides the work he is about to discuss into three groups of fifty psalms each. 'Per instinctum inspirationis divinae' [By the instinct of divine inspiration], these respectively deal with the 'status poenitentiae' [role of penitence], the 'status iustitiae' [role of justice], and the 'laus gloriae [...] aeternae' [praise of eternal glory].[57] The correlations between, on the one hand, this evaluation of the Book of Psalms and, on the other, the *Commedia*, its moral and artistic structure, and its relationship to the divine will are imposing. The importance of the Psalms for an understanding of the *Commedia*'s textuality and structure is further confirmed when we learn that *canticum*, not least in the guise of *canticum novum*, was often used as a variant for *psalmus*.[58]

That of all the books of the Bible, Dante should have decided to establish particular metaliterary links, thanks also to *cantica*'s connotative range, between his poem and the Book of Psalms and the Song of Songs has a precise cultural significance. From the twelfth century onwards, exegetes had paid increasing attention to the literal sense of the Bible. Indeed, it was widely acknowledged that, while God was the source of Scripture's moral, figural, and analogical meanings, its earthly authors were responsible for its surface values, including its stylistic elaboration. God had chosen certain human beings as his *scribae* not only because of their moral worth but also because of their literary abilities. And David and Solomon were precisely

---

56   On biblical *divisio*, see Beryl Smalley, *The Study of the Bible in the Middle Ages*, 3rd edn (Oxford: Blackwell, 1983). On the Psalter and the Song of Songs, see Ann W. Astell, *The Song of Songs in the Middle Ages* (Ithaca, NY: Cornell University Press, 1990); James Kugel, *The Idea of Biblical Poetry: Parallelism and History* (New Haven, CT: Yale University Press, 1981); Minnis, *Medieval Theory*, pp. 42–58.

57   Thomas Aquinas, *In Psalmos Davidis expositio*, in *Opera omnia*, XIV, 149–50, and see pp. 344 & 351. See also Pertile, 'Cantica', p. 408.

58   See 'Canticum', in *TLL*, III, 284–85. Dante underscored the proximity between *canticum* and *psalmus* by opening *Purgatorio* XXXIII, the canto that closes with the reference to 'questa cantica seconda' (140), with an allusion to Psalm 78 as 'dolce salmodia' (2).

two of the *scribae* who especially fascinated medieval exegetes.[59] Dante was well aware of these trends in biblical scholarship. He presented himself as an artistically responsible *scriba Dei*, and also recognized a similar role for David, who, in Paradise, is rewarded for, and able to appreciate, the worth of his poetic endeavours, the 'effetti' of his own 'consiglio':

> Colui che luce in mezzo per pupilla,
> fu il cantor de lo Spirito Santo,
> che l'arca traslatò di villa in villa:
> ora conosce il merto del suo canto,
> in quanto effetto fu del suo consiglio,
> per lo remunerar ch'è altrettanto. (*Par.* xx. 37–42)

However, rather than simply place himself on a par with David, Dante, as he did with secular authors, measures himself against him and suggests his own artistic superiority. David's poetic powers were limited to the writing of a 'teodía', while Dante was the *auctor* of a 'comedía', one of whose many literary purposes, and not its exclusive intent, was that of celebrating God.[60] Dante similarly challenged Solomon, whose canticle was often presented as the supreme form of poetry:[61]

> Salomon inspiratus divino spirito, composuit hunc libellum de nuptiis Christi et Ecclesiae [...]. Unde et Cantica Canticorum vocavit hunc libellum: quia omnia alia Cantica superexcellit [...]. dicuntur Cantica Canticorum ob excellentiam et dignitatem. Est autem in hoc obscurissimus iste liber, quia nullae ibi commemorantur personae, cum tamen stylo quasi comico sit compositus.[62]

> [Solomon inspired by the divine spirit, composed this little book on the marriage of Christ and the Church [...]. Thus he called this book the Song of Songs: because it rose above all other songs [...]. It is called the Song of Songs

---

59   See Minnis, *Medieval Theory*, pp. 40–51, 88–97, 103–12, 129–30. The Lamentations of Jeremiah was another Scriptural book that the Middle Ages deemed to be poetic and hence labelled a *canticum*; see for instance, Hugh of St Victor, *Didascalicon*, ed. by Charles H. Buttimer (Washington, DC: Catholic University Press, 1939), iv. 8. Thanks to its association with the Lamentations, 'cantica' also indicates the *Commedia*'s prophetic and apocalyptic dimensions. On the *Commedia* and the Lamentations, see Ronald L. Martinez, 'Dante between Hope and Despair: The Traditions of *Lamentations* in the *Divine Comedy*', *Logos. A Journal of Catholic Thought and Culture*, 5 (2002), 45–76, and 'Dante's Jeremiads: The Fall of Jerusalem and the Burden of the New Pharisees, the Capetians, and Florence', in *Dante for the New Millennium*, ed. by Teodolinda Barolini and H. Wayne Storey (New York: Fordham University Press, 2003), pp. 301–19.

60   On Dante and David, see especially Theresa Federici, 'Dante's Davidic Journey: From Sinner to God's Scribe', in *Dante's 'Commedia': Theology as Poetry*, ed. by Vittorio Montemaggi and Matthew Treherne (Notre Dame, IN; University of Notre Dame Press, 2010), pp. 180–209. See also Barolini, *Dante's Poets*, pp. 275–79; Sergio Cristaldi, 'Dante e i salmi', in *La Bibbia di Dante: esperienza mistica, profezia e teologia biblica in Dante*, ed. by Giuseppe Ledda (Ravenna: Centro Dantesco dei Frati Minori Conventuali, 2011), pp. 77–120; Robert Hollander, 'Dante's Use of the Fiftieth Psalm (A Note on *Purg.* xxx, 84)', in his *Studies in Dante*, pp. 107–13; Antonio Staüble, '*Paradiso* xxv. 38 e i salmi dei pellegrinaggi', *Versants*, 5 (1983), 3–21. Of limited use: Michel David, 'Dante et sa théodie', in *Omaggio a Gianfranco Folena*, i, 429–46.

61   On Dante and Solomon, see in particular Paola Nasti, *Favole d'amore e 'saver profondo': la tradizione salomonica in Dante* (Ravenna: Longo, 2007).

62   *In Canticum Canticorum expositio*, attributed to Thomas Aquinas but probably written by Haimo of Auxerre, in, *Opera omnia*, xiv, 354.

for its excellence and dignity. But this book is now mostly unknown, because no person is commemorated in it, even though it is composed in an almost comic style.]

Once again, in comparison to Solomon's 'comedy', the greater stylistic complexity and narrative range of Dante's 'comedía' is apparent, not least because, unlike the Scriptural 'libellum', his work is not just a 'cantica' but also a 'canzon'. Where all this leaves the *Commedia* in the poetic pantheon is more than self-evident.

7. The Problem of the *terza rima*

By examining the metrical structures of the *Commedia* and the designations that the poet assigned to these, considerable information about the work and its composition can be unearthed. And the bulk of this knowledge derives from the *novitas* of the forms, whose metrical innovativeness is not restricted, as is widely believed, simply to Dante's invention of the *terza rima*.[63] As we have seen, every tier of the *Commedia* is notable for its originality — an originality whose implications can only be appreciated by assessing each structure's relationship both to the other parts of the poem and to the literary tradition in general. Thus, as a final example of this process, what is formally most significant about the *terza rima* is the manner in which it synthesizes different rhyme schemes: for instance, those of the *serventese caudato* and of the *sestina* together with the tercets of the sonnet (especially those with alternate rhyme as in the *Fiore*) and the triple rhyme patterns that characterize so many of Dante's own *canzoni*. The *Commedia*'s rhyme, too, indicates its ability to absorb and transcend any kind of poetry, thereby revealing its differences from conventional writing and its ideological continuity with the poem's other structures. In addition, the *terza rima* is formally integrated with these. For instance, the solitary last line of each canto serves as a means of hooking on to the next one, while the *rime rilevate* are the necessary demarcatory boundaries without which the canto cannot exist as an independent unit. Indeed, the *terza rima*, the *canto*, and the *cantica*, on account of the 'unbreakable' determinacy of their forms, come together

---

63   On the *terza rima*, see Adoyo, pp. 48–58; Baldelli, 'Terzina', pp. 583–94; Beltrami, pp. 109–12; Tommaso Casini, 'Per la genesi della terzina e della *Commedia* dantesca', in *Miscellanea di studi storici in onore di Giovanni Sforza* (Lucca: Tip. Ed. Baroni, 1920), pp. 689–97; Gianfranco Contini, 'La questione del *Fiore*', *Cultura e scuola*, 13–14 (1965), 768–73 (p. 773); Freccero; Mario Fubini, *Metrica e poesia* (Milan: Feltrinelli, 1962), pp. 168–200; Franco Gavazzeni, 'Approssimazioni metriche sulla terza rima', *Studi danteschi*, 56 (1984), 1–82; Guglielmo Gorni, 'Sull'origine della terzina e altre misure: appunti di metrica dantesca', *Metrica*, 2 (1981), 43–60, and 'Postilla sull'ottava e sulla terza rima', in his *Metrica e analisi letteraria* (Bologna: il Mulino, 1993), pp. 295–310; Leonardi, 'Sonetto e terza rima'; Giovanni Mari, 'La sestina d'Arnaldo. La terzina di Dante', *Rendiconti dell'Istituto Lombardo di Scienze e Lettere*, ser. II, 32 (1899), 953–85; Aldo Menichetti, 'Una lezione sulla terzina di Dante', in *'In principio fuit textus': studi di linguistica e filologia offerti a Rosario Coluccia in occasione della nomina a professore emerito*, ed. by Vito Luigi Castrignanò and others (Florence: Cesati, 2018), pp. 111–18; Charles S. Singleton. *Dante's 'Commedia': Elements of Structure* (Baltimore and London: Johns Hopkins University Press, 1977), pp. 58–59; John S. P. Tatlock, 'Dante's *terza rima*', *PMLA*, 51 (1936), 895–903; Vanossi, pp. 219–21; Paola Vecchi Galli, 'La fabbrica della terzina', in *Dante e la fabbrica della 'Commedia'*, ed. by Alfredo Cottignoli and others (Ravenna: Longo, 2008), pp. 43–64; Tibor Wlassics, 'Le caratteristiche strutturali della terzina', in his *Interpretazioni di prosodia dantesca* (Rome: Signorrelli, 1972), pp. 9–23.

to guarantee the *Commedia*'s textual integrity, as they do to provide answers to Dante's experimentation.[64]

---

64   See John Ahern, 'Binding the Book: Hermeneutics and Manuscript Production in *Paradiso* 33', *PMLA*, 97 (1982), 800–09 (p. 804), and 'Dante's Last Word: The *Comedy* as *liber cœlestis*', *Dante Studies*, 102 (1984), 1–14 (pp. 2–3). See, more generally, Amelia E. Van Vleck, *Memory and Re-Creation in Troubadour Lyric* (Berkeley and Los Angeles: University of California Press, 1991).

PART III

Creating Canons

CHAPTER 9

Purgatorio XXV:
Creating Poetic Bodies

1. Reading/Misreading *Purgatorio* XXV[1]

Purgatorio XXV's modern critical reception can be divided into three, largely discrete, interpretive camps, each of which has tended to insist a bit too confidently on the validity of its own proposals, while taking little heed of alternative solutions and interpretations. As a result, *Purgatorio* XXV has had a lopsided, reductive, and at times contradictory critical reception, even if, by bringing together the principal exegetical suggestions, it is possible to begin to form a summary impression not only of its conceptual richness, but also of the challenges that it poses.[2] Normally,

---

1   On the relationship between human bodies and textual corpora in Dante, see James C. Kriesel, 'Allegories of the Corpus', in *The Cambridge Companion to Dante's 'Commedia'*, ed. by Zygmunt G. Barański and Simon Gilson (Cambridge: Cambridge University Press, 2019), pp. 110–26.
2   Since this *lectura* originally appeared in 2001, Dantists have paid considerable attention to *Purgatorio* XXV. The most weighty and original contribution, which, unfortunately though not surprisingly, Dantists have largely ignored, is: Patrick M. Gardner, 'Dante and the Suffering Soul' (unpublished PhD thesis, University of Notre Dame, 2009). The present, significantly rewritten version of my Italian *lettura* of nearly twenty years ago has been substantially improved as a result of taking Gardner's work into consideration. See also Leonardo Cappelletti, *'Ne le scuole de li religiosi...':* *le dispute scolastiche sull'anima nella 'Commedia' di Dante* (San Donato a Livizzano, Montespertoli, and Florence: Aleph, 2015); Sergio Cristaldi, 'Canti XXV–XXVI: potenza e atto della poesia', in *Esperimenti danteschi: Purgatorio 2009*, ed. by Benedetta Quadrio (Genoa and Milan: Marietti, 2010), pp. 253–71; Paolo Falzone, 'Canto XXV: Virgilio, Stazio e le sofferenze dell'anima nell'adilà', in *Lectura Dantis Romana. Cento canti per cento anni. II. Purgatorio. 2. Canti XVIII–XXXIII*, ed. by Enrico Malato and Andrea Mazzucchi (Rome: Salerno, 2014), pp. 745–74; Nicola Fosca, 'Dante e l'origine dell'anima umana', *Letteratura italiana antica*, 16 (2015), 253–85; Manuele Gragnolati, 'From Plurality to (Near) Unicity of Forms: Embryology in *Purgatorio 25'*, in *Dante for the New Millennium*, ed. by Teodolinda Barolini and H. Wayne Storey (New York: Fordham University Press, 2003), pp. 192–210, and *Experiencing the Afterlife: Soul and Body in Dante and Medieval Culture* (Notre Dame, IN: University of Notre Dame Press, 2005); Anne C. Leone, 'Communal and Economic Implications of Blood in Dante', *Italian Studies*, 71 (2016), 265–86; Pasquale Porro, '"Dentro dai fuochi son li spirti": Dante, il fuoco infernale e l'escatologia scolastica', in *Medioevo e filosofia: per Alfonso Maierù*, ed. by Massimiliano Lenzi and others (Rome: Viella, 2013), pp. 229–62; Giuliano Rossi, '"Ma come d'animal divegna fante": Dante tra Alberto Magno e Tommaso', *Critica del testo*, 13 (2010), 191–209; Giorgio Stabile, 'Fisiologia della riproduzione in Dante: l'eccedenza tra generazione, gola e lussuria', *Bollettino di italianistica*, n.s. 7 (2010), 35–45; Luigi Surdich, 'Dante e i "corpi aerei"', in *Unità*, ed. by Silvia Zoppi Garampi (Rome: Salerno, 2014), pp. 23–44; Heather Webb, 'Dante's Definition of Life',

however, by restricting their interpretations, scholars have produced readings that pay limited attention to the ties between *Purgatorio* XXV's various ideological and thematic interests, as well as to the possible functions of the canto's impressive *varietas* in the artistic and ideological economy of the poem. To put it somewhat differently, they have rather lost sight of the overall logic and the poetic coherence of a canto that ranges from the relationship between life and death to that between philosophy, theology, and poetry, and which, in addition, dwells on issues such as the bond between the body and the soul; the connections between the *Deus artifex*, Nature, and the human artist; the epistemological effectiveness of Scripture; the relations between the pagan world and Christianity; the 'voglia' (13) of knowledge; the generation of humans, the creation of the soul, and the resurrection of the body; and the condition of the shades in the afterlife — all key themes not just in medieval culture, but also, and more specifically, in the *Commedia*.

Despite the complexity and controversial nature of the questions raised in *Purgatorio* XXV (for example, the problem of how the soul might be united with the body was hotly debated throughout the Middle Ages), and despite the questions' obvious relevance for a 'sacrato poema' (*Par.* XXIII. 62) that deals with the realities of human salvation and damnation, the most substantial of the three critical traditions — prevalent especially in Italy — has tended drastically to restrict and to 'secularize' the canto's parameters. *Purgatorio* XXV's significance is essentially limited to its ties to medieval science and philosophy — its treatment of human generation and of the creation of the rational soul — and hence what it can reveal about Dante's familiarity with the Aristotelian tradition. The question of the aerial body, a vital and controversial issue in the poet's account of the afterlife, is pushed into the background, since, by 'embodying' the immaterial soul, it runs directly counter to the strict Aristotelian anthropology of the first part of Statius's speech. The fact that his *lectio* is a response specifically to a question about the (mutable) condition of the shades in the afterlife — 'Come si può far magro | là dove l'uopo di nodrir non tocca?' (20–21) — does not appear to have been a cause of concern and reflection.[3] The aerial body is dismissed as an artistic invention, a literary *fictio*, and hence of considerably less interest than those passages that permit a glimpse of Dante's doctrinal knowledge. According to this critical purview, to interpret *Purgatorio* XXV is largely equivalent to indicating the poet's debts to Aristotle and to his Arab and Christian commentators; and once these have been noted, the critical endeavour is deemed to be largely over. Scholars normally do not even consider how Dante's supposed ideological selections from within the welter of medieval Aristotelianism might affect the canto's meaning. As a result, the impression is

Dante Studies, 129 (2011), 47–62. See also George Ferzoco, '25. Changes', in *Vertical Readings in Dante's Comedy*, ed. by George Corbett and Heather Webb, 3 vols (n.p.p.: Open Book Publisher, 2015–17), III, 51–70.

3   As far as I am aware, Gardner is the first to have noted the precise parameters of the *viator*'s question: 'what the pilgrim in fact demands [...] is in fact quite distinct from the problem of sensation, and concerns simply how the torment which the souls do in fact experience [...] could possibly be manifested in this way, since it can hardly by nature reduce the size of a body which never eats' (p. 121).

created that *Purgatorio* XXV, rather than being a highly problematic and far-reaching canto — as I hope to illustrate in this short *lectura* — is entirely contained within and defined by its doctrinal concerns.[4] Dantists are as if mesmerized by the presence in the canto of the imposing authoritativeness of Aristotelian science. They thus do not ask whether it is actually valid to analyse *Purgatorio* XXV as if its primary function were to show off Dante's philosophical expertise — a function, I suspect, that, in the context of the canto, is of limited relevance. Reading *Purgatorio* XXV in this manner can be valuable if one intends to study Dante's intellectual formation. It is much less useful, however, if one wants to understand the canto's poetic, structural, and even ideological purpose in the *Commedia*.

Assessing *Purgatorio* XXV 'philosophically' is both popular and authoritative because it bears the imprimatur of Bruno Nardi, the major twentieth-century scholar of Dante's thought.[5] Furthermore, the fact that Nardi was followed by Dantists of the calibre of Étienne Gilson[6] and Patrick Boyde has served to confirm the validity of this approach.[7] Indeed, *lecturae* that take Nardi's proposals as conclusive consider *Purgatorio* XXV as largely unproblematic, given that, with its sources confirmed, the substantive exegetical effort has been completed. Yet, if one compares Nardi's, Gilson's, and Boyde's respective studies, it becomes quickly apparent that such a confident and tidy view of the canto is unsustainable. What in fact is immediately striking are the differences that distinguish their proposals regarding *Purgatorio* XXV's philosophical background. The study of sources, including scientific sources, is as subjective and precarious as any other field of philological and hermeneutic inquiry. Thus, in assessing Statius's lesson on physical generation and spiritual creation, Nardi emphasizes Dante's dependence on Albertus Magnus; Gilson clarifies the poet's debts to Thomas Aquinas; while Boyde, in Kenelm Foster's wake, attempts to synthesize the two positions.[8] Moreover, while Nardi and Boyde reveal little interest in the sources of the aerial body, Gilson stresses the links between Dante's

---

4   Gardner provides an insightful and persuasive overview of the critical debate on Statius's lecture — rather than on the canto as a whole — prompted by the reasonable belief that 'no one has yet provided a consistent interpretation of the entire discourse' (pp. 4–5); and it would be fair to add that, to date, his doctoral thesis is by far the best attempt at arriving at an organic analysis of *Purg.* XXV. 34–108. Gardner's evaluation of the scholarly tradition (pp. 5–6, n. 6) has various points of contact with my discussion here of the main ways in which the canto has been read. Together with a few other scholars (see below), Gardner and I are motivated by the need to offer alternative 'totalizing' interpretations of the canto in general and of Statius's *lectio* in particular as counters to the partial and restrictive ways in which these have normally been analysed.

5   See, in particular, Bruno Nardi, 'L'origine dell'anima umana secondo Dante' [1931–32], in his *Studi di filosofia medievale* (Rome: Edizioni di storia e letteratura, 1960), pp. 9–68; 'Sull'origine dell'anima umana' [1938], in his *Dante e la cultura medievale*, ed. by Paolo Mazzantini and Tullio Gregory, 2nd edn (Rome and Bari: Laterza, 1990), pp. 207–24; and 'Il canto XXV del *Purgatorio*', in *Letture Dantesche: Purgatorio*, ed. by Giovanni Getto (Florence: Sansoni, 1958), pp. 501–17.

6   See Étienne Gilson, 'Dante's Notion of the Shade: *Purgatorio* XXV', *Medieval Studies*, 29 (1967), 124–42, and 'Qu'est-ce qu'une ombre? (Dante, *Purg.* XXV)', in his *Dante et Béatrice: études dantesques* (Paris: Vrin, 1974), pp. 22–45.

7   Patrick Boyde, *Dante Philomythes and Philosopher: Man in the Cosmos* (Cambridge: Cambridge University Press, 1981), pp. 270–81.

8   Kenelm Foster, 'Tommaso d'Aquino', in *ED*, V, 626–49 (p. 635).

'ombre' (101) and Virgil's *umbrae* in *Aeneid* VI, as well as with Christian discussions of the ways in which the dead can suffer infernal pain, thereby restricting — correctly in my view — the importance and scope of the canto's Aristotelianism. Finally, unlike Gilson, neither Nardi nor Boyde are concerned with the more strictly religious dimension of Statius's explanations — the dimension which, as I intend to demonstrate, plays a fundamental role in *Purgatorio* XXV.[9]

At first glance, the second of the three critical threads — this one North American in origin — could not be more different from the 'Nardian' strand. In the wake of John Freccero,[10] American Dantists have marginalized the doctrinal character of the canto and its Aristotelian sources to underscore its metaliterary functions:[11]

9   Gardner usefully highlights the continuities between the different Aristotelian readings of Statius's disquisition: 'Etienne Gilson, Patrick Boyde, and Manuele Gragnolati [*Experiencing the Afterlife*, pp. 67–77] follow generally in this line [namely that of Nardi who 'concerned himself entirely with doctrinal debates over the origin of the soul and simply glided past Statius's conclusion despite its puzzling relationship to the rest of the discourse and to the originative question'], each offering some modifications to Nardi's polemic [with Busnelli] but also accepting the conclusion of a sensing shade-body without much explanation of how that could cohere with the foregoing embryology, regardless of its classification as Albertian or Thomistic, favoring plurality of forms or unicity' (p. 5). It goes without saying that Gardner offers a major corrective to this trend. Indeed, he proffers a radically new and distinctive interpretation of Statius's lecture (pp. 112–206). His critique of the standard explanation among Dantists of how Statius resolves the pilgrim's question regarding otherworldly suffering is impeccable: 'The common denominator for all theological treatments of the question, whether Patristic or Scholastic, is the assumption that by nature a body can only affect another body; thus presumably the simplest way to allow for a corporeal fire is to supply a new body for separated souls in the interim. If that be granted, the basic problem is solved — the fire can torment by its natural calefaction. According to an almost unanimous interpretative tradition, that is exactly what Dante does through the mouth of Statius in this crucial canto: he explains how separated souls produce new bodies for themselves which allow them to sense bodies such as fire and suffer thereby. // The trouble is that this neat solution would make no contribution to the debate at all. The theologians did not simply miss the option of interim bodies because of a lack of imagination, but because it would seem to be incoherent in the context of the problem. If the bodies supplied to separated souls in the interim are of flesh and blood, then the Resurrection to come has been preempted or trivialized; if they are not of flesh and blood, then the human soul has no proportion to union with such a body and could not sense by means of it. Thus given the universal assumption that Statius means to account for sensation as the mode of the *poena ignis*, it is quite understandable that several commentators on this passage have seen futility in the explanation and attributed it to poetic necessity. // But to read *Purgatorio* XXV in such a way is to miss Statius's real meaning and Dante's true contribution to and reformulation of the debate over the nature of the interim state' (pp. 112–13). See n. 38 below for a discussion of what Gardner demonstrates to be 'Statius's real meaning and Dante's true contribution to and reformulation of the debate'. Gardner's thesis constitutes the major corrective to Nardi's views. Marc Cogan, *The Design in the Wax: The Structure of the 'Divine Comedy' and its Meaning* (Notre Dame, IN, and London: University of Notre Dame Press, 1999) also convincingly revises some of Nardi's claims (pp. 119–47).

10   John Freccero, 'Manfred's Wounds and the Poetics of the *Purgatorio*', in his *Dante: The Poetics of Conversion*, ed. by Rachel Jacoff (Cambridge, MA: Harvard University Press, 1986), pp. 195–208.

11   See, for instance, Rachel Jacoff, '"Our Bodies, Our Selves:" The Body in the *Commedia*', in *Sparks and Seeds: Medieval Literature and its Afterlife: Essays in Honor of John Freccero*, ed. by Dana E. Stewart and Alison Cornish (Turnhout: Brepols, 2000), pp. 119–37 (p. 129); Nancy Lindheim, 'Body, Soul, and Immortality: Some Readings in Dante's *Commedia*', *MLN*, 105 (1990), 1–32; Giuseppe Mazzotta, *Dante, Poet of the Desert: History and Allegory in the 'Divine Comedy'* (Princeton: Princeton University Press, 1979), pp. 211–26. See also Dino Cervigni, 'XXV', in *Dante's 'Divine Comedy': Introductory Readings. II. 'Purgatorio'*, ed. by Tibor Wlassics (Charlottesville: University of Virginia

Statius' discussion about conception and reproduction in Canto XXV also serves
as a gloss on Canto XXIV, where the subject is literary creation and conception.
More than that, it seems to suggest strongly an analogy between the act of
writing and the act of procreation [...]. As the soul is inspired in the fetus, so
the inspiration of the poet comes from God. The body, however, is the work
of parenthood. In the same way, the poetic corpus is sired by the poet, who
provides the vehicle for God's message. (Freccero, p. 202)

Freccero's suggestion is alluring and acute. It convincingly integrates *Purgatorio*
XXV's scientific interests with the metapoetic concerns that dominate in the surrounding cantos: from the celebration of Virgil and classical culture in *Purgatorio*
XXI and XXII to the critique of 'comic-realist' forms in *Purgatorio* XXIII, and then
to the definition of the 'dolce stil novo' (57) in *Purgatorio* XXIV — a literary thread
that continues to unwind until it arrives at the assessment of the Romance lyric
tradition in *Purgatorio* XXVI (and in the early cantos of the Earthly Paradise). At the
same time, like the 'philosophical' *lettura* of the canto, the American metaliterary
reading is unnecessarily reductive. By focusing solely on a single aspect of *Purgatorio*
XXV, it fails to offer a broad-based evaluation of the canto. As far as I am concerned,
what crucially needs to be clarified are the reasons why, during the course of his
sustained analysis of literature in *Purgatorio* XXI–XXVI, Dante decided to dedicate a
whole canto to assessing the contacts between poetry and doctrine.[12]

The beginnings of an answer may be glimpsed in the third critical current that
includes readings by Vittorio Russo,[13] Giorgio Padoan,[14] and Anna Maria Chiavacci
Leonardi.[15] Although less compact than the other two, what unites these scholars is
a lucid sense of the canto's connotative richness and of its intricate ramifications in
the structure of the *Commedia*. Russo stresses the need to go beyond *Purgatorio* XXV's
Aristotelian sources and to investigate its ties to literary traditions intent on tackling
scientific and philosophical matters — most notably Cavalcanti's *stilnuovo*. Padoan
explores the reasons why, by means of Statius, who is both saved and a poet, Dante
decided to discuss the body and soul at this point in the poem. He argues that this
is part of Dante's strategy to establish his providentially ordained responsibilities. In
her turn, Chiavacci Leonardi refines Padoan's arguments, illustrating the manner in
which the canto establishes poetry's capacity to deal with highly complex subjects
to which philosophy cannot offer adequate explanation, thereby underlining the
close ties between poetry and (divine) truth.

Printing Service, 1993), pp. 362–79. For an important attempt to blend the metaliterary and the
scientific, see Paola Ureni, 'Human Generation, Memory and Poetic Creation: From *Purgatorio* to
the *Paradiso*', *Quaderni di italianistica*, 31 (2010), 9–33.

12   On the general question of 'philosophical poetry' in Dante, see Zygmunt G. Barański, '"Per
similitudine di abito scientifico": Dante, Cavalcanti, and the Sources of Medieval "Philosophical"
Poetry', in *Literature and Science in Italian Culture: From Dante to Calvino. A Festschrift in Honour of
Patrick Boyde*, ed. by Pierpaolo Antonello and Simon Gilson (Oxford: Legenda, 2004), pp. 14–52.

13   Vittorio Russo, 'A proposito del canto XXV del *Purgatorio*', in his *Esperienze e/di letture dantesche
(tra il 1966 e il 1970)* (Naples: Liguori, 1971), pp. 101–58.

14   Giorgio Padoan, 'Il canto XXV del *Purgatorio*', in *'Purgatorio': letture degli anni 1976–'79*, ed. by
Silvio Zennaro (Rome: Bonacci, 1981), pp. 577–600.

15   Anna Maria Chiavacci Leonardi, 'Introduzione al canto XXV', in Dante Alighieri, *Commedia. II.
Purgatorio* (Milan: Mondadori, 1994), pp. 727–33.

It is thus obvious that literature has at least as important a function as doctrine in *Purgatorio* XXV. What remains unexplored, however, is the nature of their relationship, as well as what the canto may reveal about Dante's views regarding both literature and doctrine considered in themselves. If the doctrinal section of *Purgatorio* XXV goes beyond strictly scientific concerns to become part of the *Commedia*'s metaliterary system, the question arises how human generation, the creation of the intellectual soul, and the formation of the aerial body might have meaningful poetic reverberations.[16] Finally, it is worth asking how these specific philosophical and theological *quaestiones* might relate to the broad metaliterary discourse that Dante developed in *Purgatorio* XXI–XXVI.

2. Purgatorial Poetry

To answer these questions, it is useful to start by noting the main literary issues addressed in the upper *gironi* of Purgatory: the connections between pagan Latin literature and Christian vernacular writing; poetic and authorial hierarchies; poetry's salvific functions, as emerges from Statius's personal account of the *Aeneid*'s restorative effects (*Purg.* XXII. 64–73); and the link between literature, ethics, and the need to write clearly. On this last point, the technical value of each of the terms constituting the phrase 'dolce stil novo' highlights the need for expressive clarity[17] — a fact confirmed by what the pilgrim and Bonagiunta say about writers' responsibilities towards their sources of inspiration:

> E io a lui: 'I' mi son un che, quando
> Amor mi spira, noto, e a quel modo
> ch'e' ditta dentro vo significando'.
>   'O frate, issa vegg'io', diss'elli, 'il nodo
> che 'l Notaro e Guittone e me ritenne
> di qua dal dolce stil novo ch'i'odo!
>   Io veggio ben come le vostre penne
> di retro al dittator sen vanno strette,
> che de le nostre certo non avvenne;
>   e qual più a gradire oltre si mette,
> non vede più da l'uno a l'altro stilo'. (*Purg.* XXIV. 52–62)

More significant than the general declaration regarding the bond between ethics and writing lucidly are two other literary notions embedded in these lines that have a direct, if not actually an exclusive, bearing on Dante and his poem. In the first place, and in line with standard contemporary thinking, it is almost certain that God is the 'Amor' that 'inspires' the poet (see the next paragraph).[18] Second,

---

16   Lindheim offers a good analysis of the ways in which Dante's reflections on the relationship between body and soul have a bearing on the *Commedia*'s structure.

17   See Zygmunt G. Barański, '"nfiata labia" and "dolce stil novo": A Note on Dante, Ethics, and the Technical Vocabulary of Literature', in *Sotto il segno di Dante: scritti in onore di Francesco Mazzoni*, ed. by Lionella Coglievina and Domenico De Robertis (Florence: Le Lettere, 1998), pp. 17–35 (pp. 27–31).

18   See Barański, '"nfiata labia"', pp. 31–32; Robert Hollander, *Studies in Dante* (Ravenna: Longo, 1980), p. 82, and 'Dante's "dolce stil novo" and the Comedy', in *Dante: mito e poesia*, ed. by

whatever the function of lines 52–62 in elucidating Dante's thinking about the history and character of Italian lyric poetry, what the lines most fittingly define is the *Commedia* itself. Indeed, various scholars have maintained that both the metaliterary observations that precede *Purg.* XXIV. 52–62 and those that follow serve primarily to define the unique features of the 'sacrato poema' (*Par.* XXIII. 62). Thus, coming immediately after the somewhat allusive affirmation of the *Commedia*'s divinely inspired character, *Purgatorio* XXV offers concrete clarification of the nature of the collaboration between 'cielo e terra' (*Par.* XXV. 2) and legitimates the *Commedia*'s status as a 'sacred poem'.

The canto introduces several cases of divine 'art', the key example being the creation of Adam: 'Formavit igitur Dominus Deus hominem de limo terrae, et inspiravit in faciem eius spiraculum vitae, et factus est homo in animam viventem' [The Lord God created man from the mud of the earth, and breathed into him the spirit of life, and man became a living being] (Genesis 2: 7). The formation of the first man lies behind and serves as the matrix for the divine act of creation of every human being, as Dante reveals by modelling his description of the formation of the rational soul, another instance of the activity of the *Deus artifex*, on the passage from Genesis:

> lo motor primo a lui [the foetus] si volge lieto
> sovra tant' arte di natura, e spira
> spirito novo, di vertù repleto,
>   che ciò che trova attivo quivi, tira
> in sua sustanzia. (*Purg.* XXV. 70–74)

Moreover, according to Dante, the *Commedia*'s coming into being also depends on the same model of divine creativity that shaped Adam and every human individual. This is evident not only on account of the presence of the verb *(in)spirare* in all three accounts, but also because the same process and end determine the accomplishment of the three 'works' of the *digitus Dei*. In each case, God *ispira* a lower form — the mud of the earth, the vegetative and sensitive soul, the human *auctor* — a process that results in an entity that integrates *cielo* and *terra* — Adam, the rational soul, the *Commedia* — each of which, like all that God creates, functions as a *vestigium Dei*.[19] In *Purgatorio* XXV, therefore, by integrating the genesis of his poem with the Creator's other 'artistic' activities, Dante renders explicit the divine character of the *Commedia*. In addition, he reiterates that the definition proffered in the previous canto ('I' mi son un che, quando | Amor mi spira, noto, e a quel modo | ch'e' ditta dentro vo significando') needs to be interpreted in light of the creativity of 'Colui che volse il sesto | a lo stremo del mondo' (*Par.* XIX. 40–41).

Michelangelo Picone and Tatiana Crivelli (Florence: Cesati, 1999), pp. 263–81 (pp. 267–70); Ronald Martinez, 'The Pilgrim's Answer to Bonagiunta and the Poetics of the Spirit', *Stanford Italian Review*, 3 (1983), 37–63; Mazzotta, pp. 192–211.

19   On the *Deus artifex* and related notions, see at least Ernst Robert Curtius, *European Literature and the Latin Middle Ages* (Princeton: Princeton University Press, 1990), pp. 544–46; Marie-Thérèse d'Alverny, 'Le Cosmos symbolique du XIIe siècle', *Archive d'histoire doctrinale et littéraire du Moyen Âge*, 20 (1953), 31–81; Kent Emery Jr, 'Reading the World Rightly and Squarely: Bonaventure's Doctrine of the Cardinal Virtues', *Traditio*, 39 (1983), 183–218; Friedrich Ohly, *Geometria e memoria* (Bologna: il Mulino, 1985), pp. 189–247.

However, *Purgatorio* xxv does more than confirm that God inspired the *auctor* of the *Commedia* and that His 'mano' (*Par.* xxv. 2) is discernible in its make-up. The canto also reveals that God offered the poet the textual model he was to imitate as he wrote — a fundamental clarification concerning the nature of the 'new' poem theorized in *Purgatorio* xxiv. Beginning in the twelfth century, it was commonplace for Scriptural exegesis to affirm that God 'dictates' what the *scriba Dei* is supposed to write. At the same time, it was the human author who was recognized as responsible for giving literary form — 'vo significando' — to the substance of divine inspiration.[20] In *Purgatorio* xxv, Dante refined this concept, suggesting that the sacred writer who properly wants to discharge his divinely ordained responsibilities cannot simply rely on his own creative abilities but must also attempt to imitate the work of the Supreme Artist. At a basic level, this is implicit in the fact that, since Dante's poem is originally produced like other expressions of the *Deus artifex*, then it cannot but bear traces of their fundamental formal features.

The *Commedia*'s divine credentials, however, are considerably more complex than matters of vague formal consonance. Unlike the entirely passive contributions of the mud and of the vegetative and sensitive soul to the creative process, Dante plays an active role in the making of the *Commedia*. He is able to do this because of the divine element inside him, an element that the earth and the vegetative and sensitive soul lack since they are works exclusively of Nature ('tant'arte di natura', 71; and see 60). Yet, given his intellectual limitations, it is not clear how Dante might in fact imitate the *Deus artifex*. *Purgatorio* xxv's role in resolving the impasse is vital. Thanks to the *exemplum* of the formative activity of the 'alma' (96) that combines and 'porta seco e l'umano e 'l divino' (81), the canto reveals that it is entirely possible for a creature to imitate the model offered by the divine Creator. The rational soul, 'la virtù formativa', acts on, 'raggia intorno' (89), an inferior element, the air, that it 'suggella' (95) to shape the aerial body, which, in its turn, bears the marks of its double origin and, therefore, functions as a celestial sign, in particular of divine justice. Similarly, Dante, a rational but still living soul, exerts a formative influence on what, as a writer, 'circumscribes' him (88), namely, on the literary tradition, whose 'inferiority' in relation to himself is firmly established in the cantos that surround *Purgatorio* xxv. Dante is thus able to produce ''l poema sacro | al quale ha posto mano e cielo e terra' (*Par.* xxv. 2–3), by means of which he proclaims God's will to a world weighed down by sin. Nor is it mere coincidence that the definition of the 'alma' that 'porta seco e l'umano e 'l divino' should return in the definition of the *Commedia* presented in *Paradiso* xxv. As Dante is about to introduce another important explanation concerning the divine nature of his poem, the repetition serves as a reminder of the key justifications that he had already given regarding the sacred character of his text. Likewise, it is not by chance that the poet attended to the divine nature of the *Commedia* in cantos distinguished by the same number. This is typical of Dante's strategy to organize his poem according to balanced and mnemonically effective structures that reproduce the perfect *ordo*

---

20   See Alastair J. Minnis, *Medieval Theory of Authorship*, 2nd edn (Aldershot: Scolar Press, 1988), pp. 73–117. See also Chapter 7, pp. 318–19.

of the Creator's art — the divine formal feature that he most strikingly attempts to replicate (see the previous chapter).

As he regularly did, especially when defining the *Commedia*, Dante radically adapted a cultural commonplace, invigorating standard, 'lifeless' ideas about divine and human artistry. Boldly, yet orthodoxly, he evoked God's act of 'inspiring' life, as well as the *suggello* of the aerial body, in order to clarify the distinctive, precisely because celestial, features of his poem. In the economy of the *Commedia*, the poem is essentially an analogue of the works of the *Deus artifex*. Conversely, the description of the generation of the vegetative and sensitive soul is an instance of 'non-divine' art whose relationship to the 'sacrato poema' (*Par.* XXIII. 62) is at best tenuous. Moreover, in establishing the inspired character of the *Commedia* in light of divine creation, Dante reprises the main points of *Purgatorio*'s reflection on literature, thereby underscoring the coherence and rigour of his metaliterary discourse. Thus, in *Purgatorio* XXV, he alludes to the hierarchical association between different writers and texts; he touches on the theme of salvation; and he stresses the need to communicate in accessible ways, given that the 'poetics' of the *Deus artifex* finds expression in the *sermo humilis*. As far as I am concerned, the metaliterary character of *Purgatorio* XXV's doctrinal elements is incontrovertible. And one basic fact would seem to confirm this. For Dante, the problem of the survival of the soul and of the body in the afterlife was not, as it was for many Christian thinkers, an essentially abstract theological *quaestio* (as I discuss below). It was also a profoundly literary, and therefore practical, issue. If he had been unable to find a 'logical' solution for the necessary presence in the other world of *ombre* who *parlano, ridono, piangono*, and *sospirano* (101, 103–04), rather than an afterlife, as the majority of theologians believed (see n. 22), inhabited by separated souls without bodily traits, the *Commedia*'s artistic and ideological infrastructure would have collapsed. In Dante's masterpiece, it is impossible artificially to separate doctrine (not to say 'structure') from poetry. *Purgatorio* XXV illustrates this with noteworthy efficiency and sophistication. Thus, in the remainder of the present *lectura*, I propose to highlight other aspects of the rich interaction between doctrine and literature.

The key feature regarding the *Commedia*'s divine origins is its status as *vestigium Dei*. Consequently, as with all divine signs, the poem is able to communicate the truth about salvation. In making this claim, Dante pushed poetry into areas that had long been the traditional preserve of biblical exegesis and theology. The fact that, in *Purgatorio* XXII, Statius acknowledges that the *Aeneid* played a crucial role in his salvation serves to underline — whatever the other implications of such an extraordinary admission — that the bond between God and poetry is not limited to the *Commedia*. Although Dante's poem demonstrates the link in a particularly explicit and effective manner, it is, in reality, an element inherent, at least potentially, in poetry in general. At the same time, that Virgil should fail to offer an adequate explanation of 'Come si può far magro | là dove l'uopo di nodrir non tocca' (20–21) — a failing that should be associated with his ignorance of the inspired dimension of his epic poem (*Purg.* XXII. 67–69) — and that he should ask Statius, a saved soul, and therefore a 'Christian poet', for help, emphasizes that God forges different relationships with different poets. Even if Statius is able to explicate divine mysteries in the afterlife, there is no suggestion in the *Commedia* that the works that he wrote when alive are in any way repositories of divine truths. Among poets, only Dante, by means of the *Commedia* — as *Purgatorio* XXV documents — deals with salvation in a fully cognizant and involved manner. In addition, in light of *Purgatorio* XXV's doctrinal character, Dante seems to imply that there are questions — for example, how separated souls can suffer the pains of Hell and Purgatory, or 'come d'animal divegna fante' (61) — that poetry, particularly that of a *scriba Dei*, can better illuminate than theological, never mind philosophical, prose.

3. Real Flames, Airy Bodies: Virgilian Premonitions

It is time, given its import in the *Commedia*, to concentrate on the condition of the individual in the afterlife and the ways in which s/he experiences the otherworld, a problem that, in Dante, is centred on the aerial body.[21] Although some early Church Fathers had argued otherwise, scholastic theologians agreed that, once the soul separated from the body, the *anima exuta* was completely spiritual and without traces of corporeity.[22] This position inevitably jarred against the related belief that the fires of Hell — accepted as real on the authority of Scripture — caused suffering to immaterial souls: 'tunc dicet et his qui a sinistris erunt discedite a me maledicti in ignem aeternum qui paratus est diabolo et angelis eius' [then he shall say even to those who will be on his left side: depart from me, you damned, into the eternal fire which was prepared for the devil and his angels] (Matthew 25: 41).[23] The explanations that learned theologians proposed were ingenious and convoluted. On the other hand, there also existed a rich visionary tradition that, largely unproblematically, presented the inhabitants of the afterlife as if they were living beings.[24] Such representations had an extensive oral, written, and iconographic

---

21   In his noteworthy book, Manuele Gragnolati contextualizes Dante's thinking against the background of the 'new sense of eschatological experience that emerged in the twelfth century and developed thereafter', and which 'concerns [...] the individual destiny of the separated soul and is closely related to the emergence of a new attitude toward physical death', whereby, 'personal death began to be considered the decisive moment of the individual's existence, when the actual judgment of his or her life takes place, and after which the separated soul's experience either of pain (in hell or purgatory), or of joy (in heaven) begins immediately, even without the body' (*Experiencing the Afterlife*, p. xii).

22   See Gardner, pp. 7–12 and 16–111; J. Bainvel and others, 'Âme', in DTC, I:1, cols 968–1042. See also Sergio Cristaldi, 'Territori d'oltremondo', in *'Il mondo errante': Dante tra letteratura, eresia e storia*, ed. by Marco Veglia and others (Spoleto: Fondazione Centro italiano di studi sull'alto Medioevo, 2013), pp. 385–470 (pp. 385–403); Caroline Walker Bynum, *The Resurrection of the Body in Western Christianity 200–1336* (New York: Columbia University Press, 1995).

23   See Albert Michel, 'Feu de l'Enfer', in DTC, V:2, cols 2196–239. Gardner is especially informative on the tensions that arose between the two views.

24   See Cristaldi, pp. 404–30; Peter Dinzelbacher, 'Il corpo nelle visioni dell'aldilà', *Micrologus*, I (1993), 301–26; Gragnolati, *Experiencing the Afterlife*, pp. 1–51; Aron Gurevich, 'The *Divine Comedy* before Dante', in his *Medieval Popular Culture: Problems of Belief and Perception* (Cambridge: Cambridge University Press, 1988), pp. 104–52, and 'Perception of the Individual and the Hereafter in the Middle Ages', in *Historical Anthropology of the Middle Ages*, ed. by Jana Howlett (Cambridge: Polity Press,

dissemination. Dante is likely to have appreciated the allure and the flaws of both traditions. Theologians offered strictly theoretical explanations, which necessarily stripped the afterlife of its drama, and hence its 'narratability'. In contrast, the visionaries focused on the drama without endeavouring to illuminate the principles underlying the world that they were evoking. Dante's ambition in *Purgatorio* XXV was to synthesize the two traditions: his aim, to narrate and clarify.[25] At the same time, Dante knew that such a reconciliation had already been attempted, and, significantly, by a poet. In lines 724–51 of the sixth book of the *Aeneid*, Virgil's Anchises expounds a scientific theory of the origin, the condition, and the experiences of the *umbrae* who inhabit Avernus. It is obvious that Dante wants the reader to keep Anchises's explanation in mind when reading Statius's *lectio*. Thus, the 'cantor di Tebe' (*Purg.* XXI. 92) borrows from 'pater Anchises' (*Aen.* VI. 713). In particular, 'Quindi parliamo e quindi ridiam noi; | quindi facciam le lagrime e ' sospiri' (103–04) depends closely on 'Hinc metuunt cupiuntque, dolent gaudentque' [here they fear and long for, they suffer and rejoice] (733). Equally, despite their different subject-matter, Dante's 'Or si spiega, figliuolo, or si distende | la virtù ch'è dal cor del generante, | dove natura a tutte membra intende' (58–60) echoes Virgil's 'Spiritus intus alit totamque infusa per artus | mens agitat molem et magno se corpore miscet' [The spirit nourishes it on the inside and, spread through all the limbs, the mind moves the body's mass and joins itself to it] (726–27).

By alluding to *Aeneid* VI, Dante celebrates Virgil, who, although a pagan, had tried to solve a problem that would challenge the best Christian minds. Furthermore, the echoes serve to emphasize the capacity of poetry to address intellectually challenging issues. In the Middle Ages, among his attributes as *auctor* supreme, Virgil, poet and philosopher, represented the far-from-negligible intellectual potential of poetry.[26] It is of course this dimension of poetry that, in *Purgatorio* XXV, Dante highlighted to legitimate the *Commedia*'s divine attributes. Yet, elsewhere in the canto, Dante seems to challenge the positive image of poetry's capabilities that he was steadily forging. Perplexingly, Virgil, Dante's illustrious predecessor in developing a theory of otherworldly being and, therefore, in creating a poetry rich in doctrinal possibility, and who is celebrated in *Purgatorio* XXV because of this attempt, capitulates, as he had already done in Ante-Purgatory

1992), pp. 65–89; Carol Zaleski, *Otherworld Journeys* (New York and Oxford: Oxford University Press, 1987), pp. 50–52. See also Alison Morgan, *Dante and the Medieval Other World* (Cambridge: Cambridge University Press, 1990).

25   'The poet's engagement with this point of friction between Aristotelian anthropology and Christian eschatology is no fanciful poetic escape from the problem, but a philosophically coherent defense of the possibility of separated souls manifesting themselves physically. If taken in earnest, this discourse also forms part of a larger defense of the legitimate role of poetic vision within *doctrina*, such that testimony of visions of the afterlife might to some extent be complementary to the discursive theological accounts of the state of souls after death, not merely a popular or credulous tradition belonging to a separate sphere of Christian belief — and this connection recovers a crucial aspect of the Patristic sources on the *poena ignis* which was left behind in the Scholastic debate' (Gardner, pp. 11–12).

26   See also Christopher Baswell, *Virgil in Medieval England: Figuring the 'Aeneid' from the Twelfth Century to Chaucer* (Cambridge: Cambridge University Press, 1995).

(*Purg.* III. 31–45), when faced with the problem of the aerial body. Indeed, when he attempts to give the pilgrim an idea of the nature of the problem, he does not repeat the solution he had presented in the *Aeneid*, but uses two *exempla*, that of Meleager and that of the 'image' in the 'specchio' (22–26), which are of limited explanatory efficacy.[27] Unexpectedly, poetry no longer seems a powerful intellectual tool. Such an impression, however, is misleading. The apparent contradiction is in fact readily resolved when it is seen in terms of the opposition that Dante sets up between himself and Virgil as representatives of two different types of sacred poetry. *Sub specie aeternitatis*, the Latin poet recognizes that his ideas on the *anima mundi*, on the netherworld, and on the transmigration of souls, fruits of a mind lacking divine inspiration, had been incorrect. With due humility, he avoids repeating his earthbound errors.[28] As Dante demonstrates elsewhere in the *Commedia*, all that Virgil had achieved was ultimately a heroic failure.[29] Thus, the *Aeneid* offers a glimpse, but only a glimpse, however alluring, of poetry's remarkable resources. It is instead the *Commedia*, *vestigium Dei* and *aemulatio* of the Latin poem, as *Purgatorio* XXV affirms, especially as regards its revelation of the 'true' doctrine of the aerial body (see the following subsection), that successfully manages to realize poetry's rich artistic and intellectual potential. The 'poema sacro' (*Par.* XXV. 1) owes its unique success to the active collaboration between 'l'umano e 'l divino' (*Purg.* XXV. 81), a matter that constitutes one of *Purgatorio* XXV's key themes. Conversely, when Virgil composed the *Aeneid*, he left no sign that he was aware of the 'fiamma divina' which in fact *allumava* (*Purg.* XXI. 95–96) his text. Virgil's failure is, of course, superseded by Dante's success, so that ('modern' Christian) poetry emerges enriched and improved. The poet explains the singularity of the *Commedia* not only in terms of its sacredness, but also by (contrastively) associating it with the rest of the literary tradition. This strategy reaches a climax in *Purgatorio* XXI–XXVI, where, specifically in *Purgatorio* XXV, Dante introduced a vibrant and inventive clarification of the vital yet varied contacts between God's 'books' and human poetry — contacts that find remarkable expression in the 'wondrous' synthesis that constitutes the providential prerequisite for the *Commedia*'s coming into being.

4. The 'Wondrous' Aerial Body

Yet, as we have begun to see, in *Purgatorio* XXV, Dante did not restrict himself to evaluating the *Commedia* in exclusively divine and literary terms but assessed it too in light of other intellectual systems, such as philosophy and theology. Dante's purpose was not simply to define his poem. His broader aim was to investigate poetry's communicative potential and to establish its status within the contemporary

---

27   For an extended discussion of the exegetical limitations of the two images, which 'offer little explanation of the phenomenon in question', and their effects on Dante's presentation of Virgil, see Gardner, pp. 122–25 (pp. 122–23).

28   On Virgil as a 'posthumous Christian' in Purgatory, see Robert Hollander, 'Canto II: Dante's Authority', in *Lectura Dantis. 'Inferno'*, ed by Allen Mandelbaum and others (Berkeley: University of California Press, 1998), pp. 25–35 (p. 32).

29   In particular, see Robert Hollander, *Il Virgilio dantesco* (Florence: Olschki, 1983).

hierarchical system of the 'sciences' (although the *Commedia* is never in fact far from the centre of this more general investigation). The canto's generalizing ambitions emerge with particular vigour in Statius's speech on generation and creation (37–78), thereby consolidating the bond that unites doctrine and metapoetic reflection in *Purgatorio* XXV.[30] Statius's lesson is divided into four parts: lines 37–51, 52–60, 61–66, and 67–75. Lines 37–51 describe the process of the descent of the sperm into the womb and the union of the two 'bloods' (37 and 45). Scholars have not established precise sources for the passage. It seems to repeat information that can be found in several thirteenth-century commentators on Aristotle's *De generatione animalium* who read the philosopher's work in light of the writings of Galen and Avicenna.[31] On the other hand, it has long been accepted that lines 52–60, which clarify the formation of the vegetative and sensitive soul, follow a recognizable *auctoritas*: Albertus Magnus's *De natura et origine animae*.[32] Gardner, however, has convincingly demonstrated that Statius's treatment is compatible with 'both the Thomistic and Albertian accounts of the origin of the soul' (p. 152, n. 46). Up to this point, the general thrust of Dante's presentation is conventional — he accepts the authority of the Aristotelian tradition in the field of natural science. However, as Dante himself admits, substantive problems emerge if Aristotle and his followers are relied upon to understand the 'passaggio dall'animalità alla razionalità' (Chiavacci Leonardi, II, 742), namely, the passage from matter to spirit:[33]

> Ma come d'animal divegna fante,
> non vedi tu ancor: quest'è tal punto,
> che più savio di te fé già errante,
>   sì che per sua dottrina fé disgiunto
> da l'anima il possibile intelletto,
> perché da lui non vide organo assunto. (*Purg.* XXV. 61–66)

By alluding to the error of the great Arab commentator of Aristotle, Averroes, whose shade the pilgrim had seen in Limbo, Dante metonymically recalls the difficulties that the whole Aristotelian tradition — whether philosophical or theological — with its confidence in the capabilities of reason, had in clarifying the mystery of

---

30   Gardner notes as regards Statius's elucidation of the aerial body: 'As to the content of the explanation, surely it is as much a part of the poet's art as the invention and illustration of the torments themselves' (pp. 2–3).

31   Boyde, pp. 271–73. 'The first half of Statius's explication of "la veduta etterna" [31] will follow closely Aristotle's account in *De generatione animalium*, the key source for the Stagirite's embryology. One brief passage captures most of the essential elements which will feature in the discourse [II. 1. 54–55]' (Gardner, p. 133; but see also pp. 139–40 on the mediating effects of commentary). On the passage's Galenic dimension, see Vittorio Bartoli and Paola Ureni, 'Controversie medico-biologiche in tema di generazione umana nel XXV del *Purgatorio*', *Studi danteschi*, 68 (2003), 83–111, and 'La dottrina di Galeno in "sangue perfetto" (*Purg* . XXV 37)', *Studi danteschi*, 70 (2005), 335–43.

32   Nardi, 'L'origine dell'anima umana secondo Dante', pp. 22–33 & 50–54, and 'Il canto XXV', pp. 145–47. However, now see the fuller and more nuanced discussion in Gardner, pp. 136–52.

33   'Up to that point [line 72], the Aristotelian embryology need not be thought of as new to the pilgrim; it is given as a sort of refresher course, calling to mind already-known principles so that something further might be established on their basis, just as Dante is at times admonished to remember the teaching of Aristotle, not to learn it for the first time' (Gardner, p. 183).

'come d'animal divegna fante' (61; and see Gardner, p. 153). In the last part of his speech, Statius reveals that the 'truth' (67) on the *quaestio* does exist, but that this is to be found not in the writings of the Aristotelians but in a quite different text:

> Apri a la verità che viene il petto;
> e sappi che, sì tosto come al feto
> l'articular del cerebro è perfetto,
>   lo motor primo a lui si volge lieto
> sovra tant' arte di natura, e spira
> spirito novo, di vertù repleto,
>   che ciò che trova attivo quivi, tira
> in sua sustanzia, e fassi un'alma sola,
> che vive e sente e sé in sé rigira. (*Purg.* XXV. 67–75)

Although Aristotelian elements persist in Statius's explanation, the lines' primary sources, because most prominent and accessible, are Scriptural — something that Dante scholarship appears to have missed.[34] The opening line clearly reveals its biblical origins: 'cuius Dominus aperuit cor intendere his quae dicebantur a Paulo' [whose heart the Lord opened to attend to what Paul was saying] (Acts 16: 14), and 'Tunc aperuit illis sensum ut intelligerent Scripturas' [Then he opened their mind to understand Scripture] (Luke 24: 45). Furthermore, as we might have expected, it is the description of the act of divine creation that most obviously depends on the Bible. Lines 70–72 integrate several Scriptural passages that address divine joy ('Laetabitur Dominus in operibus suis' [The Lord will delight in his works], Psalm 113: 31), creative inspiration ('Formavit igitur Dominus Deus hominem de limo terrae, et inspiravit in faciem eius spiraculum vitae, et factus est homo in animam viventem' [The Lord God created man from the mud of the earth, and breathed into him the spirit of life, and man became a living being], Genesis 2: 7) and 'Et qui inspiravit illi animam quae operatur, | Et qui insufflavit ei spiritum vitalem' [and who inspired in him the spirit that operates, and who breathed into him the spirit of life], Wisdom 15: 11), and the 'replete' condition of the 'spirito novo': 'Ave gratia plena: Dominus tecum' [Hail full of grace; the Lord is with thee] (Luke 1: 28) and 'et repleti sunt omnes Spiritu Sancto' [and they were all filled with the Holy Spirit] (Acts 2: 4).[35] The products of human reason are incapable of clarifying a miracle of the calibre of the union of matter with spirit. Only God, by means of his *vestigia*, such as the Bible and the *Commedia*, can do this. Again, poetry, in the guise of the 'sacrato poema' (*Par.* XXIII. 62), which humbly follows and imitates the lessons of Scripture, proves to be a superior conduit to knowledge than scholastic philosophy and theology, whose deficiency is probably a consequence of their over-reliance on logical structures. Indeed, it is noteworthy that, in closing his biblically circumscribed presentation of the creation of the intellectual soul, Dante should underline the special ties that associate poetry to Scripture. Thus, when offering a final explanation of 'come animal divegna fante', Statius relies not on a biblical

---

34   Chiavacci Leonardi, II, 743–45; Gardner, pp. 154–57. Once more, Gardner makes clear the partiality of Nardi's explanation of these lines; see especially p. 156, n. 48.

35   On the significance of the *auctoritas* in the *Commedia*, see Gardner, pp. 174–79.

auctoritas but on an elegant poetic image:

> E perché meno ammiri la parola,
> guarda il calor del sol che si fa vino,
> giunto a l'omor che de la vite cola. (*Purg.* xxv. 76–78)[36]

Purgatorio xxv is tightly focused on establishing the *Commedia*'s unique credentials. Both the general analogies that Dante institutes between his poem and divine making and its connections to specific matters of doctrine reinforce the miraculous character of the 'poema sacro | al quale ha posto mano e cielo e terra' (*Par.* xxv. 1–2).

In the *Commedia*, Dante repeatedly stressed that the best way for humanity to arrive at knowledge of the divine was by interpreting the Bible and other transcendental *signa*.[37] Thanks to its ideological and formal complexity and its explicitly doctrinal ambitions, *Purgatorio* xxv is able to make this point in a particularly effective way. Indeed, the canto's emphasis on the necessary role of Scripture in elucidating the problem of the creation and survival of the intellectual soul is bolstered by two other Dantean passages connected to the *quaestio* — passages that can be read as a sort of *avant la lettre* 'gloss' on Statius's words. In the *Convivio*, when he examined the formation of a human being, Dante had found himself perplexed, in line with other philosophers, by how the 'anima in vita' might receive 'lo intelletto possibile':

> E però dico che quando l'umano seme cade nel suo recettaculo, cioè nella matrice, esso porta seco la vertù dell'anima generativa e la vertù del cielo e la vertù delli elementi legati, cioè la complessione; [e] matura e dispone la materia alla vertù formativa, la quale diede l'anima [del] generante; e la vertù formativa prepara li organi alla vertù celestiale, che produce della potenza del seme l'anima in vita. La quale, incontanente produtta, riceve della vertù del motore del cielo lo intelletto possibile; lo quale potenzialmente in sé adduce tutte le forme universali, secondo che sono nel suo produttore, e tanto meno quanto più dilungato dalla prima Intelligenza è.
>
> Non si maravigli alcuno s'io parlo sì che pare forte ad intendere; ché a me medesimo pare maraviglia come cotale produzione si può pur conchiudere e collo intelletto vedere. Non è cosa da manifestare a lingua, lingua, dico veramente, volgare. Per che io voglio dire come l'Apostolo: 'O altezza delle divizie della sapienza e della scienza di Dio, come sono incomprensibili li suoi giudicii e investigabili le sue vie!' [Romans 11: 33]. (*Conv.* iv. 21. 4–6)

According to Dante, the union is a 'maraviglia' that the human 'intelletto' cannot fathom. Yet, as Statius will reveal, the mystery is 'comprehensible' when trust is placed in the *vox Dei*. Remaining entangled in reason's earthbound constraints, as had happened to Dante in the *Convivio*, results in needless, because resolvable, ignorance. What distinguishes Statius's otherworldly lecture from the philosophical elucidation is of course the determining presence of the Bible. In the *Convivio*, after relying on Aristotelian *scientia*, Dante passively cites Scripture to seal his failure of understanding. In the *Purgatorio*, on the other hand, he resolves the same problem

---

36   On the effectiveness of the image, see Cogan, p. 138; Gardner, p. 185.

37   See Zygmunt G. Barański, *Dante e i segni: saggi per una storia intellettuale di Dante* (Naples: Liguori, 2000).

by actively weaving together biblical *sententiae* in a manner reminiscent of much religious discourse.

The second passage too — Virgil's despondent yet honest admission of his inability to understand how souls might suffer pain in the afterlife — is centred on the contrast between the flawed capacities of human reason and the infinite power of divine revelation:

> A sofferir tormenti, caldi e geli
> simili corpi la Virtù dispone
> che, come fa, non vuol ch' a noi si sveli.
>   Matto è chi spera che nostra ragione
> possa trascorrer la infinita via
> che tiene una sustanza in tre persone.
>   State contenti, umana gente, al *quia*;
> ché, se potuto aveste veder tutto,
> mestier non era parturir Maria;
>   e disïar vedeste sanza frutto
> tai che sarebbe lor disio quetato,
> ch'etternalmente è dato lor per lutto:
>   io dico d'Aristotile e di Plato
> e di molt' altri. (*Purg.* III. 31–44)

Given the controversial and unresolved nature of the problem of otherworldly being, it is thus appropriate that, more than any other element in *Purgatorio* XXV's richly connotative and culturally resonant structure, it should be Statius's explanation of the 'wonder' of the aerial body that validates the canto's crucial concerns, thereby affirming the centrality rather than the marginality, as Dante scholarship has tended to maintain, of lines 79–102:

> Quando Làchesis non ha più del lino,
> solvesi da la carne, e in virtute
> ne porta seco e l'umano e 'l divino:
>   l'altre potenze tutte quante mute;
> memoria, intelligenza e volontade
> in atto molto più che prima agute.
>   Sanza restarsi, per sé stessa cade
> mirabilmente a l'una de le rive;
> quivi conosce prima le sue strade.
>   Tosto che loco lì la circunscrive,
> la virtù formativa raggia intorno
> così e quanto ne le membra vive.
>   E come l'aere, quand' è ben pïorno,
> per l'altrui raggio che 'n sé si reflette,
> di diversi color diventa addorno;
>   così l'aere vicin quivi si mette
> e in quella forma ch'è in lui suggella
> virtüalmente l'alma che ristette;
>   e simigliante poi a la fiammella
> che segue il foco là 'vunque si muta,
> segue lo spirto sua forma novella.

Però che quindi ha poscia sua paruta,
è chiamata ombra; e quindi organa poi
ciascun sentire infino a la veduta. (*Purg.* XXV: 79–102)[38]

It is a critical commonplace to assert that Dante invented the doctrine of the

38   Gardner analyses the lines at pp. 186–206. He notes: 'Surely it must have appeared from the first that at some point, Statius would have to go somewhat afield from the permissible paths of theological and philosophical treatments of the separate existence of the soul or the requirements for sensation, and in what follows [beginning at line 85] he apparently does so with abandon' (p. 189). Gardner is especially good at highlighting the difficulties that Statius's *lectio* presents for Aristotelianism. Nonetheless, Gardner goes on to present a philosophically and theologically coherent reading of the Dantean aerial body: 'If the shade-bodies are not produced for sensation but for manifestation, moved rather than informed, then they are produced for the only one who can see them, the only subject of sensation. At the end of his discourse, Statius has in effect hinted that the shades are all for the pilgrim's sake' (p. 199); and he goes on to conclude: 'Under this rereading of the discourse, the same may be said, but now with at least some accuracy, and of a rather different conclusion. If the discourse indeed argued, according to the common reading, that the separated soul becomes the form of air and actually exercises sensory power through it, this would not be a new appropriation of Aristotelian principles under any interpretation, but a rather obvious disregard for them; the discourse as a whole would then be, at best, somewhat incoherent. There is, however, room to improvise, if one wishes to argue that the separated soul is the mover alone of such a body, and uses the body purely for physical manifestation. // In this case it would really be true that basic physical principles are not violated. Theologians such as Bonaventure and Thomas saw no logical impossibility in such a body being moved either by an angel (and that was a matter of historical occurrence according to Scripture, thus demanding explanation), or indeed by a separated soul, granting divine intervention (and that had somewhat less authority, needing only a brief hypothetical remark). Certainly Statius says nothing of the influence of divine power in the production of the shade bodies, and there is much yet to answer for regarding the coherence of the narrative under this understanding' (p. 205).
    I will be frank: I am persuaded by Gardner's interpretation. The problem thus arises of how his reading impacts on my argument. First and foremost, it supports my point that Statius's lecture on the aerial body should not be read as a poetic fiction. Second, as Gardner himself notes with reference to the Italian version of this *lectura*, Dante is effecting a synthesis: 'by Statius's argument, Dante makes a Herculean effort to draw together two modes of speculation on the interim state which had grown farther and farther apart since Gregory's *Dialogues*: strict theological consideration of what is logically possible for that state, and accounts of miraculous visions which cast aside all rational critique for the moving reality of what has been seen' (p. 206). Our arguments are complementary and not exclusive, their differing emphases the result of our differing perspectives: Gardner's aim is to establish the coherence of Statius's speech in its entirety, mine that of the canto.
    In any case, I would encourage anyone seriously interested in Dante to read Gardner's excellent thesis and not rely on my digests and selective quotation, although I should like to close this overlong yet necessary note by citing him one last time, since Patrick best summarizes his position: 'both the question and the answer of the discourse of *Purgatorio* XXV concern the shades' capacity for self-manifestation rather than sensation, on the grounds that such an understanding is not only permitted by the precise language of that canto, but also yields a more theologically coherent explanation of it — especially in light of the creation-passages of *Paradiso*. As a result, this interpretation would allow for a more meaningful dialogue between Dante's claims for the nature of the otherworld he portrays and the late medieval tradition of Catholic theological speculation on the afterlife using the terms and tools of Aristotelian anthropology. Understanding Statius's final assertion in terms of *movens* and *motum*, rather than *formans* and *formatum*, allows that the sensitive and vegetative powers remain 'tutte quante mute' without formal union to flesh and blood, and thereby preserves some continuity between the embryology with which he begins and the skialogy with which he concludes' (p. 207).

aerial body, and that, consequently, it is a matter of secondary importance, given that, as a literary fiction, its significance is inevitably limited. I find this claim quite unpersuasive. The import of the doctrine of the shade for arriving at an appropriate artistic and ideological assessment of the *Commedia* has already been noted. Indeed, in structural terms, *Purgatorio* XXV is constructed around the last, climactic part of Statius's speech. Equally, the proposition that the aerial body is a poetic invention is unconvincing. How likely is it that Dante would have reduced a doctrinally complex notion involving a fundamental aspect of divine creation to a simple *fictio*? In fact, as occurs with another passage where the poet deals with a key feature of the universe that, until recently, scholars had also dismissed as mere artistic fancy — the formation of Hell in *Inferno* XXXIV (see Barański, *Dante*, pp. 199–219) — when he presented the aerial body, Dante actually invented very little. Statius's doctrine of the shade, like Virgil's explanation of how Hell came into being, synthesizes and is based on a range of authoritative texts.

Most obviously, the creation of the aerial body mirrors the process of the formation of the human being described in lines 37–75. Dante evokes two 'births', thereby underlining the intimate relationship between life and death: a bond that constitutes one of the key elements that undergirds the artistic and ideological structure of the *Commedia*. Once again, in *Purgatorio* XXV, doctrinal and poetic aspects overlap; and the sources of the aerial body, like those of the physical body, not only elucidate the nature of the miracle, but also contribute to the canto's exploration of the relative value of different epistemologies and of the sacred character of the *Commedia*.[39]

To shape, but also to legitimate, the aerial body, Dante mainly and appropriately drew on texts that, like the *Commedia*, enjoyed the status of *vestigia Dei*.[40] In addition to what these works reveal about the nature of the aerial body, they contribute to defining the ideological and textual parameters of Dante's poem. Given that the *Commedia* shares their same divine imprint, it has no difficulty, unlike rationally based traditions, in assimilating and repeating their lessons. In *Purgatorio* XXV, the poet makes clear how we should evaluate his poem, as well as which texts we need to consult if we want to grasp the meaning of God's 'giudicii' and 'vie' (*Conv.* IV. 21. 6). Accordingly, Dante's aerial body can be linked to contemplative texts, to the literature on the resurrection of the body at the Last Judgment, and to the commentary tradition on passages in Genesis that deal with the creation of Adam. For example, in the *De diligendo Deo*, when Bernard of Clairvaux describes how, in the fourth degree of love, the spiritual body's human affections are transformed and lose themselves in the divine will while at the same enduring in the act of union — a description that immediately precedes the analysis of the relationship between the soul and the body after death (XI. 30–33) — he employs similes illustrating a process of ineffable, divinely prompted metamorphosis that return in the images Dante uses

39   The points made in this paragraph are now reinforced by Gardner's work on the doctrinal dimension of Statius's lecture on the aerial body.

40   Gardner himself stresses the serious interpretive difficulties involved in arriving at his reading of *Purg.* XXV. 79–102 (p. 206). It thus remains that the contemplative texts and commonplaces that I discuss would have been rather more readily accessible to a contemporary audience than the aerial body's abstruse philosophical-cum-theological ramifications.

to delineate the formation of the aerial body.[41] In both writers we find references to the effects of fire (97–99; and see also 22–23) and of the sun on the air (91–93), as well as an evocation of the reality of the body after death:

> Sic affici, deificari est. Quomodo stilla aquae modica, multo infusa vino, deficere a se tota videtur, dum et saporem vini induit et colorem, et quomodo ferrum ignitum et candens igni simillimum fit, pristina propriaque exutum forma, et quomodo solis luce perfusus aer in eamdem transformatur luminis claritatem, adeo ut non tam illuminatus quam ipsum lumen esse videatur, sic omnem tunc in sanctis humanam affectionem quodam ineffabili modo necesse erit semetipsa liquescere, atque in Dei penitus transfundi voluntatem. Alioquin quomodo omnia in omnibus erit Deus, si in homine de homine quidquam supererit? Manebit quidem substantia, sed in alia forma, alia gloria, aliaque potentia. Quando hoc erit? [...] Itaque in corpore spirituali et immortali, in corpore integro, placido placitoque, et per omnia subiecto spiritui, speret se anima quartum apprehendere amoris gradum, vel potius in ipso apprehendi, quippe quod Dei potentiae est dare cui vult, non humanae industriae assequi. (Bernard of Clairvaux, De diligendo Deo, x. 28–29)

> [To be in such a state is to become godlike. As a little drop of water, poured into much wine, seems to disappear completely, while it assumes the taste and colour of wine; and as the iron, heated and glowing, is very much like fire, despoiled of its own previous form; and as the air, filled with sunlight, is transformed into that same brightness of light, thus it looks not lit but a light itself; so in the saints all human affections must have melted away in some unspeakable way and been transferred completely into God's will. For how will God be everything in everything, if something human remains in man? His substance will endure, but in a different form, a different glory, and a different power. When will this happen? [...] thus only in a spiritual and immortal body, a perfect, peaceful, and lovely body, and in everything subjected to the spirit, shall the soul hope to reach, or rather be captured into, the fourth degree of love, which is in God's power to grant whom He will, not an achievement of the human effort.]

Moreover, it is common in Bernard, just as occurs in Dante's presentation of the aerial body, to find light, fire, air, and water united to describe the estranging impact of the divine on the human. It is, however, St Augustine who provides an explanation of the soul's effects on air, light, and fire in forming the body that has strong ties to Dante's description of how the aerial body comes into being:

> Quapropter non est quidem humanae animae naturae nec de terra nec de aqua nec de aere nec de igne quolibet; sed tamen crassioris corporis sui materiam, hoc est humidam quandam terram, quae in carnis uersa est qualitatem, per subtiliorem naturam corporis administrat, id est per lucem et aerem. Nullus enim sine his duobus uel sensus in corpore est uel ab anima spontaneus corporis motus. Sicut autem prius esse debet nosse quam facere, ita sentire prius est quam mouere. Anima ergo quoniam res est incorporeal corpus quod incorporeo uicinum est, sicuti est ignis uel potius lux et aer, primitus agit et per haec cetera quae crassiora sunt corporis, sicuti humor et terra — unde carnis corpulentia solidatur — quae magis sunt ad patiendum subdita quam praedita ad faciendum.[42]

---

41 Bernard of Clairvaux, De diligendo Deo, in Opera, III, 104–54.

42 Dante may be alluding to Augustine's phrase at Purg. XXV. 47: 'l'un disposto a patire, e l'altro a

Non mihi ergo uidetur dictum: factus est homo in animam uiuam, nisi quia sentire coepit in corpore: quod est animatae uiuentisque carnis certissimum indicium. (*De Genesi ad litteram* VII. 15. 21–16. 22; see also VII. 19. 25–20. 26)

[There is, accordingly, no particle of earth, water, air, or fire, in the nature of the human soul; nonetheless the soul administers the heavier elements of its own body — that is this kind of moist soil that has been transformed into flesh, through thinner components of the body, that is through light and air. Without these two there is in fact no physical sense in the body and no spontaneous motion of the body guided by the soul. Just as knowing must precede doing, so feeling precedes moving. Therefore the soul, which is incorporeal, first moves an element which is close to the incorporeal, just as fire, or rather as light and air, and through these the heavier elements of the body, as water and earth — which form the solid mass of the flesh — that are subject to enduring rather than made for acting.

I do not see why the text should say: man was created into a living being, if not because man starts to have sensation in his body: which is the most obvious sign of an animated and living flesh.]

Significantly, this passage is part of Augustine's extended gloss on Genesis 2: 7, a verse — as I have noted — that plays a key role in the structure of *Purgatorio* XXV.

Contemplative ecstasy, the action of the soul on the physical body, and the nature of the risen body, which was also frequently identified with light, do not quite correspond to Dante's aerial body. At the same time, to establish the authoritativeness and truthfulness of his *ombre* — we might say their 'reality' — Dante drew on descriptions of the externalization of the God-soul-body complex taken from works whose *auctoritas* as divine *signa* was incontestable. In this way, the poet ensured the coherence and orthodoxy of the *Commedia*'s doctrine of the aerial body. *Purgatorio* XXV, in fact, offers a rare and 'unique' (Gardner, p. 112) sustained explanation of the nature of the spiritual body. As a result, the status of the *Commedia* as a *vestigium Dei* crucially depends on the credibility of its presentation of the aerial body, since, by revealing this truth, the 'sacrato poema' (*Par.* XXIII. 62) casts new light on an aspect of divine creation. The *Commedia*'s standing as 'divine' is inextricably entwined with the validity of its revelations regarding the nature and reality of the aerial body. The remainder of the canto refers to its inspired status only *per analogiam*, through that system of metaphor and allusion that I dicussed earlier. In a final analysis, the fact that the poem imitates the forms of the *Deus artifex*, or that it absorbs *auctoritates* taken from the Bible and from other sacred texts,

fare'. In his turn, the Bishop of Hippo was adapting Cicero's words: 'aer et ignis movendi vim habent et faciendi, reliquae partes accipiendi et quasi patiendi, aquam dico et terram' [The air and the fire are able to move and act, and the remaining parts — I mean water and earth — can receive and, as it were, endure]: *De natura deorum. Academica*, trans. by H Rackham (Cambridge: Harvard University Press, 1979), I. 7. 26. The standard commentaries normally cite a passage from Thomas Aquinas as the line's likely source: 'In generatione distinguitur operatio agentis et patientis. Unde relinquitur quod tota virtus activa sit ex parte maris, passio autem ex parte feminae' [In generation there are two distinct operations — that of the agent and that of the patient. Thus it follows that the whole active power is on the part of the male, whereas the passive is on the part of the female] (*ST* III. q. 32. a. 4). It is noteworthy that, in terms of its content, line 47 is closer to Thomas, while, in its form, it recalls Augustine.

does not, in itself, guarantee its providentiality. It is only by unveiling to the world a *mirabile* that had hitherto remained shrouded in mystery that the *Commedia*'s special ties, and more generally those of poetry, to God are incontrovertibly established. The aerial body allows Dante to carry out successfully this risky strategy. However, in developing the doctrine of the *corpus spirituale*, he could not deviate too far from texts and codified elements that were able to give support and cogency to his treatment of the survival of the body in the afterlife. The aerial body is of course a Dantean 'invention'. However, not in the straightforward manner in which Dante scholarship has used the term to equate it with *fictio*. If the aerial body were no more than a literary artifice, then *Purgatorio* XXV's carefully crafted ideological structure would collapse, and the *Commedia* would lose its divine credentials. It is the 'sacred' sources of the aerial body, chosen with unerring precision, that transform 'invention' into divine 'fact' and the *Commedia* into a poetic *vestigium Dei*.

5. Beyond the Aerial Body

The aerial body stabilizes and anchors the main issues around which *Purgatorio* XXV revolves: from the relationship between the human and the divine to that between doctrine and poetry, and from the 'sacredness' of the *Commedia* to the primacy of inspired forms of knowledge. Yet, in keeping with his customary syncretism, Dante also introduced into the mix of his aerial body elements belonging to the Aristotelian tradition. Thus, when he constructed Statius's speech, Dante may well have recalled Aquinas's words on the bodies of angels:

> Dicendum quod licet aer, in sua raritate manens, non retineat figuram, neque colorem; quando tamen condensatur, et figurari et colorari potest, sicut patet in nubibus. Et sic angeli assumunt corpora ex aere, condensando ipsum virtute divina, quantum necesse est ad corporis assumendi formationem. (*ST* I. q. 51. art. 2. ad 3)[43]

> [It must be said, of course, that air, when rarified, does not keep a shape, nor a colour; but when it is condensed, it can take shape and colour, as it is clear in the clouds. And so the angels take their body from the air, by condensing it through a divine power, as far as it is necessary for the formation of a body that they can take up.]

Like the Bible, which, according to a standard exegetical trope, embraced and hierarchized the sum of knowledge, so the omniverous *Commedia* too, as *Purgatorio* XXV illustrates, brings together and evaluates different epistemologies.[44] Few

---

43   The same idea was present in other scholastic theologians; see Gardner, pp. 192–93 & 198–201, who emphasizes that 'the theologians are careful to note that the angel is not the form of the aerial body; to suggest this would be a category mistake, for a simply spiritual being cannot be the form of any body. Granted divine dispensation, an angel can take over the shape and movement of such an aerial body, a condescension for the sake of men who so often need to see in order to believe. Such bodies could simulate, to the eye, any human form or activity; but they could not have the activities actually belonging to composite life' (p. 192).

44   It is possible that, through his aerial bodies, Dante was also indicating his debts to the visionary tradition. Already in the seventh-century *Visio Baronti* we find the visionary being granted a body

other cantos clarify and legitimate the *Commedia*'s singularity with *Purgatorio* XXV's efficiency and range. Thus, there is more to the canto than its fundamental synthesis of doctrine, literature, and divine creation. For instance, the link that can be forged between the 'scientific' description of the generative act and the allusion, towards the end of the canto, to 'donne | [...] e mariti che fuor casti | come virtute e matrimonio imponne' (133–35) introduces the thorny question of the nature and ends of sexual relations between women and men.[45] Indeed, the same 'scientific' description alludes to the problem, also widely discussed in the Middle Ages, of the legitimacy of speaking about matters deemed to be *obscena* (see Chapter 19). As is fitting for a canto that illustrates the *Commedia*'s divine origins and that functions almost as a microcosm of the poem, the scope of its interests is imposing. Moreover, the problem of the relationship between God and humanity, and therefore of the ways in which we can know the divine will — the problem which is at the basis of *Purgatorio* XXV — touches every aspect of our existence. Consequently, the canto cannot but endeavour to offer at least a sense of the all-encompassing nature of our debts to God. It is because the bonds between the human and the divine, on account of our intellectual limitations, are so precarious that we are deeply dependent on the *vestigia Dei* and, specifically, on the *Commedia*. As *Purgatorio* XXV makes clear, we need to rely on the 'sacrato poema' (*Par.* XXIII. 62) if we want to have some idea of the divine will and, therefore, if we are serious about saving our soul and body or, to put it poetically, if we would rather 'laugh' than 'weep' in the afterlife.

of air and light similar to his physical body so that he might travel in the other world. See *Visio Baronti Monachi Longoretensis*, in *Monumenta Germaniae Historica, Scriptores Rerum Merovingicarum*, ed. by Wilhelm Levison, 7 vols (Hannover and Leipzig: Impensis Bibliopolii Hahniani, 1884–1910), v, 368–94 (pp. 380 & 392).

45   See Dyan Elliott, *Spiritual Marriage: Sexual Abstinence in Medieval Wedlock* (Princeton: Princeton University Press, 1993); Ferzoco, p. 58.

CHAPTER 10

Petrarch, Dante, Cavalcanti

1. Reading Petrarch Reading Dante

'Petrarca e Dante'; 'Dante in Petrarca'; 'Tra Dante e Petrarca': conjunctions and prepositions have played an unexpectedly vital role in determining the critical history of Petrarch's relationship to Dante.[1] The elimination of both grammatical

---

1   On Petrarch's relationship to Dante, see Claudio G. Antoni, 'Esperienze stilistiche petrose da Dante al Petrarca', *Modern Language Studies*, 13 (1983), 21–33; Marco Baglio, 'Presenze dantesche nel Petrarca latino', *Studi petrarcheschi*, n.s. 9 (1992), 77–136; Aldo S. Bernardo, 'Petrarch's Attitude toward Dante', *PMLA*, 70 (1955), 488–517, and 'Petrarch, Dante and the Medieval Tradition', in *Renaissance Humanism: Foundations, Forms and Legacy. 1. Humanism in Italy*, ed. by Albert Rabil Jr. (Philadelphia: University of Pennsylvania Press, 1988), pp. 115–37; Rosanna Bettarini, 'Perché "narrando" il duol si disacerba (Motivi esegetici dagli autografi petrarcheschi)', in *La critica del testo* (Rome: Salerno, 1985), pp. 305–20; Guido Capovilla, 'Petrarca e l'ultima canzone di Dante', *Lectura Petrarce*, 14 (1994), 289–358; Emilia Chirilli, 'Di alcuni dantismi nella poesia volgare di Francesco Petrarca', *L'Alighieri*, 16 (1975), 44–74; Annalisa Cipollone, ' "Né per nova figura il primo alloro...": la chiusa di *Rvf* XXIII, il Canzoniere e Dante', *Rassegna europea di letteratura italiana*, 11 (1998), 29–46; Michel David, 'Une réminiscence de Dante dans un sonnet de Pétrarque', in *Miscellanea di studi offerta a Armando Balduino e Bianca Bianchi per le loro nozze* (Padua: Seminario di Filologia moderna dell'università, 1962), pp. 15–19; Domenico De Robertis, 'Petrarca petroso', *Revue des études italiennes*, 29 (1983), 13–37, 'A quale tradizione appartenne il manoscritto delle rime di Dante letto dal Petrarca', *Studi petrarcheschi*, n.s. 2 (1985), 131–57, and 'Petrarca interprete di Dante (ossia leggere Dante con Petrarca)', *Studi danteschi*, 61 (1989), 307–28; Enrico Fenzi, 'Tra Dante e Petrarca: il fantasma di Ulisse', in his *Saggi petrarcheschi* (Fiesole: Cadmo, 2003), pp. 492–517; Michele Feo, 'Petrarca, Francesco', in ED, IV, 450–58; Giulio Ferroni, 'Tra Dante e Petrarca', in *Ulisse: archeologia dell'uomo moderno*, ed. by Piero Boitani and Richard Ambrosini (Rome: Bulzoni, 1998), pp. 165–85; Simon Gilson, *Dante and Renaissance Florence* (Cambridge: Cambridge University Press, 2005), pp. 32–40; Claudio Giunta, 'Memoria di Dante nei *Trionfi*', *Rivista di letteratura italiana*, 11 (1993), 411–52; Bernhard König, '*Dolci rime leggiadre*: zur Verwendung und Verwandlung stilnovistischer Elemente in Petrarcas *Canzoniere* (Am Beispiel des Sonnetts *In qual parte del ciel*)', in *Petrarca 1304–1374: Beiträge zu Werk und Wirkung*, ed. by Fritz Schalk (Frankfurt am Main: Klostermann, 1975), pp. 113–38; Peter Kuon, *L'aura dantesca: metamorfosi intertestuali nei 'Rerum vulgarium fragmenta' di Francesco Petrarca* (Florence: Cesati, 2004); Robert E. Lerner, 'Petrarch's Coolness toward Dante: A Conflict of "Humanisms" ', in *Intellectuals and Writers in Fourteenth-century Europe*, ed. by Piero Boitani and Anna Torti (Tübingen: G. Narr, 1986), pp. 204–25; Bortolo Martinelli, 'Dante nei *Rerum vulgarium fragmenta*', *Italianistica*, 10 (1981), 122–31; Giorgio Orelli, 'Dante in Petrarca', in his *Il suono dei sospiri: sul Petrarca volgare* (Turin: Einaudi, 1990), pp. 124–62; Gioacchino Paparelli, 'Due modi opposti di leggere Dante: Petrarca e Boccaccio', in *Giovanni Boccaccio editore e interprete di Dante* (Florence: Olschki, 1979), pp. 73–90; Emilio Pasquini, 'Dantismo petrarchesco: ancora su *Fam.* XXI 15 e dintorni', in *Motivi e forme delle 'Familiari' di Francesco Petrarca*, ed. by Claudia Berra (Milan: Cisalpino, 2003), pp. 21–38; Manlio Pastore Stocchi, 'Petrarca e Dante', *Rivista di studi danteschi*, 4 (2004), 184–204; Jennifer Petrie, 'Dante and Petrarch', in *Dante*

Comparisons, ed. by Eric Haywood and Barry Jones (Dublin: Irish Academic Press, 1985), pp. 137–45; Mario Petrini, 'Petrarca e Dante', *Critica letteraria*, 23 (1995), 365–76; Michelangelo Picone, 'Riscritture dantesche nel *Canzoniere* di Petrarca', *Rivista europea di letteratura italiana*, 2 (1993), 115–25; Paolo Possiedi, 'Petrarca petroso', *Forum italicum*, 8 (1974), 523–45; Ezio Raimondi, 'Petrarca lettore di Dante', in his *Le metamorfosi della parola: da Dante a Montale*, ed. by J. Sisco (Milan: Bruno Mondadori, 2004), pp. 173–232; Gerhard Regn, ' "Allegorice pro laurea corona": Dante, Petrarca und die Konstitution postmittelalterlicher Dichtungsallegorie', *Romanistisches Jahrbuch*, 51 (2000), 128–52; Luca Carlo Rossi, 'Petrarca dantista involontario', *Studi petrarcheschi*, n.s. 5 (1988), 301–16, and 'Presenze di Petrarca in commenti danteschi fra Tre e Quattrocento', *Aevum*, 70 (1996), 441–76; Marco Santagata, *Per moderne carte* (Bologna: il Mulino, 1990), pp. 25–91, and *I frammenti dell'anima* (Bologna: il Mulino, 1992), pp. 199–217; Gennaro Sasso, 'A proposito di *Inferno* XXVI 94–98: variazioni biografiche per l'interpretazione', *La cultura*, 40 (2002), 377–96; Sara Sturm-Maddox, 'Transformations of Courtly Love Poetry: *Vita Nuova* and *Canzoniere*', in *The Expansion and Transformations of Courtly Literature*, ed. by Nathaniel B. Smith and Joseph T. Snow (Athens: University of Georgia Press, 1980), pp. 128–40, and *Petrarch's Metamorphoses: Text and Subtext in the 'Rime sparse'* (Columbia: University of Missouri Press, 1985); Giuliano Tanturli, 'Il disprezzo per Dante dal Petrarca al Bruno', *Rinascimento*, 25 (1985), 199–219; Paolo Trovato, *Dante in Petrarca* (Florence: Olschki, 1979); Aldo Vallone, *Storia della critica dantesca dal XIV al XX secolo*, 2nd edn, 2 vols (Milan: Vallardi, 1981), I, 133–47; Giuseppe Velli, 'Il Dante di Francesco Petrarca', *Studi petrarcheschi*, n.s. 2 (1985), 185–99, and 'Petrarca, Dante, la poesia classica: *Ne la stagion che 'l ciel rapido inchina* (RVF, L) *Io son venuto al punto de la rota* (Rime, C)', *Studi petrarcheschi*, n.s. 15 (2002), 81–98; Nancy J. Vickers, 'Re-membering Dante: Petrarch's "Chiare, fresche et dolci acque" ', *MLN*, 96 (1981), 1–11, and 'Widowed Words: Dante, Petrarch, and the Metaphors of Mourning', in *Discourses of Authority in Medieval and Renaissance Literature*, ed. by Kevin Brownlee and Walter Stephens (Hanover: University Press of New England, 1989), pp. 97–108; Germaine Warkentin, 'The Form of Dante's "libello" and its Challenge to Petrarch', *Quaderni d'italianistica*, 2 (1981), 160–70; Tiziano Zanato, 'San Francesco, Pier delle Vigne e Francesca da Rimini', *Filologia e critica*, 2 (1977), 177–216. During the ten or so years since I completed this study, the following studies on Petrarch and Dante have appeared: Valentina Atturo, 'Dalla pelle al cuore: la "puntura" e il "colpo della pietra" dai trovatori a Petrarca', *Studj romanzi*, n.s. 8 (2012), 61–117 (esp. pp. 85–117); Giusi Baldissone, ' "Vera beatrice": Petrarca e il nome rinnegato', in her *Benedetta Beatrice: nomi femminili e destini letterari* (Milan: Franco Angeli, 2008), pp. 13–42; Claudia Berra, 'Appunti per una cronologia del Petrarca "petroso" ', in *Estravaganti, disperse, apocrifi petrarcheschi*, ed. by Claudia Berra and Paola Vecchi Galli (Milan: Cisalpino, 2007), pp. 99–116; Stefano Carrai, 'Petrarca lettore della *Vita nova* dantesca', *Atti e Memorie dell'Accademia Galileiana di Scienze, Lettere ed Arti in Padova*, 125 (2012–13), 203–11; K. P. Clarke, 'Boccaccio and the Poetics of the Paratext: Rubricating the Vernacular', *Le tre corone*, 6 (2019), 69–106; Martin Eisner, *Boccaccio and the Invention of Italian Literature: Dante, Petrarch, Cavalcanti and the Authority of the Vernacular* (Cambridge: Cambridge University Press, 2013); Peter Kuon, 'Petrarca lettore di Dante', *Letture classensi*, 37 (2008), 47–60, and ' "Tutte le lingue son mute" — prestiti danteschi nella lode di Laura (*Rvf* 325)', in *Francesco Petrarca: 1304–1374* (Merano/Meran: Accademia di studi italo-tedeschi/ Akademie deutsch-italienischer Studien, 2011), pp. 3–19; Irene Maffia Scariati, 'Petrarca lettore dell'*Iliade* di Giuseppe di Exeter e il primato del poema epico', *Studi mediolatini e volgari*, 54 (2008), 115–48; Nicolò Maldina, 'Dante, Petrarca e la cornice visionaria del *De casibus*', *Heliotropia*, 11:1 (2014), 79–104; Alice Malzacher, *'Il nodo che me ritenne': riflessi intertestuali della 'Vita Nuova' di Dante nei 'Rerum vulgarium fragmenta' di Petrarca* (Florence: Cesati, 2013); Mira Mocan, ' "Lucem demonstrat umbra": la serie rimica "ombra": "adombra" e il lessico artistico fra Dante e Petrarca', *Critica del testo*, 14:2 (2011), 389–423; Paolo Rigo, '*Fragmenta* danteschi e non solo: alcune riflessioni su due libri recenti e un "nuovo" metodo d'indagine del rapporto fra Dante e Petrarca', *Scaffale aperto. Rivista di italianistica*, 6 (2016), 123–39; Andrea Severi, 'Ancora sul rapporto tra Dante e Petrarca: il paragone materno di *Inf.* XXIII in *Epyst.* I, 14', *L'Alighieri*, 52 (2011), 141–49; Paola Vecchi Galli, 'Dante e Petrarca: scrivere il "padre" ', *Studi e problemi di critica testuale*, 79 (2009), 57–82. See also *Petrarch and Dante: Anti-Dantism, Metaphysics, Tradition*, ed. by Zygmunt G. Barański and Theodore J. Cachey Jr (Notre Dame, IN: University of Notre Dame Press, 2009).

categories in the title of my study marks a deliberate attempt to go beyond the parameters which, to date, have largely defined and, I believe, constrained discussions of Petrarch's attitude toward his great predecessor. The use of the 'neutral' comma to link the two poets' names is meant to suggest, first and foremost, a degree of exegetical independence from the scholarly mainstream. Indeed, it implies that Petrarch's view of Dante can be assessed outside the interpretive limits imposed by nearly two hundred years of scholarship — a possibility which, as I shall have occasion to explain, the introduction of Guido Cavalcanti's name into the title is also designed to indicate.

As is well known, Petrarch's relationship to Dante was, to say the least, complicated and ambiguous. If, on the one hand, he made few direct references to his father's companion in exile — references whose principal overt aim appears to have been to assert that, in artistic and intellectual terms, little connected him to Dante — on the other, as modern scholarship has so overwhelmingly demonstrated, his writings, beginning with the *Canzoniere*, resound powerfully with Dantean echoes. As a result of such contradictory evidence, critics have been able to put forward radically contrasting explanations of the nature of Petrarch's stance on Dante. Since the fourteenth century he has been accused of harbouring ill-concealed feelings of envy, of disdain, even of hatred toward the author of the *Commedia*. In general, such psychologizing interpretations are based on, and are supposed to account for, the suggestion, first circulated by Petrarch himself, that he had deliberately avoided reading Dante and hence was largely untouched by his influence.[2] More recently, however, scholars have definitively discredited the notion that Petrarch was somehow immune to Dante by diagnosing the extent to which his predecessor's poetry had infected his artistic system. As a result, scholars have largely left behind the longheld view of a resentful and embittered Petrarch. Instead, those who have continued to judge Petrarch's reaction to the poet of the *Commedia* as problematic have either talked generically of the 'distacco che lo separava da Dante',[3] or have explained his recourse to Dante as essentially agonistic in character.[4] Contributions that have stressed Petrarch's dissatisfaction with and 'separation' from the 'divine poet' can loosely be subsumed under the designation 'Petrarch and Dante', where the 'and' functions as an adversative preposition: 'Petrarch *against* Dante.' It was in the decade 1969–79 that perceptions began to change. Thanks to careful intertextual

---

2   'Odiosum ergo simulque ridiculum intelligis odium meum erga illum nescio quos finxisse [...]. Ea vero michi obiecte calumnie pars altera fuerat [...] nunquam librum illius habuerim [...]. Factum fateor, sed eo quo isti volunt animo factum nego. Eidem tunc stilo deditus [...] verebar ne si huius aut alterius dictis imbuerer [...] vel invitus ac nesciens imitator evaderem' [You see, therefore, that my hate against him which I do not know who invented is offensive and of course ridiculous [...]. The other utterly false accusation made against me is that [...] I have never had a book of his [...]. I admit that this is so, but I deny that it was done with that intention which those people claim. Since I was then devoted to the same style [...] I was afraid that, were I to immerse myself in his, or any other's, writings [...] I would end up an unwilling or unconscious imitator] (Petrarch, *Fam.* XXI. 15. 9–11).

3   Giuseppe Billanovich, 'L'altro stil nuovo: da Dante teologo a Petrarca filologo', *Studi petrarcheschi*, n.s. 11 (1994), 1–98 (p. 92).

4   See Lerner; Paparelli; Sasso; Tanturli; Warkentin.

analyses, most notably those of Marco Santagata and of Paolo Trovato,[5] Petrarch's persistent reliance on Dante's poetry and prose — specifically the *rime*, the *Vita nova*, and the *Commedia* — was unveiled for all to see; and, in the ensuing forty or so years, other critics have added significantly to these pioneering discoveries.[6] In its turn, this fundamental research can be catalogued under the tag 'Dante in Petrarch', where the weighty significance of that preposition 'in' is more than obvious. This is research of undoubted importance that has irreversibly altered our understanding of Petrarch's dependence on Dante. At the same time, however (and I shall soon return to these matters in greater detail), I find a number of its conclusions somewhat perplexing. In particular, it has encouraged the notion that, since Petrarch, especially in his vernacular writings, borrowed freely from Dante, his standpoint on his illustrious precursor must necessarily have been largely positive, and hence free of ambiguity and criticism. Indeed, it is claimed that Petrarch's relationship to his predecessor was so bereft of tension that the majority of his borrowings from Dante was spontaneously unconscious — marks of an effortless familiarity.[7] As a result,

5   Marco Santagata, 'Presenze di Dante "comico" nel Canzoniere', *Giornale storico della letteratura italiana*, 146 (1969), 163–211, reprinted in Santagata, *Per moderne carte*, pp. 25–78; Trovato, *Dante in Petrarca*; Marco Santagata, 'Dante in Petrarca', *Giornale storico della letteratura italiana*, 157 (1980), 445–52, reprinted in Santagata, *Per moderne carte*, pp. 79–91. See also Chirilli; Feo; Kuon (especially *L'aura dantesca*); Possiedi; Zanato. For important precursors of this type of study, see Lorenzo Mascetta-Caracci, *Dante e il 'Dedalo' petrarchesco* (Lanciano: Carabba, 1910), pp. 7–236; David.

6   There is a lack, in my view, of compelling evidence to support claims that Petrarch had read Dante's remaining Latin and vernacular prose works. Nonetheless, on Petrarch's possible knowledge of Dante's Latin prose writings, see Giuseppe Billanovich, *Petrarca letterato. I. Lo scrittoio del Petrarca* (Rome: Edizioni di 'Storia e letteratura', 1947), pp. 16 & 239, n. 2; Corrado Bologna, 'Occhi, solo occhi (*Rvf* 70–75)', in *Lectura Petrarcae Turicensis. Il Canzoniere. Lettura micro e macrotestuale*, ed. by Michelangelo Picone (Ravenna: Longo, 2007), pp. 183–205 (pp. 189–91); Lerner; Sara Sturm-Maddox, 'Dante, Petrarch, and the Laurel Crown', in Barański and Cachey, pp. 290–319; Velli, 'Il Dante di Francesco Petrarca', pp. 187, n. 3, & 190–91. At the same time, Albert Ascoli makes a sustained and persuasive case as regards Petrarch's likely knowledge of the eclogues in his 'Blinding the Cyclops', in Barański and Cachey, pp. 114–73. Several other scholars had previously mooted this possibility; for a brief survey of these suggestions, see Baglio, p. 94, n. 24. While there is no doubt that Petrarch was intimately familiar with the *Vita nova* and with the *Commedia*, it is harder to establish with the same degree of certainty how many of the *rime* he had actually read (Baglio, p. 94, n. 24). The fragmented and mediated nature of the poems' transmission, as well as the dependence of many of these on erotic and lyric commonplaces, makes such a task difficult, if not actually impossible. At the same time, we can be confident that Petrarch knew a fair number of the *rime*, including distinctive texts such as the *petrose*; see Bologna, p. 196; De Robertis, 'A quale tradizione'. As we shall see, what can be asserted rather more confidently is that Petrarch often conflated the 'lyric' and the 'comic' Dante to construct a reductively generic 'vernacular' Dante, whom he then further reduced merely to a love poet. In doing this, he 'unphilologically' conflated different moments of his predecessor's poetic career. This operation of *deminutio*, as I shall also attempt to demonstrate, should not be allowed to conceal Petrarch's overwhelming preoccupation with the Dante of the *Commedia*.

7   'L'*imitatio* [di Dante] del P. sarebbe per gli ultimi indagatori un evocare disinteressato della memoria, un riaffiorare naturale, spontaneo, di ritmi e timbri alle zone in cui la liricità si tramuta in onde sonore di parole e sospensioni, di arsi e di tesi. [...] La presenza della *Commedia* nel canzoniere sarebbe dunque soprattutto inconsapevole' (Feo, pp. 454–55). This critical tradition has its origins in Hermann Gmelin, 'Das Prinzip der *Imitatio* in den Romanischen Literaturen', *Romanische Forschungen*, 46 (1932), 83–360, and in Gianfranco Contini's famous 1965 essay 'Un'interpretazione di Dante', now in his *Varianti e altra linguistica* (Turin: Einaudi, 1970), pp. 369–405 (especially pp. 385–88). Its aim

rather than treating Petrarch's rare public statements on Dante as sly declarations of malice — the predominant perspective at least since Foscolo's day[8] — we should read them instead, in harmony with the proof apparently offered by the formal fabric of his poetry, as primarily expressions of appreciation.[9]

The effort to minimize, if not actually to neutralize, the tensions in Petrarch's treatment of Dante conforms well to a deep-seated trend in Italian literary historiography. The idea that Dante and Petrarch represent two distinct yet complementary intellectual and artistic alternatives, which together cover the field

is to confirm Petrarch's claim that any echo from Dante discernible in his poetry was unintended: 'Hoc unum non dissimulo, quoniam siquid in eo sermone a me dictum illius aut alterius cuiusquam dicto simile, sive idem forte cum aliquo sit inventum, non id furtim aut imitandi proposito, que duo semper in his maxime vulgaribus ut scopulos declinavi, sed vel casu fortuito factum esse, vel similitudine ingeniorum, ut Tullio videtur, iisdem vestigiis ab ignorante concursum' [This one thing I do wish to make clear, for if any of my vernacular writings resembles, or is identical to, anything of his or anyone else's, it cannot be attributed to theft or imitation, which I have avoided like reefs, especially in vernacular works, but to pure chance or — as Cicero thinks — because by similarity of mind one follows unintentionally the same path] (*Fam.* XXI. 15. 12). Several scholars who favour the view that Petrarch's *dantismo* was both largely unconscious and pacific have, surprisingly, made recourse to the Freudian notion of repression, and even to Harold Bloom's influential theory of 'anxiety of influence', to support their position. See De Robertis, 'Petrarca interprete di Dante', p. 319; Pasquini, pp. 34–38; Santagata, *I frammenti dell'anima*, p. 199; Trovato, p. 19. What critics who have done this fail to appreciate is that, by introducing concepts such as repression and anxiety into the exegetical mix, they undermine their own case regarding Petrarch's relaxed attitude towards Dante. Intriguingly, though with rather better justification, scholars who consider the poets' relationship to have been largely problematic have also drawn on Bloom's theory; see Roberto Antonelli, 'Perché un Libro(-Canzoniere)', *Critica del testo*, 6 (2003), 49–65 (p. 63); Lucia Battaglia Ricci, 'Il culto per Dante, l'amicizia con Petrarca', in *Dante e Boccaccio: Lectura Dantis Scaligera 2004–2005 in memoria di Vittore Branca*, ed. by Ennio Sandal (Rome and Padua: Antenore, 2006), pp. 21–54 (p. 37); Vickers, 'Widowed Words', p. 99.

8   See Ugo Foscolo, 'Parallelo fra Dante e Petrarca', in his *Saggi e discorsi critici*, ed. by Cesare Foligno (Florence: Le Monnier, 1953), pp. 279–97.

9   See Bettarini, p. 316; Capovilla, p. 296; Chirilli, pp. 72–74; De Robertis, 'Petrarca interprete di Dante'; Fenzi, 'Tra Dante e Petrarca', p. 515; Feo, pp. 456–57; Giunta; Martinelli; Pasquini; Santagata, 'Presenze di Dante "comico" nel Canzoniere', and 'Dante in Petrarca'; Velli, 'Il Dante di Francesco Petrarca', and 'Petrarca, Dante, la poesia classica'. At most, within this critical tradition, some scholars are willing to acknowledge that Petrarch's declarations on Dante were coloured by fundamentally respectful 'emulative' ambitions (Chirilli, p. 73) and by his new cultural ideas. I quote one of the most forceful expressions of the latter view: 'Le velate allusioni petrarchesche a Dante e lo stesso senso di disagio che pare accompagnarne i pochi frangenti di diretta menzione, vengono così oggi ricomposti nella prospettiva di un'innegabile distanza di progetti culturali che porta Petrarca a una sorta di difesa della propria autonomia letteraria di fronte all'imbarazzante poesia dantesca, comunque ampiamente compulsata nonché personalmente filtrata nei propri scritti' (Baglio, p. 95, n. 25). Such views have obvious points of contact with the positions of those who, preferring to highlight the problems relating to Petrarch's attitude towards Dante, have talked of his *distacco* from his precursor. In the light of this last observation, this would seem to be the appropriate point to acknowledge that my schematization of the scholarship on Petrarch and Dante — a scheme which adapts suggestions first made by Santagata in his pioneering research (*Per moderne carte*, pp. 79–84) — is precisely that, a schematization, an attempt to offer a broad, though I hope not entirely inaccurate, presentation of the essential features of a long-established and complex critical debate. Especially in recent years, the differences between the two main opposing interpretations have begun to diminish.

of literary endeavour, has its roots once more in the Trecento. It is enough to remember Benvenuto da Imola's lapidary distinction: 'Sed certe quanto Petrarcha fuit maior orator Dante, tanto Dantes fuit maior poeta ipso Petrarcha' [But as undoubtedly Petrarch was a greater orator than Dante, so Dante was a greater poet than Petrarch].[10] As a result, it is a critical commonplace to consider Italian literature as delicately, though reassuringly, caught between the contrasting possibilities offered by its two great exemplary 'founding fathers' — 'Tra Dante e Petrarca' — a condition which not even the third of the *tre corone* could, or wished to, escape.[11] Consequently, Boccaccio too is neatly assigned a representative role. In this grand historiographical narrative, Dante and Petrarch are presented as alternatives, *not* as antagonists. Conversely, however, interpretations that portray Petrarch as motivated by rancour in his judgments of Dante inevitably undermine the cosy picture of a national literary tradition harmoniously guided by its two greatest writers. Such troublesome and disturbing interpretations introduce doubt, strain, and imbalance into the idealized, tidy world of histories of literature, and so, as sources of unease, are prime candidates for elimination. More specifically, as far as the precise argument of this chapter is concerned, the perception of Dante and Petrarch as colossi bestriding Italian literature tends to isolate both them and their contacts from the cultural environment in which their relationship perforce developed. At most, that other 'giant', Boccaccio, is allowed to intrude into their lofty solitude.[12] Thus, the presence of Guido Cavalcanti's name in my title serves as an emblematic reminder of the fundamental importance of that elided context. Indeed, as we shall see, fourteenth-century culture cannot be ignored if we wish to understand Petrarch's reactions not simply to Dante but also to Cavalcanti.

Yet, as a rule, regardless of whether Petrarch's approach to Dante is deemed to have been negative or positive, both critical positions do just that: they tend to discuss the nature of the poet's *dantismo* in a vacuum. In fact, their exegetical rigour and hence their interpretive effectiveness are additionally weakened by other serious shortcomings of method. In general, psychologizing explanations are largely conjectural, unless documentary evidence can be adduced to support their essentially speculative claims. Such proof, in Petrarch's case, is conspicuously lacking. Indeed, the poet vehemently denied being prey to strong adverse sentiments with respect

---

10   Benvenuto da Imola, *Comentum super Dantis Aldigherii Comoediam*, ed. by James Philip Lacaita, 5 vols (Florence: Barbera, 1887), IV, 309.

11   See in particular Natalino Sapegno, 'Tra Dante e il Petrarca', in *Storia letteraria del Trecento* (Milan and Naples: Ricciardi, 1963), pp. 169–96; Giuseppe Billanovich, 'Tra Dante e Petrarca', *Italia medioevale e umanistica*, 8 (1965), 1–44, a reduced and revised version of which appeared with the title 'Il vecchio Dante e il giovane Petrarca', in *Letture classensi*, 11 (1982), 99–118. Fenzi's study of the same main title, 'Tra Dante e Petrarca: il fantasma di Ulisse', is not a historical survey, but, as its subtitle suggests, it examines Petrarch's views on Ulysses in the light of Dante's treatment of the classical hero. Equally, Giulio Ferroni's 'Tra Dante e Petrarca' explores the treatment of Ulysses in the works of the two writers. Theodore J. Cachey's 'Between Petrarch and Dante: Prolegomenon to a Critical Discourse', in Barański and Cachey, pp. 3–49, provides a convincing 'against the grain' (p. 3) deconstruction of the deeply rooted critical approach highlighted here.

12   For an interesting attempt to revise standard perceptions of the relationship between Dante, Petrarch, and Boccaccio, see Eisner.

to Dante.[13] To dismiss the significance of his assertions simply by invoking the Freudian unconscious does not seem to me to be the best way of corroborating a problematic, because philologically unsubstantiated, viewpoint. Rather, if we wish to arrive at some idea of Petrarch's attitude toward Dante, we need to start by trying to pick up, however faintly these may reach us, the possible cultural resonances of his comments on his predecessor. To put it a bit differently, before attempting more risky interpretations, we ought first to do our best to consider the possible literal meanings of Petrarch's words, thereby following the sensible example of our medieval forebears who stressed that every reading had to begin from a careful elucidation of the *lictera*.[14] However, a lack of interest in the 'letter' of Petrarch's declarations has characterized the debate on his possible ties to Dante. If some scholars have wanted to recognize a profound resentment behind his words, others, behind the very same words, have preferred to hear the strains of admiration — an admiration not necessarily supported by what Petrarch actually says but by the fact that, elsewhere, his writing is rich in borrowings from Dante.

The latter approach seems a strange way to proceed. To equate uncritically the simple fact that an author borrows heavily from a single source with endorsement for that same source does not smack of philological commonsense. Such an approach is especially problematic when used as the basis for establishing what a Trecento writer might have thought about Dante. In the light of the pervasiveness and variety of Dante's impact on fourteenth-century poetry, it is important to move with caution when making claims about the status, and hence possible meaning, of echoes from his writings overheard in the texts of his fellow poets. Thus, some borrowings, or Dantisms, are almost certainly indirect, having been mediated, and so largely neutralized, through the verses of others (in Petrarch's case, it is enough to think of the intervening role of Cino).[15] Likewise, Dante's uniquely personal poetic language became closely associated with the general language of Trecento poetry and culture, thereby further loosening its ties to its author. For much of the fourteenth century, Dante's Italian was the literary vernacular of Italy, and as such constituted a common resource. Dante was 'everywhere'. As Petrarch put it, Dante's *liber* was 'sine difficultate parabilis' [easily available] (*Fam.* XXI. 15. 10), and the *Commedia* was appreciated even by *fullones, caupones,* and *lanistae* [fullers, tavern keepers, and woolworkers] (*Fam.* XXII). Therefore, if we wish to establish the nature

13   'In primis quidem odii causa prorsus nulla est erga hominem nunquam michi nisi semel, idque prima pueritie mee parte, monstratum' [First of all, I have never had any reason at all to hate a man, whom I have never seen, except for once in the first part of my childhood] (*Fam.* XXI. 15. 7). In fact, as we shall see, the image that Petrarch was keen to project as regards his attitude to Dante was one of respectful yet detached objectivity.

14   On the *lictera* in medieval literary criticism, see Alastair J. Minnis, *Medieval Theory of Authorship*, 2nd edn (Aldershot: Scolar Press, 1988), pp. 73–159.

15   On Petrarch and Cino, see Armando Balduino, 'Cino da Pistoia, Boccaccio e i poeti minori del Trecento', in *Colloquio Cino da Pistoia* (Rome: Accademia Nazionale dei Lincei, 1976), pp. 33–85; Edward L. Boggs, 'Cino and Petrarch', *MLN*, 94 (1979), 146–52; Santagata, *Per moderne carte*, passim; Franco Suitner, *Petrarca e la tradizione stilnovistica* (Florence: Olschki, 1977), pp. 99–156; Guido Zaccagnini, 'Il Petrarca e Cino da Pistoia', in *Convegno petrarchesco*, 2 vols (Arezzo: Accademia Petrarca, 1936), I, 2–21.

of Trecento reactions to Dante, we ought to try to discriminate, on the basis of their effects and 'markedness', between different types of intertextuality. The mere fact of a high incidence of borrowings from Dante, even in a writer as meticulously reflective and as sophisticatedly versed in the ways of *imitatio* as Petrarch, may point to little more than the older Florentine's remarkable contemporary popularity.[16] Moreover, there is no necessary correlation between approval (or, in fact, disapproval) and the degree to which one poet repeats another.[17] Similarly, authors' explicit statements on their peers can be at odds with the recourse they actually make to the works of those same writers. In any case, it is notoriously difficult to be precise about the significance of intertextual evidence. As a norm, therefore, when assessing the relationship between two writers, it would appear prudent to begin by considering any declarations each may have made about the other. Once these have been elucidated, reference points exist against which intertextual practices can be tested and evaluated. This is the approach I intend to pursue in this study by focusing on Petrarch's direct references to Dante in the *Canzoniere*, the *Triumphi*, and the letters.[18] My approach, therefore, is in stark contrast to the tack taken by proponents of 'Dante in Petrarch', who, keen to hear everywhere the same tones of admiration, expend little effort in distinguishing between the different ways in which Petrarch had recourse to Dante. In fact, there has been a generalized tendency among scholars of Petrarch, regardless of their take on the specific question of his response to Dante, to 'banalize' the poets' relationship either by forcing its multiform aspects — from the intertextual borrowing to the metrical and generic imitation (the *Triumphi*) to the direct comment (*Rer. mem.* II. 83; *Rvf.* 287. 10; *Tr. Cup.* IV. 31; *Fam.* XXI. 15; *Sen.* V. 2) — into an 'unproblematic' totalizing characterization, or by considering individual aspects of his reaction to Dante in isolation.[19] There have thus been limited attempts to explore, first, the possible inter-relationships and differences between the different textual forms that record Petrarch's encounter with Dante; second, how in practice Petrarch assembled 'his' Dante; third, the implications of this process; fourth, whether Petrarch's construction of Dante is actually as one-dimensional as has been widely assumed;

16   If Petrarch's borrowings from Dante were mostly of this type, then it would be difficult to challenge the view that his *dantismo* was largely unconscious. It is one of the aims of this study to explore the extent to which Petrarch's recourse to Dante was culturally unreflective.

17   In his excellent article, Manlio Pastore Stocchi notes that 'la misura documentabile delle ricorrenze memoriali non è, per sé, correlata a una effettiva disponibilità del Petrarca a riconoscere la grandezza di Dante o a fargli ammettere una reale sintonia d'ingegno e di gusto' (p. 192).

18   I do not intend to examine Petrarch's presentation of Dante in the *Rerum memorandarum libri*, since their 'two *novelle* about Dante at the court of Cangrande della Scala, [...] though emphasizing his excellence in vernacular poetry, [...] essentially modulate some traditional motifs of novelistic literature on the "proud and disdainful poet"' (Gilson, p. 37), and hence are somewhat eccentric to his normal treatment of Dante. A few other traces of Petrarch's reaction to Dante have reached us. For his fleeting polemical annotation against Dante in a manuscript of Pomponius Mela, see Billanovich, 'Tra Dante e Petrarca', pp. 39–40; on the hitherto undeciphered autograph annotation to *Inf.* II. 24–26 in Vat. lat. 3199, see Armando Petrucci, *La scrittura di Francesco Petrarca* (Vatican City: Biblioteca Apostolica Vaticana, 1967), pp. 48, n. 8, & 118. See also n. 49 below.

19   Petrarch also refers to Dante in a variant of *Tr. Cup.* III. 99; see Subsection 3, 'Delimiting Dante: *Triumphus Cupidinis* IV. 28–38', below.

and finally, the extent to which the Petrarchan Dante relates to the different, often conflicting, strands of fourteenth-century reaction to the poet of the *Commedia*. As I hope is becoming evident, by emphasizing matters of context, whether textual, historical, or cultural, the primary aim of this study is to attempt to redress these and related critical shortcomings — shortcomings that have unnecessarily constrained our appreciation of Petrarch's *dantismo*.[20]

2. Delimiting Dante: 'Sennuccio mio, benché doglioso et solo'

> Sed esto; non sim dignus cui credatur. Quam tandem veri faciem habet ut invideam illi qui in his [vernacular studies] etatem totam posuit, in quibus ego vix adolescentie florem primitiasque posuerim? ut quod illi artificium nescio an unicum, sed profecto supremum fuit, michi iocus atque solatium fuerit et ingenii rudimentum? Quis hic, precor, invidie locus, que ve suspitio est? Nam quod inter laudes dixisti, potuisse illum si voluisset alio stilo uti, credo edepol — magna enim michi de ingenio eius opinio est — potuisse eum omnia quibus intendisset; nunc quibus intenderit, palam est. (Petrarch, *Fam.* xxi. 15. 21–22)

> [But let us assume that for some I am deemed unworthy of belief. Yet how true can it be that I am envious of a man who devoted his entire life to those things that were only the flower and first fruits of my youth? How, when what was for him, if not his only occupation, surely his principal one, was for me mere sport, a pastime, a mental exercise? What ground, I ask, could there be for envy or mistrust? In praising him you suggest that he could, if he wished, have used another style; I heartily agree, since I have the highest esteem for his ability, that he could do anything he undertook; but what he did choose to attempt is clear.]

What is immediately striking about Petrarch's assessment of Dante's intellectual and literary achievements is that it does not seem appropriate to regard it, in straightforward terms, as either damning or sympathetic. It is even less appropriate to view it as exclusively about Dante. On the one hand, it seems hard to dispute that Petrarch is comfortable recognizing Dante's eminence as a vernacular writer of remarkable *ingenium*; at the same time, however, he is also clearly bent on distinguishing himself from his predecessor. In essence, he, Petrarch, quite early on in life, realized that pursuing a career as a vernacular intellectual was markedly inferior to dedicating himself to Latin studies — a fact that Dante never succeeded in grasping. Thus, as *Fam.* xxi. 15 demonstrates, it is important to remember, first, that when Petrarch spoke about Dante he was invariably, if not primarily, also speaking about himself; and, second, that he elaborated his two-sided presentation

---

20   Naturally, there have been some previous attempts, particularly outside Italy, to assess and explain Petrarch's treatment of Dante without downplaying too much the tensions and contradictions that characterize their encounter; see Bernardo, 'Petrarch's Attitude toward Dante'; Gilson, pp. 32–40; Kuon's three contributions; Pastore Stocchi; Warkentin. In particular, Pastore Stocchi declares: 'mi avventurerò a suggerire che anche il sofferto rapporto del Petrarca con Dante non possa essere colto nei suoi aspetti piú complessi e storicamente significativi attraverso le mere coincidenze e reminiscenze formali, e vada affrontato invece in una piú integrale visone storico-culturale e persino civile' (p. 192).

in such a manner that it normally ended up by working to his advantage.[21] To put it a bit differently, Petrarch was not really interested in considering Dante on his merits, though, as we shall see, he was keen to create the impression that this was precisely what he was doing. To attempt to understand Petrarch's attitude to Dante is to be faced with layer upon layer of complication and ambiguity; and, to be sure, there is significantly more that can be said about the passage under discussion — and indeed about the letter as a whole — and I shall return to both in due course. What I should like to stress here, however, is that there is nothing unreflective or emotional, never mind 'unconscious', about the way Petrarch carefully evaluated himself and Dante. His rhetorical and discursive structures point to a writer in firm control of his argument — one, in fact, pursuing a deliberate strategy. In the face of Dante's overwhelming contemporary *auctoritas*, Petrarch's intent was not so much to query his 'authoritativeness' as to raise questions about its nature and remit.[22] In the fourteenth century, it would have been quite absurd to deny Dante's standing; or, as Petrarch declared, it would have been ridiculous to be envious of him. Petrarch was far too sophisticated a cultural operator and ambitious an intellectual to place himself in direct, and so outlandish, opposition to Dante. Equally, and for the same reasons, he was unwilling to place himself in a condition of passive imitation and

21   Kuon is especially good on the ways in which Petrarch used Dante in order to define himself and establish his own cultural superiority: '[i]l concetto di "riscrittura" implica l'idea di un'imitazione attiva che rovescia la prospettiva dantesca' (*L'aura dantesca*, p. 52). Other critics too, intent on countering the idea that Petrarch's appropriation of Dante was largely unconscious, have explored the ways in which the poet explicitly used Dantean elements to stress the differences between himself and his predecessor — a strategy that invariably highlights the superiority of his own ideological and artistic solutions; see Gilson, pp. 33–34; Picone, 'Riscritture dantesche'; Roberto Mercuri, 'Genesi della tradizione letteraria italiana in Dante, Petrarca e Boccaccio', in *Letteratura italiana. Storia e geografia. I. L'età medievale*, ed. by Alberto Asor Rosa (Turin: Einaudi, 1987), pp. 229–455 (pp. 334–44 & 360–76); Pastore Stocchi, p. 188; Sturm-Maddox, *Petrarch's Metamorphoses*. See also Subsection 5, ' "Disguising" Dante', below.
22   On Dante's fourteenth-century reception, see at least Gian Carlo Alessio, 'La *Comedìa* nel margine dei classici', in *Studi di filologia medievale offerti a D'Arco Silvio Avalle* (Milan and Naples: Ricciardi, 1996), pp. 1–25; Zygmunt G. Barański, '*Chiosar con altro testo*': leggere Dante nel Trecento (Fiesole: Cadmo, 2001); Saverio Bellomo, 'La *Commedia* attraverso gli occhi dei primi lettori', in *Leggere Dante*, ed. by Lucia Battaglia Ricci (Ravenna: Longo, 2002), pp. 73–84, and 'Introduzione', in his *Dizionario dei commenti danteschi* (Florence: Olschki, 2004), pp. 1–49; Elisabetta Cavallari, *La fortuna di Dante nel Trecento* (Florence: Perrella, 1921 (this study needs to be read with a degree of caution)); Guido di Pino, 'L'antidantismo dal Trecento al Quattrocento', *Letture classensi*, 5 (1976), 125–48; Gilson, pp. 21–83; Gioacchino Paparelli, 'Dante e il Trecento', in *Dante nel pensiero e nell'esegesi dei secoli XIV e XV: Atti del III Congresso Nazionale di Studi Danteschi* (Florence: Olschki, 1975), pp. 31–70; Marco Petoletti, 'La fortuna di Dante fra Trecento e Quattrocento', in *La Divina Commedia di Alfonso d'Aragona re di Napoli: commentario al codice*, ed. by Milvia Bollati, 2 vols (Modena: Panini, 2006), I, 159–86; Antonio Enzo Quaglio, Andrea Ciotti, and Bruno Basile, 'Commedia', in *ED*, II, 83–86 & 99–103; Vittorio Rossi, 'Dante nel Trecento e nel Quattrocento', in his *Scritti di critica letteraria: saggi e discorsi su Dante*, 2 vols (Florence: Sansoni, 1930), I, 293–332; Bruno Sandkühler, *Die frühen Dantekommentare und ihr Verhältnis zur mittelalterlichen Kommentartradition* (Munich: Max Hueber Verlag, 1967); Aldo Vallone, *Antidantismo politico nel XIV secolo: primi contributi* (Naples: Liguori, 1974), and *Storia della critica dantesca*, I, 51–230; *Interpreting Dante: Essays on the Traditions of Dante Commentary*, ed. by Paola Nasti and Claudia Rossignoli (Notre Dame, IN: University of Notre Dame Press, 2013), pp. 17–327.

doting discipleship in respect of the poet of the *Commedia*. Neither position, it goes without saying, would have done him many favours. He presents himself instead as willing to acknowledge Dante's achievements, though, at the same time, as decidedly unwilling to judge these as absolute, namely, as unreservedly 'authoritative'. His aim, therefore, appears to have been to redimension and delimit Dante's enormous cultural prestige, thereby opening up a space in which to locate himself and his own work; and much of what follows focuses on just these matters. Contrary, therefore, to what scholars have long and reductively maintained, the issue when examining Petrarch's relationship to Dante is not whether Petrarch was for or against his fellow poet; rather, the vital issue — one much more attuned to the cultural circumstances of the Trecento — is what precisely did Petrarch suggest were Dante's achievements and, by extension, what exactly did he think were his failings; and, furthermore, how did he relate his assessment of Dante's strengths and weaknesses, namely, 'his' image of Dante, to that other image — of himself — that he was simultaneously and obsessively constructing. I believe that, by offering answers to these questions, we can begin to have a sense of Petrarch's largely self-serving view of his illustrious yet oppressive precursor, as well as an effective yardstick with which to measure his persistent borrowing from Dante.

Given Petrarch's emphasis on Dante's vernacular prowess, it seems reasonable to begin by attempting to establish what kind of vernacular writer he considered the older poet to have been. Only once, and then fleetingly, did Petrarch explicitly name Dante in each of his two major vernacular works, the *Canzoniere* and the *Triumphi* — a reticence which straightway cannot but make one suspicious that, as in *Fam.* XXI. 15, the Dante presented in their pages will be stripped of a large part of his *auctoritas*. In November 1349, ten years before he penned his famous epistle to Boccaccio refuting accusations that he harboured negative feelings toward Dante, Petrarch commemorated the death of his close friend, Sennuccio del Bene, with the sonnet 'Sennuccio mio, benché doglioso et solo', number 287 in the *Rerum vulgarium fragmenta*.[23] Remembering one poet, Petrarch alluded to four others, among whom is Dante:

> Ma ben ti prego che 'n la terza spera
> Guitton saluti, et messer Cino, et Dante,
> Franceschin nostro, et tutta quella schiera. (*Rvf.* 287. 9–11)

His strategy is obvious. By locating Dante 'in the third sphere', namely the heaven of Venus, and associating him with these particular poets, Petrarch restricted Dante's cultural status to that of a love poet.[24] More specifically, he reduced Dante

---

23   Joseph A. Barber, 'Il sonetto CXIII e gli altri sonetti a Sennuccio', *Lectura Petrarce*, 2 (1982), 21–39; Daniele Piccini, *Un amico del Petrarca: Sennuccio del Bene e le sue rime* (Rome and Padua: Antenore, 2004), pp. xxv–xxxi, xxxiii–xxxix. See also Billanovich, 'L'altro stil nuovo', pp. 5–17, 19–22, 24–27, 48–50, 52–67, 74–78, 90.

24   That Petrarch limits Dante to love poetry both in sonnet 287 and in the *Triumphi* (see the following subsection) has been previously noted by Gilson, pp. 37–38, and by Trovato, p. 19. Feo underplays the negative implications of Petrarch's reductive definition: 'Omaggio d'occasione che non mira certo a deprimere l'Alighieri confondendolo con altri di minor levatura, ma che è circoscritto senza equivoci al rimatore d'amore' (p. 450). As regards Petrarch's attempt to 'diminish'

simply to one such poet among a large 'schiera' of erotic versifiers — a radical
curtailment of his contemporary image. Nor did Petrarch stop there. He went on to
delimit even Dante's standing as a poet of love. Thus, if one compares his treatment
of the Florentine with that of the other poets he mentions, Dante emerges yet more
dramatically diminished: 'Guitton saluti, et messer Cino, et Dante, | Franceschin
nostro' (10–11).[25] It is immediately striking that, unlike his presentation of Cino and
Franceschino degli Albizzi, poets of undoubted less burnished lustre than the author
of the *Commedia*, Dante's name is not qualified by a positive term of appreciation.
Furthermore, if, at first sight, the polemical implications of this omission seem
to be counterbalanced by the fact that Petrarch placed Dante's name in rhyme
position, that is to say in the most privileged part of the line, the polemical intent
of his operation returns with all its force when one notes the name, also introduced
without an epithet, that is located in the line's other stressed position, namely in
its opening. To bracket Dante with Guittone, especially if the aim is to challenge
and impose limits on the Florentine's *auctoritas*, is an extremely effective stratagem.
It cleverly succeeds in turning Dante against himself: the objections that he had
so publicly levied against the Aretine are made to sound hollow and self-serving,
given that the two of them are now presented as poetic partners. As a result, and
more seriously for Dante's reputation as an 'authority', Petrarch raises doubts not
just about his critical acumen and self-awareness, but also about his literary prowess.
Finally, beyond its direct implications for Dante, Petrarch's approach in sonnet 287
confirms once more his intimate knowledge of his precursor's major vernacular
works, the *Vita nova* and the *Commedia* — a knowledge, in fact, without which it
would have been impossible for him to carry out his delicately destructive strategy
of revision, reduction, and aspersion.[26]

By restricting Dante to love poetry, especially in a poem set in the afterlife, the
principal and actual target of Petrarch's attack comes clearly into sight. His intent
was to challenge the contemporary obsession with and canonization of the *Commedia*
as a text whose 'authority' not only matched but also actually outstripped that of the
great poets of antiquity. From Petrarch's perspective, he was well within his rights
to do this; indeed, as a man whose cultural views had been shaped and refined by
his detailed and historically sensitive study of the classics, it was his intellectual duty

Dante, Gennaro Sasso writes: '"Letteraria perfidia" sarà espressione troppo cruda; e si dica allora di
una tal quale, nei riguardi di Dante, *voluntas minuendi*, quasi che il nascosto proposito fosse di ridurre
il grand'uomo nell'ambito di una sua vicenda familiare, in un quadro domestico, dominato bensì
dall'esilio, e quindi tragico, ma, appunto, domestico, e richiamato al di qua del suo significato morale
e politico' (pp. 391–92).

25   On Petrarch's relationship to the three poets mentioned, see Laura Paolino, '"Ad acerbam
rei memoriam": le carte del lutto nel codice Vaticano Latino 3196 di Francesco Petrarca', *Rivista di
letteratura italiana*, 11 (1993), 73–102 (pp. 86–92); Daniele Piccini, 'Franceschino degli Albizzi, uno
e due', *Studi petrarcheschi*, n.s. 15 (2002), 129–86; Decio Pierantozzi, 'Il Petrarca e Guittone', *Studi
petrarcheschi*, 1 (1948), 145–65; Suitner; Santagata, *Per moderne carte*, pp. 128–37.

26   In sonnet 287, Petrarch is not exclusively curtailing Dante's artistic status. His presentation also
diminishes the poetic achievements of Guittone and Cino — an operation that he repeats elsewhere,
most notably in the *Triumphi* (a point which I address below). At the same time, it is undoubtedly the
case that Petrarch's assault on Dante is of a quite different order from his attack on other poets.

to unmask the *Commedia* as a middling vernacular love poet's inevitably flawed attempt at writing an epic; and the *Triumphi* make the same criticism, albeit in a much more sustained manner.[27] In particular, sonnet 287 calls into question the claims Dante makes throughout the 'sacrato poema' (*Par.* XXIII. 62) as regards the truth and the divinely inspired character of his account of the other world. When Petrarch described Sennuccio's condition in eternity, he quite deliberately recalled an emblematic moment of Dante's celestial journey:

> Alteramente se' levato al volo.
> Or vedi insieme l'un et l'altro polo,
> le stelle vaghe et lor viaggio torto. (*Rvf.* 287. 4–6)

After arriving in the heaven of the fixed stars, the pilgrim, like Sennuccio, casts an all-embracing look at the wonder and vastness of creation — a glance which also serves to confirm the miraculous, and hence true, nature of his experience (*Par.* XXII. 103–05 for the theme of flight; 118–20 for the divinely sanctioned character of his ascent; and 128–29 & 133–53 for the look at the heavens and down to earth). Yet, it is these fundamental features of the *Commedia* that Petrarch energetically disputes, underlining unambiguously that only Sennuccio, as an inhabitant of Paradise, can actually enjoy such a marvellous vision. This is a privilege that lies beyond the possibilities of the living: 'et vedi il veder nostro quanto è corto' (*Rvf.* 287. 7). This line too is a calque on Dante:

> Or tu chi se', che vuo' sedere a scranna,
> per giudicar di lungi mille miglia
> con la veduta corta d'una spanna? (*Par.* XIX. 79–81)

Once again the borrowing is highly revelatory. The eagle of justice accuses the *viator* of intellectual presumption; and, by repeating the words of the divine bird, Petrarch accuses Dante of having committed the same error when he composed the *Commedia* — or rather, since the words are Dante's, and as occurs with his association with Guittone, it is the accused who, ironically, charges himself. The subtlety of Petrarch's operation is impressive. Nor does it end here. That Petrarch should have chosen precisely Dante-*personaggio*'s entry into the starry heaven to criticize the *Commedia* has further consequences. The hero who, after rising skywards, looks back was a well-established medieval commonplace — it is enough to think of the *Somnium Scipionis* or even of Petrarch's backward glance on reaching the top of Mount Ventoux (*Fam.* IV. 1) — and was closely linked to the idea of the journey of knowledge and enlightenment.[28] By denying the truth of Dante's account, Petrarch concurrently denied both the theological and philosophical claims of the poem; and to undermine the intellectual bases of the *Commedia* was to destroy one of the key elements of Dante's fourteenth-century *auctoritas*. As we have just seen, Petrarch was also intent on contesting the other principal foundation upon which

27   See Barański, pp. 153–73. See also Bernardo, 'Petrarch's Attitude toward Dante', pp. 506–10, and the following subsection.
28   For a reading of *Paradiso* XXII from this perspective, see Chapter 4. On the influence of *Par.* XXII in the *Triumphi*, see Giunta, pp. 416–18, 449.

Dante's 'authority' was built — his standing, thanks to the *Commedia*, as a poet of exceptional ability. Petrarch's goal is obvious: to dismantle the contemporary image of Dante, divine poet of the afterlife, font of wisdom, and disseminator of truths. As a result, the *Commedia* is no longer a text that readers can trust; and 'untrustworthy' authors and texts are most certainly not 'authoritative'.[29] Specifically, given the immediate context of the *Canzoniere* in which sonnet 287 is located — a context dominated by the death of Laura — Petrarch is most explicitly calling into question Dante's assertions regarding his encounter with the dead Beatrice. By means of sonnet 287's clear-sighted realism, the poet demonstrated, and hence criticized, the inevitably deceptive character of his own visions of and contacts with the deceased Laura — illusory experiences that he had vividly described as real events in the preceding eight sonnets (279–86). In these fantasies, Laura, like Beatrice in the Earthly Paradise, inhabits a *locus amoenus*.[30] Thus, by criticizing himself for having presented illusion as fact, Petrarch extends his criticism to Dante, accusing him of having deceived both himself and his readers when he asserted that he had been reunited with a dead woman (see Chapter 12).

In sharp contrast, Petrarch portrays himself as a paragon of honesty, as someone with the moral and intellectual strength to acknowledge his mistakes — a clear-sightedness and firmness that are beyond the powers of 'his' Dante. By means of sonnet 287, Petrarch not only shattered his and Dante's illusions, but also, and more weightily, endeavoured both to expose the 'fantasy' of his predecessor's *auctoritas* and to reject the idea, so actively championed by Dante in the *Commedia*, as part of his strategy of 'self-authorization', that poetry could go beyond *fictio* — a claim which Dante's own son Pietro also denied.[31] As we shall soon see, the same polemical intent, frequently centred on the same general and specific points as those addressed in 'Sennuccio mio, benché doglioso et solo', though naturally with differing emphases, marks Petrarch's approach to Dante elsewhere in his *œuvre*. For the moment, however, I should like to stay a bit longer with sonnet 287, and consider further what else it might reveal, especially in broad terms, about Petrarch's relationship to Dante. If Petrarch really was as absorbed in destroying

29   On medieval notions of 'authority', see Mary Carruthers, *The Book of Memory* (Cambridge: Cambridge University Press, 1990), pp. 189–220; Marie–Dominique Chenu, 'Auctor, actor, autor', *Bulletin du Cange*, 3 (1927), 81–86; Alastair J. Minnis, *'Magister Amoris': The 'Roman de la Rose' and Vernacular Hermeneutics* (Oxford: Oxford University Press, 2001), and *Medieval Theory of Authorship*; *'Auctor' et 'auctoritas': invention et conformisme dans l'écriture médiévale*, ed. by Michel Zimmermann (Paris: École des Chartes, 2001); *MLTC*; *The Cambridge History of Literary Criticism. II. The Middle Ages*, ed. by Alastair Minnis and Ian Johnson (Cambridge: Cambridge University Press, 2005). On Dante and 'authority', see Albert R. Ascoli, *Dante and the Making of a Modern Author* (Cambridge: Cambridge University Press, 2008); Zygmunt G. Barański, *'Sole nuovo, luce nuova': saggi sul rinnovamento culturale in Dante* (Turin: Scriptorium, 1996), and *'Chiosar con altro testo'*.
30   On Petrarch's recourse to the episode of Dante's reunion with Beatrice in the Earthly Paradise, see Kuon, *L'aura dantesca*, pp. 85–144. On the different functions of Beatrice and Laura in their authors' works, see Mariarosaria Spinetti, 'Beatrice e Laura: due mondi a confronto', in *Beatrice nell'opera di Dante e nella memoria europea, 1290–1990*, ed. by Maria Picchio Simonelli (Florence: Cadmo, 1994), pp. 279–91.
31   See Steven Botterill, 'The Trecento Commentaries on Dante's *Commedia*', in *The Cambridge History of Literary Criticism*, pp. 590–611 (pp. 602–03).

Dante's 'authority' as I have maintained, the problem arises as to why he borrowed so heavily, and there is no doubt that he did, from the poet of the *Vita nova* and the *Commedia*. The question is highly pertinent, not least because it is pivotal in any interpretation of Petrarch's attitude to Dante. Having raised it, however, I will desist from dealing with it until I have had the chance to discuss in some depth the *Triumphi* and, probably more importantly, poem 70, 'Lasso me, ch'i' non so in qual parte pieghi', of the *Canzoniere* — though, as we have just noted, one reason why Petrarch did make such recourse to Dante was to turn Dante's own words against him.

Although this is not the right place to linger on *Rerum vulgarium fragmenta* 70, it does nevertheless have an important bearing on the present discussion of sonnet 287. *Canzone* 70, the famous *canzone cum auctoritatibus*, in which each of the first four stanzas ends with the opening line of a love poem written by an eminent vernacular poet, constitutes the *Canzoniere*'s major, if not actually sole, explicit statement of poetic genealogy, therefore making it a key point of reference for sonnet 287's metaliterary suggestions. The bonds uniting the two texts are immediately obvious, and not simply because Cino and Dante — naturally, the erotic Dante — are present in both. *Canzone* 70 defines the *Rerum vulgarium fragmenta* as essentially a Romance amorous poetic collection, if not actually a specifically Italian one, but one with few, albeit culturally noteworthy, models: Arnaut, Cavalcanti, Dante, and Cino. Yet, given the way that their verses easily and 'naturally' merge with Petrarch's poetry, functioning essentially as mere adjuncts to his poem, the impression is created, even as regards this quartet, of an influence that is largely fleeting and unproblematic, and therefore of little consequence. Indeed, when Petrarch, in 'Sennuccio mio, benché doglioso et solo', introduces, almost *en passant*, another poetic quartet, one which can be seen as a kind of partial complementary addendum to the quartet evoked in the *canzone*, exactly the same effect is produced. The idea that the poetry of others holds minimal and inconsequential sway over the *Canzoniere* fits neatly with the claim Petrarch made in *Fam.* XXI. 15 that Dante and other vernacular poets — and it is worth noting how again he fails to discriminate between Dante and the rest — had barely influenced him:

> Hoc unum non dissimulo, quoniam siquid in eo sermone a me dictum illius [Dante] aut alterius cuiusquam dicto simile, sive idem forte cum aliquo sit inventum, non id furtim aut imitandi proposito, que duo semper in his maxime vulgaribus ut scopulos declinavi, sed vel casu fortuito factum esse, vel similitudine ingeniorum. (*Fam.* XXI. 12)

> [This one thing I do wish to make clear, for if any of my vernacular writings resembles, or is identical to, anything of his or anyone else's, it cannot be attributed to theft or imitation, which I have avoided like reefs, especially in vernacular works, but to pure chance or similarity of mind.]

It is vital, I believe, to recognize the consistency — a complex and nuanced rather than one-dimensional consistency, which stretched across many years — of Petrarch's treatment of Dante (and this will become even better apparent once I have examined the letter and the *canzone*), since it highlights the care with which he undertook the task of dismantling his predecessor's *auctoritas*. And he did this with seemingly logical rigour. Thus, given that, as Petrarch implies in sonnet 287, even the most celebrated of vernacular poets is deeply flawed, it is obvious that, if he had not done his best to avoid the influence of such dubious models, he would have been in breach of his intellectual and artistic duties. The extent to which Dante dominated Petrarch's thinking can be espied not just in the persistence but also in the purposeful precision with which he built himself up while taking his rival apart. Yet, the rigour and logic of Petrarch's operation are ultimately more apparent than real, and I am not just thinking here of the complications introduced into his manoeuvre by the enormity of his intertextual debt to Dante. Petrarch found himself in the awkward position of attempting simultaneously to conceal his dependence on Dante and to conduct a critique that, as we saw in sonnet 287, was dependent on evoking both the older poet and his poetry, while at the same time suggesting that he was appreciative of his precursor's accomplishments. The tensions inherent in his approach were considerable, since the danger constantly existed that the contradictions in his treatment of Dante would stymie both his revisionary and his self-celebratory goals, thereby seriously damaging his own cultural standing. In such circumstances, the irritation with which Petrarch reacted to those, like Boccaccio, who continued to extol Dante or to accuse him of behaving dishonestly toward his predecessor is understandable. If Dante had not enjoyed the remarkable prestige that he did in the Trecento, it is just about certain that Petrarch would not have been exercised by him, just as he was not especially exercised — as I shall explain in due course — by Cavalcanti. As sonnet 287 adumbrates, it was the weight, absoluteness, and 'authority' of the *Commedia* that more than anything troubled Petrarch. In composing the *Canzoniere*, he aimed to create a major vernacular poetic structure that was both independent from and could stand comparison with Dante's 'summatic' poem, which, during the fourteenth century, had by and large become normative. Thus Petrarch's hope was to present an alternative mode of writing vernacular poetry. As a result, one way to read the *Rerum vulgarium fragmenta* is as an 'anti-*Commedia*'.[32] By stressing that Dante's achievement was exclusively as a love poet — a sphere which, at best, had a restricted role in defining his 'authority' — and that, in any case, this achievement was fairly limited, Petrarch tried to reduce Dante to such an extent that, as *canzone* 70 confirms, he could relatively easily subsume him into his 'new' lyric model of vernacular literature — the genre where the preeminent voice was of course his own. Paradoxically, in the light of all the energy that Petrarch expended in curtailing Dante's *auctoritas*, it was nevertheless very much to his advantage to be able to suggest that he could absorb and supersede a figure as 'authoritative' as the great Florentine. Complexity, self-interest, cultural politics, and contradiction are inescapably intertwined in Petrarch's reaction to Dante; and so it is not at all surprising that scholars should have described his *dantismo* in such sharply contrasting ways.

---

32   See Michelangelo Picone, 'Tempo e racconto nel *Canzoniere* di Petrarca', in *Omaggio a Gianfranco Folena*, 3 vols (Padua: Editoriale Programma, 1993), I, 581–92 (pp. 588–92), and 'Riscritture dantesche'. See also Kuon, *L'aura dantesca*, pp. 147–48, 213–14; Bortolo Martinelli, 'L'ordinamento morale del "Canzoniere"', in his *Petrarca e il Ventoso* (Bergamo: Minerva Italica, 1977), pp. 217–300.

3. Delimiting Dante: *Triumphus Cupidinis* IV. 28–38

There seems little doubt that Petrarch's primary tactic in relation to Dante was to restrict as much as possible the *Commedia*'s cultural power, if not actually to 'eliminate' the poem as the defining point of reference in the intellectual and artistic world of Trecento Italy. As long as the *Commedia* was accorded a position of almost absolute dominance, Dante's 'authority' was guaranteed and Petrarch could not hope to consolidate his own standing as a vernacular poet. Nor was he alone in thinking this. Others in the fourteenth century, including even Boccaccio, felt the oppressive weight of the poem's and its author's *auctoritas* (see Chapter 15). It was of course in the *Triumphi*, a visionary epic poem written in *terza rima* and chock-full of borrowings from the *Commedia*, that Petrarch most openly grappled with Dante's masterpiece, hoping to bend it to his sway.[33]

The fact that in the *Triumphi*, a work so obviously dependent on the *Commedia*, Petrarch should have referred only once, and then rather curtly, to Dante immediately points to the controversial thrust of his approach:

> Così, or quinci or quindi rimirando,
> vidi gente ir per una verde piaggia
> pur d'amor volgarmente ragionando:
>   ecco Dante e Beatrice, ecco Selvaggia,
> ecco Cin da Pistoia, Guitton d'Arezzo,
> che di non esser primo par ch'ira aggia;
>   ecco i due Guidi che già fur in prezzo,
> Honesto Bolognese, e i Ciciliani,
> che fur già primi, e quivi eran da sezzo;
>   Sennuccio e Franceschin, che fur sì humani,
> come ogni uon vide; e poi v'era un drappello.
>
> (*Tr. Cup.* IV. 28–38)

The polemical character of his presentation becomes quite explicit when it is noted that, in naming his predecessor, Petrarch made no effort to acknowledge Dante as the author of the *Commedia*, the text that so obviously lies at the basis of his own epic poem. Instead, as in the *Canzoniere*, he portrays Dante as one among a group of Italian love poets — 'gente [...] d'amor volgarmente ragionando' — a blatant lapse in literary protocol, that would have been flagrant to any medieval reader accustomed to the respectful manner in which epic poets in particular dutifully celebrated their predecessors and admitted the debts they owed them.[34] Petrarch's transgression was glaring since it was committed against an *auctoritas* of such singular standing; nor is

33   On the presence of Dante in the *Triumphi*, see Marco Ariani, 'Introduzione', in Francesco Petrarca, *Triumphi*, ed. by Marco Ariani (Milan: Mursia, 1988), pp. 11–45; Feo, pp. 455–56; Giunta; Marina Riccucci, 'L'esordio dei *Triumphi*: tra *Eneide* e *Commedia*', *Rivista di letteratura italiana*, 12 (1994), 313–49; Marco Santagata, 'Introduzione', in *Tr.*, pp. xi–lii (pp. xxv–xxx, xliv–xlviii). See also n. 27. In the light of the *Triumphi*'s complex and lengthy genesis and composition, it is difficult to date its two references to Dante, and hence to locate these chronologically in relation to Petrarch's other explicit allusions to the poet of the *Commedia*. Scholars now generally agree that Petrarch's main engagement with the *Triumphi* began in the early 1350s.

34   See Kevin Brownlee and others, 'Vernacular Literary Consciousness c. 1100–c. 1500: French, German and English Evidence', in Minnis and Johnson, pp. 422–71 (pp. 424–31).

there much doubt that the omission was deliberate. It allowed Petrarch to establish effectively and concisely that, however much his poem might resound with echoes of the *Commedia*, the relationship between his and Dante's text was anything but straightforward. As will become apparent, the impression he was keen to foster was that the *Triumphi* stand in clear and direct opposition to the *Commedia*, thereby bringing to the fore those criticisms of Dante's abilities as an epic writer that remain largely implicit in the *Canzoniere*. Nor does his coupling of Beatrice's name to Dante's — a notable addition with respect to 'Sennuccio mio, benché doglioso et solo' — benefit the poet of the *Commedia*. In fact, the opposite is almost certainly true. By fixing Beatrice as simply a love poet's lady, the equal of Cino's Selvaggia, Petrarch, as he had done in sonnet 287, denied her role as heavenly guide, and hence once again challenged the *Commedia*'s metaphysical claims. Moreover, when made from within an epic poem, such criticism obviously carries that much greater weight than when adumbrated in a lyric collection. Indeed, by presenting his own eschatological experience as a dream-vision — 'vinto dal sonno, vidi una gran luce' (*Tr. Cup.* I. 11)[35] — Petrarch placed himself in open rivalry to Dante and overtly challenged the idea that his predecessor could have gone bodily on a 'viaggio' (*Inf.* I. 91) through the afterlife.[36]

In keeping with the precedent set in sonnet 287, the manner in which Petrarch integrated Dante into his brief procession of Italian love poets constitutes a key factor in his programmed *deminutio* of his adversary. A variant of *Tr. Cup.* III. 99 — 'ché tutti siam macchiati d'una pece' — is extremely revealing in this respect. In the 'codice degli abbozzi', line 99 reads as follows: 'ecco qui Dante co la sua Beatrice'. From once having had a complete line given over to them, in *Triumphus Cupidinis* III, Dante and his lady are squashed into a hemistich: 'ecco Dante e Beatrice'. In contrast, Cino and Selvaggia, who immediately follow, comfortably and elegantly spread themselves over a half-line each: 'ecco Selvaggia, | ecco Cin da Pistoia'. And I will not even attempt to sound the implications in line 99 of 'pece' [sin] replacing 'Beatrice'. In this instance, I am happy to concede that the problem is best left to the hermeneutic scrutiny of psychoanalytic criticism. It is thus questionable whether the fact that Dante's name appears first in the list is really meant to underline his poetic primacy. On the surface at least, Petrarch seems conventionally to show respect for the foremost poet of the century, as he was to do, with equally studied ambiguity, in *Fam.* XXI. 15: 'Iam qui me aliis iudicandum dabam, nunc de aliis in silentio iudicans, varie quidem in reliquis, in hoc ita, ut facile sibi vulgaris eloquentie palmam dem'

---

35   Despite their undoubted importance, I do not have the space here to explore further the role played by visionary experiences in Petrarch's response to Dante. It is enough to remember the dramatic appearance of Veritas at the beginning of the *Secretum* — an appearance accompanied by a host of easily recognizable allusions to the *Commedia*, and in particular to its opening *canti*; see Mercuri, pp. 334–44; Fenzi's notes in *Secretum*, pp. 287–90. In this context, it should also not be forgotten that the dream-vision was the tradition to which, in the fourteenth century, many commentators and manuscript illustrators assigned the *Commedia*.

36   On medieval distinctions between otherworldly voyages and visions, see Alison Morgan, *Dante and the Medieval Other World* (Cambridge: Cambridge University Press, 1990); Cesare Segre, *Fuori del mondo* (Turin: Einaudi, 1990), pp. 25–48; Carol Zaleski, *Otherworld Journeys* (New York and Oxford: Oxford University Press, 1987), pp. 26–94. See also Gilson, p. 39.

[I used to submit my work to the judgment of others, whereas now I judge others in silence, varying in my opinion of them but deeming him the one to whom I would readily grant the palm for vernacular eloquence] (13). It should never be forgotten that Petrarch was keen to present himself as objectively respectful towards, if not entirely persuaded by, Dante's attainments, while concurrently working hard to spread an ever-thicker veil of uncertainty around those same attainments and their author. In a context where issues of literary supremacy are to the fore ('che di non esser primo par ch'ira aggia'), Dante's established predominance is undermined not just by the tension that is forged between him and Cino — and, as sonnet 287 confirms, this is not the only time that Petrarch appears to favour Cino over Dante — but also by the fact that, among all the Italian poets mentioned, the two most positively treated are, 'shockingly', Sennuccio del Bene and Franceschino degli Albizzi: 'Sennuccio e Franceschin, che fur sì humani, | come ogne uon vide'. Nor is it likely by chance that Petrarch placed his friends at the end of the sequence.[37] Thus, since the precise logic of the series remains ambiguous — neither strict chronological nor evaluative criteria appear consistently to hold good in it — Sennuccio and Franceschin's strategic placement encourages the thought that, on account of their exclusive 'humanity', they can be viewed as moving beyond the poets who precede them. And the pair receives a further boost thanks to their proximity to the 'drappello | di portamenti e di volgari strani' (38–39), that is to say the Occitan poets, whose broad superiority over their Italian counterparts is made transparent as a result of the sympathetic manner of their treatment and the generosity with which space is allocated to them: nineteen and a half lines (38–57) as against seven and a half (31–38). This celebration of Occitan poetic prowess strikes yet another blow against Dante's already shaky vernacular poetic standing and preeminence, as well as the reputation of the Italian lyric in general.[38] Thus, Petrarch's perfunctory nod in his direction is in stark and telling contrast to the powerful, sustained, and unqualified encomium he delivered extolling the lasting legacy of Arnaut's artistic supremacy:

> fra tutti il primo Arnaldo Daniello,
> gran maestro d'amor, ch'a la sua terra
> ancor fa honor col suo dir strano e bello. (*Tr. Cup.* IV. 40–42)[39]

---

37   It is interesting to note that Petrarch was prepared to acknowledge Dante's poetic vernacular primacy in both *Fam.* XXI. 15 and *Sen.* V. 2 but not in either the *Canzoniere* or the *Triumphi*. When he himself was engaged in writing vernacular poetry, it would seem that Petrarch was unwilling to declare Dante's primacy, something which he found less difficult to assert when composing Latin prose and addressing cultural and historical issues.

38   On Petrarch and Occitan poetry, see Atturo; Alessio Fontana, 'La filologia romanza e il problema del rapporto Petrarca-trovatori (Premesse per una ripresa del problema secondo nuove prospettive)', in Schalk, pp. 51–70; Giuseppe Frasso, 'Petrarca, Andrea da Mantova e il canzoniere provenzale N', *Italia medioevale e umanistica*, 17 (1974), 185–205; William Paden, 'Petrarch as Poet of Provence', *Annali d'Italianistica*, 22 (2004), 19–44; Maurizio Perugi, 'Petrarca provenzale', *Quaderni petrarcheschi*, 7 (1990), 109–92; Nicola Zingarelli, 'Petrarca e i trovatori', in *Provenza e Italia*, ed. by Vincenzo Crescini (Florence: Bemporad, 1930), pp. 97–139. See also Olivia Holmes, 'Petrarch and the Vernacular Lyric Past', in *The Cambridge Companion to Petrarch*, ed. by Albert R. Ascoli and Unn Falkeid (Cambridge: Cambridge University Press, 2015), pp. 154–66.

39   On Petrarch and Arnaut Daniel, see Maurizio Perugi, *Trovatori a Valchiusa: un frammento della*

However much, in *Triumphus Cupidinis* IV, Petrarch may have been eager to celebrate love poetry in general, there is also no question that he was just as eager to establish that, to-date, Italy had only made a relatively minor contribution to the genre. Thus, he further emphasized the relative insignificance of poetry in Italian by presenting it as dwarfed not only by the Occitans but also, and less problematically, by the poets of antiquity, on whom, conventionally, he lavished the most fulsome praise (13–27). Consequently, love literature in Italian is reduced to a minor tradition uncomfortably lodged, as Petrarch's actual presentation iconically reveals, between the greats 'di chiara fama, | o per antiche, o per moderne carte' (*Tr. Cup.* IV. 11–12). It is a tradition, therefore, in urgent need of a major boost if it is ever to stand favourable comparison with the best that the past and the present have produced; and such a boost of course was what Petrarch, who significantly prefaced the pageant by associating himself with its participants (*Tr. Cup.* IV. 4–9), planned to provide with the *Canzoniere*. Despite their generic differences, the ideological and metacultural ties and the communality of purpose uniting his two vernacular works are noteworthy. Thus, in direct dialectical tension with *Triumphus Cupidinis* IV, *canzone* 70 establishes in its very first stanza that Petrarch, unlike other Italian poets, has no difficulty in transcending the Occitan 'gran maestro d'amor'.[40]

The harmful repercussions for Dante, flawed poet of a flawed tradition, of Petrarch's compressed 'history of erotic literature' are more than obvious — and historical systematization and qualitative evaluation were undoubtedly one of the functions that medieval culture assigned to catalogues such as that in *Triumphus Cupidinis* IV.[41] Indeed, when Petrarch put together his poetic procession, I strongly suspect that he was less interested in defining the tradition of erotic literature and even in establishing his own standing than he was in doing as much damage as possible to Dante's reputation. In intertextual terms, the parade is unambiguously constructed with Dante as its primary point of reference.[42] It is Dante, therefore, more than any other poet in *Triumphus Cupidinis* IV, who is being assessed in relation to his peers; and it is his position in the poetic order — and medieval catalogues of authors, I repeat, were invariably hierarchical in character — that is crucially at stake. For instance, just before Dante and Beatrice are introduced, Petrarch writes 'vidi gente ir per una verde piaggia' (29), a hendecasyllable that openly recalls the

cultura provenzale del Petrarca (Padua: Antenore, 1985), pp. 292–314, and 'A proposito di alcuni scritti recenti su Petrarca e Arnaut Daniel', *Studi medievali*, ser. 3:32 (1991), 369–84; Santagata, *Per moderne carte*, pp. 157–211.

40   Although modern scholarship has established that the poem cited at the end of the first stanza of 'Lasso me' was not actually penned by Arnaut, what is important is that Petrarch considered it to have been composed by the great Occitan poet; see Pietro G. Beltrami, 'Appunti su "Razo e dreyt ay si ·m chant e ·m demori"', *Rivista di letteratura italiana*, 5 (1987), 9–39; Carlo Pulsoni, 'L'attribuzione della canzone *Drez et rayson es qu'ieu ciant e· m demori*', in his *La tecnica compositiva nei 'Rerum vulgarium fragmenta': riuso metrico e lettura autoriale* (Rome: Bagatto, 1998), pp. 239–57. See Subsection 5, ' "Disguising" Dante', for a fuller discussion of 'Lasso me'.

41   On medieval catalogues of *auctores*, see Birger Munk Olsen, *I classici nel canone scolastico altomedievale* (Spoleto: Centro Italiano di Studi sull'Alto Medioevo Italiano, 1991).

42   See Vinicio Pacca's notes to *Tr. Cup.* IV. 13–57 for a general idea of the lines' dependence on Dante.

pilgrim's arrival with the 'savi' (*Inf.* IV. 110), the five classical poets, inside the 'nobile castello' (105): 'giugnemmo in prato di fresca verdura' (111). Petrarch is deliberately evoking the memory of Dante's Limbo, where notoriously the poet had had the temerity to crown himself 'sesto tra cotanto senno' (102). Therefore, it is unlikely to be a coincidence that, in the *Triumphus Cupidinis* too, we should discover, a mere few lines earlier, another quintet of poets accompanied by an unexpected sixth:

> Virgilio vidi; e parmi intorno avesse
> compagni d'alto ingegno e da trastullo,
> di quei che volentier già 'l mondo lesse:
>   l'uno era Ovidio, e l'altro era Catullo,
> l'altro Propertio, che d'amor cantaro
> fervidamente, e l'altro era Tibullo.
>   Una giovene greca a paro a paro
> coi nobili poeti iva cantando,
> ed avea un suo stil soave e raro. (*Tr. Cup.* IV.19–27)

Not only is Dante not a member of this elite of love poets — never mind being the 'sixth' member and the symbol of comedy in a pantheon of writers who, by being associated with the major *genera*, embody literature as a whole — but the position he had originally claimed for himself is now reassigned to a woman. The cultural implications of such gender reversal, regardless of Sappho's fame, especially given the ambiguities surrounding women and language in the Middle Ages, do not need further elucidation.[43] Indeed, the deliberately polemical character of Petrarch's operation becomes even more apparent if the links between *suavitas* and comedy are remembered, as well as those between Sappho's 'stil soave e raro' and Dante's 'dolce stil novo' (*Purg.* XXIV. 57).[44] The subtle skill and precision with which Petrarch dismantled, even ridiculed, Dante's *auctoritas* are striking. Without seeming to show overt disrespect for the much admired older poet, Petrarch nevertheless made it more than plain to readers with the right degree of intellectual and cultural preparation — precisely that elite audience whose opinion he wished to influence, and among whom were others who had voiced reservations about the author of the *Commedia* — what he thought both of the contemporary cult of Dante and of the poet's campaign of self-authorization.

Attacking the *Commedia*'s elaborate metaliterary structure, Petrarch had accurately pinpointed the principal means by which Dante had decided to establish and legitimize his *auctoritas*. Thus, by showing up the vanity of Dante's declarations of

---

43   On medieval attitudes to women and language, see Barański, '*Sole nuovo, luce nuova*', pp. 102–03; Carla Casagrande and Silvana Vecchio, *I peccati della lingua: disciplina ed etica della parola nella cultura medievale* (Rome: Istituto della Enciclopedia Italiana, 1987); Helena L. Sanson, '*Ornamentum mulieri brevíloquentia*: donne, silenzi, parole nell'Italia del Cinquecento', *The Italianist*, 23 (2003), 194–244. See also Eric Jager, *The Tempter's Voice: Language and the Fall in Medieval Literature* (Ithaca, NY, and London: Cornell University Press, 1993). However, now see also Elena Lombardi, *Imagining the Woman Reader in the Age of Dante* (Oxford: Oxford University Press, 2018).

44   See Claudia Villa, *La 'Lectura Terentii'* (Padua: Antenore, 1984), pp. 39–42. See also Zygmunt G. Barański, '"'nfiata labia" and "dolce stil novo": A Note on Dante, Ethics, and the Technical Vocabulary of Literature', in *Sotto il segno di Dante: scritti in onore di Francesco Mazzoni*, ed. by Leonella Coglievina and Domenico De Robertis (Florence: Le Lettere, 1998), pp. 17–35 (p. 34).

artistic preeminence and literary 'authority', Petrarch compromised the credibility of both the poet and his *œuvre*. In addition, and this is important, having unmasked his predecessor's unsustainable pretensions, Petrarch was that much freer to recreate him in terms that could both serve his own purposes of self-authorization and appear to evaluate Dante in a balanced manner. Consequently, if Petrarch emerges as a model of intellectual probity, Dante, on the contrary, appears mired in self-interest. From this perspective, whatever claims Dante had made for himself inevitably sound expedient and exaggerated. Specifically, as Petrarch implies in sonnet 287, Dante's judgments of his fellow writers need to be approached with considerable caution. The poetic pageant in *Triumphus Cupidinis* IV can therefore be read as a 'disinterested' counter to Dante's 'selfish' presentation of many of the same poets in the *Commedia*. Indeed, the fact that so much of the procession, as we have begun to see, is openly dependent on some of the poem's most openly metaliterary cantos — *Inferno* IV, *Purgatorio* XI and XXVI — underlines its corrective character. Thus, if Dante had referred to Guinizzelli and Cavalcanti in order to promote himself ('così ha tolto l'uno a l'altro Guido | la gloria de la lingua; e forse è nato | chi l'uno e l'altro caccerà del nido', *Purg.* XI. 97–99), Petrarch recalls 'i due Guidi che già fur in prezzo' for purely literary-historical reasons. Similarly, his definition of Arnaut is more positive and categorical than Dante's ambiguous appreciation filtered through Guinizzelli's inevitably restricted and subjective point of view:

> 'O frate', disse, 'questi ch'io ti cerno
> col dito', e additò un spirto innanzi,
> 'fu miglior fabbro del parlar materno.
>   Versi d'amore e prose di romanzi
> soverchiò tutti; e lascia dir li stolti
> che quel di Lemosí credon ch'avanzi.' (*Purg.* XXVI. 115–20)

In any case, unlike Petrarch's sober — I am almost tempted to say 'scholarly' — review of Occitan poets, Dante's Arnaut and Giraut de Bornelh are introduced with an acidly polemical intent.[45] Once again, suspicions swarm around Dante's motives for naming other writers; and increasingly the *Commedia* looks like a work written primarily, if not exclusively, so that its author can accumulate literary glory for himself at the expense of his peers. Trapped in its own literary self-absorption, it is a hardnosed exercise in artificially, and therefore improperly, assigning *auctoritas* to the self. It is thus a poem lacking moral purpose — and in the Middle Ages, when literature was regularly defined as a branch of ethics, no more damning a charge could be levied against a text.[46] On the other hand, the *Triumphi* are presented as quintessentially driven by ethical concerns. Petrarch seamlessly passes from the erotic, and hence potentially selfish, poetics of the Occitans — a selfishness of a

---

45   In the context of Petrarch's overall presentation of classical and vernacular poetry, his description of Guittone — 'che di non esser primo par ch'ira aggia' (*Tr. Cup.* IV. 33), with its emphasis on the Aretine's frustration at his lowly poetic standing — reads less like a polemical barb than an insightful assessment of the attitude of a poet who, over time, has lost the position of prestige he had once enjoyed.

46   See Judson Boyce Allen, *The Ethical Poetic of the Later Middle Ages* (Toronto: University of Toronto Press, 1982).

quite different order, of course, to Dante's egoism — to his own poetics of *charitas*:

> e molti altri ne vidi, a cui la lingua
> lancia e spada fu sempre, e targia ed elmo.
>   E, poi conven che 'l mio dolor distingua,
> volsimi a' nostri, e vidi 'l bon Thomasso,
> [...]
> senza 'l qual non sapea movere un passo.
> [...]
>   Poco era fuor de la comune strada,
> quando Socrate e Lelio vidi in prima:
> con lor più lunga via conven ch'io vada.
>   O qual coppia d'amici! [...]
> [...]
>   Con questi duo cercai monti diversi,
> andando tutti tre sempre ad un giogo.
>   (*Tr. Cup.* IV. 56–59, 63, 67–70, 73–74)

Friendship, study, ethics: these are the forces that inspire and characterize the *Triumphi*. Petrarch's epic, for all its visionary qualities, is a poem about life rather than literature; and in it literature is never allowed to gain the upper hand on life:

> che né 'n rima
> poria, né 'n prosa ornar assai, né 'n versi,
> se, come dee, vertù nuda se stima. (*Tr. Cup.* IV. 70–72)

There is nothing calculated and artificial about Petrarch's writing; and it is 'living' poetry that brings success and recognition to its author. With a sharp knowing dig at Dante's failure to 'prendere 'l cappello' (*Par.* XXV. 9), Petrarch remembers his own poetic crowning, the reward, once again, for having loved and lived disinterestedly:

> Con costor colsi 'l glorïoso ramo
> onde forse anzi tempo ornai le tempie
> in memoria di quella ch'io tanto amo.
>   Ma pur di lei che 'l cor di pensier m'empie,
> non potei coglier mai ramo né foglia,
> sì fur le sue radici acerbe ed empie. (*Tr. Cup.* IV. 79–84)[47]

Then again, the epic is not poetry of the private sphere; and, if literary decorum is to be maintained, Petrarch must needs leave personal matters, however all-consuming, to one side (or better to his lyrics) and focus, as literary convention required, on matters of universalizing interest — the God of Love and not his love for Laura:

> onde, benché talor doler mi soglia
> come uom ch'è offeso, quel che con questi occhi
> vidi, m'è fren che mai più non mi doglia:
>   materia di coturni, e non di socchi,
> veder preso colui ch'è fatto deo. (*Tr. Cup.* IV. 85–89)

---

47   On poetic crowning, see Michelangelo Picone, 'Il tema dell'incoronazione poetica in Dante, Petrarca e Boccaccio', *L'Alighieri*, 46 (2005), 5–26. See also Ascoli, 'Blinding the Cyclops'; Sturm-Maddox, 'Dante, Petrarch, and the Laurel Crown'.

Speaking of *cothurni*, which, in both the ancient and the medieval worlds, served as a learned metonymy for tragedy, the *stilus* of epic poetry, Petrarch underscored that he was professionally in control of the *Triumphi*, and that he knew precisely the correct manner in which to elaborate its epic subject-matter, as well as the appropriate technical vocabulary with which to discuss his work.[48] Furthermore, to leave no doubt about his competence, he also deferentially acknowledged Homer and Orpheus as his epic 'authorities' (93). Conversely, the poet who had shown little sensitivity and even less learning when writing epic poetry was, naturally, Dante, who inexcusably had committed the bewildering solecism of turning to comedy — evoked here through the mention of *socci* — when he came to pen his epic, an elementary lack of judgment which many of his Trecento readers lamented.[49] Far from representing the contemporary vernacular epic at its best, the *Commedia* was yet another instance of the arrogant presumptuousness of the *moderni*. Thus, rather than being a literary model respectfully to be imitated, the *Commedia* is in fact the embodiment of the *vitia* that writers need to shun. The *Triumphi*, on the other hand, offer a shining example of a vernacular text written according to the hallowed conventions of tradition;[50] and their author stands as an *exemplum* of how the modern man and the modern writer ought to behave: combining Christian charity with classical learning.[51]

Petrarch pushed hard to dislodge Dante and the *Commedia* from their position of 'authority'; and it is not hard to imagine the poet, the *Triumphi* in hand, ready to claim for himself their vacated space. That Petrarch did not succeed in usurping his rival, or at least not during his lifetime, since Dante's *auctoritas* was just too powerful, does not in any way invalidate the allusive subtlety of his corrosive and delimiting revision of the Trecento Dante.[52] Behind a seemingly appreciative veil — the veil of the respectable vernacular love poet — the author of the *Commedia*

48   On tragedy and epic, see Vincent Gillespie, 'The Study of Classical Authors from the Twelfth Century to c. 1450', in Minnis and Johnson, pp. 207–23. On tragedy, see also Henry A. Kelly, *Ideas and Forms of Tragedy from Aristotle to the Middle Ages* (Cambridge: Cambridge University Press, 1993). See also Chapters 6 and 7.

49   On fourteenth-century reactions to Dante's definition of his masterpiece as a comedy, see Barański, *'Chiosar con altro testo'*, pp. 41–97; Henry A. Kelly, *Tragedy and Comedy from Dante to Pseudo–Dante* (Berkeley, Los Angeles, and London: University of California Press, 1989). On medieval ideas of comedy, see also Chapter 7, as well as Barański, *'Sole nuovo, luce nuova'*, pp. 129–51; Karl Heinz Bareiss, *Comoedia: die Entwicklung der Komödiendiskussion von Aristoteles bis Ben Jonson* (Frankfurt and Bern: Peter Lang, 1982). In his commentary to the *Commedia*, Francesco da Buti, quoting a now lost letter, presents important evidence which confirms Petrarch's dissatisfaction with Dante's choice of *comedía* as his poem's *titulus*: 'Messer Franciesco Petrarcha, in una sua epistola che incomincia *Ne te laudasse peniteat*, muove questa quistione et dice: "Nec cur comediam vocet video"': Francesco da Buti, 'Il "Commento" di Francesco da Buti alla "Commedia". "Inferno"', ed. by Claudia Tardelli (unpublished PhD thesis, Scuola Normale Superiore di Pisa, 2010–11), p. 851.

50   See Barański, *'Chiosar con altro testo'*, pp. 153–73.

51   As is well known, this is the image of himself that Petrarch consistently presented in his *œuvre*.

52   Luca Rossi's claim that Petrarch's growing authority in the second half of the fourteenth century 'sembra in qualche modo inibire la stesura dei commenti danteschi' ('Presenze di Petrarca', p. 443) is incorrect, as is immediately clear if one consults Bellomo's chronological list of Trecento and Quattrocento commentaries on the *Commedia* (Bellomo, 'Introduzione', pp. 17–19).

looms as a monster of incompetence and egoism, ready to trample over the truth and over the reputation of others in order to achieve his ends. Petrarch's Dante is most certainly not an 'authority'. If anything, he is that most dangerous of figures, the 'false *auctoritas*'.[53] As Petrarch recognized in *Fam.* XXI. 15, Dante had undeniably managed to dupe the untutored and even many a naively enthusiastic intellectual. Conversely, the truly learned not only were able to see through him, but also had the duty, regardless of the opprobrium that their honesty might bring down on their heads, to make their views public (see the following subsection). The same pose of scholarly objectivity with respect to Dante thus unites Petrarch's self-presentation in both the epistle and the *Triumphi*. It goes without saying that such a stance was the poet's best bulwark against potential accusations of hypocrisy: namely, that, in denouncing Dante for being selfishly opportunistic, he was just as selfishly looking after his own interests. In any case, further to deflect possible accusations of double standards, Petrarch also underscored that, unlike Dante, he had no need to justify and safeguard his poetic reputation. Others were publicly willing to celebrate his standing, as the brief mention of his crowning in the *Triumphus Cupidinis* confirms.

A common perspective on Dante also unites the *Canzoniere* and the *Triumphi*. Both texts reject as untenable the *Commedia*'s extraordinary metaphysical and literary claims. As a result, they restrict Dante's proficiency to vernacular love poetry, the one area in which Petrarch was prepared to grant his precursor a degree of distinction.[54] What differentiates the *Canzoniere* from the *Triumphi*, however, is the degree of ferocity with which each attacks the *Commedia*. The lyric collection is rather less forceful than the epic. The latter, on account of its generic communality with the 'poema sacro' (*Par.* XXV. 1), is appropriately more aggressive and open about its polemical intentions. As tradition required, Petrarch critically evaluated Dante's epic from within epic structures. In this respect, rather than being unconscious repetitions or marks of a respectful *aemulatio*, the many borrowings from across the *Commedia* discernible in the *Triumphi* constitute the battleground where Petrarch

---

53   It is noteworthy that, in *Sen.* v. 2, Petrarch should have attacked false modern 'authorities': 'Quanquam quid indoctum vulgus arguo, cum de his quoque qui se doctos vocant tanto et gravior et iustior sit querela, qui, preter multa ridicula, odiosum illud in fine, ignorantie summam superbiam addidere? [...] Sed quid, queso, literatos homines excusabit, qui cum veterum non ignari esse debeant, in eadem opinionum cecitate versantur? [...] Et hi quoque novis freti ducibus pudendisque' [Why, however, do I blame the unlearned crowd, when a much more severe and just accusation may be made against those who call themselves learned, who, after many buffooneries, finally have that offensive habit of adding extreme arrogance to their ignorance? [...] But what will excuse, I ask, men of letters, who, although they ought not be unaware of the ancient writers, fall into the same blindness of opinion? [...] And they too rely on authorities of which they should be ashamed] (56, 63, 67).

54   The fact that Petrarch introduced the epic Latin poet par excellence into his catalogue of love poets does not mean that, as he did with Dante, he also intended to limit Virgil to the sphere of the erotic. He was simply drawing on an established commonplace, first found in Servius, which interpreted Book IV of the *Aeneid* as a text concerned with *amor*, thereby associating Virgil with love. In the *Triumphi Fame*, Petrarch ensured that he recognized and celebrated Virgil's status as an epic poet by presenting him as Homer's companion and equal (III. 10–17). Servius' definition of Book IV can be read in *Servii Grammatici qui feruntur in Vergilii carmina commentarii*, ed. by Georg Thilo and Hermann Hagen, 3 vols (Leipzig: Teubner, 1881–87), I, 45, lines 2–5.

rescued Dante's 'comically' imprisoned epic formulations and restored them to their rightful 'tragic' context and register. To have done this in the *Canzoniere* would have been a solecism akin to Dante's disregard for the prescriptions of the *genera dicendi*. It is thus not surprising that the *Rerum vulgarium fragmenta*'s intertextual dependence on the *Commedia* is much more muted and less eye-catching than that of the *Triumphi*.[55] In any case, as I mentioned earlier and will amplify in due course, in the lyric collection Petrarch drew on Dante as a love poet, a decision that inevitably had a fundamental impact on how and what he chose to borrow from the *Commedia*. In addition, in the *Canzoniere*, Petrarch utilized Dante in order to enhance his own work, and therefore had to be careful not to do excessive damage to his predecessor. He was under no such obligation in the *Triumphi*. Indeed, he made it abundantly clear that, regardless of the fact that his poem boomed with echoes of the *Commedia*, Dante's poem, unlike the works of the great classical epic *auctores*, was most definitely not his model. Petrarch was steadfast in maintaining that, however paradoxical, the more he borrowed from Dante, the less he actually owed him: his task was to rewrite the *Commedia* as it ought to have been written if Dante had properly heeded the lessons of the *bella scola*.[56] The care with which the poet approached and finessed his critique of Dante, ensuring that, in each instance, it was appropriate to the text in which he was voicing his disapproval, while at the same time reiterating certain fixed large-scale censures, offers unmistakable evidence of the commitment with which he undertook the task of delimiting his burdensome predecessor.[57] If the psychological causes of Petrarch's largely negative reaction to Dante remain obscured by conjecture and fancy, the cultural ones, despite the passing of centuries, are somewhat plainer to see, as are the intricate and personal means by which the poet transformed these pressures into the stuff of literature.

4. 'Defending' Dante

It is hard to escape the conclusion that, in his vernacular poetry, Petrarch, even if obliquely, expressed serious misgivings about Dante and his masterpiece. According to Petrarch, the *Commedia* was a work of lamentable literary, moral, and intellectual misjudgment, which, rather than establishing and sustaining 'authority', was precisely the kind of flawed and deceptive text that someone whose probity was

---

55   See Subsection 5, '"Disguising" Dante', below for a discussion of the *Canzoniere*'s intertextual debts to Dante.

56   It is hard to escape the impression, however, that both the *Triumphi*'s tortuous and precarious composition and its widely recognized weaknesses as an epic poem can ultimately be explained in terms of Petrarch's unrelenting struggle with Dante. The *Triumphi*'s constant and overt dependence on the *Commedia*, rather than challenge and redimension Dante's poem, is a constant reminder of the latter's magisterial superiority. To put it somewhat differently, Petrarch failed to find his own epic voice because he was continually drowned out by the more powerful and successful tones of his predecessor. Conversely, in the *Canzoniere*, where he was able effectively to control Dante and to subordinate him to his own needs, Petrarch created a distinctly personal masterpiece.

57   'The other two direct references to Dante in Petrarch's oeuvre, which both occur in his vernacular poetry and date from the late 1340s and early 1350s, reflect more closely the critical stance found later in *Familiares* XXI, 15' (Gilson, p. 37).

open to question might write. Petrarch went on to reaffirm and further elaborate his doubts, again employing the rhetoric of indirection, in two letters to Boccaccio: *Fam.* XXI. 15 and *Sen.* V. 2. In terms of my argument, the choice of addressee is highly significant. Boccaccio was an enthusiastic pro-Dante intellectual of the sort that Petrarch was so determined to win over to his camp, since, without the backing of Dante's supporters, whose views represented the majority fourteenth-century position on the poet of the *Commedia*, he could never have hoped to reconfigure the world of Trecento *auctoritas*.[58] It is thus noteworthy, as first Giuseppe Billanovich and then Carlo Paolazzi have gone a long way to demonstrate, that, after having received *Fam.* XXI. 15, Boccaccio did indeed revise and tone down his celebration of Dante in the *Trattatello*.[59]

Intriguingly, *Fam.* XXI. 15 was actually born of a failure to persuade. As is well known, Petrarch's letter acts as a reply to a missive, now lost, that he had received from Boccaccio. The *certaldese* had written to his friend soon after their meeting in 1359 in Milan. As is evident from the 'Familiar' letter and Boccaccio's *carmen*, 'Ytalie iam certus honos' [Already the certain honour of Italy], which had accompanied the missing epistle, its subject-matter was almost certainly the thorny one of Dante's greatness — thorny, of course, only as far as Petrarch was concerned.[60] From the surviving texts of the exchange, it is not unreasonable to assume that, as had occurred when the writers had met in 1350 and in 1351, a large part of their Milanese encounter had been spent arguing and disagreeing about Dante's merits.[61] Given the enduring strength of Boccaccio's enthusiasm for Dante, Petrarch must have increasingly realized, and with some discomfort, that something more energetic than his finely allusive poetic criticisms of Dante was required if the Florentine's *auctoritas* was to be significantly disturbed. Instead of embedding his denunciations deep into the ideological nervous system of a universalizing 'tragic' *visio* and of a highly personal lyric self-analysis, a more direct approach, one which had Dante at its centre, was necessary.

---

58   On Boccaccio's complex attitude to Dante, which was not unconditionally appreciative, see at least Todd Boli, 'Boccaccio's *Trattatello in laude di Dante*, or *Dante Resartus*', *Renaissance Quarterly*, 41 (1988), 389–412; Battaglia Ricci, 'Il culto per Dante'; Clarke; Carlo Delcorno, 'Gli scritti danteschi del Boccaccio', in *Dante e Boccaccio*, pp. 109–37; Eisner; Elsa Filosa, 'To Praise Dante, To Please Petrarch (*Trattatello in laude di Dante*)', in *Boccaccio: A Critical Guide to the Complete Works*, ed. by Victoria Kirkham and others (Chicago: University of Chicago Press, 2013), pp. 213–20 & 430–37; Robert Hollander, *Boccaccio's Dante and the Shaping Force of Satire* (Ann Arbor: University of Michigan Press, 1997); James Kriesel, *Boccaccio's Corpus: Allegory, Ethics, and Vernacularity* (Notre Dame, IN: University of Notre Dame Press, 2019); Martin L. McLaughlin, *Literary Imitation in the Italian Renaissance* (Oxford: Clarendon Press, 1995), pp. 50–62; *MLTC*, pp. 453–58. To be consulted with caution: Jason Houston, *Building a Monument to Dante: Boccaccio as Dantista* (Toronto, Buffalo, and London: University of Toronto Press, 2010). See also n. 107 below.

59   See Billanovich, *Petrarca letterato*, pp. 238 & 270; Carlo Paolazzi, *Dante e la 'Comedia' nel Trecento* (Milan: Vita e Pensiero, 1989), pp. 167–81. However, see also the reservations expressed in De Robertis, 'Petrarca interprete di Dante', p. 311, n. 7.

60   See *Carmina*, ed. by Giuseppe Velli, in Giovanni Boccaccio, *Tutte le opere*, ed. by Vittore Branca (Milan: Mondadori, 1992), V:1, 386–91, 430–33, 476–80.

61   See Ugo Dotti, *Vita di Petrarca* (Bari: Laterza, 1987), pp. 221–23, 231–36, 330–32; Feo, pp. 451–52.

The moment was in fact critical. If, as has been suggestively maintained, a second text had accompanied Boccaccio's letter, namely the first and largely celebratory version of the *Trattatello in laude di Dante*, then the need for a public rebuttal of its encomiastic tones had become pressing.[62] At the same time, Petrarch must have thought that he had a reasonable chance of prevailing over Boccaccio, and so getting him to temper his assessment, since the younger writer himself seemed ready to concede that his enthusiasm was probably excessive: 'te michi excusas, idque non otiose, quod in conterranei nostri [...] laudibus multus fuisse videare' [you ask pardon, somewhat heatedly, for seeming to praise unduly a fellow countryman of ours] (1). If, on the one hand, Petrarch's treatment of Dante needed to be more vigorous than hitherto, on the other, its polemic — for the reasons I have already discussed — still had to be carefully controlled. *Fam.* XXI. 15 is thus a model of understated ambiguity.[63] Dante is assessed against the backcloth of contemporary culture, whose sordid state is sharply brought into focus. What initially read like tributes to the poet imperceptibly dissolve into their opposites, especially because they are diluted by being mingled with the corruption of the present. For instance, recognition of Dante's vernacular prowess is undercut by the fact that his use of his mother tongue increasingly appears as a device to gain the support of that uncouth *vulgus* whose shameful antics degrade current intellectual and artistic life, as it is this undiscriminating mass that most loudly celebrates him.[64] Petrarch stresses that, given his *ingenium*, Dante should not have wasted his time on an 'ingenii rudimentum' [a mental exercise] (21), which a youthful Petrarch had quickly abandoned as far too trifling. Dante should and could have aimed higher:

> Nam quod inter laudes dixisti, potuisse illum si voluisset alio stilo [Latin] uti, credo edepol [...] potuisse eum omnia quibus intendisset; nunc quibus intenderit, palam est. [...] fuisse illum sibi imparem, quod in vulgari eloquio quam carminibus aut prosa [in Latin] clarior atque altior assurgit. (*Fam.* XXI. 15. 22 & 24)[65]

---

62   The different versions of the *Trattatello* can be read in *Trattatello in laude di Dante*, ed. by Pier Giorgio Ricci, in Boccaccio, *Tutte le opere* (1974), III, 423–538.

63   'Sul fatto che la XXI 15 nasca sotto il segno dell'ambiguità credo non si possa dubitare' (Pasquini, p. 27).

64   '[P]opularis quidem quod ad stilum attinet [...] ventosisque diu vulgi plausibus agitatam [fax] atque ut sic dixerim fatigatam [...] ut vel sic michi odia vulgarium conflent quibus acceptissimus ille est [...] et stilus in suo genere optimus' [Popular for his poetic style [...] and his flame is fanned, and I shall say wearied, by the constant fickle approbation of the crowd [...] so as to inspire against me the hatred of that vulgar crowd by whom he is most appreciated [...] and his style is excellent of its kind] (1, 3, 6, 9).

65   The ambiguity that indelibly marks Petrarch's treatment of Dante is clearly apparent in these interconnected passages. On the one hand, Petrarch appears to acknowledge that Dante could have succeeded as a Latin writer; on the other, he criticizes what his predecessor actually wrote in the classical language. If we can be confident in concluding that *carmina* refers to the eclogues, it is much less clear what Petrarch might have meant by *prosa* (see n. 6 above). If one were to hazard a guess, among Dante's prose works, the *Monarchia* was the least unlikely text that he may have read. But hard evidence is lacking to bolster such an assumption. It is thus rather more likely that Petrarch's assessment is based not on a direct knowledge of any of Dante's Latin prose works, but simply on an awareness that his predecessor had written such works — a fact that, inter alia, he could have learned

[In praising him you suggest that he could, if he wished, have used another style; I heartily agree [...] that he could do anything he undertook; but what he did choose to attempt is clear. [...] his style was unequal, for he rises to nobler and loftier heights in the vernacular than in Latin poetry or prose.]

In maintaining that Dante so obviously failed to do justice to his talent, Petrarch creates the strong suspicion that his predecessor had chosen to write in the vernacular for less than honourable reasons. Just as seriously, the combination of Dante's choice of language and his apparent wish to reach his untutored audience had led him to make the most basic of writerly errors, and so further debase his *ingenium*. As Giovanni del Virgilio had first lamented several decades earlier (*Ecl.* I. 6–24), Petrarch too remarks that Dante incongruously clothed 'lofty' *materia* in a 'low' style: 'popularis quidem quod ad stilum attinet, quod ad rem hauddubie nobilis poete' [popular for his poetic style but doubtless noble for his theme] (I). Tellingly, this observation comes at the very beginning of the letter, immediately establishing its basic rhetoric of ambiguity — the *conterraneus* is perplexingly both 'popular' and 'noble' — and of allusion: the 'fellow-citizen' and his work, as happens throughout the epistle, remain unnamed, though it is obvious that, as we have come to expect, Petrarch's barbs, even more than at Dante, are unerringly aimed at the *Commedia*.[66]

---

from the *Trattatello*. In any case, Petrarch's aim is clear: to fix Dante as a vernacular writer whose commitment to composing in Latin was negligible.

66   Saverio Bellomo has recently suggested that Petrarch's failure to name Dante should not be deemed a 'segno di disprezzo' but an instance of that 'reticente retorica epistolare, che prevedeva di non nominare le persone ove fosse possibile capire egualmente di chi si parlasse': Saverio Bellomo, 'Il sorriso di Ilaro e la prima redazione in latino della *Commedia*', *Studi sul Boccaccio*, 32 (2004), 201–35 (p. 203). I am not persuaded by this suggestion, not only because it goes against the epistle's overall negative treatment of Dante, but also because Petrarch makes it clear that his decision not to name the poet is practical and not rhetorical: 'Solent enim plerique michi odium, ut dixi, alii contemptum viri huius obicere, cuius hodie nomine scienter abstinui, ne illud infamari clamitans cuncta audiens nichil intelligens vulgus obstreperet' [For many people often reproach me for hatred, as I said, and others for disdain against this man, whose name I have here omitted deliberately, lest the crowd, which hears everything but understands nothing, cry out loud that he has been insulted] (19). In any case, even this explanation is unpersuasive, since the identity of the *vir* is more than obvious. Petrarch's unwillingness to name Dante is consistent with his customary strategy of granting his precursor as little recognition as possible and of shrouding his achievements in ambiguity. Finally, in Petrarch, anonymity is usually a mark of disdain; it is enough to think of the four false friends condemned in the *De ignorantia* or the nameless 'foolish authorities' attacked in *Sen.* v. 2: 'Nolo ego nomen facere quibus ipsa res nullum fecit, etsi furor ingens faciat, nolo inter maximos ponere quos inter minimos vidi' [I do not want to make a name for those whose accomplishments have not done so, although their great madness may achieve this, I do not want to place among the greatest men those whom I saw among the least] (66). As with other aspects of Petrarch's treatment of Dante, *Fam.* XXI. 15 has elicited contrasting interpretations. Especially by reading the epistle selectively, some scholars have judged it a largely positive assessment of Dante or have attempted to minimize its contradictions; see De Robertis, 'Petrarca interprete di Dante', pp. 308–10; Feo, pp. 451–52; Martinelli, 'Dante nei *Rerum vulgarium fragmenta*', pp. 122–23; Paolazzi, pp. 135–46, 154–66; Pasquini. Others have concentrated primarily on its negative elements; see Paparelli, 'Due modi opposti', pp. 77–83; Sasso; Tanturli, pp. 200–05. There have been few attempts, in fact, to examine the rhetorical and ideological implications — as I endeavour to do in this section — of the interplay between the letter's positive and negative declarations; notable exceptions to this critical trend are Kuon, *L'aura*

Petrarch, who throughout the letter presents himself as a sympathetic, intellectually sophisticated, and disinterested admirer of Dante, is, as such, naturally well within his rights to raise questions regarding his forerunner's recourse to the *vulgaris*. This seems to have been essentially dictated by an all-absorbing Ulyssean desire for glory: 'exilio [...] ille obstitit, et tum vehementius cepto incubuit, omnium negligens soliusque fame cupidus' [he resisted exile and began devoting himself all the more vigorously to his literary pursuits, neglecting all else and desirous only of glory] (7). Dante, like his Greek anti-hero, was prepared to sacrifice everything and everyone to achieve his aim: 'non amor coniugis, non natorum pietas ab arrepto semel calle distraheret' [nothing [...] not his wife's love or his devotion to his children diverted him from his course once he had embarked upon it] (8).[67] Indeed, by appealing so blatantly to the *ineptissimi laudatores* — to the extremely silly admirers — rather than to the intellectual elite, he revealed not just the all-consuming strength of his obsession, but also, more worryingly (and unlike Petrarch), his lack of discrimination and his naked opportunism: 'novi enim quanti sit apud doctos indoctorum laus' [for I know how little the praise of the ignorant multitude carries weight with learned men] (22). We are once more in familiar territory. Petrarch is rehearsing again the same accusations as those he had levied against Dante in his poetry. These may very well still be carefully circumscribed; for instance, Petrarch seems to praise his precursor's singlemindedness: 'In quo illum satis mirari et laudare vix valeam' [In this I can scarcely admire and praise him too highly] (8); however, his indictments are also unmistakably less allusive. Thus, Petrarch is almost explicit in charging Dante with immorality, lightly concealing his indictment behind the veil of an optative: 'ita dico si quantum delectat ingenio, tantum moribus delectaret' [that is, if his conduct were to please me as much as his genius] (15). Equally, Dante's pursuit of glory, of wanting to receive the recognition of others (and what others), points to a profound lack of virtue: 'quod quamvis meritorum gloria ad merendi studium animos excitet, vera tamen virtus, ut philosophis placet, ipsa sibi stimulus, ipsa est premium, ipsa sibi cursus et bravium' [while the glory of deserving men stimulates in the mind an enthusiasm for such glory, true virtue, as philosophers like to say, is its own spur and its own reward, its own way and its own goal] (5).[68]

The letter leaves little doubt that Dante cannot be numbered among the *meriti*. Neither his behaviour nor his art are worthy of such an accolade. Indeed, Petrarch is at pains to underscore that Dante is rather less exceptional than is generally believed. Thus, he was not really very different from Petrarch's father ('ut quibus

---

dantesca, pp. 16–21; McLaughlin, pp. 35–37; Pastore Stocchi, pp. 184–86; Gilson, pp. 32–37.

67   On the letter's recourse to Dante's Ulysses, see Umberto Bosco, *Dante vicino: contributi e letture* (Caltanissetta and Rome: Sciascia, 1966), pp. 173–96; Fenzi, 'Tra Dante e Petrarca', pp. 509–10; Gilson, pp. 33–34; Pasquini, pp. 23–27; Sasso, pp. 393–96. See also Michelangelo Picone, 'Il sonetto CLXXXIX', *Lectura Petrarce*, 9 (1989), 151–77.

68   Petrarch expresses a similar opinion, albeit implicitly, regarding Dante's pursuit of literary fame as proof of his lack of virtue both in the *Triumphi* (see pp. 363–72 above) and in *Sen.* V. 2 (see pp. 380–81 below). Boccaccio, too, in the *Trattatello* — Petrarch's possible source on this point especially as regards Dante's striving after the 'vano favor popolesco' — notes the poet of the *Commedia*'s strong desire for glory. In general, however, Boccaccio is rather more indulgent toward Dante's aspiration than his friend; see first redaction pars. 22. 63 (from where the quotation is taken), and 125.

esset preter similem fortunam, studiorum et ingenii multa similitudo' [in addition to a similar fate, they were very similar in studious interests and intellectually], 7);[69] nor can he serve as a positive role model, as is evident from the fact that, despite being the youthful Boccaccio's 'primus studiorum dux et prima fax' [first guide and the light of his youthful studies] (2), he failed to provide his ward with the moral and intellectual wisdom that would have prevented him from committing those many errors which Petrarch feels compelled to list in *Fam.* XXI. 15; nor, as the young Petrarch had quickly realized, revealing greater acuity than Boccaccio, is he a poet who deserves to be imitated: 'sed verebar ne si huius aut alterius dictis imbuerer, ut est etas illa flexibilis et miratrix omnium, vel invitus ac nesciens imitator evaderem' [but I was afraid that, were I to immerse myself in his, or any other's, writings, being of an impressionable age so given to indiscriminate admiration, I would end up an unwilling or unconscious imitator] (11). Petrarch's Dante is a poor teacher, a flawed literary model, a man of dubious ethical standards; he almost stands as an emblem, if not actually a cause, of the corruption of the present. Yet despite all this, there are those who deem him an *auctoritas*. And it is not only the *vulgus* who pays tribute to him in this way. There are intellectuals like Boccaccio, who, showing a remarkable lack of discrimination, ally themselves to the mob, thereby besmirching their standing as men of learning: 'novi enim quanti sit apud doctos indoctorum laus' [for I know how little the praise of the ignorant multitude carries weight with learned men] (22). Boccaccio — Petrarch is quick to recognize — has an almost sacred duty to recognize his debts to his mentor; however, in acknowledging these, he was not supposed to abandon his critical and ethical faculties. We have at last reached the nub of Petrarch's argument in *Fam.* XXI. 15. It is less Dante and the *Commedia* that aggravate him than their reception, hence the persistent denigration of the present and the flow of reprimands directed at Boccaccio.[70] Dante was a blatant and unscrupulous seeker after fame. However, for all his efforts at self-authorization, it is his readers who, nearly half a century after his death, are ultimately responsible for allowing him to continue to exert unjustified sway over the contemporary world.[71]

69   See Gilson, pp. 33–34; Tanturli, p. 201.
70   On the 'highly partial construction' that is Petrarch's account of the *Commedia*'s reception, see Gilson, pp. 35–37.
71   Petrarch's criticism of Dante's reception cannot but include the commentary tradition on the *Commedia* (although, in the light of our present knowledge, it is impossible to say which, if any, specific commentators the poet might have had in mind when he voiced his censures). Indeed, in *Sen.* V. 2, Petrarch condemns contemporary men of letters who not only do not dedicate themselves to the study of the classics but also undermine these by drawing on modern 'authorities': 'Sed quid, queso, literatos homines excusabit, qui cum veterum non ignari esse debeant, in eadem opinionum cecitate versantur? Scito me, amice, acri stomaco hec iratum loqui. Surgunt his diebus dyaleticuli non ignari tantum, sed insani et quasi formicarum nigra acies nescio cuius cariose quercus e latebris erumpunt omnia doctrine melioris arva vastantes. Hi Platonem atque Aristotilem damnant, Socratem ac Pythagoram rident. Et, Deus bone, quibus hec ducibus, quam ineptis agunt! Nolo ego nomen facere quibus ipsa res nullum fecit, etsi furor ingens faciat, nolo inter maximos ponere quos inter minimos vidi, horum tamen isti nominibus gloriantur, relictisque fidis ducibus hos sequuntur, qui nescio an post obitum didicerint, certe vivi nec scientiam nec famam ullam scientie habuerunt. Quid de his dicam qui Marcum Tullium Ciceronem, lucidum eloquentie solem, spernunt? Qui Varronem, qui Senecam contemnunt? Qui Titi Livi, qui Salustii stilum horrent, ceu asperum atque

incultum? Et hi quoque novis freti ducibus pudendisque' [But what will excuse, I ask, men of letters, who, although they ought not be unaware of the ancient writers, fall into the same blindness of opinion? Know, my friend, that I speak these words out of indignation and anger. Some minor dialecticians have sprung up these days who are not only ignorant, but senseless, and almost like a dark line of ants they spring forth from the holes of who knows what withered oak, devastating all the fields of better/true learning. They condemn Plato and Aristotle, they ridicule Socrates and Pythagoras. And, good Lord, they do this with what ill-suited guides/authorities! I do not want to make a name for those whose accomplishments have not done so, although their great madness may achieve this; I do not want to place among the greatest men those whom I saw among the least, however, the senseless vaunt their names and, leaving behind trustworthy authorities, they follow these, who I do not know if they became knowledgeable after death, but certainly while living did not have knowledge or any fame of knowledge. What shall I say of those who scorn Marcus Tullius Cicero, the bright light of eloquence? Who despise Varro and Seneca? Who are horrified at the style of Titus Livy and of Sallust, as if rough and uncultivated? And they too rely on new authorities of which they should be ashamed] (63–67). It is not difficult to recognize in these words an attack on Dante's literary and cultural canonization. The 'esigua tradizione che attribuisce a Petraca un commento al poema dantesco, collocabile tra la fine del XIV secolo e la prima metà del successivo' (Rossi, p. 303) is certainly not based on fact. If its claims were true, this would mean that 'Francesco Petrarca, qualificato coi titoli che gli competono [...], accetta di farsi servo del poema dantesco e, per di più, di soggiacergli nella scelta del volgare; dal momento che il poeta laureato si piega a un compito tanto umile, Dante è degno di tanto omaggio e, dunque, poeta supremo' (Rossi, p. 308). Equally fictitious is Guglielmo Maramauro's claim that 'E tanto con l'aiuto de questi exposituri, quanto con l'aiuto [...] de miser Francesco Petrarca [...] io me mossi a volere prendere questa dura impresa [of composing a commentary on Dante]': Guglielmo Maramauro, *Expositione sopra l''Inferno' di Dante Alligieri*, ed. by Pier Giacomo Pisoni and Saverio Bellomo (Padua: Antenore, 1998), Prologo 13. Although Maramauro was certainly in contact with Petrarch, as evidenced by *Sen.* XI. 5 and XV. 4, the claim that he wrote his commentary with the poet's help represents a typical example of his strategy of exaggerated and fabricated self–aggrandizement; see Barański, '*Chiosar con altro testo*', pp. 117–52.

As regards Petrarch's attitude to the Dante commentary tradition, *Sen.* IV. 5, in which the poet instructs Federigo Aretino on how to read and interpret the *Aeneid*, and which was written in the same years as *Sen.* V. 2, both acts as a reminder of which poets deserve to be celebrated, and serves as a model of how they ought to be studied. It is surprising, therefore, that Michele Feo should have seen in *Sen.* IV. 5 'uno degli sforzi più umanisticamente impegnati a conciliare classico (Virgilio) e moderno (Dante), o meglio a capire, ad assorbire, a sistemare il moderno entro una visione classica' (p. 453). Feo bases his claim on the fact that Petrarch pays considerable attention to the wood of *Aeneid* I, which in the original is only fleetingly considered (164–68, 312–14) — a fact which he sees as positively allusive to the 'selva oscura' (*Inf.* I. 2). In particular, '[i]l tocco più scopertamente dantesco è l'interpretazione del "media...silva" come *mezzo del cammin di nostra vita* ("circa tempus vitae medium")' (p. 453). Petrarch's full description of the wood runs as follows: 'Silva vero vita hec, umbris atque erroribus plena perplexisque tramitibus atque incertis et feris habitata, hoc est difficultatibus et periculis multis atque occultis, infructuosa et inhospita et herbarum virore et cantu avium et aquarum murmure, idest brevi et caduca specie et inani ac fallaci dulcedine rerum pretereuntium atque labentium accolarum oculos atque aures interdiu leniens ac demulcens, lucis in finem horribilis ac tremenda adventuque hiemis ceno feda, solo squalida, truncis horrida frondibusque spoliata. Venus obvia silve medio ipsa est voluptas circa tempus vite medium ferventior atque acrior; os habitumque virgineum gerit ut illudat insciis; nam si quis eam qualis est cerneret, haud dubie visu solo tremefactus aufugeret; ut enim nichil blandius, sic nichil est fedius voluptate' [But the wood represents this life, filled with shadows and errors, confusing and uncertain paths, and inhabited by wild beasts, that is by many unexpected obstacles and perils; barren and inhospitable, yet with lush grass, the song of birds, and the murmuring of waters, that is, with brief and vain appearance and with the empty and deceptive sweetness of transitory things that whither, it soothes and allures the eyes and ears at daytime; but at the end of the day the wood becomes horrible

Consequently, they fail to give credit to a more worthy 'authority' figure humbly working in their midst; in fact, they attack him without justification and accuse him of harbouring feelings of envy and hatred toward their fatally defective idol. Their judgment is, of course, profoundly flawed: 'hos ineptissimos laudatores, qui omnino quid laudent quid ve improbent ex equo nescio' [these extremely silly admirers who never know why they praise or censure] (16). Among current readers of Dante, only Petrarch is able properly to evaluate him, since, far from blinded by resentment, he neither owes him a debt nor has been taken in by his blandishments: 'cum unus ego forte, melius quam multi ex his insulsis et immodicis laudatoribus, sciam quid id est eis ipsis incognitum quod illorum aures mulcet, sed obstructis ingenii tramitibus in animum non descendit' [when perhaps I alone, more than many of these tasteless and immoderate admirers, know the nature of that unknown quality that charms their ears without penetrating their minds since the pathways of intelligence are closed to them] (14). He can estimate both Dante's merits and demerits, praising the former and chastising the latter. Dante's merits, restricted as they are to 'immature' and 'slight' achievements in the vernacular, cannot but be limited; yet, within this marginal tradition, Dante is the best, and Petrarch is pleased to praise his success and even potentially to defend him: 'que ego forsitan, nisi me meorum cura vocaret alio, pro virili parte ab hoc ludibrio vendicarem' [if my many concerns were not so pressing, I might even strive to the best of my powers to rescue him] (16).[72] Petrarch thus comes across as the very ideal of intellectual fair play, approaching others in a spirit of *charitas* but also of moral rectitude. He, not Dante, is the model that the dissolute present ought to be heeding.[73]

and fearful, and with the coming of winter loathsome with mud, squalidly barren, bristling with trunks, and stripped of its foliage. Venus who comes forward in the middle of the wood represents lust, which is more impetuous and keener around midlife; and assumes a maidenly semblance and dress to deceive the ignorant; for if anyone saw her for what she actually is, he would no doubt flee just at the sight of her; as nothing is in fact more alluring than lust, so nothing is more repulsive] (25–26). The weaknesses in Feo's case clearly emerge when Petrarch's complete text is taken into consideration. Thus, the allusion to 'vitae medium' refers not so much to the wood as to Venus-*voluptas*; similarly, the differences between Petrarch's rewriting of the Virgilian wood and Dante's 'selva selvaggia' (*Inf.* I. 5), are obvious and striking, implying, if anything, a polemical response to the opening of the *Commedia*. Furthermore, the kind of amplification of a relatively minor detail which Feo deems as especially significant is, in fact, typical of medieval exegesis. There is nothing in the epistle to support the idea that it constitutes 'uno degli sforzi più umanisticamente impegnati a conciliare classico (Virgilio) e moderno (Dante)'. On the other hand, Feo's analysis reveals much about modern scholarship's increasingly frantic efforts to establish that Petrarch had managed to achieve 'riconciliazione con Dante' (p. 453).

72   It is striking that Petrarch, as is typical of his ambiguous allusiveness in the epistle, fails to be specific as regards Dante's vernacular achievements. The failure explicitly to refer to the *Commedia* is a constant in his writing. It thus does not come as much of a surprise that 'quando ottenne quel codice [of the *Commedia*] dal Boccaccio dimenticò le sue abitudini di postillatore zelantissimo e appena depositò su tante e mirabili pagine un unico, microscopico segno di lettura' (Billanovich, 'L'altro stil nuovo', pp. 90–91). See also Billanovich, *Petrarca letterato*, p. 175; Carlo Pulsoni, 'Il Dante di Francesco Petrarca: Vaticano latino 3199', *Studi petrarcheschi*, n.s. 10 (1992), 155–208.

73   Antonelli is undoubtedly correct to assert that 'la sufficienza con cui Petrarca risponde a Boccaccio circa le sue letture dantesche [...] rivela [...] la coscienza di una consapevole, forte e *autonoma* diversità: quella di un umanista che è poeta volgare ma anche nuovo frequentatore dei

Fam. XXI. 15 is a skilful, tightly constructed piece of writing. It is perfectly pitched to unsettle with its powerful mix of *laus* and *vituperatio* — a mix that is the key to understanding Petrarch's attitude to Dante, and that we as scholars must do our best not to distill, eliminating what we find troubling and unsatisfactory.[74] Yet despite the epistle's impact on Boccaccio — an impact, nevertheless, that should not be exaggerated — its views failed to have a broader effect on Trecento intellectual opinion. *Sen.* V. 2, written between 1365 and 1366 and once more addressed to Boccaccio, offers unambiguous evidence of this state of affairs. It is an even more violent attack on the intellectual, moral, and cultural corruption of the present than the 'Familiar' letter — a present in which the triumphs of the ancients are scorned and the foremost intellectual continues to be Dante, 'ille nostri eloquii dux vulgaris' [the master of our vernacular literature] (30).[75] This is the only point in the missive where reference is openly, albeit periphrastically, made to Dante, though other elements in it are recognizable as typical of Petrarch's effort to destabilize the poet's contemporary image. Thus, we find mention of the limitations of vernacular culture; of those who 'vulgi quoque suffragiis annixi' [rely on the votes of the crowd] (29); and of the fact that 'vix quisquam iustus sui operis extimator' [scarcely anyone is a fair judge of his own [creations]] (4), and that 'melius tutiusque est operose virtutis auxilio niti quam otiose fame praeconio fidere' [it is better and safer to rely upon the support of active virtue than to count on the praises of idle fame] (39).[76] However, probably the most revealing, one might say, the most emblematic, instance of this subterranean collection of Petrarchan anti-Dante commonplaces is

classici' (p. 63).

74   On the centrality of *laus* and *vituperatio* in medieval poetics, see *MLTC*, pp. 282–84. See also the close of Dante's *De vulgari eloquentia* (II. 14. 2) together with Mengaldo's notes (*Dve*, pp. 236–37).

75   For instance, when providing an explanation for Boccaccio's decision to destroy his works, Petrarch writes: 'sed indignatione quadam clara, et nobili, aetati inutili ac superbe nihil intelligenti, omnia corrumpenti, quodque est intollerabilis contemnenti, tui iuditium ingenii, surripere voluisset' [but that by a sort of illustrious and noble indignation, you have decided to withdraw any judgment on your talent from a worthless and arrogant age that understands nothing but corrupts and — this is intolerable — disdains everything] (50).

76   '[A]t hic, modo [stilus vulgaris] inventus, adhuc recens, vastatoribus crebris ac raro squalidus colono, magni se vel ornamenti capacem ostenderet vel augmenti. Quid vis? Hac spe tractus simulque stimulis actus adolescientie magnum eo in genere opus inceperam iactisque iam quasi edificii fundamentis calcem ac lapides et lignam congesseram, dum ad nostram repiciens etatem, et superbie matrem et ignavie, cepi acriter advertere quanta esset illa iactantium ingenii vis, quanta pronuntiationis amenitas, ut non recitari scripta diceres sed discerpi. Hoc semel, hoc iterum, hoc sepe audiens et magis magisque mecum reputans, intellexi tandem, molli in limo et instabili arena perdi operam meque et laborem meum inter vulgi manus laceratum iri' [but this [vernacular style], just invented, still recent, debased by frequent ravagers and cultivated by few husbandmen, showed itself capable of great development and embellishment. What shall I say? Attracted by this hope and driven by the spurs of youth I had begun a great work in that style, and after laying the foundations of the building, as it were, I gathered lime and stones and wood; I then began looking at our age, mother of pride and idleness, and I started keenly to notice how vigorous were the talents of those show offs in this style, how great the charm of their delivery, to the point that I should say that those writings were not recited but mutilated. Hearing this once, twice, then often, and pondering it more and more, I finally understood that a work built on soft mud and shifting sand is a waste of effort, and that I and my labour would have been torn to shreds by the hands of the crowd] (52–54).

the letter's lapidary title: 'de appetitu anxio primi loci atque impatientia secundi deque superbissima modernorum ignorantia' [concerning the obsessive appetite for first place and the dissatisfaction for second place and concerning the arrogant ignorance of the moderns].[77]

The time has come to acknowledge that, for all Petrarch's claims of independence, objectivity, and appreciation, he squarely belonged within the tradition of Trecento anti-*dantismo*, just as, in general, his reaction to the poet of the *Commedia* cannot be detached from Dante's overall fourteenth-century reception. Petrarch most certainly had personal reasons for wanting to redimension his precursor's reputation and *auctoritas*. At the same time, however, he was extremely careful to voice his criticisms in a manner that would find immediate and clear resonance in his world. In this way, not only could he expect his censures to find a receptive audience, but, more astutely, he could also ensure that his opinions, by being grounded in contemporary *dantismo*, would not be dismissed as the jaundiced accusations of an embittered rival, thereby safeguarding that much sought-after pose of 'objectivity'. That things did not really work out as Petrarch had intended, as evidenced by the ongoing consolidation of Dante's standing in the Tre- and Quattrocento, is, of course, quite another matter, though it does confirm the difficulties that he faced in attempting to challenge Dante's *auctoritas*. Petrarch thus drew on, and to a large extent hid behind, the doubts and criticisms — which, like his, stretched from poetics to ethics and from scholarly competence to behaviour — voiced by other contemporary readers. Although the tradition served as the legitimating basis of Petrarch's operation, in practice he adapted it to his own purposes, amplifying, developing, and, most tellingly, bringing together reservations that, normally, not only were kept apart but also were overshadowed by significantly more generous evaluations of Dante than his. He thus cleverly transformed the communal into the personal. Ultimately, Petrarch's was an extreme form of anti-Dantism, in which idiosyncrasy and tradition merged, and where 'defence' was actually attack.

5. 'Disguising' Dante

Having reached this point in my argument, I hope that both the principal lineaments of Petrarch's Dante and the cultural and ideological pressures that helped shape the younger poet's reactions to his illustrious predecessor are becoming apparent. However, given the strength of Petrarch's reservations, what is still far from clear is why, beyond the desire to give a conventional nod in Dante's direction and to exploit his 'authority' to his own advantage, the poet granted him so much space in the formal fabric of the *Canzoniere*. The answer, not surprisingly, lies in Petrarch's description of Dante as a certain kind of vernacular love poet. Given the dominant stylistic tenor and the principal thematic and narrative concerns of the *Rerum vulgarium fragmenta*, one instinctively thinks that the Dante who would

77   On *Sen.* v. 2 see Monica Berté, "Introduzione', in Francesco Petrarca, *Senile V 2*, ed. by Monica Berté (Florence: Le Lettere, 1998), pp. 2–31; Feo, p. 452; McLaughlin, pp. 37–38; Carla Maria Monti, 'Per la *Senile* v 2 di Francesco Petrarca', *Studi petrarcheschi*, n.s. 15 (2002), 99–128.

best fit the demands of the lyric collection is the author of the *Vita nova*. The *libello* and the *Canzoniere* share a preference for formal *dulcedo*, and are lyric love stories centred on a woman who is the source of both crisis and salvation, and whose death has a fundamental impact on her lover, as well as having a profound effect on the narrative and structural organization of each text. Yet, almost certainly because of such similarities, Petrarch, as we shall see, was at pains to conceal and minimize the possible ties between his collection and Dante's 'anthology'.[78] What Petrarch was never willing to acknowledge was that he owed Dante any kind of significant debt. As a result, there are few readily recognizable echoes in the *Canzoniere* from the stilnovist Dante. In fact, most borrowings from the *Vita nova*, as well as from lyrics belonging to this phase of Dante's poetic career, that scholars have highlighted in the *Rerum vulgarium fragmenta* are either erotic clichés or widely circulating lyric *dantismi*.[79]

To discover the physiognomy of Petrarch's erotic Dante, we need to turn to the evidence offered by the *Canzoniere*'s most open statement of erotic poetics and of literary definition, namely *canzone* 70, 'Lasso me, ch'i' non so in qual parte pieghi', which I have already had occasion to discuss briefly. The poem's importance is immediately obvious both from its strategic position in the Correggio version of the collection and,[80] more significantly, from its being constructed around the opening lines of five *canzoni* written by five different eminent poets.[81] The incipit of each of these *canzoni* is cited as the explicit of one of the five stanzas of 'Lasso me'. Accordingly, each stanza becomes emblematic of the writer whose line it includes. The poets, in the order in which they are alluded to in the *canzone*, are Arnaut Daniel, Guido Cavalcanti, Dante, Cino da Pistoia, and Petrarch himself, who closes his poem by citing *canzone* 23 of the *Canzoniere*, 'Nel dolce tempo de la prima etade'. *Canzone* 70, like Petrarch's other Dante-centred texts, is highly

78   On the structural and ideological similarities and tensions between the *Vita nova* and the *Canzoniere*, see in particular Malzacher's excellent book. See also Antonelli, pp. 56–63; Carrai; Picone, 'Tempo e racconto'; Kuon, *L'aura dantesca*, pp. 147–48, 213–14; Martinelli, 'L'ordinamento morale'; Regn; Sturm-Maddox, 'Transformations of Courtly Love Poetry'; Warkentin. See also De Robertis, 'A quale tradizione', pp. 136–37.

79   See, for instance, Capovilla, p. 338; however, now see also Malzacher.

80   'È dunque ipotizzabile che anche 70, come i principali testi di cornice della redazione Correggio (1, 142, 264), sia stata composta espressamente in funzione della raccolta che P. progetta dopo la morte di Laura e di cui Co sembrerebbe essere la prima organica sistemazione. Dei testi di cornice la canzone ha la rilevanza strutturale: collocata, insieme alle "cantilene oculorum", a metà delle rime in vita della redazione Co, e subito a ridosso dei testi romani, segna un netto discrimine nella vicenda narrata in quella redazione [...]. La svolta consiste in un passaggio da una concezione sensuale e pessimistica dell'amore (che ha nel Dante petroso la sua marca stilistica) a una visone spiritualeggiante che potremmo chiamare stilnovistica, con il conseguente muntamento di segno del personaggio di Laura' (Santagata, pp. 347–48). As I discuss below, 'Lasso me' does not simply mark this *svolta* but also explores it through its system of poetic quotations and reminiscences.

81   On *canzone* 70, see Corrado Bologna, 'PetrArca petroso', *Critica del testo*, 6 (2003), 367–420, and 'Occhi, solo occhi', pp. 194–97; Claire Cabaillot, 'La chanson *Lasso me* de Pétrarque ou l'écriture de la différence', *Cahiers d'études romanes*, 2 (1999), 39–49; Rino Caputo, *Cogitans fingo: Petrarca tra 'Secretum' e 'Canzoniere'* (Rome: Bulzoni, 1987), pp. 119–70; Istvàn Frank, 'La Chanson "Lasso me" de Pétrarque et ses prédécesseurs', *Annales du Midi*, 66 (1954), 259–68; Santagata, *Per moderne carte*, pp. 327–62.

complex. As regards its metaliterary connotations, it can be considered from at least three interconnected perspectives: first, it offers an account of the development of Petrarch's attitude to love and poetry about love; second, it reveals the nature of his relationship to the four poets quoted and to that earlier phase of his artistic career symbolized by *canzone* 23; and third, thanks especially to the stanza in which a particular poet is recalled, it provides a definition of each of his four precursors. As might be expected, this last perspective offers the best insight into the literary erotic identity that Petrarch was keen to allot to Dante.

It is useful to begin by citing the canzone's third, 'Dante' stanza in its entirety:

> Vaghi pensier' che così passo passo
> scorto m'avete a ragionar tant'alto,
> vedete che madonna à 'l cor di smalto,
> sì forte, ch'io per me dentro nol passo.
> Ella non degna di mirar sì basso
> che di nostre parole
> curi, ché 'l ciel non vòle
> al qual pur contrastando i' son già lasso:
> onde, come nel cor m'induro e 'naspro,
> *così nel mio parlar voglio esser aspro.* (*Rvf* 70. 21–30)

What is immediately striking about this stanza in comparison to the other four is its anomalousness. Dante is being deliberately isolated and tagged as 'abnormal'. Thus, although in 'Lasso me' Petrarch carefully alludes to specific poems, Dante's *petrosa* is the only one of the five *canzoni* cited whose subject-matter and formal qualities find obvious resonance in the stanza that incorporates it. While the other poets' verses seem open to transformation and to being adapted, Dante's poetry, on the other hand, like the 'stony lady', seems fixed and unable to change. The inflexibility of the Dantean state is emphasized by a hugely revelatory detail. The fifth line of each stanza, apart of course from the third, opens with a conditional *se* clause, which expresses the wish for a different and improved situation from that sketched in the *fronte*, thereby acknowledging that change is at least a possibility. Indeed, the hope of a better future expressed in the Arnaut and Cavalcanti stanzas — a hope that is absolutely denied in the Dante one — finds reassuring confirmation in the last two stanzas.[82] Here, as the lover begins to take responsibility for his behaviour, the aspiration that he might one day be able to exert greater control over his life becomes a very real prospect.[83] For Dante, no such escape from a bleakly depressing condition presents itself. If anything, and again uniquely, his circumstances deteriorate as 'his' stanza progresses. The lineaments of Petrarch's erotic Dante are unmistakable. He is represented as the embodiment of a doomed

---

82 'Ma s'egli aven ch'anchor non mi si nieghi | finir anzi 'l mio fine | queste voci meschine, | non gravi al mio signor perch'io il ripreghi | di dir libero un dì tra l'erba e i fiori: | *Drez et rayson es qu'ieu ciant e· m demori*' (5–10); 'Et s'io potesse far ch'agli occhi santi | porgesse alcun dilecto | qualche dolce mio detto, | o me beato sopra gli altri amanti! | Ma più, quand'io dirò senza mentire: | *Donna mi priegha, per ch'io voglio dire*' (15–20).

83 'e chi m'inganna, | altri ch'io stesso e 'l desir soverchio? | Già s'i' trascorro il ciel di cerchio in cerchio, | nessun pianeta a pianger mi condanna' (31–34).

negative sense of love — a sentiment to which he gives expression in a suitably harsh language: 'onde, come nel cor m'induro e 'naspro, | così nel mio parlar voglio esser aspro'. Dante's complex experience as a love poet, indeed as a vernacular poet, is thus drastically limited to his brief 'stony' moment. This is the one point in Dante's career that Petrarch seems willing to acknowledge as being both valid and distinct in terms of the tradition, and as having relevance for his own poetry. Yet, as we have started to see, he ensured that even this, ever so narrow instance of Dante's artistic and intellectual life was heavily circumscribed. Petrarch's Dante is no longer the poet of hope, reform, and salvation, namely the poet of the *Commedia*, but is the damned and eccentric poet of erotic despair, of a lonely hell-like stasis. 'Lasciate ogne speranza, voi ch'intrate' (*Inf.* III. 9) — the inscription over the gate of Hell seems to have been written exclusively for him. The universalizing *auctoritas* has been transformed into an embittered, self-centred symbol of isolation.

Petrarch was unrelenting in his effort to demolish Dante's Trecento fame. If, on the one hand, fixing his predecessor as *petroso* conformed to his trusted general strategy of *deminutio*, which combined large dollops of *vituperatio* with a sprinkling of *laus*, on the other, such a characterization of his rival also offered specific advantages to the *Canzoniere* and its author. By presenting Dante in this manner, Petrarch was able to distract attention from, if not actually to conceal, the influence that the *Vita nova* had indubitably exercised over his collection. Dante *stilnovista* is overwhelmed by Dante *petroso*; and the *libello*'s formal and ideological features become the exclusive preserve of the *Canzoniere*, thereby allowing Petrarch to enjoy total dominance over the field of vernacular love poetry.[84] In addition, the stress on Dante's 'stoniness' further served to sever his ties to the *Commedia*. Indeed, given the obvious equation between the *petrose* and the *Inferno*, the 'sacrato poema' (*Par.* XXIII. 62) is essentially reduced to its infernal 'rime aspre e chiocce' (*Inf.* XXXII. I). Thus, it is not surprising that the most marked borrowings from Dante in the *Rerum vulgarium fragmenta* are those taken from the *canzoni* about the *donna petra* and from the first canticle;[85] nor that, as regards the latter, *Inferno* V, that paradigm of negative love, is the canto most heavily ransacked.[86] Throughout the *Canzoniere*, the same forbidding image of Dante is relentlessly reiterated; and its negativity is further underscored as a result of the infernal and 'stony' intertexts being largely

---

84   And it is important to stress that this dominance is presented as total. Although Petrarch closely associated Dante with the 'stony' style, this does not mean that he accorded him artistic primacy in this manner. Quite the contrary. By absorbing Dante *petroso* into his own poetry, Petrarch made it clear that, as with other lyric registers, he was the master of the 'stony' one too.

85   On Petrarch's debts to the *petrose*, see Antoni; Berra: Bettarini, 'Perché "narrando" il duol si disacerba', p. 315; Cipollone, pp. 39–41; De Robertis, 'Petrarca petroso', and 'A quale tradizione', pp. 139–41; Ferdinando Neri, 'Il Petrarca e le rime dantesche della pietra', *La cultura*, 8 (1929), 389–404; Possiedi; Velli, 'Petrarca, Dante, la poesia classica'. Petrarch also drew significantly on another of Dante's 'negative' *canzoni*, one in fact with considerable ties to the *petrose*, namely the *montanina*; see Capovilla, p. 27.

86   See David, p. 16; Kuon, *L'aura dantesca*, pp. 57–83; Pastore Stocchi, pp. 188–90; Zanato, pp. 186–213. On the impact of *Inferno* V on the *Triumphi*, see Giunta, pp. 434–52; Pastore Stocchi, pp. 190–91.

used to describe moments of spiritual and psychological crisis.[87] As *canzone* 70 relates, Dante represents the 'other', all that Petrarch has to transcend if he is to reach literary, intellectual, and spiritual maturity. While it is appropriate for him to draw on his own artistic past and on the writings of others in order to continue to develop as a poet and a man, at the same time, if he wants to be artistically and morally successful, he has to shun Dante's Medusan lure.[88] And Petrarch leaves no doubt about this by publicly rejecting Dante's 'harshness': '*così nel mio parlar voglio esser aspro.* || Che parlo?' (30–31). Suggestively, when the poet finally draws explicitly on Dante, it is to highlight the fact that he must cease doing so. Petrarch reduces the great poet of plurilingualism to a flinty, arid, dangerous monotony, while displaying his own skill at controlling the 'vario stil' (*Rvf* 1. 5) necessary to tell his multifaceted story.[89] In this respect, Dante's overwhelming *petrosità* permits the *Canzoniere*, as with its camouflaging of the *Vita nova*, to hide its significant and now well-documented reliance on the *Commedia*'s rich array of 'non-harsh' elements, which, as a consequence, rather than recall their original author, appear as a natural part of Petrarch's personal lexicon;[90] and when the origin of such elements in Dante is actually highlighted, this is usually done, as we have seen, to turn them against their creator.[91]

Rather than repression or unconscious repetition, what we are faced with is calculation; and of a very high order at that, as a rapid *explication* of the third stanza of *canzone* 70 quickly confirms. The stanza, especially if read in Dantean terms, begins ominously and becomes ever more negative. Petrarch's Dante is immediately accused of erroneous thinking ('Vaghi pensier', 21), of intellectual presumption and irrationality ('ragionar tant'alto', 22). The targets of the attack are familiar: the *Commedia*'s intellectual ambitions and its eschatological claims ('Vaghi

---

87   See Stefano Benassi, 'La vertigine del sublime: moralità della poesia e razionalità della morale in F. Petrarca', in *Petrarca e la cultura europea*, ed. by Luisa Rotondi Secchi Tarugi (Milan: Editrice Nuovi Orizzonti, 1997), pp. 181–201 (p. 184); Bettarini, 'Perché "narrando" il duol si disacerba', pp. 319–20; Petrie, pp. 138–39.

88   On the importance of the myth of Medusa in Petrarch, see Theodore J. Cachey, Jr., 'From Shipwreck to Port: *Rvf* 189 and the Making of the *Canzoniere*', MLN, 120 (2005), 30–49 (pp. 44–48); Kenelm Foster, 'Beatrice or Medusa', in *Italian Studies Presented to E. R. Vincent*, ed. by Charles Peter Brand and others (Cambridge: W. Heffer & Sons, 1962), pp. 42–56; Sara Sturm-Maddox, *Petrarch's Laurels* (University Park: Pennsylvania State University Press, 1992), pp. 118–19, 164, 220–21. See also Remo Ceserani, ' "Petrarca": il nome come auto-reinvenzione poetica', *Quaderni petrarcheschi*, 4 (1987), 121–37. The possible links in Petrarch between the petrifying Medusa and the 'stony' Dante still need to be properly explored.

89   From this perspective, the *Rerum vulgarium fragmenta* can be read both as a classicizing challenge and as an orthodox corrective to the *Commedia*'s transgressive plurilingualism. Considerable research still needs to be undertaken on the *Canzoniere*'s plurilingual character and on the relationship of this to Dante.

90   See Capovilla, pp. 332–33; Chirilli, pp. 44–48, 54–55; De Robertis, 'Petrarca interprete di Dante', pp. 314, 324–28; Feo, p. 455; Petrini, p. 372; Trovato, *Dante in Petrarca*, pp. 19–20, 31, 157; Zanato, pp. 177, 183, 196.

91   This strategy is close to Petrarch's programmed use of Dantean elements to underscore the differences between himself and Dante. As I have just mentioned, it is vital to recognize the degree to which Petrarch constructed Dante as the negative antithesis of himself.

pensier' che così passo passo | scorto m'avete a ragionar tant'alto').[92] And Petrarch intensifies his assault: the 'Dantean' woman is coldhearted and uncaring, the very antithesis of Beatrice. She refuses to come to her lover's aid, not least because this is forbidden on high: 'Ella non degna di mirar sì basso | che di nostre parole | curi, ché 'l ciel non vòle' (25–27). The precise object of Petrarch's polemic is obvious, and it too is a commonplace of his anti-Dantism: the idea, propagated by both the *Vita nova* and *Inferno* II, that Beatrice had descended from Heaven to rescue Dante and to confirm him as one of God's chosen. Thus, during the course of the stanza, Petrarch explicitly and repeatedly borrows from the first two cantos of the *Inferno*, beginning with the 'passo'-'basso'-'lasso' rhyme (21, 24, 25, 28).[93] In fact, he only appropriates negative elements, carefully excluding any echo that might recall the cantos' salvific strains.[94] He appears to want to rewrite the opening of the *Commedia* in an exclusively negative key.[95] In *canzone* 70, therefore, Dante is presented as trapped in a kind of existential hell, alone, and with neither Beatrice nor Virgil, never mind God, ready to come to his rescue. This is a 'stony' poet's lonely fate — one that cuts him off from both God and his fellow humans, as well as from the full range of language. Authorization and 'authority' cannot but lie far beyond his possibilities. If Petrarch failed to impose his view of Dante in the real world, it was not through want of trying; and, at any rate, within the confines of his own imaginative universe, there is no doubt that the poet of the *Commedia* is unreservedly put in his place. Yet there is also something absurd about Petrarch's effort to bend a whole culture to his will; or perhaps not, given that this is what Dante had so irksomely succeeded in doing.[96]

6. Petrarch's Cavalcanti (and Dante)

It surely cannot have gone unnoticed, not least given the remit of this study, that

---

92   As characterizes Petrarch's overall approach to Dante, ambiguity stalks the opening of the third stanza. Thus, on first reading, the opening two lines can seem positive, since *vago* in Petrarch can mean 'beautiful' and *alto* 'sublime'. However, the rest of the stanza quickly dismisses this possibility, since its 'stony' content requires that the two epithets be assigned negative meanings.

93   The order of the rhyme words in *Inferno* I is slightly different: 'passo'-'lasso'-'basso' (26, 28, 30).

94   The following negative elements, which recall *Inferno* I, are found in stanza three, line 21: 'pensier rinova la paura' (6); line 22: the lion's 'test' alta' (47) and 'perdei la speranza de l'altezza' (54) as a result of the *lupa*'s appearance; line 24: 'esta selva selvaggia e aspra e forte' (5); line 25: 'rimirar lo passo | che non lascia già mai persona viva' (26–27) and 'basso loco' (61); line 28: 'il corpo lasso' (28); line 29: 'cosa dura' (4), 'esta selva selvaggia e aspra e forte' (5), 'di paura il cor compunto' (15), and 'la paura [...] | che nel lago del cor m'era durata' (19–20). Santagata's commentary makes no mention of any of the borrowings from *Inferno* I. He does, however, note two echoes from the *petrose* and one from *Inferno* XI (pp. 351–52).

95   Peter Kuon concludes his analysis of madrigal 54, 'Perch'al viso d'Amor portava insegna', by asserting that '[i]l fatto che il ritorno dell'io petrarchesco sia modellato sul "prologo" della *Commedia* [...] sottolinea l'intenzione di portare sulla terra un evento che in Dante si verifica nei regni ultraterreni dell'Inferno e del Purgatorio' (*L'aura dantesca*, p. 53).

96   My reading of the third stanza of 'Lasso me' is diametrically opposed to those interpretations which consider its treatment of Dante as either positive or unproblematic; see, for instance, De Robertis, 'Petrarca interprete di Dante', p. 314.

Petrarch's Dante has all the air of that great, self-acknowledged erotic pessimist, Guido Cavalcanti. The association is suggestive, especially in light of the now widely-held view that, in the *Vita nova* and the *Commedia*, Dante expended much energy to distance himself from his 'first friend'. Is the confusion between the two, therefore, another instance of Petrarch's deliberate ploy to ruin Dante's reputation, especially given his criticisms of the way in which the older poet had unscrupulously exploited his fellow writers? Was Petrarch, in fact, as a further rebuff to Dante, keen to re-examine Guido's standing after the poet of the *Commedia* had accused him of heresy in *Inferno* x? The answers to these questions are not as straightforward as they might seem to us today. In the Trecento, Guido's status did not need protecting. Dante's charges had gone almost unnoticed. Indeed, not only was Cavalcanti deemed a figure worthy of reverence, if not actually an *auctoritas*, but also he and Dante, on account of their friendship and similarities of temperament, were considered to have been extremely close and to have complemented each other as intellectuals: Guido expert in philosophy, Dante in poetry (see Chapter 13). In these circumstances, it is obvious that we need to approach Petrarch's treatment of Dante and Cavalcanti in a manner that is sensitive both to the realities of fourteenth-century vernacular culture and to Francesco's idiosyncratic *dantismo*.

Petrarch twice alluded to Cavalcanti in his *œuvre* — once by name, the other time metonymically by citing 'Donna me prega'. This is more recognition than he afforded to most *moderni*, and, at first sight, it could be perceived as a mark of respect, an acknowledgment of poetic indebtedness, even an expression of rivalry. However, as so often with hasty impressions, especially as regards Petrarch, things are in fact rather different. Cavalcanti's naming in *Triumphus Cupidinis* IV — 'ecco i due Guidi che già fur in prezzo' (34) — is essentially a device, as we saw, to attack Dante's attitude toward the literary tradition, a state of affairs which thus brings scant personal credit to the two poets being evoked. Furthermore, the use of the past historic — 'già fur in prezzo' — underlines the fact that neither Guido is now deemed to be 'of value'. Equally, Cavalcanti's reappearance in the second stanza of canzone 70 earns him only limited individual advantage. Petrarch certainly does present him as a poet who is part of his vernacular heritage. However, he also portrays him as a 'weak' poet, whom he has assimilated, bent to his own needs, and surpassed. More seriously, and as in the *Triumphi*, the main reason why Guido is evoked in the canzone has little to do with his intrinsic merits, but everything with Petrarch's wish to wound Dante. Cavalcanti, in fact, is principally evoked in 'Lasso me' as a rhetorical and ideological 'strategem' with which Petrarch might delimit the poet of the *Commedia* and constrain him as *petroso*. It is thus striking that in the second stanza we find no trace of the pessimistic Guido. Instead, he is the protagonist of an essentially hopeful mini-narrative. His negative characteristics have all been transferred to Dante. In Petrarch's world, only Dante is the poet of that love from whose 'potenza segue spesso morte'; and in his effort to transform the poet of the *Commedia*, he had no misgivings about also misconstruing Cavalcanti's poetic identity.[97] Indeed, he took away from Guido his most distinctive features; and the

---

97   Guido Cavalcanti, 'Donna me prega, — per ch'eo voglio dire', line 35, in Guido Cavalcanti,

fact that he cited 'Donna me prega', that manifesto of destructive love, in no way undermines his strategy. Quite the contrary: Cavalcanti's great philosophical canzone is actually made to serve as the stanza's optimistic highpoint, thereby putting a seal on the programmed partisanship of Petrarch's approach. There is little here that smacks of disinterested critical appreciation. Everything revolves around polemical and subjective goals. Thus, Guido's loss of his darker qualities is compensated by his eccentrically acquiring Dantean positive traits. Cavalcanti, therefore, is used not only to emphasize Dante's 'stony' isolation, but also to confiscate his archetypically 'sweet' features, such as the 'occhi santi' (15) and the 'dolce mio detto' (17), which now become a mark of Guido's erotic and poetic experience.[98]

At Petrarch's hands, Dante is metamorphosed into Cavalcanti; Cavalcanti into Dante. However, the problem remains whether, beyond helping to fix Dante as *petroso*, other polemical intentions lurk behind their rapprochement in canzone 70. Thus, given the customary presentation of Guido and Dante as Florence's 'two eyes', the one complementing the other, Petrarch's treatment of them as antagonists is eccentric, implying at the very least that he had some sense of Dante's animus against his former friend.[99] Interestingly, the first recorded fourteenth-century instance of such an awareness is to be found in the ninth story of the sixth day of the *Decameron*, the famous *novella* of Guido leaping over the *arche*, the 'case dei morti', in order to flee Betto Brunelleschi and his vacuous companions.[100] Given the impact Boccaccio had on Petrarch's knowledge of and thinking about Dante, it is extremely tempting to hypothesize that it was the *novelliere* who had enlightened Petrarch about the fate that had befallen Guido in the *Commedia*.[101] If this were actually the case, the dialectic that Petrarch had set up between Dante and Cavalcanti would have constituted a subtle and private dig at his friend, reminding him that his beloved Dante was not above acts of selfish calumny, as Boccaccio himself knew better than anyone else. Naturally, as sophisticated a reader as Petrarch did not need Boccaccio to reveal to him Dante's insidious treatment of Guido.[102] If this were a personal

---

Rime con le Rime di Iacopo Cavalcanti, ed. by Domenico De Robertis (Turin: Einaudi, 1986).

98   See 'Volgi, Beatrice, volgi li occhi santi' (*Purg.* XXXI. 133) and 'E io a lui: "Li dolci detti vostri"' (*Purg.* XXVI. 112).

99   'son due [*Inf.* VI. 73] vel jus civile et canonicum quibus justitia ministratur sed falsum est nam intelligit de se et guidone cavalcante qui erant duo oculi florentie' [or the civil and canon law with which justice is administered, but it is wrong: for he refers to himself and Guido Cavalcanti, who were the two lights of Florence]: *Commento della Divina Commedia d'anonimo fiorentino del secolo XIV*, ed. by Pietro Fanfani, 3 vols (Bologna: Gaetano Romagnoli, 1866–74), I, 254. See also Chapter 13, pp. 453–54.

100   See Chapter 13, 454–55. See also Chapter 15.

101   On the complex ways in which Petrarch and Boccaccio affected each other's thinking about Dante, see Battaglia Ricci, 'Il culto per Dante'; Billanovich, *Petrarca letterato*, pp. 57–294, and 'L'altro stil nuovo', pp. 85–90; Francesco Bruni, *Boccaccio: l'invenzione della letteratura mezzana* (Bologna: il Mulino, 1990), pp. 405–77; Eisner; Francesco Mazzoni, 'Giovanni Boccaccio fra Dante e Petrarca', *Atti e memorie dell'Accademia Petrarca di Lettere, Arti e Scienze di Arezzo*, 42 (1976–78), 15–42; Paolazzi, pp. 130–221.

102   I am not persuaded, therefore, by Pulsoni's suggestion that, when Petrarch, in 'Qui dove mezzo son, Sennuccio mio' (*Rvf* 113), calques Dante's 'Guido, i' vorrei', the poet 'crea una sorta di

discovery, transforming Dante into his reviled 'primo amico' was a means for Petrarch to confirm, if only to himself, the absolute control that he could exert over his awkward predecessor — a private, sweetly malicious satisfaction.[103] However, the metamorphosis could also serve more public ends. It was a way to ensure that generations of the future would appreciate how insightful he had been, since it was inevitable that other readers would arrive at a recognition of what Dante had done to Cavalcanti. And 'posterity', as we know, was always close to Petrarch's heart.

No one is more aware than I am that my arguments have become increasingly hypothetical, and that they have even begun to skirt around that psychologizing type of criticism about which I had something to say earlier. The time is overdue for the philologist to reassert himself. In examining Petrarch's complex interplay between Dante and Guido, one thing is clear: he makes no attempt to deal with Cavalcanti in terms of his typical contemporary standing. As I adumbrated, in the late Middle Ages, Guido's fame resided not in his poetry but in his philosophical abilities. His 'authority' was firmly in the field of *scientia*; and Dante's attack, as is obvious from the accusations of heresy, was largely directed at his intellectual reputation and, more specifically, at his identity as a philosophical poet.[104] In fact, Petrarch too seems to have been discomfited by Guido's philosophical prowess. His Guido is a love poet and not a philosopher; and 'Donna me prega', the text on which Cavalcanti's *auctoritas* was based, is presented as a celebration of the lover happy at being able to do his lady's bidding. It is hard to imagine a more drastic misrepresentation of Guido's canzone. Unlike Dante, who was convinced that poetry could serve as a vehicle for philosophy, Petrarch was equally adamant that the two must not be confused.[105] His refashioning of Guido, therefore, is not simply a result of his preoccupation with Dante; it is conditioned by other cultural and ideological reasons — the same reasons, in fact, that lie behind one of his principal objections to the *Commedia*.[106] The Cavalcanti that emerges from canzone 70 is the poet of *dulcedo*. This is not an erroneous image of Guido — he undoubtedly did write some poems in the 'sweet' register — just a terribly reductive one. As with Petrarch's Dante, so his Cavalcanti too maintains ties with the historical person.

---

parallelismo di "primi amici" fra il suo Sennuccio e il dantesco Guido' (p. 138). In keeping with the fact that 'Petrarca ricontestualizza alla propria esperienza personale la vicenda di *Guido i' vorrei*' (p. 138), it is rather more likely that he established the equation in order to stress the moral gulf that divided his attitude to friendship from that of Dante.

103 This ploy is similar to the way in which, in *Rvf* 287, Petrarch bracketed Dante with Guittone.

104 See Zygmunt G. Barański, ' "Per similitudine di abito scientifico": Dante, Cavalcanti, and the Sources of Medieval "Philosophical" Poetry', in *Science and Literature in Italian Culture: From Dante to Calvino. A Festschrift for Pat Boyde*, ed. by Pierpaolo Antonello and Simon Gilson (Oxford: Legenda, 2004), pp. 14–52.

105 See Concetta Carestia Greenfield, 'The Poetics of Francis Petrarch', in *Francis Petrarch, Six Centuries Later: A Symposium*, ed. by Aldo Scaglione (Chapel Hill: Department of Romance Languages, University of North Carolina; Chicago: The Newberry Library, 1975), pp. 213–22.

106 Furthermore, as we saw earlier, Petrarch's treatment of Guido conforms to his general intent to reduce all Italian vernacular poetry to love poetry — a strategy that allowed him to present the whole of the preceding poetic tradition as subordinate to his achievements in the *Rerum vulgarium fragmenta*.

Petrarch was too much of a philologist to reshape the tradition more than was absolutely necessary to achieve his personal ends.

At this juncture, it is appropriate to ask how much of Cavalcanti's poetry, whose transmission was erratic and often piecemeal,[107] Petrarch actually knew. Had he only read the 'sweet' Guido, thereby nullifying all that I have been saying in this subsection? The idea that he only knew sonnets such as 'Biltà di donna' and 'Chi è questa che vèn' seems unsustainable, given that he had so publicly quoted 'Donna me prega'. Nevertheless, I am far from convinced that Petrarch had in fact read the canzone. There is nothing in Canzoniere 70 to suggest that he had; while the very few borrowings from 'Donna me prega' that commentators have noted in Petrarch's poetry are all lyric clichés.[108] Before it is objected that I have been deliberately and unnecessarily misleading in raising the question of Petrarch's unease at Guido the philosopher, allow me to stress that he did not have to be familiar with 'Donna me prega' to be aware of its philosophical prestige. This was a widely established commonplace.[109] Thus, in canzone 70, when Petrarch challenged Cavalcanti's reputation as *saggio*,[110] all he needed to ensure was that no philosophical overtones could be heard in stanza 2. And this is of course what he did. The problem remains, though, whether or not Petrarch knew Guido's pessimistic verses — and, in the light of what I argued earlier as regards the 'petrification' of Dante, this problem is central to the larger question of Petrarch's attitude to his precursor. The simple fact that in canzone 70 he so effectively plays stanzas 2 and 3 off against each other, implies that Petrarch had probably read more than just Cavalcanti's 'lighter' poetry; and this is confirmed when Guido's intertextual impact on his vernacular poetry is considered.[111] At the same time, I believe that scholars have grossly exaggerated the extent of Petrarch's debts to Cavalcanti, since, as with their claims regarding the influence of 'Donna me prega', they have failed to distinguish between erotic *topoi* and precise textual borrowings. This is a question, however, that needs a much fuller treatment than I have the space to dedicate to it here.

7. 'Petrarch's Dante'

Unlike Dante, Guido did not constitute a major cause of concern for Petrarch, though, as he reflected upon the nature of contemporary vernacular culture and his own standing within it, Cavalcanti, or rather Cavalcanti the philosopher, did trouble him enough that he felt obliged to challenge his *auctoritas*. In general, however, Petrarch's public stance toward the *moderni*, beginning with Dante, was one of haughty aloofness. The fact that he referred to his great predecessor so infrequently

---

107 See Domenico De Robertis, 'Nota al testo', in Cavalcanti, *Rime*, pp. 241–50.

108 See Raffaella Pelosini, 'Guido Cavalcanti nei *Rerum vulgarium fragmenta*', *Studi petrarcheschi*, n.s. 9 (1992), 9–76 (p. 37); Santagata, pp. 9, 509, 594, 599–600.

109 See Chapter 13, pp. 447, 452, and 455.

110 On Cavalcanti's philosophical standing in the Trecento, see Chapter 13, pp. 451–57.

111 Bettarini, 'Perché "narrando" il duol si disacerba', p. 308; Pelosini; Suitner, pp. 45–63. See also Santagata's commentary to the *Canzoniere* (references to Cavalcanti are listed in *Indice dei nomi, dei toponimi e dei luoghi letterari*, pp. 1531–32).

is a sign of this attitude; and the impression that he was striving to create is obvious. The contemporary world might very well be obsessed with the *Commedia* and its author; he, however, had other, more important matters to address. Furthermore, precisely because he had not permitted Dante to dominate his attention, he had been able to judge him in a balanced and reflective manner. And what he had discovered was troubling. Rather than an *auctoritas*, Dante was of dubious moral standing and limited as a poet and an intellectual. Indeed, his 'authority' was a self-fabricated illusion bolstered by a crowd of ignoramuses. At least, this is the myth that Petrarch was keen to propagate. The reality, of course, was very different. The fabric of Petrarch's poetry reveals both the degree to which Dante was continually present in his mind, and the impact that, despite his protestations to the contrary, his predecessor had had on him ever since the 1320s, when, as a student in Bologna, he probably first read the *Commedia*.[112] Given the sophistication with which, in his vernacular poetry, Petrarch manipulated Dantean elements, it is certain that he was acutely aware that his reaction to Dante, based as it was on a mix of limited public interest and substantial covert poetic appropriation, was precariously balanced. Nevertheless, he considered his high-risk strategy a chance worth taking. On the one hand, his approach allowed him to mount a subtle critique of Dante in the present; on the other, it offered him the opportunity to demonstrate to his future readers, as well to the more refined among his contemporaries, that, despite the Trecento's exaggerated canonization especially of the *Commedia*, he had been able to establish intellectual, literary, and moral mastery over his precursor. Ultimately, it was because, in talking about Dante, Petrarch was invariably also talking about himself that his treatment of the older poet was so complex and tense. Petrarch's was, in fact, an extreme reaction to the severe disturbance that hit fourteenth-century Italian culture in the wake of Dante's claims for poetry, for the vernacular, for *scientia*, and most of all for himself. It is thus not at all surprising that Petrarch was extremely sensitive to the multifaceted forms of Trecento *dantismo*. Ironically, he stands as the best confirmation we have of Dante's fourteenth-century *auctoritas*, and of the care with which anyone who wanted to engage with the poet of the *Commedia* had to proceed. Our responsibility as historians of literature is to elucidate the intricacies of Petrarch's response to Dante. In particular, we need to underscore the artificiality and expediency of his response, as well as its calculated subtlety. In speaking of Petrarch and Dante, we are not actually dealing with the relationship between two poets, but rather with one poet's construction of the other: 'Petrarch's Dante', to propose a new designation representative of their encounter.[113] Yet, given that it is probably impossible to think about Petrarch's career without also reflecting on the sway that Dante exerted on his development as a writer and as an intellectual,

---

112 Feo, p. 450. See also Billanovich, 'L'altro stil nuovo', pp. 89–90.

113 The designation 'Petrarch's Dante' is not completely new. In its Italian form, 'Il Dante di Francesco Petrarca', it had been used by Giuseppe Velli in an article of the same name, which appeared in the 1985 issue of *Studi petrarcheschi*. By having recourse to the phrase, Velli did not intend to define Petrarch's reaction to Dante in the tense and complex terms that I have outlined in this study. His aim was to suggest a largely harmonious relationship centred upon the possibility that Petrarch's Dante was (astonishingly) '[u]n Dante classico' (p. 199).

I nearly wrote, and as a Dantist not without a touch of malice, 'Dante's Petrarch'. To have done so, however, would have been bad philology, or perhaps not.

CHAPTER 11

'Io mi rivolgo indietro a ciascun passo' (*Rvf* 15. 1): Petrarch, the *fabula* of Eurydice and Orpheus, and the Structure of the *Canzoniere*

Please don't you ever die,
You ever die,
You ever die.
(The Felice Brothers, 'Radio Song')[1]

1. 'Come Euridice Orpheo sua'

Since the 1990s, a growing number of scholars has begun to recognize the significance of the myth of Orpheus as a structuring and ideological motif in Part II of the *Rerum vulgarium fragmenta*.[2] They generally concur that, drawing on the canonical accounts of the 'Threicius vates' [Thracian poet] (*Met.* XI. 2) in Virgil's *Georgics* and Ovid's *Metamorphoses*, Petrarch established meaningful correspondences between his and Orpheus's reactions to the deaths of their respective beloveds, and hence, by extension, between Laura and Eurydice.[3] As a matter of fact, several

---

1 Track 14, The Felice Brothers, *The Felice Brothers* (Team Love Records, B0012IWHKK, 2008). This essay was originally written to mark my decades-long friendship with Martin McLaughlin.
2 See Giuseppe Mazzotta, 'Orpheus: Rhetoric and Music in Petrarch', in *Forma e parola: studi in memoria di Fredi Chiappelli*, ed. by Dennis J. Dutschke and others (Rome: Bulzoni, 1992), pp. 137–54; Nicola Gardini, 'Un esempio di imitazione virgiliana nel Canzoniere petrarchesco: il mito di Orfeo', *MLN*, 110 (1995), 132–44; Ingrid Rossellini, *Nel trapassar del segno: idoli della mente ed echi della vita nei 'Rerum vulgarium fragmenta'* (Florence: Olschki, 1995), pp. 53–102; Federica Brunori, 'Il mito ovidiano di Orfeo e Euridice nel *Canzoniere* di Petrarca', *Romance Quarterly*, 44 (1997), 233–44; Thérèse Migraine-George, 'Specular Desires: Orpheus and Pygmalion as Aesthetic Paradigms in Petrarch's *Rime sparse*', *Comparative Literature Studies*, 36 (1999), 226–46; Maria Elisa Raja, 'Per Euridice (nel Trecento)', in her *Il dolce immaginar: miti e figure della poesia trecentesca* (Piacenza: Vicolo del Pavone, 2005), pp. 97–120; Zygmunt G. Barański, '"Piangendo e cantando" con Orfeo (e con Dante): strutture emotive e strutture poetiche in *Rvf* 281–90', in *Il Canzoniere: lettura micro e macrotestuale*, ed. by Michelangelo Picone (Ravenna: Longo, 2007), pp. 617–40 (pp. 637–39; Chapter 12 in this collection); Francesco Giusti, 'Le parole di Orfeo: Dante, Petrarca, Leopardi, e gli archetipi di un genere', *Italian Studies*, 64 (2009), 56–76 (pp. 64–68), and *Canzonieri in morte: per un'etica poetica del lutto* (L'Aquila: Textus, 2015), pp. 92–100. For a reliable overview of the myth in Petrarch's œuvre, see Luca Marcozzi, *La biblioteca di Febo: mitologie e allegoria in Petrarca* (Florence: Cesati, 2002), pp. 219–33.
3 Virgil, *Georg.* IV. 453–527 and Ovid, *Met.* X. 1–154 and XI. 1–66.

common elements unite the anguished stories of the two bereaved lovers: the untimely demise of both women, the natural settings that the poets inhabit, their obsessive weeping, the shift in poetic style occasioned by their tragedies, their appeals to a higher power, and the irreversibility of their loss (in Orpheus's case after Eurydice's 'second death'). What is surprising, therefore, is not that Petrarch should have had recourse to the *fabula*, but that his readers should have been so slow to acknowledge its presence and function in the *Canzoniere*.[4] Indeed, the poet's keen propensity to illuminate and ennoble his experiences, whether autobiographical or fictional, by equating them to classical mythology ought to have served, long before it actually did, as a trustworthy spur to seek out the *Fragmenta*'s Orphic reverberations.[5]

Anyhow, in the *Parte in morte*, Petrarch explicitly drew attention to similarities between his and Orpheus's tragic circumstances:

> Or avess'io un sí pietoso stile
> che Laura mia potesse tôrre a Morte,
> come Euridice Orpheo sua senza rime,
> ch'i' viverei anchor piú che mai lieto! (*Rvf* 332. 49–52)

The double sestina 'Mia benigna fortuna e 'l viver lieto', especially in its ninth stanza, brings to a climax and seeming close Petrarch's recourse to the myth in Part II. For the only time in the *Canzoniere*, and with fitting refinement, the poem openly unites Orpheus and Eurydice, intimately placing their names next to each other in a manner that never occurs in Virgil or in Ovid. Indeed, Petrarch's syntax and wording most precisely recall those of another of his favourite *auctores*, Boethius, in his short reworking of the myth: 'Orpheus Eurydicen suam' (*Cons.* III. met. 12. 50). At the same time, the poet only very occasionally drew on Boethius's account. I suspect that this was because the heavily allegorized character of the *metrum* restricted the story's connotative possibilities. (As ought to become clear during the course of this chapter, what Petrarch found so appealing and useful about the fable was its semantic and narrative malleability.) Even if Petrarch carefully distinguished himself from Ovid, he structurally followed the Latin poet's example. The couple's concluding syntactic 'reconciliation' in the *Canzoniere* alludes to their eternal reunion 'beneath the earth' at the end of Ovid's two-part account of their tormented love story: 'hic modo coniunctis spatiantur passibus ambo | [...] | Eurydicenque suam iam tuto respicit Orpheus' [here they now both walk side by

---

4   In truth, the myth's status in the *Canzoniere* continues to remain largely unacknowledged as evidenced by the notes to recent editions of the collection (Fenzi, Dotti, Santagata, Bettarini, Stroppa, Vecchi Galli). Bettarini's commentary is the most sensitive to the *fabula*, and see her *Lacrime e inchiostro nel Canzoniere di Petrarca* (Bologna: CLUEB, 1998), pp. 10–14, 19–20.

5   See in particular Luca Marcozzi, 'Petrarca lettore di Ovidio', in *Testimoni del vero: su alcuni libri in biblioteche d'autore*, ed. by Emilio Russo, special issue of *Studi (e testi) italiani*, 6 (2000), 57–106, and *La biblioteca*; Carlo Vecce, 'Francesco Petrarca: la rinascita degli dèi antichi', in *Il mito nella letteratura italiana*, ed. by Pietro Gibellini and others (Brescia: Morcelliana, 2003–), I: *Dal Medioevo al Rinascimento*, ed. by Gian Carlo Alessio (2008), 177–228. See also Anne-Marie Telesinski, 'Pétrarque: le poète des métamorphoses', 2 vols (unpublished PhD thesis, University of Paris 3, 2014), who discusses Orpheus and Eurydice at I, 17–18, 240, 246, 262–64, 266, 271–72.

side and Orpheus now safely looks back at his Eurydice] (*Met.* XI. 61, 64, and 66).
In truth, one cannot but wonder whether the poet's decision to pen that 'variante
strana', the sestina 'doppia o raddoppiata' (Bettarini commentary, p. 1465), may not
owe something to Ovid's exceptional 'doubling' of the myth across two books. As
Orpheus and Eurydice take their leave in the *Fragmenta*, so Boethius bleeds into
Ovid and both flow into Virgil — 'Eurydicenque suam iam luce sub ipsa' [his
Eurydice now on the brink of light] (*Georg.* IV. 490) — in keeping with Petrarch's
ideas on *imitatio* that Martin McLaughlin has masterfully illustrated.[6] And there is
more. Thanks to the subtlety of his composition, Petrarch concurrently refers to
different moments and inflexions of the myth — first small proof of that malleability
of which I have already made mention. While in Virgil and Boethius the phrase
'his Eurydice' melancholically confirms her 'second death', the event that marks
the beginning of Orpheus's desperate weeping, in Ovid, as we have just seen, it
touchingly crowns the lovers' everlasting companionship in death. The ambivalence
captures well Petrarch's state at this juncture of the *Canzoniere*. He bemoans Laura's
passing, but he is also increasingly confident that he will soon join 'Laura mia' —
the unique coupling of beloved's name and possessive clearly calques the tradition's
Euridicen sua[7] — in Paradise (2 and 14) and not 'beneath the earth' (2 and 4), where
only her mortal remains lie 'scattered' (7), as sonnet 333, 'Ite, rime dolenti, al duro
sasso', that may be read as a 'Christianized' Orphic coda to stanza nine of the
preceding sestina, memorably affirms.[8] Petrarch points to similarities between his
condition and Orpheus's, while at the same time stressing that their experiences are
also fundamentally different. In addition, if, on the one hand, the poet's avowed
hope for an effective 'pietoso stile' highlights Orpheus's key role in Part II as the
section's ideal elegiac model — a role that raises the perplexing question how in
practice Petrarch might 'imitate' the vanished 'vatis Apollinei vocalia [...] ora' [the
melodious mouth of Apollo's poet] (*Met.* XI. 8) — on the other, the nature of the
poet-prophet's artistic accomplishment is moot.[9] In fact, he did not actually succeed
in 'taking [Eurydice] away from Death'. His victory was brief and transitory; his
defeat definitive. Ultimately, Orpheus's unrepeatable fleeting achievement is less an
emblem of the power of poetic song than a bitter affirmation of its powerlessness
in the face of *Morte* — a view Petrarch regularly affirms in the *Canzoniere*'s later
stages. Thus, in the opening of stanza nine, poetry's agonizing failure is memorably
captured in the mood of the verbs, the 'congiuntivo ottativo che scivola nel periodo
ipotetico dell'irrealtà', that confirms the vanity of the poet's aspiration: 'S'esser non

---

6   See Martin L. McLaughlin, *Literary Imitation in the Italian Renaissance* (Oxford: Clarendon Press,
1995), pp. 22–48.
7   Laura is very rarely named in the *Rerum vulgarium fragmenta* (239. 8 & 23; 291. 4; see also 225. 10).
Petrarch names Eurydice on five other occasions in his *œuvre*: *Africa* VI. 56; *Secretum* III. 146; *Sen.* IX.
1. 7; XV. 3. 65; *Tr. Cup.* IV. 13.
8   Appropriately, the sonnet reverses several Orphic motifs connected to Eurydice's 'second death':
the beloved's otherworldly abode is not a 'loco oscuro et basso' (4) as in the myth; it is the male
lover who follows his beloved (8); and his journey will successfully end not in an earthly but in an
otherworldly reunion (13–14). See below on the myth's Christian interpretations.
9   I return to this question below; see pp. 408–09.

pò' (332. 53).[10] Orpheus, for Petrarch, is beginning to look as if he may actually be an ambiguous artistic and existential model. Indeed, I should like to go a bit further. Unlike what most other scholars maintain, and as I shall endeavour to document here, I do not believe that, in the *Canzoniere*, Orpheus and Eurydice can be tidily superimposed on to Francesco and Laura.[11] Their purpose in the *Fragmenta* is much more nuanced and complex.

I shall have more to say about Petrarch's presentation of the myth's shortcomings in due course. For the moment, I wish to continue to explore the ways in which Part II of the *Rerum vulgarium fragmenta* is overtly placed under the sign of Orpheus and Eurydice.

After a sequence of fifty-two sonnets (271–322), the metrical monotonalism is broken by the *canzone delle visioni*, 'Standomi un giorno solo a la fenestra' (323). *Rerum vulgarium fragmenta* 323 is usefully placed alongside 332, since, together, they serve as 'grandiosi testi-guida' (Vecchi Galli, p. 1104) especially with respect to Part II. As befits the canzone's striking entry into the make-up of the *Canzoniere*, it has summatic functions. The components comprising the six visions — a 'fera [...] | con fronte humana' [possibly a doe] (4–5), a boat (with ties to Ulysses), a laurel tree, a fountain, a phoenix, and Eurydice — are 'legate alla mitografia poetica petrarchesca dopo la morte di Laura e dopo l'avvio del *Fragmentorum liber*', whereby 'i miti classici, ormai "criptati", [sono] fusi in un compiuto sistema autoreferenziale' (Vecce, pp. 227–28). It is immediately striking that, by bringing the visionary sequence to a close, of the symbols, only Eurydice, and by implication Orpheus, mirrors her actual position in the mythological development of the *Fragmenta*. She is further privileged by being the only human being with whom Laura is associated.[12] Even the laurel appears to play a subordinate part to Eurydice, evocatively signalling the vitality of Orphic elements in Part II; and this is confirmed by the fact that, beyond their common concern with 'lo scacco della poesia, l'incapacità di questo strumento, che il poeta umanista aveva creduto divino, a fare fronte alla morte', what first and foremost unites the two 'guiding texts' is, of course, the myth of Orpheus and Eurydice.[13] Indeed, it is not simply the only myth treated in the canzone to return in the sestina, but, more tellingly, it is also the sole myth present in the latter.

Although the 'canzone of the visions' mentions neither lover by name, the scene evoked in the sixth stanza, unambiguously calques Eurydice's physical death in

10   Francesco Petrarca, *Canzoniere*, ed. by Paola Vecchi Galli, 2nd edn (Milan: Rizzoli, 2013), p. 1111; henceforth Vecchi Galli. On the issue of Orpheus and 'irreality', see Subsection 4 below.

11   See, for instance, Brunori, p. 240; Gardini, pp. 135, 138, & 141–43; Marcozzi, *La biblioteca*, p. 227; Migraine-George, pp. 226–27; Raja, pp. 97 & 99, but see also 107 & 113; Rossellini, pp. 69–71, 100. See also Loredana Chines, ' "Doppi" del Petrarca: Perseo, Orfeo, Pigmalione', in her *'Di selva in selva ratto mi trasformo': identità e metamorfosi della parola petrarchesca* (Rome: Carocci, 2010), pp. 31–41.

12   In a similar vein, Maria Elisa Raja notes: 'Nella serie dei sonetti precedenti [317–21] la canzone "delle visioni" manca soltanto la figura di Euridice, cosicché la sua presenza nell'ultima stanza della canzone 323 diviene ancora più significativa, perché inattesa e inedita' (p. 107).

13   Marco Santagata, 'Il lutto dell'umanista', in his *Amate e amanti: figure della lirica amorosa fra Dante e Petrarca* (Bologna: il Mulino, 1999), pp. 195–221 (p. 211).

Ovid, as Giovanni Gesualdo had already recognized in the sixteenth century:[14]

> Alfin vid'io per entro i fiori et l'erba
> pensosa ir sí leggiadra et bella donna,
> [...]
> punta poi nel tallon d'un picciol angue. (*Rvf* 323. 61–62 & 69)

and compare:

> [...] nam nupta per herbas
> dum nova naiadum turba comitata vagatur,
> occidit in talum serpentis dente recepto. (*Met.* x. 8–10)

[For while the newly wedded bride wandered through the grass accompanied by a crowd of Naiads, she was struck down, having received a serpent's bite on her ankle.]

As in 332, Petrarch adroitly sketches the vignette so that it encapsulates Eurydice's two deaths and integrates both his principal Orphic sources.[15] There is no question that the description of the demise of the 'beautiful woman' has its roots in the *Metamorphoses*. The *Georgics*'s dark and disturbing account of her death is strikingly different in tone:

> illa quidem, dum te [Aristaeus] fugeret per flumina praeceps,
> immanem ante pedes hydrum moritura puella
> servantem ripas alta non vidit in herba. (*Georg.* iv. 457–59)

[She, to escape you, in headlong flight along the river, did not see in the tall grass before her feet, doomed girl, the monstrous water-serpent that guarded the banks.]

It is not difficult to appreciate why Petrarch would have felt that Virgil's lines would have jarred with the elegant melodiousness and refined mannerism of the ninth stanza. At the same time, however, the portrayal of the woman's 'parti supreme' that 'eran avolte d'una nebbia oscura' (67–68) is Virgilian in origin. Rather than recall the portent of Marcellus's death — 'sed nox atra caput tristi cicumvolat umbra' [but night's black shadow flies mournfully around his head] (*Aen.* vi. 866) — as scholars have claimed since Gesualdo's annotation (fol. cccxliv^r), its more likely and appropriate source is to be found in Eurydice's 'live' depiction of her second descent into the afterlife ('feror ingenti circumdata nocte' [I'm taken away wrapped around by huge night], *Georg.* iv. 497) combined with the image evoking her disappearance: 'ceu fumus in auras | commixtus tenuis' [like smoke intermingled with rarified air] (*Georg.* iv. 499–500),[16] a line which may also have exercised some passing influence on 'sí texta, ch'oro et neve parea inseme' (66).[17] As

---

14   *Il Petrarcha colla spositione di Misser Giovanni Andrea Gesualdo* (Venice: Giovann' Antonio di Nicolini & fratelli da Sabbio, 1533), fol. cccxliv^r.

15   Rather too often scholars have unhelpfully overemphasized one source over the other. In some instances, they have entirely ignored one of the two intertexts (customarily the *Georgics*).

16   See Fredi Chiappelli, *Studi sul linguaggio del Petrarca: la canzone delle visioni* (Florence: Olschki, 1971), p. 167.

17   Petrarch is also recalling his own distillation in *Laurea occidens* (1348 and revised several times until 1366) of the long list of poets presented in Ovid's *Epistula ex Ponto* iv. 16: 'Vultus densissima

in 332, Petrarch stresses the myth's ambiguities, pointing not so much to similarities between his and Laura's circumstances and those of Orpheus and Eurydice, but to the fact that, in a Christian universe, the beloved's death is not the doomed tragedy of the ancients. Nothing underlines this better than the manner of the passing of the 'bella donna' — 'lieta si dipartio, nonché secura' (71) — when compared to Eurydice's desperate departure: 'invalidasque tibi tendens, heu! non tua, palmas' [stretching out towards you feeble hands, alas, no longer yours] (*Georg.* IV. 498; but see the full account 491–502, as well as *Met.* x. 57–63). Instead of cruel, unfeeling pagan deities, the shadow of a loving and salvific God spreads out over the close of the canzone's final stanza and its congedo.[18] Petrarch, like Orpheus, cannot but weep for his loss ('Ahi, nulla, altro che pianto, al mondo dura!', 72); however, unlike Orpheus, he can also hope that, once dead, not only will he be reunited with his beloved but that their relationship will also be enriched: 'Queste sei visïoni al signor mio | àn fatto un dolce di morir desio' (74–75).

Rerum vulgarium fragmenta 323 and 332 form a perfectly calibrated and harmoniously complementary Orphic diptych that discernibly illustrates the myth's key guiding functions in the *Canzoniere's Parte in morte*. In fact, the poems stand in balanced yet sharp contrast to the two direct references to Orpheus in Part I: 'perché d'Orpheo leggendo et d'Amphïone | se non ti meravigli' (28. 68–69) and 'Ché d'Omero dignissima et d'Orpheo, | o del pastor ch'anchor Mantova honora' (187. 9–10). Both allusions, unlike those in Part II, are highly conventional. They recall in a compressed manner Orpheus's extraordinary poetic talents: in 28 the marvellous effects of his song on nature, which were generally interpreted as an *integumentum* of the civilizing power of poetry, and in 187 his exemplary status as an 'authoritative' (elegiac) poet, the equal in his *stilus* of Homer and Virgil. Both representations are long-established commonplaces for which no precise antecedent can be established.[19] In measured opposition to the two earlier evocations, Petrarch's

---

nubes | Texerat ambiguos' [A very dense cloud had covered the uncertain faces] (*Buc. carm.* x. 191–92). The *Bucolicum carmen* is cited from Francesco Petrarca, *Il Bucolicum carmen e i suoi commenti inediti*, ed. by Antonio Avena (Bologna: Forni, 1969).

18   'The story of Orpheus weaves through the double sestina, but there is no indication of his losing Eurydice for the second and last time. His myth recalled through the positive exempla connotes eternity triumphant over ending, loss, and closure': Marianne Shapiro, *The Hieroglyph of Time: The Petrarchan Sestina* (Minneapolis: University of Minnesota Press, 1980), p. 139. Santagata ('Lutto', pp. 219–20) has written well on the Christian character of the final version of the canzone. See also Raja, p. 105, as well as pp. 108–17 that examine the poem's Scriptural substratum. For a different interpretation, see Michelangelo Picone, 'Morte e temporanea rinascita dei miti dell'eros (*Rvf* 321–30)', in Picone, pp. 701–23 (pp. 721–22).

19   See Virgil, *Ecl.* IV. 55–57; Horace, *AP* 391–96 and *Odes* III. 11. 13–24; Quintilian, *Instit. orat.* I. 9. 9; Augustine, *De civ. Dei* XVIII. 37; Boethius, *Cons.* III. *met.* 12. 7–9; Isidore, *Etym.* III. 22. 8–9. For medieval expressions of these views, see the examples cited in Zygmunt G. Barański, 'Notes on Dante and the Myth of Orpheus', in *Dante mito e poesia*, ed. by Michelangelo Picone and Tatiana Crivelli (Florence: Cesati, 1999), pp. 133–62 (pp. 139, 143–46). Petrarch made regular recourse to both topoi: *Africa* v. 675–78; *Buc. carm.* II. 75 and 110; *Contra medicum* I. 153; *De vita solitaria* II. 12. 3; *Ep.* III. 35. *Fam.* I. 9. 7; VIII. 10. 25; *Tr. Cup.* IV. 91–93. On Orpheus in the Middle Ages, see Klaus Heitmann, 'Orpheus im Mittelalter', *Archiv für Kulturgeschichte*, 45 (1963), 253–94; John Block Friedman, *Orpheus in the Middle Ages* (Syracuse, NY: Syracuse University Press, 2000; original edn

subjective reworking of the tale and rewriting of his sources, as well as the crucial introduction of Eurydice, underscores the transformation that the *fabula* undergoes in Part II. From cultural cliché, Orpheus is converted into one of the *Canzoniere*'s key personalized mythic tropes that control the collection's structure, development, and meaning. At the same time, the fact that Orpheus is introduced into the first of the *Fragmenta*'s political canzoni and into one of its principal statements on Petrarch's relationship to the poetic tradition hints that even in Part I, and regardless of the general critical insensitivity to this section's Orphic reverberations, the *vates* may have functions that are not entirely negligible.

2. 'Vox forte sequetur Orphea'

It is in fact possible to reconstruct on reasonably solid foundations the process whereby Orpheus and Eurydice became key to the *Canzoniere*'s organizational logic. The evidence unambiguously indicates that Petrarch came to appreciate their value for systematizing his vernacular lyric 'book' only during its last evolutionary stages.[20] The first of the Orphic poems that can be located with certainty as part of the anthology is 28, which, as the internal historical references indicate, Petrarch composed in late 1333 or early 1334, and which appears in the *forma Chigi*, the first of the forms of the *rime sparse* for which we have definitive manuscript proof, and which was assembled between 1359 and 1363.[21] At this stage, Orpheus is essentially a one-off and isolated allusion. He appears in a guise, that of the civic poet, which, while appropriate for a canzone on the crusades, never returns again in the *Canzoniere*. Indeed, the *vates* is not even connected to Petrarch but to the poem's anonymous dedicatee. The situation begins to change somewhat with the *forma di Giovanni* of Vat. Lat. 3195 that was copied between 1366 and 1367 and incorporates 187, whose reference to Orpheus is of course connected to Petrarch and Laura.[22]

Cambridge, MA: Harvard University Press, 1970); Eleanor Irwin, 'The Songs of Orpheus and the New Song of Christ', in *Orpheus: The Metamorphoses of a Myth*, ed. by John Warden (Toronto: University of Toronto Press, 1982), pp. 51–62; Patricia Vicari, '*Sparagmos*: Orpheus among the Christians', in Warden, pp. 63–83; Elizabeth A. Newby, *A Portrait of the Artist: The Legends of Orpheus and their Use in Medieval and Renaissance Aesthetics* (New York: Garland, 1987).

20   While I generally concur with those who have warned against placing too much weight on the conjectured forms of the *Fragmenta*, it is also the case that, over many years, Petrarch did 'make' and 'remake' the collection of his vernacular *nugae*. Consequently, any assessment of the *Canzoniere* and its evolution must needs take this obsessive revising into consideration even when the evidence for a particular form is circumstantial. In what follows I shall concentrate as much as possible, although not exclusively, on the documented forms of the *Rerum vulgarium fragmenta*. On the formation of the collection, see in particular Ernest Hatch Wilkins, *The Making of the 'Canzoniere' and Other Petrarchan Studies* (Rome: Edizioni di Storia e Letteratura, 1951); Marco Santagata, *I frammenti dell'anima: storia e racconto nel Canzoniere di Petrarca* (Bologna: il Mulino, 1992).

21   Canzone 28 does not contain Petrarch's earliest extant reference to Orpheus. It is anticipated, possibly by a matter of weeks, by another political poem, 'Ursa peregrinis modo' ('Orpheus [...], dum flectere Tartara credit, | squalidus in ripa Cereris sine munere sedit' [Orpheus, while he believes he can move the underworld, sits filthy on the shore without Ceres's gift], 35–36) which was composed between Autumn and Winter 1333; see Giuseppe Billanovich, 'Un carme ignoto del Petrarca', *Studi petrarcheschi*, n.s. 5 (1988), 101–26 (p. 110); the poem is printed on pp. 118–25.

22   The sonnet cannot be dated with any degree of certainty; however, see Vincenzo Fera, 'I sonetti

Consequent to this second allusion, a first, albeit slight and not especially cogent, Orphic intratextual system is created in the collection. At this stage, although the *Canzoniere* was clearly divided into two halves, the *Parte in morte*, constituted by 264–318, did not have distinct and programmed Orphic characteristics (and see below Subsection 3).

Things change, possibly between 1371 and 1372, if one accepts the existence of the *forma Malatesta*, when both 323 and 332 enter into the universe of the *Fragmenta*.[23] I would like to suggest, however, that it is feasible that Petrarch grasped the potential of the myth, especially its Eurydicean dimension, a few years earlier. In the *Codice degli abbozzi* (Vat. Lat. 3196, fol. 2^v), the poet transcribed stanzas 3–6 and the congedo of 323, which he prefaced with the following annotation: '1368 octobris 13, veneris, ante matutinum. Ne labatur contuli ad cedulam plusquam triennio hic inclusa[m] [that contained stanzas 1 and 2], et eodem die, inter primam facem et concubium, transcripsi in alia papiro quibusdam et cetera' [1368 October 13, Friday, before morning. So that this was not lost, I juxtaposed what is written here below to a sheet that had been inserted here for more than three years, and on the same day, between when it grew dark and the dead of night, I transcribed everything on to another sheet, making some changes].[24] Despite its concision, the phrase 'ne labatur', as Rosanna Bettarini helpfully elucidates, 'sembra alludere a una labescenza mentale e a un progetto che precipita dalla mente' (p. 1409). Consequently, one cannot but wonder whether Petrarch's sudden insight concerned the potential of the Orpheus myth, especially when due prominence was granted to Eurydice, to capture the existential, spiritual, and poetic prerogatives of Part II.[25] Indeed, the fact that Eurydice should constitute the canzone's culmination would appear to support this hypothesis; as would the stanza's formal construction. Unlike the other symbols, the poet delays revealing the mythic identity of the 'bella donna' until the final line of the first sirma: 'punta poi nel tallon d'un picciol angue', when, at the point of death, her Eurydicean traits are finally unveiled. Furthermore, by witholding her name, Petrarch ensures that we focus not so much on the character, but on those aspects of her story that he deems noteworthy for his collection. Equally, the strategy allows him to refigure 'his' Orpheus — no longer simply a great poet as in Part I but also the man beset by misfortune — , while leaving no doubt about the crucial significance of Eurydice's entry into the *Canzoniere*.[26]

CLXXXVI e CLXXXVII', *Lectura Petrarce*, 7 (1987), 219–43 (pp. 221–23).

23   Wilkins claims that Petrarch 'copied No. 323 [into 3195] within the period October 13–31, 1368' (p. 142). The canzone would thus have entered into the second of Wilkins's Pre-Malatesta forms ('Probably September–October, 1368'; p. 173); see also Francesco Petrarca, *Canzoniere*, ed. by Marco Santagata, 4th edn (Milan: Mondadori, 2010), pp. 1244–45. Sestina 332 belongs to Wilkins's third Pre-Malatesta form ('Probably May–December 1369') and was copied after 27 June (pp. 174–75).

24   *Il codice Vaticano latino 3196*, ed. by Laura Paolino, in Francesco Petrarca, *Trionfi, Rime estravaganti, Codice degli abbozzi*, ed. by Vinicio Pacca and Laura Paolino, 2nd edn (Milan: Mondadori, 2000), pp. 755–889 (p. 792).

25   The question also arises whether a relationship might exist between the Orphic intuition and the fact that 'la decisione di collocare al centro del libro la morte di Laura [...] sopravvenne tardi, se non all'ultima ora': Santagata, *I frammenti dell'anima*, p. 306.

26   Further evidence of Petrarch's effort to establish the importance of the myth for Part II emerges

Unfortunately, we are unable to date 332, and so cannot conjecture about its possible compositional ties to 323. On the other hand, however, when considered in Orphic terms, it is not difficult to appreciate the reasons for the sestina's inclusion in the *Fragmenta*, especially once 323 had entered into the collection's system. In addition to fashioning, together with the *canzone delle visioni*, an elegant and meaningful contrastive balance between the *Canzoniere*'s two parts that signals and grants substance to Orpheus and Eurydice's prominence within the collection, sestina 332, as we have seen, climactically unites the names of the doomed lovers in a manner that further distinguishes the *vates* from his commonplace one-dimensional appearance in Part I. Likewise, by concentrating on Orpheus's otherworldly singing, Petrarch amplified the remit of the story that he had begun to evoke in 323's final stanza, while forging a clear link not just between Laura and Eurydice but also between himself and the bereaved poet. Emphasizing the myth's forceful resonance in the *Canzoniere*, the *sestina doppia* thus brings to a final and cogent fulfilment the intuition of 13 October 1368, when Eurydice and Orpheus entered so decisively into Vat. Lat. 3196. Indeed, I suspect that it was not only Ovid's double redaction of the myth that inspired Petrarch to invent the sestina's unusual form, but also Eurydice's 'double death' — 'quo se rapta bis coniuge ferret?' [where could he turn, twice robbed of his wife?] (*Georg.* IV. 504); and 'iterum moriens' [dying a second time] and 'gemina nece coniugis' [by his wife's double death] (*Met.* X. 60 & 64) — which, as we saw, is delicately intimated in both 323 and 332: 'et doppiando 'l dolor, doppia lo stile' (332. 39).

The structural and ideological consequence of the *fabula* of Orpheus and Eurydice in the *Rerum vulgarium frgmenta* is beyond question. Yet, it is also important to recognize that, albeit in a lesser key, approximately twenty years before he began work on the post-Giovanni sections of Vat. Lat. 3195, Petrarch had already begun to test the myth's effectiveness as an organizing trope. The *Canzoniere*'s Orphic intuition had sprung from deep roots.

Towards the middle of the century, Petrarch composed two Latin poems — the eclogue *Parthenias* (*Buc. carm.* 1; 1346–47) and the first of the Horatian *epystolae* to the musician Floriano da Rimini (*Ep.* III. 15; 1352) — whose organization is substantially controlled by the myth. Indeed, Orpheus frames each text, exerting a major sway on their development and content. This strategy is quite explicit in the *epystola*. The poem opens with the *vates*'s name, conventionally rehearses the miraculous effects of his song on nature, and recalls his glorious lineage:

---

if the sixth stanza is compared to its earlier drafts. Rather than conceal his sources as was his avowed custom, the poet makes these more explicit. In line 62, he eliminated the adjective 'sola' applied to the 'bella donna' since, in Virgil (*Georg.* IV. 517), the epithet is associated with Orpheus; in line 68, he substituted 'coperte' with 'avolte', since the latter translates 'circumdata' (*Georg.* IV. 497), an alteration that appears to confirm the *Georgics* and not the *Aeneid* as the primary source for the line (see p. 397 above); finally and most tellingly, he eliminated his original line 71 ('in terra cadde ove star pur sicura') and replaced it with 'lieta si dipartio, nonché secura' which stresses the moment of the woman's final departure that is key both to the myth and to the *Canzoniere*. All quotations are from *Il codice*, p. 789. On Petrarch's reworking of the canzone, see Bettarini, *Lacrime*, pp. 113–36; Chiappelli, who dedicates a whole chapter to 'La strofa di Euridice', pp. 139–83.

> Orpheus Euxinios solitus vel carmine fluctus
> Vel Tracum mulcere feras, truncosque sequentes,
> Clarus avis proavisque fuit. (*Ep.* III. 15. 1–3)

[Orpheus, who used to calm with his song the waves of the Black Sea and the beasts of Thrace and the trees that followed him, was illustrious thanks to his ancestors.]

It then returns to the extraordinary power of his art in the explicit: 'tum currere quercus | Saxaque mota sono, blandosque videbimus ursos' [then we will see the oak trees run, the rocks move, and the bears become tamed] (34–35).[27] The myth's framing functions, in keeping with what I deem to be the eclogue's greater consequence and sophistication (see below), are more subtly introduced into *Parthenias*. Silvius-Petrarch's final speech ends on a note of modest Orphic hope: 'vox forte sequetur | Orphea, promeritum [of Scipio Africanus] modulabor harundine parva' [perhaps an Orpheus-like voice will follow, I will play on a small flute to celebrate him] (122–23). On the surface, the poem's incipit appears to have no ties to Orpheus. Intertextually, however, the opening lines owe considerable debts to the myth, and in particular to *Georgics* IV's treatment of the events surrounding Eurydice's 'second death':

> *Silvius*
> Monice, [...] solus
> [...]
> Ast ego dumosos colles silvasque perrero
> Infelix! Quis fata neget diversa gemellis?
> [...]
>
> *Monicus*
> Silvi, quid quereris? Cunctorum vera laborum
> Ipse tibi causa es. Quis te per devia cogit?
> Quis vel inaccessum tanto sudore cacumen
> Montis adire iubet, vel per deserta vagari?
>   (*Buc. carm.* I. 1, 3–4, & 6–9)

[*Silvius*: Oh Monicus, alone [...] while I, wretch that I am, wander over hills full of thorn-bushes and through forests. Who could ever deny the different fates of two brothers? [...] *Monicus*: Oh Silvius, why do you complain? You yourself are the cause of all your travails. Who forces you to go to out-of-the-way places? Who makes you reach with so much sweat the inaccessible peak of a mountain, or wander deserted places?]

There are several points of contact, especially if one recalls Petrarch's imitative predilection creatively to rework his sources (McLaughlin, pp. 26–32). Silvius's lines 1 and 3 are a variation on 'solus Hyperboreas glacies Tanaimque nivalem | arvaque Riphaeis numquam viduata pruinis | lustrabat' [alone he wandered the icy North,

---

27   The lines primarily draw on Ovid (*Met.* X. 89, 143–44, and XI. 1–2, 44–48, & 54), although the influence of *Cons.* III. *met.* 12. 8–9 and of *Georg.* IV. 510 is also recognizable. The *Epystole* are quoted from Franceco Petrarca, *Poëmata minora quae extant omnia*, ed. by Domenico Rossetti, 3 vols (Milan: Societas Typographica Classicorum Italiae Scriptorum, 1829–34); *Ep.* III. 15 may be read at II, 112–15, where it is numbered 14.

snowy Tanais and fields that are never free of Riphaean frost] (*Georg.* IV. 517–19); while line 4 recalls 'illa "quis et me" inquit "miseram et te perdidit, Orpheu, | quis [...]?' [she said, 'what is this that has lost my wretched self and you, oh Orpheus, what?'] (494–95) combined with 'a miseram Eurydicen!' [ah wretched Eurydice!] (526) and 'miserabilis Orpheus' [wretched Orpheus] (454). In the *Georgics*, the latter designation is immediately followed in the next line by the interjection 'ni fata resistant' [unless the fates oppose it] (455) that exercises some pull on the remainder of line 4. More generally, Petrarch replays Virgil's anaphoric repetition of questions beginning in *Quis* in lines 4, 7, and 8, as well as the older poet's recourse to exclamation. In his turn, Monicus, who stands for Petrarch's brother Gherardo, merges Virgilian and Ovidian elements with the heavily moralizing interpretations of Orpheus's error that had their origins in commentaries to Boethius's *Consolation*.[28] Specifically, lines 6–9 fuse Virgil's 'victusque animi respexit. ibi omnis | effusus labor' [and his resolve overwhelmed, he looked back. In that moment all his effort was squandered] (491–92) and 'rupe sub aëria deserti ad Strymonis undam | flevisse' [beneath a high rock, by the wave of deserted Strymon he wept] (508–09) with Ovid's 'esse deos Erebi crudeles questus, in altam | se recipit Rhodopen pulsumque aquilonibus Haemum' [after having complained that the gods of the underworld were cruel, he retreated to lofty Thrace and to Haemus buffetted by north winds] (*Met.* x. 76–77) — all quotations that refer to Orpheus's 'mad' (*Georg.* IV. 488) behaviour that first led to, and then followed on from, Eurydice's 'second death'.

The Orphic patina of *Parthenias*'s opening exchange is certainly striking. At the same time, as with *Ep.* III. 15, it is the reasons why Petrarch may have resorted to the myth, as well as its subsequent unfolding during the course of each poem, that deserve especial attention, not least if these also help us better appreciate the *fabula*'s function in the *Canzoniere*. As is well known, the introductory eclogue of the *Bucolicum carmen*, via the dialogue between Petrarch and his brother Gherardo, assesses the merits of two ways of life, the active and the contemplative, and of two types of literature, classical and classicizing secular poetry as against Biblical verse, specifically the Psalms. The discussion seemingly ends in an impasse, with both brothers remaining firm in their contrasting opinions regarding life and literature. But what role might Orpheus, long-associated with harmony, play in this drama of brotherly intransigence? Although Orphic allusions recur throughout the eclogue, these are principally concentrated in the second part of Silvius's poetic autobiography and self-justification (29–45) and in Monicus's sharp response to his brother (46–49), namely, *Parthenias*'s key section, not simply because in it Petrarch

---

28   In line with Boethius's admonition in the *metrum*'s explicit ('Nam qui Tartareum in specus | Victus lumina flexerit, | Quidquid praecipuum trahit | perdit, dum videt infernos' [For he who overwhelmed should turn his eyes towards the Tartarean cave, he loses whatever superiority he has achieved, when he looks at those below], 55–58), his commentators explained Orpheus's descent to Hades and subsequent despair as signifying the allure of and dedication to *temporalia*; see Friedman, pp. 98–114. Surprisingly, not least in light of Petrarch's friendship with Pierre Bersuire, author of the influential *Metamorphosis Ovidiana*, which offers a heavily Christianized interpretation of the story of Orpheus and Eurydice, several scholars have denied the impact of the exegetical tradition on the poet's view of the myth. For further examples of Petrarch's indebtedness to the medieval reception of the *fabula*, see Subsection 3 below.

speaks of himself as a poet, but also because it includes ideological legitimation for the brothers' respective positions. Indeed, Petrarch forcefully signals the importance of the 'Rhodopeius [...] heros' [Thracian hero] (*Met.* x. 50) for his self-portrait by unusually following his source in Ovid with greater precision than usual; and this more than once. Silvius's melodramatic conclusion — 'Si fata viam [...] negarit, | Stat, germane, mori' [If the fates will deny the way, it is better, oh brother, that I die] (44–45) — repeats Orpheus's valiant altruistic declaration: 'quodsi fata negant veniam pro coniuge, certum est | nolle redire mihi: leto gaudete duorum' [For if the fates deny this favour to my wife, it is certain that I will not return: enjoy the death of two people] (x. 38–39). Equally, as occurs with Orpheus's 'flebile lingua murmurat' [tongue mournfully murmuring] to which 'respondent flebile ripae' [the riverbanks mournfully respond] (xi. 52–53) so 'arentes respondent undique cautes' [from every side the arid rocks respond] (34–35) to Petrarch's 'song'. Around these two quotations, the poet distributes an array of Orphic motifs. Silvius mentions following his poetic masters but without losing contact with them (29), as well as poetry's impact on the environment (30–31, 34–35, & 41–42), and the fluctuating nature of his existence ('Sic eo, sic redeo' [Thus I go, thus I return], 40), which succinctly captures the logic of events culminating in Eurydice's 'second death'. As he would do in the *Parte in morte* of the *Fragmenta*, Petrarch filters his poetic and human experiences through those of Orpheus, who, together with Homer and Virgil, is presented as one of his three seminal literary models.[29] Yet, in the *Canzoniere*, as we saw, while extolling the *vates*, the poet also highlights the limits of his predecessor's verse. Similarly, in the eclogue, returning to his opening Orphic gambit (6–9), Monicus stresses the error of his brother's exclusive dedication to secular poetry, once more implying parallels between Silvius's conduct and Orpheus's looking back at Eurydice, an unconscionable action (*Georg.* iv. 491) that both marked the start of the bard's unrelieved suffering and erratic behaviour, and resulted in the beloved being confined for eternity in Hell:

> O! si forte queas durum hoc transcendere limen.
> Quid refugis? Turpesque casas et tuta pavescis
> Otia? Quid frontem obducis? Nemo ante coactus
> Nostra petit. (*Buc. carm.* I. 46–49)

[Oh, if by chance you could cross the hard threshold. Why do you flee? Why do you fear the base houses and calm leisures? Why do you furrow your brow? Nobody is forced to seek our caves.][30]

The danger to which Silvius is exposing his immortal soul in Monicus's warning is obvious, although for the moment he leaves his brother's admonition unheeded.

---

29   In an important study, Albert Russell Ascoli has demonstrated that, intertextually, in *Parthenias*, Petrarch is critical of Dante as a poetic *auctoritas* by censuring his exchange of eclogues with Giovanni del Virgilio: 'Blinding the Cyclops: Petrarch after Dante', in *Petrarch and Dante: Anti-Dantism, Metaphysics, Tradition*, ed. by Zygmunt G. Barański and Theodore J. Cachey, Jr. (Notre Dame, IN: University of Notre Dame Press, 2009), pp. 114–73.
30   Monicus's response integrates and refashions (in particular contrastively: the 'tranquillity' of the monastery as against the horrors of Hades) *Georg.* iv. 467–69, 500, 502–03 and *Met.* x. 13, 29, 32–35, 55, 72.

Subsequently, as I hope to have clarified above, in Part II of the *Rerum vulgarium frgmenta*, Petrarch accepts Gherardo's criticism and will acknowledge the error of the hero's (and by extension of his own earlier) exaggerated faith in poetry, especially when this is considered *sub specie aeternitatis*.

The basic Orphic characteristics of the second section of the *Canzoniere*, namely, the myth's key structural functions and the *vates*'s status as a great yet flawed poetic and existential model, are thus already evident in the proemial poem of the *Bucolicum carmen*. In addition, the eclogue appears to reveal that what attracted Petrarch to the myth was its semantic and symbolic flexibility: first, its 'reversibility', the way in which elements from the myth can be assigned different, even contrasting, values (Orpheus's singing and the act of following as having both positive and negative connotations), and second, its 'universalism', the manner in which Eurydice's and Orpheus's experiences can be simultaneously embodied by a single character and are not gender-specific (Silvius who commits an error reminiscent of Orpheus's, but who concurrently, like Eurydice, faces the dire consequences of the misstep). These elements too would become constants in Petrarch's treatment of the *fabula* in the *Fragmenta*. Crucially, however, what is still missing is proper recognition of Eurydice's importance. It will be canzone 323, of course, that finally acknowledges her indispensable status in the story.[31] Indeed, I wonder whether my hypothesis regarding Petrarch's intuition of 13 October can be refined further. The insight may have involved an understanding not so much of the *fabula*'s ideological and creative efficacy — *Parthenias* offers proof that Petrarch was well aware of this by the late 1340s — but of Eurydice's rich and decisive potential.

By diverting to the *Canzoniere*, I have failed adequately to address Orpheus's status in the eclogue. On the one hand, I had begun to establish his significance as an emblem, together with Homer and Virgil, of the allure, success, and spectacular potential of secular poetry at its best, as well as his aptness to serve as an ideal for Petrarch to imitate. To put it simply, as far as Silvius is concerned, Orpheus legitimates his choice of life and art.[32] On the other, however, Monicus highlights the myth's pitfalls and ambiguities, and goes on to propose and celebrate an alternative literary and existential model, David the psalmist (53–58, 70–71, & 91–109). Scholars correctly read the brothers' claims in antithetical terms. In addition, they generally also maintain that, in *Parthenias*, Petrarch asserted the autonomy of the greatest poets and their achievements, and, in contrast to other contemporary intellectuals, most notably Dante and Mussato, denied that meaningful contacts might exist

---

31   It was not uncommon for Eurydice to be marginalized in the myth's medieval reception; see Friedman, pp. 99–100, 113.

32   Petrarch's embracing of Orpheus as a poetic model is further developed in *Laurea occidens*, the first version of which has been dated to 1348. The *vates* is not just given special prominence in the long catalogue of ancient writers (147–56), but, suggestively, of all the poets he had previously mentioned, Petrarch chose to close the eclogue in an Orphic key that, differently from *Parthenias*, began to give prominence to Laura-Eurydice, as well as to Petrarch-Orpheus, and that anticipates one of the woman's key functions in Part II: 'Vestigia [*lauri sacrae*] suplex | consequere, atque precare aditum, verbisque caveto | Invidiam conflare dejs' [Follow beseeching the tracks [of the sacred laurel], and beg that you be allowed to draw close, but beware not to enflame the envy of the gods with your words] (407–09).

between theology and poetry, thereby also criticizing the connected notion of the *poeta-theologus*.[33] The presence of Orpheus in the eclogue, however, calls these latter interpretations into question. Unlike Homer and Virgil, whose poetic achievements the fourteenth century largely deemed beyond reproach, Orpheus, for all his artistic prowess, did raise questions about the efficacy of poetry, as Monicus avers.[34] Equally, in the late Middle Ages, if there was one poet who more than any other embodied the figure of the *poeta-theologus*, that poet was Orpheus, who praised the gods and civilized humanity.[35] Moreover, it is interesting that, in *Parthenias*, David too is presented as having Orphic attributes: 'Semper habet lacrimas et pectore raucus anelat' [He always has tears and draws hoarse breaths from his breast] (74) and 'Omnia [riverbanks and seashores] iam resonant pastoris carmina nostri' [all now resound with the songs of our shepherd] (109). In itself, the association between the two singers, since it was widely present in medieval culture (Friedman, pp. 148–55, 188–89), is little more than a commonplace. In terms of the first eclogue, however, it further blurs the distinction, but without obliterating it, between theology and poetry. By dexterously insinuating Orpheus as his poem's controlling mechanism, Petrarch undermined the intransigence of both brothers, and furthermore introduced a third position that recognized both the achievements and limitations of secular poetry, as well as its points of contact with the sacred.[36] While placing the emphasis on profane literature, the 'Orphic' idea of poetry that emerges from *Parthenias* is one of possible and useful contacts between secular and religious writers that does not unbalance or overwhelm either tradition. In terms of mid-Trecento poetics, Petrarch's nuanced view of poetry constitutes a compromise between the claims of those who insisted on literature's glorious self-sufficiency and the contentions of those who were intent on excessively 'theologizing' it. It is the type of compromise, in fact, that will also be apparent in Part II of the *Fragmenta*, where Petrarch increasingly leavens his distinctly secular lyric poetry with Christian intertexts and values, a process that reaches a climax with 'Vergine bella'. My reading is actually not that dissimilar from the explanation that Petrarch

---

33   Ascoli; Aldo S. Bernardo, 'Petrarch's Attitude toward Dante', *PMLA*, 70 (1955), 488–517 (pp. 501–06); Thomas M. Greene, 'Pertrach *Viator*', in his *The Vulnerable Text: Essays on Renaissance Literature* (New York: Columbia University Press, 1986), pp. 18–45 (pp. 22–23); Giuseppe Mazzotta, 'Humanism and Monastic Spirituality', in his *The Worlds of Petrarch* (Durham, NC, and London: Duke University Press, 1993), pp. 147–66 (pp. 153–58).

34   See in particular Augustine, *Contra Faustum* XIII. 15; Boethius, *Cons.* III. *met.* 12. 14–17; John Scot Eriugena, *Annotationes in Marcianum*, ed. by Cora E. Lutz (Cambridge, MA: Medieval Academy of America, 1939), pp. 192–93; Remigius of Auxerre, *Commentum in Martianum*, ed. by Cara E. Lutz, 2 vols (Leiden: Brill, 1962–65), II, 310. See also J. Keith Atkinson, 'Orpheus, vates threicus et la transgression', in *Le metamorfosi di Orfeo*, ed. by Anna Maria Babbi (Verona: Fiorini, 1999), pp. 83–102.

35   See Quintilian, *Instit. orat.* I. 10. 9; Augustine, *De civ. Dei* XVIII. 14 & 37 (and see Petrarch, *Contra medicum* III. 197); Thomas Aquinas, *Comm. De anima* I. 12 and *Comm. Metaph.* I. 3. See also Friedman, pp. 100, 112, 120–21, 130–31, 157.

36   'It is clear that Petrarch [...] was aware that both Monicus and Silvius represented extremes. What he is declaring is, in effect, that the true poet lies somewhere between these extremes' (Bernardo, p. 505). I believe that Bernardo's basic insight continues to be valid; however, the presence of Orpheus in the eclogue complicates the idea that Petrarch was attempting to mediate between extremes.

offers as his framework for interpreting *Parthenias* in the *Familiaris*:

> Theologie quidem minime adversa poetica est. Miraris? parum abest quin dicam
> theologiam poeticam esse de Deo: Cristum modo leonem modo agnum modo
> vermem dici, quid nisi poeticum est? mille talia in Scripturis Sacris invenies que
> persequi longum est. Quid vero aliud parabole Salvatoris in Evangelio sonant,
> nisi sermonem a sensibus alienum sive, ut uno verbo exprimam, alieniloquium,
> quam allegoriam usitatiori vocabulo nuncupamus? Atqui ex huiusce sermonis
> genere poetica omnis intexta est. Sed subiectum aliud. Quis negat? illic de Deo
> atque divinis, hic de diis hominibusque tractatur, unde et apud Aristotilem
> primos theologizantes poetas legimus. (*Fam.* x. 4. 1–2)

> [In fact poetry is barely in opposition to theology. Are you surprised? I might
> almost say that theology is God's poetry: when Christ is called a lion or a
> lamb or a worm, what is it if not poetry? You will find thousands of such
> cases in Sacred Scripture that are too many to treat here. In truth what else do
> the Saviour's parables in the Gospel resound if not a discourse different from
> its customary meaning or, to put it simply, other speech, which in everyday
> language we term allegory? Nevertheless all poetry is woven from this type of
> discourse. But its subject is different. Who'd deny it? The first discourse treats
> God and divine things, the other gods and men, so that even in Aristotle we
> read that the first theologians were poets.]

Petrarch indicates the points of contact between theology and poetry, while also
clearly discriminating between them; although it is suggestive that, albeit to
different degrees, a divine dimension, as well as similarities in style, characterizes
both. Yet, nowhere in its exegesis, does the letter refer to Orpheus. The omission
cannot but be deliberate. Now that Petrarch himself is openly clarifying the poem's
meaning — the task that the *vates* performs allusively in the weave of the eclogue
— his presence is predictably redundant.

In cultural terms, *Bucolicum carmen* I effects a valid compromise on a matter
of significant intellectual concern. Yet, if read 'autobiographically', it is doubtful
whether the eclogue displays a similar conciliatory equilibrium with respect to the
poet's personal engagement with poetry. Petrarch confusingly associates himself
with both Silvius and Orpheus. He is caught between the shepherd's intransigent
pursuit of self-satisfying poetic glory and the hard lessons regarding poetry's
shortcomings taught by the bard's harsh experiences. Importantly, both alternatives
are present in the myth: the former in Orpheus's wondrous authority over his
earthly and otherworldly surroundings, the latter in Orpheus's loss of the almost
regained Eurydice. It is indicative that, in lines 29–47, Silvius should stress the bard's
triumphs, while Monicus his failures, although, more revealingly, both also allude
to the contrary experience.[37] Petrarch's personal dilemma is all here: his inability
to resolve in his own life tensions that, at a purely intellectual and external level,
he was able to reconcile satisfactorily. As occurs time and again in his *œuvre*, the
poet presents himself trapped between the two possibilities — a predicament whose
implications Monicus pithily summarizes in the eclogue's closing line: 'I sospes,

---

37   See for instance, Silvius: l. 34 and compare *Met.* I. 53; Monicus: l. 46 and compare *Georg.* IV.
467–69.

variosque vie circumspice casus' [Go safely, and look out for the journey's many dangers] (124). In Orphic terms, Petrarch is incapable of accepting and usefully integrating the myth's full implications. His Orpheus is a poet who is 'sundered' from his own history. Yet, when, towards the end of his life, in Part II of the *Canzoniere*, Petrarch returned to the *vates* to help him make sense of Laura's death, it was because he had finally begun to acquire a clear and balanced appreciation of the fabled poet's successes and failures — an acquisition that was largely due to the recovery of Eurydice that first and foremost represented a belated acceptance of Orpheus's limitations. It was the coming together of all these factors, I would like to think, that most likely constituted the stuff of Petrarch's sudden intuition.

Before returning definitively and conclusively to the *Fragmenta*, I need to say something about the Horatian *epystola* to Floriano. The poem lacks the layered complexity of *Parthenias*. As a political *satyra*, it aims to make its polemical points rather more directly.[38] Nevertheless, its recourse to the *vates* is anything but uninteresting. Behind the veil of hyperbolically praising the addressee as a modern-day Orpheus (compare *Ep.* III. 16. 1–2; *Sen.* XI. 5. 1) and pleading with him to abandon the corrupt environment in which he resides — surroundings that are largely described in mythological terms — Petrarch launches yet another scathing attack on the papal court at Avignon. His condemnation of the present, as is evident from the opening allusion to Orpheus, is achieved in part through a starkly unfavourable comparison with classical antiquity. As in *Rerum vulgarium fragmenta* 28, another political poem, the bard is exclusively evoked as a great civic poet whose song morally improves its listeners. Yet, even he would be unable to affect and improve the 'monstrous' Avignonese clergy (compare *De remediis* I. 24. 10), an affirmation that contrastively alludes to Orpheus mesmerizing even the most fearsome horrors of Hades (*Georg.* IV. 481–84 and *Met.* X. 40–47):

> Nisi quod modo surda canenti
> Monstra parit tellus; redeat licet ille, nec iram
> Nec luxum frenare queat, victusque tenaci
> Cedet avaritiae. (*Ep.* III. 15. 6–9)

> [Except that now the earth brings forth monsters that are deaf to the singer; even if he [Orpheus] were to return, he would not be able to curb their wrath and debauchery, and overcome by stubborn greed he will withdraw.]

As Petrarch muses about Orpheus's return from the dead, the hero metamorphoses into Eurydice, underlining again her occasional 'exploitable' status for much of the poet's career.[39] More significantly, the bard also rehearses her 'second death'. Orpheus's defeat in a hypothetical present is associated with his murder at the

---

38   On *satyra* see at least Charles A. van Rooy, *Studies in Classical Satire and Related Literary Theory* (Leiden: Brill, 1965); Udo Kindermann, *Satyra: die Theorie der Satire im Mittellateinischen. Vorstudie zu einer Gattungsgeschichte* (Nuremberg: Hans Carl, 1978); Ben Parsons, '"A Riotous Spray of Words": Rethinking the Medieval Theory of Satire', *Exemplaria*, 21 (2009), 105–28. What is striking about Petrarch's satirical style is his recourse to allegory and its rhetorical refinement, both attributes that medieval definitions of the genre presented as anithetical to the *stilus*.

39   Later in the poem, Eurydice is once more absorbed into other figures: 'senes, Stygiaque datum sit valle reverti' [if the ancients were permitted to return from the Stygian valley] (12).

hands of the savage Bacchantes, the myth's horrific climax, that Ovid describes in detail (*Met.* XI. 1–60), but which, in his *oeuvre*, Petrarch never directly remembers. Orpheus, 'overcome by deaf and stubborn greed', relives the women's unrelenting attack (13–14), their insensitivity to his song, and his cruel death:[40]

> In illo tempore primum
> inrita dicentem nec quicquam voce moventem
> sacrilegae perimunt. (*Ep.* III. 15. 39–41; and cf. 15–18)

[Then for the first time he spoke without effect and his voice did not move any of them, the impious women killed him.]

Indeed, the clergy's 'bloody hands' ('dextrasque cruentas', *Ep.* III. 15. 13) explicitly calque those of the Maenads who 'cruentatis vertuntur in Orphea dextris' [with their bloody hands they turn on Orpheus] (*Met.* XI. 23).

Although, during the remainder of the *epystola* and before its explicit, Orphic elements occasionally reappear (12, 18–21, 23, 29), Petrarch relies on a very different source to depict the curia's perversions:

> Semiviros per prata boves, perque atria cernas
> Semiboves errare viros. Non unus opacam
> Minotaurus habet perplexi tramitis aulam;
> Plurima permixtae caecaeque libidinis extant
> Signa per infames partus sobolemque nefandam
> Et natos furor exagitat, rabiesque famesque
> Dira, nec immites cessant a sanguine fauces.
> Nec septena virum, sed iam millena vorantur
> Corpora iustorum; nec solae urgentur Athenae,
> Sed cupidis totus laceratur dentibus orbis. (*Ep.* III. 15. 23–32)

[You see half-men wander through the fields like bulls and half-bulls through the houses like men. Not only is the Minotaur found in the dark hall of the unintelligible labyrinth; many signs of intermingled and blind lust are visible, the result of disreputable births and abominable progeny, and fury torments the offspring, and anger and dreadful hunger, and their savage jaws never cease from craving blood. Not seven men, but now thousands of bodies of the just are devoured; nor is Athens alone oppressed, but the whole world is torn to pieces by greedy teeth.]

We are back in Dante's Hell. At first sight, Avignon, the home of the blood-crazed Minotaur and *semiviri*, appears to have been transformed into the circle of violence. Yet, express intertextual links with *Inferno* XII are hard to find. Instead, while undeniably evoking the region of 'la riviera del sangue in la qual bolle | qual che per vïolenza in altrui noccia' (47–48), Petrarch increases the infernal intensity of his Hell-on-earth by deftly combining a series of interconnected Dantean passages

---

40 Suggestively, *victus* recalls both Orpheus's last success and his greatest failure. The 'lapis' [stone] thrown by one of the Cicones 'concentu victus vocisque lyraeque est' [is vanquished by the harmony of song and lyre] (*Met.* XI. 10–11). However, the past participle also appears, when, 'on the very verge of light', Orpheus 'immemor heu! victusque animi respexit' [forgetful alas! and his resolve overwhelmed, he looked back] (*Georg.* IV. 490–91). Petrarch's knowing manipulation of his sources is impressive.

drawn from different parts of the the first canticle. *Inferno* XXV — canto of thieves, abominations, and sexually inflected perverse transformations (compare *Ep.* III. 15. 26–27) — provides the key to the *epystola*'s Dantean intertextual system:

> Per tutt' i cerchi de lo 'nferno scuri
> non vidi spirto in Dio tanto superbo [Vanni Fucci],
> non quel che cadde a Tebe giù da' muri.
> El si fuggì che non parlò più verbo;
> E io vidi un centauro pien di rabbia.
> (*Inf.* XXV. 13–17; and see *Ep.* III. 15. 28)

Petrarch's passage yokes together *Inferno* XII, XIV, and XXV, namely, violence by introducing Cacus the centaur, blasphemy through the figure of Capaneus, and thievery — a potently apt *permixtum* (*Ep.* III. 15. 26) that captures and condemns the clergy's principal sins. Indeed, the latter two canti provide the sources for some elements in Petrarch's description. Thus, 'fuor che la tua [Capaneus's] rabbia | sarebbe al tuo furor dolor compito' (*Inf.* XIV. 65–66) anticipates 'Et natos furor exagitat, rabiesque famesque' [And fury torments the offspring, and anger and dreadful hunger] (*Ep.* III. 15. 28);[41] while 'nec immites cessant a sanguine fauces' [their savage jaws never cease from craving blood] (*Ep.* III. 15. 29) fuses 'di sangue fece spesse volte laco' with 'onder cessar le sue opere biece' (*Inf.* XXV. 27 and 31). In addition, at least one other, 'extraneous', Dantean intertext is present in the mix: 'cagne, bramose [...] | miser li denti, | e quel dilacerâro' (*Inf.* XIII. 125 & 127–28) which returns in line 32, 'Sed cupidis totus laceratur dentibus orbis' [but the whole world is torn to pieces by greedy teeth]. As in *Parthenias*, Petrarch brings Orpheus and Dante together in a move that he repeats elsewhere. I shall very soon briefly address the coupling of the two great poets. At this point, I simply wish to note that, while Orpheus is presented in all his glory as he seduces the natural and the other world, Dante is reduced to the poet of *monstra* (Chapter 10, pp. 384–85); and it is of course in the footsteps of Orpheus the civilizer that Petrarch the political poet follows, cherrypicking Dante along the way.

3. 'Bella donna punta poi nel tallon'

The poems that I have discussed so far document both the pliability of the *fabula* of Orpheus and Eurydice and Petrarch's formal, narrative, and ideological skill at exploiting the myth's possibilities. Especially in *Parthenias* the poet displayed its organizational, cultural, and semantic potential. However, as we have begun to recognize, it is in Part II of the *Canzoniere* that Petrarch most fully develops the story and adapts it to his personal needs and preoccupations. I do not have the space here to trace the myth's imposing advancement and rich elaboration in

---

41   The line also depends on the lion's 'rabbiosa fame' (*Inf.* I. 47). In addition, Petrarch's 'septena virum' (30) may relate to Dante's 'sette regi | ch'assiser Tebe' (*Inf.* XIV. 68–69), although seven is also associated with Orpheus (*Georg.* IV. 507 and *Met.* X. 73). Equally, *furor* is the term that Eurydice uses to describe her husband's looking back: 'Orpheu, | quis tantus furor' [Oh Orpheus, what frenzy] (*Georg.* IV. 494–95).

the later reworkings of the second half of the *Fragmenta* (never mind its far from inconsequential presence in the *Parte in vita*). At most I can allude to a few large-scale elements that help confirm its importance in the lyric collection; and it is precisely the *fabula*'s significance — its range and adaptability — that Petrarch scholarship has either almost entirely ignored or minimized.

Let us begin with some numbers. I have recognized Orphic elements, that range from generalized allusions, such as the theme of looking back, to more specific suggestions, such as nature's lament that involves trees, rivers, birds, and to precise evocations — thus, among the birds, 'Quel rosignuol' (311. 1) is the vernacular progeny of Virgil's distraught 'philomela' (*Georg.* IV. 511; and see 511–15 to 311. 1–5) — in thirty-five poems from Part I and in just about half the lyrics, fifty-one out of 103, in Part II. The poems are: in Part I, 1, 10, 15, 23, 28, 49, 50, 51, 53, 54, 58, 59, 93, 97, 99, 110, 123, 125, 129, 130, 135, 143, 152, 156, 170, 180, 187, 188, 190, 195, 203, 212, 222, 237, 239; and in Part II, 264, 265, 267, 268, 269, 270, 271, 273, 275, 276, 277, 278, 279, 281, 282, 283, 286, 288, 290, 291, 292, 294, 296, 297, 298, 301, 302, 304, 305, 306, 310, 311, 316, 318, 320, 323, 324, 325, 332, 333, 334, 336, 342, 346, 347, 349, 353, 357, 358, 359, 366. Simply in themselves, the statistics are eye-catching and confirm the myth's weight in the *Fragmenta*. They are even more impressive when placed against Peter Hainsworth's '51 poems in which allusions are made to Daphne or to the laurel in a readily recognizable manner'.[42] I am not trying to suggest that Orpheus and Eurydice are more significant than Apollo and Daphne or that the two doomed lovers trump all the *Canzoniere*'s other myths. I am simply underscoring their vitality and persistence in the collection. Indeed, a first inkling of their import can come from the fact that, before Petrarch, Orpheus is not named in the Occitan and Italian lyric tradition, something which the poet is very likely to have known and which confirms the highly personalized character of the myth in the *Rerum vulgarium fragmenta*.[43]

I am thus tempted to wonder whether Petrarch's *Canzoniere* may not in fact be the great overlooked Orphic text of the Western tradition, with Part II as its apogee.[44] Petrarch immediately imprints the tragic lovers on to the section: sixteen of the first twenty poems — the exceptions are 266, 272, 274, 280 — include elements drawn

---

42   Peter R. J. Hainsworth, 'The Myth of Daphne in the *Rerum vulgarium fragmenta*', *Italian Studies*, 34 (1979), 28–44 (p. 29). The comparison between the figures of my friend and former teacher and mine can only be approximate, since it is just about certain that we arrived at our totals employing different criteria — something that Peter confirmed after reading an earlier draft of this chapter. Nevertheless, despite its inadequacies, the comparison is instructive. Furthermore, sixteen of our poems (23, 28, 51, 129, 180, 188, 190, 195, 269, 270, 291, 318, 323, 325, 333, 359) contain both Daphneic and Orphic elements, which raises the question of the inter-relationship between two of the great foundational myths of the *Fragmenta*. Not dissimilarly, it would be worth investigating the extent to which Ovidian myths associated with Orpheus (for instance, Cyparissus) or recounted by the bard (say, Pygmalion) in *Met.* x ought to be considered as Orphic. The serious study of Orpheus in Petrarch is very much in its infancy.

43   See Valeria Bertolucci Pizzorusso, 'Orfeo "englouti" nelle letterature romanze dei secc. XII e XIII: prime attestazioni', in Babbi, pp. 135–54 (pp. 138–40).

44   It is conspicuous that neither Friedman nor Charles Segal, *Orpheus: The Myth of the Poet* (Baltimore and London: Johns Hopkins University Press, 1989) in their generally excellent books refer to Petrarch.

from the myth, and this sudden Orphic outpouring is all the more visible given that the close of Part I is devoid of references to the myth. The last allusions are strategically located in a sestina, 'Non à tanti animali il mar fra l'onde' (237), that does not appear in the *Canzoniere* until the Malatesta form, namely, the version, as we saw, that definitively marks the entry of Orpheus and Eurydice as key players in the collection. By accumulating a range of motifs that specify its programmed Orphic function, the sestina both anticipates the myth's dominant presence in the *Parte in morte* and emphasizes its disappearance in 238–63: 'né tanti augelli albergan per li boschi' (4) calques the simile of the souls flocking to listen to Orpheus, 'quam multa in foliis avium se milia condunt' [as many as the thousands of birds that shelter among the leaves] (*Georg.* IV. 473); variations on Virgil's 'te [Eurydice] veniente die, te decedente canebat' [he sang about you as the day approached, about you as it departed] (466) appear several times (12, 14, 20); woods are affected by the poet's sad condition (11 & 24); and he finds himself alone in wild places (9, 12, 15, 25–26, 37–38; and see *Georg.* IV. 507–09 & 517–19). In focusing on the Malatesta form, I should not like to create the impression that, before it, Part II was bereft of references to the myth. The opposite is in fact the case. Twenty-one out of the twenty-nine Correggio poems (264–92) assigned to the *Parte in morte* embrace Orphic elements; while, in the Chigi (264–304), the numbers are twenty-eight out of forty-one and, in Giovanni (264–318), thirty-four from fifty-five. Petrarch had long appreciated the relevance of the *fabula* when representing himself as a bereaved poet-lover, not least because he had already seriously engaged with it elsewhere. What was missing in his treatment until the inclusion of 323 and 332, but also 237, was an articulated structural and ideological Orphic system that could grant coherence to the disparate manifestations of the myth in the individual poems. I believe, as I have already stated, that this move to formal symmetry and intellectual orderliness was the result of the intuition of 13 October 1368 — an intuition which, for the first time, revealed to Petrarch the capacity of Eurydice to exert the necessary shaping function on the second part of his collection. As a result, for him, the myth became no longer simply that of Orpheus, but of Orpheus and Eurydice. Indeed, to put it more accurately, it became the *fabula* of Eurydice and Orpheus.[45]

I am keenly aware that I am dealing with complex matters in a cursory and unsatisfactory manner. Substantial research needs to be done before we can begin to understand the processes whereby the myth became ever more crucial for the construction of the *Fragmenta*.[46] As with this study as a whole, I am simply mapping out a few co-ordinates that might offer some directions to an in-depth investigation. Many issues would need to be taken into consideration. As I have adumbrated, attention would first need to be given to the Orphic make-up of individual forms of the *Canzoniere* and their inter-relationship, in particular to the processes whereby the myth entered into their systems, which would also entail, wherever possible, as in the case of 323, an assessment of the different phases of the Orphic construction

---

45   Petrarch's position recalls 'the Fulgentian approach to the myth which makes Eurydice the equal of or the superior to Orpheus' (Friedman, p. 113; and see also pp. 89–90).
46   For the moment, see Brunori.

of individual poems. For instance, the relative weight, prominence, and intratextual import of elements drawn from the myth in 'I' vo pensando, et nel penser m'assale' (264), the first poem of Part II, cannot but vary between versions: in the *forma Chigi* they play a secondary role, while in the post-Malatesta forms they help to introduce major structural and ideological concerns.[47] Furthermore, the potential sources — from Horace to Servius and from Statius to Claudian — of Petrarch's knowledge of the myth need to be evaluated much more efficiently and widely than I have been able to do here. In particular, much more can be said about the likely impact on the poet of the hermeneutic tradition. The myth's flexibility is at the core of its medieval reception, not least because its protagonists, like Petrarch and Laura in the *Canzoniere*, can represent both positive and negative values, as well as much else that comes between these two poles.[48] It is the commentators that stress the rapprochement in the *fabula* between art and ethics, vice and virtue, *sapientia* and *eloquentia* — all concerns that also haunt the *Canzoniere*. Finally, and it is the aspect of the medieval engagement with the myth that I find most suggestive for Petrarch, exegetes consistently read it in expressly Christian terms.[49] Indeed, I believe that such interpretations aided the poet in his endeavour to integrate secular and religious elements in Part II. A couple of examples ought to suffice. Scholars normally cite Job 30: 31 — 'versa est in luctum cithara mea et organum meum in vocem flentium' [my harp is turned to mourning and my organ into the voice of those that cry] — as the source for:

> Or sia qui fine al mio amoroso canto:
> Secca è la vena de l'usato ingegno,
> Et la cetera mia rivolta in pianto. (*Rvf* 292. 12–14)

However, the reference is also Orphic: from the lyre, to abandoning a former style, and to finding a new poetic register to express sorrow. What makes the sonnet's close so powerfully apposite, especially as a declaration of the *Parte in morte*'s poetics, is the manner in which it no longer posits, unlike for much of the *Canzoniere*, the Christian and the classical as contrasting alternatives but presents them as coming together to illuminate the poet-mourner's condition, while also offering him models to imitate in his effort to give voice to his predicament. *Mutatis mutandis*, the commentators had recognized in the story of Orpheus and Eurydice elements that could neatly dovetail with Christian situations, from the Fall to Christ's salvific

---

47 Just in the opening stanza, Petrarch introduces wandering, weeping, self-pity, divine indifference to his appeals, and outstretched arms (14–15; and compare *Met.* x. 58). The canzone as a whole, but especially in its last two stanzas, is dependent on moralizing Boethian interpretations of the myth (103, 111–12).

48 'Between the extremes of Christ and sinner are other figures with whom the hero of this legend can be compared' (Friedman, p. 130). See also Michel Zink, 'Le Poète désacralisé: Orphée médiéval et l'*Ovide moralisé*', in Babbi, pp. 15–27.

49 See Friedman, pp. 38–85, 125–28, 130, 147–55; Penelope B. R. Doob, *Nebuchadnezzar's Children: Conventions of Madness in Middle English Literature* (New Haven, CT, and London: Yale University Press, 1974), pp. 173–74, 181–84; Irwin; Vicari; Maria Tabaglio, 'La cristianizzazione del mito di Orfeo', in Babbi, pp. 65–82.

power,[50] thereby serving to legitimate the myth's Christianizing overtones in the *Canzoniere*.[51] As a result, Laura-Orpheus may lead Petrarch-Eurydice-the human 'soul' to Heaven:

> Ché, come i miei pensier' dietro a lei vanno,
> cosí leve, expedita et lieta l'alma
> la segua, et io sia fuor di tanto affanno. (*Rvf* 278. 9–11)

The tercet successfully captures the myth's potent and valuable adaptability in the *Fragmenta*. Throughout Part II, as I have indicated, its details are moved back and forth between Petrarch and Laura depending on the context of individual poems. Furthermore, to appreciate Petrarch's reworking of his Orphic borrowings, it is necessary, as 323 establishes, to recognize the functions of both lovers in the *fabula*. Indeed, if Eurydice's original attributes, as in sonnet 278, are now reassigned to a male character, this is no longer a mark of her inconsequentiality, as in *Epystola* III. 15, but of her indispensable vitality and uniqueness. Indeed, since elsewhere in the *Canzoniere*, she is regularly linked to Laura, Eurydice is not simply the saved soul but, Christologically, also the means by which that same soul achieves salvation. The myth's subtle complexity in the *Canzoniere* is neatly captured, if far from resolved, in its paradoxes.

4. In Conclusion: *Ille*

As far as I am aware, in the medieval tradition, Eurydice was never linked to Christ. This new connotation originates with Petrarch. Indeed, however much the Middle Ages may have acknowledged the myth's malleability, Petrarch energetically and deliberately 'deconstructed' it to serve his own ends. To put it somewhat differently, he appropriated and personalized the *fabula* and its exegesis, so that its values and circumstances became potentially applicable, whether *per analogiam* or contrastively, to any of the different moments, convolutions, and demands of his own story. I posed the question at the outset how Petrarch might imitate a writer whose texts he could never read. The answer, I believe, beyond following him at the general level of adopting the same (elegiac) genre, was by personally and creatively rewriting his story so that it became part of his own narrative of self-presentation. The myth ceases to be part of a common cultural heritage but becomes Petrarchan.[52] With

50   See Sara Sturm-Maddox, 'Petrarch's Serpent in the Grass: The Fall as Subtext in the *Rime sparse*', *The Journal of Medieval and Renaissance Studies*, 13 (1983), 213–26 (esp. pp. 216–17); see also Friedman, pp. 122, 125, & 127.

51   In his *Metamorphosis Ovidiana moraliter explanata* (Paris: Ascensianis et sub Pelicano, 1509), Pierre Bersuire offers an especially suggestive interpretation of Orpheus as a Christian penitent — 'Solus enim timor infernalis supplicii facit de vitiis poenitere & et sic facit uxorem per gratiam rehaberi [...] ipsam uxorem scilicet animam recuperatam' [Only the fear of infernal suffering made him repent his sins and thereby he regained his wife through grace [...] his wife namely the recovered soul], fol. LXXIII^r) — that dovetails neatly with interpretations of Part II as 'penitential' (see Santagata, *I frammenti dell'anima*, p. 305).

52   'La lirica petrarchesca si comporta insomma, [...] con grande libertà: scopre che il mito non esiste una volta per sempre, con una veste immutabile, ma è sempre di chi lo riscrive e lo reinterpreta; ed è questa, in fondo, la più alta innovazione che Petrarca apporta all'uso lirico del mito: la possibilità non

no originary text by Orpheus to deflect attention, the reader's focus is entirely on Petrarch and his poetry, which, as is well known, is not infrequently the poet's goal. As I have noted, Orpheus is put into contact with other authors, who, whether together or individually, allow Petrarch to define his own identity as a poet — and this feature too of Petrarch's Orphism needs to be evaluated properly. As well as the conventional association with *auctores* of the calibre of Homer and Virgil, or with ancient singers such as Amphion and Linus, another poet is regularly associated with Orpheus.[53] That poet, of course, is Dante, 'ille qui in his [vernacular studies] etatem totam posuit' [the one who dedicated his whole life to these], and hence whom Petrarch could never have 'envied' (*Fam.* XXI. 15. 21). This is most certainly not the place even to begin to enter into the tangled thicket of Petrarch's attitude to his predecessor (but see Chapter 10). Suffice it to say that, the rapprochement to Orpheus, as in *Epystola* III. 15, and in general to other poets, does Dante few favours. Yet, as has now been definitively established, Petrarch owed much to Dante. For instance, the assigning of Christological qualities to Eurydice-Laura is almost certainly filtered through Dante's sacralizing treatment of Beatrice in the *Vita nova* and in the Earthly Paradise. However, in Part II of the *Canzoniere*, being placed in Dante's ambit, also has negative effects on Orpheus. Time and again, Petrarch challenged Dante's central claim in the *Commedia* that he had been providentially granted direct knowledge of the other world. By denying the truthfulness of the poem, Petrarch denied too its intellectual claims, one of the key elements on which Dante's Trecento *auctoritas* was being constructed. He thus returned the *Commedia* to the realm of *fictio*, whence, by 'theologizing' it, Dante had striven to distance his masterpiece. Rather more energetically than in *Parthenias*, in the *Fragmenta*, Petrarch repudiated the idea of a transcendental poetry, replacing it with his exquisitely literary fusion of lyric and Scriptural and of classical-secular and Christian. Equally, by insisting on the autobiographical nature of the experiences that he was describing, Petrarch was also implying that, unlike the *Commedia*, the *Canzoniere* was *historia* and not *fictio*. By denying that the living Dante had been miraculously reunited with the dead Beatrice, Petrarch also rejected that Orpheus had descended to Hades and, however briefly, had spent time with his deceased spouse (see Chapter 12, pp. 432 and 438), hence the reason why, as in 278, the poet regularly reversed the *fabula*'s central situation.[54] In the *Fragmenta*, Eurydice no longer futilely follows Orpheus back to life and damnation. Instead Orpheus now beneficially trails Eurydice to death and deliverance. The ancient poet's endeavours are criticized, called into question, and rebuffed. Only the *Canzoniere* faces up honestly to the loss of a loved one, while also ensuring that poetry's rhetorically refined self-sufficiency is never compromised by its encounter with the transcendent. The greater were Petrarch's

---

solo di *usare* e di *interpretare* il materiale mitologico, ma in assoluto di *riscriverlo*, anche contaminando passi diversi' (Marcozzi, 'Petrarca lettore', p. 104; and see also *La biblioteca*, p. 104).

53   See *Ep.* II. 10. 231–33; *Fam.* XXIV. 12. 22 and 44. Although Petrarch recognized Orpheus's marvellous attainments as fictional (*Contra medicum* I. 153), like all his contemporaries, he accepted his historical reality; see Barański, 'Notes'.

54   See also Peter Hainsworth, *Petrarch the Poet: An Introduction to 'Rerum vulgarium fragmenta'* (London and New York: Routledge, 1988), p. 169.

debts to a writer, the more likely that that writer would be radically transformed at the poet's hands. Petrarch is intent on making it manifest that, in the last analysis, he did not need Orpheus's 'sí pietoso stile | che Laura mia potesse tôrre a Morte'; and this was not so much because the 'style' was ultimately no more than a consolatory delusion, but because, in the *Canzoniere*, he had forged his own decidedly 'realistic' and highly effective 'vario stile in ch'io piango et ragiono' (5).[55]

---

55   In addition to the passages already cited, Petrarch directly referred to Orpheus in *Fam.* XII. 9. 5; *Sen.* X. 4, where he confuses him with Morpheus.

CHAPTER 12

'Weeping' and 'Singing' with Orpheus (and with Dante): Emotional and Poetic Structures in *Rerum vulgarium fragmenta* 281–90

1. To Dream or Rather to 'Remember'?

My task, at least in theory, is to comment on ten sonnets — I say in theory, because in the structure of the *Canzoniere* these ten poems are not conveniently organized in a self-contained microsystem. Rather, as I will have occasion to indicate, they belong to several different microsystems that embrace not only sonnets 281–90, but also 279–80 and 291–92. Consequently, these four 'extravagant' poems also need to be considered here.

Sonnets 281–90 have not generated much interest among Petrarch's readers, despite the fact that sonnet 287 includes the only explicit reference to Dante in the *Rerum vulgarium fragmenta*: 'Ma ben ti [Sennuccio] prego che 'n la terza spera | Guitton saluti, et messer Cino, et Dante' (9–10). On consulting the annotated editions of the *Canzoniere* and the relevant critical studies, it is obvious that *communis opinio* holds that the sonnet series 279–92 evokes minor and largely repetitive moments that record Petrarch's reactions following Laura's death and his return to Valchiusa.[1] In particular, and in a quite non-controversial manner, scholars maintain that the sonnets throw light on the psychological world of the lover and on the new awareness that he acquires of how much the beloved had done for him before her premature ascent to Paradise. Recently, and in this instance rather more problematically, while at the same time — appropriately in my view — upgrading the poems' significance, it has been suggested that these fourteen sonnets constitute the episode of the 'return of Laura', an expression that explicitly calques the more

---

[1]   I have consulted the following annotated editions of the *Canzoniere*: Bettarini; Bezzola; Carducci-Ferrari; Contini-Ponchiroli; Dotti; Fenzi; Santagata; Stroppa; Vecchi Galli. See also Peter Hainsworth, *Petrarch the Poet: An Introduction to the 'Rerum vulgarium fragmenta'* (London and New York: Routledge, 1988); Patrick Boyde, 'Esercizi di lettura: i sonetti 272–279', *Lectura Petrarce*, 10 (1990), 179–99; Enzo Quaglio, 'Il sonetto CCXCII', *Lectura Petrarce*, 12 (1992), 213–34; Laura Paolino, '*Ad acerbam rei memoriam*: le carte del lutto nel codice Vaticano Latino 3196 di Francesco Petrarca', *Rivista di letteratura italiana*, 11 (1993), 73–102.

famous 'return of Beatrice' in the Earthly Paradise. Indeed, this key moment is assigned a vital role in the critical purview that sees in the collection 'Laura's *Canzoniere*'. From this perspective, the main character of the love story is not the poet but the woman, who, as our sonnets would appear to confirm, acts, during this difficult period of the lover's life, as his 'guide' by means of a succession of 'vere e proprie apparizioni'.[2]

Let me immediately confess that I find all the above interpretations of sonnets 279–92 too restrictive. In truth, in some cases, I find them problematic if not actually misleading. Thus, it does not seem to me that one can confidently assert that the sonnets present 'vere e proprie apparizioni', namely, miraculous interventions on the part of Laura, similar to Beatrice's in the *Vita nova* and the *Commedia*.[3] (The presence of Dante in the *Canzoniere*, as I will contend throughout the course of this chapter, is obviously crucial; however, with regard to the nature of the relationship between the poet and Laura presented at this point of the *Rerum vulgarium fragmenta*, rather than following in Dante's footsteps, Petrarch, as I hope to demonstrate, deliberately chooses a completely different path.)[4] It is specifically in sonnets 282–86 that Laura is supposed to 'appear' to her devotee. Yet, in none of these poems is there any trace of a divine and miraculous dimension to the ways in which Laura 'torna' to 'rallegrar' (282. 1 & 6) the weeping Francesco. If, on the one hand, referring to the incipit of 282 ('Alma felice che sovente torni | a consolar le mie notti dolenti', 1–2), it is at the very least debatable whether one can declare with a degree of certainty that 'Laura appare effettivamente in sogno all'amante' (as stated by Santagata in his commentary, p. 1121); on the other, it seems to me that one can legitimately state that, in talking about the beloved's nocturnal returns, Petrarch totally avoids the technical language used in the Middle Ages to refer to dreams.[5] That some may want to see in lines 1–2 of 282 a reference to dreams, given their associations with divine providence, is quite understandable if the purpose is to argue that Laura's 'return' is of a marvellous nature. However, the very fact that the poet has chosen to be highly allusive and vague in evoking the nocturnal returns of the dead woman should induce caution in classifying them rigidly, and particularly as miraculous manifestations. Furthermore, there is no evidence to suggest that sonnets 282–86 form a compact group in which we find 'una serie di apparizioni notturne' (Santagata's commentary, p. 1134), miraculous or not, of Laura. Despite the fact that, after appearing twice in 282 (lines 1 & 13), the verb *tornare* is also present in three of the following four sonnets (283. 9; 285. 7; 286. 7), in none of these, and the same is true of sonnet 284, are there any indications to suggest that

2   See Marco Santagata, *I frammenti dell'anima* (Bologna: il Mulino, 1992), p. 247.

3   The idea that Laura descends from Heaven to earth, either in a dream or in a vision, has deep roots in the critical tradition on the *Canzoniere*, stretching back at least as far as De Sanctis.

4   On Dante's impact on Petrarch, see Chapter 10.

5   On dreams in the Middle Ages, see Marie-Dominique Chenu, '*Imaginatio*: notes de lexicographie philosophique médiévale', *Harvard Theological Review*, 28 (1935), 69–133; Steven R. Fischer, *The Complete Medieval Dreambook* (Berne and Frankfurt am Main: Peter Lang, 1982); *I sogni nel Medioevo*, ed. by Tullio Gregory (Rome: Edizioni dell'Ateneo, 1985); Steven F. Kruger, *Dreaming in the Middle Ages* (Cambridge: Cambridge University Press, 1992). See also Giuliana Crevatin, '*Quid de nocte?* Francesco Petrarca e il sogno del conquistatore', *Quaderni petrarcheschi*, 4 (1987), 139–66.

the woman returns at night. That 282–86 are part of the same microstructure does not seem to me to be in doubt (the strategic repetition of *tornare* offers a first and explicit clue of this); just as there is no doubt that the poems dramatically record the powerful presence of the dead Laura in the life of her mourning lover. However, what seems difficult to maintain is that this presence belongs to the tradition of divinely inspired apparitions.

Moreover, there are clues that allow a more precise assessment of the nature of Laura's presence at this difficult time in Francesco's life. In fact, Petrarch clearly states that the Laura he is talking about is a creature that is born exclusively from his mind: 'Sì breve e 'l tempo e 'l penser sì veloce | che mi rendon madonna così morta' (284. 1–2), and 'membrando il suo bel viso et l'opre sante' (287. 14).[6] From this point of view, the careful contrast that the poet establishes between himself and the 'felice Titon' (291. 5), who is glad 'ch'almen di notte suol tornar colei [Aurora]' (10), while he, Francesco, finds himself in the diametrically opposite situation, is of course illuminating. Tithonus regularly enjoys the nocturnal company of his beloved; for the poet, however, whether during the day or at night, there is nothing left of the woman but a mental construct, a word:

> Le mie notti fa triste, e i giorni oscuri,
> quella che n'à portato i penser' miei,
> né di sé m'à lasciato altro che 'l nome. (*Rvf.* 291. 12–14)

Therefore, this sonnet can suggestively be read also as a gloss to the opening lines of 282: a gloss that reveals how, unlike the nocturnal returns of the goddess — and the repetition of the verb *tornare* is emblematic in this respect — those of Laura are without substance, emerging as they do from the psyche of the lover in crisis. Laura, dead, is a ghost, a word, a memory. On earth she can now exist only as a product of the poet's mind; and Petrarch further emphasizes this fact by focusing on how his imaginings of Laura not only represent moments of emotional relief, but are also the source of poetic inspiration:

> Ben torna a consolar tanto dolore
> madonna [...]
> Et se come ella parla, et come luce,
> ridir potessi. (*Rvf* 283. 9–10 & 12–13)

That Laura is only a 'name' is undeniable; but, paradoxically, it is thanks to words, that is, to the intellectual faculties of the poet, that she can continue to 'live' on earth. Other possibilities do not exist, given that, as Petrarch does not fail to repeat, once she is dead, the real Laura resides exclusively in Paradise: '[...] colei che qui fu mia | donna, or è in cielo, et anchor par qui sia' (286. 2–3; see also 279. 8; 280. 12; 285. 6). As revealed by the tension between the different tenses and moods of the verb *essere* — a tension made more precise by the implications of the phrase 'anchor par' and by the locative references — to think that, here on earth, Laura can be

---

6   See Sandro Benini, 'L'inattingibile realtà dell'illusione: presenza ed assenza di Laura nel *Canzoniere*', in *Petrarca e i suoi lettori*, ed. by Vittorio Caratozzolo and Georges Güntert (Ravenna: Longo, 2000), pp. 91–107 (pp. 97–103).

present outside the emotional and artistic sensitivities of the poet is pure vanity:

> È gita al cielo [...],
> [...] di lontano
> gli occhi miei stanchi lei cercando invano. (*Rvf* 288. 5–7)

Just as it is useless to hope to find her again in the 'dolce piano' (2), that is, in the external world. And Petrarch reaffirms this reality, as painful as it is unavoidable, noting that only Sennuccio, because he too resides ''n la terza spera' (287. 9), can actually communicate with Laura: 'A la mia donna puoi ben dire' (12). Petrarch is more than clear: contact with the dead Laura is only possible in his imagination. The abyss that separates this world from the afterlife is insurmountable. Petrarch not only demonstrates a singular clarity — a state of acute awareness, as we shall see, that the poet reaches with great difficulty[7] — but also challenges all those, with Dante at their forefront, who have claimed to have had in life miraculous interactions with a dead beloved.[8] Petrarch denies the possibility of this kind of consolation, recognizing that the dead woman can at most survive in the mind and feelings of those who loved her, but also that this survival is entirely precarious. Our sonnets tell the story of how the lover reaches this revelation and the effects of this insight on him. The *Canzoniere* focuses, therefore, not on Laura but on the poet, not least because the woman is nothing but a projection of the self's imagination.

2. Narrating Lyrically

Sonnets 279–92, therefore, attest to a key moment in Francesco's psychological, emotional, and intellectual *iter*. However, before investigating in depth the evolution of this story, I need to clarify other general and methodological points to ensure that the detailed analysis, which should also offer specific proof of the validity of my overarching assertions, is based on sufficiently solid foundations.

It is entirely legitimate to ask why, if our group of poems is as important as it appears to me, their significance has not been noticed by others. The reason for this omission may be found in the fact that, traditionally, little attention has been devoted to the structure of this part of the *Canzoniere*. As I must admit, it was only thanks to the stimulus of the *Lectura Petrarcae Turicensis* that I had the opportunity to see sonnets 279–92 with new eyes.[9] The logic of the *Lectura* shifts the critic's gaze from the single poem to the *Rerum vulgarium fragmenta* as a whole, that is, from the coherence and structure of the single microtext in itself to that of the macrotext as a whole. Perhaps more than coherence, given the 'fragmentary' nature of the *Canzoniere*, as well as its 'precarious' and 'temporary' character, one should speak rather of the ways in which the collection functions as a system, or a series

---

7   See sections 3 and 5 where I provide further evidence in support of the claims made in this opening section. In addition, I examine there the question of the relationship between the lover and his beloved in narrative terms, namely in their unfolding.

8   See sections 4 and 6.

9   See *Il Canzoniere: lettura micro e macrotestuale*, ed. by Michelangelo Picone (Ravenna: Longo, 2007).

of systems. From this perspective, the meaning of our group, like that of any other segment of the *Canzoniere*, emerges in all its complexity especially when the poems are read in series and as constitutive elements of overlapping microsystems. Reading the collection in this way, we come across the critical problem, increasingly pressing in recent years, of its narrative character: the ways in which the story is told.[10] Michelangelo Picone is undoubtedly correct in asserting that, at the macrostructural level of the *Canzoniere*, rather than of a story, we must speak of a 'non-story', given the lack in the collection of a providential view of human life.[11] The *Rerum vulgarium fragmenta* describes the unresolved and arbitrary nature of our existence. It is not surprising, therefore, that scholarly traditions accustomed to thinking of literature in terms of harmonious systems have wanted to impose, with limited success one might add, large totalizing structures on to the collection — calendrical, mythological, and oppositional structures, such as those that oppose death to life or this world to the next — in order to ascribe to the collection, and to the story it tells, a sense of stability, coherence, and evolution. At the same time, such attempts to bring the *Canzoniere* to order are continually undermined, as Petrarch continually reveals, by the surprises that time introduces into life, and by the fact that any new moment can put into crisis everything that has come before.

Despite the fundamental 'non-organization' of the *Rerum vulgarium fragmenta*, I wonder — and drawing on sonnets 279–92 to exemplify my arguments — whether the issue of the *Canzoniere*'s narrative dimension cannot be considered from at least two other, intentionally flexible, perspectives, which are specifically based on the 'disorganization' of the macrotext. As noted earlier when evaluating the suggestion that Laura functions as a structural key in the logic of the *Rerum vulgarium fragmenta*, the story narrated by Petrarch recounts the workings of a human mind and its sensitivities — an account of an emotional and intellectual world, with all its complications, contradictions, meandering thoughts, and lack of resolution. The story is told from what has been termed a 'modern' perspective; more significantly, however, it is a perspective that has profound effects on the narrative course of the collection. Thus, the wandering of the mind is mirrored in the 'erratic' organization of the poems. In particular, the difficulty, not to say the impossibility, of enclosing the *Canzoniere* in balanced and easily recognizable structures is to be explained in terms of the clear contrast that Petrarch wanted to establish between his 'human' poetic collection, so full of doubts and pitfalls, and the precise numerological structures, modelled on the *ordo* of creation, of that monument to certitude

---

10   See in particular Germaine Warkentin, 'The Form of Dante's *libello* and its Challenge to Petrarch', *Quaderni d'italianistica*, 2 (1981), 160–70; Teodolinda Barolini, 'The Making of a Lyric Sequence: Time and Narrative in Petrarch's *Rerum vulgarium fragmenta*', in *MLN*, 104 (1989), 1–38; Santagata, *I frammenti dell'anima*; Michelangelo Picone, 'Tempo e racconto nel *Canzoniere* di Petrarca', in *Omaggio a Gianfranco Folena*, 2 vols (Padua: Editoriale programma, 1993), 1, 581–92, 'Riscritture dantesche nel *Canzoniere* di Petrarca', in *Pour Dante: Dante et l'Apocalypse. Lectures humanistes de Dante*, ed. by Bruno Pinchard and Christian Trottmann (Paris: Champion, 2001), pp. 333–43, and 'Petrarca e il libro non finito', *Italianistica*, 33 (2004), 83–93. See also Hainsworth, pp. 49–77; Christoph Niederer, 'La bipartizione "in vita/in morte" del *Canzoniere* di Petrarca', in Caratozzolo and Güntert, pp. 19–41.
11   Picone, 'Tempo e racconto nel *Canzoniere* di Petrarca', p. 591.

represented by Dante's 'divine' poem. In the *Canzoniere*, we have the story of a mind which, with enormous effort, tries to understand not only its erotic experiences but also the wider world in which it finds itself, thereby hoping to bring some order to its own existence. Consequently, the various microsystems that mark the *Rerum vulgarium fragmenta*, both horizontally and vertically, on the one hand, are signs of brief moments of coherence in the life of the protagonist. However, on the other, their proliferation is the disenchanted sign of the impermanence and fragility of such moments of resolution. Advancing the hypothesis that the *Canzoniere* presents an all-encompassing point of view, even if highly subjective and fragmented — a perspective that once again establishes a noteworthy and revealing opposition to the *Commedia*, in particular with its 'encyclopaedic' ambitions — it is possible to explain the presence in the collection of non-Lauran elements. In this regard, sonnet 287 introduces into the diegesis of the *Canzoniere* themes of friendship, of literature, of the relationship with the tradition that cannot easily arise from Laura's story. At the same time, if, beyond the sensibilities of the protagonist, there is another dominant narrative reference point in the *Rerum vulgarium fragmenta*, this is of course Laura, as confirmed, once again, by 'Sennuccio mio, benché doglioso e solo', a poem that plays a vital role in our sequence of sonnets: 'A la mia donna puoi ben dire' (12). The obsession that dominates, but which also continuously destabilizes the logic of the *Canzoniere* is the love for Laura. Nevertheless, the lover has also other interests, other concerns, other affections. And the *Rerum vulgarium fragmenta* does not neglect to deal with these as well. After all, the story that the *Canzoniere* narrates, and that is embodied in its structure, is the story of the difficulty, if not actually of the impossibility, given the complications and the fleeting nature of human life, of telling any story, starting with one's own.

At most, from Petrarch's perspective, what can be fixed narratively — and I am now addressing the second of the two closely related narratological perspectives that I mentioned earlier — are moments of the larger, ever-fleeting history, even if the ultimate desire, perpetually frustrated, remains that of being able to understand and present this impossible whole. The *Canzoniere*, therefore, is made up of a large number of 'microstories' — a characteristic, as we shall see shortly, that clearly circumscribes our block of sonnets. Each microstory belonging to this textual grouping depicts different emotional and intellectual reactions, but all triggered by the same event — the death of the beloved — ranging from fantastic flights to the relief of acceptance, which then collapses again into despair. Every microstory has its own beginning and its own ending. Each one is complete in itself, thus revealing how complicated, if not misleading, it is to try to discover a dominant controlling structure in the collection. At the same time, however, and as I hope to show in what follows, an emotional state can offer the starting point for another. Thus, it is sometimes possible to recognize, in the unfolding of the *Canzoniere*, a narrative and psychological 'logic'; it is even possible to have the impression of 'progress'. These aspects attenuate the sense of 'arbitrariness' that surrounds the story narrated in the *Rerum vulgarium fragmenta*, making explicit that we are dealing with a mind that not only feels but also thinks; a mind, as already mentioned, that manages to reach moments of control and reflection, even if any progress can always turn into its opposite.

Taking into consideration the narrative functions of the poems of the *Canzoniere* allows us to appreciate the complexity, sophistication, and importance of texts often considered, and then set aside, as 'minor'. Moreover, the implications of this exegetical approach to the *Rerum vulgarium fragmenta* confirm why I am unable to concentrate exclusively on sonnets 281–90. The structures of the collection itself, the story that unfolds in this section, impose the need to broaden the critical perspective both forward and backwards. In particular, while sonnet 279 takes us back to Valchiusa, 292 has the explicit aim of marking a moment of completion and closure:

> Ora sia qui fine al mio amoroso canto:
> secca è la vena de l'usato ingegno,
> et la cetera mia rivolta in pianto. (*Rvf* 292. 12–14)

The sonnet's concuding functions become even more marked if we remember that the Correggio form of the *Canzoniere* was to end with 292. This fact, however, raises a further problem of method — namely, the question of whether and to what extent the meanings of the poems change in the passage from one form of the collection to another. Thus, in the Correggio form, as they brought the poetic collection to a close, our sonnets could not but enjoy a more significant role, at least structurally, to the one they now play in the *Canzoniere*. In particular, their crowning organizational function, of serving as the collection's culmination, almost completely disappears. Consequently, the many links that commentators have highlighted between sonnets 279–92 and previous parts of the *Canzoniere* can no longer be judged from a strictly conclusive point of view. Nevertheless, in these reprises, we can still recognize the original attempt, with all its suggestiveness, to conclude the collection by reconsidering situations belonging to the time when Laura was alive from the vantage point of the new reality of her death. In fact, with elegant symmetry between narrative and structure, the protagonist is also actively engaged in a similar process. As is dramatically recorded in compositions such as sonnets 279–86, the lover imagines seeing the dead Laura move as she once did in the landscape of Valchiusa. At the same time, however, it is inevitable that, in the *Rerum vulgarium fragmenta*, our poems' retrospective elements have neither the connotative breadth nor the formal vigour that they had in the Correggio form. Indeed, this situation can help clarify why critics have generally paid little attention to our sonnets. In the larger and more complex structures of the last version of the *Canzoniere*, at least at first sight, the original functions and meanings of our group of poems can largely vanish; and the critical indifference that has met the sonnets would seem to confirm this state of affairs. Seemingly 'marginalized' by the *Rerum vulgarium fragmenta*'s macrosystem, the poems have suffered the same fate at the hands of the majority of their readers, who have put them to one side. Yet, the fact that the sonnets have lost their original logic does not mean that, as a result, they have been voided of presence and meaning. Quite the opposite, in fact. A key element of my argument is that they retain something of their original semantic force. Thus, what they reveal especially about the psychological state of the protagonist continues to be significant in the new system of the *Rerum vulgarium fragmenta*.

The poetic, ideological, and structural wealth of our poems is noteworthy. As I hope to have begun to show, there is no lack of proof of this. In any case, it is enough to distinguish the main parts into which block 279–92 can be divided to have an immediate idea of this. The fourteen poems fall into four distinct microsystems: 279–86, 287, 288–90, and 291–92. Moreover, the first series, which is also the most substantial, is further broken down into three subsystems: 279–81, 282, and 283–86.[12] In the following paragraphs, I elucidate the mechanisms of this textual system, together with the various stories that the microsystems tell of how the poet reacted after Laura's death. In fact, both the number of distinct units into which sonnets 279–92 can be divided and the variability of the microsystems offer a first indication of the rapid succession of psychological changes that assail the protagonist. However, the relevance of our poems, as well as their original strategic position, does not emerge solely from the ways in which they function as a syntagmatic chain located in a specific and well-defined point of the *Canzoniere*'s macrotext. Many of the sonnets of the subsystem 279–92, as we have already observed regarding the connections between the parts 'in life' and 'in death', establish structural relationships with the most varied areas of the *Rerum vulgarium fragmenta*; and the number of such transversal links is remarkable. Hence, for example, sonnets 279–82 belong to the group of poems on Valchiusa; sonnets 279–81 to that group of sonnets which use, in their quatrains, alternate rhymes rather than the usual enclosed ones;[13] sonnet 285 is part of the small group of sonnets consisting of a single sentence,[14] while 287 belongs to the poems addressed to Sennuccio del Bene; sonnet 291 is related to poems that have as their theme the myth of Aurora; finally, 287 is linked to those texts whose purpose is to call into question Dante's *auctoritas*.[15] Our sonnets, therefore, seem to dialogue with the whole *Canzoniere* — a more than obvious proof of their importance. And Petrarch tried to underline the fact that we are dealing with a key moment in his collection, accumulating, in a small and compact space, and in a strikingly atypical manner, 'eccentric' formal elements, ideological issues of weighty import, and highly suggestive and intriguing intratextual echoes.

---

12   It is a critical commonplace to tie 282 to the preceding three sonnets. However, this association is questionable on metrical grounds. Differently from 279–81, sonnet 282's quatrains do not employ alternating rhymes. In truth, both formally and in its content, 282 is closer to the four sonnets that follow it. Nonetheless, as I clarify below, 282, since it functions as a bridge between them, should be kept distinct from the two subsystems that surround it.

13   Carla Molinari, 'Appunti sui quattordici sonetti a quartine anomale dei *Rerum vulgarium fragmenta*', in *Le tradizioni del testo: studi di letteratura italiana offerti a Domenico De Robertis*, ed. by Franco Gavazzeni and Guglielmo Gorni (Milan and Naples: Ricciardi, 1993), pp. 49–67.

14   Lorenzo Renzi, 'La sintassi continua: i sonetti d'un solo periodo nel Petrarca: C, CCXIII, CCXXIV, CCCLI', *Lectura Petrarce*, 8 (1988), 187–220.

15   Joseph A. Barber, 'Il sonetto CXIII e gli altri sonetti a Sennuccio', *Lectura Petrarce*, 2 (1982), 21–39.

3. The Stories of Sonnets 279–92: Part One

But what is the story — or rather, what are the stories — that sonnets 279–92 tell? The first 'chapter', as I have noted, consists of the group 279–86, a group whose limits and whose compactness Petrarch establishes unequivocally. In formal terms, 279 is different from the sonnets that precede it as it is characterized, in its quatrains, by the rare use of alternate rhymes, a trait that links it closely to the two poems that follow in which we find the same rhyme scheme. The function of sonnet 279 as an 'opening' text is further emphasized because, uniquely, its alternate rhymes are also inverted (ABAB BABA). As regards its content, the sonnet, by returning to describe the natural landscape of Valchiusa, announces its difference from the poems that come immediately before. The closing functions of sonnet 286 are obvious not only because it is placed next to the 'aberrant' 287, which commemorates Sennuccio's death, but also because it represents the last poem of the entire cycle 279–92 in which Petrarch evokes the imaginary figure of Laura.

Indeed, it is the attempts to keep Laura 'alive' thanks to the poet's mental efforts that constitute the main theme of the group 279–86. Thus, in the subsystem 279–81 — a subsystem defined on the basis of the alternate rhymes — Petrarch explains how the environment of Valchiusa (another element that unites and determines the three poems) stimulates his imagination to create fantastic simulacra of Laura: 'Mai non fui in parte ove sì chiar vedessi | quel che veder vorrei poi ch'io nol vidi' (280. 1–2; see also 279. 1–8; 281. 9–14). Having established that his beloved is a creature formed by his mind, in the sonnets that follow Petrarch does not describe so much the mental processes that bring her to life, even if in passing he does not forget to allude to these (284. 1–2), but directly presents her apparitions: for example, 'Come donna in suo albergo altera vène' (284. 9). What interests the poet are the effects on him of the visions. In truth, from the start of the cycle, the poems are always focused on the lover: 'là 'v'io seggia d'amor pensoso et scriva' (279. 5). His senses, his intelligence, his feelings, his emotions are, with stilnovist nuances, the protagonists of the drama. If it were not for their actions, neither the lover nor the beloved would exist. The emphasis on the physiological and psychological conditions of Francesco underlines the fact that, unlike Laura — who, 'morendo' (279. 13), is transformed into pure spirit ('et ne l'interno lume, | quando mostrai de chiuder, gli occhi apersi', 13–14) — he is undeniably alive; and by continuing to live, he remains prey to conflicting thoughts and reactions. His existence, dominated by the trauma of the woman's death, is troubled by disorientating comings and goings that pass from despair to relief:

> et me pien di lamenti:
> quant'io veggio m'è noia, et quant'io ascolto.
> Ben torna a consolar tanto dolore
> madonna. (*Rvf* 283. 7–10; see also 284. 1–4)

A precarious state, therefore, fluctuating and ambivalent, which finds emblematic expression in the strange, troubling, and ambiguous 'doppia pietate' (285. 8) displayed by Laura, who is 'perversely' split into 'madre' and 'amante' (9). The division of the dead woman in two not only functions as a sign of the confusion in which Francesco finds himself, but also confirms, once and for all, that the Laura of which the sonnets speak is a human invention and not a blessed soul. The different metamorphoses that she undergoes in the eight poems, from 'nimpha' to 'altra diva' (281. 9) and from 'donna viva' (13) to 'Alma felice' (282. 1) — not to mention her incarnations as mother and spouse — are not miraculous manifestations but ever more frantic outbursts of a mind that cannot come to terms with the painful implications of the beloved's death. If, in the sonnets, we were reading the story of the 'return of Laura', heavenly emissary on earth, her repeated words of encouragement (279. 9–14; 280. 12–14; 285. 10–11; 286. 9) could not but have impacted more effectively and consistently on Francesco's behaviour than they actually do. Not even the awareness that Laura is in a state of bliss gives him satisfaction. Selfishly and irrationally, even if understandably, the poet wants her with him on earth. The fact that the woman continues to change her identity, that her advice has such limited effect, and that her salvation is of little weight, is the most evident proof of her subjectivity, inconsistency, and unreality — the very antithesis of the perfect and eternal condition of the blessed. Laura's changing characteristics are as much attempts by Francesco to safeguard in the here and now some minimal fragment of her being as moments of escape from the reality of his situation. He lives through illusions, because only in them can he discover some 'riposo' (282. 12). But, like any human palliative, such fantasies are of extremely brief duration; after all, they are nothing more than 'brevi sogni' (1. 14): 'Sì breve è 'l tempo e 'l penser sì veloce | che mi rendon madonna così morta' (284. 1–2). However, the lover does not want to recognize the futility of his actions and insists on finding human solutions to the absolute implications of death, refusing to accept its reality, specifically refusing to accept that death is a fundamental part of our earthly condition. Despite his assertions to the contrary (281. 12–13; 286. 3–4), the dead do not walk among the living.

With great effectiveness, sonnets 279–86 offer a double perspective on Francesco's condition. On the one hand, they present 'realistically' and with immediacy the lover's psychological state of confused repression as he struggles with emotional ups and downs; on the other, they allow attentive readers to distance themselves from the crisis in which the protagonist lives and to judge his behaviour with critical detachment. If read individually, each poem seems to have its own particular logic; however, read in parallel with the others, this logic immediately fades into the inconsistency of often irreconcilable desires and impulses. Francesco's misfortune is to be unable to go beyond the single moment (the single sonnet), and therefore to arrive at a wider and better balanced vision of life that would allow him to recognize the contradictions into which he is sinking. For his part, however, the poet, organizing the sequence of sonnets in a highly revealing and calculated manner, confirms that, contrary to what was possible for him the first time he returned to Valchiusa, he was subsequently able to find the means with which to overcome his crisis. Therefore, from a narratological point of view, the *Canzoniere* tells two stories: the first one focuses 'directly' on the individual experiences of the protagonist; while the second concentrates on the reflections that these experiences subsequently generate in him. What separates the poet of the individual texts from the poet of the collection, the lover from the artist, is the element of 'objectivity' that the act of reflection, inherent in the form of the collection, brings with it. At the same time, however, given the inconsistency and arbitrariness of the human condition, every effort exerted by Petrarch to organize, understand, and fix his existence offers only temporary solutions, hence the obsessive need to return, over and over, to the poems, reconfiguring them to restore a degree of control over life, as evidenced by the different versions of the *Canzoniere*. In any case, as is evident from the fragmentary nature of the series 279–92, these solutions never have comprehensive and definitive results, but, at most, help to resolve highly circumscribed situations: even if the poet manages to stem a crisis, this does not prevent the surge of a new wave of problems. It is only after death, as Laura strives to make him understand, that human beings, escaping the instability of the 'mondo e i suoi dolci hami' (280. 14), find peace in the eternal and the absolute. Death should be a reason for joy and not for tears. The basic problem, nevertheless — a problem that the *Rerum vulgarium fragmenta* perhaps embodies better than any other work in the canon of Western literature — is that if, on the one hand, as a believer, Francesco ought to draw comfort from the mysteries and hope of future salvation, on the other, and principally, he finds himself ensnared by his humanity, the 'enemy' of faith and source of contradictions, doubts, contingent ratiocinations, insatiable desires, tormenting pains and, above all, fears: a confused tangle of reactions whose obscure centre conceals the impossible reality of death.

Sonnets 279–86 capture particularly well the tensions and the complexity, both existential and narratological, that define the *Rerum vulgarium fragmenta*. Indeed, they can be read as a microcosm of the *Canzoniere*. Thus, we find in them the major themes of the collection: the flux between life and death, between Heaven and earth, between pleasure and suffering, between love and despair, between truth and illusion, and between reason and fantasy — themes that, as in the macrotext, coagulate around the fleeting and ambiguous figure of Laura, whose true human and spiritual essence is never attainable, given that, like everything else in the collection, she is a reflection of the subjectivity of the protagonist. In addition, like the *Rerum vulgarium fragmenta*, our block of poems — as I have already endeavoured to document — is structured with rigorous artistic sophistication. Thus, to fix the boundaries and the relative autonomy of the microseries, Petrarch has tightly linked the first and the last sonnet. In particular, the first quatrain of 286 borrows heavily from the *fronte* of 279:

> *Se* lamentar augelli, o verdi fronde
> mover *soave*mente a *l'aura* estiva,
> o roco mormorar di lucide onde
> s'*ode* d'una fiorita et fresca riva,
> là 'v'io seggia d'*amor* pensoso et scriva;
> lei che 'l *ciel* ne mostrò, terra n'asconde,
> veggio et *odo* et intendo ch'*anchor viva*
> di sì lontano a' *sospir*' miei risponde.
> (*Rvf* 279. 1–8; my emphasis)

Compare with:

> Se quell'*aura soave* de' *sospiri*
> ch'i' *odo di* colei che qui fu mia
> donna, or è in *cielo*, et *anchor* par qui sia,
> et *viva*, et senta, et vada, et *ami*, et spiri.
>   (*Rvf* 286. 1–4; my emphasis)

In addition, the closing tercet of each sonnet focuses on crying ('pianger', 279. 12 and 'piangere', 286. 14). Equally calibrated is the function of 282 as a bridge between the two main parts of the 'mini-songbook'. The sonnet redimensions one of the most conspicuous aspects of 279–81, one that is about to disappear in 283–86, namely, the importance of the natural environment of Valchiusa as a stimulus to evoke the beloved. Sonnet 282 makes a brief reference to this aspect — 'Così comincio a ritrovar presenti | le tue bellezze a' suoi usati soggiorni' (7–8). Yet, the poem prefers to concentrate on the lover's psychological condition, a theme which, like that of Laura's *tornare*, also introduced by the sonnet (lines 1 & 13), will dominate in sonnets 283–86. Furthermore, 282 picks up the fleeting metaliterary reference found at 279. 5 and begins to give it the complexity that it will have in 283. 12–14 and in 286. 1–6:

> Là 've cantando andai di te molt' anni,
> or, come vedi, vo di te piangendo:
> di te piangendo no, ma de' miei danni. (*Rvf* 282. 9–11)

Indeed, and as further proof of the importance of this section of the *Rerum vulgarium fragmenta*, the opposition between *piangere* and *cantare* accurately synthesizes the dialectic between immediate experience and critical reflection that is one of the loadbearing structures of the *Canzoniere*.

Sonnet 286 closes the microsystem 279–86 announcing the first glimmers of a cognitive change, of some kind of intellectual progress. The lover begins to have some sense of the abyss that actually separates him from the dead woman — the truth that his previous fantasies endeavoured to deny. Therefore, even if he continues to evoke Laura's comforting 'tornar ov'io son' (7), he not only emphasizes with greater vigour the fact that she 'or è in cielo' (3), but also, and more significantly, that now her apparitions are not intended to give him a deceptive fleeting relief, but rather to offer him concrete help in saving his soul: 'Ir dritto, alto, m'insegna' (9). This is a noteworthy step forward in Francesco's attempt to come to terms with the implications of the death of the beloved — a progress confirmed by the fact that he begins to judge her disappearance not exclusively in negative terms. Therefore, sonnet 286 suggests that thinking of Laura can be not only a form of spiritual support, but also a source of poetic inspiration. The 'dolce mormorar pietoso et basso' (11) of the blessed woman, whose 'dolcezza' (13), with explicit Orphic overtones, 'avria vertù di far piangere un sasso' (14), constitutes a privileged literary model with which the poet can hope to face and overcome the artistic block that he confesses in the sonnet's first five lines.[16] The relationship between the self and the

---

16   See section 6, below, for an analysis of the presence of a significant Orphic component in sonnets 279–92. See also Chapter 11.

woman is about to enter, as confirmed by sonnets 287 and 288–90, a more realistic phase and, at times, even a more positive one. Not only does 286 conclude the story begun with 279, but also prepares the way for new stories, or rather, presents new directions in which the macrostory of the protagonist's life — and hence the macrostructure of the collection — can move.

Inserting itself into the breach created by the poems that precede it, sonnet 287 explodes once and for all the great illusion of the series 279–86, namely, that it might be possible on earth to see and maintain contact with the dead woman. Only the blessed enjoy this benefit: 'Ma ben ti [Sennuccio] prego che 'n la terza spera | [...] | A la mia donna puoi ben dire [...]' (9 & 12). Sonnet 287 works like a sort of reawakening to reality, whose 'violence' is confirmed by the shock that comes from the decision to commemorate his friend Sennuccio del Bene in the course of intimate Lauran reflections. The main effect of this interruption is to contextualize in a balanced and realistic manner both the woman's passing and the lover's reactions to the tragedy — a consequence, moreover, which reveals that 287 is only apparently anomalous in the framework of our group of poems. The sonnet, evoking together with Sennuccio four other deceased poets (10–11), emphasizes that dying is universal, thereby challenging the selfish and self-indulgent solipsism that had characterized most of the poems which, from 246 to this point, had dealt with Laura's death. Private melancholic introspection, as noted in the series 279–86, is full of pitfalls, because it irrationally restricts the sense of the real, isolating individuals within themselves, and thus separating them from the divine will. This is particularly worrying in Francesco's case: his introspection prevents him from arriving at a balanced assessment of death. It is highly noteworthy, therefore, that, for the first time, in sonnet 287, Petrarch declares orthodoxly that, for Christians, death provides moral support and liberation:

> i' pur mi riconforto,
> perché del corpo ov'eri preso et morto
> alteramente se' levato a volo.
> [...] onde col tuo gioir tempro 'l mio duolo. (*Rvf* 287. 2–4, 8)

The atmosphere of orthodoxy touches other areas of the text. The poet affirms that it is thanks to prayer — 'ben ti prego' (9) —, and not imaginings, that the living can hope to have some relationship with the blessed. Recognizing the reality of the death of his five fellow vernacular poets, Petrarch also comes to affirm in a disenchanted way the reality of Laura's death, his solitude, the importance of memory rather than imagination in thinking of the dead, given that only memory, free of fallacious visions, preserves the truth of the dead person:

> A la mia donna puoi ben dire in quante
> lagrime io vivo; et son fatt' una fera,
> membrando il suo bel viso et l'opre sante. (*Rvf* 287. 12–14)

It is the microsystem 288–90 that in particular expands the intuitions with which sonnet 287 closes. However, for now, I must leave to one side the unfolding of the love story. Our sonnet not only brings a degree of clarity to the problem of death, but, via the allusion to Sennuccio, and then to Guittone, Cino, Dante, and Franceschino degli Albizzi (10–11), it also contextualizes the *Rerum vulgarium fragmenta*, and especially the story of the death of the beloved, in terms of the literary tradition.

4. A Dantean Digression

My digression is obviously inspired by Petrarch himself. It acknowledges the interruption that, by means of sonnet 287, the poet introduces into the evolution of the *Canzoniere*. As I have tried to clarify, and as I will further elucidate in the next subsection, the sonnet in memory of Sennuccio is closely linked to the texts that surround it. At the same time, by broadening the perspective, the poem also serves as a 'pause', a moment to catch a breath, along the course of the lover's claustrophobic reflections regarding the loss of the woman. Sonnet 287 instead draws attention to universalizing themes: salvation, death, the contrasting conditions of the blessed and the living, and most especially poetry. It is clear that, by mentioning the five poets, Petrarch expects the reader to draw comparisons between the *Canzoniere* and their works. Although important links unite the *Rerum vulgarium fragmenta* to all five authors, it is clearly with one of them, given the latter's overwhelming cultural *auctoritas*, that Petrarch principally engages in critical and emulative dialogue.[17]

Although this is not the place to illustrate in depth the reasons for my opinion (but see Chapter 10), since I need to remain within the remit of the evidence provided by sonnet 287, I also need to make clear that, in light of the textual evidence, ranging from the *Familiares* to the *Seniles* and from the *Rerum vulgarium fragmenta* to the *Triumphi*, I find it difficult to understand how one might insist that Petrarch felt strong resentment towards Dante — a resentment that occasions symptoms of what has been termed 'anxiety of influence' — or, on the contrary, that their relationship was essentially untroubled. I therefore dissent from the two viewpoints that, until recently, have overwhelmingly controlled the debate on Dante's impact on Petrarch's artistic and intellectual career.[18] On the one hand, psychologizing readings inevitably end up by forcing (and unnecessarily complicating) the meanings of texts (for instance, the fact that Petrarch energetically denies nurturing negative feelings towards his great predecessor ought not to be lightly dismissed). On the other, to consider the simple fact of Dante's massive presence in the

17   See Decio Pierantozzi, 'Il Petrarca e Guittone', *Studi petrarcheschi*, 1 (1948), 145–65; Franco Suitner, *Petrarca e la tradizione stilnovistica* (Florence: Olschki, 1977); Edward L. Boggs, 'Cino and Petrarch', *MLN*, 94 (1979), 146–52; Armando Balduino, *Boccaccio, Petrarca e altri poeti del Trecento* (Florence: Olschki, 1984), pp. 141–206; Santagata, *Per moderne carte*, pp. 128–37; Paolino, pp. 86–92; Daniele Piccini, 'Franceschino degli Albizzi, uno e due', *Studi petrarcheschi*, n.s. 15 (2002), 129–86, and *Un amico del Petrarca: Sennuccio del Bene e le sue rime* (Rome and Padua: Antenore, 2004), pp. xxv–xxxi, xxxiii–xxxix. On Petrarch and Dante, see Chapter 10, n. 1.

18   As has been widely recognized, the collective volume *Petrarch and Dante: Anti-Dantism, Metaphysics, Tradition*, ed. by Zygmunt G. Barański and Theodore J. Cachey Jr (Notre Dame, IN: University of Notre Dame Press, 2009) marks a major shift in the study of the relationship between Petrarch and Dante. The essays both contextualize Petrarch's responses to Dante in light of the latter's fourteenth-century reception and tend to concentrate on assessing the literary and cultural implications provided by the textual evidence.

Canzoniere and elsewhere as a sign of a problem-free relationship has all the air of an interpretive oversimplification — let us not forget that we are talking about contacts between poets in a literary context dominated by *imitatio*, *aemulatio*, and *auctoritas*. In my view, the textual and philological evidence, with sonnet 287 at the forefront, all moves in the same direction — a direction, in fact, that does not coincide with the predominant trends identified by the critical tradition. Petrarch's aim, I believe, was to reduce the scope of Dante's ambitions and success, thereby undermining his 'authority', and hence opening a space in which to establish his own *auctoritas* and his ethical and cultural superiority. Sonnet 287 presents various examples of this key strategy. As he does in the *Triumphus Cupidinis* (IV. 31), in 287 too, by placing Dante ''n la terza spera' (9), that is, in the sphere of Venus, Petrarch essentially reduced him to the rank of love poet. Similarly, the comparisons that the sonnet establishes between Dante and the other poets do not work to his advantage: 'Guitton saluti, et messer Cino, et Dante, | Franceschin nostro [...]' (10–11). Thus, it is striking that Dante's name, unlike that of Cino and Franceschino, poets of undoubted inferior ability, is not accompanied by a positive epithet. At first sight, the polemical implications of this omission seem to be attenuated by the fact that Petrarch places Dante's name in rhyme position. Yet, its polemical intent returns with considerable force when one recognizes the name, also introduced without an epithet, placed at the beginning of the same line, namely, in the line's other position of emphasis. To associate Dante with Guittone, especially if the intention is to undermine the Florentine, is not a trifling matter. What is more, it reveals a profound knowledge of Dante's work, without which it would have been difficult for Petrarch to undertake a revisionary strategy of such delicacy.

In light of the emphasis he placed on Dante as a love poet, it is reasonable to conclude that the real target of Petrarch's attack is the *Commedia*, in particular Dante's claims regarding the veracity and the divinely inspired character of his account of the afterlife. In describing Sennuccio's otherworldly condition, Petrarch deliberately recalls an emblematic moment of Dante-character's journey in the otherworld:

> Alteramente se' levato al volo.
> Or vedi insieme l'un et l'altro polo,
> le stelle vaghe et lor viaggio torto. (*Rvf* 287. 4–6)

On arriving in the heaven of the Fixed Stars, the pilgrim casts a totalizing look at creation, which also serves to confirm the miraculous, and hence true, nature of his voyage (for the theme of flight, see *Par.* XXII. 103–05; see also 118–20 for the divinely sanctioned nature of his ascent; and 128–29 & 133–53 for the look back at the heavens and the earth).[19] Yet, it is precisely this fundamental aspect of the *Commedia* that Petrarch strongly calls into question, emphasizing that only a blessed soul like Sennuccio can enjoy extraordinary sights. Such a privilege is not part of the experience of the living: 'et vedi il veder nostro quanto è corto' (7). Even this line is modelled on Dante:

---

19   For a reading of *Paradiso* XXII from this perspective, see Chapter 5.

> Or tu chi se', che vuo' sedere a scranna,
> per giudicar di lungi mille miglia
> con la veduta corta d'una scranna? (*Par.* xix. 79–81)

Again, the borrowing is highly revealing. The eagle of justice accuses the *viator* of intellectual presumption. By repeating the words of the divine bird, Petrarch accuses Dante — or rather, as the words are his own, it is Dante who, ironically, accuses himself — of the same fault for having composed the *Commedia*. Petrarch's criticism is subtle and barbed. And this is not all. That Petrarch should have chosen precisely Dante's entry into the heaven of the Fixed Stars to criticize the *Commedia* has further implications. The topos of the hero who, having risen high into the sky, gives an overarching look at creation was widely disseminated (it is enough to think of the *Somnium Scipionis*) and was intimately connected to the idea of the journey of knowledge. Denying the truth of Dante's account, Petrarch also denies the intellectual, philosophical, and theological foundations of the poem — foundations which, in the fourteenth century, constituted one of the key aspects of Dante's *auctoritas*.[20] Petrarch, as he also does, for example, in *Fam.* xxi. 15, dismantles the contemporary image of Dante as poet of the afterlife, source of wisdom, and propagator of truths. The *Commedia* is thus not a text that readers can trust. More specifically, as regards our sonnets, so absorbed by the loss of Laura, what the *Canzoniere* cannot accept are Dante's claims about his relationship with the dead Beatrice. Having demonstrated, and thus criticized, by means of sonnet 287, which therefore functions as a sort of disenchanted 'gloss' to the series 279–86, the unreal character of his visions of the dead Laura, who, like Beatrice in the Earthly Paradise, inhabits a *locus amoenus*, Petrarch extends his criticism to Dante, accusing him of having deceived himself and his readers by insisting that he had had contact with his dead beloved. With sonnet 287 Petrarch shatters not only his own illusions but also those of other poets, with Dante at their forefront, by bringing poetry back to the realm of *fictio*, from where Dante had endeavoured to remove it. It is the *Canzoniere*, and not the *Commedia*, which, in its *lictera*, succeeds in offering a glimmer of truth. Yet, as a work of poetry and as a subjective account, the glimmers that the collection can offer are rare and dim, and its truths belong to this world and not to the transcendent.[21]

---

20   See Zygmunt G. Barański, *'Chiosar con altro testo': leggere Dante nel Trecento* (Florence: Cadmo, 2001).

21   'Petrarch's refusal to rebuild any of the fragments that he took from Dante or any other writer as a coherent whole means that any impulse to transcendentalism cannot be carried through. [...] The self and poetry absorb into their own sphere what is tendentially transcendent whilst leaving open whether or not questions of ultimate truth can be answered or even seriously asked in poetry' (Hainsworth, p. 155).

5. The Stories of Sonnets 279–92: Part Two

The impact of the end of the poet's illusion fundamentally affects the development of the love story in microsystems 288–90 and 291–92. Petrarch begins by making clear that, with sonnet 288, he is taking up again the threads of the story begun in sonnet 279. Thus, in 'I' ò pien di sospir' quest'aere tutto', the poet repeats elements taken from the two poems that open and close microsystem 279–86. To make the narrative and poetic concatenation as evident as possible, and as he had done previously by linking the initial quatrains of 279 and 286, with almost mathematical rigour, Petrarch makes sure that the first five lines of 288 include terms already present in the first quatrain of 286:

> I' ò pien di *sospir'* quest'*aere* tutto
> d'aspri colli mirando il dolce piano
> ove nacque *colei ch'*avendo in mano
> meo cor in sul fiorire e 'n sul far frutto,
> è gita al *cielo* ed àmmi a tal condutto.
> > (*Rvf* 288. 1–5; my emphasis)

Compare with:

> Se quell'*aura* soave de' *sospiri*
> ch'i' odo di *colei* che qui fu mia
> donna, or è in *cielo,* et anchor par qui sia,
> et viva, et senta, et vada, et ami, et spiri.
> > (*Rvf* 286. 1–4; my emphasis)

The links between sonnets 288 and 279 are organized with less structural precision than those between 288 and 286. However, they are equally marked: they occur with greater frequency and involve lines 1–11 of each poem: 'sospir' (288. 1 | 279. 8); 'aere' (288. 2) | 'aura' (279. 2); 'fiorire' (288. 4) | 'fiorita' (279. 4); 'cielo' (288. 5) | 'ciel' (279. 6); 'di lontano' (288. 8 | 279. 6); 'gli occhi' (288. 7 | 279. 11 & 14); 'fronda verde' (288. 10) | 'verdi fronde' (279. 1); 'fiore' (288. 11) | 'fiorita' (279. 4). Petrarch's purpose is obvious: to underline that the interruption caused by sonnet 287 has not disturbed the development of the *Canzoniere*'s principal narrative, and that he has not (and had not) ceased to probe the effects on himself of Laura's death. In particular, after demystifying his consolatory fantasies, the painful question of how he might deal with the ruthless reality of death insistently emerges.

Petrarch reiterates the continuity between microsystems 279–86 and 288–90 not only thanks to lexical repetitions, but also through narrative reiterations. Again, in sonnet 288, and as occurs in subsystems 279–81 and 282, the protagonist finds himself in a natural environment. However, the poet immediately confirms that he is now contemplating his own situation and that of the dead woman from a new perspective. He is no longer confined within the Lauran *locus amoenus* but scrutinizes it from afar and, bleakly, does not detect in it any trace of the beloved:

> D'aspri colli mirando il dolce piano
> ove nacque colei ch'avendo in mano
> meo cor in sul fiorire e 'n sul far frutto,

> è gita al cielo, ed àmmi a tal condutto,
> col sùbito partir, che, di lontano
> gli occhi miei stanchi lei cercando invano. (*Rvf* 288. 2–7)

The condition, between alienation and loneliness, in which the lover now exists has its 'objective correlative' in the *asprezza* of the 'colli' (2), whose harshness heralds the corresponding and wide-ranging negative representation of nature that dominates the tercets of the sonnet — a representation so different from the idyllic descriptions of Valchiusa in 279 and 281 — which now revolves around the repetition, anaphoric on occasion (9–11), of *non*. Moreover, and according to the universal intuitions to which he had arrived in sonnet 287, but which he now applies to himself, Francesco recognizes without hesitation the painful implications of his condition of earthly exile, far away from the benefits of eternal life. He has shifted from a period of fantasizing solipsism to a phase, still highly self-reflective, of acute clarity of vision ('Or comincio a svegliarmi, et veggio', 289. 5). This disenchanted realism, as we shall see shortly in the last microsystem of our group of poems, the one that includes sonnets 291 and 292, is potentially as full of dangers as it is a source of despair, as the darkest elements of 288 menacingly insinuate.

For the moment, however, the lover treats his new intellectual lucidity, however painful ('quanto è mia pena acerba', 288. 14), as something to be treasured. Thus, sonnets 289 and 290 reach the highest ethical and religious point of sequence 279–92, confirming the advantages, especially with regard to salvation, of assessing our human condition realistically. The poems do not focus on the misleading relief offered by a Laura born from the lover's 'fallace' (290. 5) imagination, but on the realistic and reassuring, but also sad, memory of all that Laura had objectively done for his spiritual growth while on earth:

> Lei ne ringratio, e 'l suo alto consiglio,
> che col bel viso et co' soavi sdegni
> fecemi ardendo pensar mia salute. (*Rvf* 289. 9–11; see also 5–8)

> Come va 'l mondo! or mi diletta et piace
> quel che più mi dispiacque: or veggio et sento
> che per aver salute ebbi tormento,
> et breve guerra per eterna pace. (*Rvf* 290, 1–4; see also 5–14)

With a polemical eye directed towards those poets who assert the opposite, Petrarch leaves no doubt that only living women, and not those who are dead, have the power to help their devotees. The dead beloved who comes back to guide her lover towards salvation is a myth (even if reflecting in a balanced manner on the woman's death can have positive results). Thus, like any illusion, beginning with the chimera of 'ceco Amor', one's own 'desir sempre fallace, | et degli amanti più ben per un cento' (290. 9, 5–6; see also 289. 5–8) needs to be rejected. Sonnets 289 and 290 constitute a sort of confession, not in front of a Laura miraculously restored to her lover in a privileged place, as occurs in Dante's Earthly Paradise, but in the recesses of the individual conscience, down here among the snares of the 'mondo' (290. 1). Petrarch admits to having loved imperfectly; to having allowed his desire

— 'l'empia voglia ardente' (290. 13) — to generate illusions, as much of Laura dead as alive; and to having created, in each instance, images of her that did not correspond to the truth. He has betrayed her. However, as a form of redemption, rather than concentrating on the dead woman, as Dante had done, and therefore on a being whose reality exists beyond his intellectual abilities, Petrarch, thanks to an appropriate use of his intelligence, realistically recovers the living woman. Sonnets 289 and 290 mark a moment of considerable intellectual and emotional maturity — and one can therefore understand why our group of poems should have been so dear to the poet. The lover reaches this degree of sophistication by adjusting his personal history to the truths of providential history, truths that the key sonnet 287 establishes with clarity and precision. Indeed, the implications of the positive outcomes of this existential success are not limited exclusively to the mental and emotional state of the lover, but also have a positive influence on the poet:

> O leggiadre arti et lor effetti degni,
> l'un co la lingua oprar, l'altra col ciglio,
> io gloria in lei, et ella in me virtute! (*Rvf* 289. 12–14)

In truth, these lines evoke something extremely rare in the *Canzoniere*: the lover and the beloved who collaborate harmoniously, each one *oprando* for the good of the other according to their own abilities. By equating his *arte* with Laura's salvific power, Petrarch affirms the value of poetry, particularly when his *stilo de la gloria* is inspired not by illusion but by truth and 'virtute' (14).

However, given the fragility of human nature, to which not by chance a cautionary mention is made in the initial quatrain of the optimistic 290, Francesco cannot maintain a balanced and clearsighted state of calm for long. That his situation is about to worsen is unequivocally signalled by the explicit return, in his reflections, of myth, which has immediate negative effects on his sentimental and intellectual reactions (note the violent martial metaphor):

> Quand'io veggio dal ciel scender l'Aurora
> co la fronte di rose et co' crin' d'oro,
> Amor m'assale. (*Rvf* 291. 1–3)

However, illusion can no longer offer a form of escape: having recognized the weight of reality, the lover can no longer free himself from its burden. Therefore, evoking the myth serves only to reaffirm the actual conditions of his existence following Laura's death:

> O felice Titon, tu sai ben l'ora
> da ricovrare il tuo caro tesoro:
> ma io che debbo far del dolce alloro?
> che se 'l vo' riveder, conven ch'io mora. (*Rvf* 291. 5–8)

There is nowhere for Francesco to escape, and he begins to appreciate that confronting reality brings with it significant dangers. The feeling of bitter frustration that comes from this new insight is more than evident:

> Le mie notti fa triste, e i giorni oscuri,
> quella che n'à portato i penser' miei,
> né di sé m'à lasciato altro che 'l nome. (*Rvf* 291. 11–14)

In the *fronte* of the sonnet that follows, Petrarch attempts to counter this gloomy conclusion. He presents a long description of the physical attributes of the woman as if to demonstrate that something more than just the 'nome' of the beloved is left to him. However, the seven elegant lines of the *descriptio personae* are peremptorily shattered by the harsh realism of the eighth line: 'poca polvere son [Laura's bodily beauty], che nulla sente' (292. 8).

The situation is tragic. The same conclusions about the nature of existence to which the poet had arrived with considerable difficulty, and which seemed to offer a glimmer of relief and hope, now turn into sources of bitterness. If, on the one hand, to appreciate clearly both what Laura had given him and the reality of the relationship between the living and the dead are important acquisitions, on the other, the same intuitions make him understand that the woman's support is something that belongs irrevocably to the past. He is alone and can no longer count on her help:

> Et io pur vivo, onde mi doglio et sdegno,
> rimaso senza 'l lume ch'amai tanto,
> in gran fortuna e 'n disarmato legno. (*Rvf* 292. 9–11)

Francesco must rely on his own strength. He must continue to benefit as much as possible, and at any cost, from having succeeded to contemplate reality with disenchanted eyes. Thus, if, in general, he feels aimless and confused, he can at least exercise a degree of control over his poetry: the area of his life — as we have seen — where, thanks to his efforts, he has been most successful, not least because it is the activity that is most natural to him (289. 12–14). With exemplary honesty, therefore, Petrarch declares that, given the new situation in which he finds himself, he cannot persist with the kind of poetry that he had written when Laura was alive and when he still believed in illusions, but must change style:

> Or sia qui fine al mio amoroso canto:
> secca è la vena de l'usato ingegno,
> et la cetera mia rivolta in pianto. (*Rvf* 292. 12–14)

This declaration does not represent, as has been asserted, a 'rifiuto della poesia'.[22] Rather, it is an assertion of faith in poetry (as was to be expected after its celebration in the explicit of sonnet 289) — of the fact that poetry can adapt to different situations. It is to Petrarch's merit that he has understood this fundamental fact

---

22   See Santagata's commentary, p. 1158. It is a widely held view that, at the end of sonnet 292, Petrarch announces his wish to abandon poetry. This idea results from having ignored the Orphic overtones of the last tercet and from having posited the Scriptural line 'Versa est in luctum cithara mea, et organum meum in vocem flentium' [my harp is turned to mourning and my organ into the voice of those that cry] (Job 30: 31) as the intertext behind line 14. Although, like Petrarch in 292, Job laments the misfortunes that assail him in the present, his story does not touch on matters of the heart and of loss, never mind of poetry, which are all elements that unite Francesco to Orpheus. At best, Job functions as a secondary model.

and that he has drawn the appropriate conclusions from it. The 'cetera', the poet's traditional instrument, 'rivolta in pianto' announces that Petrarch is about to leave love poetry for elegy, the only 'manner' that, realistically, can capture the implications of Laura's death and its effects on the abandoned lover.[23] In addition, the new style not only helps resolve the artistic difficulties that he had previously complained about (283. 12–14; 286. 1–6), but also, as he had suggested in passing, it conforms his poetry to Laura's rhetorical lesson. The 'dolce mormorar pietoso e basso' (286. 11) of the beloved presents an excellent model of the *stilus elegiacus*, particularly if the epithet 'dolce' is interpreted as meaning 'low style', one of the many values that this semantically rich term had in the Middle Ages, that is, the *genus*, as we also know from Dante (*Dve* ii. 4. 5), under which elegiac poetry was included.[24] Again, Petrarch and Laura seem to collaborate. However, we must not allow ourselves to be deceived by this enticing image: the 'elegiac' Laura, as I had emphasized when examining sonnet 286, is the poet's invention. In the realistic atmosphere of the close of series 279–92, the alignment of 286 and 292 serves mainly to emphasize that the source of the *Canzoniere*'s poetry is Petrarch himself.

6. Orphic structures

As much as the lyre unites all poets, the lyre 'in tears', from classical times onwards, is first of all a symbol of Orpheus mourning the death of Eurydice: 'Ipse [Orpheus] cava solans aegrum testudine amorem' [He with a hollow lyre soothes his sorrowful love] (*Georg.* iv. 464), as Virgil sang in one of the most influential and touching rewritings of the myth.[25] The basic bonds between Petrarch's state of widowerhood and that of Orpheus are obvious. However, the implications of the rapprochement between the two great lyricists are substantially more complex than Petrarch scholarship has hitherto recognized, and involve not only sonnet 292 and,

23   On the *Canzoniere*'s stylistic shifts, see Maria Serena Sapegno, *Petrarca e lo 'stile' della poesia* (Rome: Bagatto Libri, 1999). See also Rossanna Bettarini, 'Perché "narrando" il duol si disacerba (Motivi esegetici dagli autografi petrarcheschi)', in *La critica del testo: problemi di metodo ed esperienze di lavoro* (Roma: Salerno, 1985), pp. 305–20 (p. 315), and now in her *Lacrime e inchisotro nel Canzoniere di Petrarca* (Bologna: CLUEB, 1998), pp. 161–76 (p. 171).

24   See Claudia Villa, *La 'Lectura Terentii'* (Padua: Antenore, 1984), pp. 39–42. See also Zygmunt G. Barański, '"'nfiata labia" and "dolce stil novo": A Note on Dante, Ethics, and the Technical Vocabulary of Literature', in *Sotto il segno di Dante: scritti in onore di Francesco Mazzoni*, ed. by Lionella Coglievina and Domenico De Robertis (Florence: Le Lettere, 1998), pp. 17–35. Laura's 'dolce mormorar pietoso e basso' (286. 11) calques a widely disseminated moral and linguistic commonplace: 'prudentissimus vero est ille qui modum seruat in verbis qui scilicet dulciter loquitur absque clamore et asperitate quod non parum est vtile [...] non potest esse sermonis moderacio absque cordis moderacio' [Most wise is he who observes a measure in his words, namely, who speaks sweetly and without shouting and harshness what is most useful [...] there cannot be moderation of speech without moderation of heart]: Peraldus, *Summa de vitiis* (Cologne: Quentell, 1479), F1ᵛ. Interestingly, in the Middle Ages, Job was presented as the supreme example of the *prudens*. Thus, it starts to become clear how and why, in Petrarch's memory, Orpheus, Job, Laura, poetic 'sweetness', and elegy should have become associated.

25   On the complex classical and medieval ramifications of the myth of Orpheus and Eurydice, see Chapter 11.

by extension, the poems 'in death', but the *Rerum vulgarium fragmenta* as a whole. Given that I examine the Orphic dimension of the *Canzoniere* in Chapter 11, here I should simply like to point out some aspects that have particular relevance for our group of poems, or rather, for the *lectura* of these that I have undertaken.

The importance of the myth of Orpheus in the *Canzoniere* is immediately evident when we recall that it was supposed to close not only the Correggio form of the collection, but also that of the Chigi:

> Di rime armato, ond' oggi mi disarmo,
> con stil canuto avrei fatto parlando
> romper le pietre, et pianger di dolcezza. (*Rvf* 304. 12–14)

These lines explicitly allude to one of the most famous and repeated instances of the power of Orpheus's singing after the death of his beloved. Therefore, it does not seem exaggerated to assert that, at least in the early versions of the 'in death' part of the *Canzoniere*, a prominent role was assigned to the story of Orpheus and Eurydice. In truth, as I have mentioned, we find references to the myth throughout the 'second part'. We thus find significant echoes in our series of sonnets, which combines a range of Orphic topoi: the descriptions of nature, the effects of singing on the natural world, the changing circumstances of the poet-lover, and the loss and return of the woman.[26] With regard to this last Orphic echo, and in terms of what I noted earlier about Petrarch's attitude towards the claims of other poets concerning the return of their dead beloveds, it is clear that, on the one hand, he aspires to act as a 'modern' Orpheus, while, on the other, he also wants to distinguish himself from his illustrious predecessor. But Petrarch does not want to distance himself only from Dante and Orpheus. The lines 'or di madre or d'amante, or teme or arde | d'onesto foco, et nel parlar mi mostra | quel che 'n questo viaggio fugga o segua' (285. 9–11) evoke Creusa's prodigious apparition to Aeneas, while he is desperately seeking her in the burning city of Troy, at the end of the second book of the *Aeneid*.[27] Creusa, wife and mother, announces to her husband his predestined voyaging: 'Longa tibi exilia et vastum maris aequor arandum' [You shall long wander and plough the vast surface of the sea] (780). Even Virgil, 'l'altissimo poeta' (*Inf.* IV. 80), had been fascinated by the illusion that the living could have contact with their dead, especially if, on earth, they were bound by a great love. On his part, Petrarch categorically rejects the consolatory myth of a poetry that is able to revive the dead. Death is absolute; and poetry can only commemorate the life of the dead person and make public the pain of those who live on. Consequently, Petrarch presents himself as the spokesperson of a new 'realistic' and anti-Orphic poetry of death that rejects the fantastic consolatory illusions of the tradition, even at its highest moments. On

---

26   See, for instance, 279. 1–4 and *Met.* XI. 44–48; 279. 5 and *Met.* X. 146; 283. 14 and *Georg.* IV, 510; 288. 1–4, 9–11 and *Met.* X. 76–77, 86–87, 90–92, 143–44, XI. 1–2, 4, 27–30, 41–42.

27   It is with love and gratitude that I thank our daughter Anna for having made me aware of this echo. When she noted Petrarch's borrowing, Anna was about to leave for Oxford, where, unsurprisingly, she read Classics. Since graduating, she has swapped Aristotle and Virgil for developing policy strategies for NHS England. And there are those who wonder what one might do with a humanities degree...

the other hand, he accepts the lesson of the ancient bard concerning the need to find a truthful style to counteract the effects of death: 'si licet et falsi positis ambagibus oris | vera loqui sinitis' [if it is permitted and you allow me to set aside false and ambiguous speech and to speak the truth] (*Met.* x. 19–20). Petrarch's relationship to Orpheus is complex. Its oscillating character of contact and separation allows the poet to establish both his ties to the tradition and the novelty of his art. Moreover, it allows him to declare his superiority over his peers. Ultimately, as happens throughout the *Canzoniere*, it allows him to talk about himself.

7. Musings in Conclusion

Whenever we dwell on a section of a text, we run the risk of exaggerating its merits and meanings. When drafting this *lectura*, I often feared falling into this trap. However, the connotative, ideological, and formal wealth of this handful of sonnets that my late-lamented friend Michelangelo Picone assigned to me has encouraged me to persist in emphasizing their importance. In doing so, I also found encouragement in Marco Santagata's words, not least because in many other instances our interpretations of the poems are so radically different, when he declares that 'la "morale" del libro è contenuta nei sonetti 289 e 290' (Santagata, *I frammenti dell'anima*, p. 249) — an opinion that I share unreservedly. On other matters, the ways in which Santagata and I read sonnets 279–92, and therefore the whole 'in death' part of the *Rerum vulgarium fragmenta*, are diametrically opposed. He states:

> Ora, Petrarca avrebbe potuto incentrare la sezione in morte, coerentemente con quanto suggerito dalle prime battute del libro e dalla canzone terminale di quella in vita, sul ruolo del soggetto. La preminenza della vicenda penitenziale dell''io' non avrebbe negato alla donna beata un ruolo positivo, ma l'avrebbe imprigionata entro una dimensione memoriale, di testimone di una età trascorsa. Petrarca, invece, sceglie una via completamente diversa: di Laura morta egli fa un personaggio presente ed attivo, anzi, ancora più attivo di quanto non lo fosse stato in vita, e questo perché la morte non recide i legami interpersonali fra i due protagonisti. (Santagata, *I frammenti dell'anima*, p. 246)

For my part, on the contrary, I believe that, in the 'second part', the 'I' continues to dominate and control the course of the story; that Laura survives only in the psyche of the lover and, at best, in his memory; and that death has definitively dissolved the bonds that united on earth the man and the woman. It will be up to our readers to choose between Marco's and my conflicting interpretations, and, more importantly, to propose yet new ones. The richness of poetry, especially that of a great poet like Petrarch, cannot, fortunately, be resolved by any single explanation. It is precisely poetry as a place of *pianto* and canto, of pressing emotions and intellectual and artistic reflections, of the present and the past, that these sonnets celebrate. It is the poetry that preserves in words — the Petrarchan 'nome' — the crumbs of life that memory manages to rescue, offering them a minimum of 'permanence'. It is poetry that gives the poet the chance to distinguish himself from others, especially from his peers, and to commemorate not only his beloved but also himself. It is poetry, 'leggiadra arte' of 'effetti degni' (289. 12), that ultimately has the responsibility, as sonnets 279–92 reveal so emblematically, to preserve, ordering them, the shifting truths of the 'I'.[28]

28   I agree with Michelangelo Picone as to poetry's status in the *Canzoniere*: 'La poesia di Petrarca si può veramente definire [...] come la guerra contro il tempo. In effetti, l'unico debole argine che il poeta possa tentare di opporre contro il dilagare incontrollabile del tempo è la parola, è la poesia: alla labilità della realtà storica egli può solo rispondere con l'assoluto della parola poetica' ('Tempo e racconto', p. 586). See also Sara Sturm, 'The Poet-Persona in the *Canzoniere*', in *Francis Petrarch, Six Centuries Later: A Symposium*, ed. by Aldo Scaglione (Chapel Hill: Department of Romance Languages, University of North Carolina Chapel Hill; Chicago: Newberry Library, 1975), pp. 192–212.

PART IV

Exploiting Epicurus

CHAPTER 13

Guido Cavalcanti and his
First Readers

1. Inventing Guido

It is not an exaggeration to suggest that, generally speaking, Guido Cavalcanti's fourteenth-century *fortuna* appears to be encapsulated and resolved in two contrasting yet closely connected portraits.[1] As most scholars now agree, behind the forlorn figure of Cavalcante dei Cavalcanti, trapped for eternity in a fiery tomb on the sixth circle of Hell, punished for having blindly followed the false teachings of Epicurus, there lurks the son[2] — still physically alive in the Spring of 1300, though

---

1   The original version of this chapter bore the following commemorative dedication: 'In memory of Robert Dombroski, my first friend from America'.

2   As I will discuss, no independent contemporary evidence exists that might reliably support the view that Guido Cavalcanti was a follower of Epicurus. This would seem to have been an invention of Dante's. On the implications of this accusation, see below, pp. 454 & 463–67, and especially Chapter 15, pp. 494–98. As regards Dante's unfounded, yet delicately allusive and calibrated representation of Guido as intellectually unorthodox, the key problem is whether or not, in medieval culture, as has been regularly asserted, the designation 'Epicurean' could embrace that of 'Averroist'. The simple answer is that it could not, even though both ideologies called individual salvation into doubt (see Chapter 14, pp. 470–72). Consequently, the fact that, in 'Donna me prega', Cavalcanti appears to espouse Averroistic positions cannot in itself, despite what many scholars have maintained, be sufficient to transform him into an Epicurean, even though, in the Middle Ages, the tag *epicureus* embraced a wide range of meanings (see Chapters 14–17). In any case, many of Averroes's views were regularly accepted and propounded by Christian thinkers (see Chapter 3, pp. 120–22). Thus, as Durling correctly notes, 'it is still a long way from there [his association with Averroism] to establishing that Guido was actually a heretic or that he died outside the faith': Robert M. Durling, 'Boccaccio on Interpretation: Guido's Escape (*Decameron* VI.9)', in *Dante, Petrarch, Boccaccio: Studies in the Italian Trecento in Honor of Charles S. Singleton*, ed. by Aldo S. Bernardo and Anthony L. Pellegrini (Binghamton, NY: MRTS, 1983), pp. 273–304 (p. 297). Durling's point is well made, especially in light of Guido's burial in holy ground in Santa Reparata, which would confirm that his fellow-citizens did not deem him a heretic or an unbeliever: Guido Favati, *Inchiesta sul dolce stil nuovo* (Florence: Le Monnier, 2975), p. 193; but now see Francesco Velardi, 'I "due Guidi" Cavalcanti e la data di morte del necrologio di Santa Reparata', *Studi danteschi*, 72 (2007), 239–63, and 'I due Cavalcanti e il diverso Giubileo di Dante', *Sotto il velame*, 8 (2007), 7–76. On the reductive and problematic manner in which *dantismo* has made recourse to both Averroes and Averroism, see Luca Bianchi, 'L'averroismo di Dante: qualche osservazione critica', *Le tre corone*, 2 (2015), 71–110. See also Angelo M. Mangini, 'Guido, Averroè e il "granchio" di Platone: considerazioni sull'averroismo in Cavalcanti e in Bruno Nardi', in *'Il mondo errante': Dante tra letteratura, eresia e storia*, ed. by Marco Veglia and others (Spoleto: Fondazione Centro italiano di studi sull'alto Medioevo, 2013), pp. 243–56.

spiritually 'dead' in the harsh estimation of his former friend — condemned, like his father, for having expended his extraordinary mental energies on sinful intellectual pursuits.[3] A few decades later, we find the now long-dead Guido very much 'alive' as he vaults over one of the *arche* located in the vicinity of San Giovanni in order to escape unwelcome inquisitors whom he baffles with the acuity of his intellect; and who, in Getto's famous phrase, embodies in his 'resurrected' guise 'quell'ideale di vita armonica in cui si riassumono e si compongono in equilibrio perfetto tutti i valori della vita'.[4]

Two very different images of Cavalcanti: the first judged by the iron laws of a 'divine comedy'; the second celebrated according to the more relaxed tenets of a 'commedia umana'.[5] Yet, what unites the two portraits, or rather their standard critical interpretations, is the idea that both evocations of Guido are fundamentally determined by their authors' particular views of life and death — views, whose stark divergence, led Boccaccio deliberately and polemically to subvert, and hence to correct, Dante's treatment of Cavalcanti in *Inferno* X.[6] To put it somewhat differently, the impression has been created that the shadowy presence of *Inferno* X

---

3   The question of Guido's supposed Epicureanism raises an important methodological issue, namely, the need to distinguish between the historical Cavalcanti and his textual 'constructions' — something which scholars have largely failed to do, thereby contaminating the academic study of the poet with the 'prejudices' of his contemporaries. The present chapter is largely concerned with medieval images of Guido and their cultural implications. It has its point of origin in the fleeting observations of two great scholars of medieval Italian literature. Domenico De Robertis noted that 'Non c'è forse esempio, nella storia delle nostre lettere, tanto più ai loro inizi, di fortuna pari a quella di cui ha goduto Guido Cavalcanti già da vivo': Domenico De Robertis, 'Introduzione', in *Guido Cavalcanti, Rime*, ed. by Domenico De Robertis (Turin: Einaudi, 1986), pp. xi–xxiv (p. xi; all quotations from and references to Cavalcanti's poems are taken from this edition). In her turn, Maria Corti observed that 'quando il Boccaccio o il Sacchetti da un lato, Filippo Villani, Giovanni Villani, Dino Compagni, Bevenuto da Imola dall'altro abbozzano un ritratto di Guido Cavalcanti [...] subito affiora il sospetto che dietro quella frequenza di giudizi affini non ci sia [...] una fonte unica di informazione': Maria Corti, *La felicità mentale* (Turin: Einaudi, 1983), p. 4. A further secondary aim of this study is to provide as full a list as possible of such medieval 'fonti [...] d'informazione'. On Cavalcanti's early reception, see also Claudio Giunta, 'La "giovanezza" di Guido Cavalcanti', *Cultura neolatina*, 55 (1995), 149–78.
4   Giovanni Getto, *Vita di forme e forme di vita nel 'Decameron'* (Turin: Petrini, 1958), p. 158.
5   The designation 'commedia umana' was successfully applied to the *Decameron* by Vittore Branca; see, for instance, Vittore Branca, 'Una chiave di lettura per il *Decameron*', in *Dec.*, pp. vii–xxxix (p. viii).
6   See, in particular, Fabian Alfie, 'Poetics Enacted: A Comparison of the Novellas of Guido Cavalcanti and Cecco Angiulieri in Boccaccio's *Decameron*', *Studi sul Boccaccio*, 23 (1995), 171–96 (pp. 176–77, 180); Durling; Guglielmo Gorni, 'Invenzione e scrittura nel Boccaccio: il caso di Guido Cavalcanti', *Letteratura italiana antica*, 3 (2002), 359–73; Roberto Mercuri, 'Guido Cavalcanti o la metafora della cultura in Dante e Boccaccio', *Esperienze letterarie*, 4 (1979), 55–58. Obviously, Boccaccio's reaction to Guido's supposed Epicureanism takes on much more suggestive hues, if, as has been claimed, he himself had Epicurean leanings; see Lucia Battaglia Ricci, *Boccaccio* (Rome: Salerno, 2000), pp. 32–34, 161; Antonio Gagliardi, *Giovanni Boccaccio: poeta, filosofo, averroista* (Soveria Mannelli: Rubbettino, 1999); Marco Veglia, 'Giovanni Boccaccio: *Decameron* (novella VI, 9)', in *Breviario dei classici italiani* (Milan: Bruno Mondadori, 1996), pp. 44–56 (pp. 46–50), *Il corvo e la sirena: cultura e poesia del 'Corbaccio'* (Pisa and Rome: Istituti Editoriali e Poligrafici Internazionali, 1998), pp. 35–36, 46, *'La vita lieta': una lettura del 'Decameron'* (Ravenna: Longo, 2000), pp. 15–56. For a refutation of Boccaccio's presumed Epicurean sympathies, see Chapter 16.

and the leaping sinewy figure of *Decameron* VI. 9 essentially owe their existence to the artistic and intellectual preoccupations of their respective authors. They are the inventions of the imaginative 'closed worlds' of two outstanding writers. Indeed, the highly particularized nature of Dante's and Boccaccio's recourse to Cavalcanti appears to be confirmed by the fact that, in each instance, Guido is utilized as a vehicle through which both authors attempt to establish their own literary identity. In Boccaccio's case — it is claimed — he serves as the means through which the *certaldese* acknowledges his debts to Dante, while, at the same time, both passing judgment on his literary 'hero', and establishing his own artistic and ideological credentials. As regards Dante, the situation is deemed to be rather more complicated and ambiguous. Cavalcanti is called to account as the poet endeavours, *sub specie aeternitatis*, both to distance his literary and intellectual experiences from Guido's, and to define, and hence resolve to his own advantage, his troubled relationship with his 'primo amico' (*Vn* XXIV. 6). If, in the 1290s, their relationship had become uncomfortably fraught as a result of the *Vita nova*, 'Donna me prega', the sonnet of the *rimenata* 'I' vegno 'l giorno a te 'nfinite volte', and other flashpoints, this had turned darker and more problematic with Guido's untimely death as a result of his having been exiled by Dante and the other priors.[7] Given that Cavalcanti's

7   The critical literature on Dante and Cavalcanti is now extensive: see, in particular, Roberto Antonelli, 'Cavalcanti e Dante: al di qua del Paradiso', in *Dante: da Firenze all'aldilà*, ed. by Michelangelo Picone (Florence: Cesati, 2001), pp. 289–302, and '"Per forza convenia che tu morissi"', in *Guido Cavalcanti laico e le origini della poesia europea, nel 7° centenario della morte: poesia, filosofia, scienza e ricezione*, ed. by Rossend Arqués (Alessandria: Edizioni dell'Orso, 2004), pp. 203–16; Maria Luisa Ardizzone, *Guido Cavalcanti: The Other Middle Ages* (Toronto: University of Toronto Press 2002), pp. 94–102 and passim; Armando Balduino, 'Cavalcanti contro Dante e Cino', in *Bufere e molli aurette: polemiche letterarie dallo Stilnovo alla 'Voce'*, ed. by Maria Grazia Pensa (Milan: Guerini e Associati, 1996), pp. 1–19; Zygmunt G. Barański, '"Per similitudine di abito scientifico": Dante, Cavalcanti, and the Sources of Medieval "Philosophical" Poetry', in *Literature and Science in Italian Culture: From Dante to Calvino. A Festschrift in Honour of Patrick Boyde*, ed. by Pierpaolo Antonello and Simon Gilson (Oxford: Legenda, 2004), pp. 14–52, 'Guido Cavalcanti *auctoritas*', in Arqués, pp. 163–80, and 'La canzone "anomala" di Dante: *Io sento sì d'Amor la gran possanza*', in *Dante Alighieri. Le Quindici Canzoni. Lette da diversi. 1, 1–7* (Lecce: Pensa Multimedia, 2009), pp. 145–211; Teodolinda Barolini, *Dante's Poets: Textuality and Truth in the 'Comedy'* (Princeton: Princeton University Press, 1984), pp. 123–53, 'Dante and Cavalcanti (on Making Distinctions in Matters of Love): *Inferno* v in its Lyric Context', *Dante Studies*, 116 (1998), 31–63, and '"Amicus eius": Dante and the Semantics of Friendship', *Dante Studies*, 133 (2015), 46–69; Corrado Bologna, 'Beatrice e il suo "ánghelos" Cavalcanti fra *Vita Nova* e *Commedia*', in *'Per correr miglior acque...': bilanci e prospettive degli studi danteschi alle soglie del nuovo millennio*, 2 vols (Rome: Salerno, 2001), I, 115–41, and 'Canto XXXI', in *Lectura Dantis Turicensis. Purgatorio*, ed. by Georges Güntert and Michelangelo Picone (Florence: Cesati, 2001), pp. 473–93; Danilo Bonanno, *La perdita e il ritorno: presenze cavalcantiane nell'ultimo Dante* (Pisa: ETS, 1999), and 'Guido in Paradiso: "Donna me prega" e l'ultimo canto della *Commedia*', *Critica del testo*, 4 (2001), 223–43; Corrado Calenda, 'Due? Quali due? Più di due? Ancora sui "Guidi" di *Purgatorio* XI', *Rivista di studi danteschi*, 7, (2007), 355–64; Davide Canfora, 'Sul canto X del *Paradiso*', *L'Alighieri*, 50 (2009), 65–80; Federico Casari, 'Piccolo arrangiamento fra Dante, Francesca e Paolo, i due Cavalcanti', *Fronesis. Semestrale di filosofia letteratura Arte*, ser. 3, 5 (2007), 65–78; Letterio Cassata, 'Con Dante dalla parte di Guido', in Guido Cavalcanti, *Rime* (Rome: Donzelli, 1998), pp. vii–xxxii; Marcello Ciccuto, *Il restauro de 'L'Intelligenza' e altri studi dugenteschi* (Pisa: Giardini, 1985), pp. 11–138, 'Una figura del disamore in Guido Cavalcanti', in his *L'immagine del testo: episodi di cultura figurativa nella letteratura italiana* (Rome: Bonacci, 1990), pp. 15–31, 'Il disdegno di San Giacomo: per una diversa

assenza di Cavalcanti dalla *Commedia*', *Letteratura italiana antica*, 3 (2002), 311–18, 'Lo sdegno di Guido e l'umiltà di Dante: percorsi dell'interpretazione', in Arqués, pp. 255–71, and 'Guido Cavalcanti laico ed eretico?', in *Les deux Guidi, Guinizzelli et Cavalcanti: mourir d'aimer et autres ruptures*, ed. by Marina Gagliano and others (Paris: Presses Sorbonne Nouvelle, 2016), pp. 171–79; Gianfranco Contini, 'Cavalcanti in Dante', in *Un'idea di Dante* (Turin: Einaudi, 1976), pp. 143–57; Alison Cornish, 'Sons and Lovers: Guido in Paradise', *MLN*, 124:5 (2009), 51–70; Marco Cursietti, 'Dante, Guido e l'"annoiosa gente" (a proposito della 'paternale' di un presunto sonetto di Guido Cavalcanti e di un libro recente)', *L'Alighieri*, 39 (1998), 105–12; Nievo Del Sal, 'Cavalcanti in Dante "comico"', *Rivista della letteratura italiana*, 9 (1991), 9–52; Domenico De Robertis, *'Arcades ambo* (osservazioni sulla pastoralità di Dante e del suo primo amico', *Filologia e critica*, 10 (1985), 231–38, and 'Un altro Cavalcanti?', in *Guido Cavalcanti: l'altro Medioevo*, ed. by Maria Luisa Ardizzone (Fiesole: Cadmo, 2006), pp. 13–25; Guido Di Pino, 'Così ha tolto l'uno all'altro Guido', in his *Temi di critica dantesca* (Bari: Editrice Adriatica, 1973), pp. 103–22; Robert M. Durling, 'Boccaccio on Interpretation', '"Mio figlio ov'è?" (*Inferno* X.60)', in Picone, *Dante: da Firenze all'aldilà*, pp. 303–29, and 'Guido Cavalcanti in the *Vita nova*', in Ardizzone, *Guido Cavalcanti: l'altro Medioevo*, pp. 177–85; Paolo Falzone, 'Sentimento d'angoscia e studio delle passioni in Cavalcanti', in Gagliano and others, pp. 181–97; Enrico Fenzi, 'Conflitto di idee e implicazioni polemiche tra Dante e Cavalcanti', in his *La canzone d'amore di Guido Cavalcanti e i suoi antichi commenti* (Genoa: Il melangolo, 1999), pp. 9–70; Francesco Fioretti, *Ethos e leggiadria: lo stilnovo dialogico di Dante, Guido e Cino da Pistoia* (Rome: Aracne, 2012), pp. 103–66; Antonio Gagliardi, *Guido Cavalcanti e Dante: una questione d'amore* (Catanzaro: Pullano, 1997); Alberto Gessani, *Dante, Guido Cavalcanti e l'"amoroso regno"* (Macerata: Quodlibet, 2004); Noemi Ghetti, *L'ombra di Cavalcanti e Dante* (Rome: L'Asino d'oro edizioni, 2010); Guglielmo Gorni, 'Guittone e Dante', in *Guittone d'Arezzo nel settimo centenario della morte*, ed. by Michelangelo Picone (Florence: Cesati, 1995), pp. 309–35 (pp. 326–34), and *Guido Cavalcanti: Dante e il suo 'primo amico'* (Rome: Arachne, 2009); Giorgio Inglese, ' "...illa Guidonis de Florentia" "Donna me prega" (tra Cavalcanti e Dante)', *Cultura neolatina*, 55 (1995), 179–210; Lino Leonardi, 'Cavalcanti, Dante e il nuovo stile', in Picone, *Dante: da Firenze all'aldilà*, pp. 331–54; Enrico Malato, *Dante e Guido Cavalcanti: il dissidio per la 'Vita nuova' e il 'disdegno' di Guido* (Rome: Salerno, 1997); Angelo M. Mangini, 'Dante, Guido, il corpo e l'anima', *Studi e problemi di critica testuale*, 69 (2004), 53–102, and 'Pride and Friendship: On Cavalcanti's Role in the *Commedia*', in *Dante and the Seven Deadly Sins: Twelve Literary and Historical Essays*, ed. by John C. Barnes and Daragh O'Connell (Dublin: Four Courts Press, 2017), pp. 47–71; Raffaele Manica, 'Il giovane Dante e l'ombra di Guido', *Paragone*, 516–18 (1993), 14–32; Mario Marti, ' "L'una appresso de l'altra maraviglia" (*V.N.*, XXIV, 8): stilnovo, Guido, Dante nell'ipostasi vitanovistica', in *'La gloriosa donna de la mente': A Commentary on the 'Vita Nuova'*, ed. by Vincent Moleta (Florence: Olschki, 1994), pp. 141–59, and 'Acque agitate per "Donna me prega"', *Giornale storico della letteratura italiana*, 177 (2000), 161–67; Ronald L. Martinez, 'Cavalcanti "Man of Sorrows" and Dante,' in Ardizzone, *Guido Cavalcanti: l'altro Medioevo*, pp. 187–212; Filippa Modesto, *Dante's Idea of Friendship: The Transformation of a Classical Concept* (Toronto: University of Toronto Press, 2015), pp. 75–92; Gabriele Muresu, 'Con gli increduli della città di Dite (*Inferno* X)', *Rassegna della letteratura italiana*, 113 (2009), 383–414; Bruno Nardi, 'Dante e Guido Cavalcanti', in his *Saggi e note di critica dantesca* (Milan and Naples: Ricciardi, 1966), pp. 191–219; Nicolò Pasero, 'Dante in Cavalcanti: ancora sui rapporti fra *Vita nuova* e "Donna me prega"', *Medioevo romanzo*, 22 (1998), 388–414; Emilio Pasquini, 'Il mito dell'amore: Dante fra i due Guidi', in *Dante: mito e poesia*, ed. by Michelangelo Picone and Tatiana Crivelli (Florence: Cesati, 1999), pp. 283–95, and 'Dalla specola del X dell'*Inferno*: Dante e Guido', in *'Il mondo errante': Dante tra letteratura, eresia e storia*, ed. by Marco Veglia and others (Spoleto: Fondazione Centro italiano di studi sull'alto Medioevo, 2013), pp. 1–17; Daniele Piccini, 'Proposta per *Purg.* XI, 97–99: l'"uno" e l'"altro Guido"', *L'Alighieri*, 49 (2008), 95–111; Michelangelo Picone, 'Guittone, Guinizzelli e Dante', in *Intorno a Guido Guinizzelli*, ed. by Luciano Rossi and Sara Alloatti Boller (Alessandria: Edizioni dell'Orso, 2002), pp. 69–84 (pp. 83–84); Raffaele Pinto, 'La *simiglianza* come decostruzione/ricostruzione espressiva nel dialogo intertestuale fra Guido e Dante', in Arqués, pp. 27–47; Donato Pirovano, ' "Contra questo avversario de la ragione": Dante, *Vita Nuova* XXXIX, e Guido Cavalcanti, *Rime*, XV', in *Per beneficio e concordia di studio: studi danteschi offerti a Enrico Malato per i suoi ottant'anni*, ed. by Andrea Mazzucchi (Cittadella:

function in the *Inferno* and in the *Decameron* has increasingly been posited in such highly personalized terms, it is not surprising that the Guido who stares out at us from their pages should appear so totally dependent on the imaginative powers and on the artistic and ideological needs of his two illustrious creators.

In terms of Cavalcanti's function within the ideological and artistic economy of the first canticle and within that of the short story collection, it is difficult to find fault with the general directions of the interpretive solutions that I have been sketching. However, there are other, equally valid ways in which the implications of Cavalcanti's powerful presence in the two works can be addressed and unravelled. What is ultimately least satisfactory about the standard readings of both episodes is precisely their 'insularity'.[8] They remove Dante's and Boccaccio's presentations from the broad cultural context in which Cavalcanti was read, copied, and, most significantly, fashioned into a figure of quite considerable authority during the course of the Trecento. Cavalcanti, as even a cursory glance at his first reception immediately reveals, was never simply the private preserve of other writers. He enjoyed, instead, as the commentaries written on 'Donna me prega' so conspicuously confirm, a position of some standing in the intellectual and cultural life of the fourteenth century.[9] As the author of the most intellectually demanding, yet also the most popular canzone of the period — at least in terms of extant copies[10] — his

Bertoncello Artigrafiche, 2015), pp. 755–67; Roberto Rea, 'La *Vita nuova* e le *Rime*: "Unus philosophus alter poeta". Un'ipotesi per Cavalcanti e Dante', in *Dante: fra il settecentocinquantenario della nascita (2015) e il settecentenario della morte (2021)*, ed. by Enrico Malato and Andrea Mazzucchi, 2 vols (Rome: Salerno, 2016), II, 351–81; Barbara Rodà, 'Sul "disdegno di Guido": note dal carteggio D'Ovidio-Rajna', in *Carte private: taccuini, carteggi e documenti autografi tra Otto e Novecento*, ed. by Luca Bani (Bergamo: Moretti & Vitali, 2010), pp. 183–96; Selene Sarteschi, '"Donna me prega" — *Vita Nuova*: la direzione di una polemica', *Rivista europea di letteratura italiana*, 15 (2000), 9–35; Rosario Scrimieri, 'Dante y Cavalcanti: a propósito de la balada del capítulo XII de la *Vita Nuova*', *Tenzone*, 2 (2001), 67–103; Donatella Stocchi-Perucchio, 'The Knot of Cavalcanti in the *Commedia*', in Ardizzone, pp. 213–40, and 'Amore, eresia e poesia: concordanze cavalcantiane nella *Commedia*', *Atti e Memorie dell'Accademia Petrarca di Scienze, Lettere ed Arti*, n.s., 67–68, (2005–06), 97–144; Giuliano Tanturli, 'Guido Cavalcanti contro Dante', in *Le tradizioni del testo: studi di letteratura italiana offerti a Domenico De Robertis*, ed. by Franco Gavazzeni and Guglielmo Gorni (Milan and Naples: Ricciardi, 1993), pp. 3–13; Francesco Tateo, 'Ancora sul peccato di Guido', *L'Alighieri*, 50 (2009), 39–45; Marco Veglia, '"Lucerna ardens": appunti su Cavalcanti, Virgilio e il problema del "disdegno"', *Italianistica*, 26 (1997), 9–21. See also the standard *lecturae* of *Inferno* X and *Purgatorio* XI.

8   This 'insularity' is especially apparent in readings of *Inferno* X. Conversely, recent analyses of Boccaccio's short story, in the wake of Mario Baratto, *Realtà e stile nel 'Decameron'* (Vicenza: Neri Pozza, 1970), p. 337, have begun to reveal themselves sensitive to the influence on the *certaldese* of contemporary views of Guido; see Giorgio Inglese, 'Per Guido "filosofo" (*Decameròn* VI, 9)', *La Cultura*, 30 (1992), 75–95; Gorni, 'Invenzione e scrittura', as well as Chapter 15.

9   For an excellent edition of these, see Fenzi, *La canzone d'amore*, pp. 86–174, 177–219. As well as the two surviving commentaries, by Dino del Garbo and by the pseudo-Egidio Romano, a third, now lost, was probably written by Ugo dal Corno (pp. 180–81). On the commentaries, see also O. Bird, 'The "canzone d'amore" of Cavalcanti according to the Commentary of Dino del Garbo, Text and Commentary', *Mediaeval Studies*, 2 (1940), 150–203, and 3 (1941), 117–60; Guido Favati, 'La glossa latina di Dino del Garbo a "Donna me prega" del Cavalcanti', *Annali della Scuola Normale Superiore di Pisa*, 21 (1952), 70–103; Antonio Enzo Quaglio, 'Prima fortuna della glossa garbiana a "Donna me prega" del Cavalcanti', *Giornale storico della letteratura italiana*, 141 (1964), 336–68.

10   See De Robertis, 'Introduzione', p. xiii.

views on love became canonical.[11] Furthermore, his standing was especially high in his native Florence, a fact which, in itself, would strongly imply that both Dante's and Boccaccio's treatment of Guido had to be more than just a 'private affair'. As we shall see, the Trecento bedecked the figure of Cavalcanti with yet other significant traits. It is precisely Guido's cultural and ideological construction by his first readers that I should like to begin to examine in this chapter — and no one is more aware than I am of its many lacunae and oversimplifications. The topic is complex; and, in what follows, I can do little more than highlight some key moments and trends.

2. Cavalcanti *auctoritas*

Cavalcanti's earliest reception is fascinating. On the one hand, it casts important light both on how vernacular culture was assimilated and canonized during the fourteenth century, and on the ways in which vernacular *auctoritas* began to be envisaged and constructed.[12] Indeed, given the widespread contemporary view regarding Guido's antipathy towards classical literature and the Latin language — a view which may have had its origins in the *Vita nova*: 'E simile intenzione so ch'ebbe questo mio primo amico a cui io ciò scrivo, cioè ch'io li scrivessi solamente volgare' (XXX. 3) — it seems reasonable to imagine that the 'first friend', implicitly at least, would have been seen as the vernacular intellectual par excellence, something which certainly would not have gone down too well with Dante. On the other hand, as we shall see, the poet's first reception also enriches our understanding both of *Inferno* X and of *Decameron* VI. 9. However much both Cavalcantian episodes may be said to be structured around 'private' concerns, they also have an obvious 'public' dimension, as befits their protagonist, who, as Dino Compagni memorably described in his *Cronica*, was not afraid actively to involve himself in his city's factional violence:

> Uno giovane gentile, figliuolo di messer Cavalcante Cavalcanti, nobile cavaliere, chiamato Guido, cortese e ardito ma sdegnoso e solitario e intento allo studio, nimico di messer Corso, avea più volte diliberato offenderlo. Messer Corso forte lo temea, perché lo conoscea di grande animo; e cercò d'assassinarlo, andando Guido in pellegrinaggio a San Iacopo; e non li venne fatto. Per che, tornato a Firenze e sentendolo, inanimò molti giovani contro a lui, i quali li promisono esser in suo aiuto. E essendo un dì a cavallo con alcuni da casa i Cerchi, con un dardo in mano, spronò il cavallo contro a messer Corso, credendosi esser

11   See below for a fuller discussion of this important point, pp. 461–65.
12   On vernacular 'authority', see Albert R. Ascoli, *Dante and the Making of a Modern Author* (Cambridge: Cambridge University Press, 2008); Zygmunt G. Barański, '*Chiosar con altro testo': leggere Dante nel Trecento* (Fiesole: Cadmo, 2001); *MLTC*, pp. 439–519; Alastair J. Minnis, ' "De vulgari auctoritate": Chaucer, Gower and the Men of Great Authority', in *Chaucer and Gower: Difference, Mutuality, Exchange*, ed. by Robert F. Yeager (Victoria, BC: University of Victoria, 1991), pp. 36–74, and *'Magister Amoris': The 'Roman de la Rose' and Vernacular Hermeneutics* (Oxford: Oxford University Press, 2001). On the concepts of *auctor* and *auctoritas*, see Mary Carruthers, *The Book of Memory* (Cambridge: Cambridge University Press, 1990), pp. 189–220; Marie-Dominique Chenu, '*Auctor, actor, autor*', *Bulletin du Cange*, 4 (1927), 81–86; Alastair J. Minnis, *Medieval Theory of Authorship*, 2nd edn (Aldershot: Scolar Press, 1988); *'Auctor' et 'auctoritas': invention et conformisme dans l'écriture médiévale*, ed. by Michel Zimmermann (Paris: Écoles des Chartes, 2001).

segulto da' Cerchi, per farli trascorrere nella briga: e trascorrendo il cavallo, lanciò il dardo, il quale andò in vano. Era quivi, con messer Corso, Simone suo figliuolo, forte e ardito giovane, e Cecchino de' Bardi, e molti altri, con le spade; e corsongli dietro: ma non lo giugnendo, li gittarono de' sassi; e dalle finestre gliene furono gittati, per modo fu ferito nella mano.[13]

There is no doubt that, in medieval Italy — as the commentaries to 'Donna me prega' affirm — the only Duecento vernacular author, naturally besides Dante, on whose behalf serious effort was expended in order to elevate him to the rank of an *auctoritas*, was Guido Cavalcanti.[14] This important fact has been largely ignored by historians of Italian literature. Nonetheless, while noteworthy, the omission is not especially surprising. It mirrors the longtime failure to appreciate the cultural significance of Dante's much more substantial fourteenth-century reception. Thus, it is only quite recently, as research in the field of medieval literary theory and criticism has grown, that scholars have begun to appreciate the radical implications of a 'modern' writer, and a vernacular 'modern' at that, being treated as if he were on a par with the 'ancients': namely, that his writings were deemed to be deserving of commentary; that his views could be used to substantiate and illustrate an argument; and that his personal experiences were worthy of attention on account of their exemplary character.[15] For over a thousand years such a privilege had been restricted almost exclusively to the great classical *auctores*. Late-medieval Italy, spurred on by its vernacular poets, found the confidence to question this age-long ossified tradition of reading. That Dante should have served as the key stimulus to this revolution does not come as a surprise. At the same time, it is important to recognize that Cavalcanti too, in part, I suspect, because of his perceived personal aloofness and the conceptual difficulty and ambition of some of his poetry, was instrumental in inspiring such a fundamental change in attitude.

Although the hard proof of Cavalcanti's 'authoritativeness' remains visible to this day, beginning with the two surviving commentaries to 'Donna me prega', Dino del Garbo's 'scriptum super cantilena Guidonis de Cavalcantibus' [commentary on the canzone of Guido Cavalcanti] and pseudo-Egidio Romano's 'Esposizione' — and other elements indicating the poet's privileged status will be highlighted in due course — what, conversely, remains unclear, and this is in stark contrast to Dante's case, are the processes and circumstances that led to Cavalcanti being deemed worthy of such an unusual honour.[16] In the absence of firm evidence, all I can do to help untangle this knotty problem is tentatively to suggest a few hypotheses as to

---

13   Dino Compagni, *Cronica delle cose occorrenti ne' tempi suoi*, ed. by Fabio Pittorru (Milan: Rizzoli, 1965), I. 20 (p. 54). Compagni fleetingly alludes to Cavalcanti twice more in his *Cronica*: first, Guido is listed among the allies of the Cerchi exiled in 1300 (I. 21; p. 56), and later he is referred to as a supporter of the family: 'Fu ancora di loro parte Guido di messere Cavalcante Cavalcanti, perché era nimico di messer Corso Donati' (I. 22; p. 57).

14   Since I originally wrote this sentence around 2001, I have increasingly wondered whether Guittone d'Arezzo's many imitators were intent on establishing his poetic and moral 'authority'. I am not aware of any discussion of this point, although it is a question that deserves serious critical attention.

15   Barański, 'Chiosar', pp. 38–39; *MLTC*, pp. 373–75, 444–45.

16   Fenzi, *La canzone d'amore*, pp. 86 & 187.

how his canonization may have come about.

As has been noted by many scholars, Cavalcanti's poetry is marked by considerable novelty and intellectual rigour, something which, during his lifetime, other poets were also not slow to recognize, as is obvious from the complex interconnections that his verses establish with his immediate contemporaries. His poetry seems to exist in an almost constant dialogue with the writings of his fellow-poets, who, in their turn, addressed their compositions to Guido. The list of these correspondents is impressive: Guittone, Dante, Cino, Dino Compagni, Guido Orlandi, Niccola Muscia, Gianni Alfani, Bernardo da Bologna, Lapo Farinata degli Uberti, and Nuccio da Siena. It is difficult to think of another Duecento lyric poet whose art had such a conspicuous public profile; and this aspect is further strengthened by Cavalcanti's decision to address poems to friends and family members.[17] However much Guido may have been judged by his contemporaries to be 'sdegnoso e solitario' — to use Compagni's handy designation — and however much we may now refer to his elitism, his intellectual and poetic experiences had a fundamental collective character, which went well beyond the boundaries of any presumed stilnovist 'school'.[18] His poetry, his ideas, and his behaviour — as is apparent from the ways in which he was talked about in the fourteenth century (I will shortly summarize the main features of this discourse) — were judged by his contemporaries to be of interest and of value: an obvious sign of the prestige in which he was held. Indeed, Cavalcanti's personal aloofness and the public reverberations of his life and art are far from mutually exclusive. The opposite, in fact, holds good. Like all noteworthy individuals, and the *vitae* of the greats of antiquity offer ample confirmation of this fact,[19] Guido's 'otherness' would have been seen as an expression of his singular

17   On the significance of correspondence poetry in the Duecento, see especially Claudio Giunta, *Versi a un destinatario: saggio sulla poesia italiana del Medioevo* (Bologna: il Mulino, 2002), and *Due saggi sulla tenzone* (Rome and Padua: Antenore, 2002), See also Balduino, pp. 2–3.

18   When describing Guido other writers refer to one or both these character traits: Boccaccio, *Dec.* VI. 9. 9–10, and *Esposizioni sopra la Comedia di Dante*, ed. by Giorgio Padoan (Milan: Mondadori, 1965), X. 62 (p. 526; see note 27 below); Dino Compagni, 'Se mia laude scusasse te sovente', in Cavalcanti, *Rime*, pp. 212–14: 'Se mia laude scusasse te sovente, | dove se' negligente' (1–2). Elsewhere, in 'Qua' son le cose vostre ch'io vi tolgo' (in Cavalcanti, *Rime*, pp. 215–17), Cino declares that, unlike Guido, he 'né cuopro mia ignoranza con disdegno' (10). On Cavalcanti's *disdegno* as 'un contrassegno suo' (De Robertis's annotation in Cavalcanti, *Rime*, p. 216), see Guglielmo Gorni, 'Cino "vil ladro": parola data e parola rubata', in his *Il nodo della lingua e il verbo d'amore* (Florence: Olschki, 1981), pp. 125–39 (p. 134). See also Balduino, pp. 18–19; Ciccuto, 'Per una diversa assenza', p. 316. It is clear that some of Cavalcanti's standard character traits had their origins as much in his poetry as in the nature of his possible relations with others (though, in a community of poets, the two largely overlap). For instance, De Robertis has correctly termed 'S'io fosse quelli che d'Amor fu degno' as an expression of Guido's 'invalicabile solitudine' (Cavalcanti, *Rime*, p. 148). See also nn. 27 & 28 below.

19   On the tradition of the *vitae*, see at least *Accessus ad auctores Bernard d'Utrecht Conrad d'Hirsau*, ed. by R. B. C. Huygens (Leiden: Brill, 1970); Giuseppe Billanovich, 'La legenda dantesca del Boccaccio: dalla lettera di Ilaro al *Trattatello in laude di Dante*', *Studi danteschi*, 28 (1949), 45–144; Margarita Egan, 'Commentary, *vita poetae*, *vida*: Latin and the Old Provençal "Lives of Poets"', *Romance Philology*, 37 (1983), 36–48; Fausto Ghisalberti, 'Medieval Biographies of Ovid', *Journal of the Warburg and Courtauld Institutes*, 9 (1946), 10–59. See also *Creative Lives in Classical Antiquity: Poets, Artists and Biography*, ed. by Richard Fletcher and Johanna Hanink (Cambridge: Cambridge University Press, 2016).

genius (Boccaccio's *novella* is especially good on this point);[20] that same genius, in fact, which granted both him and his works a didactic and exemplary function vis-à-vis ordinary mortals (once again *Decameron* VI. 9 effectively highlights this fact: 14–15). In addition, his family's important social standing and his political activities would also have strengthened and confirmed his uniqueness and superiority.[21] Finally, beyond the efforts of others, Cavalcanti himself played no small role in establishing a high-powered public persona for himself. His attack on Guittone, 'Da più a uno face un sollegismo', is most economically interpreted as an attempt to

20   'Tralle quali brigate n'era una di messer Betto Brunelleschi, nella quale messer Betto e' compagni s'erano molto ingegnato di tirare Guido di messer Cavalcante de' Cavalcanti, e non senza cagione: per ciò che, oltre a quello che egli fu de' miglior loici che avesse il mondo e ottimo filosofo naturale (delle quali cose poco la brigata curava), si fu egli leggiadrissimo e costumato e parlante uom molto e ogni cosa che far volle e a gentile uom pertenente seppe meglio che altro uom fare; e con questo era ricchissimo, e a chiedere a lingua sapeva onorare cui nell'animo gli capiva che il valesse. Ma a messer Betto non era mai potuto venir fatto d'averlo, e credeva egli co' suoi compagni che ciò avenisse per ciò che Guido alcuna volta speculando molto abstratto dagli uomini divenia; e per ciò che egli alquanto tenea della oppinione degli epicuri, si diceva tralla gente volgare che queste sue speculazioni erano solo in cercare se trovar si potesse che Iddio non fosse' (*Dec.* VI. 9. 7–9). Giorgio Inglese correctly notes that 'nel Boccaccio [...] il filosofare [di Guido] è posto [...] come cagione di preferenza per la solitudine' ('Per Guido', p. 77).
21   It is thus not surprising that Guido should be mentioned in the three major Florentine chronicles. I have already examined his treatment in Compagni's *Cronica*. He is also present in the historical writings of Giovanni and Filippo Villani. Giovanni writes: 'Ma questa parte vi stette meno a' confini, che furono revocati per lo 'nfermo luogo, e tornonne malato Guido Cavalcanti, onde morìo, e di lui fue grande damaggio, perciò ch'era come filosafo, virtudioso uomo in più cose, se non ch'era troppo tenero e stizzoso': Giovanni Villani, *Nuova cronica*, ed. by Giuseppe Porta, 3 vols (Parma: Fondazione Pietro Bembo-Guanda, 1991), IX. 42. 2 (p. 70); and see also VIII. 15. 1 (p. 437); IX. 41. 2 (p. 68). In his turn, Filippo Villani wrote: 'Guido alterius Guidonis filius ex nobili stirpe de Cavalcantibus, liberalium artium peritissimus, Danti contemporaneus, illique familiarissimus, fuit homo sane diligens et speculativus, atque auctoritatis non contemnendae in physicis, si opinioni patris Epicurum secuti parum modicum annuisset, morigeratus, alias gravis, et omni dignus laude et honore in rhetoricis delectatus studiis, eandem artem ad rithmorum vulgarium compositionem eleganter traduxit, secundum siquidem locum in vulgaribus odis post Dantem tenuisse perperiti artis hujuscemodi voluere, nisi Petrarcha illi praeripuisset eundem. Hic de amore, qui in sensualitate potius quam in ratione versatur, ejusque natura, motibus, et affectu subtilissime disputando elegantissimam et mirabilem edidit cantilenam, in qua physicae inaudita hactenus ingenosissime et copiose tractavit; cuius mirabilem intellectum mirati Dinus de Garbo physicus, de quo supra habui mentionem, et Aegidius Romanus insignis physicus commentare dignati sunt' [Guido, son of the other Guido of the noble family of the Cavalcanti, most experienced in the liberal arts, Dante's contemporary, and very close to him, was a very diligent and thoughtful man, and of no little authority in natural philosophy, even if he somewhat approved of his father's opinion, who was a follower of Epicurus; affable, at times serious, he delighted in the study of rhetoric in a manner worthy of every praise and honour, and elegantly applied this same art to the composition of vernacular poems, and indeed the experts of this art declared he would hold the second place after Dante in vernacular poetry, had Petrarch not taken it away from him. He composed a most refined and marvellous canzone on love, which dwells in sensuality rather than in reason, and on its nature, its motions, and the accurate explanation of the condition it causes; in this canzone he discussed very skilfully and abundantly aspects of natural philosophy unheard of up to that point. Admiring his admirable genius, the natural philosopher Dino del Garbo, whom I mentioned above, and the famous natural philosopher Aegidius Romanus deemed it worthy to comment on it]: Filippo Villani, *Le vite d'uomini illustri fiorentini*, ed. by Giammaria Mazzuchelli (Florence: Sansone Coen Tipografo-Editore, 1847), p. 57.

take over the Aretine's mantle as the leading philosophical poet of the age. Equally, 'Donna me prega', regardless of the specific doctrines it expresses, is structured as the definitive and irrefutable statement on love.[22] It is enough to remember the ways in which Cavalcanti, in the first stanza, ensures that the canzone's definitions are firmly anchored in an intellectually rigorous framework:

> eo voglio dire
> [...]
> sì chi lo nega — possa 'l ver sentire!
> Ed a presente — conoscente — chero,
> [...]
> ché senza — natural dimostramento
> non ho talento — di voler provare. ('Donna me prega' 1–9)

Paradoxically, given the famously fraught nature of their relationship, it is ultimately difficult to escape the impression that, possibly more than anything, Cavalcanti owed his public fame and success to Dante's celebratory remarks in the *Vita nova*:[23]

> A questo sonetto fue risposto da molti e di diverse sentenzie; tra li quali fue risponditore quelli cui io chiamo primo de li miei amici, e disse allora un sonetto, lo quale comincia *Vedeste, al mio parere, onne valore*. E questo fue quasi lo principio de l'amistà tra lui e me, quando elli seppe che io era quelli che li avea domandato. (*Vn* III. 14)

> Io vidi venire verso me una gentile donna, la quale era di famosa bieltade, e fue già molto donna di questo primo mio amico. (*Vn* XXIV. 3)

> Onde io poi, ripensando, propuosi di scrivere per rima a lo mio primo amico (tacendomi certe parole le quali pareano da tacere), credendo io che ancor lo suo cuore mirasse la bieltade di questa Primavera gentile (*Vn* XXIV. 6)

> E questo mio primo amico e io ne sapemo bene di quelli che così rimano stoltamente. (*Vn* XXV. 10)[24]

Since, especially inside Florence's walls, Guido was recognized and treated as a

---

22   For important instances of different and often conflicting readings of the ideological parameters of 'Donna me prega', see Mario Casella, 'La Canzone d'amore di Guido Cavalcanti', *Studi di filologia italiana. Bullettino dell'Accademia della Crusca*, 7 (1944), 97–160; Maria Corti, *La felicità mentale: nuove prospettive per Cavalcanti e Dante* (Turin: Einaudi, 1983), pp. 3–37; Guido Favati, 'La canzone d'amore del Cavalcanti', *Letterature moderne*, 3 (1952), 117–41; Bruno Nardi, 'L'averroismo del "primo amico" di Dante', and 'Di un nuovo commento alla canzone del Cavalcanti sull'amore', in his *Dante e le cultura medievale*, ed. by Paolo Mazzantini, 2nd edn (Bari: Laterza, 1990), pp. 81–107 & 109–24; Ferdinando Pappalardo, 'Per una rilettura della canzone d'amore del Cavalcanti', *Studi e problemi di critica testuale*, 13 (1976), 47–76; James Eustace Shaw, *Cavalcanti's Theory of Love: The 'Canzone d'Amore' and Other Related Problems* (Toronto: University of Toronto Press, 1949). See also Domenico Chiodo, *'Donna me prega': La Caporetto dell'italianistica* (Manziana: Vecchiarelli Editore, 2016); Rossana Sodano, *Cavalcanti restituito agli Epicuri* (Manziana: Vecchiarelli Editore, 2018). For an important and acute re-reading of the canzone, see Gregory B. Stone, 'Animals Are from Venus, Human Beings from Mars: Averroës's Aristotle and the Rationality of Emotion in Guido Cavalcanti's "Donna me prega"', *PMLA*, 130 (2015), 1269–84.

23   On Cavalcanti in the *Vita nova*, see in particular Domenico De Robertis, *Il libro della 'Vita Nuova'*, 2nd edn (Florence: Sansoni, 1970); Marti; Michelangelo Picone, *'Vita Nuova' e tradizione romanza* (Padua: Liviana, 1979). See also the works cited in n. 7.

24   See also *Vn* XXX. 3 quoted above, p. 448.

litterato of consequence, that he should have been so openly canonized by the city's other great intellectual and poet, and in a work of the ambition of the *libello*, must have carried considerable weight and exerted a powerful influence. As regards this last point, it is vital to remember one key aspect. Although, increasingly, it has become a critical commonplace today to view the *Vita nova* as constituting a major attack on Dante's mentor (Antonelli, 'Cavalcanti e Dante', p. 295) — and it is an interpretation with which I concur — there is no documentary evidence to suggest that the *prosimetrum* was read in this manner in the Due- and Trecento. Indeed, it was a cultural cliché, whose origins are obviously to be sought in the *Vita nova*'s declarations of friendship, and which the early commentators of the *Commedia* repeated throughout the Trecento, that the two poets, on account of their great friendship and similarities of temperament, formed an intimate pairing.[25] The

25   Benvenuto da Imola, *Comentum super Dantis Aldigherij Comoediam*, ed. by James P. Lacaita, 5 vols (Florence: Barbèra, 1887), I, 340–41: 'Iste fuit pater Guidonis Cavalcantis, qui fuit alter oculus Florentiae tempore Dantis [...] Hoc fingit autor quia videbatur verisimile Cavalcanti quod Guido filius suus deberet esse cum Dante, quia fuerunt duo lumina Florentiae, unus philosophus, alter poeta, eodem tempore, de eadem parte, amici et socii' [This man was the father of Guido Cavalcanti, who was the other eye of Florence at the time of Dante [...] The author represents this because it seemed likely to Cavalcanti that his son Guido would be with Dante, because there were two lights in Florence, one a philosopher, the other a poet, at the same time, of the same faction, friends and companions]; Boccaccio, *Esposizioni*, x. 62 (p. 526; see n. 27 below); *Chiose cassinesi* (I quote from DDP): '*son due*. vel jus civile et canonicum quibus justitia ministratur sed falsum est nam intelligit de se et guidone cavalcante qui erant duo oculi florentie' [*son due*: or civil law and canon law with which justice is administered, but this is false, because he is talking about himself and Guido Cavalcanti who were the two eyes of Florence]; *Commento della Divina Commedia d'anonimo fiorentino del secolo XIV*, ed. by Pietro Fanfani, 3 vols (Bologna: Gaetano Romagnoli, 1866–74), I, 254 (see n. 38 below). Filippo Villani, p. 57 (see n. 21 above); Francesco da Buti, 'Il "Commento" di Francesco da Buti alla "Commedia". "Inferno"', ed. by Claudia Tardelli (unpublished PhD thesis, Scuola Normale Superiore di Pisa, 2010–11), p. 585: 'Questi fu messer Cavalcante dei Cavalcanti, padre di Guido, amico grande et compagno di Dante'; Graziolo Bambaglioli, *Commento all'Inferno' di Dante*, ed. by Luca Carlo Rossi (Pisa: Scuola Normale Superiore, 1998), p. 83: 'Hec umbra fuit pater Guidonis Cavalcantis, nobillissimi et prudentissimi viri, amici specialis et sotii Dantis, qui, cum vidisset Dantem carissimum amicum et sotium Guidonis filii sui' [This soul was the father of Guido Cavalcanti, a very noble and very learned man, close friend and fellow poet of Dante's, who, when he saw Dante, the dearest friend and companion of his son Guido]; Guido da Pisa, *Expositiones et glose*, ed. by Michele Rinaldi, 2 vols (Rome: Salerno, 2013), I, 448 (see n. 31 below); Iacomo della Lana, *Commento alla 'Commedia'*, ed. by Mirko Volpi with the collaboration of Arianna Terzi, 4 vols (Rome: Salerno, 2009), I, 334: 'Or intercide qui Dante lo processo de questa novella ed introduxe, como apar nel testo, lo padre di Guido Cavalcanti, lo qual fue molto suo compagno'; *L'ottimo commento della Divina Commedia*, ed. by Alessandro Torri, 3 vols (Pisa: Niccolò Capurro, 1827–29), I, 177–79: 'onde è da notare, che l'Autore e Guido Cavalcanti figliuolo di Messer Cavalcante, furono contemporanei, cioè ad uno tempo, e amicissimi; la quale amistade si creò in loro per similitudine d'abito scientifico, e per similitudine di costumi, e di passioni d'animo, e di vita, e di parzialitade, e di cittadinanza: le quali similitudini tennero in amistade congiunti li animi de l'Autore e di Guido, tanto quanto Guido visse; amendue studiarono in Firenze, amendue amarono per amore, amendue parlaron in rime, canzoni, e altre spezie di dire con misura di piedi, e di tempi sillabitati, amendue seguitaron un volere in governare la Repubblica di Firenze, per la quale con gli altri furon chiamati Bianchi, e per quello volere cacciati furono di Firenze con gli altri [...] L'Autore dice: due cose il mi fecero conoscere, ciò furono le sue parole, nelle quali dimostrò due cose, cioè speziale familiaritade e conversazione tra l'Autore, e 'l figliuolo di colui che parlava, abito di scienza, e sottilitate d'ingegno'. See also the following note.

common fourteenth-century identification of the enigmatic 'giusti son due' of *Inf.* VI. 73 with Dante and Guido is an obvious instance of this widely held belief.[26] Not even *Inferno* X, as far as most medieval readers of the *Commedia* were concerned, casts doubts on the healthy and lasting nature of their friendship. Boccaccio seems to have been the first to recognize Dante's polemical animus towards his former friend in *Inferno* X, as evidenced by the fact that, in the *Decameron*, but, tellingly, not in the more sober and scholarly *Esposizioni*, he highlighted Guido's supposed ties to Epicureanism.[27] However, unlike Boccaccio, who, during the course of the *novella*, undermines the idea that Guido was a heretic (see Chapter 15), his 'imitators'

---

26   Benvenuto da Imola, I, 236: 'Nam cum peto simpliciter et absolute si aliquis est iustus in civitate, secundum communem modum loquendi non debet intelligi nisi de homine. Dicendum est ergo quod autor loquitur de se et Guidone Cavalcante, qui de rei veritate tempore illo erant duo oculi Florentiae, sed autor non exprimit nomen, sed relinquit intelligi iudicio prudentum. De se enim nullus sapiens dubitabit; de Guidone autem et laudibus eius dicetur infra Inferni capitulo X et Purgatorii capitulo XI, tamen latenter tangit dicens: *e non vi sono intesi*, quia pars regens non adhaesit consilio istorum duorum: imo Guido fuit missus ad confinia ex quo mortuus est; et consilium Dantis spretum' [When I ask simply and unquestionably if there is somebody among the citizens who is just, this should be understood only of a man, according to common language. It must therefore be said that the author is talking about himself and Guido Cavalcanti, who in truth at that time were the two eyes of Florence, but the author does not write the name, and leaves it to the judgment of the wise to understand. For no learned person will doubt [that he is talking] about himself; about Guido and his praises he will talk between *Inferno* X and *Purgatorio* XI, nonetheless here he touches on him when he says: *e non vi sono intesi*, because the ruling faction did not follow the advice of these two: indeed Guido was sent into exile and thus died; and Dante's advice was rejected]; Boccaccio, *Esposizioni* VI (I). 45 (p. 355): 'Quali questi due si sieno sarebbe grave lo 'ndovinare; nondimeno sono alcuni li quali, donde che egli sel traggano, che voglion dire essere stato l'uno l'autor medesimo e l'altro Guido Cavalcanti, il quale era d'una medesima setta con lui; *ma non vi sono intesi*, cioè non è alcun lor consiglio creduto'; *Commento della Divina Commedia d'anonimo fiorentino*, I, 171–72: 'Però che quali fussono questi due non si può comprendere, se non per imaginarsi, puossi errare in discivergli: pure pare che alcuno voglia dire che l'uno fu l'Autore, et l'altro Guido Cavalcanti, che più volte consigliaro i Cerchi, ch'erano di loro parte, ch'egliono si ponessono mente alle mani, ché questi loro nimici non gli cacciassono, monstrando loro delle vie giuste et ragionevoli, che, se l'avessono tenute, non sarebbono stati cacciati'; Francesco da Buti, p. 285: 'risponde qui al secondo dimando dicendo che in Firense son du' iusti; quali siano questi du' disse frate Guido del Carmino ne lo scripto che fé sopra XXVII canti de la prima cantica, che questi du' erano Dante et messer Guido de' Cavalcanti'; Guido da Pisa, I, 378: 'Sed nos istos duos iustos intelligere possumus primum Dantem, autorem istius altissime et profundissime *Comedie*; secundum vero Guidonem de Cavalcantibus, qui duo soli illo tempore, quo civitas Florentie fuit intus et extra bellis conquassata civilibus, iusti et amatores patrie sunt reperti et rei publice defensores' [But we can understand these two just men as follows: the first one, Dante, author of the highest and most profound *Comedia*; and the second one, Guido Cavalcanti; at that time only these two were found to be just, to love their homeland, and to defend the common good, when the city of Florence was shaken inside and outside by civil war].

27   'E fu questo cavaliere padre di Guido Cavalcanti, uomo costumatissimo e ricco e d'alto ingegno, e seppe molte leggiadre cose fare meglio che alcun altro nostro cittadino: e, oltre a ciò, fu nel suo tempo reputato ottimo loico e buon filosofo, e fu singularissimo amico dell'autore, sì come esso medesimo mostra nella sua *Vita nuova*, e fu buon dicitore in rima; ma, per ciò che la filosofia gli pareva, sì come ella è, da molto più che la poesia, ebbe a sdegno Virgilio e gli altri poeti. E per ciò che messer Cavalcante conosceva lo 'ngegno del figliuolo e la singulare usanza la quale con l'autore avea, riconosciuto prestamente l'autore, senza alcuna premessione d'altre parole, nella prima giunta gli fece la domanda che di sopra si disse': Boccaccio, *Esposizioni* X. 62–63 (p. 526; and compare this passage with that from the *Decameron* quoted in n. 20).

— Benvenuto da Imola,[28] Filippo Villani,[29] and Domenico Bandino d'Arezzo[30] — assert the poet's unorthodoxy as a matter of fact, almost certainly bolstered by Boccaccio's authority (Parodi). In any case, all four writers, who constitute an isolated tradition on this point, are exceptions to the unproblematic, one might say, 'amicable', reading of the episode. Thus, the Trecento commentators, who interpreted Guido's 'disdegno' as being directed against poetry and Virgil — two things, as they were well aware, that were close to Dante's heart — did not consider this disagreement as having a damaging effect on their relationship.[31] In fact,

28   'Ad cuius cognitionem est sciendum, quod iste secundus spiritus fuit quidam miles florentinus nomine Cavalcante de Cavalcantibus. Iste omnino tenuit sectam epicureorum, semper credens, et suadens aliis, quod anima simul moreretur cum corpore; unde saepe habebat in ore istud dictum Salomonis: *Unus est interitus hominis et iumentorum, et aequa utriusque conditio.* Iste fuit pater Guidonis Cavalcantis, qui fuit alter oculus Florentiae tempore Dantis [...] *Forse cui Guido vostre ebbe a disdegno.* Et hoc nota quod iste Guido non est delectatus in poeticis, licet fuerit actus philosophus et subtilis inventor, qui fecit inter alia unam cantionem de amore ita profunde quod Aegidius romanus non erubuit facere comentum super eam, et Dinus florentinus, magnus physicus, similiter glosam fecit. Modo ad propositum, Guido, sicut et aliqui alii saepe faciunt, non dignabatur legere poetas, quorum princeps est Virgilius; sed certe Dantes alium honorem et fructum consecutus est ex poetari, quam Guido de solo philosophari, quia errorem quem pater habebat ex ignorantia, ipse conabatur defendere per scientiam' [To identify him, we must know that this second soul was a Florentine knight named Cavalcante de' Cavalcanti. He firmly belonged to the Epicurean sect, always believing, and persuading others, that the soul will die with the body; thus he often repeated Solomon's saying: *One is the death of man and of animals, and equal is their condition.* This was the father of Guido Cavalcanti, who was the other eye of Florence at Dante's time [...] *Forse cui Guido vostro ebbe a disdegno.* And here he suggests that this Guido did not delight in poetry, nonetheless he was a shrewd philosopher and a refined creator, who composed — among other things — a canzone on love so profound that, without embarrassment, Egidio Romano wrote a commentary on it, and likewise Dino Fiorentino, a great natural philosopher, glossed it. But to this end, Guido — as others often do — did not deem it worth to read the poets, among whom the leading authority is Virgil; and certainly Dante achieved a different honour and satisfaction from writing poetry than did Guido from doing only philosophy, because the mistake that his father made out of ignorance, he tried to defend by means of knowledge]: Benvenuto da Imola, I, 340 & 342. Indeed, Benvenuto translates almost verbatim into Latin the closing paragraphs of Boccaccio's short story (III, 314).
29   Filippo Villani, p. 57 (see n. 21 above).
30   'Guido filius alterius Guidonis ex nobili florentina stirpe de Cavalcantibus, liberalium artium peritissimus, Dante poete contemporaneus et familiarissimus fuit. Hic de amore libidinoso, eiusque natura, motibus et effectibus adeo preacute mirabilem edidit cantilenam, quod Dinus de Garbo phisicus et Egidius Romanus, in orbe unicus suo evo, commentando aperire dignati sunt. Erat nempe Guido vir omni virtute clarus, ni paterna opinione secutus fuisset Epycuriorum dogma, prout monstrat Dantes c. [x] prime partis. Tandem Florentie moritur et cum majoribus sue domus sepultus est' [Guido, son of the other Guido from the noble Florentine family of the Cavalcanti, most expert in the liberal arts, was Dante's contemporary and very close to him. He composed such a wondrous canzone on carnal love, on its nature, on its motions and effects that the philosopher Dino del Garbo and Egidio Romano, unique in the world of his time, deemed it worth explaining through a commentary. Guido was of course a man renowned for every virtue, if only he had not followed the doctrine of the Epicureans as a result of his father's belief, as Dante shows in canto x of the first part. He died in Florence and is buried with his ancestors]: Domenico Bandino d'Arezzo, *Fons Memorabilium*, ms. Laur. Edili 172, fol. 183r., quoted in Ernesto G. Parodi, 'La miscredenza di Guido Cavalcanti e una fonte del Boccaccio', *Bullettino della Società dantesca italiana*, n.s. 22 (1915), 37–47 (p. 40, n. 1).
31   Benvenuto, I, 343 (see also I, 342; see n. 26 above): 'quod Guido filius eius habuit ad indignationem Virgilium, et sic fuerat usus verbo praeteriti temporis, non quod vellet dicere Guidonem

fore mortuum, sed quod Guido a iuventute congruo tempore non vacaverat poetis sicut ipse Dantes' [that his son Guido disdained Virgil, and that he had consequently used the past tense, not because he wanted to say that Guido was dead, but because Guido, since the time fit of youth, had not occupied himself with the poets, as Dante himself had done]; Boccaccio, *Esposizioni* x. 62 (p. 526; see n. 27 above); *Le chiose ambrosiane alla 'Commedia'*, ed. by Luca Carlo Rossi (Pisa: Scuola Normale Superiore, 1990), p. 34: '*Desdegno* — Quia non studuit poesi' [Because he did not love poetry]; *Chiose cassinesi*: '*un'ombra*. domini cavalcantis de cavalcantibus de florentia patris Guidonis acutissimi ingenii et socii contemporanei. hujus auctoris. qui quamvis magnus rimator fuerit in materno stilo tamen non delectabatur in poesia sed potius in phylosophia ut colligitur in textu in eo quod dicit quod dedignatus fuerat studere super Virgilio' [*un'ombra*. Of *dominus* Cavalcante de' Cavalcanti of Florence, father of the supremely talented Guido, who was a contemporary companion of this author. Guido who, although he was a great versifier in his maternal style, nonetheless did not delight in poetry but in philosophy, as can be gathered from that text in which he says that he had refused to study Virgil]; *Commento della Divina Commedia d'anonimo fiorentino*, I, 254 (see n. 38 below); Francesco da Buti, pp. 450–51: '*mio fillio* cioè Guido, *ov'è, et perché non è teco?*, quasi dicesse così: "Era d'alto ingegno elli come tu, come non à facto qualche simile opera come tu?" [...] *forsi cui Guido vostro ebbe ad disdegno*, questo dice l'autore perché Guido dispregiava li poeti et Virgilio come li altri [...] quando dice che Virgilio l'aspectava vuole intendere che a parlamentare con questi suoi fiorentini non usava la ragione pratica de la poesi perché finge che parlasseno di cose che non si stendeno ad poesi. Et così si dé intendere, quando dice che Guido ebbe a disdegno Virgilio'; Guglielmo Maramauro, *Expositione sopra l''Inferno' di Dante Alligieri*, ed. by Pier Giacomo Pisoni and Saverio Bellomo (Padua: Antenore, 1998), pp. 213 & 216: 'Il qual misser Cavalcanti ebbe un figlio chiamato Guido, gioveno assai virtuoso e literato, dotato de nobilissimi costumi, pregiato da tuti' Fiorentini perfecto filosofo; e fo nel tempo de D., e delectossi multo de dir in rima vulgare e disse assai bene. Verò è che esso non se delectò sapere poesia, per la qual cossa non li fo opo studiare V[irglio]. [...] Qui D. li risponde: "Io non vegno da me. Colui che aspetta là mi mena qui. E Guido to non volse sapere V."'; Guido da Pisa, p. 448: 'Iste enim fuit quidam miles florentinus, qui fuit vocatus dominus Cavalcante de Cavalcantibus, pater illius mirabilis viri in quo omnis nobilitas et probitas relucebat: scilicet Guidoni de Cavalcantibus. Fuit enim iste Guido scientia magnus et moribus insignitus, sed tamen in suo sensu aliqualiter inflatus; habebat enim scientias poeticas in derisum; unde autor notanter dicit in subsequentibus rithimis ipsi domino Cavalcanti: *colui* — hoc est Virgilius — *ch'attende là per qui mi mena | forse cui Guido vostro ebbe a disdegno*. [...] Et quia isti duo, scilicet Dantes et Guido, erant quasi in omnibus socii sibi ad invicem predilecti miratus fuit quod filius suus Guido in isto itinere tam alti ingenii non associabat autorem' [He was indeed a Florentine knight, who was called *dominus* Cavalcante de Cavalcanti, father of that admirable man in whom all nobility and honesty shone: namely, Guido Cavalcanti. Guido was of great knowledge and of distinguished manners, but nonetheless quite proud of his own views; he scorned the art of poetry; hence the author in the following lines says to *dominus* Cavalcanti: *colui* — that is Virgil — *ch'attende là per qui mi mena | forse cui Guido vostro ebbe a disdegno*. And because these two — namely, Dante and Guido — were close in almost everything and held each other in high esteem, he was surprised that his son Guido was not going with the author on this journey of such lofty intelligence]; Pietro Alighieri, *Commentarium*, second redaction (I quote from DDP): 'Qui Guido adhesit libris phylosophicis magis quam poeticis: et hoc est quod tangit hic auctor dum dicit quod ipse Guido, vilipendendo Virgilium, idest eius poema, et alios per consequens vates, solummodo secuto est phylosophos' [Guido who adhered to philosophical more than to poetical writings: and this is what this author touches on when he says that Guido, despising Virgil, that is his poem, and consequently other poets, exclusively followed philosophers]; Pietro Alighieri, *Commentarium*, third redaction (I quote from DDP): 'patris Guidonis, viri acutissimi ingenii et comitis contemporanei huius auctoris qui, quamvis fuerit magnus rimator in materno stilo, nullatenus tamen delectabatur in poesia, sed potius in phylosophia, ut colligitur hic in textu in eo quod dicit sibi auctor quod dedignatus fuerat studere super Virgilio' [of the father of Guido, man of the highest intellect and contemporary companion of this author; Guido who, although he was a great versifier in his maternal style, by no means however delighted in poetry, but rather in philosophy, as can be gathered in the text in which this author says about himself that he had refused

they deemed it as strengthening their association, since it served to establish their differences and similarities. Benvenuto's position is typical: 'fuerunt duo lumina Florentiae, unus philosophus, alter poeta, eodem tempore, de eadem parte, amici et socii' [there were two lights in Florence, one a philosopher, the other a poet, at the same time, of the same faction, friends and companions] (I, 341). Furthermore, not even Guido's exile could cast a shadow over the cosy picture of their intimacy, since there is no mention in fourteenth-century accounts of the role that Dante played in his friend's banishment.[32] Everything would thus seem to suggest that Cavalcanti's association with Dante was vital first in establishing, and then in sustaining and reconfirming his key cultural position; and not just during the Trecento but right up to the present.[33]

3. Priorities

It is necessary at this juncture to open a small parenthesis. When I began work on this study, it was my firm intention to avoid becoming embroiled in the then current, almost certainly unresolvable (and indeed still unresolved), controversies regarding the chronological relationship between 'Donna me prega' and the *Vita nova*.[34] However, as my work progressed, I increasingly felt that not to say anything about the problem, given my effort to reconstruct, however cautiously, the context in which Cavalcanti wrote and was read, might be construed as an act of scholarly pusillanimity. Yet, given my doubts — doubts that firmly persist as, nearly twenty years later, I prepare the present collection of essays — regarding the possibility that the issue can be satisfactorily resolved, my contribution to the debate is simply to pose a question that arises directly from the subject-matter here under discussion: If 'Donna me prega', whose tones towards its opponent(s) are more cuttingly biting than the *libello*'s more subtle and nuanced criticisms, had been composed as a

to study Virgil]; *L'ottimo commento*, I, 179: 'E dice l'Autore, che forse Guido ebbe a disdegno questo libro di Virgilio, e li altri suoi'.

32   Benvenuto, I, 236 (see n. 26 above); Giovanni Villani, IX. 42 (see n. 21 above); *L'ottimo commento*, I, 178 (see n. 25 above).

33   There are dangers in tying Cavalcanti too closely to Dante. Guido's importance can only be properly appreciated if his undoubted achievements are considered on their own terms rather than through the distorting filter of Dante. It is reassuring to note that a number of critics has recently stressed the need to reconsider the ways in which Cavalcanti has traditionally been studied. By explaining how Guido's contemporaries, with Dante at their head, constructed a series of 'subjective' images of the poet-philosopher to serve a variety of cultural ends, my hope is that I can help clear some of the clutter surrounding his poetry, thereby permitting a more 'direct' access to his verse.

34   The controversy is unresolvable because, as Barolini has energetically and convincingly explained, no hard evidence is available with which to establish the texts' chronology: Barolini, 'Dante and Cavalcanti', pp. 60–63; and see also Pasero, pp. 410–11. The debate has its origins in hints dropped by De Robertis in his introduction to 'Donna me prega' (Cavalcanti, *Rime*, p. 94), which were then developed a few years later by Tanturli, who overturns the traditional sequence 'Donna me prega'-*Vita nova*. For a bibliography on what has become an increasingly acrimonious dispute, see Antonelli, 'Cavalcanti e Dante', pp. 290–91. Given that philological proof with which to resolve the conundrum is unavailable, we can only rely on 'circumstantial' evidence. For what it's worth, I feel that such evidence points to the *Vita nova* having been written after Cavalcanti's doctrinal canzone.

polemical response to the *Vita nova*, how likely is it that the idea of the two poets as 'amici et socii' [friends and companions] would have persisted with the vigour and for the length of time that it actually did?

4. Cavalcanti *filosofo*

Returning to the main drift of my argument: if the account that I have been delineating of the first reactions to Guido, as well as the stress that I have been placing on these, is at all approximate to what the actual situation may have been at the end of the thirteenth century — and I have tried to remain as conservatively faithful as possible to the surviving documentary evidence — then, it is clear that, by the time of his death in the summer of 1300, many of the elements that were traditionally associated with an *auctoritas,* such as exceptional public standing and acknowledged intellectual superiority, had become ascribed to Cavalcanti and to his writings. His untimely death, I suspect, would also have helped to confirm and consolidate his reputation, especially among those in the city who shared his political sympathies. However, I should not like to create the perception that Guido somehow owes his authority to his tragic demise, even though this was loudly lamented in some versions of his 'life'.[35] Indeed, it is important to recognize that it is almost certain that, already during his lifetime, Cavalcanti had achieved the status of an 'authority' at least in his native city. This is vitally important since it would imply that the first Italian vernacular poet unquestionably to attain the rank of an *auctoritas* was not Dante, as is commonly assumed, but his 'primo amico' — something that would help cast further light on the reasons for Dante's polemical treatment of Guido in the *Vita nova*, in some of his lyrics (Barański, 'La canzone "anomala"'), in the *De vulgari eloquentia,* and, most notably, in the *Commedia.*[36] In the years that followed his death, Cavalcanti's standing continued to grow. The commentaries to 'Donna me prega' are eloquent testimony to this fact. More importantly, the gloss of the 'magnus physicus' [the great natural philosopher] (Benvenuto, I, 346) Dino del Garbo unambiguously reveals that Guido's authoritativeness was accepted and supported not just by other *litterati* (the pseudo-Egidio Romano commentary is an expression of this group), but also by philosophers. Indeed, given Cavalcanti's personal contacts with the university of Bologna and with so-called radical Aristotelian circles, as evidenced by Jacopo da Pistoia's dedication of his *quaestio* on happiness to the 'Viro bene nato et mihi dilecto et pre aliis amico carissimo Gwidoni' [well-born man and my dear and closest friend of all, Guido], it is not unlikely that the prestige which

35   Giovanni Villani, IX. 42 (see n. 21 above); Guido da Pisa, I, p. 378 (see n. 26 above).
36   Dante grants Guido a secondary role in his account of the development of the vernacular love lyric in the *De vulgari eloquentia.* He mentions him as belonging to the group of Florentine poets using an 'excellent' form of the vernacular — 'nonnullos vulgaris excellentiam cognovisse sentimus, scilicet Guidonem, Lapum et unum alium, Florentinos, et Cynum Pistoriensem' [we have heard that some knew the excellence of the vernacular, that is Guido, Lapo and another one, Florentines, and Cino da Pistoia] (I. 13. 4); he lists Cavalcanti's canzone 'Poi che di doglia cor conven ch'i' porti' among those that exhibit the best type of *constructio* (II. 6. 5–6); and he presents 'Donna me prega' as being exclusively made up of hendecasyllables (II. 12. 3), while incorporating trisyllabic lines as internal rhymes (II. 12. 8).

came from such contacts would also have played an important role in establishing his position of cultural privilege during his life.[37] After his death, as the disputes on the relative merits of poetry and the sciences intensified, it is not difficult to imagine Cavalcanti being appropriated by the philosophers in order to underline his identity as a poet who had rejected literature in favour of *scientia* — this was, in fact, the most common image of Guido in the Trecento.[38] Once again, Dante's 'anti-poetic' presentation of his *amico* in *Inferno* x, as the episode was interpreted in the fourteenth century, would have helped fix Cavalcanti in this pose. I am tempted to take my present line of reasoning one step further and hypothesize that one of the principal motives why the philosophers would have been so keen to promote the idea of Cavalcanti the poetic philosopher 'disdainful' of poetry was to counter the growing popularity and authoritativeness of Dante, who not only had never reneged on his poetic loyalties, but whose *Commedia* was also an obvious challenge to rationalist epistemologies, as Guido da Pisa had quickly recognized.[39]

37   Jacopo da Pistoia's text was first published in Paul O. Kristeller, 'A Philosophical Treatise from Bologna Dedicated to Guido Cavalcanti: Magister Jacobus de Pistorio and his *Questio de felicitate*', in *Medioevo e Rinascimento: studi in onore di Bruno Nardi* (Florence: Olschki, 1955), pp. 425–63 (p. 442); but now see Irene Zavattero, 'La *Quaestio de felicitate* di Giacomo da Pistoia: un tentativo di interpretazione alla luce di una nuova edizione critica del testo', in *Le felicità nel Medioevo*, ed. by Maria Bettetini and Francesco D. Paparella (Louvain-La-Neuve: Féderation Internationale des Instituts d'Études Médiévales, 2005), pp. 355–409, the new critical edition may be found at pp. 395–409. On Cavalcanti's links to the University of Bologna, see Maria Corti, *Dante a un nuovo crocevia* (Florence: Libreria Commissionaria Sansoni, 1981), pp. 9–31.

38   See n. 31 above. In addition, see Benvenuto, I, 342 (see n. 26 above) and III, 313 (see n. 54 below); Boccaccio, *Dec.* VI. 9. 8 (see n. 20 above) and *Esposizioni* x. 62, p. 526 (see n. 27 above); *Commento della Divina Commedia d'anonimo fiorentino*, I, 254: 'Mio figlio ov'è: Se tu vai, disse questa anima all'Auttore, per l'inferno per altezza d'ingegno, mio figlio, che fu tanto ingegnoso (et ancora perché mentre visse fu conto dell'Auttore) perché non è teco? [...] Et però che Guido suo figliolo fu valente uomo, grande loico et gran filosofo [...] Fece Guido Cavalcanti molte cose in rima et fra l'altre una canzone morale, dove mostra bene intendere filosofia che comincia: *Donna mi priega perché io voglia dire D'uno accidente* ec. Ora, o perché Guido gli paresse che la scienzia sua fosse sì alta che'ella avanzasse molto quella de' Poeti, o ch'egli non legessi mai loro libri, parve ch'egli sdegnasse il libro di Virgilio; et per tanto rispose l'Auttore: Io non vengo qui per mia virtù, ma per quella di Virgilio, il quale Guido vostro sdegnò'; and also II, 189; Dino Compagni, 'Se mia laude scusasse te sovente': 'e come assai scrit[t]ura sai a mente | soffisimosamente' (7–8); Domenico Bandino d'Arezzo, fol. 183r. (see n. 30 above); Filippo Villani, p. 57 (see n. 21 above); Giovanni Villani, IX. 42 (see n. 21 above); Guglielmo Maramauro, p. 213 (see n. 31 above); Guido da Pisa, p. 448 (see n. 31 above); Franco Sacchetti, *Il Trecentonovelle*, ed. by Valerio Marucci (Rome: Salerno, 1996), LXVIII. 1. 8 (pp. 198–99): 'Guido Cavalcanti, essendo valentissimo uomo e filosofo, è vinto dalla malizia d'uno fanciullo. [...] Quanto fu questa sottil malizia a un fanciullo, che colui che forse in Firenze suo pari non avea per cosí fatto modo fusse da un fanciullo schernito e preso e ingannato!'. See also Inglese, 'Per Guido'.

39   See Paola Nasti, 'Autorità, topos e modello: Salomone nei commenti trecenteschi alla *Commedia*', *The Italianist*, 19 (1999), 5–49 (pp. 25–39), and 'A Friar Critic: Guido da Pisa and the Carmelite Heritage', in *Interpreting Dante*, ed. by Paola Nasti and Claudia Rossignoli (Notre Dame, IN: University of Notre Dame Press, 2013), pp. 110–79. See also Zygmunt G. Barański, *Dante e i segni* (Naples: Liguori, 2000), pp. 199–219.

5. Cavalcanti *auctoritas*?

If, as I am suggesting, Cavalcanti had indeed achieved the status of an *auctoritas,* a new problem arises. Why is his manuscript transmission uneven and fragmented, and why is his influence on Trecento lyric poetry relatively limited?[40] Thus, for instance, despite his obvious sympathy for Guido, Boccaccio's poetry, both lyric and narrative, remains largely untouched by the older poet's verses.[41] Equally, the Trecento poets who are most commonly cited as having been significantly influenced at the formal level by Cavalcanti, such as Nicolò de' Rossi[42] and Petrarch,[43] tend not so much to assimilate the poet at first hand, but to absorb him either as part of a commonplace language whose original links with Guido had been all but entirely severed or via Dante's and Cino's verses — the two writers who have unquestionable debts to Cavalcanti's poetic lessons.[44] Dante, in fact, is the writer who more than any other might be termed a 'Cavalcantian'; and an important aspect of his career can be explained in terms of his attempt to shed his early 'Cavalcantianism'. Yet, remaining unread was not in itself a bar to being deemed an *auctoritas* — it is enough to think of Homer's status in the Middle Ages. What was vital was to have the trappings of 'authority', such as being glossed, presented as exceptional, and acknowledged as having special expertise in a particular area of human intellectual endeavour — trappings that can certainly be said to have become associated with Cavalcanti. Furthermore, given Guido's increasing cultural success as a philosopher and not as a poet, the status and influence of his poetry were not really at issue as far as his authoritativeness was concerned. The limited impact which the overwhelmingly literary commentary mistakenly attributed to Egidio Romano appears to have had is a mark of the lack of concern regarding Cavalcanti's poetic standing.[45] One text was, of course, exempt from such disinterest. 'Donna me prega' was widely read, copied, and cited. Yet, the interest it generated had ultimately little to do with its literary qualities, but everything to do with its philosophical character.

---

40   On Guido's manuscript transmission, see Domenico De Robertis, 'Nota al testo', in Cavalcanti, *Rime*, pp. 241–50.

41   See Quaglio, pp. 346–49. The contrary view is asserted by Vittore Branca, *Giovanni Boccaccio: profilo biografico* (Florence: Sansoni, 1977), p. 32, but see Jonathan Usher, 'Boccaccio, Cavalcanti's Canzone "Donna me prega" and Dino's Glosses', *Heliotropia* 2:1 (2004), 1–19: 'textual traces of Cavalcanti in Boccaccio's fictional and creative works are rare and tantalising' (p. 7; but see pp. 7–8).

42   See Furio Brugnolo, *Il Canzoniere di Nicolò de' Rossi*, 2 vols (Padua: Antenore, 1974–77), II, 66–73.

43   See Raffaella Pelosini, 'Guido Cavalcanti nei *Rerum vulgarium fragmenta*', *Studi petrarcheschi*, 9 (1992), 9–76; Franco Suitner, *Petrarca e la tradizione stilnovistica* (Florence: Olschki, 1977), pp. 45–63. On Petrarch's subtle reworking of Cavalcanti as a foil against Dante, see Chapter 10. See also Furio Brugnolo, 'Il "desio che seco non s'accorda": sintonie, rispecchiamenti e fraintendimenti (*Rvf* 70–75)', in *Il Canzoniere: lettura micro e macrotestuale*, ed. by Michelangelo Picone (Ravenna: Longo, 2007), pp. 115–40 (p. 134); Claire Cabaillot, 'La Chanson "Lasso me" de Pétrarque ou l'écriture de la différence', *Cahiers d'études romanes*, 2 (1999), 39–49; Stefano Prandi, 'Ritorno a Laura (*Rvf* 141–50)', in Picone, pp. 335–60.

44   See Corrado Calenda, 'Un'accusa di plagio? Ancora sul rapporto Cavalcanti–Cino', in *Da Guido Guinizzelli a Dante: nuove prospettive sulla lirica del Duecento*, ed. by Furio Brugnolo and Gianfelice Peron (Padua: Il poligrafo, 2004), pp. 291–303; Maria Corti, 'Il linguaggio poetico di Cino da Pistoia', *Cultura neolatina*, 12 (1952), 185–223; Gorni, 'Cino "vil ladro"', pp. 125–39. See also Giunta, 'La "giovanezza" di Guido Cavalcanti'.

45   On the commentary's *fortuna*, see Fenzi, pp. 177–86.

It served to confirm Guido's reputation as a great *loico*, especially in the sphere of love, while the 'scientific' toughness of its form would have appeared to confirm the poet's 'disdegno' for literary niceties. As with other authoritative figures, it was not the specifics of what Guido had actually said that were important. What was vital instead was that reference could be made to him to substantiate, bolster, and embellish an argument in the field of his acknowledged expertise. It did not even matter whether, when referring to an *auctoritas*, there existed in practice a communality of opinion between the writer doing the citing and the 'authority' being cited, as is immediately evident as regards Petrarch's quotation of 'Donna me prega' in his canzone, 'Lasso me, chi' non so in qual parte pieghi':

> Ragion è ben ch'alcuna volta io canti,
> però ch'ò sospirato sí gran tempo
> che mai non incomincio assai per tempo
> per adequar col riso i dolor' tanti.
> Et s'io potesse far ch'agli occhi santi
> porgesse alcun dilecto
> qualche dolce mio detto,
> o me beato sopra gli altri amanti!
> Ma piú, quand'io dirò senza mentire:
> *Donna mi priegha, per ch'io voglio dire. (Rvf 70. 11–20)*[46]

The same disjuncture between the actual views of an *auctoritas* and his cultural reutilization is apparent in Boccaccio's allusion to Cavalcanti's poem in his gloss to the *Teseida*:

> E poi che egli [the author of the *Teseida*] ha disegnato quelle cose le quali generalmente possono, secondo le forze naturali, provocare a l'atto venereo ciascuno, disegna le quali provocano alcuni, li quali noi chiamiamo volgarmente innamorati. E queste pone in forme di persone, e ponle di diverse maniere, perciò che alcune ne pone naturali e sì come cagioni eccitative. E queste sono: Vagheza, la quale dice che è la prima che si truova nello 'ntrare di questo luogo di Venere; per la quale intende quello disiderio naturale il quale ciascuno uomo e donna ha di vedere e di possedere o acquistare più tosto le belle e le care cose che l'altre; e questa Vagheza è quella che tira i giovani alle feste e nelli luoghi ove donne sieno adunate, acciò che tra molte n'elegga alcuna, secondo il suo giudicio più degna del suo amore; e ancora di queste eccitative: Bellezza, Giovaneza, Leggiadria, Gentileza, Piacevolezza, e simiglianti. Alcune ne pone quasi confermative dello appetito eccitato per le sopradette: tra le quali pone Cupido, il quale noi volgarmente chiamiamo Amore. Il quale amore volere mostrare come per le sopradette cose si generi in noi, quantunque alla presente opera forse si converrebbe di dichiarare, non è mio intendimento di farlo, perciò che troppa sarebbe lunga la storia: chi disidera di vederlo, legga la canzone di Guido Cavalcanti *Donna mi priega, ets.*, e le chiose che sopra vi fece Maestro Dino del Garbo.[47]

---

46 Petrarch also refers to Cavalcanti when he presents his canon of Italian vernacular love poets in *Triumphus Cupidinis*: 'ecco Dante e Beatrice, ecco Selvaggia, | ecco Cin da Pistoia, Guitton d'Arezzo, | che di non esser primo par ch'ira aggia; | ecco i due Guidi che già fur in prezzo, | Honesto Bolognese, e i Ciciliani, | che fur già primi, e quivi eran da sezzo' (IV. 31–36).
47 Giovanni Boccaccio, *Teseida*, ed. by Alberto Limentani (Milan: Mondadori, 1964), p. 222. Cecco d'Ascoli also cites 'Donna me prega', but to question its authoritativeness: 'Amore è passïon

In both instances, major discrepancies separate Guido's actual views on love from those attributed to him by the two younger writers. To be cited without regard for meaning, but simply on account of cultural standing, was to be authoritative indeed.

However, the principal manner in which Cavalcanti was established as an *auctoritas* was by means of his 'lives', namely the brief pseudo-biographical accounts describing his many positive attributes, which, as is apparent from both the chronicles and the commentaries to the *Commedia*, must have circulated widely. Given that, as I have attempted to argue, Guido's 'authoritativeness' was firmly in place before his death, it is likely that both the chronicles and the commentaries drew on older, possibly oral versions of his *vita*. There is still considerable work to be done on the links between Cavalcanti's biographies and the *vitae* of the great established *auctoritates*. I do not have the space here to undertake such a task. My aim is to present a rapid summary of the main elements constituting his portrait. The ways in which these traits would have established, enhanced, and confirmed his 'authoritativeness' should be easily apparent. Guido was presented as one of the very best Florentines, in some areas, especially in that of speculative endeavour, as the best.[48] Together with Dante, as we have seen, he was deemed one of the two

di gentil cuore | Che vien dalla virtù del terzo cielo | Che nel crear la forma al suo splendore. | Errando scrisse Guido Cavalcanti: | "non so perchè si mosse e per qual zelo". | Qui ben mi spiego lo tacer di Danti. | "Donna mi prega perch' io debba dire" | Dimostra che l'amor muove da Marte, | Dal qual procede l'impeto con l'ire, | Che strugge p̈ietà con la mercede, | Unita cosa per disdegno parte, | Corrompe amore con la dolce fede': Francesco Stabili [Cecco d'Ascoli], *L'Acerba*, ed. by Achille Crespi (Ascoli Piceno: Casa Editrice di Giuseppe Cesari, 1927), III. 1, 1935–46 (p. 247); the line that Cecco cites at line 1939 belongs to a poem that has not reached us. In the passage quoted, it is interesting to note the appearance, in a context that evokes Cavalcanti, of the noun *disdegno*, which, especially thanks to Dante, had become closely tied to the poet, particularly as, in this instance, the noun is not directly linked to him. The same occurs in Niccola Muscia, 'Ècci venuto Guido ['n] Compostello', where St James 'becomes indignant' with Cavalcanti's behaviour: 'Sa̓ Iacopo sdegnò quando l'udìo' (9) (Cavalcanti, *Rime*, pp. 119–20); and see Ciro Di Fiore, 'Il controverso viaggio di Guido Cavalcanti a Santiago di Compostela', *Linguistica e letteratura*, 35 (2010), 229–47. See also *Le chiose ambrosiane*: 'L'uno — Scilicet dominus Guido de Cavalcantis qui composuit cantilenam amoris que incipit: "Amor"' [*L'uno* — that is *dominus* Guido de Cavalcanti who composed a canzone on love that starts: 'Amor'] (p. 34); Gianni Alfani, 'Ballatetta dolente', in *Poeti del Ducento*, ed. by Gianfranco Contini, 2 vols (Milan and Naples: Ricciardi, 1960), II, 610: 'Po' fa' sì ch'entri ne la mente a Guido, | perch' egli è sol colui che vede Amore' (18–19); Filippo Villani, *Expositio seu Comentum super 'Comedia' Dantis Allegherii*, ed. by Saverio Bellomo (Florence: Le Lettere, 1989), II. 179 (p. 120): 'Di quella fera. Audi quid de amore venereo dicat Guido de Cavalcantibus de Florentia in quadam sua cantilena in qua mirabiliter et physice de amore tractavit, et incipit: *Donna mi prega, perch'io voglio dire | d'uno, accidente, ch'è sovente fero | ed è sì altero, chè chiamato amore*' [*Di quella fera*. I have heard that the Florentine Guido Cavalcanti may refer to carnal love in a canzone of his where he speaks wondrously and in terms of natural philosophy of love, and it begins: *Donna mi prega, perch'io voglio dire | d'uno, accidente, ch'è sovente fero | ed è sì altero, chè chiamato amore*].

48   See n. 31 above. See also *Chiose anonime alla prima cantica della Divina Commedia*, ed. by Francesco Selmi (Turin: Stamperia Reale, 1865), pp. 62–63: 'Questi che surse a la vista scoperchiata fu messer Cavalcante, il padre di Guido Cavalcanti, il qual Guido fu tenuto del maggiore ingegno e più alto che allora fossse uomo di Firenze. E conoscendo la boce di Dante, e sappiendo ch'era di sua usanza e di suoi costumi, credette che Guido fosse con Dante, e levossi alto per desiderio di vedere il figliuolo. Poi che vide che non v'era, domandò Dante, e disse: poi che per ingegno tu vai per lo inferno, e

lumina or *oculi* of the city. He was also praised for the excellence of his manners and behaviour, which were not affected by a certain aloofness and preference for his own company (see n. 18).[49] He was *nobilissimus, prudentissimus, excellens, mirabilis, costumatissimo, valente, assai virtuoso e literato.*[50] He was wealthy, the scion of a noble and important family, and politically astute, even if his sound advice was not heeded and he himself ended up a victim of political in-fighting (the blame in this account of his political activity always falls on others and never on Cavalcanti).[51] Also, like any human being, he had flaws (the listing of weaknesses was a commonplace of the *vitae*, though, as in Guido's case, they were never allowed to submerge the *auctoritas's* virtues). He was irascible and *sdegnoso* (that key epithet),[52] and there were occasional hints of homosexuality, of avarice and materialism, and of arrogance.[53] Of what there is no trace, other than in Dante, and after him in Boccaccio and his imitators, is any suggestion of intellectual unorthodoxy, never mind of Epicureanism. Most significantly, while some reference was made, especially in the context of *Purgatorio* XI, to his poetic skills, his greatness lay — as I have already noted — in his philosophical abilities, most notably in the sphere of love; abilities which, to a large

Guido mio è ingegnoso come tu, e suole essere teco, come non è ora teco?'; Guido Orlandi, 'Amico, i' saccio ben che sa' limare', in Cavalcanti, *Rime*, pp. 204–05: 'Amico i' saccio ben che sa' limare | con punta lata maglia di coretto, | di palo in frasca come uccel volare, | con grande ingegno gir per loco stretto' (1–4).

49   *Dec.* VI. 9. 8 (see n. 20 below); Compagni, 'Se mia laude scusasse te sovente': 'come se' saggio, dico, intra la gente, | visto, pro' e valente, | e come sai di varco e di schermaglie' (4–6), and *Cronica* I. 20 (p. 54; see pp. 448-49); Domenico Bandino d'Arezzo, fol. 183r. (see n. 30 above); Maramauro, p. 213 (see n. 30 above); Guido da Pisa, I, 448 (see n. 31 above); *L'ottimo commento*, I, 178 (see n. 25 above).

50   Graziolo Bambaglioli, p. 83 (on the first two attributes; see n. 24 above); Benvenuto da Imola, I, 340: 'de isto Guidone viro excellente' [on this Guido, an excellent man]; Guido da Pisa, I, 448 (see n. 31 above); Boccaccio, *Esposizioni*, IX. 62 (p. 526; see n. 27 above); Compagni, 'Se mia laude scusasse te sovente' (see the preceding note); Maramauro, p. 213 (see n. 30 above).

51   *Dec.* VI. 9. 8 (see n. 20 above); *Commento della Divina Commedia d'anonimo fiorentino*, I, 171–72 (see n. 26 above); Compagni, 'Se mia laude scusasse te sovente': 'ver' te provo neente | appo ben canoscente | che nobeltate ed arte insieme aguaglie. | E grande nobiltà non t'ha mistiere | né gran masnad' avere: | c[hi] ha cortesia ma[n]tien leggera corte. | Se' uom[o] di gran corte' (10–16), and *Cronica* I. 20 (p. 54; see pp. 448–49); Domenico Bandino d'Arezzo, fol. 183r. (see n. 30 above); Guido da Pisa, I, 378 (see n. 24 above); *L'ottimo commento*, I, 178 (see n. 25 above). On Guido's wealth, see also Giunta, 'La "giovanezza" di Guido Cavalcanti', pp. 164–65.

52   See n. 18 above. On Guido's irascibility: Giovanni Villani, *Nuova cronica* IX. 42 (see n. 21 above); Sacchetti, *Il Trecentonovelle* LXVIII. 3 (p. 198): 'ed egli [Guido], come aviene, forse venendo al peggior del giuoco, levasi furioso e dando a questo fanciullo disse'.

53   On homosexuality, see Lapo Farinata degli Uberti, 'Guido, quando dicesti pasturella', in Cavalcanti, *Rime*, pp. 182–83. On avarice and materialism, see Guido Orlandi, 'Amico, i' saccio ben che sa' limare': 'e largamente prendere e donare, | salvar lo guadagnato (ciò m'è detto), | accoglier gente, terra guadagnare' (5–7); Niccola Muscia, 'Ècci venuto Guido ['n] Compostello'; see also also Giunta, 'La "giovanezza" di Guido Cavalcanti', p. 159. On arrogance, see Benvenuto da Imola, III, 314 (see the next note); Guido da Pisa, I, 448 (see n. 31 above). Boccaccio's reference to Guido's longlasting dedication to love rather than a criticism is further evidence of Cavalcanti's exemplary status: 'E quegli che contro alla mia età parlando vanno, mostra mal che conoscano che, perché il porro abbia il capo bianco, che la coda sia verde: a' quali, lasciando il motteggiar da l'un de' lati, rispondo che io mai a me vergogna non reputerò infino nello stremo della mia vita di dover compiacere a quelle cose alle quali Guido Cavalcanti e Dante Alighieri già vecchi e messer Cino da Pistoia vecchissimo onor si tennero, e fu lor caro il piacer loro' (*Dec.* IV. Introduzione 33)

extent, were seen as bolstered by his rejection of Virgil, and hence of poetry, and by his closeness to contemporary doctrinal developments.[54] In a period of social, political, and cultural uncertainty such as late Due- and Trecento Italy, Cavalcanti emerged as the model of the archetypal 'modern man', involved in the life of his city, suspicious of the past, and willing to engage with and contribute to the intellectual concerns of the present. In short, a worthy *auctoritas* to place next to, and even in opposition to, the greats of antiquity.

54   *Anonymous Latin Commentary of Dante's 'Commedia'*, ed. by Vincenzo Cioffari (Spoleto: Centro Italiano di Studi sull'Alto Medioevo, 1989), p. 164: 'Vult dicere quod Guido de Cavalcantibus extinxit famam domini Guidonis de Guiniçellis, qui rethoricis affatibus modo usi ambo fuerunt excellenter' [He means that Guido Cavalcanti ended the glory of master Guido Guinizzelli, both of whom at any rate were exceptionally skilled in rhetorical discourse]; Benvenuto da Imola, III, 313–14: 'Alter vero vocatus est Guido de Cavalcantibus de Florentia, sine comparatione excellentior eo, quia fuit magnus philosophus, de quo jam multa dicta sunt Inferni capitulo X, ubi poeta commendavit eum a scientia; hic vero commendat eum ab eloquentia [...] dicendi in lingua materna. Et hic nota, quod iste Guido, sicut et Dantes, fuit homo multum speculativus, tardiloquus, faciens subtilia et subita scommata' [The other was called Guido Cavalcanti from Florence, incomparably more exceptional than him, because he was a great philosopher, about whom many things have already been said in canto X of the *Inferno*, where the poet praised him for his knowledge; but here he praises him for his eloquence [...] in his use of his mother tongue. And he observes that this Guido, just like Dante, was a very thoughtful man, slow to speak, capable of subtle and ready taunts]; *Commento della Divina Commedia d'anonimo fiorentino*, II, 188–89: 'Similmente dice che ha tolto la fama e nominanza del dire in rima Guido Cavalcanti da Firenze a messer Guido Guinizegli da Bologna. [...] Guido Cavalcanti fu filosofo et morale et naturale, et fece assai scritti in filosofia, approvati et tenuti di grande ingegno; fu dicitore in rima, et lo stilo innovato di messer Guido Guinizzelli alzò molto, et acconciò, et ebbe di quella arte maggiore fama di lui. Fece, fondata tutta in filosofia, una canzona morale che piacque molto agl' intendenti, et fecevisi scritti per valenti uomini. Cominciò quella canzone morale: *Donna mi priega perch' io voglia dire D'uno accidente che sovente è fero, Et è si altero ch' è chiamato amore*. Fece altre canzonele, et sonetti, et ballate, fra l'altre: *In un boschetto trovai pastorella, Più che la stella bella al mio parere* etc.'; Francesco da Buti, *Commento di Francesco da Buti sopra la Divina Commedia di Dante Allighieri*, ed. by Crescentino Giannini, 3 vols (Pisa: Fratelli Nistri, 1858–62), II, 262: 'ecco che adduce l'altro esemplo, come la fama dura pongo ne la gloria del dire in rima: imperò che uno tempo durò la fama di messere Guido da Bologna, possa lie la tolse messere Guido da Fiorensa'; Iacomo della Lana, II, 1160: 'po' venne uno Guido Cavalcanti da Fiorença che disse meio del primo Guido. E cusí romaxe a questo Guido tutta la fama e del primo poco se desea'; *L'ottimo commento*, II, 188: 'ed esemplificando due Guidi, cioè messer Guido Guinizzelli da Bologna, e Guido Cavalcanti di Firenze, e' dice similemente, com' io dissi, che Giotto aveva tolta la fama della eccellenza del dipingere a Cimabue; dico, che così ha tolto Guido Cavalcanti a Guido Guinizzelli'. On Cavalcanti's poetic abilities, see also Boccaccio, *Esposizioni* X. 62 (p. 526; see n. 27 above); *Chiose cassinesi* (see n. 31 above); Benvenuto da Imola, I, 343 (see n. 29 above); *Commento della Divina Commedia d'anonimo fiorentino*, II, 429: 'pur la fama di frate Guittone tenea il campo, infino a tanto che 'l vero fu conosciuto di quelli che dissono meglio di lui. Poi questa verità fu confermata per Guido Cavalcanti, per messer Cino da Pistoja, et per Dante Alleghieri, et per molti altri valenti uomini et buoni rettorici et morali'; *L'ottimo commento*, I, 178 (see n. 25 above); Filippo Villani, p. 57 (see n. 21 above); Maramauro, p. 213 (see n. 29 above); Pietro Alighieri, *Commentarium*, second redaction: 'patris Guidonis probissimi inventoris in materna rima contemporanei ipsius Dantis' [of the father of Guido, most skilful composer in vernacular poetry and a contemporary of Dante himself], and third redaction (see n. 29). However, also contrast Iacomo della Lana, I, 335: 'Quasi a dire: Guido mio figliuolo come non fa comedia anch' elli? Qui mostra che trasse da Virgilio questa comedia, e che Guido preditto non seppe Virgilio, e però non la può fare'.

6. Dante's Guido

It goes without saying that Dante's reactions to Guido were different to those of his contemporaries, even though they were still deeply affected by the standard images of his former friend. In saying as much, I have conveniently returned to the opening premises of my chapter: the tension between the public and the personal in Dante's and, as we shall soon see, in Boccaccio's presentations of Cavalcanti. What emerges from Dante's treatment of Guido in the *Commedia* is the sense that he is systematically dismantling the main foundations upon which the *auctoritas* of his 'first friend' had been constructed, while, at the same time, establishing his own superior 'authoritativeness'. Dante's antagonism towards Cavalcanti is not simply the product of a 'private' disagreement, but emanates also from a deep preoccupation with both Guido's and his own public personae. Thus, it has been convincingly demonstrated that, in *Inferno* v, Dante calls into question Cavalcanti's philosophy of love, and hence, by extension, his status as an 'authority' on matters relating to love (Barolini, 'Dante and Cavalcanti'). Furthermore, whatever else *Inferno* x may signify, I am convinced that one of its functions is to cast doubt on certain key features of the contemporary image of Dante's 'primo amico' — an image, lest we forget, that had begun to be codified a number of years before Dante began to pen the 'sacrato poema' *(Par.* XXIII. 62). Hence, by associating Guido with Epicureanism, widely considered as among the very worst of errors and rejected by 'tutti li savi e li filosofi', Dante challenged his philosophical competence, his 'altezza d'ingegno' *(Inf.* x. 59).[55] If he had simply accused Guido of Averroism, it would have been more than likely that he would have ended up by bolstering, rather than by weakening, the philosophical standing of his 'first friend'. Averroism, which, let me repeat, was not associated with Epicureanism, was regarded in medieval intellectual circles as a highly recherché set of ideas. Furthermore, Dante openly related Cavalcanti's intellectual lapse to his 'disdainful' and arrogant character, which, when combined with the popular notion — I cite the Ottimo's words — that Epicureans believed that 'la filicità delli uomini fosse nella delettazione della carne' *(L'ottimo commento*, I, 172), effectively casts doubt on the many positive personal and social attributes with which Guido was adorned. Equally, Cavalcante's question and the pilgrim's reply can, at one level, be explained in terms of the traditions of the Cavalcantian *vitae*:

> 'Se per questo cieco
> carcere vai per altezza d'ingegno,
> mio figlio ov' è? e perché non è teco?'
>   E io a lui: 'Da me stesso non vegno:
> colui ch'attende là, per qui mi mena,
> forse cui Guido vostro ebbe a disdegno'. *(Inf.* x. 58–63)

---

55 *L'ottimo commento*, I, 172; but see the Ottimo's full condemnation of Epicureanism (pp. 172–75). See also: 'Est et alius error pessimus, non manicheorum, sed epycureorum, qui hodie regnat in multis' [And there is another extremely bad error, not of the Manicheans, but of the Epicureans, which today reigns among many]: Servasanto da Faenza, *Liber de virtutibus et vitiis*, II. 20, in Antonio Del Castello, 'La tradizione del "Liber de virtutibus et vitiis" di Servasanto da Faenza: edizione critica delle 'distinctiones' I–IV' (unpublished PhD thesis, Università degli Studi di Napoli Federico II, 2013), p. 64.

Cavalcante expresses the popular notion of the intimate bond uniting Dante and his son. Conversely, the pilgrim rejects such an idea in no uncertain terms by underlining, via reference to his new companion, all that separates him from his former friend.[56]

Dante's is a neat hatchet job. However, as a result of the strength of the myths that sustained Cavalcanti's *auctoritas*, Dante's operation remained largely unrecognized in the fourteenth century. Nevertheless, given that Epicureanism and Averroism were not synonymous, the problem remains of the grounds on which, even if invented, Dante might have based his grievous accusation of heresy against his 'first friend'. Indeed, it is clear that Dante, in line with his contemporaries, did not eccentrically believe that Epicureanism and Averroism were equivalent, since he placed Averroes in Limbo (*Inf.* IV. 144) and not in a fiery tomb.[57] At the same time, as *Purg.* XXV. 61–66 makes abundantly dear, he regarded Averroes as having been mistaken when he denied individual immortality. Yet, and this is crucial, Averroes's error had not prevented him from recanting his mistake and leading a virtuous life, as his position in Limbo eloquently attests. On the other hand, accepting Averroes's ideas if one lacked the Arab philosopher's moral rigour and self-corrective capabilities was, naturally, quite another matter. Indeed, the consequences could be disastrous. Thus, what I believe Dante attempted to do in *Inferno* X was to present Guido as an exemplum of the concrete dangers of embracing unorthodox positions on immortality by someone who did not have Averroes's ethical values and strength of character. This allowed the poet cleverly to absorb a private animosity into a general religious principle. Using the well-known Averroism of 'Donna me prega', especially in Florence, as his point of departure (several Dantists have noted allusions to the canzone in *Inferno* X), Dante implied that, between writing his canzone and the spring of 1300, Cavalcanti had undergone a fundamental ideological shift.[58] His 'first friend' had moved from Averroistic philosophical speculation about the separation of the soul from the possible intellect (*Purg.* XXV. 61–66) to the Epicureans' firm belief that 'the soul dies together with the body' (*Inf.* X. 15). This shift resulted from a weakness of the will, which inevitably had a direct impact on his behaviour. Flirting with unorthodoxy, if one lacked a compensating moral code, could lead to seriously sinful behaviour. Thus, in medieval culture, what distinguished the Averroist from the Epicurean were the ethical implications of their philosophizing. Consequently, 'epicureo e chi non crede nell'anima immortale. Ma in tutti i testi che ne parlano e sempre aggiunta la conseguenza etica e pratica di questo fatto: la dissipazione mondana' (Gorni, 'Invenzione e scrittura',

56   I have no intention of entering here into the dense debate surrounding the identity of the notorious *cui* (*Inf.* X. 63), not least because the point I am trying to make regarding the close ties that Dante wanted to establish between himself and Virgil in opposition to his supposed links with Guido is clearly expressed in lines 61–62. On the *cui* and other related cruces, see Chapter 17.

57   In this regard, Rossana Sodano makes the valid observation, rejecting the supposed medieval equation between Epicureanism and Averroism, that 'l'intelletto per Averroè è sostanza separata e immortale, ed è soltanto in quanto esso è unico per tutti gli uomini che si ha, come conseguenza, che non se ne dia sopravvivenza individuale' (p. 268, n. 198).

58   See, for instance, Luigi Surdich, 'Dante e i "corpi aerei"', in *Unità*, ed. by Silvia Zoppi Garampi (Rome: Salerno, 2014), pp. 23–44.

p. 369).[59] Indeed, while the Epicureans exploited their philosophizing to legitimate their hedonistic lifestyle, the Averroists, on the contrary, rejected baser needs and strove to achieve purely intellectual satisfaction, even if, at times, their speculations, as in the matter of the soul, could fall into error. Averroists were most certainly not Epicureans, even if, according to Dante, their philosophy, as the case of Cavalcanti seems to confirm, was not without its potential pitfalls if it were embraced by the wrong type of person. Dante's allusive account of Guido's doomed descent from Averroist thinker into practicing Epicurean is a subtle synthesis of fact, theological orthodoxy, innuendo, and personal rancour. It is a wretched portrait of human and philosophical weakness, which, for all its bias, has the powerful appearance of a divinely sanctioned 'truth'. Indeed, Cavalcanti's moral and intellectual inability properly to react to Averroes's thought dramatically undermines his supposed status as an *auctoritas*.

If, in *Inferno*, Dante goes a long way towards discrediting the common public image of Cavalcanti, it is in *Purgatorio* that he attacks the older poet from a perspective that is rather more personal (Contini, 'Cavalcanti in Dante', p. 155). As far as Dante was concerned, and regardless of *communis opinio*, Cavalcanti's reputation as a thinker never eclipsed his poetic achievements. *Purgatorio* XI is a clear sign of his sense of Guido's literary prowess and of the 'threat' that this represented to his own artistic standing:

> Cosí ha tolto l'uno a l'altro Guido
> la gloria de la lingua; e forse è nato
> chi l'uno e l'altro caccerà del nido. (*Purg.* XI. 97–99)[60]

For Dante, Cavalcanti the poet and the philosopher were intimately intertwined. By fashioning his own doctrinal poetry in *Purgatorio* XXV on a topic of serious disagreement between himself and his 'primo amico', Dante issued a challenge not just to Guido's beliefs but also to his abilities as a philosophical poet. Once again, I do not have the possibility here of developing this point further. Suffice it to say that *Purgatorio* XXV is a direct reply to 'Donna me prega'. Indeed, it is modelled on a conventional *tenzone*-like riposte *per le rime*, since about a quarter of the canto's rhymes repeat those of the canzone (Barański, '"Per similitudine di abito scientifico"', pp. 29–33, and see also pp. 38–40).[61]

7. Conclusion

There is no doubt, as many scholars have shown, that, time and again, Dante expressed a deep antipathy towards Cavalcanti.[62] Yet, it was an antipathy that

59   On the complex medieval reception of Epicurus and Epicureanism, see Chapter 3, n. 87.
60   I am not persuaded by those who argue that, when he introduced the two Guidos, Dante was referring to Guittone and Guinizzelli rather than to Guinizzelli and Cavalcanti, as this would weaken that critique of Guido the poet that I deem to be central to Dante's treatment of his 'first friend' not just in the *Commedia* but throughout his *œuvre*.
61   Chapter 15 further examines Dante's contrived transformation of Guido into an unorthodox, and hence seriously flawed thinker.
62   Nonetheless, it is important to remember that Dante was not alone in being irked by Cavalcanti,

overflowed the private to flood the public spaces of late-medieval Italian culture. When Boccaccio wrote *Decameron* VI. 9, he was conscious not just of Cavalcanti's 'authoritative' status, but also of Dante's efforts to undermine the older poet's *auctoritas*. His short story too is in part made up of elements drawn from the Cavalcantian *vitae*. We thus find mention, *inter alia*, of the *loico*'s great intellectual and personal gifts, his uniqueness, and his aloofness. These are precisely the elements that Dante had called into doubt or presented negatively in *Inferno* X. As he did with the tombs of the heretics, Boccaccio reappropriated such components of the Cavalcantian persona and re-presented them in a positive light, publicly reaffirming, and against Dante, Guido's standing as an *auctoritas*. He similarly discredited the idea that Cavalcanti was tainted with Epicureanism, and hence that he lacked philosophical acumen, by imputing such an opinion to the 'gente volgare' *(Dec.* VI. 9. 9), thereby, removing the possibility that such a view could be ascribed to Dante. We have an interesting instance here whereby Boccaccio is both personally criticizing Dante and protecting the poet from the potential criticisms of others (see Chapter 15 for an in-depth analysis of these matters).

There is, of course, much more to *Decameron* VI. 9 than merely a statement regarding Cavalcanti's *auctoritas*. However, as in Dante's portrait of Guido, so, too, in Boccaccio's, it is the interplay between the private and the public that enriches our understanding of the two texts, of their authors, and, naturally, of Cavalcanti's impressive first *fortuna*. Admiring Guido, which has been such a feature of his modern critical reception, thus finds its roots not just in the poet's independent intellectual rigour and in the formal 'perfection' of his best verses, but also in the reactions of his contemporaries. We may grant Cavalcanti a position of privilege in our scholarly endeavours; his first readers, for their part, by raising him to the rank of an *auctoritas*, granted him rather more: a unique place both in their culture and in their lives.[63] However much Dante may have strained against his being

even if his negative feelings appear to have been more deeply ingrained and longer-lasting than those of others who came into contact with the 'great logician'. Thus, Cino, too, reacted with annoyance towards Guido in his ironic yet firm sonnet 'Qua' son le cose vostre ch'io vi tolgo' (in Cavalcanti, *Rime*, pp. 215–17). In addition, it is clear that for all his 'authoritativeness', or better, because of it, Cavalcanti not only inspired respect in others but also a certain degree of ridicule, as is clear from the sonnets addressed to him by Lapo Farinata degli Uberti, Guido Orlandi, and Niccola Muscia. Cecco Angiolieri, too, in several of his sonnets, pokes fun at Guido's views on love by treating them from the perspective of the 'low' register; see Fabian Alfie, *Comedy and Culture: Cecco Angiolieri's Poetry and Late Medieval Society* (Leeds: Northern Universities Press, 2001), pp. 68–72. Interestingly, such debunkings would appear to be further evidence of Cavalcanti's standing as an *auctoritas*, since it was a longstanding cultural commonplace comically to undermine great men (Sacchetti's *novella* clearly belongs to this tradition). Revealingly, in Compagni's *Cronica* I. 20, we find Corso Donati giving vent to his 'hatred' of Cavalcanti through the medium of mockery: 'Cominciò per questo l'odio a multiplicare; e messer Corso [...] chiamava Guido Cavicchia' (p. 54).

63   In order better both to comprehend and to define the nature of Cavalcanti's standing as an *auctoritas*, it will be necessary to compare his medieval presentation to that of other vernacular poets, in particular Guittone and Guinizzelli. It is also important to measure his treatment against that of the great classical, Scriptural, and Christian 'authorities' (see Chapter 15, pp. 496–507 & 515–25). In this respect, it is interesting to note that I have found only one instance, and this a late one, of the term *auctoritas* being explicitly linked to Guido: 'fuit homo sane diligens et speculativus, atque

coupled with his erstwhile friend, and however much he may have striven to lodge all contemporary 'authority' in himself, we, his readers across the centuries, have steadfastly refused to allow him to break away from his 'primo amico'. There is, in fact, something more than fitting that medieval Italy's two outstanding vernacular 'authorities' — whose 'authoritativeness' is a mark of a world that was rapidly changing — should, despite their ceaseless struggling, have remained so fatefully intertwined.

auctoritatis non contemnendae in physicis' [was a very diligent and thoughtful man, and of no little authority in natural philosophy]: Filippo Villani, p. 57 (see n. 21 above). Despite according him many of the trappings of an 'authority', the thirteenth and fourteenth centuries, mindful of the weight of tradition, were still wary of openly granting him the tag. It was only at the end of the Trecento, when Guido's 'authoritativeness' had become deeply embedded in Italian culture, that Filippo Villani had the confidence to do this.

CHAPTER 14

The Ethics of Ignorance:
Petrarch's Epicurus and Averroes
and the Structures of
De sui ipsius et multorum ignorantia

1. Averroes the Epicurean?

One might imagine, from the chapter's title, that its aim, in keeping with much Italian literary scholarship on the Middle Ages, especially of the kind practised by scholars of Dante, is to suggest that Petrarch, like other *medievali*, took advantage of the commonplace whereby the two philosophers were yoked together as a result of their overlapping views on the immortality of the soul. In truth, nothing could be further from its purpose, given that, despite the many assertions to the contrary, there is no documentary evidence — with one notable exception to which I shall shortly return — to support the contention that, to cite the words of one of the most eminent supporters of the traditional view regarding the medieval synthesis of Epicureanism and Averroism:

> Il vocabolo 'epicureo' è applicabile a qualsiasi posizione filosofica che metta in dubbio l'immortalità dell'anima e, a maggior ragione, all'aristotelismo radicale che ha fra i suoi temi fondamentali quello, averroista in senso stretto, dell'esistenza di un intelletto universale e 'perpetuo', 'sostanza separata', con la conseguente negazione della sopravvivenza di un'anima individuale.[1]

I have arrived at this conclusion after consulting a significant and varied array of authors from Bonaventure to Thomas Aquinas, from Albertus Magnus to Ramon Llull, and from Brunetto Latini to Giles of Rome, as well as a host of others.[2] Indeed,

---

1   Maria Corti, *Dante a un nuovo crocevia* (Florence: Libreria Commissionaria Sansoni, 1981), pp. 81–82.

2   I have also been encouraged to insist on the untenability of this claim by the observation of an eminent historian of medieval thought: 'Il tentativo di Maria Corti [...] di far corrispondere all'accusa generica di epicureismo, rivolta a Guido [da Dante], specifiche dottrine averroiste e aristotelico-radicali è certamente interessante, ma dovrebbe essere approfondito con riscontri più puntuali, che allo stato attuale degli studi non è possibile': Francesco Bottin, 'Introduzione', in *Ricerca della felicità e piaceri dell'intelletto. Boezio di Dacia, 'Il sommo bene', Giacomo da Pistoia, 'La felicità suprema'* (Florence: Nardini Editore, 1989), pp. 7–41 (p. 35). See also Ilario Anzani, *Cavalcanti in Boccaccio: per un'interpretazione critica di 'Decameron' VI, 9*, Lizenziatsarbeit der philosophischen Fakultät der

I have so far come across just two passages where the names of Epicurus and Averroes are simply in close proximity to each other.[3] In both instances, they are introduced as part of a much longer list of thinkers who have contributed to the debate on the nature of the human intellect and soul; and they do this without establishing any particular links between Epicurus and Averroes. In the first of these, Albert the Great's *De quindecim problematibus*, the renowned Doctor carefully distinguishes between the 'Graeci sapientes' [learned Greeks] and the 'Arabum philosophi' [Arab philosophers], recognizing both their historical and cultural differences and their ideological points of contact, while dedicating a discrete sentence to each group.[4]

Universität Zürich, May 2002, pp. 46–49; Luca Bianchi, *Il vescovo e i filosofi: la condanna parigina del 1277 e l'evoluzione dell'aristotelismo scolastico* (Bergamo: Lubrina, 1990), pp. 154–55; Ernesto G. Parodi, 'La miscredenza di Guido Cavalcanti e una fonte del Boccaccio', *Bullettino della Società dantesca italiana*, n.s. 22 (1915), 37–47 (pp. 37–40).

3   The three passages from Albertus Magnus (*De natura et origine animae* II. 5. 30–35 and 11. 45–52; *De anima* I. 1. 8) and the one from Jacobus de Benevento (*De praeambulis ad judicium*, in Thomas Aquinas, *Opera omnia*, XVII, 456) that George Corbett puts forward as possibly linking the two traditions neither openly associate the two pagan mortalist philosophers nor actually mention them together. In any case, Corbett himself concludes that 'there is [...] little evidence [...] that the Averroistic position on the soul was conveniently identified with Epicureanism in the scholastic milieux of the thirteenth century': George Corbett, *Dante and Epicurus: A Dualistic Vision of Secular and Spiritual Fulfilment* (Leeds: Legenda, 2013), pp. 17–18. Corbett's is the best discussion I know of Dante's complex treatment of Epicurus and Epicureanism.

4   Albertus Magnus, *De XV problematibus*, I, 32, 62–71: 'Hoc igitur omnium Peripateticorum antiqua est positio, secundum quod eam Alfarabius determinavit. Ex qua sequitur intellectum possibilem intelligibilium omnium esse speciem et non omnino potentiam esse materialem ad ipsa [*sic*]. Et quia ad philosophos loquimur, qui talibus perfecte debent esse instructi, his amplius non insistimus. || Post hos Graeci sapientes, Porphyrius scilicet et Eustratius, Aspasius et Michael Ephesius et quam plures alii venerunt praeter Alexandrum, qui Epicuro consentit, qui omnes intellectum hominis intellectum possessum et non de natura intelligentiae existentem esse dixerunt. Et quem Graeci sapientes possessum, eundem Arabum philosophi Avicenna, Averroes, Abubacher et quidam alii esse dicebant, quia id quod possessum est, aliud est et alterius naturae a possidente' [This then is the long-standing position of all Peripatetics, as Alfarabi determined it. From it results that the possible intellect is the species of all intelligibles and it is not entirely in material potency in regard thereto. And since we are speaking to philosophers, who must be perfectly instructed on these topics, we shall not insist on this any further. || After these came the learned Greeks, namely, Porphyry and Eustratius [of Nicaea], Aspasius and Michael of Ephesus, and how many more came after Alexander [of Aphrodisias] — who agrees with Epicurus — who all said that the human intellect is an *intellectus possessus* and not dependent upon the nature of intelligence. And what the learned Greeks call *possessus*, is the same as what the Arab philosophers Avicenna, Averroes, A[l]bubacher [Abū Bakr ibn Bāgga] and certain others call *adeptus*, because what is owned is something different and of a different nature from the owner]. The terms *possessus* and *adeptus* require clarification: '"Possessus" is, according to Albert, a term peculiar to the Greek philosophical tradition. However, Albert makes it clear that the term "possessus" employed by the Greeks has the same meaning as the term "adeptus" used by Arabic philosophers in regard to the same status of the human intellect. Both terms, "possessus" and "adeptus", refer to one and the same idea: that which is "possessus" is other and different in nature from the subject possessing this or that disposition (*aliud est et alterius naturae a possidente*)': Michele Trizio, '"Qui fere in hoc sensu exponunt Aristotelem": Notes on the Byzantine Sources of the Albertinian Notion of "Intellectus Possessus"', quoted from: <https://www.academia.edu/1520547/_Qui_fere_in_hoc_sensu_exponunt_Aristotelem_._Notes_on_the_Byzantine_Sources_of_the_Albertinian_Notion_of_Intellectus_Possessus_> p. 4 [accessed 21 August 2019]. What is most important for my present discussion is that the point on which

In the second, Petrarch, in Book II of the *Invective contra medicum*, does something similar. Reproducing the secret irreligious musings of his opponent, he has his *stultus* catalogue those who have made differing and contradictory interventions on the soul. While 'Epycurus', who 'mortalem animam [facit]' [considers the soul to be mortal], is simply one among many holding — in Christian terms — eccentric views on the soul, Averroes is deliberately set apart from this larger group: 'fuit et qui mirabilius quiddam dicere auderet, siquidem unitatem intellectus attulit dux noster Averrois' [there was also someone who dared to state something more extraordinary, if indeed our master Averroes upheld the unity of the intellect].[5] As I shall shortly examine, Petrarch's 'extreme' presentation of the Arab commentator — he who '[Cristum] diffamavit impune' [he who insulted Christ with impunity] (*Invective*, p. 878) — was driven by a highly personalized antipathy. Yet, despite this, his treatment of Averroes can also serve to confirm my general point that no special ties united the Arab philosopher to Epicurus in the Middle Ages. It was only Dante, specifically the Dante of the *Commedia*, who suggested that, among the many who have held dubious opinions regarding the individual soul, a privileged kinship marks the speculations of Epicurus and Averroes.

It should immediately be stressed that Dante did no more than imply this affinity, and that, in addition, he essentially restricted it to one, in his eyes, deeply problematic contemporary individual. That individual, of course, is Guido Cavalcanti, whom Dante first tangentially numbered among Epicurus's 'seguaci, | che l'anima col corpo morta fanno' (*Inf.* x. 14–15), and then, many cantos later, even more obliquely, through repeated allusions to 'Donna me prega' in Statius's lecture on the immortality of the soul in *Purgatorio* xxv, he associated with Averroes, the 'savio' who 'fé disgiunto | da l'anima il possibile intelletto' (63–65).[6] This is all that we have to substantiate that now unquestioned truism that, in the Middle Ages, Epicurus and Averroes had become synonymous — the highly subjective, polemical, opportunistic insinuation of a poet keen to destroy a rival's reputation as 'un de' miglior loici che avesse il mondo e ottimo filosofo naturale' (*Dec.* VI. 9. 8), as Boccaccio put it in the *Decameron* echoing a well-established tradition.[7] As is typical of him, Dante's elusive rapprochement between past and present thinkers is more than well made: both pagan philosophers do deny the immortality of the

Epicurus, Averroes, and many other Greek and Arab thinkers agree has nothing to do with the immortality of the individual soul.

5   Francesco Petrarca, *Invective contra medicum*, in Francesco Petrarca, *Opere latine*, ed. by Antonietta Bufano, 2 vols (Turin: UTET, 1975), II, 818–980 (pp. 876–78). Citations from Petrarch's other works not listed in 'Abbreviations and Editions' are to the following editions: *Bucolicum carmen*, ed. by Luca Canali (San Cesario di Lecce: Manni, 2005); *De otio religioso*, in Petrarca, *Opere latine*, I, 568–808; *De remediis utriusque fortune*, ed. by Christophe Carraud, 2 vols (Grenoble: Editions Jérôme Millon, 2002); *De vita solitaria*, in Petrarca, *Opere latine*, I, 262–564; *Sine titulo*, in *Opera quae extant omnia* (Basel: Henrichus Petri, 1554).

6   See Chapters 13, 15, and 17, as well as Zygmunt G. Barański, '"Per similitudine di abito scientifico": Dante, Cavalcanti, and the Sources of Medieval "Philosophical" Poetry', in *Science and Literature in Italian Culture: From Dante to Calvino. A Festschrift for Pat Boyde*, ed. by Pierpaolo Antonello and Simon Gilson (Oxford: Legenda, 2004), pp. 14–52 (pp. 29–33).

7   On Guido's reputation in the Middle Ages as a major philosopher, see Chapter 13, pp. 458–60.

individual soul, while Cavalcanti, regardless of how we interpret his great canzone, undoubtedly did have good and public contacts with Bolognese and Tuscan Averroistic circles. Yet all this in no way changes the fact that Dante's equation is not just idiosyncratic and self-serving, but is also no more than lightly, even slyly, adumbrated. That, over time, it should have become so canonical as to become assigned to a whole culture — despite the fact that it failed to register with any of Dante's fourteenth-century readers, just as most of them failed to realize that the poet was accusing his 'primo amico' of being a heretic and an Epicurean (see Chapter 13, pp. 454–55) — is obvious testimony to the power and longevity of Dante's 'authority'. At the same time, we should not permit the equation's modern, and so thoroughly anachronistic, canonicity to mask its status, in the Middle Ages, as a subtle, though eccentric smear.

2. 'Titulus [...] stupendus'[8]

It goes without saying that a historically informed idea of the medieval reception of Epicurus and Averroes helps us better appreciate Petrarch's attitude towards both philosophers, and hence their functions in his *œuvre*, starting with the *De ignorantia*, which, begun in 1367, and hence less than ten years before his death in 1374, stands as the poet's major summative statement of his ideological sympathies and aversions. Indeed, by using Epicurus and Averroes as my touchstones, I hope to be able to say something about the status, function, and character of Petrarch's investigation of 'ignorance', as well as about his views on the intellectual life.[9] The book's title is an appropriate place where to begin my analysis of the 'libellus exiguus' [paltry little book] (*De ign.* VI. 195); and this is the first of the work's overarching structures that I assess during the course of this chapter.[10] What is immediately striking about the title, *De sui ipsius et multorum ignorantia*, is that the text does not explicitly define itself as a polemic — the genre to which a far from insignificant part of Petrarch scholarship would like to assign it. In fact, its *titulus* recalls nothing as much as that tradition of works which, from Roman times, had investigated a specific issue, and which, with the proliferation of *quaestiones*, had become especially popular

8   On difficulties raised by the invective's title, as well as its cultural density, see Christophe Carraud, 'Notes, remarques sur le titre', in Petrarch, *Mon ignorance et celle de tant d'autres*, trans. by Juliette Bertrand, rev. by Christophe Carraud (Grenoble: Editions Jérôme Millon, 2000), pp. 219–27.
9   The best general analysis of the *De ignorantia* is Enrico Fenzi, 'Introduzione', in *De ign.*, pp. 5–104. See also William J. Kennedy, 'The Economy of Invective and a Man in the Middle (*De sui ipsius et multorum ignorantia*)', in *Petrarch: A Critical Guide to the Complete Works*, ed. by Victoria Kirkham and Armando Maggi (Chicago and London: University of Chicago Press, 2009), pp. 263–73; Christian Trottmann, 'Pétrarque à la fracture de la philosophie dans le *De sui ipsius et multorum ignorantia*', in *Ut philosophia poesis: questions philosophiques dans l'œuvre de Dante, Pétrarque, Boccace*, ed. by Joël Biard and Fosca Mariani Zini (Paris: Vrin, 2008), pp. 171–90, and 'Philosophie, médecine et rhétorique dans l'*Invective contre un médecin* et le *De suis ipsius et multorum ignorantia*', in *Frontières des savoirs en Italie à l'époque des premières universités (xiii–xv siècles)*, ed. by Joël Chandelier and Aurélien Robert (Rome: École française de Rome, 2015), pp. 351–85. See also Francesco Bausi, *Petrarca antimoderno* (Florence: Cesati, 2008), pp. 109–29 & 193–224.
10   In the dedicatory epistle to Donato Albanzani, Petrarch describes his work as *liber parvus* [little book]: *De ign.*, pp. 172–75 (p. 172).

in scholastic circles. It presents itself as a text 'on ignorance', a fact confirmed not just by its evaluation of a rich variety of different forms of *ignorantia*, from *stultitia* [foolishness] to *inscitia* [inexperience] and from *sine literis* [illiteracy] to *insania* [insanity], but also by its investigation of ignorance's equally multifaceted opposite — wisdom. In fact, Petrarch himself, towards the end of the book, nudges us in this direction, suggesting that his 'libellus exiguus' might serve as a first tentative step towards a much grander work on ignorance, which, given the condition's ubiquity, would be made up of 'ingentes [...] libri' [substantial books] (VI. 195). Petrarch goes further in these closing paragraphs. He explicitly, albeit partially, associates his title with Marcus Antonius's lost *De sua ebrietate*, which examined *ebriositatis vitium*: 'Videri autem prima fronte potuerit *De mei ipsius ignorantia*, nisi aliud addidissem, novus libri titulus, non stupendus tamen ad memoriam revocanti ut de ebrietate sua librum scripsit Antonius triumvir' [Had I not added anything else, the title *On My Own Ignorance* might appear new at first sight, however it would not be impressive for someone who recalls that the triumvir Antonius wrote a book on his drunkenness] (VI. 196). The association and contrast which Petrarch drew between his own book and the triumvir's are instructive — not so much as regards their specific relationship, but, more suggestively, as regards that between the *De sui ipsius et multorum ignorantia* and the contemporary obsession with logically structured *quaestiones* on a wide and seemingly randomly chosen range of subjects. By introducing himself into the title, Petrarch acknowledged the subjective nature of his presentation in stark opposition to the 'pseudo-scientific' investigations of his detested scholastics. At the same time, by transforming the original first-person pronoun into a third-person one, he attempted to delimit somewhat the personalized thrust of his work, implying instead that 'his own ignorance' had more general, exemplary connotations; and Petrarch confirmed this generalizing ambition by associating himself with the 'many others' who share and have shared his same state. Indeed, against the abstracting and theorizing analyses of the blinkered mass of the *aristotelici*, namely, against the 'peregrinorum dogmatum ventoseque disputationis improbitas' [depravity of strange doctrines and of bombastic disputation] (IV. 126), his assessment of ignorance makes it obvious that its focus is real people, beginning with himself. His work is born from experience and examines ignorance in history (and, simply by taking this latter purview, Petrarch straight away lets us know that he is not 'sine literis').[11] His book is the precise opposite of the useless prattlings of those who 'tumentes inauditis ambagibus [...], quod cum nichil sciant, profiteri omnia et clamare de omnibus didicerunt' [swelling with unheard-of sophistries [...], even though they know nothing, have learned to lecture on any subject and to boast about everything] (IV. 124). More than anything, his *liber*, by concentrating on people's lives, will take an ethical and not a 'scientific' approach to ignorance.

---

11   The primary overt stimulus for the *De ignorantia* is the accusation made by four Aristotelian intellectuals, friends of the poet, that, despite his reputation as a man of culture, he is in fact 'sine literis virum bonum' [a good man lacking in learning] (II. 32; and see 16 & 38). One of the treatise's main aims is to debunk the charge of ignorance while confirming that its author is indeed 'good'. On the Scripturally positive connotations of the description, see Carraud's annotations, pp. 247–48.

The primary polemical intent of the *De ignorantia* is here: in its opposition not so much to the four false friends — though, of course, in its pages, Petrarch also mercilessly unmasks their perfidious stupidity and envy as he 'confesses' his own ignorance — but to an entire system and method of thought and to an ethics, or rather, a lack of ethics, of what it means to be an intellectual and more generally a human being.[12] Just because Petrarch fails to term his work an *invectiva*, this does not mean that it has no controversial ambitions. Quite the contrary, in fact. Nevertheless, as its title so effectively reveals, the aim of the *De sui ipsius et multorum ignorantia* is not so much to polemicize but to demonstrate an alternative mode of argumentation, and thus of life, to the empty, futile syllogizing and sinfulness of the 'ceci ac surdi' [blind and deaf] (IV. 116). As his choice of *stupendus* to talk about his *titulus* would seem to suggest, Petrarch, despite all the formulas of humility with which he circumscribed his text, was also keen to emphasize its 'extraordinariness', namely its 'unusualness' and 'novelty', both attributes which can be appreciated only in terms of the typical argumentative forms of his contemporaries. Rejecting all pretensions to 'scientificity', the *De ignorantia*'s ideological 'uniqueness' is to be sought in its reliance on both the particular — and specifically the subjective — and the general, on both the history of the individual and that of the community, and on the strains that arise and the bonds that are created between any two coupled elements and within each of them, as well as, naturally, all that might distinguish and unite ignorance and non-ignorance.

As I shall go on to argue, Petrarch's recourse both to relativized contrastive structures and to relational comparisons — closely complementary devices, among several such, emblematically captured in the tension and the ties between 'sui ipsius' and 'multorum' — is what most characteristically defines the *De ignorantia* and formally distinguishes it from the bogus procedures of the 'false philosophers' (IV. 137–38). It is important to recognize the highly relativized character of what it means to be human in Petrarch's ontology — a fact that the poet himself stresses frequently and explicitly as occurs, for instance, in the *Seniles*: 'siquidem actus idem pro intentione agentis nunc laudabilis nunc infamis est' [for indeed an act itself is now praiseworthy now disreputable according to the agent's intention] (V. 2. 50). Relativism is inescapable on account of the fundamental instability and limitations of the human, especially before the mysterious absoluteness of the divine, where ultimately all earthly relativism finds its resolution. It was the scholastics' absurd behaviour in following a human *auctoritas* who they maintained was all-knowing and above error, and in trusting blindly in a philosophical method that presumed to be able to establish 'truths', that Petrarch, with his profound faith in divine providence, found entirely unacceptable.[13] He thus organized his own thinking in

---

12   On Petrarch's opinion of contemporary intellectual life, see *De ignorantia* II. 13–16, 22–38. By aiming to analyse the *De ignorantia* in relation to specific contemporary historical figures, places, and institutions, Kennedy, in his useful article, downplays the treatise's generalizing and summative scope.

13   On Petrarch's attitude to contemporary scholastic culture, see Olivier Boulnois, 'Scolastique et humanisme: Pétrarque et la croisée des ignorances', in Petrarch, *Mon ignorance et celle de tant d'autres*, pp. 5–43; Eugenio Garin, 'La cultura fiorentina nella seconda metà del 300 e i "barbari britanni"',

such a manner that it could constitute a candid declaration both that divergence and relativism are inescapable, and that no logical sleight of hand can ever hope to conceal this fact. Furthermore, by relying so heavily on something as potentially volatile as contrast and the duality of things, Petrarch was able to grant a distinctiveness to the style of his critical discourse which dramatically and iconically, and hence more than conveniently, distinguished his eloquence from the arid 'scientific' prose of his adversaries. Indeed, Petrarch's recourse to contrast and binarism stands in stark opposition to the scholastics' reliance on the syllogism — the discrete structures of the former openly challenge the deceptive structural coherence of the latter.[14]

3. Petrarch and Epicurus

The functions and standing of Epicurus and Averroes — like those of every other historical personage mentioned in the *De ignorantia* — are controlled by those broad structures and concerns that the book's title so effectively, even if allusively, evokes. In addition, the philosophers' status in the *liber parvus* is further circumscribed by the lineaments that both had acquired in Petrarch's *œuvre* and thought in the years before he started to pen his remarkably erudite, wide-ranging, and sophisticated contribution 'on ignorance' in 1367. The case of Epicurus is particularly indicative of this state of affairs.

Another largely unsatisfactory critical commonplace has until recently distorted our understanding of Petrarch's attitude to Epicurus. In keeping with his 'proto-humanistic' profile, Petrarch's treatment of the Greek philosopher was deemed to introduce, in opposition to medieval distortion, a new, better-balanced, and historically more nuanced appreciation of Epicurus, which, in subsequent centuries, would become the norm.[15] It is certainly the case that Epicurus is a figure of some prominence in Petrarch's writings and is present at some crucial junctures in his *œuvre*,[16] perhaps most notably, even if not acknowledged by name, in the

---

Rassegna della letteratura italiana, 64 (1960), 181–95, and 'Petrarca e la polemica con i "moderni"', in his *Rinascite e rivoluzioni* (Rome and Bari: Laterza, 1975), pp. 71–88; Pietro Paolo Gerosa, *Umanesimo cristiano di Petrarca* (Turin: Bottega d'Erasmo, 1966), pp. 181–223; Robert E. Lerner, 'Petrarch's Coolness Toward Dante: A Conflict of "Humanisms"', in *Intellectuals and Writers in Fourteenth Century Europe*, ed. by Piero Boitani and Anna Torti (Cambridge: Brewer, 1986), pp. 204–25; David Lummus, 'Boccaccio's Hellenism and the Foundations of Modernity', *Mediaevalia*, 33 (2012), 101–67 (pp. 120–23, 130–33); Giuseppe Mazzotta, *The Worlds of Petrarch* (Durham, NC, and London: Duke University Press, 1993), *passim*; Cesare Vasoli, 'Intorno al Petrarca ed ai logici "moderni"', in *Antiqui und Moderni: Traditionsbewusstsein und Fortschrittsbewusstsein im späten Mittelalter*, ed. by Albert Zimmermann (Berlin and New York: de Gruyter, 1974), pp. 142–54, and 'Petrarca e i filosofi del suo tempo', *Quaderni petrarcheschi*, 9–10 (1992–93), 75–92.

14   On Petrarch's extremely negative attitude to the syllogism, see *Invective*, pp. 876 & 880–82.

15   See for instance, Giuseppe Saitta, 'La rivendicazione di Epicuro nell'Umanesimo', in *Filosofia italiana e Umanesimo* (Venice: 'La Nuova Italia' Editrice, 1928), pp. 55–82 (pp. 55–57). On Petrarch and Epicurus, see also Mazzotta, pp. 38–39, 43, 55, 89, 160; Maria Rita Pagnoni, 'Prime note sulla tradizione medievale ed umanistica di Epicuro', *Annali della Scuola Normale Superiore di Pisa. Classe di Lettere e Filosofia*, ser. 3, 4 (1974), 1443–77 (pp. 1455–57). See n. 20 for a brief discussion of the likely sources of Petrarch's knowledge of Epicurus.

16   For Petrarch's references to Epicurus, see *De ign.* II. 18, IV. 113–14, 127–29, VI. 212; *De otio*, pp. 776–78; *De rem.* I. 12. 22, 18. 10 & 18, 69. 38, II. 10. 16, 40. 6, 53. 10, 114. 36; *Fam.* I. 1. 20, 2. 17, 8. 3,

Prologue of the *Secretum*, where he finds himself sharing a privileged stage with such luminaries as Virgil, Seneca, Augustine, Boethius, and Dante.[17] At the same time, there is nothing in what Petrarch said about Epicurus or the kind of contexts into which he introduced him to distinguish the poet's position from the ways in which the Middle Ages had long considered the philosopher.[18] At most, what can be sustained is that Petrarch's *œuvre* may serve as a handy *summa* of what the Middle Ages knew and thought about Epicurus. This is not surprising. On the one hand, Petrarch drew for his knowledge of the Greek philosopher from the same authors — Cicero, Horace, Seneca, Lactantius, Augustine, and John of Salisbury[19] — as generations of intellectuals had done before him.[20] On the other hand, he was also

---

III. 6. 1 & 3–4, IV. 3. 6, VIII. 4. 3, 7. 22, IX. 8. 3, X. 3. 48–49, XII. 8. 8, XVIII. 9. 2, XXIV. 4. 3; *Invective*, pp. 876–78, 904; *Rer. mem.* III. 51. 1, 77, 79, IV. 22. 3; *Sen.* II. 1. 117–18, XIV. 1. 161, XV. 3. 34, 38; *Tr. fam.* III. 106–09, IIa. 34–36; *Vita solit.* p. 324. In *Bucolicum carmen* VI and VII, we find the character Epy who functions as a Petrarchan adaptation of the tradition which depicted Epicurus as a wanton seeker after pleasure.

17   On the complex web of references that structure the *Prohemium* to the *Secretum*, see Enrico Fenzi's notes in Petrarca, *Secretum*, p. 287.

18   On medieval attitudes to Epicurus and Epicureanism, see Corbett; Tullio De Mauro, 'Porci in Paradiso, un motivo epicureo in Dante, *Par.* XXVI, 124–38', in *L'occhio e la memoria: miscellanea di studi in onore di Natale Tedesco*, 2 vols (Milan: Lussografica, 2004), I, 59–70; Michael Erler, '"Et quatenus de commutatione terrenorum bonorum cum divinis agimus...": Epikureische Diesseitigkeit und christliche Auferstehung bei Augustinus und Lorenzo Valla', in *Abwägende Vernunft*, ed. by Franz-Josef Bormann and Christian Schröer (Berlin and New York: De Gruyter, 2004), pp. 78–90; Eugenio Garin, 'Ricerche sull'epicureismo nel Quattrocento', in his *La cultura filosofica del Rinascimento italiano: ricerche e documenti* (Milan: Sansoni, 1994), pp. 72–92; Howard Jones, *The Epicurean Tradition* (London and New York: Routledge, 1989); Richard I. Jungkuntz, 'Christian Approval of Epicureanism', *Church History*, 31 (1962), 279–93; Valerio Lucchesi, 'Epicurus and Democritus: The Ciceronian Foundations of Dante's Judgement', *Italian Studies*, 42 (1987), 1–19; Simone Marchesi, '"Epicuri de grege porcus": Ciacco, Epicurus and Isidore of Seville', *Dante Studies*, 117 (1999), 117–31; Joseph A. Mazzeo, 'Dante and Epicurus: The Making of a Type', in his *Medieval Cultural Tradition in Dante's 'Comedy'* (Ithaca, NY: Cornell University Press 1960), pp. 174–204; Alexander Murray, 'The Epicureans', in Boitani and Torti, pp. 138–63; Pagnoni; Ilaria Ramelli, 'The Rejection of the Epicurean Ideal of Pleasure in Late Antique Sources: Not Only Misunderstandings', *Mirabilia*, 18 (2014), 6–21; Giovanni Santinello, 'Storia della filosofia e storia dei filosofi: il commento di Alberto al libro I della *Metafisica*', *Medioevo*, 16 (1990), 43–70; Wolfgang Schmid, *Epicuro e l'epicureismo cristiano* (Brescia: Paideia, 1984). See also Chapters 15, 16, and 17.

19   The key role that John of Salisbury played in Petrarch's career is clear evidence that the poet's attack against the *barbari britanni* (see Garin, 'La cultura fiorentina') was not conditioned by their place of origin but by their intellectual sympathies and methods. Indeed, John's critique of his world in the *Policraticus* has many points of contact with Petrarch's similarly negative assessment of his own society in the *De ignorantia*.

20   Although Fenzi has persuasively demonstrated the extensive influence of the *De natura deorum* on the *De ignorantia*: Enrico Fenzi, 'Nota al testo', in *De ign.*, pp. 105–27 (pp. 121–27)), and specifically on Petrarch's presentation of Epicurus (notes to *De ign.* pp. 423, 432, 530–31), Cicero's work is far from being the poet's only major source on the Greek philosopher either in the treatise or elsewhere. Indeed, in Petrarch's *œuvre*, the *De finibus* probably exerted greater sway on his view of Epicurus than did the *De natura deorum*. In any case, Petrarch's Epicurus is a composite figure made up of elements taken from Seneca's *Letters to Lucilius*, Horace's poetry, Lactantius's *Institutions*, a broad swathe of Augustine's writings, Scriptural exegesis, John of Salisbury's *Policraticus*, and a wealth of other texts given Epicurus's ubiquity in late-medieval culture. Considerable research still needs to be done to establish the texts that lie behind each of Petrarch's explicit references to the classical philosopher. Furthermore, as in the Prologue to the *Secretum*, Petrarch alluded indirectly to Epicurus. In rewriting

heir to popular perceptions of the philosopher. While such views were exclusively negative and largely restricted to Epicurus's porcine wallowing in pleasure, the educated had frequently attempted to distinguish between the positive and the negative in the philosopher's thought and behaviour, even if their academic sense of the negative was inescapably in part affected by popular clichés. Petrarch's position was exactly the same, as is immediately obvious from the major assessment of Epicurus he undertook in Book III of the *Rerum memorandarum*. The Greek is both the proponent of that 'Effeminatum dogma [...] et infame, inter hominem et pecudem nullum statuens discrimen' [Effeminate [...] and dishonourable doctrine, which establishes that there is no difference between man and beast] (III. 77. 1), and the source of 'tam multa [...] et consulta sapienter et dicta suaviter, ut eis Seneca, tantus vir, epystolas suas et farciat et exornet' [so many [...] wise reflections and elegant words, that with these Seneca, such great a man, filled and adorned his own epistles] (III. 77. 2). What is significant, therefore, as regards Petrarch's relationship to the Greek philosopher, is not so much what he says about him but the reasons why he chose to make such regular recourse to him. At the most basic level, he did this because two of his key intellectual mentors, Cicero and Seneca, had done this. Equally, the 'magnifice voces Epycuri' [Epicurus's noble thoughts] (*Rer. mem.* III. 77. 18) that he was able to read in their texts served to amplify his knowledge of classical, and specifically, Greek culture. However, I should like to suggest that the principal reason why Petrarch returned with such regularity to Epicurus was because he so emblematically and perfectly embodied that contrastive, relativized, and relational dualistic model which, I believe, the poet judged to be an especially efficacious argumentative and rhetorical tool, because it so tellingly captured our human condition. Thus, the explicit of his analysis of Epicurus in the *Rerum memorandarum* freezes the philosopher in just this state of ambivalence, as the incarnation — and the term Petrarch utilized is more than revelatory — of 'una [...] regula': 'sententia placet, auctor displicet. Quamvis enim "illum" ut ait Cicero, "et bonum virum et comem et humanum fuisse" nemo neget, bonum tamen philosophum nullus affirmat' [a [...] rule: the ideas please, the author displeases. For although nobody denies that 'he', as Cicero says, 'was a good, friendly, and compassionate man', no one claims that he was a good philosopher] (III. 77. 18).

Although the *De ignorantia* does not contain an appraisal of Epicurus on the lines of that presented in the *Rerum memorandarum*, it is Petrarch's work that, along its length, includes the most interesting and wide-ranging treatment of the Greek thinker. Within the first few paragraphs, Petrarch fixes him once again in his emblematic pose: 'quod de Epycuro sentit Cicero, cuius cum multis in locis mores atque animum probet, ubique damnat ingenium ac doctrinam respuit' [what Cicero feels about Epicurus: although in many passages he praises his behaviour and his spirit, he always condemns his intellectual attitude and rejects his doctrine] (II. 18). The measured manner in which Petrarch approaches the philosopher is

passages that mention the Greek, he eliminated his name while maintaining the substance of the original text. As far as I am aware, almost no effort has been made to catalogue and study these instances of Petrarchan *imitatio*. The history of Petrarch's relationship to Epicurus is far from being written. This chapter is no more than a minor contribution to such a project.

underscored not just by the equation he establishes between Cicero's treatment of the Greek and Augustine's reaction to 'his Ambrose' (II. 18), but also by the fact that Epicurus stands as a kind of alter ego of himself. Petrarch too has been defined in a 'brief and definitive' antinomial distinction: 'sine literis virum bonum' [good man without learning] (II. 32; and see 16 & 38). Therefore, just like the Greek philosopher in Cicero's description in the *De finibus*, which Petrarch had cited in the *Rerum memorandarum* and paraphrased in the *De ignorantia*, he was, according to some, a 'good man' but a 'bad philosopher'. Indeed, one, admittedly tightly focused, way of viewing the remainder of the treatise is in terms of the strategies that Petrarch employed to prove that the opening equation between Epicurus and himself is, in fact, at best extremely partial if not actually misleading. Thus, while he went on to confirm the Greek's speculative inadequacies by recalling his ideas on creation, on God, on the plurality of worlds (IV. 113–14, 127–29), as well as his philosophical arrogance and envy (VI. 212), he equally endeavoured to rectify the mistaken judgement of his four accusers by revealing his own intellectual gifts and prowess, not least as these are reflected in the 'stupendous' *De ignorantia*. If he is 'ignorant', it is not in the same way that Epicurus was so woefully inadequate as a philosopher. He is 'ignorant' according to a new, Christ-centred way of judging 'ignorance' which ends up by revealing both the humility of his wisdom and the morality of his behaviour — precisely the synthesis that Epicurus had failed to achieve in his own life.

If, when compared to Petrarch (or equally to a Plato or to a Cicero), Epicurus ends up negatively marked — and it does not seem to be mere coincidence that his last appearance, right at the end of the book, is also his most unappealing: 'Quis ergo in primis Epycurum intoleranda superbia, sive invidia, sive utraque detrahentem omnibus non audivit?' [Who then did not hear at first that Epicurus, through unbearable arrogance or envy or both, took away from all?] (VI. 212) — he emerges much less badly scathed when matched against other thinkers. In particular, when measured against the mass of stupid modern philosophers, or even against Aristotle as regards matters relating to creation, the Epicurus of the *De ignorantia* has undoubted merits. Indeed, he is granted an exemplary role in distinguishing between pagan and Christian possibilities of knowing, a distinction which, on account of contemporary arrogance, is entirely to the advantage of the ancients: 'Fecit [...] Deus igitur mundum verbo illo, quod Epycurus et sui nosse non poterant, nostri vero philosophi non dignantur; eoque sunt priscis illis inexcusabiliores' [God therefore made the world by that word, which Epicurus and his followers could not know, but which our philosophers do not deem worthy to know; and for this reason they are far less forgivable than the ancients] (V. 129). Epicurus's shifting, refracted identities, like those of any human being, though enhanced in his case on account of the fundamental binarism of his established portrait, so that he almost acquires the traits of an Everyman, or at least of an 'Everyintellectual', figure in the *De ignorantia*, offer handy confirmation of the dualistic argumentative structures of the *libellus*. Time and again, the book reaffirms that everything depends on the perspective from which something is evaluated in the light of something else, regardless of whether the elements being equated are regarded synchronically, in relation to an idea, a mode of behaviour, an event, or diachronically, from the point of view of history, which itself is far from stable.[21] Such an approach cannot but 'fragment' — and I use the term advisedly — the overall organization of the argument. It draws attention to each individual self-contained equation and to the elements constituting it, underscoring, thanks to its comparative relativism, the pervasiveness of ethics in every single sphere of human life.[22] Thus, each association is resolved in itself, though obviously also contributing to the larger effect of which it is a part. As a result, each rapprochement represents a rhetorical problem in its own right, permitting Petrarch to show off the range and efficacy of his eloquence, hence the stylistic wealth of the De ignorantia. Nothing could be further from the illusory rigour, coherence, and, yes, monotony of the logical prose of the scholastics.[23] In Petrarch's ethically-centred sense of reality, each person, like Epicurus, can be assessed ex bono or ex malo — it all depends on who or what is also being evoked.

4. The 'enemy of Christ' and the sin of envy

Yet, there is one notable exception to this state of affairs. Though only rarely remembered in Petrarch's œuvre, Averroes, the 'howling' 'enemy of Christ', is irredeemably evil.[24] '[T]emerarii virus Averrois ac venenata convitia et sputa ad celum putido ore transmissa', as the poet declared with epigrammatic force in the De otio religioso (p. 622; The poison of reckless Averroes and his venomous insults and his spitting at heaven through a fetid mouth). Petrarch's attack is in line with other similar condemnations of the great commentator circulating during the thirteenth and fourteenth centuries.[25] It is certainly also sharpened by his strong antipathy

---

21   On Petrarch's view of history, see Mazzotta, pp. 14–35: 'history [is] where distinct individualities frankly oppose each other' (p. 35).

22   On the centrality of ethics in the De ignorantia, see Fenzi, 'Introduzione', pp. 34–56, 61–62.

23   On the relationship between rhetoric and philosophy in Petrarch, see Etienne Anheim, 'Pétrarque: l'écriture comme philosophie', Revue de Synthèse, 129 (2008), 587–609; Trottmann, 'Pétrarque à la fracture de la philosophie'.

24   For Petrarch's allusions to Averroes, see De ign. IV. 155–58; De otio, p. 622; Invective, pp. 622–24, 842, 878–80; Rer. mem. I. 26. 5; Sen. V. 2. 75, XIII. 6. 20, XV. 6. 58; Sine titulo, p. 812. Averroes 'howls' ('latrat' and related forms) in a number of the preceding passages; he is described as 'Christ's enemy' in Sen. XIII. 6. 20.

25   See, for instance, Charles Burnett, 'The "Sons of Averroes and the Emperor Frederick" and the Transmission of the Philosophical Works of Ibn Rushd', in Averroes and the Aristotelian Tradition, ed. by Gerhard Endress and Jan A. Aertsen (Leiden, Boston, and Cologne: Brill, 1999), pp. 259–99 (esp. pp. 261–62); Alain de Libera, 'Introduction', in Thomas Aquinas, Contre Averroès, ed. by Alain Libera (Paris: Flammarion, 1994), pp. 9–73, and 'Pétrarque et la romanité', in Figures italiennes de la rationalité, ed. by Christiane Menasseyre and André Tosel (Paris: Kimé, 1997), pp. 7–35; Édouard H. Wéber, 'Les Apports positives de la noétique d'Ibn Rushd à celle de Thomas d'Aquin', in Multiple Averroès, ed. by Jean Lolivet and Rachel Arié (Paris: Les Belles Lettres, 1978), pp. 211–48 (pp. 211–12); Gerosa, p. 221. See also Fenzi, 'Introduzione', p. 94; Paul Renucci, 'Pétrarque et l'Averroisme de son temps', in Mélanges de philologie romane et littérature médiévale offerts à Ernest Hoepffner (Paris: Les Belles Lettres, 1949), pp. 339–46. See also Lummus, pp. 114

towards Arab culture.[26] However, its extreme shock, its seeming 'unreasonableness' are primarily the effect of its absoluteness. Petrarch's Averroes becomes the total embodiment of evil. Intriguingly, in Petrarch, he takes on the kind of extreme lineaments that the popular tradition had ascribed to Epicurus. He is a commonplace. Thus, the poet is not really interested in or even troubled by his ideas, as Albert or Thomas had been so profoundly a few decades earlier. For Petrarch, Averroes is an exemplary figure: the heretic, the blasphemer, the embodiment of the worst excesses of self-sufficient intellectual arrogance. It is thus obvious why, as in the passages just cited, the poet should have described him according to the traditional imagery of sin.[27] However, where we might have expected the assault to have been at its most violent, Petrarch's treatment of Averroes is at its most muted in the *De ignorantia*.[28] Nonetheless, it is still negative: Averroes represents the 'primary' example of the excesses of the commentator — the 'suspect' intellectual who 'ransacks' the works of others, uncritically embracing an *auctoritas*.[29] We should not allow ourselves, however, to be duped by Petrarch's measured tones. Within the economy of the

26   See Nancy Bisaha, 'Petrarch's Vision of the Muslim and Byzantine East', *Speculum*, 76 (2001), 284–314; Enrico Cerulli, 'Petrarca e gli arabi', *Rivista di cultura classica e medioevale*, 7 (1965), 331–36; Francesco Gabrieli, 'Petrarca e gli arabi', *Al-Andalus*, 42 (1977), 241–48; Gerosa, p. 221; Karla Mallette, *European Modernity and the Arab Mediterranean: Toward a New Philology and a Counter-Orientalism* (Philadelphia: University of Pennsylvania Press, 2010), pp. 34–63. See also C. H. L. Bodenham, 'Petrarch and the Poetry of the Arabs', *Romanische Forschungen*, 94 (1982), 167–78; Charles Burnett, 'Learned Knowledge of Arabic Poetry, Rhymed Prose and Didactic Verse from Petrus Alfonsi to Petrarch', in *Poetry and Philosophy in the Middle Ages: A Festschrift for Peter Dronke* (Leiden: Brill, 2001), pp. 29–62; Richard Lemay, 'De l'Antiarabisme — ou rejet du style scolastique — comme inspiration première de l'humanisme italien du Trecento', in *Filosofia, scienza e astrologia nel Trecento europeo*, ed. by Graziella Federici Vescovini and Francesco Barocelli (Padua: Il poligrafo, 1992), pp. 105–20.

27   See Graziella Federici Vescovini, 'L'aristotelismo "secolare" in Italia. 4. La reazione di Francesco Petrarca alla filosofia e alla teologia delle scuole: il suo ritratto del medico averroista', in *Storia della teologia nel Medioevo*, ed. by Giulio d'Onofrio, 3 vols. (Casale Monferrato: Edizioni Piemme, 1996), III, 577–600 (pp. 597–99); Carmen Polito, '"Inter cuntas eminens obliqui causa iudicii livor": annotazioni in margine al *De ignorantia* petrarchesco', *Studi e problemi di critica testuale*, 41 (1990), 5–28. On Petrarch and Averroes, see also Charles Burnett, 'Petrarch and Averroes: An Episode in the History of Poetics', in *The Medieval Mind: Hispanic Studies in Honour of Alan Deyermond*, ed. by Ian Macpherson and Ralph Penny (Woodbridge: Tamesis, 1997), pp. 49–56; Carraud's notes in Petrarch, *Mon ignorance et celle de tant d'autres*, pp. 282–83; Libera, 'Pétrarque et la romanité', pp. 16–19, 24–35; Fenzi's notes in *De ign.*, pp. 330–31, 482; Garin, 'La cultura fiorentina', pp. 184–86; Gerosa, pp. 221–23; Robert Irwin, 'Petrarch and "that Mad Dog Averroës"', in *Re-Orienting the Renaissance: Cultural Exchanges with the East*, ed. by Gerald MacLean (Basingstoke: Palgrave Macmillan, 2005), pp. 108–26; Mazzotta, p. 42.

28   See Fenzi, 'Introduzione', pp. 8, 58, 94.

29   'Nam quod Averrois omnibus Aristotilem prefert, eo spectat, quod illius libros exponendos assumpserat et quodammodo suos fecerat; qui quanquam multa laude digni sint, suspectus tamen est laudator. [...] Quanta vero sit multitudo — aliena dicam exponentium, ad aliena vastantium?' [That Averroes did in fact prefer Aristotle over everyone else is clear from the fact that he had resolved to write a commentary on the philosopher's books and somehow had made them his own; and even if these are worthy of great praise, nonetheless a eulogizer raises suspicion. [...] But how many are the persons — should I say 'who comment' or 'who ransack' the works of others?] (*De ign.* IV. 155 & 157). On Petrarch's critique of commentators, see Boulnois, pp. 26–27.

De ignorantia, to be an uncritical follower, especially of Aristotle,[30] represents the worst of intellectual sins, as evidenced by the harshness of its treatment of the four Aristotelians and not, as now has been largely recognized, Averroists.[31] And yet, the four are 'Averroists' — at least in so far as they take over that emblematic imagery of sin that elsewhere in Petrarch defines Averroes: 'Cupide igitur et audacter, et importune, contra preceptorem [Cristum] contraque discipulos eius clamant, imo latrant et insultant' (IV. 121; Eagerly, therefore, audaciously, and savagely they cry out — or rather howl and insult — against the teacher [Christ] and his disciples). In the *De ignorantia*, Averroes can take a back seat because his epigones — epigones of an epigone... — are shown to be rabidly doing his work. Petrarch's recourse to conventional religious language in describing his enemies points to another of the 'little book's' vital structures: its heavy dependence on the conventions of popular religion. Yet, much work still needs to be done to clarify its debts to the traditions of the vices and virtues, of the 'sins of the tongue', and of *imitatio Christi*, all of which grow out of the text's rich Scriptural substratum.[32] Indeed, the principal point of reference for and the major structuring element behind the *De ignorantia*'s first two parts are to be found in a clearly delimited area of the medieval concern with sin.

Although both the work's title and the dedicatory letter declare that its topic is ignorance, this fact is far from apparent in its first thirty-eight paragraphs. In the light of these, the *De ignorantia* actually appears as a work about envy — *invidia, livor*. This is the sin that dominates the book's opening pages; and it does this to the extent that these can be read as a compendium of many of the commonplaces which, in the Middle Ages, had come to characterize this most corrosive of sins.[33] The first two paragraphs set the scene (and almost all the following thirty-six paragraphs make some reference to envy): 'Quotidie amicorum laudibus, quotidie emulorum iurgiis respondendum erit? Nec invidiam aut latebre excluserint aut tempus extinxerit? [...] O venenum pertinax! Que me pridem rei publice [etas] excusasset, nondum excusat invidie, cumque illa cui multum debeo me absolvat, hec, cui nil debeo, me molestat' (I. 1–2; Shall I reply every day to the praises of friends and the reproaches of rivals? Will hiding not shut out or time not extinguish envy? [...] Oh obstinate poison! Long after my age would have excused me from public duty, but does not still excuse me from envy, and although the state, to which I owe a lot, discharges

---

30   On Petrarch's attitude to Aristotle in the *De ignorantia*, see Fenzi, 'Introduzione', pp. 7–17, 33–48; Trottmann, 'Pétrarque à la fracture de la philosophie', pp. 375–79.

31   See Paul Oskar Kristeller, 'Petrarch's "Averroists": A Note on the History of Aristotelianism in Venice, Padua, and Bologna', *Bibliothèque d'Humanisme et Renaissance*, 14 (1952), 59–65.

32   See Polito; in addition see Fenzi's notes in *De ign.*, which list and discuss a large number of Scriptural echoes. I do not have the space here to examine Petrarch's recourse to the concept of *imitatio Christi* in the *De ignorantia*. On its presence in Petrarch, see Dina De Rentiis, 'Sul ruolo di Petrarca nella storia dell'*imitatio auctorum*', in *Dynamique d'une expansion culturelle: Pétrarque en Europe XIVᵉ–XXᵉ siècle*, ed. by Pierre Blanc (Paris: Champion, 2001), pp. 63–74.

33   On envy in the Middle Ages, see Carla Casagrande and Silvana Vecchio, *I sette vizi capitali: storia dei peccati nel Medioevo* (Turin: Einaudi, 2000), pp. 36–53; L. Desbrus, 'Envie', in DTC, V:1, cols 131–34; Édouard Ranwez, 'Envie', in DSAM, IV:1, cols 774–85; Mireille Vincent-Cassy, 'L'envie au Moyen Âge', *Annales E.S.C.*, 35 (1980), 253–71. On envy in the *De ignorantia*, see Polito, pp. 9–25. See also n. 51.

me, envy, to which I owe nothing, torments me). Describing envy as a poison and stressing its tenaciousness are both traditional tropes;[34] equally conventional is the reference to spiteful rivals and to loyal friends.[35] Even the image of Petrarch seeking refuge in his hiding-place is connected to the contemporary discourse on envy. On the one hand, it points to envy's ability to penetrate every corner of the world and every area of social existence;[36] on the other, the poet's recess, the just reward for his labours, stands in stark contrast to envy's malevolent lurking in dark places.[37] Petrarch immediately establishes himself both as a victim of *invidia* and as an expert on the sin. In unmasking and condemning envy, Petrarch's voice is doubly 'authoritative' — his *auctoritas* stemming both from direct personal experience and from his scholarly knowledge of the subject. As he does throughout the rest of the treatise, Petrarch begins by bringing together *ethica* and *scientia*, while also calling into question the charge of ignorance that has been laid against him. At least as far as envy is concerned the poet is clearly a specialist. With consummate rhetorical skill, thereby preparing for the *De ignorantia*'s subsequent celebration of *eloquentia*, the poet traces in its first few sentences some of the work's key preoccupations and strategies; and for the remainder of the treatise's first two parts, Petrarch presents overwhelming confirmation of how sophisticated is his intellectual and moral understanding of envy.[38] He thus pens a veritable treatise *de invidia*. He offers a rich selection of the images which in Christian writing had accrued around *impius livor* (I. 8): envy is a monster, blind and indiscriminate (I. 5); like a rabid dog, it barks, shows its tongue, and bites (I. 8 and II. 10, 22); it lurks in the dark (I. 8) and remains hidden (II. 19), yet its noxiousness spreads forth;[39] it is both cross-eyed (II. 20) and blind (II. 22); it is a source of bitterness (I. 8) and a type of madness (II. 22, 23).[40] As occurs in the tradition, Petrarch compares the behaviour of his four

34   On envy and poison see, for instance, John of Salisbury, *Policraticus*, ed. by Clement Charles Julian Webb, 2 vols (Oxford: Clarendon Press, 1909), VII. 24; Ovid, *Met.* II. 777, 784, 800–01. On envy's tenaciousness see Gulielmus Peraldus, *Summa virtutum ac vitiorum* (Brescia: A. et J. de Britannicis de Pallazolo, 1494), II. 7. 1; see also Casagrande and Vecchio, p. 37.

35   On envy as antithetical to friendship and as arising from rivalry, see Carla Casagrande and Silvana Vecchio, *I peccati della lingua: disciplina ed etica della parola nella cultura medievale* (Rome: Istituto della Enciclopedia Italiana, 1987), pp. 337–38, 347; Casagrande and Vecchio, *I sette vizi capitali*, pp. 41, 45–49; Desbrus, 'Envie', cols 133–34; Fenzi's notes in *De ign.*, pp. 323–25, 328–29.

36   See Casagrande and Vecchio, *I sette vizi capitali*, pp. 37, 44–45.

37   See Ovid's hugely influential description of Envy's cave in *Met.* II. 760–64.

38   In penning such an effective introduction to the *De ignorantia*, Petrarch not only demonstrated his control over his text, but also revealed his mastery of rhetorical convention. According to medieval poetics, an author, in the opening of his work, was expected to offer a synthesis of its principal concerns; see Ernest Gallo, 'Matthew of Vendôme: Introductory Treatise on the Art of Poetry', *American Philosophical Society Proceedings*, 118 (1974), 51–92 (59–60); Heinrich Lausberg, *Handbuch der literarischen Rhetorik*, 2 vols (Munich: Max Hueber Verlag, 1960), I, 150–63. The way in which, as we saw earlier, the treatise's title too provides valuable insight into its aims is also in keeping with medieval literary thinking; on the exegetical functions of the *titulus*, see Alastair J. Minnis, *Medieval Theory of Authorship*, 2nd edn (Aldershot: Scolar Press, 1988), pp. 19–20.

39   Petrarch refers to envy as both *virus* (I. 8; and see Ovid, *Met.* II. 800) and *pestis* (II. 21).

40   On the imagery of envy, see in particular Vincent-Cassy, especially pp. 255–56. See also Casagrande and Vecchio, *I sette vizi capitali*, pp. 38–39, 48; Edwin D. Craun, *Lies, Slander, and Obscenity in Medieval English Literature: Pastoral Rhetoric and the Deviant Speaker* (Cambridge: Cambridge University Press, 1997), p. 149; Fenzi's notes in *De ign.*, pp. 323–29; Polito, pp. 11–21. For

accusers to that of envious women (II. 35)[41] and describes the workings of envy by having recourse to martial (I. 3, 5; II. 10, 21)[42] and sexual (I. 8) metaphors.[43] Equally conventionally, he presents *invidia* as a vice that arises among people who are close to each other and that is particularly prevalent in intellectual circles (II. 11–12, 23–26, 37).[44] In this regard, it is therefore not surprising that, as Petrarch stresses in line with many other thinkers, envy should destroy friendship and undermine charity (I. 3, 5, 8).[45] Furthermore, to ensure that his treatment is as wide-ranging and balanced as possible, he even makes fleeting reference to that type of envy for spiritual improvement, theorized in particular by Thomas Aquinas, which, as a form of zealous imitation, leads to an increase in virtue: 'virtutem ipsam, optimam haud dubie, invidiosissimamque rerum omnium' (II. 16; virtue itself, without doubt the best, is the most enviable of all things) — though it goes without saying that the poet's four false friends feel no envy for his virtue.[46]

In addition to describing envy, and in keeping especially with scholastic reflection on the sin, Petrarch explores the psychology of the envious, those who, on account of their own inadequacies and *superbia*, are deeply resentful of the successes of others. This *passio* is the source of considerable internal suffering, which the envious often mask behind a hypocritical façade, but which — and Petrarch once again draws on a traditional metaphor to describe its effects — furiously burns inside them, since it is an uncontrollable and irrational sentiment that causes tremendous harm to those who fall prey to it.[47] Petrarch's analysis, like the whole of his presentation, firmly follows mainstream opinion. Its erudite orthodoxy is definitively confirmed by the emphasis it places on two elements that the Middle Ages deemed fundamental to any serious discussion of *invidia*. After a lengthy dramatic build up, Petrarch reveals that what the four resent so profoundly is his *fama* — that fame which was universally judged to be the principal source of envy's animosity,[48] and which, it was just as widely believed, could be most effectively sullied by *detractio*, namely, 'denigratory words, frequently lies, which are spoken in envy about someone absent with the intention of injuring her reputation'.[49] Unsurprisingly, *detractio* was the

a wide-ranging medieval discussion of envy, see Alexander Neckam, *De naturis rerum*, ed. by Thomas Wright (London: Longman, Green, Longman, Roberts, & Green, 1863), II. 189.

41   See, for instance, Andreas Capellanus, *On Love*, ed. by Patrick G. Walsh (London: Duckworth, 1982), III. 73–77. See also Ranwez, col. 776.

42   On the tradition of martial metaphors to describe envy, see Casagrande and Vecchio, *I peccati della lingua*, p. 342, and *I sette vizi capitali*, pp. 36–37.

43   On envy and sexual imagery, see Dante, *Inf.* XIII. 64–67.

44   See Casagrande and Vecchio, *I sette vizi capitali*, pp. 43–49.

45   See Casagrande and Vecchio, *I peccati della lingua*, p. 338, and *I sette vizi capitali*, pp. 44–45; Fenzi's notes in *Secretum*, pp. 323–25. On the importance of friendship in *De ignorantia*, see Kennedy.

46   See Casagrande and Vecchio, *I sette vizi capitali*, pp. 51–52.

47   See *De ign.* II. 11–12, 16–17, 19, 23; and see Casagrande and Vecchio, *I sette vizi capitali*, pp. 38–43; Ranwez, cols 778–80.

48   See *De ign.* II. 20–22, 26; and see Carla Casagrande, 'Fama e diffamazione nella letteratura teologica e pastorale del sec. XIII', *Ricerche storiche*, 26 (1996), 7–24; Casagrande and Vecchio, *I peccati della lingua*, pp. 332, 335, 339, and *I sette vizi capitali*, p. 47; Polito, pp. 21–23.

49   Craun, pp. 136–37. On *detractio*, see Casagrande and Vecchio, *I peccati della lingua*, pp. 331–51; T. Ortolan, 'Diffamation', in DTC, IV:1, cols 1300–07; A. Thouvenin, 'Médisance', in DTC, X:1, cols 487–94.

'sin of the tongue' most intimately associated with *invidia*, so that the two sins were normally assessed together.[50] Although Petrarch does not actually use the term *detractio* or its cognate forms to define the four's offense against him, there is no doubt that this is the wrongdoing of which they are guilty.[51] Thus, his accusers are quintessentially linguistic sinners — 'nec internis pulsas stimulis linguas frenant' (II. 19; they do not restrain their tongues urged on by internal impulses) — and, as the poet announces in the incipit of the second section, the section which establishes the four as 'detractors', their specific fault is *murmur* (II. 10), a sin with extremely close ties to *detractio*.[52] Furthermore, and in line with the literal meaning of *detrahere* — 'detraction' was understood as a 'taking away of a good'[53] — , Petrarch employs the verbs *eripere* (II. 16, 34, 39) and *auferre* (II. 37), both of which signify 'to take | snatch away', in order to describe the effects of the four's lies on his reputation; and, in the normal way of 'detractors', the four speak ill of Petrarch when he is not present (II. 10, 26–27).[54] As mediocre yet arrogant *studiosi* (II. 23), and hence as emblematic incarnations of envy, they cannot stomach Petrarch's *fama* as an intellectual, and so rail against his reputation. Consequent on the four's behaviour, envy and ignorance, as they did in the tradition, come together, thereby ensuring that the *De ignorantia*'s first two parts are efficiently restored to the treatise's argumentative mainstream. The four's backbiting is clear proof of their limitations as 'philosophers' — a fact confirmed by their predilection for knowledge as a form of ostentation rather than as means of understanding the truth (II. 24–25): 'naturam hominum, ad quod nati sumus, unde et quo pergimus, vel nescire vel spernere' (II. 25; they ignore or disdain the nature of man, what we were born for, the beginning and end of our journey).

Petrarch is careful to provide as much verifiable and culturally acceptable confirmation as possible that his accusations against the four are well founded, and therefore are not a sign that he too is guilty of 'detraction' — not naming his critics is the most obvious means of avoiding such a charge.[55] In fact, his conduct is the precise opposite of *detractio*. By denouncing their faults, he practices *correptio*. Like any good Christian, whenever he recognizes evil, he has the duty openly and truthfully to denounce it, thereby offering the wrongdoers the possibility to

---

50 See Casagrande and Vecchio, *I peccati della lingua*, p. 336; Craun, pp. 136–37.

51 Petrarch was of course more than familiar with the term and its technical meanings and connotations, not least its close association with envy; see *De ign.* VI. 212. Interestingly, in this passage, Petrarch applied the word to Epicurus: 'Quis ergo in primis Epycurum intoleranda superbia, sive invidia, sive utraque detrehantem omnibus non audivit?' [Who then did not hear at first that Epicurus, through unbearable arrogance or envy or both, took away from all?]. By associating the philosopher with his four enemies, Petrarch leaves no doubt that, despite superficial similarities, little, in fact, unites him to the Greek. Indeed, the final condemnation of Epicurus underscores that the parallels the poet had established between himself and the classical thinker were first and foremost an elegant rhetorical and argumentative ploy — the comparison was, in fact, another type of contrastive device.

52 See Casagrande and Vecchio, *I peccati della lingua*, pp. 243–44, 247–49, 338, and *I sette vizi capitali*, p. 50.

53 See Casagrande and Vecchio, *I peccati della lingua*, p. 332; Thouvenin, cols 492–93.

54 See Casagrande and Vecchio, *I peccati della lingua*, pp. 331–33; Thouvenin, col. 490.

55 Not revealing the names of his four accusers has, in fact, primarily negative implications. It is a particularly effective and radical form of condemnation and of *damnatio memoriae*.

mend their ways.[56] Petrarch further underscores his virtuousness by asserting that, as the literature on 'detraction' recommended, he does not intend to counter their lies (II. 16), but has decided to suffer in silence (III. 39).[57] Although it is certainly the case that Petrarch does not directly challenge the opinion expressed by the four that he is ignorant, the *De ignorantia* as a whole, as we have seen, is actually a sustained, albeit indirect, affirmation of the unfairness of their allegations. Indeed, in a highly original and paradoxical move, Petrarch goes so far as to declare that he accepts and concurs with their assessment that he is 'sine literis bonus' (II. 38; and see 32–33, 36–38; a good man without learning). If, on the one hand, this permits him to underscore the importance he places on his relationship to God and on the role of humility and ethics in his life, on the other, it is a means to draw attention to his rhetorical and dialectical skills, as well as to the dangers inherent in language and disputation, whereby lies can be transformed into truths while still being lies, and 'detractors' metamorphose into speakers of truth whose truthfulness, however, remains open to question: 'modo ne id [regarding his goodness] quoque mentiti sint, et michi preriperent quod volebant, quod non erat dederint' (II. 34; provided they have not lied about this too, and taken from me what they wanted, and given me what was not mine).[58] For all his dependence on the commonplaces of *invidia* and *detractio*, Petrarch, in a typical manoeuvre, brings his discussion to a close by introducing a highly personalized development into the tradition. In the same way, the extended legal metaphor that the poet employs to structure his treatment of the workings of envy (I. 3; II. 26–32, 34), and which returns throughout the treatise, constitutes an individual amplification of an image on the margins of discussions of *invidia*.[59] Eloquence, 'science', and ethics coalesce in order to damn his 'detractors' and to present irrefutable proof of the reasons for his fame and their envy.

5. Conclusion

Given its concern with salvation and with the relationship between God and humanity, it is entirely appropriate for the *De ignorantia* to be run through with elements taken from both academic and popular Christianity. More interestingly, its reliance on religious tropes and on binary equations offers a revealing glimpse of that intellectual and stylistic eclecticism to which I have already referred. And let me stress that there is nothing arbitrary about Petrarch's eclecticism.[60] The control

56   See Casagrande and Vecchio, *I peccati della lingua*, pp. 334–35.

57   Ibid., p. 341.

58   By highlighting the instability between truth and falsehood in human discourse, and hence its fundamental relativism, Petrarch confirms that the truth and true knowledge reside only in God (II. 32, 35).

59   To date I have found only one example of envy being coupled with the law: *Policraticus* VIII. Prologue. There are other original elements in Petrarch's presentation of envy: for instance, deliberately avoiding the term *detrahere*; the rich elaboration of martial imagery to describe the sin (Polito, pp. 10–11); and the claim that, despite the four's envious calumnies, he still considers them friends (see Fenzi's note in *De ignorantia*, pp. 323–24).

60   Petrarch himself points to the *De ignorantia*'s eclecticism in the dedicatory epistle, whose functions as an *accessus* have been almost entirely ignored by scholars: 'Nam que latior loquendi area,

he exerted over his disparate material is a defining mark of his sophistication and critical acumen. Thus, the *De ignorantia*'s formal breadth, which, in keeping with its constantly changing *materia*, smoothly shifts between analogy, the full gamut of the 'flowers of rhetoric', the learned quotation, *laus* and *vituperatio*, accumulation, *variatio*, repetition, dramatic shifts in tone, is testimony to Petrarch's eloquence, discrimination, intelligence, and faith, determined as these are by his confidence in and 'imitation' of the best of classical and Christian culture. The poet's eclecticism is further apparent in other aspects of his great polemical treatise. Thus, by exploring the potential, the responsibilities, and the inanities of the human mind, Petrarch ensured that the *libellus* is both a major statement 'on ignorance' and a sort of 'history' of pagan and Christian philosophy, thereby affirming its author's intellectual prowess and erudition. Finally, by gathering together in one place his many, frequent, and scattered laments and fulminations about the state of the modern world, Petrarch was able to establish his moral and intellectual 'uniqueness'. His is the lonely voice in the wilderness attempting to make itself heard amidst a storm of stupidity and malice.

Yet, as so much else in the *De ignorantia*, this last representation too is a rhetorical construct. Petrarch — we now know — was far from alone at the close of the Middle Ages in criticizing scholasticism and Aristotelianism. He was part of a major and well-established tradition, which also included the Dante of the *Commedia*; a tradition whose arguments and language too are granted space in Petrarch's richly layered book 'on ignorance'.[61] However, thanks to its historical range and moral ambition, to its erudition, to its ability stylistically to draw on a wide array of sources, to its powerful personal stamp, to its keenness to present itself as 'other', the *De sui ipsius et multorum ignorantia* is a quintessentially Petrarchan work, a *summa* of so much that, throughout his life, caused the poet disquiet. As its title declares, it is a book that tells us much about both its author and 'many others'; or, rather, about the former's naturally 'non-detractive' views of 'many others', thereby further drawing attention to the self. Among these many *ex bono* and *ex malo* refractions of the self who populate his highly personalized drama, Petrarch assigned not entirely negligible roles to those two archetypal, though unrelated 'baddies' of the medieval world, Epicurus and Averroes.

---

quis campus ingentior, quam humane tractatus ignorantie, et presertim mee?' [For what subject of discussion is wider, what field more vast than a treatise on human ignorance, and especially on mine?] (p. 172).

61   See Luca Bianchi, '"Aristotile fu un uomo e poté errare": sulle origini medievali della critica al "principio di autorità"', in *Filosofia e teologia nel Trecento: studi in ricordo di Eugenio Randi*, ed. by Luca Bianchi (Louvain-la-Neuve: FIDEM, 1994), pp. 509–33; Boulnois, pp. 7–19, 36; Fenzi, 'Introduzione', pp. 20–22, 57; Gerosa, pp. 201–05; Edward P. Mahoney, '"The Worst Natural Philosopher" (*pessimus naturalis*) and "The Worst Metaphysician (*pessimus metaphysicus*)": His Reputation among Some Franciscan Philosophers (Bonaventure, Francis of Meyronnes, Antonius Andreas, and Joannes Canonicus) and Later Reactions', in *Die Philosophie im 14. und 15. Jahrhundert: in memoriam Konstanty Michalski*, ed. by Olaf Pluta (Amsterdam: Grüner, 1988), pp. 261–73; François-Xavier Putallaz, 'La Connaissance de soi au Moyen âge: Vital du Four', *Collectanea franciscana*, 40 (1990), 505–37. On Dante's critique of scholasticism, see Zygmunt G. Baranski, *Dante e i segni* (Naples: Liguori, 2000).

CHAPTER 15

'Alquanto tenea della oppinione degli epicuri': The *auctoritas* of Boccaccio's Cavalcanti (and Dante)

1. 'Ottimo loico e [...] buon dicitore in rima'[1]

It is a critical commonplace to assert that Guido Cavalcanti had a significant impact on Boccaccio's poetic formation.[2] At the same time, textual evidence for this claim is anything but readily available. Scholars have managed to recognize few explicit borrowings from Cavalcanti's poetry in Boccaccio's *œuvre*.[3] Indeed, unlike Dante and Petrarch, Boccaccio himself makes scant reference to Cavalcanti's standing as a poet; and, when he does, his comments raise questions both about the extent of his knowledge of his predecessor's poetry and about his opinion of Guido's achievements as a poet. Boccaccio first alludes to Cavalcanti in his self-commentary

---

1   All quotations from and references to Boccaccio's works are taken from the following editions: Giovanni Boccaccio: *Teseida*, ed. by Alberto Limentani (Milan: Mondadori, 1964); *Dec.* (the quotation in the title is found at VI. 9. 9); *Trattatello in laude di Dante*, ed. by Pier Giorgio Ricci, in Giovanni Boccaccio, *Tutte le opere*, ed. by Vittore Branca (Milan: Mondadori, 1974), III, 423–538; *Esposizioni sopra la Comedia di Dante*, ed. by Giorgio Padoan (Milan: Mondadori, 1965). The quotation in the subtitle is found at Esposizioni X. 62 (p. 526).

2   See, for instance, Lucia Battaglia Ricci, *Boccaccio* (Rome: Salerno, 2000), p. 25; Vittore Branca, 'Introduzione', in Giovanni Boccaccio, *Rime*, ed. by Vittore Branca (Milan: Mondadori, 1992), pp. 1–32 (pp. 5–10); Stefano Carrai, 'Esercizi petrarcheschi (con implicazioni cronologiche) del Boccaccio lirico', *Studi sul Boccaccio*, 28 (2000), 185–97 (p. 196); Rosario Ferreri, 'Studi sulle *Rime*', *Studi sul Boccaccio*, 7 (1973), 213–37 (pp. 235–36); Antonio Lanza, *Studi sulla lirica del Trecento* (Rome: Bulzoni, 1978), pp. 84, 105, 109–11, 117; Luigi Russo, *Letture critiche del 'Decameron'* (Bari: Laterza, 1956), p. 222. For a contrary view, see Armando Balduino, *Petrarca, Boccaccio e altri poeti del Trecento* (Florence: Olschki, 1984), p. 184; Antonio Enzo Quaglio, 'Prima fortuna della glossa garbiana a "Donna me prega" del Cavalcanti', *Giornale storico della letteratura italiana*, 141 (1964), 336–68 (pp. 346–49); Jonathan Usher, 'Boccaccio, Cavalcanti's Canzone "Donna me prega" and Dino's Glosses', *Heliotropia* 2:1 (2004), 1–19 (pp. 7–8). See more recently Matteo Pace, 'L'amore di Cimone: tradizione medica e memoria cavalcantiana in *Decameron* V 1', *Studi sul Boccaccio*, 44 (2016), 251–75.

3   See Branca, 'Introduzione', pp. 6–10; Lanza, pp. 109–11. In their annotations, editors of Boccaccio's poetic works and of Cavalcanti's poetry not infrequently quote passages that they claim demonstrate the *novelliere*'s debts to Guido. However, in just about every instance, the borrowings they propose are lyric commonplaces. As a result, it is difficult to see how these might serve as evidence of Boccaccio's dependence on Cavalcanti. Even high-calibre editions reveal marks of this tendency; see, for instance, Giovanni Boccaccio, *Filostrato*, ed. by Luigi Surdich (Milan: Mursia, 1990); Guido Cavalcanti, *Rime*, ed. by Letterio Cassata (Anzio: Rubeis, 1993).

to the *Teseida*, when he cites 'Donna me prega' in order to circumvent the need to discuss how the *innamorati* fall in love:

> Il quale amore volere mostrare come per le sopradette cose si generi in noi, quantunque alla presente opera forse si converrebbe di dichiarare, non è mio intendimento di farlo, perciò che troppa sarebbe lunga la storia: chi disidera di vederlo, legga la canzone di Guido Cavalcanti *Donna mi priega, ets.*, e le chiose che sopra vi fece Maestro Dino del Garbo. (*Teseida*, p. 222)

Yet, if we compare Boccaccio's presentation of the workings of the *appetito eccitato* with Cavalcanti's account of the nature of love in his great philosophical canzone — regardless of whether we read this with or without Dino's Latin commentary — obvious and significant discrepancies emerge between their respective accounts.[4] Mentioning Guido and his poem, Boccaccio was conventionally drawing on their 'authoritative' status in matters of love — a fact confirmed by the allusion to their commentator — an 'authoritative' status which, since the late-thirteenth century, had been accorded to both especially in Tuscany (see Chapter 13). As is well known, quoting an *auctoritas* in the Middle Ages did not mean having first-hand familiarity with the cited author and his texts. Thus, in light of the textual evidence, it is very likely that, between 1339 and 1341, when he composed the *Teseida*, Boccaccio was not directly familiar with 'Donna me prega', though he was clearly aware of its prominent cultural prestige and its efficacy as an intellectual point of reference.[5]

A few years later, in a famous passage of the *Decameron*, the Introduction to Day IV, Cavalcanti reappears as an exemplary lover:

> Io mai a me vergogna non reputerò infino nello stremo della mia vita di dover compiacere a quelle cose [feminine attributes] alle quali Guido Cavalcanti e Dante Alighieri già vecchi e messer Cino da Pistoia vecchissimo onor si tennero, e fu lor caro il piacer loro. (*Dec.* IV. Introduzione 33)

Once again, there is no evidence in this claim of anything more than, at best, anecdotal knowledge of Cavalcanti the love poet — that is, if the verb *compiacere*, 'to take pleasure in', actually refers to the writing of poetry. In the months before his death in 1375, Boccaccio made a last, though highly revealing, mention of Cavalcanti as a poet. When he came to gloss *Inferno* X, and specifically Cavalcante dei Cavalcanti's presence among those whom God had damned for heresy, while offering information about the father, Boccaccio also talked about the son:

> [Guido] fu nel suo tempo reputato ottimo loico e buon filosofo, e fu sing-ularissimo amico dell'autore, sì come esso medesimo mostra nella sua *Vita nuova*, e fu buon dicitore in rima; ma, per ciò che la filosofia gli pareva, sì

---

4   All quotations from and references to Cavalcanti's poetry are taken from Guido Cavalcanti, *Rime*, ed. by Domenico De Robertis (Turin: Einaudi, 1986). Dino's *chiose*, together with other commentaries on the canzone, may be read in Enrico Fenzi, *La canzone d'amore di Guido Cavalcanti e i suoi antichi commenti* (Genoa: Il melangolo, 1999).

5   Although the only surviving copy of Dino del Garbo's *chiose* comes from Boccaccio's pen, he did not transcribe this until around 1366 (Quaglio, p. 354), thus many years after he had composed the *Teseida*. At the same time, as Usher convincingly demonstrates, 'the evidence for Boccaccio having read Dino del Garbo early on in his career, earlier than the *Teseida*, is quite strong' (p. 19). It is thus noteworthy that Boccaccio first knew the gloss and then the canzone.

come ella è, da molto più che la poesia, ebbe a sdegno Virgilio e gli altri poeti.
(*Esposizioni* x. 62)

Boccaccio's brief pen-sketch of Guido is far from original. As is the case with the two passages already discussed, Boccaccio's Cavalcanti in the *Esposizioni* is a cultural cliché — in this instance, an amalgam of some of the widely circulating stock notions which, since the end of the Duecento, had collected around his name.[6] What is more significant for our present purpose is that Boccaccio, in line with most of his contemporaries (Dante and Petrarch were exceptions in this respect), chose to place strict boundaries around Guido's artistic abilities. Cavalcanti is no more than a 'buon dicitore in rima', a competent wordsmith in comparison to Virgil and the other true *poeti*.[7] His real calling, the source of his *auctoritas*, is philosophy, and, as a consequence, his poetic limitations — as Boccaccio makes clear — are more than understandable. It should not come as a surprise, therefore, that Cavalcanti did not exert a major literary sway over Boccaccio, as he similarly did not over the majority of medieval Italian poets, who, in general, seemed to be aware of the man rather than of his poems (Chapter 13, pp. 460–61). Yet, modern scholarship has been reluctant to accept this fact. Spurred on by Dante's and Petrarch's emphasis on Guido as a poet of note, and largely unaware of the intricacies of his medieval reception, it has granted him, understandably though problematically — problematically because the hard intertextual evidence is lacking to support their case — a position of determining influence in accounts of the origins of vernacular poetry in Italy.[8] In particular, critics have striven to emphasize the wealth of his contacts with other leading literary figures at the close of the Middle Ages — something that is undoubtedly true as regards Dante, but which is far more difficult to sustain as regards Boccaccio, and even Petrarch. That Cavalcanti is a poet of considerable significance, as Dante and Petrarch had not failed to appreciate, is now almost certainly beyond question. However, the fact remains that this was not an assessment widely shared by his contemporaries. For them, first and foremost, Cavalcanti was a philosopher of some standing — 'fu nel suo tempo reputato ottimo loico e buon filosofo' (*Esposizioni* x. 62) — arguably the greatest thinker of his day.[9] And, in keeping with *communis opinio*, it was as

6   Chapter 13, pp. 462–64. For a discussion of the commonplaces associated with Cavalcanti's name and of Boccaccio's recourse to these, see Subsection 3 below entitled 'Rewriting "Authority"'.
7   On the fundamental cultural and semantic differences and tensions between the concepts of *poeta* and *dicitore in rima*, see at least Barbara Bargagli Stoffi-Mühlethaler, '*Poeta, poetare* e sinonimi: studio semantico su Dante e la poesia duecentesca', *Studi di lessicografia italiana*, 8 (1986) 5–299; Mirko Tavoni, 'Che cos'è la poesia? Chi è poeta?', in his *Qualche idea su Dante* (Bologna: il Mulino, 2015), pp. 295–334.
8   On Petrarch's debts to Guido's poetry, see Chapters 10 and 13, n. 43. On Dante's relationship to Cavalcanti, see n. 6 in the latter chapter. The other medieval Italian poet with obvious debts to Guido is Cino da Pistoia; see Chapter 13, n. 44.
9   See, for instance, Benvenuto da Imola, *Comentum super Dantis Aldigherij Comoediam*, ed. by James P. Lacaita, 5 vols (Florence: Barbèra, 1887), I, 342; Boccaccio, *Esposizioni* x. 62; *Chiose anonime alla prima cantica della Divina Commedia*, ed. by Francesco Selmi (Turin: Stamperia Reale, 1865), pp. 62–63; *Commento della Divina Commedia d'anonimo fiorentino del secolo XIV*, ed. by Pietro Fanfani, 3 vols (Bologna: Gaetano Romagnoli, 1866–74), I, 254. For further examples, see Chapter 13.

an emblematic intellectual, rather than as a poet, that Guido interested Boccaccio — a state of affairs, as we shall see, that in no way detracts from the intricacy and fascination of their inter-relationship.[10]

Thus, it is clear that, both in the *Teseida* and in Day IV of the *Decameron*, Boccaccio is not actually drawing on Cavalcanti as a poet but as an expert on love. He cites 'Donna me prega' in the former work not for its literary qualities but as a source of reliable information: 'chi disidera di vederlo, legga la canzone di Guido Cavalcanti *Donna mi priega, ets.*'. The thinker, the established contemporary 'authority' on the philosophy of love, these are the attributes that Boccaccio prizes in Cavalcanti, a fact eloquently confirmed in his most detailed portrait and assessment of Guido, namely, the penultimate story of Day VI of the *Decameron*. Not only does Boccaccio make no reference in it to Cavalcanti as a poet, but the whole story is centred on the excellence and range of his intellectual, moral, and rhetorical gifts:

> Oltre a quello che egli fu un de' miglior loici che avesse il mondo e ottimo filosofo naturale [...], si fu egli leggiadrissimo e costumato e parlante uom molto e ogni cosa che far volle e a gentile uom pertenente seppe meglio che altro uom fare; e con questo era ricchissimo, e a chiedere a lingua sapeva onorare cui nell'animo gli capeva il valesse. (*Dec.* VI. 9. 8)

Boccaccio's Guido, bolstered by the accumulation of superlatives and by the eagerness of the *brigata* to include him among their number (7 & 9), emerges as a supreme individual, a more than worthy *auctoritas* for the world of the fourteenth century; and Cavalcanti's 'authoritative' status is further signalled by the moral-didactic reverberations of his caustic reply to the *brigata* (12–15) — a pithy phrase whose standing as a valuable *sententia* is confirmed by Betto Brunelleschi, the leader of the *brigata*, who accords it an explicatory gloss: 'Allora ciascuno intese quello che Guido aveva voluto dire e vergognossi, né mai piú gli diedero briga, e tennero per innanzi messer Betto sottile e intendente cavaliere' (12).[11] Indeed, the issue of how 'authority' might be achieved and maintained by a 'modern', especially when faced by the imposing edifice, crafted over centuries, of Scriptural, classical, and patristic *auctoritas*, lies at the core of Cavalcanti's medieval reception.[12] *Decameron* VI. 9, as we

---

10   See also the recent Jelena Todorović, 'Guido Cavalcanti in Boccaccio's *Argomenti*', *Heliotropia*, 11:1–2 (2014), 1–15. As this and other chapters in this volume demonstrate, I find untenable the claim that 'the key for understanding Boccaccio's favourable attitude towards Guido in his introductions and rubrics to the *Inferno* must be attributed to no thing but his Epicureanism on the one hand and to the high esteem in which he held love poetry on the other' (p. 12).

11   On Betto's role as an exegete, see Francesco Bruni, 'Comunicazione', in *Lessico critico decameroniano*, ed. by Renzo Bragantini and Pier Massimo Forni (Turin: Bollati Boringhieri, 1995), pp. 73–92 (pp. 82–83); Giuseppe Velli, 'Seneca nel *Decameron*', in his *Petrarca e Boccaccio: tradizione memoria scrittura* (Padua: Antenore, 1995), pp. 209–21 (p. 218). On the *novella*'s profound concern with matters of exegesis, see Robert M. Durling, 'Boccaccio on Interpretation: Guido's Escape (*Decameron* VI.9)', in *Dante, Petrarch, Boccaccio: Studies in the Italian Trecento in Honor of Charles S. Singleton*, ed. by Aldo S. Bernardo and Anthony L. Pellegrini (Binghamton, NY: Center for Medieval & Early Renaissance Studies, 1983), pp. 273–304; Guglielmo Gorni 'Invenzione e scrittura nel Boccaccio: il caso di Guido Cavalcanti', *Letteratura italiana antica*, 3 (2002), 359–73.

12   On Cavalcanti's status as a 'modern' *auctoritas*, see Chapter 13, p. 464. On 'authority' in the Middle Ages, see Mary Carruthers, *The Book of Memory* (Cambridge: Cambridge University Press

shall see, makes a compellingly profound contribution to this question, engaging not just with Guido, but also with the key figure regarding all matters of 'authority' in fourteenth-century Italy, Dante Alighieri.[13] Though much critical attention has quite rightly already been paid to the *novella di Guido*,[14] its concern with *auctoritas* has generally been ignored.[15] This has led, as I hope to demonstrate, to a failure properly to appreciate the complexity both of the short story and of Boccaccio's interest in Cavalcanti. In *Decameron* VI. 9, Guido, the idealized individual, is presented as a man worthy of respect and as a model worthy of imitation. He stands as a paradigm and teacher both for the community (as embodied in the *brigata*) and, given the story's (and the Day's) well-documented metaliterary implications, for Boccaccio himself — an exemplary role Cavalcanti had previously been fleetingly assigned in the Introduction to Day IV.[16] By concentrating almost

1990), pp. 189–220; Marie-Dominique Chenu, 'Auctor, actor, autor', *Bulletin du Cange*, 4 (1927), 81–86; Alastair J. Minnis, *Medieval Theory of Authorship*, 2nd edn (Aldershot: Scolar Press, 1988); 'Auctor' et 'auctoritas': invention et conformisme dans l'écriture médiévale, ed. by Michel Zimmermann (Paris: Écoles des Chartes, 2001).

13   On Dante's *auctoritas* and vernacular 'authority' in general, see Albert R. Ascoli, *Dante and the Making of a Modern Author* (Cambridge: Cambridge University Press, 2008); Zygmunt G. Barański, *'Chiosar con altro testo': leggere Dante nel Trecento* (Fiesole: Cadmo, 2001); Alastair J. Minnis, '"De vulgari auctoritate": Chaucer, Gower and the Men of Great Authority', in *Chaucer and Gower: Difference, Mutuality, Exchange*, ed. by Robert F. Yeager (Victoria, BC: University of Victoria, 1991), pp. 36–74, and *'Magister Amoris': The 'Roman de la Rose' and Vernacular Hermeneutics* (Oxford: Oxford University Press, 2001); *MLTC*, pp. 439–519.

14   See Fabian Alfie, 'Poetics Enacted: A Comparison of the Novellas of Guido Cavalcanti and Cecco Angiulieri in Boccaccio's *Decameron*', *Studi sul Boccaccio*, 23 (1995), 171–96; Ilario Anzani, *Cavalcanti in Boccaccio: per un'interpretazione critica di 'Decameron' VI, 9*, Lizenziatsarbeit der philosophischen Fakultät der Universität Zürich, May 2002, and 'Cavalcanti tra Dante e Boccaccio: fenomenologia della leggerezza in *Dec.* VI 9', *Rassegna europea di letteratura italiana*, 26 (2005), 21–50; Francesco Bausi, 'Lettura di *Decameron* VI.9: ritratto del filosofo averroista', *Per leggere*, 9 (2005), 5–19; Durling; Gorni; Giorgio Inglese, 'Per Guido "filosofo" (*Decameròn* VI, 9)', *La Cultura*, 30 (1992), 75–95; Roberto Mercuri, 'Guido Cavalcanti o la metafora della cultura in Dante e Boccaccio', *Esperienze letterarie*, 4 (1979), 55–58; Carlo Muscetta, 'Prefazione alla VI giornata del *Decameron*', in Giovanni Boccaccio, *Decameron*, 3 vols, ed. by Mirko Bevilacqua (Rome: Editori Riuniti, 1980), II, 503–18; Kristina M. Olson, '*Concivis meus*: Petrarch's *Rerum memorandarum libri* 2.60, Boccaccio's *Dec.* 6.9, and the Specter of Dino del Garbo', *Annali d'italianistica*, 22 (2004), 375–80; Ernesto G. Parodi, 'La miscredenza di Guido Cavalcanti e una fonte del Boccaccio', *Bullettino della Società dantesca italiana*, n.s. 22 (1915), 37–47; Luca Carlo Rossi, 'Sul motto di Cavalcanti in *Decameron* VI 9', in *L'antiche e le moderne carte: studi in memoria di Giuseppe Billanovich*, ed. by Antonio Manfredi and Carla Maria Monti (Rome and Padua: Antenore, 2007), pp. 499–517; Marco Veglia, 'Giovanni Boccaccio: *Decameron* (novella VI, 9)', in *Breviario dei classici italiani*, ed. by Gian Mario Anselmi, Alfredo Cottignoli, and Emilio Pasquini (Milan: Bruno Mondadori, 1996), pp. 44–56; Paul F. Watson, 'On Seeing Guido Cavalcanti and the Houses of the Dead', *Studi sul Boccaccio*, 18 (1989), 301–18. See also Silvia Contarini, 'La voce di Guido Cavalcanti: Jolles interprete di *Decameron* VI 9', *Studi sul Boccaccio*, 24 (1996), 209–30. On Boccaccio and Guido, see also Patrizia Grimaldi Pizzorno, 'La metafora della "sepoltura" in *Decameron* IV 1: fra Cavalcanti e Tino da Camaino', *Studi e problemi di critica testuale*, 53 (1996), 5–28; Quaglio; Marco Veglia, *'La vita lieta': una lettura del 'Decameron'* (Ravenna: Longo, 2000), pp. 10, 17, 20–21, 41.

15   Even if scholars do not highlight the issue of 'authority' when discussing Boccaccio's Guido, they normally stress that the *novelliere* praises him as an ideal intellectual; see, for instance, Anzani, *Cavalcanti in Boccaccio*, pp. 38 & 54; Carlo Muscetta, *Boccaccio* (Bari: Laterza, 1972), p. 252; Velli, p. 219.

16   See Anzani, *Cavalcanti in Boccaccio*, pp. 34–35; Franco Fido 'L'*ars narrandi* di Boccaccio nella sesta giornata', in his *Il regime di simmetrie imperfette* (Milan: Franco Angeli, 1988), pp. 73–89; Alan

exclusively on Guido's literary influence on Boccaccio (regardless of the premises for this perspective), modern scholarship could not but distort the nature of their relationship. At the same time, having recognized the significance for the *certaldese* of Cavalcanti the 'ottimo filosofo', the exemplary intellectual, and the morally upright individual par excellence, it is equally important not to then dismiss the issue of Boccaccio's poetic debts to Guido.[17]

These debts, however, and not just for reasons of space, must needs remain beyond the remit of this chapter. The ways in which Boccaccio reacted to Cavalcanti were extremely complicated. As I have begun to explain, Boccaccio was primarily interested in Guido as an intellectual and moral *auctoritas* rather than as a poet; and, in *Decameron* VI. 9, he expended considerable effort in establishing and clarifying the nature of Cavalcanti's standing. Thus, Boccaccio pointed to Guido's 'authoritativeness' both at the 'literal', narrative level of the story and through his choice of laudatory terminology. Yet, it is not at the 'surface' of the *novella* that Boccaccio primarily undertook his tribute to Cavalcanti. He did this instead in two other, rather more complex and suggestive ways: first, through the mosaic of quotations out of which he fashioned his Guido,[18] and which colours his description of the self-absorbed *filosofo*'s encounter with the disruptive *brigata*; and second, through a system of intricate structural and ideological links that he forged between the penultimate story of Day VI and other areas of the *Decameron*.[19] The present chapter addresses the first, intertextual stage of Boccaccio's operation — the 'sources' of Cavalcanti's *auctoritas*, that careful synthesis of key and, important to note, widely circulating texts which to a large extent both determine the story's narrative logic and its linguistic finish, and provide the necessary cultural and ideological support for its claims regarding its protagonist's 'authority'.[20] Thus, briefly to return once more to the matter of Boccaccio's poetic debts to Guido, it is clear that their import and extent can only be satisfactorily assessed once Cavalcanti's significance for the *novelliere* has been better established.

Freedman, 'Il cavallo del Boccaccio: fonte, struttura e funzione della metanovella di madonna Oretta', *Studi sul Boccaccio*, 9 (1975–76), 225–41; Michelangelo Picone, 'Madonna Oretta e le novelle *in itinere* (Dec. VI. I)', in *Favole parabole istorie: le forme della scrittura novellistica dal Medioevo al Rinascimento*, ed. by Gabriella Albanese and others (Rome: Salerno, 2000), pp. 67–83.

17   Cavalcanti's poetry did affect Boccaccio's versifying, though rather less seminally than normally has been claimed; see nn. 3 & 4 above.

18   Michelangelo Picone has aptly noted with reference to the 'problema spinoso delle "fonti" o dei modelli letterari' of the *Decameron* that 'la situazione degli studi in questo campo è a dir poco allarmante': Michelangelo Picone, 'Leggiadri motti e pronte risposte: la sesta giornata', in *Introduzione al 'Decameron'*, ed. by Michelangelo Picone and Margherita Mesirca (Florence: Cesati, 2004), pp. 163–86 (p. 174). Two useful overarching studies of Boccaccio's use of his sources in the *Decameron* are Costanzo Di Girolamo and Charmaine Lee, 'Fonti', and Giuseppe Velli, 'Memoria', both in Bragantini and Forni, pp. 142–61 & 222–48 respectively.

19   On the problem of the structure of the *Decameron*, see Franco Fido, 'Architettura', in Bragantini and Forni, pp. 13–33.

20   When I wrote the original version of this chapter, I had hoped to be able to follow it up fairly quickly with a complementary study on VI. 9's intratextual functions in the *Decameron*. Alas, as new and more pressing commitments distract me, my original notes and good intentions continue to gather dust. However, see my 'The Tale of Forese da Rabatta and Giotto (VI.5)', in *The 'Decameron' Sixth Day in Perspective*, ed. by David Lummus (Toronto: University of Toronto Press, forthcoming).

2. The Sources of *auctoritas*

Boccaccio scholarship has highlighted two principal sources for *Decameron* VI. 9. Cavalcanti's quickfire allusion to the 'houses of the dead', uttered to fend off the unwelcome intrusion and inane questioning of the members of the *brigata*, who had trapped him among the marble tombs around San Giovanni, has, quite correctly, been recognized as a widely circulating cliché which associated intellectual torpor with death:[21]

> Ser Betto con sua brigata [...] cominciarongli a dire: 'Guido, tu rifiuti d'esser di nostra brigata; ma ecco, quando tu avrai trovato che Idio non sia, che avrai fatto?'
>
> A' quali Guido, da lor veggendosi chiuso, prestamente disse: 'Signori, voi mi potete dire a casa vostra ciò che vi piace' [...].
>
> Alli quali [his companions] messer Betto rivolto, disse: 'Gli smemorati siete voi, se voi non l'avete inteso: egli ci ha onestamente e in poche parole detta la maggior villania del mondo, per ciò che, se voi riguarderete bene, queste arche sono le case de' morti, per ciò che in esse si pongono e dimorano i morti; le quali egli dice che son nostra casa, a dimostrarci che noi e gli altri uomini idioti e non letterati siamo, a comparazion di lui e degli altri uomini scienziati, peggio che uomini morti, e per ciò, qui essendo, noi siamo a casa nostra'. (*Dec.* VI. 9. 10–12, 14)

It is not difficult to appreciate how Boccaccio's reworking of the saying both organizes the close of the *novella* and serves as an effective means to underscore Cavalcanti's intellectual stature. It is equally fairly straightforward to grasp the relevance of the second of the two main sources of the story hitherto indicated by critics, namely, canto X of *Inferno*, the canto in which Cavalcante de' Cavalcanti inquires about the whereabouts of his son:[22]

> [Cavalcante] piangendo disse: 'Se per questo cieco
> carcere vai per altezza d'ingegno,
> mio figlio ov' è? e perché non è teco?'.
>   E io a lui: 'Da me stesso non vegno:
> colui ch'attende là, per qui mi mena
> forse cui Guido vostro ebbe a disdegno'. (*Inf.* X. 58–63)

Scholars have noted how Dante's stress on Cavalcanti's haughtiness and on his intelligence are both crucial elements that return in Boccaccio's portrayal (Alfie, p. 180). In addition, and more importantly, they have emphasized that his reference to the heretical tenor of Guido's Epicurean-inspired speculations regarding the existence of God (Alfie, p. 176; Veglia, 'La vita lieta', p. 21) — and I would add the story's overall eschatological atmosphere — have their origins, too, in the

---

21   On the 'houses of the dead' topos and on its functions in *Decameron* VI. 9, see Branca's annotation in *Dec.*, p. 753, n. 1; Elena Landoni, 'Strutture lessicali ricorrenti nel modello del motto verbale arguto: il caso di *Decamerone* VI.9 e dell'*Antica vita iacoponica*', *Testo*, 22 (1991), 74–81; Parodi, pp. 42–45; Quaglio, pp. 366–68; see also Subsection 4 below, 'The "Houses of the Dead"'.
22   See, for instance, Alfie, pp. 176–77, 180; Anzani, *Cavalcanti in Boccaccio*, p. 19; Francesco Bruni, *Boccaccio: l'invenzione della letteratura mezzana* (Bologna: il Mulino, 1990), pp. 298–301; Durling, pp. 281–84; Gorni, pp. 365–66.

Commedia.[23] Dante, of course, did not actually consign Cavalcanti *fils* to the circle of heresy (this was not an option open to him as Guido was still alive, even if for not much longer, during Easter-time 1300, the period of time during which he set the *Commedia*). Nonetheless, there has long been widespread agreement (though, as we shall soon see, for not as long nor as unanimously as many of today's Dantists imagine) that, first by damning Cavalcanti's father, and then by evoking Guido himself in the sixth circle, Dante was fairly openly charging the *filosofo* with being an Epicurean, a member of the heterodox 'sect' (*Inf.* IX. 128) that he presented as emblematic of the sin of heresy:

> Suo cimitero da questa parte hanno
> con Epicuro tutti i suoi seguaci,
> che l'anima col corpo morta fanno. (*Inf.* x. 13–15)

When Dante called into question Guido's religious orthodoxy, it is very likely that his charge was without foundation.[24] It was a carefully crafted calumny, a memorable and disconcerting instance of the growing bitterness of his feelings towards his former 'primo amico'.[25] His accusations are all the more disturbing since, given Guido's untimely death on 29 August 1300, namely, a matter of months after the date of Dante's supposed otherworldly voyage, they seem to imply that, with so little time to mend his ways and with no evidence to suggest such an intention on his part — indeed the opposite would appear to be more likely given his 'disdainful' attitude — Cavalcanti can already be counted among the damned. This is condemnation of the harshest kind in a religious culture which envisaged the possibility of repentance *in extremis*.[26] And critics have stressed that Boccaccio was clearly troubled by Dante's intransigent lack of *charitas* towards not just someone whom he had once called a friend, but also towards someone who was widely acknowledged to be one of Florence's leading lights (and Day VI as a whole is a celebration of past Tuscan and in particular past Florentine customs and wit; the opening three paragraphs of our story (4–6), which dwell on the fact that 'ne' tempi passati furono nella nostra città assai belle e laudevoli usanze' (4), are a telling

---

23   By raising matters relating to the afterlife in a context profoundly marked by Dante's *Commedia* (see below, pp. 501–02, for other Dantean elements in the *novella*), Boccaccio was almost inevitably introducing an eschatological atmosphere into *Decameron* VI. 9. Boccaccio makes use of this same ploy in *Dec.* III. 4. 8, 10; V. 8.

24   To put it simply, Dante's attack is baseless because no independent evidence exists to corroborate it. Dantists have attempted to legitimate the poet's charge by pointing to Cavalcanti's presumed Averroistic sympathies. However, there is once again no documentary proof to suggest that, in the Middle Ages, Epicurus and Averroes, and hence their respective followers, were ever associated or seen as counterparts; see Chapter 13, pp. 470–72; Parodi, pp. 37–40. See below for further discussion of these points, pp. 497–502 & 509, and in particular Chapter 3, n. 94.

25   Dante terms Cavalcanti his 'primo amico' in *Vn* III. 14; XXIV. 3 and 6; XXV. 10; XXX. 3. The critical literature on Dante and Cavalcanti is now substantial; see Chapter 13, n. 6.

26   Dante normally laid great store on this possibility as is evident from his treatment of the late repentant in Ante-Purgatory. At the same time, Guido is not the only living person whom the poet condemns to Hell. Pope Boniface VIII and Branca d'Oria share a similar fate. On this last point, see Chapter 3, pp. 96–102.

instance of this perspective).[27] Thus, *Decameron* VI. 9 has normally been interpreted as Boccaccio's attempt to counter Dante's negative treatment of Cavalcanti. The *novelliere* — as we have seen — paints a highly flattering portrait of Guido. More significantly, however, he does not simply allude to *Inferno* X to highlight his difference of opinion with Dante, but, in order to 'save' Cavalcanti, directly subverts the *Commedia*'s association between the *filosofo* and heresy, thereby vouchsaving his intellectual integrity.[28] Boccaccio's most obvious borrowing from the sixth circle is his story's sepulchral setting. Dante's heretics are trapped for eternity in fiery tombs, specifically in 'arche' (*Inf.* IX. 125), and the same recherché term is twice employed by Boccaccio to describe his cemetery. However, while Dante's Guido seems likely to be doomed to remain in his *arca* in perpetuity, Boccaccio's Guido, having fired off his cutting retort, dramatically escapes both from the clutches of the *brigata* and from the restrictions of the 'arche grandi di marmo' (10):

> A' quali Guido, da lor veggendosi chiuso, prestamente disse: 'Signori, voi mi potete dire a casa vostra ciò che vi piace'; e posta la mano sopra una di quelle arche, che grandi erano, sí come colui che leggerissimo era, prese un salto e fusi gittato dall'altra parte, e sviluppatosi da loro se n'andò. (*Dec.* VI. 9. 12)

It is difficult to find fault with the general interpretive directions taken by critics when examining the functions in *Decameron* VI. 9 of its two traditionally recognized sources. Nevertheless, scholarly work on the story's intertexts has tended to be overly cautious. In saying this, I am not broadly alluding to the fact that, as shall be my aim to demonstrate, it is possible to discern other important influences on its composition; nor am I specifically referring to the implications for Boccaccio's story of sidelining its preoccupation with Cavalcanti's 'authority'. My concern here is to highlight the critical tentativeness with which even *Inferno* X and the 'houses of the dead' *sententia* have been treated.

3. Rewriting 'Authority'

The most striking aspect of Dante's and Boccaccio's respective presentation of Cavalcanti is not, as has normally been maintained, the dependence of the short story on *Inferno* X, but the fact that both writers depend on a common well-spring of sources. As with Boccaccio's other passages in which Guido makes an appearance, so too the *Commedia* and *Decameron* VI. 9 are constructed out of elements taken from the impressive body of largely overlapping texts in which Cavalcanti's life and exploits were recorded, and which constitute the most obvious mark of the enormous respect in which he was held by his contemporaries. Boccaccio revisited this shared

27   See Mario Baratto, *Realtà e stile nel 'Decameron'* (Vicenza: Neri Pozza, 1970), pp. 31 & 336; Nicolò Mineo, 'La sesta giornata del *Decameron* o del potere delle donne', *Rassegna europea di letteratura italiana*, 3 (1994), 44–69 (p. 66); Velli, 'Seneca nel *Decameron*', p. 219.

28   See, for instance, Alfie, pp. 176–77 & 180; Durling; Franco Fido, *Il regime di simmetrie imperfette* (Milan: Franco Angeli, 1988), pp. 119–20; Gorni; Mercuri. Some critics, while accepting Boccaccio's sympathetic treatment of Cavalcanti, nevertheless also claim that, like Dante, the *novelliere* too deemed him an unorthodox thinker. I find this position unpersuasive. If Boccaccio had presented Guido as in any way heterodox, this would have completely undermined his efforts to confirm the *filosofo* as a major 'authority'. For further discussion of these points, see below pp. 505–11.

cultural heritage because he fervently disagreed with the ways in which Dante had earlier exploited it. Thus, in his short story, he was not simply drawing on *Inferno* x's portrait of Cavalcanti so as to call this into question, but was actually involved in a rather more subtle operation. By going back to and then reproposing the textual bases of Dante's Guido, Boccaccio, first and foremost, was passing judgement on the manner in which the poet had chosen to inflect the conventional likeness of the 'buon filosofo'. It was not just Dante's view of Cavalcanti that Boccaccio was challenging; more precisely and suggestively, he was expressing disquiet at how his great predecessor had realized his portrayal of an illustrious contemporary.

Indeed, the extent of his disquiet must have been considerable. Boccaccio had recognized something in *Inferno* x which no one before him had appreciated. In discussing the relationship between *Decameron* VI. 9 and *Inferno* x, modern scholars assume that, since Boccaccio, in harmony with their preferred interpretation, see in the canto an attack on Cavalcanti, this was a widely held view in medieval Italy. Nothing, in fact, is further from the truth. On the basis of the available evidence, it is obvious that not only was *Inferno* x not read in this manner (Chapter 13, pp. 454–55; and n. 42 below), but that the idea of any kind of tension between Dante and Guido was equally not current. The common perception was actually the opposite.[29] The realization that Dante was intent on distancing himself from Cavalcanti must have troubled Boccaccio. However, this was as naught compared to the realization that the poet was accusing his former friend — the contemporary paragon of philosophical acumen — of being a heretic. As confirmed by *Decameron* VI. 9, Boccaccio is the first recorded reader of the canto to recognize both Dante's insinuations regarding Guido's Epicureanism and his general fault-finding with his 'first friend'. This was almost certainly a shocking discovery — a discovery, in fact, that placed the *novelliere* in a difficult predicament. Thus, the unease left by the poet's calculated malice vied with the powerful admiration for all that the author of the *Commedia* had achieved; and both sentiments became confused with the worry over the implications for Guido's reputation of Dante's charges, as well as with the concomitant anxiety over the implications of these same charges for Dante's standing (the accusation of Epicureanism was potentially damaging to both accuser and accused).[30] *Decameron* VI. 9, I believe, constitutes Boccaccio's attempt

---

29   See Benvenuto, I, 340–41; Boccaccio, *Esposizioni*, p. 526; *Commento della Divina Commedia d'anonimo fiorentino*, I, 254; Filippo Villani, *Le vite d'uomini illustri fiorentini*, ed. by Giammaria Mazzuchelli (Florence: Sansone Coen Tipografo-Editore, 1847), p. 57; Francesco da Buti, 'Il "Commento" di Francesco da Buti alla "Commedia". "Inferno"', ed. by Claudia Tardelli (unpublished PhD thesis, Scuola Normale Superiore di Pisa, 2010–11), p. 284; Graziolo Bambaglioli, *Commento all'*'Inferno' *di Dante*, ed. by Luca Carlo Rossi (Pisa: Scuola Normale Superiore, 1998), p. 83; Guido da Pisa, *Expositiones et glose*, ed. by Michele Rinaldi, 2 vols (Rome: Salerno, 2013), I, 448; Iacomo della Lana, *Commento alla* 'Commedia', ed. by Mirko Volpi with the collaboration of Arianna Terzi, 4 vols (Rome: Salerno, 2009), I, 334; *L'ottimo commento della Divina Commedia*, ed. by Alessandro Torri, 3 vols (Pisa: Niccolò Capurro, 1827–29), I, 177–79.

30   On Boccaccio's complex attitude to Dante, see at least Todd Boli, 'Boccaccio's *Trattatello in laude di Dante*, or *Dante Resartus*', *Renaissance Quarterly*, 41 (1988), 389–412; Martin Eisner, *Boccaccio and the Invention of Italian Literature: Dante, Petrarch, Cavalcanti and the Authority of the Vernacular* (Cambridge: Cambridge University Press, 2013); Robert Hollander, *Boccaccio's Dante and the Shaping Force of Satire* (Ann Arbor: University of Michigan Press 1997); James Kriesel, *Boccaccio's Corpus: Allegory, Ethics,*

to resolve and draw advantage from the predicament in which *Inferno* x had left him, rather than — as critics have long claimed — simply serving as a rebuttal of the canto. The operation was extraordinarily complex and arduous. As we shall soon see, it involved strongly reaffirming Guido's traditional *auctoritas*; criticizing, albeit with care, aspects of Dante's presentation while attempting to conceal others, and endeavouring to protect and acknowledge the poet's prestige; and, finally, integrating his treatment of Cavalcanti and Dante into a broad assessment of the role of 'authority' in contemporary culture.[31]

It is not surprising that little of all this should have emerged in modern scholarship. The failure adequately to address Dante's and Boccaccio's debts to medieval accounts of Guido has inevitably constrained discussion.[32] Thus, Dantists have tended to present *Inferno* x as offering a distinctly individual, private even, representation of Cavalcanti — a representation, therefore, that has its origins in the two poets' actual contacts, in what is perceived to have been an increasingly acrimonious personal relationship.[33] Yet, apart from the idiosyncratic charge of Epicureanism, the remainder of Dante's depiction correlates fairly explicitly to some of the most popular elements that had accrued around the figure of Guido. Ultimately, even the eccentric accusation that the *filosofo* was a 'follower of Epicurus' can essentially be explained in terms of Cavalcanti's contemporary reception. By tying Guido to Epicureanism, widely deemed the very worst of intellectual errors and, as such, rejected by 'tutti li savi e li filosofi' (*Ottimo commento*, I, 172), Dante raised serious doubts about his former friend's famed philosophical acuity, his 'altezza d'ingegno' (*Inf.* x. 59). Developing his denunciation, Dante unambiguously presented Cavalcanti's intellectual blunder as a consequence of his 'disdainful' and arrogant nature (*Inf.* x. 61–63) — character traits that had become closely associated with Guido, but which, in keeping with the conventions of the *vitae* of

---

and Vernacularity (Notre Dame, IN: University of Notre Dame Press, 2018); Martin L. McLaughlin, *Literary Imitation in the Italian Renaissance* (Oxford: Clarendon Press, 1995), pp. 50–62; *MLTC*, pp. 453–58. To be consulted with caution: Jason Houston, *Building a Monument to Dante: Boccaccio as Dantista* (Toronto, Buffalo, and London: University of Toronto Press, 2010).

31   For an excellent analysis of Boccaccio's ideas on 'authority', history, and modernity, see David Lummus, 'Boccaccio's Hellenism and the Foundations of Modernity', *Mediaevalia*, 33 (2012), 101–67.

32   This flaw is especially apparent in readings of *Inferno* x. A few recent analyses of *Decameron* VI. 9, in the wake of Baratto, p. 337, have begun to appreciate the influence on Boccaccio of contemporary views of Guido; see Anzani, *Cavalcanti in Boccaccio*, pp. 19 & 95; Inglese; Gorni.

33   Scholars have long tended to explain the nature of Dante and Guido's difficult relationship in highly personalized and psychologizing terms. There is, in fact, little evidence to support such an interpretation. What evidence has come down to us suggests that the conflict between the two poets was fundamentally cultural, revolving around the intellectual and artistic standing, the 'authority', that each had acquired or was hoping to attain. See Zygmunt G. Barański, ' "Per similitudine di abito scientifico": Dante, Cavalcanti, and the Sources of Medieval "Philosophical" Poetry', in *Literature and Science in Italian Culture: From Dante to Calvino. A Festschrift in Honour of Pat Boyde*, ed. by Pierpaolo Antonello and Simon Gilson (Oxford: Legenda, 2004), pp. 14–52. By focusing, in *Decameron* VI. 9, on contemporary writing about Cavalcanti, Boccaccio was recognizing both his societal import and, more pertinently for my present argument, the cultural rather than the biographical reverberations of Dante's treatment of Guido.

great men, were normally treated positively, as marks of his superiority.[34] Finally, by depicting a selfishly haughty Cavalcanti against the backdrop of the Epicureans' rejection of the immortality of the soul, the primary cause, as was popularly believed, for their also subscribing to the view that 'la filicità delli uomini fosse nella delettazione della carne', Dante efficiently and tellingly undermined the many positive personal and social attributes with which the figure of Guido had become adorned.[35] In sharp contrast to his ignoble image of Cavalcanti, the poet introduced himself as closely tied to an intellectual and spiritual tradition with salvation as its end:

> 'Se per questo cieco
> carcere vai per altezza d'ingegno,
> mio figlio ov' è? e perché non è teco?'.
>   E io a lui: 'Da me stesso non vegno:
> colui ch'attende là, per qui mi mena
> forse cui Guido vostro ebbe a disdegno.' (*Inf.* x. 58–63)

It is readily apparent that, in the *Inferno*, Dante was deliberately undermining the principal supports on which Cavalcanti's *auctoritas* had been built. At the same time, in direct and open opposition to his 'first friend', he was also engaged in establishing his own superior 'authoritativeness', and, by extension, that of his thought and of his writings, most notably the divinely sanctioned *auctoritas* of the *Commedia*. As is well known, throughout his career, Dante was intent to establish himself as the supreme, probably unique, modern and vernacular 'authority'; and one way in which he did this was to denigrate those who in any way threatened his position. Thus, Dante's antagonism towards Guido — at least in terms of the evidence that has come down to us — is not something 'private', but arises from concerns about Cavalcanti's and his own public standing. Indeed, even the seemingly most intimate moment of the pilgrim's exchange with Cavalcante, the latter's appeal to the ties of companionship binding Dante to his son — 'mio figlio ov' è? e perché non è teco?' (60) — is less a reminiscence of their life together in Florence than yet another cultural commonplace that the poet was keen to rebut. In addressing his frantic question to Dante-*personaggio*, Cavalcante expresses the idea, extensively present in texts celebrating Guido, that his son and the poet were not just close, but also that they complemented each other (see n. 30 above). Dante immediately dismissed such a suggestion. By having the pilgrim point to his new companion, while at the same time emphasizing Guido's 'disdegno', Dante definitively declared that not even the most fragile thread still connected him to his former friend.

In fourteenth-century terms, Dante's treatment of Cavalcanti is unusual not only on account of its unremitting negativity, but also because of its selectiveness. His portrait, while effective in painting an unappealing image of Guido, is actually

---

34   See, for instance, Boccaccio, *Esposizioni*, p. 526; Dino Compagni, *Cronica delle cose occorrenti ne' tempi suoi*, ed. by Fabio Pittorru (Milan: Rizzoli, 1965), I. 20 (p. 54). Dante is described with these same attributes by Boccaccio, *Trattatello*, p. 163, and by Giovanni Villani, *Nuova cronica*, ed. by Giuseppe Porta, 3 vols (Parma: Fondazione Pietro Bembo-Guanda, 1991), x. 136. See also Chapter 13, pp. 450–51. On the tradition of the *vitae*, see the same chapter, n. 19.

35   *Ottimo commento*, I, 172. See Chapter 13, pp. 462–64.

based on a very limited number of the elements which, in the Middle Ages, had become associated with the 'philosopher'. Boccaccio signalled his disapproval of Dante's strategy not just by the overwhelmingly positive tenor of his presentation of Cavalcanti, but also by its comprehensiveness. He, thus, challenged *Inferno* x for its selective bias. Conversely, *Decameron* VI. 9 appears as a kind of 'objective' *summa* of the motifs traditionally used to define Guido, and hence serves as an overarching assessment and confirmation of the nature of his 'authority'. As a consequence, the short story ranges from the key commonplaces of Cavalcanti's presentation, for instance, his intelligence, to singular and idiosyncratic claims, such as Dante's charge of Epicureanism; and, within the boundaries of the *novella*, the validity of each claim is carefully weighed. After Dante's potentially damaging intervention, Boccaccio was keen to counter any unflattering suggestions that had or might become associated with Guido's name. Thus, apparently negative details introduced into his short story are shown to be without substance. They either are expressions of ignorance (the *gente volgare*'s misunderstanding of Cavalcanti's 'speculazioni', 9) or are actually evidence of his exceptional wisdom (the fact that 'molto abstratto dagli uomini divenia', 9). Furthermore, to ensure that *Decameron* VI. 9 was not read simply, or even primarily, as a criticism of *Inferno* x, but that instead it was treated as a balanced and judicious assessment, Boccaccio not only corrected Dante, but also rectified other misapprehensions regarding Cavalcanti. Thus, the emphasis on Guido's wealth and his generosity — 'e con questo era ricchissimo, e a chiedere a lingua sapeva onorare cui nell'animo gli capeva che il valesse' (8) — is meant to counteract accusations of avarice that were occasionally levied against Cavalcanti.[36] Indeed, Boccaccio underlined this point by noting that 'avarizia' was generally absent from the Florence of Guido's day: 'ne' tempi passati furono nella nostra città assai belle e laudevoli usanze, delle quali oggi niuna ve n'è rimasa, mercé della avarizia che in quella con le ricchezze è cresciuta' (4).

Detail after detail of Boccaccio's description of Guido finds a precedent in other, earlier accounts:

> Guido di messer Cavalcante de' Cavalcanti [...] oltre a quello che egli fu un de' miglior loici che avesse il mondo e ottimo filosofo naturale [...], si fu egli leggiadrissimo e costumato e parlante uom molto e ogni cosa che far volle e a gentile uom pertenente seppe meglio che altro uom fare; e con questo era ricchissimo, e a chiedere a lingua sapeva onorare cui nell'animo gli capeva che il valesse. Ma a messer Betto non era mai potuto venir fatto d'averlo, e credeva egli co' suoi compagni che ciò avvenisse per ciò che Guido alcuna volta speculando molto abstratto dagli uomini divenia; e per ciò che egli alquanto tenea della oppinione degli epicuri, si diceva tralla gente volgare che queste sue speculazioni erano solo in cercare se trovar si potesse che Iddio non fosse. (*Dec.* VI. 9. 8–9)

Thus, the allusions to Cavalcanti's parentage, to his logical and philosophical

---

36   See Guido Orlandi, 'Amico, i' saccio ben che sa' limare', in Cavalcanti, *Rime*, pp. 204–05: 'e largamente prendere e donare, | salvar lo guadagnato (ciò m'è detto), | accoglier gente, terra guadagnare' (5–7); Niccola Muscia, 'Ècci venuto Guido ['n] Compostello', in Cavalcanti, *Rime*, pp. 119–20.

abilities, to the excellence of his behaviour, to his linguistic skills, to his *gentilezza*, to his wealth, to his abstraction, to his disdain for the company of others, to his speculative tendencies are all well-established characteristics of his medieval portraiture (see Chapter 13, pp. 462–64). Equally, the use of superlatives is conventional; while even his physical prowess, which permits him to escape the *brigata*, has a basis in the tradition, just as the motif of an attack by horsemen followed by a getaway also finds a precedent in contemporary writing about Guido (Compagni, I. 20; p. 54). The Florentine setting, too, is typical, given the frequent stress on the intimate ties between Cavalcanti and his city (see Chapter 13, pp. 452–53). In fact, Boccaccio creates an idealized setting, an urban *locus amoenus*, in which to locate and honour his idealized 'hero'; and idealization is, of course, a fundamental aspect of every portrayal of an *auctoritas*.

Boccaccio's knowledge of Cavalcanti the 'authority', as distinct from Cavalcanti the poet, was impressive; as was the subtle manner in which he wove the varied threads of Guido's medieval renown into a new and highly suggestive tapestry. Beneath this, however, it is possible to espy a much older pattern of venerability. The short story is stitched on to the weave of the long-established tradition of the wise man behaving eccentrically — at least in the eyes of the majority or of those who do not share his intelligence — and who often confirms his superiority thanks to an unerringly apposite observation.[37] As with other of its constituent elements, critics have once again paid little attention to *Decameron* VI. 9's debts to this tradition (the fact that they have underplayed the *novella*'s interest in 'authority' stems in part from this omission). They have been too intent to read the short story essentially as a moment in Boccaccio's rich reaction to Dante, thereby, as we have seen, seeking to explain its genesis largely in terms of the *Commedia*. Yet, by locating *Decameron* VI. 9's originary point of departure in the wise man tradition, Boccaccio was choosing the ideal structure on to which to graft his own story of 'authority'. In order to substantiate and defend Cavalcanti's wisdom, he could legitimately range widely across the typical, culturally sanctioned elements that defined Guido's exceptional intellectual prowess, and which were, ultimately, also the best protection against *Inferno* X's accusations.

Nevertheless, for all Boccaccio's determined and notable effort in *Decameron* VI. 9 equitably to synthesize and celebrate the tradition on Cavalcanti, it is difficult to deny that *Inferno* X is the *novella*'s most obvious source.[38] This is not surprising

---

37   See for instance stories LXI and LXVI in the *Novellino*, ed. by Alberto Conte (Rome: Salerno, 2001); for further references to this tradition see pp. 351, 358–59 of this edition.

38   There are other Dantean elements, besides those taken from *Inferno* X, in the *novella*: the figure of Betto Brunelleschi, as the recipient of one of Dante's sonnets, cannot but call to mind the poet; the evocation of past Florentine glories recalls the celebration of the Florence of Cacciaguida's day in *Paradiso*; lamenting present-day Florentine decadence is a commonplace in Dante; finally, several details recall the cantos of barratry (in particular *Inferno* XXII): thus, the devils that both capture Ciampolo and attempt to attack Virgil and the pilgrim are compared to 'cavalier' (XXII. 1), while Ciampolo, having uttered his *motto* (106), leaps to safety: '"Odi malizia | ch'elli ha pensata per gittarsi giuso!" | [...] | fermò le piante a terra, e in un punto | saltò e dal proposto lor si sciolse' (107–08, 122–23), and compare 'e posta la mano sopra una di quelle arche [...] prese un salto e fusi gittato dall'altra parte, e sviluppatosi da loro se n'andò' (12). See also n. 41 below. On Boccaccio's recourse

given that, in the first instance, the short story is a reaction to Dante's assault on his 'first friend'. However, drawing so visibly on *Inferno* x, Boccaccio faced the danger of ending up by having the poet dominate his representation, and thereby distorting his critical and corrective ambitions. At the same time, it was only by engaging properly with Dante's claims that Boccaccio could feel confident that he was effectively tackling the poet's allegations. In a somewhat circular manoeuvre, the tradition on Cavalcanti served him both as the yardstick with which the soundness of his and Dante's accounts of the *filosofo* were to be measured, and as the institution whose own validity, under pressure from Dante's revisionism, was in need of protection. The *novella*, whose 'truthfulness' is bolstered by its carefully constructed historical and geographical setting, provides compelling evidence for the legitimacy of the conventional image of Cavalcanti not only by recalling the range of his excellence, but also by offering, via the anecdote of his encounter with the horsemen, a concrete and documented instance of his intelligence — the primary mark of his distinction — and of its beneficial effects on others. Conversely, by immersing references to *Inferno* x into the unrelentingly positive and culturally homogeneous context of *Decameron* vi. 9, Boccaccio ensured that Dante's portrait of Guido could not appear but at odds with the tradition. Attention is directed towards its subjectivity and towards the disturbing fact, that, unlike Boccaccio, Dante, in *Inferno*, apart from the allusion to Cavalcanti's 'disdain',[39] did not actually provide corroborating evidence to support his damaging reading of the conventional bases of Guido's 'authority', and hence was unable to verify his claims against either his 'primo amico' or the tradition.[40] More specifically, the poet could not authenticate his most shocking and unexpected claim — Cavalcanti's involvement with heresy. Under Boccaccio's scrutiny, Dante's charge that Guido had misused his 'altezza d'ingegno' (*Inf.* x. 59), thus appears without substance. As a result, any doubts that the poet had raised regarding Cavalcanti's cultural standing are fairly definitively dispelled. It is, in fact, Dante's (not to mention the *Commedia*'s) *auctoritas*, and not Guido's, that ends up coming under critical scrutiny.

to Dante in his treatment of Florentine history, see Kristina M. Olson, *Courtesy Lost: Dante, Boccaccio, and the Literature of History* (Toronto, Buffalo, and London: University of Toronto Press, 2014).
39   In any case, as we have seen, a disdainful attitude was not necessarily a negative trait — it could be the mark of a lofty intellect. Indeed, several medieval Dante commentators, intererpreting Guido's 'disdain' as directed at Virgil, saw this as a reference to Cavalcanti favouring the higher pursuit of philosophy over poetry. See Chapter 13, p. 456.
40   To underscore *Inferno* x's flawed vision, Boccaccio not only criticized its treatment of Cavalcanti, but also called into question other aspects of the canto. Thus, his presentation of the Florence of the recent past paints a picture of a morally upright city rather than of one riven by factionalism; similarly, when mentioning 'messer Cavalcante de' Cavalcanti' (7), Boccaccio offers no criticism of Guido's father. It is also noteworthy in this respect that the condition of the infernal damned, with whom Dante's Guido is implicitly associated, whereby 'tutto è vano | nostro intelletto [...] | [...] | [...] tutta morta | fia nostra conoscenza' (103–04, 106–07), recalls the intellectual 'death' of Betto and the other horsemen. Finally, as yet another example of the degree to which Boccaccio's short story depends on Dante's canto, it is suggestive that the incipit of *Inferno* x — 'Ora sen va' — is re–echoed at the beginning of the description of the encounter between Cavalcanti and the *brigata*: 'Ora avenne' (10).

The manner in which Boccaccio involved the whole Cavalcantian tradition in constructing *Decameron* VI. 9 provides the key to the way in which he had decided to deal with *Inferno* X. His aim was to focus on Guido rather than on Dante. In this way, he could both bolster Cavalcanti's *auctoritas* and redimension Dante's criticisms. He wanted to point to *Inferno* X's accusations, but without exaggerating their import. They were simply part of a minority position regarding Guido that expressed a degree of criticism of the great man. By assessing Dante's views against those of the tradition, Boccaccio both contextualized the poet's opinion, and removed any suspicion that his own revisionary tactic was somehow orchestrated for personal ends. Even though there is little doubt that, in the last analysis, Boccaccio was unrelenting in his rejection of Dante's view of Guido — I return below and in greater detail to the tensions characterizing the *novelliere*'s attitude to his illustrious predecessor — his immediate intent was to create the impression that he was simply restoring proper order among the proliferation of discourses that had accrued around a venerable figure, and not aggressively targetting any particular individual or stance. The one aspect of Dante's presentation, however, that he could not neutralize so easily was, of course, the startling indictment of heretical Epicureanism. It is thus not surprising that, although Boccaccio was able to imply that the charge of heresy — like Dante's lesser charges against Cavalcanti — was baseless, it was of such seriousness that he felt compelled to fashion a special and specific *escamotage* in order to deal with it.

Notwithstanding that, in the middle of the fourteenth century, he was probably alone in recognizing what the poet had done, and despite his own best efforts to stress the positive and marginalize the negative as regards Cavalcanti, Boccaccio is likely to have felt that Dante's accusation of heresy cast a heavy and threatening shadow over his former friend's exalted public standing. It was only a matter of time before someone else interpreted *Inferno* X as he had done.[41] As a result of his insidious insinuation, Dante had created the potential for a serious disturbance in the overwhelmingly positive appreciation of Guido. By suggesting that Cavalcanti was intellectually and morally bankrupt, and hence unfit to be treated as an *auctoritas*, the poet was not just criticizing his 'first friend', but also anyone who saw merit in Cavalcanti. To put it simply and more directly, given Guido's cultural prestige, Dante was calling the tradition into question. However, as far as Boccaccio was concerned, the tradition was precisely what confirmed and guaranteed Guido's exemplary greatness. In standing up to Dante, therefore, Boccaccio was also taking on the tricky role of defender of his culture's dominant values; and, in the Trecento, to do so in opposition to the author of the *Commedia*, the paragon, according to

---

41 Ironically, in the wake of Boccaccio's *novella*, this is exactly what happened. Thus, the *certaldese*'s 'imitators', Benvenuto da Imola (I, 340 & 342), Filippo Villani (p. 57), and Domenico Bandino d'Arezzo (*Fons Memorabilium*, ms. Laur. Edili 172, fol. 183r., quoted in Parodi, p. 40, n. 1), treat Guido's heterodoxy as a matter of fact, almost certainly bolstered by Boccaccio's authority. All four writers, who constitute a tradition apart on this point, are exceptions to the customarily unproblematic reading of Dante's allusion to Guido in the episode of the infernal Epicureans. In any case, apart from Boccaccio, no one else deems Cavalcanti's Epicureanism as a reason for calling into question the closeness of his relationship with Dante.

many, of all that was best and most respectable in 'modern' intellectual and artistic life, was no small matter.

That *Decameron* VI. 9 is profoundly interested in resolving and rectifying (cultural) conflict and misinterpretation is apparent from the fact that this concern is not the exclusive product of its intertextual relationship with *Inferno* x. The same idea is centrally present at the story's narrative level. Indeed, in harmony with its other metacritical implications, the *novella* can be read as a kind of 'allegorization' of the cultural tensions which, by alluding to Dante, Boccaccio was attempting to evoke, examine, and resolve. It tells how, during his life, Cavalcanti's ideas and behaviour had been misconstrued and not properly appreciated: 'delle quali cose [Cavalcanti's intellectual successes] poco la brigata curava' (8); 'si diceva tralla gente volgare che queste sue speculazioni erano solo in cercare se trovar si potesse che Iddio non fosse' (9); 'Costoro rimaser tutti guatando l'un l'altro, e cominciaron a dire che egli era uno smemorato e che quello che egli aveva risposto non veniva a dir nulla' (13). It had needed an insightful interpreter of Guido's words, Betto Brunelleschi, to come to his support and to restore his reputation. The parallels between the narrative content of *Decameron* VI. 9 and the ways in which, intertextually, Boccaccio organized the triangular relationship between himself, Cavalcanti, and Dante are more than self-evident. Indeed, the remedial and restorative character of the *novelliere*'s cultural strategy integrates neatly with the unifying topic of Day VI: 'incomincia la Sesta, nella quale [...] si ragiona di chi con alcun leggiadro motto, tentato, si riscotesse, o con pronta risposta o avvedimento fuggí perdita o pericolo o scorno' (Intro. VI. 1).[42] Given the prestige of the problems raised by *Decameron* VI. 9 — vernacular *auctoritas*, cultural memory, the role of the intellectual, Dante's and the *Commedia*'s status — it is not unreasonable to recognize in Cavalcanti the structural and ideological fulcrum around which the whole of Day VI revolves.[43]

---

42   *Mutatis mutandis*, and in very general terms, the *motto*, if considered rhetorically, is not dissimilar in function and status to the *novella*, especially when the latter is judged in relation to the other main medieval prose genres. More specifically, the improvements that the *motti* bring about in the narrative unfolding of each of the tales of Day VI. parallels our short story's effort to restore and safeguard Guido's reputation in fourteenth-century Italy. On the tradition of the *motto*, see Luisa Cuomo, 'Sillogizzare motteggiando e motteggiare sillogizzando dal *Novellino* alla VI giornata del *Decameron*', *Studi sul Boccaccio*, 13 (1982), 217–65. See also Matteo Palumbo, '"I motti leggiadri" nella sesta giornata del *Decameron*', *Esperienze letterarie*, 33:3 (2008), 3–23, and, but to be consulted with caution, Filippo Andrei, 'The *Motto* and the Enigma: Rhetoric and Knowledge in the Sixth Day of the *Decameron*', *Heliotropia*, 10:1–2 (2013), 17–45.
43   On the structure of Day VI, see Giancarlo Alfano, 'Scheda introduttiva: Giornata VI', in Giovanni Boccaccio, *Decameron*, ed. by Amedeo Quondam and others (Milan: Rizzoli, 2014), pp. 949–74; Gilbert Bosetti, 'Analyse "structurale" de la sixième journée du *Décaméron*', *Studi sul Boccaccio*, 7 (1973), 141–58; Fido, '*L'ars narrandi*'; Eugenio L. Giusti, 'La novella di Cesca e "intenderlo come si conviene" nella sesta giornata del *Decameron*', *Studi sul Boccaccio*, 18 (1989), 319–46; Ronald Martinez, '*Scienze delle cittade*: Rhetoric and Politics in the Sixth Day of the *Decameron*', *Mediaevalia*, 34 (2013), 57–86; Franziska Meier, 'Day Six of the *Decameron*: Language's Polysemy or the Importance of Being Understood', *Annali d'Italianistica*, 31 (2013), 289–313; Mineo; Cecilia Oesch-Serra, 'Il motto di spirito: istruzioni per l'uso. Appunti per una lettura pragmatica della VI giornata del *Decameron*', *Versants*, 17 (1990), 3–16; Picone, 'Leggiadri motti'; Pamela D. Stewart, 'La novella di madonna Oretta e le due parti del *Decameron*', in her *Retorica e mimica nel 'Decameron' e nella commedia del Cinquecento* (Florence: Olschki, 1986), pp. 19–38; Cok Van Der Voort, 'Convergenze e divaricazioni tra la Prima e la Sesta Giornata del *Decameron*', *Studi sul Boccaccio*, 11 (1979–80), 207–41.

In this respect, the centrality accorded to the *ottimo filosofo* in the organization of the *Decameron* is yet another vital element in Boccaccio's celebration of Guido as the exemplary embodiment of human and intellectual values (and, as we shall soon have occasion to detail, his celebration does not end simply by correcting Dante, but goes on to establish precise connections between Cavalcanti and other great emblematic individuals).

Decameron VI. 9 not only has important implications for the cultural standing of Cavalcanti, but also, as I have been adumbrating, for that of Dante. Even more interestingly, for all Boccaccio's stress on the 'objectivity' of his short story, its implications for his own artistic and intellectual standing are anything but insignificant. Thus, if one simply considers the ways in which the *novelliere* positioned himself in respect of *Decameron* VI. 9's metanarrative structure, it is obvious that he was intent on creating parallels between Betto and himself, especially as regards their roles as active and influential participants in the intellectual life of their day. Much more intriguing, though, is the manner in which, metanarratively, Dante's judgement is equated, however implicitly, with that of the 'gente volgare' (9) and the 'uomini idioti' (14) of the *brigata*. For the greatest vernacular 'authority' of his age to be treated in this manner is startling. At the same time, the absurdity of the equation diminishes, if not actually dissipates, its force. The whole cultural thrust of fourteenth-century Italy meant that it was just about inconceivable that credence might be given to any claim which seriously suggested that Dante concurred with the attitudes of the untutored and the ignorant.[44] The reputation of anyone championing such a far-fetched idea would have been in immediate and serious danger. Boccaccio was once more relying on traditional perceptions to make and bolster his point. He lucidly appreciated how problematic and precarious were the ideological structures underlying his short story. At every stage, he carefully circumscribed his censure of Dante — not least because he had an enormous, if not unconditional, respect for the poet — by developing his criticisms first allusively and then 'objectively', at a clear remove from the 'letter' of *Decameron* VI. 9. Boccaccio found himself in the ambiguous position of wishing both to sustain and to challenge Dante. Thus, as regards the central charge that Cavalcanti was an Epicurean atheist, by attributing such an accusation to the 'gente volgare', the *novelliere* largely removed the possibility that such a view could be ascribed to any intellectual, including Dante, thereby, significantly reducing the likelihood that *Inferno* X might be read as an attack on Guido's orthodoxy. Boccaccio was disturbed by Dante's ominous accusation that Cavalcanti was a heretic. However, he was equally troubled by the consequences for Dante if others, like he had done, formed the idea that the poet was intent on damning his former friend. The situation was especially serious since, as I noted earlier, Dante did not appear to provide any hard proof to substantiate his indictment. He was behaving, in fact, like the hypocritical 'avaro religioso' of *Dec.* I. 6. 3 who falsely accused a 'valente uomo' (3) of 'miscredenza' (6), treating him 'quasi costui fosse stato Epicuro negante

---

44   At the same time, it should not be forgotten that it was not unusual for Dante to be criticized for having written the *Commedia* in the vernacular, and hence for an uneducated audience.

l'eternità dell'anime' (9), before the 'good man' shows up his 'wickedness' 'con un bel detto' (1). Boccaccio's aim was both to countermand Dante's negative intimation and to distance it as far as possible from its source. He wanted both to criticize the poet and to protect him from the possible criticisms of others. As a result, he acknowledged that *Inferno* x was less appreciative of Guido than it might have been, while camouflaging as best he could its most controversial charge. Consequently, Boccaccio's main goal was to fashion as positive an image of Cavalcanti as he was able, rather than to perform a swingeing frontal attack on Dante. Indeed, the more effective his portrait of Guido, the more it conformed to established views of the great man, the less likely that others would recognize and then be persuaded by the negative overtones that he had heard in *Inferno* x. Thus, as we shall see, Boccaccio was notably less concerned with undermining the canto's insinuations regarding Guido's unorthodoxy than with establishing a fruitful relationship, on the one hand, between Cavalcanti and Epicurus based on a constructive interpretation of the Greek philosopher and, on the other, between Guido and Christian orthodoxy — both relationships that could significantly further enhance the *filosofo*'s *auctoritas* and neutralize Dante's potentially damaging insinuations.[45]

There were considerable dangers in criticizing Dante, not least for someone like Boccaccio who had frequently expressed public support and admiration for the poet; however, this did not mean that Dante was beyond criticism. Indeed, as early as the 1290s and throughout the Trecento, the poet engendered strong negative reaction, though this rarely brought advantage to his detractors (Barański, *'Chiosar con altro testo'*, especially pp. 13–76). At the same time, it is obvious that, in *Decameron* VI. 9, Boccaccio was keen to raise legitimate questions regarding the nature and extent of Dante's increasingly overwhelming, not to say, totalizing 'authoritativeness'. The problem was how to do this in a manner that was both effective and judicious. Boccaccio's solution was to create that subtle interaction between the different levels of his short story that has served as the hub of the analysis in this subsection. First and foremost, he explicitly recalled and reconfirmed Cavalcanti's status as an 'authority', thereby countermanding the idea that Dante had so energetically fostered and which, in the poet's wake, had become increasingly prevalent, that contemporary *auctoritas* was located exclusively in the author of the *Commedia*.[46] Then, rather more cautiously, he posed questions about the limits of Dante's eminence and judgement, as he did both elsewhere in the *Decameron* and even in the different versions of the *Trattatello*.[47] Though, in general terms, Boccaccio's approach to Dante has elements

45   See Subsections 5, 'Guido the Epicurean', and 6, '"Saint" Guido', below.

46   Petrarch too was profoundly disturbed by this state of affairs. Differently from Boccaccio, his critique of Dante and his contemporary cultural standing, was uncompromising and ungenerous. It recalls nothing as much as Dante's treatment of Guido. Indeed, one of the ways in which Petrarch endeavoured to downplay Dante's status and influence was to transform him into Cavalcanti's epigone. See Chapter 10.

47   Boccaccio's career is marked by his complicated and ambivalent attitude to Dante. Thus, in the 1350s, and therefore in the years immediately after completing the *Decameron*, through his work as biographer and copyist of the poet, he was the key figure in consolidating and enhancing Dante's reputation. See most recently Laura Banella, *La 'Vita nuova' del Boccaccio* (Rome and Padua: Antenore, 2017); K. P. Clarke, 'Boccaccio and the Poetics of the Paratext: Rubricating the Vernacular', *Le tre corone*, 6 (2019), 69–106.

in common with that broad trend which, in the fourteenth century, sought to reassess and raise doubts about long-established *auctoritates*, his perspective, in fact, is quite tightly focused. Boccaccio's attention is firmly on the present, on the inter-relationship between 'moderns'.[48] Unless Dante's stranglehold on contemporary culture could be eased, there was little possibility for others, including Boccaccio, to establish themselves as significant writers and intellectuals in their own right. The *novelliere* was attempting to create a space in which he and his peers might pursue their work without constantly finding themselves in the shadow of Dante. By having recourse to Cavalcanti, he was able to recall that, at no stage, had Dante held exclusive sway over contemporary culture. If anything, as the younger of the two, his 'authority' had followed on from that of Guido. At the same time, Boccaccio had to be careful not to do decisive damage to Dante. If he seriously undermined the poet's 'authority', he was potentially undermining the very idea — already rejected by many — that a 'modern' might achieve 'authoritativeness'.[49] Paradoxically, Dante was both the principal obstacle to Boccaccio becoming an *auctoritas* and the best guarantor that his ambition was not beyond the bounds of possibility. The *novelliere* had every right to hope that, like 'messer Betto', he too would be deemed 'sottile e intendente' (15). Criticizing Dante was dangerous. However, such bold daring also held out the promise of considerable rewards.

4. The 'Houses of the Dead'

It is ironic that a tale so profoundly concerned with interpretation, and in particular with the need for interpreting sensitively and correctly, should have engendered so many disappointing readings. If it is hard to argue against the conclusion that, in direct opposition to Dante, Boccaccio presented Cavalcanti as a reputable intellectual, critical suggestions regarding the kind of thinker the *novelliere* deemed Guido to have been, especially in light of the fact that egli 'alquanto tenea della oppinione degli epicuri' (9), have been less convincing. On this latter issue, two main exegetical trends are discernible. In the wake of Cavalcanti's athletic escape from the 'arche', and hence from Dante's charges of heretical Epicureanism, scholars have dismissed the possibility that, when he composed *Decameron* VI. 9, Boccaccio may have believed that Guido was in any way sympathetic to Epicurus and his philosophy (Durling, p. 283; Gorni, pp. 367–70). They judge the reference to his supposed Epicurean leanings as conveying only the malicious gossip of the ignorant, and not the studied views of the *novelliere*, even though the logic of the text makes it abundantly clear that the reference to Cavalcanti's Epicureanism, like the remainder

---

48   See Luca Bianchi, '"Aristotele fu un uomo e poté errare": sulle origini medievali della critica al "principio di autorità"', in *Filosofia e teologia nel Trecento: studi in ricordo di Eugenio Randi*, ed. by Luca Bianchi (Louvain-La-Neuve: Fédération internationale des instituts d'études médiévales, 1994), pp. 509–33.

49   See Concetta Carestia Greenfield, *Humanist and Scholastic Poetics, 1250–1500* (Lewisburg, PA: Bucknell University Press, 1981); *MLTC*; Giorgio Ronconi, *Le origini delle dispute umanistiche sulla poesia* (Rome: Bulzoni, 1976); Francesco Tateo, *Retorica e poetica fra Medioevo e Rinascimento* (Bari: Adriatica Editrice, 1960).

of the presentation in paragraphs 8 and 9, is part of Boccaccio's 'objective' and encomiastic description of Guido. On the other hand, what should not be taken as 'objective' — though it is 'objectively' reported — is the erroneous manner in which the 'common herd' had interpreted Cavalcanti's Epicurean 'opinions':

> Guido alcuna volta speculando molto abstratto dagli uomini divenia; e per ciò che egli alquanto tenea della oppinione degli epicuri, si diceva tralla gente volgare che queste sue speculazioni erano solo in cercare se trovar si potesse che Iddio non fosse. (*Dec.* VI. 9. 9)[50]

Critics rejecting the idea that Boccaccio could have considered Cavalcanti an Epicurean fail to appreciate the nuanced manner in which the *novelliere* expresses his estimation of Guido's intellectual sympathies. He is careful not to present the *loico* as an absolute and intransigent follower of the Greek philosopher. 'Egli alquanto tenea della oppinione degli epicuri', and the extent to which Boccaccio believed that Cavalcanti subscribed to such views, depends on how one chooses to interpret that crucially delimiting 'alquanto'. It shall be the purpose of the following subsection to establish which aspects of the rich tradition of Epicurean 'opinion' current in the Middle Ages, Boccaccio actually associated with Guido. What can safely and usefully be said here is that there can be no doubt that the *certaldese* did indeed reckon that Cavalcanti had indeed embraced some Epicurean principles. Furthermore, and just as categorically, unlike the 'gente volgare', he did not number among such principles any that called orthodox Christian doctrine into doubt.

The alternative critical position, faithful to the text, accepts that Boccaccio presents Guido as a supporter of Epicurus (Bruni, *Boccaccio*, pp. 300–01; Inglese, pp. 79–86; Muscetta, pp. 252–53). However, having done so, it then surprisingly runs counter to the 'letter' of the tale and aligns itself both with the *vulgus* and with Dante, and argues that the *novelliere* too believed in Cavalcanti's ideological heterodoxy. According to this view, what distinguished Boccaccio from the poet of the *Commedia* was not simply the sympathy he felt for Guido, but also the fact that, having recognized his intellectual and human worth, he was not interested in passing judgment on his 'opinions'.[51] The general reasons why I might find this position deeply problematic ought to be obvious from the directions of my argument so far. At the same time, however, supporters of this view and I are united in the belief that the allusion to the 'houses of the dead' plays a vital role in establishing Boccaccio's take on Guido. What unites us is the conviction that Cavalcanti's 'motto' (1) is more than just an effectively proffered cliché, an ephemeral instance of his cleverness, but the very ideological nub of the *novella*. As is appropriate for an 'authoritative' intellectual, Guido defines himself through his own mouth. Suggestively, it is no coincidence that 'Signori, voi mi potete dire a casa vostra ciò che vi piace' (12) are the only words he actually speaks during the course of the story.

50   The passage is constructed around the opposition between Boccaccio's reliable 'telling' and the fanciful 'gossip' of the uninformed: 'si diceva tralla gente volgare che [...]'. Inglese too highlights the partiality of 'la diceria popolare' (p. 82).

51   See, for instance, 'la simpatia che circonda il filoepicureo Cavalcanti nella novella, [...] in fondo il Cavalcanti ritratto dal *Decameron* è considerato dall'esterno, come uomo d'ingegno e cultura superiore, nonché pronto alla battuta, e una sentenza sulle sue idee sarebbe stata fuor di luogo': Bruni, *Boccaccio*, p. 300.

Those who see in Boccaccio's Cavalcanti a problematic thinker cite his reply to the *brigata* as proof of his Epicurean-inspired religious unorthodoxy. In particular, they note that variations on the cliché were an Epicurean commonplace, as evidenced by Salimbene's partisan portrait of Frederick II of Hohenstaufen, in which the Emperor has recourse to a Scriptural form of the saying:[52] 'Erat enim epycurus, et ideo quicquid poterat invenire in divina Scriptura, per se et per sapientes suos, quod faceret ad ostendendum quod non esset alia vita post mortem, totum inveniebat, ut illud Ps.: [...] "Sepulchra eorum domus illorum in eternum [48:12]"' [He was in fact an Epicurean, and anything that he could find — either by himself or thanks to his wise men — in divine Scripture that served to demonstrate that there was no other life after death, he found, as that Psalm [...] 'Their tombs will be their home in eternity'].[53] Indeed, the whole of this section of the *Cronica* is primarily constructed out of Scriptural extracts (512–14). Salimbene quotes these to show how Frederick and his ilk, the so-called *carnales*, misinterpret the Bible. They fail to grasp that the holy book does not support their claims. The passages they favour are simply *exempla* of their own erroneous thinking: 'Quod Salomon multa dixit in persona carnalium hominum, de quibus aliter fuit opinio sua' [That Solomon said many things about the character of men given to pleasure, from whom his opinion was different] (513. 1–2). In fact, like Psalm 48: 12, another of the cited 'carnal' excerpts — 'Item: "Quodcumque potest facere manus tua, instanter operare, quia nec opus nec ratio nec sapientia nec scientia erunt apud inferos, quo tu properas" [Ecclesiastes 9: 10]' [Similarly: 'Whatever your hand can do, do it at once, since there will be no work nor reason nor wisdom nor knowledge in Hell, to where you are hastening'] (513. 6–8) — also serves as a fairly obvious subtext to Cavalcanti's 'case de' morti' in which the 'uomini idioti e non letterati' (14) reside. I shall assess the significance of the Scriptural tenor of Guido's words very shortly. For the moment, however, I intend to linger a bit longer in the company of Salimbene. As well as using the Bible to unmask the false ideology of the *carnales*, the chronicler had recourse to Scriptural quotation in order to describe the behaviour of this class of sinner:

> Sicut enim stoyci ponunt felicitatem hominis in sola animi virtute, sic epycuri in sola corporis voluptate. Unde et vita eorum optime describitur Sapientie II [...].
> De vita carnalium hominum.
> Isti tales sicut dicit Apostolus, I ad Cor. XV [32], sunt qui dicunt: 'Manducemus et bibamus, cras enim moriemur'. (*Cronica* 513. 26–28; 514. 14–16)

---

52 There is, in fact, no evidence to support the view that having recourse to the 'houses of the dead' was a mark of Epicureanism. It was a highly popular saying associated both with a 'sinner' like Frederick and with a 'saint' like Iacopone da Todi; see Landoni; Parodi, pp. 42–45. To bolster their case regarding the peculiarly Epicurean connotations of the phrase, some scholars cite Averroistic texts in which versions of the cliché are present; see Bruni, *Boccaccio*, pp. 300–01; Veglia, '*La vita lieta*', pp. 41–42. However, as I have mentioned, the equation they claim between Epicureanism and Averroism — for all its popularity in modern (Dante) scholarship — has no basis in medieval culture. I know of no text in the Middle Ages that explicitly coupled the two ideologies; it is an equivalence idiosyncratically and exclusively implied by Dante as part of his highly personal attack on Cavalcanti in the *Commedia*; see nn. 25 & 34 above, and Chapter 14, pp. 472–73.

53 Salimbene de Adam, *Cronica*, 2 vols, ed. by Giuseppe Scalia, CCCM CXXV and CXXVa (Turnhout: Brepols, 1998–99), 512. 13–18 (II, 537–38).

[Just as the Stoics place man's happiness exclusively in the virtue of the soul, so the Epicureans place it exclusively in the pleasure of the body. Thus their life is perfectly described in Wisdom II.

About the life of men given to pleasure.

Men of this type, as the Apostle says in I Cor. xv, are those who say: 'Let us eat and drink, for tomorrow we will die'.]

It is at the least intriguing that, in addition to Epicureanism and to the 'houses of the dead', *Decameron* VI. 9 should, like Salimbene, also make reference to feasting: 'e oggi l'uno, doman l'altro, e cosí per ordine tutti mettevan tavola, ciascuno il suo dí, a tutta la brigata' (5).

In order to avoid possible misunderstanding as regards what follows, I should like to state at the outset that I do not believe that the chronicler directly influenced the *novelliere*. The implications of the elements they share are rather more intricate and revealing than a matter of straightforward literary borrowing. In fact, as will become apparent, their points of contact are evidence of a complex and wideranging cultural discourse. If one accepts the Scriptural reverberations of Cavalcanti's reply to Betto and his companions, then it is immediately obvious that Frederick and Guido use the same passages of the Bible for quite different ends, thereby confirming that the latter's equation between *sepulchra* and *domus* ought not be taken as a sign of his sinful allegiance to Epicurus. If the Emperor attempted to legitimate his materialism by drawing on Scriptural *auctoritates*, Cavalcanti used those very same *auctoritates* in order to make a quintessentially anti-materialist point. By associating the *brigata* with the *carnales* of Scripture, Guido could not have been more explicit about the dangers that their hedonistic lifestyle posed. It was they, and not he, who had ties with that most notorious group of pleasure-seekers, the *epycuri*; indeed, it was they, and not he, who were denying God as a result of their dedication to *voluptas*.[54] Since nowhere in the *novella* does Cavalcanti actually express any religiously eccentric opinions — it is always others of highly dubious standing who ascribe these to him — it is not unreasonable to surmise that Guido's message, however much it may be read as an appeal to pursue the life of the intellect, given its fundamental dependence on the Bible, is also meant, in keeping with convention, to have more specifically spiritual connotations. Depicting a Cavalcanti who actually manages unproblematically to touch on matters of salvation and to warn others of the dangers of the *inferi*, it is hard to imagine how much further Boccaccio could have gone to distance his Guido from the threat of Dante's fiery tombs of heresy.[55]

---

54   Other scholars have commented on the Epicurean character of the *brigata*; see Anzani, *Cavalcanti in Boccaccio*, p. 78; Durling, p. 283; Gorni, p. 369.

55   *Decameron* VI. 9's obvious and heavy reliance on Dante, and specifically on the *Commedia*, makes it likely that contemporary readers, encouraged also by the story's overt nods towards the afterlife, would have sought eschatological, and hence spiritual, meanings in it. By the middle of the fourteenth century, the religious character of the 'sacrato poema' (*Par.* XXIII. 62) had become a commonplace, as had the poet's 'divine' qualities. Indeed, around 1351–55, Boccaccio definitively consolidated both these attributes in the first redaction of the *Trattatello* (in particular 179–89). See Pio Rajna, 'Il titolo del poema dantesco', *Studi danteschi*, 4 (1921), 5–37. Like the Bible, Dante was a convenient and 'authoritative' means to bolster and confirm the *novella*'s (and Guido's) concern with matters of the spirit.

Establishing an orthodox religious identity for Cavalcanti was undoubtedly the best way in which Boccaccio could defuse the destructive menace of Dante's insidious accusation.[56] It was also a highly effective means further to strengthen and enrich Guido's 'authoritativeness', not least because his doom-laden warning to the *brigata* is expressed in the very same language used by *scribae Dei* to define those who fail to see beyond the pleasures of this world. Boccaccio's Cavalcanti thus imitates and draws on the lessons of the highest moral and spiritual *auctoritates* of his culture, so that something of their standing passes to him. Nor is it accidental that the *novelliere* should have established particular ties between his 'modern' intellectual and the loftiest exponents of divinely inspired wisdom, such as Solomon and Paul. Indeed, in the context of the *novella*'s reassessment of Dante's *auctoritas*, it is hard not to think that the manner in which Boccaccio brought Guido close to the writers of Scripture was, in part, also done to delimit and reformulate Dante's powerful and troubling affirmation that, when he composed the *Commedia*, he was performing the duties of a *scriba Dei*.[57] Thus, in stark contrast to Dante's extraordinary self-canonization, Boccaccio was careful to avoid any suggestion that Cavalcanti was somehow divinely inspired just because, similarly to the author of the *Commedia*, he had addressed a spiritual question. When, in *Decameron* VI. 9, Guido has recourse to the Bible, unlike Dante, he is not attempting to define himself: he is simply behaving in a time-honoured manner and drawing on the best 'authorities' to make his point.[58] At the same time, to stress Cavalcanti's intellectual prowess and independence, Boccaccio ensured that Guido did not passively follow his Biblical models. When Cavalcanti redeploys the Old Testament examples of the arguments rehearsed by the *carnales* to substantiate their ideology, he brings to the fore what remains implicit in the Bible and condemns the sinners by overtly turning their own words against them. In clarifying and making explicit the *lictera* of Scripture, Guido is acting like a dutiful and insightful Biblical commentator, thereby re-establishing,

---

56   I provide further evidence of Boccaccio's recourse to religious elements in his presentation of Cavalcanti in Subsection 6, '"Saint" Guido', below.

57   On fourteenth-century reactions to Dante's claims to be a *scriba Dei*, see Barański, '*Chiosar con altro testo*', pp. 22, 66–75, 120–25; *MLTC*, p. 387; Paola Nasti, 'Autorità, topos e modello: Salomone nei commenti trecenteschi alla *Commedia*', *The Italianist*, 19 (1999), 5–49 (pp. 25–39), and 'A Friar Critic: Guido da Pisa and the Carmelite Heritage', in *Interpreting Dante*, ed. by Paola Nasti and Claudia Rossignoli (Notre Dame, IN: University of Notre Dame Press, 2013), pp. 110–79. Though Boccaccio rejected the idea that Dante, or indeed any poet, was divinely inspired, he was nevertheless keen to establish links not only between poetry and Scripture and theology, but also between the 'sacred page' and other forms of intellectual endeavour, most notably philosophy; see especially Kriesel. See also Boli; *MLTC*, pp. 387–92, 455; Ronald G. Witt, 'Coluccio Salutati and the Conception of the *poeta theologus* in the Fourteenth Century', *Renaissance Quarterly*, 30 (1977), 538–63.

58   On Dante's self-presentation as a latter-day *scriba Dei*, see, for instance, Zygmunt G. Barański, *Dante e i segni* (Naples: Liguori, 2000); Peter S. Hawkins, *Dante's Testaments: Essays in Scriptural Imagination* (Stanford: Stanford University Press, 1999); Robert Hollander, 'Dante's *dolce stil novo* and the *Comedy*', in *Dante mito e poesia*, ed. by Michelangelo Picone and Tatiana Crivelli (Florence: Cesati, 1999), pp. 263–81; Paola Nasti, *Favole d'amore e 'saver profondo': la tradizione salomonica in Dante* (Ravenna: Longo, 2007); Lino Pertile, *La puttana e il gigante: dal Cantico dei Cantici al Paradiso Terrestre di Dante* (Ravenna: Longo, 1998).

in opposition to Dante, the properly subservient relationship between the 'modern' intellectual and the authors of the holy book.[59]

The emphasis on exegesis, however, does more than just help define Cavalcanti's status as a contemporary *auctoritas* and underscore yet again the importance of interpretation in the story's ideological make-up. It also points to Boccaccio's own reliance on Scripture and its explication, as well as to his skill in respectfully adapting the Biblical tradition to his needs as a writer — all elements that could not but enhance his cultural standing. Thus, it was thanks to Scriptural commentary — specifically, some of those same threads of the exegetical tradition that Salimbene had bound together when presenting the *epycuri* — that the *novelliere* was able to elevate the local spat between Guido and the *brigata* onto the universalizing level of the conflict between the *spirituales* and the *carnales*. Even more significantly, at least in literary terms, he imaginatively transformed the knot of texts on the *carnales* and their entwined exegesis into one of *Decameron* VI. 9's major constituent strands. The import of the Scriptural tenor of Guido's words is irresistible.

As I have already noted, two 'carnal' texts and their exegesis exerted a particular influence on Cavalcanti's words: 'Et sepulchra eorum domus illorum in aeternum' [And their tombs will be their home in eternity] (Psalm 48: 12) and 'Quodcumque facere potest manus tua instanter operare, quia nec opus, nec ratio, nec sapientia, nec scientia erunt apud inferos, quo tu properas' [Whatever your hand can do, do it at once, since there will be no work nor reason nor wisdom nor knowledge in Hell, to where you are hastening] (Ecclesiastes 9: 10).[60] Indeed, the degree to which the passage from Ecclesiastes made a powerful impression on Boccaccio is obvious from the fact that, in describing Cavalcanti's qualities, he translated and adapted the first part of the phrase: 'e ogni cosa che far volle' (8). However, it is not only verse 10 that affected the *novelliere* but the whole of the chapter of which it is part. Thus, *Decameron* VI. 9's basic narrative structure — the opposition between the *sapiens* and a community entirely concerned with earthly matters to whose rescue the *sapiens* comes — has a clear precedent in Solomon's chapter (see *Dec.* IX. 1, 13–18), as does the stress on the need for a change in behaviour and attitude in order to avoid the negative effects of 'death' (IX. 2–4, 10–12). In addition, several details of the *novella* find their equivalent in Ecclesiastes 9 — for instance, the allusions, in close proximity to each other, to the enjoyment of food (5 and see 9: 7, 9) and elegant clothing (6 and see 9: 8), and, most notably, the description of an assault that is successfully countered by a wise man (10–12 and see 9: 14–15). In fact, more than the book of the Old Testament, it is the gloss to chapter 9 that leaves a mark on the description

---

59   On the exegesis of the 'literal sense' of the Bible, see Minnis, *Medieval Theory of Authorship*, pp. 73–159.

60   In what follows, I shall concentrate on these two key passages, given their obvious links to *Decameron* VI. 9. To attempt to examine the inter-relationship between the *novella* and the many other Biblical texts the tradition associated with the *carnales* would not be especially illuminating since there is considerable overlap between such passages and their interpretation. Unlike our two excerpts, it is much more difficult to establish the extent to which other 'carnal' texts actually had an impact on Boccaccio, though it is more than likely that he was aware of at least some of them, since they are cited in commentaries to Psalm 48 and to Ecclesiastes 9 which, as I am about to demonstrate, he had read, as well as in works of compilation such as Salimbene's *Cronica*.

of the *brigata*'s attack and Guido's escape, since it is this, rather than Solomon's text, that places repeated emphasis on the brisk succession of attack, enclosure, timely wisdom, and liberation that are the hallmark of Boccaccio's episode.[61] In truth, the gloss's heavy influence is felt throughout the *novella*. It is exegesis that clarifies and develops the opposition between the *sapiens* and the *stulti*, between the spirit and the flesh, between life and death, between knowledge and ignorance.[62] It is exegesis that specifically mentions Epicurus in connection with a life of pleasure and unbelief: 'fruere uoluptate [...]. Non est enim aliqua in morte sapientia; nullus post dissolutionem uitae huius sensus. Et haec, inquit, aliquis loquatur Epicurus' [Enjoy pleasure [...]. For there is not any wisdom in death; and no sensation after the end of this life. And let a certain Epicurus claim such things, he says].[63] It is the gloss that contrasts the good man to the heretic (St Jerome, *Commentarius* IX. 7–8. 205–08; 11. 291–92; Rupert of Deutz, *In librum*, col. 1284); and finally, it is the gloss that establishes the positive attributes of 'colui che leggerissimo era' (12):

> Qui uinctus est compedibus ferreis et grauibus plumbi nexibus praegrauatur: 'Iniquitas enim sedet super talentum plumbeum' [Zachariah 5: 7]; et in psalmo loquitur: 'Quasi onus graue grauatae sunt super me' [37: 5]. Non est aptus ad cursum illum, de quo dicitur: 'Cursum consummaui, fidem seruaui' [11 Timothy 4: 7]. Qui autem leuis est et anima illius non grauatur, nihilominus et ipse absque adiutore Deo ad calcem not potest peruenire. (Jerome, *Commentarius* IX. 10. 243–50)

> [One who is tied with iron fetters and is oppressed with heavy lead chains: 'For iniquity stands on a talent of lead'; and the Psalm says: 'As a heavy weight [my iniquity] hangs over me'. He is not suitable for that course, of which it is said: 'I have finished my course, I have kept my faith'. But even one who is light and his soul is not oppressed, without God's help could not ever reach his goal.]

Decameron VI. 9 thus emerges as a 'modern' variation on Ecclesiastes 9, and Guido as a Florentine version of the Biblical *sapiens*.[64] In an unimpeachable manner,

---

61   See St Jerome, *Commentarius in Ecclesiasten*, in *Opera*, ed. by Marc Adriaen, part I, vol. I, CCSL LXXII (Turnholt: Brepols, 1959), IX. 13–15. 309, 317–46; Rupert of Deutz, *In librum Ecclesiastes Commentarius*, in PL CLXVIII, cols 1285–86; St Bonaventure, *Commentarium in Ecclesiasten*, IX. 14, 15, 16–17.

62   See St Jerome, *Commentarius* IX. 5–6. 63–66, 100–04; 7–8. 126–44, 166–69, 177–80; 9. 213–16, 221–25; 10. 229–30; 11. 253–63, 274–83; 13–15. 352–54; Rupert of Deutz, *In librum*, cols 1278–86; St Bonaventure, *Commentarium* IX. 2, 4, 5, 7–10.

63   St Jerome, *Commentarius* IX. 7–8. 131, 141–43. See also Rupert of Deutz, *In librum*, cols 1280–81; St Bonaventure, *Commentarium* IX. 9–10, Quaestiones.

64   At first sight, on account of the precise parallel it establishes between 'sepulchra' and 'houses', the incipit of verse 12 of Psalm 48 — 'Et sepulchra eorum domus illorum in aeternum' [And their tombs will be their home in eternity] — and, by extension, the complete text of which it is a part, would appear to be more likely and precise sources for *Decameron* VI. 9 than any aspect of Ecclesiastes 9. Yet, in reality, except for the opening of verse 12, whose tombs, like Boccaccio's 'arche grandi di marmo' (10), the commentators described as being of marble (see St Augustine, *Enarrationes in psalmos*, in *Opera*, ed. by Eligius Dekkers and Jean Fraipont, part X, vol. I, CCSL XXXVIII (Turnholt: Brepols, 1956), XLVIII. 1. 15–16; Cassiodorus, *Expositio psalmorum*, in *Opera*, ed. by Marc Adriaen, part II, vol. I, CCSL XCVII (Turnholt: Brepols, 1958), XLVIII. 12), there are no other specific points of contact between the *novella* and the psalm. There are a number of general connections between the

Boccaccio asserts both the eternal truth of Scripture and the Christian ethical worth of his much maligned protagonist. As is clear from the story's (and the Day's) restricted contemporary setting and the highly respectful manner in which it rewrites Ecclesiastes 9, *Decameron* VI. 9 is keen to acknowledge the 'humility' of its standing in relation to the Bible.[65] As a consequence, first and foremost, Cavalcanti

story and Psalm XLVIII and its exegesis: criticism of the *stulti*; celebration of the gift of the intellect; warnings against materialism and against exaggerated concern with the things of the world; the nature of death; and sinners' misunderstanding of the wise. Furthermore, perhaps a faint echo of the verse 'Iniquitas calcanei mei circumdabit me' [The iniquity of my heels will surround me] (6) together with its gloss — 'Magis ergo debet timere, si iniquitas calcanei eius circumdabit eum. Non enim timeat, inquit, homo quod non habet in potestate deuitare. [...] Dicat mihi qua euadat quod debet Adam [...] Si ergo uitet iniquitatem calcanei sui, et ambulet per uias Dei, non perueniet ad diem malam' [He must fear more, therefore, if the iniquity of his heels will surround him. For a man, he says, who has no capacity of avoiding it, shall not fear. [...] He should tell me how he would avoid Adam's fall [...] But if he shuns the iniquity of his heel, and walks on God's path, he shall not arrive at damnation] (St Augustine, *Enarrationes* 48. 1. 6. 4–16) — can be heard in the description of Guido's encirclement and escape. It should be remembered, however, that these are all elements also present in Ecclesiastes 9 and its tradition. Given that, as we have seen, the two passages were not infrequently associated in the Middle Ages, it is not unreasonable to conclude that the two had also become combined in Boccaccio's memory, even though it was Solomon's text that held sway, not least because the *novelliere* was keen to forge links between his Florentine thinker and the supreme embodiment of Scriptural wisdom.

65   I naturally do not recognize any kind of parodic intent in Boccaccio's recourse to Scripture in *Decameron* VI. 9, though parody of the sacred is present elsewhere in the collection. This is largely a feature of the presentation of transgressive religious figures such as ser Ciappelletto and frate Cipolla. My reading of the story is predicated on its profound and sincere engagement with Christianity. In fact, and in harmony with my arguments here, it has justly been noted that 'i registri morali del *Decameron*, che ci riportano a definizioni giuridiche e scolastiche, hanno un modello primario nelle Sacre Scritture': Victoria Kirkham, 'Morale', in Bragantini and Forni, pp. 249–68 (p. 263). Although modern readers have stressed — far from unreasonably, even if at times somewhat too heavyhandedly — that the *Decameron* is a markedly 'secularizing', 'anthropocentric' work, it should not be forgotten that Boccaccio himself was a man of considerable theological knowledge and committed religious faith; see, Francesco Bausi, 'Gli spiriti magni: filigrane aristoteliche e tomistiche nella decima giornata del *Decameron*', *Studi sul Boccaccio*, 27 (1999), 205–53; Aldo S. Bernardo, 'The Plague as Key to Meaning in Boccaccio's *Decameron*', in *The Black Death: The Impact of the Fourteenth–century Plague*, ed. by Daniel Williman (Binghamton, NY: Center for Medieval and Early Renaissance Studies, 1982), pp. 39–64; Vittore Branca, *Boccaccio medievale e nuovi studi sul 'Decameron'* (Florence: Sansoni, 1990), pp. 17–20, 93–109; Florinda M. Iannace, *La religione del Boccaccio* (Rome: Trevi, 1977); Victoria Kirkham, *The Sign of Reason in Boccaccio's Fiction* (Florence: Olschki, 1993); Paolo Valesio, 'Sacro', in Bragantini and Forni, pp. 372–418. It should not come as a surprise, therefore, that Boccaccio's masterpiece does not restrict itself simply to earthly matters. Furthermore, it would be wrong to surmise that Betto offers an exclusively lay, nevermind 'humanistic', interpretation of Cavalcanti's answer — 'le quali [the tombs] egli dice che son nostra casa, a dimostrarci che noi e gli altri uomini idioti e non litterati siamo, a comparazion di lui e degli altri uomini scienziati, peggio che uomini morti' (14). Indeed, the generic term *uomo scienziato* cannot be restricted simply to secular knowledge (*scientia*, as is clear, for instance, from the commentaries on Ecclesiastes 9, was widely employed in the Middle Ages to refer to both human and divine knowledge). Equally, the *brigata*'s ignorance covers all areas of understanding: they are indiscriminately 'idioti e non litterati'. Boccaccio constructs Betto's explanation in such a manner that Guido's words can be taken to refer to any and every kind of wisdom. In fact, the overt eschatological dimension of the story, its concern to countermand those who deny, or accuse others of denying, the existence of God, its recognizable Scriptural character, and its preoccupation with matters of ethics, all make it likely that, since Cavalcanti is replying to a

is presented as a model for fourteenth-century Tuscany. At the same time, however, given how illustrious is his pedigree as an *auctoritas* — and there is more to be said about this — there is strong evidence to believe that, with Cavalcanti, Boccaccio's ultimate aim was to fashion a figure who could successfully hold his own among the great *auctoritates* of the past. In this respect, it is suggestive that the one significant change that the *novelliere* made to the Scriptural model should have involved Guido. Unlike the *sapiens* of Ecclesiastes, who is forgotten and ignored by his fellow-citizens (14–15), Cavalcanti has a lasting and beneficial effect on his listeners: 'Allora ciascuno intese quello che Guido aveva voluto dire e vergognossi, né mai più gli diedero briga' (15).

5. Guido the Epicurean

Nevertheless, for all Boccaccio's celebratory fervour, the problem remains of how and why someone of Cavalcanti's apparent virtues and *auctoritas* — virtues and 'authority' that integrate the religious with the lay — might feel impelled to subscribe, however 'alquanto', to the 'oppinione degli epicuri'. Once again, Guido's reply provides the beginnings of a solution, thereby affirming its key ideological function in the story. Indeed, and quite appropriately, it is Cavalcanti's own words that best reveal him as delicately poised between the human and the divine — a pose emblematically captured in the 'lightness' of his 'leap'.

The Scriptural hallmark of the 'houses of the dead' is impressed next to a highly prestigious secular counterpart. Offering advice to Lucilius on how best to lead his life, Seneca noted: 'deinde idem delicati timent, [morti] cui vitam suam fecere similem. [...] Puto, aeque qui in odoribus iacet mortuus est quam qui rapitur unco; otium sine litteris mors est et hominis vivi sepultura' [then all those voluptuaries fear the same thing, [death] on which they have modelled their life. [...] One who lies in perfumes, I think, is as dead as someone who is dragged by the [executioner's] hook; leisure without study is death and the burial of a living man].[66] As in the Scriptural texts discussed earlier, we find the opposition between the intellectual and pleasure-seekers expressed in terms of the motif of 'death-in-life', the same motif that provides the basic narrative and ideological structure of *Decameron* VI. 9. Akin to what occurs in Boccaccio's *novella*, it is the study of philosophy that marks out Seneca's wise man (82. 5–7), not least because his *meditatio* (8) leads to self-knowledge (6), precisely what the *brigata* lacks until Guido's intervention. In addition, the key moment of the story, the confrontation between the 'filosofo' and 'Betto e' compagni' (7), finds a precedent not only in Ecclesiastes 9 but also in Seneca's letter. Yet again, a thinker besieged by his tormentors — similar martial imagery connects the three texts — relies on his wisdom to counter their verbal

---

theological question, he should primarily accuse the *brigata* of lacking spiritual wisdom. The resulting 'shame' ('e vergognossi', 15) felt by the horsemen thus has suggestive penitential overtones.
66   Lucius Anneus Seneca, *Epistulae morales ad Lucilium*, ed. by Leighton Durham Reynolds (Oxford: Clarendon Press, 1965), X. 82. 2–3. Giuseppe Velli too stresses the importance of this passage for our *novella* ('Seneca nel *Decameron*', pp. 218–20).

and physical assault:[67]

> Quae tam emunita et in altum subducta vitae quies quam non dolor territet? quacumque te abdideris, mala humana circumstrepent. Multa extra sunt quae circumeunt nos quo aut fallant aut urgeant, multa intus quae in media solitudine exaestuant. Philosophia circumdanda est, inexpugnabilis murus, quem fortuna multis machinis lacessitum non transit. In insuperabili loco stat animus qui esterna deseruit et arce se sua vindicat; infra illum omne telum cadit. (*Epistulae morales ad Lucilium* 82. 4–5)

> [Which peaceful life is so fortified and so remotely withdrawn that pain cannot terrify it? Wherever you will hide yourself, human sufferings will resound all around. There are many external things that surround us either to deceive us or to oppress us, and many internal things that froth even amidst solitude. Wrap yourself around with philosophy, an unbreachable wall, which even if assailed by many engines of war fortune cannot break through. The mind that has abandoned external preoccupations and protects itself in its fortress stands on unassailable ground; every weapon falls below it.]

Just as it had done for the Bible, *Decameron* VI. 9 presents concrete and specific confirmation of Seneca's general points, as well as evidence of their lasting relevance for the 'modern' world.[68] Indeed, there seems little doubt that Boccaccio selected the basic conflictual narrative structure and its attendant metaphor of the 'tombs of the living', because, thanks to their genealogy, they allowed him conveniently and efficiently to bring together Christian and pagan culture, religious and secular values, and the past and the present.[69] It is not difficult to recognize in this mix a rudimentary model of the world of the mid-fourteenth century — a world, according to Boccaccio, rich in potential but seriously marred by venality, self-interest, and expediency: 'ne' tempi passati furono nella nostra città assai belle e laudevoli usanze, delle quali oggi niuna ve n'è rimasa, mercé della avarizia che in quella con le ricchezze è cresciuta, la quale tutte l'ha discacciate' (4). At the same time, and as confirmed by the Scriptural and classical 'authorities' to whom Guido alludes and by the behaviour of the *brigate* of recent Florentine history, the problems of the present are in fact no different from those of the past.[70] More importantly, as

---

67   On Boccaccio's skill at intertwining different sources, see Lucia Battaglia Ricci, '*Decameron*: interferenze di modelli', in *Autori e lettori di Boccaccio: Atti del Convegno internazionale di Certaldo*, ed. by Michelangelo Picone (Florence: Cesati, 2002), pp. 179–94; Velli, 'Seneca nel *Decameron*'.

68   Velli offers a not dissimilar reading of *Decameron* VI. 9: 'Quello che in ogni caso mi pare la novella suggerisca è che la cultura è fatta di tradizione, di memoria e trasmissione di valori' ('Seneca nel *Decameron*', p. 219).

69   Regarding Boccaccio's sense of the complex relationship between the past and the present, David Lummus writes that in 'Boccaccio, who was just as self-conscious [as Petrarch] of his age's historical isolation from antiquity, modernity can be understood in terms of the fluid, generative relationship that he establishes between past and present through a process of critical historicization [that involves] [h]is willingness to integrate new phenomena [...] within a holistic vision of culture that nonetheless reflects historical difference' (p. 103).

70   At first sight, it may seem that contradictions exist between Boccaccio's celebration of the Florentine past and its *brigate* and his condemnation of one of these, as well as between his emphasis on Guido's wealth and the anti-materialist force of his reply to the horsemen. The contradictions in fact are only apparent and can be resolved thanks to Epistle 82: 'Omnia ista per se non sunt

his illustrious precedents also reveal, such evils are not insurmountable. Through the exemplary tale of Cavalcanti, Boccaccio offered 'realistic' and culturally guaranteed proof that excessive materialism could be countermanded and then replaced by an ethically rigorous set of principles.[71] It was the responsibility of the *tempi presenti* to learn from the 'tempi passati'; and Guido Cavalcanti, who almost belonged to the present while also embodying the lessons of the past, was the perfect *auctoritas* from whom to draw comfort and inspiration.

Although there can be little doubt concerning the importance of Seneca's Epistle 82 in *Decameron* VI. 9, the question remains how it might cast light on the nature of Guido's Epicureanism. In itself, Epistle 82 cannot do this. However, the compilation of which it is a part is able do this effectively and appositely. The *Epistolae morales ad Lucilium*, which Boccaccio knew in their entirety, excerpted in the *Zibaldone magliabechiano*, and drew on especially around the time he composed the *Decameron*, make regular and largely approving recourse to Epicurus and his philosophy.[72] They can thus serve as an apt and illuminating guide to Cavalcanti's Epicurean sympathies, not least because it is Guido himself who indicates their relevance when he adapts one of the collection's most famous *dicta* to instruct the *brigata* in the advantages of seeking wisdom and of practicing restraint in the pursuit of sensory delight — teachings that are quintessentially Epicurean in character.[73]

honesta nec gloriosa, sed quidquid ex illis virtus adiit tractavitque honestum et gloriosum facit: illa in medio posita sunt. Interest utrum malitia illis an virtus manum admoverit' [All these things are not honourable and glorious per se, but any of these which virtue approaches and manages, it makes honourable and glorious: they stand on neutral ground. The difference is whether wickedness or virtue has laid hands upon them] (12). Wealth and belonging to a *brigata* are in themselves without value; what can be judged positively or negatively, however, is the moral attitude with which these are approached: Guido's and that of many of the *brigate* of the past are 'virtuous', while Betto's and that of his companions are 'malicious'.

71   On Boccaccio's ethical concerns in the *Decameron* and, in particular, his desire for contemporary civic renewal, see Kirkham, 'Morale'. For other important studies of the complex and contentious issue regarding the ethics of the *Decameron*, see Bausi; Kurt Flasch, *Poesia dopo la peste: saggio su Boccaccio* (Rome and Bari: Laterza, 1995); Walter Haug, 'La problematica dei generi nelle novelle di Boccaccio: la prospettiva di un medievista', in *Autori e lettori di Boccaccio*, ed. by Michelangelo Picone (Florence: Cesati, 2002), pp. 127–40; Robert Hollander, '*Utilità* in Boccaccio's *Decameron*', *Studi sul Boccaccio*, 15 (1985–86), 215–33, and 'The *Decameron* Proem', in *The 'Decameron' First Day in Perspective*, ed. by Elissa B. Weaver (Toronto, Buffalo, and London: University of Toronto Press, 2004), pp. 12–28; Marilyn Migiel, *The Ethical Dimension of the 'Decameron'* (Toronto: University of Toronto Press, 2015); Giuseppe Mazzotta, *The World at Play in Boccaccio's 'Decameron'* (Princeton: Princeton University Press, 1986); Roberta Bruna Pagnamenta, *L'ambiguità come strategia narrativa* (Ravenna: Longo, 1999). On the story's 'realism', see Watson, pp. 306–08. See also Pier Massimo Forni, 'Realtà/ verità', in Bragantini and Forni, pp. 300–19.

72   See Aldo M. Costantini, 'Studi sullo Zibaldone magliabechiano. II. Il Florilegio senechiano', *Studi sul Boccaccio*, 8 (1974), 79–126; Antonia Mazza, 'L'inventario della "parva libraria" di Santo Spirito e la biblioteca del Boccaccio', *Italia medioevale e umanistica*, 9 (1966), 1–74 (p. 16). Velli persuasively argues that the *Epistolae* play an especially important role in Day VI ('Seneca nel *Decameron*', pp. 212–15, 217–20). See also Jonathan Usher, 'Apicius, Seneca, and Surfeit: Boccaccio's Sonnet 95', *MLN*, 118:1 (2003), 46–59.

73   A further section of the *Epistles to Lucilius* appears to have had a bearing on Guido's reply and Betto's interpretation: 'Hos itaque, ut ait Sallustius, "ventri oboedientes" animalium loco numeremus, non hominum, quosdam vero ne animalium quidem, sed mortuorum. Vivit is qui multis usui est, vivit is qui se utitur; qui vero latitant et torpent sic in domo sunt quomodo in conditivo. Horum

Among the many problematic effects of Dante's monumental regulating influence is its distorting impact on perceptions of medieval Epicureanism among present-day scholars of Italian literature. Too many have taken the poet's partial and negative characterization in *Inferno* x as definitive and all-encompassing:

> Suo cimitero da questa parte hanno
> con Epicuro tutti suoi seguaci
> che l'anima col corpo morta fanno. (*Inf.* x. 13–15)

Although the Middle Ages predominantly judged Epicurus's philosophy in negative terms, it is also the case that it had a rather broader and, at times, also more favourable sense of Epicureanism than the narrowly unorthodox doctrine that emerges from the *Commedia*. Indeed, it is enough to consult Dante himself to find confirmation of this fact. In the *Convivio* he writes:

> Per le quali tre virtudi [faith, hope, and charity] si sale a filosofare a quelle Atene celestiali dove li Stoici e Peripatetici e Epicurî, per la 'luce' della veritade etterna, in uno volere concordevolmente concorrono. (*Conv.* III. 14. 15)

> Altri filosofi furono, che videro e credettero altro che costoro, e di questi fu primo e prencipe uno filosofo che fu chiamato Epicuro; che, veggendo che ciascuno animale, tosto ch'è nato, è quasi da natura dirizzato nel debito fine, che fugge dolore e domanda allegrezza, quelli disse questo nostro fine essere voluptade (non dico 'voluntade', ma scrivola per P), cioè diletto sanza dolore. E però [che] tra 'l diletto e lo dolore non ponea mezzo alcuno, dicea che 'voluptade' non era altro che 'non dolore', sì come pare Tullio recitare nel primo di Fine di Beni. (*Conv.* IV. 6. 11–12)

> Per queste tre donne [the three holy women who go to Christ's tomb mentioned in Mark 6: 1–2] si possono intendere le tre sette della vita attiva, cioè li Epicurî, li Stoici e li Peripatetici, che vanno al monimento, cioè al mondo presente che è recettaculo di corruttibili cose, e domandano lo Salvatore, cioè la beatitudine, e non lo truovano; ma uno giovane truovano in bianchi vestimenti, lo quale, secondo la testimonianza di Mateo e anche delli altri [Evangelisti], era angelo di Dio. (*Conv.* IV. 22. 15)[74]

What is immediately striking about these passages is not just the respectful manner in which Dante treats the 'Epicurî', but also the fact that, like Boccaccio after him, he is perfectly prepared to integrate Epicureanism with Christianity. For all the charges of impiety that many Christian writers had laid against Epicurus and his supporters since their clash with Paul (Acts 17: 18), others, as early as Clement

---

licet in limine ipso nomen marmori inscribas: mortem suam antecesserunt' [We should number these who are 'subjected to their belly' — as Sallust says — among animals, not among men, and in fact not even among animals, but among the dead. He lives who is of use to many, he lives who makes use of himself; but those who hide and lie idle live in their house as in a tomb. You may write their name on their marble threshold: they have anticipated their own death] (VI. 60. 4). On Boccaccio's recourse to this passage, see Usher, 'Apicius'.

74   See also *Conv.* IV. 22. 4. This is not the place to explore the implications of Dante's radical change of view as regards Epicurus. I should, however, like to note two points. First, in the *Convivio*, when he condemned those who do not believe in the afterlife, Dante made no mention of Epicurus or of his followers (II. 8. 7–8); second, it is not unreasonable to surmise that the poet's shift in attitude had at the very least something to do with his polemical hostility towards Cavalcanti.

of Alexandria, had taken a more tolerant line, highlighting the positive aspects of Epicureanism as a moral philosophy; and among those who persuaded them to do so, as occurred with Boccaccio, was Seneca.[75]

Boccaccio's Guido is a modern-day Senecan Epicurus; and his actions offer ample evidence of this fact.[76] He leads his life according to Epicurean principles anthologized and lauded in the *Epistolae* (principles that serve as another of the *novella's* rich assortment of structuring sources). Thus, when he rejected Betto's invitation to be part of the *brigata*, Guido was following Epicurus's maxim: 'Ante [...] circumspiciendum est cum quibus edas et bibas' [First [...] you must consider carefully with whom you eat and drink] (II. 19. 10–11), thereby avoiding inappropriate companions. Similarly, his ability to discriminate, especially when granting favours — 'e a chiedere a lingua sapeva onorare cui nell'animo gli capeva che il valesse' (8) — confirms him as an attentive follower of the 'consilio sapientium: "beneficia non parant amicitias?" parant, si accepturos licuit eligere, si conlocata, non sparsa sunt' [a maxim of the wise: 'Don't favours obtain friendships?' they do, if one has been able to choose the beneficiaries, and if they are conferred judiciously, not scattered] (12). Guido's cautiously reflective attitude, like Epicurus's, has its origins in his suspicion of the mass and in his sense of his fundamental difference from the *populus*:

'Numquam volui populo placere; nam quae ego scio non probat populus, quae probat populus ego nescio.' 'Quis hoc?' inquis, tamquam nescias cui imperem. Epicurus; [...] Quis enim placere populo potest cui placet virtus? malis artibus popularis favor quaeritur. Similem te illis facias oportet: non probabunt nisi agnoverint. (Seneca, *Epistolae* III. 29. 10–11; and compare *Dec.* VI. 9. 14, and in particular 'delle quali cose — Guido's intellectual achievements — poco la brigata curava', 8)[77]

[I have never wanted to please the crowd; for the things that I know the crowd does not approve, and the things that the crowd approves I do not know. 'Who says this?' you ask, as if you did not know whom I am calling upon. It is Epicurus; [...] Who in fact can love virtue and please the crowd? Popular approval is sought through wicked artifices. You ought to make yourself like them: they will not approve of you unless they recognize you as one of them.]

75 On the complex inter-relationship between Epicureanism and Christianity, see Wolfgang Schmid, *Epicuro e l'epicureismo cristiano* (Brescia: Paideia, 1984), pp. 137–97.

76 Boccaccio's assessment and rehabilitation of Epicurus at the service of Cavalcanti constitutes an exemplary instance of his Hellenism as has been persuasively elucidated by David Lummus: 'Boccaccio's Hellenism, derived both from direct and indirect knowledge of the Greek language and culture, was not only the foundation of his perspective on the past, but also the basis for his defense of *novitas*, or modernity, *tout court*, from Greek and Arab science to vernacular poetry' (p. 102).

77 And compare: 'Cum hoc effeceris et aliqua coeperit apud te tui esse dignatio, incipiam tibi permittere quod idem suadet Epicurus: "tunc praecipue in te ipse secede cum esse cogeris in turba". Dissimilem te fieri multis oportet, dum tibi tutum [non] sit ad te recedere. [...] Tunc praecipue in te ipse secede cum esse cogeris in turba — si bonus vir <es>, si quietus, si temperans' [When you will have done this, and you start to hold yourself in some esteem, I shall begin to allow you what even Epicurus recommends: 'when you are forced to be in a crowd, then especially you must withdraw into yourself'. You must be different from the multitude, when it is not safe for you to retreat into yourself. [...] When you are forced to be in a crowd, then especially you must withdraw into yourself — if you are, that is, a good, peaceful, and moderate man] (Seneca, *Epistolae* III. 25. 6–7).

Furthermore, in keeping with Epicurus's plea to Idomeneus, Cavalcanti knows exactly the right moment to flee danger: 'ut quantum potest fugiat et properet, antequam aliqua vis maior interveniat et auferat libertatem recedendi. Idem tamen subicit nihil esse temptandum nisi cum apte poterit tempestiveque temptari: sed cum illud tempus captatum diu venerit, exiliendum ait' [to flee and hasten as fast as possible, before some greater strength should intervene and take away the freedom to withdraw. But he also suggests that nothing should be attempted except when it can be attempted suitably and in a timely manner: but when that long-desired time shall come, let him leap up — he says] (III. 22. 5–6). Time and again, Seneca presented Epicurus as the embodiment of the wise man par excellence (I. 8. 8; 12. 11; II. 14. 18; 16. 7; 21. 9). Equally, by having Guido follow in the Greek philosopher's wake, Boccaccio made similar claims for his outstanding 'loico' and 'filosofo naturale', who, like his mentor, achieved freedom thanks to his dedication to philosophy (I. 8. 7); deemed the philosopher to be self-sufficient (I. 9. 1); was critical of obsessive materialism (II. 14. 17–18; 16. 7–9); and revealed both a proper attitude to being 'ricchissimo' (II. 20. 9–13) and a correct appreciation of the benefits of study (II. 21. 2–3). Thus, 'ut ait Epicurus' [as Epicurus says], Cavalcanti behaves 'tamquam spectet Epicurus' [as if Epicurus was watching] (III. 25. 4–5). He is Epicurus's *vir bonus*, society's moral arbiter: ' "aliquis vir bonus nobis diligendus est ac semper ante oculos habendus, ut sic tamquam illo spectante vivamus et omnia tamquam illo vidente faciamus". Hoc [...] Epicurus praecepit' ['We must choose and always have in front of our eyes some virtuous man, so that we may live as if he were watching us and act always as if he could saw us'. This is what [...] Epicurus taught] (I. 11. 8 9).

By evaluating Guido's behaviour against that of Seneca's Epicurus, a clear picture emerges of the former's Epicureanism. There is no hint in it of hues of atheism or of religious unorthodoxy. Indeed, one has the impression that, thanks to his portrait of Cavalcanti, Boccaccio was 'humanistically' restoring to Epicurus his rightful identity in opposition to the anachronistic distortions of so much 'vulgar' medieval opinion.[78] Epicureanism, in fact, adds to rather than detracts from Guido's *auctoritas*, since it helps to define his identity as a great philosopher and to define his status as 'un de' miglior loici che avesse il mondo e ottimo filosofo naturale' (8). However, as one might expect from a wise man of Cavalcanti's standing, his relationship to Epicurus is not of uncritical and passive adherence. He only accepts from his *magister* what is in keeping with contemporary orthodoxy. Thus, there is no hint in *Decameron* VI. 9 that he might subscribe to Epicurus's troubling theory of *voluptas* to which Seneca refers several times.[79] That delimiting 'alquanto' is once more the key to understanding Boccaccio's Guido.

---

78   On Boccaccio's attitude to Epicurus, see Chapter 16.

79   Guido's rejection of *voluptas* cannot but augment his Christian credentials. Basing himself on the delimiting character of 'alquanto', Anzani, *Cavalcanti in Boccaccio* (p. 56), also stresses that Guido embodies positive Epicurean characteristics. Unfortunately, he weakens his case by anachronistically turning Cavalcanti into an Averroistic philosopher on the basis of his sympathy for Epicurus. See also Inglese, pp. 79–81.

6. 'Saint' Guido

In fact, the 'alquanto' not only serves to delimit Cavalcanti's Epicureanism, but also to highlight that he has other, non-Epicurean, ideological sympathies; and foremost among these is, of course, Christianity. Once more, *Inferno* x offers a useful yardstick with which to measure the intricate ramifications of Boccaccio's operation. Despite his efforts to deflect attention away from Dante's accusation that Cavalcanti was an Epicurean heretic, it is unlikely that Boccaccio thought that his strategy would be completely successful. Thus, showing the kind of deference towards Dante that had become widespread in the Trecento, he agreed with him that Guido had Epicurean leanings. Strange as this might seem at first blush, to concur with Dante on this point was actually a highly effective way of nullifying the negative impact of the poet's attack on Cavalcanti. By going along with Dante's suggestion, Boccaccio neither called his *auctoritas* into doubt nor raised suspicions about his motives. He simply questioned the accuracy of Dante's definition of Epicureanism. He reduced the whole issue to one of philology — a perfectly legitimate and dispassionate position, especially in the new cultural climate in which Boccaccio was writing. Using Seneca as his 'historical' guide, Boccaccio corrected Dante's error regarding Epicurus's philosophy. As a result, Dante's characterization of Cavalcanti as an Epicurean heretic could not be seen as driven by personal rancour. It was merely the result of flawed knowledge. Furthermore, thanks to his re-assessment of Epicurus, Boccaccio was able to point to his own intellectual 'authoritativeness', to confirm that Guido's *auctoritas* was in no small part due to his Epicureanism, and, most importantly, to dispel the possibility that Cavalcanti's commitment to Epicurus was in any way heretical.

To confirm Guido's strict religious orthodoxy, Boccaccio also took care to envelop him in an aura of Christian values and reminiscences. Not only does Cavalcanti propound a Christian message of reform and salvation, but, as I have indicated, he also takes on the guise of the Scriptural *sapiens*. Moreover, this is not the exclusive Christian identity that Boccaccio conferred on his champion. Most strikingly and suggestively, Cavalcanti's experiences evoke various moments of Christ's time on earth. Thus, his being pressed and surrounded before managing to escape recalls similar situations befalling Jesus (for example, Matthew 15: 30; Luke 4: 42; John 10: 39); equally, Guido's fatuous interrogation by the horsemen brings to mind Jesus being challenged by Pharisees and other Jewish religious figures.[80] In particular, Cavalcanti's encounter and exchange with the *brigata* establishes links with the famous episode, present in all three synoptic Gospels, of the Sadducees facetiously questioning Jesus on the resurrection of the dead. I quote Matthew's account:

> In illo die accesserunt ad eum sadducaei, qui dicunt non esse resurrectionem:
> et interrogaverunt eum, dicentes: Magister, Moyses dixit: Si quis mortuus
> fuerit non habens filium, ut ducat frater eius uxorem illius, et suscitet semen

---

80   See, for instance: Matthew 16: 1–4 (this is an especially interesting passage since Boccaccio translates its close — 'Et [Iesus] relictis illis, abiit' [And Jesus left them, and went away] — when he describes Guido's departure: 'e sviluppatosi da loro se n'andò' (12), 22: 15–21; Luke 7: 5–8.

fratri suo. [...] In resurrectione ergo cuius erit de septem uxor? omnes enim habuerunt eam. Respondens autem Iesus, ait illis: Erratis nescientes Scripturas, neque virtutem Dei. (Matthew 22: 23–29; and see Mark 12: 18–24; Luke 20: 27–34)

[On that day he was approached by some Sadducees, who say that there is no resurrection: and questioned him, saying: 'Master, Moses said: if one dies without children, let his brother marry his widow, and raise up offspring for his brother. [...] At resurrection, then, whose wife will she be of the seven? Since all of them were married to her.' Then Jesus answered and said: 'you are wrong because you do not know Scripture nor God's power'.]

The points of contact between Matthew and Boccaccio are not difficult to appreciate. Furthermore, as occurs with the two Old Testament passages discussed earlier, thereby confirming the rigorous coherence of the *novella*'s Biblical sources, the Scriptural text once again clarifies that it is not Guido who has an improper attitude to salvation but Betto and his companions. The exegetical tradition on the passage in fact leaves no doubt as to the fact that it is the questioner and not the questioned who should be deemed a heretic; and, interestingly, in doing so, Jerome had recourse to metaphorical 'houses':

'In illo die accesserunt ad eum Sadducaei qui dicunt non esse resurrectionem.' Duae erant hereses in Iudaeis, una Pharisaeorum et altera Sadducaeorum. [...] Istae sunt duae domus de quibus Esaias manifestius docet quod offensurae sint in lapidem scandali [Isaiah VIII. 14]. [...] [Sadducaei] Qui resurrectionem corporum non credebant et animam putabant interire cum corporibus.[81]

['On that day he was approached by some Sadducees'. There were two heretical sects among the Jews, that of the Pharisees and that of the Sadducees. [...] These are the two houses about which Isaiah even more openly declares that they would offend against the stone of scandal. [...] The Sadducees who did not believe in the resurrection of the body and believed that the soul was buried with the body.]

Naturally, associating Cavalcanti with Jesus could not but add to the former's *auctoritas*, just as his humble *imitatio Christi* made him an exemplary figure for other Christians to follow, and hence the very antithesis of the heretic. There is nothing comically parodic, never mind desecratory, in Boccaccio's representation.[82] Indeed, the respectful and orthodox manner in which the *novelliere* alluded to Christ in order to highlight Guido's worth stands in stark opposition to the way in which, in *Inferno* x, Dante had grotesquely reversed Christological elements in order to emphasize the heretics' sin.[83] In 'saving' Guido, Boccaccio revealed himself a sensitively subtle, if somewhat obsessive, reader of Dante's canto.

---

81   St Jerome, *Commentarii in Mathaeum*, in *Obras Completas*, vol. I (Madrid: Biblioteca de Autores Cristianos, 2002), III. 204–05 (p. 310).

82   See n. 66 above. Durling notes that 'Boccaccio has unmistakably used the imagery of resurrection in Guido's escape' (p. 282). See also Watson, p. 317.

83   See Anthony K. Cassell, *Dante's Fearful Art of Justice* (Toronto: University of Toronto Press, 1984), pp. 23–28.

In composing *Decameron* VI. 9, Boccaccio was particularly drawn to one aspect of the medieval reception of Jesus. The most memorable (and famous) moment of the short story is, of course, Guido's getaway: 'e posta la mano sopra una di quelle arche, che grandi erano, sí come colui che leggerissimo era, prese un salto e fussi gittato dall'altra parte, e sviluppatosi da loro se n'andò' (12). We have already seen that the end of the sentence is closely based on Matthew 16: 4 — 'Et relictis illis, abiit' [And he left them, and went away] — which describes Jesus's escape from the 'pharisaei et sadducaei tentantes' [the Pharisees and Sadducees who had come to tempt him] (1). However, it is the most striking detail of Cavalcanti's flight, his leap — for which, as far as I am aware, no source has hitherto been proposed — that firmly establishes his Christological credentials. Since the time of the Church Fathers, two Scriptural passages, which had become closely associated, were interpreted as presenting a shorthand allegorical version of Jesus's life. The leaping giant of Psalm 18: 6 ('Exsultavit ut gigas ad currendum viam' [he leapt like a giant to run his course]) and the equally agile Bridegroom of Song of Songs 2: 8 ('ecce iste venit | Saliens in montibus, transiliens colles' [behold he comes leaping on mountains, jumping over hills]) came together to offer the basis for a dramatically energetic metaphorization of Christ's ministry constructed around the topos of the 'leaps of the Word'.[84] The image was widespread in medieval culture, passing from commentary to commentary and playing an important role in the liturgy. I quote two of the most influential versions of the representation:

> 'Ecce', inquit, 'iste advenit'. Adhuc ego eum quaero et ille iam venit [...] Ego dixi 'veni', ille salit et transilit. [...] Salit super excelsa, ut ascendat super sponsam — sponsae enim thalamus tribuna est Christi — , salit super Adam, transilit super synagogam, salit super gentes, transilit super Iudaeos. Videamus salientem: salit de caelo in virginem, de utero in praesepe, de praesepio in Iordanem, de Iordane in crucem, de cruce in tumulum, in caelum de sepulchro. Proba mihi, David, salientem, proba currentem; tu enim dixisti: 'Exultavit tamquam gigas ad currendam viam'.[85]

> ['Behold,' he said, 'here he comes'. I am yet calling him and he comes already [...] I said 'come', he jumps and leaps. [...] He jumps over the height of the mountains, to go up to his bride — for the marriage-bed of the bride is the tribunal of Christ — , he jumps over Adam, leaps over the synagogue, jumps over the peoples, leaps over the Jews. Let us see him jump: he jumps from Heaven into a virgin's womb, from the womb into the stable, from the stable into the river Jordan, from the Jordan onto the cross, from the cross into the tomb, and to Heaven from the sepulchre. Show him to me as he jumps, David, show him to me as he runs; for you yourself have said: 'He leapt like a giant to run his course'.]

> 'Ecce iste venit saliens in montibus'. Veniendo quippe ad redemptionem nostram, quosdam, ut ita dixerim, saltus dedit. Vultis, fratres charissimi, ipsos

---

84   See Alexandre Olivar, 'Varia Patristica. 1. "Los saltos del Verbo": una interpretación patrística de Cant. 2,8', *Analecta Sacra Tarraconensia*, 29 (1956), 3–15; Pertile, pp. 205–13, 219–21.

85   St Ambrose, *Expositio Psalmi CXVIII*, 2 tomes, ed. by L. Franco Pizzolato, in *Sancti Ambrosii Episcopi Mediolanensis Opera*, ed. by Biblioteca Ambrosiana, vol. VIII (Milan and Rome: Città nuova, 1987), VI. 6 (pp. 244–45).

eius saltus agnoscere? De coelo venit in uterum, de utero venit in praesepe, de praesepe venit in crucem, de cruce venit in sepulcrum, de sepulcro rediit in coelum. Ecce, ut nos post se currere faceret, quosdam pro nobis saltus manifestata per carnem veritas dedit; quia 'exsultavit ut gigas ad currendam viam suam', ut nos ei diceremus ex corde: 'Trahe nos post te, curremus in odorem unguentorum tuorum'.[86]

['Behold, he comes jumping over mountains'. For indeed coming for our redemption, he gave, as it were, some leaps. Do you want, dearest brothers, to know what his leaps were? From Heaven he came into the womb, from the womb he came into the stable, from the stable he came to the cross, from the cross he came to the tomb, from the tomb he went back to Heaven. Behold, in order to let us run the same course after him, the truth made manifest in the flesh gave some leaps for us; because 'he leapt like a giant to run his course', so that we may speak to him from our heart: 'Draw us after you, and we shall run following the scent of your ointments'.]

It is my contention that, in a *novella* replete with Christological allusion, behind Guido's 'salto' lies Christ's *saltus*. Thus, the Song of Songs's coupling of 'Saliens [...] transiliens' (2: 8) is repeated in *Decameron* VI. 9's 'prese un salto e fussi gittato dall'altra parte' (12), thereby ensuring that the entire close of Boccaccio's description of Cavalcanti's athletic escape is based on Scriptural intertexts. Furthermore, like Christ, Guido offers an example for others to follow ('post se currere').[87] Indeed, in a passage from the *Confessions*, which has extremely suggestive links to *Decameron* VI. 9, St Augustine yokes together the giant and the Bridegroom in order to present Christ as a means of saving those who seek life in a place of death:

Beatam vitam quaeritis in regione mortis: non est illic. Quomodo enim beata vita, ubi nec vita?

Et descendit huc ipsa vita nostra et tulit mortem nostram et occidit eam de abundantia vitae suae [...] et inde 'velut sponsus procedens de thalamo suo exultavit ut gigas ad currendam viam'.[88]

[You seek life's happiness in the reign of death: it is not there. How could it be a happy life, when it is not even life?

Our life itself came down here and took away our death and destroyed it with the abundance of his own life [...] hence 'as a bridegroom going forth from his marriage-bed he leapt like a giant to run his course'.]

---

86   Gregory the Great, *Expositio in Canticum Canticorum*, in PL LXXVI, col. 1219.

87   This feature of the tradition of the 'leaping Christ' emerges with particular emphasis in the influential writings of Bernard of Clairvaux, such as the *Brevis Commentatio*: 'Vel "Trahe me" [Cant. I. 3], id est, spiritualem me fac post te, id est ad imitationem tuam [...]. Cum enim thalamo virginali processit Sponsus, "exsultavit ut gigas ad currendam viam" per omnem dispensationem conversationis suae, quasi quamdam vivendi viam nobis sternens et ordinans, per quam nos post se et exemplis, quasi quibusdam vestigiis, dirigeret, et amore traheret' ['Draw me', that is, make me spiritual after you, that is, in your likeness [...]. When indeed the Bridegroom proceeded to the marriage-bed, 'he leapt like a giant to run his course' through each teaching he gave, preparing and disposing, as it were, a way of life for us, through which he may lead us after him by examples, as if in his own footprints, and draw us through love]: *Brevis Commentatio in Cantica*, in PL CLXXXIV, col. 420.

88   St Augustine, *Confessionum libri XIII*, ed. by Martin Skutella and Aimé Solignac, 2 vols (Bruges: Desclée de Brouwer, 1962), IV. 12. 18–19.

Guido's pedigree is more and more extraordinary. Nor is even the merest whiff of heresy allowed to linger. Thus, like Christ who leaps from his tomb to reach Heaven ('salit [...] in caelum de sepulchro' [he leapt [...] to Heaven from the sepulchre]), so Cavalcanti 'posta la mano sopra una di quelle arche, che grandi erano, sí come colui che leggerissimo era, prese un salto' (12) — a leap which, while it permits him to break away from his immediate earthly oppressors, also prefigures, as befits an intellectual and moral *auctoritas* of his illustrious standing, his future otherworldly salvation.[89] More even than his *imitatio Christi*, it is his extreme lightness and agility, as well as his speed ('prestamente disse [...] e posta', 12), that point to Guido's upcoming state of blessedness. To describe the mechanics of Cavalcanti's flight, Boccaccio drew on yet another contemporary religious cliché. The resurrected body in Paradise — it was widely believed — would enjoy the advantages of four dowries (*dotes*): *impassibilitas* [the absence of any suffering], *claritas* [beauty], *subtilitas* [lightness or penetrability], and *agilitas* (a kind of weightlessness allowing for great swiftness of movement).[90] Consequently, popularizing descriptions of the blessed, such as that by Giacomino da Verona, underscore their leaping feet: 'li pei ge ne saio';[91] while others, such as that by Bonvesin da la Riva, highlight their speed and nimbleness: 'Ma el g'è zascun adorno, vïaz e intendevre, | Cortes e temperao e lev e ben desevre'.[92] Describing his athleticism, Boccaccio not only saved Guido from the puerile pressures of the *brigata* and from the cruel insinuations of Dante's pen, but also saved his immortal soul. There is nothing in *Decameron* VI. 9 to tie Cavalcanti to those 'che l'anima col corpo morta fanno' (*Inf.* X. 15).

7. Conclusion

Boccaccio's Guido is a highly recherché cultural synthesis — an *auctoritas* constructed out of *auctoritates*, namely, in keeping with the term's double meaning (see n. 13), he is the product of a powerful mix of 'authoritative' individuals and 'authoritative' statements. By extension, and quite appropriately, given its metaliterary connotations, the story is also a compelling emblem of the complexity of Boccaccio's writing in the *Decameron*. Just as the *novella* calls into question Dante's reductive judgment of

---

89 Ambrose, *Expositio* VI. 6. Guido's *saltus* only faintly recalls the commonplace, that has its origins in Plato (*Timaeus* 47a–c; *Republic* IX. 586a), and that was widely current in classical and Christian culture, whereby, among earthly creatures, human beings are unique in their capacity and responsibility to look upwards and heavenwards. In presenting Cavalcanti's leap, Boccaccio was intent on underlining its specifically Christian rather than generically humanistic connotations.

90 On the *dotes*, see Caroline Walker Bynum, *The Resurrection of the Body in Western Christianity, 200–1336* (New York: Columbia University Press 1995), pp. 131–32, 335–37; Joseph Goering, 'The *De dotibus* of Robert Grosseteste', *Medieval Studies*, 44 (1982), 83–101; Nikolaus Wicki, *Die Lehre von der himmlischen Seligkeit in der mittelalterlichen Scholastik von Petrus Lombardus bis Thomas von Aquim* (Freiburg: Universitätsverlag, 1954), pp. 202–37. On beatitude, see Chapter 4.

91 Giacomino da Verona, *De Ierusalem celesti et de pulcritudine eius et beatitudine et gaudia sanctorum*, 187, in *Poeti del Duecento*, ed. by Gianfranco Contini, 2 vols (Milan and Naples: 1960), I, 634. *Saio*, infinitive *sagire*, is the vernacular equivalent of Latin *saliunt*.

92 Bonvesin de la Riva, *Libro delle Tre Scritture*, in *Le opere volgari di Bonvesin da la Riva*, ed. by Gianfranco Contini (Rome: Presso la Società, 1941), pp. 629–30.

Cavalcanti, so, in light of its classicizing and humanistic ambitions and of its overt Christian roots, it cannot but at least make us pause and think about the exegetical efficacy of such over-used present-day critical tags as *Boccaccio medievale* and *Boccaccio secolare*. Nevertheless, despite his tale's literary sophistication, in fashioning his remarkable champion, in whom active and contemplative virtues converge, to ensure that there could be no ambiguity as regards the values he wished others to appreciate in Guido, Boccaccio drew heavily, if not quite exclusively, on widely circulating texts and notions. It was vital that *Decameron* VI. 9's ideological points of reference were clearly recognizable. For all Cavalcanti's culturally powerful identity and the 'heroic' role he plays in his own story, ultimately, he remains a means — even if a highly attractive one — to a broader end. Indeed, Cavalcanti's composite, culturally wide-ranging, and exemplary identity highlights better than anything the principal focus of Boccaccio's attention. He is preoccupied not so much with a single individual but with contemporary society as a whole, as the opening paragraphs of the story establish and the concern with 'authority' confirms. In systematizing Guido, Boccaccio was systematizing his culture.[93] In particular, as he does throughout the *Decameron*, he was reminding his contemporaries that, despite all the difficulties of the present, the 'modern' world had within itself the potential for renewal. This was a potential, however, that was neither self-sufficient, as the early allusion to 'avarice' (4) makes abundantly obvious, nor a natural given, but which — like his tale — in order to achieve fulfillment, had to be meticulously crafted by drawing on the great achievements of the past, whether pagan or Christian, secular or religious. The story is a powerful plea for balance and tolerance, as well as an affirmation of hope, both in the possibilities of this life and in the expectations of the next. Looked at from a slightly different perspective, I do not believe it is exaggerated to suggest that it can be read, naturally in minor key, as an attempt to give a somewhat different, more earthly emphasis to Dante's not dissimilar synthesis of Christian and classical values in the *Commedia*. The overwhelming presence of the 'divine poet' in the *novella* would seem to allow for such an interpretive possibility. And mentioning Dante, we are back, for one last time, at *Decameron* VI. 9's ideological and cultural centre. Dealing with contemporary reality meant dealing with that reality's emblematic individuals and the processes whereby such individuals achieved and maintained their 'authoritativeness', and exerted their sway over their world. *Decameron* VI. 9 not only explores such issues but itself also becomes a means for questioning, reconfirming, and establishing *auctoritas*: it questions Dante's 'authority', reconfirms Guido's Dante-ravaged reputation, and raises the possibility of Boccaccio's 'authoritativeness'. *Auctoritas* is not something fixed but is renewed across generations. It is also an attribute which each generation, as the succession Cavalcanti-Dante-Boccaccio underlines, can decide to accord to its exemplary representatives. At the same time, new

---

93   One cannot but wonder whether Boccaccio's decision to make no reference to Guido's prowess as a poet — something that he was happy to mention elsewhere in his writings — was conditioned by the social and ethical emphasis he wanted to give his *novella* and its protagonist. On the story's social implications, see Giovanni Getto, *Vita di forme e forme di vita nel 'Decameron'* (Turin: Petrini, 1958), pp. 155–58.

'authorities' are deeply indebted to their predecessors. Indeed, Boccaccio's hoped-for 'authority' is largely the result of his careful challenge to Dante and his aligning himself with Cavalcanti — to put it simply, Guido's existential ideology is also that of the author of the *Decameron*, who, in addition, acts as the older man's defender, apologist, and eulogist.[94] In this way, as Sallust had declared in a passage which, in Boccaccio, had become closely associated with the Senecan texts discussed earlier, the *novelliere* attempted to guarantee both Cavalcanti's and his own fame: 'Pulchrum est bene facere rei publicae, etiam bene dicere haud absurdum est; vel pace vel bello clarum fieri licet. Et qui facere et qui facta aliorum scripsere, multi laudantur' [It is honourable to act for the good of the state, and even to write for its good is not at all inglorious; one may become famous either in peace or in war. And many are praised, both who did glorious deeds and who have written the deeds of others] (*Bellum Catilinae*, III. 1).

Yet, for all the *novella*'s scope and ambition, it is hard to escape the impression that, in a final analysis, it is a 'failure'. Despite Boccaccio's best efforts to safeguard Cavalcanti's reputation and to curtail Dante's influence, the poet's false charge of Epicureanism has become 'authoritative'. At the same time, despite Dante's own far from inconsiderable effort to do Cavalcanti down, he too 'failed' in his endeavour. Over the centuries, thanks in part to Boccaccio's celebration in *Decameron* VI. 9, Guido's reputation has grown to the extent that he has become what most in his own time wanted him to be: a great canonical figure. And perhaps nobody wanted this as much as Boccaccio; nor managed to give expression to this desire with the same skill. Though Boccaccio thrusts on to Cavalcanti's shoulders a cultural burden of considerable bulk, like a true 'hero', he never wavers under the weight of its allusions and expectations.[95] Thanks to the 'lightness' of his author's touch, Guido's lasting glory is his liberating 'leggerezza'.

---

94   On Boccaccio identifying himself with Cavalcanti, see Battaglia Ricci, *Boccaccio*, p. 178; Contarini, p. 217; Velli, 'Seneca nel *Decameron*', p. 219.

95   I do not have the space here to consider whether Boccaccio's relatively perfunctory presentation of Guido in the *Esposizioni*, twenty years after celebrating him so memorably in the *Decameron*, marks an actual shift in attitude towards the 'philosopher', or whether the muted treatment simply stems from the fact that he was writing a commentary on Dante's *Commedia*.

CHAPTER 16

Boccaccio and Epicurus:
from Epy to Tito and Gisippo

1. Branca, Boccaccio, Epicurus[1]

Boccaccio marked Petrarch's death in 1374 with a sonnet, 'Or sei salito, caro signor mio', which he modelled closely on his friend's 1349 sonnet in memory of Sennuccio del Bene, 'Sennuccio mio, benché doglioso et solo' (*Rvf* 287).[2] Given the two friends' mutual love of poetry and their public status as poets, Boccaccio's was a fitting, as well as an honest acknowledgement of the debts he owed his *preceptor*. Yet, in the very act of commemoration, and there is nothing to suggest that Boccaccio's feelings of loss were anything but heartfelt, he nevertheless asserted his own individuality and even his dissent from Petrarch. Boccaccio was typically more generous and less self-centred than Petrarch, who had used the death of Sennuccio to bemoan his own condition and to strike a new blow in his personal campaign against Dante.[3] Indeed, as he had done in life, it was his friend's jaundiced attitude towards their great predecessor that Boccaccio could not refrain from disputing in his poem of remembrance:[4] not only are Petrarch and Dante presented as reconciled in Heaven, but his sonnet also harmoniously integrates reminiscences from both poets.[5] *Mutatis mutandis*, we too, like Boccaccio, are intent on remembering and paying tribute to our friend, colleague, and 'teacher'; and, like Giovanni, we have chosen to express our emotions, obligations, and respect through professional forms which, as they had done in life, continue even in death to define our relationship to Vittore and to bind us to him. However, if once more like Boccaccio, we do not intend our contributions to be passively celebratory, and hence quintessentially anti-intellectual, in performing our duty as scholars, and regardless of the extent

1   This chapter was originally written for a volume to honour the memory and achievements of Vittore Branca who had died on 28 May 2004.
2   Giovanni Boccaccio, *Rime*, ed. by Vittore Branca, in *Tutte le opere*, ed. by Vittore Branca, 12 vols (Milan: Mondadori, 1964–), v, 97.
3   See Chapters 10, pp. 355–62, and 12, pp. 429–32.
4   See Gioacchino Paparelli, 'Due modi opposti di leggere Dante: Petrarca e Boccaccio', in *Giovanni Boccaccio editore e interprete di Dante* (Florence: Olschki, 1979), pp. 73–90. On Petrarch's complex attitude to Dante, see Chapters 10 and 12; and for a critical bibliography, see Chapter 10, n. 1. On Boccaccio's complex attitude to Dante, which was not unconditionally appreciative, see Chapter 15, n. 31.
5   See Branca's notes to his edition of the sonnet in Boccaccio, *Rime*, pp. 302–03.

to which our work might depend on Branca's magisterial contributions in so many areas of Italian literary studies, a creative dialogue cannot but be set up between ourselves and the man we wish to honour, or rather, between our work and his. It is the basic nature of research to refine and alter what is known, and hence to make us see previous discoveries, approaches, and interpretations with new and quizzical eyes. I am confident that Vittore, who reflected on the nature of our profession with such sensitivity, would smile indulgently at our difficulty, and would be far from surprised that, in endeavouring to recognize the importance of his critical and philological legacy, our aim is not to limit ourselves to restate its findings.

As I began to gather my thoughts on the question of Boccaccio's knowledge of and attitude towards Epicurus, I felt the ambiguities inherent in what I was doing with particular keenness, poised as my reflections were between appreciation and scholarship. My career as an academic owes much to Vittore Branca; at the same time, my work on Boccaccio — little of it that there is — has tended, respectfully I hope, to distinguish itself from his, and my current topic was going to be no exception. My situation was especially poignant as my last contact with Vittore — mediated as so often by Giulio and Laura Lepschy — concerned none other than Epicurus. I had been keen to learn the *maestro*'s views on recent claims regarding a 'Boccaccio epicureo', claims that had received a sympathetic hearing especially in Italy, but about which I had serious reservations.[6] Vittore was typically forthright in dismissing their validity, not simply because they appeared to affirm that for most of his career Boccaccio was almost exclusively concerned with earthly issues, and from a materialist 'Epicurean' perspective at that, but because no single label could ever define a writer of Boccaccio's stature and heterogeneous intellectual interests.

'Boccaccio epicureo' marks the extreme expression of a deep-rooted secularizing tendency in Boccaccio studies. On the basis of the poet's apparent confession in the fifteenth eclogue of his *Buccolicum carmen*, the *Phylostropos*, that he had been drawn to the ideas of 'pastor Epy' (132) — a Petrarch-coined abbreviation for the name of the Greek philosopher Epicurus to which I shall return in due course — it has been argued that '*l'amor vitae*, esibito a suo luogo dalla *Phylostropos* come radice dell'epicureismo (e, quindi, di una visione "terrena" della vita), torna ovunque nelle opere del Boccaccio, dalle prime alle ultime, campeggiando nel *Decameron*' (Veglia, '*La vita lieta*', p. 25).[7] More specifically, it is maintained, Boccaccio's

---

6   See Marco Veglia, 'Giovanni Boccaccio: *Decameron* (novella VI, 9)', in *Breviario dei classici italiani*, ed. by Gian Mario Anselmi and others (Milan: Bruno Mondadori, 1996), pp. 44–56 (pp. 46–50), *Il corvo e la sirena: cultura e poesia del 'Corbaccio'* (Pisa and Rome: Istituti Editoriali e Poligrafici Internazionali, 1998), pp. 35–36, 46, and '*La vita lieta': una lettura del 'Decameron'* (Ravenna: Longo, 2000), pp. 15–56. See also Sandra Debenedetti Stow, 'Gli sviluppi del concetto dell'*otium* epicureo: dal *Roman de la Rose* a Dante e Boccaccio', *Testo*, 23 (2002), 115–26. More cautious and better-balanced observations on the problem may be found in Lucia Battaglia Ricci, *Boccaccio* (Rome: Salerno, 2000), pp. 32–34, 161, and 'La villa come luogo narrativo', in *La letteratura di villa e di villeggiatura* (Rome: Salerno, 2004), pp. 33–64 (pp. 44–45, 50–51, 56–58, 63–64). Closely linked to this critical current are those studies which seek to define Boccaccio as an 'Averroist'; see Antonio Gagliardi, *Giovanni Boccaccio: poeta filosofo averroista* (Soveria Mannelli: Rubbettino, 1999). See also Jonathan Usher, 'A *ser* Cepparello Constructed from Dante Fragments (*Decameron* I, I)', *The Italianist*, 23 (2003), 181–93.

7   Giovanni Boccaccio, *Buccolicum carmen*, ed. by Giorgio Bernardi Perini, in Boccaccio, *Tutte le opere*, V:2, 880–93.

'Epicureanism' had precise and highly indicative contemporary cultural and ideological characteristics, given that it was synonymous with 'Averroism': '[u]na tale parola [epicureo] evocava [...] nella cultura del Due e del Trecento, il fondamento aristotelico e diffusamente laico (secondo l'interpretazione che ne diede Averroé) di una filosofia ampiamente fondata sull'autorità della ragione' (Veglia, *Il corvo*, p. 35), namely, '*la* cultura più moderna e spregiudicata [...] (quella, nel suo intreccio di astrologia, cortesia e filosofia naturale, già condannata dall'arcivescovo Tempier nel 1277)' (Veglia, '*La vita lieta*', p. 17). The exact equivalence of the two intellectual systems in the Middle Ages, whereby 'Averroism' had become the contemporary version of 'Epicureanism', is taken as a given by scholars of Italian literature on the basis of the fact that both ideologies denied the immortality of the soul, as Dante makes clear when referring to Epicurus in *Inferno* x and to Averroes in *Purgatorio* xxv.[8] Nevertheless, while concurring with Branca's sensible broad criticisms of the notion of a 'Boccaccio epicureo', what, for me, irreversibly damages the idea as this has been defined and developed by colleagues in Italy is precisely its absolute dependence on the flawed conviction that, in medieval culture, Epicureanism and Averroism were essentially indistinguishable (see Chapter 14, pp. 470–72).

2. 'Boccaccio epicureo'?

It goes without saying, therefore, that if I am correct as regards the lack of even the faintest Averroistic trace in medieval perceptions of Epicureanism, then, the elaborate construct that is 'Boccaccio epicureo' quickly fades to naught. At the same time, however, the disappearance of 'Boccaccio epicureo' should not lead us to dismiss equally quickly the possibility that Epicurus and his philosophy could have exerted an influence on Boccaccio, not least because Giovanni openly referred to the philosopher and his ideas four times in his *œuvre* (in two stories of the *Decameron*, in the *Buccolicum carmen*, and in the *Esposizioni*), and had certainly read about both the man and his views in authoritative classical works such as Cicero's *De finibus* and Seneca's *Epistulae ad Lucilium*.[9] Nor should we forget, as supporters of 'Boccaccio epicureo' have justly stressed, that it was none other than Boccaccio who first established a direct link between himself and Epicurus. It is strange therefore, especially given Giovanni's customary reluctance to talk about himself, that the vast majority of scholars, even ones of the stature of Vittore Branca, should not have felt the need to explore the implications of this revelation. In his letter to Martino da Signa, Giovanni stressed that the *Phylostropos*'s Typhlus, who had declared his sympathy for Epy, was none other than himself.[10] The problem thus

8   In addition to Veglia (Battaglia Ricci is careful not to suggest such an equivalence between Epicureanism and Averroism), see, for instance, Francesco Bausi, 'Lettura di *Decameron VI.9*: ritratto del filosofo averroista', *Per leggere*, 9 (2005), 5–19 (p. 7); Maria Corti, *Dante a un nuovo crocevia* (Florence: Libreria Commissionaria Sansoni, 1981), pp. 81–82; Giorgio Inglese, 'Per Guido "filosofo" (*Decameròn* VI, 9)', *La cultura*, 30 (1992), 75–95 (pp. 79–81).
9   *Dec.* I. 6. 9; VI. 9. 9; *Bucc. carm.* XV. 132; *Esposizioni sopra la Comedia di Dante*, ed. by Giorgio Padoan (Milan: Mondadori, 1965), X. 10–13.
10   Giovanni Boccaccio, *Epistole*, ed. by Ginetta Auzzas, in *Tutte le opere*, V:1, 712–23 (p. 720).

arises how best to understand this confession. In countering Phylostropus's warning about the dangerous advances of the 'infames [...] nymphe' [disreputable nymphs] (127), Typhlus speaks of 'placid*i* lud*i*' [gentle games] (130), confirming their value seemingly by drawing on the authority of the Athenian philosopher: 'Memini: cantabat inesse | pastor Epy [...], | interitum menti pariter cum corpore cunctis' [I remember: the shepherd Epy sang that for everybody the death of the soul happened simultaneously with [that of] the body] (131–33). The admission is both shocking and absurd; and one can understand why colleagues have preferred to ignore it. Yet, regardless how troubling and ridiculous the implications, we cannot escape the fact that Boccaccio did publicly associate himself with Epy. However, given that, when he did this, he could not, as has been claimed, have been declaring his Averroistic *amor vitae*, then, what is the likelihood that, in 1367, Boccaccio was actually owning up to a life of pleasure, the direct result of his not believing in the immortality of the soul? Such a possibility seems highly unlikely, not least because it finds no support in the rest of his work. Indeed, evidence of Boccaccio's orthodoxy is not difficult to discover.[11]

Two alternative interpretations of the eclogue suggest themselves at this juncture: first, despite the epistle to Martino da Signa, the poem is pure fiction and should not be read autobiographically; second, and as is not unusual in symbolic writing, behind what by the late 1360s was a centuries-old cliché linked to Epicurus, Boccaccio was actually alluding to a relationship with some other, less problematic aspect of the Epicurean tradition. Scholars have largely forgotten that Epicurus's medieval reception, as had already occurred in the classical world, was complex, confused, and contradictory (see Chapter 14, n. 18). Thus, if on the one hand, he was deemed a bad thinker, a dangerous materialist, a wanton pleasure-seeker, and an enemy of all things divine, on the other, and even among some Christian thinkers, Epicurus was judged very differently, and was in fact appreciated as an ethical teacher of note who had led an exemplary life of asceticism. Boccaccio, as we know from the *Esposizioni*, was aware of the contradictions and misunderstandings characterizing contemporary thinking about the philosopher from Athens, and in his exegesis of *Inferno* x constructed a *vita* which, judiciously, or better, humanistically, corrected error and took into consideration both the positive and the negative.[12] The opening of the *vita* is exemplary in this respect: 'Epicuro fu solennissimo filosofo e molto morale e venerabile uomo [...] È il vero che egli ebbe alcune perverse e detestabili oppinioni' (*Esposizioni* x. 10). Boccaccio's presentation is a model of balance and scholarly fairness. Even though he does not openly cite any source, the confidence with which he discusses different proposals and rebuts those he finds unacceptable — 'E perciò non fu ghiotto, come molti credono' (*Esposizioni* x. 13) — makes it clear that his knowledge of Epicurus is extensive and authoritative. If sympathy is too strong a term to describe the tone in which Boccaccio composed the 'life', there is little doubt that he treats Epicurus with interest and respect. The philosopher is most certainly not someone whose behaviour and system of beliefs are summarily to be dismissed and condemned.

---

11   See Chapters 14 and 15; for a critical bibliography see n. 66 in the latter chapter.
12   Petrarch's treatment of Epicurus is very similar to Boccaccio's, see Chapter 14.

Given both the lateness of the *Esposizioni*'s composition and their reflective, classicizing, and summative character, the manner in which Boccaccio treated Epicurus is perhaps not surprising. The commentary, therefore, should not be taken as indicative of Giovanni's attitude towards the philosopher at other, earlier moments in his career. Such a view, however, would be mistaken. In fact, over twenty years previously, Boccaccio had already evaluated Epicurus in a similarly evenhanded manner. Two stories in the *Decameron*, both of which tellingly deal with intellectuals, VI. 9, whose subject is Guido Cavalcanti, and X. 8, the tale of Tito and Gisippo, can be read, both singly and together, as thoughtful, even if indirect assessments, of Epicurus and Epicureanism. That VI. 9 might have such a function is not really so unexpected, given that Guido is described as having Epicurean leanings: 'egli alquanto tenea della oppinione degli epicuri' (9). Conversely, even though I believe that X. 8 engages more widely with the philosopher than does VI. 9, its concern with matters Epicurean, since no explicit reference is made to these during the course of the story, is less immediately obvious. However, I am getting ahead of myself. It is probably best to follow the *novelliere*'s own order of presentation when endeavouring to unveil his thinking about Epicurus.

3. Epicurus in the *Decameron*

As is well known, *Decameron* VI. 9 is a eulogy of Guido Cavalcanti, who is depicted as an ideal 'modern' intellectual. One aspect of this celebration is a sophisticated rebuttal of Dante's charge that his former 'first friend' had subscribed to heretical 'Epicurean' beliefs.[13] The intricacy and ambition of Boccaccio's presentation is apparent from the fact that, although he denied the validity of Dante's accusation, he nevertheless still described Guido as 'somewhat' sharing in the 'opinions' of Epicurus and his followers. The tale's attitude towards Epicureanism obviously emerges from the way in which it resolves this apparent tension. Thus, it is vital to recognize that it is exclusively the untutored, beginning with Betto and his companions, who accuse Cavalcanti of being an 'Epicurean' atheist: 'e per ciò che egli alquanto tenea della oppinione degli epicuri, si diceva tralla gente volgare che queste speculazioni erano solo in cercare se trovar si potesse che Iddio non fosse' (9). Tellingly, no support for the validity of this tittle-tattle comes from either Boccaccio or the story's protagonist. Indeed, given their dedication to pleasure and their anti-intellectualism, both traits which fundamentally distinguish them from Guido, it is the members of the *brigata* who behave like the proverbial 'Epicuri de grege porci' [pigs from Epicurus's herd] (Horace, *Ep.* 1. 4. 16). It is therefore safe to conclude that, according to the author of the *Decameron*, Cavalcanti's Epicureanism had embraced neither heresy nor materialist sensuality. Yet, in the Middle Ages, these were Epicureanism's generally accepted seminal characteristics. Just as he was intent to challenge Dante's view of Guido, so Boccaccio was also keen to call into question his culture's predominant perception of Epicurus. The two operations were of course inextricably intertwined. Thus, to construct his image of Cavalcanti,

13   This paragraph schematically presents some of the conclusions that constitute the core of Chapter 15.

the *novelliere* drew on positive Epicurean elements that he found in one of his favourite authors, the Seneca of the letters to Lucilius. In particular, Boccaccio's Guido is a modern-day Epicurean wise man, since, like the Senecan version of Epicurus, he achieves freedom thanks to his dedication to philosophy; deems the philosopher to be self–sufficient; is critical of obsessive materialism; and reveals both a proper attitude to being 'ricchissimo' (8) and a correct appreciation of the benefits of study. Moreover, Boccaccio did not stop at this. His Cavalcanti is in fact an amalgam of Seneca's Epicurus and great Biblical and Christian thinkers such as Solomon and Paul. He even has Christological attributes. Boccaccio's portrait of Guido redeems both the poet and the Greek philosopher from the erroneous prejudices of the 'moderns', whether these are voiced by the foremost artist of the age or by the 'vulgar mass'. As long as one is only 'alquanto' an Epicurean, then, this can bring distinct ethical, spiritual, and intellectual advantages. What is important, Boccaccio stresses, is to draw on the appropriate aspects of Epicurus's legacy — a legacy that the contemporary world has forgotten and perverted, but whose true identity, and even its compatibility with Christianity, can be recovered by drawing on the authority of the classics.

Although Boccaccio's approach to Epicurus in VI. 9 is reminiscent of the scholarly manner that he would employ in the *Esposizioni*, the *novella*, as an assessment of Epicurus, has two major flaws: it is dependent on only one authoritative source and it exclusively presents the philosopher in positive terms. *Decameron* VI. 9 ultimately lacks balance; and Boccaccio leaves it to X. 8 to restore the necessary critical and historical equilibrium. The latter is a richly complicated story.[14] Set during Caesar Octavian's time as triumvir and moving between Rome and Athens, it stands as the *Decameron*'s major assessment of classical culture. In particular, the story can be read as an evaluation of Cicero's contribution as a thinker, moralist, and orator (Hyatte). Taking the archetypically Ciceronian notion of friendship as its key structuring motif, X. 8 transforms into narrative some of the *De amicitia*'s key precepts.[15] Most notably it addresses the question of 'quatenus amor in amicitia progredi debeat' [how far love should advance in friendship] (Cicero, *De amicitia* XI. 36). However, while Cicero decreed as the basic 'law' of friendship that friends 'neither ask dishonourable things, nor do them, if asked', Tito and Gisippo's relationship, with its calculated duping of Sofronia, her family, and the citizens of Athens, is fundamentally based on a cynical disregard for the 'prima lex amicitiae' [the first

14   See B. L. Blackbourn, 'The Eighth Story of the Tenth Day of Boccaccio's *Decameron*: An Example of Rhetoric or a Rhetorical Example', *Italian Quarterly*, 27 (1986), 5–13; Reginald Hyatte, *The Arts of Friendship: The Idealization of Friendship in Medieval and Early Renaissance Literature* (Leiden: Brill, 1994), pp. 142–63; Victoria Kirkham, *The Sign of Reason in Boccaccio's Fiction* (Florence: Olschki, 1993), pp. 237–48; Alexander Lee, *Petrarch and St. Augustine: Classical Scholarship, Christian Theology and the Origins of the Renaissance in Italy* (Leiden: Brill, 2012), pp. 266–71; Howard I. Needler, 'Song of a Ravished Nightingale: Attitudes toward Antiquity in *Decameron* x,8', *Literary Review*, 23 (1980), 502–18.

15   On Boccaccio and friendship in general, see Ginetta Auzzas, '"Quid amicitia dulcius?"', in *Miscellanea di studi in onore di Vittore Branca. II. Boccaccio e dintorni* (Florence: Olschki, 1983), pp. 181–205.

law of friendship] (*De amicitia* xiii. 44).[16] It will be clear from what I have just said that I agree with those — *pace* Vittore — who in recent years have claimed that the last day is anything but a 'splendido crescendo' of the 'highest' human values, but explores instead behaviour that is troubling and morally dubious.[17]

Boccaccio, however, did not limit Cicero simply to serving as an authoritative guide to classical thinking about the ethics of friendship. He drew on him to explore other aspects of the ancient world in x. 8; and among these, probably unsurprisingly given Cicero's very public antipathy towards the doctrine, was Epicureanism. Tito and Gisippo are Epicurean intellectuals, since they acquired their education 'sotto la dottrina d'un filosofo, chiamato Aristippo' (6). Already in Roman times, Aristippus's brand of hedonistic philosophy had become conflated, not least by Cicero in the *De finibus* and the *De officiis*, with Epicurus's: 'Atqui ab Aristippo Cyrenaici atque Annicerii philosophi nominati omne bonum in voluptate posuerunt virtutemque censuerunt ob eam rem esse laudandam, quod efficiens esset voluptatis. Quibus obsoletis floret Epicurus, eiusdem fere adiutor auctorque sententiae' [And the Cyrenaics, of the philosophical school of Aristippus, and the followers of Anniceris placed all good in pleasure and valued virtue as something to be praised for this, that it was a cause of pleasure. Now that these philosophers are out of date, Epicurus is eminent, as promoter and founder of practically the same doctrine].[18] In fact, and it is with great pleasure that I note this, the first person to recognize an '[a]ccenno alle teorie epicuree' in Tito's speech to the Athenians was none other than Vittore Branca (note to paragraph 59 in *Dec.* p. 1193). As he had done with the *De amicitia*, Boccaccio narratively adapted abstract elements from the first two books of the *De finibus* in order to reveal, through Tito and Gisippo's 'dishonourable' actions, the dangers inherent in subscribing to Epicurus's theory of *voluptas*, especially when, in contrast to what Cicero and Seneca recount about Epicurus, its proponents lack moral fortitude.[19] Tellingly, in order to leave no doubt about their lack of virtue, Boccaccio's two Epicureans are condemned in terms both of Torquatus's exposition and defence of Epicureanism in the first book of the *De finibus* and of Cicero's rebuttal in the second. Thus, contrary to Epicurus's teachings, Tito and Gisippo choose the wrong pleasures and act unjustly: 'At vero accusamus et iusto odio dignissimos ducimus qui blanditiis praesentium voluptatum deleniti atque corrupti quos dolores et quas molestias excepturi sint occaecati cupiditate non provident' [But we accuse and deem most deserving of legitimate disdain those who, captivated and corrupted by the allurements of present pleasures, do not foresee what

16   'Haec igitur lex in amicitia sanciatur, ut neque rogemus res turpis nec faciamus rogati' (*De amicitia* xii. 40).

17   See, in particular, Robert Hollander and Courtney Cahill, 'Day Ten of the *Decameron*: The Myth of Order', *Studi sul Boccaccio*, 23 (1995), 113–70. The quotation from Branca appears in his *Boccaccio medievale e nuovi studi sul 'Decameron'* (Florence: Sansoni, 1990), p. 17. Branca's position is energetically supported by Giorgio Cavallini, *La decima giornata del 'Decameron'* (Rome: Bulzoni, 1980); Marga Cottino–Jones, *Order from Chaos: Social and Aesthetic Harmonies in Boccaccio's 'Decameron'* (Washington, DC: University Press of America, 1982), pp. 170–90.

18   Cicero, *De officiis* iii. 33. 116. See also *De fin.* i. 7. 23; ii. 6–7. 18–20; 11–12. 35; 13. 39–41.

19   See *De fin.* i. 20. 65; 31. 99; Seneca, *Epistulae morales ad Lucilium*, ed. by Leighton D. Reynolds (Oxford: Clarendon Press, 1965), i. 9. 20; ii. 21. 9.

trouble and vexation they will receive, because they are blinded by their cupidity]
(*De fin.* I. 10. 33; and see also I. 13. 43–44; 14. 47; 18. 57; 19. 62–63). Furthermore,
by behaving immorally, the two also make a mockery of Epicurus's supreme faith
in the benefits of friendship: 'de qua Epicurus quidem ita dicit, omnium rerum quas
ad beate vivendum sapientia comparaverit nihil esse maius amicitia, nihil uberius,
nihil iucundius' [about which Epicurus states that, of all the things which wisdom
provided for a blessed life, nothing is greater than friendship, nothing more fruitful,
nothing more delightful] (*De fin.* I. 20. 65).[20] More pertinently, the youths' plot to
trick Sofronia is a textbook example of Cicero's view in book II that Epicureanism
legitimates base sensual activity such as adultery, particularly when the guilty party
expects to escape detection:

> An potest cupiditas finiri? Tollenda est atque extrahenda radicitus. Quis est
> enim in quo sit cupiditas, quin recte cupidus dici posit? Ergo et avarus erit,
> sed finite, et adulter, verum habebit modum, et luxuriosus eodem modo.
> Qualis ista philosophia est quae non interitum afferat pravitatis sed sit contenta
> mediocritate vitiorum? [...] Sed tamen ex eo quod eam voluptatem quam omnes
> gentes hoc nomine appellant videtur amplexari saepe vehementius, in magnis
> interdum versatur angustiis, ut hominum conscientia remota nihil tam turpe sit
> quod voluptatis causa non videatur esse facturus. (*De fin.* II. 9. 27–28; and see
> II. 16. 52–53; 19. 60; 22. 73)

> [Can cupidity be limited? It ought to be removed and eradicated altogether. For
> if there is anyone who has a desire for pleasure, why not call him virtuously
> desiring for pleasure? He will then be greedy, but within limits, and adulterous,
> but he will have moderation, and lustful in the same manner. What is this
> doctrine that does not contribute to the end of depravity but is content with a
> measure in vices? [...] But since he seems to approve ever more eagerly of that
> pleasure which everybody calls with this name, he sometimes finds himself in
> a difficult situation, in that it looks as if there is nothing so base that he is not
> ready to do, provided nobody know.]

Unlike the *De finibus*, however, *Decameron* X. 8 is ultimately less an attack on
Epicurus and his philosophy, than an investigation of how two individuals might
pervert this tradition to satisfy their own misguided desires. That such an outcome
is not an inevitable consequence of Epicureanism, as Cicero had maintained (*De fin.*
II. 7. 22; 17. 56; 22. 71), is clear when X. 8 is read together with VI. 9, or rather when
the *De finibus* is read together with the letters to Lucilius. Boccaccio, and not just as
regards Epicurus, carefully weighed the evidence left by antiquity in order to arrive
at a balanced, rather than at an idealized or a corrupted vision of the classical world.
In the 1350s, such an approach was not without some cultural import.

In the light of Boccaccio's careful treatment of Epicurus in the *Decameron*, the
question arises whether the *novelliere*'s interest in the philosopher constitutes simply
another instance of his omnivorous intellectual and historical curiosity, or whether
the ancient thinker plays a more fundamental role in the collection's ideological
structure. In this respect, it is at the very least suggestive to read in the author's

20   On Epicurus and friendship, see Benedino Gemelli, 'L'amicizia in Epicuro', *Sandalion*, 1 (1978),
59–72; John M. Rist, 'Epicurus on Friendship', *Classical Philology*, 75 (1980), 121–29.

Introduction that most Florentines reacted to the plague by abandoning themselves to sensuality:

> Altri [...] affermavano il bere assai e il godere e l'andar cantando a torno e sollazzando e il sodisfare d'ogni cosa all'appetito che si potesse e di ciò che avveniva ridersi e beffarsi esser medicina certissima a tanto male: e così come il dicevano il mettevano in opera a lor potere, il giorno e la notte ora a quella taverna ora a quella altra andando, bevendo senza modo e senza misura. (*Dec.* I. Introduction 21)

> E ho sentito e veduto più volte, se pure alcuni ce ne sono, quegli cotali [those still able to leave the city], senza fare distinzione alcuna dalle cose oneste a quelle che oneste non sono, solo che l'appetito le cheggia, e soli e accompagnati, di dì e di notte, quelle fare che più di diletto lor porgono; e non che le solute persone, ma ancora le racchiuse ne' monasteri, faccendosi a credere che quello a lor si convenga e non si disdica che all'altre, rotte della obedienza le leggi, datesi a' diletti carnali, in tal guisa avvisando scampare, son divenute lascive e dissolute. (*Dec.* I. Introduction 61–62)

In the face of death, Florence has become a city of Epicureans, or rather, what the Middle Ages generally believed Epicureans to be: 'gli epicurî: credettero che fosse in mangiare e in bere e in diletti di carne, e chi assai n'avesse potesse essere beato'.[21] Even more suggestively, as Jon Usher established in an important article, the protagonist of the opening story, ser Ciappelletto, embodies several Epicurean characteristics (pp. 186–89). The *Decameron* thus opens in the shadow of the Athenian philosopher; and, given the vital role played by the proemial parts of a medieval text in establishing its concerns and directing its exegesis, it is hard to escape the conclusion that, in Epicurus, Boccaccio saw a figure of some relevance as regards the substance of his masterpiece.

In bringing this short chapter to a close, I should like briefly to suggest some reasons why Boccaccio may have wanted to associate the ancient thinker with his *Decameron*. Given the *certaldese*'s philologically sensitive reconstruction and rehabilitation of Epicurus in VI. 9 and X. 8, it is very likely that, despite appearances to the contrary, in the *Decameron*'s opening, the philosopher is not evoked solely, or even primarily, to characterize and condemn the lascivious behaviour of the Florentines and Ciappelletto. Thus, in I. 1, if, on the one hand, the notary — '[g]ulosissimo e bevitor grande' (14) — behaves like an Epicurean of contemporary popular imagination, on the other, when he 'confesses' to fasting (41; and see Usher, pp. 186–87), Boccaccio cleverly alludes to the asceticism, rather than the licentiousness, that is actually at the core of Epicurus's philosophy. Ciappelletto, therefore, mocks and degrades not just Christianity but also Epicureanism, an important clue to how seriously Boccaccio was prepared to treat Epicurus's ideas. By beginning with a tale where nothing is as it seems — 'e per Ciappelletto era conosciuto per tutto, là dove pochi per ser Cepparello il conoscieno' (9) — Boccaccio warns us to keep our wits about us as readers and not to allow ourselves to be 'da oppinione ingannati' (5),

---

21   Giordano da Pisa, *Quaresimale fiorentino*, ed. by Carlo Delcorno (Florence: Sansoni, 1974), 75, p. 360.

thereby encouraging us to look beyond the apparent and immediate surface of what we know and read, an issue to which he returns explicitly at the beginning of the fourth day and in the 'Conclusione dell'autore'. The meticulousness with which, during the course of the *Decameron*, Boccaccio sifts and evaluates the information he has about Epicurus becomes an interpretive model for us to imitate. Indeed, if our first impression of the *novelliere*'s recourse to Epicurus is that he is using the philosopher in a trite and clichéd manner, the error of this first 'deceptive opinion' is vigorously unmasked in VI. 9 and X. 8, though a first hint of our mistake is already present in I. I.

As Boccaccio acknowledges in the Conclusion, what preoccupies him is that the *Decameron* should not be perceived as work that legitimates immoral sensual conduct. As has unfortunately occurred to Epicurus, he does not want to be misrepresented as an advocate of pleasure. He wants instead to be judged fairly.[22] Rather than foster dissoluteness, both in the Introduction and throughout the *Decameron*, Boccaccio places great emphasis on the need for reason to be properly and morally exercised — a fact that is immediately apparent in Pampinea's stirring speech in Santa Maria Novella, 'a niuna persona fa ingiuria chi onestamente usa la ragione' (I. Introduction 53) — a speech that establishes that the grounds for the *brigata*'s departure are rational and ethical, and that moreover their actions stand in stark contrast to that mindless satisfaction of the 'appetites' that has become the norm among their fellow-citizens (53–72). Thus, as occurs emblematically in VI. 9, Boccaccio consistently celebrates the life of the intellect, while decrying that of unbridled sensuality which transforms humans into 'beasts' and 'uomini morti' (VI. 9. 14). Yet, as is well known, Boccaccio is not against either pleasure or recognizing the dictates of nature, as long as such fulfillment of the senses conforms to the appropriate moral standards: 'onestamente a' nostri luoghi in contado [...] ce ne andassimo a stare, e quivi quella festa, quella allegrezza, quello piacere che noi potessimo, senza trapassare in alcuno atto il segno della ragione, prendessimo' (I. Introduction 65; and see 98; 110–15). Like Epicurus before him, Boccaccio too has a philosophy of pleasure to impart. Thus, by 'rehabilitating' Epicurus, the *novelliere* encourages us to assess soberly what he, in his turn, has to say about the complex interaction between the mind and the senses, and about the dangers inherent in both — dangers that are magnified, as the exemplary cases of Ciappelletto and of Tito and Gisippo reveal, when the intellect is placed at the service of illicit desire. Epicurus, who, as Cicero and Seneca made evident, acknowledged the tensions between the mind and the body, celebrated the intellectual life, and was guided by a profound ethical sense, must have seemed to Boccaccio an ideal point of reference in relation to whom to develop and present his own thinking about issues that had long been surrounded in controversy. In addition, by measuring himself against a pagan predecessor, Boccaccio was able usefully to stress that his own thought conformed to Christian standards — a point which, thanks to Panfilo, he highlights both at the beginning and at the end of the *novella* of the false saint (I. I. I–6, 89–91) — thereby affording his ideas a legitimacy and a moral force which Epicurus's views, for all that might be valuable in them,

22   See the next paragraph for a discussion of this point in the light of the Author's Conclusion.

could never have. Yet, despite Epicurus's limitations, limitations that Boccaccio did not attempt to conceal, the *novelliere* nevertheless felt confident that alluding to the Athenian philosopher would help him illuminate both the *Decameron*'s poetics and its ideology — a remarkable rehabilitation for someone who was widely deemed a thinker of almost no merit.[23]

At the same time, it is the indisputably Christian dimension of the *certaldese*'s thinking that, more than anything, confirms that 'Boccaccio epicureo' is a historical impossibility. Indeed, after evoking the ghost of Epicurus at the beginning of the *Decameron*, the *novelliere* also quickly establishes the ideological and spiritual gulf that separates him from the ancient philosopher. In the Proemio, he presents himself as a man of orthodox religious belief whose life is in harmony with the divine will: 'Ma sì come a Colui piacque il quale, essendo Egli infinito, diede per legge incommutabile a tutte le cose mondane aver fine, il mio amore [...] per se medesimo in processo si diminuì in guisa' (5). Conversely, however much the phrase is laced with irony, and however much the force of the condemnation falls not on Epicurus but on the corrupt inquisitor, the fact remains that the first direct reference to the philosopher in the *Decameron*, in the sixth story of day one, does allude to his heterodoxy: 'E con queste e con altre parole assai, col viso dell'arme, quasi costui [the 'valente uomo'] fosse stato Epicuro negante la eternità dell'anima, [the 'frate minore inquisitore'] gli parlava' (I. 6. 9). It is naturally on account of such intellectual eccentricities that a Christian sage can only 'hold' 'alquanto [...] della oppinione degli epicuri' (VI. 9. 9). More generally, it is because of the unenlightened nature of pagan culture that, as in the case of Cavalcanti, the Christian *sapiens* must countermand any debts he incurs with the ancient world by drawing on the example of the great figures of Christianity (see Chapter 15, pp. 521–25). As x. 8 demonstrates, dangers lurk in Epicureanism. Yet, the *Decameron* too can be a source of peril. However, as regards both the philosophical system and the short-story collection, their menace is the fault not of their progenitors, but of the ways others — like Tito and Gisippo — have chosen to exploit them: '[l]e quali [the 'novelle'], chenti che elle si sieno, e nuocere e giovar possono, sì come possono tutte l'altre cose, avendo riguardo all'ascoltatore' (Concl. 8). Indeed, given that '[n]iuna corrotta mente intese mai sanamente parola' (11), even the Bible has been 'perversely' (12) interpreted. As Boccaccio tellingly observes: 'Ciascuna cosa in se medesima è buona a alcuna cosa, e male adoperata può essere nociva di molte' (13). This is just as true of his own 'novelle' (13), as of Epicurus's ideas. Instead of seeking in the philosopher, as so many had done, 'malvagio consiglio e malvagia operazion', Boccaccio, by shunning anachronism and prejudice, and by returning, through his reading of Cicero and Seneca, to the pre-Christian world for which Epicurus had written, attempted to establish the 'utilità e frutto' (14) of the pagan thinker's philosophy. As with his own 'novelle', so, regarding Epicurus too, Boccaccio implied that context is everything: 'né sarà mai che altro che utile e oneste sien dette o tenute, se a que' tempi o a quelle persone si leggeranno per cui e pe' quali state son raccontate' (14) — a lesson in philology close to Vittore's heart.

23   Wolfgang Schmid, *Epicuro e l'epicureismo cristiano* (Brescia: Paideia, 1984), pp. 165–73.

4. Conclusion

Boccaccio's historical Epicurus sits uncomfortably with his bucolic Epy, not least because the 'shepherd' is intimately associated with religious unorthodoxy, materialism, and sensual pleasure (*Bucc. carm.* XV. 114–33), the very aspects which *Decameron* VI. 9 had presented as 'modern' misunderstandings and banalizations of Epicureanism. Indeed, Boccaccio knew from having read Cicero and Seneca that Epicurus was neither an atheist nor a libertine (*De fin.* II. 34. 115; *Ep. Ad Lucilium* II. 18. 9). Epy, as the strange abbreviated form of his name implies, is not Epicurus. He embodies in fact just about everything that the historical Epicurus, whose figure lurks in the poem's background, was not. Specifically, he is a literary construct based first and foremost on the character of the same name from Petrarch's *Bucolicum carmen*, the debauched lover of eclogues VI and VII, who stands for the corrupt Church.[24] Indeed, it comes as no surprise that such a figure, as occurs in the *Phylostropos*, should hold heretical views (VI. 184–206). Although indirectly constituting a moment in Boccaccio's rehabilitation of Epicurus, Epy primarily belongs to his literary engagement with Petrarch, the eclogue's Phylostropos. As a consequence, the poem should not be read as autobiography but as literature. In simple terms, I believe it presents an account of the struggle between the earthly and the spiritual, constructed both as a confession narrative and as a dialogue centred on the poetic self — an account, therefore, that closely and respectfully imitates certain well-known Petrarchan narrative and formal archetypes. Yet, while in the *Phylostropos* the idea that Epicureanism rejects the immortality of the soul loses much of its venom by being part of a system of literary allusion, just as in the *Decameron* the same idea had been downplayed by being humorously associated with the antics of a corrupt cleric, in the *Esposizioni*, and for the first time in Boccaccio, this is soberly presented as a key component of Epicurus's doctrine: 'egli negò del tutto l'eternità dell'anima' (*Esp.* X. 10).[25] Even if there never was a 'Boccaccio epicureo', it certainly is the case that Giovanni had felt drawn to the Senecan *sapiens*, some of whose attributes he transferred to his alter ego, Guido Cavalcanti, and that, for at least the last twenty-five or so years of his life, he kept returning to Epicurus and philologically refining and modifying his view of the philosopher.[26] In hinting at this, however obliquely, the *Phylostropos* can thus be said also to have an autobiographical substratum. Epicurus was a living part of Boccaccio's life as

---

24   Petrarch, *Bucolicum Carmen*, ed. by Luca Canali (San Cesario di Lecce: Manni, 2005), pp. 97–129.

25   This is entirely appropriate and consistent with Boccaccio's approach to Epicurus elsewhere in his *œuvre*. It is only in the *Esposizioni*, and as befits his responsibilities as a commentator, that he presents a disinterested scholarly assessment of the philosopher, hence, for instance, his sharp criticism of the inappropriate reasons for his decision to fast. In the other cases discussed, Boccaccio, for all his philological sensitivity, always subordinates Epicurus to some other purpose, though none as 'extreme' as his transformation into Epy in the *Phylostropos*.

26   See Chapter 15, pp. 517–21; Battaglia Ricci, *Boccaccio*, p. 178; Silvia Contarini, 'La voce di Guido Cavalcanti: Jolles interprete di *Decameron* VI 9', *Studi sul Boccaccio*, 24 (1996), 209–30 (p. 217); Giuseppe Velli, 'Seneca nel *Decameron*', in his *Petrarca e Boccaccio: tradizione memoria scrittura* (Padua: Antenore, 1995), pp. 209–21 (p. 219).

an intellectual and as an artist. And, once again taking our cue from Giovanni, it behoves us to ensure that Vittore too continues to be a living force not just in our lives as scholars, but also in the wider world of Italian literary studies.[27]

27 It goes without saying that the story of Tito and Gisippo and the *Phylostropos* deserve a fuller and more careful analysis of their engagement with Epicureanism and of their sources than I have been able to undertake here. Indeed, as regards both these matters, interesting links unite the two texts.

PART V

Writing Reality

Guido Cavalcanti Among the Cruces of *Inferno* IX–XI, or Dante and the History of Reason

1. 'Disdain' and Exegesis

It has become something of a critical commonplace, when speaking of 'Guido's disdain', to observe that the question is among the most controversial and most debated in the field of Dante studies.[1] In order to resolve the challenge posed by *Inf.* x. 61–63, scholars have normally focused on the rapid exchange of questions and answers that characterizes the encounter between Cavalcante de' Cavalcanti and the pilgrim. At most, they then integrate these with Dante-*personaggio*'s subsequent explanations to Farinata, whose purpose is to reassure Guido's father and to elucidate the reasons why he had failed to respond to Cavalcante's frantic second set of questions:

> Allor surse a la vista scoperchiata
> un'ombra, lungo questa, infino al mento:
> credo che s'era in ginocchie levata.
>   Dintorno mi guardò, come talento
> avesse di veder s'altri era meco;
> e poi che 'l sospecciar fu tutto spento,
>   piangendo disse: 'Se per questo cieco
> carcere vai per altezza d'ingegno,
> mio figlio ov' è? e perché non è teco?'.
>   E io a lui: 'Da me stesso non vegno:
> colui ch'attende là, per qui mi mena
> forse cui Guido vostro ebbe a disdegno'.
>   Le sue parole e 'l modo de la pena
> m'avean di costui già letto il nome;
> però fu la risposta così piena.

---

1   For critical surveys of the debate that include extensive bibliographies, see Letterio Cassata, 'Il disdegno di Guido (*Inf.* x, 63)', *Studi danteschi*, 46 (1969), 5–49; Pier Luigi Cerisola, *Il canto x dell''Inferno' nella storia critica* (Turin: Giappichelli, 1977); Enrico Malato, *Dante e Guido Cavalcanti: Il dissidio per la 'Vita nuova' e il 'disdegno' di Guido*, 2nd edn (Rome: Salerno, 2004), pp. 75–109; Mirko Tavoni, 'Contributo sintattico al "disdegno" di Guido (*Inf.* x, 61–63)', in *Leggere Dante*, ed. by Lucia Battaglia Ricci (Ravenna: Longo, 2003), pp. 217–40.

> Di súbito drizzato gridò: 'Come?
> dicesti "elli ebbe"? non viv' elli ancora?
> non fiere li occhi suoi lo dolce lume?'.
>   Quando s'accorse d'alcuna dimora
> ch'io facëa dinanzi a la risposta,
> supin ricadde e piú non parve fora.
> [...]
>   Allor, come di mia colpa compunto,
> dissi: 'Or direte dunque a quel caduto
> che 'l suo nato è co' vivi ancor congiunto;
>   e s'i' fui, dianzi, a la risposta muto,
> fate i saper che 'l fei perché pensava
> già ne l'error che m'avete soluto. (*Inf.* X. 52–72 & 109–14)

The analysis, both of the interpretive conundrum centred on *il disdegno di Guido* (63) and of this group of tercets as a whole, is further integrated with the intricate (and intriguing) question of the relationship between Dante and Guido and their contrasting attitudes towards Virgil and Beatrice.[2] The critical tendency is to isolate not only the specific question of the 'disdegno', but also the wider one of Dante's attitude towards Guido. The Cavalcantian episode is separated from the rest of the canto. It is treated as if it were a self-standing micro-narrative: an interlude, a distraction even, despite the fact that it augments the drama surrounding the titanic figure of Farinata. In truth, I find it difficult to read the meeting between the pilgrim and Cavalcante as if it were an aside in the structure of *Inferno* X; and not only because, for Dante, Guido was never an 'aside', but also, and more significantly, because the structure of the canto prevents us from reading it in this manner. The episode of the 'disdegno' is placed at the centre of *Inferno* X; and as is well known, in Dante, matters of structure are never to be taken lightly. Thus, Cavalcante does not simply find himself at the heart of the canto. He is also located at the centre of the circle of heresy which, as is rarely noted, extends over three cantos: the ninth, tenth, and eleventh of the *Inferno*.[3]

Relying on the fact of the 'centrality' of the two Cavalcantis, my aim is to begin to re-examine the infernal episode, and consequently the specific issue of Guido's 'disdegno', first, in light of the principal structures, and hence the main questions, that determine the three cantos of heresy, and second, in relation to the cultural and intellectual context in which Guido's and Dante's contacts developed. This was an environment, of course, in which the two poets enjoyed positions of prominence and to which they contributed in decisive ways. The 'disdegno' — like the whole tangled history of their contacts — can only be judged in terms of what is 'publicly' available, namely, what can be discovered in the *Commedia*, or in the medieval

---

2   On the complex relationship between Dante and Guido, see Chapters 13 and 15, and in particular the bibliography listed in Chapter 13, n. 7.

3   The events described in the opening of *Inferno* IX obviously begin in the previous canto, and there is no doubt that elements of continuity unite *Inferno* VIII to the following three cantos. However, I have decided not to include the canto as part of my analysis since heresy is not part of its narrative purview. In addition, as I discuss in the next subsection, Dante appears to have structured *Inferno* IX–XI as a single episode.

world, or in both simultaneously. These are the only traces of their relationship that we have: the only ones, in truth, that could have reached us.

The problem of Guido's 'disdegno', which in any case is not primarily an issue regarding the nature of his 'disdain' but how best to qualify the 'cui': 'forse cui Guido vostro ebbe a disdegno' (63), is not the sole hermeneutic challenge that *Inferno* x throws up. In fact, exegetical problems proliferate not just in *Inferno* x but also in the two cantos that frame it (a new element that, together with heresy, clearly serves to unite them). It is enough to recall the disconcerting identity of the *messo celeste*; the meanings to be attributed to the mythological figures that gather at the gates of Dis; the 'versi strani' (IX. 63), namely, the phrase's remit as regards the text of the *Commedia*; the reasons why the two wayfarers, once inside the infernal city, move 'a la man destra' (134) and not leftwards as has been their custom; the problem of the relationship between magnanimity and sin, or that of the relationship between heresy and politics; whether the punishment of seeing exclusively 'come quei c'ha mala luce' (*Inf.* x. 100) is restricted to the heretics or affects all sinners in Hell; the ideological contradictions that are created between the 'malizia' that embraces 'forza' e 'frode' (*Inf.* xi. 22 & 24), namely the whole of lower Hell, and that other 'malizia' which, together with 'matta bestialitade' (82–83), structures in an unspecified way the last three infernal circles. Furthermore, given that, in the Middle Ages, heresy was essentially considered an error of hermeneutics — obstinately maintaining, despite unambiguous evidence to the contrary, the validity of heterodox interpretations of Scripture and of matters relating to faith — it is clear that, as a consequence of the accumulated presence of interpretive posers in *Inferno* IX–XI, Dante has suggestively introduced into the fabric of his text an element that brings the reader into close proximity with the basic attitude underpinning the sin at the centre of the episode.[4]

In this regard, it is striking that, at various points of the three cantos, Dante should stress the importance of exegesis. His emphasis, and in clear contrast to the behaviour of heretics, is on the benefit of correct interpretation, not only of his own poem, but also generally. And in saying this, I am not thinking, in the first instance, of the well-known appeal to the readers of the *Commedia*:

> O voi ch'avete li 'ntelletti sani,
> mirate la dottrina che s'asconde
> sotto 'l velame de li versi strani. (*Inf.* IX. 61–63)

Rather more arresting and pertinent are the several occasions in the diegesis when Dante describes situations in which a character is faced with the need to interpret, and reveals himself to be more or less capable of undertaking the task. The most notable example is naturally Cavalcante de' Cavalcanti, who misrepresents — as in life he had misunderstood the doctrine of the salvation of the soul — the words of the pilgrim: 'Come? | dicesti "elli ebbe"? non viv'elli ancora?' (*Inf.* x. 67–68). Cavalcante, who represents the despair that is the inexorable result of incorrect exegesis, functions as the emblem of the heretic, thereby confirming the

---

4   On heresy in the Middle Ages, see Chapter 3, n. 35.

reasons for his centrality in the structure of *Inferno* X and in that of the episode of intellectual heterodoxy.[5] Differently from Cavalcante, who, in death just as in life, never acknowledges his hermeneutic errors, Dante-*poeta* does not fail to confess the interpretive mistake that he had made outside Dis when he too was obliged to elucidate an ambiguous phrase:

> 'Pur a noi converrà vincer la punga',
> cominciò el, 'se non... Tal ne s'offerse.
> Oh quanto tarda a me ch'altri qui giunga!'.
>   I' vidi ben sì com' ei ricoperse
> lo cominciar con l'altro che poi venne,
> che fur parole a le prime diverse;
>   ma nondimen paura il suo dir dienne,
> perch' io traeva la parola tronca
> forse a peggior sentenzia[6] che non tenne. (*Inf.* IX. 7–15)

That this little exegetical drama should be placed at the beginning of the episode of heresy is anything but fortuitous. Dante immediately alludes to the ideological and behavioural parameters that define the new sin, and to our duties as responsible readers who, in contrast to the heretics, strive, by exercising our ''ntelletti sani' (61), to arrive at the appropriate 'sentenzia' not just of the *Commedia* but also of any system of signs, beginning obviously with divine ones.[7] In truth, thanks to this carefully crafted antithesis, Dante presents in a nutshell one of the key aspects of *Inferno* IX–XI: the dialectic between good and bad readers. In a context dominated by heresy, 'reading' well or badly, that is, exercising one's reason (the *intelletto*) 'healthily' or 'vainly' ('tutto è vano | nostro intelletto'; *Inf.* X. 103–04), is the same as saving or damning one's soul. The reader, Dante-character and Dante-poet, the heretics, the entire episode are thus all enclosed within the same hermeneutic circle.

The emphasis on interpretation is likely to have a bearing on how best to clarify the enigmatic 'cui'. However, before evaluating the possible ties between the most famous pronoun of Italian literature and the medieval and Dantean obsession with interpreting, there are other problems that need to be addressed. There is more in fact to say about the weighty hermeneutic character of *Inferno* IX–XI.

---

5   Cavalcante's centrality and his emblematic status raise questions regarding the weight and value to be assigned to Farinata (see below for some further discussion of this issue). In saying this, I hope that I will not be misunderstood. Farinata is undoubtedly of great significance in *Inferno* X, in the episode of heresy, and in the *Commedia* as a whole. At the same time, by relegating Cavalcante to a secondary position, something that the text militates against, the importance of 'quell'altro magnanimo' (73) has been somewhat exaggerated. This has affected the balance of the canto, which rather too often has been reductively read as *il canto di Farinata* and in a predominantly political key.

6   The meaning of 'sentenzia' here is technical: namely, the 'sense' that emerges from an act of interpretation. It thus serves as the first indication of the important role that exegesis plays in *Inferno* IX–XI. See also Chapter 2, n. 88.

7   On Dante's relationship to the symbolic tradition, see Zygmunt G. Barański, *Dante e i segni* (Naples: Liguori, 2000); for bibliographies on medieval symbolism and allegoresis, see pp. 3–4, 15, 42, 46, 50, 53–54. See also Chapter 9.

The identity of the *messo celeste*, like that of the 'cui', has long fascinated Dante's readers.[8] I will briefly return to the question of the mysterious divine messenger's identity. Here, however, I should like to focus on some of his other aspects. Since the *messo* has been sent from Paradise to help a person in serious spiritual danger, he functions first of all, and before any other meaning that might be attributed to him, as an emblematic example of the providential intervention of the divine in earthly life. To put it simply, he is a *signum coeleste*, a *vestigium Dei*. He serves as a medium through which God reveals himself to us. We, in our turn, have the responsibility of interpreting the 'senses' that lie behind the external appearance — the *lictera* — of the divine sign. In strict accordance with the standard way in which, in the Middle Ages, the relationship between God and human beings was considered as symbolic in nature, Dante prefaces the arrival of the celestial messenger with an appeal to readers to interpret the new miraculous intervention, namely, the new divine sign, that he is about to describe:[9]

> O voi ch'avete li 'ntelletti sani,
> mirate la dottrina che s'asconde
> sotto 'l velame de li versi strani. (*Inf.* IX. 61–63)

At the same time, having recognized the heavenly provenance of the *messo*, his precise identity still remains hidden behind a 'veil' of question marks. However, this should not be the cause of surprise. As the *commentaria* on Scripture regularly affirmed, divine signs are necessarily polysemous and can, at best, only partially be interpreted by the human mind. In presenting *vestigia Dei* in the *Commedia*, Dante always endeavoured to fashion symbolic figures to which it is not easy to assign obvious and exclusive values (see Barański, pp. 47–53, 63–65). This is what occurs too in the case of the *messo*: his identity and the 'dottrina' that he conveys are neither simple nor easy to decipher. The trap into which modern readers often fall is that of wanting to restrict Dante's divine *signa* within a single set of meanings. It is enough to consider the critical literature on the *messo* immediately to recognize the prevalence of such critical reductionism. At the same time, it is also the case that a fair number of the solutions proposed are entirely reasonable — confirmation, I would suggest, of the care with which the poet created, following the example of the *Deus artifex*, a deliberately polysemous figure. In approaching what Dante signals as markedly divine, we need to move with care. We need to remember the exegetical, intellectual, and spiritual expectations that, in the presence of God, would have conditioned the poet's attitude, as well as that of the orthodox medieval *lector*, who was the type of 'reader' for whom Dante was writing.

In the Middle Ages, it was axiomatic that correct interpretation was only possible if the ''ngegno', even the most 'lofty', was in harmony with the lessons coming from Heaven. This, of course, was the vital lesson that the heretic rejected. For the medieval Christian, especially when matters of salvation were at stake ('il viaggio' of our 'vite', *Inf.* X. 132), *leggere* meant allowing oneself humbly to be guided by that which 'era da ciel messo' (*Inf.* IX. 85). Thus, the divine too is pulled inside that hermeneutic circle which, like the walls of Dis, encloses the episode of heresy. As the *lector* 'opens' a text so as to see what lies behind the 'door' of the *lictera*, the *messo*, by opening the gates of Dis, makes visible the 'senses' that the infernal 'text' wishes to keep hidden — a 'text', let us not forget, that the 'divina podestate' has also 'created' (*Inf.* III. 5 & 7), and which therefore requires the interpretive energies of a divine *lettore*. Furthermore, thanks to his act of disclosing, the *messo* also takes on the typical traits of the exegete. Both guises underline the centrality that hermeneutics play in the life of the Christian. The *messo* is not simply a *signum*; he is also an interpreter of *signa*, who, through his symbolic and exegetical efforts, strengthens the faithful and defeats the heretic. In allowing the two poets to proceed on their journey of salvation, which, as the doctrinal character of *Inferno* XI confirms, is in large part a journey of knowledge, the *messo*'s intervention endorses that it is only thanks to divine mediation that humanity can come to a full understanding of sin ('la condizion', *Inf.* IX. 108), and hence go on to defeat it. Moreover, he stands as the emblem par excellence of the episode's fundamental interest in interpretation which, as an intellectual and spiritual system that integrates exegesis, ethics, and knowledge, leads to salvation or to damnation. Indeed, the *messo*'s extensively documented traits associating him with Mercury definitively confirm his ties to hermeneutics, since it was conventional to gloss the deity's name as 'interpreter': 'Hermes autem dicitur graece apo tes hermeneias, latine interpres' [In Greek he is called *Hermes* [messenger/interpreter] from *tes hermeneias* [interpretation], in Latin interpreter].[10]

Positioned at a prominent and dramatic moment in the narrative structure of the three cantos, the *messo*, if interpreted 'healthily', offers a set of keys with which to 'open' the cantos. He confirms that, at its best, hermeneutics must allow itself to be guided by Heaven, according to that miraculous process whereby a divine sign illuminates other (divine) signs. Then, by encouraging us to explicate both his literal and symbolic meanings, the *messo*, or rather Dante, directly involves us in heresy's exegetical and intellectual atmosphere, reminding us of the need to interpret orthodoxly. It should thus not come as a surprise that *Inferno* IX–XI are chock-full with problems to be solved. The crux is a key element of the rhetorical and ideological system controlling the three cantos. Moreover, it is difficult to imagine that the different cruces, whatever their individual solutions might entail, do not also function as a single system, and hence need to be considered together. The critical weakness that has undermined studies of *Inferno* IX–XI, and in particular the analyses of controversial passages, has been the tendency to treat each problem in itself, isolating it from all the other hermeneutic challenges. If, on the one hand, there is no doubt that each crux poses its own difficulties and requires its own solutions, on the other, it would seem to make sense to try to solve an individual problem also by keeping an eye on all the other enigmas that surround it. The solution to a particular crux may thus in part also be found both in the solutions to the other puzzles and in those general elements, with heresy to the fore, that

---

10   On the connections between the *messo* and the pagan god, see Giuseppe Mazzotta, *Dante, Poet of the Desert: Poetry and Allegory in the 'Divine Comedy'* (Princeton: Princeton University Press, 1979). There are a number of points of contact between my analysis of heresy and that proposed by Mazzotta; see in particular pp. 275–95. The Latin quotation is taken from *Le Premier Mythographe du Vatican*, ed. by Nevio Zorzetti (Paris: Les Belles Lettres, 1995), II. 17. 8 (p. 68).

constitute them into a single system centred on interpretation. To assert as much does not mean to deny that some problems are of greater weight than others — among the former, the 'cui', and the relationship between Dante and Guido unquestionably hold pride of place. My point, rather, is that, in unravelling the knot of the 'disdegno', we should not restrict our attention solely to *Inferno* x. 61–63, or to the meeting with Cavalcante. When it comes to deciphering the 'cui', as I hope to demonstrate, valuable clues are present in all three cantos.

2. The Structures of Heresy

That Dante intended *Inferno* IX–XI to be read in a cohesive manner is evident from the many elements that serve to amalgamate them.[11] The most striking proof of this fact, as has been noted, is that, from a narrative point of view, heresy stretches across the boundaries of the three cantos. This feature, which we might term 'macrostructural', is accompanied by a range of microstructural elements. For example, the explicit of *Inferno* IX dovetails neatly with the incipit of *Inferno* x to suggest an effect akin to *coblas capfinidas*: 'E poi ch'a la man destra si fu volto, | passammo tra i martíri e li alti spaldi (132–33); a close that has its seamless continuation in the first lines of the following canto:

> Ora sen va per un secreto calle,
> tra 'l muro de la terra e li martíri,
> lo mio maestro, e io dopo le spalle.
>   'O virtù somma, che per li empi giri
> mi volvi'. (*Inf.* x. 1–5)

The end of the tenth and the start of the eleventh cantos are not marked by a similarly rigorous formal bond. At the same time, as between *Inferno* IX and x, the shift between the two cantos is characterized by perfect narrative continuity: an uninterrupted transition whereby the diegetic elements of the two cantos are integrated and coherently complete each other:

> Appresso mosse a man sinistra il piede:
> lasciammo il muro e gimmo inver' lo mezzo
> per un sentier ch'a una valle fiede,
> che 'nfin la sú facea spiacer suo lezzo.
>
> In su l'estremità d'un alta ripa
> che facevan gran pietre rotte in cerchio,
> venimmo sopra piú crudele stipa;
> e quivi, per l'orribile soperchio
> del puzzo che 'l profondo abisso gitta. (*Inf.* x. 133–36 & XI. 1–5)

The stench, moreover, a traditional symbol of sin, was already present in *Inferno* IX: 'questa palude che 'l gran puzzo spira' (31).[12] Indeed, the verbal echoes between the

---

11 Although I am convinced of the advantages of reading *Inferno* IX, x, and XI as though constituting a single entity, it is also the case that each canto, as is the norm in the *Commedia*, is distinguished by its own narrative, stylistic, and thematic identity.

12 Past commentators have judged this section of Virgil's speech as 'un po' oziosa' (Sapegno, with

cantos — like the repetition of *puzzo* — which often involve key matters, constitute the most conspicuous element of Dante's unifying strategy. It is enough to think of the *disdegno* that characterizes both the *messo* (*Inf.* IX. 88) and Guido (*Inf.* X. 63); or the *dispetto* that links the 'cacciati del ciel' (*Inf.* IX. 91) and Farinata (*Inf.* X. 36). Returning to the *capfinida*-type connection between *Inferno* IX and X, it is striking that Dante further tightens the links between the two passages by employing the same Virgilian source for both the explicit and the incipit:

> Hic locus est, partis ubi se via findit in ambas:
> Dextera, quae Ditis magni sub moenia tendit,
> Hac iter Elysium nobis: at laeva malorum
> Exercet poenas et ad impia Tartara mittit. (*Aen.* VI. 540–43)

> [This is a place where the path splits in two: The right, which stretches under the walls of great Dis, And through that is our way to Elysium: but the left punishes the evil souls and descends to wicked Tartarus.]

As occurs in this instance, Dante's intertextual choices in *Inferno* IX–XI are often used to consolidate the cantos' unitary identity. The poet's borrowings — and this in an episode full of textual echoes — come from a fairly limited number of classical and Christian sources. Thus, first and foremost, Dante makes regular recourse to Book VI of the *Aeneid*, which is then immediately followed in frequency by Matthew's gospel. Other texts used across the three cantos with similar connecting functions include Ovid's *Metamorphoses*, the Psalms, Ecclesiastes, John's gospel, the Acts of the Apostles, and some of Paul's letters.[13]

It needs to be acknowledged that, however evocative, the means by which Dante unites the three cantos are, in general, of an 'external', formal nature, and hence that such links can only fleetingly touch on ideologically complex questions. Yet, even if they are more difficult to recognize on account of their 'internal' relationship to the text, such questions do fundamentally bracket together *Inferno* IX–XI. In truth, they probably constitute the prime motive for the cantos' amalgamation. For example, as we have seen, the three cantos develop a fairly thorough analysis of the centrality of exegesis in human life — an analysis that Dante integrates and enriches with a series of related questions, ranging from the contacts between God and humanity to the cognitive effectiveness of different epistemological systems, and from heresy to the appropriate use of intelligence, thereby developing a broad assessment of the role of human intellectual activity. In the final analysis, it is the human intellect rather than exegesis — heresy functions as an apt metonymy for our capacity to reason — that functions as the main organizational, ideological, and unifying fulcrum of the three cantos. Consequently, they are filled with references to human mental activity: 'mente', 'conoscenza', 'intelletto', 'ingegno', as well as thought,

references to Torraca and Porena). My sense, however, is that the lines are anything but 'otiose', since they serve important structural functions.

13   I do not have the space here to examine this important structural element in detail. However, see Subsections 3 and 5 for some examples of the ways in which Dante exploits intertextual elements in *Inferno* IX–XI.

reasoning, and so on.[14] Nor is it by chance that, in bringing the episode to a close, Dante should have contrasted the many examples of faltering human mental effort to the 'divino 'intelletto e la sua arte' (*Inf.* XI. 100); or that, with similar strategic purposes, in *Inferno* XI, he should have introduced the first great doctrinal lesson of the *Commedia* — a lesson that he interspersed with learned references to the works of the 'maestro di coloro che sanno' (*Inf.* IV. 131). Human intellectual activity, with all that defines and delimits it, is at the heart of the episode of heresy.

The poet skilfully adapted the different formal, narrative, cultural, symbolic, and ideologicial elements that make up the three cantos to the needs of the dominant problem of the 'intelletto'. He thus fused the text's *lictera*, the 'polisemia che si svolge interamente entro la lettera, per molteplicità di richiami interni e di allusioni culturali', according to Contini, with its *allegoria*.[15] Furthermore, from the perspective of the *Commedia*'s structure, and particularly that of the *Inferno*, it would have been difficult for Dante to have located his assessment of human reason at a more effective juncture of the poem. On the one hand, heresy is a quintessentially intellectual sin. On the other, the two wayfarers are about to cross the threshold separating the sins of the senses from those of the intellect — a vital event whose importance and implications are sharply brought into focus by Virgil's doctrinal contribution in *Inferno* XI. Virgil's lecture also complements and helps to bring to the surface the episode's broader albeit 'submerged' concern with reason. Dante's analysis of the role and function of the human intellect in *Inferno* IX–XI is impressively wide-ranging. It ranges from general and abstract allusions and remarks to specific questions. It is an investigation undertaken with care and precision, even if, appropriately, the reader-exegete, evoked by the poet almost at the start of the episode, is then responsible for untangling its various threads. Nevertheless, the main emphasis of Dante's treatment of reason, in line with the *Commedia*'s self-proclaimed responsibility of having been written 'in pro del mondo che mal vive' (*Purg.* XXXIII. 103), is practical, as is confirmed by the stress given to allegoresis. The scholastics' philosophical and theological speculations on the mind and knowledge, often of a highly theoretical nature,[16] find very little space in Dante's first survey of human reason.[17] In his *lectio*, thanks to references to Aristotle's *Ethics* and *Physics* (*Inf.* XI. 80 & 101), Virgil conventionally underlines that our reasoning has concrete ends.

---

14   See *Inf.* IX. 14–15, 30, 34, 43, 61–62; X. 16–18, 36, 41, 51, 57–58, 63, 95–96, 103–04, 106–08, 113–14, 122–23, 127–28; XI. 15, 20–21, 33, 67–68, 76–78, 93, 97.

15   Gianfranco Contini, 'Filologia e esegesi dantesca', in his *Un'idea di Dante* (Turin: Einaudi, 1976), pp. 113–42 (p. 119).

16   See *The Cambridge Translations of Medieval Philosophical Texts. III. Mind and Knowledge*, ed. by Robert Pasnau (Cambridge: Cambridge University Press, 2002).

17   When assessing the nature and range of Dante's analysis in *Inferno* IX–XI, it is important to remember that we are still in the early stages of the otherworldly journey. Consequently, the questions raised need to emerge from and be consistent with the logic and development that constrain the poem at this juncture, as well as its narrative and ideological unfolding. As the action moves forward, so the problems addressed increase in complexity. Exegesis and practical reason are excellent points of departure for the *Commedia*'s engagement with matters of doctrine. They deal with fundamental issues that affect any thinking subject grappling with the demands of the 'cammin di nostra vita' (*Inf.* I, I).

Thought for Dante cannot be separated from the demands of earthly life, namely, from our responsibilities to God and to others. This explains why, in *Inferno* IX–XI, the poet brought together politics, ethics, and heresy. Thinking, for Dante, always had historical and social implications and constraints. From this point of view, the 'disdainful' speculations of the heretics represent the apex of a type of ahistorical thinking which is simply a sterile end in itself. Indeed, it is difficult to imagine, in orthodox medieval terms, a more 'useless' form of speculation, given its disconnect from reality, than that which, by repudiating the immortality of the individual soul, denied that ties united humanity to God which reason could perceive, enlighten, and strengthen.

3. Moments in the History of Reason

In light of the above, it is just about axiomatic that, in *Inferno* IX–XI, Dante should have examined the connection between history and the intellect. The poet focuses on two historical issues in particular. The first, whose grand sweep goes to the very core of providential history, concerns human intellectual potential before and after the Incarnation, and, by extension, the connections between pagan and Christian thought. The other, narrowly focused and acting as a counterpoint to *Inferno* X's political concerns, addresses contemporary intellectual life.

In treating the first question, Dante has recourse to that sophisticated network of intertextual references discussed earlier. The echoes are not randomly distributed, but are deployed in a carefully calculated manner along the three cantos. Thus, *Inferno* IX is distinguished from the other two cantos as a result of its high number of classical borrowings. At the narrative level, it is enough to recall the press, in front of the walls of the infernal city, of monsters, figures, places, and events taken from pagan mythology: Erichtho, the three Furies, Persephone (or Hecate),[18] Medusa, Theseus, Cerberus, Hercules, Styx, and, of course, Dis itself. Moreover, as the commentaries to the canto document, the environment in which the action takes place is based not only on *Aeneid* VI, but also on passages of the *Pharsalia* and of the *Metamorphoses* that deal with the underworld. Even the protagonist of the episode, the *messo celeste*, albeit a messenger of the Christian God, is adorned with classical traits that associate him with Mercury, with epic descriptions of woods and winds, with the famous Ovidian representation of frogs, and with Aeneas.[19] It is this impressive accumulation of pagan material that, alongside the *messo*'s miraculous characteristics, Dante prompts us to interpret when he draws our attention to the 'versi strani' (63). Therefore, it does not seem appropriate, as has been done, to restrict the scope of the poet's appeal solely to the arrival and actions of the celestial messenger given that the main value of classical culture for Christians was precisely the 'dottrina' that the 'velame' of the pagan *lictera* 'ascondeva' (62–63).

---

18   It is not clear to which of the two characters from myth Dante is alluding with the periphrasis 'regina dell'eterno pianto' (44).

19   See *Aen.* II. 416–19, VI. 179–82, 369, XII. 451–55; *Georg.* I. 242–43, II. 440–41; *Metam.* VI. 370–81; *Theb.* II. 1–3, VII. 65; *Phars.* I. 389–672.

Although I have indicated precise sources for the classical infrastructure of *Inferno* IX, what is immediately striking about the pagan gallery evoked in the canto is that it consists of figures and places that are not exclusive to a particular text or author. Thus, the Furies are present in epic and lyric poetry, in mythographical works, and in the encyclopeadic and compilatory traditions. For Dante and his world, such elements functioned as emblems of pagan culture — specifically, as the intertextual allusions confirm, they are representatives of epic poetry, of the 'alta [...] tragedìa' (*Inf.* XX. 113), and hence of the most refined literature that classical culture had transmitted to the Christian era (see also Chapter 18, pp. 587–93). If, thanks to his 'imitative' skills, in *Inferno* IX and elsewhere, Dante confirms the vitality of this tradition for the 'modern' poet, it is the *utilitas* and the ideological values of the ancient world, and specifically of Latin (and Greek) poetry, that, in the present 'rationalist' context, concern him most.

What then, at least in general terms, is the 'dottrina' transmitted by the pagan *fabulae* that can benefit the Christian? Dante's answer is highly conventional. As the fourteenth-century commentators of the *Commedia* recognized when they glossed *Inferno* IX's classical elements, ancient literature was a source of valuable ethical teaching. The *monstra*, for example, symbolized various manifestations of evil; and, in *Inferno* IX, Dante drew on these meanings to offer a first all-encompassing idea of the nature and variety of sin, a question that he would philosophically refine in *Inferno* XI. In fact, without wanting to deny the dramatic, narrative, and literary functions of the canto's *mirabilia*, the principal logic underpinning Dante's choices is the fact that, as commonplaces, they all enjoyed a rich and widespread cultural reception. Together, they symbolize the ethical acquisitions of paganism — acquisitions which, from the point of view of salvation history, represent the best that the ancient world could offer to Christianity. *Inferno* XI, so obviously indebted to the ancient world's two greatest *ethici*, Aristotle and Cicero, confirms this fact. It also emphasizes that, in moral terms, there was no divergence between classical poetry and *scientia*, and therefore between ancient *fictio* and *philosophia*, as the synergy between the classical elements present in *Inferno* IX and XI confirms. Dante does not hesitate to recognize and celebrate the solidarity of pagan intelligence around ethical issues. At the same time, it is noteworthy that, with repect to *Inferno* IX–XI, the moral lessons of the ancients have much more to say about the reality of evil than of good — a first indication of the ideological and historical limitations of a philosophy lacking divine illumination. In addition, even concerning sin, as the lacunae and errors in Virgil's *lectio* on the moral structure of Hell reveal (Barański, pp. 127–46), the reflections of pagans were not without flaws. All this is of course confirmed at the level of the story by Virgil's inability to defeat the intransigent arrogance of the denizens of Hell (and we can only stand back and admire the deftness with which Dante integrates and harmonizes the different levels of his polysemous text).

As Dante's Limbo, too, affirms, the ethical thought of the ancients cannot in itself lead to salvation. At best, it can provide the Christian believer with what might be termed secondary support. Yet, Dante also recognizes that, in spite of their undoubted cognitive limits — limits that Providence had imposed — there were pagans who succeeded in coming closer than many Christian intellectuals to aspects of divine truth. By alluding to passages on the netherworld present in the 'tragedies' of Virgil, Ovid, and Lucan, Dante emphasized that, unlike the 'disdainful' Christians, who 'l'anima col corpo morta fanno' (*Inf.* x. 15), the ancients believed in the afterlife and in the survival of the soul.[20] Moreover, through the reference to Aristotele's *Physics* at the end of *Inferno* XI, the poet also highlighted the ability of classical *scientia* to intuit truths about the nature of creation and of the relationship between God and humanity:

> 'Filosofia', mi disse, 'a chi la 'ntende,
> nota, non pure in una sola parte,
> come natura lo suo corso prende
>   dal divino 'ntelletto e da sua arte;
> e se tu ben la tua Fisica note,
> tu troverai, non dopo molte carte,
>   che l'arte vostra quella, quanto pote,
> segue, come 'l maestro fa 'l discente;
> sí che vostr' arte a Dio quasi è nepote'. (*Inf.* XI. 97–105)

And it is just this type of problem that heretics, swollen with intellectual arrogance and with their eyes fixed only on earthly things, refuse to consider.

Yet, thanks to the advent of Christ, it was possible for heretics to reach a degree of understanding of these matters that went far beyond the intellectual possibilities of even the greatest pagan thinkers. The absurdity of heretical behaviour is encapsulated in this self-injurious act of obstinate blindness. The Incarnation had occasioned the strengthening of human ratiocinative capacities, especially with regard to the divine, but only if human beings, in contrast to the egocentric inflexibility of the sinful 'magnanimo' (*Inf.* x. 73), behaved humbly as befits Christian *magnanimi*.[21] As is made evident by the appearance and actions of the *messo celeste*, as well as by the behaviour of the two wayfarers, human reason must subordinate itself to divine revelation, entrusting itself to the guidance and enlightenment that comes from above. After the predominance of classical material at the beginning of *Inferno* IX, and in conformity with the historical logic of Dante's presentation, the arrival of the 'da ciel messo' (85) is accompanied by the first major entry of explicitly Christian intertexts and values into the poetic and exegetical structures controlling the episode of heresy. With the touch of a 'verghetta' (89), these succeed in removing what seemed an unsurmountable obstacle to pagan culture and ethics when faced by the recalcitrance of evil. I have already noted the ideologically orthodox implications of the *messo*, and in particular his heavenly symbolic connotations. However, the most conspicuous way in which poetically Dante announces the entrance of the divine and its effects is the concomitant increase in Scriptural

---

20   See Anna Pegoretti, 'Filosofanti', *Le tre corone*, 2 (2015), 11–70 (p. 22, n. 7).
21   On the concept of magnanimity in the ancient world and in Christianity, as well as on the deep divergences between pagan and Christian views of the virtue, see René A. Gauthier, *Magnanimité: l'idéal de la grandeur dans la philosophie païenne et dans la théologie chrétienne* (Paris: Vrin, 1951). For Dante's idea of magnanimity, see n. 42 below.

allusions that attend the celestial *mirabile*. The *messo* recalls Moses; Daniel's 'man dressed in linen'; Christ walking on the water and descending into Hell; and the Holy Spirit.[22] And further biblical quotations envelop the divine messenger.[23] The appearance of a divine *signum* evokes a wealth of other related *signa*: a process that calques the conventions of Scriptural exegesis, whereby a passage was explained in light of other passages taken from the sacred book. In a context in which classical and biblical intertexts follow one another, the call to 'mirare la dottrina' (62) is also an appeal to distinguish between different types of texts, and, therefore, to apply the appropriate hermeneutical forms to the works in question. Thus, the conventions of *allegoria in verbis*, appropriate for classical literature, could not be transferred to the Bible, which needed to be read according to the conventions of *allegoria in factis*.[24] Lines 61–63, which strategically separate and unite the 'pagan' and 'Christian' sections of *Inferno* IX, and whose appeal to interpret extends along the whole canto and the whole episode, underline the key distinction between sacred and human books that controlled medieval exegesis. The distinction not only impacts on *Inferno* IX–XI's concern with interpretation, but also the canto's sense of history. The 'dottrina' that lies behind the Scriptural *lictera* is not limited to revealing moral and scientific truths, but permits access, however obscurely, to divine truths.

As in the unfolding of providential history, so also in the *Commedia*, the Bible takes precedence over pagan culture and its literature. Once more, Dante proceeds in a strictly conventional manner, as might be expected in a context in which matters of orthodoxy and unorthodoxy predominate. Yet, while recognizing the key differences that separate the world before and after the Incarnation, the poet nonetheless seems to have felt the need to soften the tensions and contrasts that fissure human history in two. Although Christian thinkers had for centuries tried to reconcile the best of pagan culture with Christianity, such conciliatory ambitions have a particular urgency in Dante. The *messo* offers immediate proof of this, harmoniously combining classical and Christian elements. Dante's syncretistic representation highlights the respective achievements of the two eras and the possibility of their fruitful interaction, as well as, and more significantly, the presence of the divine along the entire course of history. On the one hand, Dante legitimates the association between paganism and Christianity in light of Providence's constant presence in the world; while, on the other, he presents the continuity of human reason as the further element that unites pagan to Christian. When speaking of Dante's 'humanism', we should depart, I believe, from his confidence in the possibilities of the human mind, a confidence, however, that,

---

22   See Daniel 10–11; Matthew 3: 7, 14: 25; Acts 2: 2. See also Amilcare A. Iannucci, 'Dottrina e allegoria in *Inferno* VIII, 67–IX, 105', in *Dante e le forme dell'allegoresi*, ed. by Michelangelo Picone (Ravenna: Longo, 1987), pp. 99–124; Nicolò Mineo, 'Lettura del canto VIII dell'*Inferno*', *L'Alighieri*, 24 (2004), 53–77 (pp. 70–73); Pasquazi.

23   See Ezechiel 1: 4; Daniel 12: 7; Matthew 23: 13; Mark 4: 9; Luke 3: 7; Acts 9: 5 & 26: 14; Romans 9: 19. See also Mineo, pp. 70–73.

24   On medieval allegory, see Chapter 2, n. 25. On Dante's relationship to this tradition, see Barański, pp. 103–26; James C. Kriesel, 'Allegories of the Corpus', in *The Cambridge Companion to Dante's 'Commedia'*, ed. by Zygmunt G. Barański and Simon Gilson (Cambridge: Cambridge University Press, 2019), pp. 110–26.

unlike the *superbia* of the *disdegnosi*, is acutely aware of both our intellectual limits and possibilities.

Inferno ix serves almost as a 'prologue' to the two cantos that follow, and therefore to the episode of heresy as a whole. It raises and synthesizes problems, concerning reason, exegesis, the relationship between God and humanity, the points of contact and divergence between the classical and the Christian era, that cantos x and xi ponder more precisely and in greater depth. *Inferno* x focuses on the working of the human intellect in the Christian epoch, while *Inferno* xi investigates the role of reason in antiquity, as is evident from the former's emphasis on heresy, and the latter's on ethics and Aristotelian *scientia*. Leaving aside the immediate narrative environment, inhabited by 'modern' heretics, intertextuality is once more the primary mechanism through which Dante emphasizes the Christian character of *Inferno* x. The canto is rich in Scriptural echoes.[25] By first identifying the quotations that Dante has woven into the fabric of his text, and then relying on their established exegesis, we can exercise our intelligence in ways that the heretic rejects.[26] Thus, the biblical passages and their gloss are the means by which to recognize, judge, and condemn heretical behaviour. The Bible's substantial presence in the poetic weave of *Inferno* x constitutes a sort of 'external *contrapasso*' that the text imposes on sinners who, in life, had ignored, refused, or, worst of all, had deliberately misunderstood Scripture's truths. In the episode of heresy's heavily exegetical atmosphere, the biblical *sententiae* function as 'glosses' on the sin.

At the narrative level, and hence as part of their eternal punishment, the obstinate *lectores* of the *sacra pagina* are 'serrati' (*Inf.* x. 10), as they are by the 'sepulcri' (115), by the memory of biblical quotations and their canonical interpretations. The heretics are thus prompted to recall and ponder texts that, if they had read them correctly in life, could have saved their souls. The Scriptural provenance of the 'tombe' (129) is a telling case in point. Psalm 48 provides both the site and the torment of the Epicureans' eternal state: 'Et sepulchra eorum domus illorum in aeternum' [And their tombs will be their home in eternity] (12). The personal pronoun 'eorum' refers to the 'insipiens et stultus' [unwise and foolish], whom the psalmist contrasted to the 'sapientes' [wise] (11), whose souls God saves 'de manu inferi' [from the grasp of Hell] (16). The Psalm not only offers the basic framework for the sixth circle of Dante's Hell, but also alludes to the condition of the 'wise' pilgrim, who, spiritually and intellectually, is placed in direct opposition to the heretics. Thus, the most

25   See, for example, Anthony K. Cassell, *Dante's Fearful Art of Justice* (Toronto and Buffalo: University of Toronto Press, 1984), pp. 15–31; Robert M. Durling, 'Farinata and the Body of Christ', *Stanford Italian Review*, 2 (1981), 5–35, and ' "Mio figlio ov'è?" (*Inferno* x. 60)', in *Dante da Firenze all'aldilà*, ed. by Michelangelo Picone (Florence: Cesati, 2001), pp. 303–29; Durling-Martinez, pp. 162–64; Vincent Moleta, 'Dante's Heretics and the Resurrection', *Medioevo romanzo*, 7 (1980), 247–84; Michelangelo Picone, ' "Iacob dilexi..."': Dante, Cavalcanti e la predestinazione', *L'Alighieri*, 47 (2006), 5–23.

26   'Dante claimed that the *Com.* could teach its readers how to shape their relationship to God through a correct understanding and use of the Bible. In this regard, the poet presented himself as someone who "umilmente con essa [Scripture] s'accosta" (*Par.* xxix. 93), namely someone who practices a method of reading the Bible that avoids error by respecting both the literal meaning of the text and the views of authoritative past interpreters': Paola Nasti, 'Religious Culture', in Barański and Gilson, pp. 158–72 (p. 159).

obvious explanation for the unexpected direction — 'a la man destra' — towards which Virgil 'turned' so as to 'passare tra i martíri e li alti spaldi' (*Inf.* IX. 132–33) should be sought in the long-standing view that saw *sinister* as indicating intellectual error and *dexter* as embodying the correct use of reason. Consequently, on entering the realm of heresy, the two wayfarers are straightaway symbolically distinguished from its sinful inhabitants. And further elements from Psalm 48 exert an influence on *Inferno* x: for instance, Dante's misbelievers recall those:

> Qui confidunt in virtute sua
> et in multitudine divitiarum suarum gloriantur
> frater non redimit redimet homo
> non dabit Deo placationem suam
> et pretium redemptionis animae suae
> et laboravit in aeternum et vivet adhuc in finem.
>
> (Psalm 48: 7–10)

[Those who trust in their own strength, and boast of the abundance of their riches, no brother redeems, nor shall man redeem: he will not pay God his due and the price for the redemption of his soul, and will labour in eternity and will live unto the end.]

Equally, Farinata and his personal drama have suggestive links with the Psalm's close:

> Nec timueris cum dives factus fuerit homo
> et cum multiplicata fuerit gloria domus eius
> quoniam cum interierit non sumet omnia
> neque descendet cum eo gloria eius
> quia anima eius in vita ipsius benedicetur
> confitebitur tibi cum benefeceris ei
> introibit usque in progenies patrum suorum
> usque in aeternum non videbit lumen
> homo in honore cum esset non intellexit
> conparatus est iumentis insipientibus
> et similis factus est illis. (Psalm 48: 17–21)

[Do not fear when a man shall be made rich and when the glory of his house shall be multiplied, because when he dies he shall carry nothing with him, nor shall his glory descend with him. Since his soul will be blessed in his lifetime, he shall trust you when you will do well to him. He will enter the generations of his fathers and will never see the light. When the man was in honour, he had no understanding: he was compared to senseless beasts and was made similar to them.]

However, rather than the *lictera* of the Bible, it is its canonical allegoresis that, appropriately, both weighs upon the sinners and elucidates their sinfulness. Thus, Psalm 48: 12 was commonly associated with the behaviour of the *epicuri* — proof, once more, of the centrality of exegesis in our cantos and of the care with which Dante was guided by hermeneutic structures and suggestions.[27] More generally, the gloss on Psalm 48 examines some of the same questions that the poet explores

27   See Chapter 15, pp. 512–15.

in *Inferno* IX–XI: the condemnation of the *stulti*; the celebration of the gift of the intellect; the dangers of materialism and of an exaggerated interest in the things of this world; and the inability of the sinner to understand who is truly wise (see Chapter 15, p. 513). These were the problems that heretics typically misunderstood. According to the Scriptural tradition, which Dante is closely following, the *stultus* and the heretic are extreme rationalists, who, like Farinata and Cavalcante, direct their reason only to the things of this world, and whose intellectual extremism is a mark of pride. Indeed, it is noteworthy that, in *Inferno* IX–XI, they are condemned not only by Christianity, but also by pagan culture. Virtuous ancient intellectuals, although they were totally dependent on their unenlightened reason, had nonetheless recognized their own ratiocinative limits and accepted the implications of the existence of higher intelligences. Again Dante stresses the connections that unite the best of paganism and Christianity, whereby the two historical epochs come together to condemn the intellectual arrogance that has beset humanity from the time of Epicurus right up to the present.

The *Commedia* too is the fruit of this collaboration across history. By simultaneously 'imitating' biblical and classical forms, the poem transmits a complex and multifaceted 'dottrina'. In *Inferno* IX–XI, its focus is both on the achievements and dangers of reason, and, thanks to a strategy that might be termed metaexegetical, on the functions and responsibilities of hermeneutic intelligence throughout time, as well as at single moments, such as the one evoked in the episode of heresy. If, in Limbo, Dante had mainly emphasized the excellence of the pagan world in itself, in *Inferno* IX–XI he contextualizes this greatness. On the one hand, he redimensions the accomplishments of antiquity with respect to Christianity; on the other, he exalts these not only in light of the errors committed by pagans and Christians, but also by recognizing the constraints within which such successes had been attained. When presenting the major achievements of Christianity in *Inferno* IX and X, Dante grants pride of place to the Bible. Given that Dante's attention is firmly on human reason, this means highlighting the literary abilities of the *scribae Dei* in composing the Scriptural *lictera*, as well as the skill of exegetes in deciphering God's signs. These two Christian intellectual traditions can be aligned, *mutatis mutandis*, with those poetic and interpretive activities that Dante had indicated as constituting some of the finest results realized by the pagan mind. It is clear, therefore, what Dante considered to be a constant of human rationative endeavour at its best. At the same time, it is also striking that the poet decided not to mention the intellectual contributions that constituted the new and most advanced point of contemporary thought. In an account of reason written at the beginning of the fourteenth century, such an omission could only have been deliberate and eyecatching. Thus, there are no explicit allusions to the interest either in logic or in rationalist epistemologies and argumentative forms that defined a considerable number of thirteenth- and fourteenth-century intellectuals, both lay and religious. In this regard, it is equally important to recognize that Dante was not being polemical against scholasticism as a whole. When he referred in a respectful manner to Aristotle's *Ethics* and *Physics*, Dante was also recalling the impressive recent exegetical and doctrinal tradition that the philosopher's works had inspired. In particular, Dante was alluding to those interpretations that had illuminated Aristotle's congruence with Christianity, and which, naturally, legitimate and underpin his own 'Christianization' of the pagan philosopher in *Inferno* XI.

As is evident from *Inferno* IX–XI, Dante was not opposed to rationalism in itself. What he most certainly was against was any sort of selfish and unabashed rationalism. The heretic, who refuses to subjugate reason to faith and who proposes untenable hypotheses and interpretations, represents the extreme example of such dishonestly self-sufficient rationalism. The heretic uses intelligence not for the good of the community, but solely as a means of self-satisfaction. Rather than contributing to the sum of human knowledge, s/he fractures *sapientia*'s cohesion. The heretic is a sectarian (*Inf.* IX. 128) who foments partisan struggle. By bringing together intellectual and political discord, Dante subtly affirmed that the ideological roots of contemporary political tensions and violence were deep and complex. For Dante, to think badly is akin to acting badly. The 'practical' implications of reasoning constitute a fixed point of Dante's thought. Empty speculation can only be sinful. The gift of reason and responsibilities towards God and others that are its consequences cannot be squandered in 'private' and abstract rumination.

In terms of the evolving logic of the three cantos, *Inferno* XI provides the main counterweight to the heretics' fanaticism and the 'disdainful' thinking. Aristotle functions as the alternative not just to eccentric pagan thinkers such as Epicurus, but also, and more significantly, to heterodox Christian and 'modern' intellectuals. While the latter denied the existence of the afterlife, the philosopher presents facts with which to understand the reality of the other world. *Inferno* XI brings Dante's investigation into human reason to an end by celebrating the potentialities of the human mind. It is emblematic that Aristotle should stand for self-sufficient, yet virtuous intelligence which, even if not divinely enlightened, is capable of discriminating between right and wrong — intelligence that is 'independent' yet 'orthodox'. In direct opposition to heretics, who are bad rationalists, Aristotle represents the good rationalist. At the same time, *Inferno* XI, and by extension the entire episode, does not uncritically exalt the ancient thinker and his rationalism. In presenting Aristotle, Dante interweaves praise with criticism. *Inferno* XI ends with a direct reference to the Bible, to 'lo Genesí dal principio' (107), thereby highlighting that, for human reason fully to actualize its potential, it needs divine *signa* much more than intelligence's ratiocinative capabilities. Where Aristotle fails, the Bible elucidates without difficulty. Consequently, in order to illustrate properly why 'usura offende | la divina bontade' (95–96), Virgil abandons the philosopher and instead cites the divine book:

> Da queste due [Nature and art], se tu ti rechi a mente
> lo Genesí dal principio, convene
> prender sua vita e avanzar la gente;
>   e perché l'usuriere altra via tene,
> per sé natura e per la sua seguace
> dispregia, poi ch'in altro pon la spene. (*Inf.* XI. 106–11)

In Virgil's *lectio*, Aristotle and Scripture, namely rationalism and symbolic exegesis, meet. And when they meet, there is no doubt as to which of the two epistemological traditions is the most effective. In an essentially orthodox religious writer like Dante, it is of course unremarkable that 'reading' the Bible is presented as the best way to arrive at the truth. Yet, at the beginning of the fourteenth century, and in particular as regards issues relating to reason and human knowledge, such a stance, in fact, was neither obvious nor without polemical implications.

The second half of the thirteenth century and the first decades of the fourteenth century were marked by ideological conflicts.[28] One of the main effects of the medieval recovery of Aristotle was a renewed interest in human reason and its possibilities, including its autonomy. Dante's analysis in *Inferno* IX–XI cannot be separated from these disputes which, in broad terms, involved the relative merits of symbolism and rationalism as means of knowing. The traditional idea of human intelligence as subjected to divine enlightenment was challenged by the notion of reason as self-sufficient, confident in its own intellectual powers, and convinced that 'il sapere può rendere pienamente felici, anche se di quella felicità finita e limitatata che è possibile in terra'.[29] Logic, as I mentioned earlier, was the preferred epistemological tool. Unlike what occurs in *Inferno* XI, as well as throughout the *Commedia*, in the late Middle Ages, symbolism and rationalism tended to function as two contrasting intellectual systems. Always ready to counter and remedy any form of factionalism in his great poem, in *Inferno* IX–XI Dante emphasized that symbolism and rationalism most certainly could and should cooperate. Antiquity offered illustrious confirmation of this. According to the poet, the division between the two epistemologies had disastrously occurred only in the contemporary world. Unlike the situation facing the pagan who 'nasce a la riva | de l'Indo, e quivi non è chi ragioni | di Cristo né di chi legga né che scriva' (*Par.* XIX. 70–72), there were no obstacles to impede Christians from concentrating their minds (*ragionare*) on the interpretation and dissemination (*leggere* e *scrivere*) of the Bible. The three verbs here are technical: they indicate that God had primarily granted humanity the gift of reason so that it might decipher His *signa*. Yet, 'i terreni animali' ignore 'la Scrittura' that God has placed 'sovra' them and which allows tham to *consuonarsi* with the 'prima volontà'; instead, the 'menti grosse' prefer to squander their intellects in pointless *assottigliarsi* (82–83, 85–86, 88).

28   See Chapter 2, n. 65. On Dante's reactions to these conflicts, see Barański; Giuseppe Mazzotta, *Dante's Vision and the Circle of Knowledge* (Princeton: Princeton University Press, 1992); Angela Meekins, 'Reflecting on the Divine: Notes on Dante's Heaven of the Sun', *The Italianist*, 18 (1998), 28–70. See also Chapters 2–5, and 9.

29   Francesco Bottin, 'Introduzione', in *Ricerca della felicità e piaceri dell'intelletto. Boezio di Dacia 'Il sommo bene'. Giacomo da Pistoia 'La felicità suprema'*, ed. by Francesco Bottin (Florence: Nardini Editore, 1989), pp. 7–41 (p. 13). On the concept of happiness in the Middle Ages, see Luca Bianchi, 'La felicità intellettuale come professione nella Parigi del Duecento', *Rivista di filosofia*, 78 (1987), 181–99, and 'Moral Philosophy', in *Dante in Context*, ed. by Zygmunt G. Barański and Lino Pertile (Cambridge: Cambridge University Press, 2015), pp. 159–72; *La felicità nel Medioevo: Atti del Convegno della Società Italiana per lo Studio del Pensiero Medievale (SISPM)*, ed. by Maria Bettetini and Francesco D. Paparella (Louvain-La-Neuve: Fédération internationale des instituts médiévales, 2005); Irene Zavattero, 'Felicitas — beatitudo', in *Mots médiévaux offerts à Ruedi Imbach* (Porto: FIDEM, 2011), pp. 291–302.

The divine eagle's condemnation has deep roots in the *Commedia*, and, of these, few are as vital as *Inferno* IX–XI. Although Dante tends to criticize his intellectual environment in general, as well as lament the widespread doctrinal disharmony it has engendered, he also deems one current to be especially blameworthy for the present state of ideological disarray. Dante's heretics, who deny the immortality of the soul and who refuse to focus their intelligence on the divine, represent extreme rationalists and materialists. They are, as far as Dante is concerned, modern-day 'Epicureans'.[30] And, in *Inferno* X, Dante's attention is very much on the present, since, apart from the mention of Epicurus, the other sinners, Farinata, Cavalcante, ''l secondo Federico | e 'l Cardinale' (119–20), all belong to the contemporary world. They are emblems of the intransigence of contemporary rationalism. It is thus both appropriate and indicative that the doctrinal questions that Dante placed at the centre of *Inferno* X — the soul and nobility — were two of the most thorny and controversial matters debated in philosophical circles at the dawn of the fourteenth century. The centrality of the soul is self-evident.[31] Equally, it is not difficult to appreciate that Dante is taking aim at those contemporary intellectuals who, in the wake of Averroes's theory of the unicity of the possible intellect, namely the so-called neo-Averroists or radical Aristotelians, questioned the survival of the individual soul. The same 'radical' circles also developed the idea of philosophical nobility, the preserve of 'quidam homines contemplativi bene nati ad scientias ex parte corporis sui et animae' [certain contemplative men well-born for the sciences as part of their own body and soul].[32] Such men were intellectually 'magnanimous'.

30   In the wake of John Freccero, 'Ironia e mimesi: il disdegno di Guido', in *Dante e la Bibbia*, ed. by Giovanni Barblan (Florence: Olschki, 1988), pp. 41–54, and 'Ancora sul disdegno di Guido', *Letture classensi*, 18 (1988), 79–92, Albert A. Ascoli concludes: 'in *Inferno* 10 [...] Dante systematically attacks and subverts the perspective of those Epicureans who, like Farinata and Cavalcanti, sustain the autonomy of human history as a field of action. Their commitment to historical temporality has led to blindness and damnation. In other words, Dante pointedly rejects secularism and its modes of representing earthly existence': *Dante and the Making of a Modern Author* (Cambridge: Cambridge University Press, 2008), p. 49.
31   On medieval debates on the soul, see Andrew Arlig, 'The Complexity of the Soul and the Problem of Unity in Thirteenth-century Philosophy', in *Philosophy of Mind in the Early and High Middle Ages*, ed. by Margaret Cameron (London: Routledge, 2018), pp. 197–218; Alain de Libera, *'L'Unité de l'intellect': commentaire du 'De unitate intellectus contra averroistas' de Thomas d'Aquin* (Paris: Vrin, 2004); Richard C. Dales, *The Problem of the Rational Soul in the Thirteenth Century* (Leiden: Brill, 1995); J. De Raedemaker, 'Une ébauche de catalogue des Commentaires sur le *De anima* parus aux XIII, XIV et XV siècles', *Bulletin de philosophie médiévale*, 5 (1963), 149–83 and 6 (1964), 119–34, and 'Informations concernant quelques commentaires du *De anima*', *Bulletin de philosophie médiévale*, 8–9 (1966–67), 87–110 and 10–12 (1968–70), 194–211; Benoît Patar, *Le Traité de l'âme de Jean Buridan: édition, étude critique et doctrinale* (Louvain-La-Neuve: Éditions de l'Institut supérieur de philosophie, 1991); Kara Richardson, 'Soul and Agent Intellect: Avicenna and Aquinas', in Cameron, pp. 178–96. See also Patrick M. Gardner, 'Dante and the Suffering Soul' (unpublished PhD thesis, University of Notre Dame, 2009); Manuele Gragnolati, *Experiencing the Afterlife: Soul and Body in Dante and Medieval Culture* (Notre Dame, IN: University of Notre Dame Press, 2005); Bruno Nardi, 'L'origine dell'anima umana secondo Dante', in his *Studi di filosofia medievale* (Rome: Edizioni di storia e letteratura, 1960), pp. 9–68, and 'Sull'origine dell'anima umana', in *Dante e la cultura medievale*, ed. by Paolo Mazzantini and Tullio Gregory (Rome and Bari: Laterza, 1990), pp. 207–24. See also Chapter 9.
32   Boethius Dacus, *De somniis*, ed. by Nicolaus G. Green-Pedersen (Copenhagen: F. Bagge, 1976), p. 382.

And it is through Farinata, 'quell'altro magnanimo' (73), that Dante is able to interweave the question of nobility into the fabric of *Inferno* x:

> La nozione aristotelica di *'bene nasci'* indica nell'ordine: un talento intellettuale, anzitutto logico; un equilibrio 'genetico' tra ragione e sensibilità, una sorta di continenza ereditaria, tale da favorire il talento suddetto; il perfezionamento intellettuale legato allo studio della filosofia e, finalmente, alla contemplazione delle sostanze nobilissime. [...] Codesto nucleo si può, a sua volta, combinare con altre caratteristiche 'nobili' (capacità di governo, antichità di casato, ma anche possesso di ricchezze o notorietà).[33]

The focus is entirely on the *bene natus* and his earthly status and attainments rather than on the needs of the community and our obligations to the divine. Such a view of intelligence and personal merit is both earthbound and elitist. It fosters a sense of self and of individual 'nobility' that is perfectly captured in Farinata's 'disdainful' (*Inf.* x. 41) attitude. The infernal *magnanimus* is a failed materialist intellectual, blindly obsessed with problems of lineage and with the fate of his family and his own reputation.

Dante's decision to have recourse to the heretic as a general symbol of the arrogant and non-believing rationalist, as well as, more specifically, of the 'modern' philosopher smugly satisfied with his own cleverness and ruminations, is well made. Moreover, the fact that, traditionally, the heretic was deemed to be someone who wilfully misunderstood the senses of Scripture — and, from this perspective, the 'sequestered' presence of 'Anastasio papa [...] | lo qual trasse Fotin de la via dritta' (*Inf.* xi. 8–9) plays an exemplary role — allows Dante, in a spirit of non-partisanship, to criticize the symbolic tradition too. Yet, Dante's confidence in divine and human *signa* and in the worth of their exegesis, coupled to the *Commedia*, the 'poema sacro | al quale ha posto mano e cielo e terra' (*Par.* xxv. 1–2), constituting a privileged space where the two semiotic systems meet, constrains him from treating the exegetical-symbolic tradition too negatively, not least because, as the *messo* reveals, it is the one that best leads to salvation.

Ideological struggles between traditionalist intellectuals secure in the word of God and new philosophers confident in the powers of reason and logic; providential history; the relationship between paganism and Christianity, which are not reduced to two worlds in contrast, but are each evaluated *ex bono* and *ex malo*, so that their respective merits and demerits, as well as their points of contact, can become apparent; the ties and tensions between the two great human epistemologies, symbolism and rationalism; and, finally, at the heart of this imposing accumulation of fundamental questions, human reason, divine gift that conditions our commitment to God and others, as well as our sense of self — these are the issues that allegoresis can help uncover behind the 'velame' (*Inf.* ix. 63) of the episode of heresy. Dante's ambitious treatment of reason in the three cantos, as I have endeavoured to illustrate, is rigorously constructed. Poetic form and execution are marks of his intellectual

---

33   Andrea A. Robiglio, 'Dante "bene nato": Guido Cavalcanti e Margherita Porete in *Par.* v, 115', *L'Alighieri*, 46 (2005), 45–62 (p. 58); and see also his 'The Thinker as a Noble Man (*bene natus*) and Preliminary Remarks on the Medieval Concepts of Nobility', *Vivarium*, 44 (2006), 205–47.

abilities, of the *Commedia*'s capacity to transmit 'doctrina' (62), and of its moral-didactic seriousness. At the same time, given its openly philosophical character, it is *Inferno* xi that primarily highlights and historically contextualizes the doctrinal dimension of the two preceding cantos. The third act of the great drama of heresy encourages reconsideration of the many references to the intellect and intellectual activity already present in the episode. *Inferno* xi is anything but a mechanistic digression — as has been averred — whose sole function is stolidly to explicate the moral structure of Hell. In reality, the canto offers the first clear indication of the *Commedia*'s highly original doctrinal character, together with its commitment to assess human thought in relation to both providential and intellectual history.[34] It also signals the sophistication with which *scientia* will be treated. The *Inferno*, contrary to another critical commonplace, is far from being a cantica without doctrinal ambition.

4. Epicureans and not Aristotelians?

A final general problem before, at last, returning to Guido, the 'cui', and the 'disdegno': why does Dante, if he is in fact concerned to evoke the contemporary intellectual scene, term his heretics 'Epicureans' rather than, as would be reasonable to expect, 'Aristotelians'?

It is useful to begin with a fact. In the late Middle Ages, the term 'Epicurean' was not synonymous with 'Averroist', as scholars of Italian literature have long and erroneously maintained, despite the lack of documentary evidence for their claim. The two pagan philosophers, whose names inspired the above designations, despite the eccentric ideas that each held about the eternity of the soul and which, superficially at least, united them, were always presented and assessed separately in medieval texts (see Chapter 14, pp. 470–72; and Part iv, 'Exploiting Epicurus', in general). It is enough to recall that, in the *Commedia*, Averroes is in Limbo, while Epicurus is punished in the sixth circle of Hell. And their 'seguaci' (*Inf.* x. 14) too were differentiated in the same manner. Consequently, in itself, the tag *epicureus* did not also embrace that of *aristotelicus*, as is confirmed by the well-established distinction, present too in the *Convivio*, whereby the ancient world had produced three great philosophical schools: the Epicurean, the Stoic, and the Peripatetic: 'Per le quali tre virtudi si sale a quelle Atene celestiali dove li Stoici e Peripatetici e Epicurî, per la "luce" della veritate etterna, in uno volere concordevolmente concorrono' (iii. 14. 15).

At the same time, as emerges, for example, from commentaries on the Psalms and Ecclesiastes, *epicuri* was used as a general term with which to refer not just to heretics (for medieval Christians, heretics were those whose beliefs, regardless of when they lived, did not conform to the principles of the faith; see n. 4 above), but

---

34   On the *Commedia*'s novelty as a 'philosophical' poem, see Zygmunt G. Barański, '"Per similitudine di abito scientifico": Dante, Cavalcanti, and the Sources of Medieval "Philosophical" Poetry', in *Literature and Science in Italian Culture: From Dante to Calvino. A Festschrift in Honour of Patrick Boyde*, ed. by Pierpaolo Antonello and Simon Gilson (Oxford: Legenda, 2004), pp. 14–52.

also to whoever used their intelligence erroneously, in particular for exclusively materialist ends (see Chapter 3, p. 113). In other words, Epicurus and his 'setta' (*Inf.* IX. 128) represented philosophizing at its worst. As Dante illustrates in the *Inferno*, they were extreme rationalists interested exclusively in worldly things, while showing *disdegno* for eveything else. For many, including Dante in the *Commedia*, their intellectual *habitus* had little or nothing to do with philosophizing in the true sense of the word.[35] That Epicurus and his followers could effectively embody the (ir)rationalist 'anti-philosopher' was a notion deeply rooted in medieval culture. Their reputation as unbridled hedonists, sceptical about the gods, and pessimistic about the conditions of existence were commonplace notions. In *Inferno* IX–XI, the Epicureans' rejection of the immortality of the soul emblematically serves as a sort of synecdoche for all their errors. Thus, while 'Epicuro [e] tutti suoi seguaci' (*Inf.* X. 14) are literally themselves, they also stand for anyone who abuses her or his reason. As ought to be clear from this brief account, *epicurus* was a highly elastic term. It could be applied to a wide range of sinful behaviour and suspect ideological attitudes (even if Averroes and the Averroists do not seem to have been tagged with the designation). On account of the term's connotative flexibility, it was entirely appropriate for Dante to equate the Epicureans with heresy and with misguided thinking in general. Moreover, in stark opposition to Virgil and Aristotle, Epicurus could represent the dangers inherent in paganism from which Christians needed to shield themselves. Equally, the 'modern' Epicurean inhabitants of *Inferno* X recall those Christians who, unlike Dante, misunderstand or exploit classical culture for erroneous and immoral ends. Finally, thanks to the close association between Epicurus and the question of the survival of the soul, Dante was able to introduce a problem of great contemporary relevance; and he could do this without directly attacking those radical Aristotelians who doubted the immortality of the individual soul. Celebrating, but also 'protecting', Aristotle and his intellectual legacy is almost certainly one of the main functions of *Inferno* IX–XI.

In dealing with heresy, Dante was involved in a complex operation. Rather than dwell on individual issues, his aim was to examine human reason from a broad perspective, highlighting major tendencies. As regards the present, his principal focus was on the clash between supporters of rationalist epistemologies and those who preferred to rely on Scripture and revelation. At the same time, he was keen to avoid condemning either side in absolute terms. As far as Dante was concerned, the fundamental problem was not inherent in the two intellectual systems, but in their conflict. More explicitly, associating the death of the soul with the radical Aristotelians meant not only concentrating on a single moment of the unfolding of the 'history of reason', but also, and more problematically, it meant criticizing Aristotle, whose *De anima* was at the basis of the controversy around the immortality of the soul. Such criticism would have put into crisis the positive presentation of the 'maestro di color che sanno' (*Inf.* IV. 131), of pagan culture, and of rationalism that the poet was carefully constructing. Dante therefore transferred responsibility for the belief in the death of the soul exclusively to Epicurus and the Epicureans,

---

35   On the medieval reception of Epicurus, see Chapter 14, n. 18.

who, for the Middle Ages, were unquestionably guilty of the error. In addition, as a result of the range and pliability of the cultural and ideological connotations that had accrued around them, Epicurus and the Epicureans could also act as pointers to other intellectual issues which Dante was keen to stress. In this regard, it is noteworthy that, in presenting his heretics, the poet omits almost all the descriptive elements that normally accompanied heresy in the Middle Ages, such as metaphors of disease, the image of poison, references to sexual perversion, and the cataloguing of heterodox sects. Dante's intent was not to deal exclusively with heresy, but, as the wayfarers do in *Inferno* XI, to move on to issues of greater scope. Epicureans, and not Aristotelians, as I have endeavoured to explain, were culturally and ideologically best placed to serve as the spool from which Dante could spin out the different threads of his ambitious and multifaceted analysis of earthly intellectual life.

Indeed, his treatment of the Epicureans reveals further nuances. In keeping with the balanced analytical approach with which Dante carried out his inquiry into reason, even the *epicuri* are not represented solely in negative terms. As is evident from the *Convivio*, where Epicurus and his philosophy are always treated with respect (III. 14. 15; IV. 6. 11–13; 22. 4 & 14–15), a tradition also existed that, ever since antiquity, as in Seneca's *Epistles to Lucilius*, had emphasized the positive aspects of Epicurean ethics. Thus, in the circle of heresy, we actually find an Epicurean who not only does not deny the immortality of the soul, but also serves as a guide to Christians. In the *Convivio*, Dante had implicitly acknowledged that Epicurus had believed in the eternity of the soul — an idea that he had possibly found in Albertus Magnus (*De natura et origine animae*, p. 36).[36] In a similar vein, several apologists had recognized points of contact between Epicurean and Christian asceticism.[37] The good *epicurus* is of course Virgil, who had a reputation, both in his *vitae* and in the commentaries to his works, of having had Epicurean sympathies,[38] of having lived 'pluribus annis [...] liberali in otio secutus Epicuri sectam' [for many years [...] in abundant leisure following the sect of Epicurus].[39] That Dante was likely intent on

36   'Ma però che della immortalità dell'anima è qui toccato, farò una digressione ragionando di quella; perché di quella ragionando, sarà bello terminare lo parlare di quella viva Beatrice beata, della quale più parlare in questo libro non intendo per proponimento. Dico che intra tutte le bestilitadi quella è stoltissima, vilissima e dannosissima, chi crede dopo questa vita non essere altra vita; però che, se noi rivolgiamo tutte le scritture, sì de' filosofi come delli altri savi scrittori, tutti concordano in questo, che in noi sia parte alcuna perpetuale. E questo massimamente pare volere Aristotile in quello dell'Anima; questo pare volere massimamente ciascuno Stoico; questo pare volere Tulio, spezialmente in quello libello della Veg[li]ezza; questo pare volere ciascuno poeta che secondo la fede de' gentili hanno parlato; questo vuole ciascuna legge, Giudei, Saracini, Tartari e qualunque altri vivono secondo alcuna ragione. Che se tutti fossero ingannati, seguiterebbe una impossibilitade che pure a ritraere sarebbe orribile' (*Conv.* II. 8. 7–9).

37   See Richard I. Jungkuntz, 'Christian Approval of Epicureanism', *Church History*, 31 (1962), 279–93.

38   See *Servii grammatici qui feruntur in Vergilii carmina commentarii*, ed. by Georg Thilo and Hermann Hagen, 3 vols (Leipzig: Teubner, 1881–87), glosses to *Aen.* II. 536, 689; IV. 34; VI. 264, 272, 376; X. 467, 487; to *Buc.* VI. 13; *Scholia bernensia ad Vergilii Bucolica atque Georgica*, ed. by Hermann Hagen (Hildesheim: Georg Olms, 1967), gloss to *Georg.* II. 248.

39   Probus, *Vita*, 10–11, in *Vitae vergilianae antiquae*, ed. by Colin Hardie (Oxford: Clarendon Press, 1957), p. 23.

evoking Virgil's Epicurean leanings would seem to be confirmed, in *Inferno* IX and X, by his recourse to at least two of the passages that Servius had glossed as providing evidence of Virgil's Epicureanism.[40] As occurs elsewhere in the episode of heresy, its intertextual system helps map the directions of Dante's thinking. In the spirit of providential syncretism and intellectual anti-factionalism that distinguishes *Inferno* IX–XI, Dante felt it appropriate to 'save' even the extreme fringes of paganism. Yet, as soon ought to become apparent, when considered in light of 'Guido's disdain', an Epicurean Virgil has carefully calibrated polemical ends.

5. The Polysemous 'cui'

The 'cui' presents a range of different, albeit interconnected, interpretive problems. In general, scholars have focused on the meaning of the pronoun, namely, on the identity of the figure to which it refers. A question of 'content', one might say; and three principal names have been proposed: God, Beatrice, and Virgil. Less attention has been paid to the implications of the form of the sentence in which the pronoun appears: 'colui ch'attende là, per qui mi mena | forse cui Guido vostro ebbe a disdegno' (62–63). The standard view is that the 'cui' should be read as a direct or indirect object pronoun. Once again, three interpretations are proffered: (i) 'colui ch'attende là' whom 'Guido vostro ebbe a disdegno'; (ii) 'to him/her whom 'Guido vostro ebbe a disdegno'; and (iii) 'to him/her to whom Guido disdained to go. As with the identity of the disdained character, no convenient single solution presents itself. Naturally, not all solutions fit each figure equally well. However, it is also the case that the syntax of the sentence permits all three interpretations. In fact, the grammatical and syntactic structure of lines 62–63 is open to a further reading.

---

40   Compare: (i) 'Perché recalcitrate a quella voglia | a cui non puote il fin mai esser mozzo, | [...] | Che giova nelle fata dar di cozzo?' (*Inf.* IX. 94–95, 97) and '(neque enim, credo, sine numine divum | flumina tanta paras Stygiamque innare paludem) | [...] | "unde haec, o Palinure, tibi tam dira cupido? | tu Stygias inhumatus aquas amnemque severum | Eumenidum aspicies ripamve iniussus adibis? | desine fata deum flecti sperare precando"' [for not, I think, without the help of the gods you dare cross this dreadful river and the Stygian lake [...] whence, Palinurus, such impious desire? Will you, unburied, behold the Stygian waves and the stern river of the Eumenides, will you, unbidden, approach its shore? Hope not to change by prayer the fate given by the gods] (*Aen.* VI. 368–69, 373–76); Servius annotates line 376 as follows: 'fata quae semel decreverunt. Et locutus est secundum Epicureos, qui dicunt nec bene promeritis capitur neque tangitur ira' [the fate that they had once decreed. And he spoke following the Epicureans, who say that it is neither acquired by services not touched by wrath]; and (ii) 'Noi veggiam, come quei c'ha mala luce' (*Inf.* X. 100) and 'quale per incertam lunam sub luce maligna | est iter in silvis, ubi caelum condidit umbra | Iuppiter, et rebus nox abstulit atra colorem' [as beneath a misty moon's malignant light the traveller journeys into the woods, when Jupiter shades the heaven with clouds, and the dark night hides the colour of things] (*Aen.* VI. 270–72); Servius glosses line 272 thus: 'hoc et videmus et tractatur ab Epicureis, rebus tollere noctum colorem varietatem: unde etiam apud inferos omnia nigra esse dicuntur. Contra hos Academici una re pugnant: nam squamas piscium dicunt lucere per noctem' [this is what we see and is also discussed by the Epicureans, that the night takes away the variety of colours: thus in the underworld all things are said to be dark. But the Academics reply against this with one single element: they say that the scales of fish shine in the night].

The 'cui' can be taken as a subject pronoun: 'he/she who disdained Guido'.[41] Given Dante's subtlety as a writer, it is difficult to imagine that the ambiguity surrounding the phrase is anything but intentional. The poet is prodding our exegetical skills, involving us in the central problems of *Inferno* ix–xi. It is a renewed appeal to exercise our "ntelletti sani' (*Inf.* ix. 61). Nor does it seem to me a coincidence that the perplexing passage concerning Guido has the same length, of a tercet, and the same collocation in the canto, lines 61–63, as the appeal to interpret correctly in *Inferno* ix. And the terzina's interpretive tangle becomes further entwined, when we ponder the meaning of 'forse' and 'ebbe'. Lines 61–63, I'm tempted to say, constitute the very essence of what a crux should be.

By integrating ambiguity with the crux and the demands of exegesis, Dante affirms the importance of their combined role in the episode of heresy. In fact, their interaction offers the key with which to 'open the door' through which to access the key problems addressed in *Inferno* ix–xi. Ambiguity's contribution is crucial as is evident from its return with respect to Farinata's magnanimity, *Inferno* x's other major interpretive problem. Dante thus envelops in uncertainty the two figures who would have primarily attracted the attention of contemporary (Florentine) readers. As uncertainty demands explanation, the poet once again emphasized the importance of exegesis. The 'disturbing' phrase, 'Ma quell'altro magnanimo' (73), can be read in at least three ways: (i) 'Magnanimo' can be taken in apposition to 'quell'altro', and it would therefore refer narrowly to Farinata; (ii) as distinguishing 'magnanimous' Farinata from Cavalcante de' Cavalcanti who is also 'magnanimo'; and (iii) as differentiating Farinata from all the other *magnanimi* surrounding him, namely, from the rest of the heretics. My aim here is not to engage with the problem of *magnanimitas*, not least because the problem has been effectively tackled by scholars of the calibre of Fiorenzo Forti and John Scott.[42] The point I should like to make is that, in line with the episode of heresy's determining concerns, regardless which interpretation of 'quell'altro magnanimo' is preferred, attention falls on the fateful relationship between intellectual arrogance, which has connections to non-Christian forms of magnanimity, and heterodox ideas. Equally, as I'm about to discuss, *Inferno* ix–xi's deep ideological structures are yet again left unaffected whether the 'amorphous' 'cui' is taken as subject or object, and regardless of the figure one believes the pronoun conceals.

Dante placed *Inf.* x. 61–63, as well as the other elements that constitute the encounter among Florentines, in a subsidiary position with respect to the three cantos' main theme. Human reason and not qualifying the 'cui' takes pride of place. This does not mean that the 'cui', Guido Cavalcanti, and the 'disdegno' are unimportant. To put it simply, *Inf.* x. 61–63 is at the service of the episode of heresy and not vice versa — a perspective that overturns the one that, rather too frequently, Dantists have employed. The cruces and their resolution are not the

41   See Paolo Cherchi, 'Il disdegno per Guido', *L'Alighieri*, 9 (1970), 73–77, and ' "Da me stesso non vegno" (*Inf.* x, 61)', *Rassegna europea di letteratura italiana*, 18 (2001), 103–06; Picone, ' "Iacob dilexi…" '.
42   See Fiorenzo Forti, *Magnanimitade: studi su un tema dantesco* (Bologna: Patron, 1977); John A. Scott, *Dante magnanimo* (Florence: Olschki, 1977). See also Massimo Seriacopi, *La dialettica magnanimità–prudenza in Dante* (Reggello: FirenzeLibri, 2006).

episode's main focus and function. They are instead the means by which to arrive at *Inferno* IX–XI's ideological centre, in relation to which, consequently, they need to be assessed.

Given that the three cantos are centred on reason as a divine gift, on the relationship between humanity and its Maker, and on heresy as an act of presumptuous intellectual rebellion against faith and revelation, the immediate reaction is to think that Guido's disdain is directed against God. Moreover, the fact that Guido Cavalcanti had close ties with Bolognese radical Aristotelian circles, and hence, like the inhabitants of the sixth circle, was likely sympathetic to rationalist and materialist positions, would seem to bolster this 'automatic' interpretation. Finally, the biblical antecedents of the tercet's two key elements, the mode of journeying and the disdain — in Scripture, it is always sinful disdain for God — would confirm that the 'cui' alludes to the Lord.[43] Then, if the pronoun is treated as the subject of the phrase, seeing in it a reference to God becomes almost unavoidable. As Michelangelo Picone has demonstrated ('"Iacob dilexi…"'), there is a disturbing Scriptural tradition which presents God as disdainful *ab aeterno* towards certain individuals. The key text is the story of Jacob and Esau, since God declares that 'Iacob dilexi, Esau autem odio habui' [I have loved Jacob, but I have hated Esau] (Malachi 1: 2–3; Romans 9: 13). In Paul's wake, exegetes deemed the declaration as relating to 'il mistero della divina predestinazione' (Picone, p. 21). In particular

> La lotta dei due fratelli nel seno della madre in qualche modo annuncia la lotta che caratterizzerà le loro vite future: lotta che Giacobbe è destinato a vincere e Esaù a perdere; l'uno scelto da Dio a guidare il Suo popolo verso la salvazione, l'altro categoricamente escluso da tale storia salvifica. (Picone, pp. 22–23).

Reading the 'cui' as the subject, unlike when it is taken as the object, also attenuates the interpretive problems associated with the preterite 'ebbe' (63). If instead we consider the pronoun as the object, the verb can only refer to a particular, albeit unspecified, moment, known both to the pilgrim and to Cavalcante, when Guido definitively disdained God. This would be a 'private' and recherché allusion which refers to a series of assumptions that are difficult, if not impossible, to imagine. On the contrary:

> Se il soggetto del disdegno è Dio […] allora il ricorso ad una forma perfettiva del verbo diventa obbligatoria. Dio infatti ha stabilito *ab aeterno* che il titolare del privilegio di compiere il viaggio della cristianità moderna fosse Dante e non Guido. (Picone, p. 23)

The implications of this interpretation for Dante's account of his 'friendship' with Cavalcanti are weighty and disconcerting (see the next subsection). Indeed, whatever grammatical value is given to the 'cui', its association with God has highly negative effects for Guido. He represents either the archetypal arrogant and

---

43   Regarding the journey, see John 7: 35–36, 8: 12–59, in particular, verse 42: 'dixit ergo eis Iesus si Deus pater vester esset diligeretis utique me ego enim ex Deo processi et veni neque enim a me ipso veni sed ille me misit' [then Jesus said to them: if God were your father, you would love me too, for I proceeded from God, and came from Him; for I came not of myself, but He sent me], and see too John 3: 2. On the 'disdegno', see Romans 1: 16–32, 2: 1–10.

sinful (modern) intellectual, or the person whom God 'held in disdain', or indeed a combination of the two. Even more significant is the fact that each of the three images of Cavalcanti lurking behind the *viator*'s answer conforms to the primary issues that Dante introduced into his 'history of reason'.

At the same time, if the 'cui' is deemed to be the object and if the tercet's most obvious syntactic development is accepted, the pilgrim's words would seem 'naturally' to refer to Virgil:

> Da me stesso non vegno:
> colui ch'attende là, per qui mi mena
> forse cui Guido vostro ebbe a disdegno. (*Inf.* x. 61–63)

This was in fact how fourteenth-century *lectores* of the *Commedia* interpreted the 'cui'. In addition, their reading was bolstered by historical and cultural evidence. Standard medieval views of Cavalcanti presented him not as a poet but as a philosopher. Thus, like other *magistri*, given poetry's perceived epistemological limitations, it was entirely appropriate for Guido to disdain it, and, by extension, its loftiest *auctoritas*, Virgil (see Chapter 13, pp. 455–56). Moreover, the related idea also circulated that Cavalcanti disdained Latin as a literary language (*Vn* xxx. 3). In this case, too, Guido stands for the haughty intellectual whose attention is solely fixed on philosophical nobility and happiness. By identifying the 'cui' with Virgil, the pronoun is limited to its function as object, while the problem of how best to interpret the preterite is left unresolved. Conversely, a Guido who treats Virgil with disdain is anything but an implausible figure, especially since, as we have come to expect, it would not disturb the episode's dominant interests. Indeed, Dante strengthens the logic of the syntax of lines 61–63, and thus directs our attention towards his guide, by modelling Cavalcante's anxious questions on Andromache's frantic interrogation of Aeneas:

> piangendo disse: 'Se per questo cieco
> carcere vai per altezza d'ingegno,
> mio figlio ov'è? e perché non è teco? (*Inf.* x. 58–60)

> 'vivisne? Aut, si lux alma recessit,
> Hector ubi est?' dixit, lacrimasque effudit et ominem
> implevit clamore locum. (*Aen.* iii. 311–13)

['You live? Or, if the white light withdrew, where is Hector?' she said, and poured out tears and the whole place she filled with wailing.]

For about a century, the explanation of the 'cui' that Dantists have widely championed identifies Beatrice as the figure behind the pronoun. I'll be frank. Among the various suggestions, I find this proposal the least satisfactory. My scepticism derives from George Corbett's acute claim that the pilgrim's answer is honestly given.[44] Dante-character is not deliberately trying to confuse or deceive Cavalcante. If the contrary were the case, then he would be behaving in an intellectually disreputable manner that would associate him perilously closely with

---

44   See George Corbett, *Dante and Epicurus: A Dualistic Vision of Secular and Spiritual Fulfilment* (Leeds: Legenda, 2013), pp. 65–120.

the heretics. That the pilgrim is not in fact acting dishonestly is evident from the care with which the poet distances him from the sinners of the sixth circle. It is thus not unreasonable to assume that the *viator* believes that his reply is intelligible to his interlocutor, as is confirmed by the 'colpa' (108) that he subsequently feels. It is not the pilgrim's fault that Cavalcante is incapable of understanding what he says. This is a consequence of Cavalcanti *père*'s intellectual erring and presumption which find confirmation in his inability to interpret correctly. Accepting the validity of this perspective with regard to lines 61–63, it becomes difficult to defend the position that Guido disdained Beatrice. While it is unproblematic to imagine Dante-character assuming that Cavalcante de' Cavalcanti would be able to grasp an allusion to God or to Virgil, the same cannot be said for the woman.

Let us start from two incontrovertible facts. First, when the pilgrim speaks to Cavalcante, he is unaware that his former friend's father, like his companions in sin, has no knowledge of the present. Second, here and elsewhere in the *Commedia*, Dante intends the poem's *lictera* to be read as if it were historically true. To put it differently, we need always to remember the date of the journey, and hence the historical constraints affecting its characters. According to medieval convention, the 'literal sense' serves as the basis for any act of interpretation. When the pilgrim replies to Guido's parent, he is almost certainly aware of the crucial fact that Cavalcante had died around 1280, when Beatrice would have been fourteen years old. Talking to him, and allusively at that, about a young woman who, at best, given the social conventions of the time, Cavalcante may have fleetingly known, makes little sense. For a Florentine who had died in 1280, Beatrice, unlike God and Virgil, was a figure of no significance. It was only thanks to the *Vita nova*, written more than ten years later, that the woman's miraculous nature was made public. If the pilgrim were in fact referring to Beatrice, this would mean that, while suffering the pains of Hell, Cavalcante had also found time to appreciate Dante's 'libello', and, further, that the *viator* was cognizant of this infernal *lectura*... In reality, in the *Inferno*, there is no suggestion that the damned either know the *Vita nova* or are aware of Beatrice's divinity. Scholars have of course realized that, to identify the 'cui' with Beatrice, seriously distorts the *lictera* of the story. To rectify the problem, they have maintained that, when he alludes to Beatrice, Dante-character is only referring to her symbolic values as a representative of the divine, and that, as a result, the sentence should not be taken literally. The proposal fails to persuade since it undermines the fundamental coherence of the poem's *lictera*. It would constitute a unique case in the *Commedia*. Nor are the reasons why Dante should have wished to do violence to his poem readily apparent, especially as this would occur in an episode in which allegoresis is granted pride of place.[45]

Although it seems unlikely that, responding to Cavalcante, the pilgrim is alluding to Beatrice, the fact remains that, as Virgil announced at the beginning of

---

45   In any case, since Cavalcante de' Cavalcanti is unfamiliar with Beatrice, it is impossible for him to appreciate her divine attributes. Besides, even if he had known her, as a bad and impious exegete, would it be reasonable for the pilgrim to assume that Guido's father would be able to interpret Beatrice as a divine *signum*?

the journey (*Inf.* I. 121–23), the person to whom he would 'lead' his ward is none other than his deceased lady. Ambiguity follows on ambiguity; and it is no surprise that we should be exhorted to exercise our 'intelletti sani', even though the appeal does not mean that tidy solutions are always readily to hand. Even if the *viator* has no wish to confuse or deceive Cavalcante, it is nevertheless the case that his reply is far from transparent. Yet, despite the opacity of his words, their general sense is not only clear, but also remains essentially unchanged whichever of the three candidates proposed as solutions to the enigmatic 'cui' is granted pride of place (with respect to Beatrice, *signum coeleste*, and regardless whether the 'cui' is treated as a subject or an object pronoun, what has already been said about God is valid for her too). What the pilgrim is unambiguously stating is that Guido has sinned gravely. The poet-philosopher has abused his gift of reason, his 'altezza d'ingegno' (59), and has thus transgressed against someone towards whom he ought to have behaved humbly and not disdainfully. Evoking Guido among the tombs of heresy leaves no doubt that his sin constitutes a gross misuse of his intelligence. Taking the pronoun as the subject of the phrase clarifies why God (or possibly Beatrice) 'would hate him' *ab aeterno*. On the other hand, treating the 'cui' as the object, attention falls on Guido's sinful action — an offence against God, but also against Virgil (and perhaps even against Beatrice) — rather than on the attitude of the person that Cavalcanti's behaviour has offended. Lines 61–63 are caught in a connotative tension, between what remains unresolved and what cannot be called into doubt; and I have increasingly come to believe that this is ultimately their most conspicuous and crucial feature.

I am well aware that my line of argument runs counter to the long-standing established exegesis of the passage, which has concentrated on restricting the scope of the pilgrim's words. Yet, it does not seem possible to enclose his reply within a single and undisputed explanation. Consequently, our responsibility as 'healthy' readers (*Inf.* IX. 61) is to acknowledge the ambiguities and the strains surrounding the sentence, and then to draw appropriate conclusions. In line with the corresponding lines of *Inferno* IX, lines 62–63 of *Inferno* X ('colui ch'attende là, per qui mi mena | forse cui Guido vostro ebbe a disdegno'), given their enigmatic density, are also an appeal, even if an indirect one, to 'mirare la dottrina che s'asconde | sotto 'l velame de li versi strani' (*Inf.* IX. 62–63). I should like to suggest, therefore, that the wayfarer's response functions as an emblem of the key standing of the *crux* — a kind of *crux crucum* — and of allegoresis in Dante's treatment of the circle of heresy, especially as the pilgrim's answer is so profoundly involved with the pivotal question of the relationship between God and humanity and with the role of reason in this. The central position accorded to the meeting between the *viator* and Cavalcante de' Cavalcanti in the structure of the canto and of the episode as a whole would appear to support such an interpretation. There are also 'literal' narrative reasons for the tone of the pilgrim's response. As is clear from the 'forse' (63), the pilgrim's words are marked by *reticentia*. Once more, the implications of this choice of register do not change whether the adverb is associated with the verb *menare* or with the subordinate clause that follows it. In both cases, and in contrast to Guido's 'disdain', Dante-*personaggio* speaks with noteworthy humility. He is either alluding circumspectly to his divinely sanctioned mission or refraining from passing judgment in absolute and smug terms on the faults of another. He displays the traits of the Christian *magnanimus*, traits that distinguish him from the 'magnanimity' of the heretic. If the pilgrim makes plain to Cavalcante that his son had abused his 'alto ingegno' (*Inf.* x. 59), and so could not accompany him on his otherworldly journey, he does this sensitively without dwelling on the details of Guido's sin. Dante-character is a model of Christian reticence; and, appropriately, his response is a model, both in its form — it is enough to recall its biblical overtones — and its content, of how to use one's 'ingegno' correctly.[46]

The highly nuanced manner in which Dante constructed *Inf.* x. 61–63 has far-reaching narrative and ideological consequences. Its polysemy also brings to mind, though I say this with all due caution, the 'senses' of the Scriptural *lictera*. From the opening canto (Barański, *Dante e i segni*, pp. 103–26), the poet suggests that the 'letter' of the *Commedia* needs to be interpreted according to the conventions of the *allegoria in factis*, since his journey, like the events recorded in the Bible, is part of providential history. It is thus not unreasonable to hypothesize that there are moments, as occurs in *Inferno* xix, where the *viator* takes on the guise of an Old Testament prophet (Barański, *Dante e i segni*, pp. 147–72), when his *vox*, especially when it openly draws on Scripture, may be regarded as divinely inspired. In an episode such as ours that focuses on exegesis, it would be understandable if Dante had wanted to hint at the *Commedia*'s allegorical status, as well as the *viator*'s special relationship to God, his privileged role as *signum coeleste* (see also Chapter 9).

6. 'Guido vostro'

Drawing attention to the *Commedia*'s uniqueness and to the miraculous nature of his otherworldly voyage, Dante ran the risk of destroying the halo of humility he had constructed around the *viator*, and which, by extension, he wished to extend to his poetic self. The potential dangers further increased when he presented himself as a *scriba Dei* who has the duty to 'make manifest the whole of his vision' (*Par.* xvii. 128). At the same time, insisting that the journey and the 'poema sacro | al quale ha posto mano e cielo e terra' (*Par.* xxv. 1–2) had been endorsed by God, and that pilgrim and poet do their best to behave as Christian *humiles*, Dante was endeavouring to distance from himself possible accusations of arrogance. Among the various crucial elements that emerge from the episode of heresy, and specifically from the meeting with Cavalcante, we should not ignore that, unlike Guido, Dante's attitude towards God (and Beatrice), but also Virgil, is anything but disdainful. Yet, as is evident from Cavalcante's questions, in late-medieval Florence Dante and Guido were often associated and celebrated together (see Chapter 13, pp. 453–54). When he criticized his friend, Dante opened himself up to charges of arrogance, selfishness, and 'disdegno'. As a counter, in *Inferno* ix–xi, Dante strenuously challenged the *communis opinio* that he and Guido were intellectually and ethically close. His

---

46   By concentrating exclusively on his misreading of 'ebbe', Cavalcante fails to acknowledge what the pilgrim has just told him, just as, in life, he had misused his reason and had refused to recognize the reality of his situation.

attacks on his former friend were not outbursts of malice, jealousy, and presumption but expressions of unimpeachable moral and religious probity. And, according to Dante, Guido's faults were grievous and more than worthy of censure.

As I have already suggested, Dante's condemnation of Guido deliberately implicates every aspect of his person. Another effect of the polysemy of the pilgrim's reply to Cavalcante, as well as its structural prominence, is to confer on Guido exemplary traits. Given the complex indeterminacy of the 'cui', which allows for different imposing figures to coexist in the pronoun, Guido ends up embodying different instances of intellectual pride. He is almost certainly the sinner who disdains God, and who equally scorns divine realities and human *auctoritates*. He is also the sinner who, because of intellectual vanity ('tutto è vano | nostro intelletto', *Inf.* x. 103–04), deserves to be disdained by Heaven. Guido's image becomes even more negatively multifaceted by being associated with heresy and with contemporary rationalism. Against the backdrop of the history of reason sketched in *Inferno* IX–XI, and because of the many sins of the intellect with which he is connected, Guido is inexorably transformed into the intellectual sinner par excellence. Dante reinforces this feature by having Guido seemingly 'absorb' into himself the two canonical protagonists of *Inferno* X. It is fairly uncontroversial to maintain that Dante introduced Cavalcante de' Cavalcanti into the *Commedia* so as to 'locate' his son among the heretics. In this regard, Cavalcante functions as a figure for Guido, who, in Easter week 1300, was still alive. Despite the aura of *reticentia*, it is difficult not to conclude that, for someone as emblematically disdainful as Guido, the tag of 'follower' of Epicurus (14) is far from unbecoming. In light of Dante's unrelenting censure, the 'primo amico' is, to all effects, damned.

The idea that Farinata may be 'subsumed' into Guido is controversial. I'm encouraged in my hypothesis by *Inferno* IX–XI's complexity and ambition. Equally, to suggest that there may be circumstances in which Farinata is 'subordinate' to Guido does not mean denying the key role that the great Ghibelline plays in the *Commedia*. An inevitable effect of any polysemous text is that the relative value of the single constituent elements changes. Looked at politically, Farinata is certainly more significant than Guido. However, from the point of view of the history of reason, the philosopher has primacy over the party man. It is also far from a given that, for a fourteenth-century reader, Farinata would have been more important than Guido. There is no doubt that, particularly in Florence but also elsewhere, the latter was considered a remarkable modern *auctoritas* (see Chapter 13, pp. 448–57). If, on the one hand, Dante is challenging the nature of Guido's 'authoritativeness' — a question to which I shall shortly return — on the other, by turning him into an emblematic sinner, the poet was taking advantage of his status as an 'anima [...] di fama nota' (*Par.* XVII. 138). The suggestion that Farinata may at times defer to Guido would seem to go against the expectations of post-romantic critics rather than of medieval readers.

How, in *Inferno* X, might Farinata depend on Guido? The answer is actually both surprisingly simple and culturally pointed. Dante's representation of Farinata draws on some of the key features of Guido's medieval portrait. 'Disdain', as Guglielmo

Gorni has rightly noted, is Guido's 'contrassegno'.[47] It is thus highly suggestive that Farinata should be described as 'quasi sdegnoso' (*Inf.* x. 41) and 'com'avesse l'inferno a gran dispitto' (36). Both Guido and Farinta are arrogant and haughty, preferring self-centredly to cut themselves off from others. Both also actively participated in factional struggle, driven by an exaggerated sense of loyalty to their own family.[48] Dante goes so far as to grant Farinata an intellectual dimension that sits uneasily with the man of action, but that fits well with Guido, the consummate modern intellectual. The Ghibelline is more than an Epicurean thinker, like Guido (*Vn* XXX. 3) he is sensitive to his own vernacular (*Inf.* x. 22–23) and, as a 'magnanimo', is interested in nobility and philosophical happiness. Farinata is a key figure in the *Commedia*; and his importance is due in part to his association with Guido. Next to the two 'ombre' (53), there is a third shade in the 'arca' (29): the ghost of Guido Cavalcanti lurks among the damned.

In *Inferno* x, Dante pronounces a terrible condemnation against someone whom he had once considered his 'primo amico'. Throughout his œuvre, from the *Vita nova* (not to mention from the *Fiore*) to the highest spheres of the *Paradiso*, Dante developed an insidious and wide-ranging anti-Cavalcanti polemic. The problem remains why Dante was so fiercely opposed to Guido. I feel uncomfortable constructing psychologizing hypotheses dependent on possible clashes between the two in life, as some Dantists have done, not least because evidence is lacking to support this type of reading. Conversely, cultural clues do exist that may aid us understand why Dante levied reproaches and accusations against his former friend.

It goes without saying that Dante's presentation of Cavalcanti runs counter to that of his contemporaries, who treated Guido with great respect and appreciation, even if, as I noted earlier, the poet's views are visibly marked by standard images of his 'primo amico'. What most conspicuously emerges from the *Commedia*'s portrait of Cavalcanti is the ways in which Dante systematically demolishes Guido's *auctoritas*, while concurrently establishing his own superior 'authoritativeness': Dante-Jacob against Guido-Esau. Dante's antagonism towards Cavalcanti is not simply the result of a 'private' disagreement about the nature of love, as is frequently asserted, but is also connected to their respective public images. Dante does not seem to have wanted to share with anyone, and particularly not with Cavalcanti, the mantle of vernacular *auctoritas*. Thus, one of the key functions of *Inferno* x, and especially of lines 61–63, is to call into question basic elements of Cavalcanti's contemporary image. Associating Guido with Epicureanism, commonly judged among the most grievous of intellectual errors and rejected by 'tutti li savi e li filosofi', not least because of its rampant materialism, whereby 'la felicità delli uomini fosse nella delettazione della carne', Dante directly challenged Cavalcanti's famed philosophical abilities.[49] He then further undermined Guido's abilities as a thinker by stressing his arrogant and disdainful temperament, thereby neatly subverting the many positive

47   Guglielmo Gorni, 'Cino "vil ladro": parola data e parola rubata', in his *Il nodo della lingua e il verbo d'amore* (Florence: Olschki, 1981), pp. 125–39 (p. 134).

48   On Guido's political activities, see Chapter 13, pp. 451 & 463.

49   *L'ottimo commento della Divina Commedia*, ed. by Alessandro Torri, 3 vols (Pisa: Niccolò Capurro, 1827–29), I, 172.

philosophical, social, and personal attributes that were a mark of Guido's *auctoritas*. Although his contemporaries celebrated Cavalcanti's philosophical prowess rather than his poetic achievements, Dante regularly extended his attack to his poetry. His criticisms touch the whole person. Thus, *Inferno* IX opens with clear echoes from the fourth stanza of 'Donna me prega'. From the very beginning of the episode of heresy, Guido's poetry, as will soon happen to its author, is closely associated with sin, error, and recalcitrance.[50] Moreover, by referring to the Medusa (*Inf.* IX. 52–57), Dante evoked, to condemn them, his 'stony rhymes', the most explicitly Cavalcantian moment of his lyric experience.[51] For Dante, even if not for the Middle Ages, Guido the poet and Guido the philosopher were one.

Yet, in keeping with contemporary sensitivities, first and foremost, the episode of heresy allowed Dante to condemn Guido's intellectual abilities. He thus highlighted how the heretic conceals himself behind the reassuring lineaments of the learned. It is deeply ironic that the only totally negative Epicurean that appears in *Inferno* IX–XI is not the ancient philosopher but the modern Florentine. If only Guido had followed rather than disdained Virgil, in particular because the ancient poet had been able to get the best out of Epicurus, he may 'perhaps' have saved his soul. Against the same universalizing background that serves to historicize and legitimate the condemnation of his former friend, Dante makes it apparent that, since he has not disdained divine authority but has willingly submitted to it, he has succeeded in attaining true *auctoritas*. Dante presents their individual experiences, modelled on the story of Isaac's two sons, as antithetical. Although the two 'brothers' had a common origin inside the walls of Florence, they in fact embody two contrasting ways of life, of cultural engagement, and of wisdom. Nothing unites them. 'Guido' is literally 'vostro' (*Inf.* X. 63): he has nothing to do with Dante, but everything with the murky world of sin. According to the poet, contemporary Florentines had the duty to choose between the alternatives that he and Guido represented: between the divinely sanctioned humble *auctoritas* and the disdainful heretic. The city's tragedy, like that of the 'modern' world in general, was not only to have confused them, but also to have chosen badly: 'calcando i buoni e sollevando i pravi' (*Inf.* XIX. 105).

7. In Conclusion

As readers of the *Commedia* we have the responsibility not to imitate Dante's fellow-citizens. Instead we need to react appropriately to the incentives to 'read' correctly and to behave well that the poet has left in the text. The crux, in this regard, is a refined and valuable incentive; and the system of cruces that controls the

---

50   Compare 'Quel **color** che viltà di fuor mi pinse | **veggendo** il duca mio **tornare** in volta, | piú tosto dentro il suo **novo** ristrinse. | Attento si fermò com' **uom** ch'ascolta' (*Inf.* IX. 1–4) to 'L'essere è quando — lo voler è tanto | ch'oltra misura — di natura — **torna**, | poi non s'adorna — di riposo mai. | Move, cangiando — **color**, riso in pianto, | e la figura — co paura — storna; | poco soggiorna; — ancor di lui **vedrai** | che 'n gente di valor lo più si trova. | La **nova** — qualità move sospiri | e vol **ch'om** miri — 'n non formato loco': Guido Cavalcanti, *Rime con le rime di Iacopo Cavalcanti*, ed. by Domenico De Robertis (Turin: Einaudi, 1986), XXVII. 43–51.
51   John Freccero, 'Medusa: The Letter and the Spirit', in his *Dante: The Poetics of Conversion* (Cambridge, MA: Harvard University Press, 1986), pp. 119–35.

organization of the cantos of heresy serves to involve us directly in the *Commedia*, making us personally responsible for the correct elucidation of the *vestigia Dei* that appear in its tercets. As with every divine *signum*, the 'senses' of Dante's poem too are multiple. Following Augustine and the rich tradition of Christian Scriptural exegesis, when interpreting, it is vital to remain within the limits imposed by faith, and so not to be seduced by the disdainful example of the heretic.[52] Such a 'humble' attitude in fact allows for considerable hermeneutic freedom that, at the same time, respects the unbounded polysemy of divine signification. We too should not unnecessarily restrict the 'orthodox' scope of the 'sacrato poema' (*Par.* XXIII. 62). Rather we should recognize the implications of the religious, intellectual, cultural, and poetic divinely-inflected polysemy of Dante's masterpiece. That, for centuries, the 'cui' has attracted such attention is more than understandable: Dante and Guido are fascinating figures; and they are even more so when brought together. At the same time, both the 'cui' and the portrait of Dante's Guido are impoverished if they are detached from the episode's system of *cruces* and from the 'dottrina' (*Inf.* IX. 62), the providential history of reason, concealed behind ''l velame' of the cantos' lines. The legitimacy for Dante's potentially risky presentation of himself and his arch-rival comes from God. If the judgments expressed in the *Commedia* were not in harmony with the divine, the poet would join Guido in disdaining God. It may seem to us today that, driven by a Luciferian pride, Dante has done just that. However, 'reading' with medieval eyes, it is evident that, adhering strictly to orthodox positions, Dante succeeded in painting a portrait of himself adorned with the features of a *humilis*, of a *scriba Dei*, and of an *auctoritas*, while, simultaneously, damning Cavalcanti both in this world and in the next. Dante's greatness, alas, can also be recognized in his ability to manipulate religious beliefs for questionable purposes. The *Commedia* is a poem that demands our total involvement, and even our negative reactions may have 'positive' results. And, the crux is one of the key mechanisms that Dante employs to immerse us in his extraordinary poem. The crux is not a 'defect' that disfigures Dante's masterpiece, as some scholars maintain, and which they feel they must 'heal'. The poet's highly wrought cruces are nuggets rich in connotative possibilities that first enthrall us and then lead us to the *Commedia*'s artistic, moral, and doctrinal treasures. 'O voi ch'avete li 'intelletti sani'...

---

52   On Augustine and exegetical freedom, see. *De Gen. ad litt.* I. 18. 37–21. 41; *In Johannis Evangelium Tractatus CXXIV*, ed. by Radbodus Willems (Turnhout: Brepols, 1954), LXIV. 2; *Confessionum libri XIII*, 2 vols. ed. by Martin Skutella and Aimé Solignac (Bruges: Desclée de Brouwer, 1962), XII. See also Martin Irvine, 'Interpretation and the Semiotics of Allegory in Clement of Alexandria, Origen, and Augustine', *Semiotica*, 63:1–2 (1987), 33–71 (pp. 63–66).

CHAPTER 18

'E cominciare stormo':
Notes on Dante's Sieges

1. Dante's 'Lost' Sieges

> così vid'ïo già temer li fanti
> ch'uscivan patteggiati di Caprona,
> veggendo sé tra nemici cotanti. (*Inf.* XXI. 94–96)

In modern Dante scholarship, the siege and fall of the Ghibelline castle of Caprona in August 1289 — a matter of months after the battle of Campaldino — to which the poet succinctly alludes in the tercet above, have been largely overshadowed by the alluring admission that he had taken part in the attack.[1] 'La similitudine militare, di grande evidenza, è l'unica ma decisiva testimonianza che Dante ci ha lasciato della sua partecipazione a fatti d'arme', declares Anna Maria Chiavacci Leonardi in her important commentary (I, 643–44). Given the relative paucity of reasonably reliable biographical information on Dante, it is not surprising that, ever since the Trecento, *dantisti* have drawn attention to this fleeting glimpse into an intriguing moment in the poet's life: 'Caprona a Tuscis fuit obsessa. In qua quidem obsidione fuit iste autor, et vidit oculis propriis id quod in textu ad comparationem inducit' [Caprona was besieged by the Tuscans. And this author took part in that siege, and saw with his own eyes what he introduces in his text as a comparison];[2] 'Pone sua similitudine alla quale conoscere si è da sapere che nel .mcclxxxviiii. del mese d'agosto li Luchesi con li cavalieri et pedoni fiorentini, tra li quali cavalieri fue Dante [...] la quale cosa vide Dante, la paura che coloro [the castle defenders] mostrarono. Et così dice qui di sé';[3] 'Et hic nota quod autor fuit personaliter in isto exercitu [lucani cum florentinis equitibus et peditibus]; erat enim tunc juvenis viginti quinque annorum, et ibi vidit istum actum; ideo libentius fecit talem comparationem, ut de se memoriam faceret, quia aliquando tractaverat arma; quamvis comparatio, etiam non habito isto respectu, sit valde propria'.[4]

---

1   For a major reassessment of Dante's involvement in the battle of Campaldino, see Silvia Diacciati, 'Dante a Campaldino', *Le tre corone*, 6 (2019), 11–25.

2   Guido da Pisa, *Expositiones et Glose. Declaratio super 'Comediam' Dantis*, ed. by Michele Rinaldi, 2 vols (Rome: Salerno, 2013), I, 661.

3   *L'ultima forma dell'Ottimo commento. Chiose sopra la Comedia di Dante Alleghieri fiorentino tracte da diversi ghiosatori. Inferno*, ed. by Claudia Di Fonzo (Ravenna: Longo, 2008), p. 198.

4   Benvenuto da Imola, *Comentum super Dantis Aldigherij Comoediam*, ed. by James Philip Lacaita,

[And here the author indicates that he himself was in this army [the Lucchese together with the Florentine knights and infantry]; for he was then a young man of twenty-five-years, and here he saw this event; thus he deliberately made such a comparison, in order to create a memory of himself, since he had occasionally taken up arms; although the comparison, even without such concern, would be absolutely apt.]

However, it is not just the siege of Caprona that, since the nineteenth century, has attracted little attention among Dante's readers. Indeed, it is safe to say that sieges in general have been of little interest to Dantists.[5] This is probably because the poet's direct references to sieges are brief and allusive.[6] Even famous sieges are dealt with cursorily, 'poi che 'l superbo Ilïon fu combusto' (*Inf.* I. 75),[7] or partially, 'Ecco | la gente che perdé Ierusalemme, | quando Maria nel figlio diè di becco' (*Purg.* XXIII. 28–30).[8] At the same time, the fact that Dante could refer to the destruction of Troy and to the fall of Jerusalem to Titus's army in such concise ways indicates the popularity, and hence too the importance, of the two sieges and of their cultural traditions, respectively, the *excidium Troiae*[9] and the *vindicta*

5 vols (Florence: Barbera, 1887), II, 115.

5   It is telling that sieges barely figure in two excellent books on Dante and the city: Claire E. Honess, *From Florence to the Heavenly City: The Poetry of Citizenship in Dante* (Leeds: Legenda, 2006); Catherine Keen, *Dante and the City* (Stroud: Tempus, 2003).

6   See, for instance, the description of the siege of Forlì as 'lunga prova' (*Inf.* XXVII. 43). Equally, the assault on the fortress of Penestrino is reduced to the deception that led to its capture — 'lunga promessa con l'attender corto | ti farà trïunfar ne l'alto seggio' (*Inf.* XXVII. 110–11) — while the sieges of Lerida and Marseille, despite the latter's length, are barely touched on: 'e Cesare, per soggiogare Ilerda, | punse Marsilia' (*Purg.* XVIII. 101–02). Even the taking and destruction of Florence merit only a single line: ''l cener che d'Attila rimase' (*Inf.* XIII. 149).

7   Dante again mentions the ruin of Troy in not too dissimilar terms at *Purg.* XII. 61–62: 'Vedeva Troia in cenere e in caverne; | o Ilïón, come te basso e vile'.

8   Dante's other references to the siege of Jerusalem are equally telegraphic: 'Nel tempo che 'l buon Tito, con l'aiuto | del sommo rege, vendicò le fóra | ond' uscì 'l sangue per Giuda venduto' (*Purg.* XXI. 82–84), and '[the Roman eagle] poscia con Tito a far vendetta corse | de la vendetta del peccato antico' (*Par.* VI. 92–93). The story of the mother who eats her child, which seems to have its origins in Josephus's *De bello judaico*, became a commonplace in accounts of Titus's siege of Jerusalem. In fact, acts of cannibalism are a standard motif in siege narratives; see, for instance, Boncompagno da Signa, *Liber de obsidione Ancone*, ed. by Paolo Garbini (Rome: Viella, 1999), p. 140. See also Bonnie Millar, *The Siege of Jerusalem in its Physical, Literary and Historical Contexts* (Dublin: Four Courts Press, 2000), pp. 76–104; Merrall Llewelyn Price, 'Imperial Violence and the Monstrous Mother: Cannibalism at the Siege of Jerusalem', in *Domestic Violence in Medieval Texts*, ed. by Eve Salisbury and others (Gainesville: University Press of Florida, 2002), pp. 272–98.

9   See Malcolm Andrew, 'The Fall of Troy in *Sir Gawain and the Green Knight* and *Troilus and Criseyde*', in *The European Tragedy of Troilus*, ed. by Pietro Boitani (Oxford: Clarendon Press, 1989), pp. 75–93; C. David Benson, *The History of Troy in Middle English Literature* (Woodbridge: D. S. Brewer, 1980); Alfonso D'Agostino, *Le gocce d'acqua non hanno consumato i sassi di Troia: materia troiana e letterature medievali* (Milan: CUEM, 2006); Malcolm Hebron, *The Medieval Siege: Theme and Image in Middle English Romance* (Oxford: Clarendon Press, 1997), pp. 91–111; Arianna Punzi, 'Sulle fonti dell'*Excidium Troiae*', *Cultura neolatina*, 51 (1991), 5–26, and 'La circolazione della materia troiana nell'Europa del '200: da Darete Frigio al *Roman de Troie en Prose*', *Messana*, 6 (1991), 69–108; Andreola Rossi, *Contexts of War: Manipulation of Genre in Virgilian Battle Narrative* (Ann Arbor: University of Michigan Press, 2004); Andrew Sprung, 'The "townes wal": A Frame for "fre chois" in Chaucer's *Troilus and Creseyde*', *Medievalia*, 14 (1988), 127–42.

Salvatoris, for the medieval world.[10] Dante scholars' particular neglect of sieges is mirrored by their widespread disinterest in the *Commedia*'s treatment of martial themes in general. Despite the centrality of *arma* in classical and medieval literature, a fact confirmed by Dante himself in the *De vulgari eloquentia*,[11] the opinion has prevailed that the poet 'did not work in the tradition of martial epic'.[12] This view has now been effectively challenged by Robert Hollander, who has established that, even if Dante's references to war and warring are, as with his mentions of sieges, normally brief and allusive, they are neither infrequent nor inconsequential.[13] More significantly, he has demonstrated that, albeit often indirectly, the poet did in fact substantially rework classical epic military material from a Christian perspective in order to fashion a 'better form of martial epic' as 'sacred narrative'.[14] The question

10   See in particular Ronald S. Martinez, 'Lament and Lamentations in *Purgatorio* and the Case of Dante's Statius', *Dante Studies*, 115 (1997), 45–88. See also Hebron, pp. 112–35; Amnon Linder, 'Jews and Judaism in the Eyes of Christian Thinkers of the Middle Ages: The Destruction of Jerusalem in Medieval Christian Liturgy', in *From Witness to Witchcraft: Jews and Judaism in Medieval Christian Thought*, ed. by Jeremy Cohen (Wiesbaden: Harrasowitz, 1996), pp. 113–23, and *Raising Arms: Liturgy in the Struggle to Liberate Jerusalem in the Late Middle Ages* (Turnhout: Brepols, 2003); Millar, especially pp. 42–56; Suzanne M. Yeager, *Jerusalem in Medieval Narrative* (Cambridge: Cambridge University Press, 2008), and 'Jewish Identity in *The Siege of Jerusalem* and Homiletic Texts: Models of Penance and Victims' Vengeance for the Urban Apocalypse', *Medium Aevum*, 80 (2011), 56–84.

11   'Quare hec tria, Salus videlicet, Venus et Virtus, apparent esse illa magnalia que sint maxime pertractanda, hoc est ea que maxime sunt ad ista, ut armorum probitas, amoris accensio, et directio voluntatis. Circa que sola, si bene recolimus, illustres viros invenimus vulgariter poetasse; scilicet Bertramum de Bornio, arma [...]. Arma vero nullum latium adhuc invenio poetasse. Hiis proinde visis, que canenda sint vulgari altissimo innotescunt' [Therefore these three, that is Well-being, Love, and Virtue, appear to be those most important subjects that are to be treated in the highest style, this means the topics that are most closely associated with these, such as mastery in arms, ardour of love, and control of the will. And if I recall correctly, I have found that illustrious men composed vernacular poetry on these subjects alone, namely, Bertran de Born on arms, [...]. But I find that no Italian has yet composed poetry on arms. Having seen this, what should be sung in the highest form of vernacular becomes clear] (*Dve* II. 2. 8–10).

12   Robert Hollander, 'Dante and the Martial Epic', *Medievalia*, 12 (1986), 67–91 (p. 70).

13   For instance, Hollander refers to 'the series of visitations of classical epic in *Inferno* IX, the presentation of Farinata as a sort of modern "epic hero" in *Inferno* X, the references to arms in *Inferno* XII, the gallery of epic presences in *Inferno* XX, the "war simile" in *Inferno* XXII, 1–2, and Nimrod's Roland-recalling horn-blast in *Inferno* XXXII, 18' (Hollander, p. 87, n. 7). As Hollander himself acknowledges, his argument has points of contact with Jeffrey T. Schnapp, *The Transfiguration of History at the Center of Dante's 'Paradise'* (Princeton: Princeton University Press, 1986), pp. 14–69.

14   Hollander, p. 81. Given the validity of Hollander's contribution, it is a pity that Dantists have largely ignored his findings, and so have continued to misunderstand the status of the martial in the *Commedia*. Michelangelo Picone, in 'I trovatori di Dante: Bertran de Born', *Studi e problemi di critica testuale*, 19 (1979), 71–94, demonstrated that, in his treatment of the Occitan poet in *Inf.* XXVIII, Dante adapted and modified troubadour writing on war in light of Christian values. Three important recent studies have begun to re-examine the martial in Dante: Anne C. Leone, '"L'ardor del sacrificio": Epic and Christian Blood in the *Commedia*', in her '"Sangue perfetto": Scientific, Sacrificial and Semiotic Blood in Dante' (unpublished PhD thesis, University of Cambridge, 2010), pp. 68–121; Luca Marcozzi, 'La Guerra del cammino: metafore belliche nel viaggio dantesco', in *La metafora in Dante*, ed. by Marco Ariani (Florence: Olschki, 2008), pp. 59–112; and Sebastiana Nobili, '"Al taglio de la spade": immagini di guerra nella *Commedia*', *Studi e problemi di critica testuale*, 90:1 (2015), 173–90. See also Anne C. Leone, 'Communal and Economic Implications of Blood in Dante', *Italian Studies*, 71 (2016), 265–86, and 'Women, War and Wisdom: the 18s', in *Vertical Readings in Dante's Comedy*, ed. by

thus arises whether, as with matters of war in general, Dante's engagement with sieges is actually also rather more considered, interesting, and extensive than has normally been assumed.

During the course of his reminiscences about the Florence of his time, Cacciaguida tells the pilgrim how it was typical for a woman 'favoleggiare con la sua famiglia | d'i Troiani, di Fiesole e di Roma' (*Par.* xv. 125–26). The tales of course relate to Florence's origins. However, they are also stories of sieges, of cities destroyed and refounded. Sieges, as Cacciaguida recognizes, hold, or rather should hold, since he laments the forgetful corruption of the present, a vital place in the cultural memory of each Florentine. Given that he enjoys the privilege of gazing on 'il punto | a cui tutti li tempi son presenti' (*Par.* xvII. 17–18), Cacciaguida is indisputably correct about the neglect into which the retelling of Florence's past had fallen by the close of the thirteenth century. At the same time, even if Dante's self-serving fellow-citizens were ignorant of the history of their own city, it is almost certain that the same could not be said about their knowledge of sieges, beginning with that of Troy. Descriptions and depictions of sieges were everywhere. They had fascinated the *auctores*. They were a literary commonplace that spanned across *stili*, languages, and religious and secular writings. They were a mainstay of manuscript illustrators, painters, and sculptors. They made an appearance in the schoolroom. Indeed, they were even re-enacted at public events.[15] Furthermore, the representation of sieges had become highly codified.[16] To put it slightly differently: however much sieges constituted a violent and far from uncommon reality of medieval warfare — in fact, assaults on fortified places were largely synonymous with war in the Middle Ages — they were also, and primarily, an extraordinarily potent cultural trope.[17]

George Corbett and Heather Webb, 3 vols (Cambridge: Open Book Publishers, 2015–17), II, 151–71.
15   See in particular Hebron. See also R. Howard Bloch, *Medieval French Literature and Law* (Berkeley: University of California Press, 1977), pp. 81–90; Franco Cardini, 'Introduzione', in San Bernardino da Siena, *La battaglia e il saccheggio del Paradiso, cioè della Gerusalemme celeste*, ed. by Franco Cardini (Siena: Edizioni Cantagalli, 1979), pp. 5–62; Roger S. Loomis, 'The Allegorical Siege in the Art of the Middle Ages', *American Journal of Archaeology*, 2nd ser., 23 (1919), 255–69; Lyn Pemberton, 'The Narrative Structure of the Siege', *Olifant*, 12 (1987), 95–124; Claude Roussel, 'Le Siège de Rome dans les chansons de geste tardives', in *La Chrétienté au péril sarrasin: Actes du colloque de la section française de la société internationale Rencesvals* (Aix-en-Provence: Publications de l'Université de Provence, 2000), pp. 219–30; Helen Solterer, 'States of Siege: Violence, Place, Gender: Paris around 1400', in *New Medieval Literatures II*, ed. by Rita Copeland and others (New York: Clarendon Press, 1998), pp. 95–132; Jean-Claude Vallecalle, 'Remarques sur l'emploi des machines de siège dans quelques chansons de geste', in *Mélanges de langue et littérature françaises du Moyen-âge offerts à Pierre Jonin* (Aix-en-Provence: Publications du CUERMA Université de Provence, 1979), pp. 689–702; *The Medieval City under Siege*, ed. by Ivy A. Corfis and Michael Wolfe (Woodbridge: Boydell Press, 1995).
16   'Les plus caractérisées de ces séquences [narratives stéréotypées] [...] sont celles qui ont pour sujet une action guerrière: siège, bataille, combat singulier de tout type [...] les récits du siège: il s'agit là en effet d'une séquence très définie': Marguerite Rossi, 'Les Séquences narratives stéréotypées: un aspect de la technique épique', in *Mélanges de langue*, pp. 593–607 (pp. 596 & 598). See also Pemberton.
17   For historical assessments of the siege and warfare in the Middle Ages, see Jim Bradbury, *The Medieval Siege* (Woodbridge: Boydell Press, 1992); Philippe Contamine, *War in the Middle Ages* (Oxford: Basil Blackwell, 1984).

As such, they gained much of their connotative force from, first, being associated with some of the key ideological concerns of the day, from the salvation of the soul to the crusades, and from matters of love to divine providence, and second, from finding important expression in the works of many of the leading *auctoritates*. In such circumstances, it would be remarkable indeed if as culturally sensitive a writer and intellectual as Dante were to have deemed the siege unworthy of his sustained attention; and all the more so, if he had decided to marginalize it in a work of the totalizing cultural ambition and purview of the *Commedia*.

2. From Devils and Sieges to Besieging Dis

In the *Inferno*, devils are closely connected with the martial. Lucifer is introduced as the leader of an advancing army, '*Vexilla regis prodeunt inferni* | verso di noi' (XXXIV. 1–2), so that Virgil urges his ward to 'arm' himself — 'convien che di fortezza t'armi' (21) — in preparation for the encounter with 'Dite' (20). The devil of the schismatics brutally wields a sword with which he inflicts gruesome wounds on the damned (XXVIII. 37–39), and is bracketed by the memorable list of four bloody battles (7–21) and the decapitated presence of the greatest Occitan poet of arms (118–42). The devils of barratry are presented as an armed unit, 'la decina' (XXI. 120) led by a 'decurio' (*Inf.* XXII. 74), which acts as a 'scorta' (128) and whose 'duca' (138) employs a most eccentric 'cennamella' (10) to give the off to his men (XVI. 139–XXII. 1–12) — a 'wind instrument' which inspires the poet to open *Inferno* XXII with a complex simile that evokes a range of military events and activities. Although the ties between the 'demon cornuti con gran ferze' (*Inf.* XVIII. 35) who beat the panders and seducers and the martial are weaker than in the other episodes, the devils are once again instruments of violence and are immediately preceded by Dante's portrayal of a fortified castle (10–15). Interestingly, as well as establishing links between the devils and warfare in general, in each instance, Dante also associates them with sieges. Thus, the depiction of the stronghold with which *Inferno* XVIII opens is reminiscent of descriptions of the fortifications of besieged cities:

> Dove per guardia de le mura
> più e più fossi cingon li castelli,
> [...]
> e come a tai fortezze da' lor sogli
> a la ripa di fuor son ponticelli. (*Inf.* XVIII. 10–11 & 14–15)

In the cantos of barratry, the poet refers both to the siege of Caprona and to the start of an assault ('cominciare stormo', *Inf.* XXII. 2); in *Inferno* XXVIII, Mohammed prophesies the fall of fra Dolcino's mountain redoubt after a long siege:

> Or dì a fra Dolcin dunque che s'armi, [...]
> sì di vivanda, che stretta di neve
> non rechi la vittoria al Noarese,
> ch'altrimenti acquistar non saria leve. (*Inf.* XVIII. 55 & 58–60)[18]

18 The fourteenth-century commentators of the *Inferno* regularly describe the attack on Dolcino as a siege; see, for instance, Benvenuto da Imola, *Comentum*, II, 361. In addition, the image of

And the climb along Lucifer's body — 'Attienti ben, ché per cotali scale' (*Inf.* XXXIV. 82) — hints at attackers successfully scaling the wall of a castle (Andreola Rossi, pp. 180–81 & 184), a suggestion which appears to be confirmed by the unexpected and strange declaration that '[n]on era camminata di palagio | là v'eravam, ma natural burella' (*Inf.* XXXIV. 97–98), since it was typical of conquerors of cities to head for palaces which, suggestively, were often located at the 'centro' (107) of the built space.[19] Furthermore, in keeping with the perverse and distorted nature of Hell and its inhabitants, and as revealingly occurs with the paradoxical assertion that the victorious Virgil and the pilgrim found themselves not in a grand hall but in a 'dungeon', when alluding to the martial in light of the demonic, Dante ironically reverses the normal order of military practice.[20] Thus, the entombed Lucifer is quite unable to 'advance'; Barbariccia is anything but a 'gran proposto' (*Inf.* XXII. 94) and his troop lacks any sort of soldierly discipline.[21] Even the simile of the siege of Caprona, evoked to describe the *viator*'s fear, reverses the actual historical event, since Dante is now connected to the defeated rather than, as had been the case in reality, to the victors; and, finally, the appearance of Malebolge, despite its layout recalling a fortified castle, is, in actuality, the opposite of a 'fortezza' (*Inf.* XVIII. 14) since, rather than rising upwards, it plummets downwards without enclosing and defending anything.

Although some scholars have claimed that, in Dante's Hell, devils are restricted to the circles of fraud, if not actually just to Malebolge, the fundamental paradigm, often grotesquely ironic, which unites devils, war, and sieges, is in fact initially established and finds its major expression some distance away from the 'luogo [...] detto Malebolge' (*Inf.* XVIII. 1). As a number of critics has noted, the events before 'la città c'ha nome Dite' (*Inf.* VIII. 68), at whose gates mingle 'più di mille [...] da ciel piovuti' (82–83) — namely fallen angels, and hence devils — have a strong militaristic tenor. Indeed, canto VII, in which one of the city's structures, 'una torre' (130), is first evoked in its explicit, makes several preliminary allusions to acts of war: from the war, recalled in the Book of Revelation, fought in Paradise between the army of the archangel Michael and that of the 'draco [...] magnus', the 'great dragon', Satan (12. 7–9, and compare 'là dove Michele | fé la vendetta del superbo strupo', 11–12)[22] to the close-quarter combat between the avaricious and

---

the 'armour of conscience' — 'se non che cosci̇enza m'assicura, | la buona compagnia che l'uom francheggia | sotto l'asbergo del sentirsi pura' (*Inf.* XXVIII. 115–17) — is a commonplace of religious siege writing.

19   See Andreola Rossi, p. 179. See also Pemberton, pp. 101 & 123.

20   On *burella* as an underground prison, see Paget Toynbee, *Dante Studies* (Oxford: Clarendon Press, 1921), pp. 85–91 (pp. 87–91).

21   The events described in *Inferno* XXII 'pongono tutto il canto e la sua vicenda sotto il segno — già anticipato nel XXI — di una parodia di vicende e atti della vita militare sulla terra' (Chiavacci Leonardi, I, 655).

22   Dantists disagree as to the meaning of *strupo*. Although a majority interprets the term as signifying 'violence' or 'rebellion', and a few assign it a sexual denotation, namely 'rape' or possibly 'violation', in light both of the account in Revelation 12: 7 — 'et factum est proelium in caelo Michahel et angeli eius proeliabantur cum dracone et draco pugnabat et angeli eius' [and there was a great battle in heaven: Michael and his angels fought against the dragon and the dragon fought,

the prodigal, reminiscent of similar struggles in epic narratives:

> Queste [the 'genti fangose'] si percotean non pur con mano,
> ma con la testa e col petto e coi piedi,
> troncandosi co' denti a brano a brano. (*Inf.* VII. 112–14)[23]

Furthermore, in *Inferno* VIII too, perplexingly 'assai prima | che noi fossimo al piè de l'alta torre' (1–2), martial references loom large. The 'due fiammette' (4) atop the tower recall 'usi militari dell'epoca';[24] the speed of Phlegyas's boat is equated to that of an arrow (13–15); the pilgrim's betterment of Filippo Argenti has been seen as a victory over an adversary;[25] and the attack on ''l fiorentino spirito bizzarro' (62) is a 'strazio' (58) heralded by a battle cry: ' "A Filippo Argenti!" ' (61). Even the *viator* is the victim of an act of violence: 'ma ne l'orecchie mi percosse un duolo' (65) — suggestively, the poet employs the same verb, *percuotere*, as he had done twice in the previous canto to describe the clash between the prodigal and the avaricious.

Once our two travellers at last arrive outside the city of Dis, the number, the concentration, and the consistency of direct allusions to matters military increase substantially. Not only: the majority of the references are linked to one specific type of warfare. As I am sure will be self-evident by this point in my argument, that type of warfare is, unsurprisingly, the siege. And yet, astonishingly, despite the overwhelming nature of the evidence in this regard, as I will start to document momentarily, the fact that Dante was intent on recounting the siege of Dis has been almost entirely missed by generations of *dantisti*.[26] The reason for this failure, I believe, can be traced firmly to the parodic nature of the assault on the infernal stronghold. If, on the one hand, the poet's perspective on the proceedings before the walls of Dis conforms perfectly to his customary grotesque treatment of his

---

and his angels too] — and of the emphasis placed on combat in the episode of Dis, I prefer the interpretation which deems *strupo* to be derived from medieval Latin *stropus*, 'troop', 'host'.

23   See, for instance, *Aen.* x. 354–61; *Theb.* II. 590–93. Before describing the fighting souls in detail, Dante notes that they '[p]ercotëansi 'ncontro' (*Inf.* VII. 28), and that they were involved in a 'zuffa' (59) and in a 'giostra' (35) — the same term returns in *Inf.* XXII. 6 ('correr giostra'). As we have begun to see, close ties unite the diabolic martial episodes of the first canticle. Furthermore, *Inf.* VII's concentration on Fortune links it to the epic commonplace that deemed military success a consequence of Fate; see Sprung.

24   Sapegno, I, 88. Sapegno also usefully notes that '[a] tali *cenni di castella* Dante allude anche in *Inf.*, XXII, 8'. See also Hollander, I, 158–59.

25   Sergio Cristaldi, 'Canti VII–VIII–IX: verso Dite', in *Esperimenti danteschi. Inferno*, ed. by Simone Invernizzi (Genoa and Milan: Marietti, 2009), pp. 81–94 (p. 87).

26   Among the Trecento commentators, Francesco da Buti is the most sensitive to the presence of siege motifs in the poet's treatment of Dis: '*qual c'a la difension dentro s'aggiri*, cioè benché dentro s'aggiri intorno a le mura per quelli dentro a la difensione come si fa dalli assediati ne le castella et ne le citadi'. I cite Francesco's commentary to *Inferno* not from Giannini's nineteenth-century text, but from the excellent new critical edition: Francesco da Buti, *Commento alla 'Commedia'. 'Inferno'. Nuova Edizione*, ed. by Claudia Tardelli, 2 vols, Tesi di Perfezionamento (Pisa: Scuola Normale Superiore di Pisa, 2010–11), I, 376. Among modern Dante scholars, Robert Hollander has come very close to recognizing that Dante is describing a siege: 'This whole passage, from *Inferno* VII.130 to now [*Inf.* IX. 106], the moment of successful entry of the walled City of Dis, narrates a military campaign' (Hollander, I 164); but see also Giuseppe Acciani, 'L'ingresso di Dante nella città di Dite', *L'Alighieri*, 19 (1978), 45–58 (pp. 47–48).

militarized devils, on the other, by incongruously reversing in *Inferno* VIII and IX the normal order of things when a 'fortezza' (*Inf.* IX. 108) is besieged, Dante has ended up — unintentionally of course — by misdirecting most readers of the *Commedia* as regards the exact identity of the event he describes. Thus, the basic situation that he evokes is the precise opposite of what invariably took place, as countless accounts and representations of sieges had codified, at the start of a blockade whether in life or in art.[27] To put it bluntly, the idea that a 'città' (*Inf.* VIII. 68) provided with robust defences (76–78) and protected by a 'grande stuolo' (69), including 'più di mille in su le porte' (82), would slam shut its gates at the approach of two unarmed travellers is unquestionably ridiculous. The devils' behaviour is a hallmark of the irrationality of evil and the 'otherness' of Hell, key concerns especially of *Inferno* IX. In contrast, relying on our ''ntelletti sani' (*Inf.* IX. 61), our responsibility is to look beyond the literal and to decipher the poem's 'versi strani' (63; see Chapter 17). Thus, all the signs in the text do point to the fact that, absurd as it might appear — and as we shall see, the poet deliberately inverts other standard elements normally associated with *obsidiones* — Virgil and Dante-character are indeed 'laying siege to' Dis. As a consequence, the second half of *Inferno* VIII, from line 67 onwards, and most of *Inferno* IX, at least as far as line 123, ought to be read as the poet's major sustained engagement with one of the great essential motifs of classical and medieval culture. The evidence in this respect, as I have already mentioned, is overwhelming.

At the most basic level, Dante employs terminology and alludes to circumstances that can be judged typical of contemporary representations of sieges. As had been established in the founding siege narrative, the assault on Troy, the 'attackers' arrive by water.[28] As was conventional too, their 'approach' ('s'appressa la città c'ha nome Dite', *Inf.* VIII. 68) is accompanied by a description of the city which focuses on its defences:

> L'alte fosse
> che vallan quella terra sconsolata:
> le mura mi parean che ferro fosse. (*Inf.* VIII. 76–78)[29]

Equally, the 'meschite' (70) that the pilgrim discerns recall the burgeoning literature, both historical and fictional, on the crusades and on the conflicts between Christians and Muslims, large parts of which were dedicated to accounts of sieges.[30] However, an odd note is struck by the fires that burn within the walls (72–74), since such fires were a determining trait of the fall of cities and not of

---

27   In order to illustrate Dante's engagement with siege commonplaces in *Inferno* VIII and IX, I shall primarily draw on classical examples since, for centuries, these controlled the parameters of epic siege writing. In what was a highly codified tradition, medieval Latin and vernacular epics closely followed classical precedents. When I employ the designation 'classical epic', I normally refer to this tradition as a whole.

28   See also G. D. West, 'The Description of Towns in Old French Verse Romances', *French Studies*, 11 (1957), 50–59 (pp. 53–55, 57).

29   See David Cowling, *Building the Text: Architecture as Metaphor in Late Medieval and Early Modern France* (Oxford: Clarendon Press 1998), pp. 55 & 59; Marguerite Rossi, p. 598.

30   See Bernard Guidot, *Chanson de geste et réecritures* (Orleans: Paradigmes Edition, 2008); Hebron, p. 6; Pemberton; Roussel.

the start of hostilities.[31] Furthermore, Dante introduces a distinctly Scriptural component to his description, which, in general, as we shall see, is based primarily on Latin epic precedents, by highlighting the 'grande aggirata' (79) that Phlegyas's boat had made around the city. This manoeuvre calls to mind Joshua's circling of Jericho that preceded the miraculous capture of the city: 'dixitque Dominus ad Iosue [...] circuite urbem' [and the Lord said to Joshua [...] go around the city] (Joshua 6: 2–3, and compare 4, 7, 11, & 14–16).[32] Equally, the moment when 'chiuser le porte que' nostri avversari | nel petto al mio segnor, che fuor rimase' (115–16) calques the start of the siege of Jericho: 'Hiericho autem clausa erat atque munita timore filiorum Israhel et nullus egredi audebat aut ingredi' [But Jericho was shut and feared the children of Israel and nobody dared go out or enter] (Joshua 6: 1). The Biblical reference, while hinting at the culturally composite nature of Dante's treatment of the assault on Dis — a matter to which I will need to return in some detail — also looks forward to the similarly miraculous and astonishing breaching of the infernal city by the *messo celeste*. It is thus indicative that, among his many antecedents, Dante's celestial envoy should also count the 'prince of the army of the Lord' who appeared to Joshua outside the walls of Jericho. Thus, the messenger's coming ('E già venia', *Inf.* IX. 64) and his divine provenance ('elli era da ciel messo', 85), as well as Virgil's admonition that the pilgrim ought 'drizzare il nerbo | del viso' (73–74) so as to see the marvellous apparition, evoke 'cum autem esset Iosue in agro urbis Hiericho levavit oculos et vidit virum stantem contra se [...] qui respondit [...] sum princeps exercitus Domini et nunc venio' [when Joshua was in the field of the city of Jericho, he lifted up his eyes and saw a man standing in front of him [...] who replied [...] I am the prince of the army of the Lord and I now come] (Joshua 5: 13–14).

The opening salvoes of the siege continue to unfold according to convention. The pilgrim, ludicrously of course, is treated by the demons as an aggressive invader: 'e quei sen vada | che sì ardito intrò per questo regno' (90, and compare 84–85); the 'attackers' and the defenders parley[33] ('E 'l savio mio maestro fece segno | di voler lor parlar segretamente', 86–87), with the unsuccessful outcome of the negotiation marking the effective start of the assault (112–16); and Virgil as 'duca' (97) rallies and reassures his 'troop' (103–08 & 121–30). The martial atmosphere is enhanced by the 'combat' going on in the pilgrim's mind — 'che sì e no nel capo mi tenciona' (111) — yet another siege commonplace, in this instance taken from the metaphorical armoury of erotic, moral, and religious literature.[34] In fact, 'le dolenti case' (120) too can be returned to the tradition of siege writing since threatened

31   It is probable that Dante introduced this unexpected feature as a first indication that his blockade, for all its dependence on the siege tradition, was going to be distinguished by unusual and unique elements. See Andreola Rossi, pp. 24–30, 181, 185.
32   The circling of a city is a commonplace in the siege tradition; see, for instance, St Cyprian, *Liber de zelo et livore* II, in PL IV, col. 639.
33   Pemberton, pp. 115–18 and 123; Marguerite Rossi, p. 599; Roussel, pp. 338–39.
34   See Heather Arden, 'The Slings and Arrows of Outrageous Love in the *Roman de la rose*', in Corfis and Wolfe, pp. 191–205 (p. 195); Hebron, pp. 140–41.

domus are a constant in the classical epic, as well as in Christian literature.[35] The canto closes, first, with a clear reference to the basic pattern of any siege, namely, to an outside force attempting to overwhelm opponents inside a defensive structure ('io vincerò la prova, | qual ch'a la difension dentro s'aggiri', 122–23), and, second, with a direct and sustained allusion to probably the most famous successful assault against a fortification in Christian culture, the Harrowing of Hell (124–30).[36] Finally, as confirmation of how profoundly *Inferno* VIII is involved with the tenets of siege literature, even the pilgrim's state of panic and irrational fear (*Inf.* VIII. 94–102, 109–11 and IX. 1, 13–15), which cause him to imagine non-existent dangers since, as Statius put it in the *Thebaid*, 'nil falsum trepidis' [nothing is false to those who are afraid] (VII. 131), have an obvious precedent in the motif of the 'panic-stricken city', a sub-genre of the *urbs capta* tradition.[37] However, in line with his personal reworking of the conventions of siege literature, Dante modifies the motif in two significant ways. Even though, as was the norm, he describes such extreme behaviour as occurring at the beginning of the siege, custom had it gripping defenders rather than attackers, and it was never limited to a single individual.[38]

   Inferno IX extends and takes forward the account of the siege of Dis, once again introducing unexpected twists to well-known situations and developments. Dante thus is careful to establish clear continuities between the close of canto VIII and the start of canto IX, beginning with similarities in the rhyme sounds. The *-erta* (128 & 130) and *-orta* (125, 127, & 129) rhymes of the former are in part re-echoed by the *-olta* (2, 4, & 6) rhyme of the latter; while *Inferno* VIII's *-orse* (110, 112, & 114) and *-ase* (116, 118, & 120) rhymes partially anticipate *Inferno* IX's *-inse* (1 & 3) and *-erse* (8, 10, & 12) rhyme endings. Narratively, the opening of *Inferno* IX conforms precisely to the situation delineated at the end of canto VIII. After presenting Virgil's reaction to having the gates slammed in his face (VIII. 115–30), the poet, logically, next focuses on the pilgrim's response and the effect of this on his guide (IX. 1–15). In addition, lexical similarities and recurring elements draw the explicit and incipit together: 'il duca mio tornare in volta' (IX. 2) recalls 'mio segnor, che [...] | rivolsesi a me' (VIII. 116–17); in both cantos (VIII. 128–30 and IX. 8–9), Virgil ruminates on a divinely ordained 'tal' (VIII. 130 and IX. 8); and, finally, his repeated insistence on 'winning the fight' — 'io vincerò la prova' (VIII. 122) and 'converrà vincer la pugna' (IX. 7) — reasserts the primacy of the martial in the events uniting the two cantos. More specifically, Virgil closes his account of his earlier voyage to the depths of Hell by reminding the pilgrim that they must now take the city by violence:

35   Dante's phrase especially recalls 'at domus interior gemitu miseroque tumultu | miscetur' [but the house inside resounds with groans and miserable laments] (*Aen.* II. 486–87). See also Cowling, pp. 27–29.

36   I return to the Harrowing of Hell at various points during the remainder of my analysis.

37   See George M. Paul, '*Urbs capta*: Sketch of an Ancient Literary Motif', *Phoenix*, 36 (1982), 144–55; Andreola Rossi, pp. 17–53.

38   On the 'panic-stricken city', see Statius, *Thebaid VII: A Commentary*, ed. by Johannes J. L. Smolenaars (Leiden, New York, and Cologne: Brill, 1994), pp. 199–210. See, for instance, *Theb.* IV. 369–82; VII. 452–69 (an episode in which, as in *Inferno* IX, Tisiphone plays a vital role); X. 552–79. A not dissimilar state of irrational panic overwhelms the Argive army on its way to Thebes (*Theb.* VII. 105–32).

> 'Questa palude che 'l gran puzzo spira
> cigne dintorno la città dolente,
> u' non potemo intrare omai sanz' ira.' (*Inf.* IX. 31–33)[39]

Virgil is of course wrong about the outcome of the siege. No aggression will be needed for the gates of Hell to be opened to the two travellers. As the author of dramatic and brutal sieges in the *Aeneid*, Virgil is incapable of imagining a situation where a city might be captured peacefully and bloodlessly. And the lack of bloodshed is another feature which drastically distinguishes Dante's account from those of the Latin and vernacular epic traditions. As a pagan, Virgil is ultimately unable to comprehend the power and mercy of the Christian God.[40] Indeed, it is not unreasonable to surmise that, inter alia, what motivates Dante's overturning of key motifs of the siege tradition is the desire to censure the customarily lengthy, detailed, and over-indulgent treatment of carnage characteristic of epic writing — a perspective which obviously went against Christian attitudes regarding the sanctity of life and respect of others.[41] That Dante judged such literary wallowing in gore as problematic, and hence unnecessary, is confirmed by the restraint and brevity with which, in *Inferno* XXVIII, he presents four of the bloodiest battles on record (7–20), which, in any case, are 'nulla' (20) when compared to 'il modo de la nona bolgia sozzo' (21). And yet, despite the unspeakable horrors 'del sangue e de le piaghe' (2) that he had witnessed, the poet carefully curbs and curtails his descriptions: Mohammed's wounds are depicted in six lines (22–27), Ali's in one (33), Pier da Medicina's in five (64–66 & 68–69), Curio's again in one (101), Mosca dei Lamberti's in three (103–05), and Bertran's in seven (119–25). Indeed, with the possible exception of the portraits of Mohammed, Mosca and perhaps Pier, Dante's approach is a model of illustrative *reticentia*.

The poet's desire to distinguish his siege narrative from the epic tradition — an approach which, as I have noted, is not without its critical reverberations — becomes increasingly evident as the battle for Dis moves inexorably to its predestined conclusion. Having been reminded by Virgil that the city must be taken by force, the pilgrim's 'occhio' (35) is relentlessly drawn to the battlements, 'ver l'alta

39   Given my reading of *Inferno* VIII and IX as offering an account of a siege, it ought not come as a surprise that I favour the reading of 'ira' as the 'anger', namely the violence, needed to breach the city, rather than the alternative suggestions which interpret the noun as 'divine righteous anger' or as the wrath of the defenders.

40   As is well known, the events before the gates of Dis place into sharp relief the limitations of paganism, especially when this is considered in relation to Christianity.

41   On Christian attitudes to war and violence in the Middle Ages, see Cardini, 'Introduzione'; Michael Walzer, *Just and Unjust Wars: A Moral Argument with Historical Illustrations*, 4th edn (New York: Basic Books, 2006); *Ethics, Nationalism, and Just War: Medieval and Contemporary Perspectives*, ed. by Henrik Syse and Gregory M. Reichberg (Washington, DC: Catholic University of America Press, 2007). By closely tying the martial to the devils, Dante was expressing a clear condemnation of war and violence, which associated him with contemporary pacifist Christian positions. At the same time, the poet was not against divinely sanctioned warfare, most notably, the wars that led to the creation of the Roman empire. Dante thus reflects the ambiguities and contradictions regarding war that dogged medieval Christianity. It lies well beyond the remit of this study to examine these fascinating questions; just as I do not have the space here to assess the extent to which the poet's 'military' devils are part of his critique of chivalric culture.

torre a la cima rovente' (36). What he sees is disturbing:

> In un punto furon dritte ratto
> tre furïe infernal di sangue tinte,
> che membra feminine avieno e atto,
>   e con idre verdissime eran cinte;
> serpentelli e ceraste avien per crine,
> onde le fiere tempie erano avvinte.
>   E quei, che ben conobbe le meschine
> de la regina de l'etterno pianto,
> 'Guarda,' mi disse, 'le feroci Erine.'
> [...]
>   Con l'unghie si fendea ciascuna il petto;
> battiensi a palme e gridavan sì alto. (*Inf.* IX. 37–45 & 49–50)

The portrayal of the Furies combines and subverts a series of fundamental epic siege commonplaces that had received canonical status thanks to their deployment in the *Aeneid*. In addition, Dante's description subtly heralds the imminent and inevitable fall of Dis, since the topoi he chooses to meld were all normally associated with the destruction of cities. Fires blazing;[42] bloodstained defenders standing on the summit of towers or other buildings;[43] women weeping and screaming — these were among the tell-tale signs of the *urbs capta*.[44] In fact, the rhetoricians, as they codified these and similar siege topoi, recognized their power to create scenes of great pathos:

> Sic et urbium captarum crescit miseratio. Sine dubio enim qui dicit expugnatam esse civitatem complectitur omnia quaecumque talis fortuna recipit, sed in adfectus minus penetrat brevis hic velut nuntius. At si aperias haec, quae verbo uno inclusa erant, apparebunt effusae per domus ac templa flammae et ruentium tectorum fragor et ex diversis clamoribus unus quidam sonus, aliorum fuga incerta, alii extremo complexu suorum cohaerentes et infantium feminarumque ploratus et male usque in illum diem servati fato senes: tum illa profanorum sacrorumque direptio, efferentium praedas repetentiumque discursus, et acti ante suum quisque praedonem catenati, et conata retinere infantem suum mater, et sicubi maius lucrum est pugna inter victores. Licet enim haec omnia, ut dixi, complectatur 'eversio', minus est tamen totum dicere quam omnia.[45]

> [In this way the compassion for a conquered city grows. For certainly one who says that a city was seized includes all that this outcome entails, but this brief statement, as it were, barely touches the emotions. But if you unfold the implications of this single word, flames will appear running through houses and temples, and the crashing sound of tumbling roofs, and a single echo of many cries, some wavering in flight, others embracing their beloved one last

---

42   Fire was the quintessential trademark of the defeated city; see n. 31.

43   See, for instance, *Aen.* II. 315–16; 458–61. On the tower as the archetypal siege building, see Andreola Rossi, pp. 182–83, 186.

44   See Andreola Rossi, pp. 40–44, 46. Battles notes that 'all of [the *Thebaid*'s] chief episodes are punctuated by laments by women, often quite lengthy' (p. 185, n. 65); see for instance *Theb.* III. 53–57.

45   Quintilian, *Instit. orat.* VIII. 3. 67–69. See also *Ad Her.* IV. 39. 51.

time, and the weeping of women and children, and the old men spared by a cruel fate to see this day: then will appear the plundering of things sacred and profane, the running to and fro of those who carry away their booties and come back for more, the prisoners, each driven chained before his captors, a mother trying to keep her baby, and fights among the victors where the spoils are richer. For all these things, as I said, may be included within the 'conquest of a city' [eversio], but to tell the whole [event] is less effective than to describe it part by part.]

On the other hand, unlike Aeneas's heart-wrenching account of the destruction of his home in Book II of the *Aeneid*, the very last thing Dante wants his readers to feel for the inhabitants of Dis is any sort of compassion — 'Qui vive la pietà quand' è ben morta' (*Inf.* XX. 28). As a result, Virgil's deceived heroic defenders and doomed noblewomen of Troy are metamorphosed into the Furies, who traditionally were linked with the ruin of households and communities rather than with their protection.[46] It is for this reason that Aeneas terms Helen 'Troiae et patriae communis Erinys' [The common Fury of both Troy and the fatherland] (*Aen.* II. 573); and the Virgilian 'Fury' inside the lost city may very well have encouraged Dante to place his three Furies on the walls of Dis. Given their bent for destruction, the Erinyes prove to be extremely poor guardians. Paradoxically, they are defenders who are also attackers. Their appearance and behaviour recall some of the more horrific aspects of the final Greek assault against Troy. Thus, beyond constituting part of their typical iconography, the three species of reptiles on their heads connect them to the three instances in Book II where the Greeks are associated with snakes: the two sea serpents that kill Laocoön and his sons (203–27);[47] the angry rearing snake which appears in the simile describing Androgeos's startled reaction when he realizes that he has stumbled on Aeneas and his men (379–85); and the gruesome comparison between Pyrrhus and a vicious snake awakening from hibernation (469–75).[48] Indeed, like the barbaric, *furens* (499) Pyrrhus, who is 'multo Priami de sanguine' [covered in Priam's blood] (662), the Furies too are 'di sangue tinte' (*Inf.* IX. 38) and 'feroci' (45).

There is little doubt that, when, in a strikingly original manoeuvre, Dante transformed the Furies into the guardians of Dis, he deliberately and quite radically destabilized the time-honoured logic of a tradition of siege writing that, in the wake of Virgil's seminal account of the fall of Troy, had increasingly become ossified and rhetorically conservative; and, in broad terms, the same subversive intent clearly lies behind his rendering of the siege of the infernal city in general. Almost certainly,

46   It is enough to remember Alecto's part in fomenting war between the Latins and the Trojans in *Aeneid* VII, incitements which result in the sieges of the Trojan camp and of the city of Latinus.

47   Aspects of Dante's portrait of the Furies recall *Aen.* II. 206–07, 210, 218–19, 222. In particular, lines 206–07, 'pectora quorum inter fluctus arrecta iubaeque | sanguineae superant undas' [and their breasts rose up in the flowing tide and their bloody crest rose above the waves], re–echo in *Inf.* IX. 37–38 & 49.

48   Once again, the upward thrusting of the snake, the movement that unites Virgil's three passages, returns in Dante's description of the Furies. 'Dritte ratto' (*Inf.* IX. 37), as well as the rhyme words 'avvinte' (2) and 'petto' (49), connect with the *Aeneid*'s 'lubrica convolvit sublato pectore terga | arduus ad solem' [lifting its breast it unfolds its gliding length challenging the sun] (II. 474–75).

one major reason for the poet's parodic reworking was to underscore the perverted nature of Hell and the abnormality of evil. Everything about his Furies overturns confirmed perceptions — even of the Furies themselves. Sin destroys rational and natural distinctions: defenders and attackers, like the thieves and reptiles of the seventh bolgia, become confused. The Furies can be both Greek and Trojan, male and female, aggressor and victim, divine and human. The 'meschine | de la regina de l'etterno pianto' (*Inf.* IX. 43–44) recall sadistic Pyrrhus, but also, albeit contrastively, the distraught Trojan women — 'penitusque cavae plangoribus aedes | femineis ululant' [and inside the hollow houses howl with women's cries] (*Aen.* II. 486–87) — and the huddled figures of Hecuba and her entourage (501 & 515–17). Yet, by the same token, they can merge with Minerva championing the Greek assault on Troy: 'iam summas arces Tritonia [...] Pallas | insedit nimbo effulgens et Gorgone saeva' [now Minerva Tritonia on top of the citadel sits flashing out from a cloud and a terrible figure with her Gorgon-shield] (615–16), and their implicit intertextual association with the Gorgon Medusa is obviously suggestive in the context of canto IX, where, as with the Erinyes, the chthonic *monstrum* is made to 'switch sides', as she is now required to repulse rather than support an 'assalto' (54). Dante's operation is sophisticated, ingenious, and skilfully controlled. Yet, it is open to question whether he could have achieved his innovatory ends as efficiently and effectively as he did if Virgil's retelling of the siege of Troy had not acquired authoritative status. For all its unconventionality, Dante's treatment of the besieged Furies ultimately testifies, even if microcosmically, both to the canonicity of Book II of the *Aeneid* and to the pedestrian conventionality of siege literature. More importantly, his Erinyes highlight Dante's mastery over the tradition — an expert control that allowed him to challenge and reformulate established practices.

It is obvious that the metaliterary consequences of Dante's rewriting of the epic siege are far from insignificant. However, since the issues involved are best considered in light of the overall standing of the siege in medieval literature and culture, I shall examine them in greater depth after establishing, first, that, right up to their close, the poet insistently portrays the events before Dis as an attack against a fortified city, and second, that Dante's depiction, for all its Virgilian patina, also reveals the unmistakable signs of a broad engagement with the tradition of siege writing.

The conventional climax of any siege narrative is the extended and overwrought description either of the successful defence of the fortification or, more typically, of its emotionally charged, violent, and destructive fall.[49] Conversely, though entirely in line with his general parodic approach to the episode, Dante's presentation of the taking of Dis is brief, subdued, and devoid of effort and aggression. The gate to the 'fortezza' (*Inf.* IX. 108) — the poet strategically closes his account with a term which leaves in no doubt the type of conflict that he has been depicting — is breached thanks to the lightest of touches:[50] 'Venne a la porta e con una verghetta

---

49   See Aeneas's account of the fall of Troy in Book II of the *Aeneid*.

50   Dante makes two further allusions to the defensive walls: the first at the end of canto IX ('li alti spaldi', 133) and the second at the beginning of canto X ("l muro de la terra', 2).

| l'aperse, che non v'ebbe alcun ritegno' (90–91). The revelation that the *messo* had met absolutely 'no resistance' goes against the most basic of siege topoi.[51] Indeed, Dante reiterates this remarkable fact when he declares that Virgil and he '[d]entro li 'ntrammo sanz' alcuna guerra' (106); and, having entered, what they observe also contradicts the spectacle which invariably greeted attackers pouring into a defeated city. Although, as was common, our two 'victors' find themselves in a place 'pieno di duolo e di tormento rio' (111) and ablaze with flames (118–20), they do not see either people or buildings — just 'ad ogne man grande campagna' (110). To the very end, Dante's siege defeats expectations. Its anticlimactic finale is, first and foremost, an undeniable affirmation of God's absolute might.[52] For Dante to have concluded his siege in an exciting and intense key would have meant suggesting that evil had some power, and was thus able, even if minimally, to resist divine authority — something which, in the *Commedia*, the poet never concedes. The sense of anticlimax is a final reminder too of Dante's highly personalized and unique interpretation of one of the great narrative set pieces of his world. In fact, the poet displays his total mastery over the tradition by not neglecting to provide his version of the siege with a dynamic climax. However, instead of mechanically tying this to the entry into, and hence the conquest of, the doomed city, he linked it adroitly to the moments just before the stereotypical high point.

We need to return one last time to the Furies. Both warring sides, as was typical, call for and await the coming of reinforcements. The Erinyes appeal to Medusa (52–54), while Virgil and Dante place their wavering trust in the 'descent' (*Inf.* VIII. 128) of the 'tal che per lui ne fia la terra aperta' (130, and see IX. 9). Dis's 'biggest defensive weapon', yet another sign of the futile ineffectiveness of evil, never appears. On the other hand, 'God's own siege-breaker'[53] majestically arrives and easily scatters the forces of Hell, which flee 'before their enemy' (*Inf.* IX. 75) in panic: 'vid' io più di mille anime distrutte | fuggir così dinanzi ad un' (79–80). If, as I have noted, the *messo*'s conquest of the city is drained of tension, the same is certainly not true of his advent. The divine emissary's approach is gripping, tense, sensational. Indeed, as befits the closing stages of a siege, his arrival is dominated by violence.[54] There is little doubt that his powerful appearance, which Dante suitably evokes in a vigorous and lengthy simile, serves as the dramatic acme of the siege of Dis:

> E già venìa su per le torbide onde
> un fracasso d'un suon, pien di spavento,
> per cui tremavano amendue le sponde,
>   non altrimenti fatto che d'un vento

---

51 Alexander and his army too take a city, Babylon, without meeting serious resistance; see Galteri de Castellione, *Alexandreis*, ed. by Marvin L. Colker (Pavia: Antenore, 1978), V. 534–37. I am grateful to Ambrogio Camozzi for this reference.

52 In Christian culture, given the close association between sin and the siege (see the following subsection), the fall of a city was 'regarded as the just end for a morally corrupt' place (see Hebron, p. 138), and hence divinely willed (see Roussel, p. 328).

53 Both designations may be found in Hollander, I, 162.

54 See Denise Heilbronn, 'Dante's Gate of Dis and the Heavenly Jerusalem', *Studies in Philology*, 72 (1975), 167–92 (pp. 182–83 & 189).

> impetüoso per li avversi ardori,
> che fier la selva e sanz'alcun rattento
>   li rami schianta, abbatte e porta fori;
> dinanzi polveroso va superbo,
> e fa fuggir le fiere e li pastori. (*Inf.* IX. 64–72)

The description of the *messo*'s advent has its roots in Virgil. In particular, it is constructed out of elements drawn from two of the *Aeneid*'s similes.[55] Significantly, both images are associated with the imminent fall of a city: Troy in the first instance, the city of Latinus in the second:

> Adversi rupto ceu quondam turbine venti
> confligunt, Zephyrusque Notusque et laetus Eois
> Eurus equis; stridunt silvae saevitque tridenti
> spumeus atque imo Nereus ciet aequora fundo. (*Aen.* II. 416–19)

[And at once when a whirlwind breaks the winds clash, western, southern, and eastern delighted with its morning steeds; the woods shriek and foaming Nereus rages with his trident and stirs the deep dark sea.]

And:

> Ille volat campoque atrum rapit agmen aperto.
> Qualis ubi ad terras abrupto sidere nimbus
> it mare per medium (miseris, heu, praescia longe
> horrescunt corda agricolis: dabit ille ruinas
> arboribus stragemque satis, ruet omnia late),
> ante volant sonitumque ferunt ad litora venti. (*Aen.* XII. 450–55)

[But he [Aeneas] dashes ahead and drags his dark cohort into the open field. As when a storm from the torn sky flies towards land over the open sea (alas, recognizing it from afar, the hearts of pitiable farmers shudder: for it will tear the trees asunder and kill the crops, and bring ruin far and wide), the winds fly and carry their roar to the shore.]

Although it is not impossible, as we have seen, to recognize distinguishable if faint traces connecting the siege of *Inferno* VIII and IX with those of the *Aeneid*, until the fearsome, crashing intervention of the *messo*, the elements uniting the two texts do not point to a close association. Their links are essentially commonplaces characteristic of the epic siege whose parameters had been largely set by the *Aeneid* and especially by the poem's second book. Conversely, when Dante depicted the mysterious 'da ciel messo' (85), the dramatic fulcrum of the assault on Dis, in terms which explicitly recalled not just Virgil's poem but also his descriptions of attacks against a fortification, the poet dutifully acknowledged his 'maestro's' (58 & 124) *auctoritas* as regards the epic treatment of the siege. At the same time, by ensuring that, unlike Aeneas, the divine Christian hero remains unscathed and

---

55   See Erich Auerbach, *Literary Language and its Public in Late Latin Antiquity and in the Middle Ages* (Princeton: Princeton University Press, 1993), p. 229, n. 42: Dante Alighieri, *La Divina Commedia*, ed. by Niccolò Tommaseo and with an introduction by Umberto Cosmo (Turin: UTET, 1927), quoted from the DDP, annotation to lines 70–72. The simile also incorporates other Virgilian borrowings; see *Aen.* VI. 296; VII. 586–89.

is inconvenienced 'only' (84) by the irritation of the 'aere grasso' (82), is never defeated, and wins his battles without effort, Dante vividly underscored the *novitas* of his siege narrative. The distinctiveness of his account stems directly from its being the record of an extraordinary supernatural action willed in Heaven. Thus, it is far from unsurprising that, when Dante composed his 'versi strani' (63), the pagan poet, just as had occurred before the walls of Dis, can only grant him limited assistance. Even if, however briefly, the pilgrim had had serious doubts about the outcome of his journey (*Inf.* VIII. 101–02), its success was never in question, as Virgil had properly tried to remind him: 'ché 'l nostro passo | non ci può torre alcun: da tal n'è dato' (104–05). The fall of Dis, unlike that of other cities, was inevitable and the traveller-'attackers' were always going to be able 'passar più oltre' (101). Yes, the infernal city is besieged, but it is a siege like no other — and particularly so when judged in light of the sieges of classical epic literature.[56]

3. Sacred Sieges

In order to depict his miraculous otherworldly siege — the fact that it is an assault upon a stronghold in the afterlife immediately confirms its uniqueness in relation to the epic tradition — Dante had to find solutions which could offer a sense of the distinctiveness of the remarkable event in which he had participated. Thus, by integrating similes belonging to two separate sieges in the *Aeneid*, the poet offered a hint as to the complexity of the siege of Dis, which could not straightforwardly be equated with any one particular siege, not even if that assault could be numbered among the most notable sieges of the past. Instead, by conflating and reworking different siege narratives, Dante hoped that the singularity of the attack on Lucifer's 'empire' (*Inf.* XXXIV. 28) could begin to emerge. The poet's reliance on and overturning of a broad range of siege commonplaces serve the same function; as does his reference to the 'meschite' (*Inf.* VIII. 70), since it brings to mind, especially for a contemporary readership, the increasingly popular crusade narratives, whether literary, historiographical or religious, in which sieges, beginning with that of Jerusalem, were given pride of place.

As the siege of Dis unfolds, Troy merges into Latinus's city, and both melt into Jerusalem and the other sieges involving Christians and Muslims. Such syncretism, as we well know, is typical of Dante and his 'comic' style, and so it is far from unexpected that another notorious siege, that of Thebes, together with its attendant wars and general aura of bloody violence, should also be discernible in the weave of *Inferno* VIII and IX. Indeed, there is substantial evidence to confirm that Statius's Thebes, together with its medieval reworkings, serves as 'the principal dystopian model for the city of Dis in Dante's Hell'.[57] However, for all Dante's calculated

---

56   Conventionally, 'the outstanding impression cultivated by the siege is suspense' (Solterer, p. 107).

57   See in particular Ronald L. Martinez, 'Dante, Statius, and the Earthly City' (unpublished PhD thesis, University of California, Santa Cruz, 1977). The quotation comes from Schnapp, p. 18, and see also pp. 16–17 & 36–37. On Thebes in the Middle Ages, see Dominique Battles, *The Medieval Tradition of Thebes: History and Narrative in the Old French 'Roman de Thèbes', Boccaccio, Chaucer, and*

dependence on the rich tradition of the classical epic siege and on contemporary siege narratives to determine the intricate originality of the attack on the infernal stronghold, the most important and illuminating precedents, as he makes quite clear, both for the event itself and for his treatment of this, come from a very different direction. Thus, his evocation of the miraculous fall of Jericho and its Heaven-sent envoy provides a first, though far from exclusive, indication that the most significant precursors of the siege of Dis are to be sought in the Bible and in religious literature more generally, especially as, unlike his recourse to secular models, the poet avoids parodying his Scriptural source in the Book of Joshua. Furthermore, by integrating classical and Christian motifs in his presentation of the assault, Dante ensured that the episode contributed to *Inferno* VIII and IX's overarching assessment of the differences and continuities between paganism and Christianity (see Chapter 17).

In fact, Dante unambiguously affirms the pre-eminent archetype, both literary and historical, for the siege of Dis. To allay both his own and the pilgrim's anxieties, Virgil declares:

> Questa lor tracotanza non è nova;
> ché già l'usaro a men segreta porta,
> la qual sanza serrame ancor si trova.
> Sovr' essa vedestù la scritta morta. (*Inf.* VIII. 124–27)

The reference of course is to the *Descensus Christi ad inferos*, a story which, ever since the *amplificatio* in the fifth-century Latin version of the *Gospel of Nicodemus* of the fleeting New Testament allusions to the Harrowing of Hell, had burgeoned in popularity during the course of the Middle Ages.[58] Dante followed and adapted the apocryphon as regards the shutting of the gates of Hell, the fear generated among Hell and its ministers by the advent of Christ, and the ease with which the Saviour opened the locked portals. At the same time, although the episode has a martial veneer — Satan is presented as a 'mighty man of war' and Jesus is termed a 'warrior' — the assault on Hell, which is described as a prison, is rapidly sketched, no more than a detail which serves to give narrative coherence to the liberation of the patriarchs and to the celebration of Christ's triumph over death and sin.[59] The connections between the Harrowing of Hell and Dante's poetic treatment of the siege of Dis are thus fairly limited, not least because at no point is the harrowing treated as a siege. On the other hand, the 'descent' is absolutely

---

Lydgate (New York: Routledge, 2004); Arianna Punzi, '*Oedipodae confusa domus*': la materia tebana nel *Medioevo latino e romanzo* (Rome: Bagatto Libri, 1995).

58   On the Harrowing of Hell in cantos VIII and IX and in the *Inferno* more generally, see Peter S. Hawkins, *Dante's Testaments* (Stanford: Stanford University Press, 1999), pp. 99–124; Amilcare A. Iannucci, 'Beatrice in Limbo: A Metaphoric Harrowing of Hell', *Dante Studies*, 97 (1979), 23–45, 'Dottrina e allegoria in *Inferno* VIII, 67–IX, 105', in *Le forme dell'allegoresi*, ed. by Michelangelo Picone (Ravenna: Longo, 1987), pp. 99–124, and 'Canto IX: The Harrowing of Dante from Upper Hell', in *Lectura Dantis: Inferno*, ed. by Allen Mandelbaum and others (Berkeley and Los Angeles: University of California Press, 1998), pp. 123–35; Tobias Foster Gittes, '"O vendetta di Dio": The Motif of Rape and Retaliation in Dante's *Inferno*', *MLN*, 120 (2005), 1–29.

59   *Evangelium Nicodemi cum epistolis Pilati* XXI–XXIV, in *Codex Apocryphus Novi Testamenti*, ed. by Johannes Karl Thilo (Leipzig, Vogel, 1832–), I, 487–802 (pp. 715–47).

fundamental to defining the providential character of the pilgrim's salvific journey and to guaranteeing its success.

It is far from unusual for Dante openly to indicate a source but then only to make limited use of it.[60] The precise logic of this strategy has remained largely unstudied, though, in very general terms, it seems to be directed at underlining the importance of that part of the text where the indication is given, at involving the reader in its interpretation ('Pensa, lettor', *Inf.* VIII. 94), and at designating its broad cultural context. Thus, it is suggestive that, beyond the bonds uniting the siege of Dis to the fall and destruction of Biblical cities, such as Jericho and Jerusalem, two New Testament passages and their legacies appear specifically to bear on Dante's episode: 'Ipse [Jesus] intravit in quoddam castellum' [and He came into a certain town] (Luke 10: 38) and 'Ite in castellum quod contra vos est' [Go into the town that is before you] (Matthew 21: 2).[61] The ideological and narrative import of these verses for *Inferno* VIII and IX is immediately evident. However, what makes them especially significant is that, in the Middle Ages, they were widely circulating and interconnected *sententiae*,[62] the exegetical tradition on which both developed the verses' association with the siege and related them to key moments in providential history — moments which are afforded a key position in the *Commedia* in general and in cantos VIII and IX in particular.[63]

60   See, for instance, Zygmunt G. Barański, 'Notes on Dante and the Myth of Orpheus', in *Dante: mito e poesia. Atti del secondo Seminario Dantesco Internazionale*, ed. by Michelangelo Picone and Tatiana Crivelli (Florence: Cesati, 1999), pp. 133–62; Ambogio Camozzi Pistoja, 'Ugolino and the Oneirocritical Practice — Dream Divination in *Inferno* 32–33', in *Dante's Volume from Alpha to Omega*, ed. by Cristina Purdy and Carol Chiodo (Tempe: ACMRS, forthcoming).

61   On the meaning of the term *castellum*, see Abigail Wheatley, *The Idea of the Castle in Medieval England* (Woodbridge and Rochester: York Medieval Press, 2004), pp. 19–43. Despite Christianity's claims to being a religion of peace, violence and war are deeply engrained in its imaginary. Martial images have been used to illustrate a wide range of Christian experiences, from the *Christus triumphans* to the idea of earthly life as soldiering: 'militia est vita hominis super terram' [the life of man on earth is warfare] (Job 7: 1). The siege is simply one element of this fertile metaphorical system. In order properly to appreciate Dante's reliance on Christian treatments of the siege, it would be necessary to consider the assault on Dis in light of the status accorded to war and violence both in Christian culture and in the poet's *œuvre* in general — a task which lies well beyond the remit of this narrow introductory study. In any case, one cannot but wonder the extent to which the mix of violence and non-violence that surrounds the *messo* results from the tension in Christianity between peace and aggression, which, inter alia, found expression in the liturgical formula 'Sis miles pacificus' [Be a peaceful soldier]. The celestial messenger certainly embodies the characteristics of the 'soldier of peace'; however, in their own way, so do Virgil and Dante-*personaggio*, who are archetypical pilgrims 'in pugna semper' [always battling]: Jacobus a Voragine, *Legenda aurea*, ed. by Theodor Graesse (Osnabrück: Otto Zeller, 1965), Preface.

62   On the two *sententiae*, see Cowling, pp. 58–60, 62; Roberta D. Cornelius, *The Figurative Castle: A Study in the Medieval Allegory of the Edifice with Especial Reference to Religious Writings* (Bryn Mawr: n.pr., 1930), pp. 37–48; Hebron, pp. 142–46; Wheatley, pp. 28–30, 88, 94, 106. Exegetes glossing one passage frequently cited the other. Both Mark and Luke also record Jesus's words to the two disciples: 'ite in castellum quod est contra vos' [Go into the town that is before you] (Mark 11: 2) and 'ite in castellum quod contra est' [Go into the town that is ahead] (Luke 19: 30). The commentary tradition on these verses is almost identical to that on Matthew 21: 2. Though Matthew was more frequently cited than the other two evangelists, the three passages were basically interchangeable.

63   See Chapter 17; Heilbronn; Mark Musa, 'Rereading '*Inferno* IX', *Rivista di studi italiani*, 11 (1993), 1–27.

The corrupt city that turns against the good person or persons, the *iustus* or *iusti*, is a Scriptural commonplace. Indeed, it is one that Dante exploited to define his relationship to Florence. More unusual, however, is the idea of the just attempting to enter a sinful habitation, or, as a commentator on Matthew 21: 2 put it, of 'duo discipuli' [two disciples] 'being sent' 'ad vicium' [to vice].[64] Other Scriptural *lectores* were more precise about the nature of the sinfulness of the city and its inhabitants: 'contra apostolos enim erat, nec jugum doctrinarum volebat accipere' [for it was against the apostles, and did not want to accept the yoke of their teachings][65] and 'id est, Jerusalem, quae contra legem Evangelii repugnabat' [that is, Jerusalem, which fought against the law of the Gospel].[66] Furthermore, it was customary to represent the *castellum* as a fortified place whose defences needed to be breached by Christ's two emissaries: 'Ne autem absconderetur civitas supra montem hunc posita, mittit discipulos in castellum, quod contra eos est, ut per illos totius contra positi orbis munitiones penetret' [Lest the city that was on this mountain be forgotten, He sends his disciples into the town that was before them, so that through them he may breach the means of defence of the whole town][67] and:

> Duo autem missi sunt propter scientiam veritatis, et munditiam operis, vel in sacramento geminae dilectionis, quibus bene fulgere debent Ecclesia doctores, et dixit eis: 'Ite in castellum quod contra vos est', id est penetrate barbara et indocta mundi loca, quasi contra positi castelli moenia. Erat enim mundus prophetica [philosophica?] ratione, et pharisaica traditione adversus Christum armatus.[68]

> [Two then were sent on account of their knowledge of truth, and for the purity of their work, or as a sacred oath of mutual love, things with which the doctors of the Church should shine, and He said to them: 'Go to the town which is before you', that is, penetrate the barbaric and unlearned places of the world, as if through the walls of a town. For the world was armed against Christ with prophetic [philosophical?] reason, and with the Pharisaic tradition.]

Indeed, Matthew 21: 2 was specifically associated with the siege and fall of Jerusalem.[69] Finally, if doubts were to persist about the relevance of the two *sententiae* for *Inferno* VIII and IX, or even about the legitimacy of treating the events outside Dis as a siege, it is enough to note that both verses and their traditions were intimately involved with the popular motif of the siege of the soul, namely, of the soul of the Christian attacked by the forces of iniquity.[70] The devils' assault was invariably repulsed, often after a long and bitter struggle, thanks to the efforts of the virtues and the intercession of the divine. Dante effectively adapted the conceit to his infernal context and to his overall treatment of evil. By presenting Satan and

---

64   Hilarius Pictaviensis, *In Evangelium Matthaei Commentarius* XXI. I, in PL IX, col. 1034.
65   Jerome, *Commentarium in Evangelium Matthaei* III, in PL XXVI, col. 146.
66   Anon., *Expositio Evangeliorum*, in PL, XXX, col. 556.
67   Wernerus S. Blasii, *Libri deflorationum sive excerptionum. Dominica in palmis*, in PL CLVII, col. 899.
68   Hildebertus Cenomanensis, *Sermones* XXXII, in PL CLXXI, col. 500.
69   Ordericus Vitalis, *Historia Ecclesiastica*, in PL CLXXXVIII, col. 48.
70   See Cornelius; Hebron, pp. 137–50. See also Cowling, pp. 23–33, 54–82; C. L. Powell. 'The Castle of the Body', *Studies in Philology*, 16 (1919), 197–205.

his minions as cowardly defenders and not as aggressive attackers, and by having the representatives of good besieging and, thanks to the intervention of the *messo celeste*, entering the citadel of malice, he diminished, once again, the active power of sin and asserted God's absolute dominion.[71]

The situation facing Virgil and Dante-*personaggio* before the walls of Dis is thus similar to that which, according to Christian culture, confronted Christ's two disciples. A fortified city, den of every kind of iniquity, confronts two divinely sanctioned envoys: 'sapientes sunt isti discipuli, et a sapientissimo magistri instructi' [these disciples are wise, and taught by the wisest teacher] — a designation that is especially fitting for the 'mar di tutto 'l senno' (*Inf.* VIII. 7).[72] In addition, just as the exegetical tradition saw in the *castellum* a symbol of intellectual presumption that challenged the word of God, so, fittingly, the first sinners whom our two travellers encounter once they enter Dis also refused 'to accept the yoke of the doctrines' of faith.[73] For the Middle Ages, heretics were those who, because of intellectual arrogance, persisted in erroneously and irrationally challenging divine authority.[74] More specifically, a heavily ironic judgment weighs down on Dante's Epicureans 'che l'anima col corpo morta fanno' (*Inf.* X. 15), since, in light of the tradition of the siege of the soul, they find themselves in the very same position, behind defensive walls, as the soul, whose immortality they had rejected and which, in life, they had failed to protect. And there is more: the medieval exegesis of Matthew 21: 2 helps to clarify the status of the pilgrim and, to a lesser extent, of Virgil as God's chosen who are called to participate in the workings of divine providence. Thus, as we have already seen, they are aligned with the *doctores* and the *praedicatores*, whose responsibility it is to lead others to salvation, a duty which Virgil is fulfilling to the best of his limited abilities with respect to Dante-character, who is going on the journey not just to save his own soul but also spiritually to enlighten others.[75] Thus, just as the poet's reworking of epic siege commonplaces helps to establish the uniqueness of the *Commedia*, so the Scriptural tradition of the *castellum* points to the poem's providential character. Indeed, both New Testament passages firmly set Dante's otherworldly and writerly experiences in the context of divine history, a major concern especially of *Inferno* IX (see Chapter 17). 'Ipse [Jesus] intravit in quoddam castellum' [He entered a certain town] in particular was interpreted as referring to the Incarnation: the castle standing for the Virgin's womb into which Christ entered. More generally, the line was allegorized as the 'human soul':

71 Although Dante overturns an established commonplace, this is not done either for parodic, self-authorizing ends, as happens with his recourse to classical siege elements, or for grotesque ironic ones, a typical Dantean manoeuvre in *Inferno*, whereby an aspect of Hell is presented as a perversion of the sacred (Lucifer's three heads as a distorted Trinity). The reversal in this instance is used straightforwardly to highlight God's supremacy and the futility of evil.

72 Bruno Astensis, *Commentaria in Matthaeum* IV. 85, in PL CLXV, col. 243.

73 The commentary tradition too asserted that sinners confronted the two disciples once they had entered the *castellum*: 'Introeuntes mundum praedicatores invenerunt populum nationum perfidiae vinculis irretitum' [When the preachers entered the world they found the people of the nations ensnared in the fetters of perfidy]: Bede, *In Lucae Evangelium expositio* v. 19, in PL XCII, col. 567.

74 On heresy in the Middle Ages, see Chapter 3, n. 35.

75 See, for instance, St Bede, *In Lucae Evangelium expositio* v. 19, in PL XCII, col. 567.

Quod est autem hoc castellum, nisi cor humanum, quod prius quam Dominus
ad illud veniat, cupiditatis fossa vallatur, muroque obstinationis clauditur,
atque in interiori latitudine sua, Babylonica turre erigitur? Tria certe in omni
oppido sunt maxime necessaria: victualia, quibus sustententur; munitio, qua
protegantur; arma, quibus hostibus resistant. Sic ergo et hujus castelli incolae
victum habent, voluptatem corporis, et saeculi vanitatem, quibus pascuntur.
Habent et qua teguntur, proprii cordis duritiam; ut verbi Dei sagittis potentibus
vix, aut nunquam penetrari valeant. Accincti sunt armis, carnalis scilicet
sapientiae argumentis, quibus contra hostes repugnant.[76]

[What then is this town, if not the human heart, which before the Lord comes
for it is surrounded by the moat of cupidity, and enclosed by the wall of
obstinacy, and within its own inner space is fortified by the tower of Babylon?
In every town three things are certainly essential: food thanks to which citizens
may be sustained; means of defence, through which they may be protected;
arms, through which they may resist their enemies. Thus the citizens of this
town have food, carnal pleasure, and vanity of the age, on which to feed. They
have the means of defence, the harshness of their heart, so that they will hardly
be won over, or perhaps never, by the powerful arrows of God's word. They are
surrounded by arms, that is, the arguments of carnal knowledge, with which
they fight against their enemies.]

Again, the relevance of a passage such as this one from St Bernard's sermons in
praise of Mary for Dante's treatment of the siege of Dis is self-evident, not least
because, like the saint from Clairvaux, the poet too concentrates on 'l'alte fosse |
che vallan' (*Inf.* VIII. 76–77), on 'le mura' (78), and on 'l'alta torre' (2). Furthermore,
the *castellum* tradition confirms and defines the symbolic value of the episode, a
fundamental feature of its configuration to which the poet explicitly draws our
attention:[77]

> O voi ch'avete li 'ntelletti sani,
> mirate la dottrina che s'asconde
> sotto 'l velame de li versi strani. (*Inf.* IX. 61–63)

The siege of Dis is not simply an instance of classicizing moral allegory — the
standard way in which, since the Trecento, scholars have tended to react to it (see
Chapter 17) — but, thanks to its Scriptural genealogy, it constitutes a vital moment
in Dante's fashioning of the *Commedia* as a work that should be read according
to the principles of the 'allegory of the theologians'. Conventional moralizing
personification allegory, of the type epitomized by the siege of the soul or other
types of psychomachia, offered a concrete general symbolic representation of the
psychological and spiritual struggle going on inside the soul and mind of the
Christian.[78] On the other hand, Dante describes a unique actual event that is self-

---

76   Bernard of Clairvaux, *Sermones in assumptione beatae Mariae Virginis* V. 1, in PL CLXXXIV, col.
1001.

77   On the symbolism of the *castellum*, see Hebron, pp. 136–65; Wheatley, pp. 78–111. See also
Cowling, pp. 57–61.

78   See Morton W. Bloomfield, *The Seven Deadly Sins* (East Lansing: Michigan State College Press,
1952); Adolf Katzenellenbogen, *Allegories of the Virtues and the Vices in Medieval Art from Early Christian
Times to the Thirteenth Century* (London: Warburg Institute, 1939); Jennifer O'Reilly, *Studies in the*

evidently external to both Virgil and the pilgrim. The infernal city and its inhabitants, as well as the values they embody, stand in stark contrast to the two *iusti*, whose individual and differing emotional and spiritual reactions to being confronted by malice's many forms are separately recorded. To put it slightly differently, the siege is not a *fictio* whose significance is to be sought exclusively in its 'dottrina' and not in its *lictera*. It is instead a true event that occurred during the course of a providentially willed experience. The attack on Dis is *allegoria in factis* and not *in verbis*, so that, given their 'facticity', both the 'versi strani' and what lies 'beneath their veil' are worthy of attention.[79] Thus, if, in strictly literary and narrative terms, Dante's siege depends, however obliquely, more on classical precedents than on Biblical ones, its ideological underpinnings, thanks to the *castellum* tradition, are overwhelmingly Christian. Given that the Christian siege also has a far from insignificant bearing on the formal treatment of the blockade, it is clear that the religious reverberations of the siege motif are in the foreground of *Inferno* VIII and IX.

4. Besieging Virginity

However, it would be a mistake to restrict the assault on the infernal city to the interplay between epic pagan and Scriptural Christian elements in its construction, even if the episode as a whole is profoundly concerned with the effects on humanity of the Incarnation (see Chapter 17). As I mentioned at the start of this chapter, the siege was an extraordinarily popular, potent, and polysemous subject in medieval culture. It is not my intention here to review all the various traditions in which the siege played a role, not least because these, as with the allusion to crusade writing via the rapid reference to the 'meschite', have at best a minor part to play in our two cantos.[80] At the same time, there is a third tradition that does appear to have a not inconsequential bearing on the siege of Dis.

Mary's virginity was regularly celebrated in terms of the fact that her *castellum* had remained unbreached:

> Mystice vero castellum in quo Dominus intravit, uterus est beatae Virginis. Quod bene congruit ei et nomine et significatione. Nomine, quoniam castellum sive castrum dicitur a castrando, eo quod propter vigilias et laborem armorum omnis libide eliminetur a castro. Ab utero quoque beatae Virginis omnis libido propter labores et honestas exercitationes exclusa fuit. Significatione, quoniam castellum dicitur quod est muris et propugnaculis circumvallatum, custodibus munitum, necessariis repletum. Castrum quoque beatae Virginis fuit propugnaculis vallatum, ut abstinentia contra ingluviem, castitate contra luxuriam, munificentia contra avaritiam, patientia contra iram, humilitate contra superbiam Unde in Canticis canticorum: 'Hortus conclusus soror mea sponsa, hortus conclusus, fons signatus' [IV. 12]. Item: 'Collum tuum sicut turris David, quae aedificata est cum propugnaculis. Mille clypei pendent

Iconography of the Virtues and Vices in the Middle Ages (New York and London: Garland, 1988).
79   On medieval allegory, see Chapter 2, n. 25.
80   On Dante's dependence on the literature of the crusades, see Zygmunt G. Barański, '"Without any Violence": *Inferno* IX, *Purgatorio* IX, *Paradiso* IX', in *Vertical Readings in Dante's 'Comedy'*, ed. by George Corbett and Heather Webb, 3 vols (Cambridge: Open Book Publishers, 2015–17), I, 181–202.

ex ea, omnis armatura fortium' [IV. 4]. Fuit enim beata Virgo collum, per quod exiit ad nos Verbum Dei. Fuit etiam custodibus munitum, utpote quam Gabriel caeterique angeli, et sancti homines, ut Joseph et Joannes evangelista, ut Dei templum, sanctissime custodierunt. Fuit et necessariis repletum, utpote in qua fecit sibi cellarium panis vitae et aqua sapientiae. Fuit igitur beata Virgo castellum, et quoddam, id est singulare, quia, quamvis caeterae virgines possint esse mundae et castae, tamen nulla potest esse similis, et Virgo et Mater. Quod et si concedamus posse fieri, nulla tamen alia potest esse mater Filii Dei. Qui sicut est unico Patri, ita est unicus unicae matri. In hoc igitur castissimum castellum intravit Jesus. Porta vero per quam intravit, fides est. Quia enim credidit, perfecta sunt ei omnia quae dicta sunt ei a Domino. Nec intrans Jesus hoc castellum violavit; Jesus enim salvat, non violat. Secundum nomen ejus, ita et opus ejus.[81]

[But mystically the castle into which the Lord entered is the womb of the blessed Virgin. And this is coherent both in terms of the word and of its meaning. In terms of the word (*lictera*), since 'castle' [*castellum*] or 'fort' [*castrum*] comes from 'removing' [*castrando*], in that by means of night-watches and effort of arms all passions are removed from the fort. So too all passions were kept out of the womb of the blessed Virgin through effort and virtuous practices. In terms of its meaning (*allegoria*), since a castle is a place that is surrounded by walls and ramparts, defended by guards, and equipped with the necessary accoutrements. Even the fort of the blessed Virgin was surrounded by ramparts, such as fasting against gluttony, chastity against lust, liberality against avarice, patience against wrath, humility against pride. Thus in the Song of Songs: 'My sister, and spouse, is an enclosed garden, an enclosed garden and a guarded fountain'. And moreover: 'Your neck is like the tower of David, built with ramparts. A thousand shields hang from it, all the armours of valiant men'. For the blessed Virgin was the neck, through which the Word of God came to us. She was also a fort defended by guards, since Gabriel and the rest of the angels, and the saints, such as Joseph and John the evangelist, guarded her most sacredly as the temple of God. The fort was also equipped with the necessary accoutrements, since the bread of life and the water of wisdom made His receptacle in her. The blessed Virgin was then a castle, and a particular, that is unique, castle, since although other virgins may be pure and chaste, they cannot however be like her, both Virgin and Mother. And even if we allowed for it to be possible, no other woman could be the mother of the Son of God. And as He comes from one single father, so He is the only one of His only mother. In this most chaste of castles, therefore, entered Jesus. And the door through which He entered is the faith. Because she believed, all the words that the Lord said to her were perfect in her. And by entering, Jesus did not violate this castle; for Jesus saves, he does not violate. As was His name, so was His work.]

The figure of the blessed Virgin as a castle that has remained 'inviolate' stands in obvious contrast to the erotic commonplace of the woman whose *castellum* is penetrated by the lover, as occurs in the *Roman de la rose* and in the *Fiore*.[82] As

---

81   Ralph Ardent, *Homiliae*. I. *Homiliae de tempore*. XXXI. *In festo assumptionis beatae Mariae*, in PL CLV, col. 1429.

82   On the erotic siege, see Arden; Thérèse Bouché, 'Burlesque et renouvellement des formes: l'attaque du château dans le *Roman de la rose* de Jean de Meun', in *Hommages à Jean-Charles Payen: farai chansoneta novele. Essais sur la liberté créatrice au Moyen âge* (Caen: Centre de Publications de l'Université

John Freccero has demonstrated, the Medusa connects Dis to *luxuria*. In particular, the highly negative presentation of the Gorgon also involves a rejection of the *petrose*, which, suggestively, rely heavily on martial and violent imagery, and are explicitly recalled in *Inferno* IX's poetic fabric.[83] In fact, the idea of negative and impure femininity that dominates in the *petrose* returns in *Inferno* IX not solely via the allusion to ''l Gorgón' (56), but also via the evocation of 'Eritón cruda' (23) and of the 'feroci Erine' (45). If, at the narrative level, their threat is countered by the memory of Beatrice, 'Tal ne s'offerse' (8), intertextually and culturally, the poet condemns them thanks to the references to Mary's virtues. In addition, for Dante to repudiate the poems for the *donna petra* meant also to reject the authority of his *primo amico*, since the *canzoni* constitute the most overtly Cavalcantian moment of his lyric production — a subtle anticipation of the severe charges that he would lay against the older poet in the following canto. Moreover, thanks to the Marian character of the siege, Dante extends his criticism of vernacular erotic literature beyond Guido to take in not just a certain type of 'materialist' love lyric but also 'naturalist' narrative love poetry. Dante's censure of the authors of the *Rose* and the *Fiore*, and if he were the author of the *poemetto*, the critique would assume hugely significant proportions, allows him once again, as occurs with his parodic manipulation of the classical epic and his respectful *imitatio* of the Scriptural tradition, to establish the literary uniqueness of the *Commedia* — a vernacular narrative poem which, as its treatment of the siege confirms, succeeds in integrating and reworking classical, Scriptural, and Romance literature for rigorously ethical and divinely sanctioned ends.

Without wishing in any way to underplay the religious implications of the siege as a topic through which Dante defined the sacred character both of his otherworldly journey and of his *comedía*, I suspect that it was probably its syncretic qualities that most appealed to him.[84] For medieval culture, as for the classical age, the siege was a great literary motif — possibly among the greatest. It enjoyed a prominent position in the Bible, in the classical, Christian, and medieval epic, in chronicles, in love literature, and in a wide array of Christian texts, from homilies to exegesis. The topos of the *obsidium*, which bound together paganism and Christianity, and which transcended the boundaries of the single *genera dicendi*, could serve as a convenient and recognizable microcosm both of the complex vision of creation and of providential

---

de Caen, 1989), pp. 87–98; Hebron, pp. 150–65; Barbara Kurtz, 'Allegory and/of Memory: Allegories of Amorous Imprisonment in Medieval Spanish Literature', *Medievalia et Humanistica*, n.s. 16 (1988), 133–51; Helaine Newstead, 'The Besieged Ladies in Arthurian Romance', *PMLA*, 63 (1948), 803–30; Wheatley, pp. 94–97, 103.

83   John Freccero, 'Medusa: The Letter and the Spirit', in *Dante: The Poetics of Conversion* (Cambridge, MA: Harvard University Press, 1986), pp. 119–35. See also Maria Cristina Meschiari, 'Da Medusa a Beatrice: il rituale del pentimento', *Italianistica*, 24 (1995), 9–27; Marco Veglia, 'Beatrice e Medusa dalle "petrose" alla *Commedia*', *Tenzone*, 11 (2010), 123–56; Carla Rossi, '*Inferno, IX*, 51–57: Medusa, lo sguardo che fa peccare', *Rassegna europea di letteratura italiana*, 35 (2010), 37–49.

84   The syncretism of the siege dovetails perfectly with the overall syncretic character of the episode of Dis. Dante's treatment of the siege also needs to be considered in light of another syncretic element, the classical and Christian *descensus ad inferos*, which has an important presence in *Inferno* VIII and IX. This problem too lies beyond the limits of the present study.

history that Dante endeavoured to present throughout the *Commedia*, as well as of the poem's plurilingual sense of 'comedy'. Like the siege, Dante's Christian epic cannot be restricted within a single 'manner of writing'. It ranges across languages, registers, *stili*, and the richness of the universe. By evoking the different traditions in which the siege was represented, Dante highlighted the weakness of a poetics that was based on the idea that reality could be neatly organized into distinct and self–sufficient literary categories.[85] Thanks to its ability to shift between *genera*, the siege, from the very heart of the medieval literary system, underscored the absurdity of such artificial reductionism. Only the *Commedia*, well aware of its limits, but also confident in its syncretic capacities, could hope, following in the wake of the Bible and of Scriptural *sermo humilis*, to lead humanity to salvation by revealing the organic complexity of God's creation. In establishing and legitimating the 'poema sacro's' (*Par.* XXV. 1) *novitas*, Dante not infrequently relied on cultural elements that his world deemed to be of especial significance. Scholars have long acknowledged the importance of the events outside Dis for defining the unique literary and religious character of the *Commedia*, not least because 'the entire episode focuses sharply on the nature of Dante's poem as a text' (Durling-Martinez, I, 150). What has not been adequately recognized, however, is that the basic, culturally determined reason why the episode is so vital is because it is a siege.[86]

---

85   See Franz Quadlbauer, *Die antike Theorie der 'Genera dicendi' im lateinischen Mittelalter* (Vienna: Hermann Böhlaus Nachf., 1962). See also Chapters 6–8.
86   Indeed, Virgil and the pilgrim's journey through Hell is consistently associated with sieges. Thus, their passage into each major infernal area is distinguished by allusions to cities and sieges: the shattered gate of Hell in *Inferno* III; the siege of Dis; Malebolge being compared to a fortification; and the giants guarding Cocytus being presented as city towers (*Inf.* XXXI. 19–21, 31–33, & 40–45).

CHAPTER 19

Scatology and Obscenity
in Dante

1. Reading Shit and Sex, Poorly

Dante scholars, good bourgeois that they are, have normally taken considerable care to avoid the mix of sex and excrement that is *Inferno* XVIII. Indeed, as far as I have been able to ascertain, it is the only canto of the *Commedia* that, until quite recently, had never inspired an overarching critical reading independent of the demands of the cycles of *lecturae Dantis*.[1] When 'obliged' by the conventions of the *lectura* to confront the sinful inhabitants of the first two bolgias, Dantists have

---

1   See Salvatore Accardo, 'Il canto XVIII dell'*Inferno*', in *Inferno: letture degli anni 1973–'76*, ed. by Silvio Zennaro (Rome: Bonacci, 1977), pp. 443–59; Marino Barchiesi, 'Arte del prologo e arte della transizione', *Studi danteschi*, 44 (1967), 115–207; Giulio Bertoni, 'Il canto dei lenoni e degli adulatori', *Archivum romanicum*, 12 (1928), 288–302; Lanfranco Caretti, 'Canto XVIII', in *Lectura Dantis Scaligera: Inferno* (Florence: Le Monnier, 1971), pp. 583–616; Raffaello Fornaciari, *Il canto XVIII dell'*'*Inferno*' (Florence: Sansoni, 1902); Fulco Tommaso Gallarati Scotti, 'Il canto XVIII dell'*Inferno*', in *Letture dantesche: Inferno*, ed. by Giovanni Getto (Florence: Sansoni, 1964), pp. 331–44; Gianni Grana, *Il canto XVIII dell'*'*Inferno*' (Turin: SEI, 1959); Georges Güntert, 'Canto XVIII', in *Lectura Dantis Turicensis: Inferno*, ed. by Georges Güntert and Michelangelo Picone (Florence: Cesati, 2000), pp. 243–57; Mario Martelli, *Canto XVIII dell'*'*Inferno*' (Naples: Loffredo, 1981); Edoardo Sanguineti, 'Il canto XVIII dell'*Inferno*', in *Nuove letture dantesche*, 8 vols (Florence: Le Monnier, 1968–76), II, 137–60; H. Wayne Storey, 'XVIII', in *Dante's 'Divine Comedy': Introductory Readings. I. 'Inferno'*, ed. by Tibor Wlassics (Charlottesville: University of Virginia Printing Service, 1990), pp. 235–46. During the last twenty or so years, the canto has begun to attract the interest of scholars independently from the needs of 'readings' of the *Inferno*; see Stefano Carrai, 'Attraversando le prime bolge: *Inferno* XVIII', *L'Alighieri*, 37 (2011), 97–110; Roberto Mercuri, 'Trame metalinguistiche nel canto XVIII dell'*Inferno*', *Annali dell'Istituto Universitario Orientale. Sezione Romanza*, 32 (1990), 201–11; Francesco Tateo, 'Il canto XVIII dell'*Inferno*', *L'Alighieri*, 12 (1998), 33–43; Pasquale Tuscano, *Dal vero al certo: indagini e letture dantesche* (Naples: Edizioni scientifiche italiane, 1989), pp. 39–52; Tiziano Zanato, 'Lettura del canto XVIII dell'*Inferno*', *Per leggere*, 6 (2004), 5–47, which is by far the best analysis of the canto that I have read. See also Zygmunt G. Barański, '*Inferno* XVIII', in *Lectura Dantis Bononiensis*, ed. by Emilio Pasquini and Carlo Galli, 14 vols (Bologna: Bononia University Press, 2011–), III, 81–110; Vittorio Celotto, 'Canto XVIII: la menzogna e il comico', in *Lectura Dantis Romana. Cento canti per cento anni. I. Inferno. 2. Canti XVIII–XXXIV*, ed. by Enrico Malato and Andrea Mazzucchi (Rome: Salerno, 2013), pp. 575–613; Paolo Chiesa, 'Canti XVIII–XIX–XX. Il comico e il politico', in *Esperimenti danteschi: Inferno 2008*, ed. by Simone Invernizzi (Genoa and Milan: Marietti, 2009), pp. 141–55; Anne C. Leone, '18: Women, War and Wisdom', in *Vertical Readings in Dante's 'Comedy'*, ed. by George Corbett and Heather Webb, 3 vols (Cambridge: Open Book Publisher, 2015–17), II, 151–71.

reacted with disdain, embarrassment, and discomfort, as if afraid of being tainted and overwhelmed by the 'alito' (107) emanating from the 'sterco | che da li uman privadi parea mosso' (113–14), seemingly forgetting that they were confronting words on a page rather than an actual open sewer. The critics' squeamishness and sense of propriety, which, as regards Italian scholars, is exacerbated by the fact that, scandalously, it is Dante, *poeta nazionale e cattolico*, who is talking about shit and sex, have, in my view, led to bad criticism.[2] Thus, Dantists have tended to concentrate on the panders and seducers, only summarily commenting on the flatterers, since the punishment of the former merely involves whips on bare flesh, and the sexual character of the bolgia is somewhat less explicit when compared to that of the second 'pouch' of the *adulatores*, where prostitutes move provocatively in 'merda' (116). At the same time, however, considerable attention has been paid to Thais in order to explain the implications of her misquoting Terence's Eunuchus — a concentration of critical effort that has yielded some excellent historically and philologically sensitive results.[3]

The pity is that the same approach, which is predicated on acknowledging *Inferno* XVIII's status as an early fourteenth-century literary text, has not been taken with the canto as a whole. Other parts of the *Commedia*, such as the descriptions of the naked soothsayers, of the mutilated Mohammed, and of the leader of the Malebranche who 'avea del cul fatto trombetta' (*Inf.* XXI. 139), which also include overt scatological references, have equally been treated with little critical and historical sensitivity. Scholars have generally judged Dante's treatment of the flatterers to be 'extreme', and have struggled to forge a critical framework and vocabulary able to accommodate, and hence explain and validate, the episode's presumed 'extremism'. To talk about *Inferno* XVIII's problematic subject-matter and language, they have used terms such as 'realistic', 'objective', and 'farcical', as well as definitions such as 'avantgarde poetics of vulgarity', 'infernal humour', and 'stylistic-poetic process of degradation'.[4] What is immediately striking about all these epithets and descriptions is their anachronism. Notions such as 'realism', 'farce', 'humour', 'vulgarity', 'avantgarde' either were not current in the Middle Ages or had quite specific culturally determined meanings that may or may not be relevant to the context of *Inferno* XVIII (for instance, given the deep ethical preoccupations with the dangers of laughter in much medieval moral writing, it is extremely unlikely that *risus* was something that Dante wanted to provoke with his evocation of the *adulatores*).

2   However, see the recent Leonardo Cappelletti, '"Uno sterco | che dagli uman' privadi parea mosso" (*Inf.* XVIII 113–14): adulatori dissenterici?', in *Letteratura italiana antica*, 18 (2017), 303–05.

3   See Marino Barchiesi, *Un tema classico e medievale: Gnatone e Taide* (Padua: Antenore, 1963). See also Chapter 7, pp. 289–92. In addition, much of the scholarly bibliography relevant to various aspects of this essay may be found in Chapter 7, as well as in Zygmunt Barański, *Language as Sin and Salvation: A 'lectura' of 'Inferno' XVIII* (Binghamton, NY: MRTS, 2014), which also develops several of the points sketched here.

4   Though I take all the terms and phrases just quoted either from *lecturae* cited in n. 1 or from standard commentaries to the *Commedia*, I purposely do not give references to specific studies. It is not my intention in this short chapter to criticize individual scholars. My aim is simply to highlight what I deem to be a general flaw in Dante criticism. I take a similarly broad perspective when I go on to assess what critics have said about *Inferno* XVIII's stylistic register and its ethical character.

Dantists reveal somewhat greater historical sensibility when they assert that canto XVIII, like much of Malebolge, is an exercise in the 'low style'. Nevertheless, assertions of this kind, at least as they have been couched to date, are at best unnecessarily reductive. On the one hand, they assume that the *genus humilis* is a monolithic form of expression, when, in fact, it embraced a large variety of different literary types, only some of which are directly relevant to Dante's treatment of the panders, seducers, and flatterers — a point to which I shall return in due course. On the other, from a medieval rhetorical point of view, it is quite incorrect to characterize *Inferno* XVIII as 'low'. It is undoubtedly the case that both the use of scatological language and the presence of a *meretrix* unambiguously indicate the *humilis* register. Indeed, by the fourteenth century, Thais had become a stock character of 'comedy' and, like Davus, served as a metonymy for the *stilus* as a whole. At the same time, however, Dante's prostitute leaves the scene shedding her 'low' associations. Virgil's presentation carefully translates her supposed exchange with Thraso into the vernacular, while maintaining the Latinate flavour of the original: a textbook instance of the 'tragic', 'high style':

> Taïde è, la puttana che rispuose
> al drudo suo quando disse 'Ho io grazie
> grandi apo te?': 'Anzi maravigliose!' (*Inf.* XVIII. 133–35)

Inferno XVIII stands as a classic example of Dante's syncretic plurilingual style, as many other elements in the canto clearly demonstrate, beginning with its opening line — 'Luogo è in inferno detto Malebolge' — which combines a Latin epic formula, *locus est*, with a 'low' vernacular proper noun, Malebolge, that has its roots in the *Roman de la rose* and in the *Fiore*. At the juncture in the *Commedia* when the poet has begun systematically to define and justify his new 'comedy' (the term *comedía* makes its first appearance towards the end of *Inferno* XVI), he is careful to underscore the differences between traditional forms of the *genus humilis* and his divinely inspired 'comic' poem. This, not some conventional exercise in the 'low' style, seems to have been Dante's primary aim in composing the cantos of Malebolge; and I shall have something further to say about this point too.[5]

Building on their belief regarding the canto's 'low' status, interpreters of *Inferno* XVIII also make the far from invalid claim that a close correlation exists between the sins depicted and Dante's formal and linguistic choices. Yet, the ways in which they have developed this insight reveal, once again, that lack of historical awareness which has dogged analyses of the canto. Thus, they frequently allude to the sinners' 'extreme moral degradation', which they see 'objectively' or 'realistically' reflected in the poet's recourse to the language of the gutter. However attractive such an interpretation may appear at first sight, it signally fails to explain why Dante felt it necessary and appropriate to bring together the erotic, the excremental, and the three particular sins of fraud with which he opens Malebolge. Similarly, the idea that the panders, seducers, and flatterers represent an excessive form of moral debasement which has to be treated in an appropriately excessive manner goes against the logic

---

5   On the 'low' register, comedy, and the *stili* in general, as well as their impact on Dante, see Chapters 6–8.

of the ethical structure of Dante's Hell, where much more grievous, and hence extreme, sins exist — sins that, nevertheless, are overwhelmingly depicted without the poet having to resort to the language of the 'uman privadi' (114). Somewhat naively, and revealing rather more of their own attitudes than Dante's, critics appear to assume that because the poet is presenting matters dealing with sex and deceit, he is inevitably dealing with a 'degraded' and 'degrading' subject-matter that he would have felt obliged to present through an abject vocabulary and imagery. Yet, when proffering this view, they provide no evidence based on medieval sources to substantiate their conviction. Equally reductively, and driven by their desire to establish the 'objectivity' of Dante's treatment, scholars equate the *genus humilis* both with what is generally deemed immoral and, more particularly, with matters relating to sex, thereby forgetting the Scriptural pedigree of the *sermo humilis*, the poet's predominantly 'tragic' treatment of the lustful in *Inferno* v, and the fact that, if the 'low' and immorality were as closely associated in the Middle Ages as they claim, then the whole of the first canticle should have been composed in this register.

What Dantists have failed to do when analysing *Inferno* xviii, as well as the other episodes to which I referred earlier, is explain the interaction between Dante's linguistic and ethical choices in terms of medieval culture, the only yardstick with which the 'objectivity' — or 'subjectivity' — of the poet's presentation can be measured. They have allowed the disgust they personally feel to control their reactions as exegetes, forgetful that their repugnance is an effect of Dante's verse, and that the poet, obviously through different rhetorical means, also wants us to feel disdain for the rest of Hell's inhabitants. Disgust, to put it plainly, is, ultimately, what we are always meant to feel when confronted by sin. It is not something peculiar to the *adulatores*. What is especially disconcerting, since such behaviour goes against the critic's age-old duty to interpret texts, is that Dantists have not only distanced themselves, quite reasonably, from the sinners of canto xviii, but also, quite unreasonably, from the words that Dante chose to evoke the three sets of fraudsters. As a result, problems of style, of rhetoric, of literary tradition, and of intellectual history have been reduced to mere emotive effects at the service of generalizing moral ends — excrement as a sign of the 'degradation' of the *adulatores* and of the need to shun their sin — a viewpoint that reveals almost nothing about flattery's specific medieval characteristics. In addition, such emotive effects have been presented in absolute terms, as if, in every epoch and in every culture, 'l'unghie merdose' (131) of a 'sozza e scapigliata fante' (130) inevitably lead to the same psychological and ethical reactions. To put it a bit differently: Dantists have read and assessed *Inferno* xviii without ever posing the question of the role played in the Middle Ages by obscenity and scatology, elements that — whether one likes it or not — fundamentally delimit the canto; and hence they have failed to address the issue of the status and the impact on the poet of the texts in which such matters were discussed and presented. As far as I am concerned, the real 'scandal' of *Inferno* xviii is to be found not in Dante's linguistic expressionism but in this critical failure.

2. Defining and Historicizing Shit and Sex

Before offering what I hope is a historically warranted hypothesis for the interplay between language, ethics, and literature in *Inferno* XVIII, it is incumbent on me to say something, however fleetingly, about the highly complex problem of the position of obscenity and scatology in medieval culture. Let me begin by dealing with some questions of terminology, normally an illuminating point of departure. So far in this chapter, I have been careful to distinguish between 'obscenity' and 'scatology', even though, in present-day usage, 'obscenity' is often used as a blanket term that conflates the scatological with the sexual. For reasons that should become clear, I prefer to keep the two notions separate, although, as in *Inferno* XVIII, there is no doubt that the erotic and the excremental have long overlapped in Western culture. Put simply: I employ 'obscenity' to designate base and/or explicit discourse relating to sex, while I utilize 'scatology' to mean base and/or explicit discourse relating to excretory functions. Although the term *obscenitas* was current in both classical and medieval Latin, it was very rarely used to refer to the sphere of the lewd. Instead, the Middle Ages employed a whole series of other terms, all of which were negatively marked, and unambiguously defined *obscena verba* as sinful. First and foremost among these was *turpiloquium* [lewd talk] though this was flanked, inter alia, by designations such as *scurrilitas* [scurrilous joking] and *multiloquium* [loquacity]. On the other hand, as far as I have been able to ascertain, no equivalent technical term to our 'scatology' was current in medieval culture. This terminological discrepancy is highly suggestive. The proliferation of references to obscenity highlights a deep moral concern with and anxiety over matters relating to sex, or, better, with talking about sexual topics. A similar ethical preoccupation would appear not to have affected the use of scatological language, given the lack of a tag with which to describe this type of discourse. However, this fact in itself should immediately counsel caution when, as has regularly happened, we feel impelled to treat the erotic and the scatological elements of *Inferno* XVIII as if they were somehow equivalent. Instead, it would seem rather more likely that, as far as the Middle Ages were concerned, the two spheres were viewed as distinct rather than as coterminous, even though they could both be present in the same text.[6]

6   Though much has been written, especially in recent years, on sexuality in medieval culture, rather too little of this work takes a philological or historically informed approach to the question or considers this in relation to what I term 'obscenity'. The problem of scatology has been largely ignored. Considerable research in both areas still needs to be undertaken. In preparing this essay and developing my research on scatology and obscenity in medieval culture and in Dante, I have found the following studies particularly useful: John W. Baldwin, *The Language of Sex: Five Voices from Northern France around 1200* (Chicago and London: University of Chicago Press, 1994); Pierre Bec, *Burlesque et obscénité chez les troubadours* (Paris: Stock, 1984); Howard R. Bloch, *The Scandal of the Fabliaux* (Chicago and London: University of Chicago Press, 1986); John Boswell, *Same-Sex Unions in Pre-Modern Europe* (New York: Villard Books, 1994); James A. Brundage, *Law, Sex, and Christian Society in Medieval Europe* (Chicago and London: University of Chicago Press, 1987); William Burgwinkle, *Sodomy, Masculinity, and Law in Medieval Literature: France and England, 1050–1230* (Cambridge: Cambridge University Press, 2004); Joan Cadden, *Meanings of Sex Difference in the Middle Ages* (Cambridge: Cambridge University Press, 1995); Edwin D. Craun, *Lies, Slander, and Obscenity in Medieval English Literature* (Cambridge: Cambridge University Press, 1997); Dyan

Indeed, evidence for such a sense of their distinctiveness is apparent in *Inferno* XVIII. It has not been previously noted that, in the canto, Dante actually treats the excremental and the erotic in quite different ways. In very schematic terms, the poet is prepared to talk openly about the former but not about the latter, a diversifying approach that interestingly correlates with the suggestions coming from medieval terminological practice relating to scatology and obscenity. Thus, Dante graphically evokes the disgusting environment of the second bolgia of the eighth circle by drawing on strikingly explicit locutions, namely, 'sterco' (113), 'uman privadi' (114), 'di merda lordo' (116), 'unghie merdose' (131), which he combines with harsh-sounding plebeian terms in rhyme position, such as: 'si nicchia' (103), 'scuffa' (104), 'stucca' (126). All these elements are then effectively moulded into highly vivid descriptions of the sinners and of their place of eternal punishment. In this respect, it is more than understandable why modern critics should have turned to a concept such as 'realism' in order to define Dante's technique for presenting the *adulatores*. Conversely, the poet is coy when describing the sinners' libidinous conduct. The most explicit word he utilizes is 'puttana' (133), though only after he has used the decidedly more neutral 'fante'.[7] In any case, the term fixes Thais's profession rather than evoking the erotic activities in which she may have indulged. Elsewhere in the canto, Dante is carefully constrained and, in general, formally elegant, relying on concision, periphrasis, antonomasia, and allusion — textbook instances of *reticentia* — to indicate transgressive sexual behaviour and attitudes. Thus, the sordid tale of a brother prostituting his sister is reduced to the stark phrase 'la sconcia novella' (57) and to the characterization of the pander-sibling, Venedico Caccianemico, as 'colui che la Ghisolabella | condusse a far la voglia del marchese' (55–56); 'femmine da conio' (66), on the other hand, is an expression whose precise meaning ultimately cannot even be pinned down, and hence whose sexual force is dissipated, since it can designate either 'women for sale' or 'women to deceive', just as Thais's movements, 'e or s'accoscia e ora e in piedi stante' (132), may have sexual connotations or may simply describe the discomfort of her otherworldly condition; finally, Jason's shameful treatment of Hypsipyle is cloaked in Dante's own 'ornate words':

> Con segni e con parole ornate
> Isifile inganno
> [...] Lasciolla [...] gravida, soletta. (*Inf.* XVIII. 91–92, 94)

Elliott, *Fallen Bodies: Pollution, Sexuality, and Demonology in the Middle Ages* (Philadelphia: University of Pennsylvania Press, 1999); Lucia Lazzerini, *Il testo trasgressivo* (Milan: Franco Angeli, 1988); Pierre Payer, *The Bridling of Desire: Views of Sex in the Latter Middle Ages* (Toronto: University of Toronto Press, 1993); Anthony Weir and James Jerman, *Images of Lust: Sexual Carvings in Medieval Churches* (London: Batsford, 1986); *Obscenity: Social Control and Artistic Creation in the European Middle Ages*, ed. by Jan Ziolkowski (Leiden: Brill: 1998); *Sex in the Middle Ages*, ed. by Joyce E. Salisbury (New York and London: Garland, 1991). See also Eduardo Crisafulli, 'Dante's "Shameless Whore": Sexual Imagery in Anglo-American Translations of the *Comedy*', *TRR: Traduction, Terminologie, Rédaction*, 14 (2015), 11–38.

7   Chiavacci Leonardi defines *fante* as a 'donna di condizione modesta, vile' (vol. I, p. 557) and provides compelling proof against the term having sexual connotations as many Dantists have claimed in Barbi's wake: Michele Barbi, *Con Dante e i suoi interpreti* (Florence: Sansoni, 1941), p. 321.

In formal terms, there is nothing here, as will be confirmed shortly, to cause either moral or stylistic offence.

It is clear that Dante deals with the scatological and the obscene as if the two belonged to different ethical, literary, and ideological traditions. In doing so, as my earlier discussion of the relevant terminology implies, the poet's practice accurately reflects medieval attitudes regarding the treatment of the erotic and the excremental. Ever since Paul's epistles, Christian moral writing had constantly warned against the dangers of *verba obscena*, of indulging in unbridled lewd speech. Basically, two major positions evolved on the question: a hardline viewpoint that had its origins in the apostle's letters, and a more flexible approach that drew on the authority of Saint Augustine. Paul categorically forbids all reference to *immunditia*: 'Fornicatio autem, et omnis immunditia, aut avaritia, nec nominetur in vobis, sicut decet sanctos: aut turpitudo, aut stultiloquium, aut scurrilitas, quae ad rem non pertinet' [Fornication however, and all uncleanliness, or greed, let it not be named among you, as befits saints, or filthiness, or foolish talk, or scurrilous joking, which are not befitting] (Ephesians 5: 3–4). The Bishop of Hippo, however, as he does elsewhere in his *œuvre*, proposes a rather more pragmatic solution to the problem:

> Quisquis ergo ad has litteras inpudicus accedit, culpam refugiat, non naturam; facta denotet suae turpitudinis, non verba nostrae necessitatis; in quibus mihi facillime pudicus et religiosus lector vel auditor ignoscit. [...] Legit enim haec sine offensione [...], sed in explicandis, quantum possumus, humanae generationis effectibus verba tamen, sicut ille [Paul; Romans 1: 26], obscena vitamus. (*De civ. Dei* XIV. 23)

> [Thus if anyone approaches with impure thoughts what I am writing, he should shun his own guilt, not nature; he should stigmatize the actions of his own depravity, not the words imposed on us by necessity. The chaste and religious reader or listener will easily forgive my use of such words [...]. He will read these without taking offence [...], yet, in explaining as best I can, the process of human generation, I must try, like him, to avoid obscene words.]

Augustine acknowledges the need to talk about erotic activity, not least because it is a fact of nature — the passage quoted refers to the thorny and much-debated problem regarding Eve and Adam's sexual relations before and after the Fall. At the same time, however, he stresses the obligation to shun salacious language, and places responsibility on the reader to avoid arousal when confronted by the author's carefully and modestly chosen words. Indeed, the rhetorical tradition supported the saint's standpoint by proscribing lewdly explicit language, while highlighting the usefulness of circumlocution when needing to address sexual matters.

Dante's practice in the *Commedia* conforms strictly to the Augustinian rhetorical position (though, if the poet is the author of the *Fiore* and of the sonnets to Forese, it is obvious that he was not consistent in this throughout his life). The passages already examined from *Inferno* XVIII bear testimony to the fact of Dante's adherence to Augustine's precepts, as does the rest of the poem. For instance, Dante employs textbook periphrases to allude to the male and female reproductive organs: 'lo membro che l'uom cela' (*Inf.* XXV. 116) and '[sangue perfetto] scende ov' è più bello | tacer che dire' (*Purg.* XXV. 43–44), while, when obliged to speak about human generation in *Purgatorio* XXV, he uses dryly scientific language, eliminating not just any reference to desire, but also to the human agents (37–60). After having criticized colleagues' work, it cheers me at this juncture to be able to correct my own earlier research — something that always gives me a salutary satisfaction since it reminds me how little I know and how provisional our discoveries inevitably are. Before completing the present study, I often asserted that a key feature of the plurilingual *Commedia* is its all-embracing character. I should now like to refine my earlier statement and declare that Dante was careful to establish a limit to his poem's linguistic and thematic encyclopaedism. In keeping with contemporary ethical attitudes, Dante considered overt references to the sexual as sinfully transgressive, and hence unsuitable for his 'sacrato poema' (*Par.* XXIII. 62). At the same time, as I hope is becoming manifest, and as I shall soon document further, obscenity and scatology have an important role to play in the *Commedia*'s metaliterary infrastructure. Indeed, this is especially evident when we explore Dante's treatment of the excremental.

The reason why both the poet and Christian culture, unlike their response to the sexual, were quite sanguine about the scatological is straightforward. The Bible makes significant recourse to it. For instance, there are over twenty instances of *stercus* [excrement] and related forms in the Vulgate.[8] These then inspired, especially through the commentary tradition, a massive use of the term in the writings of both the Fathers and the Doctors. Searching the Corpus Christianorum database, I was overwhelmed by around a thousand references. Drawing on scatological language was part of religious writing, as a cursory glance at the works of Iacopone da Todi, for instance, immediately confirms. This fact is immensely important when considering the use Dante makes of excremental terminology in the *Commedia*: it constitutes yet another sign that he is doing God's work, that he is a *scriba Dei*. It also confirms how inadequate are those interpretations that banally trivialize Dante's 'merda' as merely an expression of disgust. On the other hand, secular, classically grounded literary-critical opinion was rather more wary of scatology. For instance, it was accepted that authors writing in the 'low style' could mention the breaking of wind, though it does not appear that they were granted license to refer to other excretory functions.[9] In this context, Dante's farting devil cannot but take on metaliterary trappings. Malacoda appears in a group of cantos that, as I have already observed, define Dante's experimental *comedía* in opposition to established 'comic' practices. Hence, the tension between Thais's 'shit-filled nails' and the devil's trumpeting 'ass' can be seen to indicate the poet's rejection of traditional Terentian 'low' poetics in favour of the more flexible conventions of biblical *sermo humilis*. Indeed, as some of the fourteenth-century Dante commentators were quick to recognize, it is precisely from Scripture that the poet took the idea of bringing together prostitution and excrement: 'omnis mulier, quae est fornicaria, quasi

8   See Deuteronomy 28: 27; Judges 3: 22; I Kings 2: 8; IV Kings 6: 25, 9: 37, 18: 27; Tobias 2: 11; Psalms 82: 11, 112: 7; Ecclesiastes 9: 10, 22: 2; Isaiah 5: 25, 36: 12; Jeremiah 9: 22; Lamentations 4: 5; Joel 1: 17; Sophonias 1: 17; Malachi 2: 62; I Maccabees 2: 62; Luke 13: 8; Philemon 3: 8.
9   Claudia Villa, La 'Lectura Terentii' (Padua: Antenore, 1984), pp. 89–90.

stercus in via conculcabitur' [every woman, who is promiscuous, will be trodden in the road as if she were excrement] (Ecclesiastes 9: 10).[10]

As ought to be apparent from the variety of texts already alluded to during the course of this short study, scatology and sex found space in a large number of different medieval works. The number and diversity of these is, in fact, remarkable. They include the Bible, Scriptural commentary, religious verse, sermons, confessional manuals, treatises on sins, mystical literature, medical and scientific texts, encyclopaedias, legal tracts, works of rhetoric, poetics, and criticism, and a variety of 'low' literary genres. Any half-thorough investigation of Dante's attitudes toward obscenity and scatology must engage with all of these — a task beyond the remit of this rudimentary sketch. But I should like to close by briefly considering the poet's relationship to a couple of these classes of texts, specifically the 'low' literary forms and the treatises on sins.

There were several vernacular discrete *humilis* forms — it is enough to think of the *fabliaux* and the *fatrasies* — that presented the sexual, often in association with the excremental, in an explicit manner. It is thus safe to assume that Dante was intent on ensuring that his 'divine comedy' should not be confused with traditions that both he and the religious-cum-literary culture of his day deemed immoral and lacking in merit as literature. Confirmation of this orientation comes, once again, from the devils of barratry. As Michelangelo Picone demonstrated, the Malebranche can be interpreted as representing medieval jongleurs, those *scurrae* whose activities were closely associated with *scurrilitas*.[11] Though the majority of their largely orally performed works have not come down to us, we can arrive at a good sense of the nature of these from legal and religious texts describing the jongleurs' performances. Indecency, played for laughs and accompanied by obscene gesturing, appears to have been commonplace. Dante's condemnation of the devils' antics thus serves also to pass judgment on the *scurrae*, authors who talked openly about sex purely to amuse and for material gain. Their transgressive works were without moral *utilitas*, their sole aim was *delectatio*, entertainment based on laughter — a fact that underscores that *risus* could not have been one of *Inferno* XVIII's goals. On the other hand, the *Commedia*, too, is a text that transgresses established literary norms, but it does this for divinely inspired ethical ends and with a proper awareness — based, as we have seen, on the *sermo humilis* — of what should or should not be expressed. In defining his poem's plurilingual 'comic' qualities, Dante ensured that the *Commedia* would not be confused either with conventional Terentian forms of the 'low' or with the 'style's' most extreme forms. He rejected both the constraints of the *genera dicendi* and the false freedom of *turpiloquium*.

The question of the proper and improper use of language lies at the heart of *Inferno* XVIII; and it is high time that I returned to my point of departure and said something about the medieval bases of Dante's treatment of the first two groups of

---

10   See especially Pietro Alighieri, *Il 'Commentarium' nelle redazioni ashburnhamiana e ottoboniana*, ed. by Roberto Della Vedova and Maria Teresa Silvotti (Florence: Olschki, 1978), pp. 290–91.
11   See Michelangelo Picone, 'Canto XXI', in *Lectura Dantis Turicensis. Inferno*, ed. by Georges Güntert and Michelangelo Picone (Florence: Cesati, 2000), pp. 291–304.

the fraudulent. *Inferno* XVIII, as is the case with Malebolge as a whole, to which the canto, revealingly, stands as a *prooemium*, is heavily dependent on a branch of the treatises on sins, namely, that which dealt with the so-called Sins of the Tongue, which, beginning in the twelfth century, had become increasingly popular and influential.[12] Obviously, the linguistic and semiotic character of fraud has long been recognized by Dantists. Nevertheless, the Sins of the Tongue provide a historically appropriate framework within which to consider the poet's presentation of the eighth circle of Hell. Indeed, both the unambiguously linguistic character of the panders', seducers', and flatterers' wrongdoing and their association with sinful sexuality were almost certainly dictated by the widely recognized ties that connected such sinners and lasciviousness to the *peccata linguae*. Dante wanted to ensure that his cultural signals were clearly received. Starting with the canto's opening image of the fortified castle (7–18), many elements in *Inferno* XVIII can also best be explained in terms of the conventions of the Sins of the Tongue. It was a commonplace of the tradition that good people 'guarded' their tongues: 'Qui custodit os suum: custodit animam suam' [Whoever guards his mouth, guards his soul] (Proverbs 3: 31) and:

> Hance bestiam [the tongue] inclusit deus in palato
> uallauit muro dencium
> clausit hostiis labiorum et obserauit seribus preceptorum ut bene teneretur et custodiretur.[13]

> [God shut this beast in the palate; he surrounded it with a wall of teeth; he closed it with the gates of the lips; and he bolted it with the bars of precepts so that it should be well defended and guarded.]

Dante's allusion to city walls, therefore, provides a first indication of the general *contrapasso* governing the otherworldly condition of the inhabitants of Malebolge. As an eternal reminder of their sinfulness, those who in life had failed to 'guard' their tongues are punished by being 'enclosed', not within city walls, since, metaphorically speaking, they had rejected their protection when alive, but, tellingly, within 'fossi' (17) lying outside the 'mura' (10). More significant, the Sins of the Tongue provide the punishments for both *Inferno* XVIII's sets of sinners. The image of language as a whip is a memorable topos originating in Job (5: 21), a book important, as we shall soon see, in the context of *Inferno* XVIII, and which, together with the Psalms, the Sapiential Books, Paul's letters, and the Epistle of James, served as the key Scriptural *auctoritates* in assessments of verbal sins. Equally, the *contrapasso* of the *adulatores* indelibly marks them, in light of the treatise *Duplex est abstinentia, detestabilis et commendabilis*, as archetypal linguistic sinners:

> Loquens debet attendere quid dicat, quomodo dicat, cui dicat et quando dicat. Quid debet homo loqui docetur I Pe. 4 [11], *Si quis loquitur quasi sermones dei,*

---

12   See Carla Casagrande and Silvana Vecchio, *I peccati della lingua* (Rome: Istituto della Enciclopedia Italiana, 1987); Craun. See also Katie L. Walter, *Middle English Mouths: Late Medieval Medical, Religious and Literary Traditions* (Cambridge: Cambridge University Press, 2018).

13   Étienne de Bourbon, *Tractatus de diversis materiis predicabilibus*, Oriel College, Oxford, MS. 68, fols 15r–434v (fol. 153v).

et Eph. 4 [29], *Omnis senno malus non procedat ex ore uestro: sed qui bonus est ad edificacionem fidei ut det gratiam audientibus.* Qui enim non timet coinquinare linguam suam plus quam alia membra pocius porcus uidetur quam homo. Porcus enim in cito ponit rostrum suum in luto sicut pedem. Item porcus semper habet os apertum ad stercora et non ad flores, sic mali ad stercora peccatorum non ad flores uirtutum [...]. De ore latrini et sepulcri non egreditur nisi fetor.[14]

[A speaker should pay attention to what he ought to say, to how he should speak, to whom and when he should speak. What a person should say is taught in I Peter 4: *If anyone speaks let him do it as if with the words of God,* and Eph. 4: *Allow no evil speech to come forth from your mouth, but that which is beneficial for the edification of faith so that it may grant grace to those who hear it.* Whoever is not afraid of fouling his tongue more than his other members seems to be a pig rather than a human being. For a pig places its snout in dirt as readily as its foot. Equally a pig always has its mouth open to excrement and not to flowers, just like evil people keep their mouths open to the excrement of sins and not to the flowers of virtues [...]. Nothing comes out of the mouth of a toilet or a sepulchre except for stench.]

The *contrapassi* of the panders, seducers, and flatterers are not the result, as Dantists have for too long maintained, of the poet's disgust for their sexual deceptions and practices, but are clear and rigorous — one might even be tempted to say 'objective' — moral assertions of the ways in which their sinfulness had perverted the divine gift of speech.

Dante-pilgrim and Dante-poet stand in direct opposition to such debasers of language. Discussions of the *peccata linguae* also dealt with those who employ their tongues virtuously, namely, the prudent and patient person: 'prudens est qui futura prouidet, et premia et tormenta; et talis non murmurat de flagello. Libenter enim virgam tolerat qui a gladio pene eterne eum conseruat. Patienter eciam sustinet ab eo flagellari a quo celestem hereditatem expectat' [the prudent person discerns future things, both rewards and sufferings; and such a person does not grumble about the whip. For he freely bears the rod who saves himself from the sword of eternal punishment. And furthermore he patiently endures being scourged by him from whom he expects the heavenly inheritance].[15] A key trait of the *prudens* is the way he uses language in a manner pleasing to God:

Prudens est qui loquitur quando loquendum est. Unde ecclus xx [7], *Homo sapiens tacebit vsque ad tempus.* Prudentior est qui loquitur talia qualia debet loqui, vt qui loquitur verba pura a falsitate et a proximi nocumento et a contumelia dei. Unde prouerbiorum xv [26], *Sermo purus pulcerrimus est.* Prudentissimus vero est ille qui modum seruat in verbis qui scilicet dulciter loquitur absque clamore et asperitate quod non parum est vtile [...] non potest esse sermonis moderacio absque cordis moderacio. (Peraldus, *Summa de vitiis*, F1v)

[The prudent person speaks when he ought to speak. Thus Ecclus. 20: *The wise man will be silent until the time is right.* More prudent is the person who says those things which he ought to say, like him who speaks words pure from falsehood

14   Oxford, Bodleian Library, MS. 185, fols 25v–114v (fol. 70v).
15   Gulielmus Peraldus, *Summa de vitiis* (Cologne: Quentell, 1479), G1r.

and from injury to others and from abuse of God. Thus Proverbs 15: *Pure speech is most beautiful*. Most prudent in fact is the person who maintains a measure in words, namely, who speaks sweetly and without noise and harshness what is rather useful [...] there can be no moderation in speech without moderation of the heart.]

The similarities between the torments endured by the *prudens* and those suffered by the panders and seducers are self-evident, though the moral context is, naturally, completely different. The *adulatores*, too, are the negative anti-type of this prudent person, since Job, who was presented as the supreme example of prudence and patience, was traditionally depicted as *in stercore sedens* [sitting in excrement]. As often occurs elsewhere in Dante's Hell, the punishment of the sinners grotesquely parodies the ethically upright condition that they should have embraced in life. The complexity of the poet's vision in *Inferno* XVIII is striking. Via the reference to the pilgrim's 'chiara favella' (53), the poet establishes a firm link between his own language and the *sermo purus* of the *prudens*, both of which stand in obvious contrast to Jason's lying 'parole ornate' (91). In the *Commedia*, in order effectively to communicate his divine message, Dante rejects the standard rhetorical conventions of the *genera dicendi*, not least because, as Jason reveals, 'tragic' elegance is no guarantee of moral rectitude. Instead, like the other *scribae Dei*, he is prepared to approach language ethically and, hence, flexibly — a stance that permits him to have recourse, when appropriate, even to the language of the 'human privies'. By highlighting the poem's relationship to both scatology and obscenity, *Inferno* XVIII and the other early cantos of Malebolge define its divinely ordained *humilis* parameters. Rather than being something marginal which needs to be dismissed swiftly to avoid embarrassment, the sexual and the excremental not only confirm the *Commedia*'s Scriptural character, though they do this in conjunction with many other elements performing a similar function, but also, and in this respect quite uniquely, reveal its linguistic and thematic limits.

LIST OF PUBLICATIONS

excluding reviews

Books

'Chiosar con altro testo': leggere Dante nel Trecento (Florence: Cadmo, 2001)
Dante e i segni: saggi per una storia intellettuale di Dante (Naples: Liguori, 2000)
'Luce nuova, sole nuovo': saggi sul rinnovamento culturale in Dante (Turin: Scriptorium, 1996)

Edited Books

(With Theodore J. Cachey Jr and Luca Lombardo) *Dante e la cultura fiorentina tra Bono Giamboni e Brunetto Latini* (Rome: Salerno, 2019)

(With Simon Gilson) *The Cambridge Companion to Dante's 'Commedia'* (Cambridge: Cambridge University Press, 2019)

(With Andreas Kablitz and Ülar Ploom) *'I luoghi nostri': Dante's Natural and Cultural Spaces* (Tallinn: TLU Press, 2015)

(With Lino Pertile) *Dante in Context* (Cambridge: Cambridge University Press, 2015)

(With Theodore J. Cachey Jr, Teresa Kennedy, and Walter Stephens), *'Tra amici': Essays in Honor of Giuseppe Mazzotta*, supplement to *MLN*, 127:1 (2012)

(With Martin McLaughlin) *Dante the Lyric and Ethical Poet* (Leeds: Legenda, 2010)

(With Theodore J. Cachey Jr) *Petrarch and Dante: Anti-Dantism, Metaphysics, Tradition* (Notre Dame, IN: University of Notre Dame Press, 2009)

(With Martin McLaughlin) *Italy's Three Crowns: Moments in the Reception of Dante, Petrarch, and Boccaccio* (Oxford: Bodleian Library, University of Oxford, 2007)

(With Rebecca West) *Cambridge Companion to Modern Italian Culture* (Cambridge: Cambridge University Press, 2001)

Pasolini Old and New: Surveys and Studies (Dublin: Four Courts Press, 1999)

(With Lino Pertile) *In amicizia: Essays in Honour of Giulio Lepschy*, special supplement to *The Italianist*, 17 (1997)

(With Gino Bedani, Anna Laura Lepschy, and Brian Richardson) *Sguardi sull'Italia: Miscellanea dedicata a Franceco Villari* (Leeds: Society for Italian Studies, 1997)

Seminario Dantesco Internazionale/International Dante Seminar 1 (Florence: Le Lettere, 1997)

(With Patrick Boyde) *The 'Fiore' in Context: Dante, France, Tuscany* (Notre Dame, IN, and London: University of Notre Dame Press, 1997)

'Libri poetarum in quattuor species dividuntur': Essays on Dante and 'Genre', special supplement 2 to *The Italianist*, 15 (1995)

(With Patrick Boyde and Lino Pertile) *Lettura del 'Fiore'* (Ravenna: Longo, 1993)

(With Lino Pertile) *The New Italian Novel* (Edinburgh: Edinburgh University Press, 1993)

(With Shirley W. Vinall) *Women and Italy: Essays on Gender, Culture and History* (London: Macmillan, 1991)

(With Robert Lumley) *Culture and Conflict in Postwar Italy: Essays on Mass and Popular Culture* (London: Macmillan, 1990)

(With John R. Short) *Developing Contemporary Marxism* (London: Macmillan, 1985)

Published Lecture

Language as Sin and Salvation: A 'lectura' of 'Inferno' XVIII (Binghamton: MRTS, 2014)

Articles

'The Classics', in *The Oxford Handbook of Dante*, ed. by Manuele Gragnolati and others (Oxford: Oxford University Press, forthcoming)

'*Paradiso* I', in *Lectura Dantis Bononiensis*, ed. by Emilio Pasquini and Carlo Galli, 14 vols (Bologna: Bononia University Press, 2011–), x (forthcoming)

'L'esperienza di Dio nella *Commedia*', in *'Vedi lo sol che 'n fronte ti riluce': la vista e gli altri sensi in Dante e nella ricezione artistico-letteraria delle sue opere*, ed. by Maria Maślanka-Soro (Florence: Aracne, forthcoming)

'The Tale of Forese da Rabatta and Giotto (VI. 5)', in *The 'Decameron' Sixth Day in Perspective*, ed. by David Lummus (Toronto: University of Toronto Press, forthcoming)

'*Inferno* I: "In principio operis"', in *Lectura Dantis Andreapolitana*, ed. by Claudia Rossignoli and Robert Wilson (Notre Dame, IN: University of Notre Dame Press, forthcoming)

'*Commedia*: Genesis, Dating, and Dante's "Other Works"', in *The Cambridge Companion to Dante's 'Commedia'*, ed. by Zygmunt G. Barański & Simon Gilson (Cambridge: Cambridge University Press, 2019), pp. 208–28

'Dottrina degli affetti e teologia: la rappresentazione della beatitudine in *Paradiso*', in *Dante poeta cristiano e la cultura religiosa medievale: in ricordo di Anna Maria Chiavacci Leonardi*, ed. by Giuseppe Ledda (Ravenna: Centro Dantesco dei Frati Minori Conventuali, 2019), pp. 259–312

'"Oh come è grande la mia impresa" (*Conv.* IV. vii. 4): Notes towards Defining the *Convivio*', in *Dante's 'Convivio', or, How to Restart Writing in Exile*, ed. by Franziska Meier (Bern: Peter Lang, 2018), pp. 9–26

'"Io mi rivolgo indietro a ciascun passo" (*Rvf* 15. 1): Petrarch, the *fabula* of Eurydice and Orpheus, and the Structure of the Canzoniere', in *Cultural Reception, Translation and Transformation from Medieval to Modern Italy: Essays in Honour of Martin McLaughlin*, ed. by Guido Bonsaver, Brian Richardson, and Giuseppe Stellardi (London: Legenda, 2017), pp. 1–24

'On Dante's Trail', *Italian Studies*, 72 (2017), 1–15

'Textual Transmission', in *Dante in Context*, ed. by Zygmunt G. Barański and Lino Pertile (Cambridge: Cambridge University Press, 2015), pp. 509–17

'Early Reception: 1290–1481', in *Dante in Context*, ed. by Zygmunt G. Barański and Lino Pertile (Cambridge: Cambridge University Press, 2015), pp. 518–37

'The *Triumphi*', in *The Cambridge Companion to Petrarch*, ed. by Albert R. Ascoli and Unn Falkeid (Cambridge: Cambridge University Press, 2015), pp. 74–84

'*Purgatorio* I', in *Lectura Dantis Bononiensis*, ed. by Emilio Pasquini and Carlo Galli, 14 vols (Bologna: Bononia University Press, 2011–), v (2015), 105–33

'"With Such Vigilance! With Such Effort!": Studying Dante "Subjectively"', *Italian Culture*, 33 (2015), 55–69

'"Con quanta vigilanza! Con quanto impegno!": studiare Dante "soggettivamente"', in *Dante e la critica letteraria: una riflessione epistemologica*, ed. by Thomas Klinkert and Alice Malzacher (Freiburg: Rombach Verlag, 2015), pp. 75–98

'Sulla formazione intellettuale di Dante: alcuni problemi di definizione', *Studi e problemi di critica testuale*, 90:1 (2015), 31–54

'"Without any Violence": *Inferno* IX, *Purgatorio* IX, *Paradiso* IX', in *Vertical Readings in Dante's 'Comedy'*, ed. by George Corbett and Heather Webb, 3 vols (Cambridge: Open Book Publishers, 2015–17), I, 181–202

'Studying the Spaces of Dante's Intellectual Formation: Some Problems of Definition', in '*I luoghi nostri': Dante's Natural and Cultural Spaces*, ed. by Zygmunt G. Barański and others (Tallinn: TLU Press, 2015), pp. 257–82

'Reading the *Commedia*'s 1xs "Vertically": From Addresses to the Reader to the *crucesignati* and the *Ecloga Theoduli*', *L'Alighieri*, 44 (2014), 5–35

'*Inferno* XVIII', in *Lectura Dantis Bononiensis*, ed. by Emilio Pasquini and Carlo Galli, 14 vols (Bologna: Bononia University Press, 2011–), III (2014), 81–110

'The Temptations of a Heterodox Dante', in *Dante and Heterodoxy: The Temptation of Radical Thought in the Thirteenth Century*, ed. by Maria Luisa Ardizzone (Newcastle upon Tyne: Cambridge Scholars Publishing, 2014), pp. 164–96

'Dante and Doctrine (and Theology)', in *Reviewing Dante's Theology*, ed. by Claire Honess and Matthew Treherne, 2 vols (Bern: Peter Lang, 2013), I, 1–63

'(Un)Orthodox Dante', in *Reviewing Dante's Theology*, ed. by Claire Honess and Matthew Treherne, 2 vols (Berne: Peter Lang, 2013), II, 253–330

'"E cominciare stormo": Notes on Dante's Sieges', in '*Legato con amore in un volume': Essays in Honour of John A. Scott*, ed. by John Kinder and Diana Glenn (Florence: Olschki, 2013), pp. 175–203

'*Magister satiricus*: Preliminary Notes on Dante, Horace and the Middle Ages', in *Language and Style in Dante*, ed. by John C. Barnes and Michelangelo Zaccarello (Dublin: Four Courts Press, 2013), pp. 13–61

'"Lascio cotale trattato ad altro chiosatore": Form, Literature, and Exegesis in Dante's *Vita nova*', in *Dantean Dialogues: Engaging with the Legacy of Amilcare Iannucci*, ed. by Maggie Kilgour and Elena Lombardi (Toronto: University of Toronto Press, 2013), pp. 1–40

'*Inferno* IX', in *Lectura Dantis Bononiensis*, ed. by Emilio Pasquini and Carlo Galli, 14 vols (Bologna: Bononia University Press, 2011–), II (2012), 100–26

'*Inferno* I', in *Lectura Dantis Bononiensis*, ed. by Emilio Pasquini and Carlo Galli, 14 vols (Bologna: Bononia University Press, 2011–), I (2011), 11–40

'Dante poeta e *lector*: "poesia" e "riflessione tecnica" (con divagazioni sulla *Vita nova*)', in *Dante oggi*, vol. I, ed. by Roberto Antonelli, Annalisa Landolfi, and Adriana Punzi, special issue of *Critica del testo*, 14:1 (2011), 81–110

'The Roots of Dante's Plurilingualism: "Hybridity" and Language in the *Vita nova*', in *Dante's Plurilingualism, Authority, Knowledge, Subjectivity*, ed. by Sara Fortuna, Manuele Gragnolati, and Jürgen Trabant (London: Legenda, 2010), pp. 98–121

'Appunti su Guglielmo Maramauro, sull'*auctoritas* e sulla "lettura" di Dante nel Trecento', in '*Accessus ad Auctores': Studies in Honor of Christopher Kleinhenz*, ed. by Fabian Alfie and Andrea Dini (Tempe: ACMRS, 2011), pp. 223–37

'"Valentissimo poeta e correggitore de' poeti": A First Note on Horace and the *Vita nova*', in *Letteratura e filologia tra Svizzera e Italia: miscellanea di studi in onore di Guglielmo Gorni*, ed. by Maria Antonietta Terzoli, Alberto Asor Rosa, and Giorgio Inglese, 3 vols (Rome: Edizioni di Storia e Letteratura, 2010), I, 3–17

'Dante Alighieri', in *The Classical Tradition*, ed. by Anthony Grafton, Glenn W. Most, and Salvatore Settis (Harvard: Harvard University Press, 2010), pp. 250–52

'La canzone "anomola" di Dante: *Io sento sì d'Amor la gran possanza*', in Dante Alighieri, *Le quindici canzoni: lette da diversi. I, 1–7* (Lecce: Pensa Multimedia, 2009), pp. 145–211

'Petrarch, Dante, Cavalcanti', in *Petrarch and Dante*, ed. by Zygmunt G. Barański and Theodore J. Cachey Jr (Notre Dame, IN: University of Notre Dame Press, 2009), pp. 50–113

'Guido Cavalcanti tra le *cruces* di *Inferno* IX–XI, ovvero Dante e la storia della ragione', in *Versi controversi: letture dantesche*, ed. by Domenico Cofano and Sebastiano Valerio (Foggia: Edizioni del Rosone, 2008), pp. 39–112

'Boccaccio and Epicurus', in *Caro Vitto: Essays in Memory of Vittore Branca*, ed. by Jill Kraye and Anna Laura Lepschy, special supplement to *The Italianist*, 27 (2007), 10–27

'Petrarca, Dante, Cavalcanti: la formazione dell'*auctoritas* volgare', *Deutsches Dante-Jahrbuch*, 82 (2007), 119–45

'"Piangendo" e "cantando" con Orfeo (e con Dante): strutture emotive e strutture poetiche in *Rerum vulgarium fragmenta* 281–90', in *Il Canzoniere: lettura micro e macrotestuale*, ed. by Michelangelo Picone (Ravenna: Longo, 2007), pp. 617–40

'"Honour the Loftiest Poet"': Dante's Reception in Fourteenth-century Italy', in *Italy's Three Crowns: Moments in the Reception of Dante, Petrarch, and Boccaccio*, ed. by Zygmunt G. Barański and Martin McLaughlin (Oxford: Bodleian Library, University of Oxford, 2007), pp. 9–22

'The Ethics of Ignorance: Petrarch's Epicurus and Averroes and the Structures of the *De sui ipsius et multorum ignorantia*', in *Petrarch in Britain: Interpretations, Appropriations, Translations*, ed. by Martin McLaughlin and Letizia Panizza (London: British Academy, 2007), pp. 39–59

'Dante e Orazio medievale', *Letteratura italiana antica*, 7 (2006), 187–221

'"Alquanto tenea della oppinione degli Epicuri": The *auctoritas* of Boccaccio's Cavalcanti (and Dante)', in *Mittelalterliche Novellistik im europaischen Kontext*, ed. by Mark Chinca, Timo Reuvekamp-Felber, and Christopher Young (Berlin: Erich Schmidt Verlag, 2006), pp. 280–325

'Dante Alighieri: From Experimentation to Canonization', in *Visible Language: Dante in Text and Image. An Exhibition in Cambridge University Library, 17 January–1 July 2006* (Cambridge: Cambridge University Library, 2006), pp. 3–4

'Dante Commentaries', in *Medieval Italy: An Encyclopedia*, ed. by Christopher Kleinhenz, 2 vols (New York and London: Routledge, 2004), I, 286–90

'Dante i kategorie literatury', *Pamiętnik Literacki*, 95 (2004), 43–72

'"Per similitudine di abito scientifico": Dante, Cavalcanti, and the Sources of Medieval "Philosophical" Poetry', in *Literature and Science in Italian Culture: From Dante to Calvino. A Festschrift in Honour of Patrick Boyde*, ed. by Pierpaolo Antonello and Simon Gilson (London: Legenda, 2004), pp. 14–52

'Il *Convivio* e la poesia: problemi di definizione', in *Lectura Dantis Federiciana*, ed. by Francesco Tateo and Daniele M. Pegorari (Bari: Palomar, 2004), pp. 9–64

'Guido Cavalcanti and his First Readers', in *Guido Cavalcanti*, ed. by Maria Luisa Ardizzone (Fiesole: Cesati, 2003), pp. 149–75

'Guido Cavalcanti *auctoritas*', in *'Donna me prega': Guido Cavalcanti e le origini della poesia europea*, ed. by Rossend Arqués (Alessandria: Edizioni dell'Orso, 2003), pp. 1–18

'Scatology and Obscenity in Dante', in *Dante For the New Millennium*, ed. by Teodolinda Barolini and H. Wayne Storey (New York: Fordham University Press, 2003), pp. 259–73

'Dante Alighieri: Experimentation and (Self-)Exegesis', in *The Cambridge History of Literary Criticism. II. The Middle Ages*, ed. by Alastair J. Minnis and Ian Johnson (Cambridge: Cambridge University Press, 2005), pp. 561–82

'The Epistle to Cangrande', in *The Cambridge History of Literary Criticism. II. The Middle Ages*, ed. by Alastair J. Minnis and Ian Johnson (Cambridge: Cambridge University Press, 2005), pp. 583–89

'Un monumento a Dante', *El Pais*, 15 November 2002

'Canto XXII', in *Lectura Dantis Turicensis: Paradiso*, ed. by Georges Güntert and Michelangelo Picone (Florence: Cesati, 2002), pp. 339–62

'Le riviste di italianistica britanniche', in *Riviste d'italianistica nel mondo*, ed. by Marco Santoro (Pisa and Rome: Istituti Editoriali e Poligrafici Internazionali, 2002), pp. 243–52

Entries on 'Ars dictaminis', 'Cronica di Anonimo romano', 'Cursus', 'De vulgari eloquentia', 'Fiore', 'Horace', 'Italy and the Middle Ages', 'Literary Theory (–1400)', 'E. G. Parodi', 'Plurilinguismo', 'Questio de aqua et terra', 'A. M. Ripellino', 'Ritmo laurenziano', 'Strumenti *critici*', 'S. Vassalli', 'Translations' (with Giulio Lepschy), in *The Oxford Companion to Italian Literature*, ed. by Peter Hainsworth and David Robey (Oxford: Oxford University Press, 2002), pp. 32–33, 162–63, 187–88, 230, 295, 339–40, 381–84, 438, 469, 493, 516–17, 570, 594–95, 612–13

'Three Notes on Dante and Horace', in *Dante: Current Trends in Dante Studies*, ed. by Claire E. Honess, special issue of *Reading Medieval Studies*, 27 (2001), 5–37

'*Purgatorio* XXV', in *Lectura Dantis Turicensis: Purgatorio*, ed. by Georges Güntert and Michelangelo Picone (Florence: Cesati, 2001), pp. 389–406

'Lo studio delle fonti e l'esegesi medievale del testo della *Commedia*', in *Bilanci e prospettive degli studi danteschi*, ed. by Enrico Malato, 2 vols (Rome: Salerno, 2001), I, 569–600

'Introducing Modern Italian Culture', in *Cambridge Companion to Modern Italian Culture*, ed. by Zygmunt G. Barański and Rebecca West (Cambridge: Cambridge University Press, 2001), pp. 1–15

'Cantica', 'Canto', 'Comedy (genre)', '*Commedia*: Title and Form', '*Detto d'Amore*', '*Dolce stil novo*', in *The Dante Encyclopedia*, ed. by Richard Lansing (New York and London: Garland, 2000), pp. 137–38, 139–40, 180–81, 184–88, 299–300, 308–11

' "Il poema sacro [...] che m'ha fatto per molti anni macro": Notes on the Genesis of Dante's *Commedia*', in *La Lotta con Proteo: Essays in Memory of Glauco Cambon*, ed. by Joseph Francese (Rome: Bordighera, 2000), pp. 58–81

'*Inferno* XI', in *Lectura Dantis Turicensis: Inferno*, ed. by Georges Güntert and Michelangelo Picone (Florence: Cesati, 2000), pp. 151–64

'*Inferno* XIX', in *Lectura Dantis Turicensis: Inferno*, ed. by Georges Güntert and Michelangelo Picone (Florence: Cesati, 2000), pp. 259–75

'Notes on Dante and the Myth of Orpheus', in *Dante: mito e poesia. Atti del secondo Seminario Dantesco Internazionale*, ed. by Michelangelo Picone and Tatiana Crivelli (Florence: Cesati, 1999), pp. 133–62

'The Importance of Being Pier Paolo Pasolini', in *Pasolini Old and New: Surveys and Studies*, ed. by Zygmunt G. Barański (Dublin: Four Courts Press, 1999), pp. 13–40

'Pasolini, Friuli, Rome (1950–51): Philological and Historical Notes', in *Pasolini Old and New: Surveys and Studies*, ed. by Zygmunt G. Barański (Dublin: Four Courts Press, 1999), pp. 253–80

'The Texts of *Il Vangelo secondo Matteo*', in *Pasolini Old and New: Surveys and Studies*, ed. by Zygmunt G. Barański (Dublin: Four Courts Press, 1999), pp. 281–320

' "'nfiata labbia" and "dolce stil novo": A Note on Dante, Ethics, and the Technical Vocabulary of Literature', in *Sotto il segno di Dante: scritti in onore di Francesco Mazzoni*, ed. by Domenico De Robertis and Leonella Coglievina (Florence: Le Lettere, 1998), pp. 17–35

'Bibliography of Giulio C. Lepschy's Publications: 1960–1997', in *In amicizia: Essays in Honour of Giulio Lepschy*, ed. by Zygmunt G. Barański and Lino Pertile, special supplement to *The Italianist*, 17 (1997), 21–51

'The Mystery of Dante's *Questio de aqua et terra*', in *In amicizia: Essays in Honour of Giulio Lepschy*, ed. by Zygmunt G. Barański and Lino Pertile, special supplement to *The Italianist*, 17 (1997), 146–64

' "Orpheus id est pulchra vox": Philological Notes on Dante, Orpheus, Horace, and Other Writers', in *Sguardi sull'Italia: miscellanea dedicata a Francesco Villari*, ed. by Zygmunt G. Barański and others (Leeds: Society for Italian Studies, 1997), pp. 1–18

'Pier Paolo Pasolini: teoremi e teorie', in *Lezioni su Pasolini*, ed. by Tullio De Mauro and Francesco Ferri (Ripatransone: Sestante, 1997), pp. 99–111

'The Ethics of Literature: The *Fiore* and Medieval Traditions of Re-writing', in *The 'Fiore' in Context*, ed. by Zygmunt G. Barański and Patrick Boyde (Notre Dame, IN, and London: Notre Dame University Press, 1997), pp. 207–32

'Teoria musicale e legittimazione poetica nella *Commedia* di Dante', in *Letteratura italiana e la musica*, ed. by Jørn Moestrup, Palle Spore, and Conni-Kay Jørgensen, 2 vols (Odense: Odense University Press, 1997), I, 75–82

'Dante and Medieval Poetics', in *Dante: Contemporary Perspectives*, ed. by Amilcare A. Iannucci (Toronto: University of Toronto Press, 1997), pp. 3–22

'"Tu numeris elementa ligat": un appunto su musica e poetica in Dante', *Rassegna europea di letteratura italiana*, 8 (1996), 89–95

'The "New Life" of "Comedy": The *Commedia* and the *Vita Nuova*', *Dante Studies*, 113 (1995), 1–29

'Il *Fiore* e la tradizione delle *translationes*', *Rassegna europea di letteratura italiana*, 5–6 (1995), 31–41

'Introduction', in *'Libri poetarum in quattuor species dividuntur': Essays on Dante and 'Genre'*, ed. by Zygmunt G. Barański, supplement 2 to *The Italianist*, 15 (1995), 5–6

'"Tres enim sunt manerie dicendi...": Some Observations on Medieval Literature, Dante, and "Genre"', in *'Libri poetarum in quattuor species dividuntur': Essays on Dante and 'Genre'*, ed. by Zygmunt G. Barański, supplement 2 to *The Italianist*, 15 (1995), 9–60

'Dante, the Roman Comedians, and the Medieval Theory of Comedy', in *'Libri poetarum in quattuor species dividuntur': Essays on Dante and 'Genre'*, ed. by Zygmunt G. Barański, supplement 2 to *The Italianist*, 15 (1995), 61–99

'Dante's Signs: An Introduction to Medieval Semiotics and Dante', in *Dante and the Medieval World*, ed. by John C. Barnes and Cormac Ó Cuilleanáin (Dublin: Irish Academic Press, 1995), pp. 139–80

'Dante, America, and the Limits of "Allegory"', *Italian Studies*, 50 (1995), 139–53

'*Paradiso* XIX', in *Dante's 'Divine Comedy': Introductory Readings. III. 'Paradiso'*, ed. by Tibor Wlassics (Charlottesville: University of Virginia Printing Service, 1995), pp. 277–99

'The Poetics of Meter: *terza rima*, "canto", "canzon", "cantica"', in *Dante Now*, ed. by Theodore Cachey Jr (Notre Dame, IN, and London: Notre Dame University Press, 1995), pp. 3–41

'Dante commentatore e commentato: riflessioni sullo studio dell'*iter* ideologico di Dante', in *Letture classensi*, 23 (1994), 135–58

'Dante fra "sperimentalismo" e "enciclopedismo"', in *L'enciclopedismo medievale*, ed. by Michelangelo Picone (Ravenna: Longo, 1994), pp. 383–404

'Dante Alighieri', in *Johns Hopkins Guide to Literary Theory and Criticism*, ed. by Michael Groden and Martin Kreiswirth (Baltimore: Johns Hopkins University Press, 1994), pp. 183–85

'La diffusione della letteratura italiana contemporanea in Gran Bretagna', *The Italianist*, 13 (1993), 255–65

'A Note on Italian Culture in North America', *The Italianist*, 13 (1993), 269–71

'La *Commedia*', in *Manuale di letteratura italiana. I. Dalle origini alla fine del Quattrocento*, ed. by Franco Brioschi and Costanzo Di Girolamo (Turin: Bollati Boringhieri, 1993), pp. 492–560

'A Note on the Trecento: Boccaccio, Benvenuto, and the Dream of Dante's Pregnant Mother', in *Miscellanea di studi danteschi in memoria di Silvio Pasquazi*, ed. by Alfonso Paolella, Vincenzo Placella, and Giovanni Turco, 2 vols (Naples: Federico & Ardia, 1993), I, 69–82

'"Sordellus qui patrium vulgare deseruit": A Note on *De vulgari eloquentia* I, xv, 2–6', in *The Cultural Heritage of the Italian Renaissance: Essays in Honour of T. G. Griffith*, ed. by Clive Griffiths and Robert Hastings (Lampeter: Edwin Mellen Press, 1993), pp. 19–45

'Dante e i comici latini', in *Dante e la 'bella scola' della poesia*, ed. by Amilcare A. Iannucci (Ravenna: Longo, 1993), pp. 225–45

'Lettura dei sonetti I–XXX', in *Lettura del 'Fiore'*, ed. by Zygmunt G. Barański, Patrick Boyde, and Lino Pertile (Ravenna: Longo, 1993), pp. 13–35

'The Literary Lives of Sebastiano Vassalli', in *The New Italian Novel*, ed. by Zygmunt G. Barański and Lino Pertile (Edinburgh: Edinburgh University Press, 1993), pp. 239–57

'Canto VI', in *Dante's 'Divine Comedy': Introductory Readings. II. Purgatory*, ed. by Tibor Wlassics (Charlottesville: University of Virginia Printing Service, 1993), pp. 80–97

'Luigi Meneghello: bibliografia (1948–1991)', in Ernestina Pellegrini, *Nel paese di Meneghello: un itinerario critico* (Bergamo: Moretti & Vitali, 1992), pp. 155–79

'Giuliana Morandini', *The Italianist*, 11 (1991), 230–31

'"Primo tra cotanto senno": Dante and the Latin Comic Tradition', *Italian Studies*, 46 (1991), 1–31

'Benvenuto da Imola e la tradizione dantesca della *comedía*: appunti per una descrizione del *Comentum*', in *Benvenuto da Imola lettore degli antichi e dei moderni*, ed. by Pantaleo Palmieri and Carlo Paolazzi (Ravenna: Longo, 1991), pp. 215–30

Review article based on Bernard Delmay, *I personaggi della 'Divina Commedia'* (Florence: Olschki, 1986), *Romance Philology*, 44 (1991), 508–16

'*Comedía*: Notes on Dante, the Epistle to Cangrande, and Medieval Comedy', *Lectura Dantis Virginiana*, 8 (1991), 26–55

'Rassegna sullo studio di Dante nell'America del dopoguerra', *Lettere italiane*, 42 (1990), 626–56

'Reflecting on Dante in America', *Annali d'Italianistica*, 8 (1990), 58–86

(With Shirley W. Vinall) 'Introduction', in *Women and Italy*, ed. by Zygmunt G. Barański and Shirley W. Vinall (London: Macmillan, 1990), pp. 1–7

'The "Marvellous" and the "Comic": Towards a Reading of *Inferno* XVI', *Lectura Dantis Virginiana*, 7 (1990), 72–95

(With Robert Lumley) 'Turbulent Transitions: An Introduction', in *Culture and Conflict in Postwar Italy*, ed. by Zygmunt G. Barański and Robert Lumley (London: Macmillan, 1990), pp. 1–17

'Pier Paolo Pasolini: Culture, Croce, Gramsci', in *Culture and Conflict in Postwar Italy*, ed. by Zygmunt G. Barański and Robert Lumley (London: Macmillan, 1990), pp. 139–59

'The Constraints of Form: Towards a Provisional Definition of Petrarch's *Triumphi*', in *Petrarch's 'Triumphs': Allegory and Spectacle*, ed. by Konrad Eisenbichler and Amilcare A. Iannucci (Ottawa: Dovehouse, 1990), pp. 63–83

'Reading the Real Dante [Obituary: Gianfranco Contini]', *Guardian*, 7 February 1990, p. 39

'Dante's Three Reflective Dreams', *Quaderni d'italianistica*, 10 (1989), 213–36

'Meneghello scrittore', *The Italianist*, 9 (1989), 9–10

'Luigi Meneghello: A Select Bibliography', *The Italianist*, 9 (1989), 28–31

'Dante's Biblical Linguistics', *Lectura Dantis Virginiana*, 5 (1989), 105–43

'Divine, Human, and Animal Languages in Dante: Notes on *De vulgari eloquentia* I i–ix and the Bible', *Transactions of the Philological Society*, 87 (1989), 205–31

'Dante's (Anti-)Rhetoric: Notes on the Poetics of the *Commedia*', in *Moving in Measure: Essays Presented to Brian Moloney*, ed. by Judith Bryce and Doug Thompson (Hull: Hull University Press, 1989), pp. 1–14

'Cinquant'anni di riviste di italianistica in Gran Bretagna', *Revue des Études Italiennes*, 34 (1988), 96–104

'Per una bibliografia di/su Luigi Meneghello', *Quaderni veneti*, 8 (1988), 75–102

'Crises and Cultures in Postwar Italy', *The Italianist*, 8 (1988), 120–29

'Re-viewing Dante', *Romance Philology*, 42 (1988), 51–76

'Tra storia e metafora: letteratura italiana e arti figurative', in *Letteratura italiana e arti figurative: Atti del XII Convegno dell'Associazione Internazionale per gli studi di Lingua e*

Letteratura Italiana, ed. by Antonio Franceschetti, 3 vols (Florence: Olschki, 1988), I, 207–25

'La lezione esegetica di *Inferno* I: allegoria, storia e letteratura', in *Dante e le forme dell'allegoresi*, ed. by Michelangelo Picone (Ravenna: Longo, 1987), pp. 79–97

'Dante Poet of History', in *Chronicles of the Age of Chivalry*, ed. by Elizabeth Hallam (London: Weidenfeld & Nicholson, 1987), pp. 154–55

'"Significar per verba": Notes on Dante and Plurilingualism', *The Italianist*, 6 (1986), 5–18

'The Power of Influence: Aspects of Dante's Presence in Italian Twentieth-century Culture', *Strumenti critici*, 52 (1986), 343–76

'Structural Retrospection in Dante's *Comedy*: The Case of *Purgatorio* XXVII', *Italian Studies*, 41 (1986), 1–23

'Pasolini's Radicalism', *Journal of the Association of Teachers of Italian*, 47 (1986), 43–48

'The Texts of *Il Vangelo secondo Matteo*', *The Italianist*, 5 (1985), 77–106

'Notes Towards a Reconstruction: Pasolini and Rome 1950–51', *The Italianist*, 5 (1985), 138–49

Editor of Pier Paolo Pasolini, 'L'accelerato Venezia-Udine' and 'Domenica al Collina Volpi', *The Italianist*, 5 (1985), 150–61

(With John R. Short) 'Developing Contemporary Marxism', in *Developing Contemporary Marxism*, ed. by Zygmunt G. Barański and John R. Short (London: Macmillan, 1985), pp. 1–7

'Literary Theory', in *Developing Contemporary Marxism*, ed. by Zygmunt G. Barański and John R. Short (London: Macmillan, 1985), pp. 229–67

'Report on the 12th AISLLI Congress', *The Bulletin of the Society of Italian Studies*, 18 (1985), 46–54

'The Threads of Influence: Dante and Montale', in *Dante Comparisons*, ed. by Eric Haywood and Barry Jones (Dublin: Irish Academic Press, 1985), pp. 11–48

'Dante tra dei pagani ed angeli cristiani', *Filologia e critica*, 9 (1984), 293–302

'Dante nell'opera narrativa di Meneghello', *Studi novecenteschi*, 11 (1984), 81–102

'On Texts and Authors', *The Italianist*, 4 (1984), 135–49

'Alle origini della narrativa di Meneghello', in *Su/Per Meneghello*, ed. by Giulio Lepschy (Milan: Edizioni di Comunità, 1983), pp. 97–108

'Zygmunt Krasiński', 'Adam Mickiewicz', 'Cyprian Norwid', in *Makers of Nineteenth-century Culture*, ed. by Justin Wintle (London: Routledge Kegan & Paul, 1982), pp. 341–42, 425–27, 464

'Antithesis in Fellini's *I vitelloni*', *The Italianist*, 1 (1981), 24–42; reprinted in *Critical Perspectives on Federico Fellini*, ed. by Peter Bondanella and Cristina Degli-Espositi (Boston: G. K. Hall & Co, 1993), pp. 70–86

'*Inferno* VI. 73: A Controversy Re-examined', *Italian Studies*, 36 (1981), 1–26

'Italian Literature and the Great War: Soffici, Jahier, and Rebora', *Journal of European Studies*, 10 (1980), 155–77

'Nad notatnikiem teatralnym Jana Kotta', *Wiadomości*, 1793 (1980), 2

'A Note on Montale's Presumed Dantism in "Meriggiare pallido e assorto"', *Italica*, 56 (1979), 394–401

'Leopardi, Ungaretti, Montale: Three Recent Studies', *Forum for Modern Language Studies*, 15 (1979), 86–90

'Varsavia Boinego', *Wiadomości*, 1758 (1979), 2

'Czytajac szkice Jana Kotta', *Wiadomości*, 1720 (1979), 22

(With John C. Barnes) 'Dante's "Canzone Montanina"', *Modern Language Review*, 73 (1978), 297–307

'Marcello Cora, *La Ronda* i Polska', *Wiadomości*, 1685 (1978), 2

'Dante's Starling Simile', *Aberdeen University Review*, 47 (1978), 326–28

'Leopardi o Kościuszce', *Wiadomości*, 1641–642 (1977), 3

GENERAL INDEX

❖

INDEX OF REFERENCES TO
DANTE, BOCCACCIO, AND PETRARCH

Boccaccio, Giovanni

Petrarca, Francesco

INDEX OF MANUSCRIPTS